Elgar Encyclopedia of Food and Society

ELGAR ENCYCLOPEDIAS IN THE SOCIAL SCIENCES

Elgar Encyclopedias in the Social Sciences serve as the definitive reference works to their fields. Each *Encyclopedia* is overseen by an editor internationally recognised as a leading name within the field, and contains a multitude of entries written by key scholars, providing an accessible and condensed overview of the key topics within a given subject area. Volumes in the series are commissioned across the breadth of the social sciences, and cover areas including, but not limited to, Political Science, Sociology, Human Geography, Development Studies, Social Policy, Public Management and Public Policy. Individual entries present a concise and logical overview of a given subject, together with a list of references for further study. Each *Encyclopedia* will serve as an invaluable resource for practitioners, academics, and students, and should form an essential part of any research journey.

For a full list of Edward Elgar published titles, including the titles in this series, visit our website at www.e-elgar.com.

Elgar Encyclopedia of Food and Society

Edited by

Lewis Holloway

School of Environmental Sciences, University of Hull, UK

Michael K. Goodman

Department of Geography and Environmental Science, University of Reading, UK

Damian Maye

Countryside and Community Research Institute, University of Gloucestershire, UK

Moya Kneafsey

Centre for Agroecology, Water and Resilience, Coventry University, UK

Alexandra E. Sexton

Department of Geography, Durham University, UK

Ana Moragues-Faus

Food Action and Research Observatory (FARO), Faculty of Economics and Business, University of Barcelona, Spain

ELGAR ENCYCLOPEDIAS IN THE SOCIAL SCIENCES

 Edward Elgar
PUBLISHING

Cheltenham, UK · Northampton, MA, USA

Published by

Edward Elgar Publishing Limited
The Lypiatts
15 Lansdown Road
Cheltenham
Glos GL50 2JA
UK

Edward Elgar Publishing, Inc.
William Pratt House
9 Dewey Court
Northampton
Massachusetts 01060
USA

Authorised representative in the EU for GPSR queries only: Easy Access System Europe – Mustamäe tee 50, 10621 Tallinn, Estonia, gpsr.requests@easproject.com

A catalogue record for this book
is available from the British Library

Library of Congress Control Number: 2025938910

This book is available electronically in the **Elgar**online
Geography, Planning and Tourism subject collection
https://doi.org/10.4337/9781800887435

ISBN 978 1 80088 742 8 (cased)
ISBN 978 1 80088 743 5 (eBook)
ISBN 978 1 0353 6956 0 (ePub)
Printed and bound by CPI Group (UK) Ltd, Croydon, CR0 4YY

Contents

Contributors

Helen Addison-Smith, RMIT University, Australia

Raquel Ajates, Universidad Nacional de Educación a Distancia, Spain

Emanuele Amo, Aberystwyth University, UK

Colin R. Anderson, University of Vermont, Canada

Molly D. Anderson, Middlebury College, USA

Lucy Aphramor, Public Scholar, UK

Sabrina Arcuri, University of Pisa, Italy

Kirsten Ayris, University of Reading, UK

Jane Battersby, University of Cape Town, South Africa

Dave Beck, University of Salford, UK

Melanie Bedore, McMaster University, Canada

David Bell, University of Leeds, UK

Ellen Bishop, University of Glasgow, UK

Megan K. Blake, University of Sheffield, UK

Albert Boaitey, Newcastle University, UK

Rob Booth, University of Birmingham, UK

Fernando Bosco, San Diego State University, USA

Silvia Bottinelli, Tufts University, USA

Gianluca Brunori, University of Pisa, Italy

Karly Burch, Waipapa Taumata Rau University of Auckland, Aotearoa New Zealand

Matthew Canfield, Leiden Law School, Netherlands

Martin Caraher, City St. George's, University of London, UK

Enric Castelló, Universitat Rovira i Virgili, Spain

Martha Caswell, University of Vermont, Canada

Kin Wing (Ray) Chan, Royal Agricultural University, UK

Jennifer Clapp, University of Waterloo, Canada

Beth Clark, Newcastle University, UK

Marta Coll, Institute of Marine Sciences (ICM-CSIC)

Rachel Colls, Durham University, UK

Jonas Cromwell, University of Leeds, UK

Laura Cuch, Goldsmiths, University of London, UK

George Cusworth, University of Oslo, Norway

Anna Davies, Trinity College Dublin, Ireland

Mariela de Amstalden, University of Basel, Switzerland

Michaela DeSoucey, North Carolina State University, USA

Sanchia deSouza, University of Toronto Scarborough, Canada

Jonathan Deutsch, Drexel University, USA

Brian Dowd-Uribe, University of San Francisco, USA

Jessica Duncan, Wageningen University, the Netherlands

Ferne Edwards, City, University of London, UK

Gareth Enticott, Cardiff University, UK

Sally Everett, Kings College London, UK

Pam Farrell, University of Calgary, Canada

Giuseppe Feola, Utrecht University, the Netherlands

Isabel Fletcher, University of Edinburgh, UK

Jérémie Forney, University of Neuchâtel, Switzerland

Paul Freedman, Yale University, USA

Harriet Friedmann, University of Toronto, Canada

Sinéad Furey, Ulster University, Northern Ireland, UK

Francesca Galli, University of Pisa, Italy

Dieter Gerten, Potsdam Institute for Climate Impact Research, Germany

David Goodman, University of California, Santa Cruz, USA

Michael K. Goodman, University of Reading, UK

Santiago Gorostiza, Universitat Autònoma de Barcelona, Spain

Cristina Grasseni, University of Leiden, the Netherlands

Mikelis Grivins, Riga Stradins University, Latvia

Mascha Gugganig, Ludwig-Maximilians University of Munich, Germany

Neva Hassanein, University of Montana, USA

Allison Hayes-Conroy, Temple University, USA

Jessica Hayes-Conroy, Hobart & William Smith Colleges, USA

Jack A Heinemann, University of Canterbury, New Zealand

Agatha Herman, Cardiff University, UK

Jennifer Hodbod, University of Leeds, UK

Lewis Holloway, University of Hull, UK

Philip H. Howard, Michigan State University, USA

Alex Hughes, Newcastle University, UK

Aqeel Ihsan, York University, Canada

Julie Ingram, University of Gloucestershire, UK

Lisa Jack, University of Portsmouth, UK

Hannah Kass, University of Wisconsin-Madison, USA

Kathleen Kevany, Dalhousie University, Canada

Jakob A. Klein, University of London, UK

Laurens Klerkx, Universidad de Talca, Chile

Moya Kneafsey, Coventry University, UK

Andrzej Kowalczyk, University of Warsaw, Poland

Stinne Gunder Strøm Krogager, Aalborg University, Denmark

Anna Krzywoszynska, University of Oulu, Finland

Magdalena Kubal-Czerwińska, Jagiellonian University in Kraków, Poland

Sharron Kuznesof, Newcastle University, UK

Gurpinder Singh Lalli, University of Wolverhampton, UK

Claire Lamine, INRAE ACT-Ecodéveloppement, France

Geoffrey Lawrence, The University of Queensland, Australia

Jonatan Leer, University of Örebro

Stephen Leitheiser, Wageningen University, the Netherlands

Ronan Le Velly, Institut Agro Montpellier, France

John Lever, Manchester Metropolitan University, UK

Tania Lewis, RMIT University, Australia

Carolynne Lord, UK Centre for Ecology and Hydrology, UK

Jessica Loyer, William Angliss Institute, Australia

Norah MacKendrick, Rutgers University, USA

Siobhan Maderson, Aberystwyth University, UK

Niamh Mahon, James Hutton Institute, UK

Jose Martini Costa, University of Toronto, Canada

Sonia Massari, Pisa University, Italy

Damian Maye, University of Gloucestershire, UK

Andrew McGregor, Macquarie University, Australia

Will McKeithen, University of Washington at Tacoma, USA

Jane Midgley, Newcastle University, UK

Kushang Mishra, University of Auckland, New Zealand

Denise Misleh, UNU-FLORES, Chile

Ana Moragues-Faus, University of Barcelona, Spain

Kevin Morgan, Cardiff University, Wales, UK

Oona Morrow, Wageningen University, the Netherlands

William G. Moseley, Macalester College, USA

Oli Mould, Royal Holloway, University of London, UK

David Nally, University of Cambridge, UK

Anitra Nelson, University of Melbourne, Australia

Kate J. Neville, University of Toronto, Canada

Nicholas Nisbett, University of Sussex, UK

Samatha Noll, Washington State University, USA

Patricia Northover, The University of the West Indies, Jamaica

Miquel Ortega, CSIC- Institute of Marine Sciences

Alissa Overend, MacEwan University, Canada

Ronalda S. Pairman, Chieftainess of Yamaye Guani Taino Peoples, Jamaica

Laxmi Prasad Pant, University of Greenwich, UK

Luca Panzone, Newcastle University, UK

Noelia Parajuá, University of Santiago de Compostela, Spain

Barbara Parker, Lakehead University, Canada

Kelly Parsons, University of Cambridge, UK

Jack Pickering, University of Sheffield, UK

Hannah Pitt, Cardiff University, UK

Paolo Prosperi, CIHEAM-IAMM, UMR MoISA, Montpellier F-34093, France

Katerina Psarikidou, University of Sussex, UK

Dana-Marie Ramjit, St Mary's University, Canada

Krishnendu Ray, New York University, USA

Gabrielle Reagan, Temple University, USA

Marta Guadalupe Rivera-Ferre, INGENIO (CSIC-Universitat Politècnica de València), Spain

Alice Rizzuti, University of Hull, UK

Emma Roe, University of Southampton, UK

David Rose, Harper Adams University, UK

Colin Sage, Independent research scholar, Portugal

Eric Sarmiento, Texas State University, USA

Lopamudra Patnaik Saxena, Coventry University, UK

Joshua Sbicca, Colorado State University, USA

Sergio Schneider, Federal University of Rio Grande do Sul, Brazil

Alexandra E. Sexton, University of Sheffield, UK

Amanda Shankland, Toronto Metropolitan University, Canada

Emma Sharp, Waipapa Taumata Rau | University of Auckland, Aotearoa New Zealand

Rosalind Sharpe, University of Hertfordshire, UK

Philippa Simmonds, University of Gloucestershire, UK

Jasber Singh, Coventry University, UK

Sarah Ruth Sippel, Münster University, Germany

Elizabeth Smythe, Concordia University of Edmonton, Canada

Sarah Snuggs, University of Reading, UK

Neil Stephens, University of Birmingham, UK

Elaine Swan, University of Sussex, UK

Laura Terragni, Oslo Metropolitan University, Norway

Ana Tominc, Queen Margaret University Edinburgh, UK

Christopher Turner, University of Greenwich, UK

Stefan Wahlen, University of Giessen, Germany

I-Liang Wahn, Tunghai University, Taiwan

Chi-Mao Wang, National Taiwan University, Taiwan

Rebecca Wells, City St. George's, University of London, UK

Harry G. West, University of Exeter, UK

Richard White, Sheffield Hallam University, UK

Andrew Williams, Cardiff University, UK

Lauren T. Williams, Griffith University, Australia

Marisa Wilson, University of Edinburgh, UK

Han Wiskerke, Wageningen University, the Netherlands

Tai Wright, University of Auckland, New Zealand

Adele Wylie, University of Reading, UK

Christopher Yap, City St. George's, University of London, UK

Lukáš Zagata, Czech University of Life Sciences, Czechia

Acknowledgements

The editors of the *Elgar Encyclopedia of Food and Society* would like to acknowledge the involvement of the following in the production of this volume.

We offer our deepest thanks to all those who have contributed entries to the Encyclopedia. We are delighted to have such breadth of coverage in the volume from a diverse range of authors, and we are very grateful to every one of them for writing informative, accessible and interesting accounts of their topics. Contributors faced a stream of editorial reminders and requests, and we thank them for their responses and efforts throughout.

In the early stages of planning the Encyclopedia we consulted with a number of colleagues to seek their advice and thoughts on our initial attempts to scope out the volume and to create a set of possible entries.

Their input was invaluable and has significantly shaped the Encyclopedia. We thank Colin Anderson, Jane Battersby, Megan Blake, Michael Carolan, Dan Crossley, Gareth Enticott, Julie Ingram, Josée Johnston and Colin Sage.

Daniel Mather at Edward Elgar Publishing, who first approached us with the idea of creating this Encyclopedia, has been a great source of advice as we have progressed through this project, and we thank him for his continual support and encouragement.

Alexandra Sexton would also like to acknowledge that her contributions to this Encyclopedia were supported by the Leverhulme Trust (Early Career Research Fellowship, ECF-2020-105).

Introduction to *Elgar Encyclopedia of Food and Society*

Lewis Holloway, Michael K. Goodman, Damian Maye, Moya Kneafsey, Alexandra E. Sexton and Ana Moragues-Faus

Recent years have seen a rapid expansion of interest in studies of the relationships between food and society, covering a highly diverse range of thematic and empirical perspectives and engaging with many of the key issues of our time, including the climate emergency, global inequalities and the persistence of poverty alongside wealth, and imbalances of power at global and local scales. Preparing the *Elgar Encyclopedia of Food and Society* has provided an opportunity to take stock of what can be a bewildering array of ideas, materials, topics and examples, to highlight key connections between different themes and approaches, and to provide some signposting towards future directions for research into food and society. In this brief introduction, we contextualise the volume's entries by commenting on how food–society relationships have been studied, the approach and underlying principles that informed our own thinking, our aims and intentions for the Encyclopedia and the process of putting the volume together, and, finally, how the Encyclopedia can be used.

Food and society

The scale, diversity and complexity of food issues in contemporary society makes approaching a project like this a daunting task. Consider, for example, the following list of food-related books from the editors' bookshelves. We have – and this is just a sample! – books such as *Sustainable Diets* (Mason and Lang, 2017); *The Climate Book* (Thunberg, 2022); *Food Security* (McDonald, 2010); *The School Food Revolution* (Morgan and Sonnino, 2008); *Geographies of Meat* (Neo and Emel, 2018); *Waste* (Stuart, 2009); *Environment and Food* (Sage, 2012); *Hungry City* (Steel, 2008); *The Food System* (Tansey and Worsley, 1995); *Feeding Britain* (Lang, 2020); *Ravenous* (Dimbleby and Lewis, 2023); *Regenesis* (Monbiot, 2022); *Alternative Food Networks* (Goodman et al.,

2012); *Food and Development* (Young, 2012); the *Routledge Handbook of Landscape and Food* (Zeunert and Waterman, 2018); and *Geographies of Food* (Kneafsey et al., 2021). So many books, topics, arguments and ideas. How best to organise a project like this? Where even to begin? Moreover, what to say about food and society? We explain the more procedural aspects of our work and thinking in the following section, but here we first provide a sense of how we, as editors, approach and think about food and society as a topic, including influences from previous studies.

There is a popular saying that 'you are what you eat'. This phrase connects food to our bodies and the visceral process of eating for nutritional need, but also signifies connections to cultures, places, ecosystems, habits, identities, practices and possibly even social stereotypes. The phrase also gets used in popular TV programmes and food-related books alerting us, for example, to the dangers of eating too many of the 'wrong' (unhealthy) foods, or reworking the sentiment to, as Alice Waters (2021) implores, ditch fast food cultures and embrace slower modalities of living and eating.

This seemingly simplistic phrase – 'you are what you eat' – and its embodiment in traditional and new forms of media, culture and debate, can be thought of as summarising food–society relations that actually take multiple forms, have deep historical roots and diverse trajectories of change, are essential but often taken-for-granted, are sometimes bad for us, and intersect with much wider social, cultural and political debates. They are open also to arguments that they should be radically transformed to improve our health, protect the environment or address socio-economic inequalities. It is this multiplicity that symbolises in many respects the essence of what we seek to retain and achieve in our approach to food and society in this Encyclopedia: i.e., to recognise, problematise and celebrate foods in varied forms as material objects and sets of socio-ecological relations that are, as Annemarie Mol (2008) puts it, 'ontologically multiple'. Kneafsey et al. (2021: 298) express this multiplicity as 'material-semiotic', recognising a simultaneous material quality to foods alongside their social embeddedness in multiple layers of meaning and cultural significance. We need to add another layer to this in terms of the economic models and power relations that increasingly determine who eats what and when, and the framing of food as (for example) an 'economic good' or a 'universal human right' (Vivero Pol, 2017). In this sense, food and society relations provide a window onto wider market and society dialectics (Polanyi, 1944) – with food an object of routine and ever-increasing 'commodification' and 'marketisation', but also a site of resistance, as symbolised by 'counter movements' built on underlying principles of food as 'a human right' or 'a commons' (see Jackson et al., 2021).

This suggests that there can sometimes be a need to conceptualise food and society relationships outside of the more commonly applied agri-food framings, such as those that examine these relations through the lens of 'sustainability'. Such frameworks typically cover the social, economic and environmental dimensions of food systems and wider links to, for example, the United Nations' Sustainable Development Goals. These approaches are valuable, but they can have an element of normativity about them. What we mean by that is that they can risk representing complex and multiple food production and consumption practices and relationships as part of a single, somehow abstracted, rather homogeneous system. And that a set of 'best' practices and relationships might be universally prescribed. Instead, what we take from the ideas discussed above is the idea that diverse actual, on-the-ground food practices and relationships in practice are embedded within and connected to wider social, economic and environmental systems in many different ways. Rather than prescribe too narrow a framing of the relationships between food and society we prefer to embrace the language of complexities (Mol and Law, 2002), multiplicity (Mol, 2008) and projects such as Anna Tsing et al.'s *Feral Atlas* (2021). These languages and approaches highlight relations within and between entities and systems, and crucially fully acknowledge the diverse roles of non-human elements of food–society relationships.

We note below a set of principles that worked, then, as a guiding framework in the creation of this volume, and that helped not only to organise the entries (more on that in the next section) but to express 'food and society relationships as complex and multiple', reflected in how they are studied, conceptualised, debated, measured, known, expressed, fought over and so on. In this spirit, the study of the many and varied relationships between food and society is necessarily interdisciplinary (i.e., involving different academic approaches) and transdisciplinary (i.e., in drawing on concepts and knowledges from outside of academia), something which is also reflected here in the diverse disciplinary backgrounds and approaches of the contributors of the Encyclopedia's entries. The set of entries thus reflects perspectives emanating from areas including, for example, geography, sociology, anthropology, psychology, epidemiology, economics, nutrition and public health, politics, philosophy, history and many others, as well as from inherently interdisciplinary areas like food policy and food studies. The plurality of voices that results from this disciplinary diversity offers the opportunity to view and explore food–society relationships in different ways, and to think about the interconnections between perspectives as well as their divergent ways of conceptualising, problematising and prioritising food–society issues. This diversity allows the Encyclopedia to embody and reflect a multitude of intellectual, empirical and conceptual pathways through which to understand food–society relationships.

The Encyclopedia's entries reflect the complexities of both food production and food consumption, while also spanning and disrupting that binary polarisation through paying attention to a plurality of production–consumption related practices, movements, structures and representations. Entries go beyond the production–consumption dualism, for example through the inclusion of an entry addressing the increasingly important topic of food 'waste' (Reynolds et al., 2020). Also included are entries which describe many of the concepts which have been used to try and frame or capture the nature of food–society relations, for example through the deployment of terminologies describing food chains, systems, regimes, networks, environments and assemblages. There are also entries which focus on the struggle to intervene in and sometimes radically change what are presented as unjust, ecologically damaging, insecure and fragile food systems, by exploring, for example, social movements involving food production and consumption practices, alternative and sustainable food networks, and alternatives to the dominant representation of 'food as a commodity' (Vivero Pol, 2017; Jackson et al., 2021).

Many of the entries in the collection cohere around the attention they pay to a set of urgent, multiple and intersecting ecological and social food-related crises. The climate emergency is especially prominent here, alongside and related to issues such as food security, social inequalities and injustices, biodiversity, poverty and health. Necessarily, some of these issues have become individual entries in themselves; however, many other entries refer to these issues as important touch points for the discussion of their own specific themes. At the same time as this crucial focus on crises, however, entries also pay attention to the social, cultural, embodied and sensual pleasures associated with growing, consuming, learning about, imagining and representing food. Many entries also conclude by looking forward, with authors setting out research pathways that they see as offering hope amidst this age of planetary crisis. This is important as the Encyclopedia seeks to document the positive and emotional, affective, more-than-representational, and hopeful dimensions of food–society relations alongside the problematic structural issues embedded in current food systems.

The format of the Encyclopedia means that it includes entries on broad substantive themes that provide a particular inflection on food (and where food provides a particular inflection on a theme), entries where food intersects with other significant issues and shorter entries on more specifically food-related topics. Thus, for example, food provides a lens through which to examine broader themes of race, gender and social class, and how food production–consumption both is affected by racial, gendered and classed relationships, and at the same time can reproduce these categories and relationships. On the other hand, the Encyclopedia includes focused entries on topics such as food banks, nutrition and food deserts, which, of course, are inter-related with those social categories. In between, other entries show how food is entangled with a wide range of other issues and concerns, including biodiversity, policymaking, health and conflict.

Food–society relationships can be both intensely local and expansively global, while both differentiating and connecting places at all scales. The entries thus engage with issues at a variety of scales, from the bodily and the local, through to the global. Entries also address food–society relations across different geographical arenas and institutions, including urban spaces, the school and the prison and, using a range of spatial metaphors such as the food desert, they draw on examples and issues from diverse parts of the world. Food–society relations have a history as well as a geography, and many of the entries attempt to give a sense of the emergence over time, as well as over space, of the issues they address. In some cases, entries draw heavily on historical examples and references, while others develop engagements with more contemporary contexts and events and suggest how these food–society issues might change and be engaged with in the future.

Although the focus in studies of food–society relationships tends to be on people (for example as food producers and consumers), and on human institutions and structures, in this Encyclopedia we wanted to ensure that the role and significance of nonhuman actors in food systems was also acknowledged (i.e., to see food–society relationships as 'more-than-human'). Living nonhumans, both plants and animals, and the ecosystems and wider environmental systems they are part of, are profoundly important to the relationships between food and society, and are, clearly, significantly impacted by food systems centred around differential human needs and imperatives. At the same time, other components of our food systems, especially technologies of different kinds, need to be fully considered in the conceptualisations of food–society relationships. We have thus ensured that the selection of entries represents different kinds of nonhuman entities, such as soils, animals and technologies, considering how they play a role in the formation of different relationships between society and food, and are in turn affected by those relationships.

Creating the Encyclopedia

An encyclopedia cannot claim to provide completely comprehensive coverage of its topic. This *Elgar Encyclopedia of Food and Society* is not a complete synthesis of modern food–society studies, and neither is it a neutral reflection of the world. The Encyclopedia is necessarily incomplete, as it could never include an entry on everything about food and society. It is a product of the time and places it was produced in and of the different perspectives of the authors of each entry, and it was constructed around editorial intentions regarding what we as editors wanted the book to do and how we hoped it would be used. We briefly outline here what our intentions for the Encyclopedia were from the outset, and how we constructed the volume.

As an editorial collective, we wanted the Encyclopedia to have a critical, reflective edge. This influenced our approach to drawing up lists of prospective entries. We wanted it to include potentially contentious and/or critical perspectives, and to include some unconventional and new, emergent themes, as well as covering those key, more traditional, themes and ideas that our hoped-for wide readership would expect to find. In particular, and drawing on the metaphor of the food chain, we wanted to ensure that the volume provided coverage of all the different nodes and linkages included in and between food production and (post-)consumption. In addition, we wished to include reference to the key nonhuman actors involved in and affected by food–society relations, to ensure coverage of issues in many different parts of the world that involved a diverse range of social groups, to provide a sense of the history of food–society relations, and to capture, as much as possible, the ongoing processes of change across both water environments and the more usually focused-on terrestrial environments associated with food.

Drawing on the editors' own diverse academic interests and experiences, we thus constructed an initial long list of potential themes and entries. We then refined and prioritisedthese into what would become longer, medium length and shorter entries. We instigated a process of field-testing our list with a group of colleagues, some of whom went on to contribute entries as well. We are hugely grateful for the enormously valuable feedback we received from all those colleagues who were involved in this early stage of sifting and sorting our potential entries. They made a significant and very positive difference to the eventual set of entries, and to the scope and impact of the encyclopedia.

Following this, we began to identify and approach prospective authors for each entry. We tried to identify contributors from different career stages and different geographical locations beyond the UK, US and Western Europe in order to encompass a range of voices and perspectives. Identification of contributors was inevitably shaped by the reach of our collective networks, experience and subject knowledge and the limitation of publishing a work in English only. At later stages, we were also approached by colleagues with proposals for additional entries. Many of these excellent entry suggestions we took up and have incorporated into the volume.

Although there were some stylistic constraints on the presentation of entries to ensure some consistency, we also wanted the contributors of different entries to bring their distinctive perspectives and voices to bear in their writing. Thus, although we provided editorial guidelines to each contributor, the Encyclopedia embodies a diverse range of voices, coming from different disciplinary perspectives, within the volume's wider intention of providing a framework of critical takes on food–society relationships of all kinds.

How to use the Encyclopedia

We have endeavoured to ensure that the Encyclopedia is a useful resource for a wide range of readers, including students at different stages of their studies, as well as researchers and other groups interested in food and society.

As an encyclopedia, entries are arranged alphabetically rather than thematically, which risks producing a fragmented sense of the volume's subject, despite the possible serendipitous advantages of encountering unexpected juxtapositions of topics. Moreover, the topics that the various entries address are entangled with each other. To try to represent this entanglement during the production of the entries we have systematically identified interconnections between them: these are highlighted within each entry. This will help readers to navigate between sometimes disparate entries and contribute to creating an enriched sense of different specialist areas of food–society relationships, as well as (we hope) sometimes taking readers off in unexpected directions.

HOLLOWAY, GOODMAN, MAYE, KNEAFSEY, SEXTON AND MORAGUES-FAUS

Entry authors have in addition provided recommended readings and references, which will guide readers to further, more detailed resources relating to each topic. Finally, the detailed index at the end of the Encyclopedia will help readers to identify entries addressing the specific topics they are interested in.

It is our hope that this *Elgar Encyclopedia of Food and Society* – and all the hard work invested in it by the entry authors, along with the editors of the volume – not only makes a substantial contribution to the study of food and society, but also inspires readers of all proclivities and interests to pursue their own interests in food-related research and also work for more socially and environmentally sustainable food systems the world over.

References

Dimbleby H and Lewis J (2023) *Ravenous: How to Get Ourselves and Our Planet into Shape*. London, Profile Books

Goodman D, DuPuis E M and Goodman M (2012) *Alternative Food Networks: Knowledge, Practice and Politics*. London, Routledge

Jackson P, Rivera Ferre M G , Candel J, Davies A, Derani C, de Vries H, Dragović-Uzelac V, Hoel A H, Holm L, Mathijs E, Morone P, Penker M, Śpiewak R, Termeer K and Thøgersen J (2021) Food as a commodity, human right or common good. *Nature Food* 2, 132–134

Kneafsey M, Maye D, Holloway L and Goodman M K (2021) *Geographies of Food: An Introduction*. London, Bloomsbury

Lang T (2020) *Feeding Britain: Our Food Problems and How to Fix Them*. London, Penguin

Mason P and Lang T (2017) *Sustainable Diets: How Ecological Nutrition Can Transform Consumption and the Food System*. Abingdon, Earthscan Routledge

McDonald B L (2010) *Food Security*. Cambridge, Polity Press

Mol A (2008) I eat an apple: on theorising subjectivities. *Subjectivity* 22, 28–37

Mol A and Law J (2002) Complexities: an introduction. In: Law J and Mol A (eds) *Complexities: Social Studies of Knowledge Practices*. Durham, NC, Duke University Press, pages 1–23

Monbiot G (2022) *Regenesis*. London, Allen Lane

Morgan K and Sonnino R (2008) *The School Food Revolution*. London, Earthscan

Neo H and Emel J (2018) *Geographies of Meat*. London, Routledge

Polanyi K (2024/1944) *The Great Transformation: The Political and Economic Origins of Our Time*. London, Penguin

Reynolds C, Soma T, Spring C and Lazell J (eds) (2020) *Routledge Handbook of Food Waste*. London, Routledge

Sage C (2012) *Environment and Food*. London, Routledge

Steel C (2008) *Hungry City: How Food Shapes Our Lives*. London, Chatto and Windus

Stuart T (2009) *Waste: Uncovering the Global Food Scandal*. New York, WW Norton and Company

Tansey G and Worsley A (1995) *The Food System*. London, Earthscan

Thunberg G (2022) *The Climate Book*. London, Penguin

Tsing A, Deger J, Saxena A K and Zhou F (2021) *Feral Atlas: The More-Than-Human Anthropocene*. Redwood City, CA, Stanford University Press

Vivero Pol L (2017) The idea of food as commons or commodity? Exploring the links between normative valuations and agency in food transition. *Sustainability* 9, 1–23

Waters A (2021) *We Are What We Eat: A Slow Food Manifesto*. New York, Penguin

Young E M (2012) *Food and Development*. London, Routledge

Zeunert J and Waterman T (2018) *Routledge Handbook of Landscape and Food*. London, Routledge

1. Advertising and food

MOLLY D. ANDERSON

Introduction

Advertising for food and beverages is omnipresent in industrialised societies through billboards, social media, television, radio and print media. It is the primary way that food manufacturers persuade people to purchase their products, and its effectiveness is demonstrated by the increasing amounts that companies are willing to spend on marketing. Food and beverage advertising is a multi-billion-dollar business: in 2021, food businesses spent US$2.54 billion on advertising (Faria, 2023) and food, beverage and restaurant companies spent almost US$14 billion on advertising in 2017 (Rudd Center, n.d.). Fast food advertising increased 9% between 2019 and 2021 (Harris et al., 2021). Foods that are advertised are seldom the most nutritious options: most advertising dollars promote fast foods and junk foods (those that are high in salt, sugar, fat and calories).

Current concerns

Some populations are especially vulnerable to advertising. Children are of greatest concern, since they often cannot make good judgments yet about whether advertising claims are plausible and they are susceptible to cheap tricks such as bright colours, animation and toys packaged with food. Children's obesity rates are rising around the world and fast food, ultra-processed food and sugar-sweetened beverages are largely to blame. These are precisely the products that are heavily advertised. The World Health Organization posted guidelines (WHO, 2023) to protect children from food marketing, including that policies should be mandatory; protect children of all ages; use a government-led nutrient profile model to classify foods to be restricted from marketing; be sufficiently comprehensive to minimise the risk of migration of marketing to other media, to other spaces within the same medium or to other age groups; and restrict the power of food marketing to persuade. Previously, many food and beverage companies had adopted voluntary policies to restrict marketing to children, but these were largely ineffective as companies simply switched their venue from television to social media.

While obesity was once a problem primarily in industrialised countries that had adopted high meat and dairy consumption, now it has risen in a majority of countries across all age levels. The highest obesity rates in 2022 were found in the Pacific Islands and in countries in the Middle East. North American and European food manufacturers that have saturated the US and EU market have increasingly gone overseas. For example, even though Burger King's advertising budget in the US decreased in 2021 to its lowest level since 2010, its global advertising expenditures increased by 12% (Gitnux.com, 2023). Some manufacturers and fast food companies, such as Coca-Cola and McDonald's, have had an international presence for decades. Industry websites announce that Coca-Cola entered the global market in the 1920s and McDonald's opened a restaurant in British Columbia (Canada) in 1967.

Many countries have attempted to restrict consumption of junk food and fast food by prohibiting their sale in certain places: for example, not allowing fast-food restaurants near schools; imposing taxes on their sale; or mandating 'stop signs' on foods with high salt, fat, sugar and caloric content. Chile was the first country to launch the stop-sign system, and this has resulted in lower sales of these foods. However, the US will not allow products from other countries with 'stop sign' warnings on them into US markets. And food and beverage companies have launched expensive campaigns against taxation of products such as sugar-sweetened beverages as soon as taxes appear on ballots, trying to convince consumers that they will put these products out of reach of low-income customers or that the government is overreaching its responsibilities to protect the public.

An additional concern about advertising is the way that many fast-food restaurants and junk food manufacturers target people of colour. Black and Hispanic youth in the US are exposed to more food advertising in the media and their communities compared with white youth and food companies target Black and Hispanic youth with advertising for their least healthy products (Harris et al., 2022).

Emerging concerns and what is needed

Food manufacturing companies have gained political power as they have become more concentrated through mergers and acquisitions.

They have moved into domestic and international forums that set guidelines on diets; for example, in the US, 95% of the 2020 Advisory Committee on Dietary Guidelines has ties with the food industry (Mialon et al., 2022). Not surprisingly, they use this political power to weaken or evade strict guidelines and many domestic and international agencies lack conflict of interest policies that would prohibit companies with a financial interest from participating in governance about diets and food trade. Unless governments are willing to break up food companies using anti-trust laws, they will continue consolidating and growing in power. Strong conflict of interest policies would keep food businesses out of governance forums. And governments could prohibit the sale of unhealthy foods or impose high taxes on them. This is not easy to implement, but would take the onus off the harried consumer in a retail market to make decisions to protect the health of themselves and their families.

References

Faria J (2023) U.S. food and kindred products ad spend 2020–2021, https://www.statista.com/statistics/470418/food-and-kindred-products-industry-ad-spend-usa/

Gitnux.com (2025) Fast food advertising statistics in 2023: The latest statistics and trends, https://blog.gitnux.com/fast-food-advertising-statistics/

Harris J L, Fleming-Milici F, Phaneuf L, Jensen M, Choi Y Y, McCann M (2021) Fast food facts 2021. Rudd Center for Food Policy and Obesity, University of Connecticut

Harris J L, Fleming-Milici F, Mancini S, Kumanyika S and Ramirez A G (2022) Targeted food and beverage advertising to Black and Hispanic consumers: 2022 update. Rudd Center for Food Policy and Health, University of Connecticut

Mialon M, Serodio P, Crosbie E, Teicholz N, Naik A, Carriedo A (2022) Conflicts of interest for members of the U.S. 2020 Dietary Guidelines Advisory Committee. *Public Health Nutrition* (21 March 2022). Published online. DOI 10.1017/S1368980022000672

Rudd Center for Food Policy and Health (n.d.) Food marketing, https://uconnruddcenter.org/research/food-marketing/

World Health Organization (2023) Policies to protect children from the harmful impact of food marketing: WHO guideline, https://www.who.int/publications/i/item/9789240075412?lctg=103724728

Further reading

Nestle, Marion (2013) *Food Politics: How the Food Industry Influences Nutrition and Health. Revised and Expanded Tenth Anniversary Edition.* Davis, University of California Press
This is an excellent entry point into Nestle's work on how the food industry, and its advertising, are subverting health.

Gilmore, AB, A Fabbri, F Baum, A Bertscher, K Bondy, H-J Chang, S Demaio, A Erzse, N Freudenberg, S Friel, KJ Hofman, P Johns, S Abdool Karim, J Lacy-Nichols, C Maranha Paes de Carvalho, R Marten, M McKee, M Petticrew, L Robertson, V Tangcharoensathien, AM Thow (2023, April 8) Defining and conceptualising the commercial determinants of health. *The Lancet* 401(10383), 1194–1213 DOI: https://doi.org/10.1016/S0140-6736(23)00013-2
This reading introduces the ways that commercial determinants increasingly affect health outcomes.

2. Aesthetics and food

KRISHNENDU RAY

Introduction: food in aesthetic discourse

When aesthetics appeared as a word in 18th-century European languages and philosophy, food was excluded from the discussion. Dominant Western aesthetic theory recommends the methodical separation of palatal senses and proximate taste – the salty, sweet, or savoury qualities of food – from the higher order of aesthetic taste mostly elaborated in the domain of the visual and auditory senses and arts. Aesthetics was used to unify disparate fields of activities from painting to music, later architecture and photography, focusing on questions of form, beauty, and emotion. Food was viewed as something too subjective, sensuous, intimate, and ephemeral to generate useful, reasoned, and durable arguments about 'good taste'. Out of the attempt to separate mind from body, everyday work of feeding and caregiving from thinking, and pleasure from reason was born a certain kind of rational ambition exemplified by the 18th-century philosopher Immanuel Kant, who wanted to make taste a faculty of aesthetic judgement which could make "universally valid discriminations" (Korsmeyer 2017: 208). Yet the emerging consensus is that aesthetics, far from being universal, has both a history and a geography. Both palatal taste (on-the-tongue taste) and aesthetic taste, according to the philosopher David Hume, are subjective, but shared by cultivation among critical experts, drawing no distinction between the lowly taste for food and the elevated taste for art.

Just as the relationship between senses and aesthetic judgement has varied over time, so it varies by location. The conception of aesthetic engagement entangles the subject and the object, for instance, in the rasaesthetics of Bharata-muni's *Natyasastra*, a Sanskrit manual of performance coming out of India (between the 6th century BCE and the 2nd century CE). This mutual attunement of subject and object also abounds in Perso-Arabic theories in the court cultures of the Middle East (Pollock 2016, Schechner 2001, Janer 2022, Puerta-Vilchez 2017). Such conceptions posit a savouring of emotions evoked at the moment of affective engagement with a performance, in contrast to the distant, rational, intellection recommended by the dominant Western tradition of high aesthetics. Bahauddin Dagar, the venerable Indian musician, writes that it is not surprising to hear a Pandit or an Ustad say, "Usey khanna hi theek say nahin ata hai, woh sangeet kaise bajayega" (How will he ever play music; he doesn't even know how to eat well?) (Dagar 2022). That startling claim connecting mundane eating and the making of elevated music underlines how far Western high aesthetic has come from the everyday sensory realm. This kind of philosophy of high aesthetic theory in the West, breaks down "time and again on the question of the body," adds Judith Butler, as "it tends to separate what is called thinking from what is called sensing, from desire, passion, sexuality, and relations of dependency" (2015: 15). In Dagar's conception, eating well is necessary in developing an aesthetic sensibility. Rasa is the savouring of the aesthetic experience, where savouring is not just a metaphor. The relationships between the senses and modalities of perception, and their hierarchies, depend on cultural training in place and time, and what is considered 'good to eat' is equally contingent upon the aesthetic arguments of a particular moment in time.

Aesthetic evaluation

Shifting characteristics of haute cuisine

The sociologist Pierre Bourdieu debunked good taste as just another form of cultural domination by the upper classes in his book *Distinction* (1984). He concentrated on aesthetic judgement – and specifically its class basis – without saying much about the nature or quality of aesthetic attention or the formal nature of the object. In doing so, he reconnected the taste for the most refined objects – art, architecture, music – to the elementary tastes for food flavours.

That dynamic can be illustrated in the way spices used in cooking have flowed in and out of fashion. The term 'spice' itself takes on two distinct meanings depending on use: the aromatics of the East, mostly dried fruits such as pepper, the inner bark of trees such as cinnamon, aromatic flower buds such as clove, seeds such as nutmeg and its aril such as mace; and heat from New World chillies. The spice trade in highly valued commodities from the East is more than two thousand years old across the Indian Ocean and the Mediterranean world. Spices were considered the curative superfoods of their time, essential to rebalancing the 'humours', the historical theory of health in Europe for over a millennia.

In Europe, spices were prestigious because they were expensive since the places they came from were distant from the places they were consumed. For instance, in the early 15th century, the long unruly logistical chain, coupled with elite demand and profiteering, raised the Venetian price of some spices to 100 times that paid in the Moluccas, one of the sources of nutmeg and mace. As long as prices were very high and could be afforded only by the super elites, the commodity retained its prestige.

With increased supply, delivered by various European East India Companies (founded ca. 1600 CE), the European appetite for spices and aromatics peaked, as access to the flavouring agents reached wider strata of society. As supply continued to expand, prices subsequently fell and the status of these commodities was eventually reduced. In *The French Cook* (1651), Francois Pierre de La Varenne called for reduced use of sugar, saffron, and spices to restructure notions of refinement. Nicholas de Bonnefons (ca. 1650s) asserted the new orthodoxy most clearly: "cabbage soup should taste of cabbage, leeks of leeks, turnips of turnips" (Freedman 2008). The rejection of spices and vinegar-based sauces in lieu of more butter-and-cream-based herbed combinations marked the shift within French gastronomy towards a new essentialism at the apex of European haute cuisine. It took generations to normalise the new standard of good taste with decreasing spices and increasing 'naturalness' of the flavour of the thing in itself (Janer 2022: 98). The gourmand, gastronome, and writer Alexandre Balthazar Laurent Grimod de la Reyniere (1758–1837) solidified the new standard of using local herbs over exotic Oriental spices. The exit of spices from European haute cuisine was interpreted as a good thing by ideologues of a new aesthetic, such as chefs, gourmands, restaurant critics, and food writers in modern Europe (Mennell 1996).

European haute cuisine was born with the rise of the West, exactly when other parts of the world were out-stripped by Euro-American powers in terms of military and capital accumulation. This transformation moved the taste of elite Europeans away from those of the upper classes in Arab, Persian, and South Asian courts, who would continue to prefer complex aromatic and sweet-and-sour culinary constructions. This also coincided with a newly directed disgust at eating directly with the hands, a method that everyone in Europe had practised until late into the 18th century.

Historian Ken Albala writes that if you put an urban European woman from ca. 1500 CE with another from ca. 1800 CE at the dinner table they would be unable to comprehend each other's taste in food, style of eating, and format of the meal, although they would be recognisable to each other in terms of attire and comportment: "One would reach with her hand for a gobbet of meat, the other gesturing toward the knife and fork. One would look around for the bowl of sauce, something spicy, sour and thickened with bread crumbs, the other would expect it on her plate, rich with butter, stock and garnished with something elegant like truffle slices. They would never agree when to eat or what order the food should appear" (2003: 245).

In the East, distinction was not in the use of spices, per se, but in the selection of more expensive ones – saffron as opposed to the cheaper turmeric to lend a vibrant colour – and labour-intensive techniques, such as rice dishes jewelled with pomegranate seeds, stuffed and layered breads, hand-squeezed sherbets, and finely ground koftas and kebabs as found, for instance, in the *Ni'matnāma* of the Sultans of Mandu (in India), and *Kār-nāme (The Manual)* compiled by Hāji Mohammad Ali Bāvarči Baqdādi (in Persia), in the 16th century. The layered aromatic constructions of these court cuisines, where camphor, ambergris, cardamom, and clove ruled, would filter down the societal stratum to create versions of perfumed biryanis, pilafs, kebabs, and stews that would eventually find homes in restaurants everywhere, including migrant enclaves in 20th century Euro-American worlds. But by then, 'spiciness' would be seen by Euro-American commentators as a metonym for the food of poor migrants – as "ethnic food," not haute cuisine – in the wake of mass migration from the Mediterranean and Ottoman periphery, followed by Asia and Latin America, the very sources of spices and chillies: "The decline was gradual, but inexorable and finally quite extreme. What took place was a seismic shift in taste. The wealthy people of Europe no longer liked fiery and perfumed food. To this day Italian,

Spanish, and French foods still use almost no spices" (Freedman 2008: 222). Even Sicilians would be scorned for their garlicky food, said to increase cravings for alcohol. Olive oil was dismissed as greasy and spicy deep into the 20th century until the upward mobility of Italians in the capitalist world economy. Eventually other peoples' foods would be dragged into this structure of Western elite disdain that would include spiced and stewed foods that did not segregate cereals, legumes, vegetables, roots, and animal proteins, which is also the food of their own poor and domestic female cookery. Increasingly, spices came to be associated with strong and irritating pungency, not very subtle or sophisticated.

Hierarchies of taste in the 20th and 21st centuries

As Asian countries such as Japan, South Korea, Taiwan, and China have become the new centres of capital accumulation since the last quarter of the 20th century, their cuisines have acquired new visibility and prestige in global cities such as New York, Los Angeles, London, Frankfurt, Paris, Shanghai, Seoul, Taipei, and Tokyo. Some of the most expensive Michelin-starred restaurants in these cities often bring together ingredients, idioms, techniques, shape of dishware, terminology, and alcoholic drinks from these parts of the world.

In the 21st century, as changes move faster, spurred by networks of information and exchange across social media platforms, especially Instagram, the evaluative criteria of old fashioned Western haute cuisine is increasingly suspect. Nevertheless almost all of these new Michelin-consecrated Asian haute cuisine restaurants serve substantial servings of endangered fish and ecologically unsustainable large animal proteins. The climate emergency is in part perpetrated by those diets over the last two centuries, which are beginning to be challenged. The intrusion of aesthetic notions of immigrant consumers, entrepreneurs, and their upwardly mobile populations are altering the acceptable standards of good taste. These new idioms are often centered on street foods such as kebabs, pani puri, and pho.

The future of food and aesthetics: food as art

The consensus at one point that food could not be art had fallen apart by the late-20th century even among Western cultural elites, which is illustrated here by three examples. Rikrit Thiravanija, the conceptual artist, cooked and served pad thai at the opening of his exhibition at New York's Paula Allen Gallery (1990) posing the questions: what is art and can it be an interactional experience, such as cooking and serving food? "I have, more or less, used the kitchen and cooking as the base from which to conduct an assault on the cultural aesthetics of Western attitudes toward life and living," Thiravanija says. "In the communal act of cooking and eating together, I hope that it is possible to cross physical and imaginary boundaries" between life and art.

Even more dramatically, Cara Walker (2014) exhibited what she characterised as a *subtlety*, a term for a sugar-based dessert, at an old Domino Sugar Factory in Brooklyn, NYC, from May to July 2014. It was a monumental white mammy-sphinx with archetypical Black features that both paid homage to the glories of Egyptian civilization, and forcefully critiqued the institutional foundation of modern sweetness, built on the stolen labour of enslaved Africans who produced, processed, and represented its new power and reach. Food, especially in the form of cooking, baking, and confectionery, is connected here to the idiom of early modern European labour as ice sculptures and subtleties (Korsmeyer 1999).

A final example of the return of food-centered aesthetics in contemporary art is Paul Ramirez Jonas' *Eternal Flame* (2020). In its simplest iteration it is a stylised barbeque grill with five cooking spaces arrayed around a 11 x 11 x 20 feet (approx. 3.4 x 3.4 x 6m) high chimney stack in Socrates Sculpture Park, Queens This installation, with its openings and spaces, is analogous to so many mouths, where food is taken in and language comes out. These two forms of orality are what make the private act of eating into something social. There is the language of words and of gestures embodied from long practice. On the tongue it is an accent, the memory of another language, and in the limbs it is the memory of kneading dough, churning butter, flipping burgers, skewering kebabs, making tamales. Communities remember by cooking, most often without books or writing things down. Until TV and new forms of social media such as Instagram and TikTok emerged, the art of cooking was contained in people's bodies in ways that could not be accessed over long distances and gaps in time. Cookbooks only approximated the action. Televisuality allowed cooking to be born as a public image. Now we can see and hear it. The age of social media is the age of consciousness of the unconscious. What lay hidden in the inarticulate language of our limbs has been exposed to light and can be shared. That is how societies remember: by doing and by talking, by sharing and by learning, by watching and smelling and tasting.

The taming of fire gestures towards transformative moments in human history. On a very large scale, fire was a tool to regulate landscapes of hunting and gathering, and on a much smaller scale it marked important transitions in human social organisation of the household and the group. Fire makes hunting and gathering more efficient. Fire at the hearth enables humans to access more nutrients from their food, and soften it enough to make our small mouths adequate for the calories we need for our brains, reshaping the human physique by the diminution of jaws and gut. It is probably the most important tool we have sought to master without getting burnt by it.

The hearth can be a place of care but it can also invite discordant notes as people gather and quarrel with each other. Stereotypes of what others eat and smell like abound in every culture. The hearth is also a reminder of the gender and class inequalities in cooking that expose millions of women and children to chronic respiratory illness due to indoor pollutants. Smoke that filled our nostrils for days after cooking, and infused our clothing, was a reminder that some people pay the price of our cultures and carry the burden of that responsibility unfairly.

The *Eternal Flame* is a new kind of monument that eschews monumentalism. It is a performance space that brings a memorial down to human size by inviting people to cook – that most quotidian, most humble, of life-sustaining activities. It inverts the usual injunction of an aesthetically important space such as a museum, a library, or a performance theatre, where no food or drinks may have been allowed previously.

References

Bourdieu, Pierre. 2010 [1984]. *Distinction*. New York: Routledge.

Butler, Judith. 2015. *Senses of the Subject*. New York: Fordham University Press.

Dagar, Bahauddin. 2022. 'The Dagar Kitchen: Rasaa and Rasm', November 7th, *On Eating. A Multilingual Journal of Food and Eating*, 2, 7, unpaginated.

Freedman, Paul. 2008. *Out of the East: Spices and the Medieval Imagination*. New Haven, CT: Yale University Press.

Janer, Zilkia. 2022. *The Coloniality of Modern Taste: A Critique of Gastronomic Taste*. New York: Routledge.

Korsmeyer, Carolyn. 2017. The Taste Culture Reader. Experiencing Food and Drink. 2nd edition. London: Bloomsbury Academic.

Mennell, Stephen. 1996. *All Manners of Food*. Chicago: University of Illinois Press.

Pollock, Sheldon (ed.). 2016. *A Rasa Reader. Classical Indian Aesthetics*. New York: Columbia University Press.

Puerta-Vilchez, Jose Miguel. 2017. *Aesthetics in Arabic Thought: From Pre-Islamic Arabia through al-Andalusia*. Leiden: Brill.

Ramirez, Paul. 2020. 'Eternal Flame' in *Monuments Now*, Socrates Sculpture Park, pp. 90–111. https://socratessculpturepark .org/artist/paul-ramirez-jonas/.

Thiravanija, Rirkrit. 1990. 'A Lot of People', MoMa PS1, NYC. https://www.momaps1 .org/events/318-rirkrit-tirvanija-s-untitled -1990-pad-thai.

Walker, Cara. 2014. 'A Subtlety or the Marvelous Sugar Baby'. https:// southernspaces.org/2014/kara-walkers -blood-sugar-subtlety-or-marvelous-sugar -baby/.

Further reading

Korsmeyer, Carolyn. 1999. *Making Sense of Taste: Food and Philosophy*. Ithaca, NY: Cornell University Press.

Provides a history of Western theorisations on aesthetics from the 18th century onwards. She shows how cooking lacks the 'right history' to be considered an art form. Instead it has been considered a craft or among the decorative arts.

Schechner, Richard. 2001. 'Rasaesthetics', *The Drama Review* 45, 3 (T171), pp. 27–50.

Illustrates the different drivers of aesthetic judgement in early Indian idioms of singing and dancing, which are quite different from the ways we enjoy, say, a painting in a museum or an opera. Instead of watching quietly, the audience is pulled into the music performance to sing along, respond by moving their heads and hands, in synchronisation with each other, and with the performer, echoing jazz forms of call and response. This is the aesthetics of entanglement.

Albala, Ken. 2003. *Food in Early Modern Europe*. Westport, CT: Greenwood.

Shows how tastes changed in Europe between 1500 and 1800 CE.

Myhrvold, Nathan. 2011. 'The Art in Gastronomy: A Modernist Perspective', *Gastronomica*, 11, 1 (Spring), pp. 13–23.

Microsoft's chief technology officer, Myhrvold articulates a vision of a belated culinary modernism that he finds in the work of chefs Ferran Adria and Heston Blumenthal, as an aesthetically revolutionary moment, analogous to the Impressionist exhibition in 1874.

3. Agriculture 4.0

Laurens Klerkx and David Rose

Introduction

Agriculture 4.0 refers to a host of emerging technologies that are said to radically change, or disrupt, current ways of food production, processing, logistics, consumption, and waste disposal. Currently, Agriculture 4.0 remains quite openly defined, with some mainly talking about digitalisation and automation of current agri-food systems, such as precision technologies, robotics, the Internet of Things, and blockchain, whereas others also refer to radically new ways of producing food (particularly protein), such as cellular agriculture and precision fermentation (Broad and Chiles, 2022). Also, it may encompass broader concepts comprising several technologies, such as vertical agriculture, circular food systems, regenerative agriculture, nature positive agriculture, or protein transitions (Klerkx and Rose, 2020). Whereas some Agriculture 4.0 technologies do not majorly affect the way products are made and how consumers perceive them (e.g. robots picking apples), others may have effects on the way consumers perceive food (e.g., cellular meat). Agriculture 4.0 technologies are in different stages of maturity and application and are subject to 'hype cycles', and may thus have periods of heavy attention and unbounded investment and subsequent stages of realism and adjustment of expectations (Klerkx and Rose, 2020).

Agriculture 4.0 is seen as a way to make agriculture and food systems more resource efficient, reduce physical workload and labour requirements, attract a younger, differently skilled workforce, increase circularity, and enable interconnected food, fibre, and energy systems for multiple purposes (Klerkx and Rose, 2020). Despite the grand promises as regards the potential of Agriculture 4.0 to support food systems transformation, some scholars see Agriculture 4.0 as a form of extreme techno-optimism and techno-utopianism (Stock and Gardezi, 2021). There is scepticism as to whether it will help transform food systems or rather reproduce and consolidate current ways of production and concentration of power (Fairbairn et al., 2022), and negatively affect farmer, worker, consumer, and animal autonomy, and farmer and rural identity at large. Others do see this as a possibility, but then go beyond mere technological optimism and point to the need to consider issues of food systems justice, equity, and power distribution, as well as environmental impacts of novel technologies, which would lead to 'Agriculture 5.0' (Fraser and Campbell, 2019).

Current issues

Since Agriculture 4.0 is rarely about a single technology, but about connected technologies (e.g. using Artificial Intelligence to perfect the taste and texture of alternative proteins, or satellite monitoring of sustainability indicators connected to blockchain traceability schemes), these technologies constantly co-evolve. Moreover, they influence resource and energy flows in agriculture and food systems (Rijswijk et al., 2021), and change elements such as raw material production, energy use, and waste streams. Hence, there are likely to be cumulative and cascading effects of Agriculture 4.0 on (agro)ecosystems, alongside effects on social systems, such as labour arrangements, human expertise, and autonomy, as well as food cultures (Rijswijk et al., 2021). One aspect of the impacts on social systems relates to ethical concerns and specifically effects on privacy. In the case of digitalisation, for example, fears are raised that this will lead to 'surveillance agriculture', unfairness in data ownership (technology makers gather data but those that contribute data have no access to it), and increasing power concentration and dependency relationships (Stock and Gardezi, 2021). In the case of cellular meat, fears relate to issues such as affordability, food safety, place-based community economic development, and labour equity (Broad and Chiles, 2022). There may be disruptive effects on current systems which may lead to 'winners' and 'losers' as regards new forms of production (e.g., in the case of cellular and plant-based meat and dairy, they could replace or displace current systems) (Burton, 2019). Technologies to produce protein alternatives are at variegated stages of development, which points to a wider trend in that the pace and scale of Agriculture 4.0 should not be expected to be rapid and uniform everywhere; innovation in agriculture tends to be slow and influenced by socio-political-economic factors, such as skills, investment, inequality, infrastructure, and trust. Agriculture 4.0, therefore, may represent a period of continual evolution in farming, rather than the story of rapid revolution told by techno-utopi-anists (Rose et al, 2023).

Future questions

To anticipate potential risks of singular areas under Agriculture 4.0 (such as automation) and address these in an inclusive way with diverse stakeholders, rights holders, and knowledge holders, approaches such as responsible innovation are important (Klerkx and Rose, 2020). This requires scrutiny of the effects of Agriculture 4.0 on food systems, through analysis which helps unravel the complex rela-tionships that change due to the introduction of Agriculture 4.0 (Rijswijk et al., 2021). Such analysis also needs to comprise how multi-sector innovation systems are formed due to technological convergences in Agriculture 4.0, the role of start-up ecosystems, and how Agriculture 4.0 contributes to larger change narratives and transition pathways following different concepts, such as protein transitions, agroecology and regenerative agriculture, and urban and vertical agriculture, amongst oth-ers (Klerkx and Rose, 2020).

References

Broad, G.M., Chiles, R.M. (2022). Thick and thin food justice approaches in the evaluation of cellular agriculture. *Nature Food* 3, 795–797.

Burton, R.J.F. (2019). The potential impact of synthetic animal protein on livestock production: The new "war against agriculture"? *Journal of Rural Studies* 68, 33–45.

Fairbairn, M., Kish, Z., Guthman, J. (2022). Pitching agri-food tech: Performativity and non-disruptive disruption in Silicon Valley. *Journal of Cultural Economy*, 15 (5), 652–670.

Fraser, E.D.G., Campbell, M. (2019). Agriculture 5.0: Reconciling production with planetary health. *One Earth* 1, 278–280.

Klerkx, L., Rose, D. (2020). Dealing with the game-changing technologies of Agriculture 4.0: How do we manage diversity and responsibility in food system transition pathways? *Global Food Security* 24, 100347.

Rijswijk, K., Klerkx, L., Bacco, M., Bartolini, F., Bulten, E., Debruyne, L., Dessein, J., Scotti, I., Brunori, G. (2021). Digital transformation of agriculture and rural areas: A socio-cyber-physical system framework to support responsibilisation. *Journal of Rural Studies* 85, 79–90.

Rose, D., Barkemeyer, A., de Boon, A., Price, C., Roche, D. (2023) The old, the new, or the old made new? Everyday counternarratives of the so-called fourth agricultural revolution. *Agriculture and Human Values* 40, 423–439.

Stock, R., Gardezi, M. (2021). Make bloom and let wither: Biopolitics of precision agriculture at the dawn of surveillance capitalism. *Geoforum* 122, 193–203.

Further reading

da Silveira, F., Lermen, F.H., Amaral, F.G. (2021). An overview of agriculture 4.0 development: Systematic review of descriptions, technologies, barriers, advantages, and disadvantages. *Computers and Electronics in Agriculture* 189, 106405. Gives a detailed overview of how the literature on Agriculture 4.0 has developed in recent years.

4. Agroecology

COLIN R. ANDERSON, CLAIRE
LAMINE AND MARTHA CASWELL

Introduction

While agroecology as a term has been around
for almost 100 years, over the last 20 years
it has gained international recognition and
uptake in science, policy, and practice. It is
increasingly recognised for its potential to
address multiple crises in the food system,
including climate breakdown, biodiversity
loss, deteriorating rural livelihoods, food and
nutrition insecurity, environmental degradation, and inequity (HLPE, 2019). Agroecology
is defined as the application of ecological and
social principles to the design and functioning of agriculture and food systems. It is
differentiated from other related concepts
(e.g., sustainable agriculture, climate smart
agriculture, nature-based solutions, organic
agriculture) through its uncompromising
commitment to each of the ecological, social,
political, and cultural dimensions of sustainability. It directly addresses power imbalances
and centrs the agency, voice, and knowledge
of local communities, peasant farmers, and
Indigenous Peoples.

Early academic thinking on agroecology
emerged out of the careful study of socio-ecological principles of production as observed
in the practices and lives of Indigenous and
peasant communities of Africa, the Americas,
Asia, Australia, Europe, and Polynesia.
Although these groups did not use the term
agroecology, their practices are reflected in
the principles of what is now called agroecology. Thus, agroecology does not have a single
centre of origin. Instead, it is held in a deep
reservoir of practice, cultures, and knowledges that are rooted within regions across
the world where peoples, nature, and food
systems have co-evolved together interritorial
relationships.

Agroecology is grounded in a rich, transdisciplinary body of knowledge that aims
to better understand food and farming systems rooted in agroecological principles.
Early research documented the practices
of Indigenous foodways and peasant farming systems to understand the principles and
approaches that underpin their resilience
and sustainability. From these observations,
agroecology grew into a science of designing
farming systems that mimic the biodiversity,
structure and functioning of natural ecosystems. Agroecology was later broadened to
include the 'ecology of food systems', thus
emphasising the embeddedness of farming in
wider social-ecological relations.

More recently, the political dimensions
of agroecology have been articulated and
emboldened by social movements, such as
La Via Campesina, and by scholars who have
deployed theoretical approaches from critical
agrarian studies, political ecology, and social
movement studies. This approach concep-
tualises agroecology as a contested terrain
of struggle for power, control, and resources
linked with the struggle for food sovereignty.
Here, agroecology is viewed as the confluence
of a political and technical project, that aligns
with social movements working for people's
collective rights, self-determination, agency,
and emancipation from intersecting systems
of oppression. In the following sections, we
review several of the defining dimensions of
agroecology followed by an overview of several key areas of tension that will shape the
future of agroecology.

Agroecology today

Agroecology's transgressive foundation

In its most holistic and deepest expression,
agroecology is fundamentally transgressive
of the project of modernity and the trappings
of linear Western notions of development
that characterise most approaches to agricultural development. Agroecology calls for
a reterritorialisation and repeasantisation of
small-scale agriculture and food systems, and
autonomy from monopolistic agribusinesses
and other forms of external control. Through
this reorganising of social relations with land
and in territory, agroecology reconfigures
political ecological relations in ways that
subvert the extractive logics of capitalism.
Through the redesign of agricultural systems
in harmony with natural processes, circular
economies, and worldviews that position people as part of nature (rather than outside of
it), agroecology represents a process of repair
with the potential to heal the metabolic rift
between society and nature.

The agroecological approach transcends
other frameworks (e.g., sustainable agriculture) because it is viewed as incompatible and
in confrontation with existing world-systems
and food regimes. To this end, agroecology is
utopian in its imagination, but pragmatic in

its application. It calls for the pursuit of 'real utopias' (Wright 2020) within a wider system that is hostile to alternatives. By revaluing reproductive labour and valorising the knowledge of women, youth, and other marginalised peoples, and centring the goals of well-being, the good life, radical collectivism, and social justice, new futures are made possible. In this way, agroecology challenges the dominant development goals of increased productivity, profit, and technological modernisation as well as the neoclassical economic construct of individuals as purely self-interested actors. Agroecology challenges neoliberalism, racial capitalism, coloniality, patriarchy, caste, and other systems of power that prevent the realisation of thriving food systems and the good life for all. It affirms the development of pluriversal strategiesthat emerge through collective processes rooted in the cosmologies and particularities that emerge in place. Agroecology rejects the cherry-picking of technical fixes, or single dimension solutions (e.g., focusing only on ecological considerations), and instead looks for entry points to meet people wherever they are in the process of transition, facilitated by iterative learning, mutual support, and collective action (Anderson et al., 2021).

Knowledge and knowledge networks

Agroecology is sustained through knowledge networks and methods that relate to and enhance the specificities of local socio-ecological contexts. It reaffirms bottom-up approaches to knowledge co-production and valorises farmers' knowledge and expertise. The importance attached to situated and contextualised knowledge raises a key question: how can such knowledge circulate beyond the context in which it has been produced? There are multiple answers to this, including the importance of sharing and iterating through networks such as *campesino a campesino* (farmer to farmer) approaches that allow knowledge exchange among farmers, participatory action research, collective on-farm experimentation, and larger transdisciplinary approaches involving other actors. These knowledge processes have varying degrees of formalisation, and generally involve the collective identification of concerns by farmers and possibly other agrifood systems actors and workers, who develop them into problems to be addressed through the co-creation of knowledge.

Agroecology represents a shift from the "monoculture of scientific understanding" to an "ecology of knowledge" (de Sousa Santos, 2009) in which diverse forms of knowledge and ways of knowing exist and interact. Within agroecology, the roles of professionals and institutions shift away from patterns of extracting knowledge and then extending it to knowledge users, and towards cycles of facilitating knowledge co-creation with farmers and agrifood systems actors and workers. These knowledge systems, which are lighter, decentralised, and flexible at the local level, avoid the threat to autonomy that arises from centralised information and knowledge systems. Under these networked models the goal is to find the most appropriate responses within particular contexts, thus reinforcing the power of diversity and seeding healthy scepticism about solutions that are touted as a fit for all.

Re-scaling food systems and the territorial approach

Agroecology involves a re-scaling of food systems away from the prevailing emphasis on the integration of agriculture into global markets and supply chains and the deterritorialisation of peasant farmers. Regional, territorial, and local approaches have been developed through ideas such as bioregionalism or territorial ecology and concrete forms such as bioregions, ecoregions, or biodistricts. The territorial approach focuses on reconfiguring actors, networks, and rules to proactively influence agrifood systems in territories. Diverse food systems actors assess and reflect together on past trajectories, to develop shared visions and to chart transition pathways.

Working at the territorial scale reveals the interplay between ecological and social processes, highlighting concrete opportunities to align situated biophysical features with technical, organisational, market, and social forms of innovation. Such integration supports the reconnection of agriculture, food, environment, and health (Anderson et al., 2021). The territorial perspective facilitates the identification and involvement of diverse actors representing different components of agrifood systems (farmers, agrifood chain actors, public institutions, civil society, etc.), in addition to exposing competing visions and interests, which can risk the cooptation of agroecology's transformative potential, as discussed in the last section.

The territorial scale is socially constructed and may be analytically tackled according to a range of circumstances and context-specific factors, including geo-physical and environmental conditions, political and administrative structures, and cultural identities. The territory is a spatial unit in which policy and governance activities are delivered and can be a key nexus for transversality integrating agricultural, food, health, and social policies. This need for reterritorialisation has been institutionally recognised both at the international level (OECD, FAO) and at national levels, with some devoted policies such as the 'territorial food project scheme' set up in France in 2014, or municipal agroecological policies in Brazil and other countries.

While agroecology has gained much ground as a transformative approach towards more just and sustainable food systems, the future of agroecology remains contested as it is continually remade and potentially coopted by a diversity of actors and processes. The next section provides critical insights into future pathways for agroecology.

Agroecology tomorrow

Agroecology and technology

The role of technology in agroecology has been a contentious issue and a point of ongoing debate. On the one hand, appropriate technologies have a vital role to play in the deepening and expansion of agroecology. On the other hand, novel technology has been a powerful and privileged driver of injustices that arise from industrial agricultural development. From the green revolution to contemporary times, the dominant trend has been the imposition of Western agricultural technologies to raise productivity. Early distribution of technological packages focusing on hybrid seeds, fertilisers, and chemical pesticides displaced agroecological farming systems, shifted entire regions towards monocultural export-oriented farming and displaced people-natures in the Global South through processes of depeasantisation and the capitalist reorganisation of agrarian relations. Today, this technology-driven approach is further entrenched in the drive for a new green revolution in Africa, and the 4th Industrial Revolution, including through the advancement of disruptive technologies such as automation, big data, and gene editing.

Agroecology is not anti-technology, yet the values and principles of agroecology demand a critical questioning of technologies and their long-term impact on the agency and autonomy of farmers and their communities, and the health of land and nature. This implies a need for precautionary principles and participatory technological assessments that interrogate issues of power, control, and the long-term implications of technologies on the functioning of landscapes and the structure of societies. This critical examination of technology is especially important when technology is being proposed as a magic-bullet solution in crisis narratives. These quick-fix solutions allegedly solve immediate problems, yet longer-term implications of the technologies are unknown or disregarded. Further work is needed to examine what kinds of technology should be refused and which are appropriate within an agroecological approach, and how they can be wisely developed, adopted, disseminated, and governed. Critical discussions on the potential for complementarity between technologies (e.g., gene editing) and agroecology are calling for deeper analysis within the framework of technology sovereignty to understand the necessary conditions and processes to ensure technologies are aligned with agroecology (Montenegro de Wit, 2022).

Agroecological resilience in a crisis-laden present and future

As the spectre of climate collapse, political instability, and other intersecting vulnerabilities grows, diverse agroecological food systems have shown the potential to be highly resilient and relevant in a turbulent future. Recent shocks, including pandemics, floods, coups, and war, have revealed serious hazards associated with the high-input globally complex systems of agriculture and food systems. In the face of rapid and accelerating environmental degradation, agroecological approaches encourage the maintenance and/or restoration of crop varieties that are acclimatised to specific contexts, with an emphasis on biodiversity, functional redundancy, and the minimal use of external inputs. Increased levels of autonomy and lower levels of dependence on state support and industrial supply chains have contributed to impressive levels of resilience within agroecological systems after

COLIN R. ANDERSON, CLAIRE LAMINE AND MARTHA CASWELL

extreme weather events and in relation to the ongoing effects of climate change, such as in the wake of Hurricane Maria in Puerto Rico (e.g., McCune et al., 2019). Agroecological systems also demonstrate strength in response to political and economic instability, due in large part to social and cultural mechanisms intrinsic to the approach, including intentionally networked relationships, shorter supply chains, and a high value placed on collective work. Working from the ground up, using diversified and distributed approaches, agroecology offers a context-specific nimbleness that is designed for both resilience and sovereignty.

Just transitions – centring equity

As agroecology has grown and matured as a concept, nascent work to interpret agroecology through the lens of equity has led to important connections between agroecology and wider movements of people struggling for 'just transitions' (i.e., centring the dismantling of inequity and oppression in efforts to transition towards sustainable economies). In these spaces, the notion of intersectionality provides a prism through which to parse the entangled influences of patriarchy, racism, ableism, caste-ism, classism and other intersecting axes of injustice in our food systems. Connecting with fields such as decoloniality, solidarity economies, feminism, degrowth (see entries 29 and 30, this volume) and post-development alternatives, agroecology provides prefigurative influences that confront the status quo. By reimagining what is possible, agroecology offers a path away from consolidation and abuses of power and towards reciprocal and regenerative futures. A more transgressive and self-critical agroecology is being deepened by: (a) social movements, including La Via Campesina, the largest alliance of farmers, peasants, and rural workers in the world, which has argued that without feminism there is no agroecology; (b) critiquing the caste system in agroecological projects; and (c) and pursuing land reform towards the return and redistribution of previously colonised lands. Linking agroecology to these wider struggles can help to avoid the 'development mindset' often found in articulations of agroecology that emanate from institutions, NGOs, politicians, and researchers, while also forging solidarities that are needed to build momentum in transformative processes for a more just and sustainable world.

The future – centring transformation, resisting cooptation

As agroecology gains legitimacy and is taken up by different actors, there is a risk of its cooptation and depoliticisation. The contestation over the meaning of agroecology has given rise to efforts to strategically centre the emancipatory, transgressive, and transformative basis of the agroecological project. Indeed, there is no consensus around a single definition of agroecology, and there are different ideologies, framings, ontologies, and interpretations of agroecology from distinctive camps and positions. In this sense, there is a battle over the meaning of agroecology, rooted in both different diagnoses of problems and diverging theories of how to affect change. These debates revolve around questions of who the protagonists of the agroecological transition should be, and how different actors with uneven relations of power and privilege can and should be involved in advancing agroecology. These multiple positions reveal differences in the proposed pace and scope of necessary change (incremental versus transformative), the intersection with issues of power (technical versus emancipatory), and the most desirable sites of intervention (movement, institutional, etc.). For example, should the voice of scientists and policy-makers lead, or should peasant farmers and their organisations be at the helm? Is agroecology a process of development (from a liberal modern perspective) or autonomous emancipation (from a more radical post-development perspective)? Should agroecology work on reforming existing systems, institutions, and regimes, or are these very systems the root of the problems, whereby investing faith and power in them would undermine transformation? Attempts to reflexively assess the extent to which 'agroecological approaches' align with the transformative perspective requires both a critical eye and a commitment to multiple ways of knowing that avoids the traps of duality. They also require a constant analysis of power, participation, and agency, which is why explicit links to food sovereignty, the right to food, rights of nature, degrowth, and other related struggles are so important. The land-based experience of agroecology that has emerged from peasant farmers and

Indigenous stewards of the land across the globe is steeped in self-determination and connection to place. These innate understandings of agroecology need to be accompanied by political work to mobilise knowledge and build legitimacy for a fully transformative agroecology.

Acknowledgements

This work was achieved by the three co-authors in the frame of the Agroecological Transitions for TERritorial food systems (ATTER) project, funded by the European Union's Horizon 2020 research and innovation programme under the Marie Skłodowska-Curie grant agreement No 101007755.

References

Anderson, C R, Bruil, J, Chappell, M J, Kiss, C, & Pimbert, M P (2021) *Agroecology Now! Transformations Towards More Just and Sustainable Food Systems*. Cham, Palgrave MacMillan.

de Sousa Santos, B (2009) A non-occidentalist west? Learned ignorance and ecology of knowledge. *Theory, Culture & Society*, 26(7–8), 103–125 https://doi.org/10.1177/0263276409348079.

HLPE (2019) *Agroecological and other innovative approaches for sustainable agriculture and food systems that enhance food security and nutrition*. CFS High Level Panel of Experts. Rome, FAO.

McCune, N, Perfecto, I, Avilés-Vázquez, K, Vázquez-Negrón, J, & Vandermeer, J (2019) Peasant balances and agroecological scaling in Puerto Rican coffee farming. *Agroecology and Sustainable Food Systems*, 43(7–8), 810–826 https://doi.org/10.1080/21683565.2019.1608348.

Montenegro de Wit, M (2022) Can agroecology and CRISPR mix? The politics of complementarity and moving toward technology sovereignty. *Agriculture and Human Values, 39*(2), 733–755 https://doi.org/10.1007/s10460-021-10284-0.

Trevilla Espinal, D L, Soto Pinto, M L, Morales, H, and Estrada-Lugo, E I J (2021) Feminist agroecology: analyzing power relationships in food systems. *Agroecology and Sustainable Food Systems, 45*(7), 1029–1049 https://doi.org/10.1080/21683565.2021.1888842

Wright, E O (2020) *Envisioning real utopias*. Verso Books.

Further reading

Declaration of the International Forum for Agroecology (2015). Nyéléni, Mali: 27 February 2015. *Development* 58, 163–168 https://doi.org/10.1057/s41301-016-0014-4.

This declaration is the outcome of the gathering of social movements from around the world and provides an articulation of agroecology from a movement perspective.

IPES-Food (2016). From uniformity to diversity: a paradigm shift from industrial agriculture to diversified agroecological systems. International Panel of Experts on Sustainable Food Systems (IPES). https://ipes-food.org/report/from-uniformity-to-diversity/

This seminal report provides an accessible, visual, and thorough overview of the rationale for shifting away from industrial food systems towards agroecology.

COLIN R. ANDERSON, CLAIRE LAMINE AND MARTHA CASWELL

5. Alternative food networks (AFNs)

DENISE MISLEH

Introduction: the socio-political significance of AFNs

The way food is currently produced, distributed, and consumed is becoming increasingly unsustainable. The conventional food system – resting on principles of modernisation, standardisation, and industrialisation – is exhausted as a paradigm. Intensive food systems are questioned in terms of their contribution to greenhouse gas emissions causing the climate emergency, alongside the recognition of natural losses in habitats and biodiversity. At the same time, conventional food production is becoming inefficient, as it produces an enormous amount of food waste, while hunger and food poverty persist. It has failed to respond to the demands of broad segments of the population in terms of quality, safety, and sustainability.

The costs of conventional farming are being borne by society at large. While some actors try to solve these problems by intensifying the agro-industrial paradigm of food production, other more emergent forms of producing and distributing food have been proliferating. These initiatives, which seek to build more sustainable, territorially embedded, quality-oriented alternatives, are brought together under the umbrella term of 'alternative food networks' (AFNs). AFNs are inherently diverse. However, what holds AFN initiatives together is that they engage in different modes of exchange: distributing food outside the conventional chains controlled by supermarkets, employing direct marketing schemes, and/or shortening chains, such as through farmers' markets, box schemes, and community-supported agriculture.

The literature has traditionally identified two main trajectories and models, namely Western European and North American models (Dupuis et al., 2006). The first developed as a rural development tool, especially for those areas and producers that were struggling to remain competitive in the global food market; while the second emerged in connection with civic rights and organic social movements. Hence, the latter constituted a more radical variant of AFNs compared with the European version which focused more on the economic viability of farms. This distinction has been helpful for mapping the historical trajectories of AFNs. Nowadays, however, alternative food initiatives have proliferated across these geographical boundaries and have engaged in different business models and forms of social organisation, motivated by an array of values, and acquiring a socio-political significance that no longer fits these two models.

In Europe, for example, AFNs currently address issues related to food poverty or enacting more egalitarian food democracies. Newer expressions include civic food networks, city food charters, and solidarity purchasing groups. Moreover, local food and short food chains (SFCs) have acquired renewed relevance due to the coronavirus pandemic, which put severe pressure on global food chains. This has brought new impetus to the transformation of the food system in which local food networks emerge as a more resilient alternative.

AFNs are considered a strategic component of sustainable transitions that aim to build food systems based on principles of sufficiency, regeneration, distribution, commons, and care (McGreevy et al, 2022). While the socio-political significance of AFNs has been widely acknowledged, they have also been criticised for not being able to deliver the progressive goals that they intended, instead following a path of conventionalisation (Guthman, 2004), and for being in essence a neoliberal strategy supporting this political project.

The diversity, empirical complexity, and inherent contradictions of AFNs forces us to ask: 'in what sense are these initiatives alternative?' (Whatmore et al., 2003). Initially, 'alternative' as an analytical concept was built in opposition to the 'conventional', but this was criticised and revisited as it was neither true nor useful for analysing AFNs. With the inadequacy of an oppositional understanding of alterity for analysing the diversity and hybridity of AFNs, the analysis of alterity remains in a 'theoretical impasse' (Misleh, 2022). A deadlock has been created which has tended to inaccurately represent AFNs as either overly celebratory or lacking potential for radical change.

This entry discusses the different sources of alterity identified in academic research by looking at the spatial, economic, and normative dimensions of AFNs. It also points to the persistent challenges in the practice and research of AFNs, concluding by underscoring the analytical value of alterity and indicating directions for further research.

Understanding AFNs' alterity and persistent challenges

The practices of AFNs are dynamic: evolving to address different problems with conventional food production, distribution, and consumption, while seeking to remain viable economic alternatives. Research has also evolved to make sense of the socio-political significance of the variegated and hybrid character of the experiences that make up AFNs, but, despite the prolific academic literature on the subject, challenges to its conceptual definition remain. This section discusses AFNs as an object of study, identifying three interrelated dimensions of AFNs – their spatial, economic, and normative dimensions – which have been employed to conceptualise their transformative potential from different approaches. These dimensions are useful for understanding AFNs' ability to reconfigure chains, redistribute value toward primary producers, and engage with production systems that move beyond a cost-effective rationale.

AFNs originated with a strong spatial component, and ideas of scale and place have been central in constructing alternatives to the conventional food system. Geographical proximity and a clearer link between food and place were articulated as a way of overcoming 'placeless' and 'faceless' conventional food. The first generation of AFNs underscored these characteristics as part of a 'quality turn' in food production (Watts et al., 2005).

The link between food and place was also conceptualised through the notion of embeddedness, which was extended from its original meaning concerning the social embeddedness of economies (Granovetter, 1985) to describe AFNs as *territorially embedded* food networks. Once the research focus shifted from food products to distribution channels, and (more specifically) closer producer–consumer relations, the embeddedness approach was employed to analyse both the social and spatial dimensions. AFNs were characterised by more personal and direct relations in economic transactions. The embeddedness approach was widely employed in the early 2000s, through which AFNs were broadly conceptualised by their potential to re-socialise and re-spatialise food production.

This linkage between the social and spatial dimensions was also employed to develop typologies of SFCs based on social and spatial distance, in which three types were identified: face-to-face, spatially proximate, and spatially extended (Renting et al., 2003). While closer and direct relations between producers and consumers were associated with relations of trust, regard, and reciprocity (Sage, 2003), how this economic diversity was transformative remains unclear.

This stage of academic development placed particular emphasis on the re-localisation of food production and the role of closer relations between producers and consumers, favouring an interpretation of alterity based on relations of proximity. Critiques pointed to the conflation of spatial and social relations, uncritically taking localised social relations as a more positive form of economic exchange (Hinrichs, 2000). Born and Purcell (2006) described a 'local trap', which conflated the goals of alternative food initiatives with re-localisation as a strategy for achieving those goals. However, the notion of embeddedness has been further problematised, bringing nuances and contingency to the concept. For example, Zhong et al. (2022) identify different forms of fragmentary embeddedness, showing that AFNs might be embedded in one way but not in others. For instance, AFNs' actors engage in territorially embedded practices while they might be at odds with traditional local relations of farmers and residents; hence failing to be embedded in the locality.

The cultural politics of food localism have pointed to the exclusionary character of AFNs. However, the exclusionary politics of AFNs extend beyond notions of localism, also addressing their class and racial components. AFNs have been criticised for reproducing inequalities by orienting their businesses towards more affluent consumers. Slocum (2007) argues that AFNs contribute to 'white spaces', not despite their progressive politics, but as an intrinsic part of them.

At this stage, other characteristics of AFNs, such as the economic strategies beyond producer–consumer relations, were left unexplored. In broad terms, the economic dimension of AFNs addresses the strategies for capturing and adding value to food products. AFNs have been described as able to redistribute value to primary producers. The transformative potential of upward value distribution needs to be situated in the context of a neoliberal food system dominated by a handful of powerful retailers, in which this reconfiguration is considered a countermovement to conventional retail-led supply chains. The market concentration and the buying power of supermarkets have been used to extract value from upstream suppliers while primary producers who engage in less-intensive farming systems are struggling to remain competitive.

AFNs' economic strategies aim to capture value through direct selling and shorter chains which allow intermediaries to be cut out, and generally disengaging from conventional retailers that extract value. AFNs have also sought to add value to their products through the valorisation of specific attributes such as local resources, localities, and organic and even 'beyond organic' methods of production. Watts et al. (2005) distinguish between those alternative *products* belonging to the 'quality turn', and those constructing alternative *networks*. The former is considered weaker as they are more easily subject to co-optation as part of retailers' own quality turn.

A major line of criticism has come from the role that markets and voluntary labels, as a marketing strategy, play in AFNs. Alternative food strategies have been turning to the market to integrate social and environmental practices to their price formation, reflecting the 'real costs' of food (Buller and Morris, 2004). In this sense, the market has played an important role in AFNs – creating niche, ethical, or more-coordinated markets. Optimistic accounts consider this in embracing a new value system in market relations (Barham, 2002). However, sceptical scholars have interpreted AFNs' economic strategies as based on commodification and consumer choices (Guthman, 2007).

Regarding the practice of AFNs, market mechanisms also make them more vulnerable to dynamics of co-optation and 'conventionalisation'. AFNs have been described as hybrid as they employ the same distribution channels and selling outlets, or because they engage in similar production practices, 'dipping in and out' of conventional chains (Ilbery and Maye, 2005). Moreover, AFNs' products have been imitated and co-opted by major food retailers, who have identified an opportunity for profit and who are in a prime position to respond to these newer trends in food consumption.

The normative dimension of AFNs concerns the motives and goals of people engaging in AFNs. The presence of values is central in conceptualising alterity, allowing the analysis of economic practices that transcend a profit-maximisation rationale as the dominant economic logic. The recognition that the practices of AFNs are more complex and diverse than initially thought moved the research agenda to address AFNs' heterogeneity. Through engagement with diverse economies and alternative economies literature, especially Gibson-Graham's work (2006), the role of values has received more attention than previously. Inscribed in post-structuralist approaches, AFNs were described as constituted by an array of relationships, rationales, and social values (Sarmiento, 2017).

In this vein, AFNs are not only shorter or more direct, but they are also value-based, establishing more cooperative chains that create fairer and more symmetrical economic relations. While direct selling remains a relevant characteristics of AFNs' economic strategies, more heterogenous arrangements, socially and materially, have emerged for overcoming direct selling limitations, for example by aggregating and diversifying their supply. For this, different forms of partnerships emerge between producers selling collectively, producers and specialised retailers agreeing prices and quantities even before the season starts, and producer and consumer partnerships in community-supported agriculture, online platforms, and some box-schemes, in which consumers commit to advanced purchases or give up consumer choice to reduce the costs and risks of local food. These forms of coordination aim to ease competition, which is central to developing farming practices that are not structured to reduce production costs or engage in economies of scale.

The diverse economies project motivated agri-food researchers to account for community and diverse economies and the politics of possibility. These approaches underscored actors' motivations, and ethical and social values, and their role in informing alternative economic practices. Alterity is conceptualised normatively as the potential to create a more progressive outcome in terms of community development, environmental sustainability, and social justice.

DENISE MISLEH

The value of 'alternative' for future research

This section highlights the value of 'alternative' as a relational approach in future research. The underlying idea is that the broad range of experiences under the umbrella of AFNs developed in an ongoing struggle with the hegemonic food system. The relationality implicit in AFNs requires that conceptual approaches highlight the processual and contingent nature of these experiences. Currently, AFN research is better suited to distinguishing, creating nuances, and providing more clarity concerning the ways AFNs challenge dominant food practices, rather than assuming or discarding its transformative potential. In this vein, three lines of future research are identified: (i) the multiple manifestations and differential transformative potential of AFNs, (ii) the broader context in which AFNs develop, including the role of public policy in the advancement and retrenchment of alternative food initiatives, and (iii) situating AFNs as a process of social change.

Future research should address the multiple manifestations of AFNs across places and scales, including their hybridity and contradictory characteristics. This does not entail just registering or praising economic diversity – rather, hybridity needs to be interrogated in relation to the possibilities for alternatives to enact social change. In this vein, research should aim to explain the differential transformative potential of AFNs, because some of these initiatives might offer radical change, mild reform, or nothing alternative at all, as they might aim only to survive in the context of neoliberalism. This also entails avoiding ideal types of alterity, and recognising how they are shaped by the conventional, underscoring their relational contingency (Holloway et al., 2007).

The focus on socio-spatial proximity as a proxy for understanding alterity has generally omitted the broader context in which alternatives develop, ignoring political and economic relations across different scales. Therefore, a second line of future research could place AFNs in their broader context, to analyse the entrenchment and retrenchment of these initiatives. More specifically, this calls for engaging with AFNs and the public policies that affect their development. A policy-oriented focus would also address the political and economic barriers to more sustainable food systems. In this line, research should analyse the policies supporting small-scale farmers who employ alternative production methods, agri-environmental schemes, food safety regulations, and rural development programmes. Therefore, future research could employ inter-scalar and multilevel approaches for addressing how institutions at national and international scales support (or not) the development of AFNs. Such an approach would also help to reinsert the analysis of power dynamics and politics involved in the emergence, practices, and institutionalisation of AFNs.

Thirdly, AFNs should be understood as a longer process of social change. A more accurate understanding of the socio-political significance of these local, hybrid, and emerging alternatives requires moving beyond 'localising' these experiences through approaches that emphasise proximity but also engaging with its temporal dimension. Alternative food initiatives often appear to be reduced to multiple, disconnected small-scale experiences bound to places, undervaluing their overall socio-political significance. AFN initiatives have been developing in different geographical contexts and, although they are context-specific, they point to more universal claims to reassert control and social justice over the food system.

References

Barham E (2002) Towards a Theory of Values-based Labelling. *Agriculture and Human Values* 19, 349–360, https://doi.org/10.1023/a:1021152403919.

Born B and Purcell M (2006) Avoiding the Local Trap: Scale and Food Systems in Planning Research. *Journal of Planning Education and Research* 26, 195–207, https://doi.org/10.1177/0739456X06291389.

Buller H and Morris C (2004) Growing Goods: The Market, the State, and Sustainable Food Production. *Environment and Planning A* 36, 1065–1084, https://doi.org/10.1068/a35282.

Dupuis E M, Goodman D and Harrison J (2006) Between the Local and the Global Just Values or Just Value? Remaking the Local in Agro-Food Studies. *Research in Rural Sociology and Development* 12, 1–8, https://doi.org/10.1016/S1057-1922(06)12010-7.

Gibson-Graham J K (2006) *A Postcapitalist Politics*. London, University of Minnesota Press.

Goodman D, Dupuis M and Goodman M (2012) *Alternative Food Networks Knowledge, Practice, and Politics*. London, Routledge.

Granovetter M S (1985) Economic Action and Social Structure: The Problem of Embeddedness. *The American Journal of Sociology* 91, 481–510, https://doi.org/10.1086/228311.

Guthman J (2004) The Trouble with "Organic Lite" in California: A Rejoinder to the "Conventionalisation" Debate. *Sociologia Ruralis* 44, 301–316, https://doi.org/10.1111/j.1467-9523.2004.00277.x.

Guthman J (2007) The Polanyian Way? Voluntary Food Labels as Neoliberal Governance. *Antipode* 39, 456–478, https://doi.org/10.1111/j.1467-8330.2007.00535.x.

Hinrichs C (2000) Embeddedness and Local Food Systems: Notes on Two Types of Direct Agricultural Market. *Journal of Rural Studies* 16, 295–303, https://doi.org/10.1016/S0743-0167(99)00063-7.

Holloway L, Kneafsey M, Venn L, Cox R, Dowler E, Tuomainen H (2007) Possible Food Economies: A Methodological Framework for Exploring Food Production–Consumption Relationships. *Sociologia Ruralis* 47, 1–19, https://doi.org/10.1111/j.1467-9523.2007.00427.x.

Ilbery B and Maye D (2005) Alternative (shorter) food supply chains and specialist livestock products in the Scottish–English borders. *Environment and Planning A* 37, 823–844. https://doi.org/10.1068/a3717.

McGreevy S R, Rupprecht C D D and Niles (2022) Sustainable Agrifood Systems for a Post-growth World. *Nature Sustainability* 5, 1011–1017, https://doi.org/10.1038/s41893-022-00933-5.

Misleh D (2022) Moving Beyond the Impasse in Geographies of "Alternative" Food Networks. *Progress in Human Geography* 46, 1028–1046, https://doi.org/10.1177/03091325221095835.

Renting H, Marsden T K and Banks J (2003) Understanding Alternative Food Networks: Exploring the Role of Short Food Supply Chains in Rural Development. *Environment and Planning A* 35, 393–411, https://doi.org/10.1068/a3510.

Sage, C. (2003) 'Socialembeddedness and relations of regard: Altenrative "good food" networks in south-west Ireland', *Journal of Rural Studies*, 19(1), pp. 47–60. doi:10.1016/S0743-0167(02)00044-X.

Sarmiento E R (2017) Synergies in Alternative Food Network Research: Embodiment, Diverse Economies, and More-than-human Food Geographies. *Agriculture and Human Values* 34, 485–497, https://doi.org/10.1007/s10460-016-9753-9.

Slocum R (2007) Whiteness, Space and Alternative Food Practice. *Geoforum* 38, 520–533, https://doi.org/10.1016/j.geoforum.2006.10.006.

Watts D, Ilbery B and Maye D (2005) Making Reconnections in Agrofood Geography: Alternative Systems of Food Provision. *Progress in Human Geography* 29, 22–40, https://doi.org/10.1191/0309132505ph526oa.

Whatmore S, Stassart P and Renting H (2003) What's Alternative about Alternative Food Networks? *Environment and Planning A* 35, 389–391, https://doi.org/10.1068/a3621.

Zhong S, Hughes A, Crang M, Zeng G and Hocknell, S (2022) Fragmentary Embeddedness: Challenges for Alternative Food Networks in Guangzhou, China. *Journal of Rural Studies* 95, 382–390, https://doi.org/10.1016/j.jrurstud.2022.09.008.

Further reading

Goodman D, Dupuis M and Goodman M (2012) *Alternative Food Networks Knowledge, Practice, and Politics*. London, Routledge. The book offers an overview of AFNs and their different backgrounds and trajectories, but also problematises more idealised notions, offering a critical engagement with the topic.

Hinrichs C (2016) Fixing Food with Ideas of "Local" and "Place". *Journal of Environmental Studies and Sciences* 6, 759–764, http://dx.doi.org/10.1007/s13412-015-0266-4. The article gives an overview of the different ways in which ideas of locality and place have been mobilised in constructing AFNs, and some inherent problems that arise from this conceptualisation.

DENISE MISLEH

6.   Alternative proteins

MARIELA DE AMSTALDEN AND NEIL
STEPHENS

Introduction

'Alternative proteins' is a term used to collate a set of actual and emerging foodstuffs that seek to engender new protein eating practices, typically framed as replacements for industrial livestock farming. The core examples are foods using insects, 'plant-based' ingredients, single-cell proteins, and cellular agriculture: precision fermentation and cultured (aka cultivated) meat. While these examples have very different histories, they have been bound into a shared category, retaining both overlapping narratives and core actors, as well as divergent claims and pathways.

First, why is it that these disparate foods have been grouped together under the term 'alternative protein'? As with any 'alternative' label, they are defined in terms of what they are 'not' – they are not 'conventional' meat protein. As we will explain, the 'meatness' of these alternative proteins can also be a point of contention, with some plant-based meats and cultured meats looking to be meat-like, or even *be* meat, without having the same challenges as conventional meat. Either way, the concept of 'alternative protein' is inherently tied to a critique of livestock animal-based food systems – often conceptualised as de-animalisation (Morris et al., 2018) – their environmental, health, and ethical impacts.

Insects have been eaten by humans since pre-historic times, and still feature in diets in parts of the world today. However, insects as 'alternative protein' is a contemporary phenomenon. The Netherlands has been one of the key sites of this work, where insect ingredients – e.g. flour made from mealworms – have been used to produce burgers for sale in conventional supermarkets. Yet the novelty is not eating insects per se. Instead, it is repackaging them among new millennial narratives that seek to reinvent their meanings and associations (House, 2018).

Plant-based meats and milks are also similarly a modern repackaging of existing foods. Plant-based proteins are typically vegan products made from plants. Like eating insects, eating plant-protein sources has an extended history, from beans and pulses, processed products like tempeh and tofu, through to 'vegetarian' branded products of the last century – such as textured vegetable protein or veggie burgers. Important here is the attempted reimagining of these foods as 'foodtech' – most notably by US companies like Beyond Meat and Impossible Foods – who seek to use science to develop foods that are viscerally identical to meat products (Sexton, 2020, 2016).

There is also the category of single-cell proteins, the most visible and commercially successful of these in Europe being Quorn. Single-cell or microbial proteins involve the production and processing of unicellular microorganisms for food, which can include yeasts, bacteria, or algae. Quorn itself uses mycoprotein, a type of fungus. Launched in 1985, today the Quorn range includes 'mince', 'fillets', and 'pieces', all of which are designed to look and taste similar to familiar meat products.

Finally, cellular agriculture seeks to produce foods that are either very similar – or indeed identical – to existing livestock products through controlling cells in a bioreactor (Stephens et al., 2019). Milks and egg products developed this way typically use 'precision fermentation', in which yeast or a similar fermentable cell is engineered to produce specific protein molecules, e.g. casein for milk. At the time of writing – mid-2023 – these products are legally available in the US and Israel, although still in relatively small volumes. Cultured meat, in contrast, takes cells from living animals to proliferate and differentiate them in bioreactors and so produce muscle and fat to reproduce familiar meat products. These products are legal only in Singapore and the US at the time of writing, although it is expected that other countries will follow soon.

It is important to study alternative proteins to understand their inherent politics. As argued above, the very categorisation embodies a critique of the traditional meat industry. The underlying investment has been diverse, and has been part of this politics, with some areas seeing early investment from venture capital firms, including explicitly vegan venture capital firms, but increasingly also funds from governments and incumbent food and meat industry organisations. Alternative proteins also demonstrate complex entanglements of the past and the present, invoking novel and sometimes radical new futures. Indeed, if these products are as successful as their supporters hope, they may lead to revolutionary reconfigurations of our food systems, our landscapes, and our diets.

Current issues and concerns

The politics of alternative proteins can in part be traced through the narratives that surround them, as well as those narratives that challenge them. Sexton et al. (2019) identified a 'typology of promises' for alternative proteins, through five core narratives used to support their success: 'healthier bodies', 'feeding the world, now and forever', 'good for animals and the environment', 'control for sale', and 'tastes like an animal'. Collectively, these promissory narratives seek to assert the meanings associated with alternative proteins by articulating certain desirable futures should they be adopted. The narratives look to enrol supporters and invoke identity categories for potential consumers and industry stakeholders, who will in turn engage in their successful futures.

However, through these narratives, we can also see gaps and discontinuities between the various potential foodstuffs collated under the 'alternative proteins' category. For example, in contrast to eating plant-based meats, eating insects would involve many more deaths than livestock production to gain the food volume of a single cow. Insects, plant-based meats, and cultured meats all have very different health questions associated with them, with technical uncertainties and new forms of contamination risk for cultured meats, and concerns around ultra-processed foods with plant-based products. While insects and plant-based products are a well-established food technology, there are genuine questions about the feasibility of cellular agriculture at scale, which brings questions about the capacity to feed the world, or to produce food with a significantly lower environmental impact. Furthermore, discussions about food security often show that the problem relates to the political distribution of food readily available, and not to the volume thereof, opening questions about the political, social, and legal organisation of alternative proteins themselves.

Assuming technical uncertainties over the feasibility of producing these foodstuffs are overcome, questions about consumer acceptance remain. Onwezen et al.'s (2021) review of Western consumer acceptance found generally low levels of acceptance for alternative proteins compared with meat, especially insects and cultured meat, and that drivers to increase consumer acceptance are taste, healthiness, familiarity, and existing attitudes and norms about willingness to try new things. These factors are not new. Instead, they are typical and well-documented drivers of food choices that emphasise the importance of prior eating experience of, and emotional response to, novel foods, in turn impacting attitudes on their continued consumption.

Regulation is another core issue. The law acts as a reinforcement mechanism of social norms, and as such it is tasked with reflecting its society (Maidana-Eletti, 2016). There are a range of muti-layered laws and regulations that apply to food in general and alternative proteins in particular, and these tend to vary from country to country – with only a few international agreements in place that facilitate legal and regulatory harmonisation, equivalence, and cooperation. Increasing legal challenges to alternative protein products might be seen, most likely based on food quality regulations – e.g. labelling issues – rather than food safety. The French parliament passed a law restricting the use of words like 'steak' or 'burger' to label plant-based products in 2022 which was later suspended by the Council d'Etat in 2023, while in Switzerland the Supreme Court of Justice is, as of winter 2024, ruling on whether plant-based products can be labelled as vegan 'chicken' or 'pork'. Italy banned the production and marketing of cultivated meat by a significant parliamentary majority in November 2023, likely to be followed by France, too, after having tabled a similar bill in December 2023.

These developments can be traced back to the numerous and diverse food terms with legally defined meanings. Conversely, what we consider as 'alternative proteins', and the categorisation that results thereof, influences our cultural perceptions and social ability to accept new technologies, which ultimately become codified in law. As such, how the law defines 'insects', 'plant-based', and 'cellular agriculture' will directly impact new technologies' ability to display their potential benefits to the global food system, as regulations concretise our interpretation of reality in the material world (de Amstalden, 2022).

Future concerns

The healthiness, environmental impact, and ethical burden of the proteins we eat (alternative or not) is clearly important. Two concerns with alternative proteins, and the politics of any futures they might bring about, are considered here: first, questions over the feasibility of the claimed capacity for social, environmental, and food system change; and second some of the food justice and social justice issues that may arise should they prove successful.

The category of 'alternative proteins' has been framed by a set of promissory narratives about profound potential change, premised upon replacing the traditional, harmful livestock sector with more benign alternatives. A critical social science analysis must ask how feasible and likely this level of radical change may be. This will vary depending on the type of alternative protein. Insect protein has been marketed in European countries for over a decade now, both whole dried insects and less visibly in products – like crisps made of waxworm larvae. They have not had strong sales and have remained novelty foods in these markets. Plant-based meats have received much more positive media attention, and specific brands have increased their profile, but as yet have only achieved reasonable equivalence to processed meats, like burgers and sausages. Cellular agriculture still faces multiple technical challenges to be commercially viable at scale, including developing cheaper culture media and effective upscaling of the technology. All have a significant distance to travel before they can prove themselves to replace traditional livestock products at sufficient volume to materially affect the climate emergency, food security, and animal welfare.

Yet, in this context of critical questioning of feasibility, we must also retain speculative imagination about potential futures in which alternative proteins do succeed in gaining significant market share, resulting in a sizable reduction of the traditional livestock sector. Here, we can only ask questions as to the exact form such a replacement might take, which at present is entirely indeterminate. And so, if the conventional livestock sector were to shrink, in which parts of the world would this happen first? What impact may this have on local communities and cultures, and what forms of support and protection would be required? What might recovered land be used for? Who owns, controls, and profits from the various alternative proteins? Do these new products frictionlessly replace animal products, or does their adoption entail shifts in our identities, values, and cultures around food and eating? The very breadth and significance of these questions makes clear both the importance of alternative proteins and their uncertainties. It also renders clear the need for sustained social analysis of alternative proteins, whatever futures they may invoke.

Acknowledgements and funding

De Amstalden and Stephens' work on this chapter has been supported by an APEX Award funded by the British Academy, the Royal Academy of Engineering, and the Royal Society [Grant APX\R1\231024]. Stephens' work is also supported by the Wellcome Trust [Grant WT208198/Z/17/Z], and the EPSRC [Grant EPX0381141].

References

De Amstalden, M. (2016). *Global Food Governance: Implications of Food Quality and Safety Standards in International Trade Law*. Peter Lang: Berne.

De Amstalden, M. (2022). Seafood without the sea: Article 20 of the Agreement on Trade-Related Aspects of Intellectual Property Rights, the 'justifiability test' and innovative technologies in a sustainable blue economy. *Journal of World Trade and Investment*, 23, 68–94.

House, J. (2018). Insects as food in the Netherlands: Production networks and the geographies of edibility. *Geoforum*, 94, 82–93.

Morris, C., Mylan, J., & Beech, E. (2018) Substitution and food system de-animalisation. *International Journal of the Sociology of Agriculture and Food*, 25(1), 42–58.

Sexton, A. (2016). Alternative proteins and the (non) stuff of "meat". *Gastronomica*, 16(3), 66–78.

Sexton, A. (2020). Food as software: Place, protein, and feeding the world Silicon Valley–style, *Economic Geography*, 96(5), 449–469.

Stephens, N., Sexton, A. E., & Driessen, C. (2019). Making sense of making meat: Key moments in the first 20 years of tissue engineering muscle to make food. *Frontiers in Sustainable Food Systems*, 45. doi.org/10.3389/fsufs.2019.00045

Further reading

Onwezen, M. C., Bouwman, E. P., Reinders, M. J., & Dagevos, H. (2021). A systematic review on consumer acceptance of alternative proteins: Pulses, algae, insects, plant-based meat alternatives, and cultured meat. *Appetite*, 159, 105058.
This reading reviews consumer acceptance studies on alternative proteins.
Sexton, A. E., Garnett, T., & Lorimer, J. (2019). Framing the future of food: The contested promises of alternative proteins. *Environment and Planning E: Nature and Space*, 2(1), 47–72.
This reading critically analyses the promissory narratives associated with alternative proteins.
Van der Weele, C., Feindt, P., van der Goot, A. J., van Mierlo, B., & van Boekel, M. (2019). Meat alternatives: An integrative comparison. *Trends in Food Science & Technology*, 88, 505–512.
This reading reviews and compares the innovation pathways of a number of alternative proteins.

7.   Animals and food

Kin Wing (Ray) Chan

Introduction

Since the 1960s, global demand for food animals has increased more than fivefold. In 2023 the estimated amount, by weight, of animals used for food production was around 364 million tonnes (FAO, 2023). This rise in animal-based food production and consumption has shifted geographically from the Global North to the Global South, particularly in populous Asian countries. Current debates on food and animal studies are inspired by more-than-human perspectives which recognise animals' agency, vitality, and embodiment (Buller, 2014). However, there is a noticeable neglect of the burgeoning field of food and animal research in Asia. The objective of this entry is to broaden our understanding of food animal production, framed particularly through an Asian context. This argument begins by introducing relational thinking and methodologies derived from food and animal studies. It then proceeds to recognise various circumstances involving food animals, including meat production and transportation, as well as their utilisation for ceremonial and medical purposes.

Relational thinking and the agential role of human/animal interactions

Within food and animal literature, scholars challenge the anthropocentric view of animals as invisible others (Buller, 2014). Recent theoretical debates on human–animal relationships have gone beyond the notion of human mastery over animals to a relational understanding of human/animal interactions (Lorimer, 2020). Taking a relational perspective offers two advantages: first, it helps to break down the binary classification; second, it considers humans and animals as situated in the same social network, working together to co-produce heterogeneous socio-economic practices (Hinchliffe et al., 2016). Rather than emphasising species differences, this relational thinking style helps to consider how human/animal interactions enact multiple practices (Despret, 2004).

A number of concepts have emerged to make sense of multiple spatialities of human–animal interactions in different 'beastly spaces' (Philo and Wilbert, 2004). For instance, Lorimer et al. (2019) develop the 'animal atmosphere' concept to examine the affective and material aspects of human/animal interactions in the Anthropocene; while Braverman (2017) proposes a 'zoometric scale' as a way to elucidate how different hierarchical relationships are constructed along human–animal lines of inquiry. Human–animal interactions also involve shared senses of feelings and timing (Petitt and Brandt-Off, 2022). These conceptual frameworks not only celebrate the 'animal moment' but also cross-fertilise the 'animal turn' in food studies, geography, anthropology, sociology, feminist studies, and post-structural studies. Furthermore, these ontological reflections spur methodological innovations to address relational, emotional, and embodied interactions between humans and animals, ultimately influencing food and society relations.

Recalibrating animals as food: more-than-human methodologies

Food and animal studies scholarship increasingly engages with more-than-human methodologies to reduce the dependence on human representation and find better ways to represent animals in research. Inspired by Haraway's (2008) *When Species Meet*, scholars in this field are paying more attention to theoretical and methodological innovation to examine multispecies interactions (Roe and Greenhough, 2014), moving away from anthropocentric perspectives. Videos, for instance, are utilised to illustrate patterns of animal movement, while photographs are used to demonstrate the co-presence of microbes and humans within food systems (Lorimer, 2010; Roe et al., 2019). Hodgetts and Lorimer (2015) outlined three more-than-human methodologies to map out the interactions between food and animals: firstly, the utilisation of biosensing technology for monitoring, tracking, and analysing animal behaviours; secondly, the exploration of artistic and scientific experiments to assess the most effective methods of inter-species communication; and thirdly the application of molecular markers to understand the ecologies of farm animals. More-than-human methodologies allow farm animals to be represented in food systems, while also conveying a significant message that humans and animals co-create social meanings and specific practices to shape the materiality, cultural understandings, and symbolic values of foods.

Farm animal domestication as more-than-food

In the literature on food and animal studies, increasing focus is given to topics such as animal ethics, rewilding, animal justice, food security, and metabolism. These research areas are often discussed in the context of human–animal interactions in the Global North. However, food and animal studies have also become an important field of interest in Asia. The rest of the entry thus explores how food animals are involved in various contexts in Asia, such as farming, labour provision, and ceremonial and medical purposes, to broaden our understanding of animal domestication. Farm animal domestication is not unidirectional (Swanson et al., 2018, p. 15). In Asia, there is a complex domestication relationship where farm animals are not merely for food production but also provide draught power, participate in religious rites, and serve as biological remedies for medicinal purposes.

In contemporary food and animal literature in Asia, research primarily focuses on the political economy, governance, and environmental politics of farm animal production. These literatures provide insights into how rapid capitalist development processes, stimulated by the rise of middle-class, Western fast-food diets and dining-out cultures in Asia, resulted in more intensive farm animal production and environmental challenges (Hansen, 2018). Whilst the intensification of farm animal production increases the risks of spreading infectious diseases because of high livestock densities, poor animal welfare, low disease resistance, and low genetic diversity, scholars also examine the agential power and embodied practices of domesticated farm animals to provide insights for disease prevention and monitoring. Chan and Enticott (2023), for example, employ narrated mapping methods to explore the agential role of non-human life forms (i.e. infectious diseases) which shape the biosecurity practices of Hong Kong pig farmers (see also studies by Neo, 2012; Fearnley, 2020; Keck, 2020).

Domesticated food animals to co-produce ceremonial, draught, and medical purposes

The above studies examined how farm animal production leads to environmental politics and disease risks beyond farm settings. In fact, there are more entangled human/animal boundaries co-existing in Asian animal domestication as examined in this section. Under rapid capitalist development processes, domesticated animals in Asia become various forms of 'lively commodities' and 'working subjects' to provide labour and therapeutic remedies to fulfil human transportation, ceremonial, and medical needs (Barua, 2016; Porcher and Estebanez, 2019).

Ceremonial animals

In Asian religious rituals, material parts of animal bodies are used to mediate life and death, attachment (i.e. blessing and fortune), and detachment (bad luck and wrongdoing). For instance, 'holy pigs' are raised for religious rites in Taiwan, with the fattest pigs slaughtered and decorated. Pig raisers compete to raise the heaviest pigs. The weight of pigs represents sincerity, so they offer the heaviest pigs to the deities, and the pig raisers obtain blessing from the deities in return. Pig raisers compete with one another to please the deities in return for spiritual vitalities such as gaining good fortune and acquiring blessings; meanwhile, 'holy pig' bodies become 'eating machines' by devouring tonnes of feed.

In southern parts of China, domesticated roosters are used in many religious rituals. For instance, according to Liu (2008), roosters' blood will be used as a purification agent to cleanse the ritual venue in the Daoist 'Jiao' festival; roosters are also used in death rituals to recall those souls who died unnaturally. After the rituals, the ceremonial roosters will be 'rewilded'. From these religious rituals, we can see that religious practitioners regard the material animal bodies as containing transcendental spiritual power to carry human souls through the body of a living animal. Under the influences of Buddhism, many Asian countries embrace animal liberations as an act of compassion, and a means of 'saving life', enacted 'through the release of wild animals such as birds, tortoises and fish' (Shiu and Stokes, 2008, p. 186). However, the act of animal liberation is also different from the consecration of domestic animals in the context of nomadic herding, because consecration of domestic animals represents a means to counteract illness and misfortunes rather than the meaning of saving life (White and Fijn, 2020).

Draught animals

Traditionally, domesticated food animals are not only consumed, digested, and ingested by humans as protein, but they also provide draught power to assist human labour through agricultural practices. The power of draught animals assists humans in crop cultivation in numerous agricultural tasks from ploughing and harvesting to different means of transport and hauling. Draught animals, including dromedaries, donkeys, horses, buffalo, and cattle in Asia, are vital forces for agriculture, especially for smallholders (Mota-Rojas et al., 2021). Smallholders raise and feed draught animals to produce animal bodies which can generate draught power, while draught animal manure provides essential nutrients for their crops. The labour of draught animals consumes feed and turns it into power and fertiliser for the farming system in Asia.

Medical animals

In Asia, wild animals are domesticated and raised to produce traditional medicines, including wild deer, bear, turtles, civet cats, and crocodiles. The 'medicalisation of animals' is an anthropomorphic view, framing animals as a medicine to be digested and absorbed, transforming animals' vitality and energy from their flesh to enrich the vitality of human blood and human inner strength (Chee, 2021). However, consuming medical animals can lead to the suffering of captive wild animals. To balance human metabolism, animal body parts are consumed by humans to obtain vitality and energy. Ironically this also increases the chance of zoonotic spillover, which risks human health rather than rejuvenating human metabolism. For example, the consumption of civet cats has increased the spread of severe acute respiratory syndrome (SARS) in southern parts of China (Peiris and Poon, 2008).

Future directions for food and animals

Farm animals are not just consumed, digested, and ingested by humans to produce protein. They are also choreographed with humans to co-produce spiritual power in religious rites and draught power in agricultural practices, and to generate metabolic vitality in traditional medicines. The picture of domestication is far more entangled and complex in Asia. Future research can be conducted in this direction to develop theoretical and methodological understandings of the agency and situated context of farm animals' place in food and society.

Acknowledgement

I would like to acknowledge the Wellcome Trust for their funding support for the project (223592/Z/21/Z) 'The Future of One Health? The Challenges and Opportunities of Using Digital Technologies to Strengthen Infectious Disease Management and Animal Health Responses in China'.

References

Barua M (2016) Lively commodities and encounter value. *Environment and Planning D: Society and Space*, *34*(4), pp. 725-744.

Barua M (2017) Nonhuman labour, encounter value, spectacular accumulation: The geographies of a lively commodity. *Transactions of the Institute of British Geographers*, *42*(2), pp. 274–288.

Braverman I (2017) Captive: zoometric operations in Gaza. *Public Culture*, *29*(1), pp. 191-215.

Buller H (2014) Animal geographies I. *Progress in Human Geography*, *38*(2), pp. 308–318.

Chan, KWR and Enticott G (2023) Good methods for good farmers? Mapping the language of good farming with "diligent farmers" in Hong Kong. *Journal of Rural Studies*, *100*, p. 103005.

Chee L P (2021) *Mao's bestiary: Medicinal animals and modern China*. Duke University Press.

Despret V (2004) The body we care for: Figures of anthropo-zoo-genesis. *Body & Society*, *10*(2–3), pp. 111–134.

FAO (2023) Food Outlook – Biannual Report on Global Food Market: Food Outlook in June 2023. https://doi.org/10.4060/cc3020en.

Fearnley L (2020) *Virulent zones: Animal disease and global health at China's pandemic epicenter*. Duke University Press.

Hansen A (2018) Meat consumption and capitalist development: The meatification of food provision and practice in Vietnam. *Geoforum*, *93*, pp. 57–68.

Haraway D (2008) *When species meet.* University of Minnesota Press.

Hinchliffe S, Bingham N, Allen J and Carter S (2016) *Pathological lives: Disease, space and biopolitics.* John Wiley & Sons.

Hodgetts T, Lorimer J (2015) Methodologies for animals' geographies: Cultures, communication and genomics. *Cultural Geographies*, 22(2), pp. 285–295.

Keck F (2020) *Avian reservoirs: Virus hunters and birdwatchers in Chinese sentinel posts.* Duke University Press.

Liu T S (2008) Custom, taste and science: Raising chickens in the Pearl River Delta Region, South China. *Anthropology & Medicine*, 15(1), pp. 7–18.

Lorimer J (2010) Moving image methodologies for more-than-human geographies. *Cultural Geographies*, 17(2), pp. 237–258.

Lorimer J (2020) *The probiotic planet: Using life to manage life* (Vol. 59). University of Minnesota Press.

Lorimer J, Hodgetts T and Barua M (2019) Animals' atmospheres. *Progress in Human Geography*, 43(1), pp. 26–45.

Mota-Rojas D, Braghieri A, Álvarez-Macías A, Serrapica F, Ramírez-Bribiesca E, Cruz-Monterrosa R, Masucci F, Mora-Medina P and Napolitano F (2021) The use of draught animals in rural labour. *Animals*, 11(9), p. 2683.

Neo H (2012) "They hate pigs, Chinese farmers… everything!" Beastly racialization in multiethnic Malaysia. *Antipode*, 44(3), pp. 950–970.

Peiris JSM, Poon LLM (2008) Severe acute respiratory syndrome (SARS). *Encyclopaedia of Virology*, pp. 552–560. Elsevier.

Petitt A and Brandt-Off K (2022) Zoocialization: Learning together, becoming together in a multispecies triad. *Society & Animals*, 4(1), pp. 1–8.

Philo C and Wilbert C (2004) *Animal spaces, beastly places.* Routledge.

Porcher J and Estebanez J (2019) *Animal labor: A new perspective on human-animal relations* (Vol. 18). Transcript Verlag.

Roe E and Greenhough B (2014) Experimental partnering: Interpreting improvisatory habits in the research field. *International Journal of Social Research Methodology*, 17(1), pp. 45-57.

Roe E, Veal C and Hurley P (2019) Mapping microbial stories: Creative microbial aesthetic and cross-disciplinary intervention in understanding nurses' infection prevention practices. *Geo: Geography and Environment*, 6(1), e00076.

Shiu H and Stokes L (2008) Buddhist animal release practices: Historic, environmental, public health and economic concerns. *Contemporary Buddhism*, 9(2), pp. 181–196.

Swanson H A, Lien M E and Ween G B (2018) *Domestication gone wild: Politics and practices of multispecies relations.* Duke University Press.

White T and Fijn N (2020) Multispecies co-existence in inner Asia: Introduction: Resituating domestication in Inner Asia. *Inner Asia*, 22(2), pp. 162–182.

Further reading

Hinchliffe S, Blanchette A, Chan KW, Degeling C, Emel J, Leach M, Scoones I and Winter M (2024) Understanding the roles of economy and society in the relative risks of zoonosis emergence from livestock. *Royal Society Open Science*, 11(7), pp. 1–20.

Emphasises the need to integrate socio-economic and policy dimensions in zoonotic risk assessments, including understanding the interconnectedness of human, animal, and environmental health.

Davé NN (2023) *Indifference: On the praxis of interspecies being.* Duke University Press.

Examines complex human–animal relations in India through understanding the entanglement between care and violence as well as the ethics of indifference.

KIN WING (RAY) CHAN

8.   Animal rights

RICHARD WHITE

Introduction

Addressing the question "What are animal rights?" is to engage with a complex philosophy and social justice movement (Regan, 2004). As a starting point perhaps, it might be helpful to think about how we – *Homo sapiens* – are a species of animal that have rights: rights that are recognised and protected by law. These include basic rights such as the right to life, the right to bodily integrity, and freedom (from slavery or servitude).

In many ways, animal rights can be understood as a logical extension of these basic human rights. Sentience (the ability to feel pain or pleasure) is the moral cornerstone upon which these rights are given. Animal rights advocates (ARAs) argue that sentience is a characteristic that is far from unique to humans: it is shared by many other animals. Therefore, the rational conclusion is that all sentient beings have *instrinsic* moral value, and should be afforded similar basic rights (and protections). How far these rights should extend, and on what grounds, continues to provoke debate in all areas of society. Importantly, such reasoning draws an important distinction between animal rights and animal welfare approaches. From an animal welfarist perspective, it would be morally acceptable that as long as an animal's welfare is given due consideration, then they can be used *instrumentally*, for human ends.

Applying this to the question of contemporary society, food, and agricultural systems – given the centrality of animals embedded in these systems – the challenge presented by the animal rights perspective is a potentially revolutionary one. For context, it is estimated that "around 31.0 billion land animals and 38.8 to 215.9 billion fish are being farmed globally at any given time" (Anthis and Anthis, 2019: unpaginated). ARAs would argue that these systems (particularly in meat and dairy farming, and animal husbandry more generally) are entirely dependent on the routine violations of basic animal rights. If this truth-claim is correct, then it stands to reason that these systems must be abolished.

Current issues

It's not just about other animals

Recognising how acts of violence and injustice often cause harm to both humans and other animals, it is not surprising to note how many influential ARAs have also fought to advance human rights (see Salt, 1892; Regan, 2004). Both human and animal rights-violations, ARAs argue, can clearly be seen in the farming systems that inform the lived experiences of farmed animals. That farmed animals suffer direct harm is beyond question (ARAs, unlike animal welfarists, consider death – the deprivation of life, and with it any possibility of a future – to be a harm). As Nibert (2017: xi) argues:

> The physical and emotional suffering from such horrific treatment experienced by each individual being, multiplied by the billions of individual animals who undergo it, results in a degree of severe distress and pain – every second – that defies comprehension.

ARAs also highlight another deeply inconvenient truth about animal husbandry: that many humans suffer terribly too. The experiences of slaughterhouse workers (SHWs) powerfully illustrates of this. While it is well known that the animal slaughtering and processing industry has some of the highest physical injury incident rates, the psychological traumas that SHWs experience and the negative coping strategies that many turn toward , are increasingly recognised (see Slade and Alleyne, 2023).

Finally, at a time of acute anxiety about the threat and realities of climate emergency, the devastating impacts of animal husbandry on the environment are well known (Parlasca and Qaim, 2022). This provides another powerful argument that animal husbandry should be abolished, urgently, to help maintain the fundamental support systems that all life depends on.

Toward post-lethal agriculture

Thinking more broadly about food production, ARAs consider many contemporary (industrial) ways of arable farming to be irreconcilable with an AR framework. Many arable farming methods, for example, use pesticides and other agro-chemicals to destroy various insect and animal lifeforms. These in turn have devastating impacts across broader food-chains and the environment at large (see Gunderman and White, 2021).

Moving forward, ARAs point to diverse communities and farmers who are imagining and practising alternative systems of food production, in ways that seek to minimise rights-violations. In the context of agriculture, there is growing momentum and visibility around a range of 'post-lethal' ways of farming. Veganism, often associated with ARAs, can be understood as a:

> [p]hilosophy and way of living which seeks to exclude—as far as is possible and practicable—all forms of exploitation of, and cruelty to, animals for food, clothing or any other purpose; and by extension, promotes the development and use of animal-free alternatives for the benefit of animals, humans and the environment. (Vegan Society: unpaginated)

So-called veganic (veganic organic) farming – also known as 'stockfree' farming – has made particularly strong impressions here (Seymour and Utter, 2021). These alternative approaches point to a vibrant international network of successful, commercially viable veganic farms. These are located across not only the UK, Europe, and North America, but also many other countries in the world. Their success in turn is inspiring other farmers to move away from being financially reliant on animal husbandry, and provide new options for growing food in sustainable and minimally exploitative ways (Garcés, 2024).

Future concerns

ARAs argue that treating *all* sentient beings with respect is the morally right thing to do. From an AR perspective, it is unimaginable to think of animal husbandry operating in ways that would not violate the basic rights of animals (and humans). Ergo it is morally unjustifiable, and must be abolished.

The implications for contemporary agricultural systems would be far-reaching. However, ARAs also point to the existence of "post-lethal" alternative forms of agriculture. In this context we might consider the tremendous impact it would have if the billions of pounds of government subsidies currently given to industrial animal farms and environmentally unsustainable farming practices across the world, were re-directed to these forms of agriculture..

The primary concern that many ARAs share is that the steps needed to end animal husbandry will not be taken. The concern is based on the exceptional lobbying powers that the meat and dairy industries hold over governments. Compounding this is the lack of popular movements that would advocate for animal rights to be recognised and upheld. This resistance reflects the deeply engrained and widely held speciesist/human supremacist belief systems that humans have superiority over other animals simply because they are human. Individually and collectively, both factors provide significant, if not insurmountable, barriers to the transformative change needed.

References

Anthis, K. and Anthis, J.R. (2019) Global Farmed & Factory Farmed Animals Estimates, *Sentience Institute* https://www.sentienceinstitute.org/global-animal-farming-estimates.

Garcés, L. (2024) 'Transfarmation' Stories: The Farmers Switching from Animals to Crops. Plant Based News. (Available at https://tinyurl.com/56uuv4vp [last accessed 30.04.2024]).

Gunderman, H. and White, R.J. (2021) Critical Posthumanism for All: A Call to Reject Insect Speciesism. *International Journal of Sociology and Social Policy* 41, no. 3–4(2021), 489–505.

Nibert, D. (2017) Introduction. In D. Nibert (ed) *Animal Oppression and Capitalism*. Volume 1: the Oppression of Nonhuman Animals as Sources of Food. Praeger Press, xi–xxv.

Parlasca, M. C. and Qaim, M. (2022) Meat Consumption and Sustainability. *Annual Review of Resource Economics* 14, pp. 17–21. https://www.annualreviews.org/doi/10.1146/annurev-resource-111820-032340.

Regan, T. (2004) *Empty Cages: Facing the Challenge of Animal Rights*. Rowman & Littlefield.

Salt, H. (1892) *Animals' Rights: Considered in Relation to Social Progress*. George Bell & Sons Ltd.

Seymour, M. and Utter, A. (2021) Veganic Farming in the United States: Farmer Perceptions, Motivations, and Experiences. *Agricultural Human Values* 38, pp. 1139–1159 https://doi.org/10.1007/s10460-021-10225-x.

RICHARD WHITE

Slade, J. and Alleyne, E. (2023) The Psychological Impact of Slaughterhouse Employment: A Systematic Literature Review. *Trauma, Violence & Abuse* 24(2), pp. 429–440.

Vegan Society (no date). Definition of Veganism. The Vegan Society. Retrieved from https://www.vegansociety.com/go -vegan/definition-veganism.

Further reading

Hodge, P., McGregor, A., Springer, S., Véron, O. and White, R.J. (eds) (2022) *Vegan Geographies: Spaces Beyond Violence, Ethics Beyond Speciesism.* Lantern Books https://lanternpm.org/book/vegan -geographies/.

Drawing on the work of international geographers and cultural analysts, this book provides both conceptual and accessible pathways that explore ways in which we can move beyond nonhuman animal agriculture to move collectively toward less destructive worlds.

D. Nibert (ed) (2017) *Animal Oppression and Capitalism.* Praeger Press https://publisher .abc-clio.com/9781440850745.

This two-volume set makes a powerful argument for the ways in which capitalism and speciesism oppress life on earth, and how these need to be addressed if sustainable and peaceable futures are to be achieved.

RICHARD WHITE

9.   Animal welfare

EMMA ROE

Introduction

Animal welfare is a significant and complex topic found in the relationship between society and the animals that humans farm for food. Farmed animals are known as livestock. Species that have received significant attention are dairy and beef cattle, pigs, broiler chicken birds and laying hens, sheep, and farmed fish (salmon and trout). Animal welfare considerations span interests in both the animal's physical and mental health, and from birth or hatching to end of life/slaughter.

The term farm animal welfare is a phrase originating in Western societies of the Global North as a reaction to growing numbers of reports of poor animal husbandry conditions in modern industrial livestock systems. This caused rising public alarm and concern, along with an increase in concerns for food safety and food quality associated with the UK's bovine spongiform encephalopathy (BSE) outbreak, starting in 1986. What witnesses reported was described as poor animal welfare, leading to an aspiration that this could be improved, to achieve good animal welfare. Attention to poor, vulnerable citizens through providing social welfare support was a characteristic of 20th-century Britain. The invention of the term animal welfare extended this ethos of drawing attention to the plight of the vulnerable animals. We should not ignore the fact that caring for the wellbeing of farm animals has been and is practised in pre-industrial pastoralist cultures around the world (Szűcs et al., 2012; Qekwanaa et al., 2019). These practices pre-date the conceptual invention of animal welfare and its science that has since been established. In late-modern, industrialised societies in the 20th century, there was and continues to be growing public awareness of so-called 'factory farming' techniques and growing popular belief that animals have feelings and can suffer, and thus farming systems should enable them to meet their own needs and desires. Animal welfare science studies farm animal experiences in modern farming systems to support legislation for reducing harms.

From Harrison's *Animal Machines* and the Brambell Report to sentient beings

Farm animal welfare developed as a concept through the second half of the 20th century, extending from earlier concerns of cruelty to pets and animals used in science. In the UK, the realities of the rapid expansion of technologically driven livestock production following the end of World War Two rationing (Kirchhelle, 2021) were brought to a wider audience through the writing of activist author Ruth Harrison in her book *Animal Machines* (Harrison, 1964). Between 1947 and 1960, total meat production in the UK had more than doubled to 1,713,000 tonnes (Kirchhelle, 2021). For example, pig production gains were initially achieved through outdoor or hybrid indoor–outdoor systems (Woods, 2012) but then settled into typically an indoor system. For poultry, the new intensive indoor facilities that could offer all-year-round animal production with optimised feed and environmental conditions were widely taken up. Harrison described what has become known as 'factory farming'. This book captured the attention of politicians and societal groups, leading to an immediate UK government enquiry and the publication of the Brambell Report in 1965 (Brambell, 1965).

The Brambell Report detailed the plight of confined farmed animals and delivered recommendations about the (poor) conditions in which farm animals may live, as well as animals' capacity to suffer mentally and physically (Veissier et al., 2008). Recommendations included that hens should be able to spread their wings, and that routine mutilations such as pig tail-docking should be phased out. Ten years after the Brambell Report, the first European Community (the precursor to the EU) regulation to protect animals was published. A rethink to animal protection legislation was brought about across the EU and UK (then a member) with the signing of the Amsterdam Treaty Act of 1997. The Act redefined animals as sentient beings, i.e. that they have feelings that matter to them, whereas previously livestock were considered units of production, de-animalising them. The growing activity of NGOs such as the Royal Society for the Prevention of Cruelty to Animals, Compassion in World Farming and Eurogroup for Animals in the 1980s and 1990s was key to how this shift took place, alongside debates about how this legislative shift would provide an ethical enhancement for European farmers competing in a globalised food market (Buller and Roe 2018). The legal activity has not halted, but continues to identify safeguards. This is important given the ongoing intensification of livestock production through biotechnological advances. It is envisaged that precision breeding using gene editing techniques whilst supporting further production efficiencies could also include welfare improvements for livestock animals.

Thinking critically about globalising animal welfare and the food industry

There is considerable effort by animal welfare non-governmental organisations and governments based in higher-income countries to globalise engagement with the contemporary concept of farm animal welfare. Their argument is that it should be central to intensive livestock farming as it continues to spread to industrialising nations. Concern for animal welfare is argued as evidence of a culture's 'civilising process', as a step towards 'sustainable agriculture', as linked to producing healthier animals, and as offering trading opportunities with higher-income nations and global food brands, who set welfare as an ethical product specification (Buller and Roe, 2018). These arguments are well intentioned but, in places where human welfare standards are of lower regard, attention to animal welfare can jar.

There is widespread engagement with animal welfare across Europe, Australasia, and North America. Across African, Asian, and South American nations, engagement with farm animal welfare science and farm standards is increasing, supported by trading opportunities and a growing middle-class. Notably, animal welfare's narration around the world very often perpetuates colonial knowledge patterns and pathways. Animal welfare is a modern Western concept that is exported to parts of the world where it is presumed farming practices and relations to farm animals are morally inferior. Within the business of promoting progressive, intensive, high-production farming systems meeting animal welfare legislation is part of the sales pitch for intensive farming technologies and the trading opportunities that could follow.

The contemporary European approach to animal welfare is also an outcome of how the food industry structures the relation between farm animals and society. Paradoxically, the food industry both creates the conditions for poor farm animal welfare and offers market-based mechanisms for production system adjustments to improve animal welfare. These market-based mechanisms work to go beyond legal requirements to better meet the welfare needs of intensively produced animals. Hence animal welfare manifests itself as a complex interconnected achievement. These connections run between: societal expectations and imaginations about the quality of the lives of livestock; the location and level of legal requirements to care for sentient animals' wellbeing supported by animal welfare science; and animal welfare accreditation working to differentiate food product qualities within the market for animal-based food from predominantly intensive, mass-produced livestock production systems.

Farm animal welfare science

Animal welfare science has developed ever more sophisticated techniques to understand how to measure the welfare outcomes of farm animals and to provide a scientific basis for driving improvements. Approaches for assessing and scientifically studying animal welfare within food production systems include the healthy *biological functioning* of the animal; the capacity for the species to fulfil *natural behaviours* (such as sow nest-building or hen dustbathing); and awareness of animals' individual *affective or emotional states* to address negative behaviours such as intra-species injurious pecking and tail-biting. Recent years have seen an interest in applying science to assess for positive welfare as opposed to solely addressing negative welfare. Defining animal welfare has been informed by changing frameworks of what the steps to an ideal animal welfare-friendly life might be (Mellor, 2016). The Five Freedoms framework, initially outlined in the Brambell Report, was pioneering in this respect. It states that good welfare means freedom from hunger and thirst; freedom from discomfort; freedom from pain, injury, or disease; freedom to express normal behaviour; and freedom from fear and distress. They have since become a key, intuitive (Yeates, 2011) and memorable (Webster, 2016) framework for thinking about what good animal welfare is (FAWC, 2009). However, they have been criticised for their Platonic idealism and being unachievable despite placing a worthy focus on mitigating negative welfare conditions (Buller and Roe, 2018). New approaches champion positive welfare conditions, e.g. that farm animals should have a life worth living (Mellor, 2016), or a life where the animal can flourish.

Auditing farms for farm animal welfare standards

One application of animal welfare science is to work out how to incorporate animal welfare ideals into the framework of commercial farming, in such a way that it can be audited by a visiting assessor, and potentially explicitly or implicitly communicated to consumers (Buller and Roe, 2014). For example, the UK has a scheme dedicated solely to animal welfare (RSPCA Assured) and a scheme that includes animal welfare along with other standards (Red Tractor Assured). A farm assessment includes attention to animal health and veterinary records, housing, gait-analysis, and animal reactions to humans, amongst other things. The use of digital remote sensing technologies (e.g. auditory, air temperature) in animal houses, or robot milking machines, are providing additional data that can offer a longitudinal assessment of welfare that would be impossible to achieve during a ninety-minute farm visit. A farm animal welfare assessment, alongside other farming audits, is often a requirement to sell into supermarkets, fast food service, or manufacturing branded supply chains.

Commercially strategic animal welfare product labelling

Some food retailing or manufacturing brands choose to strategically place accreditation labels of farm audit companies on packaging, such as the Red Tractor (UK) or Label Rouge (France) labels. These indicate the farm animal, whose meat, milk or, eggs are in a food product, was raised on an audited farm which met certain standards. The food service sector serving un-packaged food may include logos on menu cards or boards. They may or may not be accompanied by product description that includes an animal welfare claim, like outdoor reared. But equally, food packaging can carry descriptions that could be inferred to mean the animal had a good life but with no certifying label validating that claim, unlike the regulatory requirement for organic certification. Currently, the active use of a label or a marketing claim that could infer better animal welfare only strategically features on *some* products created from the animal body, and has met animal welfare standards, never all products. This is because the animal carcass is used for many different types of meat products and not all are high value with potential to attract a premium price if carrying an animal welfare claim. Consequently, animal welfare communication to consumers is always strategic on selected products, for selected markets, since only some consumers will actively seek out animal welfare-friendlier products and are willing to pay more for this.

For example, some retailers actively use animal welfare claims, bundled with other values, to sell and differentiate a more expensive own-brand product range, e.g. Sainsbury's Taste the Difference. In other cases, a retail or manufacturer brand has a broad consumer base across many income levels and so does not choose to actively communicate about animal welfare but does want to have an answer should a shopper ask (Buller and Roe, 2014). These examples illustrate how animal welfare features in positioning a product in the market for selling food products found operating across and within food retailing outlets. Through the design of product pricing hierarchies and marketing claims, animal welfare can be actively marketed as a product quality to appeal to engaged consumers, often at a higher product price-point with the inference it is better quality food than competitor products without welfare claims. The markup can mean these products achieve a bigger profit margin for the seller. Consequently, the market, which characterises the ethical consumer as the person who is willing to pay more for higher animal welfare, prices out the many whose budgets cannot stretch that far and yet are engaged and concerned about farm animal welfare (Roe and Buser, 2016).

Societal imaginations and realities of farm animal welfare

Food industry activity around farm animal welfare and the market that supports it shows how societal expectations and imaginations about how farm animals should live, despite the fact they are often misaligned with the realities of commercial intensive agricultural systems, have spawned the active development of farm standards that go beyond legal requirements. Arguably, the most successful of these has been free-range laying hens that produce what are marketed and sold as 'free-range eggs' (Buller and Roe, 2014). However, there continues to be debate about what the welfare potential could be of a farm system, and the reality of what is achieved due to extenuating on-farm circumstances. The capacity to both deliver good welfare and improve welfare is linked to the complex demands of the commercial environment and the skills of stockpersons (Bonnefous et al., 2022). This leads to debate about whether a free-range system can in all cases provide better animal welfare for hens than an indoor loose-housed or enriched cage system. Consequently, the broad social imagination of good farm animal welfare, the critical evaluations that scientists make of welfare-friendlier intensive agricultural systems, and food packaging claims to 'sell' welfare-friendlier food products rarely cohere (Miele and Lever, 2013).

To support and maintain a market for higher-welfare food products there has been the continual need to keep the plight of farm animals in the public eye and for societal engagement with the importance of animals being able to choose according to their needs and desires. Animal welfare NGOs have figured significantly in lobbying government and putting pressure on the food industry, but there are examples where the food industry has worked with the animal welfare NGOs. Again, the example of free-range eggs is an interesting case. The EU was to introduce a ban on caged eggs in 2012, but to achieve this required considerable industry capital investment in poultry-housing infrastructure. In the UK, the egg industry, with the NGOs, collaborated to engage consumer interest in buying free-range eggs. The UK celebrity chef Jamie Oliver hosted a 2008 Channel 4 TV show *Jamie's Fowl Dinners* that revealed poor welfare in the poultry industry and advocated for free-range eggs. The consequence was that most major food retailers in the UK, following the airing of the programme and the press attention it received, took the immediate decision to stop stocking caged eggs. Overnight, a much larger market share for free-range eggs was created that could support growth and continued investment in this production system.

Future of farm animal welfare in a multi-crisis world

The future of farm animal welfare is interlinked with and co-dependent on other global challenges the food industry faces. The need to reduce carbon emissions, for example, could be tackled through reducing meat consumption, but also through more intensive, rather than extensive, livestock production systems. This is an attractive option especially for those species with a lower carbon footprint, like poultry. Higher welfare production systems also need to respond to actions to mitigate increasingly regular zoonotic disease threats – for example, UK outdoor free-range poultry were ordered to be kept inside during a serious avian influenza outbreak beginning in 2021. However, as a sector of the ethical food market, such production systems will no doubt continue to have a place where consumers have a cultivated interest in animal welfare matters.

References

Bonnefous, C., Collin, A., Guilloteau, L.A., Guesdon, V., Filliat, C., Réhault-Godbert, S., Rodenburg, T.B., Tuyttens, F.A.M., Warin, L., Steenfeldt, S., Baldinger, L., Re, M., Ponzio, R., Zuliani, A., Venezia, P., Väre, M., Parrott, P., Walley, K., Niemi, J.K., Leterrier, C., 2022. Welfare issues and potential solutions for laying hens in free range and organic production systems: A review based on literature and interviews. *Frontiers in Veterinary Science* 9. https://doi.org/10.3389/fvets.2022.952922

Brambell, F.W.R., 1965. Report of the Technical Committee to Enquire into the Welfare of Animals Kept under Intensive Livestock Husbandry Systems. Her Majesty's Stationery Office, London.

Buller, H., Roe, E., 2018. *Food and Animal Welfare*. Bloomsbury Publishing.

Buller, H., Roe, E., 2014. Modifying and commodifying farm animal welfare: The economisation of layer chickens. *Journal of Rural Studies* 33, 141–149. https://doi.org/10.1016/j.jrurstud.2013.01.005.

FAWC, 2009. FAWC Report on Farm Animal Welfare in Great Britain: Past, Present and Future.

Harrison, R., 1964. *Animal Machines. The new factory farming industry*. Vincent Stuart Ltd, London.

Kirchhelle, C., 2021. Ideals and intensification: Welfare campaigns in a nation of animal lovers, in: Kirchhelle, C. (Ed.), *Bearing Witness: Ruth Harrison and British Farm Animal Welfare (1920–2000)*. Springer International Publishing, Cham, pp. 65–78. https://doi.org/10.1007/978-3-030-62792-8_5.

Mellor, D.J., 2016. Updating animal welfare thinking: Moving beyond the "Five Freedoms" towards "A Life Worth Living". *Animals* 6, 21. https://doi.org/10.3390/ani6030021.

Miele, M., Lever, J., 2013. Civilizing the market for welfare friendly products in Europe? The techno-ethics of the Welfare Quality® assessment. *Geoforum* 48, 63–72. https://doi.org/10.1016/j.geoforum.2013.04.003.

Qekwanaa, D.N., McCrindleb, C.M.E., Cenci-Goga, D., Grace, D., 2019. Animal welfare in Africa: Strength of cultural traditions, challenges and perspectives, in: Hild, S., Schweitzer, L. (Eds.) *Animal Welfare from Science to Law*. La Fondation Droi Animal, Éthique et Sciences (LFDA) pp. 103–107.

Roe, E., 2011. Ethics and the non-human: The matterings of animal sentience in the meat industry, in: Anderson, B., Harrison, P. (Eds.), *Taking-Place: Non-Representational Theories and Geography*. Routledge, pp. 261–280.

Roe, E., Buser, M., 2016. Becoming ecological citizens: Connecting people through performance art, food matter and practices. *Cultural Geographies* 23, 581–598. https://doi.org/10.1177/1474474015624243.

Szűcs, E., Geers, R., Jezierski, T., Sossidou, E.N., Broom, D.M., 2012. Animal welfare in different human cultures, traditions and religious faiths. Asian-Australas. *Journal of Animal Science*. 25, 1499–1506. https://doi.org/10.5713/ajas.2012.r.02.

Veissier, I., Butterworth, A., Bock, B., Roe, E., 2008. European approaches to ensure good animal welfare. *Applied Animal Behaviour Science* 113, 279–297. https://doi.org/10.1016/j.applanim.2008.01.008.

Webster, J., 2016. Animal welfare: Freedoms, dominions and "A Life Worth Living". *Animals* 6, 35. https://doi.org/10.3390/ani6060035.

Woods, A., 2012. Rethinking the history of modern agriculture: British pig production, c.1910–65. *Twentieth Century British History* 23, 165–191. https://doi.org/10.1093/tcbh/hwr010.

Yeates, J.W., 2011. Is 'A Life Worth Living' a concept worth having? *Animal Welfare* 20, 397–406. https://doi.org/10.1017/S0962728600002955.

Further reading

Buller, H., Roe, E., 2018. *Food and Animal Welfare*. Bloomsbury Publishing.

This book provides a fascinating journey through animal welfare issues from farm to fork, analysing the economies, culture, and politics of food in this much debated area of the food industry. It explores how animal welfare is defined, advocated, assessed, and implemented by farmers, veterinarians, retailers, and consumers.

Kirchhelle, C. (Ed.), 2021. *Bearing Witness: Ruth Harrison and British Farm Animal Welfare (1920–2000)*. Cham: Springer International Publishing, pp. 95–124.

The biography of one of Britain's foremost animal welfare campaigners and of the world of activism, science, and politics she inhabited. In 1964, Ruth Harrison's bestseller *Animal Machines* triggered a gear change in modern animal protection by popularising the term 'factory farming' alongside a new way of thinking about animal welfare.

EMMA ROE

10. Art and food

SILVIA BOTTINELLI

Introduction

Acknowledging that definitions of art shift through time and place, and depend on cultural and disciplinary parameters, this entry addresses a diverse range of phenomena, including: representations of food production, consumption, and waste in global visual and material cultures; works created with edible materials from ancient to modern times; food-based art practices that, in recent decades, have placed taste, ingestion, and digestion as central to the viewer's experience and co-creation with the artist; and chefs who reclaim a position as artists. Today, the questioning of a hierarchy between art and cuisine has resulted, on the one hand, in the incorporation of traditional cooking practices in the realm of the visual arts and, on the other, in a thirst for recognition for chefs whose work has historically been undervalued.

This entry is mostly organised chronologically, looking at contemporaneous phenomena in different geographical areas. To underline how the legacy of past histories continues across time, the entry at times jumps forward to discuss contemporary art that reflects on a given historical moment.

Cave paintings, Ancient Egypt, and Greco-Roman civilizations: economies of food representations

Food representations often showcase the symbolic role of food in societies, reinforcing the connection between diet and wealth, religion, identity, community, intercultural exchange, and political structures and power. The first traces of images and objects produced by humans include representations of hunting scenes, edible plants, and, later, farming practices. Tools meant to gather and prepare food were among the first objects created by humans. Cave paintings from the Upper Paleolithic period (Lascaux, around 15000 BC) illustrate animals, likely game. Ancient Egyptian pictographs, limestone models (Old Kingdom), and wooden group sculptures (Middle Kingdom) demonstrate farming techniques, the processing of grains, the brewing of beer, and the baking of bread, among other foods. One of the largest collections of wooden models – the majority food-themed

– was found in the tomb of Djehutynakht (2010–1961 BC). Grain functioned as a barter unit in Ancient Egypt; painting and sculpture were used to provide accounts of existing wealth and document production techniques. Abundance of food signified prosperity across ancient civilisations; in the 2nd century BC, mosaic artist Sosos of Pergamon depicted unswept floors (asaroton) with leftover foods from feasts; mosaics with similar themes can be found in Imperial Rome's patrician homes (since the 1st century BC), where they functioned as markers of class distinction.

Late antiquity to modernity: foodstuffs and foodways as indicators of class, religion, and colonial power

Food offerings, feasts, and recipes

Food offerings arranged in spectacular and creative compositions characterise diverse cultures across the globe – including in Africa, Mesopotamia, India, and the Americas – and appear in religious traditions like Judaism and Islam. Offerings to ancestors and gods are forms of visual and material culture that celebrate spiritual beliefs, mark the passage of time, and honour the cycle of life and death.

Since late antiquity, Christian iconography has hinged on food references, including fish, wine, lamb, and bread, which are associated with Christ. The ritual of the Eucharist – the act of eating Communion wafer and drinking wine that are believed to be transubstantiated into the body and blood of Jesus – has been a subject of art for centuries; in contemporary times, Cuban artist Felix Gonzalez-Torres incorporated references to the Communion in his edible works with candy that responded to the AIDS crisis (including "Untitled (Portrait of Ross in L.A.), 1991).

During the medieval and Renaissance periods in Europe, painters often depicted biblical feasts that illustrated seminal moments of the Christian narrative (for example *The Marriage at Cana* or *The Last Supper*). These subjects exist in a myriad of variations that show cultural and stylistic changes. Similarly, in China, food was a frequent subject of art: during the Song, Liao, and Yuan dynasties (10th to 14th centuries), images of banquets stood for the continuity of life and afterlife. During the Ming dynasty (1368–1644), materia medica treaties illustrated foods with symbolic and medicinal properties, often involving women as collectors and painters to express family identity and class standing. In Renaissance Italy, treaties on art and food described the practices of painting and cooking, which influenced each other in the codification of recipes for food and art making. At the courts of Italy, France, Spain, and Britain, luxury foods like sugar were imported from North Africa from the 13th century, and sometimes were used as sculptural materials for subtleties, that is, table centrepieces to be displayed at exclusive feasts.

Colonial trades and plantation agriculture

Starting from the 1600s, sugar became increasingly more available in European courts due to colonial economies and plantation agriculture, which relied on the exploitation of lands and people, often enslaved workers forcefully taken to the Americas from Africa across the Middle Passage. Contemporary Cuban artist María Magdalena Campos-Pons and US artist Kara Walker have created installations and performances that excavate colonial histories through the use of sugar as an art material, and through references to sites and methods of sugar processing, trades, and labour.

In the early modern period, after contact with Indigenous populations in the Americas, European artists like Giovanni da Udine (Loggia of Psyche, Villa Chigi, Rome, 1517–1518) depicted what they perceived as exotic foods to indicate abundance and diversity, and signify the political power of their patrons. In Mesoamerica, collaborations between Spanish patrons and Indigenous artists led to the creation of codices like Codex Mendoza (ca. 1541) and the Florentine Codex (1540s–1570s), which document life in the Mexica Empire. The illustrations show the function of corn (maize), amaranth, chocolate, chillies, and other crops in agricultural production, everyday consumption, and ritual. Images depict, among other subjects, tribute foodstuffs stored in containers, indicative of the administrative and political system of the Mexica Empire.

In the 17th century, in the context of the Dutch Golden Age, artists like Pieter Claesz developed the genre of still life and *vanitas*. In their paintings, fruits, meats, and fish, sometimes rotting, can be seen as critiques of the overaccumulation of wealth due to global trade and colonialism, and as a reminder that everything will eventually pass away (*memento mori*).

Fruits and other foods continued to be depicted as signs of imperial power for centuries: the cultivation of coffee, tea, bananas, and more in landscape paintings often signified agricultural progress, global reach, and geopolitical economies, building the imagery of Western colonial empires until the 19th century.

Food depictions and politics, and 19th and early 20th century modernism

In the 1800s, in a phase of rapid industrialisation, artists turned to everyday subjects like food and foodways to capture shifting societal changes. European and American Impressionist artists often painted still lifes (Cézanne) and everyday dining (Monet, Renoir, Cassat) to suggest the appreciation of simple, fleeting moments of modern life.

In the early 20th century, the avant gardes questioned the boundaries of art, which for some came to encompass the realm of cooking and dining. In particular, Futurism (1909–1944) called for a totalising reconstruction of the universe according to principles of progress, technology, and even war and conflict. In 1932, Italian Futurists Filippo Tommaso Marinetti and Fillìa co-edited the *Futurist Cookbook*, combining storytelling, experimental recipes, and imagined sculptural works created out of edible and inedible ingredients. Their goal was to refuse traditional Italian diets based on pasta consumption and propose foodways for muscular and masculine bodies, aligned with the fascist and nationalist politics that they supported.

Food art: reimagining art practices after WWII

Fluxus and pop art in the 1950s and 1960s

Futurist politics were rejected after World War II, but their expanded concept of art is often considered a precedent for postwar art movements that made cooking and eating an integral component of art aesthetics. For example, for Fluxus – a loose group of international visual artists, musicians, writers, and more – art and life coincided. Contrasting with contemporaneous Pop artists like Andy Warhol or Claes Oldenburg, who in the early 1960s represented mass produced drinks and foodstuffs like Coca-Cola, Campbell's soup, and hamburgers, Fluxus artists worked with experiences. For them, processing food, eating, writing recipes, and allowing organic materials to decay in exhibition spaces all demonstrated the everyday and bodily nature of creative endeavours. These artists shared control over the work with the participants and incorporated the possibilities of chance. Iconic Fluxus pieces that revolve around food include Alison Knowles' *Make a Salad* (1962) and *Identical Lunch* (1969), and Yoko Ono's *Apple* (1966). Artists like Daniel Spoerri, Dieter Roth, and Joseph Beuys were initially related to Fluxus and engaged with food in their practice at different stages of their career. For his *Snare Pictures* (starting in 1960), Spoerri glued the remnants of meals to the table to document gestures and exchanges with guests. He later founded the Eat Art movement and opened the Eat Art gallery and the Restaurant Spoerri in Düsseldorf, Germany (1968). Roth was involved with the Restaurant Spoerri: his work with food used chocolate, seeds, candy, sausage, and more, and embodied excess, decay, and even death, often destroying the context in which it was placed. Beuys used foods like lard and potatoes and initiated planting projects to conceptualise a reinvention of human societies inspired by relationships with nature, in the name of community and creativity.

Arte Povera, farming as art, feminism in the 1960s and 1970s

Food and cooking tools were often employed as materials in the sculptural and performative pieces of several artists associated with the Italian movement of Arte Povera (1967–1972), including Giuseppe Penone, Mario Merz, and Marisa Merz. They centred bodily and domestic experience in reaction to the sudden spread of the mass media in post-WWII Italy.

During the 1970s, some artists retreated to urban or rural farms and framed their agricultural activities as a form of art, expanding on the premises of Fluxus and Arte Povera. Among others, Gianfranco Baruchello created *Agricola Cornelia S.p.A.* (1973–1981) at the outskirts of Rome, Italy, and Bonnie Ora Sherk opened *A Crossroads Community: The Farm* in San Francisco, USA (1974–1980). In the same decade, feminist artists critiqued gender role separation and the confinement of women in the home, especially the kitchen (Judy Chicago, Miriam Shapiro et al., *Womanhouse*, 1972; Martha Rosler, *Semiotics of the Kitchen*, 1975).

Identity politics, race and gender in the 1980s

By the 1980s, artists employed food as a marker of race and gender identities: Indigenous artist Jolene Rickard (Tuscarora) used photomontage and installation to point to the personal and spiritual relevance of crops like corn, squash, and beans for family and national histories, highlighting how matriarchal lineage and women's roles held power in traditional social structures. Czech-born Canadian artist Jana Sterbak denounced the objectifying representation of women in popular media and fashion by sewing a dress made of raw steaks, titled *Vanitas: Flesh Dress for An Albino Anorectic* (1987). By triggering disgust, Sterbak brought to the viewers' attention the dehumanising condition endured by women in consumer societies. Beginning in 1991, Korean artist Lee Bul displayed rotting fish decorated with baubles and beads in her piece *Majestic Splendor*, to make evident the contrast between organic decay and ever-shining artificial objects, associated with gendered labour.

Relational aesthetics and community-based art since the 1990s

While artists like Roth, Sterbak, and Bul played with decaying food to convey critiques of art institutions or social issues, in the 1990s, several artists saw cooking and dining together as a means to form communities and initiate relationships under the broad umbrella of Relational Aesthetics. Examples include Thai Argentinian artist Rirkrit Tiravanija's *Untitled (Free)* (1992), and Taiwanese American artist Lee Mingwei's *Dining Project* (1997). In the early 2000s, contemporary artists became interested in making everyday relations the subject of their practice, while chefs gained attention in the art world, as indicated by the invitation of Ferran Adrià, the inventor of molecular gastronomy, to dOCUMENTA 12 in Kassel, Germany, in 2007.

Most recently, a strong concern for the links between food production, waste, and sustainability has become central to environmental art practices that focus on agriculture in the 21st century. For example, US artists Fritz Haeg and Seitu Jones, Australian collective Artist as Family, Palestinian American Nida Sinnokrot, and British Nigerian Yinka Shonibare care for farms that experiment with adaptive forms of food sovereignty, while addressing queer, race, and decolonisation issues.

Current and future landscapes

The ethics of food production in global contexts continue to remain an open question for artists that propose alternative models in agriculture, critiquing labour exploitation, resource extraction, and monocultures. Their experiential and slow approaches counter the fast and mediated exposure to food and eating on social media.

In contemporary times, art provides critiques of mediatic representations, offers embodied forms of knowledge, and establishes possibilities of co-research and co-creation with human and non-human agents to reclaim sustainable forms of food production, consumption, and waste. Ever increasing geopolitical tensions, war, and climate change will likely escalate food's scarcity, contributing to a material, cultural, and personal sense of loss over crops, traditional recipes, and nutrition. As in the past, artists will be well positioned to help process emotions triggered by major changes in food systems; their practices will help redesign a diversity of tools and methods for imaginative adaptations to unpredictable circumstances.

References

Benish BL, Blanc N (2023) *Art, Farming and Food for the Future: Transforming Agriculture*. New York: Routledge.

Bottinelli S, D'Ayala Valva M (2017) *The Taste of Art: Cooking, Food, and Counterculture in Contemporary Practices*. Fayetteville, United States: University of Arkansas Press.

Kelley L (2016) *Bioart Kitchen: Art, Feminism and Technoscience*. London: I.B. Tauris.

Klein S (2020) *The Fruits of Empire: Art, Food, and the Politics of Race in the Age of American Expansion*. Berkeley: University of California Press.

Malaguzzi S (2008) *Food and Feasting in Art*. Los Angeles: J. Paul Getty Museum.

Morán E (2016) *Sacred Consumption: Food and Ritual in Aztec Art and Culture*. Austin: University of Texas Press.

Novero C (2010) *Antidiets of the Avant-Garde: From Futurist Cooking to Eat Art*. Minneapolis: University of Minnesota Press.

Smith S (2013) *Feast: Radical Hospitality in Contemporary Art*. Chicago: Smart Museum of Art, University of Chicago.

Varriano JL (2009) *Tastes and Temptations: Food and Art in Renaissance Italy*. Berkeley: University of California Press.

Weinryb I (2018) *Agents of Faith: Votive Objects in Time and Place*. New York: Bard Graduate Center Gallery.

Further reading

Bottinelli S (2024) *Artists and the Practice of Agriculture: Politics and Aesthetics of Food Sovereignty in Art Since 1960*. London and New York: Routledge.
Discussion of contributions by artists who reimagine the future of food production as critiques of and alternatives to exploitative global systems.

Flood C, Rosenthal Sloan M, Stephenson J (2019) *Food: Bigger Than the Plate*. London: V & A Publishing.
Critical overview of contemporary artists' political and social engagement with farming, cooking, and dining.

Riley G (2015) *Food in Art: From Prehistory to the Renaissance*. London: Reaktion Books.
Chronologically broad and contextualized analysis of historical food representations in Europe and beyond.

11. Automation and food

DAVID ROSE AND KIRSTEN AYRIS

Introduction

Automation is defined as a technology that can perform an automatic action without human intervention. There are a variety of autonomous applications at different stages of technology readiness across the food supply chain. At the farm-scale, some automated crop technologies, such as tractor autosteer, variable rate seeding, and fertiliser application have been available to farmers for many years. Some automated livestock technologies, such as robotic milking machines, automatic feeding systems, and selection gates, are also operational. Despite their technical readiness, adoption challenges related to cost, digital infrastructure, skills, performance, ease of use, and trust have limited the scalability of these technologies (Lowenberg-deBoer and Erickson, 2019). Uptake varies by region, farming sector, and scale, and between the Global North and South. Elsewhere in the supply chain, automation has been present to varying degrees in processing operations for some time, helping to standardise quality, add traceability, and perform dangerous tasks (e.g. dicing and slicing).

There is a suite of autonomous farm technologies broadly associated with the so-called fourth agricultural revolution, including those incorporating artificial intelligence and machine learning. On farms, drones can undertake autonomous surveillance of crops and soils, and facilitate spot-spraying of pests and diseases. Autonomous field robots could perform a variety of functions, including targeted weeding and pest management, harvesting, crop surveillance and forecasting, logistics support, packing, pruning, etc. (Rose and Bhattacharya, 2023). Examples of these technologies are in operation at a small scale throughout the world (e.g. DOT Technology in broadacre systems in Canada; UVC disease treatment of soft fruit in the UK; weeding, harvesting, and field surveillance in the UK and France). In processing operations, further uptake of collaborative robots could help in warehouse distribution, whilst robots could deliver food autonomously to customers (e.g. Starship robots in Milton Keynes, UK).

Current issues

Autonomous technologies in the food supply chain present a range of ethical and regulatory challenges. There are undoubted potential benefits, including greater traceability, a reduction in the need for humans to perform dull, dangerous, repetitive tasks, and a boost to skilled employment. However, for each, there exists the potential for harm to be caused, such as increased corporate control and reduction of farmer autonomy, injuries to workers, and the loss of jobs in areas where food-related employment is a lifeline (Rose et al., 2021). In terms of the structure of the farming industry, automation could enable a switch to more equitable, regenerative forms of agriculture, or facilitate ever more intensive monocultures and reduce farmer control. The debate over the role of automation in agriculture is the subject of the FAO's *State of Food and Agriculture* report 2022. This broadly argued that agricultural automation could bring many benefits to farmers in the Global South, but only if policy instruments support inclusive and accessible development for all, particularly women and small-scale farmers.

There are clear signals that the market for agricultural automation technologies is thriving. An AgFunder report found that global investment in farm robotics and automation rose by 40% from 2020 to 2021. In Europe, the UK government's Farming Transformation Fund offers grants to encourage the uptake of robotics and other emerging technologies, and the ROBS4CROPS project aims to develop and demonstrate robotic systems in four European countries. In Australia, the *Agricultural Mobile Field Machinery with Autonomous Functions in Australia* code of practice signals a clear expectation for the increasing presence of agricultural automation.

Future concerns

Given this trajectory, one of the primary ways to address the debates around the automation of agriculture and food systems now and in the future is to adopt responsible approaches. Responsible innovation, stakeholder engagement and co-design, and consideration of sustainable agricultural transitions offer a range of frameworks through which debates regarding automation may be filtered (Rose et al., 2021).

A key challenge for inclusive automation in the food system is establishing which stakeholders to include. Everyone has a stake in food. Stakeholder groups include farmers, landowners, agricultural workers, factory workers, governments, academics, communities, technology developers, and consumers. It is therefore important that consideration is given to the power dynamics inherent in the food system, avoiding a concentration of decision-making power and opening up discussion to wider communities. It is also important to consider the appropriate scale of stakeholder inclusion for food systems that are simultaneously hyper-local – connected intrinsically to physical geographies of growing crops and raising livestock – and globalised through international trade, supply chains, and global dissemination of technologies.

Inclusion of diverse stakeholders for the technical design of robotic solutions for agriculture has been conducted in several studies. However, many of the debates surrounding automation in food systems revolve not around the technical capacity of these technologies, but around their social and environmental sustainability, and their ethical impacts on society. As such, approaches to inclusion that move beyond technical questions to societal impacts are crucial. Some examples of these studies have emerged in recent years, such as the work of Ditzler and Driessen (2022) in the Netherlands, which examines how the development of agricultural robotics relates to sustainable agroecological practices; Rose and Bhattacharya (2023), who explore barriers to adoption of autonomous robotics by growers in the UK; and a body of work on robot co-design in New Zealand (Burch and Legun, 2021).

References

Burch K A and Legun K (2021) Overcoming Barriers to Including Agricultural Workers in the Co-Design of New AgTech: Lessons from a COVID-19-Present World. *Culture, Agriculture, Food, and Environment* 43, 147–160 https://doi.org/10.1111/cuag.12277.

Ditzler L and Driessen C (2022) Automating Agroecology: How to Design a Farming Robot without a Monocultural Mindset? *Journal of Agricultural and Environmental Ethics* 35, 1–31. https://doi.org/10.1007/s10806-021-09876-x.

Lowenberg-Deboer J and Erickson B (2019) Setting the Record Straight on Precision Agriculture Adoption. *Agronomy Journal* 111, 1552–1569. https://doi.org/10.2134/agronj2018.12.0779.

Rose D C and Bhattacharya M (2023) Adoption of Autonomous Robots in the Soft Fruit Sector: Grower Perspectives in the UK. *Smart Agricultural Technology* 3. https://doi.org/10.1016/j.atech.2022.100118.

Rose D C, Lyon J, de Boon A, Hanheide M and Pearson S (2021) Responsible development of autonomous robotics in agriculture. *Nature Food*. https://doi.org/10.1038/s43016-021-00287-9.

Further reading

Daum T (2021) Farm Robots: Ecological Utopia or Dystopia? *Trends in Ecology & Evolution* 36, 774–777. https://doi.org/10.1016/j.tree.2021.06.002 – gives a clear sense of the normative nature of automated future food systems.

FAO (2022) The State of Food and Agriculture 2022: Leveraging Agricultural Automation for Transforming Agrifood Systems. https://www.fao.org/documents/card/en/c/cb9479en.

Sparrow R and Howard M (2021) Robots in Agriculture: Prospects, Impacts, Ethics, and Policy. *Precision Agriculture* 22(3), 818–833 – good overview of the current and future issues associated with agricultural robots, a key automation technology.

DAVID ROSE AND KIRSTEN AYRIS

12. Babies, children and food

SARAH SNUGGS

Introduction

Consumption of a healthy diet in babies and children is associated with positive physical and mental health outcomes and improved educational attainment. Nonetheless many are not meeting basic dietary guidelines. Globally, children eat substantially fewer fruits and vegetables than the recommended guidelines and this extends to other nutrients and vitamins. The health consequences of a poor diet can be severe; in particular, they can pose as a risk factor to numerous conditions such as diabetes, heart disease and various cancers. A healthy diet is also associated with positive mood, better sleep and improved memory, and is shown to be a protective factor against some mental health challenges. Whilst these health outcomes are more typically associated with adults than children, increasingly evidence indicates that unhealthy eating behaviours in childhood are likely to track into adulthood. Further to this, infant and child malnutrition in low-income countries in the Global South is a well-established contributor to poor health outcomes, while growing numbers of children in the Global North come from families who experience food insecurity (Polland and Booth, 2019), also carrying a risk of malnutrition.

It is important to recognise that research in this area has traditionally emerged from countries like the UK, USA and Australia when considering how children's eating behaviours develop and the associated public health challenges. As such, findings from such work might not apply to all contexts. Indeed, there are many cultural and contextual differences in the influences on child nourishment both between and within countries. These differences can relate to religion, lifestyle, socioeconomic status, values and background, all of which contribute to both our attitudes and access to food.

Babies

Even in the womb, development of individual food choice has started for babies; one study showed that babies whose mothers had consumed carrot juice during pregnancy were then less likely to show aversion to carrot-flavoured food when solid foods were later introduced. Similarly, breast-feeding babies were more likely to accept these flavours if their mothers had regularly consumed them (Menella et al., 2001). This is likely because the baby is experiencing the flavours that the mother is consuming in-utero and through breast milk.

When babies are first born, they rely entirely on milk (whether breast milk, formula milk or a combination) for their nutrition. Typically developing infants will have the reflex to be able to 'self-latch' as soon as they are born. The World Health Organization (WHO) recommends that babies are exclusively breast-fed (where possible) until the age of 6 months and that mothers continue to breast-feed after that up to the age of 2 years, whilst introducing new solid foods alongside (see 'complementary feeding' below). There are many health benefits of breast-feeding for both baby (e.g. it is thought to protect against later development of obesity) and mother (e.g. reduced risk of breast cancer). Breast milk is also clean, does not cost money and contains useful antibodies for the infant. This can be particularly relevant for infants in low-income families and countries where water required for formula milk might not be clean. Not all mothers can (or want to) breast-feed though, and formula milk has been developed to be a good nutritional substitute, also allowing for other carers to feed the baby easily.

After the natural reflex of latching, all other eating skills and behaviours in babies and children need to be *learned*. This leads to the introduction of 'solid' foods (often referred to as complementary feeding or weaning). Traditionally, parents started this process with spoon-fed, low-texture blended purees and then gradually introduced textured foods. In more recent years, some people have preferred to take an approach known as 'baby-led weaning' which means that the baby is allowed to try to feed themselves from the start, with solid finger foods. Both of these approaches work and babies typically receive the food they are offered enthusiastically to start with. By the time babies are around 10 months old, they will be starting to grasp and bite food. This is a key time to introduce a wide variety of healthy foods to the baby; parents are often told 'food before one is just for fun' because the majority of nutrition during this period comes from milk but babies tend to be very receptive to trying new foods and this is a key period in which they can develop their tastes.

Toddlers

Once they reach 24–36 months old, children are anatomically developed to chew food in a similar way to adults and are much more reliant on solid food as a source of nutrition. In this sense, they can eat almost all of the things adults do. However, with toddlerhood often comes a new phase known as 'food neophobia' (the fear of new foods). Parents and carers often report that, during this time, their child becomes very reluctant to try new things, and also to try things they used to accept when younger. This happens at the same time children are learning to converse with their parents, to test boundaries and to take autonomy with some decisions. This can be a challenging time for parents and is often confused with 'picky eating' but is actually thought to be a natural phase of development. One theory as to why food neophobia is so common in this age group is 'learned safety' (Kalat and Rozin, 1973). This approach proposes that children are more happy to consume foods with which they are familiar because they have learnt that this does not result in negative consequences (e.g. being unwell). From an evolutionary perspective, some researchers believe that there is a reason why this coincides with other areas of toddler development: as a child becomes more mobile they might be more likely to find something on their own and eat it. Historically, this could be something dangerous or poisonous, so the learned safety approach could be argued to help protect against this behaviour.

Children

Following from these stages in early life, children's food preferences continue to develop and are influenced by a number of factors. Developmental models of food choice consider how these preferences progress in childhood and mostly focus on three separate processes: *exposure*, *social learning* and *associative learning*.

Repeated *exposure* refers to the concept that individuals' preferences and liking for a product increase the more times it is shown to them (i.e. the more times they are 'exposed' to it). In the context of children's food preferences, this can be applied if a child is repeatedly exposed to a food by their parent, carer or childcare setting. The term can also be applied to media and advertising approaches, where a child might repeatedly see the same food advertisement. In terms of trying to encourage a healthy diet, studies have shown that children might need to see a new vegetable ten or more times before they are familiar enough with it to taste it (Spill et al., 2019). For picky eaters, this number might be even higher.

Social learning captures the idea that we learn from others around us. Primary carers are the principal agent of change in early life food preference. Role-modelling from adults has been shown to encourage children to consume the foods their parents or carers do, and as children grow older and enter pre-school or school settings, they also start to copy what their peers eat. This peer effect might become even stronger as children approach adolescence and may be intensified by social media influences. Parents can also influence their children's food choices with encouragement, and by fostering a healthy food environment (e.g. making sure healthy food is available and accessible to their child).

Finally, *associative learning* considers how we learn by association. That is, learning from past experiences and connecting an event with its consequences. With food, this can be applied when a child consumes something palatable – they remember the positive feelings around this and they have learned that they like that food and would like to have it again. Other associations can include reward (e.g. 'if you eat this broccoli, you can go to the playground'). On the other hand, if a child is unwell shortly after consuming the broccoli, they may then associate these two events and conclude that they do not wish to have broccoli again. Associative learning can be helpful in encouraging a healthy diet, but it is not thought to be positive if food itself is the reward; studies have shown that if a child is offered, for example, a vegetable and rewarded for eating it with, for example, ice cream, the child's liking for ice cream will go up, but the liking for the vegetable in question will decrease, also lowering the likelihood of them asking for it again (Mikula, 1989).

Challenges to a healthy diet for children

It is clear that there are several key elements to a child's environment which shape their food preferences and their diets. However, there are also challenges to all of these for both parents and society. For example, repeated exposure is extensively and robustly evidenced as an approach to encouraging children to try new foods, but is reported to be burdensome for parents (Corsini et al., 2013). It is also arguably wasteful and expensive to implement if the food goes frequently uneaten. This presents a challenge to sustainable food provision and to parents' budgets. Families facing food insecurity are both particularly vulnerable to unhealthy diet and particularly unlikely to waste food. One study in this area suggested that very-low-income parents in the UK were especially likely to purchase unhealthy takeaway food because this represented a way to ensure that their child consumed as much energy as possible as cheaply as possible (Harvey, 2016). These challenges are further exacerbated in low-income, Global South countries where healthy food may not even be available to some, let alone affordable.

Despite the fact that many children grow out of food neophobia, some remain picky eaters and this is associated with poor nutrition and a possible over-reliance on sweet food. Many countries in the Global North also nurture 'obesogenic environments' (that is, an environment which promotes weight gain, or in which it is easy to gain weight) with large portions, a plethora of available and cheap ultra-processed food (which has been linked to weight gain and other health risks) and increasingly sedentary lifestyles. This is also thought to be a challenge in some countries in the Global South due to 'nutrition transition' (i.e. changes in structure of diet and physical activity). All parents face competing priorities when choosing what to feed their children; they may be led by time, convenience, cost and many other factors that are more pressing than the matter of immediate healthy food decisions. Parents in the UK, for example, report that their top motivator when planning family meals is to avoid stress and also that food rejection is problematic (Snuggs et al., 2019).

Health messages can also be confusing for individuals; for example, public health messages about whether we should consume 5, 7 or 10 fruits and vegetables per day have varied in recent years. Research also suggests that what we read on social media can impact adults' and children's attitudes towards food. For example, a recent review suggested that certain social media content might be related to unhealthier food preferences and disordered eating behaviours (Wu et al., 2024). Research consistently shows that children show an increased preference for food and brands which they have seen advertised on television compared with children who have not seen these advertisements. More concerningly, studies indicate that large, well-known food companies rely specifically on their more unhealthy products to attract children and that products which WHO recommends against marketing to children are routinely shown to them on television in numerous countries (Kelly et al., 2019). Parents report increased requests for junk food from their children as a direct response to this type of marketing. As children grow older and develop autonomy over their food decisions, they are able to purchase it themselves; not only is accessibility to ultra-processed food increasing across the globe, but there is evidence that fast food outlets and convenience stores are intentionally placed on school routes to attract a younger audience and increase sales. Collectively, this evidence suggests that some of the dietary challenges of children's health arise from the social and environmental food-based messages produced by large corporations.

Where next?

Moving forward, therefore, a key question must be how families can be supported to encourage a healthy diet in a variety of different contexts while facing numerous competing priorities. If this can be achieved, wider societal problems such as food insecurity and the 'obesity crisis' could also be eased.

Interventions are often tried and tested to support families on an individual basis and this research continues. There is a need for innovative approaches to this support as studies continue to suggest that parents and carers know *how* to feed their children healthily but often find this challenging because of stressors such as cost, family pressures and environmental factors. One example of a novel way of approaching the development of children's food preferences is the concept of 'visual exposure'. This involves repeatedly exposing young children not to the real food but to realistic images of target foods in order to familiarise them without wasting food on all the exposure episodes. This is thought to contribute to both lowered cost and more sustainable food provision. Early indications from this research suggest that after this process, pre-school-aged children are more willing to taste the food in question (e.g. Masento et al., 2023). Schools and childcare settings are also well-placed to support provision of healthy food and learning about how to live a healthy lifestyle. For example, in the UK, education about healthy eating is now included in the curriculum and free school meals are provided to eligible pupils. The important role that schools play in this context is also highlighted by emerging evidence that children perform better at school if they consume a healthy diet, as well as having improved concentration and increased confidence.

More widely, obesity, sustainability and health inequalities remain significant challenges. In the year 2021–2022, nearly 40% of 10–11 years olds were reported to have overweight or obesity in the UK. In adults, these levels have risen from around 15% of the population in the 1980s to around 60% today, placing burdens on healthcare systems. Individuals from more deprived areas are also more likely to experience obesity or overweight. As these trends continue globally, environmental changes must be implemented. The so-called 'sugar tax' which was applied in the UK specifically taxed sugary beverages and early studies indicate that there might be a consequential decrease in household purchase of sugary soft drinks and a reduction in consumption in some groups of children. If this approach appears to be effective with longer-term follow-up data, similar taxes could be applied to ultra-processed food. In terms of food insecurity, schemes such as food banks can provide food to individuals and families who otherwise could not afford it, but there are frequently limits to how often a person can use these organisations, restricting how much they can be relied upon. Additionally, they are not well placed to provide long-term support, relying on donations which vary considerably in their nutritional quality. Families who benefit from free school meals also often struggle to find similar support in school holidays. Future lines of enquiry, therefore, could explore whether there are other areas of the environment that could be changed at a policy level in order to adjust general public purchasing and eating behaviour. This could include finding ways to reduce the price of nutritious food and considering how schools and childcare providers can help further. Meanwhile families need quick, stress-free ways to create healthy meals for their children.

To conclude, the evidence base regarding how children learn about and develop preferences for certain foods, ultimately shaping their long-term diets, is well established. Next steps should consider how to support our future generations in doing so in a healthy, sustainable and enjoyable way.

References

Corsini, N., Slater, A., Harrison, A., Cooke, L. & Cox, D. (2013). Rewards can be used effectively with repeated exposure to increase liking of vegetables in 4-6 year old children. *Public Health Nutrition, 16*(5), pp. 942–951. doi: 10.1017/S1368980011002035.

Harvey, K. (2016). 'When I go to bed hungry and sleep, I'm not hungry': Children and parents' experiences of food insecurity. *Appetite, 1*(99), pp. 235–244. doi: 10.1016/j.appet.2016.01.004.

Kalat, J.W. & Rozin, P. (1973). 'Learned safety' as a mechanism in long-delay taste-aversion learning in rats. *Journal of Comparative & Physiological Psychology, 83*.

Kelly, B., Vandevijvere, S., Ng, S., Adams, J., Allemandi, L., Bahena-Espina, L. et al. (2019) Global benchmarking of children's exposure to television advertising of unhealthy foods and beverages across 22 countries. *Obesity reviews, 20*(2). doi: 10.1111/obr.12840.

Masento, N., Dulay, K., Roberts, A., Harvey, K., Messer, D. & Houston-Price, C. (2023). See and Eat! The impact of repeated exposure to vegetable ebooks on young children's vegetable acceptance. *Appetite, 1*(182). doi: 10.1016/j.appet.2022.106447.

Menella, J.A., Jagnow, M.S. & Beauchamp, G.K. (2001). Prenatal and postnatal flavor learning by human infants. *Pediatrics, 107*(6). https://doi.org/10.1542/peds.107.6.e88.

Mikula, G. (1989). Influencing food preferences of children by 'if-then' type instructions. *European Journal of Social Psychology, 19*(3). https://doi.org/10.1002/ejsp.2420190304.

Polland, C.M. & Booth, S. (2019). Food insecurity and hunger in rich countries – it is time for action against inequality. *Environmental Research and Public Health,* *16*(10). https://doi.org/10.3390/ijerph16101804.

Snuggs, S., Houston-Price, C. & Harvey, K. (2019). Development of a parental feeding goal measure: The family mealtime goals questionnaire. *Frontiers in Psychology, 10.* doi: 10.3389/fpsyg.2019.00455.

Spill, M.K., Johns, K., Callagan, E.H., Shapiros, M.J., Wong, Y.P, Benajmin-Neelon, S.E., Birch, L., Black, M.M., Cook, J.T., Faith, M.S., Menella, J.A. & Casavale, K.O. (2019). Repeated exposure to food and food acceptability in infants and toddlers: A systematic review. *The American Journal of Clinical Nutrition, 109*(1). https://doi.org/10.1093/ajcn/nqy308.

Wu, Y., Kemps, E. & Prichard, I. (2024). Digging into digital buffets: A systematic review of eating-related social media content and its relationship with body image and eating behaviours. *Body Image,* *48.* https://doi.org/10.1016/j.bodyim.2023.101650.

Further reading

Dovey, T. (2010). *Eating Behaviour.* Open University Press. (Chapter 4: Learning about food: developmental aspects of eating behaviour.)
This chapter provides a clear overview of the development of eating behaviour in children, considering the process from social, cognitive and environmental perspectives.
Holley, C.E., Farrow, C. & Haycraft, E. (2017). A systematic review of methods for increasing vegetable consumption in early childhood. *Current Nutrition Reports 6*(2), 157–170. https://doi.org/10.1007/s13668-017-0202-1.
This paper reviews 22 separate studies which aim to increase vegetable consumption in children and provides recommendations for the best ways to do so.

13. Biodiversity, food and society

Siobhan Maderson

Biodiversity and food systems: social and ecological synergies

Loss of 'biosphere integrity' is one of the nine planetary boundaries; it is critically threatened due to biodiversity loss and extinctions. Current global food systems put enormous pressures on biosphere integrity, threatening the functioning of both the immediate ecosystem where food is being produced, and the wider environment (Tamburini et al., 2020). Since the post-war rise of the industrial food system, we have seen a corresponding decrease in biodiversity both within the food system, in terms of crops grown and livestock varieties, and surrounding levels of biodiversity. Since 1970, agriculturally driven habitat loss has led to a 68% drop in species numbers of birds, mammals and fish. Farmed animals, their grazing land, and the arable land used to produce animal feed now account for over 75% of global agricultural land, with more than half of bird species mass now consisting of farmed chickens (Benton et al., 2021). Animals reared for human consumption – primarily cows and pigs – make up 60% of all mammal species by mass. In contrast, wild animals account for 4%.

As well as a loss of overall species diversity, global food systems are also driving a worrying loss of genetic diversity within plant and animal species, as some variants are prioritised for agricultural purposes. Since the early 20th century, common agricultural crops have seen a collapse in their varieties. Key staples of global diets such as wheat, corn and rice have seen a collapse in commercial cultivars; common vegetables such as peas, onions and carrots have also seen up to 90% decreases in cultivar diversity (Thrupp 2000)

Food systems are challenged by the climate emergency, population growth and increased demands on food-producing areas: addressing biodiversity loss and working to restore biodiversity in crops and the surrounding environment is crucial to food system stability and wider socio-ecological resilience.

Biodiversity within our food system can be enhanced by social factors, including communities' environmental knowledge, values and concepts of stewardship (Barthel et al., 2013). There can also be negative social and cultural impacts on biodiversity. Dietary choices have a powerful effect, due to the amount of land needed for food production, with some foods having a far larger 'ecological footprint', and the transformation of forest land to produce cash crops. Global income rises are associated with dietary changes which frequently result in increased ecological pressures and reduced biodiversity.

Diversity loss within food systems and the surrounding environment

Agricultural biodiversity loss: crops and livestock

Many staple foods have seen a collapse of genetic diversity amongst the main commercially cultivated lines. This is highly problematic, due to the resulting lack of associated resilience amongst crops. Crop variants that are chosen for commercial cultivation are often prioritised for commercial reasons rather than nutritional or cultural values. There is a large body of knowledge amongst many food-producing communities of a far wider range of crop variants. Much of this is held by Indigenous peoples, whose cultural heritage is interlinked with agricultural practices and knowledge of variants which thrive in local climatic conditions. There is a strong link between this traditional environmental knowledge (TEK) and practices that support biodiversity; areas benefiting from this stewardship have been referred to as 'biocultural refugia'. Biodiversity of fisheries, hay meadows, non-timber forest products, and agricultural and horticultural crops has been understood and enhanced with TEK throughout human history. Efforts to protect this knowledge, and associated cultural and crop diversity, are central to the global food sovereignty movement. Crops that are not cultivated on a large scale are often referred to as 'orphan crops'; these are frequently central to local community diets, and highly resilient to more-challenging environmental conditions. Seed-saving and seed-swapping groups are working to increase cultivation of commercially non-viable seed variants; this can increase biodiversity within food production systems, albeit on a relatively small scale. Work is being done by organisations such as the African Orphan Crops Consortium to promote understanding and use of such crops.

Similar efforts are being made to increase stock diversity through supporting the raising of 'rare' breeds of livestock. This is important to counter the general decline in breed diversity of farmed animals, and to highlight the importance of genetic diversity within animal species, many of which have been bred over centuries to thrive in particular microclimates and geographical regions. Within species, selective breeding for commercially desired traits such as productivity is associated with negative health impacts on animals as diverse – yet central to our food systems – as cattle, chickens and honey bees.

Surrounding biodiversity

As well as directly within agricultural regions, there is a worrying collapse of biodiversity in the surrounding landscape. This leads to disruption of ecosystems and food chains. Since the mid-20th century, the widespread use of insecticides and herbicides has led to massive pressure on invertebrates, and the birds and mammals that rely on them as a food source. Pollinators and other invertebrates that are central to agricultural productivity, as well as wider ecosystem integrity, have become severely depleted. Insecticide runoff into waterways creates problems for freshwater ecosystems. Fertiliser runoff is associated with algae blooms that threaten other species. Introduced agricultural species can lead to decreased biodiversity. Changes in agricultural management, such as the switch from hay to silage, has decreased biodiversity due to silage being harvested earlier, with a subsequent negative impact on the food chain. Agro-ecological, organic and mixed cropping systems can support increased biodiversity within agriculture systems. Some of these systems also emphasise the importance of community knowledge and changes in food governance (Horlings and Marsden, 2011).

Urban food system biodiversity

Biodiversity within urban/peri-urban food production, including urban agriculture, is also important and associated with social diversity. Positive synergistic effects between pollinator and plant diversity are commonly found within urban food production systems. Allotments and community gardens often have a greater variety of food plants grown throughout the seasons, and have become an important site for maintaining diverse food plant varieties that are not considered commercially viable. Urban food systems' biodiversity supports wider understanding about the role of food in society, and the environment (Lin et al., 2015).

Restoring biodiversity in food systems: challenges and regenerative pathways

Our current dominant food system has had a devastating impact on biodiversity, and there are concurrent challenges impacting the biosphere. When considering how our future food system will affect biodiversity, there are several important issues to consider.

Recent years have seen a notable rise in people following vegetarian and/or vegan diets. Similarly, there has been a steady increase in people changing their diets to include previously uncommon food, such as quinoa, and prioritise plant-based foods. Seaweed, and its cultivation, is also being promoted for dietary and environmental benefits, although there may be as yet unforeseen negative consequences from this development. How will changing diets, particularly decreased meat consumption ('demeatification'), impact biodiversity? Similarly, the rise in alternative proteins and plant-based alternatives to dairy, as well as controlled environment production, are also bound to impact biodiversity; the form, degree and scale of these impacts are not yet clear.

Climate change brings multiple and synergistic challenges to our food system, and biodiversity. We do not yet know how our currently limited crop, animal and wider biodiversity will respond to our rapidly changing climate. There are concerns that currently prioritised commercial variants may not be able to withstand changing conditions. A changing climate is also associated with an increase in crop pests and pathogens: will an increased cultivation of 'orphan crops' and more diverse seed variants see increased resilience to new threats to crop viability?

References

Barthel S, Crumley C L and Svedin U (2013) Biocultural refugia: combating the erosion of diversity in landscapes of food production. *Ecology and Society, 18*(4), pp. 1142–1152. https://doi.org/ 10.1016/j. gloenvcha.2013.05.001.

Benton T G , Bieg C, Harwatt H, Pudasaini R and Wellesley, L (2021) *Food system impacts on biodiversity loss: Three levers for food system transformation in support of nature.* Chatham House, London.

Horlings L G and Marsden T K (2011) Towards the real green revolution? Exploring the conceptual dimensions of a new ecological modernisation of agriculture that could 'feed the world'. *Global environmental change, 21*(2), pp. 441–452. https://doi.org/10.1016/j.gloenvcha.2011.01.004.

Lin B B, Philpott S M and Jha S (2015) The future of urban agriculture and biodiversity-ecosystem services: challenges and next steps. *Basic and Applied Ecology, 16*(3), pp.189–201. https://doi.org/10.1016/j.baae.2015.01.005.

Raven P H and Wagner D L (2021) Agricultural intensification and climate change are rapidly decreasing insect biodiversity. *Proceedings of the National Academy of Sciences, 118*(2) https://doi.org/10.1073/pnas.2002548117.

Sage C (2011) *Environment and food.* Oxford, Routledge.

Tamburini G, Bommarco R, Wanger T C, Kremen C, Van Der Heijden M G, Liebman M and Hallin S (2020) Agricultural diversification promotes multiple ecosystem services without compromising yield. *Science Advances*, 6. eaba1715. https://doi.org/10.1126/sciadv.aba1715.

Thrupp L A (2000) Linking agricultural biodiversity and food security: the valuable role of agrobiodiversity for sustainable agriculture. *International Affairs, 76*(2), pp. 265–281. https://doi.org/10.1111/1468-2346.00133.

Further reading

Gemmill-Herren B, Baker L E and Daniels P A (2021) *True cost accounting for food: Balancing the scale.* Oxford, Routledge.

This open-access compilation explores alternative ways of assessing the 'cost' of food, including the environmental impact of food production systems. As more biodiverse systems of food production are frequently dismissed within policy circles as being prohibitively expensive, changing ideas of cost can support biodiversity, and improve public health.

Saladino D (2021) *Eating to extinction: The world's rarest foods and why we need to save them.* London, Random House.

This engaging collection presents a highly readable, accessible exploration of various crops and livestock varieties throughout the world that are central to local communities, resilient to local climatic conditions and at risk of dying out due to changes in global food systems.

14. Biopolitics of food

Stefan Wahlen

Introducing biopolitics of food

Consider for a moment the connections between our everyday choices, such as what we eat, and the broader systems of power that govern our lives. Michel Foucault, the prominent French historian and philosopher, delved into these intricate relationships, introducing the concept of 'biopolitics' to explore, understand and critique them. During his lectures at the Collège de France (Foucault 2009 [1978/1979]), he framed biopolitics as a conceptual tool for scrutinising the interplay between biological processes – such as nutrition – and political structures, such as those evident in agricultural and food policies. In his wider work, Foucault particularly focussed on the governance of mental health, sexuality, and hygiene (Burchell et al., 1991), providing the groundwork for the conceptual framework of biopolitics. This framework can be used to analyse strategies and policies entangled in the governance of food, encompassing specific initiatives such as health or sustainability programmes and policies. Moreover, biopolitics lends itself to the investigation of the role of power in other societal mechanisms that influence our relationship with food, such as education, media, economic systems, or cultural practices. In essence, biopolitics facilitates reflection on the role of power in strategies and mechanisms of governance (Lemke, 2011), both enabling and disciplining those involved in producing and consuming food.

To comprehend power more thoroughly, Foucault employed the notion of 'genealogy' as an historical critique, tracing the evolution of ideas, practices, and institutions associated with power. He contrasted three modalities of power by examining their historical context and the specific conditions of their emergence. First, classical sovereignty, the traditional form of power, historically governed societies through a top-down authority, embodied by a monarch or ruler. Second, disciplinary power emerged in the modern era, emphasising regulation and organisation within specific institutions, such as schools, prisons, or hospitals. In modern societies, Foucault identified biopower as third modality of power, which governs biological life through policies, technologies, and scientific knowledge. Biopower investigates the governance of bodies (human and non-human), health (including plants and animals), and the environment. Examples are government initiatives promoting healthy eating, such as the drive for '5 a day' fruits and vegetables or sustainable food production, such as organic farming or integrated pest management. These examples highlight how political power manifests in policies guiding the behaviours and well-being of both human and non-human populations (Burchell et al., 1991). Biopower is closely related to biopolitics – the former being the specific exertion of power, while the latter entails the broader, encompassing strategies and mechanisms of governance, such as recommended daily dietary guidelines or farming regulations to control river pollution.

In essence, biopolitics serves as a lens through which we comprehend the sophisticated ways political and regulatory power operates, utilising various technologies to regulate and control populations and their behaviours and activities. It emphasises the importance of recognising and understanding how food-related practices are intertwined with broader systems of political and economic power and governing regulations. Biopolitics assists in debunking traditional views of how politics might exert power in governing conduct at the individual and/or population level. For example, biopolitics might examine how the consumer is constituted as subject or how the identities of the individual consumer are shaped in food markets. In an economic understanding, the consumer is an individual chooser, whose autonomy becomes normalised and an unquestioned central mechanism for regulating markets. In this sense, biopolitics challenges more traditional perspectives on politics, as the centrality of (bio)power uncovers processes relevant to the governing of food, extending beyond governmental institutions. Biopolitics and biopower also point toward practices of surveillance, control, and regulation in the food system. A focus on these practices emphasises aspects of the ethical dimensions of food, shedding light on human rights (e.g., food justice), social equality, and overall well-being in the food system.

The literature on biopolitics can be divided into two strands (see Lemke, 2011). The first involves its theoretical and philosophical traditions that reflect on the nature of biopolitics. The second deploys and utilises the concept for empirically investigating social phenomena. The remainder of this entry will focus on the latter, discussing key concerns of the biopolitics of food provisioning as well as eating. To conclude, it will address potential future concerns of food biopolitics.

Food system biopolitics

Biopolitics has not occupied a central position in the study of food. However, various scholars from diverse disciplines have employed biopolitics with varying interpretations to empirically examine food-related phenomena. If biopolitics is basically concerned with the role of (bio)power governing all aspects of life, the unifying theme in the biopolitical study of food is the examination of power dynamics in the politics surrounding biological processes tied to food production and consumption. Food system biopolitics inherently brings forth the controversies entangled in the governing of food and highlights ethical dimensions, considering how power mechanisms shape food systems. For instance, the power dynamics between large agribusinesses and small-scale farmers raise ethical concerns regarding equitable access, fair trade practices, and sustainability. Another example is the biopolitics of food labelling, revealing the power of information in market mechanisms designed to tell us what to eat, posing questions about transparency, truthfulness, and the right to make informed choices. These examples illustrate that, within the framework of biopolitics, food is not just sustenance but a terrain of ethical and political negotiation. The following sections provide glimpses into food's biopolitical landscape and evaluate specific examples that empirically explore biopower in the practices of provisioning and consuming food.

Biopolitics of food provisioning

Food provisioning entails the entire organisation of agriculture and food production as well as processing and distribution. A Foucauldian reading of biopolitics emphasises the role of (economic) freedom in late modern societies, including freedom in food provisioning. The laissez-faire approach of liberal economic thought has inspired an analysis of biopolitics in the political economy of food provisioning. For example, Nally (2011) traces the biopolitics of the (late) modern food economy in an historical analysis of the role of power in various food regimes. The analysis describes a gradual shift from a morality of hunger towards a political economy of food security. The shift towards industrial food systems is associated with a focus on (liberal) market economies and the introduction of economic measures. Currently, in an increasingly globalised food system, multi-national corporations are the primary actors shaping the practices and governance of food provisioning from farm to fork. Biopolitics on the farm extends beyond power concerned with human life to consider animals and plants. For example, Saxton (2015) investigated the eco-biopolitics of Californian strawberry fields as extreme environments in which power operates through the management and control of human and non-human biological life through pesticides. The chemical interventions of industrialised food production impact not only strawberry plant health, but also farm workers' bodies through the application of pesticides and accompanying illnesses and cancers. Exploited labour and farmworkers' poor health are, however, not just an outcome; they also demonstrate how power in agro-industrial food regimes impacts the multifaceted nature of agricultural knowledge and practices.

Climate mitigation policies targeted at livestock farming also point to the regulation of non-human lives. McGregor et al. (2021) use the lens of biopower to investigate contradictions in mitigation efforts reducing cattle methane emissions, including more-than-human forms of regulation from the molecular gastroenterological scale of cows (through specific diets) towards planetary climate scales and efforts made by the Food and Agriculture Organisation of the United Nations (FAO) and the Intergovernmental Panel on Climate Change (IPCC). McGregor et al. (2021) interweave agricultural practices with the broader socio-political landscape, underscoring how nonhuman resistance and agency, such as that from cows, can shape and challenge biopolitical strategies. Meat products are controversial and have led to the development of alternative proteins. Sexton (2018) explores biopolitical mechanisms associated with cultured meat. By exploring the process of how novel 'things become food' for consumers, Sexton (2018) points to the biopolitical potentialities of edibility. As such, acceptance of cultured cells as 'meat' has become the latest frontier for moralising consumers to be more ethical or environmentally friendly through their food choices.

Consumers are also put centre stage in the industrialised food system in terms of marketing, advertising, and digitalised communication. Dulsrud and Jacobsen (2009) describe how various retail techniques govern the consumer in the supermarket, influencing food choices. Various market technologies govern conduct and discipline consumers in food environments: supermarkets build environments that steer bodily movements through space and normalise shopping routines. In addition, data collection on digital platforms and datafication are gaining relevance in food provisioning (Dulsrud and Forno, 2023). New forms of governing and disciplining consumers emerge on digital platforms through their underlying algorithms shaping consumer conduct by providing individualised marketing regimes that target consumers' digitally perceived desires and tastes.

Biopolitics of consuming food

Food consumption is often understood as either food shopping or the act of ingesting food. A biopolitical take on food consumption can relate to both and even beyond, emphasising practices of surveillance, control, and regulation of the processes of consumption. The governing of food consumption involves a complex interplay of actors, including government agencies, health advocates, environmental organisations, and commercial entities, all contributing to the regulation and steering of consumption practices (Wahlen, 2012). Food knowledge and how it is used to address dietary issues are both inherently political. Mayes and Thompson's (2015) biopolitical analysis describes knowledge produced by nutrition sciences in health promotion, disease prevention, or marketing as 'nutritional scientism'. Such a perspective exposes the power dynamics and ethical implications of nutritional knowledge, pointing towards the individual responsibility, freedom, and overall well-being of consumers and allowing reflection on knowledge about physiological processes. Yet, eating transcends physiological aspects; it is embedded in the biopolitics of everyday life, where discussions often revolve around what is understood as 'good food'. Processes of differentiation are central to most food consumption. Individual and collective cultural identities are intricately

woven into the politics of food consumption especially at the intersections of migration, multiculturalism, and the globalisation of eating habits. Cultural appropriation and the authenticity of food are recurring topics on social media as well, pointing towards ethical contestations of 'good food'. In contemporary societies, food is indeed at the heart of capitalist assemblages and often communicated via the media. Goodman et al. (2017) highlight mediated foodscapes that regulate cultural politics, food identities, and evolving social constructs of 'good food'. Such a biopolitical consideration of mediated foodscapes challenges normalised notions of responsible eating, providing a more nuanced picture on responsibilities for undesired outcomes of food consumption.

Political initiatives currently underscore how food environments significantly influence our dietary choices. The perspective on marketing techniques of Dulsrud and Jacobsen (2009), outlined above, can also be extended to a consumer perspective. Du Gay's (2004) genealogical critique of self-service exemplifies the constitution of consumers as subjects disciplined by self-service approaches. Whereas in the past sales assistants would hand out products over the counter, introducing self-service has put consumers to work. From a biopolitical perspective, retail techniques serve as technologies of government, shaping the behaviour and identity of consumers, allowing critique of individual responsibilities ascribed to the autonomous consumers (Wahlen, 2012). The biopolitics of food consumption extends to normative, sometimes conflicting goals, touching on environmental concerns, health, and also food safety. Consider the example of the 'best before' date introduced as a protective measure against microbial harm and potential consumer illness. However, it now poses an environmental challenge by contributing to increased food waste (Wahlen, 2018). The 'best before' date and associated shelf life exemplifies the biopolitics of everyday life, involving governmental regulations, the food industry, and research efforts in shaping new eating practices. Various other initiatives are implemented to promote healthy eating, such as the '5 a day' fruits and vegetables campaign. Dietary recommendations emphasise individual freedom and the 'responsibilisation' of the consumer and their choices. Yet, as Coveney (2006) outlines, individuals might become anxious about what they eat and how they are disciplined through dietary advice, and in the end just feel shame and guilt over what they are eating, resulting in inaction or even resistance. Policy initiatives and measures might hence have adverse effects and might lead to the opposite of intended outcomes. Governments manage health crises, such as the so-called obesity pandemic. Understanding the reactions of populations to these measures become essential in the biopolitical landscape (see Guthman, 2011) to delineate the role of power in governing consumption.

Future concerns of food biopolitics

As demonstrated throughout this entry, the biopolitical approach to food is inherently diverse, reflecting an interdisciplinary framework that is interested in the power dynamics between biological life and how food is governed. At the core of biopolitics lies the exploration of how various forms of power intersect and operate, influencing the production and consumption of food as an integral aspect of life. While existing biopolitical analyses have delved into issues of health and environmental sustainability within the global, industrialised, and capitalist food system, several social questions warrant further investigation. For example, the precarious conditions and exploitation faced by food industry workers globally, in both the Global South and North, merit scrutiny through a biopolitical lens. Examining the role of food movements (e.g. Zhang, 2021), such as fair trade or slow food, from a biopolitical perspective could shed light on how these movements uphold standards governing worker processes, while marketing's affective, emotive, and status-based approaches often clash with public health objectives. Engaging with recent debates on food biotechnology, including CRISPR-Cas gene editing in food production, offers an opportunity to assess the ethical implications of biopolitical interventions at both the molecular and species levels. Environmental concerns, encompassing ecological sustainability, climate change, and environmental justice, provide fertile ground for biopolitical inquiry into agricultural and food policies impacting natural resources.

Moving forward, the biopolitics of food could explore trends in biologically oriented nutrition research, touching on diet and disease, nutrigenomics, obesity, chronic diseases, aging, and mental health. The burgeoning interest in the human microbiome opens avenues for microbiopolitics research. Moreover, the growing emphasis on food sustainability has sparked political debates on plant-based diets, planetary health diets, and processed as well as ultra-processed foods, inviting further investigation. The intersection of power and knowledge warrants ongoing inquiry into how nutrition science shapes political agendas and policies related to nutritional evidence. This includes examining questions of surveillance, regulation, and control over dietary choices and understanding how governing practices connect with human well-being, social justice, and environmental concerns. Alternative food networks, local food systems, and food sovereignty movements challenging dominant biopolitical practices present an opportunity to explore efforts towards establishing food democracy within the industrialised food system, addressing the rights of farmers and labourers, and understanding the impact of globalised industrialised food systems on cultural and local food habits.

References

Burchell, G, Gordon, C & Miller, P (1991) *The Foucault Effect: Studies in Governmentality.* Chicago: University of Chicago Press.

du Gay, P (2004) Self-Service: Retail, Shopping and Personhood. *Consumption Markets & Culture*, 7(2): 149–163. https://doi.org/10.1080/1025386042000246205.

Dulsrud, A & Forno, F (2023) *Digital Food Provisioning in Times of Multiple Crises: How Social and Technological Innovations Shape Everyday Consumption Practices.* London: Palgrave.

Dulsrud, A & Jacobsen, E (2009) In-store Marketing as a Mode of Discipline. *Journal of Consumer Policy*, 32: 203–218. https://doi.org/10.1007/s10603-009-9104-y.

Foucault, M (2009 [1979]) *Security, Territory, Population: Lectures at the College de France 1977-1978.* London: Palgrave Macmillan.

Goodman, MK, Johnston, J & Cairns, K (2017) Food, Media and Space: The Mediated Biopolitics of Eating. *Geoforum*, 84: 161–168. https://doi.org/10.1016/j.geoforum.2017.06.017.

Guthman, J (2011) *Weighing in: Obesity, Food Justice and the Limits Of Capitalism*. Los Angeles: University of California Press.

Guthman, J & Brown, S (2016) I Will Never Eat Another Strawberry Again: The Biopolitics of Consumer-citizenship in the Fight against Methyl Iodide in California. *Agriculture and Human Values*, 33: 575–585. https://doi.org/10.1007/s10460-015-9626-7.

Lemke, T (2011) *Biopolitics: An Advanced Introduction*. New York: New York University Press.

Mayes, CR & Thompson, DB (2015) What Should We Eat? Biopolitics, Ethics, and Nutritional Scientism. *Bioethical Inquiry*, 12: 587–599. https://doi.org/10.1007/s11673-015-9670-4.

McGregor, A, Rickards, L, Houston, D, Goodman, MK & Bojovic, M (2021) The Biopolitics of Cattle Methane Emissions Reduction: Governing Life in a Time of Climate Change. *Antipode*, 53: 1161–1185. https://doi.org/10.1111/anti.12714.

Nally, D. (2011) The Biopolitics of Food Provisioning. *Transactions of the Institute of British Geographers*, 36: 37–53. https://doi.org/10.1111/j.1475-5661.2010.00413.x.

Saxton, DI (2015) Strawberry Fields as Extreme Environments: The Ecobiopolitics of Farmworker Health. *Medical Anthropology*, 34(2): 166–183. https://doi.org/10.1080/01459740.2014.959167.

Sexton, AE (2018) Eating for the Post-Anthropocene: Alternative Proteins and the Biopolitics of Edibility. *Transactions of the Institute of British Geographers*, 43: 586–600. https://doi.org/10.1111/tran.12253.

Wahlen, S (2012) *Governing Everyday Consumption*. Helsinki: National Consumer Research Centre. http://urn.fi/URN:ISBN:978-951-698-251-2.

Wahlen, S (2018). "Foodsharing": Reflecting on Individualized Collective Action in a Collaborative Consumption Community Organisation. In: Cruz, I, Ganga, R, Wahlen, S (eds), *Contemporary Collaborative Consumption*. Kritische Verbraucherforschung. Springer VS, Wiesbaden. https://doi.org/10.1007/978-3-658-21346-6_4.

Zhang, JY (2021) (Bio)politics of Existence and Social Change: Insights from the Good Food Movement. *The Sociological Review*, 69(3): 647–663. https://doi.org/10.1177/00380261211009069.

Further reading

Coveney, J (2006) *Food, Morals and Meaning: The Pleasure and Anxiety of Eating* (2nd edition). London: Routledge.

Coveney's book delves into the societal and ethical implications of food consumption, exploring how power dynamics and cultural values influence individuals' relationships with food, intertwining perspectives on food choice and the moral significance of eating.

Carolan, M. (2011) *Embodied Food Politics*. London: Routledge.

Carolan's book emphasises the role of embodied knowledge, materialisations, and the ways individuals know, experience, and relate to the food system, considering bodies as sites of (affective) knowledge which are governed by food industries.

STEFAN WAHLEN

15. Biosecurity

GARETH ENTICOTT

Introduction

Biosecurity, in its simplest definition, is concerned with 'keeping life safe'. The simplicity of this definition, however, belies biosecurity's diversity and application, as well as its geographical relevance to both the global north and south. Biosecurity is central to the integrity of the food chain and food safety, the health and welfare of farmed animals, the practices and decisions taken by professionals and animal keepers, and the presence or absence of 'pests' – whether they be bacteria, viruses, or plant and animal species. In doing so, the concept of biosecurity raises some fundamental philosophical questions relating to food and society: what kind of lives do we find within the food supply chain, and which lives need saving? More specific definitions of biosecurity refer to its role in protecting 'against risks posed by diseases and organisms' using tools such as disease surveillance (testing), exclusion (such as zoning and restricting movements), eradication and control (such as individual or mass culling), and sharing vital information to encourage a state of readiness (Renault et al., 2022).

The importance of biosecurity to food studies lies, firstly, with its implications for food safety and public health. Although the word biosecurity only emerged in the 1980s, its core principles are common to disease management practices that have sought to eliminate bacteria and pathogens from common foods such as milk and meat. At the same time, biosecurity affects crops, trees, and animals and insects that are not farmed. Secondly, the challenges to public health have been exacerbated through globalisation and climate change. Approximately 75% of newly discovered diseases are zoonotic: that is, they are transmissible from animals to humans. Covid-19 is the most dramatic of these, affecting not just human health but the health of food supply chains. The climate emergency will also contribute to the spread of pathogens affecting the productivity of livestock. Similarly, climate change is associated with the spread of invasive species and pathogens responsible for deterioration in plant and tree health. Thirdly, biosecurity is central to international trade and the global food system. On the one hand, industrial systems of agriculture are dependent upon ever tighter layers of biosecurity, which themselves may be the cause of subsequent disease outbreaks. On the other hand, the globalisation of agriculture is increasingly reliant upon sophisticated technologies of risk assessment and traceability to ensure that countries remain disease-free, as well as systems of inspection and surveillance to prevent the entry of pathogens into disease-free countries. In doing so, however, biosecurity regulations reveal not only the biopolitics that hold global agriculture together, but also how other countries are held apart: the winners and losers of globalisation.

Current issues

Biopolitics and biosecurity

Attempts to prevent the spread of disease between and within countries focus attention on biopolitics: the different practices and technologies that define disease and shape the behaviour of farmers and publics to maintain biosecurity (Hinchliffe et al., 2016). Given the biological nature of disease threats, science and scientific practices are frequently invoked in the biopolitics of biosecurity. Studies of the politics of disease control, however, show how resorting to scientific analysis is used to delay and prevaricate decision making for contentious biosecurity concerns. Similarly, the 'antipolitical' nature of practices such as disease risk assessment are the focus of debates between nation states seeking to export agricultural produce and those seeking to protect their farmers from disease risks. Biosecurity practices invoked to manage large-scale outbreaks of disease may privilege some forms of biosecurity expertise against others: the local, specific, and contextual knowledge of field veterinarians versus the distanced, quantifiable, and placeless knowledge of disease modelling (Bickerstaff and Simmons, 2004). The reliance on computer modelling has important effects, justifying the pre-emptive culling of healthy livestock during the outbreak of foot and mouth disease (FMD) in the UK in 2001.

In this critique of the rigid application of scientific expertise, other versions of veterinary practice are shown to involve greater levels of flexibility. Biosecurity research in areas such as animal disease and food safety has come to show how 'care' and 'tinkering' are therefore essential practices to the implementation of biosecurity on the ground, resulting in an ongoing contextual negotiation of scientific knowledge and protocols to ensure they 'work' (Lavau and Bingham, 2017). Related research has shown Indigenous knowledge and practices provide alternative ways of thinking and doing biosecurity, yet these are threatened by colonialist approaches to biosecurity (Kuru et al., 2021). Contestations and negotiations of biosecurity practices also reflect disputes over veterinary identity and appropriate ways of working. These examples from animal health also reflect the geography of the veterinary profession and the physical and cultural distance between decision makers and those responsible for the implementation of disease controls. In other areas, such as tree and plant health, forms of non-scientific expertise – such as 'citizen science' – have been increasingly turned to identify and report disease incursions. Nevertheless, the reliance on volunteers to monitor biosecurity raises broader questions over the efficacy and sustainability of these neoliberal forms of governance.

The socio-economic impacts of biosecurity

The impacts of biosecurity regulations are felt not only by animals within the food system, but also by those people who look after them. Farmers may experience significant economic impacts to their businesses arising from the loss of animals and/or productivity as a result of activities such as frequent disease testing. The outbreak of FMD in 2001 in the UK, for example, caused a 60% fall in revenue from traditional farm activities, leading many farmers to consider 'rebalancing' their farm businesses to include greater income from agri-environmental schemes and tourism (Franks et al., 2003). The culling of farm animals is also associated with socio-psychological impacts amongst farmers, which are attributed to the emotional bonds with their animals, and their death at the wrong time of life, in the wrong place (Convery et al., 2005). Farmers' well-being may also be affected by the disruption to the routine of the agricultural calendar when farms are 'shut down' by biosecurity regulations. Impacts to farmers' well-being may also stem from bureaucratic procedures that accompany biosecurity regulations which are unbending and show little compassion to farmers (Jaye et al., 2021). This can contribute to a breakdown in trust between governments and farmers, which

has consequences for farmers' motivations to follow biosecurity advice. Veterinarians may also face workplace stress from culling healthy animals, which may be a key reason for exiting the profession.

Biosecurity behaviours

Changing behaviour – particularly farmers' – has been a key concern for those responsible for implementing biosecurity rules and regulations. A general approach taken by governments has been to assume that farmers and other livestock keepers require education about how best to manage disease or information to guide judgements relating to risk. For example, in New Zealand, cattle herds are categorised according to their disease risk and incentives are offered to guide farmers towards purchasing the least risky animals. The extent to which these forms of 'market instrument' are successful has been questioned: farmers' biosecurity decisions are complicated, fitting within a complex task of managing their farm as a whole and their own understandings of their land, herds, nature, and disease. Whilst farmers' biosecurity decisions may be motivated by a range of factors, the role of cultural identity can play a significant role in guiding their biosecurity decisions. The concept of 'good farming' suggests that status is achieved through farmers' ability to visibly demonstrate specific cultural symbols. In disease management, biosecurity practices such as having a clean and tidy farm may be associated with being a good farmer. Other biosecurity practices may be trumped by other symbolic goods, such as the importance of breeding or purchasing high-status stock (Enticott and Little, 2022).

The role of cultural identity is also important in shaping biosecurity citizenship: the values and duties of everyone in eliminating threats posed by disease and invasive species. Developing biosecurity citizenship is a pre-requisite in an era of constant threat and emergency, with questions over how this is achieved and how effective it is. In China, for instance, biosecurity may rest on cultural practices of gifting and relationship building (Chan and Enticott, 2019) in combination with governmental attempts to modernise the image of farmers. Elsewhere biosecurity citizenship activities may include national regulations, the alignment of border practices with national identity, and material and discursive practices that emphasise individual responsibility. In the management of avian influenza in East Asia, these attempts to prepare for and secure territory may also be reflective of wider geopolitical relations and tensions (Keck, 2020). In all of these attempts to produce biosecurity citizenship, a fundamental question is who decides and where: in the private spaces of laboratories and boardrooms, or in spaces where biosecurity decision making can be democratised and full consideration given to what kind of natures and lives are worth protecting (Barker, 2010).

Future concerns

In the aftermath of the Covid-19 pandemic, subsequent political and economic restructuring, and ongoing climate change, biosecurity will be an increasingly important issue for food systems and society. The pandemic has shown the vulnerability of food supply chains to biosecurity concerns and highlighted public responses to biosecurity crises. Whilst much of the existing focus of biosecurity research has been on farmers' activities, in future, more attention is likely to be paid to the way the public respond to biosecurity emergencies through, for example, panic buying and hoarding of food, or longer-term planning ('prepping') for biosecurity events. The pandemic has also shown how sites of food production (such as meat processing plants and markets) are themselves implicated in the incubation and spread of zoonotic disease. Of particular concern here is the extent to which the effects of biosecurity breakdowns are unequally distributed. On farms and processing sites, this leads to a concern to examine how working conditions put already marginalised workers, such as migrant workers, at greater risk of the effects of zoonotic disease. In doing so, this contributes to debates about the kinds of food systems that are desirable and resilient to future shocks, and the extent to which international agri-food corporations will seek to protect existing food production systems despite their inherent biosecurity risks. At the same time, agricultural restructuring raises other questions about biosecurity. The use of rewilding as a means of ecological restoration and climate change mitigation, for instance, raises questions about disease management within reintroduced animal populations. Whilst the presence of wild animals may provide biosecurity concerns to farmed

animals, they may also contribute to an active re-imagining of place such that their removal for biosecurity purposes becomes highly contested. This raises other questions about the potential for new digital technologies to minimise biosecurity risks as part of the fourth agricultural revolution. This could include new technologies of traceability and tracking, such as the use of wearable technologies by farm animals to monitor their health, but also limit their ranging behaviours to prevent biosecurity risks.

References

Barker K (2010) Biosecure citizenship: politicising symbiotic associations and the construction of biological threat. *Transactions of the Institute of British Geographers* 35(3): 350–363.

Barker K and Francis RA (Eds) (2021) *Routledge Handbook of Biosecurity and Invasive Species.* London: Routledge.

Bickerstaff K and Simmons P (2004) The right tool for the job? Modeling, spatial relationships, and styles of scientific practice in the UK foot and mouth crisis. *Environment and Planning D: Society and Space* 22(3): 393–412.

Chan KW and Enticott G (2019) The Suzhi farmer: constructing and contesting farming subjectivities in post-socialist China. *Journal of Rural Studies* 67: 69–78.

Convery I, Bailey C, Mort M and Baxter J (2005) Death in the wrong place? Emotional geographies of the UK 2001 foot and mouth disease epidemic. *Journal of Rural Studies* 21: 99–109.

Enticott G and Little R (2022) (Dis)Entangling livestock marketplaces: cattle purchasing, fluid engineering and market displays. *Environment and Planning E: Nature and Space.* DOI: 10.1177/25148486221120543.

Franks J, Lowe P, Phillipson J, et al. (2003) The impact of foot and mouth disease on farm businesses in Cumbria. *Land Use Policy* 20(2): 159–168.

Hinchliffe S, Bingham N, Allen J, et al. (2016) *Pathological Lives: Disease, Space and Biopolitics.* Oxford: Wiley Blackwell.

Jaye C, Noller G, Bryan M, et al. (2021) "No better or worse off": Mycoplasma bovis, farmers and bureaucracy. *Journal of Rural Studies* 88: 40–49.

Keck F (2020) *Avian Reservoirs: Virus Hunters and Birdwatchers in Chinese*

Sentinel Posts. Durham, NC: Duke University Press.

Kuru R, Marsh A and Ganley B (2021) Elevating and recognising knowledge of indigenous peoples to improve forest biosecurity. *Frontiers in Forests and Global Change* 4. https://doi.org/10.3389/ffgc.2021.719106

Lavau S and Bingham N (2017) Practices of attention, possibilities for care: making situations matter in food safety inspection. *The Sociological Review* 65(2_suppl): 20–35.

Renault V, Humblet M-F and Saegerman C (2022) Biosecurity concept: origins, evolution and perspectives. *Animals* 12(1): 63.

Further reading

Hinchliffe et al. (2016) *Pathological Lives: Disease, Space and Biopolitics*. Oxford: Wiley Blackwell.

This book provides a comprehensive overview of the biopolitics of disease control practices, and the consequences of different modes of agriculture for biosecurity.

Barker K and Francis RA (Eds) (2021) *Routledge Handbook of Biosecurity and Invasive Species*. London: Routledge.

This edited collection provides a range of chapters covering biosecurity issues facing plants and animals, across different ecosystems including invasive species, rewilding, knowledges and expertise, and Indigenous biosecurity practices.

GARETH ENTICOTT

16. Biotechnology and food

Brian Dowd-Uribe and Jack A. Heinemann

Introduction: biotechnology and food in the global food system

Biotechnology and food are best understood in relationship to the larger forces shaping the food system, which consists of its production, processing, distribution, marketing, and consumption. This entry begins by characterising the terms food and biotechnology, before connecting them to some key food system dynamics.

Food, at its most basic, is what people eat to provide sustenance. However, food is more than a conveyor belt for calories and nutrients. For this entry it is important to note that food production and access is mediated through a global food system comprised of multiple actors. Food also has important cultural values that extend beyond its capacity to nourish.

Biotechnology can be usefully classified into two categories: classical and modern (NRC, 1989). Classical biotechnology refers to the identification, selection, and then amplification of individuals with desired traits. Modern biotechnology is used to produce genetically modified or engineered (GM) organisms. It includes the direct manipulation of genetic material, usually DNA, at the cellular level. Transgenesis, where a gene from one organism is transferred to another organism, and site-directed techniques, such as genome editing, are both examples of how organisms are genetically modified. The development of new reagents since the early 2000s, such as CRISPR/Cas, has improved the efficiency of genome editing such that it can be applied at commercial scale to plants. The term GM crop is used to refer to plants with traits that were developed using this suite of modern biotechnology techniques.

Modern biotechnologies can be used to make organisms that contribute in different ways to the food system, such as in the production of micro-organisms for precision fermentation, modifying the traits of plants and animals, and constructing biological pesticides. This entry focuses on plant agricultural biotechnologies, or those seeds and plants that have been modified using modern biotechnological techniques, and which are sown in agricultural fields. The dynamics developed here to characterise plant agricultural biotechnologies are also relevant in understanding other biotechnological applications in food and in other sectors.

Several food system dynamics help to characterise the relationship between food and biotechnology. Globalisation of the food system, connecting food production and consumption across vast geographic areas, is characterised by a more concentrated private and nation-state supply pipeline. Private firms control a sizable portion of the processing, distribution, and retailing activity. A shrinking number of private firms also control the seed, chemical, animal reproduction, and farm machinery industries that develop and sell inputs to farmers. The products they make are increasingly homogenised for large-scale production across vast areas of the world.

These features of concentration are compounded by a regional specialisation in the production of particular food commodities. For example, among the top ten rice producing countries, China alone grows 91% of the sum total produced by the other nine. Likewise, the US alone grows 87% of the maize produced by the sum of the world's next nine largest producers. The production advantages can be converted into market dominating trade positions. Amongst the top 10 rice exporting countries, the US exports more than the sum of the next nine largest producers, and along with Argentina exports an amount of maize equal to the sum of the next eight largest producers (Clapp, 2021; FAOSTAT, 2023).

Globalisation has also further facilitated the transformation of food from its cultural uses into commodities that attract the highest bidder. Food commodities become defined by the relative wealth of the consumer. One implication is that an increasing proportion of agricultural products are not directly consumed by people. Examples are meat production that demands 36% of the calories produced by agriculture, and combustion engines that consume 9% of the calories that could feed people. Only just over half of the food calories made by agriculture are used to directly feed people (Cassidy et al., 2013).

Meanwhile, the use of modern biotechnology on food-producing organisms has driven the development of specific regulations. The following section first details the ways in which modern biotechnology has expanded the ways and sites in which regulations intersect with the global food system. Next, the entry discusses how the regulatory, concentration, and commodity-driven dynamics affect the geography of GM crop production, and specifically for smallholder farmers in the Global South. The entry concludes by discussing possible biotechnology and food futures.

Explaining the relationship between biotechnology and food

Regulation

Much has been written about the concentration of the agriculture biotechnology and chemistry sectors as well as in the food retail sector. This is no accident. It is the result of the economic forces acting on modern nation states. Particularly for agricultural biotechnology, a critical accelerant was the extension of the utility or process-based patent instrument to seeds and other plant reproductive material by the 1980 US Supreme Court decision in *Diamond v. Chakrabarty* and subsequent changes in the Protection of New Varieties of Plants (UPOV) convention of 1991, to 'germplasm' (Heinemann et al., 2014).

The power of the patent was de facto established through the discovery of heterosis, a process whereby the desired agronomic trait was locked into the parental generation and the (F1) offspring were sold to farmers. F1 offspring did not efficiently pass the special phenotype, or desirable characteristics, to their (F2) offspring, requiring farmers to return to the breeder each season. This practice was so effective it became known as the 'biological patent' and transformed the corn agroecosystem in the US from open-pollinated farmer-led to the hybrid breeder-controlled system dominant now.

The biological patent is limited to certain species. In the 1980s, the opportunity arose to extend the legal utility patent to other plants when they were modified using molecular biotechnology. As a result, GM plants may receive a utility patent that follows their germplasm, regardless of the trait's value. Due to the legal risk of violating patent rights through saving seed, farmers again must return to breeders for new seed each season.

The rewards of owning fundamental patent intellectual property rights (IPR) on germplasm have united biotechnology with the chemical industry; the main catalyst being (chemical) herbicide resistant staple crops.

Along with the collapse in breeder and breed stock diversity was a restructuring in public research toward 'technology transfer'. The public research sector, from government to university, aligned to produce processes and products that could attract the strongest licensable IPR instruments to industry.

Meanwhile, the public breeding capacity withered to the point where farmers must turn to the private sector for seed. Innovations that might work locally, for small farmers, lose out to innovations that can be sold to the largest market at the greatest profit. No matter how useful a new trait may be for a small market, it must compete with all the other germplasm that breeders amplify for the biggest markets each year (Clapp, 2021).

The other side of regulation is to ensure accuracy in advertising, compliance with certifications, and safety. Biosafety legislation describes how the techniques of modern biotechnology may be used (e.g. in contained laboratories), prescribes when GM organisms intended for use in food must be tested, and applies to the release of the GM organisms into the environment, such as a farm. In some jurisdictions, regulations also impose product labelling requirements to inform consumer choices. Whereas patents provide a pathway to maximising profit, labelling requirements have served to limit sales of GM crops (Bovay and Alston, 2018).

Production

In 1994, the FLAVR SAVR tomato, genetically engineered to forestall fruit softening for longer periods after harvest, became the first commercial food crop produced using modern biotechnology in the world. After receiving regulatory approval, it was sold via major market brands of tomato paste in the United States and United Kingdom. Though engineered to endure, it only lasted commercially until 1999, its downfall due to stiff consumer backlash (Bruening and Lyons, 2000).

The creation of FLAVR SAVR epitomised the hope that modern biotechnology could improve consumer experiences. It also represented how market rejection of modern biotechnology food products can limit the production and consumption of GM plants. Market rejection continues to affect where GM plants are produced and consumed. Even in the United States, the earliest and historically largest producer of GM crops, the potential for market rejection is a key factor for farmers considering the adoption of inputs derived from modern biotechnology (Ufer et al., 2022). Moreover, perceptions of GM foods as causing adverse health and environmental effects, or principally benefiting food manufacturers, continue to influence consumer preferences for non-GM foods (Rose et al., 2020).

The regulatory frameworks described above, and, crucially, the concentration in control over the IPR of biotechnology processes and traits, as well as in the agricultural seed and chemical industry, are also major ways to understand the current (and future) geographies of GM crop production. Concentration in the seed and chemical industry helps to explain the types of GM crops and traits produced. In 2022, four seed companies accounted for 51% of global seed sales. Those same four companies also accounted for 62% of global agrochemical sales (ETC, 2022), and are also the largest purveyors of GM seeds.

The coupling of seeds and chemical industries, and the concentration in IPR held by the same companies, explains the existing suite of commercialised GM crops and traits. Only four GM crops and two traits dominate GM crop production. Canola, cotton, maize, and soybean with two traits, herbicide tolerance and pest resistance, accounted for 99% of total area planted in GM crops in 2019. Seventy-one per cent of all GM crops contain herbicide tolerance traits, vastly increasing sales and use of several herbicides (Brookes, 2022).

GM crops are principally directed towards large-scale producers of commodities in specific parts of the world where a significant return on investment can be achieved. Since the mid-1990s, GM crop production has risen sharply in specific areas. Beginning in 1996 with 1.7 million hectares, the total area grown of GM crops in 2019 reached 190.4 million hectares in 2019, or approximately 12.2% of total global cropland (ISAAA, 2019; FAOSTAT, 2023).

The coverage of GM crops, however, is punctuated by a recent stagnation with significant regional and crop market concentration. Since 2014 the total global cropland devoted to GM crops has oscillated between a high of 12.3% and a low of 11.7% (ISAAA, 2019; FAOSTAT, 2023). Only three countries, the US, Brazil, and Argentina, account for 78%

of total GM crop area. Adding Canada and India brings that figure to 91%. In many of the countries listed above, GM versions of key crops have saturated their markets, helping to explain recent stagnation. For example, in 2018, 94% of total soybean production in the US is GM and 89% of total maize production in Brazil is GM.

Production data and evaluations of biotechnology products are also the outputs of interested parties creating a narrative that shapes socioeconomic/legal systems. The only global repository of GM crop production data and the only global assessment of economic impacts (both of which we draw from above) are both funded by the relevant industry. Moreover, many of the individual assessments of GM crops in particular countries are also funded by technology owners or promoters (Glover, 2009). Further compounding these issues is the primary focus on economic impacts in evaluative studies in the Global South, and expressed in a narrow suite of metrics, principally average yield and profit gains (Fischer et al., 2015). These evaluative studies have been widely critiqued given a number of biases of composition, notably time, selection, and cultivation, and counter-factual biases, often resulting in overestimations of benefits (Stone, 2012).

The most contested evaluative metric related to production is yield. Much metaphoric blood has been shed over whether GM crops yield more. No commercially available traits introduced by genetic modification specifically address improving yields. Rather, the dominant traits of pest and herbicide resistance can, in principle, improve productivity by decreasing weed competition and/or pest destruction. Many studies, which predominantly use field trial and early adoption data, show an increase in yields in comparison to conventionally bred crops. But closer evaluation of these studies shows that yields do not exceed productivity trends. This led the US National Academies to conclude that "there is no evidence ... that they have substantially increased the rate at which U.S. agriculture is increasing yields" (NASEM, 2016:7).

Smallholder farmers

Smallholder and peasant farmers, or farming households working plots less than 5 hectares in size, play a crucial role in food production. Globally they produce more than half of the world's food calories, and in the specific regions of Latin America, Asia, and Africa, they produce the vast majority of food calories (Samberg et al., 2016). But smallholder farmers, and, in particular, the food crops they produce, have remained on the fringes of GM crop development.

What limits modern biotechnology, used to create GM crops, from being a significant benefit to those smallholders, who produce a majority of our food? One key barrier has been IPR. The concentration of temporary monopoly rights among large private and public entities hinders public use of products and the ongoing transformation of smallholder crops. Moreover, large firms have not been attracted to crops that smallholder farmers use to feed families and communities, presumably for both a lack of market size and lack of a reliable means to extract a return on investment.

Even public use would still require significant investment to develop crops and bring them to farmers. Several countries with large smallholder farmer constituencies, most notably China and India, have the market size and scientific capacity to develop their own proprietary GM crops for food producers. But thus far, they have only developed and released pest resistant cotton at scale.

Recently, new institutional arrangements, most commonly referred to as public–private partnerships, have been formed to transfer proprietary technologies to public institutions for use on food crops. Funded principally by philanthropic and bi-lateral development assistance, these institutional arrangements have negotiated the licensing rights for the use of proprietary technologies in several breeding programs, principally in Africa but also in Asia. Most of these crops have yet to reach the hands of farmers, and it is unknown whether they will significantly aid smallholder farmers, and, notably, the most poor and vulnerable among them. Significant barriers remain including seed amplification, dissemination, and pricing (Schnurr and Dowd-Uribe, 2021). Moreover, concerns remain about whether these efforts will simply usher in the use of more inputs on a genetically narrow range of crop varieties. Promises aside, smallholder farmers look to remain on the fringes of modern biotechnology developments.

Biotechnology and food futures

The dynamics that have shaped the current geographies of biotechnology and food will continue to shape them in the future, with some changes. Current commercial GM crops are transgenic. One change is an expansion in the tools of modern biotechnology that extend the power of genome editing, e.g. using CRISPR/Cas, to plants.

Transgenic GM crops are made in laboratories using techniques that change the germplasm. Those changes are propagated to build stocks of seed to sell at scale to farmers. Genome editing can be used this way as well. However, new developments in chemistry extend the range of where and how genetic engineering can be done, especially by genome editing. For example, new research explores the use of genome editing reagents packaged in aerosols, gels, or sprays that can be applied out of doors, leading to the modification of entire fields of plants as they grow, or to kill pests. These same formulations could be used at points of sale, such as in grocery stores, to alter characteristics that are favoured by consumers (Heinemann and Walker, 2019).

The concentration of IPR over genome editing reagents and traits, and their uses as a means to extract value for rights holders, will impact the ways in which newer products are designed. Battles over regulation will also play a large role, with industry arguing for changes in legislation that reduces the power of consumers to reject food or food production systems that rely on at least some techniques of genetic modification. Should they prevail, then such products could have a much larger uptake than transgenic crops.

Whether uptake results in a financially and culturally more robust smallholder farmer community is an entirely different question. The future of biotechnology and food may be more of the former and even less of the latter.

References

Bovay J and Alston J M (2018) GMO food labels in the United States: Economic implications of the new law. *Food Policy* 78 14–25.

Brookes G (2022) GM crops: global socio-economic and environmental impacts 1996-2020. https://pgeconomics.co.uk/pdf/Globalimpactbiotechcropsfinalreportocto ber2022.pdf (Accessed 19 January 2023).

BRIAN DOWD-URIBE AND JACK A. HEINEMANN

Bruening G and Lyons J (2000) The case of the FLAVR SAVR tomato. *California Agriculture* 54 6–7.

Cassidy E S, West P C, Gerber J S and Foley J A (2013) Redefining agricultural yields: From tonnes to people nourished per hectare. *Environmental Research Letters* 8 034015.

Clapp J (2021) The problem with growing corporate concentration and power in the global food system. *Nature Food* 2 404–408.

ETC Group (2022) Food barons: Crisis profiteering, digitalization and shifting power. https://www.etcgroup.org/content/food-barons-2022 (Accessed 3 July 2023).

FAOSTAT (2023) https://www.fao.org/faostat /en/ (Accessed 7 February 2023).

Fischer K, Ekener-Petersen E, Rydhmer L and Edvardsson Björnberg K (2015) Social impacts of GM crops in agriculture: A systematic literature review. *Sustainability* 7 8598–8620.

Glover D (2009) Undying promise: Agricultural biotechnology's pro-poor narrative, ten years on. https://opendocs.ids.ac.uk/opendocs/handle/20.500.12413/2314 (Accessed 3 July 2023).

Grzenda D, Spreadbury T, Rock J, Dowd-Uribe B and Uminsky, D (2022) OMGMO: Original multi-modal dataset of genetically modified organisms in African agriculture. In: *Social Informatics: 13th International Conference, SocInfo Glasgow, UK, Proceedings* (pp. 414–425). Cham: Springer International Publishing.

Heinemann J A and Walker S (2019) Environmentally applied nucleic acids and proteins for purposes of engineering changes to genes and other genetic material. *Biosafety and Health* 1 113–123.

Heinemann J A, Massaro M, Coray D S, Agapito-Tenfen, S Z and Wen J D (2014) Sustainability and innovation in staple crop production in the US Midwest. *International Journal of Agricultural Sustainability* 12 71–88.

ISAAA (2019) Brief 55: Executive Summary. https://www.isaaa.org/resources/publications/briefs/55/executivesummary/default.asp (Accessed 3 July 2023).

NASEM (2016) *Genetically Engineered Crops: Experiences and Prospects.* Washington, DC: The National Academies Press.

National Research Council (1989) *Field Testing Genetically Modified Organisms: Framework for Decisions.* Washington, DC: The National Academies Press.

Rivera-Ferre M G (2008) The future of agriculture: Agricultural knowledge for economically, socially and environmentally sustainable development. *EMBO Reports* 9 1061–1066.

Rose K M, Brossard D and Scheufele D A (2020) Of society, nature, and health: How perceptions of specific risks and benefits of genetically engineered foods shape public rejection. *Environmental Communication* 14 1017–1031.

Samberg L H, Gerber J S, Ramankutty N, Herrero M and West P C (2016) Subnational distribution of average farm size and smallholder contributions to global food production. *Environmental Research Letters* 11 124010.

Schnurr M A and Dowd-Uribe B (2021) Anticipating farmer outcomes of three genetically modified staple crops in sub-Saharan Africa: Insights from farming systems research. *Journal of Rural Studies* 88 377–387.

Stone G D (2012) Constructing facts: Bt cotton narratives in India. *Economic and Political Weekly* 47(38) 62–70.

UN FAO (2022) *The State of Food Security and Nutrition in the World 2022: Repurposing food and agricultural policies to make healthy diets more affordable.* Rome, FAO

Ufer D J, Ortega D L, Wolf C A, McKendree M and Swanson J (2022) Getting past the gatekeeper: Key motivations of dairy farmer intent to adopt animal health and welfare-improving biotechnology. *Food Policy* 112 102358.

Further reading

Beumer K and de Roij S (2023) Inclusive innovation in crop gene editing for smallholder farmers: Status and approaches. *Elementa: Science of the Anthropocene* 11 00089.

Selfa T, Lindberg S and Bain C (2021) Governing gene editing in agriculture and food in the United States: Tensions, contestations, and realignments. *Elementa: Science of the Anthropocene* 9 00153.

These recommended articles specialise on the topic area of commercial and regulatory forces at the interface of biotechnology services and food. The entire special issue *Gene Editing the Food System* of *Elementa* is recommended.

Dowd-Uribe B (2023) Just agricultural science: The green revolution, biotechnologies, and marginalized farmers in Africa. *Elementa: Science of the Anthropocene* 11 00144. This recommended article provides critical social science scholarship on the interface of biotechnology and the smallholder food producer.

BRIAN DOWD-URIBE AND JACK A. HEINEMANN

17. Blue food

MIQUEL ORTEGA, SANTIAGO
GOROSTIZA AND MARTA COLL

Introduction: blue food, the not so well-known history of an essential good

'Blue foods' – encompassing fish, invertebrates, algae, and aquatic plants harvested or cultivated in freshwater and marine ecosystems – have significantly influenced human history. They have supported urban civilizations, provided food rations for armies, generated surpluses that underpinned empires, and, most importantly, played a central role in feeding billions of people. They constitute a vital element of the livelihoods, economies, and cultures of many coastal and riparian communities (Fagan, 2017). This remains true today: blue foods provide 17% of the world's animal protein intake, while per capita fish consumption is currently over 20kg per year. Official figures indicate that the global production and capture of blue foods have historically shown continuous growth. However, this trend is beginning to encounter its limits. After nearly quadrupling in the latter half of the 20th century, wild fish captures have plateaued and even slightly declined since then (FAO, 2022; Sea Around Us, 2024). In fact, the growth in blue food production over the last two decades has been driven exclusively by aquaculture, a trend that is now also beginning to experience a slowdown in its growth rate.

Official figures indicate that, in 2020, blue food capture and production reached a record of 214 million tonnes: 90 million tonnes from capture fisheries, 87 million tonnes from animal aquaculture (62% of which was inland), and 36 million tonnes from algae production (FAO, 2022). Additionally, almost 24 million tonnes of extra fishery captures were not accounted for in the official statistics (Pauly & Zeller, 2016; Sea Around Us, 2024). The blue food sector directly employs 59 million people, with over 90% working in small-scale fisheries. Although only 21% of those employed in the primary sector are women, gender parity is achieved across the entire value chain (FAO, 2022). However, there is a significant imbalance in role distribution, making gender equality a concern worldwide. When including those involved in the full value chain and subsistence fisheries, it is estimated that about 600 million people depend on this sector for their livelihoods, the vast majority residing in the Global South (FAO, 2022).

Approximately 75% of captures and production are utilised for direct human consumption, displaying varied geographical and species patterns (Naylor et al., 2021). The mismatch between areas of capture and production versus areas of consumption, coupled with the diverse objectives of fisheries (ranging from subsistence to productive systems aimed at earning international currency), means that blue food products often navigate multiple, and sometimes conflicting, food supply chains. A notable aspect of this system is its high level of integration into the global food market. Blue food global trade has doubled in the last decade, making blue food products among the most traded food commodities worldwide (Bellmann et al., 2016).

Globally, the blue food system shares many commonalities with other food systems. At the practical level, it shares its reliance on technological change, the dependence on the global market, consumption patterns, ecological limitations, corporate interests, macroeconomic and demographic factors, and the challenge of integrating rural/coastal areas into an increasingly urbanised world.

At the political level, it also faces several challenges: firstly, managing conflicts over the distribution of economic benefits and environmental and social impacts; secondly, a complex array of issues related to recognition and representation both internally (among different actors within the blue food system) and externally (with non-blue food stakeholders); and thirdly the competition between blue food uses and other sea-related interests that leads to a variety of political approaches and alliances from different actors.

While many experts predict an increase in demand for blue foods in the coming decades (Naylor et al., 2021), debates and decisions about food systems often fail to adequately consider blue food. This is most likely due to the specific sector's complexity of rules and access rights across diverse fisheries activities, combined with a dense array of customary rules and practices, and a great heterogeneity of actors often competing for the same resources (Tigchelaar et al., 2022). In the sections that follow, we briefly explore some of the most pressing issues and concerns, as well as emerging challenges that may influence the future of blue food.

Current issues, concerns, and areas of focus

The first area of concern within the blue food system is the need to reduce its associated environmental impact. Environmental impacts have always been intrinsic to fisheries, but while these impacts were historically confined to local or regional scales, they have accelerated since the Middle Ages and more sharply since the Industrial Revolution. Hand in hand with the development of technology and use of fossil fuels, this acceleration enabled more extensive, farther, and deeper fishing. Combined with its integration into capitalist frameworks (which have largely replaced self-regulating exploitation logics), the exploitation of fisheries has led to a global transformation of the seas. This transformation includes stock collapses (with their associated socio-economic impacts on local communities) and the devastation of important, vulnerable marine ecosystems, contributing significantly to the oceanic biodiversity crisis and the degradation of marine ecosystem services. Although there is substantial knowledge on how to reduce these impacts through ecosystem-based management strategies (Pikitch et al., 2004), fishing pressure on marine ecosystems remains significant. Currently, 35.4% of the stocks are overfished at the global level (FAO, 2022), with (likely) irreversible impacts still occurring worldwide.

A second environmental concern involves the need to reduce blue food loss and waste throughout the value chain, especially including minimising fishing discards. It is not uncommon for losses to amount to around 30% of the initial catches in many regions of the world (FAO, 2011; Pauly et al., 2002). Additionally, the amount of blue food that is not declared (is illegal, unregulated, or unreported, known as IUU catches) is substantial, contributing to non-sustainable and unfair fishing practices (Pauly & Zeller, 2016).

Lastly, the emissions associated with blue food, and their contribution to the climate emergency, have garnered increasing attention over recent decades (Muñoz et al., 2023). While emissions from blue food are often considered to be similar to or lower than those from other animal protein sources, this comparison overlooks significant disparities.

These disparities depend on the technology used (for instance, trawling can emit up to 10 times more CO_2eq per kg of fish than purse-seine fishing) and the processing method (e.g. refrigerated catches versus fresh local consumption).

Another concern involves the distributive conflicts associated with the blue food value chain, particularly during the extraction/production phase (Ertör, 2023). These conflicts often arise from competition over marine resources between small-scale and industrial fisheries or conflicts stemming from different fishing 'rights' allocation systems (Klein et al., 2022). They are also frequently associated with spatial issues, such as aquaculture's occupation of areas or encroachment of marine space by other blue economy sectors. Additionally, significant conflicts revolve around the distribution of monetary costs and benefits (e.g. between fishers and wholesalers). Wholesalers often hold controlling positions at the initial stages of the blue food value chain, leading in many instances to low first-sale prices and sometimes to debt or technological dependence among fishers, associated with vertical integration processes in the value chain. The distribution of environmental impacts, such as overfishing by certain fleets that affect others, or the impacts of certain aquaculture practices on other fishing practices, sometimes also becomes a significant source of distributive conflicts (Ertör, 2023). Finally, labour conflicts in some sectors of blue food production, especially in high-sea activities where labour rights are not always respected, are a major concern due to the special vulnerability of fishing crews in these fisheries.

A third topic deals with conflicts arising from issues of recognition and participation. Coastal fishing activities around the world have been managed for centuries through various formal and informal commons management practices controlled by fishers. However, the introduction of new technologies, capitalist practices, and state intervention has led to a misalignment with these traditional practices, resulting in multiple and sometimes abrupt changes in governance structures. Since the 1960s, techno-management has become the predominant approach. Empowered by advancements in scientific and technological knowledge and the simultaneous expansion of industrial fisheries, this modernisation process has altered the decision-making power structure in many fisheries. Often, this excludes local knowledge and shifts decision-making from practitioners to managers and the key market actors, even in contexts that are highly uncertain and complex, with limited data and often without proper participation and representation processes. These shifts in power are frequently expressed in fisheries conflicts, especially when existing territorial governance is weak, some coastal communities are not recognised, and the interests of powerful actors, often linked with fishing industries, are significant.

A fourth concern is the erosion of existing coastal and inland societal livelihood capabilities and capacities due to changes in the blue food value chain structures, often linked with global food trade. The most apparent examples are those processes associated with the collapse of a stock, leading to the downfall of coastal communities and specific value chains. Although many historical cases of these failures are well documented (Mullon et al., 2005), they still occur today, with coastal and small-scale fishers being the most affected, especially in countries lacking public adaptation resources.

Finally, a less understood but equally significant process is the cultural losses happening in many parts of the world. This is associated with the increasing concentration of fish consumption on a few species and the dominance of large-scale retailers. These trends lead to a decline in knowledge about fish food alternatives and diversification, a disconnection between local fishing practices and fish consumption, and growing difficulties in developing short blue-food value chains.

Future concerns, issues, and questions

Three elements emerge as key issues among the multiple concerns and questions raised by the future of blue foods.

First, there is the question of how the blue food system will adapt to climate change and the biodiversity crisis within the need to transition to a just and sustainable food system. Future projections predict global declines of fish biomass associated with changes in environmental conditions such as increases in temperature and declines in primary production (Lotze et al., 2019; Tittensor et al., 2021).

Emerging global frameworks for sustainable and just transitions, such as the planetary boundaries (Steffen et al., 2015) or the doughnut economy (Raworth, 2017), are not yet sufficiently developed conceptually in the marine arena (but see Ortega et al., 2024). Moreover, they have not yet found practical applications, political alliances, or sufficiently elaborated discourses for implementation. Political initiatives linked to 'food sovereignty' that have been developed in relation to agriculture and livestock food systems have seen little implementation in the blue food context.

Second, there is the issue of how the blue food system will be integrated into the wider blue economy. In recent decades, there has been a clear acceleration of human activities in the sea (Jouffray et al., 2020), including shipping, energy-related offshore extraction and transport, and coastal tourism activities, among many others (Halpern et al., 2019). However, the sea is not a cornucopia capable of providing infinite goods and services. This is leading to increasing tensions between different human-led activities in the sea. The place of blue food-related activities in this context is currently at stake.

Finally, the current and future role of blue food in terms of nutrition, food security, and health is a very relevant topic poised to play an important role in future public discussions (Crona et al., 2023). However, this cannot be addressed without considering the ecosystemic consequences of political decisions (Gephart et al., 2021) and the broader societal impacts of blue food choices. In this sense, the triad of health, biodiversity, and social justice can be seen as a Gordian knot.

References

Bellmann, C., Tipping, A., & Sumaila, U. R. (2016). Global trade in fish and fishery products: An overview. *Marine Policy*, 69, 181–188. https://doi.org/10.1016/J .MARPOL.2015.12.019.

Crona, B. I., Wassénius, E., Jonell, M., Koehn, J. Z., Short, R., Tigchelaar, M., Daw, T. M., Golden, C. D., Gephart, J. A., Allison, E. H., Bush, S. R., Cao, L., Cheung, W. W. L., DeClerck, F., Fanzo, J., Gelcich, S., Kishore, A., Halpern, B. S., Hicks, C. C., … Wabnitz, C. C. C. (2023). Four ways blue foods can help achieve food system ambitions across nations. *Nature*,

616(7955), 104–112. https://doi.org/10.1038/s41586-023-05737-x.

Ertör, I. (2023). 'We are the oceans, we are the people!': Fisher people's struggles for blue justice. *The Journal of Peasant Studies*, 50(3), 1157–1186. https://doi.org/10.1080/03066150.2021.1999932.

Fagan, B. M. (2017). *Fishing: How the sea fed civilization*. Yale University Press. https://yalebooks.yale.edu/9780300240047/fishing.

FAO. (2011). *Global food losses and food waste – Extent, causes and prevention*. Food and Agriculture Organization of the United Nations. https://www.fao.org/sustainable-food-value-chains/library/details/en/c/266053/.

FAO. (2022). *The state of world fisheries and aquaculture 2022*. FAO. https://doi.org/10.4060/cc0461en.

Gephart, J. A., Henriksson, P. J. G., Parker, R. W. R., Shepon, A., Gorospe, K. D., Bergman, K., Eshel, G., Golden, C. D., Halpern, B. S., Hornborg, S., Jonell, M., Metian, M., Mifflin, K., Newton, R., Tyedmers, P., Zhang, W., Ziegler, F., & Troell, M. (2021). Environmental performance of blue foods. *Nature*, 597(7876), 360–365. https://doi.org/10.1038/s41586-021-03889-2.

Halpern, B. S., Frazier, M., Afflerbach, J., Lowndes, J. S., Micheli, F., O'Hara, C., Scarborough, C., & Selkoe, K. A. (2019). Recent pace of change in human impact on the world's ocean. *Scientific Reports*, 9(1), 1–8. https://doi.org/10.1038/s41598-019-47201-9.

Jouffray, J.-B., Blasiak, R., Norström, A. V, Österblom, H., & Nyström, M. (2020). The blue acceleration: The trajectory of human expansion into the ocean. *One Earth*, 2(1), 43–54. https://doi.org/https://doi.org/10.1016/j.oneear.2019.12.016.

Klein, C. J., Kuempel, C. D., Watson, R. A., Teneva, L., Coll, M., & Mora, C. (2022). Global fishing between jurisdictions with unequal fisheries management. *Environmental Research Letters*, 17(11), 114004. https://doi.org/10.1088/1748-9326/AC97AB.

Lotze, H. K., Tittensor, D. P., Bryndum-Buchholz, A., Eddy, T. D., Cheung, W. W. L., Galbraith, E. D., Barange, M., Barrier, N., Bianchi, D., Blanchard, J. L., Bopp, L., Büchner, M., Bulman, C. M., Carozza, D. A., Christensen, V., Coll, M., Dunne, J. P., Fulton, E. A., Jennings, S., … Worm, B.

(2019). Global ensemble projections reveal trophic amplification of ocean biomass declines with climate change. *Proceedings of the National Academy of Sciences of the United States of America*, 116(26), 12907–12912. https://doi.org/10.1073/PNAS.1900194116/SUPPL_FILE/PNAS.1900194116.SAPP.PDF.

Mullon, C., Fréon, P., & Cury, P. (2005). The dynamics of collapse in world fisheries. *Fish and Fisheries*, 6(2), 111–120. https://doi.org/10.1111/J.1467-2979.2005.00181.X.

Muñoz, M., Reul, A., Guijarro, B., & Hidalgo, M. (2023). Carbon footprint, economic benefits and sustainable fishing: Lessons for the future from the Western Mediterranean. *Science of the Total Environment*, 865, 160783. https://doi.org/10.1016/J.SCITOTENV.2022.160783.

Naylor, R. L., Kishore, A., Sumaila, U. R., Issifu, I., Hunter, B. P., Belton, B., Bush, S. R., Cao, L., Gelcich, S., Gephart, J. A., Golden, C. D., Jonell, M., Koehn, J. Z., Little, D. C., Thilsted, S. H., Tigchelaar, M., & Crona, B. (2021). Blue food demand across geographic and temporal scales. *Nature Communications*, 12(1), 1–14. https://doi.org/10.1038/s41467-021-25516-4.

Ortega, M., Coll, M., & Ramírez, F. (2024). Can a "doughnut" economic framework be useful to monitor the blue economy success? A fisheries example. *Ecology and Society*, 29(1), art22. https://doi.org/10.5751/ES-14743-290122.

Pauly, D., & Zeller, D. (2016). Catch reconstructions reveal that global marine fisheries catches are higher than reported and declining. *Nature Communications*, 7(1), 1–9. https://doi.org/10.1038/ncomms10244.

Pauly, D., Christensen, V., Guénette, S., Pitcher, T. J., Sumaila, U. R., Walters, C. J., Watson, R., & Zeller, D. (2002). Towards sustainability in world fisheries. *Nature*, 418(6898), 689–695. https://doi.org/10.1038/nature01017.

Pikitch, E. K., Santora, C., Babcock, E. A., Bakun, A., Bonfil, R., Conover, D. O., Dayton, P., Doukakis, P., Fluharty, D., Heneman, B., Houde, E. D., Link, J., Livingston, P. A., Mangel, M., McAllister, M. K., Pope, J., & Sainsbury, K. J. (2004). Ecosystem-based fishery management. *Science*, 305(5682), 346–347. https://doi.org/10.1126/SCIENCE.1098222/

ASSET/4DBF3890-C9B0-436C-99FF-2B5A809287E6/ASSETS/SCIENCE.1098222.FP.PNG.

Raworth, K. (2017). *Doughnut economics: Seven ways to think like a 21st-century economist.* Random House Business Books.

Sea Around Us. (2024). Catches by reporting status in the Global Ocean. https://www.seaaroundus.org/data/#/global?chart=catch-chart&dimension=reporting-status&measure=tonnage&limit=10.

Steffen, W., Richardson, K., Rockström, J., Cornell, S. E., Fetzer, I., Bennett, E. M., Biggs, R., Carpenter, S. R., De Vries, W., De Wit, C. A., Folke, C., Gerten, D., Heinke, J., Mace, G. M., Persson, L. M., Ramanathan, V., Reyers, B., & Sörlin, S. (2015). Planetary boundaries: Guiding human development on a changing planet. *Science*, 347(6223). https://doi.org/10.1126/science.1259855.

Tigchelaar, M., Leape, J., Micheli, F., Allison, E. H., Basurto, X., Bennett, A., Bush, S. R., Cao, L., Cheung, W. W. L., Crona, B., DeClerck, F., Fanzo, J., Gelcich, S., Gephart, J. A., Golden, C. D., Halpern, B. S., Hicks, C. C., Jonell, M., Kishore, A., ... Wabnitz, C. C. C. (2022). The vital roles of blue foods in the global food system. *Global Food Security*, 33, 100637. https://doi.org/10.1016/J.GFS.2022.100637.

Tittensor, D. P., Novaglio, C., Harrison, C. S., Heneghan, R. F., Barrier, N., Bianchi, D., Bopp, L., Bryndum-Buchholz, A., Britten, G. L., Büchner, M., Cheung, W. W. L., Christensen, V., Coll, M., Dunne, J. P., Eddy, T. D., Everett, J. D., Fernandes-Salvador, J. A., Fulton, E. A., Galbraith, E. D., ... Blanchard, J. L. (2021). Next-generation ensemble projections reveal higher climate risks for marine ecosystems. *Nature Climate Change,* 11(11), 973–981. https://doi.org/10.1038/s41558-021-01173-9.

Further reading

The Blue Food Assessment (2021). *Building blue food futures for people and the planet: The report of the Blue Food Assessment.* https://doi.org/10.25740/rd224xj7484.
This report stems from an international joint initiative that assesses the multiple roles animal-sourced blue foods play in food systems around the world.

FAO (2022). *The state of world fisheries and aquaculture 2022.* FAO. https://doi.org/10.4060/cc0461en.
The FAO provides global, reliable, and up-to-date information in the fisheries and aquaculture sector.

Hamada, S., Wilk, R. (2088). *Seafood: Ocean to the plate.* Routledge. https://doi.org/10.4324/9781315640259.
Accessible book that helps readers to think about the future of the industry using case studies.

18. Bodies and food

Jessica Hayes-Conroy,
Gabrielle Reagan and Allison
Hayes-Conroy

Introduction

Bodies are ever-present in the food system and relevant to every other entry in this Encyclopedia. This entry focuses on making explicit the significance of the material body: a body that tastes, senses, feels, and experiences hunger, pain, and comfort; a body with taste buds, guts, muscles, hormones, and brain cells; a body that carries, works, sleeps, learns, and anticipates (and much more). The entry centres a concern for the body and food–body relationships within broader scholarship on food and society, while paying attention to the ways in which food scholarship considers the body as a site of politics, as a material and affective force, and as an environment of its own.

Attending to the material body has long been a feminist impulse, so it is not surprising that much early work on food and bodies is visible within feminist literature. In particular, the work of scholars Elspeth Probyn and Kyla Wazana Tompkins has prioritised a deeply visceral understanding of the eating body while calling attention to gender, race, power, and identity (Probyn, 2009; Tompkins, 2012). In geography, scholars like Becky Mansfield and Julie Guthman have offered key critical impulses, guiding food studies to consider the body and bodily health as exemplary of broader political ecological struggles (Guthman & Mansfield, 2015). Also, early food work pushing so-called "new materialist" approaches helped forge a path towards thinking about seemingly immaterial aspects of food systems as always relevant to the body and therefore always in some way material (Goodman, 2016). Finally, scholars of race and food have engaged the material body in order to explore the becoming of race, the embodied impacts of racism and racial trauma, and collective resilience/resistance (Garth & Reese, 2008; Jones, 2019)

Building upon this diverse backdrop, we highlight three current issues relevant to food and body scholarship. The first has to do with specifying body–food relationships, particularly within nutrition science and health, but also including work in epigenetics, metabolism, and the bio-social body.

This field has grown not only through critical dietetics and critical nutrition literature but also through engagement with the politics of health. Related, but in its own category, is a shift in understanding and conceptualising of food behaviour. There has been a critical turn away from the neoliberal interpretation of eating and food behaviours as individualised choices, toward a recognition of food behaviour as a relational and embodied negotiation. Third and last, the interrelated issues of bodily diversity and embodied social norms are highlighted. Queer and disability studies and embodied fat studies have pushed scholars to take seriously the ways in which bodily norms and normativity shape the way we place value on certain bodies, foods, and food–body relationships.

Current issues

The scholarly intersection of food and the body is large. This entry focuses particularly on a sample of scholarship that works to highlight the food–body relationship as situated in particular contexts, as always shifting, and as instructive for progressive social change. These themes emerge through each of the sections that follow.

The politics of healthy eating: contextualising the eating body

What does healthy eating mean? Do dietary nutritionism and the medicalisation of the food–body relationship actually promote health? Rethinking the answer to such questions has been key to the growth of fields like critical dietetics and critical nutrition studies. While the material body is not always centred in scholarship that troubles the nature and politics of healthy eating, it is always there. The affective, cultural, political, historical, and ecological relationships that bodies have with food matter to physical and mental health outcomes in myriad ways. Whether explicitly or implicitly, much work in both critical dietetics and critical nutrition studies speaks to the importance of *contextualising the eating body* in order to understand how food relationships shape health and wellness. The field of critical dietetics emerged as an attempt to rethink positivist epistemology within nutrition science and effect change in dietetic practice (Brady & Gringas, 2019); it is one of many overlapping areas of critical health scholarship that seeks to shift the way we think about and enact (healthy) bodies, such that neither health nor the body is approached as fixed, but instead understood in an always-shifting relational context.

Scholarship on food, health, and the Black body has been particularly important in drawing attention to such contextual lessons, especially in ways that emphasise Black experience and knowledge. Priscilla McCutcheon notes that "listening to one's body and listening to one's voice have always been a part of Black people's understanding of food and agriculture" (McCutcheon, 2021: 896). Bodily nourishment in this work is emergent, communal, and relational—and it is importantly *not* contingent upon "dominant notions of good food, good bodies, or sustainability" (McCutcheon, 2021: 896). Naya Jones's work also emphasises the relational quality of embodied food experiences over "hegemonic nutrition" and bad/good food binaries (Jones, 2018: 907), and similarly centres Black healing and collective agency in the production of radical, embodied resilience (Jones, 2019).

Such work helps us to move beyond positivist approaches to the food–body relationship by drawing into focus a complex material reality that is always relational, contextual, and historical. It helps us to move from seeing food as a straightforward, biomedical tool of public health to seeing it as part of a larger web that includes bodies, molecules, ideas, practices, ecosystems, histories, and more. This shift can encourage more inclusive and effective interventions in health and ecological systems, more nuanced understandings of individual agency, and more comprehensive perspectives on sustainability and ethics, among many others. In particular, scholarship on epigenetics has helped food–body scholars to "open the black box" of the body (Guthman, 2012), by disrupting the binary between meaning and matter and highlighting the ways that our material bodies are attentive.

Food behaviour as relational negotiation: sustaining the eating body

Within work that seeks to contextualise the eating body, we emphasise scholarship that attends to and reinterprets bodily behaviour. This emphasis is important because all too often, in clinical and public health contexts, the eating individual is blamed for (or assumed to be uneducated about) "bad" behaviours.

Corrective work not only looks toward the broader economic and political structures in which this behaviour takes place, but also attends to the ways that the relational, visceral body helps us to make sense of specific behaviours beyond the good/bad binary. As Brady (in conversation with Yates-Doerr and other colleagues) explains, "we do a disservice to the people whose behaviour we seek to change by disregarding the deep historical roots that shape why and what people eat or drink" (Yates-Doerr et al., 2022: 103). Those historical roots, which are also both collective and embodied, point to the need to understand behaviour not as individual choice—whether bad or good—but instead as a matter of contextual sustenance—sensical to the historically situated embodied moment.

It may be helpful, but perhaps not sufficient, to consider food behaviour as a coping mechanism of sorts—an "immediate coping with what is confronting us" (Varela, 1999: 5, quoted in Anderson, 2005). While coping may be immediate, the "feeling right" (Anderson, 2005) of the coping behaviour is born from an assemblage that is vast both temporally and spatially. In relation to eating behaviour, social theorist Lauren Berlant has described such coping as "the activity of doing what is necessary to lubricate the body's movement through capitalized time's shortened circuit" (Berlant, 2011: 115). Berlant's point is ultimately about how we inhabit agency *differently*, which is not to say unconsciously or unreflexively, but rather in the context of getting by—the mundane, often unremarkable activities of attending to what the body is immediately confronted with over the day, the week, the month (Berlant, 2011: 116). Here, bodily well-being is not a fixed point but an (often pleasurable) feeling that "spreads out for a moment … [offering] an 'episodic intermission' from life, from 'the long haul'" (Berlant, 2010, quoted in O'Flynn, 2015: 106). As Gabrielle O'Flynn (2015) suggests, this insight has significant implications for environmental sustainability, as it does for health education.

Berlant's interpretation of obesity has been critiqued in important ways, and more discussion on this critique is provided in the section below. Here, though, the importance is emphasised of bridging large-scale structural concerns of inequality with small-scale, immediate concerns of the visceral body. Indeed, a central point for scholars like Berlant is that the two are inextricable—"slow death" is reproduced in the daily, embodied living out of structural inequality (Berlant, 2011). This observation has significant and often overlooked implications for public health. As Susan Greenhalgh and Megan Carney observe, "rather than enabling Latinos and other minority groups to overcome the oppressive social, economic, and political conditions that systematically ostracize them as 'lesser' bodies that produce less value for society, anti-obesity programs frame their agency as 'destructive'" (Greenhalgh & Carney, 2014: 274). It also has implications for scholars interested in food behaviour, and for behaviour science at large. The critical work of attending to the complexity of food–body relationships, and in particular to the complex materialisations of food behaviour, helps food–body scholars to move beyond positivist approaches that provide limited views of, or even demean and blame, the eating body.

Queer and crip embodiments: (re) conceptualising the eating body

This last section highlights scholarship that has drawn important attention to normative assumptions about food–body relationships. This includes ongoing scholarship in disability studies, queer studies, and fat studies, including work that spans across these fields. While theories of the material, affective, or visceral body have helped to connect queer theoretical perspectives to food studies, theories of disability (and/or crip, which further resists normative embodiment) are still underappreciated in the field. Kim Q. Hall, however, has written convincingly about the overlaps between these fields and their relation to food and bodies (Hall, 2014). Hall uses a queer crip feminist conception of food justice to critique the "metaphysics of purity and alimentary ableism that inform assumptions about what makes a food [and bodies] good," building instead a "metaphysics of compost [that] understands bodies and food as interactively emergent" (Hall, 2014: 178–9). As Hall explains elsewhere, turning toward queer and crip perspectives is crucial for building a sustainable and just future, as it helps to build a "resistant imagination"—"an imagination that is ready to confront relational possibilities that have been lost, ignored, or that remain to be discovered or invented" (Medina, quoted

in Hall, 2017; see also Wong, 2019 on creating a "habitable world").

The interdisciplinary field of fat studies invites critical examination of attitudes, practices, and programmes related to body weight and appearance, including assumptions related to bodily health and food behaviour. Theories of the material body play a particularly important role in the field. Fat studies has intersected significantly with both queer studies and disability studies (Schalk, 2013), and has also overlapped with and influenced critical food studies a great deal. Fat studies has also intersected in important ways with Black studies, and scholars like Anna Mollow have called for fat Black disability studies by demonstrating the ways that food–body assumptions fuel anti-Black violence (Mollow, 2017). All of this scholarship demonstrates the power of intersectional analyses when seeking to understand food–body relationships. It also speaks to the power of cross-movement solidarity between the disability, queer, fat, racial, gender, and food justice movements (among others), and to the significance of the material body in justice-centred work.

Lucas Crawford's (2017) critique of Berlant in the article "Slender Trouble" is illustrative of the critical perspectives that fat studies lends to food–body analyses. One particularly helpful analysis extending from queer, disability, and fat studies relates to accounts of time, especially in relation to food and eating. Crawford demonstrates how Berlant's reading of the fat body "[attributes] causality and linear temporalities far more casually to fat bodies than to normative ones", leading to the calculus that "fat only 'is' what one 'has done'" (Crawford, 2017: 453). Indeed, although we find Berlant's concept of "slow death" itself to be very useful in drawing attention to bodily debility under conditions of capitalism, her continued decision to equate fat with (slow) death reproduces what Crawford calls "slender-normative" approaches to the food–body relationship (Crawford, 2017). Any attempt to contextualise food behaviour must take seriously the important, often intersectional work happening within queer, disability, and fat studies.

Future concerns

This brief account of scholarship relevant to food and bodies has attempted to showcase work that emphasises the food–body relationship as wholly contextual, always shifting, and deeply political. This brief conclusion offers some suggestions for how and where this trajectory of thought might play out in future research. As O'Flynn (2015) illustrates, there are important parallels between food justice and climate justice, and this discourse suggests that the body is at the centre of both. In particular, just as work on the material body helps to expand and complicate food behaviour, so too can the material body be instructive in deepening understandings of sustainable futures. As recent work on alternative proteins demonstrates (Sexton, 2016), there is much overlap between the two. At a time when combating the climate emergency means engaging in individual behavioural modifications, theories of the material body that help to bridge the personal and the structural are crucial. It is time for sustainability science and activism to begin to take the material body, in all its non-normative materialisations, seriously.

This account has also served as a critique of positivist science. While we are deeply appreciative of the (partial) knowledge gained by positivist science, we are also interested in promoting rigorous scholarship at the intersection of positivist and critical theory approaches to the body (Nichols, 2022; Hayes-Conroy et al., 2022, although see Meloni et al., 2022 for sceptical take). The theoretical, methodological, and empirical contributions mentioned above make such work not only possible but also timely and vital for our human–environment futures.

References

Anderson, B. (2005). Practices of judgement and domestic geographies of affect. *Social & Cultural Geography*, 6(5), 645–659.

Berlant, L. (2010). Risky bigness. In Metzl, J. & Kirkland, A. (eds), *Against health: How health became the new morality* (pp. 26–39).

Berlant, L. (2011). *Cruel optimism*. Duke University Press.

Brady, J., & Gingras, J. (2019). Critical dietetics: Axiological foundations. In Coveney, J. and Booth, S. (eds), *Critical Dietetics and Critical Nutrition Studies* (pp. 15–32).

Crawford, L. (2017). Slender trouble: From Berlant's cruel figuring of figure to Sedgwick's fat presence. *GLQ: A Journal of Lesbian and Gay Studies*, 23(4), 447–472.

Garth, H., & Reese, A. M. (Eds.). (2008). *Black food matters: Racial justice in the wake of food justice*. University of Minnesota Press.

Goodman, M. K. (2016). Food geographies I: Relational foodscapes and the busy-ness of being more-than-food. *Progress in Human Geography*, 40(2), 257–266.

Greenhalgh, S., & Carney, M. (2014). Bad biocitizens?: Latinos and the US "obesity epidemic". *Human Organization*, 73(3), 267–276.

Guthman, J. (2012). Opening up the black box of the body in geographical obesity research: Toward a critical political ecology of fat. *Annals of the Association of American Geographers*, 102(5), 951–957.

Guthman, J., & Mansfield, B. (2015). Nature, difference, and the body. In Perreault, T., Bridge, G. and McCarthy, J. (eds), *The Routledge handbook of political ecology* (pp. 558–570). Routledge.

Hall, K. Q. (2014). Toward a queer crip feminist politics of food. *PhiloSOPHIA*, 4(2), 177–196.

Hall, K. Q. (2017). Cripping sustainability, realizing food justice. In Ray, S.J. and Sibara, J. (eds), *Disability studies and the environmental humanities: Toward an eco-crip theory*, (pp. 422–446).University of Nebraska Press.

Hayes-Conroy, A., Kinsey, D., & Hayes-Conroy, J. (2022). Biosocial wellbeing: Conceptualizing relational and expansive well-bodies. *Wellbeing, Space and Society*, 3, 100105.

Jones, N. (2018). "It tastes like heaven": Critical and embodied food pedagogy with Black youth in the Anthropocene. *Policy Futures in Education*, 17(7), 905–923.

Jones, N. (2019). Dying to eat? Black food geographies of slow violence and resilience. *ACME: An International Journal for Critical Geographies*, 18(5), 1076–1099.

McCutcheon, P. (2021). Growing Black food on sacred land: Using Black liberation theology to imagine an alternative Black agrarian future. *Environment and Planning D: Society and Space*, 39(5), 887–905.

Medina, J. (2013). The epistemology of resistance: Gender and racial oppression, epistemic injustice, and the social imagination. Oxford University Press.

Meloni, M., Wakefield-Rann, R., & Mansfield, B. (2022). Bodies of the Anthropocene: On the interactive plasticity of earth systems and biological organisms. *The Anthropocene Review*, 9(3), 473–493.

Mollow, A. (2017). Unvictimizable: Toward a fat black disability studies. *African American Review*, 50(2), 105–121.

Nichols, C. E. (2022). Digesting agriculture development: Nutrition-oriented development and the political ecology of rice–body relations in India. *Agriculture and Human Values*, 39(2), 757–771.

O'Flynn, G. (2015). Food, obesity discourses and the subjugation of environmental knowledge. *Australian Journal of Environmental Education*, 31(1), 99–109.

Probyn, E. (2009). Fat, feelings, bodies: A critical approach to obesity. In Malson, H. and Burns, M. (eds), *Critical feminist approaches to eating dis/orders,* (pp. 135–145). Routledge.

Schalk, S. (2013). Coming to claim crip: Disidentification with/in disability studies. *Disability Studies Quarterly*, 33(2). DOI: 10.18061/dsq.v33i2.3705.

Sexton, A. (2016). Alternative proteins and the (non) stuff of "meat". *Gastronomica*, 16(3), 66–78.

Tompkins, K. W. (2012). *Racial indigestion: Eating bodies in the 19th century.* New York University Press.

Varela, F. J. (1999). *Ethical know-how: Action, wisdom, and cognition.* Stanford University Press.

Wong, A. (2019). The rise and fall of the plastic straw: Sucking in crip defiance. *Catalyst: Feminism, Theory, Technoscience*, 5(1), 1–12.

Yates-Doerr, E., Vasquez, E., Tejeda, A. S., Brady, J., & Gálvez, A. (2022). The politics and practices of representing bodies in capitalism: A discussion about public health in Mexico & beyond. *Critical Dietetics*, 6(2), 100–111.

Further reading

Jones, N. (2019). Dying to eat? Black food geographies of slow violence and resilience. *ACME: An International Journal for Critical Geographies*, 18(5), 1076–1099.
By drawing on visceral geographies, Jones highlights the need to understand memory as both collective and embodied, arguing that "tending to the visceral opens up space for Black food epistemologies that counter dominant ways of knowing food or the body" (910).

Hall, K. Q. (2017). Cripping sustainability, realizing food justice. In Ray, S.J. and Sibara, J. (eds), *Disability studies and the environmental humanities: Toward an eco-crip theory,* (pp. 422–446). University of Nebraska Press.
Hall draws attention to the heteronormative and able-bodied nature of the farm-to-table environmental imaginary. Questioning the compatibility between sustainability discourses in the US environmental movement and disability justice, Hall ultimately imagines a more inclusive sustainable future.

JESSICA HAYES-CONROY, GABRIELLE REAGAN AND ALLISON HAYES-CONROY

19. Caste and food

SANCHIA DESOUZA

Introduction: caste and the ethics of food

As environmentalist concerns around reducing emissions focus in part on industrial farming and the need to reduce meat consumption, Indian food has increasingly been touted for its possibilities for vegetarians. Vegetarian consumers and cooks focus on how Indian cuisine combines spices with legumes and vegetables for a rich flavour profile without the need for animal products, in particular meat. Absent in this narrative around Indian food, however, is an understanding of how *caste* as a system of power and exclusion undergirds all Indian cuisines and food subcultures, particularly vegetarian ones, and the ethical issues this relationship brings up.

The practice of caste through food

The caste system in South Asia is a social hierarchy and segregation that dates back between 2,500 and 3,000 years. The ascribed position in the caste hierarchy for an individual is based on a complex intertwining of ancestral occupations of their caste group and maintenance of ritual purity in all areas of life. Highest in the ritual hierarchy are castes associated with ancestral occupations that focus on the inherently "pure" scriptures, textual learning, and religious rituals; lowest are those whose ancestral occupations are seen to be inherently ritually polluting, such as sanitation work and work with the dead bodies of animals (including meat and leather production). While an individual may not practice their ancestral occupation, the position of their caste group on the purity–pollution spectrum remains determined by this ancestral status and by associated ancestral practices of daily life. The maintenance of ritual purity is carried out most significantly through endogamy – marriage only within the caste group – and avoidance of eating with and accepting food from people of lower caste groups, as well as the avoidance of certain foods. As Appadurai (1981) has argued, food in South Asia can be used to construct social relations characterised by equality and intimacy with the in-group, but it is simultaneously used to segregate and exclude those outside the caste group or lower in the social hierarchy. The preoccupation with ritual purity translates in the diet into the avoidance of various foods, the most crucial being the avoidance of meat, poultry, fish, and seafood by most upper castes, because these are classified as polluting. South Asian vegetarianism may thus not be counter-cultural and progressive but rather hegemonic in a caste-based society (Natrajan and Jacob, 2018). Conversely, dairy products such as ghee and milk, which are seen to be the gifts of the cow as mother, are eminently acceptable and purifying foods, despite their animal origins, since they are produced by a living cow. Given this complex intersection of caste power and hierarchies with the ethics of vegetarianism and veganism, no examination of vegetarian and vegan diets and their place in food justice and environmental justice globally can be complete without the examination of caste, particularly in relation to growing South Asian and Hindu populations within and outside South Asia.

Histories of caste and food

The line between vegetarianism and meat-eating has been a particularly fraught site of conflict and oppression historically and in contemporary India. In early modern South Asia, for instance, mercantile castes (third in the broad caste categorisation hierarchy) in Western India inscribed and demarcated their difference from Muslims and so-called untouchables (now referred to as Dalits) through dietary practices. The association of vegetarianism with Hinduism and meat-eating with untouchability and outcastes owes much to the solidification of caste hierarchies in this period (Cherian, 2022). In the late 19th century, beef-eating in particular came to be more strongly associated than ever before with being outside the Hindu fold, when cow protection was promoted as one facet of a consolidated Hindu identity (Adcock, 2010). The association of Indian food with the foodways of upper-caste and elite groups, including vegetarianism, became particularly strong in the 20th century globally, as a result of these groups' increased migration to and within the Global North and circulating practices of yoga and Hindu-aligned new-age spiritualism. Outcaste political assertion has drawn much more attention in the late 20th and early 21st centuries to the diet-based segregation practised by upper castes (Sathyamala, 2019). Dalit cookbooks and narratives about food have brought into focus non-elite, non-vegetarian cuisines of India and subverted the idea of Indian food as authentically and fundamentally vegetarian, while also demonstrating that vegetarianism is not in itself necessarily progressive and just (Hasnain and Srivastava, 2023).

Contemporary thinking on caste and food

Studies of food and caste in contemporary India have much to discuss in relation to increasing violence against Dalits and Muslims suspected of carrying or consuming beef, as well as the institutionalised segregation of vegetarians and non-vegetarians (Sathyamala, 2019). A crucial question is the effect of class mobility on Indian diets and how caste purity norms interact with ideas of health, environmentalism, and status as expressed through diet (Staples, 2020). Other considerations include the relationship between caste and race in the stigmatisation of food (Kikon, 2022).

References

Adcock, C. S. (2010) Sacred Cows and Secular History: Cow Protection Debates in Colonial North India. *Comparative Studies of South Asia, Africa, and the Middle East* 30 (2), 297–311.

Appadurai, Arjun (1981) Gastro-Politics in Hindu South Asia. *American Ethnologist*, 8 (3), 494–511.

Cherian, Divya (2022) *Merchants of Virtue: Hindus, Muslims, and Untouchables in Eighteenth-Century South Asia*. Berkeley: University of California Press.

Hasnain, Aseem & Abhilasha Srivastava (2023) Vegetarianism without Vegetarians: Caste Ideology and the Politics of Food in India. *Food and Foodways*, DOI: 10.1080/07409710.2023.2261721.

Kikon, Dolly (2022) Dirty Food: Racism and Casteism in India. *Ethnic and Racial Studies*, 45 (2), 278–297.

Natrajan, Balmurli & Suraj Jacob (2018) 'Provincializing Vegetarianism: Putting Indian Food Habits in Their Place. *Economic and Political Weekly*, LIII (9), 54–64.

Sathyamala, C. (2019) Meat-Eating in India: Whose Food, Whose Politics, and Whose Rights? *Policy Futures in Education* 17 (7), 878–891.

Staples, James (2020) *Sacred Cows and Chicken Manchurian: The Everyday Politics of Eating Meat in India*. Seattle: University of Washington Press.

Further reading

Kikon, Dolly (2022) Dirty Food: Racism and Casteism in India. *Ethnic and Racial Studies*, 45 (2), 278–297.
This article discusses how food, race, and caste are interlinked in the marginalisation of northeastern Indians.

Hasnain, Aseem & Abhilasha Srivastava (2023) Vegetarianism without Vegetarians: Caste Ideology and the Politics of Food in India. *Food and Foodways*, DOI: 10.1080/07409710.2023.2261721.
This piece gives a strong overview of ethical issues surrounding vegetarianism and caste politics in India.

20. Celebrities and food

Ana Tominc

Introduction: from celebrity chefs to food celebrities

Today, it is hard to imagine food without celebrities and celebrities without food. Using traditional and, increasingly, social media they guide our understanding of not only what to eat but also how to think about food, mediating and framing our perceptions around food cultures, food systems and the power ingrained in them (Johnson and Goodman, 2015). From early television 'celebrity' chefs, who appeared in the decades after the Second World War on a number of television programmes in Europe, US and across the world (Tominc, 2022) to contemporary successful Instagram influencers, activists and even film stars, the term 'food celebrities' encapsulates famous media-produced personalities who are uniquely positioned to tie themselves and their brands to fashionable food advice discourses that today penetrate most of our postmodern lives, at least in the West, where traditional ways of producing and consuming food have given way in the last decades to a less stable, more lifestyle-driven set of food practices (Johnson and Goodman, 2015).

Such development is a consequence, in part, of the expansion and interconnection of digital media into our everyday consumption practices, from food preparation to shopping and restaurant going (Lewis, 2020). Due to this, celebrity chefs have been joined by a range of other personalities who have used this global platform to provide lifestyle advice to audiences around the world, from advice on health and wellness, to critiques of the food system. Providing simplistic, individualised solutions to systemic problems of contemporary societies, such as inequality and food poverty, food celebrities act as Rojek's (2014) 'Big Citizen', where the audience is provided with a solution to a food-related problem. These are not radical changes, but might be viewed as a series of individual actions, often based on food 'choice' (Johnston and Goodman, 2015). Other developments, such as the decontextualisation of the traditionally linear television programme, through reruns and on-demand television, have added to these changes. In addition, political food programmes have been repositioned in, or even excluded from, the less-critical, lifestyle-oriented food media offerings (Phillipov, 2023).

Celebrity and the politics of food: impacts on food and society

Food celebrities profoundly impact our thinking on what is considered appropriate and inappropriate food as they frame food discourses through categories of gender, religion, class, nation and race, often repositioning the more traditional identity boundaries or transgressing them altogether. How to be a good mother, middle class consumer or member of a particular nation is communicated to the audience through a moral lens, as food media representations of appropriate 'citizenly' behaviour slide into requests for compliance with certain ethical positions. Examples include the portrayal of 'irresponsible' mothers, who do not feed their children what is generally considered healthy food, overweight people, who seemingly cannot control their food intake to conform to the desired body size, or men, for whom vegan food must be rebranded to be seen as manly enough to eat (Hollows, 2022). Similarly, such governmentality extends to consumption of sustainable diets as a badge of good citizenship for all, often without much thought for how these ideas intersect with larger underlying issues to do with poverty and inequality or how these marginalise certain groups. All of these meanings, as Lupton (2020) suggests, are often presented as opposites, as digital food media explores binary affects and morality around food, such as disgust, guilt and shame as well as pleasure and excitement.

As market-driven and often food industry-dependent cultural intermediaries, food celebrities tend to have ties to 'Big Food', although these are often not perceived critically by the audience or are just taken for granted. The relationship is, however, often worked both ways: as food celebrities rely on the food industry for financial support, the food industry, equally, relies on ideas that these food celebrities generate to sell their products, through both digital marketing channels and claims they make on food packaging (Contois, 2020). Foods are presented through the familiar frames that link certain lifestyles to healthier, more sustainable, animal-welfare-friendly lives, and repositioned to suit contemporary customers' sense of belonging.

Some food celebrities, however, have built their media presence from a counter-mainstream perspective, positioning themselves as a voice of resistance to the capitalist food system and its ills. While some mainstream discourses call for more state regulation, control of the food industry and better animal conditions (e.g. Hollows, 2022), some activist influencers and other food celebrities build their digital platform almost exclusively on critiques of the status quo demanding through digital platforms greater food transparency and a change in current (food) systems (Schneider et al., 2018). An example of such celebrity activism are calls for veganism, with TV and movie personalities and other media celebrities, such as Joaquin Phoenix and Alicia Silverstone, campaigning through their platforms for more compassion, care for the environment and increased animal rights (Doyle, 2016; Parkinson and Herring, 2023). Others, such as a group of micro-celebrity food bloggers engaged with #blackoutTuesday on Instagram, demonstrate how food influencers can engage in controversial discussions to do with food and race in a meaningful way (Dejmanee, 2023).

Who will tell us what to eat next? The future of food celebrities

Food celebrities will undoubtedly play a role in shaping future discourses around food systems, as well as promotions of food trends and global lifestyles. As hegemonic ideas around food are resisted through the rise of micro-food celebrities who provide 'alternative' digital resistance forms and formats across the world, audiences moving away from more traditional formats to social media also suggest increasing pressure for such content production, and the need to understand better the relationship between the two. For example, the possibility of co-production of content, as well as concerns around monetisation and data privacy, is common to all digital platforms. Much of the research into food celebrities, however, remains very Western-centric, even if the phenomenon in itself is global, e.g. chef Ranveer Brar based in India had more than 4 million Instagram followers and Lebanese Abir El Saghir who cooks from Turkey was followed on TikTok by almost 30 million people, both in the middle of 2025. So, although some like Kasturi (2023) have done fascinating research on village food videos in India to offer a look at a unique type of food celebrity, future research could well start by zooming in on less-explored locations and cultures to better represent the global nature of food media and food celebrities.

References

Contois, Emily (2020). *Dinners, Dudes and Diets: How Gender and Power Collide in Food Media and Culture*. University of North Carolina Press.

Dejmanee, Tisha (2023). Influencer Activism: Visibility, Strategy, and #BlackLivesMatter Discourse on Food Instagram. In Fakazis, E. and Fürsich, E. (eds), *The Political Relevance of Food Media and Journalism. Beyond Reviews and Recipes*. Routledge, pp. 19–33.

Doyle, Julie (2016). Celebrity vegans and the lifestyling of ethical consumption. *Environmental Communication*, 10:6, 777–790.

Hollows, Joanna (2022). *Celebrity Chefs, Food Media and the Politics of Eating*. Bloomsbury.

Johnston, Josee and Goodman, Mike (2015). Spectacular Foodscapes: Food Celebrities and the Politics of Lifestyle Mediation in an Age of Inequality. *Food, Culture and Society*, 18, 205–222. https://doi.org/10.2752/175174415X14180391604369.

Kasturi, Sumana (2023). Of Clay Stoves and Cooking Pots: "Village Food" Videos and Gastro-Politics in Contemporary India. In Fakazis, E. and Fürsich, E. (eds), *The Political Relevance of Food Media and Journalism. Beyond Reviews and Recipes*. Routledge, pp. 135–152.

Lewis, Tania (2020). *Digital Food: From Paddock to Platform*. Bloomsbury.

Lupton, Deborah (2020). Understanding Digital Food Cultures. In: Lupton, D. and Feldman, Z. (eds), *Digital Food Cultures*. Routledge, pp. 1–16.

Parkinson, Claire and Herring, Lara (2023). Vegan Celebrity Activism: An Analysis of the Critical Reception of Joaquin Phoenix's Awards Speech. *Celebrity Studies*, 14:4, 584–601, DOI: 10.1080/19392397.2022.2154684.

Phillipov, Michelle (2023). *Digital Food TV: The Cultural Place of Food in a Digital Era*. Routledge.

Rojek, Chris (2014). 'Big Citizen' celanthropy and its discontents. *International Journal of Cultural Studies,* 17:2, 127–141.

Schneider, Tanja, Eli, Karin, Dolan, Catherine, and Ulijaszek, Stanley (eds) (2018). *Digital Food Activism.* Routledge.

Tominc, Ana (ed.) (2022) *Food and Cooking on Early Television in Europe: Impact on Post-war Foodways.* Routledge.

Further reading

Rousseau, Signe (2012). *Food Media.* Routledge.
Although now more than a decade old, this is one of the first books that addresses the development of chefs as food celebrities and their media messages. It argues that the cacophony of messages around food in intersection with popular culture offers consumers a challenge as they decide which recommendation to follow and how they think of their own eating habits.

Contois, J. H. and Kish, Z. (eds) (2022). *Food Instagram: Identity, Influence and Negotiation.* University of Illinois Press.
This edited collection addresses the question of Instagram and how it intersects with its various users, including food influencers. Situating Instagram in its historic context as a visual medium, the book presents a number of cases from across the world that speak not only to Instagram's potential to build identities, but also to redefine what and why we eat in a contemporary world.

ANA TOMINC

21. Cheap food

GEOFFREY LAWRENCE

Introduction

'Cheap' is a relative term – cheap for whom? Under what circumstances? And with what consequences? This entry will not consider the multiple ways individuals, families, and communities gain access to basic, inexpensive, foodstuffs. Rather, it will deal with cheap food as a geopolitical and socio-economic strategy of states and businesses to shore up power – power to influence, control, and make financial gain. It will also explore the economic, social, and environmental consequences of 'cheap food' policies.

The wealthy have always profited from low-cost labour, and resultant low-cost food. In ancient times, Roman and Greek slaves worked the fields, producing more output for their owners than was required for their sustenance. Such exploitation of labour continued into feudal times, where serfs were obliged to surrender up to half their year's produce to the lord, or to work on the lord's land, without financial recompense, for a defined period of the year.

Feudalism was challenged by an emerging capitalism, the key to which was seventeenth- and eighteenth-century slavery in the British colonies. Sugar was being produced by enslaved African people who had been forced to work – in appalling conditions and under sufferance – on plantations in the Caribbean. While the trade in enslaved people and sugar made plantation owners and merchants enormously wealthy, it also provided a nascent British proletariat with cheap calories, helping to fuel British industrialisation (Mintz, 1985).

One industry especially advantaged by British, and later American, industrialisation was farming. By the turn of the twentieth century, horses were giving way to tractors, scythes to mechanical reapers, oxen to steam engines, and wagons to trucks. In concert these innovations dramatically improved both labour productivity and the volume of farm output. So too did the selective breeding of animals and seeds, the application of artificial fertilisers, the use of chemical pesticides, and the irrigation of crops. By the 1960s political economists and sociologists had come to identify what has been termed 'productivist' farming. It is characterised by *specialisation* in production, operational *intensification*, and economic *concentration* – each justified and promoted by neoliberal globalisation (Lawrence et al., 2012; Lawrence, 2024).

The productivist path to farming has created vast volumes of food for domestic consumption and export. In the US, the so-called 'cheap food policy' of subsidising farmers to stimulate production has allowed the amount of income consumers spend on food to decline significantly since the 1960s. In the early 2020s, US consumers spent 10.3% of their disposable income on foodstuffs – compared with 42.5% in 1901 (USDL, 2006; USDA, 2023). Surplus food stocks have become a problem not only for the US, but also for the EU, where, during the 1980s, 'lakes' of wine and milk and 'mountains' of butter were generated via subsidies provided to producers under the EU's Common Agricultural Policy (CAP).

The US has sought to manage its food surpluses through 'dumping' – the practice of exporting food to the Global South either as aid, or at a price below market value. This was achieved through the so-called Food for Peace strategy (P.L. 480), which claimed to be addressing world hunger. But the dumping of food solved the US problem of farm overproduction, while dampening any moves toward social disruption – and the potential rise of communism – in the poorer nations.

The so-called Green Revolution was also a vehicle for the production of cheap food – particularly in the Global South. By combining new high-yielding varieties of seeds, inorganic fertilisers, and pesticides, along with practices such as irrigation and double cropping, farmers were able to expand dramatically the output of staple foods, such as wheat and rice. However, such gains came with considerable costs, as outlined below.

Current issues and concerns

Cheap foods are those foods traded in the marketplace whose full costs of production, transportation, marketing, and consumption have not been included into their price. They are literally under-priced for one or both of two reasons. The first is that the market cannot or will not recognise the input subsidies – exploited labour, government handouts, and trade distortions – that allow their prices to be artificially low. The second is that their impacts, or 'externalities' – including environmental pollution, climate change, and poor public health – are not accounted for in their sale.

Input subsidies

Food can be made less expensive than it might otherwise be by providing farmers with subsidies, reducing their overall costs of production. Numerous schemes have been developed to support farmers including direct payments, marketing loans, counter-cyclical payments, minimum revenue schemes, disaster payments, and crop insurance. All are either funded directly, or subsidised, by governments. Subsidies are often based on a producer's output, which means the owners of the largest farms receive the greatest benefit – in the US the wealthiest 10% receive nearly 60% of the funds distributed (Green Fiscal Policy Network, 2021). Wealth moves upward to rich farmers and agribusinesses, land prices are artificially inflated, and an unsustainable productivist paradigm of agriculture is expanded.

Subsidies to assist farmers produce cheap foods in the Global North give those farmers an unfair trade advantage in the world marketplace. This impacts negatively on farmers in the Global South, who find it hard to compete with low-cost food imports. Agricultural production in the South becomes less profitable, with subsequent reductions in output. This makes people vulnerable to domestic food shortages if and when the cheap food from the North no longer flows.

Throughout the world the cost of food is cheapened through the exploitation of farm and factory labour. In the US some 75% of farm labourers are Mexican-born – a large majority of whom are undocumented workers. In Spain and Italy, farmers employ tens of thousands of undocumented workers from Morocco and West Africa. They are paid below minimum wages. In Mexico, workers producing food for the US market are housed in camps with barbed wire fences, patrolled by guards. Wages are often illegally withheld by employers to help ensure workers do not escape before the peak of the harvest. Throughout the world, agricultural workers face physical abuse, sexual violence, intimidation, debt bondage, and restriction of movement. They live in shantytowns, which are devoid of basic sanitation and health services. In 2021 over 27 million people around the globe – including children – encountered modern slavery in the form of forced labour, some 30% of whom were involved in agriculture (Walkfree, 2023).

Externalities

Foods are cheap because the full cost of producing them is not borne by the producer, with so-called 'negative externalities' being passed on to the wider community and environment. If agricultural outputs included the full costs of production, farmers would be paying for the pollution of waterways from agrochemical runoff, damage to the soil from erosion, biodiversity losses, and global heating from the release of greenhouse gases. None of this is priced into the food we eat.

In terms of global health, it is estimated that close to 40% of the world's population is overweight or obese, resulting in diseases such as type 2 diabetes, heart disease, stroke, musculoskeletal disorders, and cancer – all of which can cause disability and premature death (Elflein, 2022). The cheap ingredients derived from corporate-style industrial farming are built into cheap manufactured foods. The 'industrial diet' is one in which natural foods are adulterated with macro-ingredients like sugar, salt, and fats. The result is nutrient-poor 'pseudo foods' (junk foods) which are sold globally by supermarkets and the fast food industry (Winson, 2013; Lawrence, 2024). Foods such as burgers, pizzas, sugary drinks, carbohydrate-based desserts, and candy bars contain 'empty calories' which deliver energy but little or no nutrition. Macro-ingredients enhance the flavour of foods, which explains why people crave them. Cheap foods are unhealthy foods and are replacing higher cost, but healthier, items such as vegetables and fruit in diets. It is estimated that, globally, the hidden costs of cheap food – costs to human health and the environment – are in the vicinity of US$20 trillion annually (Hawkes, 2022).

Supermarkets occupy a dominant position in the provision of cheap food. Their *modus operandi* is to sell high volumes of fresh and manufactured products at low margins. Supermarkets have enormous power over farmers and food manufacturers. To keep foods cheap they adopt practices which impact negatively. For example, contracts with growers can 'squeeze' the producer who, in turn, cuts corners in farming operations – to the detriment of workers and the environment. Rigid product specifications mean that a large amount of what is grown is wasted. Supermarkets demand slotting fees from suppliers, alter specifications without compensation, demand retrospective payments, and threaten delisting if a supplier refuses to reduce prices. The pressures to become more efficient are passed down the supply chain, ultimately affecting worker wages and conditions, and environmental security. The supermarket store is designed to stimulate purchasing. Various food smells permeate the stores, while carefully selected music aims to relax the customer as a means of generating sales. Two-for-one deals, loss-leaders, and weekly specials entice the customer, while reinforcing the supermarket's generous 'cheap food' trope.

Future issues and concerns

The climate emergency might foreshadow the end of cheap food. Global warming will exacerbate drought conditions, flooding, cyclones, fires, and diseases making it increasingly difficult for farmers to grow food. NASA has predicted that global wheat production could decline by 17%, and corn (maize) production by 24% over the next decade (Gray, 2021). This is likely to herald increased hunger and social unrest. Furthermore, the production, distribution, and consumption of food contributes more than a third of all greenhouse gases released into the atmosphere (Charles, 2021). But demand for the most important contributor to greenhouse gas emissions from agriculture – meat – continues to surge. Can burgeoning world demand for cheap meat be met in a sustainable manner? Lab-based meats are viewed as a potential solution – but they might produce more carbon dioxide than the animals they replace (Lynch and Pierrehumbert, 2019).

At the same time agribusinesses are promoting a Second Green Revolution harnessing genetically engineered super-crops, new synthetic chemicals, and 'precision' farming utilising robotics and artificial intelligence. Others have rejected this model. Farmer and consumer movements throughout the world are arguing, instead, for locally based, environmentally benign, biodiverse, and more energy efficient food production options such as agroecological farming.

Cheap foods are foods created in exploitative and unsustainable ways. Scientists and other commentators argue what is required is a food system delivering affordable, nourishing, and ethically sourced foods produced in a sustainable manner. How to achieve this is one of the most important questions of the twenty-first century.

References

Charles K (2021) Food production emissions make up make up more than a third of global total. https://www.newscientist.com/article/2290068-food-production-emissions-make-up-more-than-a-third-of-global-total/ (Accessed 5 March 2023).

Elflein J (2022) Obesity worldwide – facts and figures. https://www.statista.com/topics/9037/obesity-worldwide/#topicOverview (Accessed 10 March 2023).

Gray E (2021) Global change impact upon crops expected within 10 years, NASA study finds. https://climate.nasa.gov/news/3124/global-climate-change-impact-on-crops-expected-within-10-years-nasa-study-finds/ (Accessed 12 March 2023).

Green Fiscal Policy Network (2021) Under Trump administration, farm subsidies soared and the rich got richer. https://greenfiscalpolicy.org/under-trump-farm-subsidies-soared-and-the-rich-got-richer/ (Accessed 5 March 2023).

Hawkes C (2022) Rising prices: Why the global drive to keep food cheap is unsustainable. https://www.marketwatch.com/story/rising-prices-why-the-global-drive-to-keep-food-cheap-is-unsustainable-11656009015 (Accessed 15 March 2023).

Lawrence G (2024) *Societal Deception: Global Social Issues in Post-Truth Times.* London, Palgrave Macmillan.

Lawrence G, Richards C, Gray I and Hansar N (2012) Climate change and the resilience of commodity food production in Australia. In: Rosin C, Stock P and Campbell H (eds) *Food System Failure.* London, Earthscan, pp. 131–146.

Lynch J and Pierrehumbert R (2019) Climate impacts of cultured meat and beef cattle. *Frontiers in Sustainable Food Systems* 3, https://doi.org/10.3389/fsufs.2019.00005 (Accessed 19 March 2023).

Mintz S (1985) *Sweetness and Power.* New York, Penguin

Statista (2023) Share of victims of trafficking for sexual exploitation worldwide between 2012 and 2020, by industry of exploitation. https://www.statista.com/statistics

/1368200/share-trafficking-victims-forced
-labor-world-industry/ (Accessed 22 March
2023).

USDA (2023) Food prices and spending.
https://www.ers.usda.gov/data-products/ag
-and-food-statistics-charting-the-essentials
/food-prices-and-spending/.

USDL (2006) 100 Years of U.S. consumer
spending. https://www.bls.gov/opub/100
-years-of-u-s-consumer-spending.pdf.

Walkfree (2023) Global estimates of modern
slavery. https://www.walkfree.org/reports/
global-estimates-of-modern-slavery-2022/
(Accessed 22 March 2023).

Winson A (2013) *The Industrial Diet*. New
York, New York University Press.

Further reading

Carolan M (2018) *The Real Cost of Cheap
Food*, Second Edition. London, Routledge.
This book explains how many of the costs
of producing food remain invisible.
Lawrence G (2024) Societal Deception:
Global Social Issues in Post-Truth Times.
London, Palgrave Macmillan.Discusses
supermarket power, the fast-food industry
and consequences of the 'industrial diet'.

Patel R and Moore J (2018) *A History of the
World in Seven Cheap Things*. London,
Verso.
This book argues that cheap food helped to
make the industrial world.

22. Class and food

DAVE BECK

Introduction

Social class is a way to understand hierarchical positioning between members of a
community. It can be related to several factors such as wealth, education, occupation,
and income. Class and food are intimately
linked as they are bound together by deep-
rooted connections that embody many other
sociological concepts. Food and class are
both intimately tied to who we are personally,
and who we identify with both individually
and collectively. Food sits at the heart of the
discussion of class, and can provide a way
to understand and examine how we relate to
'class' as part of our social identity. An intersectional approach to food and consumption
is important to examine food and class relations, looking at different structural divides
to assess how people are empowered and disempowered along multiple axes in relation to
the food system (e.g., by relating class to other
divides such as those of gender and race). The
concept of class is a key divide and food, and
more specifically food '*taste*', is a powerful way to observe class divisions in society.
This entry, therefore, brings together issues
of social class with how we understand food,
arriving at a confluence where class identity
meets the issue of taste. Placing food at the
centre, the entry argues that food is differentiated across social classes. A person's class
(however it is defined) is informed by their
history. This history is shaped by taste, i.e.
the values that have shaped and subsequently
inform our enjoyment of, not just food, but all
aspects of social life.

The entry aims to highlight this relationship between class, capital, and taste and,
in the process, reveal inequalities relating to
class and access to food within the capitalist
system, focusing especially on class, food,
and poverty.

Defining class: habitus, capital, and taste

Understanding class is fundamental in sociological studies, as the field is concerned with
the structure of society and what this means
for social life and interactions. Understandings
of social class have changed over time. For
example, Karl Marx and Friedrich Engels

(1848) understood social class and its accompanying inequality to be associated with the
exploitation of economic capital produced
by the proletarian working class, usurped
into profit for the bourgeois class. Therefore,
social class for Marx and Engels was examined through a lens of oppression and the
subjugation of one social class for the benefit of another. For Max Weber (1978), class
was identified as those individuals with a
similar economic background, shaped by
features such as income, property, or occupation. Defined as an '*Ideal Type*', this allows
us to see how the collective identity of people
shapes their social class and the value placed
on certain things such as food.

For both Marx and Weber, social class
is hierarchical: influence and power are
expressed top-down, and shape people's
food consumption practices and tastes. The
flow and reproduction of power and what
this means for developing and maintaining
a class identity was central to the work of
French sociologist Pierre Bourdieu. In his
work on habitus, Bourdieu (1986) describes
social class as determined through a process
of socialisation, showing that social class, as
an identity, is constructed around three distinctive and intersecting 'capitals'. First is
economic capital. This is the financial abilities of an individual inherent within their
social class and family background and can
be seen as a signifier of financial social status, i.e., how wealthy you are. Next Bourdieu
identifies cultural capital, typically obtained
through education but also acquired through
the process of socialisation – e.g., family out-
ings and vacations leading to the development
of cultural awareness and learning. Finally,
Bourdieu argues for the role of social capital,
identified as social connections. These can
also be inherited (along with the conditions
inherent within economic and cultural capital) through the process of socialisation – i.e.,
who you know and, more importantly, *who*
knows *you*. As Bourdieu (1986) describes it,
these capitals work together, symbiotically, to
develop individuals' sense of class, and any
change in one capital can lead to changes in
others. These understandings of class relate to
food and our consumption of it, as explored in
the next section.

Current concerns in food and class

The unpleasant taste of poverty

The impact social class has on food choice and food consumption is profound. This is because for most people in the Global North at least, food exists within a capitalist system where healthier food options tend to be more expensive than their ultra-processed or fast food counterparts, limiting choice and/or access to certain foods for some people. The capitalist system is replete with exploitation, and any form of exploitation creates winners and losers. The food system is no different. Those with higher socio-economic status are rewarded as 'winners' in terms of their food-choice–health nexus, as they can deploy their capital(s) to their benefit. At the opposite end of the spectrum, those with lower socio-economic status are more restricted in terms of their food-choice–health options and tend to suffer a worse diet. In essence, choice can be a delusion as the capitalist industrial food system produces good food for wealthy people and poor food for poor people.

Food poverty, and its implications for health and society, thus has structural causes. The sociologist David Caplovitz (1963) famously developed the term 'Poverty Premium' as a practical and grounded way to show how choice is structurally conditioned and interacts with socio-economic status and, significantly, impacts the lives of poor people. The Poverty Premium describes a multitude of ways in which those suffering from poverty typically are forced, through a lack of real choice, to pay more for the same goods and services as those not in poverty (see also Beck, 2020). In terms of food choices, this can occur due to a variety of factors such as limited access to affordable, healthy food options, being unable to save money by bulk buying, and transportation challenges limiting people's ability to reach affordable supermarkets. As a result, people living in poverty may be faced with additional costs such as having to resort to purchasing food from convenience stores or fast food outlets, which is often less healthy and more expensive than food purchased from supermarkets.

Food is an aspect of life where being in a lower social class ultimately costs more as it means spending a greater proportion of disposable income on trying to access it. Healthier food options are often more expensive than ultra-processed foods, but geography also plays an important role as living in an area lacking adequate access to food shops means more expense in travel and time. Smith and Thompson (2023: 5), for example, refer to 'food deserts' where access to healthy and affordable food is limited; these are typical of urban areas blighted by low income.

Food and the subjective nature of class

Taking Bourdieu's work on habitus and capitals, and the patterns associated with the development of class as an expression of social identity, Savage et al. (2013), in collaboration with the BBC, designed and administered the Great British Class Survey. Asking the British public about their income and assets (economic capital), the occupations of people they know on a personal level (social capital), and hobbies and interests (cultural capital) they are involved in encouraged people to think reflectively about their habitus. This suggests an additional way of understanding social class and its relationship with food on the basis of people's subjective experience, while still conceptualising this as related to habitus. As the survey illustrated, habitus is informed by an accumulation of capital, reflecting people's socialisation into a social class. Individuals develop their appreciation of socially defined styles, or their 'taste' in things, including food. However, any discussion of 'taste' when viewed through the lens of food and class inevitably brings up the value-laden duality of 'good taste' and what, to individuals, 'tastes good' (Vogler, 2020: 16). On one level, we are socialised into 'good taste'. It is a learnt characteristic that is associated with social class, an expression of a person's knowledge and awareness of what their social class represents. For example, truffles, oysters, caviar, and foie gras may reflect a palate of 'good taste' for the higher social class adult, but an appreciation of these tastes (and what they signify to others) has to be developed over time.

Something 'tasting good', however, reflects also the more subjective nature of our food desires and may be, initially, less of a socialised characteristic. What tastes good to one person may not necessarily taste good to another. Moreover, culturally, things that we appreciate as 'tasting good' may also have a geographical expression; for example, they might be tied to the idea of local cuisine, delicacies, and cultural histories.

DAVE BECK

An appreciation of what 'tastes good' may also be a learnt characteristic in our display of social class. Studies have shown how people have learnt to crave ultra-processed foods – high in salt, fat, and sugar, and often served in large proportions – and which are actively bad for us and unnecessary for our diets, but which we consume nonetheless (Albritton, 2013, Dimbleby, 2021). What is more, further research has shown that around 50% of calories consumed in the UK now come from ultra-processed foods (Yeo, 2021). This market is also specifically targeted at consumers who, on average, tend to share some characteristics of a lower social class, e.g., low income, time poor, and/or lacking food preparation skills.

Future concerns: 'food-class-appropriation' and transformation

Food, as with class, has a habit of transformation. This has been driven by the increasingly important position of food in the capitalist system. What may have been the food of one social class, over time, becomes capable of transforming into food associated with a different class identity. Mainly this is a case of what can be described as a 'class–food-appropriation' nexus; the appropriation of foods historically associated with or developed from within one class become transformed into foods now associated with a different class. For example, farmers' markets, local food retailers, foraging, and street food would have once been common for all social classes and used extensively at low cost by the working class. However, structural transformations have worked to reduce the freedom previously experienced by working-class people to benefit from local food, farmers' markets, and street foods as these have become more expensive options, and they are now associated with more affluent consumers.

Supermarkets, due to their purchasing power and economies of scale can 'stack 'em high, sell 'em cheap', and have worked to put many local independent retailers out of business since the 1960s (Jones and Mair, 2016). Through their business model of selling convenience, they are also partly to blame for facilitating a decline in consumer food skills (Jaffe & Gertler, 2006) and encouraging the development of the ultra-processed foods market. This is associated, partly, with a loss of consumer power, the centralisation of food retail into big-box stores and strengthening of the business model of supermarkets. Furthermore, structural socio-political changes at the heart of neoliberalism aim to disempower working-class people in relation to food with emphasis on individual choice and responsibility. For example, Caraher (2012) highlights how, structurally, the working class has been disempowered through the removal of taught food skills in schools following the demise of home economics in favour of a design and technology approach. The result is a multi-generational food skills deficit that may ultimately drive people towards consuming more ready meals and ultra-processed foods.

Defining 'food work' as any household task involving food, O'Connell and Brannen (2016) found that food is still divided along gendered lines. Their research finds that two-thirds of food work in UK households is done by women, especially so within working-class households, and that the childhood consumption of processed foods increases in line with maternal full-time employment. A lack of food skills and the absence of Bourdieusian cultural capital related to cooking, meal planning, and the consumption of nutritious food can have significant impacts on poverty, as it affects people's ability to make informed and healthy food choices, which can lead to diet-related health issues. A lack of food related skills may also drive an increase in the food industry attending to a consumerist culture, where a capitalist food system prioritising profit is manifested in the production of unhealthy highly processed foods that are high in calories and low in nutritional value (Albritton, 2009). This perpetuates a cycle of poor health, increased healthcare costs, and continued poverty.

As this entry has highlighted, food and class are inextricably linked. They can be united in what is 'good taste', something appreciated and extolled by one social class, yet at the same time establish social class differences in what is considered to be 'tasting good'. People are bound together in class identity through the concept of taste. As the work of Bourdieu has shown, to understand modern notions of social class identity we need to consider the intersection of social, cultural, and economic capitals, and how they work to create habitus. Sociologically, social class is more than simply an expression of occupational identity; it is something residing within *you,* and what makes you '*you*'. Whatever social class you think, believe, or feel that you belong to is a personal reflective examination of your past, your present, and your future-self in equal parts. It is where you feel comfortable in your *taste*; it is your *habitus*. However, the relationship between food and class is not always fixed, and taste can be (re) formed through processes of socialisation. Taste may be a learnt characteristic, yet one which subsequently can become appropriated by one social class from another through the application of structural power. As this entry has made clear, this power typically resides in one class and is facilitated through a complex and evolving system of capitalism which systematically disempowers those with a low socio-economic status.

References

Albritton R (2009) *Let Them Eat Junk: How Capitalism Creates Hunger and Obesity.* Pluto Press.

Albritton R (2013) Between obesity and hunger: The capitalist food industry. *Socialist Register 2010: Morbid Symptoms* 46, 342–352.

Beck D (2018) The changing face of food poverty with special reference to Wales. PhD Thesis. Bangor University.

Beck D (2020) Poverty Premiums: Cost of Being Poor. In: Leal Filho W, Azul AM, Brandli L, Lange Salvia A, Özuyar PG & Wall T (eds), *No Poverty: Encyclopedia of the UN Sustainable Development Goals.* Springer, Cham. https://doi.org/10.1007/978-3-319-69625-6_110-1.

Bourdieu P (1984) *Distinction: A Social Critique of the Judgement of Taste.* Harvard University Press.

Bourdieu P (1986) The Forms of Capital. In: Richardson J (ed.), *Handbook of Theory and Research for the Sociology of Education.* Greenwood Press, pp. 241–258.

Caplovitz D (1963) *The Poor Pay More: Consumer Practices of Low-income Families.* Free Press of Glencoe, Collier-Macmillan.

Caraher M (2012) Cooking in crisis: Lessons from the UK. https://arrow.tudublin.ie/dgs/2012/june512/6/.

Crompton R (2008) *Class and Stratification.* 3rd ed. Polity.

Dillon M (2020) *Introduction to Sociological Theory: Theorists, Concepts, and their Applicability to the Twenty-first Century.* John Wiley & Sons.

Dimbleby H (2021) *National Food Strategy Independent Review: The Plan.* https://www.nationalfoodstrategy.org.

Jaffe J & Gertler M (2006) Victual vicissitudes: Consumer deskilling and the (gendered) transformation of food systems. *Agriculture and Human Values*, 23(2), 143–162. https://doi.org/10.1007/s10460-005-6098-1.

Jones P & Mair M (2016) Genealogy, Parasitism and Moral Economy: The Case of UK Supermarket Growth. In: Whyte D and Wiegratz J (eds), *Neoliberalism and the Moral Economy of Fraud.* Routledge, pp. 98–111.

Marx K & Engels F (1848) *Manifesto of the Communist Party.* Marx/Engels Selected Works, 1, 98–137. Available: https://www.marxists.org/archive/marx/works/download/pdf/Manifesto.pdf.

O'Connell R & Brannen J (2016) *Food, Families and Work.* Bloomsbury Publishing.

Savage M, Devine F, Cunningham N, Taylor M, Li Y, Hjellbrekke J, Le Roux B, Friedman S & Miles A (2013) A new model of social class? Findings from the BBC's Great British Class Survey experiment. *Sociology*, 47(2): 219–250. https://doi/full/10.1177/0038038513481128.

Smith D & Thompson C (2023) *Food Deserts and Food Insecurity in the UK: Exploring Social Inequality.* Taylor & Francis.

Vogler P (2020) *Scoff: A History of Food and Class in Britain.* Atlantic Books.

Weber M (1978) *Economy and Society: An Outline of Interpretive Sociology* (Vol. 2). University of California Press.

Yeo G (2021) *Why Calories Don't Count.* Orion Publishing Co.

Further reading

Beck D & Gwilym H (2023) Neoliberalism, Division and Austerity: Precarity and Hunger in the UK. In: Gregory L & Iafrati S (eds), *Diversity and Welfare Provision: Tension and Discrimination in the 21st Century.* Bristol University Press.

Beck D (2020) Poverty Premiums: Cost of Being Poor. In: Leal Filho W, Azul AM, Brandli L, Lange Salvia A, Özuyar PG & Wall T (eds), *No Poverty: Encyclopedia of the UN Sustainable Development Goals.*

DAVE BECK

Springer, Cham. https://doi.org/10.1007 /978-3-319-69625-6_110-1.

These sources provide a detailed discussion of neoliberalism, its effect on food poverty, and how this has impacted social class and the role of the poverty premium.

DAVE BECK

23. Climate and food emergencies

Marta Guadalupe Rivera-Ferre

Introduction

Food and climate are closely interlinked. On the one hand, food systems are dependent on climate conditions, being severely affected by the impacts associated with climate change, mainly extreme events and gradual changes in temperature and rain patterns (Figure 23.1). Those impacts increase risks of food insecurity through changes in *food availability*, due to a reduction of global yields and agricultural productivity for major crops, and through impacts on infrastructures; *food access*, mainly through impacts on food prices; *food use*, through changes in the nutritional profile of food (e.g. protein and micronutrient content); and *food stability*, due to increasing variability (Bezner-Kerr et al., 2022; Mbow et al., 2019). On the other hand, food systems contribute to climate change through greenhouse gas (hereafter 'GHG') emissions. The land report of the Intergovernmental Panel on Climate Change (IPCC) estimated 21 to 37% of GHG emissions are linked to food systems globally (Mbow et al., 2019), which included emissions of 9 to 14% from crop and livestock activities within the farm gate, 5 to 14% from land use and land-use change, including deforestation and peatland degradation, and 5 to 10% from food supply chain activities.

Apart from climate change, current food system trajectories are also leading to transgressions of other planetary boundaries, via biodiversity loss, land and aquatic ecosystem degradation, excessive water extraction, and uncoupling of biogeochemical flows of nutrients, like nitrogen or phosphorus (Steffen et al., 2015). Furthermore, it is also essential to consider that both food and climate are embedded in social systems, and different social groups are affected differently by climate change. Among the most vulnerable social groups in food production, the IPCC identified small-scale farmers and small-scale fishers, pastoralist groups and Indigenous peoples, and women and young people within these groups, which include billions of people worldwide, while at the same time, all of us are consumers of food. Thus, issues of equity and justice need to be at the centre of decisions. It is essential, therefore, to analyse food systems and climate change together, to consider the existing interconnections between the two, and to identify actions that can contribute to deliver food security and nutrition, and sustainable and healthy livelihoods, while reducing emissions and adapting to climate change.

Current issues: climate emergency and food emergency

The emergence of a global syndemic

Every 7 to 8 years the IPCC evaluates the existing scientific evidence regarding climate change. In every report, as the complexity of the analyses increases, projections about the impacts of climate change are worsening. The first reports were mostly focused on assessing the origins of climate change to elucidate whether and to what extent it was anthropogenic. Once its anthropogenic origin was evident, the focus on the impacts, vulnerability, and adaptation options increased, mainly because climate change was having real impacts on people's lives. As a result, the contributions of social sciences to the IPCC reports increased. Indeed, with flooding, droughts, heat waves, wildfires, and other associated impacts in all parts of the planet being more evident and severe every year, concerns about climate change in society are growing. Thus, climate change is changing from being perceived as something in the future to something that is happening now, and it is widely acknowledged that we live in a climate emergency. Different countries and cities have signed climate emergency declarations, and civil society is increasingly promoting a diversity of actions worldwide to force governments to stop emissions, e.g. through civil disobedience or even bringing governments to court. In this context, some scientists argue that IPCC projections are too conservative and that the reality is even worse, asking to include some bad to worst-case scenario projections leading to catastrophe, where not only climate, but also associated crises, so-called *'climate-triggered risk cascades'*, such as conflict, political instability, or systemic financial risk, can be included in the analyses, potentially leading to social catastrophe (Kemp et al., 2022).

One of the associated risks linked to climate change is food insecurity (Figure 23.1). We are in not only a climate emergency, but also a food emergency. The food emergency

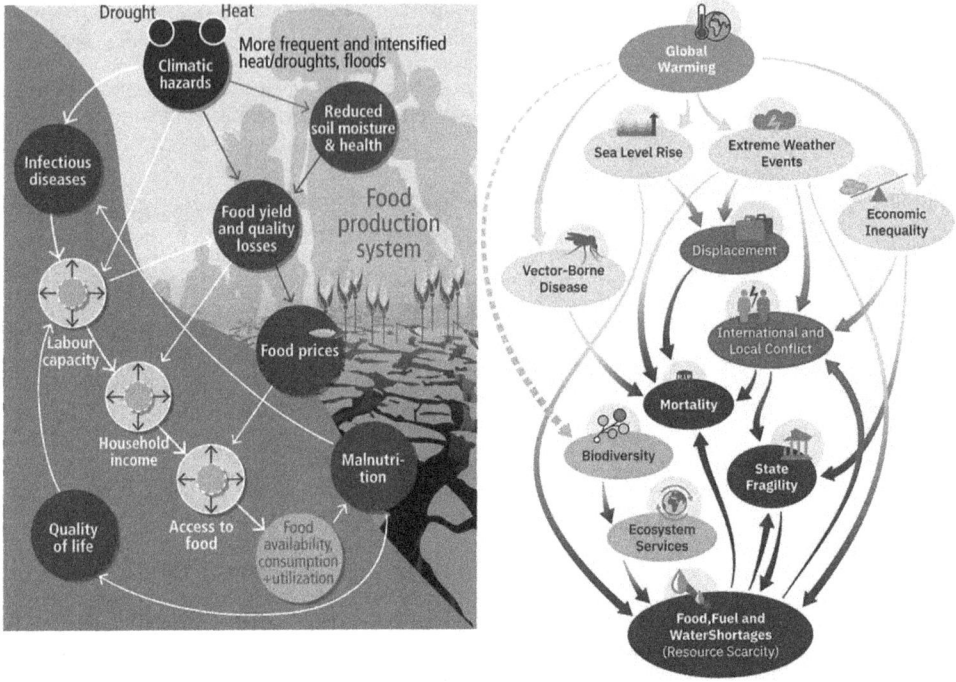

Notes: The first panel shows climate hazards and food production with impacts on food security; the second panel shows bad to worst-case projections leading to catastrophe scenarios.

Source: Bezner-Kerr et al. (2022: 724) and Kemp et al. (2022: 7).

Figure 23.1   Relations between food security and climate change

was identified even before the climate emergency, with global famine and hunger emergencies leading to starvation of millions of people for decades during the first half of the 20th century. These events led to the creation of the World Food Programme (WFP) and the Food and Agriculture Organization of the United Nations (FAO) during the 1960s. For 60 years, different actors at the global level have collaborated to address malnutrition, but we are still a long way from solving it. In fact, the food emergency has become even worse in the last decades, with issues related to undernutrition (including wasting, stunting, and micronutrient deficiencies) persisting alongside increasing trends of overconsumption leading to overweight and obesity. Currently, most of the world's population live in countries where overweight and obesity kill more people than underweight. In other

words, food insecurity has increased in the last decades as a result of the global nutrition transition and the incapacity to address hunger. The food emergency is very clear when we look at the numbers: globally, one-third of the population is moderately or severely food insecure. More than 3.1 billion people (42% of the world's population) were unable to afford a healthy diet in 2021 (FAO, 2023).

In this context, the EAT Lancet Commission published a report in 2019 which recognised the existence of a "global syndemic" of climate change, undernutrition, and obesity that affects most people in every country and region worldwide (Swinburn et al., 2019: 791) and in so doing focuses "attention on the scale and urgency of addressing these combined challenges and emphasises the need for common solutions".

Response options to tackle food and climate emergencies

Addressing food security and climate change together was the objective of the *Special Report on Climate Change and Land* (IPCC, 2019). In the report, after evaluating more than 7000 scientific publications, the authors analysed a diversity of response options that tackled food security, climate change mitigation and adaptation, and combating desertification and land degradation. They divided the options into land management, value chain management, and risk management. Response options included both supply and demand, including behaviour change actions such as dietary change (e.g. reducing the consumption of animal protein) and reduction of food loss and waste, the latter of which contributes 8 to 10% of global GHG emissions (Mbow et al., 2019).

The food chapter of the IPCC's 2022 global climate change report (Bezner-Kerr et al., 2022) provides an integrated assessment of the responses, highlighting, among the options with the highest mitigation and adaptation potential, dietary change and agroecological approaches. Options include agro-forestry, intercropping, organic agriculture, and all farm management strategies targeting soil organic carbon, cover crops, and rotational grazing that can provide mitigation and support adaption to climate change via food security, livelihoods, biodiversity, and health co-benefits. Approaches that evaluate nexus relations between land, water, energy, and food in the context of climate change are also gaining momentum.

As well as assessing particular strategies and how they can contribute to both food security and climate change adaptation and mitigation, the IPCC (2022a; 2022b) and EAT-Lancet (2019) also propose the use of international human rights law and applying the concept of a right to wellbeing. This encompasses the right to food. This is a further step to avoid fragmentation of the responses into isolated strategies that would impede the transformation needed, going beyond technical practices to introduce the social dimension into the responses, with a focus on equity and justice.

A good deal of literature exists on both climate change and food systems, demonstrating the efficiency and imperative of human-rights-based approaches in combating both emergencies in an effective and equitable manner. Furthermore, the concept of climate-resilient development, proposed by the IPCC (Roy et al., 2018; IPCC, 2022a), calls for development trajectories that integrate both adaptation and mitigation as a means to realise sustainable development goals, expanding the discussion towards issues of equity and justice. However, the representation of climate change and food security is very often technical – measuring GHG emission increases and access to technical means for adaptation in the case of climate; a lack of enough food in the case of hunger; or bad individual choice decisions in the case of obesity – leading to a favouring of technical, and often individual, solutions to address these global social problems.

The technologisation of food and climate responses: lock-in to transformation

Climate emergency and food security are often framed as technical problems, leading to technical rather than political solutions, with a technocratic and orthodox economics focus (Dewulf, 2013; Rivera-Ferre, 2012). In the climate arena, technology development and transfer have emerged as essential means of global action for mitigation and adaptation (Oh, 2020), and technological innovation is framed as a leading component to be accelerated, encouraged, and enabled. In the case of climate change adaptation, we can distinguish between a 'tame' technical problem (technoscientific perspective) versus a 'wicked' problem of governance (sociopolitical perspective). The former focuses on aspects like impact assessments or technological solutions; the latter directs attention towards the high stakes, uncertainties, communication strategies, power relations, and equity issues related to climate change adaptation (Dewulf, 2013). In the mitigation arena, the technological framing is even more compelling, and here most of the actions are focused on reducing emissions through new technologies, e.g. the use of biochar, bioenergy, and carbon capture and storage (BECCS) in the case of agriculture. This framing is complementary to the deregulatory ecological modernisation discourse described by McGee and Taplin (2014), which is characterised as: (i) technology is a central instrument to respond to climate change, (ii) a cleaner technology market is facilitated, (iii) the private sector is more empowered, and (iv) mutual relations exist between economic development and GHG emission reduction.

In the case of food security, a diversity of framings has also been identified, leading to different solutions. Rivera-Ferre (2012) identified an alternative and official framing, the latter suggesting that the problem of hunger is due to a lack of productivity, and is thus a technical problem: more food needs to be produced. This framing tends to consider only the food availability component of food security. Despite growing evidence showing that food security, and particularly hunger, is not a matter of increasing production, the field of global food security remains dominated by macro- and micro-institutions that put food availability and agricultural production at the heart of the problem and preferred solutions (Fouilleux et al., 2017). In the context of climate change, those framings promote solutions that support technologies such as precision agriculture or developing new crop varieties to ensure the production of food in adverse climate conditions. The vested interests of global corporations have been identified as barriers to change to tackle the root causes of both climate and food emergencies. They are described as potential lock-ins to transformation and path dependence (Clapp and Fuchs, 2009; IPCC, 2022b; IPES-Food, 2016, 2023).

In the climate arena, the IPCC (2022b) states that obstacles to transformation include both entrenched power relations dominated by vested interests that control and benefit from existing technologies, and governance structures that continue to reproduce unsustainable patterns of production and consumption. They discuss systemic responses that move beyond incremental responses, aiming for a society-wide transformation that will require expanding the focus of efforts beyond the technical to include people, and their behaviour and attitudes. A broader socio-political focus on mitigation leads to paying attention to degrowth and just transition narratives (IPCC, 2022b).

In the food arena, the EAT-Lancet Commission also identifies that a principal source of policy inertia related to addressing obesity and climate change is the power of vested interests, i.e. commercial actors, whose engagement in policy often constitutes a conflict of interest that is at odds with the public good and planetary health (Swinburn

et al., 2019). In a similar vein, IPES-Food (2023) reports that corporate influence over food system governance has become the new normal and that corporations have succeeded in convincing governments that they must be central in any discussion on the future of food systems. Confirming this trend, co-optation processes of transformative proposals, like agroecology, are currently on the way, separating the technical dimension of the proposal (practice and scientific knowledge) from the social and political ones (associated social movements and the contributions of peasant and Indigenous knowledge to agroecology). In this context, global corporations appear as promoting proposals that would fall under the agroecological approach, like regenerative agriculture, creating confusion and delaying the necessary action for transformation in food systems to tackle both the climate and food emergencies, while maintaining the status quo, as has happened in the past with organic and fair trade standards (Jaffee and Howard, 2010).

Future issues for climate and food emergencies

Since evidence shows that the climate and food emergencies both have common societal drivers, it is here that we need to focus energy and attention in the future in order to find those synergistic solutions that allow societies to reduce emissions, adapt to climate change, achieve food and nutrition security, and ensure the livelihoods of millions of people with a focus on equity, food justice, and rights. From a research perspective, this requires analysis of both climate and food crises from a complex perspective, analysing interactions, synergies, and trade-offs. The latest IPCC (2022a) and EAT-Lancet Commission (2019) reports have provided advances in this direction in the science–policy interface; however, vested interests and representation of food and climate crises as a technological problem can lock in and prevent the transformation required.

References

Bezner Kerr, R., T. Hasegawa, R. Lasco, I. Bhatt, D. Deryng, A. Farrell, H. Gurney-Smith, H. Ju, S. Lluch-Cota, F. Meza, G. Nelson, H. Neufeldt, and P. Thornton, 2022. Food, Fibre, and Other Ecosystem Products. In: *Climate Change 2022: Impacts,*

Adaptation and Vulnerability. Contribution of Working Group II to the Sixth Assessment Report of the Intergovernmental Panel on Climate Change [H.-O. Pörtner et al. (eds.)]. Cambridge University Press, pp. 713–906.

Clapp, J. and D.A. Fuchs. 2009. *Corporate Power in Global Agrifood Governance.* MIT Press.

Dewulf, A. 2013. Contrasting frames in policy debates on climate change adaptation. *WIRE's Climate Change,* 4(4): 321–330.

EAT-Lancet 2019. Healthy Diets from Sustainable Food Systems: EAT-Lancet Commission https://eatforum.org/content/uploads/2019/07/EAT-Lancet_Commission_Summary_Report.pdf

FAO 2023. The State of Food Security and Nutrition in the World 2023. Food and Agriculture Organization of the United Nations, Rome, Italy. https://openknowledge.fao.org/items/445c9d27-b396-4126-96c9-50b335364d01

Fouilleux, E., Nicolas Bricas and Arlène Alpha. 2017. 'Feeding 9 billion people': Global food security debates and the productionist trap. *Journal of European Public Policy,* 24(11): 1658–1677.

IPCC 2019. Special Report on Climate Change and Land. Cambridge University Press. https://www.ipcc.ch/srccl/

IPCC. 2022a. *Climate Change 2022: Impacts, Adaptation, and Vulnerability. Contribution of Working Group II to the Sixth Assessment Report of the Intergovernmental Panel on Climate Change* [H.-O. Pörtner et al. (eds.)]. Cambridge University Press.

IPCC. 2022b. *Climate Change 2022: Mitigation of Climate Change. Working Group III Contribution to the IPCC Sixth Assessment Report.* https://www.ipcc.ch/report/ar6/wg3/

IPES-Food. 2016. *From Uniformity to Diversity: A Paradigm Shift from Industrial Agriculture to Diversified Agroecological Systems.* https://www.ipes-food.org/_img/upload/files/UniformityToDiversity_FULL.pdf

IPES-Food. 2023. *Who's Tipping the Scales? The Growing Influence of Corporations on the Governance of Food Systems, and How to Counter It.* https://ipes-food.org/report/whos-tipping-the-scales/

Jaffee, D. and P.H. Howard. 2010. Corporate cooptation of organic and fair trade standards. *Agriculture and Human Values,* 27: 387–399.

Mbow, C., C. Rosenzweig, L.G. Barioni, T.G. Benton, M. Herrero, M. Krishnapillai, E. Liwenga, P. Pradhan, M.G. Rivera-Ferre, T. Sapkota, F.N. Tubiello and Y. Xu, 2019. Food Security. In: *Climate Change and Land: An IPCC Special Report on Climate Change, Desertification, Land Degradation, Sustainable Land Management, Food Security, and Greenhouse Gas Fluxes in Terrestrial Ecosystems* [P.R. Shukla et al., (eds.)]. Cambridge University Press, pp. 437–550.

Kemp, L., Chi Xu and Timothy M. Lenton. 2022. Climate endgame: Exploring catastrophic climate change scenarios. *PNAS,* 119(34): e2108146119.

McGee, J. and R. Taplin. 2014. The Asia-Pacific partnership and market-liberal discourse in global climate governance. *International Journal of Law in Context,* 10(3): 338–356.

Oh, C. 2020. Discursive contestation on technological innovation and the institutional design of the UNFCCC in the new climate change regime. *New Political Economy,* 25(4): 660–674.

Rayner, G., M. Gracia, E. Young, et al. 2010. Why are we fat? Discussions on the socioeconomic dimensions and responses to obesity. *Globalization and Health* 6: 7.

Rivera-Ferre, M.G. 2012. Framing of agri-food research affects the analysis of food security: The critical role of social sciences. *International Journal of Sociology of Agriculture and Food,* 19(2): 169–175.

Roy, S.S., M.A. Ansari, S.K. Sharma, B. Sailo, Ch. Basudha Devi, I.M. Singh, A. Das, D. Chakraborty, A. Arunachalam, N. Prakash and S.V. Ngachan 2018. Climate Resilient Agriculture in Manipur: Status and Strategies for Sustainable Development. *Current Science,* 115: 7, 1342–1350. https://www.jstor.org/stable/26978408

Steffen, W., K. Richardson, J. Rockström, S.E. Cornell, I. Fetzer, E.M. Bennett, R. Biggs, S.R. Carpenter, W. de Vries, C.A. de Wit, C. Folke, D. Gerten, J. Heinke, G.M. Mace, L.M. Persson, V. Ramanathan, B. Reyers and S. Sörlin 2015. Planetary boundaries: Guiding human development on a changing planet. *Science,* 347, 736–746.

Swinburn, B.A., A. Boyd, et al. 2019. The global syndemic of obesity, undernutrition, and climate change: The Lancet Commission report. *The Lancet,* 393(10173): 791–846.

Further reading

Kemp, L., Chi Xu, Timothy M. Lenton. 2022. Climate endgame: Exploring catastrophic climate change scenarios. *PNAS,* 119(34): e2108146119. This paper provides a useful overview of climate change scenarios, including impacts on food, fuel, and water security.

IPES-Food. 2023. Who's tipping the scales? The growing influence of corporations on the governance of food systems, and how to counter it. Provides a useful account of links between corporate governance in managing food system futures, including for climate change.

24. Commensality and food

Laura Cuch

Introduction: commensality as the basis of sociality

Commensality, or eating together, is a basic practice of human sociality, often associated with bonding and intimacy, hospitality and reciprocity, as well as cooperation and conviviality. Through embodied, material and symbolic practices of food sharing – involving choices in what people eat, where, how and with whom – commensality articulates group identities and belonging. Hierarchical norms that govern the material organisation of collective meals contribute to the transmission of cultural practices and values, and expose inequalities regarding status, class, race and gender. Therefore, anthropologists and sociologists have traditionally studied commensality as a way of understanding both the different cultural systems that inform eating practices and the organisation of "societies".

Early work within these disciplines was pivotal in studying religious food prohibitions and rituals, including sacrificial meals, but overlooked the more ordinary and everyday aspects of commensality (Fischler, 2011). However, the role and nature of household meals have recently gained interest in sociocultural research, partly due to the perceived decline of the family meal in modern Western societies. This has engendered empirical research into its possible impact on people's wellbeing, health and nutrition. Food sharing, particularly in its sensuous dimensions, is also perceived to play an important role in fostering positive multicultural relationships. Thus, commensality remains a complex, multidisciplinary and expanding research field.

Shifting understandings and key dimensions

Various definitions and typologies suggest that commensality is both complex and ambivalent. This is evident in its capacity to include and exclude, to structure everyday life and mark special events, and to enable both conviviality and conflict. Its complexity also stems from its being both individual and shared, public and private, as well as both a symbolic and a sensuous process. This can be further explored in relation to the politics, materiality and embodied dimensions of eating together.

Definitions and typologies

The word commensality derives from the Latin *commensalis*, composed of *com* (together/with) and *mensa* (table), meaning sharing the table or, more generally, eating together (Tan, 2015). Commensality is also defined through its relationality, as eating with people produces a wide range of relationships that materialise through commensal groups or circles as settings for feeding and sharing food. These convey hierarchy and dependence, through different types of food and levels of formality, as well as closeness and intimacy, for example, by eating or drinking from the same plate, glass or cutlery.

Commensality has been classified according to context and purpose – such as "domestic", "kin and communal", "ceremonial and religious", "political" and "hospitality" (Tan, 2015: 14) – and is generally understood as a positive practice of reciprocity that contributes to healthier lives. However, Grignon (2001) emphasises difference: from the power asymmetries of "domestic commensality" (between partners , and between caregivers and children), to hierarchical norms that rule "institutional commensality", such as in schools, prisons or the army. Further, commensality's ability to separate and unite groups of people defines "segregative commensality", which asserts group identities through inclusions and exclusions, and "transgressive commensality", which dissolves boundaries between different groups, if only symbolically and temporarily, while, ultimately, contributing to maintaining them. He also foregrounds temporal and rhythmic dimensions of commensality that distinguish "everyday commensality" (e.g. at home, work and other ordinary contexts) from "exceptional commensality" at significant times in the year (e.g. Easter, Ramadan, New Year, birthdays) and life events (e.g. marriages and funerals).

Politics of commensality

The dichotomy between public and private takes centre stage in the study of political commensality, to which history and literature have contributed greatly. This includes meals with kings and emperors that promote internal cohesion and external alliances, and is associated with trust, betrayal and the fear of being poisoned. Political commensality also relates to the emergence of the distinction between public and private in Greco-Roman Antiquity through public meals and sacrificial banquets, which involved representatives of institutions, and excluded women, slaves and strangers, who lacked full citizen status (Fischler, 2011).

Relatedly, Appadurai's (1981) concept of "gastro-politics", by which eating practices articulate conflict, blurs the boundaries between public and private. This is informed by understandings of commensality as part of a syntax that structures social organisation. Focusing on Hindu South Asia, Appadurai interrelates the domestic meal, the marriage feast and food in the Temple as part of an integral moral cosmology, where commensal roles and meanings are carried across these spheres. In a society where issues of rank and exclusiveness are vital between host/guest, giver/receiver and insider/outsider, food transactions, involving human and divine hierarchical relations, are the currency for contesting specific economic or cultural resources. As such, the politics of commensality are closely tied to hospitality, as is also exemplified by research on domestic dinner parties in North America (Julier, 2013). Here, the relationships between hosts and guests are mediated through expectations and rules, which are often tacit and expose race, gender and class inequalities. These manifest as differences in social, cultural and economic capital, reflected, for example, in the host's taste and performance of a social atmosphere and status – including who is invited, choices in decoration and food, and employment of staff to cook and serve it.

Recent research shows that family meals can produce challenging experiences that are very different from romanticised understandings of commensality. Nonetheless, the latter play an important political role as idealised and normative aspirational references and as part of people's imaginary (Jönsson et al., 2021). Therefore, literature and other cultural media are relevant for understanding the politics and aesthetics of cultural expressions of commensality, which can overcome the limitations of the social sciences for addressing the intellectual, symbolical, imaginative and creative functions of eating together (Goldstein, 2018).

Similarly, arts practices are well suited to the examination of normative forms of commensality by experimenting and disturbing assumed rules, hierarchies and cultural practices. For instance, Ryan's (2006) The Silent Dinners project and The Permanent Breakfasts project (Derschmidt, 1996) change commensality norms by not allowing people to speak during group meals, and by organising a chain of collective breakfasts in public spaces respectively, creating novel embodied and affective experiences of commensality. Similarly, some of Miralda's works in Made in USA (2016) (for instance, *Food Situation for a Patriotic Banquet, 1972–73/2010* and *Movable Feast, 1974*) explore political dimensions of commensality through experimentation with its performance and materiality.

Material arrangements of eating together

The material settings of commensality relate to sociocultural norms of eating around a table, including table manners. However, in many cultures and communities people do not use tables to eat, and different domestic spaces, such as the sofa or in front of a television set, are increasingly popular. The physical aspects of commensality, such as table size, shape and sitting arrangements, enable different social relations. Eating around a circular table fosters equality and empathy between sitters who have the same opportunities to address each other. Instead, long rectangular tables enable hierarchical relations, as the more privileged seats are often reserved for those with rank or status (e.g. at the top end or in the middle of one side, such as in depictions of the Last Supper) (Fischler, 2011).

Communities centred around religion constitute a rich comparative field for investigating commensality. Key here is Cuch's *Meals* (2017) a photographic series of spaces of commensality, as part of a research project, Spiritual Flavours, involving seven different faith communities in a London suburb. The series addresses the logistics and rhythms of eating together in worship places through formal image compositions and captions, which reveal the meals' recurrence and the spiritual, hierarchical and gendered relations involved in their organisation. The images foreground the embodied and affective dimensions of the material arrangements and how these perform the politics of commensality in each context. They also speak to the capacity to be moved, spiritually and collectively, by the atmosphere, including specific material and spatial qualities embodied in practices of shared eating.

Commensality as a symbolic and embodied practice

Cuch's (2022) research on religious diversity through food – particularly, the biographic photobook *Spiritual Flavours Cookbook* (2019) – demonstrates that commensality, at home and in worship places, is a powerful means of performing and passing religious values and cultural traditions to new generations. Its strength lies in its being simultaneously a representational and embodied practice. Food sharing operates as a symbolic and narrative device, where specific meals and dishes (for example, the Jewish Seder or Karah Parshad in Sikh temples) tell and represent specific scriptural passages, stories and values from religious denominations, communities and families. This is combined with the multisensory intensity of eating together, which is associated with individual, collective and embodied memory.

Commensality is central to identity formation through the principle of incorporation – by which culturally and symbolically imbued foods become part of one's body, which, in turn, "incorporates the eater into a culinary system and therefore into the group which practises it" (Fischler, 1988: 280). In this sense, community cookbooks enable a form of commensality that produces a communal sense of identity and belonging, as their recipes create both literary expressions of these identities and shared flavours or tasting experiences. This is not limited to religious contexts, and is performative of national and ethnic identities too, enabled and constructed through multiscalar commensal rituals (within households, communities and public celebrations), further supported by cookbooks of national and regional cuisines.

As global cities become increasingly diverse, there is a burgeoning interest in the material agency of food and how the embodied experience of tasting unfamiliar dishes can transform people's attitude towards cultural difference. While commercial consumption of multicultural foods is often deemed to reproduce colonial dynamics, exoticising and exploiting "other" cultures, commensality,

by contrast, is significant for understanding the potential of developing positive multicultural relationships in diverse urban settings, through the affective dimensions of cooking and eating together.

Evolving contexts of commensality

Further to taking embodied aspects more seriously, scholars call for research on commensality to combine qualitative data on socio-cultural dimensions with quantitative data on nutrition (Scander et al., 2021), to provide more robust evidence on how commensality impacts health and wellbeing in different sociocultural contexts. Moreover, questioning an assumed decline in domestic and wider commensality, research should investigate evolving configurations of food sharing (Jönsson et al., 2021), such as those emerging from new social and public initiatives, technologies and social relations.

The belief that food sharing can promote multicultural conviviality underpins increasingly popular meals endorsed by city councils. For instance, in Barcelona, alongside typical outdoor meals (e.g. "calçotades") and traditional street festive meals, there is a proliferation of multicultural meals in public spaces. Some aim to give visibility and promote acceptance of specific migrant communities, such as public Iftars, organised by Muslim communities who share a meal with local neighbours to break the fast during the month of Ramadan. Other meals, such as "Soups of the World", celebrate cultural diversity of residents who cook and share their traditional soups. Thus, public meals are fertile socio-material events for questioning the relationship between commensality and urban governance of cultural and religious diversity in public space. For instance, how does the material organisation and institutional support create political narratives; perform different forms of inclusions and exclusions; and produce affective experiences within specific urban contexts?

Other urban settings where people eat simultaneously warrant further research, such as parks in London during peak lunch hours in business districts. How do working rhythms produce specific situations and experiences of commensality in the city? Additionally, food delivery services have diversified how we might think about commensality at home, within communities and in public space. For example, youth in Barcelona increasingly get food delivered when drinking and socialising in public places, often producing tensions with residents and authorities who endure noise and rubbish on a regular basis.

Finally, social and environmental initiatives often use commensality as a tool for materialising and promoting their goals, including: food justice, social inclusion, alternative food networks, decolonial food relations, the recovery of Indigenous food cultures, sustainable cities and environmental justice. These engender evolving contexts for eating together as part of collective action – such as within self-governed community and soup kitchens, urban gardens, foraging and food waste reduction initiatives. These offer exciting research avenues on commensality vis-à-vis wider social, economic, cultural and ecological debates, which are simultaneously grappling with new technologies, the climate emergency and the more-than-human.

References

Appadurai, A. (1981) Gastro-politics in Hindu South Asia. *American ,Ethnologist* 8 (3), 494–511. doi:10.1525/ae.1981.8.3.02a00050.

Cuch Grases, L. (2017) *Spiritual Flavours: Meals.* https://www.spiritualflavours.com/page.php?series=meals. (Accessed 01/03/2024)

Cuch Grases, L. (2019) *Spiritual Flavours Cookbook*. London, Self-published.

Cuch Grases, L. (2022) *Spiritual Flavours: Reflections on using creative practice to explore food and religion in a multi-faith suburb*. Doctoral disseration. University College London. https://discovery.ucl.ac.uk/id/eprint/10144078/.

Derschmidt, F. (1996) *The Permanent Breakfasts.* https://derschmidt.com/2017/09/14/permanent-breakfast/#:~:text=On%20the%20morning%20of%201,person%20invites%20others%20to%20breakfast. (Accessed 01/03/2024)

Fischler, C. (1988) Food, self and identity. *Information (International Social Science Council)* 27 (2), 275–292. doi:10.1177/053901888027002005.

Fischler, C. (2011) Commensality, society and culture. *Social Science Information* 50(3–4), 528–548. doi:10.1177/0539018411413963.

Goldstein, D.B. (2018) Commensality. In: G.G. Shahani (ed.), *Food and Literature*. Cambridge; New York, NY, Cambridge University Press. pp. 39–58.

Grignon, C. (2001) Commensality and social morphology: An essay of typology. In: P. Scholliers (ed.), *Food, Drink and Identity: Cooking, eating and drinking in Europe since the Middle Ages*. Oxford, UK; New York, NY, Berg. pp. 23–34.

Jönsson, H., Michaud, M. & Neuman, N. (2021) What is commensality? A critical discussion of an expanding research field. *International Journal of Environmental Research and Public Health* 18 (12), 6235. doi:10.3390/ijerph18126235.

Julier, A.P. (2013) *Eating Together: Food, friendship and inequality*. Urbana, Chicago and Springfield, USA, University of Illinois Press.

Miralda, A. (2016) *Miralda Made In USA, Museu d'Art Contemporani de Barcelona* [Exhibition Catalog]. Barcelona, MACBA.

Ryan, H. (2006) *The Silent Dinners.* https://silentdinnerparty.com/. (Accessed 01/03/2024)

Scander, H., Yngve, A. & Lennernäs Wiklund, M. (2021) Assessing commensality in research. *International Journal of Environmental Research and Public Health* 18 (5), 2632. doi:10.3390/ijerph18052632.

Tan, C.-B. (2015) Commensality and the organization of social relations. In: S. Kerner, C. Chou & M. Warmind (eds.), *Commensality: From everyday food to feast*. London; New York, NY, Bloomsbury Publishing. pp. 13–29.

Further reading

Jönsson, H., Michaud, M. & Neuman, N. (2021) What is commensality? A critical discussion of an expanding research field. *International Journal of Environmental Research and Public Health,6* 18 (12), 6235. doi:10.3390/ijerph18126235.
This article offers an updated historical review of the theorisation of commensality and addresses key debates and assumptions regarding its impact on nutrition and health.

25. Concentration and power in food systems

Philip H. Howard

Introduction

Food systems in many parts of the world are becoming dominated by fewer and larger firms. This is occurring at every link in the food chain, including retailing, distribution, manufacturing, processing, and farm inputs. One indicator of these trends is that the market share held by the top four firms has been increasing in most food and agricultural industries in recent decades, when measured at either national or global levels. Another indicator is that the market capitalisation figures of the world's largest food firms are increasing, reflecting investor expectations of continued success in amassing greater amounts of power.

The consequences of the growth of these firms include fewer people making key decisions about much of the food we eat, as well as numerous negative social and ecological impacts (Howard 2021). These trends and impacts are illustrated below with a focus on beef supply chains, primarily in the United States. As dominant firms seek to increase their power, they may encounter limits to growth in their initial industries. This frequently leads to strategies of breaking previous ownership "envelopes" (Nitzan and Bichler 2009) via mergers and acquisitions to enter additional markets.

For firms in beef supply chains, this includes acquiring upstream suppliers and downstream customers in the *vertical* direction, such as animal genetics firms, livestock feed suppliers, distributors, or retailers. It may also include *horizontal* acquisitions of direct competitors, or *concentric* acquisitions of related industries at the same stage, such as chicken and pork processors, or plant-based meat alternative protein manufacturers. Another envelope is *geographic*, expanding from an initial region to break into new nations and continents.

These strategies are aided by political economic systems that have shifted away from the more stringent antitrust enforcement that characterised the middle of the 20th century. Such trends are leading to the removal of distinct boundaries between different links in the food chain, which previously involved numerous competitive market exchanges. In their place are increasingly "seamless" and centrally planned systems, controlled by a much smaller number of firms (Heffernan 1999). A close examination of these trends, however, finds that they are almost always resisted. Although this resistance is frequently hidden, such efforts have had some notable successes in recent years, illustrating that these trends are not inevitable.

Retailing

Most of the beef consumed in high income countries, such as the US, is purchased at grocery retailers and fast food restaurants. In these retail segments, the largest firms have increased their market shares substantially since the 1980s. In 2018, the leading US grocery firm, Walmart, for example, controlled approximately 25% of sales and Kroger controlled approximately 10%; in 2022 Kroger proposed to merge with the fourth ranked firm, Albertsons. Institutional economists suggest that when four firms control 40% or more of sales the market is no longer competitive. When the concentration ratio of the top four firms (abbreviated as CR4) is this high, for example, and one firm signals an intention to raise prices, other dominant firms will find it in their interest to do the same; this results in consumers paying more than they would in a market characterised by many small firms.

The US grocery sector exceeded the 40% threshold with a CR4 of 45 in 2018, and fast food retailing was approaching this mark with a CR4 of 39. At that time, McDonald's controlled approximately 17% of sales and Yum! Brands held approximately 11% of the market: these two firms together provided more than 3% of daily calories consumed in the US. Similar trends are occurring in food retail sectors in many other nations. Grocery concentration ratios were even higher in Europe, for example, with an average CR4 of 60 for 27 countries by 2018, an increase of approximately 50% compared with a decade earlier (Van Dam et al. 2021).

Beef processing

Much of the beef supplied to dominant retailers in the US is from the top four beef processors, which together accounted for 82% of the national market in 2018. These firms are JBS and Marfrig, both headquartered in Brazil, and Tyson and Cargill, both headquartered in the US; all four also have substantial shares of beef markets in many other nations.

A beef "trust" in the US in the early 1900s was broken up as a result of the passage of antitrust laws, but the original intent of such laws has since been reshaped through political efforts. These changes accelerated in the 1980s and included appointing heads of regulatory agencies who were more friendly to the interests of dominant firms, and corporate-funded think tanks influencing most federal judges to view mergers and acquisitions as beneficial due to increasing "efficiency". Very large ownership combinations have been approved by government regulators in recent decades, such as Tyson's acquisition of Hillshire Farms for $8.55 billion in 2014.

JBS also grew significantly with a global acquisition spree, fuelled by loans from the government of Brazil that allowed for payments totalling more than $20 billion from 1996 to 2016. In 2017 it was revealed that the firm had also paid nearly $220 million in bribes to 1,829 politicians, which played a significant role in access to capital, at the expense of other firms in their industry. JBS is now ranked only below the number one firm, Nestle, in global food sales.

Dominant meat processors in the US have also allegedly gone beyond price signalling by using a data sharing firm called Agri Stats, Inc. to coordinate their actions. These firms have since paid hundreds of millions of dollars in government enforced fines and court settlements for driving up prices for consumers and driving down wages and benefits for plant workers. The top executives of the world's leading meat processors are all billionaires: in the case of JBS, the founder and 5 of his 6 children are billionaires, including two who served several months in prison following the bribery scandal.

Farming and ranching

Farming and ranching produce cattle to supply them to downstream meat processors. Although this segment of the food supply chain is much less concentrated than others, there is also a trend toward fewer and larger farms. The number of farms with beef cattle in the US declined from 842,000 in 1987 to 712,000 in 2017, for example. During this same period the median herd size increased from 89 to 120 animals (MacDonald 2020). Farming and ranching require extensive amounts of land, large amounts of time, and exposure to risks that include weather, pests, and disease, which creates barriers to the entry of very large firms. Although chickens and pigs have been bred to better tolerate factory conditions, cattle are typically raised extensively in their earlier stages of life, and only move to feedlots, intensive operations designed to fatten cattle, just before slaughter. For this reason, the decline in the number of beef cattle farms has been less steep than for other livestock sectors, particularly pigs and dairy cows (Hendrickson et al. 2020).

Leading beef processors, however, have vertically integrated into feedlots, with as many as 150,000 cattle in one location. This integration provides processors with their own "captive supplies", which in turn gives them much more control over the prices they pay for cattle from independent operations. The ability to quickly shift to their own supplies for processing when cattle prices begin to rise gives them power to drive prices back down. Over the last 40 years the average profit per animal for independent cattle producers has declined from a gain of $50 to a loss of $50 (Taylor 2022). This trend has contributed to the loss of farms, with substantial impacts on rural communities, such as declines in populations, tax bases, and social cohesion.

The negative impacts of concentrating beef production also include high levels of antibiotic use, leading to antibiotic resistant diseases in humans. Another impact is concentrated waste, which contributes to the eutrophication of waters, as well as health impacts on neighbouring communities from air and water pollution. In addition, an increasing amount of the world's beef production is in Brazil, contributing to deforestation and forced labour (Hofmeister et al. 2022).

Animal feed processing

The processing of livestock feed is also highly concentrated. For soybean processing, for example, just four firms controlled 80% of industry capacity by 2011: Bunge, ADM, Cargill, and AGP. Cargill was not only the third leading soybean processor but was also in third place in beef and chicken processing. More meat processors are breaking ownership envelopes and increasing control over their supplies of livestock feed. Smithfield, for example, a division of the Chinese firm WH Group, acquired grain elevators in Ohio to supply its livestock operations in North Carolina, and increased its purchases of animal feed directly from farmers from 10% in 2010 to 65% by 2016.

International trade in this industry was once dominated by four firms that were collectively called ABCD for the first letters of their names: ADM, Bunge, Cargill and (Louis) Dreyfus. In recent years they have been joined by other giant firms, such as COFCO (owned by the government of China), Glencore (headquartered in Switzerland), and Wilmar (headquartered in Singapore). Cargill and Dreyfus are not publicly traded, which makes market shares difficult to estimate, but the CR4 for global grain trading is estimated to be 70% or more (Clapp 2022).

Farm inputs

Farm inputs have seen the most dramatic changes in recent decades, with a number of these industries now dominated by a small number of firms at the global level, not just at the national level. Animal pharmaceuticals, for example, had a global CR4 of 58% in 2018. These trends have been aided by increasing intellectual property protections, such as restrictions on seeds that prevent farmers from saving and replanting them (Howard 2015). Acquisitions that accelerated with the introduction of patented soybeans in the mid-1990s have led to just four agrochemical firms globally controlling well over half of commercial seed sales, in addition to well over half of agrochemical sales. These firms are Bayer, Corteva, SinoChem/ChemChina, and BASF, and they are the result of combining what were once more than 30 separate firms in the 1970s.

For farm equipment sales the global CR4 was 45% in 2018. Machinery and seed-chemical firms are collaborating on digital strategies that are likely to further reduce the decision-making power of farmers. Synthetic fertilisers had a global CR4 of 33% in 2018, but much higher concentration ratios in most national markets. The industry is organised in a cartel-like fashion, usually with the support of national governments (Taylor and Moss 2013). This contributed to fertiliser costs increasing 100% or more in the US in 2022.

Resistance

The increasing power of dominant firms in each of the food system segments described above does not reflect the numerous challenges they have faced, particularly resistance efforts that are beginning to obtain more traction. One example is efforts to establish labour unions for retail workers, some of which have succeeded at stores operated by the fast-food chain Chipotle and the grocery retailer Trader Joe's. Another example involves local communities that have organised to defeat government approvals for giant meat processing plants in recent years, such as a proposed Prestage pork plant in Mason City, Iowa, and a Tyson poultry plant in Tonganoxie, Kansas.

The problem with concentrating so much of the beef processing capacity of the US in so few plants was illustrated by the 2020 Covid-19 pandemic: outbreaks among workers led to plant shutdowns, followed by empty supermarket shelves for many beef and pork products. Interestingly, the leading retailer Walmart is vertically integrating into beef plants to enable more control over supply chains and become less subject to the power of dominant processors. Some government agencies, such as the USDA, have also responded by providing funds to assist with rebuilding the meat processing infrastructure that had been lost due to these trends, which has the potential to reduce the market share of dominant firms. A growing number of consumers connected directly with local farms in efforts to find sources of food that are less subject to these types of disruptions.

Other government responses have included the passage of 'right to repair' laws in some US states to give farmers the ability to fix machinery and software on their own, without being forced to pay dominant firm dealerships. Although intellectual property protections on seeds have increased in many nations, some governments have resisted pressures to move to the most restrictive international agreements (Howard 2015). In addition, grassroots initiatives to develop new seed varieties that are not subject to these types of restrictions, and that therefore can be saved, replanted, or exchanged, have been organised in countries including the US, India, Ethiopia, and Germany.

The strategies of breaking ownership envelopes have enabled dominant firms to continue to dramatically increase their power in recent decades, as well as increase their negative impacts on society and ecosystems. Growing awareness of these trends and their impacts, however, may make these strategies more difficult to implement in the near future. In addition, higher levels of concentration have contributed to food systems that are fragile and more vulnerable to numerous types of challenges; additional research is needed on the potential for disruptions such as pandemics, the climate emergency, and resource depletion to threaten future food supplies, and to derail efforts to amass power.

References

Clapp J (2022) The Rise of Big Food and Agriculture: Corporate Influence in the Food System. In: Sage C. (Ed.) *A Research Agenda for Food Systems*. Northampton, MA, Edward Elgar Publishing, pp. 45–66.

Heffernan W D (1999) Biotechnology and Mature Capitalism. Presented at the 11th Annual Meeting of the National Agricultural Biotechnology Council, Lincoln, NE.

Hendrickson M K, Howard P H, Miller E M and Constance D H (2020). *The Food System: Concentration and Its Impacts. A Special Report to the Family Farm Action Alliance*. https://farmaction.us/wp-content/uploads/2021/05/Hendrickson-et-al.-2020.-Concentration-and-Its-Impacts_FINAL_Addended.pdf.

Hofmeister N, Campos A, Harari I and Jordan L (2022) JBS Admits to Buying Almost 9,000 Cattle from 'One of Brazil's Biggest Deforesters'. Unearthed. https://unearthed.greenpeace.org/2022/11/11/jbs-cattle-brazils-biggest-deforester-amazon/.

Howard P H (2015) Intellectual Property and Consolidation in the Seed Industry. *Crop Science*, 55, 2489–2495. https://doi.org/10.2135/cropsci2014.09.0669.

MacDonald J M (2020) Tracking the Consolidation of US Agriculture. *Applied Economic Perspectives and Policy* 42, 361–379. https://doi.org/10.1002/aepp.13056.

Nitzan J and Bichler S (2009). *Capital as Power: A Study of Order and Creorder*. New York, Routledge

Taylor C R (2022). *Harvested Cattle, Slaughtered Markets?* Report to the US Department of Agriculture. http://dx.doi.org/10.2139/ssrn.4094924.

Taylor C R and Moss D L (2013). *The Fertilizer Oligopoly: The Case for Global Antitrust Enforcement*. The American Antitrust Institute. https://www.antitrustinstitute.org/wp-content/uploads/2013/10/FertilizerMonograph.pdf.

Van Dam I, Wood B, Sacks G, Allais O, and Vandevijvere S (2021) A Detailed Mapping of the Food Industry in the European Single Market: Similarities and Differences in Market Structure Across Countries and Sectors. *International Journal of Behavioral Nutrition and Physical Activity* 18, 54. https://doi.org/10.1186/s12966-021-01117-8.

Further reading

ETC Group (2022) *Food Barons: Crisis Profiteering, Digitalization and Shifting Power*. https://www.etcgroup.org/files/files/food-barons-2022-full_sectors-final_16_sept.pdf.
This report details market shares held by the largest firms in key food and agricultural sectors globally. It emphasises the importance of new digital technologies for increasing control, as well as the rising influence of firms in Asia, particularly China.

Howard P H (2021) *Concentration and Power in the Food System: Who Controls What We Eat?* Revised edition. London, Bloomsbury Academic.
This book provides substantially more detail on the topic of food and agricultural industry concentration. It analyses dominant firm strategies in numerous stages of the food chain, with a focus on additional specific foods and commodities in the United States.

26. Conflict and food

WILLIAM G. MOSELEY

Introduction: conflict and food

Global food security measures had been improving until 2014 when they began to move backward (FAO and WFP 2016). A major contributing factor to this reversal has been war, including several conflict and post-conflict situations in the early 2020s that were also hunger hotspots such as Yemen, South Sudan, Sudan, northeastern Nigeria, Afghanistan and Tigray, Ethiopia (WHH et al. 2024). The war in Ukraine also had significant food security implications as it was one of the world's major breadbaskets (historically exporting grain surpluses that were critically important to food importing countries in North Africa, the Middle East and the Horn of Africa) (Moseley 2022a). These events have reinforced the idea that there are strong linkages between conflict and hunger.

Conflict has long been entangled with food insecurity and hunger, both historically and in the present. Alas, we see war and hunger included among the Four Horsemen of the Apocalypse in ancient religious texts and in a famous 1887 painting of the same name by Viktor Vasnetsov. Armed conflict has resulted in food shortages, the destruction of farms and pastures, loss of livestock and damaged transportation infrastructure used to get food to markets. Food has also been used as a weapon of war, with food blockades and destruction used as a tactic to starve out and subjugate the enemy, an approach that is now considered a fundamental violation of human rights. There is also an active scholarly debate concerning the degree to which food, land and resource scarcity contributes to armed conflict. Lastly, in some cases, war and conflict has led to shifts in the types of food that are consumed and the way food is produced, from the use of wild foods as a coping strategy when farm fields are destroyed during conflicts, to the popularisation of SPAM, to victory gardens in the Word War II era.

Food security is often conceptualised as having six dimensions: availability, access, stability, utilisation, sustainability and agency (Clapp et al. 2022). All six of these dimensions may be impacted by conflict, which helps us understand why this is such a devastating problem for food systems. Food availability, which is a combination of local production and net imports, is often curtailed when conflict disrupts local producers or destroys the transportation systems needed to get food to markets. Access may be inhibited when conflict leads to loss of employment and people do not have the means to purchase food. Stability of food supplies and prices may be undermined when conflicts degrade local and international transit and supply chains. Utilisation, or access to the sanitation, clean water and kitchen facilities needed to prepare healthy food, may also be compromised when this type of infrastructure is destroyed in times of war and conflict. Producing food more sustainably may become more challenging if farmers, herders and fishers are confined to smaller and smaller areas. Lastly, people's agency or power over their production methods and food choices is often deeply curtailed during times of war.

Current issues

The direct effects of conflict on food production and transport

In areas of the world where food is produced, conflict and war often prevent farmers from going to their fields, herders from caring for their cattle and fishers from tending their nets. Conflict may also disrupt the transport of food from surplus to deficit areas, including urban areas. Each of these livelihood systems, as well as transport, is discussed in turn.

Many farmers shift their cultivation patterns during periods of insecurity. If they have a range of fields, they may abandon plots farther from the village in favour of those closer to where they live, which are presumed to be safer. Women farmers in particular (who grow the majority of food in some regions such as Africa) may curtail their movements and farm work in times of insecurity and conflict (Ayisi 1995). Many farm fields, granaries and pieces of equipment are also vulnerable to theft by combatants. For example, one of the lesser known aspects of the war in Ukraine was the looting of Ukrainian farms by Russian soldiers for grain, livestock and equipment (Ordonez 2022).

Pastoral livelihoods are especially impacted by conflict because their success often depends on people's ability to seasonally move widely across dryland areas. For example, during a period of protracted unrest in central Mali (West Africa) from 2012 to 2023, many herders changed their normal seasonal grazing patterns due to concerns about insecurity and cattle theft (Moseley 2017). These shifts led to the concentration of herders and their animals in certain areas and resulted in rangeland degradation. Many insurgent groups are also fond of cattle rustling (as opposed to other forms of food looting) because livestock are relatively easy to take, are a nutrition-dense food source, and may be transported on the hoof. Herders may also be targets for attacks by ruling regimes as they are sometimes viewed with more suspicion because of their mobility, especially if they are on the wrong side of an ethnic cleavage (Benjaminsen and Ba 2019).

Fishing livelihoods may also be impacted by conflict. When ports are blockaded, waters mined or boat traffic restricted, this impedes the movement of fishers. Fresh fish are also highly perishable, making the efficient transport of this product important and more vulnerable to transit disruptions. Fishing vessels are also vulnerable to attacks and piracy, especially as they venture into less travelled waters (Gupta and Sharma 2012).

Conflict can also disrupt the transport of food and grain from areas of production to markets, both within countries and between countries. Within countries, key roads, rail lines and waterways are used to move various forms of food and this infrastructure is also a frequent target for attacks during times conflict. The movement of food in and out of countries may also be impaired during times of war, resulting in declines in income for the exporters and loss of food for the importers. A recent example of such a problem at the international scale was the Russian invasion of Ukraine in 2022 which resulted in major declines in food exports from the Black Sea region. This disruption was especially challenging for those countries that had become heavily dependent on Ukrainian wheat, such as Egypt, Indonesia, Bangladesh, Turkey, Yemen and Somalia (HLPE 2022).

Ironically, the war in Ukraine and the ensuing food crisis sheds light on earlier debates about security, conflict and food. Until the late 1970s, many countries pursued food self-sufficiency policies (producing enough food within national boundaries to meet the caloric needs of a population) for national security reasons, as it was considered too risky to be reliant on another country for food supplies. Then the thinking on this began to shift. One of the early arguments in favour of trade (in

addition to economic ones) was that more trade, including trade in foodstuffs, would create a world where war was unthinkable (Clapp 2017). Unfortunately, the unthinkable did happen when one major global grain exporter decided to attack another, resulting in a serious amount of collateral damage.

Conflict and food security

Conflict is one of the major causes of food insecurity historically and in the world today. In many cases, declining food security is related to food production and transit systems degraded by war and conflict (as discussed earlier). In some cases, food may also be used as a weapon of war. There is a long history of attempting to starve out the enemy, or the use of scorched earth campaigns to destroy local food systems, during times of war. However, ever since the Universal Declaration of Human Rights was adopted by its signatories, which includes the Right to Food, using food as a weapon of war is considered to be a crime against humanity (Marchione 1996).

There is also a significant body of literature investigating the degree to which food insecurity, and scarcity more broadly, leads to conflict (e.g., Koren and Bagozzi 2016). One group of scholars, sometimes referred to as the environmental security camp, argues that scarcity and food insecurity is driving conflict (e.g., Homer-Dixon 1993). Scholars adhering to this paradigm often argue that overpopulation leads to food and resource scarcity, which drives conflict. On the other side of the debate are those who suggest that scarcity alone does not explain many of these conflicts. This group often sees the environmental security paradigm as Malthusian and having a tendency to overly simplify what are often deeply political conflicts (Turner 2004). Others are concerned that environmental security fails to account for the international dimensions of what may appear to be local conflicts (Dalby 2002). A good example of the latter is Samatar et al.'s (2010) scholarship on fisheries in Somalia, where incursions by international vessels in Somali waters is largely responsible for the decline of local fisheries and livelihoods. As such, Somali 'pirate' attacks on foreign vessels cannot simply be seen as acts of banditry.

Fear of social unrest related to high food prices, especially in urban areas, is also one of the major reasons that political leaders have often sought to keep food prices low.

Subsidising or controlling the pricing of staple food stuffs has been one approach, which the ruling regime in Egypt continues to do today (Moseley 2022c). Moreover, the United States has also had a cheap food policy supported by programmes that encourage over-production. The rationale for this policy was partly inspired by concerns about labour organising and social unrest driven by high food and living costs in the early 20th century (Miller and Coble 2007). Some have also argued that high food prices were part of what stirred the social unrest that led to the Arab spring in the early 2010s (Soffiantini 2020). Others are more sceptical of this argument. More broadly, high urban food prices that stir social unrest in urban areas is a phenomenon often labelled as 'food riots' (Patel and McMichael 2009). The challenge with this terminology is that it essentially frames these protests as spontaneous outbursts of rage and anger when, in fact, they may be carefully planned to express displeasure with the policies of a regime. As such, 'food demonstrations' may be a term that better captures and describes such events as civic engagement rather than violent outbursts.

Longer-term effects of conflict and post-conflict situations

The longer-term impact of conflict on food systems can be crippling. One of the biggest challenges related to conflict is displaced people, both internationally and within countries. Many displaced people end up in refugee camps. If conflicts are protracted, some refugee camps may exist for decades, such as the Dadaab refugee camp in northern Kenya, Africa's largest (Montclos and Kagwanja 2000). Extended periods of time in refugee camps may make it less likely that people will return to their former livelihood strategies. Children may be born and raised in such camps with little exposure to the farming or pastoral livelihoods of their parents, making it harder for them to participate in the recreation of a former food system once a conflict has ended. Food consumption and cooking practices may also change when displaced people spend long time periods in camps (Trapp 2018). In post-conflict periods, another significant roadblock to a return to normalcy may be mined fields. This challenge is significant enough that the 2023 World Food Prize winner, Heidi Kühn, was recognized for her

organisation's work on the demining of agricultural areas (World Food Prize Foundation 2023).

Conflict and changing food consumption and production patterns

In some cases, war and conflict has led to shifts in the types of food that are consumed and the way food is produced. Diets often change during periods of conflict. The disruption of normal food system practices may lead to a variety of coping strategies such as the consumption of foraged or wild foods (Sulaiman et al. 2022). War and conflict in more industrialised countries has also led to the emergence and proliferation of new processed foods and eating habits, such as the consumption of SPAM (a processed meat product produced by Hormel Foods). According to McNamee (n.d.), "SPAM did not become a household word until after World War II, for more than 100 million pounds of SPAM were consumed by Allied soldiers and, after the war, by civilians in Allied and the defeated Axis countries."

Conflict has also led to new strategies for producing food. One such example is the use of victory or war gardens in the United States, United Kingdom, Canada, Australia and Germany during World Wars I and II in order to boost domestic vegetable production (Lambert 2014). Countries facing embargoes during periods of 'hot' and 'cold' conflict (meaning active fighting versus political conflict) have also sometimes turned to systems of radical food self-sufficiency or autarky. Cuba is perhaps the most famous example of this, but this has also been the case in Burundi and Qatar (Moseley 2022b). These challenging situations have produced new agricultural paradigms, such as agroecology and 'organoponico' (a system of urban gardening involving raised beds and drip irrigation) in the case of Cuba (Miller 2007) and increased agrobiodiversity more broadly (Tamariz and Baumann 2022). Lastly, conflict has sometimes led to an increase in illicit drug related crop production as a coping strategy, such as the expanded cultivation of opium poppies in Afghanistan and coca in Columbia (Livingstone 2004).

WILLIAM G. MOSELEY

Future concerns, issues and questions

If the global community has any hope of addressing Sustainable Development Goal #2 (SDG2), or zero hunger by 2030, then tackling the challenging nexus of food insecurity and conflict must be part of the strategy. Unfortunately, this may feel like a near impossible challenge as the world in 2023 is rife with conflict and associated food insecurity problems. However, resource and food scarcity needn't lead to conflict, especially if conflict mediation processes exist and people realise that most scarcity is socially constructed, i.e., the result of unequal distribution. Moving forward, it is critical to more widely acknowledge the Right to Food, as well as to launch additional efforts to hold perpetrators accountable for using food as a weapon of war. More could also be done to better understand the characteristics of food systems that allow for them to be more resilient in times of conflict.

For researchers exploring the links between food and conflict, a number of critical questions merit further research. These include:

1) Which agrifood systems are more resilient in times of conflict and why?
2) What are promising policies and programmes that help build more resilient agrifood systems in the context of conflict?
3) What are the most promising strategies for helping communities rebuild food systems in post-conflict situations?
4) What are the steps that can be taken to reduce the likelihood that food will be used as a weapon of war in conflict situations?

References

Ayisi RA (1995) Supporting women farmers in the green zones of Mozambique. SEEDS no. 17. New York: Population Council.

Benjaminsen TA and Ba B (2019) Why do pastoralists in Mali join jihadist groups? A political ecological explanation. *The Journal of Peasant Studies* 46(1), 1–20.

Clapp J (2017) Food self-sufficiency: Making sense of it, and when it makes sense. *Food Policy* 66, 88–96.

Clapp J, Moseley WG, Burlingame B and Termine P (2022) The case for a six-dimensional food security framework. *Food Policy* 106, 102164.

Dalby S (2002) *Environmental Security.* Minneapolis: University of Minnesota Press.

Food and Agriculture Organisation (FAO) and World Food Programme (WFP) (2016) Protracted conflicts causing alarming spikes in severe hunger. 29 July. www.fao.org/news/story/en/item/427423/icode/ (Accessed May 28, 2023).

Gupta C and Sharma M (2012) *Contested Coastlines: Fisherfolk, Nations and Borders in South Asia.* Abingdon: Routledge.

High Level Panel of Experts for Food Security and Nutrition (HLPE) (2022) The impacts on global food security and nutrition of the military conflict in Ukraine. Rome. https://www.fao.org/fileadmin/templates/cfs/HLPE/reports/issues_paper/Impacts_conflict_Ukraine_FSN_HLPE_Issues_Paper.pdf (Accessed May 28, 2023).

Homer-Dixon TF (1993). *Environmental Scarcity and Global Security.* Headline Series No. 300. New York: Foreign Policy Association.

Koren O and Bagozzi BE (2016) From global to local, food insecurity is associated with contemporary armed conflicts. *Food Security* 8, 999–1010.

Lambert CA (2014) Digging for Victory Gardens: A Comparative Analysis of the UK and US World War II Gardening Campaigns. In Waters, R. (ed.), *Public Relations in the Nonprofit Sector* (pp. 249–264). Abingdon: Routledge.

Livingstone G (2004) *Inside Colombia: Drugs, Democracy and War.* New Brunswick, NJ: Rutgers University Press.

McNamee, GL (No Date) SPAM. *Encyclopedia Britannica.* https://www.britannica.com/topic/SPAM-food. (Accessed May 28, 2023).

Marchione TJ (1996) The right to food in the post-Cold War era. *Food Policy* 21(1), 83–102.

Miller JC and Coble KH (2007) Cheap food policy: Fact or rhetoric? *Food Policy* 32(1), 98–111.

Miller S (2007) *An Environmental History of Latin America.* Cambridge: Cambridge University Press.

Montclos MAPD and Kagwanja PM (2000) Refugee camps or cities? The socio-economic dynamics of the Dadaab and Kakuma camps in Northern Kenya. *Journal of Refugee Studies* 13(2), 205–222.

Moseley WG (2017) The Minimalist State and Donor Landscapes: Livelihood Security in Mali During and After the 2012–2013 Coup and Rebellion. *African Studies Review* 60(1), 37–51.

Moseley WG (2022a) Like a bad rain year: The consequences of Russia's invasion of Ukraine for African food security and the need for greater food sovereignty. *Africa is a Country*. June 29. https://africasacountry.com/2022/06/like-a-bad-rain-year (Accessed May 28, 2023).

Moseley WG (2022b) Development assistance and Boserupian intensification under geopolitical isolation: The political ecology of a crop-livestock integration project in Burundi. *Geoforum* 128, 276–285.

Moseley WG (2022c) The global food system was already unsustainable before the war in Ukraine. *World Politics Review*. March 17. https://www.worldpoliticsreview.com/articles/30403/food-security-could-be-another-casualty-of-the-ukraine-russia-war (Accessed May 28, 2023).

Ordonez F (2022) Russians wreak havoc on Ukrainian farms, mining fields and stealing equipment. May 6. National Public Radio (NPR). https://www.npr.org/2022/05/06/1096481280/ukraine-agriculture-farms-russia-war (Accessed May 28, 2023).

Patel R and McMichael P (2009) A political economy of the food riot. *Review: A Journal of the Fernand Braudel Center* 32(1), 9–35.

Samatar AI, Lindberg M and Mahayni B (2010) The dialectics of piracy in Somalia: The rich versus the poor. *Third World Quarterly* 31(8), 1377–1394.

Soffiantini G (2020) Food insecurity and political instability during the Arab Spring. *Global Food Security* 26, 100400.

Sulaiman N, Pieroni A, Sõukand R and Polesny Z (2022) Food behavior in emergency time: Wild plant use for human nutrition during the conflict in Syria. *Foods* 11(2), 177.

Tamariz G and Baumann MD (2022) Agrobiodiversity change in violent conflict and post-conflict landscapes. *Geoforum* 128, 217–222.

Trapp MM (2018)."Never had the hand": Distribution and inequality in the diverse economy of a refugee camp. *Economic Anthropology* 5(1), 96–109.

Turner MD (2004) Political ecology and the moral dimensions of "resource conflicts": the case of farmer–herder conflicts in the Sahel. *Political Geography* 23(7), 863–889.

Welthungerhilfe (WHH), Concern Worldwide, and Institute for International Law of Peace and Armed Conflict (IFHV). (2024). 2024 Global Hunger Index: How Gender Justice Can Advance Climate Resilience and Zero Hunger.Bonn/Berlin: WHH; Dublin: Concern Worldwide; Bochum: IFHV.

World Food Prize Foundation (2023) Humanitarian Heidi Kühn wins 2023 World Food Prize for restoring agriculture to de-mined land in former war zones. https://www.worldfoodprize.org/index.cfm/87428/48940/humanitarian_heidi_khn_wins_2023_world_food_prize_for_restoring_agriculture_to_demined_land_in_former_war_zones (Accessed May 28, 2023).

Further reading

Committee on World Food Security (CFS) (2015) CFS Framework for Action for Addressing FSN in Protracted Crises. Rome. https://cfs-products.ifad.org/documents/75908/78102/a-bc852e.pdf/ (Accessed May 28, 2023).

This document lays out the CFS framework for improving the food security and nutrition of populations affected by protracted crises. It focuses on building resilience, adapting to challenges and addressing underlying causes.

Collingham L (2012) *Taste of War: World War II and the Battle for Food*. New York: Penguin.

This accessible book provides a global history of food during World War II. The book draws upon a broad range of scholarship to show how food was central to the origins, experience and outcome of the conflict.

27. Consumption of food and eating

David Bell

Introduction: Consuming or eating?

The title of this entry gets us thinking about how eating figures within the consumption of food broadly understood. 'Consumption of food' and 'eating' sound like the same thing, but there are important conceptual and practical differences at work. The concept of consumption can be expanded to include planning, provisioning, preparing, eating, clearing up, disposing, and even production, since production involves consumption (of resources, say) and consumption involves production (making a meal, for example). Food consumption involves myriad practices that many of us undertake routinely. In what follows the focus is narrowed down to eating.

At its simplest, eating is the biophysical act of taking food into the body, extracting nutrients from it through the digestive process, and expelling the waste. Yet even at this alimentary level, things are far from simple. When does eating start? Only when the food enters our mouth, or does it start earlier? As Ruby Tandoh (2018: 6) writes, "In order to eat well, we need to eat with every part of ourselves. We see, feel, sense, taste, touch, predict and imagine food long before it ever arrives on our fork." There is, she adds, "so much more to eating than just eating" (5).

Food interacts with our eating body. When we eat, we are incorporating something outside of us, which becomes part of us through digestion. This boundary crossing is captured in the adage 'you are what you eat', and this incorporation challenges bodily integrity, reminding us that we depend on countless others for our very being. Research on the gut microbiome tells us that we never truly eat alone, as the digestive process is worked on by the bacteria inside us, to mutual benefit.

Beyond the biophysical, there are psychological processes involved in eating too; hunger isn't the only reason we eat, and how we think about food has been a major research agenda for nutritionists, psychologists, and social scientists. There is broad consensus that our approach to eating is largely learnt rather than innate, and this is often explained by the fact of humans' omnivorousness: because

we evolved to eat a mixed diet, our in-built food rules have to be learnt and relearnt as we encounter new potential foodstuffs. Like many explanations for how we eat, this is rooted in our ancient past and our evolutionary development, leading some food researchers and writers to argue that we should eat more like our ancestors, as in so-called paleo diets (Wilson 2016).

While there is explanatory potential and popular appeal in accounts that explain our eating through the lens of evolution, social and cultural influences have also shaped how and what we eat, while food and eating in turn have shaped human societies and cultures. This has been a major focus for research on eating, though recent work has sometimes critiqued the over-focus on cultural analysis. Drawing instead on practice theory, Alan Warde (2013: 21) writes that eating is "an elaborate domain of everyday life, an activity not understandable without reference to its social embeddedness. It is hard to give an account of eating without referring to the selecting of foodstuffs, preparing dishes, making social arrangements for meals and aesthetic judgments about taste." One aspect of practice theory that makes it useful for analysing eating is its focus on mundane questions that uncover the complexities of seemingly simple acts. To honour this, the discussion is structured around a series of mundane questions about eating.

What to eat?

This answer to this question seems obvious: we eat food. But beyond that answer lie questions of food availability and choice, likes and dislikes, and strongly normative rules. What we do and do not eat can be powerfully inclusive or exclusive, a matter of intense reflection or something we barely think about. Research reveals a highly variegated picture of the practices and meanings of eating.

At the macro level, the history of eating has been divided into a number of transitions, massive transformations reshaping our diet (Wilson 2019). Today we are at the fourth stage. The previous three stages take us back, first, to our hunter-gathering origins, then to the development of agriculture, around 20,000 BCE. Advances in farming took us into the third stage, which improved food supply but reduced the diversity of our diets. Then came stage four, arrived at through the nutrition transition. Both supply and demand radically changed, and new foodstuffs met new tastes – for fat, meat, and sugar in particular. The daily calorie count of the human diet increased and food was more processed, and with this came a rise in food-related chronic illnesses. It is also at this transition that capitalism fully took hold of food systems.

In the West, this transition took place from the 18th century to the end of the Second World War. In other parts of the world, the transition has come later, often more swiftly. The end point is the Global Standard Diet: everyone eats the same things, with the same outcomes for people and planet. Much of the human diet globally comprises meat, sugar, rice, wheat, and vegetable oil, the last two heavily processed. So what we eat has narrowed down and gone global, erasing the diverse diets of the past shaped by local conditions and traditions. Yet what we eat now is not quite this homogenous. Some parts of the world are still transitioning, and in others, active food policy has held back some aspects of the transition. Optimists see ahead a fifth transition, which looks both to the future and the past for better ways to eat. One valuable lesson from previous transitions is that dramatic change is possible.

Another principal concern of the social scientific study of eating has been its social organisation, especially in terms of the meal (Wood 1995). For more than 100 years, sociologists (and others) have sought to plot the structure, sequencing, and significance of meals. The divide here is between meals and snacks. While the meal is a socially valued form of eating, snacks are often devalued both nutritionally and socially, with 'grazing' seen as a problematic way of eating.

When to eat?

The timing and sequencing of eating is often bound up with the daily rhythm of meals. When you eat depends on what you want to eat, but also on what kind of eating fits your schedule. The conventional timings and namings of meals vary nationally, regionally, locally, and at the level of families and households, shaped by and giving shape to other aspects of life. While the triplet breakfast–lunch–dinner feels like a global standard, there are differences in what's eaten when and what it's called.

Meal times structure family life and the rhythms of the nation, as well as marking

difference, too: the English abroad can struggle with later eating times (and longer meals) in Mediterranean countries, for example. In many countries, the meal has moved from being master to servant in terms of time discipline, with fast food marking the shrinking slice of our time budget devoted to eating. In the research literature, time-use surveys draw attention to the when of eating and to the duration of meals and other eating events. Consistent patterns become eating habits or routines, and these too are expressive of eating identities.

Outside the structure of meals, there are snacks, less structured and more synced with appetites both individual and social (Twine 2015). The rise of snacking is seen by some nutritionists as a worrying trend, given the increasing dominance of the snack market with fatty, sweet, and/or salty foods. On the other hand, eating practices such as the trend for street food open up opportunities to eat outside of the conventional meal structure. Whether this contributes to the 'destructuring' of meals remains a matter of debate. The fragmentation of families/households, demands of workplace culture, time poverty, and other social forces are argued to be threatening if not eroding the practice of sharing a meal with commensals, a cause of anxiety, though studies point to the durability of the meal symbolically if not in everyday lived reality (Mäkelä 2000).

Where to eat?

Geography matters to eating in myriad ways and at different spatial scales, from the room in the house where food is consumed right up to how our eating connects us to global flows (Bell & Valentine 1997). A major division in eating geographies is eating in versus eating out, though these two apparently mutually exclusive categories are subject to considerable blurring. But if we simplify our discussion and stick to 'eating in' meaning at home and 'eating out' meaning everywhere else, we can work with these two cases to explore their imbrication with other geographies. The family meal cooked and eaten at home, shared with immediate kin, is an archetype in both research and everyday talk about eating. It is a "proper meal" (Mäkelä 2000), seen as key to socialisation and maintaining social bonds. Yet, in accommodating different tastes and appetites, different schedules, and different practices, eating in can become spatially and temporally dispersed.

Eating out means leaving the home and, in most instances, moving from domestic to commercial food consumption. In Western countries, in the space of a few decades, eating out, for example at a restaurant, has moved from an occasional treat to something practised regularly (Warde et al. 2020). Of course, this experience is not shared by everyone, and different people eat out in different ways. We enter the world of commercial hospitality when eating out, so we are provided for by others, though arrangements around who does what vary. For example, in private home dining, guests pay to come together in the host's home for a meal, whereas in potlucks participants each bring a dish to share.

We have had recent and very vivid experience of the meaning and value of eating out, thanks to the lockdowns imposed as a response to the 2020 Covid-19 pandemic. Suddenly told we could not go out to eat, consumers were faced with a foodscape marked by restriction rather than abundance (*Gastronomica* 2020). While commercial eating places reeled from a sudden loss of customers and revenue, some innovated by offering home food delivery (with suitable precautions) or 'meal kits' that provided ingredients and instructions for cooking restaurant dishes at home.

The ins and outs of eating extend to other spatial scales. The rise of locavore eating, with its focus on provisioning from our immediate locale, gives a new meaning to eating in (Pollan 2007), while gastrotourism connects us to places and cuisines across the globe (Duruz 2011). Experiences of migration can lead to a desire both to eat the homely and familiar, and to achieve cultural assimilation through eating what's available in the place of settlement (or hybridising the two). And as migrants seek to feed themselves in their new home, they often set up food outlets serving the migrant community, outlets which sometimes also offer a taste of migrant cuisines to other groups – one person's 'eating in' is another's 'eating out' at the level of collective identity.

Who to eat with?

This ethics of consuming immigrant cuisines is about where one eats, but also about who with. Some critics argue that 'eating the other' gives only a superficial engagement with other cultures, while other writers see 'intercultural eating' as a sign of cultural assimilation. Trying to find a way beyond this binary in the case of 'Indian' food eaten in the UK, Ben Highmore (2008: 396) sees the possibility of "alimentary pedagogy" in the negotiating of difference in the curry house. The British (selective) embrace of 'Indian' food does not mean the end of racism, nor does it signify unthinkingly eating the other.

The coordination of eating, for example into meals, is often about who we eat with. Commensality, the sharing of food, has attracted attention from a wide range of scholars, looking at sharing within families and households, in commercial foodspaces, and in other environments of everyday eating (Kerner and Warmind 2015). Like the meal – which is of course a *shared* meal – there is a powerful cultural norm that sees sharing food as socially beneficial. 'The family that eats together stays together', to repeat another adage. Eating well together, rather than just sharing a table, invokes the idea of conviviality, of the sociability of eating as a truly social occasion . By contrast, eating alone is seen as a symptom of our atomised modern lives.

Today we are ever more connected with both proximate and distant others, not least via mobile and social media, meaning that eating-with extends virtually. The sharing of dining experiences on social media means we can eat 'alone together'. Online food sharing initiatives, which bring strangers together to share ingredients and meals, also broaden the reach of those with whom we eat. That said, most of the literature on commensality explores the immediate and co-present sharing of food with other people, whether family, invited guests, or strangers. Julian Baggini (2014), however, encourages an expanded view of conviviality. For him, eating with someone is inclusive of the workers who produce and serve our food, the foodstuffs themselves, our culture, society, and ancestors – indeed, the entire planet.

How to eat?

Learning new tastes is one important dimension in the how of eating. Encountering new foods can be a moment of wonder or bewilderment. The process of learning to like particular foods is of major interest in interventions to encourage us to 'eat well'. At an individual and cultural level, our palates develop only through exposure to new flavours and eating experiences. Set this in the context of the Global Standard Diet and we see a paradox: while we *could* learn to eat well, we can also learn to eat poorly. How we eat is a direct record of how we have learned to eat, though tastes can and do change across our lives, for example, through the influence of media and advertising. We can make ourselves learn to eat things that at first taste we do not like, and this can be driven by trends, as when a TV chef introduces a new ingredient to viewers.

Learning how to eat is not limited to the food itself: eating is a social practice with many different dimensions, from the eating tools we use to the way to behave at table. We learn how to read a menu or a recipe, as well as how to read a food trend. How to eat is a matter of social convention, etiquette, and rules, even if we choose to ignore or subvert them. At the same time, recent research focusses on the automaticity of daily eating practice (Warde 2016). How we eat is often habitual and distracted, with consequences for our diet and health.

The question of how to eat also asks us to consider the ethics of eating. Locavores and climavores eat conscious of the impact of eating on the planet, drawing attention to how to eat in the Anthropocene, and prefiguring a fifth transition to more sustainable food futures. Eating becomes a pressing issue when faced by the climate emergency and issues of food security.

This raises a final question: why do we eat? It should be clear by now that the answer is rarely simply because we are hungry. Eating is a mundane social practice, but it is also full of meaning. What, when, where, who with, and how we eat is shaped by both habit and conscious choice, by our biography and our environment, by our values and the values around us. There is both continuity and change, and the future of eating will likely be marked by both, too. New sites for eating, novel foods, and new ways of understanding what we're doing when we're eating in a changing world will continue to make this a vibrant field for research.

References

Baggini J (2014) Real conviviality. Presentation at MAD4 Symposium, Copenhagen; available from: https://www.julianbaggini.com/2183/ (accessed 28.02.13).

Bell D and Valentine G (1997) *Consuming Geographies: We are Where We Eat.* London, Routledge.

Duruz J (2011) Quesadillas with Chinese black bean puree: eating together in 'ethnic' neighbourhoods. *New Formations* 74, 46–64.

Gastronomica (2020) Volume 20, Issue 3, August.

Highmore B (2008) Alimentary agents: food, cultural theory and multiculturalism. *Journal of Intercultural Studies* 29, 381–398.

Kerner S, Chou C and Warmind M (eds) (2015) *Commensality: From Everyday Food to Feast.* London, Bloomsbury.

Mäkelä J (2000) Meals: the social perspective. In Meiselman H (ed) *Meals in Science and Practice: Interdisciplinary Research and Business Applications.* London, Woodhead, pages 37–49.

Pollan M (2007) *The Omnivore's Dilemma: A Natural History of Four Meals.* London, Penguin.

Tandoh R (2018) *Eat Up! Food, Appetite and Eating What You Want.* London, Profile.

Twine R (2015) Understanding snacking through a practice theory lens. *Sociology of Health & Illness* 37, 1270–1284.

Warde A (2013) What sort of practice is eating? In Shove E and Spurling N (eds) *Sustainable Practices: Social Theory and Climate Change.* London, Routledge, pages 17–30.

Warde A (2016) *The Practice of Eating.* Cambridge, Polity.

Warde A, Paddock J and Whillans J (2020) *The Social Significance of Dining Out: A Study of Continuity and Change.* Manchester, Manchester University Press.

Wilson B (2016) *First Bite: How We Learn to Eat.* London, HarperCollins.

Wilson B (2019) *The Way We Eat Now: Strategies for Eating in a World of Change.* London, Fourth Estate.

Wood R (1995) *The Sociology of the Meal.* Edinburgh, Edinburgh University Press.

Further reading

Warde A (2016) *The Practice of Eating.* Cambridge, Polity.

Provides a fresh take on sociological understandings of eating through the lens of practice theory. This leads us beyond the 'cultural turn' and its emphasis on meaning, towards close accounting for how we eat as a mundane daily practical accomplishment.

Wilson B (2019) *The Way We Eat Now: Strategies for Eating in a World of Change.* London, Fourth Estate.

Comprehensive and accessible, this critical discussion of the current global food system shows how we have ended up eating as we do presently, and thinks about how to change our eating to meet the challenges ahead.

DAVID BELL

28. Cuisine

JAKOB A. KLEIN AND HARRY G.
WEST

Introduction: seminal approaches to the study of cuisine

'Cuisine' entered the English language in the 17th century from French, where it refers both to cooking and the kitchen (Mennell 1985; Higman 2011). In vernacular usage the term refers to any style of cooking, serving and eating food, or to a refined, elaborated set of culinary practices. Which practices qualify as 'cuisine' may be vigorously debated. Scholarship reflects this, with some approaching cuisine as a set of shared practices (Mintz 1996; McCann 2009), and others (sometimes casting cuisines as 'high', 'low' or 'bourgeoise') emphasising how they reproduce social class distinction and hierarchy (Goody 1982; Bourdieu 1984). Some set cuisine in a symbolic register—from structuralist and semiotic approaches that call for a holistic understanding of *discrete systems* in order to recognise the significance of their component parts (Lévi-Strauss 1966; Douglas 1972; Barthes 1979; Bourdieu 1984), to recent works exploring cuisines as systems of communication that interact with wider social, discursive and institutional frameworks, or 'culinary fields' (Ferguson 2004; Farrer 2015). Others emphasise material dimensions and cuisine's embodiment in techniques of preparing, serving and eating. Integrative approaches recognise that these techniques are shaped by food technologies and informed by cosmologies and ideologies (Goody 1982; Laudan 2013; McCann 2009). Further divides arise from approaches that see cuisines as grounded in and contributing to the reproduction of ecologies and cultures of particular *places*—for example, subregions in France and China (Mintz 1996; Lin and Waley 2022)—versus those conceiving of cuisines as reflecting the *movements* of people, goods and ideas, such as work examining linkages across the Indian Ocean region (Farrer 2015; Leong-Salobir et al. 2016).

From communities of taste to collective identity

Some authors examine how the continuity of a cuisine is produced. McCann (2009) argues that textures and sensations of fullness imparted by indigenous starchy staples such as sorghum, millet and teff shaped which non-indigenous crops were incorporated into African regional cuisines in the context of cultural contact. Evolutionary psychologists Rozin and Rozin (2005) argue that cuisines are defined by distinctive 'flavour principles' informing which new foods can safely be accepted into a group's diet. Mintz (1996: 96) insists that cuisines are actively maintained and transformed by 'communities' of eaters who 'believe, and care that they believe, that they know what it consists of, how it is made, and how it should taste'.

Cuisines may contribute to group identity and differentiation on a range of scales, from villages, to lineages, to ethnic groups, to nations (Ohnuki Tierney 1993; King 2019). Regional and national cuisines may be co-constituted through comparison and contrast in discursive forms ranging from everyday talk to printed cookbooks and digital media (Appadurai 1988; Ferguson 2004). Regional culinary complexes cutting across nation-states—such as 'rice and beans' in West Africa, the Caribbean and the Americas (Wilk and Barbosa 2012)—can foster cross-regional *and* national identities, with people subtly differentiating how they combine shared components. Increasingly, nations are expected to have a cuisine. Political elites, seeking national unity at home and 'soft power' abroad, invest in gastro-diplomacy to construct and promote national cuisines (Zubaida 2000; Kim 2017), while attempts to incorporate the cuisines of marginalised groups into a 'national' cuisine may provoke debate and resistance (Hirsch 2011).

Shared or stratified?: 'high', 'low', and 'global' cuisine

Whether cuisine is a shared property or a site of social stratification is a complex, historically contingent question (Mennell 1985). French *haute cuisine* came to represent French nationhood not because all French people ate it, but because it came to be imagined in the 19th century through textual and other media as a uniquely French form of cultural sophistication (Ferguson 2004). In another example, while elites across the Ottoman empire emulated palace cuisine, the peasantry could not (Isin 2018). Popular dishes—from 'peasant foods' to 'market foods' and 'street foods'—may be elevated to the status of 'gourmet foods' without their creators enjoying attendant status. In his examination of how a racialised class system in Belize prevented common cooking practices and taste preferences from being recognised as a shared cuisine, Wilk (2002) makes a useful heuristic distinction between the performance of cuisine in public spaces, and the practice of cuisine in everyday life. To wit, women in their roles as domestic cooks may be celebrated as the bearers of culinary heritage, while men predominate in professional kitchens (Harris and Giuffre 2015).

'High' cuisines are in part defined by their transcendence of specific places, contradicting the boundedness often imagined for regional cuisines (Mintz 1996). Elite chefs— whether working in definably 'national' or 'regional' traditions, or in avowedly cosmopolitan contexts (e.g., Antipodean cuisine, or fine dining in the Gulf States)—often seek to combine and refine the quintessence of several place-based cuisines. High cuisines have often been created through ingredients to which most lack access (Goody 1982)—luxuries imported from distant lands—even if the value of these foods is sometimes recognised as a product of local cultural ecologies (such as the contemporary celebration of 'artisan' or 'heritage' foods). In any case, high cuisines are characterised by their propensity to 'travel'. French cuisine set the standard for fine dining not only in France, but also among elites in cities across the world in the 19th and early 20th centuries, from Lisbon to Tokyo (Sobral 2014; Laudan 2013). The near-global dominance of French *haute cuisine* has given way to a plurality of cuisines used to display sophistication and confer distinction, in many cases including previously low-end, local and national foods (Johnston and Baumann 2010; Sobral 2014). Nevertheless, the contemporary culinary field of fine dining is profoundly transnational, with highly mobile restaurateurs, chefs and diners who shuttle between Dubai, Johannesburg, Lima, London, Los Angeles, Mumbai, New York, Paris, Shanghai, Singapore, Sydney, Tokyo and other global cities (Farrer 2015).

The importance of place, as well as movement, to the constitution of cuisines

It is not only 'high cuisines' that travel. Migration at global scales means that the culinary practices of diasporic communities are sustained and transformed through creative uses of locally available ingredients, the creation of 'bottom-up' transnational supply chains and, increasingly, digital media, challenging the fiction of stable ties between place, taste and culture (Chen 2014; Imbruce 2015; Hegde 2014). Cuisines also travel with colonialism and imperial projects, incorporating, transforming, marginalising or even obliterating the cuisines of subjugated peoples (Laudan 2013). Intensified transregional and transoceanic trade ensures the broad availability of, and even dependence upon, imported goods, complicating elites' claims to culinary distinction. The spread of 'industrial cuisines'—products of technoscientific innovations in food production, processing, packaging, transportation and preparation— has further weakened dependence upon local, seasonal production cycles and given rise to greater homogeneity in cooking and eating, disrupting pre-existing regional and class-based cuisines (Goody 1982).

Nuanced approaches see dynamic interaction between mobilities and place-based cuisines. Regional culinary traditions have historically been shaped through the transoceanic movement of cultivars—maize to Africa (McCann 2009), chillies to China (Dott 2020), tomatoes to Italy (Gentilcore 2010)—and are sustained through ongoing international trade (Wilk 2002). Centuries-old trade networks throughout the Indian Ocean, Southeast Asia and China have produced deep and enduring gustatory connections (Leong-Salobir et al. 2016; Farrer 2015;). Appadurai (1988) argues that post-independence middle-class women, including migrants to major cities, were instrumental in delineating India's national and regional cuisines. Diasporic communities contribute decisively to the construction of national cuisines in their countries of origin (Wilk 2002). They have also played pivotal roles in creating national cuisines in their new homes, as in the case of enslaved Africans and their descendants (Harris 2012) or Chinese cooks and restaurateurs (Chen 2014) in the US, even as continuing albeit resisted marginalisation of these communities has constrained public recognition of them as creators of modern American cuisine(s), and the symbolic and economic value of these 'ethnic' or 'minority' cuisines has frequently been appropriated by white chefs (Ray 2016; Williams 2020).

JAKOB A. KLEIN AND HARRY G. WEST

The future of cuisine

Future scholarship on cuisine may further explore tensions between approaches and practices that ground cuisines in particular places—whether nations, regions or smaller spatial communities—and those that conceive of cuisines as mobile and spatially dispersed—from diasporas, to digital communities formed through the use of social media. It must also productively engage with the increasing significance of new technologies used to grow, process, cook and serve food whilst recognising the enduring significance of direct relationships with food—such as the buoyant market for 'craft' or 'artisan' products—and with one another—exemplified by the persistent celebration of commensality and 'local' foods. While many have emphasised the collective cultural dimensions of cuisines, scholars are increasingly examining work in *la cuisine*—whether domestic or commercial kitchens or other sites of preparation—paying attention to aesthetics, creativity, skill and learning, and to the ways that cuisines are organised and produced through embodied, multi-sensory interactions with the more-than-human worlds of tools, technologies and food materials. This work is beginning to complicate simplistic oppositions between 'traditional', craft-based cuisines and technology-dependent industrial cooking (Sutton 2014; Graf 2022; de St Maurice 2018). It is also starting to challenge the idea of culinary globalisation as a process of ever-greater homogenisation, showing instead how sites of food preparation (and consumption) constitute 'culinary contact zones' defined by both 'cultural friction' and 'creativity' (Farrer 2015: 8), as well as how culinary creativity is constrained and enabled by gendered and racialised divisions of labour, socioeconomic structures and legitimating institutions (Williams 2020; Lane 2014; Harris and Giuffre 2015).

References

Appadurai A (1988) How to make a national cuisine: cookbooks in contemporary India. *Comparative Studies in Society and History* 30, 3–24 https://doi.org/10.1017/S0010417500015024.

Barthes R (1979) Toward a psychosociology of contemporary food consumption. In Forster R and Ranum O (eds) *Food and Drink in History*. Baltimore, Johns Hopkins University Press, 166–173.

Bourdieu P (1984) *Distinction: A Social Critique of the Judgement of Taste*. London, Routledge.

Chen Y (2014) *Chop Suey, USA: The Story of Chinese Food in America*. New York, Columbia University Press.

de St. Maurice G (2018) Sensing bodies at the center in today's traditional Japanese restaurant kitchens. *Japanese Studies* 38, 1–20 https://doi.org/10.1080/10371397.2018.1465803.

Dott B R (2020) *The Chile Pepper in China: A Cultural Biography*. New York, Columbia University Press.

Douglas M (1972) Deciphering a meal. *Daedalus* 101, 61–81 http://www.jstor.org/stable/20024058.

Farrer J (ed) (2015) *The Globalization of Asian Cuisines: Transnational Networks and Culinary Contact Zones*. New York, Palgrave Macmillan.

Ferguson P P (2004) *Accounting for Taste: The Triumph of French Cuisine*. Chicago, University of Chicago Press.

Gentilcore D (2010) *Pomodoro!: A History of the Tomato in Italy*. New York, Columbia University Press.

Goody J (1982) *Cooking, Cuisine and Class: A Study in Comparative Sociology*. Cambridge, Cambridge University Press.

Graf K (2022) Taste knowledge: couscous and the cook's six senses. *Journal of the Royal Anthropological Institute* (N.S.) 28, 577–594 https://doi.org/10.1111/1467-9655.13708.

Harris D and Giuffre P (2015) *Taking the Heat: Women Chefs and Gender Inequality in the Professional Kitchen*. New Brunswick, NJ, Rutgers University Press.

Harris J B (2012) *High on the Hog: A Culinary Journey from Africa to America*. New York, Bloomsbury USA.

Hegde R S (2014) Food blogs and the digital reimagination of South Asian diasporic publics. *South Asian Diaspora* 6, 89–103 https://doi.org/10.1080/19438192.2014.876172.

Higman B W (2011) *How Food Made History*. Oxford, Wiley-Blackwell.

Hirsch D (2011) "Hummus is best when it is fresh and made by Arabs": the gourmetization of hummus in Israel and the return of the repressed Arab. *American*

Ethnologist 38, 617–630 https://doi.org/10.1111/j.1548-1425.2011.01326.x.

Imbruce V (2015) *From Farm to Canal Street: Chinatown's Alternative Food Network in the Global Marketplace.* Ithaca, NY, Cornell University Press.

Isin P M (2018) *Bountiful Empire: A History of Ottoman Cuisine.* London, Reaktion Books.

Johnston J and Baumann S (2010) *Foodies: Democracy and Distinction in the Gourmet Foodscape.* New York, Routledge.

Kim C-H (2017) Let them eat Royal Court Cuisine! Heritage politics of defining global *Hansik. Gastronomica: The Journal of Critical Food Studies* 17, 4–14 https://doi.org/10.1525/gfc.2017.17.3.4.

King M T (ed) (2019) *Culinary Nationalism in Asia.* London, Bloomsbury Academic.

Lane C (2014) *The Cultivation of Taste: Chefs and the Organization of Fine Dining.* Oxford, Oxford University Press.

Laudan R (2013) *Cuisine and Empire: Cooking in World History.* Berkeley, University of California Press.

Leong-Salobir C, Ray K and Rohel J (2016) Introducing a special issue on rescuing taste from the nation: oceans, borders, and culinary flows. *Gastronomica: The Journal of Critical Food Studies* 16, 9–15 https://doi.org/10.1525/gfc.2016.16.1.9.

Lévi-Strauss, Claude (1966) The culinary triangle. *Partisan Review* 33, 586–595.

Lin J and Waley P (2022) Taste and place of Nanxiong cuisine in south China: a regional analytical framework. *Food, Culture & Society* 25, 814–830 https://doi.org/10.1080/15528014.2021.1930736.

McCann J C (2009) *Stirring the Pot: A History of African Cuisine.* Athens, Ohio University Press.

Mennell S (1985) *All Manners of Food: Eating and Taste in England and France from the Middle Ages to the Present.* Oxford, Basil Blackwell.

Mintz S W (1996) Cuisine: high, low, and not at all. In Mintz S W (ed) *Tasting Food, Tasting Freedom: Excursions into Eating, Culture, and the Past.* Boston, MA, Beacon Press, 92–105.

Ohnuki-Tierney E (1993) *Rice as Self: Japanese Identities through Time.* Princeton, NJ, Princeton University Press.

Ray K (2016) *The Ethnic Restaurateur.* London, Bloomsbury.

Rozin E and Rozin P (2005) Culinary themes and variations. In Korsmeyer C (ed) *The Taste Culture Reader.* Oxford, Berg, 34–41.

Sobral J (2014) The high and the low in the making of a Portuguese national cuisine in the nineteenth and twentieth centuries. In Klein J A and Murcott A (eds) *Food Consumption in Global Perspective: Essays in the Anthropology of Food in Honour of Jack Goody.* New York, Palgrave Macmillan, 108–134.

Sutton D E (2014) *Secrets from the Greek Kitchen: Cooking, Skill, and Everyday Life on an Aegean Island.* Berkeley, University of California Press.

Wilk R (2002) Food and nationalism: the origins of 'Belizean food'. In Belasco W and Scranton P (eds) *Food Nations: Selling Taste in Consumer Societies.* New York, Routledge, 67–89.

Wilk R and Barbosa L (eds) (2012) *Rice and Beans: A Unique Dish in a Hundred Places.* London, Berg.

Williams J (2020) The Mango Gang and New World cuisine: white privilege in the commodification of Latin American and Afro-Caribbean foods. In Garth H and Reese A M (eds) *Black Food Matters: Racial Justice in the Wake of Food Justice.* Minneapolis, University of Minnesota Press, 251–278.

Zubaida S (2000) National, communal and global dimensions in Middle Eastern food cultures. In Zubaida S and Tapper R (eds) *A Taste of Thyme: Culinary Cultures of the Middle East.* London, Tauris Parke Paperbacks, 33–45.

Further reading

Ferguson P P (2004) *Accounting for Taste: The Triumph of French Cuisine.* Chicago, University of Chicago Press

Sociologist Ferguson's study analyses how the cooking of France became established as a 'national cuisine' and continues to operate as a crucial site for the production of French identity at home and abroad, instructing us that in order to understand this process we need to situate cooking and eating within a wider 'gastronomic field' of writings and other media, institutions and culinary actors.

McCann J C (2009) *Stirring the Pot: A History of African Cuisine.* Athens, Ohio University Press.

JAKOB A. KLEIN AND HARRY G. WEST

McCann's introduction to Africa's under-researched cuisines situates these firmly in relation to global food history and offers a useful template for historical and comparative research on regional and national cuisines in Africa and beyond. The monograph explores the dynamic interaction between local geographies, transregional mobilities, political projects and the creativity and knowledge of female cooks in the shaping sub-Saharan African cuisines from the 16th century to the present.

Wilk R (2002) Food and nationalism: the origins of 'Belizean food'. In Belasco W and Scranton P (eds) *Food Nations: Selling Taste in Consumer Societies*. New York, Routledge, 67–89

Wilks' historical anthropology of Belizean food examines the role of class, race, colonialism and migration in the making of 'national' cuisines and offers important insights into the relationship between the 'practised' and 'performed' dimensions of cuisines and into the role of the 'global' in shaping 'local' food cultures and identities.

JAKOB A. KLEIN AND HARRY G. WEST

29. Decolonising food

P R M
NORTHOVER-PAIRMAN-WILSON[1]

Introduction: The paradox of food – coloniality, modernity and the quest for decoloniality

From the centrality of the sacred meal in Afro-Haitian Vodou rituals to the mystery of the Eucharist in Western Christian traditions, food works as a conduit for expressing values, cultures, and diverse spiritualities. But food also involves encounters with power, exemplified by the dark histories of sugar and slavery (Mintz, 1986) or the present cornucopia of street food cultures that creatively resist global fast food chains. The paradox of food is that it can be used to connect people but also to reproduce histories of disconnection that emerged from violent experiences of imperialism, colonialism, and globalisation (Colás, 2022; Crichlow et al., 2018).

Our global food system is shaped by what decolonial scholar Aníbal Quijano (2007) calls a modernity/coloniality relation, which reproduces relations of domination between the West and the Rest through a 'coloniality of power'. For Quijano, *coloniality* is more than just colonialism; it is a power matrix expressed through complex orders of being, knowledge, and power. The coloniality of being (re)creates 'Others' through the creation of racialised spaces and bodies, as well as 'zones of non-being' (Fanon, 2008) or dehumanising spaces where people (e.g., enslaved Africans) are subjected to exorbitant violence. The coloniality of knowledge is the hierarchical imposition of Eurocentric epistemologies and ontologies, which repress, devalue, and marginalise the understandings, practices, and world-views of non-white and Indigenous populations. Mediated through the coloniality of being and knowledge, the colonial matrix of power (CMP) seeks to dominate all dimensions of human existence, from sexuality and other forms of subjectivity, to economic and labour processes, to human relationships with nature. The CMP includes past and present forms of coloniality in violently gendered and racially entangled places, where peoples and territories bear the brunt of food and climate emergencies while contributing the least to their causes (Davis et al., 2019; Lecoutere et al., 2023).

Globally, the perpetuation of extractive, plantation-style food systems – the large-scale production of a single crop, or monoculture, for export – limits access to healthy, locally produced food. This is a CMP that weakens domestic food systems while increasing dependencies and preferences for imported, ultra-processed foods (Wilson, 2013). The global food industry's overdependence on a few staple crops in industrial food systems, such as wheat, maize, soybeans, palm oil, and rice (Clapp, 2023), continues *plantation legacies* of persistent poverty (Beckford, 1972) through the marginalisation of small-scale subsistence and local market production, coupled with the widespread denigration of locally produced foods as 'backward'. Politically and economically, this CMP depends on the perpetuation of *racial capitalism*, a mode of accumulation by dispossession (Melamed, 2015) that rests on, among other things, the appropriation of labour value from Black and Othered bodies, whether in an absolute sense (chattel slavery) or relative sense (wage labour). Culturally, it depends on the perpetuation of symbolic codes of racial difference, which '*invisibilize*' (Neeganagwedgin, 2022) non-Western forms of growing, preparing, and eating food. Ecologically, the plantation system is hastening the loss of ancestral territories and biodiversity, increasing climate risks, and multiplying food and nutritional health inequalities (HLPE, 2023).

In this entry, we consider the symbolic and material impacts of the plantation and its legacies, but also the ways it has been contested and resisted on the ground, focussing on the perspectives of Indigenous and Afro-descendant Caribbeans. We demonstrate the value of decolonial food research and practice for re-centring excluded, abjected, or marginalised peoples and their foodways by 'undoing, disobeying and delinking' (Mignolo and Walsh, 2018: 3) them from the violence of modernity/coloniality.

Decolonising food from the Indigenous and Afro-descendant Caribbean

In this section, we develop understanding of decolonising food research and practice from our own positionalities and experiences as decolonial food scholars and scholar-activists. As a grassroots food activist and Yamaye (Jamaica) Taino Indigenous spokesperson,

Chieftainess Ronalda Pairman of the Jamaica Hummingbird Taíno Peoples has made pioneering efforts to communicate the nutritional and environmental importance of Taíno ancestral foodways through her food demonstrations and advocacy. Patricia Northover is an Afro-descendant Jamaican woman whose scholarship adopts Black critical theory and a decolonial Black poethic, embracing ethics, politics, and aesthetics to explore the problem of racial power and abject blackness in globalisation and development. Working from within and beyond the colonial Westernised university, Marisa Wilson's research seeks to develop understandings of the uneven effects of plantation foodways on environments, cultures, and bodies. In each of the sections below, we demonstrate our decolonial food research and practice 'from where we stand professionally, personally and in place' (Radcliffe and Radhuber, 2020: 3).

Decolonising food from the place of Black geographies of power (Patricia Northover)

Shaped by imperial-colonial histories and reinforced by decades of neoliberal economic policies, the Caribbean is a highly unequal, food import-dependent, food insecure, and vulnerable space (FAO et al., 2023), subject to multiple waves of global food crises (Phillips, 2022; Clapp, 2023) and high rates of diet-related non-communicable diseases (Razzaghi et al., 2019). In response to these impacts of the CMP, the food sovereignty movement offers crucial pathways towards anti- and de-colonising work. These align with the ethical, political, and scholarly concerns of decolonial food researchers. In confronting colonial matrices of power, the food sovereignty movement struggles against intersectional forms of class, race, gender and other forms of discrimination in food systems, which shape the experiences of women, youth, Black, Indigenous, and LGBTQ+ communities. Food sovereignty includes efforts to revive or build foodways that disrupt, delink, or diverge from Eurocentric, patriarchal, and racially hegemonic forms of life, in order to build a 'world in which there are many worlds' (de la Cadena and Blaser, 2018; Radcliffe and Radhuber, 2020).

La Via Campesina (LVC), an international movement of peasants, rural women, Indigenous people, migrant farmworkers, fishers, and pastoralists, is a central actor in this radical space. For LVC, food sovereignty is 'the right of Peoples to healthy and culturally appropriate food, produced through ecologically sound and sustainable methods, and their right to define their own food and agriculture systems' (La Via Campesina, 2021: 1). In its focus on *food as a right* rather than a commodity, LVC counteracts those in positions of authority whose projections for the future of food reproduce plantation legacies that engender multiple global crises. Recent examples of such decolonial activism include projects to develop alternatives to the United Nations (UN) World Food Summit (held in 2021). For many, the Summit perpetuated forms of modernity/coloniality in global food policy by further entrenching corporate control over food systems (Canfield et al., 2021) and by ignoring the colonial roots of present-day food problems.

Food sovereignty organisations in the Caribbean, such as the Haitian National Peasant Organization, Tet Kole Ti Peyizan Ayisyen (Tet Kole), make sharp distinctions between their vision of the future of food and that promulgated in the 2021 Summit. In the podcast episode 'Food Sovereignty and the Peasant Declaration in Haiti', National Executive Coordinator of Tet Kole, Origéne Louis, rejects the neoliberal market discourse of 'food security' (FRIED Podcast, 2021). In light of the complex, racially distributed burdens on Haitian farmers and their communities, as evidenced in Haiti's ongoing crises of hunger and malnutrition (Steckley and Shamsie, 2015; Rasul et al., 2022), Tet Kole favours precepts outlined in the 2018 UN Declaration of the Rights of Peasants and Other Peoples Working in Rural Areas (UNDROP, 2018), which entrenches land, food, and collective rights. As a deeply racialised peasant community, Tet Kole participates in the food sovereignty movement in order to protect their communities as well as to advocate for their right to protect and revalue Afro-descendant peoples' traditional knowledge of foods and plant heritage. Their aim is to use food sovereignty to reinforce cultural identity and to heal bodies harmed by the violence of slavery and subsequent market and neoliberal regimes, opposing centuries of colonial and neo-colonial violence in Haiti.

Building on this work exploring food sovereignty from the perspective of Black farmers, I recently collaborated with farming communities in Haiti, Jamaica, and Ghana, in cooperation with the Karl Lévêque Cultural Institute, a Haitian popular education, training, research, and advocacy organisation. The resulting Afro-descendant community of farmers produced a Declaration in Defence of Decolonizing Development Cooperation (GPN Farmers' Workshop Declaration, 2022), which decried neoliberal models of development, advocating instead for equitable rights to land, seeds, water, finance, insurance, and other resources, in keeping with their right to food sovereignty. They also called for *reparatory justice* regarding the histories of racial violence and dispossession that have occurred in the Caribbean and Africa. Reparatory justice claims bring into focus the harms caused by slavery and colonialism and their ongoing effects on Afro-descendant and Indigenous populations. By contrast, *climate justice* focusses on the disproportionate burdens borne by those populations who have contributed the least to climate change. Decolonising food in the context of coloniality connects these two forms of justice and goes further than a demand for 'climate reparations' as it centres attention on colonial violence and their legacies in present-day social and environmental crises.

In the next section, Chieftainess Ronalda Pairman discusses related issues of justice in the context of her own work.

Decolonising food from Indigenous Jamaica (Kasikeiani Ronalda Pairman)

The *canoa* (boat) is a key symbol of the Taíno people; it was our way of travelling long distances across the sea. The canoa helps us to preserve the legacy of our people in food. We, the Taíno Indigenous people of Jamaica, are in charge of this *canoa,* and it is our duty to ensure that we pass on our legacy to the upcoming seven generations. This was the way our ancestors taught us to support the future of our people.

In contributing to this entry, I speak from the grassroots level. As Indigenous peoples we see ourselves as key stakeholders of the land. We build sacred relationships with the land as it offers us food, a place to live, sacred medicines, ceremonial rites, and traditional farming practices. We have been seeing and feeling the effects of the vast changes in how food is now processed. Jamaica's food has undergone significant transformations. Gone are the days of planting and cooking traditional, healthy meals at home. Instead, most of the food on our plates is outsourced due to an increase in imported, processed foods that have flooded our stores, restaurants, and homes. Traditional methods of food preparation have become distant from our hearts and minds as we venture farther from the kitchen. The prevalence of lifestyle diseases such as high blood pressure, diabetes, and cholesterol has escalated.

My community and I have been fighting this tsunami of lifestyle change by sharing stories of our natural and traditional eating practices, as a way of honouring our ancestors. In my work as a food and lifestyle coach and vegan chef, I narrate tales about our culture and customs while preparing simple meals. I encourage people to participate and inspire creativity in home cooking. I do this through live cooking demonstrations and nutrition talks, and by creating ancestral gardens in our communities. I focus on using local home-grown ingredients that are easily accessible, including those that have been crucial to our survival as a people, such as cassava.

Cassava represents resilience to the Caribbean Taíno people as it sustained us through our travels across the Americas and into the Caribbean, a long and arduous journey. For this journey, we made a preserved food called *Kasabe*, a thin bread resembling a biscuit, which was made from cassava (*Manihot esculenta*) and could last up to three years. The cassava plant itself was extremely easy to cultivate as new plants could grow from just two inches of cassava stick planted in the soil.

In addition to applying Taíno ancestral foodways to issues of nutrition, lifestyle, and farming, our work refutes the idea that our Taíno existence is extinct. This persistent narrative, which is taught in schools in the UK as well as the Caribbean, perpetuates the coloniality of being, knowledge, and power through the *invisibilisation* of our peoples (Neeganagwedgin, 2022). This is experienced in everyday life through narratives that encourage our children to prefer highly processed foods, such as tinned corn, over our own maize that is grown using traditional organic farming methods. Such forms of coloniality marginalise our ancestors' and families' time-honoured traditions of food preparation.

To counteract these forms of invisibilisation, my community and I have been engaging local and international platforms, such as the UN Committee on the Elimination of Racial Discrimination, to recognise and formalise our Indigenous rights along with the rights of other Indigenous groups in Jamaica, such as the Maroons and the Rastafarians. We are contributing to efforts to save our people's physical and mental health by maintaining our food and gardening practices and teaching the next generation to continue to maintain good relationships with the land.

In the final section, Marisa Wilson shares her account of both obstacles and opportunities for Indigenous-led, decolonising food research through her own experience applying for UK funding as a researcher based in the colonial academy.

Decolonising food research in practice (Marisa Wilson)

As Indigenous scholar Linda Tuhiwai Smith argues, research is 'probably one of the dirtiest words in the Indigenous world's vocabulary' (Tuhiwai, 2021: 1). How, then, can scholars decolonise food research from *within* the colonial academy? In this final section, I outline some of the challenges of decolonising food research from my position as a white, North American researcher working in a colonial British academy. While the story relayed here is written in the first person, it involves a collaboration with colleagues referred to in the acknowledgements (below), each of whom carved out pathways to decolonising food research and practice through their own contributions to the application process. In relaying our experience applying for UK funding, our story uncovers challenges but also opportunities for decolonising food research in practice.

A central challenge we faced was the funders' designation of our Indigenous collaborators as 'project partners'. According to the funding guidelines, project partners do not normally receive funding from a research grant to carry out the research themselves. Rather, they are collaborators who offer financial or in-kind support to the research, which is carried out by others *for their benefit*. Geographer Patricia Noxolo argues that such a 'racialized and infantilising conception of "partnership"' (Noxolo, 2017: 343) upholds colonial separations between the imperial donor and the colonial recipient (Noxolo, 2006; 2017). This kind of coloniality of being

is especially problematic in Indigenous food research, since it invisibilises the expertise of Indigenous elders and others who hold ancestral knowledge of plants as food and medicine.

In recognising persistent colonialities in the funder's designated roles, my Caribbean colleagues suggested that we override the role of 'project partners' altogether. Instead, we designated the five collaborating Indigenous elders as international co-leads, just like the academic researchers named on the project. By changing the allocated roles and responsibilities, we are beginning to co-construct decolonial pathways towards Indigenous-led food research that re-centres Indigenous peoples as co-researchers.

As this last section has demonstrated, the institutional and cultural fabric of UK funding structures creates obstacles for establishing truly horizontal or equitable project co-development. Moreover, as other scholars have argued, the weight of on-the-ground decolonising work is felt disproportionately by Indigenous and other racialised groups who continue to experience different forms of coloniality in their everyday lives. Given these obstacles to decolonising projects, it is essential that collaborators who embody more privileged positionalities, such as myself, take up decolonising work in their professional and everyday lives.

Bridging reparatory and climate justice for decolonial food futures

In this entry, we have used our own work to demonstrate the relevance of key concepts and issues related to food and its decolonisation. In keeping with decolonial practice, we have emphasised collective struggles to extricate the food system from the clutches of modernity/coloniality. We have drawn lessons from Haitian food sovereignty initiatives, Jamaican Taíno food activism and advocacy, and Indigenous-led food research practice, all of which foreground ancestral foodways and their centrality to human and non-human flourishing. Decolonialising food work should counter ongoing forms of coloniality through transformative politics and relations of ethical and political accountability. These are difficult and continuous processes that call for individual, institutional, and cultural adjustments, legislative reforms, and deeply personal forms of dedication to *reparatory climate and food justice.* As racial capitalist-driven crises deepen, the case for reparatory food and climate justice becomes central for securing decolonial food futures. It is encouraging that voices from the frontline are joining together with scholars from the academy to speak back to power, overcoming the paradox of food by emphasising its ability to connect rather than disconnect.

Acknowledgements

This chapter has drawn on collaborations developed through our wider Caribbean Food for Climate Justice Research Group. We acknowledge all the members of our group in fostering a community of practice that has inspired the chapter, with special thanks to Chieftainess Ronalda Pairman and her Taíno community. We acknowledge the practitioners and activists whose lived experiences and narratives are embodied in some of the stories contained in this chapter, including: Iya Akilah Jaramogi (Fondes Amandes Community Reforestation Project); PAYI Cristo Adonis (Santa Rosa First People Community); Prof. Diana Fox (former Director of the Institute for Gender and Development Studies, The University of the West Indies); Kemba Jaramogi (Fondes Amandes Community Reforestation Project); Caroline Mair-Toby (Institute for Small Islands), and especially Blair Gopeechan (Humanitarian and Anti-Racist Practitioner). We wish to acknowledge financial support from the Global Partnership Network (GPN) for the translation of an earlier version of this document for our Haitian stakeholders, Tet Kole, and the Karl Lévêque Cultural Institute. The GPN is funded by the German Federal Ministry for Economic Cooperation and Development (BMZ).

Note

1. Our pen name indicates joint first authorship by Patricia Northover, Chieftainess (Kasike-iani) Ronalda S. Pairman of the Jamaican Hummingbird Taíno People, and Marisa Wilson.

References

Beckford, G. (1999 [1972]). *Persistent Poverty: Underdevelopment in Plantation Economies of the Third World.* Mona, Jamaica: University of the West Indies Press.

Canfield, M C., M D. Anderson, and P. McMichael. (2021). 'UN Food Systems Summit 2021: Dismantling Democracy and Resetting Corporate Control of Food Systems.' *Frontiers in Sustainable Food Systems* 5: 66152.

Clapp, J. (2023). 'Concentration and Crisis: Exploring the Deep Roots of Vulnerability in the Global Industrial Food System.' *The Journal of Peasant Studies* 50(1): 1–25.

Colás, A. (2022). 'Food, Multiplicity and Imperialism: Patterns of Domination and Subversion in the Modern International System.' *Cooperation and Conflict* 57(3), 384–401. https://doi.org/10.1177/00108367221099802.

Crichlow, M., Northover, P., and Giusti-Cordero, J. (2018). *Race and Rurality in the Global Economy.* New York: State University of New York Press.

Davis, J., Moulton, A.A., Van Sant, L., and Williams, B. (2019). 'Anthropocene, Capitalocene, … Plantationocene?: A Manifesto for Ecological Justice in an Age of Global Crises.' *Geography Compass* 13(5): e12438.

de la Cadena, M., and Blaser, M. (Eds.). (2018). *A World of Many Worlds.* Durham: Duke University Press. https://doi.org/10.2307/j.ctv125jpzq.

Fanon, Frantz. (2008 [1952]). *Black Skin, White Masks.* Translated by Richard Philcox. New York: Grove Press.

FAO, IFAD, PAHO, UNICEF, and WFP. (2023). Regional Overview of Food Security and Nutrition – Latin America and the Caribbean 2022: Towards improving affordability of healthy diets. Santiago. https://doi.org/10.4060/cc3859en.

FRIED Podcast, (December 2021) 'Episode 4: Food Sovereignty and the Peasant Declaration in Haiti – Contesting the UN Food Summit, with Origène Louis.' Food Researchers in Edinburgh, (FRIED) Podcast Series.

GPN Farmers' Workshop Declaration (2022). https://drive.google.com/file/d/1UVtoN4oxkYPEcx_Wd31ACIasKkk_Cvqy/view (accessed 8 Dec 2023).

HLPE (High Level Panel of Experts) (2023). Reducing Inequalities for Food Security and Nutrition. Rome, Committee on World Food Security (CFS), HLPE-FSN.

Lecoutere, E., Mishra, A., Singaraju, N., Koo, J., Azzarri, C., Chanana, N., Nico, G., and Puskur. R, (2023). 'Where Women in Agri-food Systems Are at Highest Climate Risk: A Methodology for Mapping Climate–Agriculture–Gender Inequality Hotspots.' *Frontiers in Sustainable Food Systems* 7: 1197809. doi: 10.3389/fsufs.2023.1197809.

La Via Campesina (2021). La Via Campesina: The Global Voice of Peasants! https://viacampesina.org/en/international-peasants-voice/.

Melamed, J. (2015). Racial Capitalism. *Critical Ethnic Studies* 1(1): 76–85. https://doi.org/10.5749/jcritethnstud.1.1.0076.

Mignolo, W., and Walsh, C. (2018). *On Decoloniality.* Durham, NC: Duke University Press.

Mintz, S. W. (1986). *Sweetness and Power.* Harlow: Penguin Books.

Neeganagwedgin, E. (2022). 'Caribbean Indigenous Experiences of Erasure: Movement, Memory and Knowing.' *Analecta Politica* 12(22): 1–17.

Noxolo, P. (2006). 'Claims: A Postcolonial Geographical Critique of "Partnership" in Britain's Development Discourse.' *Singapore Journal of Tropical Geography* 27: 254–269.

Noxolo, P. (2017). 'Decolonial Theory in a Time of the Re-Colonisation of UK Research.' *Transactions of the Institute of British Geographers* 42: 342–344.

Phillips, W. (2022). 'Food Security in the Caribbean: A Policy Perspective. *Focus* Issue 3 (Jul–Sept). https://repositorio.cepal.org/server/api/core/bitstreams/13ca87a7-82f8-4c86-820f-85514fe63fb2/content (accessed 5 Dec 2023).

Quijano, A. (2007). 'Coloniality and Modernity/Rationality.' *Cultural Studies* 21: 168–178.

Radcliffe, S. A., and Radhuber, I. M. 2020. 'The Political Geographies of D/decolonization: Variegation and Decolonial Challenges of/in Geography'. *Political Geography* 79: 1–12.

Rasul, R., Rouzier, V., Sufra, R., Yan, L. D., Joseph, I., Mourra, N., Sabwa, S., Deschamps, M. M., Fitzgerald, D. W., Pape, J. W., Nash, D., and McNairy, M. L. (2022). 'Extreme Food Insecurity and Malnutrition in Haiti: Findings from a Population-Based Cohort in Port-au-Prince, Haiti.' *Nutrients*, 14(22): 4854. https://doi.org/10.3390/nu14224854.

Razzaghi, H., Martin, DN., Quesnel-Crooks, S., Hong, Y., Gregg, E., Andall-Brereton, G., et al. (2019). '10-year Trends in Noncommunicable Disease Mortality in the Caribbean Region.' *Revista Panamerican de Salud Publica* 43: e37. https://doi.org/10.26633/RPSP.2019.37.

Steckley, M., and Shamsie, Y. (2015). 'Manufacturing Corporate Landscapes: The Case of Agrarian Displacement and Food (In)security in Haiti.' *Third World Quarterly* 36(1): 179–197. DOI: 10.1080/01436597.2015.976042.

Tuhiwai, L. S. (2021). *Decolonizing Methodologies: Research and Indigenous Peoples.* Bloomsbury Academic & Professional.

UNDROP, United Nations, General Assembly. (2018). 'United Nations Declaration on the Rights of Peasants and Other People Working in Rural Areas.' Resolution A/RES/73/165 adopted by the Human Rights Council on 28 September 2018. https://digitallibrary.un.org/record/1650694?ln=en&v=pdf.

Wilson, M. (2013). 'From Colonial Dependency to 'Finger Lickin' Values: Food, Identity, and Globalization in Trinidad.' In *Food and Identity in the Caribbean,* edited by Hanna Garth. London and New York: Bloomsbury, pp. 107–120.

Further reading

Slocum, Rachel and Saldanha, Arun (eds.) (2013). *Geographies of Race and Food. Fields, Bodies, and Markets.* London: Routledge.

This edited volume shows that the ways humans attribute meaning to food are inextricably linked to the racialisation of bodies.

Peña, Devon G, Calvo, Luz, McFarland, Pancho, and Valle, Gabriel R. (2017). *Mexican-Origin Foods, Foodways, and Social Movements: Decolonial Perspectives.* Fayetteville: University of Arkansas Press.

This edited volume includes perspectives on decolonising Mexican-origin foods from a range of perspectives, including Indigenous peoples, farm workers, seed savers, farmers, scholar-activists, cooks, and activists.

30. Degrowth and food

FERNE EDWARDS AND ANITRA
NELSON

Introduction: degrowth and food

Degrowth food actions seek to re-orient socio-economic structures to satisfy all people's needs and to provide a regenerative approach to planet Earth – enhancing both food security and biodiversity – via modest metabolic (material and energy) flows, enhancing general well-being and instituting an holistic care economy. Degrowth food production, distribution and consumption provide opportunities to transform contemporary food provision to more socially just and environmentally sustainable states.

Degrowth is a decentralised social and environmental movement, challenging capitalist economic growth and advocating for everyday practices to meet human needs within planetary boundaries. The movement views the monetary growth-driven capitalist economy as a source of social and ecological crises. As an alternative, degrowth is defined as leading to a sustainable society "with a metabolism which has a different structure and serves new functions" (D'Alisa et al. 2014: 3f). The movement seeks to transform socio-economic structures to satisfy all people's needs, and to provide a regenerative approach to planet Earth, modest material and energy flows, and general well-being.

The degrowth movement coalesces with alternative food networks in seeking to transform the food system by recreating community production and connecting producers and consumers in local and direct ways (Edwards 2016). Distancing people from local food systems obscures social and environmental co-benefits, such as healthy diets, nature connection, collective sufficiency, social cohesion and cultural heritage. Degrowth challenges the industrial food system predicated on damaging externalities and inequalities, generating global heating and the climate emergency, by decentralising power with local food provisioning.

Degrowth food practitioners practise collective, place-based food provisioning, recognise the value of local cultures and bioregional sufficiency, create local autonomy with direct participation in decision-making, and take a regenerative approach to gardening and farming. They draw on and contribute to aligned movements such as food sovereignty, agroecology, permaculture and urban community gardening – approaches that epitomise efficient and just food practices.

Putting principles into practice: food for degrowth examples

Among the distinctive degrowth principles that apply to food practices are 'frugal abundance', 'care-full approaches' and 'commoning'.

'Frugal abundance' refers to making "frugal use of Earth while living in, and with, personal, emotional and philosophical abundance" (Nelson and Edwards 2021: 3) and is practised by celebrating local diversity through sharing goods, services, knowledge and skills while enabling social and environmental efficiencies and direct governance. Frugal abundance incorporates food sovereignty, eradicating waste and convivial eating as a social pleasure. For instance, an Australian rural household divested from monetised food and energy resources to meet 70% of their household's needs by creating a collective, community of practice approach to food provisioning (Jones and Ulman, 2021).

'Care' opens up the economy to consider caring for oneself, for other humans and for nonhuman nature. Pungas (2021) writes about dachas (garden cooperatives) in Estonia to highlight how 'care-full' collective farming practices can improve mental, physical and spiritual health. Indeed, an holistic 'care economy' fits well with degrowth literature advocating political autonomy, horizontalism and 'the commons'. Defying notions of private property, 'commoning' refers to "acts of mutual support, conflict, negotiation, communication and experimentation that are needed to create systems to manage shared resources" (Bollier 2016: 2). For example, Szakal and Balázs (2021) describe the exchange of knowledge and skills in living labs in Budapest where collective efforts employ 'co-creation' – a democratic, participatory and creative process to unite people to adapt degrowth ideas to local conditions.

But such principles can prove difficult to put into practice. Homs et al. (2021) critically consider gendered roles in degrowth cases of community supported agriculture (CSA) to find that traditional gender stereotypes and divisions of labour are hard to transform. Scaling up degrowth networks is also challenging. For example, Edwards and

Espelt (2021) draw on Kerschner et al. (2018) to ask if technology in CSAs in Catalonia is viable, feasible, convivial and appropriate to retain their goals. Alternatively, polycentric, participatory and/or multi-level governance approaches are implemented to enable equitable participation in decision-making processes, as in Edwards et al. (2021), who explore multi-level food governance in international projects to enable diverse groups to reflect and embrace opportunities across different sectors.

Future research directions for food for degrowth

Degrowth principles and practices challenge "social imaginaries of how economies and societies should work" and "the political–economic structures that uphold and reproduce these imaginaries" (Lara et al. 2023: 1) presenting opportunities for further research. Current research prioritises social and economic analyses rather than ecological research and impacts; focusing on small-scale food gardening rather than larger agricultural applications; and singular, local case studies. Of course, small and local priorities fit with degrowth approaches but it is necessary to extend into more comparative research, including non-monetary food economies and emerging degrowth food chains from farming to value-adding, distribution and consumption. Similarly, Lara et al. (2023) call for more investigations of sites within the Global South, of decolonisation approaches (which sometimes align with, and other times challenge, degrowth approaches), and policy-oriented research. Greater understanding of how food for degrowth could contribute to other sectors, disciplines and movements would also benefit understandings of the transformational capacity of food for degrowth as a social movement.

References

Bollier D (2016) Commoning as a transformative social paradigm: the next system project. https://thenextsystem.org/sites/ default/files/2017-08/DavidBollier.pdf (Accessed 30 May 2023).

D'Alisa G, Demaria F and Kallis G (2014) *Degrowth: A Vocabulary for a New Era*. Abingdon, Routledge.

Edwards F (2016) Alternative Food Networks. In: Thompson P and Kaplan D (eds) *Encyclopaedia of Food and Agricultural Ethics*. New York, Springer, pp. 1–7.

Edwards F and Espelt R (2021) Technology for degrowth: implementing digital platforms for community supported agriculture. In: Nelson A and Edwards F (eds) *Food for Degrowth*. London, Routledge, pp. 128–140.

Edwards F, Pedro S, and Rocha S (2021) Institutionalising degrowth? Exploring multi-level food governance. In: Nelson A and Edwards F (eds) *Food for Degrowth*. London, Routledge, pp. 141–145.

Homs P, Flores-Pons G and Mayor Adrià M (2021) Sustaining caring livelihoods: agroecological cooperativism in Catalonia. In: Nelson A and Edwards F (eds) *Food for Degrowth*. London, Routledge, pp. 100–112.

Jones P and Ulman M (2021) Replacing growth with belonging economies: a neopeasant response. In: Nelson A and Edwards F (eds) *Food for Degrowth*. London, Routledge, pp. 19–32.

Kerschner C, Wächter P, Nierling L and Ehlers M H (2018) Degrowth and technology: towards feasible, viable, appropriate and convivial imaginaries. *Journal of Cleaner Production* 197, pp. 1619–1636.

Lara L G, van Oers L, Smessaert J, Spanier J, Raj G and Feola G (2023) Degrowth and agri-food systems: a research agenda for the critical social sciences. *Sustainability Science* 18(4), 1–16. https://doi.org/10.1007/s11625-022-01276-y

Nelson A and Edwards F (eds) (2021) *Food for Degrowth: Perspectives and Practices*. London, Routledge.

Pungas L (2021) Caring dachas: food self-provisioning in Eastern Europe through the lens of care. In: Nelson A and Edwards F (eds) *Food for Degrowth*. London, Routledge, pp. 59–74.

Szakál D and Balázs B (2021) Co-creation for transformation: food for degrowth in Budapest Food City Lab initiatives. In: Nelson A and Edwards F (eds) *Food for Degrowth*. London, Routledge, pp. 115–127.

Further reading

Nelson A and Edwards F (eds) (2021) *Food for Degrowth: Perspectives and Practices.* London and New York, Routledge.
This edited collection explores degrowth exemplars in a range of geographic, practical and theoretical contexts along the food chain in spheres of the household, collectives, networks and narratives of broader food activism and discourses.

Schmelzer M, Vansintjan A and Vetter A (2022) *The Future is Degrowth: A Guide to a World Beyond Capitalism.* Brooklyn and London, Verso.
A sound introduction to degrowth theory and activism and the political economy critique of growth, and a constructive degrowth manifesto.

FERNE EDWARDS AND ANITRA NELSON

31. Development and food

Nicholas Nisbett

Development and food – a brief history

Ensuring people have access to adequate and diverse diets and realising their right to food is one of the most basic human needs. As such, food has always been strongly tied to both development studies and development practice, with many aid and international development agencies and NGOs still focused on ending famine and hunger. At the end of the 18th century the English demographer and economist Thomas Malthus set out a theory of how population growth would outstrip food production, leading to famine. Such thinking – never far from racist ideologies of population control – was married to imperial interests to extract wealth in the form of food and other basic commodities from countries colonised by European powers. This set in motion a number of geopolitical trends that are still present today in the many intertwined global flows of food, capital, and ideologies of the food system.

The post-war development institutions of the United Nations (UN) were designed to avoid some of the worst excesses of the 19th and 20th century famines and to help to meet growing demand from food in the majority world, but they also helped export a particular model of agri-food development to the former colonies. Imperial-led efforts to develop agricultural sectors gave way to state-led efforts but still supported by former colonial powers and by the growing power of the US. Ensuring food security in the newly independent states was seen as a bulkhead against communism and so an alliance formed between humanitarian and geopolitical interests, leveraging support by large philanthropic donors such as Rockefeller and the Ford Foundation.

Scholars focusing on 20th-century developments in the food system have characterised the key forces shaping the food system as state-led industrialisation and global market expansion, agricultural trade liberalisation, corporate concentration, and financial speculation on commodity markets (Clapp, 2020; Friedmann & McMichael, 1989). The post-war domestic food security and economic concerns of the US and the European powers structured global markets through unfair trading and subsidy arrangements. The EU's Common Agricultural Policy, for example, protected domestic (EU) producers with high subsidies and import taxes (tariffs) while encouraging low cost imports from favoured former colonies. Similar arrangements in the US (particularly subsidies) shaped humanitarian flows of international food aid, where domestic surpluses (over-production due to high subsidies) were dumped on world markets, also encouraged by the EU in the form of export subsidies. Meanwhile, 'green revolution' biotechnologies and research such as high-yielding crops and the fertilisers and irrigation needed to realise such yields were exported as part of aid packages to help increase agricultural production, but they also exported a model of fossil fuel and input heavy agricultural systems with significant environmental consequences.

A fundamental change in the global outlook in food has also occurred over the past two decades, prompted not only by these original concerns with hunger and undernutrition, but also by multiple interrelated and emerging crises of catastrophic biodiversity loss, the climate emergency, and growing risks to human health of a food system rigged to deliver unhealthy food. While development funding has arguably helped raise yields, the types of agri-food systems promoted by international development funding are also deeply implicated in all three crises. Such industrialised diets are linked with global increases in non-communicable, diet-related diseases such as diabetes, heart disease, and some cancers, and are now amongst the leading causes of death globally. Not only have these new crises emerged, but the focus of food systems on increasing production at all costs has arguably failed to counter chronic hunger and acute famine at multiple points in time. This is illustrated by continuing crises in the Sahel, the Horn of Africa, and elsewhere, but also illustrated by growing levels of hunger and food insecurity in wealthy parts of North America and Europe.

Alongside this persistence of hunger and famine, nutritional epidemiologists have charted a global dietary transition, in which a dietary shift – or 'nutrition transition' – occurs alongside the classic demographic transition, from (counter to Malthus) a situation of scarcity to a situation of abundance of food, particularly unhealthy foods high in energy content and low in nutritional content. More recently, this trend has been labelled as a 'double-' or a 'triple-burden' of malnutrition, where hunger and overweight/obesity can exist simultaneously in the same communities or families, or even an individual over a lifetime (Popkin et al., 2020).

In Guatemala, for example, in the latest survey data available in 2020, 26% of households included a woman or child with the status of being overweight and either a child with wasting/stunting or a woman too thin for her height (Popkin et al. 2020, supplementary materials: 22). The reasons for this depend greatly on poverty, marginalisation, and a lack of political power, but also cannot be separated from the role played by a rapidly industrialising Central American food system, now integrated with the US and Mexico via various Free Trade Agreements , in making unhealthy food so widely available at the cost of more nutritious diets and culinary traditions.

Development and food – rural and urban agendas

As well as focusing on the 'bigger picture' of global trends in diet and hunger, much work on food and development has been based on empirical work in a village or urban setting. Work within the critical agrarian studies (CAS) tradition, for example, has offered an important perspective on the development of rural food systems, focusing on Marx's 'agrarian question'. This considered how small-scale rural producers, many surviving via forms of subsistence or various forms of servitude to landowners, would ultimately be integrated into the capitalist system – i.e. how would the surplus value they produced through their labour be expropriated by others in more 'modern' systems and in turn how would that influence rural power relations? Similar questions have also been raised (not always within a CAS framing) of political economy, or who wins and who loses, from the types of agricultural commercialisation that have been advocated by international development agencies. In many countries, both rural and urban livelihoods have been transformed as production, retail, and consumption are incorporated into global systems. This has benefited larger agricultural and food producers – and arguably urban consumers – but at the expense of those who have exited agriculture and lost jobs and

land without decent alternative livelihoods to move to (Alobo Loison, 2015).

Perhaps because of this traditional focus on agricultural producers, urban agriculture and food systems have been neglected in much food and development policy and research (Haysom & Battersby, forthcoming). But while there might be lively forms of food production in urban settings, most urban consumers are reliant on food that is purchased, or exchanged or provided by the state or NGOs (such as subsidised food or school meals). Research on food environments – including retail and marketing – or the governance of food in urban settings, has also become an important area of research and has been linked to issues of food rights (and in some cases urban food riots), infrastructure, and broader questions of providing food for burgeoning urban populations.

Food justice, gender and intersectional equity in relation to development

A traditional focus on the needs of farmers and food producers has perhaps also outweighed attention to the needs of the food system workforce more broadly and the common problems that they face across urban and rural, production and consumption settings. Such issues might include casualisation and other aspects of financial precarity; poor wages and working conditions, including bondage and forms of slavery; the abuse of migrant workers; the health consequences of physical labour and exposure to harmful working conditions in fields/fishing vessels, factories, and retail environments; and an absence of, or a suppression of, labour rights and organised labour including trades unions.

Such factors tend to affect women more, particularly migrant women, who may earn less, have less access to formal employment or recourse in the event of a dispute, or be less likely to be supported by a trades union, in some settings, than their male counterparts. The role of gender in the broader food system has also been an important topic of study, with a large body of research concluding that in food producing regions, women are more disadvantaged than men in terms of access to a range of factors that affect livelihoods and income, from land and water rights; to finance and other inputs; to access to government led programmes, education, information, and rural agricultural extension programmes ; to programme design; to decision making within families, communities, and wider political and institutional control (Kabeer, 1999). A focus only on gender, however, can obscure other axes of difference such as caste, 'race' and ethnicity, indigeneity, disability, gender orientation, and sexuality, which are likely to lead to similar or compounded forms of discrimination and marginalisation whether in food production or access to food, including through government social protection, and food and health programmes.

Modes of resistance to the global food system and alternative pathways

Peasant movements and farmers' organisations have offered strong resistance to capitalist/industrial agriculture, in some cases drawing on earlier anti-colonial, revolutionary, or indigenous struggles. Civil society opposition coalesced and strengthened in the wake of trade deals such as NAFTA and the 2004 Uruguay Round deal at the World Trade Organization (WTO) and thus formed part of a larger, anti-globalisation backlash. Food sovereignty, or the right of self-determination in terms of healthy, culturally appropriate, and ecologically sound food has been an important discourse of resistance within more mainstream food system approaches. But it has not been without its critics, who have pointed to some of the naïve localism or romanticisation of the peasantry (Bernstein, 2014), which might disregard existing rural dynamics and power structures, including entrenched patriarchy. Nevertheless, food sovereignty remains a uniting call for many different civil society and other actors opposed to mainstream industrial agriculture and has spurred many productive debates about the need for a more fundamental transformation of the food system redrawn along agroecological principles.

Indigenous ways of knowing and being in a more interconnected relationship with other species and ecologies may present a more coherent ontology from which to envision a more sustainable future. The Quechuan Andean principle of *Ayllu*, or self-governance, for example, exemplifies these concerns in a spirit of self-determination rooted in interconnectivity with the land: "Ayllu is a community and we all share the same interests and objectives linked through shared norms and principles with respect to humans, animals, spirits, mountains, lakes, rivers, pastures, food crops, and wild life – we are all interconnected" (Huambachano, 2018: 1017). That these principles seem well aligned with agroecology has been noted by Huambachano and other Indigenous scholars, signalling, again, that a fundamental shift towards a food system drawing from agroecological values is likely to be a key part of discussions over the next couple of decades, though something that continues to draw strong resistance from the many vested interests in the global food economy.

Transforming food systems and food transitions: emerging issues

What people eat, whether in Majority or Minority World settings, has huge impacts on climate, biodiversity, labour, and justice in ways that echo around the global food system. The EAT-Lancet commission, for example, has advocated a reference diet of "a diversity of plant-based foods, low amounts of animal source foods, unsaturated rather than saturated fats, and small amounts of refined grains, highly processed foods and added sugars (Willett et al., 2019: 1). This and other similar reports' singling out of the impact of intensively reared meat on both land-use and climate has attracted controversy, as although most commentators agree on the need to significantly reduce industrialised meat consumption in the minority world (so-called 'demeatification'), this may not be the case in many parts of the Majority World, where there is lower than optimal access to animal source foods or the nutrients provided by these foods (Beal et al., 2023). Others have criticised the lack of nuance in terms of the failure to recognise that traditional livelihoods such as pastoralism are well suited to providing ecosystem services over extensive rangelands (such as in Eastern Africa) (Houzer & Scoones, 2021), while aggregated figures on emissions based on life cycle analysis drawn from industrial farming are likely to overstate the climate impact of extensive systems.

Despite calls to deal with these multiple facets or failings of food systems at national and global levels, there is a sense in which the global food system has been lurching from crisis to crisis of late. Where it once seemed that food and agriculture had been absorbed into the 'Washington consensus' of the 1980s (where the World Bank and the International Monetary Fund were advocating cuts to government services and it was assumed that economic growth would simply 'trickle-down' to poor people), the 2007 to 2008 food price crisis placed food firmly back onto the international development agenda, leading to, amongst other things, the reinvigoration of the UN Committee on Food Security (CFS). But despite this renewed attention and a number of food-related targets in the globally agreed UN Sustainable Development Goals (SDGs) sufficient progress to a more sustainable, equitable, and healthy food system has not taken place.

Alarmingly, many of the major global institutions tasked with overseeing and guiding the global food system are only paying lip-service to such broader concerns and still find it hard to switch themselves from a Malthusian modus operandi (of increasing yields at whatever cost) to systems that balance equity, sustainability, and health considerations alongside the need to meet growing demand (Béné, 2022). The 2021 UN Food Systems' Summit was convened to try to bring together different interests in food, sustainability, and nutrition, partly as an attempt to move beyond narrowly focused agri-food and productionist agends. However, the summit has been heavily criticised for its lack of attention to genuine participation and because it offered a platform for big food to influence the emerging policy agenda under the name of 'multistakeholderism' (Canfield et al., 2021).

Future work on global food and development, whether in the CFS or in other fora, will need to firmly tackle issues that may or may not look like traditional food system concerns, including resolving trade-offs between food production, livelihoods and equity, biodiversity and climate change, and the position of food security in international trading arrangements (HLPE, 2023). Given the likelihood of capital intensive systems remaining in place for some time, in addition to debates on the transition to agroecological and alternative food production systems, research and activism on other issues will be important too, including: labour rights, social protection, and other redistributive measures, such as land reform, and a broader focus on the drivers of inequity and injustice in food systems, including colonialism, racism, patriarchy, and neoliberalism.

References

Alobo Loison, S (2015) Rural livelihood diversification in sub-Saharan Africa: A literature review. *The Journal of Development Studies, 51*(9), 1125–1138. https://doi.org/10.1080/00220388.2015.1046445

Beal, T, Gardner, C D, Herrero, M, Iannotti, L L, Merbold, L, Nordhagen, S, & Mottet, A (2023) Friend or foe? The role of animal-source foods in healthy and environmentally sustainable diets. *The Journal of Nutrition, 153*(2), 409–425. https://doi.org/10.1016/j.tjnut.2022.10.016

Béné, C (2022) Why the Great Food Transformation may not happen: A deep-dive into our food systems' political economy, controversies and politics of evidence. *World Development, 154*, 105881. https://doi.org/10.1016/j.worlddev.2022.105881

Bernstein, H (2014) Food sovereignty via the 'peasant way': A sceptical view. *Journal of Peasant Studies, 41*(6), 1031–1063. https://doi.org/10.1080/03066150.2013.852082

Canfield, M, Anderson, M D, & McMichael, P (2021) UN Food Systems Summit 2021: Dismantling democracy and resetting corporate control of food systems. *Frontiers in Sustainable Food Systems, 5*(103). https://doi.org/10.3389/fsufs.2021.661552

Clapp, J (2020) *Food.* Cambridge: Polity Press.

Friedmann, H, & McMichael, P (1989) Agriculture and the state system: The rise and decline of national agricultures, 1870 to the present. *Sociologia Ruralis, 29*, 93–117. https://doi.org/10.1111/j.1467-9523.1989.tb00360.x

Haysom, G, & Battersby, J (forthcoming) Cities and food systems governance: Toward a realistic model for transformation. In Resnick, D & Swinnen, J (eds.) *Political Economy of Food System Transformation.* Oxford: Oxford University Press.

HLPE (2023) *Reducing Inequalities for Food Security and Nutrition. High Level Panel of Experts on Food Security and Nutrition, United Nations Committee on Food Security, Report No.18.* Rome: FAO.

Houzer, E, & Scoones, I (2021) Are livestock always bad for the planet? Rethinking the protein transition and climate change

debate. Brighton: PASTRES. https://doi
.org/10.19088/STEPS.2021.003

Huambachano, M (2018) Enacting food
sovereignty in Aotearoa New Zealand and
Peru: Revitalizing Indigenous knowledge,
food practices and ecological philosophies.
*Agroecology and Sustainable Food
Systems, 42*(9), 1003–1028. https://doi.org
/10.1080/21683565.2018.1468380

Kabeer, N (1999) Resources, agency,
achievements: Reflections on the
measurement of women's empowerment.
Development and Change, 30(3), 435–464.
https://doi.org/10.1111/1467-7660.00125

Popkin, B M, Corvalan, C, & Grummer-
Strawn, L M (2020) Dynamics of the
double burden of malnutrition and
the changing nutrition reality. *Lancet,
395*(10217), 65–74. https://doi.org/10.1016/
s0140-6736(19)32497-3

Willett, W, Rockström, J, Loken, B,
Springmann, M, Lang, T, Vermeulen, S, ... &
Wood, A (2019) Food in the Anthropocene:
The EAT–Lancet Commission on healthy
diets from sustainable food systems. *The
Lancet, 393*(10170), 447–492. https://doi
.org/10.1016/S0140-6736(18)31788-4

Further reading

Clapp, J (2020) *Food.* Cambridge: Polity
Press.

This is an easily accessible introduction to
the global food system and some of the
environmental, social, and economic
challenges that have emerged over the
course of the 20th and 21st centuries,
particularly in relation to the geopolitics of
food trade and subsidies, financialisaton,
and broader governance issues.

Leach, M, Nisbett, N, Cabral, L, Harris,
J, Hossain, N, & Thompson, J (2020)
Food politics and development. *World
Development*, 134, 105024. https://doi.org
/10.1016/j.worlddev.2020.105024

This is a broad review of research and
thinking on global food politics and
development, covering work on food
regimes, pervasive knowledge regimes
of science and technology in agri-food
development, research on rural livelihoods,
culture, diets, and nutrition.

Patel, R (2013) The long green revolution. *The
Journal of Peasant Studies, 40*(1), 1–63.
https://doi.org/10.1080/03066150.2012
.719224

A lengthy article, but well worth the long
read for the overview of 20th-century agri-
food development and the historical roots
of mainstream approaches to food and
development today.

NICHOLAS NISBETT

32. Digitalisation and food

TANIA LEWIS AND HELEN ADDISON-SMITH

Introduction: from Insta food to drone farming

Over the past decade, our food practices—from grocery shopping and home cookery to restaurant going, food production, and distribution—have become increasingly entangled with and reshaped by the wider world of digital media and technology. Digital technology and platforms now permeate nearly every aspect of our engagement with food, from media and communication channels like YouTube, social media, and apps, to technological applications such as serving robots, 3D food, QR codes, and agricultural drones).

For consumers, digital food may conjure up images of food influencers, food ordering through online platforms, or the plethora of instructional content on how to prepare food. For restaurateurs, digitalisation touches every aspect of their work—from the growing use of digital equipment in the kitchen, to the ever-present anxiety over negative online reviews, to the daily demands of digital marketing. For farmers, digitalisation might evoke the rise of direct-to-consumer websites , the integration of technologies like drones and sensors that enable digitally monitored food production, and the emergence of online communities of practice among producers.

We face global challenges around the climate emergency, food security, food waste, extended food supply chains, and the impact of industrial agriculture on the environment. While the growing role of digital technology in the food system presents new challenges, it also holds potential for fostering progressive alternatives.

The growing role of digitalisation across the food system: impacts on food and society

Digital technology and associated media now play a role in every aspect of the food system, a transformation that has largely unfolded under the radar, often beyond state regulation, and heavily shaped by powerful corporate interests. At the same time, we are witnessing the emergence of digital practices that challenge agri-business as usual, from open-source tools that support farmers, to community-based direct-to-consumer networks, and digital apps that enable people to assess the ethical credentials of food products. How can we understand the ways in which the digital turn across society and the economy is shaping how we grow, deliver, consume, and ultimately discard or reuse food? What concerns arise from the central role that digital media and technologies now play within the food system?

A range of significant debates have been raised by the role of digitalisation in the foodscape. A key concern is around power and the centralisation of control. The evolution of the internet from web 2.0 to web 3.0 has sparked debates about the potential for decentralised, blockchain-style systems versus the current reality, which is an internet whose interactivity and participatory capacities are constrained by the dominance of large corporate players. While the global food system reflects a rich diversity of local practices and traditions, it is also increasingly shaped by the influence of powerful multinational corporations. For these latter players food is a commodity like any other product. These corporations typically prioritise cost-cutting across production, supply and distribution often leading to extended global food chains and the exploitation of local producers, farmers and the environment. In this context, digitalisation can end up reinforcing the power of Big Food.

The rise of digitalisation in farming, however, is not all doom and gloom. Digital connectivity creates new opportunities for small-scale farmers and food producers to scale up and collabore. For example, farmers are using platforms like the Open Food Network to connect directly to consumers, shortening food chains and encouraging engagement with whole, unpackaged (often dirt covered) primary produce. The growing popularity of food box schemes which limit consumer choice and often require and often require a seasonal commitment --begins to challenge the more farmer-unfriendly extremes of free-market food capitalism.

In the hospitality and consumer space, processes of digitalisation have similarly wrought huge transformations in recent years. Restaurant chefs find themselves designing menus and dishes as much for Uber Eats and Instagram as they do for in-house customers.

Advances in digital temperature control have enabled new culinary techniques and flavour developments, including sous vide cooking (using vacuum-sealed bags) and dehydration methods.. Meanwhile the rise of online food delivery platforms and apps has seen a transformation not only in household eating and purchasing practices but also in the ebbs and flows of city life, where food delivery drivers are now a taken for granted fixture. Much of this shift has been driven by convenience, with online food deliveries soaring during (and since) the Covid-19 pandemic , and reshaping expectations and experiences for food consumers. The downside of convenience, however, isincludes the piles of food packaging generated by deliveries. . Additionally, a growing body of critical literature highlights concerns around exploitative labour conditions faced by delivery drivers and those food workers labouring behind the scenes in so-called 'dark kitchens'.

The messy future of digital food

The digital economy's affordances amplify central tensions in the politics of food. While social mediadespite being advertising driven-can empower alternative food movements by raising the visibility of local food production and promoting the consumption of 'good food', digital logistics and distribution platforms simultaneously reinforce the dominance of extended, exploitative and environmentally harmful supply chains linked toh large agri-food corporations. Such long food chains rely on food being processed into stable, transportable commodities. Consequently, most food consumers are increasingly unfamiliar with unprocessed food,--a trend intensified by digitalisation--while the loss of skills to grow and cook food becomes more deeply entrenched. Everyday cooking practices are thus increasingly shaped not by athe direct experience of tasting or touching food, but by digital images of food.

The messy, sticky and variable materiality of food cannot be fully captured or explained through digital media, though platforms like YouTube and TikTok are filled with valiant attempts to do just that. Such content can certainly democratise access to food knowledge, and foreground important ethical and environmental issues surrounding food. However, digital culture by and large largely presents images of ease and beauty, often glossing

over critical issues like waste and labour conditions. Which leaves us with the question: can the dirty, messy and imperfect realities of food production and consumption find a place within the digital realm? What would it take to foster a digital food culture that makes these inconvenient truths visible, helping us take a meaningful step towards a more just and sustainable food system? By drawing on the collaborative and sharing practices of online alternative food movements, we can begin to imagine a range of counterscenarios--such as a food and data sharing ecology grounded in the ethos of the commons, supported by cooperative digital infrastructures designed for connectivity and sharing.

References

Feldman Z and Goodman M K (2021) Digital food culture, power and everyday life. *European Journal of Cultural Studies* 24, 1227–1242. https://doi.org/10.1177%2F13675494211055501

Goodman D (2023) *Transforming Agriculture and Foodways: The Digital-Molecular Convergence.* Bristol, Bristol University Press.

Harvey F (2022) The dominance of a small number of big companies over the global food chain is increasing, aided by the rising use of "big data" and artificial intelligence, new research has found. https://www.theguardian.com/business/2022/sep/22/small-number-of-huge-companies-dominate-global-food-chain-study-finds

Lewis T (2020) *Digital Food: From Paddock to Platform.* London, Bloomsbury.

Lupton D (2020) Understanding Digital Food Cultures. In: Lupton D and Feldman Z (eds) *Digital Food Cultures.* London, Routledge, pp. 1–16.

Schneider T, Eli K, Dolan C and Ulijaszek S J (eds) (2018) *Digital Food Activism.* London, Routledge.

Further reading

Lewis T (2020) *Digital Food: From Paddock to Platform.* London, Bloomsbury.
This accessible and comprehensive book provides an introduction and in-depth treatment of digital food politics through an analysis of the tensions around digital engagement in increasingly commercialised spaces, the changing nature of politics in a social media context, the growing

naturalisation of digital devices and data monitoring, and the role and impact of digitalisation on social relations.

TANIA LEWIS AND HELEN ADDISON-SMITH

33. Diverse food economies

ERIC SARMIENTO

Introduction: homogenisation and differentiation in food systems

Since the Industrial Revolution of the 19th century, the economic structure of food production, distribution, and consumption has exhibited two countervailing tendencies: increased consolidation, homogenisation, and globalisation accompanied by continuous diversification, differentiation, and spatiotemporal reorganisation. Arguably, these trends are mutually constitutive, and while the relationships between them are complex, a principal theme in scholarship on food and society concerns the ways in which the socio-ecological, cultural, and political economic problems associated with conventional food systems can lead people to seek more just, sustainable, and desirable alternatives. A wide range of 'alternative food networks' (AFNs) and concomitant economic relationships demonstrate this trend in recent decades, from community supported agriculture to fair trade, retail cooperatives, slow food, and many others. Taken together, the proliferation of alternative food initiatives suggests that the more monolithic food systems become, the more they create both the need and the opportunities for differentiation and experimentation. As a result, food practices and food economies continue to diversify in the face of – and to an extent *because of* – the homogenising aspects of conventional food systems.

It is also important to note that, despite its extensive reach, what might be called the 'conventionalisation' of food systems remains spatially uneven and politically and economically fragile. In many areas of the world, and especially in parts of the Global South, foodways have not been highly mechanised, commoditised, or reorganised around capitalist economic principles. In such instances, people often actively resist attempts by conventional food system actors to capture and transform existing foodways, and engage in political struggles to protect food sovereignty and assert their right to self-determination. Thus, while capitalist food systems continuously strive to enclose and restructure noncapitalist foodways around the planet, this process frequently meets resistance at its expanding edges, even as alternatives multiply within the well-established centres of conventional food systems in the Global North.

The dynamic interactions between homogenisation and differentiation in food systems and foodways produce a diverse array of economic practices, relationships, and structures operating at different geographical scales. Food scholars and practitioners have worked to understand these diverse food economies, accumulating a wealth of empirical observations about ever-changing food economies and developing a range of theoretical and conceptual resources for analysis. In many respects, scholarship on diverse food economies reflects ideas and debates in broader scholarly discussions of political economy and economic diversity, where different theoretical frameworks and socio-political perspectives produce divergent interpretations of economic realities. From a neoliberal or market-oriented viewpoint, for example, the removal of barriers to trade and the elimination of agricultural subsidies are understood to encourage investment and support the 'modernisation' of food systems, which in turn is thought to increase efficiency, resulting in greater volumes of food production, potentially lowering prices, and so on. This interpretation of course mirrors the mainstream economic assumption that globalised 'free market' capitalism, though problematic, produces net benefits for humanity.

By contrast, scholars working with postcolonial theory or variants of Marxist political economic theory offer more critical assessments of capitalist expansion broadly and with respect to food systems in particular. Such accounts focus on the social and ecological tensions or contradictions of conventional food systems, raise questions about power, food justice, and equity, and investigate creative approaches to foodways that seek to depart from conventional norms. In other words, both conventional and alternative food economies have their scholarly and theoretical bases of support. Each of these scholarly and practical realms, moreover, is diverse in its own right. Critical scholarship on food economies, the focus of this entry, features a range of theoretical perspectives and empirical foci, the diversity of which is essential to understanding and supporting the rich tapestry of diverse food economies. This entry examines key themes related to diverse food economies, and explores the major debates among scholars, as well as the synergies between different perspectives on food and economic diversity.

Difference and dominance: economic diversity and a food politics of possibility

Theorising and researching economic diversity in food studies

There is a longstanding tradition of scholarship and policy research examining food economies in systemic terms, i.e. as exhibiting observable characteristics and relatively predictable, widespread patterns. The more critical strands of such research are often rooted in Marxian political economic theory, and have historically emphasised the *production* side of food economies. This has entailed examining processes such as technological development and its impacts on agricultural labour dynamics, regulatory regimes, state subsidies for agriculture, and national and international trade agreements, and their relationships to changing geopolitical contexts, farm consolidation, agro-industrial integration, and so on (Fine 1994; Goodman et al. 1987). With the 'cultural turn' of the 1980s to the 1990s, researchers expanded their analyses to encompass not only production but also distribution, retail and marketing, and consumption, integrating political economy frameworks with various types of cultural and social investigation. 'Modes of capitalist regulation', for instance, implied not just regulatory control of markets and industrial sectors but also apparatuses of social control. Working in this vein, sociologists and geographers studied the extent to which food economies were 'embedded' in social relations (Winter 2003). In political ecology, food economies were understood as the contingent result of political economic dynamics and nature–society interactions unfolding across multiple scales (Blaikie and Brookfield 1987). And food supply chain, or 'commodity chain' analyses traced the political economic and socio-ecological implications of specific food products from 'upstream' inputs such as seeds and fertilisers to marketing and consumption 'downstream' (Marsden et al. 2000). This vital research is ongoing, and provides invaluable insight into what might be thought of as largely top-down processes shaping food economies across space and time.

By the 1990s, however, responses to corporate, globalised food economies were proliferating, including organic agriculture, fair trade, state sponsored certification programmes to protect distinctive regional food products and cultures, retail cooperatives, and many other approaches that sought to provide alternatives to or bulwarks against conventional food systems. While such experiments initially met with scholarly and popular enthusiasm, critical research soon revealed a series of problems with AFNs: in the Global North, they tend to be realms of elite consumption that exclude more moderately resourced people and communities of colour, even playing roles in the displacement of such communities through urban and rural gentrification; they often rest on romanticised notions of 'nature', 'tradition', 'the local', and 'small family farms', obscuring more difficult questions about labour relations and scalability; they are prone to co-optation and annihilation by corporate food system actors; and they frequently reinforce neoliberal ideology by privileging individual consumption habits and well-being over collective forms of political struggle against systemic injustices (cf. Alkon 2012; Allen and Guthman 2006; Guthman 2014). Much of the critical scholarship on AFNs can be broadly said to focus on the ways in which conventional food system actors constrain the capacities of these alternatives to transform food systems writ large.

However, critical assessments of AFNs were complicated by scholars drawing on research in economic geography led by post-structural feminist geographer J.K. Gibson-Graham. While retaining a critical stance towards capitalist economics, Gibson-Graham combined Marxist theories of surplus value with deconstruction, discourse analysis, and other post-structural methods to argue that, while economic formations might be dominated by one mode of production or another, they are constituted by a diverse array of economic relationships (Gibson-Graham 1996). Non-commoditised domestic labour, for example, produces tremendous surplus value but is generally not measured or acknowledged as part of 'the economy' in most countries. This type of labour relation, which might be considered feudalist under a Marxist rubric, sits alongside innumerable non-capitalist relationships and practices, from gift giving to volunteering, charitable donations, and redistributive social programmes. Such economic diversity, in Gibson-Graham's view, is obscured by a fixation on capital – 'capitalocentrism', as they called it – that characterises both mainstream and Marxian economic analysis and policy. Capitalist hegemony can thus be inadvertently reinforced (discursively, at least) by even the most stridently critical research. In food studies, a number of scholars followed Gibson-Graham's lead, challenging analyses that were seen to prematurely dismiss AFNs as quixotic, duped by if not inherently part of neoliberalism, and doomed to fail.

Food scholarship informed by 'diverse economies' theory has several foci. Shedding light upon and valorising diverse food economies is paramount, as this disrupts representations of conventional food systems as inexorably expanding across the planet alongside corporate capitalism, crushing all forms of resistance and erasing all difference. Much of this disruptive work relies on the analytical stance, drawn from queer theory, of 'reading for difference instead of dominance'. In this approach, research is designed to foreground divergent and emergent phenomena, however marginal and seemingly ephemeral they may be relative to more hegemonic social and political economic structures. Thus, while community gardens, ethical trade certification schemes, food cooperatives, and other AFNs clearly face a host of challenges, they also present a wealth of knowledge and experience that is essential to systematic transformations of food economies (Sarmiento 2017). This research also emphasises questions of subjectivity, examining how people come to know and understand food, food systems, and their relationships to those systems (Harris 2009). While much critical food scholarship had hitherto tended to see AFNs as implicitly reinforcing neoliberal subject positions, diverse food economies scholars ask instead how researchers might work with research participants to explore other food subjectivities. Community-based and participatory action research are common in this work, which rests on an ethos of positioning the researcher *within* – and therefore in some sense *responsible to* – the phenomena being studied rather than as an outside observer. Its practitioners argue that such work embraces a food politics of possibility, rather than a politics of closure, failure, and resentment.

Counter-critiques of post-structuralist diverse food economies research see 'reading for difference' as a refusal to account for often vast power disparities between conventional food system actors and the proponents of AFNs. What hope do AFNs have of effecting widespread change, these scholars ask, without sufficient understanding of the structural dynamics that actively constrain such initiatives? While differences between Marxist and post-Marxist understandings of diverse food economies are important, it must be said that these approaches are designed to achieve different objectives. At risk of oversimplification, we might say that one approach focuses on the ongoing emergence of difference and the other on persistent relations of dominance. Seen in this light, these approaches are perhaps more complementary than antagonistic.

Subaltern diverse food economies: justice, sovereignty, and anti-colonialist food knowledges

While much of the research on diverse food economies and AFNs has been preoccupied with debates about the food practices of predominantly white and relatively affluent groups in the Global North, it is important to note that diverse food economies are ubiquitous among communities of colour, Indigenous peoples, rural dwellers, and other moderately resourced groups around the world (Cameron and Wright 2014). For members of these groups, economic diversity in food practices is often not a narrow response to problems with conventional food systems per se, but part of broader struggles to live well in the face of systemic marginalisation and oppression. For example, Black rural agrarian cooperatives emerged in the southern United States in the mid-20th century in response to voter suppression, land dispossession, and white supremacist terror campaigns (White 2018). In urban settings marked by racial segregation and inequitable food access, Black foodways are often an important part of cultivating community resilience (Reese 2019). For Indigenous peoples, food praxis can be tied to efforts to protect political sovereignty, attend to community health, and ensure cultural survival (Mihesuah and Hoover 2019). Agrarian reform movements in Latin America – mass uprisings with long histories – fight for food systems founded on collective land holding and governance, a radical departure from the social and political economic imaginaries of most alternative food initiatives in the Global North (Wright and Wolford 2003).

Taken together, what might be called subaltern diverse food economies foreground questions of justice, equity, sovereignty, and resistance to systemic oppression as integral to environmental goals and concerns with cultural preservation, food quality, and health. While the struggles of the landless movement in Brazil, for instance, might seem very different from those of urban food justice advocates in post-industrial Detroit – and it is important to not gloss over the distinctions between such contexts – there is common cause between these wide-ranging movements when they are understood as fighting against centuries of white settler colonialism and the ongoing global expansion of European colonial worldviews (Grey and Patel 2015). Just as importantly (if not more so), subaltern diverse food economies tend to be fighting for not only more diverse food economies, but for a world in which diverse lifeways and different ways of knowing can peacefully coexist. Subaltern diverse food economies, in other words, can be tied to profoundly different views of human progress and development agendas (Woods 2017). This calls attention to the need for both Marxist and post-Marxist theorists of diverse food economies to critically interrogate the colonialist inheritance of continental and Anglophone social and political theory, and shift their efforts to learning from and with the 'epistemologies of the South' (de Sousa Santos 2018).

Diverse food economies and contested futures

The entanglements of conventional and alternative food economies with a variety of broader political struggles are ongoing, suggesting that food praxes will continue to diversify and evolve, shaped by many factors. The pressures that the global climate emergency places on environments and societies also impact food systems in multiple ways, and this is likely to be a growing area of research in diverse food economies. It seems likely that a diverse array of approaches to food provisioning makes for a more resilient food system, and thus further exploration of the linkages between diverse food economies and resilience and adaptation is vitally needed. Additionally, while it remains uncertain at the time of writing whether the SARS-CoV-2 virus had zoonotic origins, the 2020 global COVID-19 pandemic is only the latest in a long series of health challenges that call into question the ways that human/more-than-human relationships are configured by contemporary food systems. These public health concerns sit alongside profound transformations in understandings of human health linked to growing awareness of our existential dependence on the human microbiome. This paradigm shift in health and medicine has important implications for the (micro)biopolitics of food, which will intersect with diverse food economies in various ways (Sarmiento 2020).

Questions of scaling up AFNs and warding off co-optation persist. Additional exploration of these questions will require continued theoretical development and experimentation with practical interventions at all scales. Moreover, current disconnects between relatively privileged and subaltern diverse food economies deserve not only critique but also repair and constructive experimentation in search of mutual benefit and the cultivation of solidarities between people engaged in different kinds of political struggles in wide-ranging contexts. To be effective and just, such efforts will require all parties to question and rework the epistemological foundations of food practices and subjectivities. Diverse food economies across the globe, in other words, rest on diverse ways of knowing and making sense of the world. Scholars and advocates of diverse food economies must therefore continue to develop techniques and mechanisms to democratise not only food systems but also the systems of knowledge and meaning-making that support them. This applies to all phases of food provisioning, from production to distribution and consumption, as well as the multifarious fields of inquiry tied to food, such as public health, bioengineering, agroecology, and cultural anthropology, to name a few. If the planetary expansion of conventional food systems is underwritten by the colonialist epistemologies of the North, liberatory food praxes must be accompanied by the development of pluralistic modes of knowledge production capable of producing and disseminating hybrid knowledges. Novel food subjects and diverse food economies are perpetually emerging; the question is how to support these varied, nascent phenomena and collaborate with them to produce more just and livable food worlds.

ERIC SARMIENTO

References

Alkon, A. 2012. 'The socio-nature of local organic food.' *Antipode* 45:3, 663–680.

Allen, P. and Guthman, J. 2006. 'From "old school" to "farm-to-school": Neoliberalization from the ground-up.' *Agriculture and Human Values* 23, 401–415.

Blaikie, P. and Brookfield, H. 1987. *Land Degradation and Society*. New York: Taylor & Francis.

Cameron, J. and Wright, S. 2014. 'Researching diverse food initiatives: From backyard and community gardens to international markets: Editorial for special issue'. *Local Environment* 19:1, 1–9.

de Sousa Santos, B. 2018. *The End of the Cognitive Empire: The Coming of Age of the Epistemologies of the South*. Durham: Duke University Press.

Fine, B. 1994. 'Towards a political economy of food.' *Review of International Political Economy* 1:3, 519–545.

Gibson-Graham, J.K. 1996. *The End of Capitalism (As We Knew It): A Feminist Critique of Political Economy*. Minneapolis: University of Minnesota Press.

Goodman, D., Sorj, B., and Wilkinson, J. 1987. *From Farming to Biotechnology: A Theory of Agro-Industrial Development*. Oxford: Blackwell.

Grey, S. and Patel, R. 2015. 'Food sovereignty as decolonization: Some contributions from Indigenous movements to food system and development politics.' *Agriculture and Human Values* 32, 431–444.

Guthman, J. 2014. *Agrarian Dreams: The Paradox of Organic Farming in California*. 2nd Edition. Berkeley: University of California Press.

Harris, E. 2009. 'Neoliberal subjectivities or a politics of the possible? Reading for difference in alternative food networks.' *Area* 41:1, 55–63.

Marsden, T., Banks, J., and Bristow, G. 2000. 'Food supply chain approaches: Exploring their role in rural development.' *Sociologia Ruralis* 40:4, 424–438.

Mihesuah, D. and Hoover, E. (eds). 2019. *Indigenous Food Sovereignty in the United States: Restoring Cultural Knowledge, Protecting Environments, and Regaining Health*. Norman: University of Oklahoma Press.

Reese, A. 2019. *Black Food Geographies: Race, Self-Reliance, and Food Access in Washington, D.C.* Chapel Hill: University of North Carolina Press.

Sarmiento, E. 2017. 'Synergies in alternative food network research: Diverse economies, embodiment, and more-than-human food geographies.' *Agriculture and Human Values* 34:2, 485–497.

Sarmiento, E. 2020. 'Raw Power: For a microbiopolitical ecology of fermentation.' In Myles, C. (ed.), *Fermented Landscapes: Lively processes of socio-environmental transformation*. Lincoln: University of Nebraska Press.

White, M. 2018. *Freedom Farmers: Agricultural Resistance and the Black Freedom Movement*. Chapel Hill: University of North Carolina Press.

Winter, M. 2003. 'Embeddedness, the new food economy and defensive localism.' *Journal of Rural Studies* 19:1, 23–32.

Woods, C. 2017. *Development Drowned and Reborn: The Blues and Bourbon Restorations in Post-Katrina New Orleans*. Athens: University of Georgia Press.

Wright, A.L. and Wolford, W. 2003. *To Inherit the Earth: The Landless Movement and the Struggle for a New Brazil*. Pasadena: Food First Books.

Further reading

Gibson-Graham, J.K. 2006. *A Postcapitalist Politics*. Minneapolis: University of Minnesota Press.

While not focused on food economies, this is an invaluable resource for theorising economic diversity and the political implications thereof.

Morgan, K., Marsden, T., and Murdoch, J. 2009. *Worlds of Food: Place, Power, and Provenance in the Food Chain*. Oxford: Oxford University Press.

Conceptually rich but highly readable, this text combines 'big picture' perspectives on food systems with case studies from a range of regions. A particular strength of the text is its attention to questions of food distribution, which is too often overshadwed in food studies by research focused on production or consumption.

Sbicca, J. 2018. *Food Justice Now! Deepening the Roots of Social Struggle*. Minneapolis: University of Minnesota Press.

By centring food justice rather than alterity for its own sake, this monograph examines how food systems are implicated in much wider social, political, and economic struggles, illustrating how a myopic approach to food politics is unlikely to ameliorate the problems associated with conventional food systems.

ERIC SARMIENTO

34. Empire, colonialism, and food

EMMA SHARP AND TAI WRIGHT

Introduction: the exchange and appropriation of power through food

Definitions of empire and colonialism are diverse and often used interchangeably. For Steinmetz (2014: 79–80) empires are the expansive and militarised "conquest of a foreign people followed by the creation of an organization controlled by members of the conquering polity and suited to rule over the conquered territory's indigenous population" serving to "limit the sovereignty of the peoples and polities they conquer" (79). Food systems are related to these processes through a surge in mobility and volume of global capital based on trade in land and food. Veracini (2011: 1) argues that "Colonialism is primarily defined by exogenous domination. It … has two fundamental and necessary components: an original displacement and unequal relations." In its relationships to food, this definition of colonialism can also include the displacement of Indigenous food systems, resulting in unequal relations for food outcomes.

Kumar (2021) makes distinct a definition of *settler* colonialism, whereby, ideologically, settlers "have come to stay; there is no future for them beyond the colony (unlike Europeans in imperial settings who have every hope and expectation of returning home)" (249). Where domination and displacement of Indigenous peoples is in common between colonialism and settler-colonialism, the difference is most clear in the outcome; where "colonialism *reinforces* the distinction between colony and metropole, settler colonialism *erases* it" (Veracini, 2011: 3), and operates through normalising and legitimising control over Indigenous land. This includes assumptions by settler-colonists that settler sovereignty, logics and law might be effectual or make sense in a different land or even cosmology. This lack of criticality and legitimation privileges colonial sensibilities and infrastructures. It remains relevant in terms of food systems today where, for example, some Indigenous access and rights to hunting and gathering on traditional home ranges are criminalised.

Beyond material exchange and extraction, relationships between food, empire, and colonialism are also understood through transfers of ideology and knowledge. Most colonial projects laid foundations for expanding capitalism, or an economic ideology based on productivist wage-labour to benefit asset owners. In food-producing colonies or peripheries, labour was often sustained through different forms of slavery to either export agricultural systems, enterprise, and products *out* from empire centres, or extract and import tastes like spices and staple foods *in* to colonial possession. An improved ability to feed empires' urban populations further enabled domination, which was enhanced with technological advances; for example, the simple innovation of the tin can helped facilitate empire expansion and control (Naylor, 2000).

The global modern food crisis is a product of these processes of domination through global agricultural industrialisation, financialisation, and the "restructuring of processing industries, large trading companies and supermarket chains into 'food empires'" (Van der Ploeg, 2010). The metropoles' export and imposition of territorial ideologies of 'progress' thus leaves a legacy of food, health, land, and cultural insecurity, a perpetuation of processes of empire and the accumulation of concentrated power over time.

Histories of food and power

'Progress' in/for food?

Amongst the flows of technology, capital, material, and ideas between populations who are dominated and dominating, it should be acknowledged that there have been exchanges that are generative. For example, introductions of a broader, richer diet into colonised places were welcomed. For colonists, a priority of technological development in food preservation and storage enabled 'fresh' produce exports from colonies, back to the metropoles: for example, commercial refrigeration assembled new relations between Aotearoa New Zealand and Britain, making possible meat and dairy exports to British markets. The subsequent investment by British financiers significantly shaped the political economy of food, and New Zealand's narrative today as a breadbasket for the world.

The Green Revolution involved similar strategies between the early 1900s and late 1980s. The earnest adoption of applied fertilisers, pesticides and irrigation, and mechanised methods of agrifood labour in the colonies, and in 'developing countries' through technological transfer, led to vastly increased crop yields and the subjugation of traditional farming practices. This agricultural modernisation has since extended to aspects like gene technology and a concentration of corporate power in the patenting of (terminator) seeds, preventing seed saving practices and thereforefood sovereignty efforts. While heralded at the time for its potential to feed the world, the Green Revolution created legacy issues of environmental injustices wrought through the application of fertilisers and pesticides, resulting in land contaminated with heavy metals, and poisons such as DDT.

Appropriation, domination, and transformation of Indigenous land

For the most part, relationships associated with and generated out of empire and colonial domination of food systems were experienced by the colonised as manipulative, violent, and often illegal and/or morally corrupt. European centres used various tactics that enabled individual prospectors to acquire land to develop into farms in their own name.

The colonial establishment of plantations was one of the most significant imprints on stolen land, to produce food cash crops particularly in the equatorial latitudes, for export to Europe. Plantations (large-scale monocultural agricultural enterprises) relied on forced labour of slaves or indentured labourers, and were designed to extract as much profit as possible from the land and labour. It was not just individual private owners who enacted land theft – large tracts of land were readily acquired by governments or corporations.

Corporations like the East India Trading Company, an English – and later British – company founded in 1600, formed to trade in foodstuffs such as sugar, salt, spices, and tea amongst others, in the Indian Ocean region. With its own 260,000-person-strong army, it colonised large parts of the Indian subcontinent, Southeast Asia, and Hong Kong. The Company exercised administrative functions under military rule, and trafficked slaves from West and East Africa, especially Mozambique and Madagascar, to holdings in India, Indonesia, the West Indies, and the United States as plantation workers. Meanwhile, French, English, and

Dutch traders and privateers operating in the Caribbean Sea capitalised on the Sugar Revolution of the mid 1600s, triggering the enslavement of Africans and Indigenous Caribs to labour in the fields and mills of the West Indies. In Africa, European powers were using a combination of military force, treaties, and land purchase agreements to acquire land from Indigenous communities, then mobilising them as dispensable labour. These are only a few such markets and transactions around the building of food colonies of the early empires.

Contemporary empire and colonialism in food: legacies, resurrections, and novel forms of food domination

Despite the United Nations officially declaring the end of colonialism in 1960 via the Declaration on the Granting of Independence to Colonial Countries and Peoples, there still exist places that are ruled by other nations, in theory and/or practice. Colonial imperatives and logics also continue to be reproduced through corporate capitalist and conservative state interests, transforming food systems globally.

Neocolonial endeavours have included a new fervour for land grabs (land appropriation of more than 10,000 ha), which has proliferated since the 2008–2009 global financial crisis. Jurkevics (2022: 33–34) explains that "[m]any purchases are made by the sovereign wealth funds of net food importers [seeking] arable land outside their own borders – China, the Gulf States, and South Korea. On their heels have come transnational agribusiness conglomerates, speculators, and hedge funds", all key actors in what McMichael calls the "corporate food regime" (2008) and Van der Ploeg calls "the imperial food regime" (2010). These relationships are visible in the examples of the meat and soy industries' Amazonian land grabs. Whilst colonialism, resource extraction, and conversion of the Amazon into farmland are not new, in more recent times a set of economic and political crises have led to agribusiness support for right-wing politicians, a feedback of state promotion of agribusiness, new industry expansion into the Amazon to transform it into agricultural land, and aggressive settler-colonialism causing erasures of Indigenous practice and culture. In many ways, global demands for soy (for mostly feedlot animals) and beef exports are extensions of ongoing colonial and imperial power plays. We see similar contemporary exploitation in Southeast Asian sugar land grabs for lucrative Global North snack food and soft drink manufacturers.

Global climate change has been identified as a driver as well as an outcome of intensified colonialism. Production, distribution, and waste in food systems are responsible for a third of the world's greenhouse gas emissions. Sea level rise and increased intensity and frequency of extreme weather are already directly affecting lives and livelihoods, especially in the Global South. Further, (plantation) disaster capitalism is an emerging term used to define climate-related neocolonial profiteering in the aftermath of such events, which disproportionately affects the poor..

Novel biotechnologies have also been named as colonialist in their concentration of wealth and power in food systems. Many such technologies have been eagerly launched to respond to concerns around climate change, with neoliberal movements ready to bring them to market. Examples include climate-resistant seed patents, genetically modified organisms, and the Silicon Valley-isation of food production through cell-cultured meat and dairy production. Further, the adoption of such technologies by poorer countries has been known to be a condition of food aid: in 2008, a United States deputy secretary of state "called on countries to lower their 'export restrictions and high tariffs' and eliminate 'barriers to use of innovative plant and animal production technologies, including biotechnology' ... [T]he message was clear: impoverished countries had better crack open their agricultural markets to American products and genetically modified seeds, or they could risk having their aid cut off" (Klein, 2019). Greenwashing strategies have also been seen through land grabs, with innovation conglomerates acquiring significant land for farmland and green-energy technological experiments, or for biofuel crop production. Neocolonial approaches enable the literal and figurative bulldozing of local and often Indigenous (rights to) land and foodways.

A case of recent settler-colonialism: a food assemblage of Aotearoa New Zealand

The 19th-century arrival of the British into Aotearoa New Zealand displaced Māori from their existing food growing lands, with the effect of profoundly altering Indigenous food systems and diets as they were forced to adapt to new food sources, locations, and methods of food production. Demands of white settlement and European agricultural practices led to outright violence and land confiscation. Māori land was seized and converted into large-scale sheep farms, forming the backbone of the New Zealand capitalist economy. The introduction of European farming methods and of crops, such as wheat, potatoes, and vegetables, quickly supplanted Māori food systems which relied on fishing, hunting, and extensive horticulture.

The settler-colonial impacts on Aotearoa New Zealand's food systems are visible through erasing pre-colonial practice, and normalising and legitimising settler practice, for example, through legal frameworks that constrain the hunting and collection of food through quotas, catch restrictions (of species and size), and the designation of territories as in or out of bounds. With the New Zealand landscape transformed into 'empires of grass' (Pawson and Brooking, 2008) for sheep rearing and large-scale dairy farming, space for smaller-scale, diversified food systems has been enclosed. Intensive farming regimes, particularly of dairy and beef, have had significant environmental impacts, including soil erosion, water pollution, and loss of biodiversity. A long-term environmental impact has been the reduction of native forest and wetland, diminishing native flora and fauna that constituted Māori diets, representing a loss of intergenerational and environmental connection, relationship, and knowledge. More recently, there have been other attacks on native species access and guardianship with colonial attempts to appropriate genetic sequences of flora and fauna through new intellectual property deals – a process that has been defined as biopiracy. Similarly, Indigenous knowledge and language that provide distinct avenues of value for food, for example for tāonga (endemic, treasured entities) like mānuka honey, are vulnerable to exploitation, nationally and globally.

Clearly, the historic legacy of colonialism has had impacts on the ability of

EMMA SHARP AND TAI WRIGHT

contemporary Indigenous communities to produce food for themselves. They have been forced to rely on imported food from Europe, or adapt to new food systems and sources, as has been the case in the Pacific Islands (McLennan and Ulijaszek, 2015). The island of Nauru in Micronesia offers a chilling example. In the early 1900s, the British Phosphate Commissioners (formerly the Pacific Islands Company) responded to colonial demand for farming fertiliser and began extensive phosphate mining across the island, leading to widespread environmental degradation that devastated the islanders' food provisioning. Worsening dietary trends were further compounded in the mid-1900s when discarded cuts of high-fat meat started arriving across the Pacific Islands as development aid, including turkey tails from the US and mutton flaps from New Zealand, re-enshrining colonial control under the guise of propping up food security. Since the early 2000s, Nauru has grappled with renewed colonial relations following the opening of an Australian immigration refugee detention facility as the island's primary economy. While Nauru was once one of the wealthiest nations in the world, as of 2023 the island has an unemployment rate of near 90% and has lost at least 80% of its original vegetation. It also has one of the world's highest obesity rates due to the prevalence of imported foodstuffs high in salt and sugar from processed and canned food such as instant noodles and soft drinks – all legacies of historic and ongoing colonialism.

Decolonising food and (Indigenous) food sovereignty as countermovement

Given that many contemporary food systems preserve imperial and colonial relations, efforts to change food power disparities remain relevant. Calls for decolonial food systems often articulate how the assumptions and normalisation of existing food systems have become hegemonic. "Decolonial activism including demands for the end of land grabbing, food dumping, wage exploitation, tenure insecurity, and disaster capitalism – is a crucial first step of this reorganization; along with challenging powers … to generate solidarity, resistance, and self-determination" (Marrero et al., 2023: 8). Decolonising food extends to Indigenous efforts to revitalise pre-colonial food systems spaces, and peasants advocating for greater food sovereignty

by having their rights to land, seeds, environmental protections, and fair economic outcomes protected.

Examples of decolonising food movements today involve recovering access to intergenerational knowledges and Indigenous food memories that reinvigorate the idea of food as health and wellbeing, which have been lost in much of modern food production that is focussed on volume and efficiency. Born out of peasant movements in Latin America, consumers and smallholder first-nations farmers have been buoyed by transnational coalitions like La Vía Campesina, which mobilise for radical social transformation for inclusive, just, and democratically organised food systems that counter the corporate food regime. Such movements have played important roles in stabilising food supply in times of crisis, and strongly advocating for peasant rights (Mann, 2019).

Indigenous food sovereignty movements have worked to restore culturally important foods such as salmon and wild rice in North America. In Aotearoa New Zealand, food sovereignty is exercised in everyday practices of collective and Indigenous food gardens, and distributing food outside mainstream food chains (Grey et al., 2020). Re-engaging with customary food practices and consuming food of one's ancestors seeks to retain connection to land and to people, and in respectful ways that do not endorse overuse of land or overharvest of gathered foods. Given poor health outcomes in many previously colonised places, current access to quality food that is nutritious, economically accessible in reliable and abundant supply, and culturally relevant is an ongoing challenge. Exposure to international trade is sometimes a necessary influence on what is available to populations and having a say in trade agreements is, for some, an important aspect of Indigenous agency in food systems. Nonetheless, modern food sovereignty movements have in some cases resisted international trade agreements which put at risk sovereignty over what food is produced, how, where, and by whom.

There have been responses to such movements by those who benefited from colonial legacies. For example, settler-farmers have attempted to appropriate the notion of food sovereignty to protect what they perceive as their rights of food provenance, to legitimise their ownership of stolen land. Thus, Global North interpretations of food sovereignty as concept, condition, and countermovement can risk reinforcing settler-colonial norms such as private property and the continued alienation of Indigenous land.

Overall, empire and colonial practices continue to shape food systems and a range of social and environmental outcomes. The task of responding to both colonial and imperial legacies and their contemporary manifestations within food systems is immense, with resistance playing out as struggle, decolonial aspiration, and everyday practice.

References

Grey R, Muru-Lanning C, Jones N, and Muru-Lanning M (2020) Once were gardeners: Māra and planting protest at Ihumātao. *MAI Journal* 9(3). https://doi.org/10.20507/MAIJournal.2020.9.3.4

Jurkevics A (2022) Land grabbing and the perplexities of territorial sovereignty. *Political Theory* 50(1): 32–58.

Klein N (2019) *Disaster Capitalism: State of Extortion.* Available: https://naomiklein.org/disaster-capitalism-state-extortion/ (Accessed 1 December 2023).

McMichael P (2008) Peasants make their own history, but not just as they please. *Journal of Agrarian Change* 8(2–3): 205–228.

Mann A (2019) Common Ground: Connections and Tensions Between Food Sovereignty Movements in Australia and Latin America. In: Peñaloza F and Walsh S (eds) *Mapping South-South Connections. Studies of the Americas* (pp. 81–109). Palgrave Macmillan, Cham. https://doi.org/10.1007/978-3-319-78577-6_4

Marrero A, Nicoson C and Mattei J (2023) Food laborers as stewards of island biocultural diversity: Reclaiming local knowledge, food sovereignty, and decolonization. *Frontiers in Sustainable Food Systems* 7: 1093341. https://doi.org/10.3389/fsufs.2023.1093341

Naylor S (2000) Spacing the can: Empire, modernity, and the globalisation of food. *Environment and Planning A* 32(9): 1625–1639.

Pawson E and Brooking T (2008) Empires of grass: Towards an environmental history of New Zealand agriculture. *British Review of New Zealand Studies* 17: 95–114.

Steinmetz G (2014) The sociology of empires, colonies, and postcolonialism. *Annual Review of Sociology* 40: 77–103.

Veracini L (2011) Introducing: Settler colonial studies. *Settler Colonial Studies* 1(1): 1–12.

Further reading

Kumar K (2021) Colony and empire, colonialism and imperialism: A meaningful distinction? *Comparative Studies in Society and History* 63(2): 280–309.
General text on the relationships between colonialism and empire.

McLennan A K and Ulijaszek S J (2015) Obesity emergence in the Pacific islands: Why understanding colonial history and social change is important. *Public Health Nutrition* 18(8): 1499–1505.
This text gives an historical overview of the food related socio-politics of the Pacific islands, with Nauru and the Cook Islands as case studies.

Van der Ploeg J (2010) The food crisis, industrialized farming and the imperial regime. *Journal of Agrarian Change,* 10: 98–106. https://doi.org/10.1111/j.1471-0366.2009.00251.x
An in-depth reading on the modern imperial food regime.

35. Energy and food

Jose Martini Costa and Kate J. Neville

Introduction: the tensions and intersections between the energy and agro-food sectors

In 2022, the British news outlet *Financial Times* ran a story provocatively titled "Food versus fuel", examining the impact of Russia's invasion of Ukraine on food and fuel prices (Terazono and Hodgson, 2022). With the two countries responsible for almost one-fifth of global corn and over half of sunflower oil production, among other agricultural outputs, the conflict has had major consequences for food prices and access in countries around the world. Could the crops currently being turned into biofuels—liquid bioethanol and biodiesel from plants and plant oils—fill the shortfall in global food supplies, the article asked, although it concluded that countries have not placed limits on biofuels in response to these agricultural pressures. The article contributed to renewed debates over the relationship between food and fuel production and prices. But this is not a novel issue or headline.

The food versus fuel debate reveals the deep interconnections between our energy and food systems. Food production requires enormous amounts of energy—from fertiliser inputs to running irrigation systems and farm machinery, and from harvesting and processing to transportation and storage—and with these energy inputs heavily reliant on fossil fuel power sources contributes to the climate emergency. Agriculture also feeds energy production, as seen with the expansion of biofuels. These fuels sometimes compete with food systems, when crops that could enter food supply chains are instead directed into energy. Such conversion of food crops into biofuels has been controversial since interest in low-carbon transportation fuels hit the global stage in the early 2000s.

Scholarly and policy attention on food and energy connections spans everything from agricultural technologies (Miao and Khanna, 2020) to the financing of food and fuel production (Clapp and Isakson, 2018) to social movements for food and energy access, sovereignty, and justice (Alonso-Fradejas et al., 2015). Two distinct areas of scholarship have emerged, with different analytical approaches and empirical observations at their core. The first spans economics, political economy, agrarian studies, and political ecology, where scholars consider the interlinkages of food, fuel, and financial systems, with attention to claims of land grabs, environmental degradation, corporate control, financialisation, and speculative investments in these commodities. Following the 2007 to 2008 crisis, the world saw continued price volatility for energy and food commodities, including through a global financial crisis, increasing extreme weather events, and a global pandemic. Throughout this time, energy production from food crops and the intersection with finance has continued and has been embroiled in controversy over direct food production, as well as land access and rights (Clapp and Isakson, 2018).

The second field is positioned at the intersection of public policy, resource management, and interdisciplinary environmental studies and sciences, and examines the interconnections of multiple resource systems, often considered through the conceptualisation of a "nexus", countering the silo approaches that often prevail in policy responses. Conferences on the food–energy nexus were held in Brazil and India in the 1980s, and similar meetings were expanded to include water during the 1990s and 2000s (Endo et al., 2017). This framing of sectoral connections has been widely taken up in policy circles and environmental science research.

In the years to come, we anticipate that research will attend to the growing pressures for transformation in food production systems to respond to the changing climate and extreme weather events, while responding to growing demand for both food and energy. The reduction of emissions associated with certain agricultural practices and fossil fuel-based inputs, and the emerging movements that link energy, food, and climate justice at local and global scales, will also be central elements of food and energy systems. These are intertwined relationships critical for social well-being, planetary health, and ecological integrity, and how we approach these interconnections will be one of the defining challenges of the 21st century.

Food, fuel, and the nexus

Scholars have examined the intersections between energy production and inputs from food systems into energy. Research on these connections ranges from economic and trade analyses of food and fuel prices, to critical agrarian and political economy studies of food and land sovereignty claims, to assessments of interlinked commodity chains. For technological enthusiasts, a circular, low-carbon economy can integrate food and fuel sectors, with interchangeable inputs that provide flexibility based on prices, demand, and efficiency. Through this set of analytical assumptions, crops can be directed to human or animal consumption or to fuel feedstocks as needed, and, at the same time, byproducts of energy production can be directed back into the food system as livestock feed (cf. Martin, 2020). In contrast, a wide range of scholars working on food and energy intersections have taken critical approaches to the study of land enclosures, resource exclusion, and the growing power of corporate actors in shaping these systems. It is this latter body of work that we focus on.

Food vs fuel? Industrial input interdependence and land use change

The ethics and economics of biofuels production from agricultural crops, and the impacts of the industrial transformation of food crops as energy inputs, have been key points of debate in the past decade (Popp et al., 2014). Between 2005 and 2008, prices for staple food crops spiked, with prices for maize nearly tripling, and wheat and rice also rising precipitously (Taghizadeh-Hesary et al., 2019). Price increases were so severe and sustained that the period from 2007 to 2008 was designated a global food crisis, and drove millions of people into poverty, exacerbating existing conditions of global inequality and hunger (United Nations, 2011). Some observers, seeing the rise in biofuels production and consumption targets that aligned temporally with these rising food prices, concluded that the two were directly linked: fuel production for climate goals, especially in the Global North, these analysts suggested, was compromising food security around the world, especially in the Global South (see, e.g., To and Grafton, 2015). But analyses in both policy and scholarly circles reflected different conclusions about the intersection of these two industrial sectors. Some assessments found no direct impact of biofuels production on grain prices (Ajanovic, 2011). The European Commission published a report in 2015 that

suggested these pressures differ by biofuel output and feedstock, with biodiesel associated with higher emissions and land use change, and particular concerns arising with oil palm (Valin et al., 2015). These questions remain fraught and contested, with varying answers by sector, location, and the specificities of production systems.

To determine the factors shaping food access and land use decisions, some scholars focused on financial actors. Here, distant and often indirect investments shaped commodity markets and production. Attention turned to so-called "flex fuels", where crops are able to enter either food or fuel industrial processing systems, depending on demand, price, and opportunity (Borras et al., 2016). In these malleable production systems, speculative investments have created volatility and uncertainty, with troubling consequences for both producers and consumers.

Agro-food and energy as fungible and entangled investments

At the same time as biofuels debates travelled around the world, with conflicting accounts of the consequences for both carbon emissions and hunger, the growing power of financial actors and the abstraction of food and fuel commodities gained attention. Concentration of agricultural commodity markets by a handful of corporate actors and the financialisation of food systems collided with changes in global financial instruments. These enabled large institutional investors to mitigate their risks through increasingly complex sets of index funds. Even as the geopolitics of production of both food and fuel have shifted over time, the returns across integrated investments have continued to soar, mitigating risk for large investors and providing financial incentives that uphold the oligopoly of control in food systems (Clapp and Isakson, 2018).

As debates over the direct material connections between food and fuel systems continued, they were joined—and in some cases eclipsed—by concern over the abstraction of physical food and energy commodities into financial products (Ouma, 2016). Widespread land acquisitions and speculation drove these studies. Research has examined what biofuels production has meant for access to land and for matters of sovereignty at the community level, and how distant financial actors are involved in questions of local livelihoods

JOSE MARTINI COSTA AND KATE J. NEVILLE

and political control. Whether interfering with food crops or not, and whether produced on high-quality or marginal land, external investments in land poured into countries in the Global South with plans to produce bio-fuels largely for Western and Northern markets— such as sugarcane and *Jatropha curcas* and oil palm, among other feedstocks, across the African continent, in southeast Asia, and beyond. Charges of neo-colonial "land grabs" and a global "land rush" accompanied these agricultural expansion plans, with concerns about the further dispossession of communities through social and economic exclusion (Borras and Franco, 2013). Even if food was not directed into fuel tanks, these observers saw that the enclosure of communal lands for private feedstock production would threaten livelihoods and increase precarity in places with overlapping property regimes and norms of public access.

Nexus approaches

The idea of a nexus to refer to the synergies and trade-offs between energy and food is not new. Food and energy are deeply interconnected. Irrigation, which enables agricultural expansion and regularisation when rainfall is unpredictable or insufficient, requires large amounts of energy for water pumping, diversions, and storage (Campana and Lawford, 2022). Synthetic fertilisers—credited with enabling the Green Revolution and exponential increases in agricultural yields—are petrochemical products, part of the fossil fuel industry (Pfeiffer, 2006). Fisheries, espeically as part of an extensive aquaculture or "blue food" industry, require large energy inputs, including for recirculating systems, especially given the volume of food they now produce (Klinger and Naylor, 2012).

However, while adopted by many researchers, international institutions, and states, the nexus framing has been widely critiqued. Two concerns are of particular note. First, nexus approaches are challenged as technocratic and industrialised: energy, food, and water tend to be considered as commodities that need to be used and produced efficiently and at scale, with the focus on reducing waste and removing barriers to expansion. In contrast, food, water, and energy can be considered as human rights, or as culturally embedded, or as part of ecological and more-than-human systems (Wiegleb and Bruns, 2018). And

second, nexus discourses are challenged as apolitical and narrow: they consider specific material resources needed for food production or energy production in isolation, lacking consideration for livelihoods and the environment (Simpson and Jewitt, 2019). In contrast, critical approaches point to the importance of labour relations, access to capital, land tenure arrangements, and systems of political economic exchange (Wichelns, 2017). A broader politically informed approach is needed.

Future concerns

In a world that has already surpassed a population of 8 billion people, with more than half clustered in urban centres, and more than one-third living in just two countries— China and India—the question of food and energy access and distribution are of central and growing global importance. Estimates indicate that nearly 670 million people will still be undernourished in 2030, owing to a confluence of factors from conflict situations, climate-induced disasters, and prices of food and fertiliser (FAO et al., 2022). In terms of hunger, food production is only one component of the challenge—in aggregate, nearly a fifth of food is wasted. In some developing regions, on-farm losses can reach as much as 50%. This means that the energy used to grow, process, and transport that food is also wasted. At the same time, energy insecurity continues to disproportionately affect those in low- and middle-income countries, with more than 10% of people still lacking access to electricity. Energy for food storage remains a particular challenge for addressing food access and reducing waste. And 40% of the world's population lacks access to clean fuels for cooking, relying on the indoor burning of solid fuels that cause respiratory illnesses and other health challenges (IRENA and FAO, 2021). These are significant aspects of the future research needed to advance global equity and well-being.

In the next few decades, many observers suggest that food and energy production must expand dramatically to meet growing human needs, while simultaneously transforming its high-carbon footprint. Researchers will need to examine the consequences of increased extreme weather events on existing food production and on renewable energy generation. Similarly, how floods, soil erosion, fires, and droughts reorient food and energy production will need to be considered in anticipating food prices, planning trade systems, and managing supply chains. Local food production will need to be designed to anticipate disruptions from both environmental shocks and prolonged stresses.

However, given the uneven access to existing food and energy resources, estimates of the necessary expansion of both sectors do not consider what a radical reorientation of food and energy production and distribution might enable. Ensuring equitable access to food and energy, while mitigating the impacts of human-driven climate change, is already a challenge in light of the current global economic system. Emerging research agendas on changing patterns of consumption, different valuation systems, and alternate models of global political economic organisation, from steady state economics to proposals for degrowth (Hayward and Roy, 2019), offer insights into how shifting metrics of development from growth towards those of health, nourishment, and well-being can expand possibilities and support policy shifts that prioritise equitable distribution over increased profits.

References

Ajanovic A (2011) Biofuels versus food production: Does biofuels production increase food prices? *Energy*, 36(4), 2070–2076. https://doi.org/10.1016/j.energy.2010.05.019

Alonso-Fradejas A, Borras Jr S M, Holmes T, Holt-Giménez E and Robbins M J (2015) Food sovereignty: Convergence and contradictions, conditions and challenges. *Third World Quarterly*, 36(3), 431–448. https://doi.org/10.1080/01436597.2015.1023567

Borras Jr S M and Franco J C (2013) Global land grabbing and political reactions 'from below'. *Third World Quarterly*, 34(9), 1723–1747. https://doi.org/10.1080/01436597.2013.843845

Borras Jr S M, Franco J C, Isakson S R, Levidow L and Vervest P (2016) The rise of flex crops and commodities: Implications for research. *The Journal of Peasant Studies*, 43(1), 93–115. https://doi.org/10.1080/03066150.2015.1036417

Campana P E and Lawford R (2022) Renewable energies in the context of the water–food–energy nexus. In Jurasz J and Beluco A (Eds.) *Complementarity of Variable Renewable Energy Sources*. Academic Press, pp. 571–614. https://doi.org/10.1016/B978-0-323-85527-3.00010-8

Clapp J and Isakson S R (2018) Risky returns: The implications of financialization in the food system. *Development and Change*, 49(2), 437–460. https://doi.org/10.1111/dech.12376

Endo A, Tsurita I, Burnett K and Orencio P M (2017) A review of the current state of research on the water, energy, and food nexus. *Journal of Hydrology: Regional Studies*, 11, 20–30. https://doi.org/10.1016/j.ejrh.2015.11.010

FAO, IFAD, UNICEF, WFP and WHO (2022) *The State of Food Security and Nutrition in the World 2022: Repurposing food and agricultural policies to make healthy diets more affordable*. FAO, Rome. https://doi.org/10.4060/cc0639en

Hayward B and Roy J (2019) Sustainable living: Bridging the North-South divide in lifestyles and consumption debates. *Annual Review of Environment and Resources*, 44, 157–175. https://doi.org/10.1146/annurev-environ-101718-033119

IRENA and FAO (2021) *Renewable Energy and Agri-food Systems: Advancing energy and food security towards Sustainable Development Goals*. Abu Dhabi and Rome. IRENA and FAO. https://doi.org/10.4060/cb7433en

Klinger D and Naylor R (2012) Searching for solutions in aquaculture: Charting a sustainable course. *Annual Review of Environment and Resources*, 37, 247–276. https://doi.org/10.1146/annurev-environ-021111-161531

Martin S J (2020) The political economy of distillers' grains and the frictions of consumption. *Environmental Politics*, 29(2), 297–316. https://doi.org/10.1080/09644016.2019.1565461

Miao R and Khanna M (2020) Harnessing advances in agricultural technologies to optimize resource utilization in the food-energy-water nexus. *Annual Review of Resource Economics*, 12, 65–85. https://doi.org/10.1146/annurev-resource-110319-115428

Ouma S (2016) From financialization to operations of capital: Historicizing and disentangling the finance–farmland-nexus. *Geoforum*, 72, 82–93. http://dx.doi.org/10.1016/j.geoforum.2016.02.003

JOSE MARTINI COSTA AND KATE J. NEVILLE

Pfeiffer D A (2006) *Eating Fossil Fuels: Oil, food, and the coming crisis in agriculture.* New Society Publishers.

Popp J, Lakner Z, Harangi-Rákos M and Fari M (2014) The effect of bioenergy expansion: Food, energy, and environment. *Renewable and Sustainable Energy Reviews*, 32, 559–578. https://doi.org/10.1016/j.rser.2014.01.056

Simpson G B and Jewitt G P W (2019) The development of the water-energy-food nexus as a framework for achieving resource security: A review. *Frontiers in Environmental Science*, 7. https://doi.org/10.3389/fenvs.2019.00008

Taghizadeh-Hesary F, Rasoulinezhad E and Yoshino N (2019) Energy and food security: Linkages through price volatility. *Energy Policy*, 128, 796–806. https://doi.org/10.1016/j.enpol.2018.12.043

Terazono E and Hogdson C (2022) Food versus fuel: Ukraine war sharpens debate on use of crops for energy. *Financial Times.* https://www.ft.com/content/b424067e-f56b-4e49-ac34-5b3de07e7f08 (Accessed 13 February 2023).

To H and Grafton R Q (2015) Oil prices, biofuels production and food security: Past trends and future challenges. *Food Security*, 7, 323–336. https://doi.org/10.1007/s12571-015-0438-9

United Nations (2011) *The Global Social Crisis: Report on the world social situation.* United Nations.

Valin H, Peters D, Van den Berg M, Frank S, Havlik P, Forsell N, Hamelinck C, Pirker J, Mosnier A, Balkovic J and Schmidt E (2015) *The Land Use Change Impact of Biofuels Consumed in the EU: Quantification of area and greenhouse gas impacts.* ECOFYS Netherlands.

Wichelns D (2017) The water-energy-food nexus: Is the increasing attention warranted, from either a research or policy perspective? *Environmental Science & Policy*, 69, 113–123. https://doi.org/10.1016/j.envsci.2016.12.018

Wiegleb V and Bruns A (2018) What is driving the water-energy-food nexus? Discourses, knowledge, and politics of an emerging resource governance concept. *Frontiers in Environmental Science*, 6, 128. https://doi.org/10.3389/fenvs.2018.00128

Further reading

Bjork-James C, Checker M and Edelman M (2022) Transnational social movements: Environmentalist, Indigenous, and agrarian visions for planetary futures. *Annual Review of Environment and Resources*, 47, 583–608. https://doi.org/10.1146/annurev-environ-112320-084822

This article offers an overview of a series of challenges to dominant systems of governance that devalue the natural world and prioritize profits over sustainability. Bjork-James et al. present a range of concepts that recognize the intrinsic value of the living world offered by transnational Indigenous, environmental, and agrarian social movements, from environmental justice to food sovereignty to climate debt.

Lima M G B (2022) Just transition towards a bioeconomy: Four dimensions in Brazil, India and Indonesia. *Forest Policy and Economics*, 136, 102684. https://doi.org/10.1016/j.forpol.2021.102684

Through three case studies, Lima examines how the replacement of fossil fuels and their byproducts with biological alternatives intersects with distributive, procedural, retributive, and restorative justice. Lima argues that just transitions require more than a substitution of inputs—they also need transitions in land relations and farming practices.

36. Environment and food

COLIN SAGE

Introduction

The capture and use of natural resources, such as soil and fresh water, and a host of ecosystem services (the hydrological cycle, climate stability, insect pollination, genetic diversity, wild fish stocks, etc.) has enabled food production to outstrip global population growth over the past half-century. However, the demands of feeding the world have had enormous consequences for the integrity and functioning of these resources and ecosystems. Across a range of key biophysical indicators, the consequences of food system activities – from agricultural input manufacturing through farming and food processing to retail, consumption, and waste – have increased environmental concerns (Springmann et al., 2018; Poore & Nemecek, 2018; Sage, 2012), and in-depth life cycle analyses are providing an abundance of quantitative evidence revealing multiple problematic impacts (Cucurachi et al., 2019).

One issue that has especially captured attention at a time of rising global temperatures is the quantity of greenhouse gas (GHG) emissions that are attributed to agriculture. The intensity of arable and livestock operations across many high- and middle-income countries has become one of the most important anthropogenic activities contributing to the climate emergency. It has been suggested that the entire food system is responsible for between 21 and 37 percent of global anthropogenic GHG emissions (IPCC, 2021). Yet this need not be an inevitable outcome of producing food and feeding the world. One sector that has come under particular scrutiny is ruminant livestock production, and the contribution of methane from cattle is increasingly recognised by climate scientists as a problem that needs to be tackled with some urgency. In the Republic of Ireland, for example, an agricultural sector largely based upon the production of beef and dairy is now responsible for 37.5 percent of the country's total GHG emissions (EPA 2022). Yet calls to reduce the number of cattle have been met with defensiveness and hostility by those representing the agricultural sector. Thus, while evidence of environmental deterioration appears stark,

taking appropriate measures to ameliorate and resolve these problems does not elicit consensus.

Recognising that disruption of the global climate system threatens food production in many parts of the world and thereby places in danger the lives of tens of millions of people requires urgent action, although this is hampered by powerful vested interests, policy fragmentation, and the lack of a common coherent vision (Zurek et al., 2022). Yet there are many options in reducing the food system's role in climate disruption, as well as its impacts on other ecological services and environmental resources. Embarking upon a more sustainable pathway, however, must first avoid demonising the agricultural sector and recognise that many farmers find themselves boxed into production systems because of poor policy and technical support and subject to a range of forces that operate at some remove from the land, including financial institutions, agri-technology providers, and the buying desks of corporate retailers.

Moreover, it is not possible to entirely absolve dietary choices made by individuals in wealthy countries as these drive market signals translated by others into production contracts. This is why it is necessary to take a more systemic perspective when teasing out the complex relationship between food and environment. For those with agency to choose, dietary practices have a significant bearing on what is produced and how. Improving the environmental performance of the food system, then, requires changes in eating practices and it is incumbent on rich and largely food secure countries to lead the way in developing and implementing policy in favour of sustainable diets.

This entry briefly reviews the variety of ways in which the food system is driving environmental change. Although individual problem areas are identified and discussed, these should not be regarded as existing in isolation; rather, many are deeply interconnected through the web of life with wider planetary health. Consequently, the entry proceeds through the food system and, while recognising that agriculture exercises some of the greatest environmental impacts, later stages – most directly engaging food consumers – are not insignificant (Mason and Lang, 2017).

Key environmental issues in food systems

Once human societies had moved beyond the hunting and gathering of wild foods and into the age of agriculture, land use change in favour of food growing and livestock rearing largely proceeded in step with population growth. Today it has been estimated that 50 percent of the world's habitable land is now under crop cultivation and animal grazing (Ritchie & Roser, 2022) and the global food system can be regarded as the primary driver of biodiversity loss through the conversion of natural ecosystems to crop production or pasture (Benton et al., 2021). Media coverage of deforestation in the Amazon and South-East Asia has brought to wider public attention the extension of the agricultural frontier for soybeans, palm oil, and cattle ranching. Such monocultures replace ecosystems that perform complex functions including the sequestration of atmospheric carbon, buffering the effects of adverse weather, and multiple other ecosystem services such as the purification of air and water and insect pollination of food crops. The destruction of habitats such as forests removes sources of food and shelter on which wildlife depend and has led to a catastrophic decline in populations of wild mammals, birds, plants, and insects (Goulson, 2021). Meanwhile, marine ecosystems – both those within territorial waters and those that lie outside exclusive economic zones (ocean fisheries) – are largely subject to unsustainable rates of exploitation that exceed their capacity either to replenish stocks or to remediate waste streams.

The food system's contribution to global heating has, as noted above, come under increased scrutiny in recent years. Based on current trends, food system emissions alone would prevent the achievement of the 1.5°C target established under the 2015 Paris Agreement, irrespective of fossil fuel emissions reduction in other sectors (Clark et al., 2020). While CO_2 emissions arise at all stages of the food system, the largest source of uncertainty in the remaining carbon budget relates to the short-lived GHGs, methane and nitrous oxide, both strongly linked to agricultural production. Methane is a powerful GHG that has contributed about 0.5°C of warming when assessing 2010 to 2019 warming relative to 1850 to 1900 (IPCC, 2021). Methane is a consequence of enteric fermentation, the microbial process by which ruminants digest plant matter and convert this into carcass tissue and/or milk. This source accounts for almost one-third of anthropogenic methane and two-thirds of all agricultural methane (Xu et al., 2021). If the livestock sector were to continue with business as usual, this sector alone would account for almost half of the emissions budget for 1.5°C by 2030, requiring other sectors to reduce emissions beyond a realistic or planned level. Yet methane's decade-long lifespan in the atmosphere permits relatively quick gains in atmospheric concentration if emissions were lowered. Consequently, it is becoming an unavoidable conclusion that substantially reducing, if not avoiding, meat and dairy products is the single biggest way to reduce our environmental impact on the planet (Poore & Nemecek 2018).

The expansion of high external input agriculture has resulted in the depletion and contamination of freshwater resources with two-thirds of global withdrawals from rivers, aquifers, and groundwater extracted for irrigation. The production of water-intensive commodity crops for globalised supply chains can severely exacerbate the risks of local water scarcity (Qu et al., 2018). Meanwhile, the management of soil fertility under conventional agriculture has been largely reduced to ensuring the availability of three macro-nutrients – nitrogen, phosphorous, and potassium – which are provided through copious applications of synthetic fertilisers. The development of the Haber–Bosch process early in the 20th century to synthesise atmospheric nitrogen (N_2) into the form of fertiliser and thereby provide a source of reactive nitrogen (N_r) that could be taken up by crops has had a transformative effect on the global nitrogen cycle. Together with the subsequent development of fertiliser-responsive high yielding seeds, it has been argued that without Haber–Bosch synthesis about 40 percent of the world's current population could not be fed.

With nitrogen uptake by crops worldwide estimated at 43 percent, this means that over half of the fertiliser applied is lost to the environment and global alteration of the nitrogen cycle leads to many different, cascading effects on ecosystem and human health. These include nitrate leaching into groundwater; eutrophication of aquatic ecosystems resulting in fish kills and the creation of coastal 'dead zones'; loss of terrestrial and marine biodiversity; agricultural emissions of ammonia that combine with small particulate matter to create toxic air quality; and contributions to climate change through nitrous oxide (Sage 2022b). Overall, food production creates around 32 percent of global terrestrial acidification and around 78 percent of eutrophication. These emissions threaten the biological composition and resilience of natural ecosystems (Poore and Nemecek, 2018).

The intensification of agricultural production is most closely associated with the path-dependent pursuit of industrial technologies involving the use of chemicals. The rise of glyphosate, commercially developed by Monsanto under the label 'Roundup' to become by 2015 the most widely used herbicide around the world, is an illustrative example (Clapp, 2021). Besides the emergence of glyphosate resistance in weeds, the toxicological effects on human health subsequently became more widely recognised by policy-makers and the judicial system. Yet the entrenchment of glyphosate in agriculture has proven difficult to eradicate as debates around its licensing in the European Union attest. Moreover, alongside the continuing use of toxic chemicals to protect large-scale monocultures from pests and disease – with all their attendant consequences for ecologically beneficial populations of birds, mammals, and insects – is the role of pharmaceuticals in industrial livestock production. The prophylactic use of antibiotics to accelerate weight gain and control infection in intensively reared, food-producing animals is unevenly regulated but raises important questions, not only about antimicrobial resistance, but about the complex pathways connecting human and animal health, including the risk of zoonotic spill-overs, an issue addressed by the One Health approach proposed by WHO.

Moving beyond the farm gate and into the global food chain reminds us that large volumes of primary foods are grown not for local but for distant markets. Depending upon the crop, its industrial quality, and location, food commodities may take many different routes before reaching the final consumer. The major cereal crops are likely to pass through industrial refining and manufacturing stages and, combined with other – often synthetic – ingredients, give rise to an enormous cornucopia of branded products to be found on supermarket shelves and in convenience stores. Fresh produce, on the other hand, is more susceptible to spoilage and decay and must therefore be moved through the food system and into the hands of final consumers as quickly as possible. Refrigeration is key to this process and, whether freezing, chilling, or cooling, requires an environmentally toxic chemical refrigerant, as well as energy, at every stage of the supply chain from shortly after picking to the domestic refrigerator. Over the past two decades chill-chain products and their associated technologies have become a major feature of the global food system and have created path dependencies around increased energy use and packaging.

With corporate retailers providing year-round and counter-seasonal exotic fruit and vegetables, increasing volumes of food are travelling ever-greater distances. Moreover, transportation of food – whether by ship, air freight, long-distance trucks, regional distribution vehicles, or supermarket shopping trips undertaken in the family car – rely almost entirely on petroleum with its associated CO_2 emissions. The notion of 'food miles' was coined to capture the phenomenon of extended supply chains, although Life Cycle Assessment studies caution us not to assume that greater distances travelled necessarily exceed the environmental impact of production methods (Sage 2012).

Packaging, especially the use of plastics, has become one of the most visible signals of the environmental consequences of the food system. Images of choked waterways and littered beaches demonstrate the enormous problems arising from disposable containers, most particularly beverage bottles. Packaging of food products such as liquids is, of course, essential although the degree to which the soft drinks industry has achieved a global market for nutritionally dubious material remains one of their great marketing success stories. Embedded here are such concepts as 'choice' and 'convenience', which too easily translate into disposability – to throw 'away' that which one no longer wants to hold (but recognising that on a crowded planet there is no 'away'). Replacing this with deposit-imposed, reusable glass bottles is a policy challenge indeed.

The last issue that ties together food and environment is one which has been widely discussed for more than a decade and is arguably one where there is most consensus: that of food waste. There is a strong moral argument that food should not be thrown away when people are going hungry. Yet the charitable redistribution of food surplus – most commonly witnessed through increasing numbers of people presenting at food banks – raises important questions about the human right to food (Kenny & Sage 2019). Moreover, much of the celebratory narrative about 'win–win' solutions (preventing food waste, feeding hungry people) conceals the logic of a system engaged in the industrial massification of food, continuously seeking to scale up production such that ever greater volumes of highly processed products are driven through a linear supply chain destined for supermarket shelves. This is accompanied by strong media promotion such that customers are encouraged to buy more than they require through such devices as 'buy one, get one free' ('BOGOF') and results in overconsumption and food waste creation (Messner et al., 2020).

Nevertheless, given that an estimated 1.3 billion tonnes of food – or around one-third of all food produced each year – fails to reach a human stomach remains a problem. All of this waste food embodies resources – soil nutrients, virtual water, fuel energy – and the aggregated carbon footprint arising from these inputs and waste decomposition. Together these make food waste the third largest source of greenhouse gas emissions after China and the USA (EU-FUSIONS, 2016).

Future concerns

This entry has outlined some of the key issues that connect the food system to the environment but it cannot pretend to offer a comprehensive account. It makes no mention of fisheries, for example, where a current audit would point to the depletion of wild stocks and the consequences for coastal ecosystems of intensive finfish aquaculture. While dietary advice has generally encouraged people to eat more fish, it is not clear if this can be squared with maintaining a healthy and diverse marine environment. In this regard it is becoming increasingly necessary to connect dietary practices to resource availability and to recognise that the eating patterns of hundreds of millions of people across rich and middle-income countries are not only placing enormous pressure on planetary boundaries but are themselves contributing to a rising burden of non-communicable disease. Healthier diets – comprising more vegetables, fruit, and plant-based oils rather than animal products – require less cropland, ease pressure on freshwater resources, provide more opportunities for co-existence with nature, create more potential for nutrient cycling without excessive disruption to the global nitrogen cycle and, above all, lower levels of GHG emissions. However, how are we to embark upon such a dietary transition when food governance rests largely in the hands of giant corporations and public policy merely offers 'nudges' that do not infringe consumer choice?

The pursuit of sustainable food systems will require a great deal more than the current investment surge in the development of alternative proteins. Offering consumers more choice, rather than restraint, is unlikely to achieve cuts in GHG emissions nor reduce pressure on use of land and freshwater resources, or pollution of aquatic and terrestrial ecosystems with the speed that is required. One way forward may be to restore a greater sense of the social, cultural, nutritional, and territorial dimensions of customary food practices and to communicate the ways these have been transformed as a consequence of the modern, industrial food system (Sage 2022a). Ultimately, encouraging people to exercise more agency over their dietary practices by enabling a closer affinity with the ecological basis of food supply will be critical if we are to achieve nutritional security for all within planetary boundaries.

References

Benton, T., Bieg, C., Harwatt, H., Pudasaini, R., Wellesley, L. (2021) Food System Impacts on Biodiversity Loss. London: Chatham House.

Clapp, J. (2021) Explaining growing glyphosate use: The political economy of herbicide-dependent agriculture. *Global Environmental Change* 67, 102239.

Clark, M., Domingo, N., Colgan, K., Thakrar, S. K., Tilman, D., Lynch, J., Azevedo, I. L., Hill, J. D. (2020) Global food system emissions could preclude achieving the 1.5° and 2°C climate change targets. *Science* 370: 705–708.

Cucurachi, S., Scherer, L., Guinée, J., Tukker, A. (2019) Life cycle assessment of food systems. *One Earth* 1, 3: 292–297. DOI: https://doi.org/10.1016/j.oneear.2019.10.014

EPA (2022) *Ireland's Provisional Greenhouse Gas Emissions 1990–2021*. Dublin:

COLIN SAGE

Environmental Protection Agency. https://www.epa.ie/publications/monitoring--assessment/climate-change/air-emissions/irelands-provisional-greenhouse-gas-emissions-1990-2021.php

EU-FUSIONS (2016) About food waste. www.eu-fusions.org/index.php/about-food-waste

Goulson, D. (2021) *Silent Earth: Averting the insect apocalypse*. London: Jonathan Cape.

IPCC (2021) Climate change 2021: The physical science basis. Contribution of Working Group I to the Sixth Assessment Report of the Intergovernmental Panel on Climate Change. https://www.ipcc.ch/report/ar6/wg1/ Accessed 15 August 2021.

Kenny, T., Sage, C. (2019) Food surplus as charitable provision: Obstacles to re-introducing food as a commons. In Vivero-Pol, J. L., Ferrando, T., de Schutter, O., Mattei, U. (eds) *Routledge Handbook of Food as a Commons*. Abingdon: Routledge, pp. 281–295.

Mason, P., Lang, T. (2017) *Sustainable Diets. How Ecological Nutrition Can Transform Consumption and the Food System*. Abingdon: Routledge.

Messner, R., Richards, C., Johnson, H. (2020) The "Prevention Paradox": Food waste prevention and the quandary of systemic surplus production. *Agriculture and Human Values*, 37: 805–817.

Poore, J., Nemecek, T. (2018) Reducing food's environmental impacts through producers and consumers. *Science*, 360, 6392: 987–992.

Qu, S., Liang, S., Konar, M., Zhu, Z., Chiu, A. S. F., Jia, X., Xu, M. (2018) Virtual water scarcity risk to the global trade system. *Environmental Science & Technology*, 52: 673–683.

Ritchie, H., Roser, M. (2022) Environmental impacts of food production. Published online at OurWorldInData.org. https://ourworldindata.org/environmental-impacts-of-food Accessed 23 May 2023.

Sage, C. (2012) *Environment and Food*. Abingdon, UK: Routledge.

Sage, C. (2022a) The food system, planetary boundaries and eating for 1.5°C: The case for mutualism and commensality within a safe and just operating space for humankind. In Sage, C. (ed.) *A Research Agenda for Food Systems*. Cheltenham, UK: Edward Elgar, pp. 67–88.

Sage, C. (2022b) Nitrogen, planetary boundaries, and the metabolic rift: Using metaphor for dietary transitions toward a safe operating space. In Hughes, I., Byrne, E., Mullally, G., Sage, C. (eds) *Metaphor, Sustainability, Transformation: Transdisciplinary perspectives*. Abingdon, UK: Routledge, pp. 46–64.

Springmann, M., Clark, M., Mason-D'Croz, D., et al. (2018) Options for keeping the food system within environmental limits. *Nature*, 562, 7728, 519. https://doi.org/10.1038/s41586-018-0594-0.

Xu, X., Sharma, P., Shu, S., et al. (2021) Global greenhouse gas emissions from animal-based foods are twice those of plant-based foods. *Nature Food*, 2, 724–732.

Zurek, M., Hebinck, A., Selomane, O. (2022) Climate change and the urgency to transform food systems. *Science*, 376 (6600). DOI: 10.1126/science.abo2364.

Further reading

Sage, C. (2012). *Environment and Food*. Abingdon: Routledge.
Although the data may be a little old, this book still provides a useful overview of the topic, especially Chapter 5, 'Final Foods'.

IPCC (2019). Summary for policymakers. In: *Climate Change and Land: An IPCC special report on climate change, desertification, land degradation, sustainable land management, food security, and greenhouse gas fluxes in terrestrial ecosystems*. https://www.ipcc.ch/srccl/chapter/summary-for-policymakers/.
Provides a definitive scientific evaluation on land use, climate, and food supply.

37. Ethics and food

Samantha Noll

Introduction

What we eat says a lot about us. Food choices reflect personal values, or issues that we care deeply about. For the last fifty years, the public has been grappling with larger implications and questions concerning food choice. For example, how does our dinner impact personal health, the environment, and animals? What about the hard-working people who produce our food, both locally and globally? Food systems are deeply connected to social and natural environments. Choosing to eat (or not to eat) that avocado shipped from Mexico, for example, may have consequences for the farmers who produced it, the environment where it was produced, the climate, grocers and shipping companies, and even international trade agreements. Today, it is not uncommon for eaters to "vote with their dollars", supporting food production methods that they value, while not supporting others. For those eaters committed to supporting rural communities, the farmers' market may be an ideal place to shop, even if it is less convenient. The sustainably conscious may embrace buying local, eco-friendly, or organic products. These and other ethical issues will be discussed in detail below. The food ethicist Roger King (2007) argues that recognising how our food choices impact others is the first step to eating ethically. Echoing King, the goal of this entry is to introduce readers to the diverse array of ethical issues that arise concerning food.

More specifically, this entry provides an overview of the field called food ethics. Ethics is the defence and systemisation of standards and values that are used to make ethical judgements regarding human conduct (Thompson and Noll 2015). Ethicists study how ethical norms (a) guide cultural practices and (b) can be discovered through reason. For this discipline, ethical norms are understood as an accessible part of the world that can be studied. One branch of the field particularly important for understanding ethics and food is normative ethics. Food scholars interested in normative ethics concern themselves with the development of general principles that help separate "right" actions from "wrong" actions and thus explain why some choices are better than others. When the food writer Michael Pollan argues that we should "Eat food. Not too much. Mostly plants," he is making both a descriptive and a normative argument (Pollan 2009 p. 2). It is descriptive, as it describes a diet, and it is normative, as it communicates what we should eat. Ethical issues concerning food are often complex, as food systems impact people, places, and animals. These themes will play a major role in exploration of food ethics presented in this entry.

However, before we explore ethical issues concerning food, it is important to recognise that normative issues concerning food are deeply tied to agricultural production methods. Agriculture is one of the oldest of human activities, with myriad social and environmental effects. Innovation in production has been continuous for at least the last ten thousand years, as humans learned to cultivate crops, domesticate animals, and build systems of irrigation (Thompson 2015). According to the United States Department of Agriculture (USDA), agriculture also includes the cultivation, harvesting, processing, storage, and distribution of commodities produced. Placing food ethics in this wider context is important for understanding normative issues that arise in the food sector. According to King (2007), modern food ethics deeply engages with questions that occur during production and this clearly includes agricultural systems and practices. This focus is what separates modern food ethics from historical approaches, which stressed dietetics. The organic movement and local food movement each grapple with questions concerning agriculture.

Food ethics is multi-faceted, in that it encompasses many issues related to the production, distribution, and consumption of food. Some of the key areas of concern in food ethics include the following: Impacts to (1) society, (2) individuals, (3) the environment, and (4) animal rights and welfare. First, there is large body of literature discussing social considerations, such as increasing demands that food is produced, distributed, and consumed in a way that is fair and equitable for all people. Cultural sensitivity is another socially focused topic, as communities request that cultural and traditional food practices are recognised and respected (Schanbacher 2010). Second, many consumers are worried about how food systems impact their ability to make choices and their health. One of the first ethical issues that consumers usually consider is ensuring that food is free from contaminants and/or produced in a way that does not pose a risk to human health (Singer and Mason 2007). Discussions concerning dietetics, labelling, and food safety all fall under impacts to individuals. As food systems rely on ecosystem services, environmental impacts are another important consideration, especially in an age where weather patterns are changing. Improving sustainability, maintaining native species integrity, biodiversity levels, and climate mitigation are all topics that fall under the environmental impacts category. Animal welfare is another area of concern for many, when choosing what to eat. This topic has been a public concern since at least the mid-1800s, with the rise of the anti-vivisectionist movements and the founding of the American Society for the Prevention of Cruelty to Animals (ASPCA).

Food ethics: impacts on society

The first category, or social impacts, has a long history. It featured prominently in 18th-century literature on food (Thompson and Noll 2015). For instance, the economists Adam Smith (1723–1790) and Thomas Malthus (1766–1834) were two of the first thinkers to frame hunger as a social issue. Malthus' work is important for current discussions in food ethics, as he identified the connection between agricultural technology and population growth. Here the latter tends to outstrip agricultural production, leading to famine. This discussion of hunger continued into the modern age, with Amartya Sen, Martha Nussbaum, Jeffery Sachs, and other prominent scholars engaging robustly with the topic. These thinkers pushed the literature beyond economic calculations concerning "carrying capacity" to make room for discussions engaging with the following question: What ethical duties do we have to food insecure communities? Peter Singer (1972) attempts to answer this question, arguing that we have a duty to help those in need, irrespective of distance, and this is especially the case in times of famine. However, several theorists are critical of this view. For instance, the economist Garrett Hardin (1915–2003) is highly critical of egalitarian views. He stresses the concern that population growth will outstrip agricultural productivity (1968), bringing the classic arguments of Malthus into conversation with other work, such as Peter Singer's *Famine, Affluence, and Morality* (1972).

Justice concerns also play an important role in food ethics. Rather than focusing on individual conduct, philosophers such as John Rawls (2001) argue that the appropriate place to bring about change is at the level of policy and the social institution. Another key justice concern involves deciding whether laws are justified in limiting the personal liberty of citizens (Gaus et al. 2018). The question of whether an agricultural practice is to be banned is a justice issue, as the ban would limit the farmer's liberty by constraining the choices available. Food security and hunger can also be considered matters of justice. Noll and Murdock (2020) argue that the creation of food security programmes is often guided by egalitarian conceptions of justice, or the idea that individuals have what is called a "positive right" to food (or an entitlement strong enough to compel others to act on one's behalf). For instance, The United Nations Universal Declaration of Human Rights states that all people have a basic right to access to food (UN 1948).

In recent years, the idea that people have a right to food has been expanded by international farmers groups (such as La Via Campesina) to include other rights claims. Critiques of food security frameworks sparked the development of an alternative model called food sovereignty (Morales 2011, Schanbacher 2010). For initiatives which embrace food sovereignty, food is more than just a commodity that we are entitled to—food is intertwined with political action, culture, identity, and place. This literature embraces the position that communities should not only have access to foodstuffs, but also have greater control over food systems. These expanded justice claims typically include mandates that communities should have the right to define agricultural policy, organise food production and processing, prioritise local consumption, protect farm workers from gender- and race-based violence, etc. Thus, supporters of food sovereignty embrace more holistic models of justice. Using this framework, farmers' groups around the globe are attempting to change food systems, one neighbourhood at a time.

Human and environmental health

In addition to social concerns, impacts of food and farming on human health is a prominent theme in the literature. For example, the quest to identify better dietary choices was of great social importance for historical societies (Zwart 2000). The Ancient Greeks considered thoughtful eating an important part of living a good life. A key component of morality for the Greeks was developing virtues or "habits" that help people perform well, no matter the circumstances. In all situations, we can act excessively or deficiently, but a wise person finds the "golden mean", or the middle path between the two. And there is no better opportunity to develop these habits then when we're deciding what to eat. To maintain health and train our habits, food became an item of major concern for which no universal recipes could be put forward. Rather, eaters had to discover their own best daily regimen through trial and error.

Today, eaters are increasingly worried about health impacts associated with industrial agricultural practices. Both the local food and the organic farming movements are grounded in concerns about how food systems impact human health (Delind 2011). For example, common justifications for buying organic products include claims that the food is healthier, free from contaminants, or produced in a way that does not pose a disease risk (Thompson 2015). Here, food labelling becomes an ethical issue, as consumers need information to make informed choices that align with their values. The idea that we can "vote with our dollars" is an important part of this literature. Other justifications for buying local or organic produce align with the third category of concern, namely environmental impacts. These concerns were first discussed by the founders of the organic movement in the early 20th century, but the publication of Rachel Carson's *Silent Spring* in 1962 cemented environmental concerns firmly in the public sphere. This publication included critiques of pesticide use, highlighting negative impacts on human and wildlife populations, as inputs may be harmful when improperly stored, handled, or applied. These and other ecological issues continue to play a prominent role in ethical discussions surrounding emerging agricultural technologies, such as the introduction of genetically modified organisms into food systems and surrounding environments.

Animal welfare and rights

Another important theme in the literature is animal welfare. The legal and ethical protection of animals has a long history in both the United States and Europe. Public concern rose steadily for the well-being of farm animals, especially since the publication of Ruth Harrison's *Animal Machines* in 1966. Today, the debate concerning animal use has become quite acrimonious, with some parties on both sides taking extreme positions. Few would deny that caregivers have ethical responsibilities to assure the well-being of food animals. Farmers have traditionally embraced a personal stewardship ethic, where animal health and well-being are thought to correspond closely with a producer's interest in increasing farm efficiency (Rollin 1995). However, the correlation between producer and animal interests breaks down when one of three conditions occurs (Thompson and Noll 2015). First, some products require production methods contrary to animal well-being. For example, *foie gras*, a popular delicacy in French cuisine, is produced by force feeding ducks or geese to enlarge their livers. Second, some elements of animal well-being may be realisable only under ideal conditions seldom achieved in production contexts. Third, with some large operations, the management costs of attending to the needs of a few individual animals might not be matched by returns based on aggregated sales of animal products. Animal protection organisations have criticised agricultural producers on each of these three points.

These criticisms have galvanised the public, who increasingly call for improved animal welfare standards and/or abolition of animal use in agriculture. This debate also highlights how there are multiple uses of the terms "animal welfare" and "animal rights", which can be confusing. For some eaters, the term "animal rights" implies an extreme reformist position, while "animal welfare" is taken to imply an attitude favouring moderate reform in animal agriculture. However, popular use of animal rights suggests that the term expresses support for the position that individual animals' interests deserve consideration. More formal uses of these terms have been introduced into the literature by Peter Singer and Tom Regan, two influential voices in the animal liberation movement. Regan's (1995) position is rights based, as he argues that animals who fall into the category "subjects of a life" have moral rights. For Regan, all mammals fall into this category and thus should be treated with respect. Regan's rights-based approach rejects the notion of justifying harm to animals for human benefit, regardless of the consequences. He argues that animals, as "subjects of a life," have inherent rights that must be respected, and these rights cannot be overridden by considerations of utility or human preferences. From this position, the moral wrongness of using animals for food, labor, or experimentation is not contingent on the degree of suffering involved but is instead a violation of the animals' intrinsic rights to live freely and without exploitation. In contrast, Singer's view is consequentialist and utilitarian, meaning that the right action is the one that brings about the best consequences for all those involved. For example, Singer might support animal use in certain contexts if the overall benefits outweigh the harm caused to animals. However, he also argues that animals in industrial agriculture suffer to a degree that makes it impossible to justify human consumption of animal products. As such, like Regan, he is commonly associated with animal rights groups advocating radical change. The tension concerning animal welfare and animal rights definitions reflects a wider tension in the food literature concerning animal use.

Future concerns, issues, and questions

Social impacts, human and environmental health, and animal welfare discussions will continue to play a major role in food ethics discussions going forward. However, changing environmental realities are bringing unique concerns, issues, and questions to the forefront. For instance, according to the 2013 National Climate Assessment, "many regions will experience declines in crop and livestock production from increased stress due to weeds, diseases, insect pests, and other climate change induced stresses" (U.S. Department of Agriculture, 2014, n.p.). Improving sustainability, mitigating climate impacts, increasing resilience, and strengthening ecosystems services, are all necessary for ensuring environmental health and maintaining food production in the future. In addition, maintaining global food security will continue to feature prominently in

the literature. Feeding a growing population will become a major issue as climate induced stresses potentially disrupt production. Another important topic is the application of novel agricultural technologies, such as artificial intelligence applications, to increase efficiency and address environmental issues (Thompson 2006). Finally, local food movements and food justice initiatives increasingly demand that we move away from industrial production methods and embrace equitable food systems (Alkon 2012). As such, community supported agriculture, urban farming, and other alternative production methods will play a major role in the literature—and in societies more broadly—moving forward.

References

Alkon, A.H., 2012. *Black, White, and Green: Farmers Markets, Race, and the Green Economy.* University of Georgia Press, Athens.

Carson, R., 1962. *Silent Spring.* Houghton Mifflin Harcourt Trade & Reference Publishers, Boston.

DeLind, L.B., 2011. Are Local Food and the Local Food Movement Taking Us Where We Want to Go? Or Are We Hitching Our Wagons to the Wrong Stars? *Agriculture and Human Values* 28, 273–283.

Gaus, G., Courtland, S.D., Schmidtz, D., 2018. Liberalism. In: Zalta, E.N. (ed.), *The Stanford Encyclopedia of Philosophy.* Metaphysics Research Lab, Stanford University.

Hardin, G., 1968. "The Tragedy of the Commons." *Science* 162 (3859): 1243–48.

King, R., 2007. Eating Well: Thinking Ethically about Food. In: Allhoff, F. and Monroe, D. (eds.) *Food and Philosophy.* Blackwell Publishing, New York, pp. 177–191.

Morales, A., 2011. Growing Food and Justice: Dismantling Racism Through Sustainable Food Systems. In: Alkon, A. and Agyeman, J. (eds.) *Cultivating Food Justice: Race, Class, and Sustainability.* MIT Press, Cambridge, MA, pp. 149–176.

Noll, S., Murdock, E., 2020. Whose Justice Is It Anyway? Mitigating the Tensions Between Food Security and Food Sovereignty. *Journal of Agricultural and Environmental Ethics* 33, 1–14. https://doi.org/10.1007/s10806-019-09809-9

Pollan, M., 2009. *In Defense of Food: An Eater's Manifesto.* Penguin USA, New York.

Rawls, J., 2001. *Justice as Fairness: A Restatement.* Harvard University Press, Cambridge, MA.

Regan, T., 1995. Obligations to Animals are Based on Rights. *Journal of Agricultural & Environmental Ethics* 8, 171–180.

Rollin, B., 1995. *Farm Animal Welfare: Social, Bioethical, and Research Issues.* Iowa State Press, Ames.

Schanbacher, W.D., 2010. *The Politics of Food: The Global Conflict Between Food Security and Food Sovereignty.* ABC-CLIO, Santa Barbara.

Singer, P., 2015. *Animal Liberation: The Definitive Classic of the Animal Movement.* Open Road Media.

Singer, P., 1972. Famine, Affluence, and Morality. *Philosophy and Public Affairs* 1, 229–243.

Singer, P., Mason, J., 2007. *The Ethics of What We Eat: Why Our Food Choices Matter.* Potter/Ten Speed/Harmony/Rodale.

Thompson, P.B., 2015. *From Field to Fork: Food Ethics for Everyone.* Oxford University Press, Oxford.

Thompson, P.B., 2006. Should We Have GM Crops? *Santa Clara Journal of International Law* 4, 74–95.

Thompson, P.B., Noll, S., 2015. Agriculture Ethics. In: Thompson, P. and Kaplan, D. (eds) *Ethics, Science, Technology, and Engineering: An International Resource.* Cengage Press, Independence, pp. 35–42.

United Nations, 1948. Universal Declaration of Human Rights [WWW Document]. United Nations. http://www.un.org/en/universal-declaration-human-rights/ (accessed 15.1.19).

U.S. Department of Agriculture (USDA), 2014. [WWW Document]. Our Changing Climate: Third National Climate Assessment Released. https://www.usda.gov/media/blog/2014/05/06/our-changing-climate-third-national-climate-assessment-released (accessed 9.10.23).

Zwart, H., 2000. A Short History of Food Ethics. *Journal of Agricultural and Environmental Ethics* 12, 113–126.

Further reading

Kaplan, D.M., 2020. *The Philosophy of Food.* University of California Press, Berkeley.

David Kaplan provides a succinct and accessible introduction to the philosophical dimensions of food. In the volume, he examines the meaning of food and the social role it plays, as well as its ethical and political dimensions. It's an excellent overview of the subject that helps readers to embrace a broader understanding of food.

Alkon, A.H., 2012. *Black, White, and Green: Farmers Markets, Race, and the Green Economy.* University of Georgia Press, Athens.

Local food movements are changing suburban and urban landscapes. Alison Alkon's book explores the dimensions of class and race, as they relate to local food systems and farmers markets. The volume provides an important analysis of how neighbourhoods are using community food initiatives to bring about social and environmental change.

Thompson, P.B., 2015. *From Field to Fork: Food Ethics for Everyone.* Oxford University Press, Oxford.

Paul B. Thompson applies a philosophical lens to explore the interconnections between food and many aspects of our personal and political lives. He examines the reasons behind the sudden increase in public interest in food matters. *From Field to Fork* provides an in-depth overview of the current literature on ethics and food—one that stresses how food and agricultural issues span economic, environmental, social and political, and personal spheres.

38. Fair trade and food

AGATHA HERMAN

Introducing Fair Trade and Fairtrade

> Fair Trade is a trading partnership, based on dialogue, transparency and respect, that seeks greater equity in international trade. It contributes to sustainable development by offering better trading conditions to, and securing the rights of, marginalized producers and workers – especially in the South. (FTAO, 2018: 11)

Agriculture is central to the lives and livelihoods of the majority of the global poor. Fair Trade's efforts to address longstanding, and ongoing, inequalities, injustices and volatility in global food production networks therefore play a key role in supporting sustainable and equitable socio-economic and environmental developments in rural areas. Fair Trade began as a post-World War II alternative trading system in Europe and North America; through political solidarity, collective principles and face-to-face relations it aimed to transform transnational economic activity through trade-not-aid development (Raynolds, 2012) with an initial focus on handicrafts and selected food products. The introduction of labelling in 1988 bifurcated this movement with the more formalised, standardised and professionalised certification system becoming dominant. This culminated in the establishment in 1997 of what is now Fairtrade International, a global body governing Fairtrade standards and labels.

Today, certified Fairtrade 'is about better prices, decent working conditions, local sustainability, and fair terms of trade for farmers and workers around the world, but particularly in lower income countries' (Fairtrade Foundation, 2023). While the Fairtrade mechanisms of a guaranteed minimum price (varying by region and production technique), social premium, pre-financing, democratic organising and monitoring were initially used to champion the small-scale producers most vulnerable to global trade inequalities (Trauger, 2014), subsequent market and organisational growth has been driven by the expansion of standards to new products and production spaces, including plantations. As of 2023, Fairtrade International lists 20 product categories, 14 of which are food items,

with 47% of all Fairtrade farmers producing coffee (Fairtrade Foundation, 2023). Food production is therefore central to Fairtrade, accounting for a significant proportion of the 1.9 million farmers and workers in certified producer organisations worldwide (*ibid*), with the iconic tropical products of bananas, cocoa, coffee, sugar and tea particularly framing Fairtrade debates.

Certification allowed mainstreaming, which grew markets and so impacts within the system. However, the influx of corporations and plantations on which this was built has been critiqued. While Fairtrade highlights the interconnected nature and transnational scale of conventional market inequalities, and presents a well-known platform advocating for trade justice, there remain ongoing debates around exclusions and innovations within the system as well as the future of third-party certification more generally.

The politics and impacts of Fairtrade practices

Who is Fairtrade for?

A longstanding critique of sustainability labels such as Fairtrade is that they homogenise what are diverse local systems. Although the basic principles are the same, bananas, vanilla, coffee and wine – amongst others – all have certain, unique characteristics. How to negotiate between local and international definitions and practices of equity and justice represents a key tension in experiences of Fairtrade governance and certification.

In 2011, producers became equal owners of Fairtrade International, whose standards and pricing reviews are also grounded in regular, global consultations. While this improved transparency and responsiveness, institutional hierarchies of cultural value continue to shape which producers participate and how. The shift to a 'quality economy' has excluded the most marginalised, who would arguably benefit the most from Fairtrade support, from gaining certification with the quality requirements favouring large and well-established producers, cooperatives and corporations (Herman, 2021). Other barriers such as language, IT skills, internet access and education levels also exclude some from becoming certified and others from thriving within the system. Fairtrade's homogenising global marketing and standards may be necessary to govern this multistakeholder, transnational market system but they can also mask the contingency that makes up local Fairtrade engagements (see Herman, 2020, 2021). This seeming lack of care for local context can also deter both new and existing producers (Herman, 2019).

The question 'who is Fairtrade for?' is therefore a contested one. If it is for small producers, then who is able to participate? What role do gender, disability, income, class, education and age play in individuals' and communities' capabilities to engage? If Fairtrade is for workers, then how can companies' inclusion be balanced with maintaining equitable terms of trade for smaller producers? Intra-system competition is particularly contentious given the longstanding issue of surplus supply (see Herman, 2019). Growing demand through mainstreaming into volume retailers required certifying the very global production networks Fairtrade was formed to counteract, and this burgeoning corporate participation reinforces North–South inequalities. How then can Fairtrade increase its impact while maintaining its original role as a benchmark for change?

Innovating in a changing market

The first certified Fairtrade products – cocoa, coffee and tea – launched in 1994, joined by honey (1998), bananas (2000), fruit juice (2001), oranges and table grapes (2003) and wine (2004). The latter marked a shift in approach from everyday foodstuffs to luxury consumables, which was also reflected in the increasingly premium market positioning of Fairtrade coffee and chocolate, resulting from a growing need to compete on quality and price. However, consumers are more likely to pay higher Fairtrade prices for basic rather than premium products because they perceive that 'luxury' producers are already better positioned to achieve profitable terms of trade. Fairtrade moving into sectors such as wine helps draw attention to the labour and social justice issues present in *all* value chains. While consumers may question the connection between 'fine wine' and the traditional imaginaries of small, marginalised producers, this highlights the need for – but also challenges of – extending Fairtrade beyond the North–South imaginary of its traditional, tropical foods. Fairtrade has successfully demonstrated that it is not just for everyday, or even food, commodities with standards for

gold (2011), carbon (2015) and textiles (2016) pushing the boundaries of what counts as a legitimate Fairtrade product and producer, and building the market through extending the certified range.

Nonetheless, critics argue that growing the system is diluting Fair Trade's moral economy, with the tendency for more 'minor transformations' reproducing the status quo in power and social relations (Staricco, 2017). Furthermore, engaging with multiple and diverse sectors has meant that Fairtrade has had to adapt its standards, for example there is no minimum price for sugar or cut flowers, while the latter are also solely produced on plantations. Despite these and other challenges, Fairtrade retains a strong degree of buy-in from stakeholders throughout its value networks (Herman, 2019) and its presence and advocacy has ensured that justice issues are visible, and actionable, for both producers and consumers. Fairtrade's 'living' nature means it can respond to changing contexts and emerging concerns; certification standards, for example, now include climate and deforestation requirements (Millard 2021). However, despite strong brand awareness in markets such as the UK, where 93% of adults recognise the Fairtrade mark (Fairtrade Foundation, 2023), corporations are moving away from third-party certification systems.

The rise of in-house certification

In 2009, Cadbury's Dairy Milk and Nestlé's KitKat went Fairtrade. Nestlé had already launched a Fairtrade coffee in 2005 and, together with major supermarkets establishing Fairtrade own-label lines for products such as bananas, tea and sugar, it seemed that the transparency and accountability afforded by third-party certifiers, such as Fairtrade or the Rainforest Alliance, was gaining traction in consumer markets. However, in 2016 Cadbury switched from Fairtrade to its own 'Cocoa Life' programme. In 2017 Sainsbury's own-brand tea became 'Fairly Traded' and in 2020 KitKat lost its Fairtrade status, as Nestlé expanded its in-house 'Cocoa Plan'.

Large corporations are moving away from the third-party certifiers that provided an initial, simple response to consumers' socioenvironmental concerns to in-house solutions, which can apply to their whole brand, achieve exactly what the business wants and at the desired scale (Millard 2021). Although appearing to be a maturing of the ethical market since a socio-environmental baseline has been established as important to consumers, internal standards are weaker, being more flexible and with no external oversight, raising concerns about 'virtue washing' existing practices and power relations. Millard (2021) notes that small and medium enterprises are continuing with third-party certification, but this proliferation of labels adds to consumer confusion and a drop in trust as companies engage in a 'race to the bottom' in a still growing market for ethically certified commodities. Ultimately, this highlights a key challenge for standards such as Fairtrade, which are dependent on the voluntary participation of capital-focused businesses that have very different priorities to producers and certification systems. A risk management-necessitated drive for 'responsible sourcing', ensuring that farmers can remain competitive, is not synonymous with pushing for the socio-economic and environmental changes that third-party certification systems are founded on.

Working within the market also opens Fairtrade up to critiques that it does not challenge the wider injustices of conventional trading relations and practices by still fundamentally relying on a capitalist consumerist system. For critics (see Kneafsey et al., 2021), this 'anaemic' politics based on voluntary consumer choice creates parallel 'ethical' and 'conventional' markets, which absolve both state and business of real responsibility, and reduce what should be relations of care-full justice and solidarity between producers and consumers to depoliticised commodities.

Where next for Fairtrade?

Although Fairtrade has conventionalised, it has brought many developmental and market benefits for its producers, and has institutionalised goals of fairness and value in corporate networks (Barrientos, 2013). Nevertheless, to maintain its status as an ethical market pioneer, it needs to re-engage practices with ideals, particularly across three, interconnected concerns:

1.   How to address inequalities

Fairtrade needs to acknowledge the persistence of network inequalities, and so open up the opportunity to reflect on how mainstreaming has really impacted on producers,

as well as debate the nature of the relationship between Fairtrade partners. Power remains embedded in the Global North but the regional scale offers a useful arena of contestation and opportunity to re-evaluate and co-produce the relationships that structure Fairtrade's social compact. Fairtrade needs to strengthen its internal relations and address persistent inequalities in order to ensure responsive and just commodity networks (Herman, 2019).

2.   How to ensure space for alternative ways of doing trade justice

Fairtrade is not homogeneous, and its institutionalisation has excluded certain groups and precluded individuals, communities and organisations from thinking or doing trade justice differently (Herman, 2021), which is a challenge for alternative food systems more generally. Multi-directional dialogue is essential but Fairtrade as a global organisation is too unwieldy to really practice connective and caring relations within its multiscalar networks. A global governance structure remains important for brand legitimacy but decentralisation would enable direct discussions over Fairtrade's rhetoric, practices and impacts. Nonetheless, the practical challenge remains as to how exactly Fairtrade can build such global networks of solidarity, responsibility and dialogue amongst its millions of stakeholders.

3.   How to reinvigorate the Fairtrade community

Fairtrade International needs to re-establish its foundation as a common project and demonstrate its stakeholders' shared goals, ideals and solidarity. More continual and open ways of (re)defining Fairtrade makes space for the relational, communicative and active communities that are essential to building a politics of connectivity across distance, difference and scale. Big questions remain, however. How do you promote initial and continuing participation? What are the mechanisms for participation? Who do they exclude? How do you combine responsiveness with solidarity across a diverse network (Herman, 2020)? Making space for stakeholders to become co-investigators in an ongoing and reflexive process of definition and praxis offers one potential route for Fairtrade to build a more responsive system, which is better placed to negotiate the balance between its local and global needs.

References

Barrientos S (2013) Corporate Purchasing Practices in Global Production Networks: a socially contested terrain. *Geoforum* 44, 44–51. https://doi.org/10.1016/j.geoforum .2012.06.012

Fairtrade Foundation (2023) What Is Fairtrade? https://www.fairtrade.org.uk /what-is-fairtrade/ (Accessed 09 March 2023).

FTAO (2018) The International Fair Trade Charter. https://www.fair-trade.website/the -charter-1 (Accessed 09 March 2023).

Herman A (2019) Asymmetries and Opportunities: power and inequality in Fairtrade wine global production networks. *Area* 51, 332–339. https://doi.org/10.1111/ area.12467

Herman A (2020) Building a Politics of Connectivity: intercultural in-commonness in Fairtrade. *Antipode* 52, 1310–1330. https://doi.org/10.1111/anti.12633

Herman A (2021) Governing Fairtrade: ethics of care and justice in the Argentinean wine industry. *Social and Cultural Geography* 22, 425–446. https://doi.org/10.1080 /14649365.2019.1593493

Kneafsey M, Maye D, Holloway L and Goodman M K (2021) *Geographies of Food: an introduction*. London, Bloomsbury Publishing.

Millard E (2021) How Fair Trade can stay strong as companies scale up their social and environmental programmes. *Journal of Fair Trade* 3, 54–63. https://doi.org/10 .13169/jfairtrade.3.1.0054

Raynolds L T (2012) Fair Trade: social regulation in global food markets. *Journal of Rural Studies* 28, 276–287. https://doi .org/10.1016/j.jrurstud.2012.03.004

Staricco J I (2017) Transforming or Reproducing Conventional Socioeconomic Relations? Introducing a regulationist framework for the assessment of Fairtrade. *World Development* 93, 206–218. https:// doi.org/10.1016/j.worlddev.2016.12.021

Trauger A (2014) Is Bigger Better? The small farm imaginary and fair trade banana production in the Dominican Republic. *Annals of the Association of American Geographers* 104, 1082–1100. https://doi .org/10.1080/00045608.2014.923720

Further reading

Herman A (2018) *Practising Empowerment in Post-Apartheid in South Africa: wine, ethics and development*. London, Routledge.

This monograph offers an in-depth analysis of the South African wine industry, drawing on extensive and longitudinal fieldwork with workers, farmers, distributors, regulators, civil society and government. It provides insights into the challenges but also opportunities of engaging with ethics and justice, through exploring the relations and practices of Fairtrade, organics and Broad-Based Black Economic Empowerment, in the unique, politicised and racialised context of South Africa.

Raynolds L T and E A Bennett (Eds) (2016) *Handbook of Research on Fair Trade*. Cheltenham, UK and Northampton, MA, USA, Edward Elgar Publishing.

This edited collection combines a comprehensive overview with an in-depth analysis of key perspectives, opportunities and challenges within the historical and contemporary Fair Trade movement. Bringing in producer, regulator, distributor, retailer and consumer voices, it offers insights into the diversity of initiatives, regions, products and markets that constitute Fair Trade.

39. Faith-based organisations and food

DANA-MARIE RAMJIT

Introduction

Food insecurity remains a pressing global challenge, deepened by various crises such as conflicts, natural disasters, and economic downturns. Faith-based organisations play a crucial role in addressing philanthropic issues. Particularly highlighted during the COVID-19 pandemic, these organisations have provided health support, alleviated poverty, and offered aid to those in distress, through food assistance. This is especially significant considering the ongoing global hunger challenges. The Global Hunger Index (2022) indicates that 44 countries are currently experiencing alarming levels of food insecurity, while 46 countries are projected to achieve low hunger levels by 2030. This disparity underscores the differing degrees of food security and accentuates the need for tailored interventions to address hunger.

The involvement of faith-based organisations in food relief efforts is guided by their spiritual and ethical beliefs, which stress the importance of caring for the less fortunate and addressing human suffering. Many religious faiths regard feeding the hungry as a moral obligation and a way to demonstrate love and compassion towards others. Faith-based organisations have established networks and connections within their communities, allowing them to respond rapidly and effectively to emergencies.

This entry delves into the significant role of faith-based organisations in tackling food insecurity during crises. It highlights their grassroots strategies and the lasting networks they build to withstand immediate challenges. Furthermore, it discusses the hurdles and prospects these organisations encounter in maintaining their initiatives, emphasising the crucial need for continual support and collaboration to ensure sustained impact.

Global food insecurity and crisis

Food insecurity occurs when there is limited or uncertain access to adequate food, due to economic or social conditions at the household level (Treyz et al., 2021). In many regions, food insecurity results from insufficient food production, inequitable distribution, poverty, and lack of access to resources. Vulnerable populations, including women, children, elderly people, and marginalised communities, are disproportionately affected by food insecurity.

Addressing global food insecurity requires a comprehensive approach considering the underlying causes and systemic issues. This includes investing in sustainable agriculture, improving access to education and healthcare, promoting gender equality, and building resilient food systems. It also involves supporting smallholder farmers, empowering local communities, and strengthening social safety nets to ensure food security for all, especially during times of crisis.

The role of faith-based organisations

Faith-based organisations are humanitarian relief and development entities established by or affiliated with diverse religious affiliations and motivated by social and moral values. Faith-based organisations play a crucial role in addressing food insecurity, particularly at the local community level, where they function as a social safety net when state support is insufficient, inaccessible, or non-existent.

Faith-based organisations contribute to various anti-hunger initiatives, such as food distribution, food banks, agricultural programmes, and health advocacy. In the United States, across 12 states surveyed, food pantries were mainly affiliated with Judeo-Christian organisations, with 63.2% being faith-based (Riediger et al., 2022). In Nigeria, the Catholic-based Diocesan Development Services established a network of groups called Farmer Councils, offering micro-savings and micro-credit programmes designed to support food security (Morse & McNamara, 2020). Organisations like World Vision, The Salvation Army, Samaritan's Purse, and Compassion International are some of the largest prominent Christian charities with global operations, offering extensive humanitarian aid and development programmes.

What distinguishes faith-based organisations from other entities addressing food insecurity is their community-led approach that emphasises food justice and tackles systemic inequalities. Faith-based organisations leverage local knowledge, experiences, and faith to influence food governance and promote food sovereignty. These organisations have established networks and connections within their communities, allowing them to respond rapidly and effectively to crises.

Despite these efforts, faith-based organisations are challenged by a lack of support, including inadequate funding, limited collaboration with the state, and limited resource access. These entities require recognition, legitimacy, and collaboration to enhance their work. To achieve equitable, inclusive, and sustainable food practices in countries facing severe hunger, a political shift is necessary to recognise the power of local governance. Faith-based organisations are vital in addressing food insecurity, a crucial aspect of modern humanitarian efforts. Their involvement is particularly significant today, where food availability does not guarantee equity, and global hunger remains a persistent challenge.

Future concerns

The role of faith-based organisations in addressing food-related issues is poised to remain crucial. Ethical approaches to food involve tackling social inequality, poverty, accessibility, and racial injustice alongside prioritising local capacity-building, collaboration, and moral leadership. These organisations serve vulnerable populations, aligning their interventions with cultural values. For these organisations to continue providing comprehensive food solutions, they must maintain transparency, accountability, inclusivity, and flexibility. Additionally, advocating for political restructuring is essential. The future of faith-based organisations in the food sector and civil society hinges on their ability to adapt to changing circumstances while upholding their values and serving communities.

References

Global Hunger Index (2022). *Food Systems Transformation and Local Governance.* https://www.globalhungerindex.org/

Morse, S., & McNamara, N. (2020). Role of Faith-Based Social Groups in promoting sustainable food security in Nigeria. In: Silvern, S. and Davis, E. (eds) *Religion, Sustainability and Place: Moral geographies of the Anthropocene* (pp. 173–198). Singapore: Palgrave Macmillan.

https://doi.org/10.1007/978-981-15-7646-1_8

Murrell, A. J., Jones, R., Rose, S., Firestine, A., & Bute, J. (2022). Food security as ethics and social responsibility: An application of the Food Abundance Index in an urban setting. *International Journal of Environmental Research and Public Health, 19*(16), 10042. https://doi.org/10.3390/ijerph191610042

Riediger, N. D., Dahl, L., & Biradar, R. A. (2022). A descriptive analysis of food pantries in twelve American states: Hours of operation, faith-based affiliation, and location. *BMC Public Health, 22*, 525. https://doi.org/10.1186/s12889-022-12847-0

Treyz, A., Bilecky, E. L., Zoubek, S., Hill, D., & Zuckerman, J. (2021). *The Practitioner Landscape: How Faith Communities Are Involved in Food Systems Work.* D. W. F. P. Center. https://wfpc.sanford.duke.edu/wp-content/uploads/sites/15/2022/03/Landscape-FaithPractitioners-Food-DukeWFPC-April-2021.pdf

Further reading

Tarpeh, S. S., & Hustedde, R. J. (2020). How faith-based organizations perceive their role in community development: An exploratory study. *Community Development, 52*(1), 61–76. https://doi.org/10.1080/15575330.2020.1831565

This article explores the role of faith-based organisations in community development, focusing on Christian faith-based groups. It examines how these organisations perceive and utilise concepts such as solidarity and agency in their work and their role within the Community Capitals Framework. It suggests potential partnerships with government and other organisations to strengthen the effectiveness of faith-based community development efforts.

World Food Policy Center. (2024). Duke University. https://wfpc.sanford.duke.edu/

This resource provides diverse perspectives on food systems from historical, cultural, and racial angles. As a policy think tank, the World Food Policy Center at Duke University breaks down tough questions like how a decolonised food system looks in contemporary society, how power shifts can create sustainable and equitable food systems, and what a justice-centred framework can tell us about intersections and injustices between food, colour, and faith.

DANA-MARIE RAMJIT

40. Famine, hunger and starvation

DAVID NALLY

Introduction: Malthusian origins

The modern conceptualisation and understanding of famine owes much to the thinking of Thomas Robert Malthus, a Church of England cleric, demographer and holder of the first Chair of Political Economy at Haileybury College – the institution responsible for training many of the administrators of the British Empire. Malthus's argument, articulated in his *Essay on the Principle of Population* (1798), was simple but powerful: because land is a scarce resource, food production invariably lags behind population growth, which increases at a far faster "geometric" rate. The resulting imbalance between food availability and human fertility leads to population growth with the balance between those two forces only restored when either war, disease or famine reduce the population, or the population takes it upon itself to exercise "moral restraint" regarding its own fertility. Malthus believed that voluntary restraint was uncommon, especially among the "lower orders", and thus the "positive checks" of disease, conflict and famine were necessary to draw off surplus numbers.

Malthus's *Essay* was reprinted several times during his life, and it commanded a wide readership. Even those who had not read it were familiar enough with its broad outlines and the epithet "Malthusian" was widely used to signal a position not only on population matters, but on a range of issues relating to the appropriate management of the poor. Indeed, before the success of Malthus's *Essay*, hunger and famine were widely understood as elements that the poor ought to be protected against, and to secure adequate food supplies and ward off disaster, governments frequently put in place a wide range of measures, from price controls to public granaries. If scarcity did threaten, states acted swiftly, banning the exportation of food and the use of grains to feed livestock or produce alcohol, and lowering tariffs to promote a higher volume of food imports. The poor would also enforce what has been described as a "moral economy", using riots and other forms of public protest to pressure authorities to suppress rising prices and punish hoarding (Bohstedt 2010).

In the decades after the book's publication, it was much more common to question norms and policies designed to assist the poor on the grounds that "gratuitous" or free relief not only subsidised the poor, but also taught them that they could have more children without having to bear the responsibility for their support. To reduce misery in the long run, it was now thought necessary to avoid any intervention that might minimise "nature's penalty" for improvident reproduction (Polanyi 2001 [1941]: 173).

Malthus's views found their way into policy, most notably in the revised English Poor Law (1834), but it was in Europe's colonies that his ideas found their clearest, and arguably fullest, expression (Bashford and Chaplain 2016). Citing Malthus's iron-clad "laws", colonial officials claimed that famine was the logical outcome of improvident breeding and, moreover, any attempt to intervene to mitigate its impacts would only worsen the situation. Unsurprisingly it was also in the colonies where indigenous intellectuals developed a robust counterargument to Malthus's position. Writing about nineteenth-century Ireland, for example, the republican John Mitchel insisted that it was the extractive logic of economic imperialism, not indigenous improvidence, that created the conditions for famine to flourish. "[T]he exact complement of a comfortable dinner in England," Mitchel sardonically declared, "is a coroner's inquest in Ireland" (Mitchel, 1913: xxxiv). The Nobel prize-winning economist Amartya Sen, who grew up in colonial India and retains vivid memories of the war-time famine in Bengal, attacked the claim that famine could be explained as a simple decline in the overall availability of food. Across several case studies – Bengal in 1943, Ethiopia in 1973–74, Bangladesh in 1974, and Sahelian famines in the 1970s – Sen (1981) showed that "food availability decline" was neither the original nor the primary cause of distress, and even when one group suffered a direct loss of food, other groups in the same society were often unaffected. Observing such facts, Sen argued that it is more accurate to think of famine as an outcome of a process of deprivation. Using slightly more technical terms, Sen suggested that people starve when either their "endowments" – that is, the sum of their resources – or their "entitlement set" – meaning the bundle of goods and services that an individual can exploit – shift to such an extent that they can no longer obtain adequate sustenance. The framing of famine as a process of deprivation is clearly a far more complex causal explanation than the simple Malthusian equation of population growth and food availability decline. As Sen himself clarified, "The most important denial made by the entitlement approach is ... the simple analysis in terms of 'too many people, too little food'" (Sen 1980: 616).

Conquest famines

Following Mitchel, Sen, and other critics who drew attention to distributional questions, the trend in modern famine studies is to consider famine as an outcome of a political process (Rangasami 1985; Edkins 2000), rather than the result of unvarying "natural laws". Contemporary analysts also tend to agree that famines do not necessarily begin with crop failures, droughts or climatic hazards, but rather their violence is coordinated much earlier when a population is made progressively vulnerable or reduced to a point of collapse. According to this conceptualisation, droughts, floods and crop failures are "trigger factors", although not necessarily the "underlying" or "structural" cause of famine (Rangasami 1985). This lexical shift recognises the processual nature of subsistence crises and the different degrees of exposure populations face with respect to poverty, economic shocks, physical harm or environmental distress – incidents that very often precipitate mass starvations.

The tendency then, is to *historicise vulnerability* or *exposure to famine* and to raise deeper questions concerning socio-economic inequalities and asymmetrical power relations. What then are the background factors, or enabling contexts, that render certain groups more vulnerable to shocks and hazards? Examining famine conditions in Karamoja, Uganda, Mahmood Mamdani shows how British colonialism began with the "forcible acquisition of land" leaving local people bereft of the means of production and thrust back upon precarious modes of pastoral cultivation (Mamdani 1982: 68). In Angola, Dias notes that the Portuguese took the best land for their coffee and sugar estates, squeezing local populations onto marginal plots and drastically weakening their ability to independently subsist (Dias 1981). In West Africa, the Tuaregs' "desert-side economy" was fatefully undermined by the French colonial administration. According to David Arnold (1988: 50), the people's herds were frequently "pillaged to satisfy colonial demands for meat and skins; and their customary trade in salt and grain dwindled once the railways reoriented trade away from the desert to the coast".

In central Tanzania, where perhaps 20% of the region's Gogo population succumbed to famine from 1917 to 1920, the British requisitioned goods and conscripted local workers to meet wartime demands. The drawing down of local food supplies, compounded by the demands of forced labour, acted like a pincer movement that dramatically reduced the ability of the local people to self-provision. For this reason, the Gogo people associate famine less with food shortages than a "terrifying loss of autonomy" (Maddox 1990, 189). In his influential account, *Silent Violence*, Michael Watts (1983) similarly showed how the colonial state and merchant capital combined to erode the "Sahelian moral economy" – marked by mutualism, common ownership and an ethic of subsistence – leaving Hausa peasants susceptible to ecological stresses that they had previously managed to live with. To this rollcall of destruction, we must add the catalogue of El Niño-inspired famines addressed by Mike Davis (2001) in his totemic study, *Late Victorian Holocaust*. Davis powerfully argued that devastating drought provided an "environmental stage" on which commodity markets, price speculation and the "will of the state" shaped vulnerability to famine and "determined who, in the last instance, died" (Davis 2001).

In each of these cases, the interruption or "dis-articulation" of an older agrarian dynamic was the precursor to a deadly spiral of destitution, crisis, famine and collapse (Nally 2011a; Shenton and Watts 1979; Watts 2015). In a provocative reinterpretation, Alex de Waal (2018) insists that we see these events as collective acts of violence – "mass atrocities" – that start with the conscription of colonised peoples, particularly their land and labour, into an emerging world economy centred on Europe. In other words, these fatalities, or "conquest famines", occurred in the wake of the "far-reaching social disruption" caused by colonisation (de Waal 2018: 55). It is critical to note too that for de Waal starvation was not *necessarily* the primary cause of death. Hungry and weakened bodies are more susceptible to infection, and mass migration – an age-old response to famine – often brought populations together in ways that hastened the spread of communicable diseases (Arnold 1993).

Socialist famines

Colonial or "conquest famines" have been studied more systematically than socialist famines, even though the latter have produced some of the twentieth century's most deadly events (Devereux 2000). The Great Ukraine Famine, or Holodomor (meaning "killing by hunger"), of the 1930s was the result of a "virtual war on the countryside" (Scott 1998: 201) led by Soviet planners who sought to remove prosperous farmers ("dekulakization") and rapidly collectivise agricultural production. In China, perhaps as many 30 million people died because of Mao's "Great Leap Forward" (1958–62), a campaign designed to multiply grain yields and convert China into a modern industrial society. In the mid 1990s, North Korea experienced famine conditions with lower-bound estimates suggesting 240,000 fatalities and upper-bound estimates close to half a million excess deaths (Spoorenberg and Schwekendiek 2012). The causes of North Korea's famine were complex, with the breakup of the Soviet Union (which deprived the government of its main sponsor) and heavy flooding proving to be the immediate trigger. However, the deeper underlying or "structural" causes included the government's push for *juch'e*, or national self-sufficiency, to be achieved through the expansion of agricultural lands and the rapid adoption of industrial methods, especially the "four modernisations" of mechanisation, electrification, irrigation and chemicalisation (Haggard and Noland 2007). These agrarian strategies created one of the world's most input-intensive agricultural systems, with the over-use of chemical fertilisers contributing to soil erosion, river silting and, eventually, catastrophic flooding. As agricultural production faltered, the government cut rations to the Public Distribution Systems, prioritising the needs of high-ranking officials, military personnel and urban dwellers, and cutting supplies to groups deemed to be politically expendable (Haggard and Nolan 2007).

This emphasis on expendability or "political triage" – making decisions that determine who lives and who dies – has been taken up very directly in series of studies on famine conditions in Cambodia under the leadership of the Communist Party of Kampuchea, also known as the Khmer Rouge (Tyner and Rice 2016; Rice 2020; Tyner 2023). Drawing on the theoretical insights of Michel Foucault, Tyner and Rice argue that famine deaths resulted from a "contradictory" set of biopolitical imperatives: on the one hand, the Khmer Rouge were ideologically committed to assembling a new social order – "a planned utopia" – based on the advancement of communes, worker cooperatives, factory production, public works and state-led "care centres". On the other hand, to assemble this new social order, the party's leadership continually drew distinctions between "productive" and "unproductive" forms of life. Those calculations on "living value" empowered the regime to act strategically, including letting certain individuals or groups die. In Foucauldian terms then, famines are moments when the very right to existence of certain populations is radically called into question (cf. Nally 2011b).

Ideology and famine

Famines are thus not only about economic vulnerability; they are also an outcome of political and ideological forces (Nally 2011b). With respect to Bengal, when rumours of starvation reached Winston Churchill he refused to believe them. A report commissioned by Westminster found no evidence of food scarcity, a situation that was taken to mean there was no famine. Significantly, Churchill publicly berated Indians for "breeding like rabbits", reportedly asking why Gandhi hadn't died if food was so scarce (Kineally 2011: 88, 98). Clearly, Churchill and his officials were trapped inside a Malthusian mind-set that took "scarcity" as an index of hunger; they simply could not imagine a famine occurring amidst abundance. However, equally obvious is the fact that racism was a significant factor in the decision to withhold life-saving support from Bengal. Cormac Ó Gráda's conclusion that "there has probably never been a famine where a more caring ruling elite could not have saved more lives" is a powerful reminder that the construction of differences and divisions within and between populations – hierarchies built on class, gender, race, age and ability – are central features of most starvation events (Ó Gráda 2015: 1; cf Watts 1991).

This last point is a reminder that famines have "functions as well as causes", an argument put forward by David Keen (1994) in his foundational study of famine in southwestern Sudan. Indeed, a common theme across many if not all of the famines surveyed above is the notion that human progress can be engineered into social structures and that crises can be used to root out political enemies, laggards, and misfits – those deemed to stand in the way of "modernity" (Vernon 2007; Newman 1990). Malthus thought that the poor brought misery on themselves and that efforts to ease suffering risked dragging the rest of society down to the level of common paupers. Natural laws would restore demographic balance and the role of government was to respect its disciplinary edits: "When nature will govern and punish for us," Malthus tellingly wrote, "it is a very miserable ambition to wish to snatch the rod from her hands" (James 1989: 140). In the colonies, officials concluded that subaltern populations were idle breeders and thus undeserving of basic humanitarian care. Here racial logics dovetailed with the rule of nature advanced by Malthus and his supporters (Nally 2020). However, as we saw with socialist famines, ruling elites rarely saw the population as equally deserving of succour. Whether "kulaks" in the Ukraine or aged and infirm people in North Korea, again and again governing authorities made decisions that determined who lived and who died. Even at the household level, as the work of Megan Vaughan (1987) has shown, vital rations are often distributed to men and boys first, thus sacrificing females in the interest of male survival. If famines can be defined as "wars over the right to existence", as Mike Davis (2001) has suggested, then they are also battlegrounds on which very status the "human" is contested.

References

Alfani G and Ó Gráda C Eds (2017) *Famine in European History*. Cambridge, Cambridge University Press.

Arnold D (1988) *Famine: Social Crisis and Historical Change*. Oxford, Basil Blackwell.

Arnold D (1993) Social crises and epidemic disease in the famines of nineteenth-century India. *Social History of Medicine* 6(3): 385–404.

Bashford, A and J E Chaplin (2016) *The New Worlds of Thomas Robert Malthus: Rereading the Principle of Population*. Princeton, NJ, Princeton University Press.

Bohstedt J (2010) *The Politics of Provisioning, Food Riots, Moral Economy, and Market Transition in England, c.1550–1850*. Farnham, Ashgate.

Davis, M (2001) *Late Victorian Holocausts: El Niño Famines and the Making of the Third World*. London, Verso.

Dias J R (1981) Famine and disease in the history of Angola c.1830–1930. *Journal of African History* 22(3): 349–378.

Devereux S (2000) *Famine in the Twentieth Century*. IDS Working Paper 105. Brighton, UK, Institute of Development Studies.

De Waal A (2018) *Mass Starvation: The History and the Future of Famine*. Cambridge, Polity.

Edkins J (2000) *Whose Hunger? Concepts of Famine, Practices of Aid*. Minneapolis, University of Minnesota Press.

Haggard S and Noland M (2007) *Famine in North Korea: Markets, Aid, and Reform*. New York, Columbia University Press.

James P (ed.) (1989) *T R Malthus: An Essay on the Principle of Population*. Two volumes. Cambridge, Cambridge University Press.

Keen D (1994) *The Benefits of Famine: A Political Economy of Famine and Relief in Southwestern Sudan, 1993–1989*. Princeton, NJ, Princeton University Press.

Kineally T (2011) *Three Famines: Starvation and Politics*. New York, Public Affairs.

Maddox G (1990) Mtunya: famine in central Tanzania, 1917–20. *Journal of African History*, 31(2): 181–197.

Malthus T R (1798) *An Essay on the Principle of Population, as it Affects the Future Improvement of Society with Remarks on the Speculations of Mr. Godwin, M. Condorcet, and Other Writers*. J. Johnson, London.

Mamdani M (1982) Karamoja: colonial roots of famine in north-east Uganda. *Review of African Political Economy* 9(25): 66–73.

Mitchel J (1913) *Jail Journal*. Dublin, M.H. Gill and Son.

Murton B (2000) Famine. In Kiple K F and Ornelas K C (eds) *The Cambridge World History of Food*. Cambridge, Cambridge University Press, pp. 1411–1426.

Nally D (2011a) *Human Encumbrances: Political Violence and the Great Irish Famine*. Notre Dame IN, University of Notre Dame Press.

Nally D (2011b) The biopolitics of food provisioning. *Transaction of the Institute of British Geographers* 36(1): 37–53.

Nally D (2020) Hunger and Famine. In Domosh M, Heffernan M and Withers C W J (eds) *The Sage Handbook of Historical Geography*. London, Sage.

Newman L F (eds) (1990) *Hunger in History: Food Shortage, Poverty and Deprivation*. Oxford, Blackwell.

Ó Gráda C (2009) *Famine: A Short History*. Princeton, NJ, Princeton University Press.

Ó Gráda C (2015) *Eating People Is Wrong, and Other Essays on Famine, its Past, and its Future*. Princeton, NJ, Princeton University Press.

Polanyi K (2001 [1941]). *The Great Transformation: The Political and Economic Origins of Our Times*. Boston, Beacon Press.

Rangasami A (1985) "Failure of exchange entitlements" theory of famine: a response. *Economic and Political Weekly* 20(41/42): 1747–52; 1797–1801.

Rice S (2020) *Famine in the Remaking: Food System Change and Mass Starvation in Hawaii, Madagascar, and Cambodia West*. Morgantown, West Virginia University Press.

Scott J C (1998) *Seeing Like a State: How Certain Schemes to Improve the Human Condition Have Failed*. New Haven, Yale University Press.

Sen A (1980) Famines. *World Development* 8(9): 613–21.

Sen A (1981) *Poverty and Famines: An Essay on Entitlements and Deprivation*. Oxford, Clarendon Press.

Shenton R and Watts M (1979) Capitalism and hunger in northern Nigeria. *Review of African Political Economy* 6(15): 53–62.

Spoorenberg T and Schwekendiek D (2012) Demographic changes in North Korea: 1993–2008. *Population and Development Review* 31(8): 133–58.

Tyner J A (2023) *Famine in Cambodia: Geopolitics, Biopolitics, Necropolitics*. Athens, University of Georgia Press.

Tyner J A and Rice S (2016) To live and let die: food, famine, and administrative violence in Democratic Kampuchea, 1975–1979. *Political Geography* 52: 47–56.

Vaughan M (1987) *The Story of an African Famine: Gender and Famine in Twentieth-Century Malawi*. Cambridge, Cambridge University Press.

Vernon J (2007) *Hunger: A Modern History*. Cambridge, MA, Belknap Press.

Watts M (1983) *Silent Violence: Food, Famine, and Peasantry in Northern Nigeria*. Berkeley, University of California Press.

Watts M (1984) The demise of the moral economy: food and famine in Sudo-Sahelian region in historical perspective. In Earl S (ed.) *Life Before Drought*. Boston, Allen & Unwin, pp. 124–48.

Watts M (1991) Entitlements or empowerment: famine and starvation in Africa. *Review of African Political Economy* 51(1): 9–26.

Watts M (2015) Thinking the African food crisis: the Sahel forty years on. In Herring R J (ed.) *The Oxford Handbook of Food, Politics, and Society*. Oxford, Oxford University Press, pp. 772–94.

Further reading

De Waal A (2018) *Mass Starvation: The History and the Future of Famine*. Cambridge, Polity.
Positions colonial famines as a vital episodes in the making of the modern world and looks ahead to imagine how famines might develop in the future.

Ó Gráda C (2009) *Famine: A Short History*. Princeton, NJ, Princeton University Press.
A concise introduction to famines in the present and past and an excellent overview of famine theory.

Tyner J A (2023) *Famine in Cambodia: Geopolitics, Biopolitics, Necropolitics*. Athens, University of Georgia Press.
Theorises famine as the expression of power over life and brilliantly analyses the micro-political decisions that determine mass mortality.

DAVID NALLY

41. Fast food

Jonathan Deutsch

Introduction: fast food in context

Fast food restaurants, called QSRs (Quick Service Restaurants) in the food industry, are a category of restaurant known for their affordability, quick service, and family-friendliness. As a multi-billion-dollar industry, fast food is relatively young, its rapid growth tied to the mid-20th century rise of car culture in the US (Belasco, 1979) with highway-side restaurants and hand-held meals conducive to being eaten in cars (Rozin, 1994). The items served at fast food restaurants, traditionally hamburgers, fried chicken, French fries, sodas, and milkshakes, for example, are hardly novel, having been mainstays of casual American restaurants from the earlier half of the century, found in many independently owned and operated diners and soda counters across the country (Stern and Stern, 1992). The innovations allowing for the success and scalability of fast food are generally attributed to two elements: standardisation and franchising. Ray Kroc, who bought the McDonald brothers' restaurant in 1961, is credited with creating standardised menus across multiple units, allowing for a consistent experience for customers, large purchasing power for a supply chain to help keep prices affordable, and a total transaction time measurable in seconds rather than minutes, allowing for further innovations such as the drive-through. Ritzer (2021) famously used the McDonald's fast food model to connect food, like many other things in modern society, to a 'cult of speed' and wider processes of globalisation. Powered by global food marketing, 'fast food culture' signifies standardisation and homogenisation, in this case of food items that are consumed around the world with little effort. Also key to the growth of the fast food industry and associated cultures of consumption is a franchise business model, allowing for rapid expansion domestically and globally without the need to raise capital centrally (Love, 1995).

Despite their popularity, nearing ubiquity, fast food restaurants have been criticised for their suboptimal practices from nutritional, sustainability and labour perspectives. While many bemoan the rise of the fast food industry globally as injurious to the health of people and the planet and as displacing traditional diets, the phenomenon of serving quick meals to travellers or busy workers in cities goes back millennia to Ancient Rome, China, and other cultures, where, for low cost, street foods like stews, noodle dishes, dumplings, beverages, and breads could be eaten on the run, much as they are today (Pilcher, 2023).

Societal problems in the fast food industry

Numerous critiques have been levied against the fast food industry. These include the poor nutritional composition of the menus and their hegemonic global spread; advertising fast food to children to encourage life-long habits; the race-to-the-bottom of menu prices and, accordingly, the little paid to farmers and ranchers, many from the Global South, providing the coffee, apples, oranges, beef, chicken, pork, potatoes, wheat, and other commodities necessary to meet global demand; the environmental costs associated with a globalised supply chain and meat-intensive menu with questions about who will be paying the true cost of this seemingly cheap food; horrific animal welfare practices tied to the vast demand for cheap meat; and labour practices that, even with full-time hours, may put a working family below the poverty line in the US and without affordable access to healthcare (Jayaraman, 2021; Schlosser, 2005). A counter to 'fast food', the so-called 'Slow Food Movement', first established in Italy in 1986, is now established globally as a direct challenge to fast food culture and associated systems of retail and production.

Warren Belasco (2008: 70–73) characterises fast food marketing via 'Eight Fs': 'family, fast, fried, filling, "fresh," fantasy, Fordist, and franchised.' These keywords are implicated in a number of societal problems with the industry. First, many fast food menu items are considered ultra-processed foods, meaning calorically dense and high in sodium, added sugar, total fat, and saturated fat, while being low in fibre and micronutrients. This nutritional composition, and the frequency with which menu items can be consumed affordably and conveniently, has been linked to a rise in non-communicable diet-related diseases including overweight and obesity, heart disease, diabetes, hypertension, and stroke (Jaworowska et al., 2013). Further problematising the nutritional inadequacy of fast food is its concentration in poorer communities that may lack adequate access to affordable fresh produce, healthcare, and transportation, exacerbating the health disparities among rural communities and urban communities of colour experiencing poverty and associated lack of food security (Fleischhacker et al., 2011). The large trucks needed to transport globally sourced food to these restaurants and prodigious amounts of trash from disposable packaging and used cooking oil out of these restaurants further adds to urban health concerns about congestion, poor air quality, and waste generation (Gunders and Bloom, 2017). Finally, the fast food industry and the restaurant industry more broadly has been aggressively lobbying to maintain a low minimum wage in countries like the US, necessitating that even full-time workers who make their career in the fast food industry remain eligible for public assistance benefits (Jayaraman, 2021).

Some societal fast food positives

Despite the many problems of the fast food industry for society, there are some positives that merit consideration. While many critics bemoan the negative impact of these restaurants in disadvantaged communities, the industry argues that it is investing heavily in these communities, offering opportunities for local ownership in the form of franchises, providing jobs that pay above the legally mandated minimum wage, and being consistently among the most hospitable workplaces for youth, immigrants, and citizens who have been previously incarcerated (Baskaran, 2018). The US government has been taking advantage of the community presence of fast food restaurants to allow them to provide free meals through a new SNAP (Supplemental Nutrition Assistance Program) benefit for those who cannot cook themselves due to disability or housing status (Cohen, 2022). Many scholars have also pointed out the important social and community role these restaurants can play – offering a safe, well-lit, substance-free, and welcoming environment for families and older adults, while also providing great convenience for workers on non-standard schedules (Watson, 2006). The fast food industry has also made highly visible efforts to offer healthier menu choices and to be more transparent about their sustainability practices (Creel et al., 2008).

References

Baskaran P (2018) Respect the hustle: Necessity entrepreneurship, returning citizens, and social enterprise strategies. *Maryland Law Review* 78, 323.

Belasco W J (1979) *Americans on the Road: From Autocamp to Motel, 1910–1945.* Cambridge, MIT Press.

Belasco W J (2008) *Food: The Key Concepts.* London, Berg Publishers.

Cohen E (2022) *The Restaurant Meals Program: A Guide for New York State's Successful Implementation.* New York, Rochester Institute of Technology.

Creel J S, Sharkey J R, McIntosh A, Anding J and Huber J C (2008) Availability of healthier options in traditional and nontraditional rural fast-food outlets. *BMC Public Health* 8, 1–9.

Fleischhacker S E, Evenson K R, Rodriguez D A and Ammerman A S (2011) A systematic review of fast food access studies. *Obesity Reviews* 12(5), e460–e471.

Gunders D and Bloom J (2017) *Wasted: How America is Losing up to 40 Percent of Its Food from Farm to Fork to Landfill.* Washington, DC, NRDC.

Jaworowska A, Blackham T, Davies I G and Stevenson, L (2013) Nutritional challenges and health implications of takeaway and fast food. *Nutrition Reviews* 71(5), 310–318.

Jayaraman S (2021) *One Fair Wage: Ending Subminimum Pay in America.* New York, New Press.

Love J F (1995) *McDonald's: Behind the Arches.* London, Random House Publishing Group.

Pilcher J M (2023) *Food in World History.* New York, Taylor & Francis.

Ritzer G (2021) The McDonaldization of society. In: Mofield E and Stambaugh T (eds) *In the Mind's Eye.* New York, Routledge, pp. 143–152.

Rozin E (1994) *The Primal Cheeseburger.* New York, Penguin Books.

Schlosser E (2005) *Fast Food Nation.* St. Louis, Turtleback.

Stern J and Stern M (1992) *Roadfood.* New York, HarperPerennial.

Watson J (ed) (2006) *Golden Arches East: McDonald's in East Asia.* Redwood City, CA, Stanford University Press.

JONATHAN DEUTSCH

Further reading

Schlosser E (2005) *Fast Food Nation*. St. Louis, Turtleback.
A detailed exposé of the problems of the fast food industry.

Watson J (ed) (2006) *Golden Arches East: McDonald's in East Asia*. Redwood City, CA, Stanford University Press.
Watson and contributors provide a nuanced view of the introduction and interactions between communities and Western fast food restaurants in East Asia.

JONATHAN DEUTSCH

42. Financialisation and food

SARAH RUTH SIPPEL

Introduction

There is a growing awareness that we live in 'financial times' as financial institutions and markets have gained increasing significance throughout economy and society. Beyond their 'traditional' areas of banking and capital markets, financial actors, logics, and rationales have started to profoundly shape further areas of society, including the ways in which we think about, define, and engage with, as well as produce, distribute, consume, and discard, food. These finance-driven transformations have profound implications for what food and farming look like, what they mean to us, and what they could or should be in society. Such arrangements deeply transform rural areas, reshape the connections between rural and urban spaces, and affect, in multifaceted ways, the everyday lives not only of farmers but also of people and societies more generally. This entry examines these emergent patterns and forms of financialisation in agri-food, introducing in particular three finance-driven transformation pathways and their influences and impacts on food systems and agri-foodscapes.

Food–finance intersections

Although there has been a long history of intersections between finance and agri-food, the strong power that financial actors have attained in our current food system became especially apparent during the global food price and financial crises of 2007/8. Since then, scholars have started to conceptualise the changing role of finance in agri-food as the 'financialisation' of food and farming. Some scholars have considered the financialisaton of agri-food as one of the most important recent transformations in the global food system. There are various definitions of financialisation, ranging from the increasing power and dominance of finance over processes of capital accumulation, to the shift towards shareholder value in corporations, to the way finance has been encroaching into everyday life. All these definitions converge upon the changing, rapidly expanding, and increasingly powerful role of financial actors and of the logics, practices, and rationales of finance

throughout contemporary politics, economy, and society (Mader et al. 2020). Scholars in this field have identified the financialisation of agri-food at three levels: the financialisation of agri-food businesses, speculation in agricultural investment products, and direct investment in agricultural productions (see Gertel and Sippel 2016). All these have been underpinned by the narrative that a growing population will increase demands on global resources, including food. From a financial perspective, this assumed supply and demand dynamic makes investments in the global food system valuable.

Financialisation of agri-food businesses

The financialisation of agri-business corporations, such as supermarkets or grain traders, can be considered as part of a broader process of the financialisation of non-financial companies (Gertel and Sippel 2016). This often means that companies become increasingly governed by the logic of 'shareholder value capitalism', which prioritises returns for shareholders over other values or investment goals in the company. Decades of consolidation and corporatisation have resulted in high levels of power concentration in the agri-food industry. This has made agri-food companies attractive for financial investment. For example, the UK supermarket chain Somerfield became subject to a financial takeover, which, amongst others, led to the implementation of shareholder value norms, the divestment of assets to repay debt, and the reduction of suppliers and employees to cut costs. At the same time, agri-food companies have started to act as financial players themselves. One example of this is large retailers – such as Carrefour, Ahold, Metro, or Target – that increasingly realise income and profits from financial investments and the development of financial activities. Another example are the four largest grain traders – Archer Daniels Midland (ADM), Bunge, Cargill, and Louis Dreyfus – which actively engage in financial speculation on agricultural commodity markets and index funds.

Speculation in agricultural investment products

Financial investment in agricultural investment products such as agricultural commodity futures contracts – agreements to buy or sell a commodity on a future date at a prede-termined price – or commodity index funds – which track an index that includes various commodity assets – is a second area which has increased significantly in recent decades. Importantly, these investment products allow financial investors to capitalise on gains made from agricultural assets without taking the risk of owning any of these assets (Clapp 2017). Agricultural investment products have become subject to financial speculation fol-lowing three main developments: the chang-ing regulatory framework in the US (where the majority of investors and trading activi-ties are concentrated), which relaxed exist-ing restrictions for commodity speculation; the weak performance of 'traditional' asset classes (such as equities and bonds) combined with the 'bursting' of the dot-com bubble and the US housing market in the 2000s; and financial studies of the risk–return character-istics of agricultural commodity derivatives, that is to say financial instruments based on the value of agricultural commodities. These studies touted commodity derivatives as offering non or negative correlations with traditional asset classes, suggesting that if tra-ditional asset classes suffered investments in these, 'alternative' assets would be safe and secure. Hence, such agri-food investments were promoted as valuable alternative invest-ment options. While some financial econo-mists see benefits within these investments, social scientists mostly agree that commod-ity speculation has negative implications, as it contributes to food price volatility especially felt by income-poor households. This became especially apparent when the sharp food price increase of key staple foods in 2007/8 and 2011 provoked 'food riots' in many urban cen-tres across the global south. In short, global food security has become highly complex as the livelihoods of food insecure groups in the global south are now closely tied to specula-tive financial activities on global markets (cf. Gertel and Sippel 2016).

Direct investment in agricultural productions

Direct investment in agricultural production is a third area where agri-food has become financialised. The post-2008 financial interest in farmland has been inspired by the poor per-formance of traditional asset classes coupled with neo-Malthusian arguments concerning the finite availability of land, increasing its value in light of rising global demand for food. This, combined with positive financial attributes ascribed to farmland, such as port-folio diversification and its capacity to hedge against inflation, has made investment in agri-cultural land an attractive proposition. Within financial theory, farmland returns consist of income returns (farm revenues attributed to the land as opposed to labour and manage-ment) and capital returns (the change in the market value of the land). Farmland has thus been touted as being both a productive and an appreciating asset class, or so-called 'gold with yield' (Fairbairn 2014). To more ethically concerned investors, farmland investments have also been promoted as a means to tackle land degradation, for example via regenera-tive agriculture, thereby combatting climate change. Different sources of finance capital (e.g. sovereign wealth funds, pension funds, private equity funds) have pursued differ-ent strategies of global farmland investment, including different target regions, investment timelines, and investment models. However, farmland has not lent itself easily to financial investment. Investments have been faced with substantial backlash from social movements protesting against 'land grabs', and have also provoked regulatory changes by governments. The material nature of farming itself has also presented obstacles to farmland investment.

Future directions and research questions

Moving beyond these three main areas, it will be important to understand how financial practices, logics, and rationales are becoming further enmeshed within agriculture and the food system. One important question con-cerns the implications for everyday activities of farmers. Farmers have become increasingly tied into global financial circuits through (micro-)credits, debt, insurance schemes, and financial inclusion programmes. This creates new risks and dependencies for farmers, and fosters the formation of new farmer subjec-tivities, as farmers increasingly need financial literacy to run their farms. Another important area will be the growing intersection with digitalisation processes, as financialisation and digitalisation of agri-food often mutu-ally condition and reinforce one another. These intersections are, for instance, apparent within the research and development of new agri-food technologies. Financial capital has become an important source of technology funding. This might have important consequences for the kinds, shape, and applicability of future farming technologies. Lastly, it will be important to investigate how the continued financialisation of agri-food assemblages affects the values we attribute to agri-food. Whether we consider food as a commodity, a financial asset, an essential need, or a human right makes an important difference in terms of the societal practices we find acceptable, what we consider makes food and farming legitimate, and how we 'care' for our food.

References

Clapp, J (2017) Responsibility to the rescue? Governing private financial investment in global agriculture. *Agriculture and Human Values* 34, 223–235. https://doi.org/10.1007/s10460-015-9678-8

Gertel, J and Sippel, SR (2016) The financialisation of agriculture and food. In: Shucksmith, M and Brown, D (eds.) *Routledge International Handbook of Rural Studies* (pp. 215–226). Routledge.

Mader, P, Mertens, D and Van der Zwan, N (2020) Financialization: an introduction. In: Mader, P, Mertens, D and van der Zwan, N (eds.) *The Routledge International Handbook of Financialization*, (pp. 1–16). Abingdon: Routledge.

Further reading

Bjorkhaug, B, Magnan, A and Lawrence, G (eds.) (2018) *The Financialization of Agri-Food Systems: Contested Transformations.* Routledge.

An edited volume that collects a range of geographically diverse case studies on different parts of the agri-food system.

Clapp, J and Ryan Isakson, S (2018) *Speculative Harvests: Financialization, Food, and Agriculture.* Fernwood Publishing.

A short introduction that provides an accessible overview of major dynamics and implications of increased financial involvement in agri-food.

Fairbairn, F (2020) *Fields of Gold: Financing the Global Land Rush.* Cornell University Press.

A comprehensive introduction to the financialisation of farmland, including its historical roots, major rationales, and political contexts.

43. Food anarchy

Hannah Kass

Introduction

The concept of food anarchy (Kass, 2022) is inspired by the food sovereignty movement, a counter-hegemonic resistance movement against the corporate food regime – capitalist agriculture's historical culmination in an age of neoliberal capitalism since the 1970s (McMichael, 2005). Food sovereignty asserts the right of people – rather than corporate agribusinesses – to define their own food and agricultural systems. *Food anarchy* is an offshoot of this *food sovereignty* movement in that it offers a more explicitly anarchist interpretation of a movement that is already quite anarchistic in many ways. Food anarchy follows La Via Campesina's (2007) Nyéléni Declaration definition of food sovereignty which asserts "the right of peoples…to define their own food and agriculture systems".

Current issues, concerns and areas of focus

The distinction between food sovereignty and food anarchy is critical to the success of the food sovereignty movement, which has been increasingly co-opted by states captured by authoritarian populist leadership (Tilzey, 2021). Without distinguishing itself as radical, the food sovereignty movement risks integration into neoliberalism and reformism (Holt-Giménez and Shattuck, 2011). Furthermore, the state protects and relies upon capitalist agriculture and property enclosure, generating a "state monopoly on hunger" (Kass, 2022: title). The interdependence of the state, capitalism, and property demonstrates the futility of relying on generating agrifood system change from within the capitalist state. Food anarchy seeks a pathway for change which recognizes this futility by seeking the complete destruction of all food regimes, and building a world free of hunger and dispossession.

As "food sovereignty seeks not just to tweak the existing system but to overhaul it entirely", its advocates "emphasise peasant solidarity and often assert collective rights over resources", and simultaneously "emphasise the need to relocalise both markets and governance" (Fairbairn 2010: 27). These principles and their applications are strikingly similar to the philosophies and praxes of social anarchism. Food sovereignty is rooted in decentralisation in that it builds a counter-power or 'destituent' power – an alternative form of power – seeking to attack and exit the food regime, and it creates autonomous infrastructure that invests in systems of sustenance while divesting from systems of starvation. The importance of prefigurative politics – politics focused on creating the world you wish to see in the here and now – through mutual aid and direct action in accordance with the participatory decision-making of communities defines both the social anarchist movement (Graeber, 2013) and the food sovereignty movement.

Insurrectionary anarchy is another well-represented praxis of food regime resistance – for example, when peasants riot in response to food price spikes and crises of hunger, the riots specifically target the destruction of the unjust food regime under which peasants farm and starve (Holt-Giménez, Patel, and Shattuck, 2009). During the agrarian transition of the enclosure movement in Europe, peasants resisted by seizing criminalised peasant ways of life through illegalist and anti-work disobedience: foot-dragging, theft, trespassing, sabotage or "everyday forms of peasant resistance" (Scott, 1985: xvi). Social and insurrectionary forms of food anarchy often characterise land and water struggles around the world (e.g. Dunlap, 2018; Gilbert, 2023).

Future concerns, issues and questions

Food anarchy encompasses a broad range of revolutionary reclamations of the right of all peoples to define their own agri-food systems. As the fight for food sovereignty continues worldwide, food anarchy encourages movements, scholars and advocates to look closely at the tactics and strategies used by the struggles that have managed to win – and the winnings their struggles have earned them. It is no coincidence that the anarchic aspirations of food sovereignty struggles have made way for more gratifying, and exemplary, gains – take, for example, the peasants in Indonesia who successfully defended their land from paper and rubber plantations (Gilbert, 2023), or the many folks who have benefitted from grassroots free-grocery projects in the wake of the COVID-19 pandemic (Kass, 2022). Food anarchy directs global agrarianism away from tired, ineffective ways of fighting for agri-food system change – it instead challenges us to think and act freely in the fight for food for us all.

References

Dunlap, A. 2018. Insurrection for land, sea and dignity: Resistance and autonomy against wind energy in Álvaro Obregón, Mexico. *Journal of Political Ecology*, 25(1): 120–143.

Fairbairn, M. 2010. Framing Resistance: International Food Regimes and the Roots of Food Sovereignty. In: Wittman, H., Desmarais, A.A., and Wiebe, N. (Eds.) *Food Sovereignty: Reconnecting Food, Nature, and Community*. Halifax: Fernwood Publishing.

Gilbert, D.E. 2023. Shutting down the machines of destruction: Possibilities for agrarian life on the protest blockade. *Antipode: A Journal of Radical Geography*, 55: 1433–1453. https://doi.org/10.1111/anti.12910

Graeber, D. 2013. *The Democracy Project: A History, a Crisis, a Movement*. New York: Spiegel & Grau.

Holt-Giménez, E., Patel, R., and Shattuck, A. 2009. *Food Rebellions! Crisis and the Hunger for Justice*. Oakland: Institute for Food and Development Policy.

Holt Giménez, E. and Shattuck, A. 2011. Food crises, food regimes and food movements: Rumblings of reform or tides of transformation? *The Journal of Peasant Studies*, 38(1): 109–144.

Kass, H. 2022. Food anarchy and the State monopoly on hunger. *The Journal of Peasant Studies*, 50(3): 1187–1206. DOI: 10.1080/03066150.2022.2101099

La Via Campesina. 2007. The Nyéléni Declaration on Food Sovereignty. Food and Agriculture Organization (FAO) Conference Report. https://www.fao.org/agroecology/database/detail/en/c/1253617/

McMichael, P. 2005. Global Development and the Corporate Food Regime. In: Buttel, F.H. and McMichael, P. (Eds.) *New Directions in the Sociology of Global Development*. Oxford: Elsevier Press.

Scott, J.C. 1985. *Weapons of the Weak: Everyday Forms of Peasant Resistance*. New Haven, CT: Yale University Press.

Tilzey, M. 2021. *Authoritarian Populism and Neo-extractivism in Bolivia and Ecuador: The Unresolved Agrarian Question and the Prospects for Food Sovereignty as Counter-hegemony*. In: Scoones, I., Edelman, M., Borras, S.M., Forero, L.F., Hall, R., Wolford, W., and White, B. (Eds.) *Authoritarian Populism in the Rural World*. Routledge.

Further reading

Kass, H. 2022. Food anarchy and the State monopoly on hunger. *The Journal of Peasant Studies*, 50(3): 1187–1206. DOI: 10.1080/03066150.2022.2101099

This article is the introductory article for food anarchy. It also theorises the structural underpinnings of the food regimes which justify a food anarchy framing, the state monopoly on hunger – the state's reliance on capitalism and property enclosure – and the social relationships which uphold this interdependency.

Patel, R. 2009. What does food sovereignty look like? *The Journal of Peasant Studies*, 36(3): 663–706.

This article frames the food sovereignty movement as an iteratively defined, pluralistic movement for agri-food self-determination, doing so by grounding the concept in its framing by the international peasants' rights organization La Via Campesina.

44. Food and technological convergence

DAVID GOODMAN

Introduction: food, technology and biological convergence

The topic of technology and food encompasses a vast range of entanglements, or co-productions, between nature and society, and considers the role of technological innovation in catalysing major transitions in the relationship between food and society. This range extends from the domestication of plants and animals to contemporary applications of artificial intelligence (AI) and machine-learning in crop production, and digital platforms and robotics in food distribution. Understanding the evolution of these entanglements reveals the structural issues embedded in food–society relationships and future food systems concerns.

In agriculture, these transitions have been marked by the progressive transformation of farm operations from relative self-sufficiency to heavy dependence on external, manufactured inputs. Industrial modernisation is the cumulative result of a series of historical appropriations of non-commoditised, on-farm activities, establishing specialised sectors of industrial accumulation, defining the nineteenth century origins of latter-day oligopolistic agribusiness giants, such as John Deere, Monsanto, Bayer and Astra-Zeneca. This continuity is an expression of corporate control of agricultural research and development (R&D), which holds the key to the reproduction of industrial agriculture. The extraordinary continuity of this techno-scientific paradigm reflects a constellation of technological, cognitive, epistemological and institutional factors that combine to lock in a particular technological regime which works to marginalise alternatives and follow trajectories of change that are incremental rather than radically transformative.

The interposition of industrial innovations in the agricultural production process has its counterpart in the reorganisation of food manufacturing into industrial food systems, where industrial substitution has reduced reliance on agriculture for whole foods and raw materials. Before 1914, greater autonomy for key agriculture and food companies was achieved by innovations in preservation techniques, such as canning, dehydration and refrigeration, and large-scale mechanical processing to produce basic 'intermediates'—flour, vegetable oils, animal fats, refined sugar, powdered milk—as standardised, homogenous inputs for food manufacturing. With these early steps, food companies could modify the form and composition of basic food ingredients, creating new sources of value added, opening the way toward mass food production of fabricated, highly processed products.

Analytically, two waves of technological convergence have cumulatively entrenched industrial agriculture as the hegemonic techno-scientific paradigm that defines food systems. Building on the transition from biomass and animal traction to fossil fuel-powered machines and industrial control of plant nutrient supply via ammonia synthesis, the first convergence integrated advances in the plant genetics of hybridisation with complementary mechanical and chemical innovations. This integration produced fertiliser-responsive, high-yielding crops, with greater planting densities and uniform height, extending markets for crop protection chemicals and harvesting equipment. The first technological convergence is characterised by the mechanisation of extensive space, epitomised by the tractor and combine harvester, stimulating greater farm size, concentration of land ownership and rural–urban migration which hollowed out rural communities.

These structural fault lines are now being intensified by the second, contemporary technological convergence between digital code as software and the genetic code as molecular engineering, which is the foundation of precision agriculture, alternative proteins and gene editing. The digitalisation of farm equipment and management practices—sensors, GPS-assisted spatial imaging technologies, drones and other devices—is creating miniaturised, grid-like digital space. Farm landscapes can be reproduced at high levels of resolution, generating large, complex datasets, known colloquially as 'Big Data'. With software analytics, these datasets allow corporate farm service platforms to provide algorithmic prescriptions of input requirements—such as fertiliser or pesticide applications—for subfield management zones on individual farms. The prospect of fully automated crop production systems is now on the horizon. These marketing opportunities have accelerated economic and ownership concentration in the 'seed-chemical complex' of plant science and plant protection companies, with mergers and acquisitions reducing the number of firms from 30 in the 1970s to the current 'Big Four' following a series of mega-mergers in 2016–18 (Howard, 2021). These four firms—Bayer/Monsanto, Correva Agriscience (a spin-off from the Dow/DuPont merger), ChemChina/Syngenta and BASF—control a combined 60% of global seed sales and over 70% of the plant pesticide market across the world.

Miniaturisation also characterises the digital–molecular convergence in the development of alternative proteins as corporate start-ups and agribusiness seek to replicate the molecular properties of farmed meat by screening vast proprietary databases to select proteins and compounds for predictive modelling and possible scaling up for fermentation in bioreactors. Digital–molecular convergence has long been the nexus of agricultural biotechnologies, as the introduction of new seed varieties requires the screening of the countless base pairs in a genome to identify promising traits to insert into the final plant.

Current issues

Industrial agriculture and climate change

The global climate emergency is at the crux of the food and society relationship because the food system is a major contributor to anthropogenic global climate change, the paramount existential question of planetary and human health. The United Nations Food and Agricultural Organisation estimates that the food system, including pre- and post-farm activities, generates 31% of total greenhouse gas (GHG) emissions, led by the 14.5% share of the industrial livestock sector. These causal links place the feed grains–livestock complex front and centre of the climate crisis and its cascading, multi-scale impacts, drawing attention to its technological base of intensive concentrated animal feeding operations (CAFOs), precision agriculture and gene editing.

These issues have opened a polarised debate on the role of alternative proteins in promoting more sustainable consumption as part of a wider transition to a low carbon future. This debate has been framed in terms of 'promissory narratives' (Sexton et al., 2019) regarding the speed and scale of

the mitigation of GHG emissions likely to be achieved by greater consumption of plant-based and cellular proteins as substitutes for farmed animal meat. Optimistic projections of this dietary shift have been tempered by recent evidence that consumption growth has slowed, firms have encountered technical difficulties in scaling up, price parity with farmed meat remains a medium-term goal at best, and the realisation that massive capital investment will be required to capture even a modest share of the global protein market (IPES-Food, 2022). Critics of the promissory narratives marshalled by the alternative proteins industry argue that a 'protein transition' is being confused with a systemic sustainability transition based on agroecological practices and regional and local food systems.

At a more elemental level, the lack of progress toward a broad-based sustainability transition in food and farming reflects the political economic structures that underpin industrial agriculture, notably the control that oligopolistic agribusiness corporations hold over crop production systems and agricultural R&D, ensuring the reproduction of the social structures and power relations of the dominant paradigm. The power these actors exercise in international fora can be seen in the absence of binding commitments to agricultural sustainability in recent COP meetings of the 2015 Paris Climate Accords. The primacy of techno-centric industrial approaches to global warming advocated by the agribusiness establishment is expressively demonstrated by the failure of the 2022 United Nations Food System Summit, convened to delineate pathways to achieve the United Nations Sustainable Development Goals (SDGs). This summit ended in an acrimonious stalemate when corporate interests attempted to wrest control of the international governance of the global food system from multi-lateral public agencies.

Precision agriculture

Precision agriculture (PA), the contemporary face of digitalisation, comprises GPS-assisted spatial imaging tools for yield and soil mapping and auto steer farm machinery equipped with sensors and other surveillance devices, which generate the field data needed to prescribe site-specific variable rate input applications. These innovations effectively transfer decision making power to corporate farm management platforms as the capacity to process these datasets is far beyond the reach of individual farmers. Such concerns have drawn attention to the process of diffusion of PA technologies, how it is differentiated by farm size, and reasons underlying farmer resistance to adoption. Related areas of focus include the further 'appropriationist' round of commodification as farmers rely on the algorithmic rationality of corporate prescriptions rather than the tacit knowledge of place-based personal experience. Research has explored how PA is changing the spatial nature of farm work as screen time displaces traditional outdoor practices. Such debates raise wider issues of farmer identity and autonomy, the politics of knowledge, and mechanisms of disempowerment associated with PA. These include the complex software licensing agreements embedded in digital farm machinery that transfer control over the farm data collected to corporate equipment suppliers. PA has also generated the 'Right to Repair' controversy, which has gained political economic salience in the USA as farmer unions, civil society organisations and, more recently, federal authorities challenge the exclusivity of corporate rights to service the digital machinery sold to farmers. In 2023, Colorado became the first state to respond to this challenge by passing Right to Repair legislation and similar bills have been introduced in a score of other states in the US (Kelloway, 2023).

Highly processed foods, diet and health

The industrial transformation of food manufacturing has gained momentum with the growing refinement of fractionation and separation technologies, complemented by biotechnologies. These techniques reduce food to its molecular constituents for re-assembly into products with a variety of industrial attributes, such as longer shelf-life. The sophistication of industrial formulations of whole foods is exemplified by the marketing of plant-based meat analogues on the 'meat shelf' of supermarkets. However, such 'bio-mimicry' of farmed animal meat places these analogues squarely in the category of highly processed food products, even attracting the label of 'vegan junk food' in reference to the 'molecular farming' involved, as well as the use of emulsifiers, bulking agents and other additives.

Meat analogues thus reflect a wider, more troubling dimension of the technology–food relationship, represented by the global dietary trend to displace minimally processed foods and freshly prepared meals with highly or ultra-processed foods. Industrially fabricated processed foods are now a key variable in the relationship between diet and human health. That is, rising consumption of these formulated foods is widely associated with increasing rates of non-communicable disease, including cardiovascular disease, cancer, diabetes and obesity (Lancet Commission, 2019). Typically, highly processed products are energy-intensive to produce and heavily packaged, adding to environmental problems.

Agricultural biodiversity and gene drives

The biodiversity of modern agro-ecosystems is already severely compromised by monocultural production and related dependence on industrial herbicides and insecticides in crop management. However, unlike the European Union, the US in the mid-1990s introduced crop protection systems based on genetically modified (GM) seeds endowed with herbicide and insect resistance. By the late 2000s, the diffusion of these seeds had reached saturation levels in the production of staple row crops in the American Midwest: soybeans, corn (maize) and cotton. By that time, 'superweeds' resistant to Roundup Ready, Monsanto's glyphosate-based herbicide, and insecticide-tolerant insects had emerged, leading to the widespread diffusion of GM seeds reinforced with multiple or 'stacked' traits, a toxic 'cocktail' with unknown health and ecological risks. Reviewing this first generation of plant biotechnologies, Benbrook (2018: 390) observes that '[o]verall pesticide use has about doubled, led by the huge increase in the volume of glyphosate applied'.

The adverse biodiversity impacts of chemically intensive first-generation biotechnologies are magnified by the prospective use of synthetic 'gene drive' systems to 'engineer' farm landscapes. Gene editing techniques, notably CRISPR-Cas 9 – the 'molecular scissors' – have enabled complementary advances in synthetic biology and brought gene driving to the forefront. Synthetic gene drive systems are engineered with 'selfish' genetic constructs that do not follow Mendelian principles of inheritance. When released to breed in the wild, these constructs introduce a heritable 'bias' into the target population that can drive it to extinction. Gene drives thus usurp evolutionary processes that underpin biological diversity. As Power (2021: 1) warns, 'CRISPR-Cas 9 gene editing tools have brought us to an era of synthetic biology that will change the world'.

Commercial interest in gene drives is generated by their potential to disrupt the development of herbicide and pesticide resistance by invasive species. Critics highlight the environmental risks and harms likely to follow if gene drives are incorporated into crop protection strategies in agricultural ecosystems. The main concern for the future is that farm landscapes are destined to become the leading commercial arena since '[t]he two foundational patents for gene drives are largely written with agricultural applications in mind' (ETC Group, 2018: 4). With scores of weed, insect and nematode species listed as potential targets of gene drives in these patents, the prospect arises of virtually sterile crop environments, the antithesis of agricultural biodiversity.

Digital foodways and gig workers

The technology–food relation in downstream food services, distribution and consumption centres on their rapid digitalisation and the accompanying ubiquity of digital platforms, extending from 'big box' supermarkets to fast food chains, the growing use of AI and robotics and high levels of concentration in app-based home food delivery markets. These are linked to the wider society by the COVID-19 pandemic of 2020–2021, which cut across this context in random ways, amplifying digitalisation and home food delivery but also causing economic disruption and widespread unemployment, exacerbating inequality and social injustice.

Digital food delivery platforms have grown extremely rapidly, accelerating particularly in the period of social lockdown during the COVID-19 pandemic, increasing the consumption of prepared foods and highly processed products. This deleterious nutritional shift in food practices has been reinforced by the expansion of on-demand, 'ten minutes' home delivery from neighbourhood 'dark' grocery and convenience stores, and 'ghost' kitchens that cater exclusively to online customers. In these ways, digitalisation is changing the foodways of society at large.

The major societal issues of food technologies in the downstream food sectors involve the welfare of the growing numbers of casual, piece-rate workers hired without employment benefits in the so-called 'gig economy'. These workers, mainly couriers in last mile logistics, are represented by app-based delivery platforms as self-employed independent 'contractors'. The future of this precarious and exploitative form of employment now has a geographic dimension. The passing in March 2024 of legislation by the EU would re-classify gig workers as employees eligible for employment benefits, whereas home food delivery platforms in the US are vigorously contesting similar regulatory proposals made by different state governments.

Future concerns

The reports comprising the Sixth Assessment of the IPCC, culminating in its Synthesis Report of March 2023, conclude unequivocally that humanity is facing an existential crisis and recommend that anthropogenic GHG emissions must be reduced dramatically by 2030 in order to keep global warming at less than 1.5°C above pre-industrial levels so that the planet remains liveable. If the urgency of this situation is recognised, future concerns in the realm of technology, food and society will revolve around the question of whether radical measures to reduce emissions in the food system, currently an important source of GHG emissions, are being adopted and, if not, why not? This fundamental issue raises a series of related questions. Will the hegemonic techno-scientific establishment and Big Food corporations launch a sustainability transition, and what changes are required for the 'Great Food Transformation' (Bene, 2022) to happen? How, and by what means, will the path-dependence and technological lock-in be changed to bring about an equitable, socially inclusive transition to a sustainable food system? Will the epistemologies of precision agriculture and agroecology be reconciled in the service of transition? The tensions and resistances of such root-and-branch political economic change and their mediation will inevitably become a major area of focus. In this respect, technology and food studies will be drawn into food policy debates about ways to galvanise the public sector in support of the transition to more sustainable and socially just agriculture and food systems.

DAVID GOODMAN

.

References

Benbrook, C.M. (2018) "Why regulation lost track and control of pesticide risks: lessons from the case of glyphosate-based herbicides and genetically engineered crop technology." *Current Environmental Health Reports* 5:387–395.

Bene, C. (2022) "Why the 'Great Food Transformation' may not happen: a deep dive into our food system's political economy, controversies and politics of evidence." *World Development* 154:1–14.

ETC Group (2018) *Forcing the farm: how gene drives could entrench industrial agriculture and threaten food sovereignty.* Ottawa, Ontario: ETC Group.

IPES: International Panel of Experts on Sustainable Food Systems (IPES-Food) (2022) *The politics of protein.* https://www.ipes.org

Kelloway, C. (2023) "Colorado passes first tractor Right to Repair law." Food and Power, April. https://www.openmarkets institute.org

Lancet Commission (2019) "The global syndemic of obesity, undernutrition and climate change". *The Lancet* 393(10173): 791–846.

Power, M.E. (2021) "The synthetic threads through the web of life." *Proceedings of the National Academy of Sciences*, 118(22). DOI: 10:1073/pnas2004833118

Sexton, A.E., Garnett, T. and Lorimer, J. (2019) "Framing the future of food: the contested promises of alternative proteins." *Environment and Planning E: Nature and Space*, 2(1):47–72. https://doi.org/10.1177/2514848619827009

Further reading

Goodman, D., Sorj, B. and Wilkinson, J. (1987) *From farming to biotechnology.* Oxford: Basil Blackwell.

This book analyses the origins of the industrial food system and the role of technological innovation in the rise of capitalist firms to positions of dominance in agricultural production and food manufacturing.

Goodman, D. (2023) *Transforming agriculture and foodways: the digital-molecular convergence.* Bristol: Bristol University Press.

The digital–molecular convergence is the cornerstone of a wave of innovations that is reinforcing the hegemony of the unsustainable industrial food system and the continuity of its powerful hierarchy of oligopolistic agri-business corporations.

Howard, P. (2021) *Concentration and power in the food system.* Revised edition. London: Bloomsbury Academic.

This book presents valuable empirical evidence from disparate sources to support an original analysis of corporate power, its dynamics, market concentration, and impacts on farmers, rural communities, different sectors of the US food system and society at large.

DAVID GOODMAN

45. Food assemblage

JÉRÉMIE FORNEY

Introduction

Assemblage thinking or assemblage theory (AT) refers originally to the work of Deleuze and Guatarri (1988) and their emphasis on the relational and heterogeneous nature of the social. From this original inspiration, AT has evolved in diverse directions, in dialogue with other theorisations that also focus their attention on complex socio-material relations, on the messiness of the world, and on the roles of more-than-human sociability. AT has strong ties with actor–network theory and the work of scholars such as Bruno Latour, Annemarie Mol, and John Urry, to name but a few. Recently, philosophers have produced new theorisations explicitly centred around the concept of assemblage (Buchanan, 2021; De Landa, 2016). In the social sciences, AT has progressively penetrated diverse disciplines and fields of research, particularly during the 2000s, and has also recently become influential in agriculture and food studies, notably because of a growing interest for relational approaches, more-than-human multispecies approaches and recognition of the need to better understand the fundamental role of non-humans.

Thinking and researching food in terms of assemblage reframes the objects and actors encountered in food systems. In contrast to bounded and fixed ontologies, AT defines the social as emerging from complex sets of relations, which always embody many heterogeneous elements. These elements can be human (a farmer, an eater, a company, etc.) or non-human (a cow, bacteria, an administrative form, a fork, etc.), and often assemble as a mix of both human and non-human parts. Indeed, the elements of an assemblage can generally be themselves described as assemblages. The definition and delimitation of an assemblage is not a question of scale, but an ontological perspective applicable to any scale of the social and the physical: a food assemblage can equally be a meal, a farm, or a value chain. However, an assemblage is not limited to the material. It articulates physical bodies with the enunciative dimension of narratives, representations, and meanings. Beyond this first description of food assemblages, AT's contributions to agriculture and food studies have been significant in several ways, which are acknowledged and outlined in the following sections of the entry, particularly ideas of connectedness, emergence, subjectivity, and agency.

Rhizomatic food worlds: rejections of rigid categories and linear representations

AT focuses on non-linear relations that transcend usual categorisations and spread instead in multiple directions, interconnecting all elements of an assemblage. Deleuze and Guattari (1988) use the metaphor of the rhizome to conceptualise the nature of connectedness in the assemblage, where human and non-human relations intersect and overlap. Following these relations leads agriculture and food scholars to question conventional categorisations and boundaries, notably by looking at the cross-influence and connections between realities that are generally seen as opposed and separated. For instance, Woods (2015) uses AT to conceptualise the restructuration of rural places and their adaptation to diverse processes, notably globalisation. Forney et al. (2018) employ the concept of agri-environmental governance assemblages as a way to highlight the interdependences and tensions between policy, market, and civil society-based practices of governance. In both cases, AT serves as a guide to address the messiness and connectedness of complex issues, with the objective of going past siloed and linear representations of socio-material worlds. Despite the apparent high level of abstraction, both uses of AT start from the very practical experience of actors who are confronted and must deal with this messy complexity in everyday life.

Re-assembling food and agriculture: a focus on emergence

AT suggests paying particular attention to the tensions that traverse social entities, emphasising at the same time the changing nature of the social and the efforts needed to maintain what exists. Assemblages are dynamic and therefore are defined by what they produce and what emerges from them, which is always more than the sum of their parts. In this sense, AT encourages agriculture and food scholars to concentrate their attention on the multiple outcomes of the complex interactions they observe, with an opening towards potentialities and possible futures. A particular way of engaging with emergent assemblages has been proposed by the Biological Economies Research Group in New Zealand. Defining assemblage as "a socio-spatial formation that is brought into being by knowledge production, notably by assembling economic practices, relations and trajectories of thought and action" (Lewis et al., 2013: 185), the group experimented with the challenges of making the rural and food economy otherwise, using active research participation to know and practise food differently and to challenge the way society values and gets value from the land. In this case, AT leads to a redefinition of methodology and theory, exploring novel approaches for more performative research and the production of new material, social, and cultural possibilities in food and agriculture and more-than-human approaches to 'economic life'.

Rethink subjectivity and agency

Following AT, nobody and nothing never act alone. Human and non-human actors act because of and through their connections with others. Consequently, AT contests an individualistic understanding of agency. Agency is considered through a relational lens and becomes collective and distributed. In an assemblage, it is never clear who actually is doing what. Mol (2021) discusses this inevitable relational dimension of action in her theoretical engagement with eating. Even mundane actions, like eating, are only possible through the intervention of other humans and non-humans across the food system. AT requires us to rethink actions and agency beyond notions of centralised control and individual action and to integrate as much as we can the interdependencies between distant actors: for instance, relations between the development of new habits for breakfast, such as the generalisation of take-away pastries and bakery products, the organisation of the baking industry, food processing and retail, the plough, earthworms, and manure.

References

Buchanan, I (2021) *Assemblage theory and method*. London/New York, Bloomsbury.
De Landa, M (2016) *Assemblage theory*. Edinburgh, Edinburgh University Press.
Deleuze, G and Guatarri, F (1988) *A thousand plateaus: Capitalism and schizophrenia*. London, Athlone.
Forney, J, Rosin, C, and Campbell, H (eds.) (2018) *Agri-environmental governance as an assemblage: Multiplicity, power, and transformation*. London/New York, Routledge.
Lewis, N, Le Heron, R, Campbell, H, Henry, M, Le Heron, E, Pawson, E, … Rosin, C (2013) Assembling biological economies: Region-shaping initiatives in making and retaining value. *New Zealand Geographer*, 69(3), 180–196. doi:10.1111/nzg.12031
Mol, A (2021) *Eating in theory*. Durham, NC: Duke University Press.
Woods, M (2015) Territorialisation and the Assemblage of Rural Place: Examples from Canada and New Zealand. In J Dessein, E Battaglini, and L Horlings (eds.), *Cultural sustainability and regional development: Theories and practices of territorialisation*. London, Routledge, pp. 29–42.

Further reading

Buchanan, I (2021) *Assemblage theory and method*. London/New York, Bloomsbury.
De Landa, M (2016) *Assemblage theory*. Edinburgh, Edinburgh University Press.
Two different engagements with the work of Deleuze and Guatarri that are useful to clarify and deepen the theoretical contributions of assemblage thinking.
Li, T M (2007) Practices of assemblage and community forest management. *Economy and Society*, 36(2), 263–293. doi:10.1080/03085140701254308
This article offers a useful operationalisation of AT in environmental and development studies by proposing six practices of assemblage.
Briassoulis, H (2019) Governance as multiplicity: the Assemblage Thinking perspective. *Policy Sciences*, 52(3), 419–450. doi:10.1007/s11077-018-09345-9
Briassoulis applies assemblage thinking to the question of governance, which is central to many aspects of food and agriculture. The paper develops a useful discussion on how AT can nurture other ways of governing society, including food systems.
Forney, J, Bentia, D and Dwiartama, A (2024) *Everyday agri-environmental governance: Insights into the emergence*

of sustainability through assemblage thinking. London/New York, Routledge.
This book engages with key elements of AT to renew current approaches to the governance of agriculture and food assemblages, both in academic engagements and in practice. After highlighting the unpredictable and unruly nature of assemblages and a distributive understanding of agency, it proposes four principles for a governance of emergence.

JÉRÉMIE FORNEY

46. Food banks

Andrew Williams

Introduction: the rise of food banks

While charitable food provision has a long history that connects to various religious, humanitarian and governmental attempts to manage poverty, food banks are distinctive in their modus operandi and global reach. Their origins are commonly traced to the distribution of farm surplus in the Great Depression 1930s (Poppendieck, 1998) or the development of the 'world's first food-bank' in St Mary's, Phoenix, Arizona, in the 1960s, where 'individuals and companies with excess food could "deposit" it, and those in need could "withdraw" it' (St Mary's Food Bank, 2021). This model of warehousing and redistributing surplus food to charitable organisations soon spread across the USA and Canada, and became established across the world through transnational policy and corporate networks (Riches, 2018). Despite this, there are regional variations in the nomenclature and methods used by food banks. For example, in the UK, the terminology 'food-banks' is more frequently used to refer to centres that collect, store and directly distribute food to individuals in need than it is in the USA and much of Europe where 'food banks' collect and distribute food to frontline charities such as food pantries (Lambie-Mumford and Silvasti, 2020). The rapid growth of food banking in the UK coincided with successive waves of austerity and welfare reform that followed the 2008 financial crisis and recession. Between April 2022 and March 2023, 2.98 million food parcels were provided by the 1,393 foodbanks affiliated to the Trussell Trust, a franchise that accounts for less than half of all known food aid providers (IFAN, 2023).

Controversies surrounding food banks

Food bank studies have predominantly drawn on some variation of the political economy and food security frameworks first set out by Poppendieck (1998) and Riches (1986) in the 1980s and 1990s. According to these arguments, food banks are understood as a shadow state mechanism that not only gradually supplants, and draws legitimacy for, an ever-diminishing welfare state, but also serves to cement new kinds of power relationships in which corporate agribusiness and food charity organisations are primary players in poverty management (see Warshawsky 2010; Fisher 2017). Food banks are criticised for reframing poverty and food insecurity as a matter of charity rather than a political responsibility and human right: serving as a 'moral safety valve' that releases pressure for more structural policy interventions (Poppendieck, 1998) while normalising, rather than averting, failures in the food system (Lang, 2020). Surely enough, the Global Food Banking Network and their corporate supporters have expanded operations across the world under the rubric of meeting the Sustainable Development Goals of cutting 'food waste'. In this sense, food charity 'at home' joins humanitarian food aid 'overseas' as the clearing yards for a capitalist food system that is characterised by profit and overproduction (Williams and May 2022). The logic of channelling food that would otherwise go to waste to meet the needs of food charities and people experiencing poverty is often portrayed as a 'win–win' solution, although this does little to address the root causes of food insecurity (Caplan, 2017) and moreover can entrench reliance on a broken food system that relies on exploitation – of workers, of land, of animals. Through philanthropic partnerships with food banks, supermarkets 'cash in' financially (through customer purchases for foodbank collections, tax deductions, and reduced costs of food waste disposal) and reputationally (corporate social responsibility), even when producing the injustices they purport to ameliorate. Many of the supermarkets that donate, or whose customers buy food to donate to food banks, are paying low wages to their own workers and suppliers, resulting in some supermarket employees and farmers needing to use food banks themselves (Bakers, Food and Allied Workers Union 2021).

From a neo-Marxist perspective, food banks represent the latest iteration in how the state regulates the conflict and contradictions inherent to capitalist society (Livingstone, 2015). Food charity has long been criticised as a tactic to allay the prospect of disorderly 'food riots' and the spectre of hunger brought on by market liberalisation (Thompson, 1971). The contemporary normalisation of food charity is said to represent a new regulatory settlement in capitalist society; one that replaces former mediatory institutions designed to negate precarity, such as the Keynesian welfare state, with more punitive forms of neoliberal workfare or a 'charity state' (Riches, 2018: 117) that do little to assuage economic precarity.

Related to this, critical scholars have highlighted the role of food banks in the ongoing neo-liberalisation of welfare and of welfare subjects, highlighting the ways in which the organisational modus operandi of many food banks serves to uphold and further embed discourses of dependency, deservedness and self-responsibility central to neoliberal thought. Although food banks frequently position their work as a pragmatic response to the violence of welfare reform, scholars have focused on the stigma and shame that many people encounter when they 'admit' their need for food assistance and when they use food banks themselves; while the food offered by food banks is often insufficient, nutritionally deficient and largely inappropriate to people's needs. Food banks are also understood as extensions of neoliberal governmentality that discipline destitute bodies through modes of pastoral power (Möller, 2021) and through strict eligibility requirements and restrictions on the number of times a person can access their services, which can make it difficult for those in need to consistently access food assistance (May et al., 2020). For this reason, charitable food provision is an imperfect measure of the scale of household food insecurity given the large numbers of people choosing not to use food banks, or if they do, they do so as a strategy of last resort (Garthwaite, 2016).

Beyond food banks?

The global growth of food banking increasingly is considered an inadequate and harmful policy development, unable to prevent food insecurity and entrench corporate power over the food system. Attempts to move 'beyond the food bank' have met varying success, given the causes of food insecurity are deeply structured in the capitalist economy and its gendered and racialised dynamics (on these dynamics inside food charities, see De Souza, 2019; Power, 2022). Recent years have seen the expansion of social supermarkets and food pantries which purport to tackle foodbank stigma by giving members flexibility in visits and choice of food items. Many of these initiatives in the UK proliferated during the COVID pandemic but risk cementing a two-tier food system entirely reliant upon the warehousing and redistribution of surplus food. Perhaps more hopefully, food banks in the UK and elsewhere have been at the forefront of developing coordinated political campaigns over the Right to Food, which legally requires governments not to take measures that result in increasing levels of hunger, food insecurity and malnutrition; to actively legislate to prevent third parties (individuals and corporations) from violating people's access to adequate food; to strengthen people's access to and utilisation of resources so as to facilitate their ability to feed themselves, and, as a last resort, fulfil that right directly (FAO, 2005). Foodbanks also have worked with local governments to develop *Cash First* schemes that aim to reduce footfall to foodbanks by issuing direct cash payments rather than food vouchers. Others have reorganised food provision according to cooperative and membership models, deliberately working with local food producers and community agriculture to bypass the dynamics of corporate food charity and surplus food distribution.

References

Bakers, Food and Allied Workers Union (2021) *The Right to Food: A law needed by food workers and communities across the UK*. Right to Food – Bakers, Food and Allied Workers Union (BFAWU).

Caplan, P. (2017) Win-win? Food poverty, food aid and food surplus in the UK today. *Anthropology Today*, *33*(3), 17–22.

De Souza, R.T. (2019) *Feeding the other: Whiteness, privilege, and neoliberal stigma in food pantries*. MIT Press.

FAO (Food and Agriculture Organization of the United Nations) (2005) *The Right to Food: Voluntary guidelines to support the progressive realization of the right to adequate food in the context of national food security*. https://www.fao.org/3/y7937e/Y7937E02.htm#ch1.2.2

Fisher, A. (2017) *Big hunger: The unholy alliance between corporate America and anti-hunger groups*. MIT Press.

Garthwaite (2016) *Hunger pains*. Policy Press.

IFAN (2023) Independent Food Banks Map | IFAN. foodaidnetwork.org.uk

Lambie-Mumford, H., & Silvasti, T. (Eds.). (2020) *The rise of food charity in Europe.* Policy Press.

Lang, T. (2020) *Feeding Britain: Our food problems and how to fix them.* Penguin UK.

Livingstone, N. (2015) The Hunger Games: Food poverty and politics in the UK. *Capital & Class, 39*(2), 188–195.

May, J., Williams, A., Cloke, P., & Cherry, L. (2020) Food banks and the production of scarcity. *Transactions of the Institute of British Geographers, 45*(1), 208–222.

Möller, C. (2021) Discipline and feed: Food banks, pastoral power, and the medicalisation of Poverty in the UK. *Sociological Research Online, 26*(4), 853–870.

Poppendieck, J. (1998). *Sweet charity?* Viking.

Power, M. (2022) *Hunger, whiteness and religion in neoliberal Britain: An inequality of power.* Policy Press.

Riches, G. (1986). *Food banks and the welfare crisis.* James Lorimer & Company.

Riches, G. (2018). *Food Bank Nations: Poverty, Corporate Charity and the Right to Food* (1st ed.). Routledge. https://doi.org/10.4324/9781315184012COPY

St Mary's Food Bank (2021) Filling hungry stomachs for 50 years! https://www.firstfoodbank.org/about/

Thompson, E.P. (1971) The moral economy of the English crowd in the eighteenth century. *Past & Present*, 50, 76–136.

Warshawsky, D.N. (2010) New power relations served here: The growth of food banking in Chicago. *Geoforum, 41*(5), 763–775.

Further reading

Papargyropoulou, E., Fearnyough, K., Spring, C., & Antal, L. (2022) The future of surplus food redistribution in the UK: Reimagining a 'win-win' scenario. *Food Policy*, 108, 102230. https://doi.org/10.1016/j.foodpol.2022.102230

Sets an research and policy agenda for the future of surplus food redistribution in the UK.

Spring, C., Garthwaite, K., & Fisher, A. (2022) Containing hunger, contesting injustice? Exploring the transnational growth of foodbanking – and counter-responses- before and during the COVID-19 pandemic. *Food ethics, 7*, 6.

Examines charitable food systems in North America and the UK in relation to the pandemic and its aftermath.

Williams, A., & May, J. (2022) A genealogy of the food bank: Historicising the rise of food charity in the UK. *Transactions of the Institute of British Geographers*, 47, 618–634. https://doi.org/10.1111/tran.12535

Historic perspective on the rise of food banks and surplus food distribution.

ANDREW WILLIAMS

47. Food citizenship

CRISTINA GRASSENI

Introduction

There exists a rich palette of concrete ways through which local, traditional, or natural foods may be preferred as a result or as a form of civic engagement. For example, engagement with foodscapes ranges from self-provisioning to preference for Fair Trade goods or geographical indications. Jennifer Wilkins, in her 2004 *Presidential Address to the Agriculture, Food, and Human Values Society* stated that '[t]he term food citizenship is defined as the practice of engaging in food-related behaviors that support, rather than threaten, the development of a democratic, socially and economically just, and environmentally sustainable food system'. In her article, she suggests 'ways to practice food citizenship' including 'a role for universities in fostering food citizenship' and identifies 'four barriers to food citizenship', namely 'the current food system, federal food and agriculture policy, local and institutional policies, and the culture of professional nutrition organizations' (Wilkins 2005: 269).

In Wilkins' address, 'food citizens' are imagined as (American) consumers who take responsibility for the implications of their food shopping (Gliessman 2006: 339), pursuing 'the consumer-level goal' to 'support, rather than threaten, the development of a democratic, socially and economically just, and environmentally sustainable food system' (Wilkins 2005: 271). Interestingly, however, literature that further develops the notion and practice of 'food citizenship' in diverse contexts is limited. The concept is more often than not taken for granted in support of more specific critical practices, indicating the general expectation of citizens' active engagement in the (global) food system. Even more limited literature acknowledges the idea that 'food citizenship' is a contextual notion, which will take on diverse meanings and signify diverse practices according to the diversity of 'food concerns' and the local background for different expectations and traditions of engagement with food (Kopczyńska 2018).

Easily co-opted by corporate discourse, the notion of 'citizen-consumer' (Johnston 2008) implies that citizens are first and foremost consumers of food as a market commodity (as critiqued by Welsh & MacRae 1998),

who wish to be more actively involved in the same capitalist framework, thus overlooking the relationally embedded, situated, and collective dimension of food procurement. In fact, expressing citizenship through food procurement takes distinctive routes as enabled by different contexts, their conceptualization depending on their rooting in local cultures of participation and in relevant food systems, as exemplified below (Grasseni 2020).

Towards a critical understanding of food citizenship

Different notions of food citizenship are circulating in scholarship: (a) as a shorthand for critical consumption whereby individual consumers should 'vote with their dollar' and thus encourage corporate 'good citizenship' (Goldberg 2018); (b) as a grassroots mobilisation for 'civic food networks' to emerge, through which citizens actively participate in the reformation of the (food) global economy (Renting et al. 2012); (c) as a normative framework akin to the moral imperative of 'sustainable citizenship' proposed by some European sociologists of consumption (Micheletti and Stolle 2012).

One recent monograph employing 'food citizenship' as a title keyword (Goldberg 2018) understands the concept as corporate social responsibility or 'good corporate citizenship'. Goldberg seeks a 'fair minded path to citizenship' as opposed to a polarisation between corporate actors and consumers participating in the food chain as 'second class' citizens (p. 178), despite the fact that 'critics have argued that it is impossible for food firm managers to integrate good global citizenship into earnings-oriented business practices' (p. xviii). 'Citizenship' is thus equated to responsible entrepreneurship, for example when a former Cargill chairman states that 'all aspects of good citizenship come down to a shared mindset in an organization' (p. 21). This allows a shift of responsibility onto the shoulders of specific parts of, or actors in, corporate operations. For example, regarding soda companies, a distinction is drawn between a parent company 'which is generally more interested in good corporate citizenship' and the regional 'bottlers', who are accused of being more cash-driven (p. 44).

Critics of advocates for the 'good citizenship' of food and beverage corporations note that the convergence of corporate interest and state aid has resulted in an unsustainable situation. In his landmark *Civic Agriculture* (2004), Thomas Lyson shows the historical emergence of 'global regionalisation' whereby both concentration and consolidation of land ownership (namely, declining numbers of farmers and increased area of cultivation per farm) has progressively moved away from the household and community focus of 'embedded agriculture'. While the latter was supportive of and dependent on networks of mutual help as well as local crafts, industrial agriculture places an increased focus on capital and management. Around the 1870s the average American homestead farm held about 75 acres (c. 30ha.), but by the turn of the millennium the average farm size was 500 acres (c. 200ha.). Nowadays so-called 'million dollar farms' dominate the landscape and most agricultural aid goes to industrial crop growers, which are mainly very large producers. Smallholders and edible crop growers, who serve their own communities, could do with a larger share of (tax payers') agricultural aid, but will not easily be heard unless these communities mobilise on their behalf. In fact, especially under the banner of 'food sovereignty', movements such as *La Via Campesina* have mobilised farmers opposing the transformation of farming into a mere business practice, initially in developing countries but increasingly in the 'First World' too.

According to Renting et al. (2012), citizens participating in emerging 'civic food networks' respond to the need of supporting shorter food chains and small-scale agriculture, while assuming a more political role than that of mere consumers. This would amount to a practice of active citizenship as well as of reformist economic practice. They provide a review of 'food citizenship' based on the work of Lyson and colleagues. In this discourse, food citizenship works as a semantic umbrella for a political imaginary wherein citizens are not considered only economic subjects.

Citizenship does not refer here to membership of a polity but to a form of ethical self-cultivation resulting in diverse practices of economic action, which bring about citizens' empowerment in the food chain. It is therefore not a definition but a gesture (as in Lozano-Cabedo and Gómez-Benito 2017) towards an 'ontological reframing' (Gibson-Graham 2008) of one's positionality in the global food system. This participatory politics underlines people's self-activation and mutual relationships as well as their relation to their space and environment, and constitutes therefore a basic practice of citizenship formation ('DIY Citizenship') also beyond food production and consumption (Ratto and Boler 2014).

Critiques see this discourse of self-determination of and through economic practice as in danger of hegemonic cooptation. For example, citizens practising community gardening 'can become complicit in the construction of neoliberal hegemony' because their unremunerated volunteer work can be structurally coopted to 'alleviate the state from service provision', not only in the area of food poverty but also in other traditional areas of welfare, health, and social service intervention (Crossan et al. 2016: 937). Moreover, the conceptualisation of food citizenship is based on tacit assumptions about citizenship practices and meanings in (neo)liberal democracies and affluent economies. For example, in post-socialist contexts food self-provisioning is rarely seen as a form of food activism with social justice and environmental sustainability as core motivations and goals, but rather as 'pleasure of sharing', for example, in quiet but historically robust informal networks of exchange (Jehlička and Daněk 2017).

Future concerns, issues, and questions

In conclusion, food citizenship has so far been used as a semantically flexible umbrella term to highlight the role of citizen-consumers vis-à-vis the value of food in ways that by definition exceed capitalist valuation. In capitalist societies, food is treated as a commodity. Price is the only way through which its value gets measured and exchanged. In a capitalist market, organic and sustainable foods are value-added, thus expensive, and therefore not accessible for the most fragile sectors of society. These are not only food-insecure, but their access to value-added food (such as healthy food) is impeded.

These inequalities are the focus of a number of movements and disciplinary literature (e.g. food justice, food sovereignty, food democracy, and alternative food networks). Inequality is only one of the faults of the global 'food system' that food citizens might want to tackle. Others regard, for example, 'food and the environment', 'technology and food', and 'industrial food' (see, this encyclopedia).

CRISTINA GRASSENI

For example, consumers' solidarity pacts with smallholders through community supported agriculture, solidarity economy networks, and cooperative buying groups aim to shelter farmers from unfavourable supply contracts and global market vagaries by decreasing their risk. Through this economic action, food citizens may support further political visions such as those linked to peasant agriculture, sustainable agriculture, indigenous food systems, or regenerative agriculture.

But it remains unclear who exactly these 'food citizens' are, or should be. Are they individual eaters engaging in moral and political mobilisation in a global food system, e.g. wasting less food, educating, lobbying? Are they local consumption movements who seek direct contact with smallholders and regional producers? How do they fare in practice and in different contexts? Are there societal issues that they do not tackle sufficiently (such as gender, ethnicity, income, and education diversities)? How do they position themselves vis-à-vis the historical and economic global dynamics that generate such issues? To answer these questions we need more in-depth studies of actual practices and discourse of food citizenship in diverse contexts, as well as outside so-called Western liberal democracies. Especially in light of cooptation criticisms, we need to better understand the (positive? negative?) impact of assuming an 'activist' stance with respect to sustainable food systems.

References

Crossan J, Cumbers A, McMaster R and Shaw D (2016) Contesting neoliberal urbanism in Glasgow's community gardens: the practice of DIY citizenship. *Antipode* 48, 937–955. https://doi.org/10.1111/anti.12220

Gibson-Graham J K (2008) Diverse economies: performative practices for 'other worlds'. *Progress in Human Geography* 32, 613–663.

Gliessman S R (2006) *Agroecology: The Ecology of Sustainable Food Systems.* Boca Raton, FL, CRC Press.

Goldberg, R A (2018) *Food Citizenship: Food System Advocates in an Era of Distrust.* Oxford, Oxford University Press.

Grasseni C (2020) Context-specific notions and practices of 'solidarity' in food procurement networks in Lombardy (Italy) and Massachusetts (USA). In:

Kropp C, Antoni-Komar I and Sage C (eds), *Food System Transformations: Social Movements, Local Economies, Collaborative Networks.* London, Routledge, pp. 157–174.

Jehlička P and Daněk P (2017) Rendering the actually existing sharing economy visible: home-grown food and the pleasure of sharing. *Sociologia Ruralis* 57, 274–296. https://doi.org/10.1111/soru.12160

Johnston J (2008) The citizen-consumer hybrid: ideological tensions and the case of Whole Foods Market. *Theory and Society* 37, 229–270. https://doi.org/10.1007/s11186-007-9058-5

Kopczyńska E (2018) How food fears frame criticisms of the food system: a case study of customers of farmers' market. *Studia Humanistyczne* 17, 79–95. https://doi.org/10.7494/human.2018.17.2.79

Lozano-Cabedo C and Gómez-Benito C (2017) A theoretical model of food citizenship for the analysis of social praxis. *Journal of Agricultural and Environmental Ethics* 30, 1–22. https://doi.org/10.1007/s10806-016-9649-0

Lyson T (2004) *Civic Agriculture: Reconnecting Farm, Food, and Community.* Medford, University Press of New England.

Micheletti M and Stolle D (2012) Sustainable citizenship and the new politics of consumption. *Annals of the American Academy of Political and Social Science* 644, 88–120. https://doi.org/10.1177/0002716212454836

Ratto M and Boler M (2014) DIY citizenship: critical making and social media. Cambridge, MA, The MIT Press.

Renting H, Schermer M and Rossi A (2012) Building food democracy: exploring civic food networks and newly emerging forms of food citizenship. *International Journal of Agriculture and Food* 19, 289–307. https://doi.org/10.48416/ijsaf.v19i3.206

Welsh J and MacRae R (1998) Food citizenship and community food security: lessons from Toronto, Canada. *Canadian Journal of Development Studies* 19, 237–255. https://doi.org/10.1080/02255189.1998.9669786

Wilkins J L (2005) Eating right here: moving from consumer to food citizen. *Agriculture and Human Values* 22, 269–273. https://doi.org/10.1007/s10460-005-6042-4

Further reading

Booth S and Coveney J (2015) *Food Democracy. From Consumer to Food Citizen*. Singapore, Springer.
This short co-authored volume focuses on how to start a transition towards better community and public health vis-à-vis the dominance of (unhealthy) 'Big Food' in the Australian context, building on the authors' expertise in clinical nutrition and community education.

www.foodcitizens.eu hosts a comparative ethnographic research project on collective food procurement in three European cities (Gdańsk, Rotterdam, and Turin). It includes open access publications, a blog and an i-doc analysing and contrasting citizens' initiatives in self-production, short food chains, and food governance in Poland, the Netherlands, and northern Italy.

CRISTINA GRASSENI

48. Food commons

OONA MORROW

Introduction

Food provisioning depends on a multitude of bio-physical, cultural, and knowledge 'commons' found in food itself, as well as the material and cultural resources needed to grow, harvest, process, and eat food, which are collectively created, shared, cared for, and governed by their users. Food commons are ubiquitous in our food systems. As Jose Vivero-Pol (2018: 30) writes, "When food is collectively produced, jointly transformed, distributed on the basis of its value-in-use and eaten by people in a convivial manner, we have then a commons". His work has helped to define food commons as: '1) the natural and non-material resources (foods, recipes, traditional food and agricultural knowledge, etc.), 2) the communities who share the resources (local, national or global), 3) the commoning practices people use to produce, transform and eat food, and 4) the moral narrative that sustains the main purpose of the food system (i.e. to sustainably produce healthy food for all)' (Tirado-von der Pahlen 2018: 357, see also Carceller-Sauras and Theesfeld 2021).

This expansive definition of food commons challenges economistic understandings of the commons (Vivero-Pol 2018). In Ostrom's (2010) commons typology, where resources are classified according to their shareability and the difficulty of excluding others, food commons can be hard to place. Food itself is a private good, food resources like grazing fields and fisheries are common pool resources, and food safety and public health are considered public goods. Commons scholars have sought to move beyond this rigid approach to commons that is dictated by the supposedly innate properties of a resource to focus instead on the process of *commoning* through which such resources are created (as private, public, or common goods), shared, cared for, and governed (Bollier and Helfrich 2019, Morrow and Martin 2019).

Of course, food commons are not new; they are the original social safety net. The land-based food commons of feudal England sustained peasant livelihood, while commons-based rights of use and access, such as grazing, gleaning, and foraging of wild foods, continue to help people feed themselves and maintain more-than-capitalist livelihoods

(Morrow 2020). The linear and Eurocentric history of enclosure could give the impression that food commons are a romantic thing of the past. What is different now is that scholars and activists are using the language of the commons to mobilise around existing, threatened, and emerging food commons in the context of broader food system transformations (Vivero-Pol et al. 2018).

Our current food system is interdependent with food commons. Even the most commodified foods depend on the existence of food commons and contain properties (history, culture, meaning, pleasure, nutrition, safety, health) that are not reducible to their commodity status (see also Vivero-Pol 2013, 2018). However, the historic and ongoing enclosure of food-based commons and the legal and political consolidation of the paradigm of food as a commodity have made food commons difficult to recognise, and elusive as objects of policy and governance (Rundgren 2016). At the same time, food commons are threatened by new forms of enclosure, and without legal protections the hard-won gains of activists to create new food commons in the city and countryside can be precarious. Calls for rethinking and reclaiming our entire food system as a commons (Jackson et al. 2021; Pettenati et al. 2018; Vivero-Pol 2018) encourage us to go beyond celebrating islands of commoning in a broken food system, instead linking up these various nodes to transition from a *commons extractive food system* (market based, private ownership, food as commodity) to a *pluriverse of commons regenerative food systems* (social systems that collectively meet human and more-than-human needs and expand conditions of possibility).

Current issues, concerns, and areas of focus

There is a fast-growing body of food commons scholarship. Vivero-Pol et al. (2018) have collected a diverse sample in their *Handbook of Food Commons*, which makes several offerings for what could be included in the food commons and how we might go about understanding them. However, in theorising food commons (Carceller-Sauras and Theesfeld 2021), we also run the risk of reproducing essentialist and binary forms of thinking in approaching commons as resources (noun) rather than as social relations (verb). As a noun, commons focuses on the thing or resource being shared – e.g., the fishery, field, or fridge. This frame has been criticised for reducing commons to mere resources, often material in form, to be exploited, managed, and extracted, in the process ignoring their more-than-human agency and reproducing economistic and extractive relations with nature (Bresnihan 2015). Commons as a verb, on the other hand, is a relational approach focused on the social and material practices through which communities create commons, and the process of sharing those benefits, as well as the ongoing practices of care and collective responsibility necessary to sustain them (Bollier and Helfrich 2019).

Next I will examine three tensions in the food commons scholarship around materialities, scale, and urban–rural relations.

Materialities

Commons scholars have pointed out the limitations of an approach to commons that extrapolates preferred property, governance, and social arrangements from the material properties of a resource (e.g. carrying capacity, shareability, and excludability). However, the *materiality* of food commons is unavoidable. We live in a finite material world and urgently need to reduce our use of materials (such as fossil fuels) that harm us, earth others, and exceed planetary boundaries. The materiality of food and foodscapes *matters* in personal, cultural, and bio-physical ways. We are viscerally affected by the touch, taste, and smell of foods and soils and emotionally connected to places and landscapes (Puig de la Bellacasa 2015, Tuan 2001). Moreover, our labouring, eating, and digesting bodies are sites of biophysical processes that metabolise foods and landscapes into well-being, and varied meanings, emotions, and embodiments (Slocum 2008, Hayes-Conroy and Hayes-Conroy 2010). Considering the diverse material entanglements and life forms that make up our food commons – from microbes and genes to seeds, soil, land, and distribution networks – we cannot afford to overlook the material dimensions of commoning, or the material inequalities in commoning across the food system.

Without sliding into material determinism, we can acknowledge that different concerns and more-than-human entanglements can arise around different food commons. Sharing recipes, seeds, meals, surplus food, property, or land are all quite different experiences, and each of these resources has unique demands and requirements when it comes to cultural norms, ownership, responsibility, and liability. Commoning land (in terms of access, tenure, and ownership) might require a different strategy than commoning food (in terms of access, sharing, etc.) or traditional knowledge, not least because these different materialities are *already* embedded in specific place-based cultural norms and governance regimes related to property, spatial planning, (land) zoning, food safety and health, and culinary heritage.

Scale

Not unrelated to the question of materiality is the question of *scale*. At what socio-spatial scales do we enact, research, and imagine the food commons? Although food commons discourses are gaining traction in international governance spaces (see e.g. SAPEA 2020), research on food commons has trended towards the local, the micro, and the organisational as a site of grassroots innovation, community, and resistance. Scholars and activists have documented inspiring cases of food sharing and other forms of mutual aid, as well as local and bioregional food commons, drawn from agroecology, peasant movements, slow food, Community Supported Agriculture (CSA) movements, and more (Kennedy 2020, Vivero-Pol et al. 2018). This pluriverse of local food commons is making a global impact by scaling out through decentralised replications and localised adaptations. However, food systems are vast and interdependent, and even with a significant redistribution of resources and power localising may not always be feasible or socially just. Can we conceive of a global food commons? Healy et al. (2020) attempt this in describing emergency food responses to Covid-19. Their 'planetary food commons' are a pluriverse of commons sociality. However, some of the examples they highlight, e.g. food banks, may be obstacles to food commons (Kenny and Sage 2018). Dedeurwaerdere (2012) takes on the global when it comes to a very small but globally dispersed food commons: genetic resources for agriculture, drawing inspiration from global digital information commons. Lastly, asking at what scale we can enact food commons also raises ethical and moral questions regarding how 'far' 'we' (e.g. activists, researchers, citizens) can care and extend our geographies of responsibility (Lawson 2007).

Urban–rural

The last tension in the literature is between *urban and rural food commons*. Urban areas have been significant sites for grassroots (social) innovation, and for radically expanding our political imaginary of what the commons can be and how they are created, shared, contested, and protected. Scholars and activists have diversified our conceptual vocabulary of the commons beyond land and property to everyday life, cultural practices, the right to the city, and the ongoing and imperfect work of reimagining and reclaiming the city as commons (Huron 2015). The continued existence, contestation, and emergence of urban commons, such as housing cooperatives and community spaces, is an important reminder that scarcity of land and competition over resources is not a given but a politically created reality. All commons are created by communities and do not exist independently of the communities that depend on them.

Urban food commons such as community gardens and greenery, solidarity purchasing groups, food cooperatives, food parks and food forests, community fridges, meals, and composting projects, as well as commons-based approaches to food governance like food councils, tend to be citizen-led, and organised around food provisioning in the city. Urban communities are creating new food commons in public, private, and community spaces by sharing land, trees, food, fridges, labour, knowledge, and skills. This includes collective negotiation of concerns over safety, ownership, access, care, responsibility, and shared benefits at different scales with different outcomes (Morrow 2019, 2020).

In urban food commons scholarship, few studies examine the role of the public sector in creating and financing new food commons. More often, we encounter the public sector as a tolerant, absentee, or hostile landlord or regulatory authority. However, research in Bologna, where 'the city as commons' legislation has taken effect, shows that cities can take a much more supportive and facilitative role in enabling food commons (Iaione 2016). Another limitation in urban food commons research is a bounded approach to the urban. With the exception of research on food provisioning networks like CSA, SoLaWi (solidarity agriculture), and solidarity purchasing, the linkages with rural and peri-urban food commons are less visible. Considering the outsized impact that cities have on our food system in terms of resource use, purchasing, and local and civic governance, there is also ample need for creating rural and urban food commons *with* cities.

Rural food commons, such as community-stewarded forests and fields, and their various legal and land use protections, continue to be critical to sustaining food-based livelihoods and feeding people across the rural–urban continuum. As Vivero-Pol et al. (2018) document, most of the world's land-based food commons are also in rural places. Protecting and growing food commons is therefore particularly urgent when it comes to the question of land, which has become inaccessible to small-scale and beginner farmers. New rural food commons are essential for creating sustainable food-based livelihoods for future generations.

Rural areas are also sites of governance innovation and have developed important legal and policy tools for food commons. Land trust legislation for shared land ownership, stewardship, and conservation was created in the 1890s to protect rural natures, and since the 1970s community land trust legislation has been adapted to protect and grow food commons in urban and rural areas (Morrow 2022). Another rural food commons innovation is the agricultural preservation restriction (APR), which exists in different forms across the world (Kassis et al. 2021). Under this scheme, soil, farming, and biodiversity are removed from the property market and protected as public goods. Farmers who participate in APRs are compensated by the public for giving up their right to more profitable land uses. On a more local level, zoning and planning are tools with which food commons can be preserved or hindered.

Rural and urban food commons have developed in different ways, by different communities with particular place-based needs and interests. However, if we seek to re-common the food system we can no longer approach urban and rural food commons as distinct territories and interests. This is especially evident at the peri-urban fringe, where diverse urban and rural stakeholders converge over competing visions of land and its uses as commons or commodity (Maughan and Ferrando

2018). Cities are increasingly cannibalising their last remaining rural food commons for housing, warehouses, and logistics infrastructure to feed the growing needs of their city, without taking food or environmental justice into account. This is made especially evident in the conflict over the Lutkemeerpolder, the last farm in Amsterdam (http://behoudlutkemeer.nl/). To move beyond this spatial divide, scholars and activists take a relational approach, which supports planning and reframes connections to place through the interdependencies, solidarities, and flows of care, power, and resources between the urban and rural in commons regenerative food systems.

Future concerns

Future research on food commons can meaningfully address the issues raised above by taking a feminist-materialist, multi-scalar, relational, food systems approach that works across the urban–rural continuum, is self-reflexive and critical in its solidarity with the local, and actively works to foster linkages between commoners at different locations in the food system. Moreover, transitioning from a commons extractive food system to a pluriverse of commons regenerative food systems would be aided by drawing from conceptual approaches like diverse economies which can help to break up 'the capitalist food system' monolith and in doing so unravel the diversity of economic practices and livelihoods, contradictions, and openings for doing things differently (Gibson-Graham and Dombroski 2020). This research would be especially effective by joining forces with scholars and activists working on de-growth and post-growth, who have placed commons at the centre of their visions for degrowth and food (Guerrero et al. 2023).

References

Bollier, D., & Helfrich, S. (2019). *Free, fair, and alive: The insurgent power of the commons*. New Society Publishers.

Bresnihan, P. (2015). The more-than-human commons: From commons to commoning. In Kirwan, S., Dawney, L. & Brigstocke, J. (Eds.), *Space, power and the commons* (pp. 93–112). Routledge.

Carceller-Sauras, E., & Theesfeld, I. (2021). The food-as-a-commons discourse: Analyzing the journey to policy impact. *International Journal of the Commons*, 15(1), 368–380.

Dedeurwaerdere, T. (2012). Institutionalizing global genetic resource commons for food and agriculture. In Halewood, M., Noriega, I.L., & Louafi, S. (Eds.), *Crop genetic resources as a global commons*, 368–391.

Gibson-Graham, J. K., & Dombroski, K. (2020). *The handbook of diverse economies*. Edward Elgar Publishing.

Guerrero Lara, L., van Oers, L., Smessaert, J., Spanier, J., Raj, G., & Feola, G. (2023). Degrowth and agri-food systems: A research agenda for the critical social sciences. *Sustainability Science*, 18(4), 1–16.

Hayes-Conroy, A., & Hayes-Conroy, J. (2010). Visceral difference: Variations in feeling (slow) food. *Environment and Planning A*, 42(12), 2956–2971.

Healy, S., Chitranshi, B., Diprose, G., Eskelinen, T., Madden, A., Santala, I., & Williams, M. (2020). Planetary food commons and postcapitalist post-COVID food futures. *Development*, 63, 277–284.

Huron, A. (2015). Working with strangers in saturated space: Reclaiming and maintaining the urban commons. *Antipode*, 47(4), 963–979.

Iaione, C. (2016). The CO-City: Sharing, collaborating, cooperating, and commoning in the city. *American Journal of Economics and Sociology*, 75(2), 415–455.

Jackson, P., Rivera Ferre, M. G., Candel, J., Davies, A., Derani, C., de Vries, H., … & Thøgersen, J. (2021). Food as a commodity, human right or common good. *Nature Food*, 2(3), 132–134.

Kassis, G., Bertrand, N., & Pecqueur, B. (2021). Rethinking the place of agricultural land preservation for the development of food systems in planning of peri-urban areas: Insights from two French municipalities. *Journal of Rural Studies*, 86, 366–375.

Kennedy, M. (2020). A Slow Food commons: Cultivating conviviality across a range of property forms. In Gibson-Graham, J. K., & Dombroski, K. (Eds.), *The handbook of diverse economies* (pp. 308–315). Edward Elgar Publishing.

Kenny, T., & Sage, C. (2018). Obstacles to re-introducing food as a commons. In Vivero-Pol, J. L., Ferrando, T., De Schutter, O., & Mattei, U. (Eds), *Routledge handbook of food as a commons* (pp. 281–295). Routledge.

Lawson, V. (2007). Geographies of care and responsibility. *Annals of the Association of American Geographers, 97*(1), 1–11.

Maughan, C., & Ferrando, T. (2018). Land as a commons: Examples from the UK and Italy. In Vivero-Pol, J. L., Ferrando, T., De Schutter, O., & Mattei, U. (Eds), *Routledge handbook of food as a commons* (pp. 329–341). Routledge.

Morrow, O. (2019). Sharing food and risk in Berlin's urban food commons. *Geoforum, 99*, 202–212.

Morrow, O. (2020). Gleaning: Transactions at the nexus of food, commons and waste. In Gibson-Graham, J. K., & Dombroski, K. (Eds.), *The handbook of diverse economies* (pp. 206–213). Edward Elgar Publishing.

Morrow, O. (2022). Governing and Commoning Activities around Urban Food Commons. In Moragues-Faus, A., Clark, J. K., Battersby, J., & Davies, A. (Eds), *Routledge Handbook of Urban Food Governance* (pp. 105–119). Routledge.

Morrow, O., & Martin, D. G. (2019). Unbundling property in Boston's urban food commons. *Urban Geography, 40*(10), 1485–1505.

Ostrom, E. (2010). Beyond markets and states: Polycentric governance of complex economic systems. *American Economic Review, 100*(3), 641–672.

Pettenati, G., Toldo, A., & Ferrando, T. (2018). Food system as commons. In Vivero-Pol, J. L., Ferrando, T., De Schutter, O., & Mattei, U. (Eds), *Routledge handbook of food as a commons* (pp. 42–56). Routledge.

Puig De La Bellacasa, M. (2015). Making time for soil: Technoscientific futurity and the pace of care. *Social Studies of Science, 45*(5), 691–716.

Rundgren, G. (2016). Food: From commodity to commons. *Journal of Agricultural and Environmental Ethics, 29*(1), 103–121.

SAPEA (2020). European Commission, Directorate-General for Research and Innovation, Group of Chief Scientific Advisors, *Towards a sustainable food system: Moving from food as a commodity to food as more of a common good – Independent expert report*, Publications Office, 2020. https://data.europa.eu/doi/10.2777/282386.

Slocum, R. (2008). Thinking race through corporeal feminist theory: Divisions and intimacies at the Minneapolis Farmers' Market. *Social & Cultural Geography, 9*(8), 849–869.

Tirado-von der Pahlen, C. (2018). Climate change, the food commons and human health. In Vivero-Pol, J. L., Ferrando, T., De Schutter, O., & Mattei, U. (Eds), *Routledge handbook of food as a commons* (pp. 356–370). Routledge.

Tuan, Y. F. (2001). *Space and place: Humanistic perspective*. University of Minnesota Press.

Vivero-Pol, J. L. (2013). Food as a commons: Reframing the narrative of the food system. Available at Social Science Research Network: https://ssrn.com/abstract=2255447.

Vivero-Pol, J. L. (2018). The idea of food as a commons. In Vivero-Pol, J. L., Ferrando, T., De Schutter, O., & Mattei, U. (Eds), *Routledge handbook of food as a commons* (pp. 25–41). Routledge.

Vivero-Pol, J. L., Ferrando, T., De Schutter, O., & Mattei, U. (2018). Introduction: The food commons are coming…. In Vivero-Pol, J. L., Ferrando, T., De Schutter, O., & Mattei, U. (Eds), *Routledge handbook of food as a commons* (pp. 1–21). Routledge.

Further reading

Bollier, D., & Helfrich, S. (2019). *Free, fair, and alive: The insurgent power of the commons*. New Society Publishers.

This open access book provides a warm and energising welcome into commons scholarship and activism.

Vivero-Pol, J. L., Ferrando, T., De Schutter, O., & Mattei, U. (2018). *Routledge handbook of food as a commons*. Routledge.

The chapters in this handbook offer impressive breadth spanning diverse geographies, disciplines and debates in terms of introducing interesting case studies and theoretical discussions regarding food commons.

49. Food crime

ALICE RIZZUTI

Introduction: what is food crime?

Food has always been contaminated or counterfeited. Practices such as food fraud were commonplace already in ancient Rome and Greece, where wine was adulterated with different colours and flavours. In recent decades, multiple international food scandals have renewed public and institutional interest towards this type of criminal behaviour. For example, in the 2013 'horsemeat scandal', consumers' trust was compromised when public authorities in several European countries discovered the large fraud of beef adulterated with horse meat. Food offences can also harm public health and food safety, put at risk food security, and are detrimental to the reputation of the food sector, at international and national levels.

Food crime types and criminal actors

Food crime is a recent and still under-researched area of investigation in legal and criminological studies. Some scholars have focused on issues of food safety or breaches of trading regulations. Others have focussed on the dynamics of food fraud and how to counter such criminal activities (Lord et al., 2017; Manning and Soon, 2016). Further research has questioned the food-related acts and omissions at various stages of the food supply chain that are not criminalised by law but harmful to human health and the natural environment including animals. Within a 'green criminology' perspective that focusses on crimes and harms against the environment, food crime was first broadly defined by Hazel Croall (2013) as the crimes that involve the processing, production, and sale of food. This conceptualisation incorporates criminal and harmful activities in the local and global food trades that victimise consumers physically (by harming their physical health), psychologically (by eroding their trust), and financially (by increasing the cost of food products).

Within this theoretical framework, examples of food crimes include: food frauds such as the intentional adulteration of food or counterfeiting; food poisoning, including the breach of food safety regulations or engaging in regulatory non-compliance; food mislabelling such as disregarding labelling standards; financial crimes such as tax and subsidy fraud; and the exploitation of labour in the agri-food system. Food harms are the legalised use of pesticides or additives in the food supply chain, non-criminalised anti-competition industry cartels and other food marketing practices that violate market competition, and cruelty to animals and further environmental harms caused by food industry activities.

The food sector is attractive to criminals. It is profitable, also in times of economic crisis. As humans need food for their daily survival, it is cash-intensive and often regulated in ways that make it hard to prosecute. For example, in the United Kingdom, food frauds are often prosecuted as administrative breaches of food safety regulations and usually punished with fines. The characteristics and conditions of the modern food system facilitate the commission of food crimes. In this context, Cheng (2012) refers to 'cheap capitalism' as the state of the modern trade and food business world characterised by low price, low quality, unsafe conditions of goods, services, and working conditions to maximise profits.

From small agri-food and farming businesses to medium producers as well as larger manufacturers, retailers, food consortia, food service entrepreneurs, andcorrupt veterinarians and health and safety officers, the range of criminal actors committing food crime is vast. The type of actors perpetrating food crimes as well as the opportunities offered by the food market typically make food crime a business crime (Spencer et al., 2018). However, organised crime groups are involved too as they are often operating in food and vegetables markets, or in food logistics, or running restaurants for money laundering purposes. For instance, Italian mafia groups have used food trucks and canned food to hide and transport drugs and weapons (Rizzuti, 2022).

Responses to food crime and future challenges

Since 2011, international policing bodies such as Europol and Interpol have conducted operations called 'Opson' to detect counterfeit food products and dismantle the frequently cross-border, criminal networks responsible for these practices. Similar investigative operations take place at national levels with regulatory bodies running safety and quality checks and police forces involved in investigating the criminal side of food offences. Unfortunately, food regulatory agencies are often under-resourced and food crimes go undetected and, when prosecuted, they are punished with low penalties.

In conclusion, from making people ill to financing corporate crime and enabling organised crime, food crimes can be serious. Global food supply chains are vulnerable to events like wars and, as recently seen, pandemics, as well as the unprecedented challenges posed by the climate emergency. Resulting food and water scarcity provide further opportunities for criminals to commit food crimes. To counter these challenges, national and international agencies addressing food crime should boost their cooperation. More importantly, food supply chains should be strengthened at global and local levels by protecting public interests beyond public health and national economy, such as food security, environmental sustainability, workers' rights, fair and equal access to food, and ethical consumption.

References

Cheng H (2012) Cheap Capitalism: A Sociological Study of Food Crime in China. *British Journal of Criminology* 52, 2, 254–273. https://doi.org/10.1093/bjc/azr078

Croall H (2013) Food Crime. A Green Criminology Perspective. In South N and Brisman A (eds), *Routledge International Handbook of Green Criminology*. London, Routledge, pp. 167–183.

Lord N, Flores Elizondo C J and Spencer J (2017) The Dynamics of Food Fraud: The Interactions between Criminal Opportunity and Market (Dys)functionality in Legitimate Business. *Criminology &*

Criminal Justice 17, 5, 605–623. https://doi.org/10.1177/1748895816684539

Manning L and Soon Y (2016) Food Safety, Food Fraud, and Food Defense: A Fast Evolving Literature. *Journal of Food Science* 81, 4, 823–834. https://doi.org/10.1111/1750-3841.13256

Rizzuti A (2022) Organised Food Crime: An Analysis of the Involvements of Organised Crime Groups in the Food Sector in England and Italy. *Crime, Law, and Social Change* 78, 5, 463–482. https://doi.org/10.1007/s10611-021-09975-w

Spencer J, Lord N, Benson K and Bellotti E (2018) 'C' is for Commercial Collaboration: Enterprise and Structure in the 'Middle Market' of Counterfeit Alcohol Distribution. *Crime, Law and Social Change*, 70(5), 543–560. https://doi.org/10.1007/s10611-018-9781-z

Further reading

Gray A and Hinch R (2018) *A Handbook of Food Crime: Immoral and Illegal Practices in the Food Industry and What to Do about Them*. Bristol, Policy Press.
This edited volume brings together contributions exploring food crime through discussions on food safety, fraud, insecurity, democracy and so on. It establishes the theoretical framework and debates current challenges around food crime.

Tourangeau W and Fitzgerald A (2020) Food Crime and Green Criminology. In Brisman A and South N (eds) *Routledge International Handbook of Green Criminology*. London, Routledge, 205–221.
Drawing on the theoretical framework of green criminology, this chapter focuses on food crimes defined by legal standards, such as food adulteration and counterfeiting, and food crimes that are not prohibited by law but are harmful and violate moral standards, such as cruelty to animals.

50. Food delivery

CAROLYNNE LORD

Introduction: the roots of food delivery

The movement of food from one place to another, or food delivery, has been a necessary component of social life since consumers began eating foods not grown or produced by themselves. It was relatively common in Victorian Britain, for instance, to purchase food from local grocers and have it delivered home (Graham, 2008).

Food delivery today, however, represents a diverse range of services – including grocery, takeaway and restaurant foods, and food subscription boxes (e.g., meal preparation kits). It is an important topic as it sits at the intersection of changing culinary preferences, transport systems, technologies, and employment models, with its diversification being enabled by new configurations.

Current issues: new configurations of food delivery in a changing sociopolitical landscape

Food delivery has transformed in recent years, becoming a global market worth over US$150 billion in 2021 – triple its value in 2017 (Ahuja et al., 2021). That said, the exact qualities and composition of food delivery services and infrastructure differ across countries. In the UK, for example, the landscape now includes household names like Just Eat, Deliveroo and HelloFresh, and increasing numbers of new competitors, as well as long-established businesses, like supermarkets, expanding their services into food delivery. The details of delivery depend on the service, with different infrastructural, transport and timing requirements necessary for delivering hot when compared with cold (or even frozen) foods. Because food delivery encompasses many different services, each has a particular history.

Though fish and chips dominated UK takeaway services until the 1970s, increasing numbers of working women meant that households had increased earnings but less time (Ball, 1996). A need for time-saving and convenient meals combined with the increasing popularity of American fast food chain branches led to a steady growth in home delivery and takeaway services (Cullen, 1994).

Grocery deliveries have ebbed and flowed in prominence over a longer-term history. The decline of the local grocer dovetailed with increasing urbanisation and the growth in supermarkets, reducing the availability of food delivery. In 1996, the UK's largest supermarket, Tesco, allowed customers to place orders by telephone, fax, and the internet for the first time (Enders & Jelassi, 2009). This development built on the presumed popularity of what was termed 'e-grocery', with industry predictions suggesting that consumers would replace all their offline shopping with online modes. Online grocery shopping, however, remained relatively niche, despite growth in other forms of internet-based retailing, and many early models disappeared (Leite Ferreira, 2009). Tesco, however, kept developing its fulfilment model and infrastructure (i.e., in-store picking, delivery hubs, dot.com -only stores) (Enders & Jelassi, 2009). Yet despite these developments, online grocers were supplying less than 2% of national groceries in 2007 (Competition Commission, 2007).

The 2020 Covid-19 pandemic sped up and cemented the position of food delivery, with guidance calling for households to order in where possible in many countries. Now, almost two-thirds (61.1%) of British consumers buy at least some groceries online (Spryker & Appinio, 2022), and 40% of UK households have up to three takeaways a week (Deliverect, 2022). Though there is variance, similar trends can be found elsewhere. China has the world's largest food delivery market, with 35.2% of consumers ordering takeaway one to five times a month, 27% of consumers ordering six to ten times, and 14.3% ordering between 11 and 20 times (iMedia, 2021). China is closely followed by the USA but developing markets in, for instance, India and Brazil also show rapid growth (Li et al., 2020).

As demand has grown, so too has the delivery workforce. Some businesses have expanded their own resources. Others, like some platform services, have used gig-economy couriers to keep costs down. Gig-economy workers are offered piecemeal rates for 'gigs' (i.e., deliveries), representing a more informal and flexible form of work available to anyone with a smartphone and a vehicle. Algorithms allocate gigs, making use of usually opaque metrics, leading to wage and job insecurity. With little to no training and time pressures for couriers, an increase in risk taking has been noted on roads (Christie & Ward, 2019).

The gig-economy is not specific to food delivery, but its growth has led to significant changes in European labour markets. Legal battles about the extent to which workers can be considered 'independent' or 'self-employed' have ensued, with differing results. Spain, for instance, determined that gig workers had to be recategorised as 'employees' from August 2021, and Italy issued legislation to ensure minimum protection levels (PwC, 2021).

Future concerns: path dependencies in future models

Some forms of food delivery represent a significant concern because of the path dependencies of their current development (Lord et al., 2022). Many platform-based services operate at a profit loss, held up by capital investment. The hope is that, once market domination is achieved, further innovations can take place.

Deliveroo, for instance, has presented a vision in which it not only mediates delivery, but also capitalises on restaurant and customer data to produce food too. In this envisioned model, food is produced by robots and delivered by drones (Cant, 2019) – siphoning off restaurant profits whilst reducing employment opportunities.

This future is far off, but it is in development with the creation of dark, or ghost, kitchens, which are delivery-only food preparation sites. Deliveroo, for instance, lets eateries rent spaces from its Editions sites, allowing them to expand their business for lower operational costs, or trial new menus under a different brand with no reputational risk. Industry predictions suggest that automated food preparation technologies may simply be 'plugged' into these in the future (Wolf, 2021). It is crucial, then, to question whether service convenience is worth the costs of that vision.

References

Ahuja K, Chandra V, Lord V and Peens C (2021) *Ordering in: The rapid evolution of food delivery.* McKinsey & Company Report. https://www.mckinsey.com/~/media/mckinsey/industries/technology%20media%20and%20telecommu nications/high%20tech/our%20insights /ordering%20in%20the%20rapid %20evolution%20of%20food%20delivery /ordering-in-the-rapid-evolution-of-food -delivery_vf.pdf (Accessed 17 May 2023).

Ball S (1996) Whither the small independent take-away. *International Journal of Contemporary Hospitality Management,* 8(5), 25–29.

Cant C (2019) *Riding for Deliveroo: Resistance in the new economy.* Polity Press.

Christie N and Ward H (2019) The health and safety risks for people who drive for work in the gig economy. *Journal of Transport & Health,* 13, 115–127.

Competition Commission (2007) Market investigation into the supply of groceries in the UK: Provisional findings report. http:// news.bbc.co.uk/1/shared/bsp/hi/pdfs/31 _10_07_prov_findings.pdf (Accessed 29 May 2025).

Cullen P (1994) Time, tastes, and technology: The economic evolution of eating out. *British Food Journal,* 96(10), 4.

Deliverect (2022) UK Inflation Delivery Trends. https://www.deliverect.com/en/uk -inflation-delivery-trends

Enders A and Jelassi T (2009) Leveraging Multichannel Retailing: The Experience of Tesco.com. *MIS Quarterly Executive,* 8(2), 89–100.

Graham K (2008) *Gone to the shops: Shopping in Victorian England.* Westport, CT, Praeger Publishers.

iMedia (2021) 2020–2021 *China's fast-selling food industry development status and consumer behaviour insight report.* https://report.iimedia.cn/repo2-0/39228 .html (Accessed 5 July 2023).

Leite Ferreira M (2009) (R)evolution of the e-grocery industry: Strategic implications. *SSRN.* http://dx.doi.org/10.2139/ssrn .1364117

Li C, Mirosa M and Bremer P (2020) Review of online food delivery platforms and their impacts on sustainability. *Sustainability,* 12(14), 5528.

Lord C, Bates O, Friday A, McLeod F, Cherrett T, Martinez-Sykora A and Oakey A (2022) The sustainability of the gig economy food delivery system (Deliveroo, UberEATS and Just-Eat): Histories and futures of rebound, lock-in and path dependency. *International Journal of Sustainable Transportation,* 17(5), 490–502.

PwC (2021) *The Gig economy in the EU and the UK.* https://www.pwc.co.uk/services/legal/insights/gig-economy-eu-uk-2021.html

Spryker and Appinio (2022) *The complete guide to online food retailing the UK: 2022 and beyond.* https://www.efoodinsights.com/uk-online-grocery-report/?utm_source=Spryker&utm_medium=Blog&utm_campaign=2021_Global_PR_Press%20Release%20Online%20Grocery%20Report%20UK (Accessed 6 July 2023).

Wolf M (2021) Our ghost kitchen future will be automated. *The Spoon.* https://thespoon.tech/our-ghost-kitchen-future-will-be-automated/ (Accessed 6 July 2023).

Further reading

Cant C (2019) *Riding for Deliveroo: Resistance in the new economy.* Polity Press.

This book provides an autoethnographic account of the experience of gig-economy working for Deliveroo and the algorithm that mediates job allocations. Whilst it puts forward the suggestion that this system exploits workers, it also shows how these so-called individual contractors have formed a community that is engaged in acts of resistance against the platform and labour conditions. Its analysis and commentary focus not just on the present, but also on the future of gig-economy food delivery.

Meemken E, Bellemare M, Reardon T and Vargas C (2022) Research and policy for the food-delivery revolution. *Science*, 377(6608), 810–813.

This article provides a more global representation of the delivery revolution, its consequences for the environment, nutrition, and decent work, as well as actual and potential policy responses.

51. Food democracy

Neva Hassanein

Introduction: food democracy

Who controls today's food system? Who should control it? Who makes choices about the structure and function of the food system, and how do they make those decisions? How do decision makers manage understandable conflicts that arise, given that sustainability is a contested concept with competing values and tradeoffs, and given uncertainty about desired outcomes? What processes might best promote and ensure collective benefit from the food system for current and future generations? These questions lie at the heart of the concept of food democracy (Lang, 1999; Hassanein, 2003, 2008). Food democracy, the focus of this entry, can be understood as an element of food sovereignty, although there are differences in terms of discourse, tactics, and origins (Carlson and Chappell, 2015; Anderson, 2023).

Fundamentally, food democracy refers to the concept that members of civil society can and should have meaningful opportunities to participate in food governance and make informed decisions that determine access to safe, nutritious food, produced in a way that is socially just and ecologically sound. People's active and meaningful engagement can transform them from passive consumers to food citizens. Food democracy calls for citizens – in the broad, denizen sense of the word, not the legal meaning – having the ability to determine agri-food policies and practices at a variety of scales, including local, regional, national, and global. Both activists and scholars have argued that food security, sustainability, and resilience depend on transformation of food governance through a redistribution of power and the adoption of democratic principles and practices (Hassanein, 2003, 2008; Carlson and Chappell, 2015; Behringer and Feindt, 2023).

Calls for food democracy emerged largely in response to greatly weakened government regulation of the market economy, and to the centralised and concentrated control that economic interests exert over food and agriculture. Large, multinational agribusiness firms have consolidated considerable economic power, measured by the share of industry sales held by the largest firms in a given sector of the food system. A recent analysis found that such concentration of economic power among agribusinesses in the United States has increased sharply over the last four decades, reducing competition, for example, in seed, livestock processing, and food retail markets (MacDonald et al., 2023). Most of these firms have a global reach.

The extensive market power of large agribusinesses is closely intertwined with their political power. Their considerable influence in governmental processes – from the local to the global – shapes the context within which these companies operate, typically prioritising corporate profit over collective benefit (IPES-Food, 2023). In our current food system, multinational corporations, as well as networks of scientific and administrative experts, make critical decisions without a clear democratic mandate. Instead, as Bornemann and Weiland point out, "it is citizens affected by food issues who are supposed to shape food systems in line with their ideas and interests in a democratically organised process of will formation and decision-making" (2019: 2). Food democracy exposes and challenges the anti-democratic forces of control, and claims the rights and responsibilities of food citizens to participate in decision making and to help determine our collective food future.

Dimensions of food democracy

Given major political and structural barriers, the ideals and norms associated with food democracy might seem unrealistic and out-of-touch. After all, transformation of the food system with effective democratic governance mechanisms across policy sectors and geographic scales remains elusive and limited. Yet, investigating existing spaces of resistance, struggle, and innovation – spaces where people attempt to govern and shape their relationships with food and agriculture – has yielded important insights into incremental progress and future possibilities.

For more than two decades now, scholars and activists have tried to advance, document, and understand movements towards food democracy. Building on the work of Lang (1999) and democracy theorists, Hassanein (2008) attempted to operationalise the concept's dimensions to facilitate analysis of instances where food democracy may be emergent. Since then, scholars have used those dimensions – and developed new ones – as an analytical lens to study a variety of alternative agri-food networks and their initiatives, generating a robust body of literature. For instance, Renting et al. (2012) explored consumer–producer cooperation as expressions of food citizenship within civic food networks. Other examples include empirical studies of the role of collective action and political engagement in food democracy as expressed during anti-pesticide campaigns (Zollet and Maharjan, 2021) and bans against genetically modified seeds (Daye, 2020). The framework has even been applied to sustainable gastronomy to explore how some chefs use democracy principles to promote sustainable food practices and behaviours (Richardson and Fernqvist, 2022). Perhaps most frequently, scholars have looked at "democratic innovations" intended to mitigate weaknesses in existing policy processes of established institutions and to improve the quality and legitimacy of policymaking, with food policy councils being the prime example (Candel, 2022).

These and other studies suggest that there is much to learn from an analysis of instances where food democracy might be emergent. Respect for the rights of food citizens and meaningful public participation are the basis for a more just, democratic, and sustainable food system. Food democracy requires active engagement by ordinary people who identify the problem, set the agenda, weigh risks and benefits, and creatively experiment with solutions. Opportunities for engagement must be deep, not symbolic. Characterising what food democracy does and could look like seems vital to its wider realisation, because without such an articulation the necessary processes and practices are unlikely to become the norm.

What are the key indicators of movement towards food democracy or its absence? While a full elaboration of the dimensions is beyond the scope of this entry, the following interrelated elements surface repeatedly (Hassanein, 2008; Candel, 2022; Behringer and Feindt, 2023):

1. Effective **collective action** through strategic coalitions can increase citizen power by enabling groups to effect change that they could not otherwise achieve on their own. To the extent that coalitions involve different interest groups, they can create important pathways for mutual learning among stakeholders. Food democracy cannot be achieved solely through individual decisions and choices, although those are certainly important modes of action for producers, consumers, and entrepreneurs.

2. Meaningful civic engagement depends on **knowledge** about the existing food system and alternative ways of designing and operating it. Only well-informed food citizens can participate and make decisions effectively. Currently, reliable information about the food system is often not available to the public, and is, for example, obscured through complex food supply chains that distance us from the food we eat or by laws protecting trade secrets. Food democracy initiatives should themselves have a high degree of transparency of decision making to inform nonparticipants, such as availability of the proceedings of meetings (Candel, 2022).

3. People make better decisions for themselves and others if they have shared ideas with each other, discussed values, and clarified the issues. Such **deliberation** is essential to navigating inevitable conflicts over values and trade-offs related to sustainability, to weighing risks and benefits in the face of uncertainty, and to generating innovative solutions. Candel (2022: 1484) refers to this as "considered judgment", and advocates for the use of good deliberative practices (e.g., the use of nontechnical, accessible language; well-facilitated discussions to understand varying viewpoints).

4. **Inclusiveness** refers to the degree to which a broad range of people are involved in food democracy initiatives and how accessible they are for socially disadvantaged groups. To address civic inequality, for instance, extra efforts and resources may be needed to ensure that people who have lived experience with food insecurity, and/or with work in low-wage jobs on farms, at food processors, or in food services, are able to engage and influence outcomes. In a strong food democracy, everyone should be able to be at the table, and participate to ensure their rights and interests are respected. Food citizenship should be considered in the broadest possible terms and not limited to those with a particular legal citizenship or immigration status.

NEVA HASSANEIN

5. **Actual and perceived efficacy** means people feel that they have the capacity to produce desired results, and thus that their participation is worthwhile. If people do not understand how social and political systems work and how to influence them, they cannot exercise effective agency. As a result, they often become disengaged and passive, and civic participation declines. Food democracy initiatives, such as food policy councils, can be evaluated in terms of actual efficacy – what Candel (2022: 1483) calls "popular control" – that is, the degree to which initiatives set the policy agenda and improve decision making.

6. Food democracy also depends on individual and collective agency being **oriented towards the common good**. Ideally, agency transcends self-interest to promote the well-being of current and future generations. Instilling the values that will bring about collective benefit from the food system can lead to genuine transformation.

The future of food democracy

While existing political-economic structures within (and beyond) the food system are formidable, they are not immutable or inevitable. There are alternatives. The existing literature documents numerous efforts to democratise food and agriculture, as well as the features that might characterise such movements towards democratisation. At a time when the democratic quality of political systems is under threat from extreme polarisation, disinformation, authoritarianism, and more, the centrality of food to everyone's lives makes it a good place to begin a wider systemic response to those threats.

Numerous questions remain to be explored. The following are just a few avenues for future scholarship and practice. First, can food democracy exist within a capitalist economic system? If so, what kinds of restraints must be placed on capitalism, and the existing concentration of economic and political power, to ensure food democracy produces collective benefit and protects individual rights? Does the right to food itself fundamentally reject capitalism's propensity towards commodification of all things (including life)? Second, food policy councils constitute the most common democratic innovation in the food arena, but what other participatory arrangements are worthy of experimentation to advance and deepen food democracy? Third, any existing movement towards food democracy seems focused at the local level. What other participatory approaches might be deployed to extend democratic innovations to other contexts and levels of governance? Last (but not least), given the urgency created by the climate emergency, how might food democracy facilitate adaptation within the agri-food system, as well as the potential for mitigation, regeneration, and resilience? How might a food democracy framework inform our appreciation for the soil, water, and microbiome upon which the ability to feed the world rests?

For people and organisations wanting to transform contemporary food systems, food democracy seems a long way off. The first steps, however, are articulating what it might look like and identifying where movement towards it exists already, even if those examples seem small relative to the considerable power of multinational agribusiness firms that greatly influence how food is produced and consumed. Scholars and practitioners have taken these first steps, and the developments are encouraging. Now, we also need to expand the practice of food democracy. To speak of the pressure to democratise the food system is to recognise the spaces of resistance and creativity, to learn from them, and to build on them.

References

Anderson M D (2023) Expanding food democracy: a perspective from the United States. *Frontiers in Sustainable Food Systems*, 7. https://doi.org/10.3389/fsufs.2023.1144090

Behringer J and Feindt P H (2023) Varieties of food democracy: a systematic literature review. *Critical Policy Studies*. https://doi.org/10.1080/19460171.2023.2191859

Bornemann B and Weiland S (2019) Editorial: new perspectives on food democracy. *Politics and Governance* 7(4), 1–7. https://doi.org/10.17645/pag.v7i4.2570

Candel, J J L (2022) Power to the people? Food democracy initiatives and contributions to democratic goods. *Agriculture and Human Values* 39, 1477–1489. https://doi.org/10.1007/s10460-022-10322-5

Carlson J and Chappell M J (2015) *Deepening Food Democracy*. Institute for Agriculture and Trade Policy. https://www.iatp.org/sites/default/files/2015_01_06_Agrodemocracy_JC_JC_f_0.pdf

Daye, R (2020) Competing food sovereignties: GMO-free activism, democracy and state preemptive laws in Southern Oregon. *Agriculture and Human Values* 37, 1013–1025. https://doi.org/10.1007/s10460-020-10034-8

Hassanein N (2003) Practicing food democracy: a pragmatic politics of transformation. *Journal of Rural Studies* 19(1), 77–86. https://doi.org/10.1016/S0743-0167(02)00041-4

Hassanein N (2008) Locating food democracy: theoretical and practical ingredients. *Journal of Hunger and Environmental Nutrition* 3(2–3), 286–308. https://doi.org/10.1080/19320240802244215

IPES-Food (2023) *Who's Tipping the Scales? The Growing Influence of Corporations on the Governance of Food Systems, and How to Counter It*. International Panel of Experts on Sustainable Food Systems. https://www.ipes-food.org/_img/upload/files/tippingthescales.pdf

Lang T (1999) Food policy for the 21st century: can it be both radical and reasonable? In: Koc M, MacRae R, Mougeot LJA and Welsh J (eds.), *For Hunger-proof Cities: Sustainable Urban Food Systems*. Ottawa, Ontario, International Development Research Centre, pp. 216–224.

MacDonald J M, Dong X, and Fuglie K O (2023) *Concentration and Competition in U.S. Agribusiness*. U.S. Department of Agriculture, Economic Research Service, EIB-256.

Renting H, Schermer M, and Rossi A (2012) Building food democracy: exploring civic food networks and newly emerging forms of food citizenship. *The International Journal of Sociology of Agriculture and Food* 19(3), 289–307. https://doi.org/10.48416/ijsaf.v19i3.206

Richardson L and Fernqvist F (2022) Transforming the food system through sustainable gastronomy: how chefs engage with food democracy. *Journal of Hunger and Environmental Nutrition*. https://doi.org/10.1080/19320248.2022.2059428

Zollet S and Majarjan K L (2021) Resisting the vineyard invasion: anti-pesticide movements as a vehicle for territorial food democracy and just sustainability transitions. *Journal of Rural Studies* 86, 318–329. https://doi.org/10.1016/j.jrurstud.2021.06.020

Further reading

Behringer J and Feindt P H (2023) Varieties of food democracy: a systematic literature review. *Critical Policy Studies*. https://doi.org/10.1080/19460171.2023.2191859
This review provides a comprehensive overview and analysis of existing literature.

Candel, J J L (2022) Power to the people? Food democracy initiatives and contributions to democratic goods. *Agriculture and Human Values* 39, 1477–1489. https://doi.org/10.1007/s10460-022-10322-5
Candel draws on political science, and analyses the food democracy literature for contributions to specific democratic goods.

Carlson J and Chappell M J (2015) *Deepening Food Democracy*. Institute for Agriculture and Trade Policy. https://www.iatp.org/sites/default/files/2015_01_06_Agrodemocracy_JC_JC_f_0.pdf
This highly accessible report describes existing examples of deepening food democracy, such as participatory budgeting and technology consensus conferences.

52. Food deserts

Melanie Bedore

Introduction

Landscapes are sometimes described as 'deserts' to indicate that they are empty, barren, harsh and lifeless. It is perhaps fitting, then, that the term 'food desert' was first used by the British government and policymakers in the late 1990s to describe urban areas without access to healthy food retail. People living in food deserts experience several concurrent challenges: (1) lack of nearby grocery stores and supermarkets (they may be closing while any newly opened stores are located in distant, suburban areas), (2) low income and (3) low mobility, especially living without a personal vehicle for food shopping.

An urban or rural area is undergoing 'food desertification' when retail food shops are withdrawing from poorer communities, leaving residents without healthy, affordable food close to home. Food deserts have been a concern primarily in countries of the Global North such as the United Kingdom, the United States and (to a lesser extent) Canada because they share at least four typical features of post-industrial political economies that create a 'perfect storm' of poor food access: aggressive consolidation and concentration of power in the retail food sector; the adoption of large, suburban store formats predicated on automobile-based travel for food shopping; the growth of car-oriented, suburban forms of investment and development; and persistent poverty that is often spatially concentrated (Eisenhauer, 2001). Philadelphia is a well-profiled example of such a perfect storm. In the 20th century the city became increasingly segregated because of a complex combination of 'white flight' (white people's large-scale residential relocation from urban to suburban areas) but also mortgage and housing redlining and urban disinvestment that affected inner city African American and other racial minority communities. The latter were most affected by food deserts as the city's local retail food sector simultaneously underwent consolidation, suburbanisation and other infrastructural changes that led to a decrease in food stores in the inner city (Deener, 2017).

People living in food deserts may encounter disproportionate burdens when shopping for food, such as financial costs (of taking a taxi, for example) and the loss of time (taking public transit or walking long distances). They may also experience helplessness, a loss of dignity from having fewer consumer choices and less autonomy from needing to ask family members for rides or negotiate ride shares with neighbours (Bedore, 2014). Residents of food deserts may also experience poorer health than non-residents, including higher rates of diet-related health conditions such as hypertension, heart disease and diabetes. Poor food access is also a clear food justice issue because communities where grocery stores cannot operate profitably (and hence close or relocate) may have a high proportion of racial and ethnic minority residents who also struggle with low income. Indeed, food deserts are one important manifestation of environmental racism and injustice that systemically expose poor, racialised communities to environmental and health burdens while denying those same communities environmental benefits such as healthy food, clean air and safe water. Compounding this injustice is the prevalence of 'food swamps', which are areas whose residents are exposed to too many unhealthy choices, such as fast food outlets. Areas around schools are of particular concern because corner stores and fast food vendors can easily market junk or fast food to young people. Too much junk food (swamps) and too little affordable, healthy food (deserts) can thus co-exist within one location, and again low-income and minority communities may be especially vulnerable to such spatial inequities.

Addressing food deserts

Institutions at a variety of scales have responded to food deserts. For example, local and state/provincial governments in the US and Canada have funded Healthy Corner Store Initiatives that offer grants to help small retailers such as bodegas (small convenience stores) to expand their fresh, healthy food offerings and upgrade shelving and storage to improve visibility and product presentation. Food financing initiatives in some US states provide grants to food retail enterprises that are working to increase fresh, healthy retail food offerings in low- and moderate-income communities (Lang et al., 2013). Innovative cities also engage in food-friendly land use, transportation and economic planning. Strategies can include updating zoning codes and by-laws to permit diverse local food production and sales; waiving development fees to attract new food retailers; and supporting crime prevention and public safety initiatives in underserved neighbourhoods.

By pushing back against the corporate control of food, civil society groups also administer alternative food programmes in underserved communities. Examples of collective, grassroots efforts include food trusts, community fridges and cellars, country food sharing in North American First Nations communities, community gardening, cooperative and non-profit food stores, community kitchens, community-supported agriculture and many other alternative provisioning options.

At the same time, some scholars, policy-makers and community groups question the urgency of the food desert problem. First, not all places suffer from poor retail food access. Studies of Edmonton, Montreal and Glasgow, for example, do not reveal any food deserts (e.g. Apparicio et al., 2007). Studies of San Francisco, Detroit, Erie County, New York and other cities suggest that researchers' fixation on the large grocery store overlooks the importance of mini-marts, bodegas and other small-scale retail to peoples' geographical and cultural construction of food access (e.g., Howerton and Trauger, 2017). More broadly, food deserts are not compelling problems in regions with diverse, decentralised retail food sectors. Many parts of the Global South, for example, have not (yet) experienced the store closures and retail disinvestment that create food deserts. Food access can instead be more productively analysed through the nexus of state political and economic stability, culture, religious dietary diversity, household income, the extent of local informal economies, supply chain stability, climate and more (Battersby, 2019).

Second, there are limits to focusing solely on geography. Mapping software and data visualisation techniques, for example, are helpful for visualising the problem; however, many mapping projects fixate on the proximity of retail food to one's home. This is problematic because many people do not shop at the store closest to where they live due to varied customer constraints, preferences and perceptions. Indeed, Alkon et al.'s (2013) research into the foodways of theurban poor reveal that lower-income shoppers in Oakland and Chicago adopt complex, strategic shopping habits in order to prioritise many factors, such as food freshness, price, healthfulness, store cleanliness, inventory and their own food taste preferences. Mapping efforts also may not always be attuned to fluctuations in peoples' incomes throughout the month that shift the relatively financial accessibility of food regardless of physical proximity to a grocery store. Researchers may not account for 'food mirages', which are areas in which retail food is physically present but not always affordable. Food mirages can exist in gentrifying cities (Portland, Oregon or Guelph, Ontario, for example) where premium, high-priced retail food stores such as Whole Foods give the illusion of choices that are, in fact, unaffordable for lower-income residents. The food desert metaphor, then, may obscure the reality that geography is merely one dimension of food access and that economic and cultural factors must be considered by policy-makers as well.

Third, new grocery stores in food deserts may not actually improve people's health and eating habits as might be hoped. Researchers have studied whether a new retail food store opening in an underserved community affects local people's diets and health. In some cases, research shows improved self-reported mental health, slower increases of chronic disease or other positive improvements. However, there may be only a modestly positive or negligible effect on people's fruit and vegetable consumption (Cummins et al., 2005; Wrigley et al., 2003). One study even showed that fast food consumption went up in a Flint, Michigan, community that gained a new grocery store, while fruit and vegetable consumption was unaffected (Sadler et al., 2013). These outcomes seem to confirm that people's shopping mobility and preferences are complex and defy one-size-fits-all interventions as the singular 'solution' to food deserts.

Is there a future for the food desert metaphor?

More than two decades after the 'food desert' metaphor was first used, it seems to be a crossroads: the metaphor readily invokes inequitable food environments that disproportionately affect the health of low-income, racialised communities. At the same time, critics suggest that it is time to retire the concept altogether. Has interest in the subject dried up for good or will it continue, albeit through more complex understandings and conceptualisations?

MELANIE BEDORE

Interest may be waning thanks to the recent growth of grocery and other food delivery services. Walmart, Amazon and many other businesses through Europe, North America and Asia have invested aggressively in grocery warehousing and ultra-rapid delivery infrastructure. The explosion of Uber and other driving/delivery services could also help to collapse the distance between grocery stores and underserved communities. Could online grocery shopping and delivery services make carlessness a non-issue in the future? Equity will be of key importance: are these services affordable, accessible and non-discriminatory? Do they work for everyone, including seniors, people with disabilities and people with low digital literacy?

Moreover, the food desert metaphor may be absorbed into other campaigns for food justice. For example, community activists such as Karen Washington suggest that the 'desert' metaphor may be misleading and depoliticising. If deserts can be naturally occurring landscapes, are food deserts somehow also 'natural'? 'Food apartheid', in contrast, explicitly highlights how poor food access is *produced* through systemic racism using political, economic and social tools of oppression at a variety of scales. Perhaps food apartheid will be a rallying cry of citizens wishing to create more just food provisioning landscapes that restore food access for people and communities and not simply for profit.

References

Alkon A H, Block D, Moore K, Gillis C, DiNuccio N and Chavez N (2013) Foodways of the urban poor. *Geoforum* 48, 126–135. https://doi.org/10.1016/j.geoforum.2013.04.021

Apparicio P, Cloutier M-C and Shearmur R (2007) The case of Montréal's missing food deserts: Evaluation of accessibility to food supermarkets. *International Journal of Health Geographics* 6(4). https://doi.org/10.1186/1476-072X-6-4

Battersby J (2019) The food desert as a concept and policy tool in African cities: An opportunity and a risk. *Sustainability* 11(2), 458–473. https://doi.org/10.3390/su11020458

Bedore M (2014) Food desertification: Situating choice and class relations within an urban political economy of declining food access. *Studies in Social Justice* 8, 207–228. https://doi.org/10.26522/ssj.v8i2.1034

Cummins S, Petticrew M, Higgins C, Findlay A and Sparks L (2005) Large scale food retailing as an intervention for diet and health: Quasi-experimental evaluation of a natural experiment. *Journal of Epidemiology and Community Health* 59, 1035–1040. http://dx.doi.org/10.1136/jech.2004.029843

Deener A (2017) The origins of the food desert: Urban inequality as infrastructural exclusion. *Social Forces* 95, 1285–1309. https://doi.org/10.1093/sf/sox001

Eisenhauer E (2001) In poor health: Supermarket redlining and urban nutrition. *GeoJournal* 53, 125–133. https://doi.org/10.1023/A:1015772503007

Howerton G and Trauger A (2017) "Oh honey, don't you know?" The social construction of food access in a food desert. *ACME* 16(4), 740–760.

Lang B, Harries C, Manon M, Tucker J, Kim E, Ansell S and Smith P (2013) *Healthy Food Financing Handbook*. Philadelphia: The Food Trust. https://thefoodtrust.org/wp-content/uploads/2022/07/hffhandbookfinal.original.pdf

Sadler R C, Gilliland J A and Arku G (2013) A food retail-based intervention on food security and consumption. *International Journal of Environmental Research and Public Health* 10, 3325–3346. https://doi.org/10.3390/ijerph10083325

Wrigley N, Warm D and Margetts B (2003) Deprivation, diet, and food-retail access: Findings from the Leeds 'food deserts' study. *Environment & Planning A*, 35, 151–188. https://doi.org/10.1068/a35150

Further reading

Morland K B, Lehmann, Y M and Karpyn A E (2022) *Local food environments: Food access in America* (2nd ed). Boca Raton, FL: CRC Press.
This book explores how inequities in local food environments are a product of broader economic and political forces shaping our food system. Focusing on policymaking and problem-solving, the authors profile state food retail interventions and other policy efforts to bring equity and improved health outcomes to food environments.

MELANIE BEDORE

Shannon J (2014) Food deserts: Governing obesity in the neoliberal city. *Progress in Human Geography* 38(2), 248–266.

This article critiques policymakers' tendency to address food deserts through bounded, localised spatial strategies such as incentivising the construction of new retail food stores. Such an approach skirts around broader-scale issues of residential segregation, environmental racism, and a dysfunctional food system. Moreover, policymakers too often privilege market-based solutions and the remaking of low-income communities to mimic white, middle class foodscapes.

MELANIE BEDORE

53. Food design

Sonia Massari

Introduction

Food design is an interdisciplinary field merging food with design methodologies, focusing on the creation, presentation, and experience of food. This concept dates back to the creation of tools for procuring, cultivating, harvesting, and preparing food. As humans developed increasingly sophisticated tools to ensure and prepare food, design has always been integral to this process. Progress in food preservation and transformation results from centuries of design efforts, accelerated by early industrial centres and urbanisation, leading to numerous advancements in food production and distribution (Ferrara and Massari, 2015). Industrialisation created new professions linked to food cultivation, transportation, sale, and cooking, with design central to these processes (Margolin, 2012). Industrial methods brought complex transformations to food materials, altering structures and visual aspects. The shapes of foods like biscuits, chocolates, and pasta, crafted from mouldable materials, illustrate this. Factory model registrations (i.e., the official documentation of product designs created within a manufacturing context – these ensure that unique design aspects of products, such as shapes of biscuits or pasta, can be legally protected) since 1895 reflect a search for formal values alongside industrial process research (Picchi, 2000). Despite differing approaches, food engineering and food design have significant overlaps: the former is scientific-mathematical; the latter is technical-cultural and behavioural.

Design has also advanced industrial food products through packaging, which evolved significantly from solutions for food containment and preservation to addressing transport, storage, and supermarket display issues. This sector has gone beyond functionality and usability, interpreting packaging as unconscious messaging, enhancing the visual and narrative aspects of consumption. By the late 1990s, globalisation shifted cultural attitudes towards food, emphasising the management of complexities within the global food system. Increased awareness of the gap between production and consumption created more design opportunities. In the 21st century, food design expanded to include sustainability, health, social dynamics, and technological innovation. Since 2015, several specialised master's programmes in food design and food innovation, along with courses, university curricula, and vocational programmes, have emerged globally. Concurrently, networks, associations, and alliances of professionals and scholars, such as the Red Latinoamericana de Diseño y Alimentos, North America Food Design Network, Dutch Institute of Food & Design, F.O.R.K., and FDxE, have been instrumental in promoting the discipline. These organisations facilitate information dissemination through conferences, proceedings, seminars, and workshops, enhancing awareness and understanding of food design.

The systemic focus of food design has led to a paradigm shift, incorporating a broader complexity of elements and their effects. Today, food design intersects various disciplines: from chemical engineering to genetics, anthropology to psychoanalysis, and food sociology to the design of hospitality and conviviality forms (Ferrara & Massari, 2015).

Dimensions of food design

Food design now encompasses a variety of subfields (Zampollo and Peacock, 2016), each addressing different aspects of the food experience.

Design for Food focuses on enhancing food production, preparation, and consumption through the creation of tools (forks, dishes), equipment, and appliances. Innovations like smart vending machines and drone delivery systems not only enhance accessibility but also streamline convenience. Additionally, using biomaterials and food waste to craft tools and tableware, such as forks made from potato waste, exemplifies sustainability efforts within this category.

Design with Food involves leveraging food as a design material to achieve artistic, functional, or experiential outcomes. This encompasses innovations like plant-based alternative proteins and foods produced using 3D printing technology, along with edible items such as coffee cups, all aimed at enhancing both the appeal and the functionality of food products.

Food Product Design is centred on creating new food items that emphasise taste, texture, nutrition, and marketability. This collaborative process often involves chefs, food scientists, and marketing experts, resulting in products like probiotic yogurts and fortified snacks that offer health benefits beyond basic nutrition. Sustainable packaging solutions, including edible options, further underline commitments to environmental stewardship.

Eating Design focuses on enhancing the dining experience by considering sensory, emotional, and social dimensions of food consumption. This includes designing immersive restaurant environments that use elements like lighting, sound, and scent to elevate the culinary experience, as well as creating themed culinary events that merge food, art, and design to deliver distinctive and often transformative dining encounters.

Foodscapes and Foodspaces encompass the spatial and environmental aspects of food production and consumption. This dimension encompasses the design of spaces where food is cultivated, sold, and consumed, including innovative interior designs and market formats like farm-to-fork initiatives that seamlessly integrate purchasing and dining experiences. Examples include urban farms and community gardens designed to integrate food production within urban settings, as well as the layout and ambience of food markets and grocery stores that enrich the shopping experience.

Social Food Design addresses the social impact of food through design interventions aimed at promoting food security, community cohesion, and social justice. Initiatives range from using surplus food to create meals for underserved populations to educational programmes fostering food literacy and creativity. This category also embraces participatory design approaches in communities to enhance public health and well-being.

Human–Food Interaction Design explores how people interact with food through multisensory experiences, advanced ICTs and Artificial Intelligence technologies, and cultural contexts. Beyond food preparation and consumption, it considers the broader ecosystem of interactions, encompassing emotions, habits, perceptions, and consumer behaviours. This interdisciplinary approach leverages technologies such as cooking apps, augmented reality, and smart devices to create immersive culinary experiences and enhance the food journey also for people with disabilities.

Contemporary food designers are challenged to transcend traditional boundaries by considering intangible elements like values and sustainability in their designs. They are increasingly tasked with redesigning food education models, informal food environments, and policy frameworks to foster new sustainable practices and habits. As the field evolves, these new dimensions of food design are becoming increasingly crucial, shaping a future where food is not only nourishment but also a conduit for meaningful experiences and societal change (Massari et al., 2022).

Future directions for food design

Food design is set to evolve, driven by technological advancements, changing consumer preferences, and global challenges such as the climate emergency and food security. Emerging trends include sustainable innovations like zero-waste restaurants, biodegradable packaging, and circular food systems that minimise environmental impact. Technology-driven solutions, such as artificial intelligence and big data, will optimise food production, personalise nutrition, and enhance food safety. Experiential culinary experiences using virtual reality, augmented reality, and other immersive technologies will create new ways to consume food. Inclusive design, focusing on accessibility, affordability, and cultural diversity, will be vital for advancing food design. Contemporary food design respects diverse cultural contexts, blending local and global dimensions, natural and technological elements, analogue and digital, industrial and artisanal. This expanding field allows scholars and experts from various disciplines to contribute to more sustainable and less harmful food cultures for future generations.

New frontiers include collaboration in living labs, fostering innovation with science, and redesigning urban, peri-urban, and rural food environments to promote rural innovation. The importance of inclusive design for people with disabilities should be emphasised. Solutions for the agri-food business now require designers' involvement from the start of the food supply chain, covering agriculture, agroecology, aquaculture, and pastoralism. Food design as citizen science and social activism for sustainability is rising, seen in exhibitions that reconnect consumers with the value of food. Additionally, food design plays an increasing role in political and diplomatic contexts, uniting policymakers through events and gastro-diplomacy (Parasecoli, 2017). In conclusion, food design leverages co-creativity to unite stakeholders, fostering innovative, healthier, sustainable, and regenerative systems essential for transformative change.

References

Ferrara, M.R., Massari, S. (2015). Evoluzione del concept food design: intersezioni storiche tra cibo, design e cultura alimentare occidentale. *AIS/Design Storia e Ricerche n. 5.*

Margolin, V. (2012). Design studies and food studies: Parallels and intersections. *Design and Culture, 5*, 375–392.

Massari, S., Jatwani, C., Tiriduzzi, M., Roversi, S. (2022). The role of design in the transition to sustainable diets. In: Kevany, K., Prosperi, P. (eds.), *Handbook of sustainable diets* (pp. 534–546). Routledge.

Parasecoli, F. (2017). Food, research, design: What can food studies bring to food design education? *International Journal of Food Design, 2*, 15–25. DOI 10.1386/ijfd.2.1.15_1

Picchi, F. (2000). Food design. Standard alimentari: I pionieri dell'industrializzazione. *InDomus* 823, 78–83.

Zampollo, F., Peacock, M. (2016). Food design thinking: A branch of design thinking specific to food design. *Journal of Creative Behavior, 50*, 203–210.

Further reading

Massari, S., Marti, P., Recupero, A. (2023). Designing digital technologies for sustainable transformations of food systems. *International Journal of Food Design, 8*(1).

For those interested in the intersection of technology and sustainable food systems, this special issue provides in-depth insights and innovative approaches that offer a comprehensive understanding of how digital technologies can be used to address and transform challenges within the complex landscape of food production, distribution, and consumption.

Massari, S. (Ed.) (2021). *Transdisciplinary case studies on design for food and sustainability.* Woodhead Publishing.

This book focuses on the intersection of design, food, education, and sustainability, presenting real-world cases and offering valuable insights into how design methods can drive innovation and positive impact across the food system.

Manzini, E. (2015). *Design, when everybody designs: An introduction to design for social innovation.* MIT Press.

This book provides insight into the transformative power of design in fostering social innovation. It offers a compelling exploration of how design principles can be used to address complex issues, delving into the intersection of design thinking and societal challenges.

54. Food environments

CHRISTOPHER TURNER

Introduction: food environments

Food environments form a critical link between food and society. They are the point where people meet the food system – where food supply meets demand (United Nations System Standing Committee on Nutrition, 2019). Consider the various places from where you have acquired and consumed food over the past week. Reflect on the myriad of influences that shaped your decisions around what to eat as you went about your daily life and activities. This is your food environment.

From formal and informal markets to various forms of self-provisioning, wild food harvesting, kin and communal networks, and online retail platforms, food environments span the range of food sources that we interact with to acquire and consume foods (Bogard et al., 2021; Downs et al., 2020; Turner et al., 2018). As such, food environments have become the focal point of public health nutrition research seeking to understand the physical, economic, and socio-cultural influences that shape what people eat (Swinburn et al., 2013).

The field of food environment research developed in high-income country settings in the mid-2000s in direct response to the mounting public health nutrition challenges related to overweight, obesity, and diet-related non-communicable disease (Caspi et al., 2012). The early literature was grounded in the notion of food deserts, focusing on the limited availability, accessibility, and affordability of nutritious foods, particularly in deprived neighbourhoods. By the mid-2010s, food environment research had also started to gain momentum in low- and middle-income countries (Turner et al., 2019; Westbury et al., 2021). In these settings, the longstanding challenges of undernutrition and micronutrient deficiencies were being accompanied by the growing prevalence of overweight, obesity, and diet-related non-communicable diseases, with food environments contributing to a rapidly emerging double burden of malnutrition (Popkin et al., 2020).

In response to the broadened scope of food environment research at the time, the Agriculture, Nutrition and Health Academy Food Environment Working Group was established in 2016 to develop globally applicable concepts for food environment research. Drawing from a socio-ecological approach, Turner et al.'s (2018) conceptual framework situates the food environment as a key interface within the wider food system (Figure 54.1). The external food environment domain reflects dimensions such as food availability, prices, vendor and product properties, and marketing and regulation – this can be considered as the outside world that we interact with. The personal domain captures dimensions such as food accessibility, affordability, desirability, and convenience – these are intrinsic to individuals. Interactions between these domains and dimensions play out as part of our daily lives and activities, constituting our lived experience of the food environment, and ultimately shaping our food acquisition and consumption practices.

Current issues in food environment research

Food environment research is a relatively new field of research, and as such it is evolving rapidly as emerging concepts are increasingly operationalised into methods and metrics that are being applied and tested in diverse settings across the globe. In the section that follows, I highlight three current issues that require attention.

The state of the science

At the global level, the influence of the food environment on dietary, nutrition, and health outcomes remains to be conclusively established. Systematic reviews of studies from high income countries have reported mixed results, with some reviewers finding modest evidence in support of the influence of the food environment on diets amongst adults (Caspi et al., 2012; Gamba et al., 2015) and children (Engler-Stringer et al., 2014), whilst others reported more ambiguity (Gustafson et al., 2014; Cetateanu and Jones, 2016). More recently, reviews of the emerging literature from low- and middle-income countries report consistent associations between food availability and dietary outcomes at both the community and school scales, whilst evidence on nutrition and health outcomes remains limited (Carducci et al., 2020; Turner et al., 2019; Westbury et al., 2021). The significant heterogeneity in the application of conceptual and methodological approaches is a key limiting factor in the state of the science and the

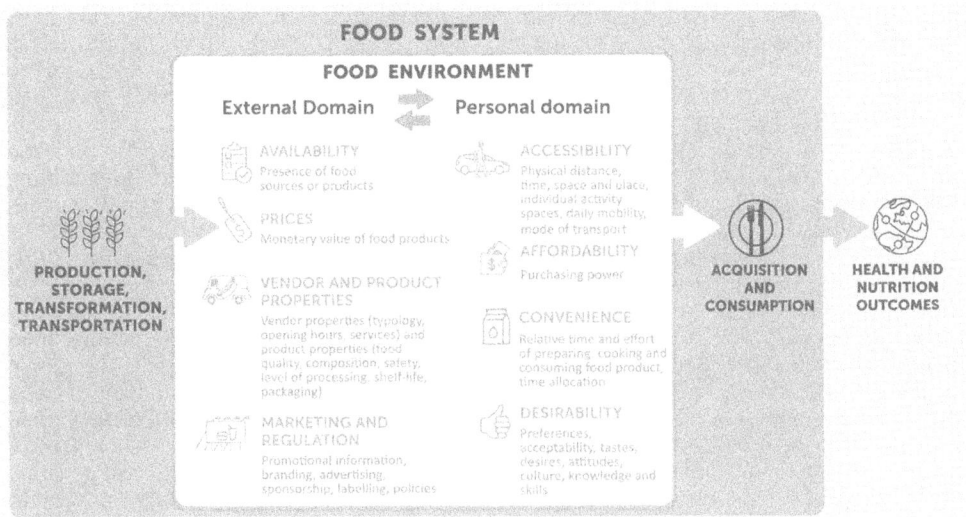

Figure 54.1   A globally applicable food environment framework developed by the Agriculture, Nutrition and Health Academy Food Environment Working Group (Turner et al., 2018)

generation of a robust evidence base. I will now turn to these two areas in the sections that follow.

Concepts and theoretical perspectives

At present, there is no gold standard definition of food environments. This poses a significant challenge to the generation of comparable evidence. Recent theoretical frameworks by Turner et al. (2018), Downs et al. (2020), and Osei-Kwasi et al. (2021) have sought to build conceptual consensus around food environment typologies and the key dimensions for consideration, building on the earlier seminal work by Glanz et al. (2007). However, the interpretation and subsequent application of these concepts has been inconsistent at best.

Terminology is an important issue. There is considerable overlap between the key terms used in the food environment and food security literature. Food availability, accessibility, stability, and utilisation are fundamental pillars in the conceptualisation and definition of food security and are well-established constructs within public health nutrition research – particularly among researchers and practitioners working in low- and middle-income country contexts (Food and Agriculture Organisation of the United Nations, 1983; Food and Agriculture Organization of the United Nations, 2001). These terms and their underlying constructs are often conflated with the terminology commonly used in food environment research, and this dialectical tension within the lexicon has yet to be resolved.

The integration of food environment concepts into wider food systems thinking is another important issue. The emphasis placed on food environments as a key interface within the wider food system in recent high-level food systems frameworks is a welcome addition (High Level Panel of Experts on Food Security and Nutrition, 2020). However, further conceptual work is needed to integrate and consolidate these frameworks, align the key concepts and typologies, and build a platform of consensus to guide and inform research and practice.

Methods and metrics

Methodologically, food environment research is developing at pace as researchers grapple with how best to study food environments and their influence on food acquisition and consumption practices. Methods can be considered in relation to the scale that they address.

At the individual scale, recent emphasis has been placed on capturing people's perceptions and experiences of their food environment in what may be termed a people centric approach. Qualitative methods such as participatory forms of photography and mapping are becoming increasingly popular ways of capturing rich accounts of the lived experiences of food environments (Spires et al., 2023; Turner et al., 2023). These approaches are inspired by participatory action research strategies (Wang, 1999) and seek to provide a collaborative mechanism for the co-design of interventions and policy actions *with* communities. At the quantitative end of the spectrum, rapid consumer surveys are becoming increasingly popular tools for the collection of perceptions and experiences of food environments (Yamaguchi et al., 2022).

At the community scale, quantitative assessments of the external food environment are the dominant approach, typically featuring the use of metrics and/or indicators that score food environments in terms of their degree of (un)healthiness. The Nutrition Environment Measurement Survey (Glanz et al., 2023) and the INFORMAS Retail module (Vandevijvere et al., 2018) are particularly notable examples of metrics that have been adapted across diverse settings. Targeting the policy scale, tools such as the Healthy Food Environment Policy Index (Food-EPI) have provided standardised approaches to benchmark food environment infrastructure and policies with a view to identifying and prioritising key actions by national governments (Sacks et al., 2021).

A current methodological issue is the need to develop comprehensive multi-scalar assessments of food environments to be able to triangulate multiple forms of evidence and fully account for the complex socio-ecological dynamics that shape food acquisition and consumption practices. The lack of consolidated mixed methods toolkits and training materials remains a key challenge (Caspi et al., 2012; Gamba et al., 2015; Turner et al., 2019).

Future issues and concerns for food environment research

This entry closes with two calls for action. Firstly, there is a need for collective consensus around how to define and conceptualise food environments. Conceptual thinking is continuing to evolve as researchers increasingly apply, test, and adapt theoretical frameworks across diverse contexts. Recent publications have highlighted the importance of aspects such as food safety (Constantinides et al., 2021; Turner et al., 2022), social capital (Turner et al., 2022), equity (Nisbett et al., 2022), gender dynamics (Constantinides et al., 2021), and sustainability (Clapp et al., 2022; Downs et al., 2020; High Level Panel of Experts on Food Security and Nutrition, 2020). In addition, the recent inclusion of agency and sustainability as pillars of food security within the right-to-food framework (Clapp et al., 2022; High Level Panel of Experts on Food Security and Nutrition, 2020) is particularly noteworthy and should be considered within food environment research. Ultimately, the global food environment research agenda must build on the foundations of a common theoretical understanding to enable the development of robust methods and metrics that can generate comparable data and strengthen the current evidence base. Secondly, the development of mixed-method, multi-scalar research designs and toolkits should be considered a priority to embrace the socio-ecological complexity of food environments and enable the integration and triangulation of multiple forms of evidence. Combining quantitative metrics with qualitative participatory methods has the potential to inform the effective co-design of more salient public health nutrition actions and policies that improve the lived experience of food environments, as well as diets, nutrition, and health.

References

Bogard J R, Andrew N L, Farrell P, Herrero M, Sharp M K, and Tutuo J (2021) A typology of food environments in the Pacific Region and their relationship to diet quality in Solomon Islands. *Foods* 10, 2592. https://doi.org/10.3390/foods10112592

Carducci B, Oh C, Keats E C, Roth D E, and Bhutta Z A (2020) Effect of food environment interventions on anthropometric outcomes in school-aged children and adolescents in low- and middle-income countries: A systematic review and meta-analysis. *Current Developments in Nutrition* 4. https://doi.org/10.1093/cdn/nzaa098

Caspi C E, Sorensen G, Subramanian S V, and Kawachi I (2012) The local food environment and diet: A systematic review. *Health and Place* 18, 1172–1187. https://doi.org/10.1016/j.healthplace.2012.05.006

Clapp J, Moseley W G, Burlingame B, and Termine P (2022) Viewpoint: The case for a six-dimensional food security framework. *Food Policy* 106, 102164. https://doi.org/10.1016/j.foodpol.2021.102164

Cetateanu A and Jones A (2016) How can GPS technology help us better understand exposure to the food environment? A systematic review. *SSM Population Health* 2, 196–205. DOI: 10.1016/j.ssmph.2016.04.001

Constantinides S V, Turner C, Frongillo E A, Bhandari S, Reyes L I, and Blake C E (2021) Using a global food environment framework to understand relationships with food choice in diverse low- and middle-income countries. *Global Food Security* 29. https://doi.org/10.1016/j.gfs.2021.100511

Downs S M, Ahmed S, Fanzo J, and Herforth A (2020) Food environment typology: Advancing an expanded definition, framework, and methodological approach for improved characterization of wild, cultivated, and built food environments toward sustainable diets. *Foods* 9, 532. https://doi.org/doi:10.3390/foods9040532

Engler-Stringer R, Le H, Gerrard A, Muhajarine N (2014) The community and consumer food environment and children's diet: a systematic review. *BMC Public Health* 14, 522. https://doi.org/10.1186/1471-2458-14-522

Food and Agriculture Organisation of the United Nations (1983) *World Food Security: A Reappraisal of the Concepts and Approaches – Director General's Report.* Rome.

Food and Agriculture Organization of the United Nations (2001) *The State of Food Insecurity in the World.* Rome.

Gamba R J, Schuchter J, Rutt C, and Seto E Y (2015) Measuring the food environment and its effects on obesity in the United States: A systematic review of methods and results. *Journal of Community Health* 40, 464–475. https://doi.org/10.1007/s10900-014-9958-z

Glanz K, Fultz A K, Sallis J F, Clawson M, McLaughlin K C, Green S, and Saelens B E (2023) Use of the nutrition environment measures survey: A systematic review. *American Journal of Preventative Medicine* 65, 131–142. https://doi.org/10.1016/j.amepre.2023.02.008

Glanz K, Sallis J F, Saelens B E, and Frank L D (2007) Nutrition Environment Measures Survey in Stores (NEMS-S): Development and evaluation. *American Journal of Preventative Medicine* 32, 282–289. https://doi.org/10.1016/j.amepre.2006.12.019

Gustafson A, Hankins S, Jilcott S, Gustafson A, Hankins S, Jilcott S (2014) Measures of the consumer food store environment: a systematic review of the evidence 2000-2011. *Journal of Community Health* 37(4), 897–911. DOI: 10.1007/s10900-011-9524-x

High Level Panel of Experts on Food Security and Nutrition (2020) *Food Security and Nutrition: Building a Global Narrative towards 2030.* The Committee on World Food Security. Rome.

Nisbett N, Harris J, Backholer K, Baker P, Jernigan V B B, and Friel S (2022) Holding no-one back: The Nutrition Equity Framework in theory and practice. *Global Food Security* 32. https://doi.org/10.1016/j.gfs.2021.100605

Osei-Kwasi H A, Laar A, Zotor F, Pradeilles R, Aryeetey R, Green M, Griffiths P, Akparibo R, Wanjohi M N, Rousham E, Barnes A, Booth A, Mensah K, Asiki G, Kimani-Murage E, Bricas N, and Holdsworth M (2021) The African urban food environment framework for creating healthy nutrition policy and interventions in urban Africa. *PLoS One* 16. https://doi.org/10.1371/journal.pone.0249621

Popkin B M, Corvalan C, and Grummer-Strawn L M (2020) Dynamics of the double burden of malnutrition and the changing nutrition reality. *Lancet* 395, 65–74. https://doi.org/10.1016/S0140-6736(19)32497-3

Sacks G, Kwon J, Vandevijvere S, and Swinburn B (2021) Benchmarking as a public health strategy for creating healthy food environments: An evaluation of the INFORMAS Initiative (2012–2020). *Annual Review of Public Health* 42, 345–362. https://doi.org/10.1146/annurev-publhealth-100919-114442

Spires M, Battersby J, Cohen N, Daivadanam M, Demmler K M, Mattioni D, Pradeilles R, Thompson C, Turner C, Venegas Hargous C, Wertheim-Heck S, Wills W, and Hawkes C (2023) "The People's Summit": A case for lived experience of food environments as a critical source of evidence to inform the follow-up to the 2021 UN Food Systems Summit. *Global*

Food Security 37. https://doi.org/10.1016/j.gfs.2023.100690

Swinburn B, Sacks G, Vandevijvere S, Kumanyika S, Lobstein T, Neal B, Barquera S, Friel S, Hawkes C, Kelly B, L'Abbe M, Lee A, Ma J, Macmullan J, Mohan S, Monteiro C, Rayner M, Sanders D, Snowdon W, and Walker C (2013) INFORMAS (International Network for Food and Obesity/non-communicable diseases Research, Monitoring and Action Support): Overview and key principles. *Obesity Reviews* 14, 1–12. https://doi.org/10.1111/obr.12087

Turner C, Aggarwal A, Walls H, Herforth A, Drewnowski A, Coates J, Kalamatianou S, and Kadiyala S (2018) Concepts and critical perspectives for food environment research: A global framework with implications for action in low- and middle-income countries. *Global Food Security* 18, 93–101. https://doi.org/10.1016/j.gfs.2018.08.003

Turner C, Bhogadi S, Walls H, Surendran S, Kulkarni B, Kinra S, and Kadiyala S (2022) Drivers of food acquisition practices in the food environment of peri-urban Hyderabad, India: A qualitative investigation. *Health and Place* 74, 102763. https://doi.org/10.1016/j.healthplace.2022.102763

Turner C, Kalamatianou S, Drewnowski A, Kulkarni B, Kinra S, and Kadiyala S (2019) Food environment research in low- and middle-income countries: A systematic scoping review. *Advances in Nutrition* 11, 387–397. https://doi.org/https://doi.org/10.1093/advances/nmz031

Turner C, Salm L, Spires M, Laar A, and Holdsworth M (2023) Capturing the moment: A snapshot review of contemporary food environment research featuring participatory photography methods. *Current Opinion in Environmental Sustaintainability* 65, 101364. https://doi.org/10.1016/j.cosust.2023.101364

United Nations System Standing Committee on Nutrition (2019) Food environments: Where people meet the food system. *Nutrition* 44.

Wang C C (1999) Photovoice: A participatory action research strategy applied to women's health. *Journal of Womens Health* 8, 185–192.

Westbury S, Ghosh I, Jones H M, Mensah D, Samuel F, Irache A, Azhar N, Al-Khudairy L, Iqbal R, and Oyebode O (2021) The influence of the urban food environment on diet, nutrition and health outcomes in low-income and middle-income countries: A systematic review. *BMJ Global Health* 6. https://doi.org/10.1136/bmjgh-2021-006358

Vandevijvere S, Waterlander W, Molloy J, Nattrass H, and Swinburn B (2018) Towards healthier supermarkets: A national study of in-store food availability, prominence and promotions in New Zealand. *European Journal of Clinical Nutrition* 72, 971–978. https://doi.org/10.1038/s41430-017-0078-6

Yamaguchi M, Praditsorn P, Purnamasari S D, Sranacharoenpong K, Arai Y, Sundermeir S M, Gittelsohn J, Hadi H, and Nishi N (2022) Measures of perceived neighborhood food environments and dietary habits: A systematic review of methods and associations. *Nutrients* 14(9), 1788. https://doi.org/10.3390/nu14091788

Further reading

Turner C, Aggarwal A, Walls H, Herforth A, Drewnowski A, Coates J, Kalamatianou S, and Kadiyala S (2018) Concepts and critical perspectives for food environment research: A global framework with implications for action in low- and middle-income countries. *Global Food Security* 18, 93–101. https://doi.org/10.1016/j.gfs.2018.08.003
This article introduces the key concepts explored in this entry, presents the globally applicable food environment conceptual framework, and outlines implications for research and practice in low- and middle-income countries.

Downs S M, Ahmed S, Fanzo J, and Herforth A (2020) Food environment typology: Advancing an expanded definition, framework, and methodological approach for improved characterization of wild, cultivated, and built food environments toward sustainable diets. *Foods* 9(4), 532. https://doi.org/doi:10.3390/foods9040532
This article presents four food environment typologies and considers aspects of sustainability in relation to food environments and diets.

CHRISTOPHER TURNER

55. Food futures

ROB BOOTH

Concerning food futures

Governmental, academic, and private sector efforts to forecast different food system futures have intensified in recent years in line with growing recognition of the unsustainability of existing agricultural and dietary practices. In turn, this growing interest in 'food futures' has amplified conflict between visions or imaginaries of what the food system could or should be (Biltekoff and Guthman, 2023; Puig de la Bellacasa, 2015). These debates have shaped and been shaped by existing paradigms around which individuals and institutions rally, including for example: degrowth or eco-modernism?; agroecology or sustainable intensification?; free trade or food sovereignty?

Scrutinising these anticipated futures can be generative for social, political, and cultural research about our food system for two reasons. Firstly, analysis of their formulation, their axioms, their outputs, and their respective advocates can offer insights about the current food system and its underlying power relations. Secondly, these envisioned food futures are themselves performative, serving to open up or foreclose different prospective future food systems from ever emerging.

Envisioning food futures

This performativity is most apparent when examining the diverse knowledge practices which attempt to anticipate both what shape the future of food and agriculture will take and how to best achieve desired outcomes. These anticipatory approaches range in scale and technique from huge environmental datasets informing work published by global collaborative institutions, such as the Intergovernmental Panel on Climate Change, to behavioural economic modelling of dietary change or participatory action research exploring scenarios for specific communities or geographies.

Each approach towards envisioning food futures arrives with its own baked-in politics of the future around what is considered possible, feasible, and/or desirable. After all, acting on information about the future implies (bio) political considerations around what or who should or should not be valued, preserved, or let go (Anderson, 2010). Historically, these exercises have served to further reproduce spatial inequalities and uneven development. Some landscapes of food production in the Global South have already become victim to processes of 'anticipatory ruination', a phrase coined by Kasia Paprocki (2022), which serves to remind us of the *presentness* of what many still call climate futures.

Modelling and envisioning food futures also often relies on anticipating technological change. For example, forecasting an agricultural future with viable pathways towards effective large-scale bioenergy, carbon capture, and storage (BECCS) has significant ramifications for possible or desirable land use patterns or emissions pathways. At the other end of the food chain, so too does the extent to which cellular agriculture (Sexton et al., 2019) or mass veganism is considered likely to prove viable and popular in transforming everyday diets the world over.

These dietary visions, and particularly those related to food processing, are frequently invoked via fictional and artistic representations of the future. Protein blocks or bioengineered sources of meat serve as instantly recognisable signifiers of a society gone awry, having 'lost touch with nature'. These tropes have become touchstones for cultural analysis by academics interested in what our imaginations tell us about the future we are seemingly heading for and speculation about how we might act otherwise (Castle and Macdonald, 2022).

However, the future of food and farming is not, and has not always been, a site of anxiety. The global ascension of industrial capitalist modernity has long brought with it predictions of, and spatial blueprints for, a cornucopian future (Belasco, 2006). This faith in the ongoing development of the productive forces of agriculture, motivated by the rapid advances of the 19th and 20th centuries, has always been entangled with speculation about the geographies, temporalities, and power relations of future societies.

As urbanists have dreamt of a mechanised agricultural hinterland feeding the metropolis, so too reformists have called for the dissolution of the boundary between the country and the city. Again, the connections between labour, spatiality, and technological change are clear and remain contemporary, as encapsulated in debates around automation, machine learning, and vertical farming.

The legacy and contingency of these historic futures can be felt in the present across the world – from tensions over housing development on green belt land in Britain to the interplay between mechanisation, agro-chemicals, and farmer suicides in Punjab.

Creating food futures

Combating the nature and climate emergency is arguably the greatest challenge of the early 21st century, and this presence haunts expectations of the future providing an altogether new epochal futurity. In the 2020s extreme weather, drought, and conflict do not have to be predicted to be intellectually confronted. Faced with this reality, those actors championing emergent or foreseen technological fixes can feel vindicated by the agricultural yield gains of the 20th century, increases in life expectancy, and the compatibility of their visions with existing institutions of finance and governance. Yet, across the Global South, those who have done least to create the political ecological conditions for their uncertain and desperate food futures to come look likely to suffer the most and benefit least from these visions. In contrast to the techno-optimists, those in the agroecological movement, or what has been more recently termed 'the long food movement' (see IPES-Food and ETC Group, 2021), advocate for a future characterised by land reform, the revitalisation of marginalised agricultural practices, and substantive global dietary change. Perhaps, they argue, we have everything we need already for future sufficiency and it's just a question of distribution (Nelson and Edwards, 2021). Despite the elegance of such a conclusion, its acceptance leads immediately to the need to confront political questions of great complexity, which reiterates the need in turn to plan for the longer term to actively enact transformative change for better food systems.

Nevertheless, the important questions, then, for food futures research remain the same foundational issues that have long defined the critical humanities and social sciences: how is the future determined? By whom and for whom? After all, the future of food will not emerge from what Marx (1990, p. 47) described as the 'recipes for the cookshops of the future' but from the present socio-ecological relations within which people struggle, feast, and starve.

References

Anderson B (2010) Preemption, precaution, preparedness: Anticipatory action and future geographies. *Progress in Human Geography* 34, 777–798. https://doi.org/10.1177/0309132510362600

Belasco W (2006) *Meals to Come: A History of the Future of Food*. Berkeley, University of California Press.

Biltekoff C and Guthman J (2023) Conscious, complacent, fearful: Agri-food tech's market-making public imaginaries. *Science as Culture* 32, 58–82. https://doi.org/10.1080/09505431.2022.2090914

Castle N and Macdonald G (2022) Introduction: Food futures. *Science Fiction Studies* 49, 209–216. https://doi.org/10.1353/sfs.2022.0021

IPES-Food and ETC Group (2021) *A Long Food Movement: Transforming Food Systems by 2045*. https://www.ipes-food.org/_img/upload/files/LongFoodMovementEN.pdf

Marx K (1990) *Capital: A Critique of Political Economy: Volume 1*. London, Penguin.

Nelson A and Edwards F (2021) *Food for Degrowth: Perspectives and Practices*. Oxford & New York, Routledge.

Paprocki K (2022) Anticipatory ruination. *Journal of Peasant Studies* 49, 1399–1408. https://doi.org/10.1080/03066150.2022.2113068

Puig de la Bellacasa M (2015) Making time for soil: Technoscientific futurity and the pace of care. *Social Studies of Science* 45, 691–716. https://doi.org/10.1177/0306312715599851

Sexton A E, Garnett T and Lorimer J (2019) Framing the future of food: The contested promises of alternative proteins. *Environment and Planning E: Nature and Space* 2, 47–72. https://doi.org/10.1177/2514848619827009

Further reading

Belasco W (2006) *Meals to Come: A History of the Future of Food*. Berkeley, University of California Press.

Warren Belasco offers an introductory history to considerations of food futures anchored around competing visions of either Malthusian or cornucopian futures.

Puig de la Bellacasa M (2015) Making time for soil: Technoscientific futurity and the pace of care. *Social Studies of Science*

45, 691–716. https://doi.org/10.1177/0306312715599851

Puig de la Bellacasa's work integrates a concern with futurity with the increasingly significant concept of care and offers an excellent introduction to feminist science and technology studies in this direction.

ROB BOOTH

56. Food governance

JESSICA DUNCAN

Introduction: why food governance matters

This entry provides an overview of food governance by discussing both traditional conceptualisations of food governance and emerging alternatives and critiques. It introduces current issues and concerns about food governance from a critical perspective, namely the wide adoption of multistakeholder governance supported by the rhetoric of the 'all-affected' principle, and calls to address pluralism, reflected in the 'most-affected' principle. The entry concludes with a reflection on transformative governance for more just and sustainable food systems.

Defining food governance

Governance is a contested and complex concept. It refers to the management functions of societies – formal and informal – that can be focused or coordinated around the state or government institutions, but also include diverse actors, including civil society, the private sector, philanthropic foundations and researchers. In this way, governance implies an arrangement of distinct but interrelated elements including: policy mandates; organisational, financial, and programmatic structures; resource levels; administrative rules and guidelines; and institutionalised rules and norms (Heinrich and Lynn 2000:4).

While this characterisation suggests an open and broad character, in practice, governance is often used to refer to two complementary dimensions: purpose (guiding and directing) and regulation (restraining, managing and controlling) (Dahlberg 2001:136). As such, food governance works to enable or constrain practices, priorities and values that translate into the mechanisms used to manage relations to food, and in this way reflect 'deeper purposes that groups and societies pursue' (Dahlberg 2001:136). These relations are organised through instruments that include, but are not limited to, public, private and hybrid (public–private) policies and rules.

In turn, a governance system can be defined as the set of instruments acting on a certain issue at a specific level of governance (Visseren-Hamakers 2018). The resulting patchwork of rules and relations is reflected in the polycentric nature of food governance (as opposed to a centric arrangement where power is centralised in one organisation). This patchwork is made visible in the way actors and processes operate at and across multiple geographic scales and sectors (e.g. agriculture, trade, health). . This fragmentation makes resistance and change difficult as there is no central power broker.

I

The emergence of food systems governance

Fragmentation at the level of global food systems governance represents a 'patchwork of international institutions that are different in their character (organisations, regimes and implicit norms), their constituencies (private and public), their spatial scope (from bilateral to global), and their subject matter (from specific policy fields to universal concerns)' (Biermann et al. 2009:16). The fragmentation of food governance and the need for a coordinated systems approach were motivations for the 2021 UN Food Systems Summit. Importantly, this summit marked a shift toward food systems governance, opening up space for new definitions and new actors to stake claims to power (Canfield, Duncan and Claeys 2021).

Food systems represent multi-scalar and cross-cutting sets of issues, which bring together diverse objectives in relation to health, equity, sustainability, resilience and inclusive economic growth, amongst many others (Leeuwis et al. 2021; Yap 2022). This shift towards food systems has been widely welcomed as a way of creating more joined-up and comprehensive approaches to food governance. However, in practice, the broad scope of food systems has arguably exacerbated existing governance challenges, opening up new areas for competition for power and influence.

Given this, food systems governance can be defined as the relations between the diverse institutions, organisations, actors, rules and norms that shape how food is produced, distributed and accessed (Margulis and Duncan 2016). It includes how diverse actors within food systems are incorporated into decision and policymaking at different levels (Canfield, Duncan and Claeys 2021). A key challenge facing food systems governance is how to adequately address the diversity of ways food influences and impacts the lives of people, all of which are marked by inequalities and ecological impacts.

Key actors in global food governance

While governance happens at all scales and levels, international organisations function as the operating arms of global food governance (Lele et al. 2021). Further, food governance is increasingly operationalised through global networks of actors and governance organisations. An overview of some of the key organizations in global food governance are provided here.

Key UN organisations active in global food governance include the so-called Rome-based agencies:

- **Food and Agriculture Organization (FAO):** The mandate of the FAO is to fight hunger worldwide and improve standards of living, especially of people in rural areas. This involves collecting, evaluating and disseminating information on agriculture, forestry, fisheries and food; performing normative tasks (e.g., setting international food standards jointly with WHO under Codex Alimentarius); and developing decision-making frameworks and strategies for agricultural development.
- **International Fund for Agricultural Development (IFAD):** IFAD provides loans at concessional rates. It also provides grants and advisory services.
- **World Food Programme (WFP):** The WFP supports people with emergency food assistance while reducing the high demand for humanitarian aid through developmental and resilience-building measures. In recent years, it has shifted from emergency response to more antici-patory humanitarian assistance.

These three organisations jointly support the Committee on World Food Security (CFS). The CFS was reformed in 2009 to work towards the elimination of hunger and promote food security and nutrition for all. The CFS promotes policy convergence and coherence on global food security and nutrition issues. Its processes ensure that the voices of all relevant stakeholders are heard, particularly those most affected by food insecurity and malnutrition. While the policy outputs of the CFS are intergovernmentally negotiated,

they are non-binding. The CFS is supported by the independent High Level Panel of Experts (HLPE), which accesses science related to food security and nutrition and provides independent and evidence-based analysis.

Another important knowledge-based actor in the governance of food is CGIAR (Consultative Group on International Agricultural Research). This is a research network supporting agricultural innovation by bringing together 15 research centres engaged in research about agriculture and food security. Its mission is to deliver science and innovation that advance the transformation of food, land and water systems in the climate emergency. It is organised around five impact areas: nutrition and food security; poverty reduction, livelihoods and jobs; gender equality, youth and social inclusion; climate adaptation and greenhouse gas reduction; and environmental health and biodiversity. CGIAR is highly influential in shaping global debates around food and agriculture, particularly in relation to science–policy interface processes (Lele et al. 2021).

There are also key trade and financial actors involved in food governance. The World Trade Organization (WTO) coordinates the global system of trade rules. It is responsible for providing a forum for negotiating trade agreements and resolving trade disputes. It governs a set of sectoral trade agreements, three of which are highly relevant to agriculture and food—the Agreement on Agriculture, the Agreement on the Application of Sanitary and Phytosanitary Measures and the Agreement on Trade-Related Aspects of Intellectual Property Rights.

The World Bank Group is the largest public lender to developing countries and to agriculture and the rural sector. In 2020, the World Bank created a dedicated Umbrella Multi-Donor Trust Fund: Food Systems 2030. The ambition of the Fund is to address systemic, pervasive development challenges and transform food systems by 2030, fostering healthy people, planet and economies.

There is a diverse range of non-governmental organisations and social movements engaged in food governance. The Civil Society and Indigenous Peoples' Mechanism to the CFS and the International Planning Committee for Food Sovereignty are two coordination mechanisms that have actively supported the participation of civil society organisations and social movements in food governance processes. In terms of specific social movements, La Via Campesina remains the largest agrarian movement in the world. It fights for food sovereignty. Food sovereignty defends peasant livelihoods and advocates for human rights and agro-ecological technologies as a matter of social justice.

Networks and public–private partnerships (PPPs) increasingly play an important role in food governance. These networks function to organise relations between these relatively autonomous but interdependent actors. Key examples of these networks include the Global Alliance for Improved Nutrition (GAIN), Scaling Up Nutrition (SUN) and the Alliance for a Green Revolution in Africa.

Finally, the World Economic Forum (WEF) has emerged as an important player in food systems governance, notably since it signed a Strategic Partnership Framework with the United Nations in 2019. The WEF hosts a Food Systems Initiative that targets multi-sectoral leadership to support collective action to accelerate food systems transformations. It also played a key role in the UN Food Systems Summit, leading to critique of the Summit's failure to address corporate influence and power (Clapp et al. 2021; Canfield, Anderson, McMichael 2021; Canfield, Duncan, and Claeys 2021; Montenegro de Wit et al. 2021; McKeon 2021).

Current issues, concerns and areas of focus

When it comes to food systems governance, the concerns are multiple. Emergent concerns include the rise of multistakeholder governance, also with consideration for the impact on multilateral governance. Pluralism, grounded in the idea of the most-affected principle, is put forward by some as a response.

Stakeholder governance and the threat of 'multistakeholderism'

When it comes to legitimate governance processes, the participation of diverse stakeholders is widely recognised as key. This has led to a rapid increase in multi-stakeholder processes (MSPs) devoted to bringing diverse perspectives together to inform and improve food policy at local, national, regional and international levels. This tendency reflects a move towards multistakeholder governance and can be seen, for example, through

standard-setting groups (e.g. the Roundtable on Sustainable Palm Oil that aims to promote the growth and use of sustainable palm oil products through global standards), policy-oriented groups (e.g. SUN, that seek to set global policy goals,) and project-oriented multistakeholder groups (e.g. GAIN's work to advance nutrition outcomes by improving the consumption of safe, nutritious food for all).

Proponents of multistakeholder governance prioritise PPPs as a way to advance policy and action (e.g. to finance infrastructure projects or to leverage funding and political will). There is, however, uncertainty about the effectiveness of such arrangements (Leigland 2018), with research from other fields documenting, for example, adverse effects of PPPs on the democratic governance of infrastructure projects and decreased political control over them (Hudon 2011). Critics claim that multistakeholder processes present threats to democratic processes and public multilateralism (e.g. Montenegro de Wit et al. 2021; McKeon 2021; Buxton and Power 2019). In particular, concerns have been raised that this form of governance threatens the legitimacy of the public sector by the corporate capture of policy spaces and narratives that assigns a lead role to private sector investment (McKeon 2021). This trend has been dubbed 'multistakeholderism'.

Multistakeholderism refers here to a trend that is increasingly visible across food governance domains, notably at the global level. It reflects efforts to bring together global actors that have a potential 'stake' in an issue to collaboratively identify solutions (Buxton and Power 2019). In multistakeholder governance, 'stakeholders' become the central actors without a clear procedure to designate who the legitimate stakeholders are, how they should engage and what happens with the outcomes of the process. In this way, multistakeholder governance arrangements are an example of the 'all-affected' principle (Kuchler 2017:195). This principle implies that 'those who are affected by a decision should be entitled to have a say in it' (Marchetti 2012:31). Regarding food, this becomes challenging as everyone is affected. At the same time, there is growing acknowledgement that not everyone is equally affected, and that governance processes need to account for asymmetries of power(Reed et al. 2009). Scholars have also warned that an effort to apply the all-affected principle could lead to cases of over-inclusion, as well as under-inclusion (Lagerspetz 2015:15). In short, when it comes to multistakeholder governance, and the rise of multistakeholderism, the main concern-relates specifically to claims of including all relevant stakeholders without due attention to who can participate and who is actually participating and what the outcome of the participation is This lack of attention to the politics of participation risks, among other things, to reinforce the status quo.

Pluralising while prioritising the 'most-affected' principle

To counter these tendencies, efforts have been made to prioritse the 'most-affected' by creating governance processes capable of managing pluralism and accounting for asymmetries of power (Duncan and Claeys 2018; Duncan et al. 2022). Pluralism is a politicising position that recognises that food system transformations include multiple and often competing visions (Duncan et al. 2022). It demands a rejection of one-size-fits-all solutions to the way future priorities are identified, and in the composition of stakeholders. Pluralism demands paying attention to uneven relations of power, by identifying and giving voice to people marginalised by food systems, and making space for disagreement and controversy (Duncan et al. 2022; Duncan and Claeys 2018).

The 'most-affected' principle has been trialled in social movement and global food security governance spaces, in different ways, for over three decades (Claeys and Duncan 2019). It aims to prioritise those most marginalised in society, and most affected by hunger and food insecurity in debates and decision-making.

The 'most-affected' principle is recognised in the UN CFS and has been key to ensuring enhanced and autonomous participation of social movements in global food governance spaces. At the same time, it has led powerful interests to dismiss or undermine the CFS on the grounds that such processes are perceived as ineffective and inefficient. This points to a lack of accountability mechansims to enhance the democratic nature of global food governance as well as to the need for innovations in governing with and for pluralism.

Future concerns, issues and questions

There is an urgent need to transform food systems. Dominant food systems are fundamentally unsustainable on environmental, economic and social grounds. Continuing with 'business as usual' will significantly endanger natural resources, human and animal health, the climate and the economy (SAPEA 2020:7). Transformation demands changes in social practices and values and as such is characterised by the destabilisation of existing behaviours, social practices, infrastructures, technological systems, and business and administration models (Duncan et al. 2022). Governance is key to such transformations.

Looking ahead, key questions include:

- How can alignment and coherence across food systems governance be balanced with the need for pluralistic transformation pathways?
- What are the opportunities and risks associated with a rise in multistakeholder food governance?
- How can the most-affected be better represented and involved in food systems governance, with a view towards supporting more just transformations across food systems?

References

Biermann F, Pattberg P, Van Asselt H, and Zelli F (2009) The fragmentation of global governance architectures: A framework for analysis. *Global Environmental Politics* 9(4), 14–40. https://doi.org/10.1162/glep .2009.9.4.14

Buxton N and Power C (2019) Multistakeholderism: A critical look. Workshop report (No. 10). Amsterdam: TNI. Available: https://www.tni .org/files/publication-downloads/ multistakeholderism-workshop-report-tni .pdf

Canfield M C, Anderson M D, and McMichael P (2021) UN Food Systems Summit 2021: Dismantling democracy and resetting corporate control of food systems. *Frontiers in Sustainable Food Systems* 5, 661552. https://doi.org/10.3389/fsufs.2021 .661552

Canfield M C, Duncan J, and Claeys P (2021) Reconfiguring food systems governance: The UNFSS and the battle over authority and legitimacy. *Development* 64(3), 181–191. https://doi.org/10.1057/s41301-021-00312-1

Claeys P and Duncan J (2019) Do we need to categorize it? Reflections on constituencies and quotas as tools for negotiating difference in the global food sovereignty convergence space. *The Journal of Peasant Studies* 46(7), 1477–1498. https://doi-org/10.1080/03066150.2018.1512489

Clapp J, Noyes I, and Grant Z (2021) The Food Systems Summit's failure to address corporate power. *Development* 64(3–4), 192–198. https://doi.org/10.1057/s41301-021-00303-2

Dahlberg K A (2001) Democratizing society and food systems: Or how do we transform modern structures of power? *Agriculture and Human Values* 18(2), 135–151. https://doi.org/10.1023/A:1011175626010

Duncan J and Claeys P (2018) Politicizing food security governance through participation: Opportunities and opposition. *Food Security* 10(6), 1411–1424. https://doi.org/10.1007/s12571-018-0852-x

Duncan J, DeClerck F, Báldi A, Treyer S, Aschemann-Witzel J, Cuhls K, Ahrné L, Bisoffi S, Grando S, Guobys L, and Kohl J (2022) Democratic directionality for transformative food systems research. *Nature Food* 3(3), 183–186. https://doi.org/10.1038/s43016-022-00479-x

Heinrich C J and Lynn L E (2000) *Governance and Performance: New perspectives*. Georgetown University Press.

Hudon P A (2011) A critique of public-private partnerships in Quebec: Democratic deficiencies and unethical procurement. *Public Integrity* 13(3), 257–274. https://doi.org//10.2753/PIN1099-9922130306

Kuchler M (2017) Stakeholding as sorting of actors into categories: Implications for civil society participation in the CDM. *International Environmental Agreements: Politics, Law and Economics* 17(2), 191–208. https://doi.org/10.1007/s10784-015-9314-5

Lagerspetz E (2015) Democracy and the All-Affected Principle. *Res Cogitans* 10(1), 6–23. https://philpapers.org/rec/LAGDAT

Leeuwis C, Boogaard B K, and Atta-Krah K (2021) How food systems change (or not): Governance implications for system transformation processes. *Food Security* 13(4), 761–780. https://doi.org/10.1007/s12571-021-01178-4

Leigland J (2018) Public-private partnerships in developing countries: The emerging evidence-based critique. *The World Bank Research Observer* 33(1), 103–134. https://doi.org/10.1093/wbro/lkx008

Lele U, Baldwin B, and Goswami S (2021) Changing global governance context for food security and nutrition. In: Lele U, Agarwal M, Baldwin B, and Goswami S (eds), *Food for All: International organizations and the transformation of agriculture*. Oxford, Oxford University Press, pp. 284–336. https://doi.org/10.1093/oso/9780198755173.003.0006

McKeon N (2021) Global food governance. *Development* 64(3–4), 172–180. https://doi.org/10.1057/s41301-021-00326-9

Marchetti R (2012) Models of global democracy: In defence of cosmo-federalism. In: Archibugi K and Marchetti R (eds), *Global Democracy: Normative and empirical perspectives*. Cambridge, Cambridge University Press, pp. 22–46.

Margulis M and Duncan J (2016) Global food governance: Institutions, actors and dynamics. In: Kok M, Sumner J, and Winson A (eds), *Critical Perspectives in Food Studies*. Toronto, Oxford University Press, pp. 270–295.

Maye D and Duncan J (2017) Understanding sustainable food system transitions: Practice, assessment and governance. *Sociologia Ruralis* 57(3), 267–273. https://doi.org/10.1111/soru.12177

Montenegro de Wit M, Canfield M C, Iles A, Anderson M, McKeon N, Guttal S, Gemmill-Herren B, Duncan J, van der Ploeg J D, and Prato S (2021) Editorial: Resetting power in global food governance: The UN Food Systems Summit. *Development* 64(3–4), 153–161. https://doi.org/10.1057/s41301-021-00316-x

Reed M S, Graves A, Dandy N, Posthumus H, Hubacek K, Morris J, Prell C, Quinn C H, and Stringer L C (2009) Who's in and why? A typology of stakeholder analysis methods for natural resource management. *Journal of Environmental Management* 90(5), 1933–1949. https://doi.org/10.1016/j.jenvman.2009.01.001

SAPEA, Science Advice for Policy by European Academies (2020) *A Sustainable Food System for the European Union*.

Berlin, SAPEA. https://doi.org/10.26356/sustainablefood

Visseren-Hamakers I J (2018) A framework for analyzing and practicing integrative governance: The case of global animal and conservation governance. *Environment and Planning C: Politics and Space* 36, 1391–1414. https://doi.org/10.1177/2399654418788565

Yap C (2022) New geographical directions for food systems governance research. *Progress in Human Geography* 47(1), 66–84. https://doi.org/10.1177/03091325221133808

Further reading

Moragues-Faus A, Clark J K, Battersby J, and Davies A (2022) *Routledge Handbook of Urban Food Governance*. Oxon, Routledge. https://doi.org/10.4324/9781003055907
This handbook focuses on urban food governance, outlining the histories, concepts and practices involved in urban food governance.

Duncan J and Claeys P (2018) Politicizing food security governance through participation: Opportunities and opposition. *Food Security* 10(6), 1411–1424. https://doi.org/10.1007/s12571-018-0852-x
This article outlines processes of de-politicisation in food security governance before analysing a case where food security governance is being politicised through the implementation of the most-affected principle.

HLPE (2020) *Food Security and Nutrition: Building a global narrative towards 2030*. A report by the High Level Panel of Experts on Food Security and Nutrition of the Committee on World Food Security, Rome: Committee on World Food Security. https://www.fao.org/3/ca9731en/ca9731en.pdf
This report sets out a theory of change for establishing a global narrative for sustainable and nutritious food systems. It outlines key trends and challenges for food governance and outlines promising policy directions to move beyond the challenges.

57. Food justice

Joshua Sbicca

Introduction: food justice foundations

Overlapping systems of oppression have long structured food systems. From settler colonialism and racial capitalism to white supremacy and heteropatriarchy, our experience of working with and eating food are inescapably bound to systems that benefit some and harm others. How this happens, who has the most to gain by changing these systems, and how communities struggle for something different are central to the study and practice of food justice. Food justice is, in effect, concerned with upending arrangements that confer power on the most privileged members of society and carving out space for more liberatory food cultures, practices, and movements.

As a contemporary social movement, food justice is rooted in similar conditions that animated the environmental justice movement in the United States. For many decades, environmentalists ignored harm to humans in favour of focusing on harm to the environment. In response to the colourblindness of the environmental movement, and the environmental racism of the industrial era, many Indigenous, Black, and Brown communities fought to elevate their concerns. The result has been the environmental justice movement, which now encompasses the experiences of many marginalised communities and forms of environmental inequality. Given the centrality of food to organising society along lines of social difference and environmental health, the food justice movement has pushed the mainstream food movement to similarly engage with the needs of the most marginalised. Due to the breadth of disparities in our food environments, a range of interrelated food justice struggles has sought to organise under one big tent. Farmworkers are fighting for toxin-free workplaces and better remuneration. Poor communities are organising to improve the quantity and quality of food in their neighbourhoods. Indigenous groups are recovering ancestral foodways and land management practices and decolonising their diets. City dwellers are building aquaponic operations to create living wage jobs and job training in communities suffering from disinvestment. Taken together, these practices reveal the creativity enlivening food-related efforts to improve where we live, work, and play.

Several prominent definitions of food justice reflect some of the history provided above, inevitably leading to different points of convergence and divergence. Gottlieb and Joshi (2010: 6) contend that food justice would be a condition under which "the benefits and risks of where, what, and how food is grown and produced, transported and distributed, and accessed and eaten are shared fairly". Alkon and Agyeman (2011:5) specify this definition with respect to the direct experiences of low-income communities and communities of colour, claiming that "[e]ssential to the food justice movement is an analysis that recognizes the food system itself as a racial project and problematizes the influence of race and class on the production, distribution, and consumption of food". In both cases there is a focus on inequity, an appreciation of the underlying structural conditions of oppression and inequality, and therefore the pressing need for food system changes.

Beyond these academic definitions, there are movement-based articulations. One of the most important convenings by activists to set out their agenda occurred at the Food + Justice = Democracy conference in 2012. Out of a series of People's Assemblies, activists from across the United States crafted six broad-based Principles of Food Justice (2012). First, with a focus on the intersectional ways in which *historical trauma* is experienced and perpetuated, the food justice movement can work collaboratively to link and undo the resulting harms. Second, food is a human right, which demands *local food system control, community-led development, and public investment*. Third, organising around racial and economic justice is necessary to *provide hunger relief and address health disparities* emerging from the industrial food system. Fourth, a fair, just, and sustainable food system is only possible if people can autonomously control *land*. Fifth, because structural racism leads to the exploitation of food chain workers, food justice is only possible if *labour and immigration* are at the centre of these concerns. Last, taking care of the environment is taking care of people, which requires creating a *toxin-free and climate-just food system*. Put succinctly, Hislop (2014: 19) offers a widely cited definition of food justice as "the struggle against racism, exploitation, and oppression taking place within the food system that addresses inequality's root causes both within and beyond the food chain".

What makes food justice a particularly important social movement is its recognition and experimentation with building up more livable worlds within and across countless differences. As a body of scholarship, then, food justice is at its most potent when grounded in critical, community, and movement spaces concerned and focused not only on how systems of oppression produce inequities, but also on how people imagine and organise for food and social systems that take care of people and the planet.

Food justice now

As Holt-Giménez (2017: 56) notes, "The food system is not broken; rather, it is working precisely as a capitalist food system is supposed to work". Namely, the contemporary food system is rooted in the history of racial capitalist and heteropatriarchal development. Endemic to capitalism is exploitation and domination based in class, ethnoracial, and gender differences. For capitalism to grow it requires ascribing and extracting value from socially marginalised groups. Food justice scholarship begins similarly from the premise that transforming the food system requires first understanding the institutions and organisations that structure our relationships to food.

Exploitation of land and labour

Beginning with colonial efforts by Europeans, the global food system evolved in part through the plunder of natural resources abroad, such as bat guano to fertilise farms at home, and the establishment of commodity exports, like sugar, in colonised countries. In other forms, colonialism meant settlers forcibly removing or killing Indigenous people, dispossessing Indigenous people of their lands, and establishing different agricultural systems, often monocultures like cotton and tobacco, with the intent to generate profit. As part of the history of how this system worked in the United States, there was the added practice of the enslavement of Africans. In places like South Carolina, this entailed stealing African labour, ingenuity, and culturally based practices to grow rice. In other places, it meant developing profitable systems of incarceration that leased prisoners of colour to white farmers or forced prisoners to work on penal plantations.

Given the longstanding political deference to white male economic interests, agriculture has also exploited the labour of many different immigrant groups in the United States. From the use of Chinese and Japanese farmworkers in California, followed by legal efforts to disenfranchise these same groups from starting their own farms, to the use of Mexican and Central American farmworkers, regardless of documentation status, agriculture relies on socially marginalised groups. And this is the case worldwide. Such conditions are furthermore managed through militarised borders and immigration regimes that produce precarity for farmworkers. Deportability is a structural condition that often quells agitating for safer working conditions, job security, access to healthcare, and better pay. Other food chain workers also experience problems. Corporate fast-food chains notoriously treat their workers poorly, whether in terms of remuneration, sexual and racial harassment, or anti-union browbeating. In meat packing and food processing facilities, workers furthermore face dangerous line speeds, lack of hygienic conditions, poor ventilation, high turnover, and more. While frontline workers in all these jobs are overwhelmingly people of colour and working class, the CEOs and managers are disproportionately white and male. Exploitation of land and labour is not experienced evenly.

Harming bodies with harmful food

There are also many food inequities experienced by eaters. Several prominent threads of research aim to identify why certain communities disproportionately lack access to healthy, affordable, and culturally appropriate food, experience higher levels of diet-related diseases, and are at greater risk of having their foods culinarily appropriated. These areas of research respond to a set of pressing conditions prevalent in many different food environments.

Focusing on cities, urban development doesn't serve everyone equitably. Communities living under food apartheid— a racist regime of segregation and relegation to the slow death of being structurally denied adequate healthy food—face several structural impediments. In many cities, housing discrimination in the form of racial covenants and redlining have led to concentrations of poverty, low tax base, and crumbling infrastructure resulting in limited food choices. Coupled with the carceral state's reliance on policing and incarceration to manage poverty, there is a set of intersecting systems of oppression that produce hunger and poor health. Moreover, the intensification of gentrification has led to the displacement of these same structurally excluded groups once their neighbourhoods are ripe for investment. This spatial removal of people furthermore disrupts what fragmented food environments existed to ensure a bare minimum means for survival.

Rural environments face their own set of concerns. Weak rural economies, low crop prices, limited health care access, corporately controlled food markets, and more have meant that living in a place with lower population density increases risk of dietary health problems. For tribal communities living on reservations in the United States there is the added history of settler colonialism. The forced removal of Indigenous people from their ancestral lands onto reservations led to the disruption of hunting, fishing, gathering, and farming practices. The federal government responded with many unhealthy food rations. Not only is there a psychological toll associated with this cultural change, but there is also physiological damage. What links many of these examples is poverty. And poverty is the manifestation of racial capitalism's imperative to produce racialised precarity, weak government social safety nets, and political efforts to maintain elite forms of social control. Harm to bodies through food undermines the conditions for human flourishing.

Organising to end food injustices

Food justice is such a pressing area of work because it does more than identify structural disparities. It compels people to act. At each point in the food system, and in the intersecting institutions that shape society, activists and food movements are experimenting with alternatives and directly challenging those in power. Food is not only a site for struggle, but also a means for struggle. In practice this has prominently entailed food justice campaigns and practices that advance the interests of food chain workers, farmers, eaters, and the environment with explicit focus on economic, racial, and gender justice. But it has also meant challenging neoliberal and colourblind

approaches to food system change efforts and using food as a mutual aid strategy that builds community and power.

One of the clearest representations of this diversity is the HEAL Food Alliance, a multi-sector and multi-racial coalition made up of fifty organisations representing over two million individuals throughout the United States. Their Ten-Point Program—a clear homage to the Black Panther Party's Ten-Point Program—reflects the diversity of the food justice movement, in an explicitly action-oriented way, in even more detail than the Principles of Food Justice mentioned above. There are three areas covered by the Ten-Point Program: the economy, health, and the environment (HEAL Food Alliance 2018). As for the economy, the Alliance aims to provide dignity for workers, opportunity for producers, fair and competitive markets, and resilient regional economies. In practice this requires ending prison slavery, legislating living wages, providing a pathway to citizenship for immigrants, debt forgiveness for farmers, land access for people of colour and women, fair pricing for growers, enforcing antitrust laws, culturally appropriate regional food systems, cooperative ownership structures, community control, and more. As for health, the Alliance aims to eliminate junk food, increase food literacy and transparency, and ensure real food in every neighbourhood. In practice this means ending subsidies for junk commodities and the marketing of junk food to children, creating visible warning labels, banning corporate influence in food and agriculture research, transparency in the food production process, worker ownership of food and agriculture businesses, land access, increasing food aid, and more. As for the environment, the alliance aims to phase out factory farming, promote sustainable farming, fishing, and ranching, and close the loop on waste and energy. In practice this means banning antibiotics and runoff, centring the health of communities and ecosystems, investing in agroecology, rewarding stewardship, enhancing biodiversity, centring Indigenous knowledge and practices, recycling nutrients, internalising the true cost of food, eliminating waste, ending overproduction, and more. Overall, it is apparent that achieving a more just food system will require robust imaginations and transformative practices.

The food justice movement is maturing as the number of people and organisations involved multiplies. In part, this is due to the organising and creativity of the movement across every sector that food touches, which is to say nearly every facet of social life. There is a dire need to completely transform our food and social systems, but what this looks like going forward will inevitably require adjustments to changing circumstances and grassroots visions.

Food justice futures

Several areas of research and movement-building portend promising futures for food justice. What they share is a commitment to intersectional analysis and action. From an engagement with the diverse needs of differently situated social groups and social movements, the various institutions, regimes, cultural conditions, and power relations, and uneven places and spaces, to creative approaches with praxis, mutual aid, policy making, state craft, and movement building, food justice is capaciously positioned to expand more radical work. In sum, there is a need to attend to the less recognised institutional forces and social movements that intersect with food justice.

Institutional intersections

The food system intersects with both human and non-human life. On the human front, every major institution demands attention. While economic and political institutions receive the most food justice research and activist focus, there are other institutions that structure food inequities. Whether it is the media, religion, health care, or more, our daily food lives are shaped by powerful social forces. The media shapes and reproduces gender, race, and class stereotypes and social relations through food. Religious traditions honour certain foods or can be undermined when adherents face repressive political persecution. Health care medicalises certain dietary health problems or can be used to revolutionise our understanding of health through food. The pressing consideration here is that mapping these and other intersections creates more inclusive and expansive terrains of food justice struggle.

On the non-human front, a just food system will require thriving ecosystems. While most research on the biological and ecological dimensions of food systems is in the natural and physical sciences, accounting for the human dimensions of changes to non-human conditions is critical. From the experience of clearcutting forests to make way for agricultural production to the poisoning of soil from pollutants, people are directly impacted, which shapes an array of food inequities. Seeing ecological and social systems as mutually constitutive of the food system therefore opens the imagination to new kinds of work.

Social movement intersections

If part of the growth of food justice is tied to the connections activists and scholars draw to institutional intersections, then there is also the need to attend to other possible or nascent social movement intersections. Several intersections are particularly noteworthy.

Indigenous food activists note the ongoing practice of settler colonialism as central to problems in the food system. Logics of private property, which seek to enclose, control, and exploit land, has led to agricultural practices that undermine human and natural conditions needed for survival. Beyond Indigenous communities already modelling agricultural practices predicated on responsibilities to nature, the Land Back Movement seeks the "rematriation" of land, that is, the restoring of a sacred relationship to and cultural harmony with the land. Sovereignty over land in this way is a precondition for achieving food justice.

Lesbian, gay, transgender, and queer food activists have been building community and advocating for how the food system operates and how we imagine the conditions needed to achieve food justice. Food is a tool to blur identity boundaries and resist gender and sexual binaries. In terms of food culture, there are cookbooks focused on the lives and views of gay and lesbian cooks, magazines that look at intersections between sexuality, gender, and food, and dinner parties and autonomous pop-up spaces for queer-identified people. There are also ongoing efforts to support queer farmers in their drive to survive and thrive in spaces traditionally coded as masculine, cis-gender, and straight.

Exploitative agricultural and food conditions in prisons have stoked organising that aims to challenge carcerality, namely those political economic and ideological regimes of social control. Prison abolitionists argue that simply reforming the farms prisoners are forced to work on or the food they eat will not ultimately rid prisons from society. Instead, there is the need for solidarity work with incarcerated people and non-reformist reforms, efforts that do not obstruct creating a world without prisons. This may take the form of supporting prisoners engaged in subversive food practices and demanding better food, divestment campaigns to rid public entities of food contracts with companies that do business with prisons, and struggles to shrink the prison industrial complex at the point of cutting ties with companies providing agricultural inputs, food, and beverages.

While this is just a sample of some of the intersections that reflect the growth of the food justice movement, it is by no means the last word. For that we need to keep looking to the streets and the increasing diversity of food justice practice in all its intersectional possibilities.

References

Alkon AH and Agyeman J (2011) *Cultivating Food Justice: Race, Class, and Sustainability.* Cambridge, MIT Press.

Gottlieb R and Joshi A (2010) *Food Justice.* Cambridge, MIT Press.

HEAL Food Alliance (2018) The HEAL Food Platform for Real Food. https://healfoodalliance.org/platformforrealfood/

Hislop D (2014) Reaping Equity Across the USA: Food Justice Organizations Observed at the National Scale. Master's Thesis, University of California–Davis.

Holt-Giménez E (2017) *A Foodies Guide to Capitalism: Understanding the Political Economy of What We Eat.* New York, Monthly Review Press.

Institute for Agriculture and Trade Policy (2012) *Principles of Food Justice.* Minneapolis.

Further reading

Alkon AH and Agyeman J (2011) *Cultivating Food Justice: Race, Class, and Sustainability.* Cambridge, MIT Press.

This foundational edited volume provides many examples of racial and class inequalities in the food system and several types of food justice responses.

Sbicca J (2018) *Food Justice Now! Deepening the Roots of Social Struggle.* Minneapolis, University of Minnesota Press.

This book offers a wide-ranging critical exploration of the expanding politics of the food justice movement.

Garth H and Reese A (2020) *Black Food Matters: Racial Justice in the Wake of Food Justice.* Minneapolis, University of Minnesota Press.

This book offers a deep dive into Black cultural foods and Black food struggles from the perspective of Black writers.

58. Food literacy

PAM FARRELL

Introduction: food literacy as a social practice

Food literacy is a multidimensional concept that traditionally encompasses the knowledge, skills, behaviours and attitudes related to food (e.g., Vidgen and Gallegos, 2014). Popular and mainstream definitions of food literacy from health and nutrition studies primarily focus on cooking skills and nutritional knowledge, neglecting the contextual and sociocultural factors that impact and influence a person's food literacy (Farrell, 2023).

Over the last decade or so, there has been a steady push to expand the definition of food literacy. These understandings include concepts related to contextual influences such as the food system, food environments, sociocultural factors, power imbalances (Azevedo et al., 2017; Cullen et al., 2015; Truman et al., 2017), a social practice approach to food literacy (Farrell, 2023) and a greater focus on the literacy aspect of food literacy (Renwick and Powell, 2019). These expanding concepts are essential to consider as food literacy education continues to be used as a strategy to promote population health in today's times of increased obesity and health-related impacts, as well as address the apparent widespread 'deskilling' of youth and adults alike (Jaffe and Gertler, 2006; Markow et al., 2012). Food literacy programmes are often turned to improve population health, change dietary behaviours and promote healthier food consumption. However, decades of focusing on improving health outcomes through food literacy education have not had the desired effects, as is evident in the high rates of obesity and diet-related illnesses such as diabetes, certain types of cancers and cardiovascular diseases.

Focusing on the literacy in food literacy

Approaching food literacy from a literacy studies rather than a health or food perspective provides a greater understanding of 'how' and 'why' food literacy is acquired, applied or practised. Within literacy studies, we can explore literacy through different traditions, one of which views literacy as a social practice. In simple terms, a social practice approach to literacy is what we do with reading, writing and texts and why we do it (Perry, 2012). This focuses on the "everyday meanings and uses of literacy in specific cultural contexts" (Street and Lefstein, 2007: 41). Literacy as a social practice describes literacy as being "located in the interaction between people" (Barton and Hamilton, 1998: 3) and as a resource for people to "draw on to make sense of events in their own lives" (Barton and Hamilton, 1998: 231). Barton and Hamilton (1998) theorised literacy as *sense making* and argued that when people make sense of the world, they connect to and produce what they referred to as vernacular or local knowledge.

Food and the practices associated with food are very personal, social and integral to an individual's life. A social practice approach to food literacy acknowledges that food literacy is not just cognitive but highly social. Most food literacy practices take place between people, such as preparing meals for family or friends, helping a parent cook or garden, and even taking a trip to the grocery store. The social connections that are formed and strengthened through food are important aspects of food literacy (Farrell, 2023). Food literacy events and practices, just like those of conventional literacy, take place between people and are purposeful, context-specific, historically situated and change, and new practices are acquired through 'sense-making' and informal learning (Barton and Hamilton, 1998). For example, food literacy practices, such as how and why we celebrate with food, are often rooted in our traditions but will also change if we are presented with barriers to implementing them or opportunities to change them (Farrell, 2023).

This understanding of food literacy is culturally sensitive and contextual. It recognises that people's food literacies are deeply informed and influenced by historical, social and contextual factors which align with a social practice view of literacy. It calls for a shift in perspective from solely focusing on health outcomes to creating environments and contexts that support individuals and communities in acting on their informal or vernacular food literacies.

The purpose of food literacy

Thinking about food literacy as a social practice presents us with opportunities to challenge how food literacy programming has been developed and delivered in recent years and provides a new understanding and application of food literacy. Viewing food literacy as a social practice allows us to recognise the real and varied factors that influence what we do with food and why we do it.

Considering the intended goal or outcomes of food literacy education, what do we as practitioners or scholars in the greater field of food studies and education hope to achieve or impact with food literacy? Beyond improving health outcomes, what should be the goal of developing food literacy in both formal and informal contexts? Should food literacy education shift its focus away from the individual and focus on analysing and understanding our food environments?

The purpose of food literacy as a social practice goes beyond improving health outcomes. It presents opportunities to challenge existing food literacy programmes and offers a new understanding and application of food literacy. While improved population health is one desired outcome, the goal of food literacy should include food sovereignty, food justice and collective action. This broader perspective considers the historical, cultural and social elements attached to food literacy.

References

Azevedo Perry, E, Thomas, H, Samra, H R, Edmonstone, S, Davidson, L, Faulkner, A, Petermann, L, Manafò, E and Kirkpatrick, S I (2017) Identifying attributes of food literacy: A scoping review. *Public Health Nutrition* 20(13), 2406–2415. https://doi.org/10.1017/S1368980017001276

Barton, D and Hamilton, M (1998) *Local literacies: Reading and writing in one community*. London, Routledge.

Cullen, T, Hatch, J, Martin, W, Higgins, J W and Sheppard, R (2015) Food literacy: Definition and framework for action. *Canadian Journal of Dietetic Practice and Research* 76(3), 140–145. https://doi.org/10.3148/cjdpr-2015-010

Farrell, P (2023) You eat what you are: Sociocultural factors that influence and inform food literacies (Doctoral thesis, University of Calgary, Calgary, Canada). https://prism.ucalgary.ca

Jaffe, J and Gertler, M (2006) Victual vicissitudes: Consumer deskilling and the (gendered) transformation of food systems. *Agriculture and Human Values* 23(2),

143–162. https://doi.org/10.1007/s10460-005-6098-1

Markow, K, Coveney, J and Booth, S (2012) Enhancing food literacy through school-based cooking programs: What's working and what's not? *Journal of the Home Economics Institute of Australia* 19(2), 2–11. https://doi.org/10.3316/aeipt.195370

Perry, K H (2012) What is literacy? A critical overview of sociocultural perspectives. *Journal of Language & Literacy Education* 8(1), 50. https://eric.ed.gov/?id=EJ1008156

Renwick, K and Powell, L J (2019) Focusing on the literacy in food literacy: Practice, community, and food sovereignty. *Journal of Family & Consumer Sciences* 111(1), 24–30. https://doi.org/1014307/JFCS111.1.24

Street, B V and Lefstein, A (2007) *Literacy: An advanced resource book*. New York, Routledge.

Truman, E, Lane, D and Elliott, C (2017) Defining food literacy: A scoping review. *Appetite* 116, 365–371. http://doi.org/10.1016/j.appet.2017.05.007

Vidgen, H A and Gallegos, D (2014) Defining food literacy and its components. *Appetite* 76, 50–59. https://doi.org/10.1016/j.appet.2014.01.010

Further reading

Farrell, P (2021) Conceptualizing food literacy: A literature review. *Canadian Journal for New Scholars in Education* 12(2), 126–134. https://journalhosting.ucalgary.ca/index.php/cjnse/article/view/72690

This literature review provides an overview of the growing conceptualisation and understanding of the term food literacy in an educational context. It describes the transition of skills and knowledge-based definitions to a broader understanding with a focus on critical and contextual aspects of food literacy.

Renwick, K and Powell, L J (2019) Focusing on the literacy in food literacy: Practice, community, and food sovereignty. *Journal of Family & Consumer Sciences* 111(1), 24–30. https://doi.org/1014307/JFCS111.1.24

This article discusses the importance of paying attention to the literacy in food literacy and highlights the connection between family, community and the (food)

environment. The authors describe how a critical approach to food literacy can lead to more socially just and ecologically sustainable food system transformation.

PAM FARRELL

59. Food movements

STEPHEN LEITHEISER

Contemporary food movements: origins and diversity

Contemporary food systems are in the midst of crisis, as calls for deliberate transformation of food systems are on the rise. Through both critique and the material construction of alternatives to dominant systems of food provisioning, social movements have played a crucial role in shaping and/or resisting the transformation of agri-food systems throughout history.

Today's food movements are highly heterogeneous, and as with other social movements, they vary in terms of ideology and goals, strategy and tactics, and structure and participants. Here we understand food movements in terms of both Polanyian-progressive and Marxist-radical traditions (see Tilzey, 2017), as various forms of collective resistance by which people attempt to take more control over their food (sometimes, as a part of social reproduction more broadly) in the face of commodification-induced crises (cf. Holt Giménez and Shattuck, 2011). Put simply, food movements emerge as negative effects of agri-food provisioning systems are experienced, people get 'fed up' and push back in various, context-dependent ways.

In order to understand the origins and nature of contemporary food movements, we can go back to crises that ruptured the stability of the post-World War II macroeconomic system in general, and food regime in particular. By the early 1970s, there was a growing recognition that the post-war regime's narrow focus on maximising production was harmful to both human health and ecological sustainability. This awareness was demonstrated by the rise of local, organic, slow food and farm-to-table movements in Europe and the US; and a worldwide wave of national environmental legislation throughout the 1960s to the 1970s. The acute food crisis of the early 1970s reached a head in 1973, marking an 'end' to the post-war regime (Friedmann and McMichael, 1989). As food prices skyrocketed worldwide, billions of people in formerly agrarian societies that had become dependent on US food aid during the post-war regime were suddenly subjected to hunger and malnutrition. In 1974, world powers adopted the Universal Declaration on the Eradication of Hunger and Malnutrition at the UN's World Food Conference, and 'food security' became the official doctrine of food policy for multilateral institutions, nation states and NGOs. However, institutional responses, such as the liberalisation of agricultural trade, have not been able to stabilise a new regime that is viewed and experienced as legitimate by many of the world's producers and consumers of food. In turn, contemporary food movements have continued to focus their resistance on the ongoing crises of health and ecology (largely led by consumers in the Global North), and marginalisation and dependency (largely led by smallholders in the Global South) that reached a breaking point in 1973.

As the post-war international monetary system of Bretton Woods officially came to an end in 1976, (more or less) sovereign national economies progressively gave way to liberalised capital movements across borders, and agri-food systems were increasingly globalised (Friedmann and McMichael, 1989). This marked a shift in ideology, goals, tactics and strategy among social movements more broadly. Prior to the 1970s, and particularly before globalisation, relatively uniform and formally organised movements oriented their efforts vertically towards attaining state power. In this 'old' movement strategy (Amin et al., 1990), attaining state power was seen as a necessary precursor to transforming society in a positive direction. The post-1968 and post-modernist zeitgeist advanced a critique of the successes of these 'old' guard movements (i.e. communist and welfare states), and shifted the ideological focus towards horizontality – from the unity of class politics to the fragmentation of cultural politics. Moreover, the terrain of struggle was considerably altered under globalisation. As transnational corporations and supranational institutions (e.g. the WTO, World Bank, and IMF) were perceived as more powerful vis-à-vis nation-states, a 'new' strategy marked by cross-border alliances and networked organisation became more salient. In contrast to food movements of the past, which exhibited a central focus on the nation state, contemporary food movements became more grounded in and built on localised alternatives and translocal networking. The primary example is La Via Campesina (LVC, in English meaning 'the way of the peasant'), formed in 1993, which "links over one hundred organisations of small- and medium-sized agricultural producers, landless, rural women, indigenous people and agricultural workers in over 60 countries in the Americas, Europe, Asia and Africa" – boasting a membership ranging from "landless peasants in Brazil, small dairy farmers in Europe, well-off farmers in South India, wheat producers in Canada and land-poor peasants in Mexico" (Edelman, 2012: 436). While LVC chapters are locally rooted, they are networked in a nested sense (e.g. nationally, regionally, internationally) for knowledge exchange, and multi-scalar confrontation and engagement with relevant institutions.

The most notable distinction among food movements both today and in recent decades can be found in their degree of anti-systemic political nature. This distinction has, generally, been drawn along the lines of relative oppression in the world capitalist system between the 'majority' and 'minority' worlds (Amin et al., 1990), that is, the neo-colonial relationships between the minority of the world's population in the 'core' capitalist countries, who own and consume the vast majority of the world's resources, and the majority of the world's relatively marginalised population in the 'periphery'.

Food movements in the capitalist core have tended to be based in middle- and working-class populations, consumer-led, and 'progressive' in a Polanyian sense of re-embedding market relations into society through the state (Holt Giménez and Shattuck, 2011). Their focus has generally been on politics *within* existing political and economic frameworks. This includes more issue-specific appeals to convince/lobby/pressure elites in the current system, or in the case of Food Policy Councils to collaborate with municipal and regional governments. Issues of interest are context-dependent, but include more generally: food justice for urban poor people, food democracy for citizens' rights to participate in and decide on food policy, generating support for local initiatives (e.g. community gardens), campaigns for healthier foods or against GMOs, and more regulation for environmentally friendly production systems.

Movements in the periphery have tended to be more producer-led and 'radical', i.e. explicitly anti-capitalist. Majority world movements have more commonly exhibited a politics against existing political and economic frameworks – sometimes through agonistic engagement with the state, and other times through extra-legal antagonistic engagement. Here food sovereignty and self-sufficiency have been the focus, as they are understood as a linchpin to both development and freedom from (neo-)imperial domination. In many cases, e.g. Brazil's Landless Workers Movement (MST) or the revolutionary movement in Burkina Faso under leadership of Thomas Sankara, peripheral food movements have continued to focus on the 'old' strategies of agrarian reform and state-socialist development (see e.g. Moyo and Yeros, 2005). In general, food movements in the periphery have tended to be more radically oppositional, militant and revolutionary.

Although the core/periphery framing provides an important lens for understanding the diversity of food movements, it is also important to note that these lines cannot be so clearly demarcated (both within and between the North and South). For example, although the Indian farmers' protests both during the 1980s and in 2020 took place in the Global South, they were split along lines of class (landless labourers and land-owning farmers), caste, ethnicity and religion (Baviskar and Levien, 2021). Such contradictions and fissures continue to characterise food movements more broadly. While these divisions remain, questions of convergence of diversity have become more salient than ever before.

Towards a great green food transformation? Opportunities and challenges for converging diversity

Many of the concerns that food movements have championed in recent decades are no longer 'alternative'. In addition to growing recognition from elite institutions of industrial agriculture's contributions to poor health, the climate emergency and biodiversity loss, the 2020 COVID-19 pandemic and 2022 war in Ukraine have made vulnerabilities in the global food system increasingly undeniable. The need for radically different food systems is hardly disputed. Institutional actors including the World Bank, the European Commission and the United States Department of Agriculture have all endorsed what food movements have demanded for decades – a *transformation* of food systems. Yet beneath this surface-level consensus on the need for 'transformative change', fissures – regarding what change should look like, who the winners and losers of change should be, and who should decide – remain as important as ever. This is demonstrated by current events which present both opportunities and challenges for contemporary food movements, including the risk of co-optation in the rise of elite agendas for agri-food systems transformation (i.e. the capture or appropriation of discourse on 'transformation' by elite actors with interest to maintain business as usual); the position of agroecology as a 'territory in dispute' between institutionality and social movements (Giraldo and Rosset, 2018); and the escalation of farmers' protests.

Crisis openings, confrontations with the mainstream and co-optation risks

The United Nations Food Systems Summit (UNFSS) in the summer of 2021 marked a distinct shift in global food governance. The summit's focus on food *systems transformation* framed the event around addressing holistic concerns of agri-food impacts on social, economic and ecological systems that have been championed by food movements for decades. Despite the summit's holistic framing and promises of inclusivity, food movements like LVC were quick to highlight its Janus-faced nature. Echoing the critiques of LVC, analysts have argued that it is "clear that the Summit [represents] an effort by a powerful alliance of multinational corporations, philanthropies, and export-oriented countries to subvert the growing power of the [UN Committee on World Food Security (CFS)] as well as to capture the narrative of 'food system transformation'" (Canfield et al., 2021: 2). To LVC and other critics, the UNFSS represented an attempt by transnational capital (embodied in organisations like the World Economic Forum) to, on the one hand, subvert the scrutiny and oversight provided by the CFS and, on the other hand, maintain its grip on the global food system. That is, to centre corporations and business-led solutions (like digitalisation) as the agents of food system transformation, rather than farmers, citizens and food movements. More than 300 organisations affiliated with food movements boycotted the UNFSS. This instance highlights that although crisis recognition has created an opening for the demands and desires of food movements to be realised, resistance efforts are far from over. The role of food movements in interrogating 'nice sounding' elite solutions has become more and more salient.

The particular confrontations of the UNFSS resonate in a more general sense with opportunities and challenges in the paradigm of agroecology. Agroecology is often described as a terrain in which practice, science and movements interface and struggle for coherence across these sometimes divergent domains. Institutional interest in agroecology is growing (e.g. in Europe and the FAO), which presents opportunities for food movements to further their agendas. However, food movements have remained steadfastly alert, calling out the selective use of certain agroecological practices and methods as a 'fix' to fine-tune and "ease the sustainability crisis of industrial food production, while the existing structures of power remain unchallenged" (Declaration of the International Forum for Agroecology at Nyéléni, 2015: 164). More than 500 representatives from organisations of "peasants/family farmers, artisanal fisherfolk, indigenous peoples, landless peoples, rural workers, migrants, pastoralists, forest communities, women, youth, consumers and environmental and urban movements" gathered in Mali in 2015, and there vowed to block, reject, fight and expose the "insidious appropriation of agroecology" by multilateral institutions, governments, universities and research institutes, corporations, etc. Yet many of these institutional actors, and those involved more in the 'science' domain of agroecology, are either unaware or dismissive of these clear claims to define agroecology as the dominion of food movements. Many in the aforementioned institutions may also be well intentioned to support an agroecological paradigm, but may have an insufficient (or politically and historically naïve) analysis of the power relations that food movements aim to challenge. Regardless of intentionality, ignoring these deeply political foundations and inherent connection to social movements may dilute agroecology's transformative potential. Growing interest in the agroecology discourse thus creates a dilemma for food movements – "give in to being co-opted and captured, or take advantage of the opening of political opportunities to push forward the transformation of the prevailing agroextractive model" (Giraldo and Rosset, 2018: 546). This again highlights a key challenge for food movements for critical engagement with existing institutions: how does one avoid becoming a closed off niche without diluting principles and transformative character?

STEPHEN LEITHEISER

The resurgence and escalation of farmer protests in the context of 'green transitions'

More recently, Europe's farmer protests, which have alternated between a smoulder and a blaze in the Netherlands and elsewhere in recent years, were reignited across Europe. Grievances are wide-ranging, but there is a sense that family farmers cannot compete in the face of institutional responses to environmental issues, which are often narrowly defined and targeted, as e.g. nitrogen pollution or greenhouse gas emissions. As they have faced lower incomes and more and more environmental restrictions, farmers perceive that they are footing the bill for 'green transitions'. In Europe two coalitions have begun to form, and these also resonate with contours drawn in other contexts. On the one hand, there are the 'big farmers' who have partnered with agribusiness organisations and corporations to oppose environmental measures in favour of the status quo. On the other hand are the 'small farmers' and food-movement-related organisations, including the European Coordination Via Campesina (ECVC), which agree that environmental measures are urgently necessary, but oppose the wider neoliberal framework (i.e. the paradigm of international economic law constituted in institutions like the WTO, IMF, World Bank, EU, etc.) in which placing the burden on farmers appears as the only option. The former group wants to continue business as usual, and is often presented in public discourse as 'the voice' of the farmers. This flattens out a much more complex and nuanced reality in which food movements can play a key role. Many farmers are, in fact, open to change, but cannot and will not change without more general support. This highlights a central challenge for food movements in this opportune crisis moment: how to develop a unifying narrative that brings farmers and citizens together around a concrete vision for an alternative food regime. And how and to what extent to engage with states and other existing institutions so as to realise this vision.

Future concerns, issues and questions

Both the critique and practical alternatives that food movements have been building for decades are ripe for consideration and action. In the midst of the crisis of intensification, food movements are presented with a historic opportunity to shape the transformation of agro-food systems and stabilisation of a new food regime.

As Samir Amin (2011), the late Egyptian French political economist and theorist of food movements argues, a primary characteristic of food movements in recent decades has been de-politicisation – here, this is understood as a lack of *universalist* struggles to transform the general conditions that shape production, distribution and consumption in food provisioning systems. Amin also points out the importance of new forms of politicisation, as new struggles work to *universalise* the particular 'successes' of dispersed practices and networks (e.g. AFNs). Here, politicisation may involve hybrid forms of the 'old' and 'new' strategies discussed above, and a contextual process of evolutionary learning and experimentation.

Going forward, food movements are challenged to both continue building and strengthening local alternative practices and find new ways to go beyond them. This highlights the importance of experimenting with various strategies and tactics, converging diversity by building alliances across disconnected domains, and, crucially, engaging critically to (radically) reform, transform and/or replace existing institutions.

References

Amin, S. (2011). Food sovereignty: A struggle for convergence in diversity. In: Holt-Giménez, E. (Ed.). *Food movements unite! Strategies to transform our food system*. Food First Books.

Amin, S., Frank, G., &. Arrighi, G. (Eds.) (1990). *Transforming the revolution: Social movements and the world system*. Monthly Review Press.

Baviskar, A., & Levien, M. (2021). Farmers' protests in India: Introduction to the JPS forum. *The Journal of Peasant Studies*, 48(7), 1341–1355.

Canfield, M., Anderson, M. D., & McMichael, P. (2021). UN Food Systems Summit 2021: Dismantling democracy and resetting corporate control of food systems. *Frontiers in Sustainable Food Systems*, 5, 661552.

Declaration of the International Forum for Agroecology, Nyéléni, Mali. (2015). *Development, 58*, 163–168.

Edelman, M. (2012). Rural social movements. In: Amenta, E., Nash, K., & Scott, A.

STEPHEN LEITHEISER

(Eds.), *The Wiley-Blackwell companion to political sociology* (pp. 431–443). Wiley-Blackwell.

Friedmann, H., & McMichael, P. (1989). Agriculture and the state system. *Sociologia Ruralis*, 29(2), 93–117.

Giraldo, O. F., & Rosset, P. M. (2018). Agroecology as a territory in dispute: Between institutionality and social movements. *The Journal of Peasant Studies*, 45(3), 545–564.

Holt Giménez, E., & Shattuck, A. (2011). Food crises, food regimes and food movements: Rumblings of reform or tides of transformation? *The Journal of Peasant Studies*, 38(1), 109–144.

Moyo, S., & Yeros, P. (Eds.) (2005). *Reclaiming the land: The resurgence of rural movements in Africa, Asia and Latin America*. Zed Books.

Tilzey, M. (2017). Reintegrating economy, society, and environment for cooperative futures: Polanyi, Marx, and food sovereignty. *Journal of Rural Studies*, 53, 317–334.

Further reading

Ajl, M. (2021). *A people's green new deal*. Pluto Press.

This book builds on the work of food movements and sketches out a vision for a global agri-food transformation linked to broader struggles of anti-imperialism, anti-capitalism and climate justice.

Moulaert, F., Jessop, B., Swyngedouw, E., Simmons, L., & van den Broeck, P. (2022). *Political change through social innovation: A debate*. Edward Elgar Publishing.

This book offers various perspectives on what new forms of politicisation from food movements might look like, and how they might navigate the current conjuncture towards more socially and ecologically sane and just futures.

STEPHEN LEITHEISER

60. Food networks

RONAN LE VELLY

Introduction

"Food networks" is a widely used term in agri-food studies, particularly through such declensions as "alternative/local/conventional food networks". Yet few efforts have been made to define precisely what these "food networks" are. Alternative food networks, local food networks and conventional food networks have all been the subject of debate. However, each time, the discussions have focused on the adjective, that is, the alternative, local or conventional nature of the network, not on what the term "food network" itself means. This entry suggests a definition of the term that will then serve as a foundation for showing the contributions that reasoning around the notion of "food networks" can make.

Food networks can be described as involving sets of entities that are connected together in order to produce, exchange or consume food in certain ways. This definition is deliberately inclusive. It strives to include food supply chains or commodity chains (composed at the very minimum of farmers and consumers, and often of processors and trade intermediaries as well), but also other forms of groups of actors, such as trade networks for sharing advice, consumers' groups, etc., in food networks. Such a definition situates food networks on an intermediate scale between individuals and food systems. Even though the terms "food systems" and "food networks" are sometimes used interchangeably, it is preferable to consider the former to include the latter. Seen from this standpoint, the functioning of urban food systems or of the global food system can be said to depend on the food networks of which the system is composed.

Current issues

This definition prompts consideration of the processes by which food networks take shape. Food networks are the result of assembling things, with intentionality. From this perspective, one must first pay attention to the motivations of the actors in food networks and their views on "good agriculture" and "good food". This is particularly relevant for "alternative" networks, given that they are marked by criticism of conventional networks and the plan of establishing other ways of organising production, trade and food consumption (Goodman et al., 2012). It is also necessary to take into account the concrete operations that make it possible to create and maintain these networks, i.e. the establishment of stabilised relationships, formal rules, material infrastructure, quality conventions, shared representations and so on. Observing these processes offers an excellent opportunity to understand the sources of the balances of power amongst the actors. For example, the study of global commodity or value chains shows that the power wielded by the importers in the Global North often stems from their ability to impose production and trade standards on farmers in the Global South (Ponte and Gibbon, 2005; Ouma, 2015).

This way of looking at food networks also implies taking account of the processes that stabilise or destabilise them. Notably, the promoters of 'alternative' initiatives often come up against the great resistance of conventional food networks. For example, in France it remains difficult to supply school cafeterias with local farm produce, given the constraints that are placed on farmers by health rules and public procurement regulations, the infrastructure and routines of the schools' central kitchens, existing logistic pathways, etc. (Le Velly et al., 2021). Nevertheless, as the research that analyses food networks as "assemblages" also shows, food networks can be fragile. For example, unexpected behaviour can destabilise existing food networks: That is the case when the spread of a virus or bacterium interrupts a well-oiled chain of international trade (Wang, 2018).

Finally, work on food networks has enabled examination of the heterogeneity of the networks' components (Le Velly and Dufeu, 2016). First, this has required a need to go beyond certain dualisms, such as those that pit the local against the global or the alternative against the conventional, to show that food networks are hybrid: school cafeterias turn to major distributors in order to buy local produce, locavore restaurant menus include quinoa that comes from halfway around the world, and so on. Second, it has required considering the entities connected in food networks to include not only human beings, but also material devices and other biological entities. Attention is then paid to the quality standards, logistic infrastructure, computational tools, information systems, etc., that are vital for the food networks to function. It is also paid to the actions of the biological entities involved, from the smallest (viruses, micro-organisms) to the largest (soil, biodiversity), with the actions of the agricultural produce and foodstuffs themselves (fish, milk) in between. Actor–network theory is a particularly influential theoretical reference for these last two points. It suggests that food networks should be analysed as hybrid collectives capable of action, with agency distributed over their various components. We can then posit that what a food network is able or unable to do (for example, offer healthy and sustainable food to low income consumers) is the result of the entangled actions of its human, material and biological components.

Future concerns

Among the many prospects for future research related to food networks, two avenues seem particularly promising. The first relates to the resilience of food networks, considered as the collective capacity of the human and non-human entities that compose them to overcome the multiple shocks they face (sanitary crises, extreme climatic events, economic downturn, etc.). The resilience of conventional food networks deserves particular attention in this respect: what arrangements allow their resistance despite crises? The second consists in deepening the analysis of the agency of biological entities in the construction and evolution of food networks. Despite efforts made over the past fifteen years to develop "more-than-human" agri-food studies, particularly by taking greater account of the action of material devices, there is still much to do to move beyond a conception of food networks centred on the agency of human beings. For this, research will benefit from a broad multidisciplinary approach, including for example ecology, soil science, animal science and agronomy.

References

Goodman D, DuPuis M and Goodman M (2012) *Alternative Food Networks: Knowledge, Practice and Politics*. London, Routledge.

Le Velly R and Dufeu I (2016) Alternative food networks as "market agencements": Exploring their multiple hybridities. *Journal of Rural Studies*, 43, 173–182.

Le Velly R, Goulet F and Vinck D (2021) Allowing for detachment processes in market innovation: The case of short food supply chains. *Consumption Markets & Culture*, 24, 4, 313–328.

Ouma S (2015) *Assembling Export Markets: The Making and Unmaking of Global Food Connections in West Africa*. Oxford, Wiley.

Ponte S and Gibbon P (2005) Quality standards, conventions and the governance of global value chains. *Economy and Society*, 34, 1, 1–31.

Wang C M (2018) Assembling lettuce export markets in East Asia: Agrarian warriors, climate change and kinship. *Sociologia Ruralis*, 58, 4, 909–927.

Further reading

Müller M (2015) Assemblages and actor-networks: Rethinking socio-material power, politics and space. *Geography Compass*, 9, 1, 27–41.

This article delves deeper into the theoretical questions opened by the mobilisation of actor–network theory and assemblage thinking.

RONAN LE VELLY

61. Food policy

REBECCA WELLS, ROSALIND SHARPE, CHRISTOPHER YAP AND KELLY PARSONS

Introduction: why food policy matters

Food policy comprises all the policies which influence the food system and what people eat (Hawkes and Parsons, 2019). It refers to statements of action or intent made by authorities such as governments and their agencies that influence how food is produced, processed, distributed, consumed and recovered or disposed of. It is 'about how policy-making shapes who eats what, when and how' (Lang et al., 2009: 21). The breadth of food policies reflects the breadth of food systems, which comprise a multiplicity of interrelated activities, actors, drivers and outcomes (Hasnain et al., 2020). In this entry, we set out what food policy is and how it has emerged as an important governance and research focus in the context of overlapping social, economic, health and environmental challenges. In the second section, we set out some critical contemporary debates in the field of food policy. In the concluding section, we reflect on emerging issues and possible questions to guide future food policy research agendas.

Defining food policy

Food policy is a primary mechanism of food systems governance, which refers to a broader set of structures, processes and relations across the public, private and civil society sectors. A wide range of policy-makers, governmental departments and their multifarious influencers, working in relation to different elements of the food system, is involved (Parsons et al., 2020). Food policies are made by intergovernmental and multilateral agencies, such as the European Union and United Nations (UN), and by governmental agencies operating at the national and subnational levels, including local authorities. These can vary significantly between countries. In the UK, for example, they include executive agencies, public bodies and non-ministerial departments, among others (Parsons, 2020). The processes through which food policies are made within this governance landscape are often political, contested and power laden.

We use the term 'food policy' to refer both to explicit food strategies and to other policies that impact food systems. Food policies can be highly specific, e.g. the 1987 Omnibus Investment Act in the Philippines, which exempted tax on imports of animal breeding stock and genetic materials to encourage investment in domestic livestock production. Or they can be broader, e.g. 'urban food policy', which involves a web of institutions, infrastructure, people and processes and is subject to the influences and interests of competing parties. Therefore, food policy takes many forms, including action plans, strategies, framework legislation, statutes, bills, laws, court decisions, directives, regulations, guidelines, standards, codes of practice, specific programmes and voluntary initiatives. The types of policy levers available to policy-makers can be summarised into types, such as: *regulatory levers*, which include mandatory and voluntary rules affecting different parts of the food chain; *economic levers*, which involve the provision of financial incentives like subsidies, or penalties such as taxes; *direct food provision levers*, which include school meals or food vouchers; and *information and communication levers*, which include media, dietary guidelines and labels (Parsons and Barling, 2021).

These levers are used by policy-makers to try to shape the food system, and its drivers and outcomes. At the national level, for example, many governments develop agricultural policies that influence what farmers in their jurisdiction produce and how they produce it; animal welfare policy influences how animals reared for food are treated; and trade policies have bearing on what is imported and exported, and thus on food prices, as well as the global competitiveness of national food businesses.

Beyond these direct policies, a range of other types of policy affects food systems indirectly. Social welfare policy determines how much money some people have for food. Energy policy affects land use and the cost of fuel and fertilisers for food production; migration policies influence who works where in the food system; planning and tax policy can encourage or discourage investments by farmers; and government investment in research influences food industry innovation (Hawkes and Parsons, 2019).

This complex governance landscape means that responsibility for food policy is often distributed across multiple decision-making authorities, leading to significant challenges in coherence, coordination and cooperation, and increasing the risk of confusion, duplication, contradiction, issues 'falling between the cracks' and unforeseen consequences (Parsons, 2019; Hawkes and Parsons, 2019).

The historical development of food policy

Control of food production, distribution and consumption has been a vital concern for societies throughout history. However, the first recognisable use of the term 'food policy' in English appears in the context of World Wars I and II, referring to the need for strategies to balance supply and demand and mitigate shortages (Boyd Orr, 1943). Concerns about food supply continued up to and through the 1970s following decades of famines throughout sub-Saharan Africa, the Soviet Union, China, India and Bangladesh. Food policy emerged as a focus of academic inquiry, and international food policy institutions were established, such as the International Food Policy Research Institute. In 1981, the Organisation for Economic Cooperation and Development (OECD) published a *Food Policy* report, which called for 'a strategy that views the food economy and policies relating to it in an integrated way and in a broad economic and political context' (OECD, 1981: 58).

Important developments from the 1970s broadened the remit of food policy beyond supply and demand. Local and national governments began to develop policy that integrated objectives around production and consumption, such as Norway's 1975 national Food and Nutrition Policy. Food policy also emerged as a mechanism to address societal challenges, such as reducing inequalities and improving food security with the creation of the Municipal Secretariat for Food Supply in Belo Horizonte, Brazil, in 1993. Mechanisms to coordinate local food policies among diverse stakeholders also emerged, such as the first Food Policy Council, established in 1982 in Knoxville, Tennessee. By 2016 there were 329 Food Policy Councils around the world (Bassarab et al., 2018).

In 1994, the Centre for Food Policy was established by academics in London to research, teach and advocate for 'joined-up food policy' to address a range of interconnected problems across institutionally separate policy areas, such as health and the environment (Barling et al., 2002). Through the 1990s and 2000s, the environmental dimensions of food systems emerged as key issues, e.g. in relation to food waste and loss, nitrogen fertiliser dependency, biodiversity loss and the contribution of food systems to global greenhouse gas emissions, estimated to be between 21% and 37% of total global emissions (Mbow et al., 2019: 439). Food policy began to encompass the need both to adapt to and mitigate these impacts.

Contemporary food policy and its challenges

The trajectory of food policy from the concern of national governments to manage production, consumption and trade towards a more multi-level, multi-actor and cross-sector set of policies represents both an important advance and a challenge. We identify three key challenges facing food policy today: fragmentation, contestation and inequality. These are addressed in turn below.

Fragmentation

Food policy is often characterised by fragmentation and incoherence across governmental departments, sectors and administrative levels. In 2020 in England, for example, at least 16 departments and government bodies were responsible for policy decisions that impacted the food system (Parsons et al., 2020). In India, responsibility encompasses 19 divisions and 15 ministries of the central government (Brown et al., 2020). These examples reflect an international trend: food policy is rarely coordinated centrally, for example by a cross-departmental committee, statutory commission or independent advisory board, though these have repeatedly been called for (e.g. National Food Strategy Independent Review, 2021).

When specific food policy solutions are implemented, the interconnections in the system mean all dimensions can be affected. In recent years 'food systems' approaches have been advocated, taking into account the interactions between the food supply chain and its economic, political, environmental, health and social dimensions (Parsons and Hawkes, 2019).

The sub-national, urban scale has been an important site for more coordinated forms of

REBECCA WELLS, ROSALIND SHARPE, CHRISTOPHER YAP AND KELLY PARSONS food policy. Since 2015, over two hundred cities worldwide have signed the Milan Urban Food Policy Pact. This calls on policy-makers to address challenges including lack of food access, unhealthy diets, food waste, environmental change and sustainable livelihoods for marginalised populations. In the UK, cross-sector food partnerships have led the development of local food strategies across the country that likewise aim to address a diversity of food system challenges (SFP, 2024).

At the supra-national level, in 2015 the UN's 193 member countries adopted the Sustainable Development Goals (SDGs) as a global development agenda. Although the terms 'food policy' and 'food system' do not appear in the document itself, the SDGs' integrated vision aligns with a more joined-up approach to food policy.

Interactions between policies made at different levels can present challenges to coherence or lead to the prioritisation of one level over another. For example, the Codex Alimentarius Commission, led by the Food and Agriculture Organization of the UN and the World Health Organization, established a 'food code' that comprises food standards and guidelines that aim to promote food safety and fair trade. However, each country develops food standards that reflect its own cultural practices, economic context and political realities. Key differences currently include labelling of genetically modified organisms, animal welfare standards and food additives such as colouring and preservatives (Campden, 2021), leading to a heterogeneous landscape of regulation. Overall, the fragmentation of food policy is hard to overcome, and realising horizontal policy coherence between governmental departments at the national level is only one part of the challenge. The other part concerns the vertical integration of food policies between levels of policy-making and governance, such as local and national, where disconnects are seen.

Contestation

Food policy-making is often political and contested. Key issues include the use of evidence, transparency and inclusion. Food policies should ideally be developed in ways that involve scrutiny and inputs from diverse food systems actors. But in practice, policy development can be opaque. Food policies are commonly presented as 'evidence-based',

but the processes through which evidence is produced, appraised and synthesised are generally not open to scrutiny (Headings et al., 2022). In 2014, the UN Special Rapporteur on the Right to Food explicitly called for wider participation of farmers and those affected by hunger and malnutrition in policy-making processes (de Schutter, 2014). In reality, there are many other influences on food policy beyond the evidence base, including political considerations and economic constraints.

Inequality

Power imbalances in food policy processes contribute to the challenges food policy-makers face today. Food production continues to reproduce productivist, colonial and corporate food regimes which are to the advantage of the global North (McMichael, 2016), while widening gaps in food security point to continuing inequalities that disadvantage the most vulnerable groups in our societies, despite attempts to address racial, gender and physical ability-related discrimination (Pimbert, 2008). This leads to inequalities of access and involvement in policy-making. While civil society organisations have been highly effective in advocacy and public campaigning to create agendas and shape food policy (Zerbian et al., 2023), civil society does not share the same level of governmental access and influence as, for example, major food retailers or corporate lobbyists. This reflects broader inequalities in the food system, which has seen power concentrated in specific actors, such as major retailers and agri-food businesses (Clapp, 2021).

Future concerns, issues and questions

The significant challenges currently facing food policy are likely to extend into the future, in the context of the nature emergency and geopolitical conflicts. For policy-makers, and those seeking to influence them, three questions emerge.

How to raise food up the political agenda and ensure action is taken?

Fundamentally, food policy-making needs to be more ambitious in its aims and approaches to meet the scale and urgency of the social, economic and ecological challenges and opportunities facing our food systems. We have seen action at local and city level, but there is a lack of action at national level, hampered by crises including geo-political tensions, conflicts, climate change and the COVID-19 pandemic. Achieving the necessary goals will require an end to 'business-as-usual' policy-making, and a greater embrace of inclusion and diversity in policy-making. Ultimately it requires food policy that enables the transition to fair and sustainable food systems.

How can a systems approach to food policy-making be effectively institutionalised?

Taking a 'systems approach' to food policy-making means identifying connections and understanding their impact across historically isolated policy areas. This means being aware that a policy intervention to address one part of the system may impact on other parts (Parsons et al., 2019). But just as the connections mean policies can have unintended consequences, they also mean policy solutions can bring multiple benefits, termed 'co-benefits' or 'synergies' (Parsons and Hawkes, 2018). For example, interventions could aim to promote foods which are generally good for people's health but also protect nature, such as by redesigning food-based dietary guidelines to take account of both human and planetary health. Institutionalising a systems approach does not mean that every policy area needs to address every element of food systems. Rather, it implies that a food systems perspective can offer a critical, cross-cutting lens to the development of all policy. And yet while advocacy of systems approaches has become widely accepted in academic, policy and practitioner circles, the ways in which they can be incorporated into day-to-day decision-making are not well understood and require further exploration and testing.

How to reduce inequalities in food policy-making processes?

Power differentials between actors in food policy-making processes mean that some groups have greater influence than others (Clapp, 2021), with some interests privileged and others marginalised. These inequalities extend to the knowledge and evidence base of food policy, which typically privileges academic knowledge at the expense of more tacit or informal forms of knowledge and 'know-how'. Reducing the power differentials

between food systems actors – promoting 'food democracy' – must involve making them visible and working proactively to support more inclusive and transparent forms of food policy-making at all levels.

Future food policy, in research and practice, must answer the above questions in order to tackle the urgent need for policies that will improve our currently unsustainable food systems.

References

Barling D, Lang T, and Caraher M (2002) Joined-up Food Policy? The Trials of Governance, Public Policy and the Food System. *Social Policy & Administration* 36(6), 556–574.

Bassarab K, Santo R, and Palmer A (2018) *Food Policy Council report 2018.* Baltimore, Johns Hopkins Centre for a Livable Future.

Boyd Orr J (1943) *Food and the people.* London, Pilot Press.

Brown K A, Sharma P, Venkateshmurthy N S, Singh S, Mohan S, and Hawkes C (2020) *Who is making food policy in India?* Centre for Food Policy Research Brief. https://researchcentres.city.ac.uk/__data/assets/pdf_file/0004/567571/WMFP-IN-Brief-v1-updated.pdf

Campden B R I for Food Standards Agency (2021) *Comparing international approaches to food safety regulation of GM and Novel Foods.* https://www.food.gov.uk/sites/default/files/media/document/comparing-international-approaches-to-food-safety-regulation-of-gm-and-novel-foods_0.pdf

Clapp J (2021) The problem with growing corporate concentration and power in the global food system. *Nature Food* 2(6), 404–408.

De Schutter O (2014) *Final report: The transformative potential of the right to food.* Report of the Special Rapporteur on the right to food. New York, UN General Assembly.

Hasnain S, Ingram J, and Zurek M (2020) *Mapping the UK food system: A report for the UKRI Transforming UK Food Systems Programme.* Oxford, Environmental Change Institute, University of Oxford. https://www.foodsecurity.ac.uk/wp-content/uploads/2009/10/Mapping-food-system-web-09-11-20.pdf

Hawkes C and Parsons K (2019) *Brief 1. Tackling food systems challenges: The role of food policy*. London, Centre for Food Policy. https://www.city.ac.uk/__data/assets/pdf_file/0005/570443/7643_Brief-1_Tackling-food-systems-challenges_the-role-of-food-policy_WEB_SP.pdf

Headings R, Doherty B, Parsons K, Heron T, and Barling D (2022) *Shifting toward healthy and sustainable diets: How to optimise evidence use for policy and practice*. Technical report for the Food Standards Agency. https://www.food.gov.uk/print/pdf/node/12616

Lang T, Barling D, and Caraher M (2009) *Food policy: Integrating health, environment and society*. Oxford, Oxford University Press.

McMichael P (2016) Commentary: Food regime for thought. *The Journal of Peasant Studies*, 43(3), 648–670.

Mbow C, Rosenzweig C, Barioni L G, Benton T G, Herrero M, Krishnapillai M, Liwenga E, Pradhan P, Rivera-Ferre M G, Sapkota T, Tubiello F N, and Xu Y (2019) Food Security. In: Intergovernmental Panel on Climate Change (IPCC), *Climate change and land: An IPCC special report on climate change, desertification, land degradation, sustainable land management, food security, and greenhouse gas fluxes in terrestrial ecosystems*. https://doi.org/10.1017/9781009157988.007

National Food Strategy Independent Review (2021) *National Food Strategy Independent Review: The Plan*. https://www.nationalfoodstrategy.org/

OECD (1981) *Food policy*. Paris, Organisation for Economic Cooperation and Development.

Parsons K (2019) *Brief 3. Integrated food policy: What is it and how can it help connect food systems?* London, Centre for Food Policy. https://www.city.ac.uk/__data/assets/pdf_file/0003/570441/7643_Brief-3_Integrated_food_policy_What_is_it_and_how_can_it_help_connect_food_systems_WEB_SP.pdf

Parsons K (2020) *Who makes food policy in England? A map of government actors and activities. Rethinking Food Governance, Report 1*. London, Food Research Collaboration. https://foodresearch.org.uk/publications/who-makes-food-policy-in-england-map-government-actors/

Parsons K and Barling D (2021) *Food systems transformation: What is in the policy toolbox?* Report for the Transforming UK Food Systems Programme. https://ukfoodsystems.ukri.org/food-systems-transformation-whats-in-the-policy-toolbox/

Parsons K and Hawkes C (2018) *Connecting food systems for co-benefits: How can food systems combine diet-related health with environmental and economic policy goals?* European Observatory on Health Systems and Policies and World Health Organization, Regional Office for Europe. https://iris.who.int/handle/10665/331979

Parsons K and Hawkes C (2019) *Brief 5. Policy coherence in food systems*. London, Centre for Food Policy. https://researchcentres.citystgeorges.ac.uk/__data/assets/pdf_file/0018/504621/7643_Brief-5_Policy_coherence_in_food_systems_2021_SP_AW.pdf

Parsons K, Hawkes C, and Wells R (2019) *Brief 2. What is the food system? A food policy perspective*. London, Centre for Food Policy. https://www.city.ac.uk/__data/assets/pdf_file/0004/570442/7643_Brief-2_What-is-the-food-system-A-food-policy-perspective_WEB_SP.pdf

Parsons K, Sharpe R, and Hawkes C (2020) *Who is making food policy in England?* Centre for Food Policy Research Brief. https://foodresearch.org.uk/publications/who-makes-food-policy-in-england-map-government-actors/

Pimbert M (2008) *Towards food sovereignty: Reclaiming autonomous food systems*. London, IIED.

SFP (2024) *Sustainable food places* https://www.sustainablefoodplaces.org

Zerbian T, Yap C, Sharpe R, and Reynolds C (2023) *Leveraging knowledge-policy interfaces for food systems transformation in the UK: Lessons from civil society*. London, UKRI-Transforming UK Food Systems Strategic Priorities Fund. https://ukfoodsystems.ukri.org/wp-content/uploads/2023/12/11010-TUKFS-Knowledge-policy-interfaces-report_VF.pdf.

Further reading

Caraher M, Furey S, and Wells R (2023) *Food policy in the United Kingdom: An introduction*. London, Routledge.

This introduction to food policy in the United Kingdom explores the development, implementation and evaluation of policies across the food system, outlining influences and current issues.

Lang T, Barling D, and Caraher M (2009) *Food policy: Integrating health, environment and society.* Oxford, Oxford University Press.

This handbook introduces food policy as an area of research and practice, outlining the history, concepts, theories and actors involved.

OECD (2021) *Making better policies for food systems.* Paris, OECD. https://doi.org/10.1787/ddfba4de-en

This report from the OECD assesses food policy's role in food systems, explores food policy coherence and outlines ways policy can navigate multiple stakeholder perspectives to improve the food system.

REBECCA WELLS, ROSALIND SHARPE, CHRISTOPHER YAP AND KELLY PARSONS

62. Food regimes

Harriet Friedmann and Noelia
Parajuá

Origins and conceptualisation of food regimes

The concept of food regimes began with an article by Friedmann and McMichael (1989) called "Agriculture and the state system: The rise and fall of national agricultures, 1870 to the present". It was written in the context of an unexpected spike in food prices in the early 1970s after a long period of low prices, launching the first of several price spikes, called "food crises". The authors responded with the aim of recovering "the role of agriculture in the development of the capitalist world economy and in the trajectory of the state system" (Friedmann and McMichael, 1989:93). They proposed an approach called "food regimes", which linked international relations of food production and consumption to rules shaping capital accumulation, especially *money* and *trade*.

Friedmann and McMichael defined a food regime as a stable set of relationships and practices in which dominant state powers and capitals reorganise agriculture with specific technologies, farming systems, and geographies. Successive regimes consist of a specific farming and food production pattern, including labour, agricultural technologies, land use, finance, trade, manufacturing, transportation, and energy. For several decades, these elements have been combined in a specific way to shape what is grown and where, and what people in different regions and social classes eat. The food regime approach considers the following fundamental questions: *Where, how and by whom is (what) food produced in the capitalist world economy? Where and how are specific foods consumed, and by which social classes? What are the social and ecological effects of international relations of food production and consumption in different food regimes?* (Berstein, 2016).

First, second, and third food regimes

The first or "diasporic-colonial" food regime (1870–1914)

Friedmann and McMichael identified two historical food regimes. The first food regime arose as a world wheat market became the

first price-governed global market for a staple food. It emerged during social unrest, hunger, and emigration in Britain, triggering a new "consensus" between the state, industrial employers, landowners, capitalist farmers, and social movements. In 1846, Britain repealed import controls (Corn Laws), which had long protected its landowners and commercial farmers, partly because of the growing power of industrial and commercial segments and increasing wheat imports from settler states (Winders, 2009). Imports from North America and Australia/New Zealand, among others, were complemented by exports of labour and capital, through which Europeans settled along railways as they were built. Food from abroad, for the first time, became critical in provisioning emerging urban industrial classes in Europe. The first food regime led to new geographies by transforming distant grassland ecosystems into grain monocultures. Eventually appearing to be the "natural breadbaskets of the world", these export regions are at most two centuries old. It created unprecedented classes of commercial family farmers completely dependent on world markets (Friedmann and McMichael, 1989; Friedmann, 2005). That food regime unravelled along with the larger imperial system of trade and money between 1914 and 1945. Falling wheat prices in the 1920s led to the Great Depression, and British power was finally ended during the Second World War.

The second or "mercantile-industrial" food regime (1947–1973)

The second food regime was characterised by a state-led model of *national* regulation of agriculture under US hegemony (Friedmann, 1993). This US-centred food regime set the norm of the national economy with contiguous territory linking agriculture and industry. International trade – i.e., exchanges *between nations* – replaced imperial exchange between metropoles and colonies. The US reshaped food regime rules in its interest as an export nation. The territorial norm, which had been based on "frontier" expansion in the 19th century, was adapted to very different national circumstances inherited from the first regime, Europe as historically dependent on imports and postcolonial states, which were largely self-sufficient in food as they gained independence in the 1950s and 60s.

The rules of the mercantile-industrial food regime were highly influenced by US domestic classes of commercial family farmers created in the former regime, while financial capitals centred in Chicago reorganised international trade. US wheat farmers, who had lost the wheat market that created them, became a large, well-organised part of the governing New Deal coalition. The US government supported them through innovative domestic and trade policies, which gave the new regime a mercantile shape.

Within the mercantile (state-managed) regime, agriculture and food became increasingly *industrial*, using chemicals (fertilisers and pesticides) and machines instead of human and animal labour. Wheat farmers in the US and elsewhere became larger and fewer in number as they shed labour and acquired land. They became dominated by corporations from both sides – those selling them machines and chemicals as inputs and those buying crops as raw materials to process into industrial foods. Soon the "wheat complex" was outpaced by two emerging agrofood complexes. Monocultural maize and soybean enterprises grew up to feed an emerging livestock industry (confined animal feeding operations or CAFOs). The "livestock complex", in turn, provided byproducts of maize and soy from feedstuff industries as raw materials for an emerging "durable foods" complex. Manufacturers of industrial foods eventually drew in many more crops as raw materials, and supermarkets spread diets of "ultra-processed foods" worldwide (Friedmann, 1992). Agrifood corporations created *transnational* supply chains of vegetables, fruits, fish, and palm oil (Friedmann, 1993).

Food regime analysts studied and debated continuing hunger and farm crises, often in tandem with food, money, and energy crises. Social movements of farmers and indigenous peoples, such as La Via Campesina, challenged both industrial agriculture and the surplus exports of the food regime. Consumers and environmentalists soon joined them to oppose genetically modified crops and ultra-processed foods. Yet agribusiness power seemed impervious to change through the World Trade Organization (Friedmann and McMichael, 1989; Friedmann, 2005, 1993; McMichael, 2009). Surpluses maintained by the US (and eventually the EU) remained captive to farm lobbies, by now dominated by corporations, which deepened and widened control through patented seeds, consolidation of farmland ("land grabs"), and expansion of supermarkets into the Global South.

A third food regime?

Consolidating a third food regime has been a contentious – and generative – debate (Jakobsen, 2021). McMichael (2005, 2009) identified a "corporate food regime" within a new moment in the political history of capital. For McMichael and Weber (2021), the corporate food regime is part of the "globalisation project" in which states promote dominance by agrifood corporations. They see it as already opposed on many fronts, led by international coalitions of farmers and indigenous peoples, notably La Via Campesina. Friedmann (2005) doubted whether a corporate food regime had stabilised and instead suggested a "corporate-environmental food regime" defined by unresolved contests over farming systems and diets. Corporate restructuring and reframing in response to "green" issues led corporations to adapt critics' language (and selected practices) to deepen industrial agriculture and food. In 2023, agribusiness corporations appeared for the first time at both climate and biodiversity negotiations, where they promoted what they called "nature-based" solutions to the problems their industries had created. Critics described this as "greenwashing" and "smoke and mirrors" (IPES-Food, 2023). At the same time, a new capitalist sector appeared that offered commodities called "meat alternatives" to replace the environmentally destructive products of CAFOs and associated monocultures of maize and soy. While still small, novel technologies, such as cellular meat, are gaining regulatory approval and appeal to social movements promoting vegetarian and vegan diets. If edible commodities from corporate laboratories gain market share, they threaten to deepen diets of ultra-processed foods.

Other authors have suggested new emphases and new names. For example, Burch & Lawrence (2009) linked the rise of the retailing sector to the transformations of financial relations, suggesting a "financial food regime". As retail capitals increasingly dominate consumers, two authors have built on food regimes to propose a "neoliberal diet" (Pechlaner and Otero, 2010) and an "industrial diet" (Winson, 2013). In response to health problems created by ultra-processed and meat-intensive diets, "nutritionism" offers individual solutions to problems caused by the displacement of cultural cuisines (Srinis, 2013). Inter-state power, so central to the original definition of food regimes, now focuses on China's geopolitical and financial power and a coalition of important agrifood countries called BRICS – Brazil, Russia (especially Ukraine), India, China, and South Africa (Belesky and Lawrence, 2019; McMichael, 2019).

Key elements of food regimes

States and state systems

The rules governing relations among states and capitals are a key debate in food regimes literature. A generative difference is between McMichael's (2005, 2013) and Friedmann's (2005) respective emphasis on the power of corporations versus states. Both agree on most empirical realities of class, social movements, hegemony, and corporate organisation. Researchers using a food regime lens can use either focus. What unifies the historical and holistic approach. The starting point of food regimes was that the *system of states* shapes and governs states, including their relative power, by governing the geography of production and consumption of specific foods. Successive state systems are the framework within which agrifood corporations came to dominate food and farming.

Commodity frontiers

Commodity frontiers is a perspective that deepens and widens the food regime approach. Moore (2015) introduced the concept as part of a shift in world-systems literature from world-*economy* to world-*ecology*. Defined as processes and sites of incorporation of territories into the expanding capitalist world-ecology, commodity frontiers enlarge the historical perspective with two kinds of study. One, later called "food supply chains", entered early food regime analysis through the French concept of "agro-alimentaire" (Malassis, 1973). It refers to all activities from agricultural production to food consumption – including transportation, packaging, processing, and distribution – constituting the agrifood system. Second, food regimes were among the first fields to introduce "commodity complexes" into inter-disciplinary world-systems literature. Commodity systems are wider than food and convert more places into "frontiers". Sugar can be considered the first commodity frontier for food. Building on Mintz's pioneering (1985) *Sweetness and Power* (itself an early influence on Friedmann and McMichael), Beckert's *Empire of Cotton* (2014) joined increasingly influential food regime research on the livestock complex (Weis, 2013, Oliveira and Schneider 2016) to align food regimes with "global history" (Bosma and Vanhaute, 2023).

Transitions

A critical contribution of food regimes studies is the reminder that the ways of producing food in the past could have been different. Understanding key choice points in former transitions can sensitise us to choices that are possible now for the future of food. Past transitions show how old regimes unravel and new possibilities emerge. Analysing them can guide understanding how to shape new relations of food and farming, hunger or its absence, cuisines, and land use. One example is how some grassland regions, notably Ukraine and Punjab, colonised to produce wheat for the UK in the late 19th century, became marginal with the end of the food regime.

Future directions

Four challenges face food regime analysts: ecocide (also called "loss of biological diversity"); combining alternative ways of knowing (ancient wisdom and formal sciences); restructuring of agrifood capitals; and crisis of the state system.

Although ecocide may be older, five hundred years ago commodity frontiers dramatically reshaped landscapes, first through "ecological imperialism" in the imperial food regime (Crosby, 2013) and then through industrial standardisation of seeds, diets, and agriculture in the US-centred regime. But within cracks of the regimes, people have also reshaped landscapes from below with regenerative gardens and new cultural cuisines. Maize, which is now a staple crop and food in much of Africa, was brought from America as part of trade in enslaved humans. The rich agronomies and cuisines of the Caribbean and North America were made by peoples from many cultures who learned together to create new biocultural landscapes from transplanted and native plants. European, African, and Asian cuisines were changed by early

HARRIET FRIEDMANN AND NOELIA PARAJUÁ

transplants of native American chilli peppers, tomatoes, and potatoes. This legacy suggests that appropriate governance could support regenerative farming, cooking, and landscapes even in degraded natural conditions, as well as knowledge exchanges across places.

Different ways of knowing are led by farmer, environmental, and indigenous movements. At the same time, formal sciences themselves diverge. Industrial agronomy emerged with reductionist sciences that measure the productivity of single crops and the availability of specific nutrients. Chemical and later genetic technologies displaced ecological interconnections guided by farmers. Practical approaches such as agroecology and permaculture show how human foodgetting can recover its ancient role as a "matrix" for natural systems (Perfecto et al., 2009).

Restructuring of agrifood capitals, however, points to what may be a new alignment of capital and states. An emerging corporate sector linking genetic and information technologies aims to replace the livestock complex with new industrial commodities. "Meat alternatives" offer industrial substitutes to live animals (cellular meat and fish) and to all animals (rapidly reproducing bacteria that can be turned into imitations of anything). By contrast, older vegetarian diets (Lappe et al., 1977) promoted the plant-centred foodways of agrarian societies, which included (fewer) animals as integral to farming systems. Industrial commodities offering to displace meat include packaged vegan commodities listing ingredients that can come only from corporate laboratories. A transition from intensive livestock could either support food sovereignty or deepen industrial foods and corporate control.

Few doubt that the state system is changing. The crisis of US hegemony is increasingly evident in both monetary instability and military conflicts. The original holistic insight of "Agriculture and the state system" may guide explorations of what will emerge from the crisis of the particular "rule-based order" under US hegemony. Like the settler-colonial and mercantile-industrial food regimes, the future depends on new ways of governing cultures and landscapes. If a democratic food regime is to emerge, it is likely to be based on governing lands and cultures that are attuned to waterways, biomes, and intentional movements of people and plants.

References

Beckert, S. (2014). *Empire of Cotton: A Global History*. Alfred A. Knopf.

Belesky, P., and Lawrence, G. (2019). Chinese state capitalism and neomercantilism in the contemporary food regime: Contradictions, continuity and change. *Journal of Peasant Studies* 46(6), 1119–1141.

Bernstein, H. (2016). Agrarian political economy and modern world capitalism: the contributions of food regimesa analysis. *The Journal of Peasant Studies* 43(3), 611–647. https://doi.org/10.1080/03066150.2015.1101456

Bosma, U., and Vanhaute, E. (2023). Commodity Frontiers: Linking Global Capitalism and Local Resilience. In J. Curry-Machado, J. Stubbs, W.G. Clarence-Smith and J. Vos (Eds.), *The Oxford Handbook of Commodity History* (pp. 85–102). Oxford University Press. DOI: 10.1093/oxfordhb/9780197502679.013.5

Burch, D., and Lawrence, G. (2009). Towards a third food regime: Behind the transformation. *Agriculture and Human Values* 26, 267–279. https://doi.org/https://doi.org/10.1007/s10460-009-9219-4

Crosby, A. (2013). *Ecological Imperialism: The Biological Expansion of Europe, 900–1900*. Cambridge University Press.

Friedmann, H. (1992). Distance and durability: Shaky foundations of the world food economy. *Third World Quarterly* 13(2), 37–83.

Friedmann, H. (1993). International political economy of food: A global crisis. *New Left Review* 197, 29–57.

Friedmann, H. (2005). From Colonialism to Green Capitalism: Social Movements and Emergence of Food Regimes. In F.H. Buttel & P. McMichael (Eds.), *New Directions in the Sociology of Global Development* (Research in Rural Sociology and Development), Vol. 11 (pp. 227–264). Emerald Group Publishing Limited.

Friedmann, H., and McMichael, P.M. (1989). Agriculture and the state system: The rise and decline of national agriculture. *Sociologia Ruralis* 19, 93117.

IPES-Food (2023). *Smoke and Mirrors: Briefing for Biodiversity COP*. https://www.ipes-food.org/pages/smokeandmirrors.

Jakobsen, J. (2021). New food regime geographies: Scale, state, labor. *World*

Development 145, 105523. https://doi.org/10.1016/j.worlddev.2021.105523

Lappe, F.M., Collins, J., and Fowler, C. (1977). *Food First: Beyond the Myth of Scarcity.* Houghton Mifflin.

Malassis, L. (1973). *Economie agroalimentaire.* Cujas.

McMichael, P. (2005). Global development and the corporate food regime. In F.H. Buttel and P. McMichael (Eds.), *New Directions in the Sociology of Global Development* (pp. 265–299). Oxford University Press. https://doi.org/10.1016/S1057-1922(05)11010-5

McMichael, P. (2009). A food regime genealogy. *The Journal of Peasant Studies* 36(1), 139–169. https://doi.org/10.1080/03066150902820354

McMichael, P. (2013). *Food Regimes and Agrarian Questions.* Practical Action Publishing. https://doi.org/http://www.jstor.org/stable/j.ctt1hj553s

McMichael, P. (2019). Does China's 'going out' strategy prefigure a new food regime? *The Journal of Peasant Studies* 47(1), 116–154. https://doi.org/10.1080/03066150.2019.1693368

McMichael, P., and Weber, H. (2021). *Development and Social Change: A Global Perspective*, 7th Edition. Sage Publications.

Mintz, S.W. (1985). *Sweetness and Power: The Place of Sugar in Modern History.* Viking.

Moore, J.W. (2015). *Capitalism in the Web of Life: Ecology and the Accumulation of Capital.* Verso.

Offer, A. (1991). *The First World War: An Agrarian Interpretation.* Oxford University Press.

Oliveira, G.D.L.T., and Schneider, M. (2016). The politics of flexing soybeans: China, Brazil and global agroindustrial restructuring. *The Journal of Peasant Studies* 34(1), 167–194. http://dx.doi.org/10.1080/03066150.2014.993625

Pechlaner, G., and Otero, G. (2010). The neoliberal food regime: Neoregulation and the new division of labor in North America. *Rural Sociology* 75(2), 179–208. https://doi.org/10.1111/j.1549-0831.2009.00006.x

Perfecto, I., Vandermeer, J., and Wright, A. (2009). *Nature's Matrix: Linking Agriculture, Conservation and Food Sovereignty.* Earthscan.

Srinis, G. (2013). *Nutritionism: the science and politics of dietary advice.* Columbia University Press.

Weis, A. (2013). *The Ecological Hoofprint: The Global Burden of Industrial Livestock.* Zed.

Winders, B. (2009). The vanishing free market: The formation and spread of the British and US food regimes. *Journal of Agrarian Change* 9(3), 315–344. https://doi.org/10.1111/j.1471-0366.2009.00214.x

Winson, A. (2013). *The Industrial Diet: The Degradation of Food and the Struggle for Healthy Eating.* University of British Columbia Press.

Further reading

McMichael, P.M. (2017). *Development and Social Change: A Global Perspective*, 6th edition. Sage.

This book provides a broader perspective on the relationship between food regimes to historical "projects" of "development" and "globalisation".

HARRIET FRIEDMANN AND NOELIA PARAJUÁ

63. Foodscapes

Norah MacKendrick

Introduction and definitions

The term foodscape was coined by geographer Gisèle Yasmeen, who drew from Appadurai's articulation of "scapes" as describing five dimensions of global cultural flow (Appadurai, 1990; Yasmeen, 1995). In general terms, foodscapes are the places and social relations that influence what a person eats, how they get their food, and the meanings they attach to food and foodways. Every person is embedded in a foodscape. It is multidimensional; it is a constellation of material, relational, and symbolic entities that make food and meals accessible, like ecosystems, families, food charities, restaurants, convenience stores, supermarkets, schools, gardens and farms, global food processors, seed and chemical companies, and food television and social media channels. In short, a foodscape is more than a food environment. It is the cultural, social, and political relations that determine what, how, and whether we eat (MacKendrick, 2014).

In academic research and policymaking, a foodscape can serve as an analytic lens to examine the (i) spatial composition of food environments (e.g., a municipal food environment), (ii) symbolic representation and meaning of food and eating (e.g., food traditions and food media), (iii) behavioural aspects of food encounters (e.g., food choices and shopping habits), and (iv) networked structures that produce food systems (e.g., relations between producers, regulators, and consumers) (Vonthron et al., 2020).

Current issues

Contemporary research explores the extent to which foodscapes influence individual- and group-level diets and health. The relative proportion of fast-food outlets, corner stores, farmers' markets, and supermarkets in urban and rural areas is thought to have some influence on what people eat. In the United States, fast food franchises site their restaurants in low-income, Black and Hispanic communities to attract potential customers and secure a labour force for low-wage and part-time jobs (Kwate, 2023). The impact of foodscapes on health is not simple nor direct, yet research does suggest that neighbourhood-level access to wholesome and culturally appropriate foods has a positive influence on public health (Kusuma et al., 2022) and that the degree of access to such foods is largely structural (MacKendrick, 2014).

Cultural production and consumption have been front and centre in foodscape research (Johnston and Goodman, 2015). The symbolic meanings that make up the digital foodscape are tangible and consumable through documentary films, food celebrities, and virtual spaces offering rich visual representations of dishes and meals, including how-to videos and "hacks" for producing a perfect dish (Johnston and Goodman, 2015; Barnes, 2017; Goodman and Jaworska, 2020). Contemporary foodscapes now incorporate online and offline elements as digital food influencers guide whether and how individuals eat, cook at home, dine out, and experiment with new flavours and recipes (Goodman and Jaworska, 2020).

The relationship between gender and unpaid labour in foodscapes is another current issue. Within the private sphere of the home and family, women (and mothers especially) continue to do most of the foodwork and interact with foodscapes in ways that differ significantly from men. In general, women do more of the food planning, shopping, and advocating for better school food, and are more active in digital spaces that address family foodwork (Yasmeen, 1996; Cairns and Johnston, 2015). Men, in contrast, are associated with gourmet culture and professional foodwork, for example, as chefs and sommeliers (Johnston and Baumann, 2009).

Future concerns

Political, social, health, and economic disasters and conflicts that disrupt and recreate foodscapes are areas for future attention from researchers and policymakers. Conflict, economic collapse, the climate emergency, and global pandemics have all disrupted the global flows of food, imperilled food security, and changed how people relate to food and agriculture. The COVID-19 pandemic (2020–2023) and the war in Ukraine (from 2022), for instance, have endangered the utilisation, access, availability, and stability of food supplies around the world (Gebeyehu et al., 2022; World Food Programme, 2022). Extreme weather events, such as major storms and heat waves, along with drought, increases in rainfall, and rising sea levels in regions of the globe pose additional challenges to food supply chains, food security, and the safety of agricultural workers (Hasegawa et al., 2021). These dynamics will be critical to future research and policy making related to foodscapes.

References

Appadurai A (1990) Disjuncture and difference in the global cultural economy. *Theory, Culture & Society* 7, 295–310. https://doi .org/10.1177/026327690007002017.

Barnes C (2017) Mediating good food and moments of possibility with Jamie Oliver: Problematising celebrity chefs as talking labels. *Geoforum* 84, 169–178. https://doi .org/10.1016/j.geoforum.2014.09.004.

Cairns K and Johnston J (2015) *Food and Femininity*. Bloomsbury Publishing, London.

Gebeyehu D T, East L, Wark S and Islam M S (2022) Impact of COVID-19 on the food security and identifying the compromised food security dimension: A systematic review protocol. *PLOS ONE* 17, e0272859. https://doi.org/10.1371/journal.pone .0272859.

Goodman M K and Jaworska S (2020) Mapping digital foodscapes: Digital food influencers and the grammars of good food. *Geoforum* 117, 183–193. 10.1016/j. geoforum.2020.09.020.

Hasegawa T, Sakurai G, Fujimori S, Takahashi K, Hijioka Y and Masui T (2021) Extreme climate events increase risk of global food insecurity and adaptation needs. *Nature Food* 8, 587–595. https://doi.org/10.1038/ s43016-021-00335-4.

Johnston J and Baumann S (2009) *Foodies: Democracy and Distinction in the Gourmet Foodscape*. Routledge, New York.

Johnston J and Goodman M K (2015) Spectacular foodscapes. *Food, Culture & Society* 18, 205–222. https://doi.org/10 .2752/175174415X14180391604369.

Kusuma D, Atanasova P, Pineda E, Anjana R M, De Silva L, Am Hanif A, Hasan M, Hossain M M, Indrawansa S, Jayamanne D, Jha S, Kasturiratne A, Katulanda P, Khawaja K I, Kumarendran B, Mridha M K, Rajakaruna V … and Miraldo M (2022) Food environment and diabetes mellitus in South Asia: A geospatial analysis of health outcome data. *PLOS Medicine* 19, e1003970. https://doi.org/10.1371/journal .pmed.1003970.

Kwate N (2023) *White Burgers, Black Cash: Fast Food from Black Exclusion to Exploitation*. University of Minnesota Press, Minneapolis.

MacKendrick N (2014) Foodscape. *Contexts* 13, 16–18. https://doi.org/10.1177 /1536504214545754.

Vonthron S, Perrin C and Soulard C-T (2020) Foodscape: A scoping review and a research agenda for food security-related studies. *PLOS ONE* 15, e0233218. https:// doi.org/10.1371/journal.pone.0233218.

World Food Programme (2022) War in Ukraine drives global food crisis. https:// www.wfp.org/publications/war-ukraine -drives-global-food-crisis.

Yasmeen G (1995) Exploring a foodscape: The case of Bangkok. *Malaysian Journal of Tropical Geography*, 2, 1–11.

Yasmeen G (1996) "Plastic-bag housewives" and postmodern restaurants? Public and private in Bangkok's foodscape. *Urban Geography* 17, 526–544. https://doi.org/10 .2747/0272-3638.17.6.526.

Further reading

Kwate N (2023) *White Burgers, Black Cash: Fast Food from Black Exclusion to Exploitation*. University of Minnesota Press, Minneapolis.

This book examines the rise of fast food in the United States with attention to how an industry that originally marketed itself to suburban White, middle class communities came to target Black and low-income communities.

Vonthron S, Perrin C and Soulard C-T (2020) Foodscape: A scoping review and a research agenda for food security-related studies. *PLOS ONE* 15, e0233218. https:// doi.org/10.1371/journal.pone.0233218.

This provides an excellent overview of the origins of the concept of the "foodscape" that maps the literature applying the concept.

NORAH MACKENDRICK

64. Food security

JENNIFER CLAPP

Introduction

The problem of food insecurity has become markedly worse over the past decade. As of 2023, up to 757 million people around the world faced chronic undernourishment, while 2.33 billion people faced moderate or severe food insecurity (FAO et al. 2024). The rising number of hungry people brings us yet further away from meeting the United Nations' Sustainable Development Goal (SDG) 2 to end hunger. Although there are metrics to measure food insecurity, be it the number of people facing chronic undernourishment or other measures that capture the extent to which people are not able to obtain a sufficient diet to meet their nutritional needs, the concept of food security – that is, the conditions necessary to ensure people can secure a sufficient and healthy diet – is often less clear.

Several hundred definitions of food security have appeared in the literature over the past 50 years (Maxwell 1996). Today, the concept of food security typically incorporates "four pillars", namely: availability, access, utilisation, and stability (FAO 2006; Webb et al. 2006). More recently, two additional dimensions have been more often included as important elements of food security: agency and sustainability (Clapp et al. 2022). These different dimensions of the concept have been proposed and adopted at different historical moments and in response to real-world events and scholarly insights, which have deepened our understanding of food security in ways that are important for improving policies that support it.

Evolution of a four-pillar food security framework

Availability

The first formal use of the term food security in a policy context dates back to the 1974 World Food Conference, where it was defined as "[the] availability at all times of adequate world food supplies of basic foodstuffs to sustain a steady expansion of food consumption and to offset fluctuations in production and prices" (FAO 1974). This definition reflected the wider context at that time, including a world food crisis marked by high food prices, market turmoil, and a sharp increase in world hunger (Upton et al. 2016). The World Food Conference definition emphasised availability, and, in turn, governments sought to address rising food insecurity through increased food production, including in developing countries that were experiencing high rates of hunger at the time.

Access

By the 1980s, there was growing understanding in both scholarly and policy circles that availability alone did not provide a complete picture with respect to food security. Amartya Sen's *Poverty and Famines* (1981) brought increased attention to the fact that access to food mattered as much as availability by showing how famines had historically occurred in contexts where food was widely available. The Bengal famine in India in the mid-1940s, for example, took place at a time of high levels of food production. In this case, people went hungry because they were not able to access food despite its availability through markets. As Sen demonstrated, a person's entitlement to food depended on a number of elements, such as their access to productive land, their employment status, whether they owned assets that could be traded for food, and their broader rights within society. If a person's entitlement fails in any of these areas, for example, due to job loss, rising food prices, or the violation of human rights, it is likely to affect their access to food (Sen 1981).

Formal understandings of food security incorporated Sen's ideas in the 1980s. A 1982 report by the director general of the UN Food and Agriculture Organization (FAO) to the United Nations Committee on World Food Security (CFS) called for an updated conceptual approach to food security. This report acknowledged that the 1974 World Food Conference definition of food security was too narrow and called for the official understanding for policy purposes to be widened to include recognition of the importance of food access. This point was especially important at this time, given major changes in the world economy, including a global recession and rising developing country debt, both of which had important implications for the ability of the world's poorest people to access food on world markets (FAO 1982).

Stability

The FAO director general's 1982 report also warned that periods of economic instability could affect food systems and food prices in ways that could lead to increased levels of hunger. It expressed concern about the potential for speculation in agricultural commodity markets as well as currency instability (FAO 1982). The report further outlined the potential for large countries to engage in global grain markets in ways that could reduce the ability of the world's poorest countries to secure adequate food supplies. As such, it outlined the need to widen the conceptual understanding of food security by stressing three key dimensions: adequate food production to ensure food availability; the free flow of food through markets to ensure stability; and enabling the poorest countries and the poorest people to secure access to the food supplies they need.

Utilisation

The definition of food security was further widened in the 1990s with growing attention to the importance of food quality for ensuring an adequate diet. This focus incorporated attention to both the nutritional makeup of food and cultural food preferences (Maxwell 1996). A report published by the International Food Policy Research Institute (IFPRI) in 1995 was instrumental in promoting the idea of a dietary quality dimension of food security by highlighting three pillars of food security where women play crucial roles: availability, access, and nutritional security (Quisumbing et al. 1995). This report was significant in establishing that food quality often depends on the availability and access to nonfood resources such as healthcare, clean water, and sanitation. In other words, this wider context affects the capacity of the human body to take up nutrients in food. This fourth pillar of food security has more recently come to be referred to as "utilisation", referring to a person's ability to uptake food nutrients.

Four-pillar framework

The 1996 World Food Summit definition of food security, which was updated slightly in 2001 to add the word "social" to the definition, refers to all four pillars: "Food security exists when all people, at all times, have physical, social and economic access to sufficient, safe and nutritious food that meets their dietary needs and food preferences for an active and healthy life" (FAO 2001). The FAO's annual reports on the state of world hunger have made use of this four-pillar food security framework in recent decades, and the CFS also embraced this framework. The four pillars are also prominent in the Integrated Food Security Phase Classification (IPC) guidelines, as is outlined in its guidance documentation: "Food must be available; households must have access to it; they must utilize it appropriately; and the whole system must be stable" (IPC 2019).

Agency and sustainability: toward a six-dimensional food security framework

While the four-pillar food security framework became the dominant approach by the early 2000s, it was not without its critics. The rise of the food sovereignty movement in the 1990s drew attention to the fact that standard understandings of food security did not emphasise rights or consider the ecological impact of food systems (Wittman et al. 2010). The fact that food sovereignty advocates call for the rights of communities to determine the shape of their own food systems, as well as the importance of ecologically sound food production, prompted some critics to see food security and food sovereignty as oppositional ideas (Fairbairn 2010). Others, however, saw them as complementary rather than competing ideas (Jarosz 2014; Clapp 2014).

At the same time, it has become increasingly clear that the translation of the four-pillar framework into policies that support food security has not been sufficient to reduce world hunger. As noted at the outset, the number of people experiencing hunger rose sharply in the decade since 2014 as an increased frequency of climate events, the 2020 COVID-19 pandemic, and the Russian invasion of Ukraine in 2022 roiled food systems and international food markets, with consequences that led to rising food prices and reduced access to food. The reasons these events have had such profound impacts on food systems include growing inequalities and power differentials within food systems, and the tight linkage between food systems and ecological systems. A growing literature over the past decade on the need to understand food security within a broader "food systems" perspective (e.g. Ingram 2011) has brought these issues more clearly into view and has prompted some to call for a further widening of our understanding of food security to incorporate two additional dimensions: agency and sustainability (Clapp et al. 2022).

Agency

Agency refers to the capacity of individuals or groups to make their own decisions about their engagement with food systems and their ability to participate in processes that shape food system policies and governance (HLPE 2020). Agency is widely viewed as an important element to address inequalities in power differentials within society. This idea draws on other work by Sen that emphasises the need to take a capabilities approach to development, which includes a focus on people's rights and capabilities to determine their own well-being (Sen 1985). In short, agency is not just about the exercise of voice to make decisions, but also people's ability to exercise their rights to act upon them in their own capacity in order to improve their own situation.

The element of agency is important for food security, as those with greater capacity to shape food systems are more able to participate in those systems on their own terms to ensure they are free from hunger and can exercise their food preferences (Burchi and de Muro 2016). Structural inequities and power differentials within societies – whether they are based on differences in gender, race, literacy, or other factors that are beyond the control of individuals – can work to preclude the exercise of voice and participation both by individuals and within communities regarding food systems, often undermining food security (Chappell 2018). Thus, working to elevate individuals and communities to give them greater agency and voice within food systems helps overcome these barriers and supports active "food citizens" rather than passive food consumers (Fernandez-Wulff 2019; Vivero-Pol 2017).

A growing number of studies have confirmed a link between food security and agency by demonstrating that the enhancement of agency through improved access to land ownership and education, especially for women facing gender-based inequities, results in improved diet quality and childhood nutrition outcomes (e.g., Malapit and Quisumbing 2015; Bezner Kerr et al. 2011). In Ghana, for example, women's empowerment in the agricultural sector has been positively associated with greater nutrient availability (Tsiboe et al. 2018; e.g., Malapit and Quisumbing 2015). Similarly, in Malawi, households engaged in participatory agroecological research that included community education on gender equity resulted in significant improvements in food security and nutrition among smallholder households (Bezner Kerr et al. 2019). In Brazil, grassroots activism led to the establishment of national food security councils that enhanced the agency of participants to shape their food systems, resulting in creative initiatives such as the Food Secretariat in the city of Belo Horizonte, which established low-cost popular restaurants that made healthy food more accessible to marginalised urban populations while also supporting farmer livelihoods in the surrounding countryside (Chappell 2018).

Sustainability

Sustainability refers to food system practices that promote the long-term regeneration of natural, social, and economic systems in a way that does not compromise the food needs of future generations (HLPE 2020). Seeing sustainability as a dimension of food security emphasises the close connections between ecosystems, livelihoods, and nutrition, and the need to ensure that food systems can continue to support food security into the distant future (HLPE 2019). The concept of sustainability has gained wide attention especially since the 1980s and 1990s, especially with growing focus in the food studies literature on the concept of "food systems", which recognises the tight interlinkages between ecological systems and food systems in an era of climate change (Ingram 2011). This approach recognises the complex ways in which a variety of systems – ecological, health, economic, political, and sociocultural – interface with food systems in ways that affect the long-term well-being of both food systems and these other systems (Berry et al. 2015; Schipanski et al. 2016).

Growing attention to sustainability coincides with growing understanding of the ways in which the dominant, industrial food system is not ecologically sustainable. Many of the technological innovations that have sought to increase food production over the past century have exacerbated the situation (Willett et al. 2019). Monocultural production systems, for example, have led to a dramatic decline in agricultural biodiversity. The growing use of synthetic fertilisers has contributed to pollution from runoff as well as greenhouse gas emissions, while large-scale irrigation systems have contributed to a decline in water availability. The rise of intensive animal farming operations has also contributed to an enormous animal waste problem that has contributed to water contamination. Industrial farming systems also are major contributors to climate change, with the IPCC estimating that between 21% and 37% of greenhouse gas emissions are associated with food systems from farm to plate (IPCC 2020).

A growing number of studies show that climate change exacerbates malnutrition by affecting food production and diversity, constraining women's time for child feeding and care, and altering environmental conditions that affect nutrient intake (e.g., Smith and Myers 2018; Fanzo et al. 2018). At the same time, other studies show that more diversified and sustainable farming practices, such as agroecology, especially when combined with initiatives to address inequities, enhance diversity of diets and contribute to more diverse food production that supports better nutritional and food security outcomes (Bezner Kerr et al. 2021). Similarly, studies have shown that there are multiple points along agrifood supply chains where environmental impacts can be reduced, suggesting that healthy diets can be made more sustainable by reducing levels of food processing, supporting more localised markets, and shifting diets to include more plant-based foods (e.g. Willett et al. 2019).

A six-dimensional approach: debates and uptake

The inclusion of agency and sustainability along with the earlier four pillars of food security suggests the need for a six-dimensional food security framework. Thinking about food security as having multiple interacting dimensions also highlights the complex ways in which each of the elements of food security interacts with the others, which better reflects reality compared with standalone pillars (Clapp et al. 2022). The FAO *State of Food Security and Nutrition in the World* report referred to the six dimensions of food security in its analysis in recent years, demonstrating that the utility of this framework is useful for understanding the persistence of food insecurity in the world today.

Although a growing number of scholars and international organisations are adopting the six-dimensional food security framework, the UN's CFS has not yet adopted agency and sustainability as part of its understanding of food security to shape international food policies. This is likely a reflection of political dynamics within that body, rather than a rejection of the need to improve the sustainability of food systems or address inequities and uphold human rights. Indeed, all six dimensions of food security are already incorporated into the UN Voluntary Guidelines on the Right to Adequate Food (also known as the Right to Food Guidelines), which were unanimously agreed by all FAO member states as early as 2004 (FAO 2005).

Worsening hunger trends since 2017 are a stark signal that the status quo in terms of food security policy – focused on the four traditional pillars of the concept – is insufficient to address the current challenges. In a context of rising inequalities and the ecological and climate emergencies that have a direct bearing on people's capacity to acquire an adequate diet, the relevance of agency and sustainability to meeting food security goals is becoming increasingly obvious and they are likely to gain further attention, including in policy contexts at all scales, in the coming years. The importance of these dimensions has long been underscored by social and environmental movements on the ground, such as the food sovereignty movement and the agroecology movement, and is reflective of a rising awareness of the need to address these issues within a broader food systems approach. Going forward, it will be important to incorporate elements of agency and sustainability into food security research agendas, documenting initiatives on the ground that seek to address inequalities and unsustainable practices within food systems and assessing the lessons for policy.

References

Berry, E M, Dernini, S, Burlingame, B, Meybeck, A and Conforti, P (2015) Food security and sustainability: can one exist without the other? *Public Health Nutrition* 18, 2293–2302. https://doi.org/10.1017/S136898001500021X.

Bezner Kerr, R, Berti, P and Shumba, L (2011) Effects of a participatory agriculture and nutrition education project on child growth in Northern Malawi. *Public Health Nutrition* 1466–1472. https://doi.org/10.1017/S1368980010002545.

Bezner Kerr, R, Kangmennaang, J, Dakishoni, L, Nyantakyi-Frimpong, H, Lupafya, E, Shumba, L, Msachi, R, Boateng, G O, Snapp, S S, Chitaya, A, Maona, E, Gondwe, T, Nkhonjera, P and Luginaah, I (2019) Participatory agroecological research on climate change adaptation improves smallholder farmer household food security and dietary diversity in Malawi. *Agriculture, Ecosystems & Environment* 279, 109–121.

Bezner Kerr, R, Madsen, S, Stüber, M, Liebert, J, Enloe, S, Borghino, N, Parros, P, Mutyambai, D M, Prudhon, M and Wezel, A (2021) Can agroecology improve food security and nutrition? A review. *Global Food Security* 29, 100540.

Burchi, F and De Muro, P (2016) From food availability to nutritional capabilities: advancing food security analysis. *Food Policy* 60, 10–19. https://doi.org/10.1016/j.foodpol.2015.03.008.

Chappell, M J (2018) *Beginning to End Hunger: Food and the Environment in Belo Horizonte, Brazil, and Beyond.* Oakland, University of California Press.

Clapp, J (2014) Food security and food sovereignty: getting past the binary. *Dialogues in Human Geography* 4, 206–211. https://doi.org/10.1177/2043820614537159.

Clapp, J, Moseley, W, Burlingame, B and Termine, P (2022) The case for a six-dimensional food security framework. *Food Policy* 106, 102164. https://doi.org/10.1016/j.foodpol.2021.102164.

Fairbairn, M (2010) Framing resistance: international food regimes and the roots of food sovereignty. In: Wittman, H, Desmarais, A A and Wiebe, N (eds) *Food Sovereignty: Reconnecting Food, Nature and Community.* Halifax, Fernwood Publishing, pp. 15–32.

Fanzo, J, Davis, C, McLaren, R and Choufani, J (2018) The effect of climate change across food systems: implications for nutrition outcomes. *Global Food Security* 18, 12–19. https://doi.org/10.1016/j.gfs.2018.06.001.

FAO (1974) *World Food and Agriculture Situation.* Rome, FAO. http://www.fao.org/3/F5340E/F5340E03.htm#ref13.

FAO (1982) *World Food Security: A Reappraisal of the Concepts and Approaches.* Director General's Report. Rome, FAO.

FAO (2001) *The State of Food Insecurity in the World 2001.* Rome, FAO. http://www.fao.org/docrep/003/y1500e/y1500e00.htm.

FAO (2005) *Voluntary Guidelines to Support the Progressive Realization of the Right to Adequate Food in the Context of National Food Security.* Rome, FAO. http://www.fao.org/3/y7937e/Y7937E00.htm#TOC.

FAO (2006) *Food Security.* Policy Brief Issue 2. Rome, FAO. http://www.fao.org/forestry/13128–0e6f36f27e0091055bec28ebe830f46b3.pdf.

FAO, IFAD, UNICEF, WFP and WHO (2024) *The State of Food Security and Nutrition in the World 2024* Rome, FAO. https://doi.org/10.4060/cd1254en.

Fernandez-Wulff, P (2019) Collective agency in the making: how social innovations in the food system practice democracy beyond consumption. *Politics and Governance* 7, 81–93. https://doi.org/10.17645/pag.v7i4.2111.

HLPE (2019) *Agroecological and Other Innovative Approaches for Sustainable Agriculture and Food Systems that Enhance Food Security and Nutrition.* http://www.fao.org/3/ca5602en/ca5602en.pdf.

HLPE (2020) *Food Security and Nutrition: Building a Global Narrative Towards 2030.* http://www.fao.org/3/ca9731en/ca9731en.pdf.

Ingram, J (2011) A food systems approach to researching food security and its interactions with global environmental change. *Food Security* 3, 417–431. https://doi.org/10.1007/s12571-011-0149-9.

Intergovernmental Panel on Climate Change (IPCC) (2020) Summary for Policymakers. In: Shukla, P R, Skea, J, Calvo Buendia, E, Masson-Delmotte, V, Pörtner, H-O, Zhai, P, Roberts, D, Slade, R, Ferrat, M, Neogi, S, Pereira, J P, Kissick, K, Connors, S, Haughey, E, Pathak, M, Vyas, P, Belkacemi, M, van Diemen, R, Luz, S, Petzold, J, Huntley, E and Malley, J (eds) *Climate Change and Land: An IPCC Special Report on Climate Change, Desertification, Land Degradation,*

Sustainable Land Management, Food Security, and Greenhouse Gas Fluxes in Terrestrial Ecosystems. https://www.ipcc .ch/site/assets/uploads/sites/4/2020/02/ SPM_Updated-Jan20.pdf.

IPC (2019) *Integrated Food Security Phase Classification: Technical Manual Version 3.0.* http://www.ipcinfo.org/fileadmin/user _upload/ipcinfo/manual/IPC_Technical _Manual_3_Final.pdf.

Jarosz, L (2014) Comparing food security and food sovereignty discourses. *Dialogues in Human Geography* 4, 168–181. https://doi .org/10.1177/2043820614537161.

Malapit, H and Quisumbing, A (2015) What dimensions of women's empowerment in agriculture matter for nutrition in Ghana? *Food Policy* 52, 54–63. https://doi.org/10 .1016/j.foodpol.2015.02.003.

Maxwell, S (1996) Food security: a postmodern perspective. *Food Policy* 21, 155–170. https://doi.org/10.1016/0306 -9192(95)00074-7.

Quisumbing, A, Brown, L, Feldstein, H, Haddad, L and Peña, C (1995) *Women: The Key to Food Security.* IFPRI Food Policy Report. https://www.ifpri.org/publication/ women-key-food-security.

Schipanski, M, MacDonald, G, Rosenzweig, S, Chappell, M J, Bennett, E, Bezner, Kerr, R, Blesh, J, Crews, T, Drinkwater, L, Lundgren, J G and Schnarr, C (2016) Realizing resilient food systems. *BioScience* 66, 600–610. https://doi.org/10 .1093/biosci/biw052.

Sen, A (1981) *Poverty and Famines: An Essay on Entitlement and Deprivation.* Oxford, Oxford University Press.

Sen, A (1985) Well-being, agency and freedom: The Dewey lectures 1984. *The Journal of Philosophy* 82, 169–221. https:// doi:10.2307/2026184.

Smith, M R and Myers, S S (2018) Impact of anthropogenic CO2 emissions on global human nutrition. *Nature Climate Change* 8, 834–839. https://doi.org/10.1038/s41558 -018-0253-3.

Tsiboe, F, Zereyesus, Y A, Popp, J S and Osei, E (2018) The effect of women's empowerment in agriculture on household nutrition and food poverty in northern Ghana." *Social Indicators Research* 138:

89–108. https://doi.org/10.1007/s11205-017 -1659-4

Upton, J, Denno Cissé, J and Barrett, C B (2016) Food security as resilience: reconciling definition and measurement. *Agricultural Economics* 47, 135–147. https://doi.org/10.1111/agec.12305.

Vivero-Pol, J L (2017) Food as commons or commodity? Exploring the links between normative valuations and agency in food transition. *Sustainability* 9, 442. https://doi .org/10.3390/su9030442.

Webb, P, Coates, J, Frongillo, E, Lorge, Rogers, B, Swindale, A and Bilinsky, P (2006) Measuring household food insecurity: why it's so important and yet so difficult to do. *The Journal of Nutrition* 136, 1404S–1408S. https://doi.org/10.1093/ jn/136.5.1404S.

Willett, W, Rockström, J, Loken B, Springmann M, Lang T, Vermeulen S, ... & Murray C J (2019) Food in the Anthropocene: the EAT–Lancet Commission on healthy diets from sustainable food systems. *The Lancet* 393, 447–492.

Wittman, H, Desmarais, A and Wiebe, N (2010) The origins and potential of food sovereignty. In: Wittman H, Desmarais A and Weibe N (eds) *Food Sovereignty: Reconnecting Food, Nature and Community.* Halifax, Fernwood Publishing, pp. 1–14.

Further reading

Burchi, F and De Muro, P (2016) From food availability to nutritional capabilities: advancing food security analysis. *Food Policy* 60, 10–19. https://doi.org/10.1016/j .foodpol.2015.03.008.

This article reviews different approaches to conceptualizing food security, including consideration of a capabilities approach.

Clapp, J, Moseley, W, Burlingame, B and Termine, P (2022) The case for a six-dimensional food security framework. *Food Policy* 106, 102164. https://doi.org/10 .1016/j.foodpol.2021.102164.

This article provides a history of the concept of food security, including the evolution of the traditional four pillars, and makes the case for the addition of agency and sustainability as dimensions of the concept.

JENNIFER CLAPP

65. Food sharing

Anna Davies

Introduction: food sharing

The sharing of food is a foundational element of human civilisation identified in historical hunter-gatherer societies and still visible today. It is a fundamental form of co-operation with multiple motivations from securing sustenance and allowing for labour specialisation to cementing a range of social relations. Contemporary scholarship has commonly set out sharing as a counterpoint to commercial capitalist forms of food production, acquisition, consumption and disposal. However, the cultural diversity and evolutionary dynamism of such practices across time and space means the boundaries of what constitutes 'sharing' are contested and highly differentiated, particularly following the emergence of commercial platform-based 'sharing economies'. As a result, expansive definitions have emerged where food sharing is seen as:

> *having* a portion [of food] *with* another or others; *giving* a portion [of food] *to* others; *using, occupying or enjoying* food [and food related spaces to include the growing, cooking and/or eating of food] *jointly*; possessing an *interest* in food *in common*; or *telling* someone *about* food. (Davies, 2019: 6)

This definition covers not only familiar acts of routine and celebratory meal sharing with friends and family, but also the sharing of seeds, unprocessed and processed foodstuff, utensils, surplus food and compost. It also incorporates the sharing of spaces for growing food (such as community gardens), food preparation (co-working kitchens), collective eating (community kitchens), and the sharing of knowledge and experiences around food across the food system. There are various mechanisms through which food and food-related activities can be shared. Termed modes of sharing, these include gifting (giving for free), bartering (trading for other products or services), collecting (such as foraging wild food and gleaning), and selling (for profit and otherwise).

Despite the definitional complexity surrounding what counts as food sharing, attention to its role and contribution (current and potential) has been amplified in the 21st century as concerns increase about the limitations of the mainstream food system to achieve a sustainable food system for all.

Current issues in food sharing

The evolution of food sharing has been shaped by changes in political economies, technological developments and shifting socio-cultural norms, as well as through increasing concerns about food systems' impacts on people and the environment. There are then diverse geographies to food sharing practices in different places; for example, there are differences between Eastern and Western Europe. As a result, issues within contemporary food sharing scholarship and practice are manifold, but at a high level revolve around the need for a more complete picture of the location, nature and scope of contemporary food sharing internationally; the impacts of food sharing and its contributions towards the achievement of sustainability; the ways in which contemporary governing structures shape food sharing practice; and how to evolve food governance and engagement with food sharing to optimise sustainability potential in the future.

Geography

Mapping the location, nature and scope of food sharing is a fundamental requirement for building greater understanding. However, this is no easy task given the diversity of sites where food sharing takes place, the blurred boundaries of what constitutes sharing and the multifaceted nature of food sharing practices themselves. As a result, research has tended to focus on one element of food sharing. For example, longstanding social research has identified trends indicating an overall decline in meal sharing within many Western societies linked to changing economic practices, gendered roles and familial structures, increased privatisation and greater disposable income (Jones, 2008). Meanwhile, research examining contemporary platform-mediated food sharing economies has emerged with international comparative mapping of urban food-sharing initiatives that use some form of information and communication technologies (ICT) to mediate their sharing (Davies, 2019). Usefully, the ICT component leaves a digital trace that can be collated and compared across locations. Elements of less visible food sharing still fly beneath the radar of public and private institutions and citizens who are not aware of activities or how they might participate in them.

Sustainability

It is often presumed that food sharing will be positive for people and the planet. While international research examining the stated goals of food sharing initiatives has confirmed that in non-commercial settings social, economic and environmental sustainability are common features of mission statements, it has also uncovered a lack of evaluation and assessment of the impacts that such initiatives create. As such, sustainability impacts of food sharing tend to be sought rather than evidenced. There are a number of reasons for this, not least the challenges of identifying, collating and analysing impacts when these may be hard to quantify. This is particularly the case in the sphere of social impacts from food sharing where mental health and well-being benefits of co-operative activities in mitigating loneliness, for instance, are often flagged as central. Nonetheless, efforts are being made to co-design appropriate metrics and mechanisms for improved sustainability impact assessment (Mackenzie and Davies, 2022).

Governance

Food sharing initiatives and activities are currently governed externally by general food system regulatory mechanisms, as well as by socio-cultural rules around when and where it is acceptable to share food. In the formal governing space, there are few policies, regulations or rules which apply only to food sharing initiatives. Instead they are treated as mainstream food businesses (where food is treated solely as a commodity) even if they are not-for-profit activities with public goals. This means food sharing initiatives have the same obligations as their commercial counterparts irrespective of their organisational structure and the size, scale and purpose of food sharing. Regulation around food donations from retailers, a growing arena for the sharing of surplus food, is emerging in certain European locations supported by guidelines from the European Commission. However, the regulatory attention is predominantly focused on reducing the liability of commercial donors in order to divert food waste from landfill. In other sectors of food sharing, such as collective growing, international research shows that activities are often accommodated in temporarily vacant spaces which means they rarely have security of tenure (Davies et al., 2019). The specific social, economic and environmental impacts created by food sharing, for individuals, communities and the wider environment, are largely undocumented and therefore remain invisible to, and undervalued by, those with the power to make land use decisions. Perhaps most significantly, the practices of food sharing often transcend the existing landscape of government departments at national and local levels, which means they have to navigate complex and fragmented policy architecture with no single department or officer to champion their causes.

Future issues for food sharing

There is clear need for more research exploring diverse food sharing activities and their potential role in a reconfigured and more sustainable food system. This requires a deeper, longitudinal understanding of engagement with food sharing internationally. The empirical research conducted to date needs to be expanded to explore implementation deficits between goals and impacts and to understand the barriers to participation and investment in sustainable food sharing. Innovative sustainability impact assessment mechanisms need to be developed and disseminated, with results communicated to food sharing initiatives, participants, funders and regulators. Finally, research needs to move beyond urban centres, where much recent work has focused, to include peri-urban and rural contexts and ensure sustainable food sharing is visible, optimal and valued across the food system.

References

Davies A R (2019) *Urban Food Sharing*. Policy Press, Bristol.

Davies A R, Cretella A and Franck V (2019) Food sharing initiatives and food democracy: Practice and policy in three European cities. *Politics and Governance* 7(4), 8–20. https://doi.org/10.17645/pag.v7i4.2090.

Jones M (2008) *Feast: Why Humans Share Food*. Oxford University Press, Oxford.

Mackenzie S and Davies A R (2022) Assessing the sustainability impacts of food sharing initiatives: User testing The Toolshed SIA.

Frontiers in Sustainable Food Systems 6. https://doi.org/10.3389/fsufs.2022.807690.

Further reading

Davies A R (2019) *Urban Food Sharing.* Policy Press, Bristol.
Explores the history, current practice and impacts of urban food sharing using international case studies to set out an agenda for research and action.
Jones M (2008) *Feast: Why Humans Share Food*. Oxford University Press, Oxford.
Documents how humans came to share food and traces the ways in which the human meal has shaped cultural evolution.

66. Food sovereignty

MATTHEW CANFIELD

Introduction

Food sovereignty is a claim for democratising and decentralising food systems. The claim was first articulated in the 1990s by La Vía Campesina (LVC), the International Peasant Movement, to oppose the liberalisation of agricultural trade. Since then, food sovereignty has been adopted as a collective action frame for rural and urban movements across the Global South and North. Over the past twenty-five years, movements mobilising food sovereignty have converged through regional and global platforms to elaborate a robust vision of food systems transformation centred on challenging neoliberal trade and agricultural policies, promoting rural livelihoods and food security, and mitigating climate change through agroecological food production.

Food sovereignty overlaps with many of the goals and values of other frameworks developed to re-order food production and provisioning such as the right to food, food security, and food justice (Anderson and Bellows, 2012; Noll and Murdock, 2020). However, what makes it distinct is its holistic approach to socio-ecological and economic transformation rooted in the autonomy of small-scale food producers and workers. Food sovereignty movements insist on reorienting food systems through the knowledges and voices of their constituents and refuse to delegate their representation to scientists, NGOs, or lawyers. Moreover, in contrast to liberal legal claims that privilege Western scientific knowledge and the nation-state as the primary site for social justice claims, food sovereignty is a claim mobilised within and beyond states to democratise epistemic, economic, and political control over food systems.

Food sovereignty does not offer a single vision for food systems. Given the wide range of constituencies that now claim food sovereignty—including peasants and family farmers, fisherfolk, food chain workers, indigenous peoples, and urban poor people across many different geographical and agroecological contexts—the organisation and boundaries of food sovereignty claims are often overlapping and contested (Schiavoni, 2017). Food sovereignty is thus best understood as a set of material and communicative practices of translation (Brent et al., 2015; Canfield, 2022) through which food sovereignty activists seek to politicise, decommodify and decolonise food systems based on shared principles and values (Trauger, 2017; Figueroa-Helland et al., 2018).

This entry reviews the history of food sovereignty and its development over the past twenty-five years. It describes three "waves" of food sovereignty mobilisation, in which movements have articulated the meaning of food sovereignty in relation to shifting political-economic conditions that have been crystallised through specific events. These include: the liberalisation of food and agricultural markets through the World Trade Organization, the 2007–8 global food crisis, and the 2021 UN Food Systems Summit. The final wave has precipitated a resurgence of global food sovereignty mobilisation in which movements are now re-articulating food sovereignty in relation to converging forces of climate chaos, rising illiberalism, and techno-utopianism. As they do so, food sovereignty continues to offer a powerful vision for more democratic and just food systems.

The origins of food sovereignty

The claim of food sovereignty was first articulated in the context of what agrarian scholars often refer to as the "corporate" food regime—a global food order characterised by trade liberalisation, privatisation, and reduced state support for the rural sector (McMichael, 2013). In the 1980s and 90s, transnational activist networks began challenging the hegemonic global actors promoting these policies, instead demanding a global order that adhered to human rights. In the 1980s, Latin American peasant movements were among the many activists forming transnational networks to challenge structural adjustment policies and trade liberalisation. These networks laid the foundation for what would become LVC (Martinez-Torres and Rosset, 2010).

LVC was officially established in 1993 at a meeting attended by movements composed of peasant, small-scale, and family farmers from around the world. They proclaimed their unity around three values: (1) the rights of small-scale farmers to maintain their livelihoods, (2) the right to diversified agriculture and quality food, and (3) the right of countries to define their own agricultural policies (Desmarais, 2007). However, it was not until their second global conference in Tlaxcala, Mexico, that LVC began using the term food sovereignty. The language of food sovereignty then gained prominence later that year at the 1996 World Food Summit.

Since then, many additional movements and constituencies have adopted the claim of food sovereignty—from fisherfolk to food chain workers. Scholars now refer to this as the global food sovereignty movement (Claeys and Peschard, 2020). Although this movement has been growing consistently since the 1990s, three major events—the liberalisation of food and agricultural systems through the World Trade Organization, the global food and financial crisis of 2007–8, and the 2021 UN Food Systems Summit—have catalysed what social movement theorists call "waves of contention" (Koopmans, 2004) of deepening food sovereignty articulation and movement growth. Analysing these waves offers a heuristic to understand the evolution of food sovereignty in relation to changing political and economic conditions.

The three waves of food sovereignty

During its first wave, food sovereignty brought together diverse movements around the shared understanding that "food is different"—that it cannot be treated as a commodity like other goods and services that were liberalised in the 1990s (Rosset, 2006). Movements sought to reframe food as a material and symbolic substance through which small-scale food producers, indigenous peoples, and other rural peoples reproduce not only their livelihoods, but also their cultural and spiritual worlds. Food sovereignty movements also sought to distinguish themselves from international NGOs, by establishing new structures of leadership and platforms to organise peasant movements and facilitate their direct representation and voice in international policy (Claeys, 2015). During this period, food sovereignty movements targeted the UN Food and Agriculture Organization (FAO) as a key institution through which to institutionalise their values. In 2002, movements formed the International Planning Committee for Food Sovereignty (IPC) to facilitate interaction between movements and organisations as well as with international institutions, particularly the FAO.

The IPC has since become a hub for food sovereignty movements to further refine the meaning and practice of food sovereignty. In 2007, the IPC organised the Nyéléni Forum held in Mali, which brought together over 500 organisations to assert their unity. The definition developed at the 2007 Forum is still the most widely circulated definition of food sovereignty. According to the Nyéléni Declaration, "Food sovereignty is the right of peoples to healthy and culturally appropriate food produced through ecologically sound and sustainable methods, and their right to define their own food and agriculture systems". As part of this definition, movements articulated six pillars of food sovereignty. Food sovereignty: (1) focuses on food for people; (2) values food providers; (3) localises food systems; (4) puts control locally; (5) builds knowledge and skills; and (6) works with nature (Nyéléni, 2007).

The second wave of food sovereignty activism emerged in 2007–8, when a global food crisis significantly increased the number of those facing food insecurity. Food sovereignty platforms and alliances expanded into a number of global regions across the Global North and South. As food sovereignty movements proliferated, they reckoned with several tensions over the *who*, the *where*, and the *how* of food sovereignty that were identified by critical scholars (for discussion of these debates see Edelman (2014) and Claeys et al. (2021)). Although these tensions continue to animate debates over food sovereignty, movement leaders have pointed to their productive role in shaping emancipatory visions. Scholars now understand food sovereignty to be a relational practice, in which negotiating necessarily overlapping and conflicting claims to food sovereignty serves as a prefigurative process through which activists are actively envisioning and building alternative forms of food system governance (Iles and de Wit, 2015).

During the second "wave" of food sovereignty activism, food sovereignty movements accrued greater legitimacy within international spaces. In 2009, the UN Committee on World Food Security (CFS) was reformed to be an inclusive multilateral arena in which food sovereignty activists established an autonomous mechanism to facilitate their participation—the Civil Society and Indigenous Peoples' Mechanism (CSIPM). The CSIPM serves as a key hub through which food sovereignty movements have developed policy positions on specific issues such as land tenure, responsible investment, food waste, and nutrition (among many others) and negotiated global policy recommendations and guidelines on these topics with Member States of the FAO (Brem-Wilson, 2015). In response to movement demands, the FAO also began to increasingly invest in agroecology through two International Symposiums on Agroecology in 2014 and 2018. This raised new debates over the institutionalisation of agroecology (Giraldo and Rosset, 2018). Finally, in 2018, after years of consistent advocacy by social movements, the United Nations General Assembly voted for the UN Declaration of the Rights of Peasants and Other People Working in Rural Areas (UNDROP). More research is now needed into the implementation and mobilisation of UNDROP on national and local levels.

A third "wave" of food sovereignty activism swelled in response to a combination of political-economic and ecological forces. The 2020 COVID-19 pandemic combined with the Russian invasion of Ukraine in 2022, and the deepening effects of climate change, sparked a third food crisis, highlighting the underlying contradictions of industrial food systems (Clapp and Moseley, 2020).

Current issues

Food sovereignty movements face a different world than the one they faced when food sovereignty was first articulated. Today, there is widespread consensus that current food systems are failing. Food insecurity and malnutrition are increasing, and food systems are a significant contributor to global greenhouse gas emissions. In 2021, the UN Secretary General organised a global Food Systems Summit to address these challenges. But food sovereignty movements ended up boycotting the summit for several reasons: its leadership included figures from philanthropic and corporate networks, it adopted a multi-stakeholder structure that sidelined human rights, and it promoted technologically driven solutions that benefitted corporations (Canfield et al., 2021). These movements strengthened their solidarity in challenging the summit. But they also recognised new challenges stemming from changing socio-ecological and political-economic conditions. These challenges are leading movements to refine the meaning once again in response to two major global forces—climate change and changing forms of neoliberalism.

First, food systems are now at the centre of debates over how to both adapt and mitigate climate change. Food systems contribute about one-third of the world's greenhouse gas, most of which stems from industrial crop and livestock production (IPCC, 2019). Food sovereignty activists have long suggested that agroecology offers a key solution to climate change. But the solutions that are being advanced by hegemonic actors primarily support corporate and agribusiness investors, rather than enabling de-fossilisation and the adaptivity of small-scale food producers and workers who themselves often face food insecurity (Center for International Environmental Law, 2022). Rather than promoting agroecology, hegemonic actors have called for "climate-smart agriculture". Many of the practices endorsed as climate-smart—such as precision farming and biotechnology—are in direct contradiction to agroecology's commitment to local and indigenous knowledge and serve to further reinforce corporate power (Montenegro de Wit, 2022; Prause et al., 2020). Therefore, food sovereignty movements are struggling to distinguish agroecology from climate-smart agriculture, and continue to demand that agroecological approaches be at the centre of climate change policy (AFSA, 2022).

Second, global geopolitical shifts and political realignments are transforming the global normative order in which food sovereignty was originally articulated. Today, scholars describe a set of political realignments that have brought together nationalist parties with neoliberals in what is now described as "neo-illiberalism" (Hendrikse, 2021). Some of these governments have even adopted the language of food sovereignty as part of their nationalist platform. For food sovereignty movements this raises significant challenges. First, food sovereignty movements must both articulate themselves in opposition to these politics and challenge their appeal to rural constituents (Scoones et al., 2018). Second, as geopolitical tensions grow and states withdraw from engaging in multi-lateral negotiations, they are promoting "multi-stakeholder processes" that tend to be dominated by the corporate sector (Manahan and Kumar, 2021). As "multi-stakeholderism" proliferates at global and national levels, movements are left with strategic questions over how to engage in these spaces. Thus, in this era when new geographies of power are once again transforming formations of state sovereignty, food sovereignty movement are reconsidering how to mobilise their visions of justice.

Food sovereignty is a justice claim that is evolving in relation to the mutations of neo-liberal governance. It combines claims for the recognition of rural peoples, the redistribution of resources to support them, and representation in policymaking. The greatest strength of the global food sovereignty movement is its diversity, which has led it to develop prefigurative social practices to maintain solidarity across competing constituencies and uneven relations of global power. Since food sovereignty was articulated by LVC twenty-five years ago, movements have won important victories including the reform of the CFS and UNDROP. Today, however, the convergence of climate change and neo-illiberalism is raising significant new challenges. As food sovereignty movements reposition themselves in relation to these forces, they continue to offer a democratic antidote to neoliberal capitalism.

References

Alliance for Food Sovereignty in Africa, 2022. Africa's climate emergency: a call for adaptation and resilience through agroecology to COP27 and beyond. Available at: https://afsafrica.org/communique-a-call-for-climate-adaptation-and-resilience-through-agroecology/ (Accessed 23 October 2023).

Anderson, M.D., Bellows, A.C., 2012. Introduction to symposium on food sovereignty: expanding the analysis and application. *Agriculture and Human Values* 29, 177–184. https://doi.org/10.1007/s10460-012-9369-7.

Brem-Wilson, J., 2015. Towards food sovereignty: interrogating peasant voice in the United Nations Committee on World Food Security. *The Journal of Peasant Studies* 42, 73–95. https://doi.org/10.1080/03066150.2014.968143.

Brent, Z.W., Schiavoni, C.M., Alonso-Fradejas, A., 2015. Contextualising food sovereignty: the politics of convergence among movements in the USA. *Third World Quarterly* 36, 618–635. https://doi.org/10.1080/01436597.2015.1023570.

Canfield, M.C., 2022. *Translating Food Sovereignty: Cultivating Justice in an Age of Transnational Governance.* Stanford University Press, Stanford, CA.

Canfield, M.C., Anderson, M.D., McMichael, P., 2021. UN Food Systems Summit 2021: dismantling democracy and resetting corporate control of food systems. *Frontiers in Sustainable Food Systems* 5. https://doi.org/10.3389/fsufs.2021.661552.

Center for International Environmental Law, 2022. *Fossils, Fertilizers, and False Solutions: How Laundering Fossil Fuels in Agrochemicals Puts the Climate and the Planet at Risk.* Center for International Environmental Law, Washington, D.C.

Claeys, P., 2015. *Human Rights and the Food Sovereignty Movement: Reclaiming Control.* Routledge, New York.

Claeys, P., Desmarais, A.A., Singh, J., 2021. Food sovereignty, food security and the right to food. In A. Haroon Akram-Lodhi, K. Dietz, B. Engels and B. McKay (Eds.), *Handbook of Critical Agrarian Studies* (pp. 238–249). Edward Elgar Publishing, Cheltenham, UK and Northampton, MA, USA.

Claeys, P., Peschard, P., 2022. Transnational agrarian movements, food sovereignty, and legal mobilization. In F. Marie-Claire Foblets, M. Goodale, M. Sapignoli and O. Zenker (Eds.), *The Oxford Handbook of Law and Anthropology.* Oxford University Press, Oxford. (online ed., Oxford Academic, 8 Oct. 2020). https://doi.org/10.1093/oxfordhb/9780198840534.013.40 (Accessed 23 Oct. 2023).

Clapp, J., Moseley, W.G., 2020. This food crisis is different: COVID-19 and the fragility of the neoliberal food security order. *The Journal of Peasant Studies* 47, 1393–1417. https://doi.org/10.1080/03066150.2020.1823838.

Desmarais, A.A., 2007. *La Via Campesina: Globalization and the Power of Peasants.* Pluto Press, London.

Edelman, M., 2014. Food sovereignty: forgotten genealogies and future regulatory challenges. *The Journal of Peasant Studies* 41, 959–978. https://doi.org/10.1080/03066150.2013.876998.

Figueroa-Helland, L., Thomas, C., Aguilera, A.P., 2018. Decolonizing food systems: food sovereignty, indigenous revitalization, and agroecology as counter-hegemonic movements. *Perspectives on Global*

Development and Technology 17, 173–201. https://doi.org/10.1163/15691497-12341473.

Giraldo, O.F., Rosset, P.M., 2018. Agroecology as a territory in dispute: between institutionality and social movements. *The Journal of Peasant Studies* 45, 545–564. https://doi.org/10.1080/03066150.2017.1353496.

Hendrikse, R., 2021. The rise of neo-Illiberalism. *Krisis | Journal for Contemporary Philosophy* 41(1), 65–93. https://doi.org/10.21827/krisis.40.2.37158.

Iles, A., de Wit, M.M., 2015. Sovereignty at what scale? An Inquiry into multiple dimensions of food sovereignty. *Globalizations* 12, 481–497. https://doi.org/10.1080/14747731.2014.957587.

IPCC, 2019. Climate Change and Land: An IPCC Special Report on Climate Change, Desertification, Land Degradation, Sustainable Land Management, Food Security, and Greenhouse Gas Fluxes in Terrestrial Ecosystems. P.R. Shukla, J. Skea, E. Calvo Buendia, V. Masson-Delmotte, H.-O. Pörtner, D. C. Roberts, P. Zhai, R. Slade, S. Connors, R. van Diemen, M. Ferrat, E. Haughey, S. Luz, S. Neogi, M. Pathak, J. Petzold, J. Portugal Pereira, P. Vyas, E. Huntley, K. Kissick, M. Belkacemi, J. Malley, (Eds.).

Koopmans, R. 2004. Protest in time and space: the evolution of waves of contention. In D.A. Snow, S.A. Soule and H. Kriesi (Eds.), *The Blackwell Companion to Social Movements* (pp. 19–46). Blackwell, Oxford.

McMichael, P., 2013. *Food Regimes and Agrarian Questions, Agrarian Change and Peasant Studies*. Practical Action Publishing, Rugby, UK.

Manahan, M.A., Kumar, M. (Eds.) 2021. *The Great Takeover: Mapping of Multistakeholderism in Global Governance*. People's Working Group on Multistakeholderism, Amsterdam.

Martinez-Torres, M.E., Rosset, P.M., 2010. *La Via Campesina: The Evolution of a Transnational Movement*. Available at: https://www.globalpolicy.org/social-and-economic-policy/world-hunger/land-ownership-and-hunger/48733-la-via-campesina-the-evolution-of-a-transnational-movement.html (Accessed 23 October 2023).

Montenegro de Wit, M., 2022. Can agroecology and CRISPR mix? The politics of complementarity and moving toward technology sovereignty. *Agriculture and Human Values* 39, 733–755. https://doi.org/10.1007/s10460-021-10284-0.

Noll, S., Murdock, E.G., 2020. Whose justice is it anyway? Mitigating the tensions between food security and food sovereignty. *Journal of Agricultural and Environmental Ethics* 33, 1–14. https://doi.org/10.1007/s10806-019-09809-9.

Nyéléni, 2007. *Forum for Food Sovereignty Report*. Available at: https://nyeleni.org/DOWNLOADS/Nyelni_EN.pdf (Accessed 23 October 2023).

Prause, L., Hackfort, S., Lindgren, M., 2020. Digitalization and the third food regime. *Agriculture and Human Values* 38, 641–655. https://doi.org/10.1007/s10460-020-10161-2.

Rosset, P., 2006. *Food Is Different: Why the WTO Should Get Out of Agriculture*. Zed Books, London.

Schiavoni, C.M., 2017. The contested terrain of food sovereignty construction: toward a historical, relational and interactive approach. *The Journal of Peasant Studies* 44, 1–32. https://doi.org/10.1080/03066150.2016.1234455.

Scoones, I., Edelman, M., Borras Jr, S.M., Hall, R., Wolford, W., White, B., 2018. Emancipatory rural politics: confronting authoritarian populism. *The Journal of Peasant Studies* 45, 1–20. https://doi.org/10.1080/03066150.2017.1339693.

Trauger, A., 2017. *We Want Land to Live: Making Political Space for Food Sovereignty*. University of Georgia Press, Athens.

Further reading

Perfecto, I., Vandermeer, J.H., Wright, A.L., 2009. *Nature's Matrix: Linking Agriculture, Conservation and Food Sovereignty*. Earthscan.
This book describes the critical role of agroecology in enabling food sovereignty for small-scale food producers. It reveals the connections between agro-biodiverse landscapes and the social, political, and ecological systems that enable them.

Rock, J.S., 2022. *We Are Not Starving: The Struggle for Food Sovereignty in Ghana*. MSU Press.
This book examines the struggles for food sovereignty in Ghana and offers insight into

MATTHEW CANFIELD

the specific challenges of food sovereignty movements in the face of neo-colonialism and the Green Revolution on the African continent.

Canfield, M.C., 2022. *Translating Food Sovereignty: Cultivating Justice in an Age of Transnational Governance.* Stanford University Press.

This book explores how food sovereignty activists based in the Pacific Northwest of the United States mobilise for food sovereignty across local, regional, and global arenas of governance. It elaborates the social practices that food sovereignty activists have cultivated as they translate food sovereignty across different contexts and geographies.

MATTHEW CANFIELD

67.   Food supply chains

Alex Hughes

The food supply chain concept

Tracing the journeys our food takes from settings of production, processing, and packaging, through distribution, logistics, and retail, to consumption spaces of the home and hospitality, has become both a popular and an academic endeavour. Through an era of intensifying globalisation from the 1980s to the present, piecing together the links in the chains between production and consumption has become particularly important given the often distanced and complex relationships between food suppliers and those consuming the final products. Urban food consumers, for example, can be significantly removed from the materiality and cultures of food production (Jackson, 2010). Connections to production are sometimes made most apparent to consumers when supply chains break down, such as in the case of the horse meat scandal in the UK in 2013 (Atkins, 2013).

The notion of the commodity chain informing understandings of these food supply chain journeys refers to "the progressive movement of a commodity through the sequential phases of production, distribution, and consumption" (Hughes and Reimer, 2004: 2). Emphasis is placed on the vertical relations between upstream (supplying) and downstream (buying) actors. The chain can, and arguably should, also be extended to capture post-consumption phases involving waste and recycling. For social scientists from diverse backgrounds including political economy, science and technology studies, cultural studies, and business management, tracking the connections between sites of food production, consumption, and waste helps to capture and explain food's embeddedness in projects of development, processes of commercialisation, geographies of inequality, cultural practices and ethics of everyday life, and environmental challenges, as well the relationships between these fields. In contemporary times, digitalisation, automation, shifting geopolitics including increasing protectionism, climate crisis, and the COVID-19 pandemic have all in various ways altered topologies and workings of food supply chains, with implications for their conceptualisation.

Theoretical perspectives on food supply chains

Perspectives on agri-food supply chains

Commodity chain, network-based, and systems approaches to understanding the links between food production, consumption, and waste are varied. They include food regimes perspectives addressing macro-scale regulatory shifts affecting trade (Friedmann, 1993), systems of provision (Fine et al., 2018), the global value chain (GVC) framework (Gereffi, 2018), global production networks (GPNs) (Coe, 2021), and assemblage thinking on the heterogeneous associations between human and non-human elements of production networks (Freidberg, 2017; Ouma, 2015). Also worthy of mention are the more applied approaches of supply chain management associated with business management and informing strategic operations (Mentzer et al., 2001). An influential set of these perspectives is outlined below.

Global value chains and global production networks

The GVC and GPN frameworks are part of a family of political-economic approaches capturing the morphology and governance of production–consumption chains through a period of global economic liberalisation, structural adjustment, deregulation, and export-oriented industrialisation since the late 1980s. They essentially map and evaluate the organisation and influence of "spatially dispersed yet centrally coordinated production and distribution networks" (Ponte et al., 2019: 135). The GVC conceptual framework evolved from an earlier global commodity chains approach, focusing mainly on inter-firm governance within the supply chain (Gereffi, 2018). Since its inception in the early 2000s, the framework has evolved from initially concentrating on the coordinating roles played by firms, particularly lead firm buyers, to capturing the influences of a wider array of organisations from states to civil society organisations and trade unions (Gereffi, 2018). The GPN perspective associated with economic geographers is similar but attends more closely to spatiality and complex webs of connection in production–consumption chains (Coe, 2021).

Food supply chains and assemblage

The concept of assemblage has also significantly influenced scholarship on food supply chains (see, for example, Freidberg, 2017; Ouma, 2015). The value of assemblage thinking for theorising food supply chains lies in its engagement with inter- and intra-actions between human and non-human elements in a network (Anderson et al., 2012). Rather than seeing agency in food supply chains as concentrated into the hands of identifiable institutions like the state and corporations, as more vertically orientated GVC and GPN perspectives do, an assemblage perspective views agency as being more distributed in practice and working through these complex non-human–human connections (Henry and Roche, 2013).

Food supply chains and circuits of knowledge

Also influential in scholarship on food supply chains is a body of work embracing commodity cultures and meanings attached to food in different times, places, and phases of commodity circulation. Much of this work has its roots in economic anthropology, studies of material culture, and critical ethnography (Appadurai, 1986; Miller, 1998). It has inspired projects seeking to investigate the geographies of production and supply behind the goods we consume, known as an approach of "follow the thing" (Cook et al., 2017). Whilst some of this scholarship follows a Marxist objective of revealing economic processes and labour conditions at sites of production, other work has considered the complex and culturally inflected ways in which goods may be displaced from one site in the production–consumption chain to another and the ways in which various cultural and geographical knowledges are integral to that process (Crang, 1996).

Applications of food supply chains perspectives: some examples

Power and space in the production–consumption chain

Informed by the frameworks and perspectives outlined above, there has been widespread critical attention in the literature on food supply chains to questions of power and governance. Little and Watts' (1994) major edited work, *Living Under Contract*, for example,

identified power imbalances between influential corporate supply chain actors, farms, and workers in the case of contract farming in low- and middle-income counties, with a special issue of the *Journal of Agrarian Change* edited by Vicol et al. (2022) revisiting that work and considering changes over the past twenty-five years. From a different, GVC-inspired, perspective, German et al. (2020) reflect on a broad range of policy-focused work around these questions. They show how value chain governance structures favouring agribusiness enable and constrain inclusion of regions and locales in GVCs with (often problematic) implications for land and labour. Lang et al. (2022) also apply the GVC framework to understand inequalities between supply chain actors, specifically examining the South African hake value chain.

Food supply chains and labour issues

Kissi and Herzig (2020) present a systematic review of literature on food supply chains and work showing a tendency for research to focus on private rather than public forms of regulating labour standards, on trading dynamics and pressures rather than contextual issues at sites of production, and on male workers in large commercial settings more than on smallholders and female workers. The different commodity chain approaches outlined above have been applied in research. Matheis and Herzig (2019), for example, use GVC notions of economic and social upgrading to address how ethical initiatives and learning in the supply chain can facilitate improvements in labour conditions that can help to meet the United Nations Sustainable Development Goals. And Barrientos (2020) has critically evaluated both the capacity and limitations of private voluntary labour codes of conduct to deliver improvements for women workers in global food supply chains.

Pye's (2021) work takes a Marxian perspective to conceptualise current forms of agricultural work and labour agency in supply chains as a part of wider class struggle. And also on the theme of labour agency, but working explicitly with GVC perspectives, Mieres and McGrath (2021: 1) study "worker-driven" approaches to improving the rights and conditions of agricultural workers embodied in the US-based Fair Food Program. At the other "end" of the chain, socio-cultural perspectives on ethical food consumption consider the influence of consumer knowledge and action on ethical trading initiatives and Fairtrade, which focus on labour codes of conduct and improving the livelihoods of farming communities respectively (Clarke, 2008).

Food supply chains and environmental issues

Much of the work applying GVC and GPN perspectives to questions of how environmental issues are apprehended and addressed in food supply chains has considered forms of environmental governance associated with voluntary, private initiatives and standards (see Bush, 2010, for a critical analysis of initiatives in the seafood sector). Empirical studies of organic food supply chains involving certification particularly abound (Raynolds, 2004). On the theme of the organic food sector, however, as well as appreciating the value of organic production for addressing environmental issues, Cook (2019) presents a critical account. Using the example of Jordanian olive oil, Cook explores some of the contradictory tendencies of the global organic food trade that can sometimes encourage intensive production and internationally stretched supply chains rather than locally and environmentally sensitive forms of production and supply.

Ponte (2022) also takes a critical stance on environmental governance at a broad level, alerting us to how environmental sustainability itself can become commodified in value chains, regularly benefiting the corporate bottom-line, whilst Freidberg (2017) critiques the use of metrics in an increasingly data-driven global economy when it comes to addressing environmental sustainability in food commodity chains. Strube et al. (2021) provide an example of these issues, looking at how sustainability metrics can themselves become commodified, favouring corporate capital, using the case of the "field to market" multi-stakeholder initiative in the USA.

Reflecting scholarship on the links between social and environmental dimensions of food supply chains, Werner (2022) reviews how recent geographical scholarship on production networks and the environment considers not only environmental governance and impact, but also ways in which "nature" itself is a constituent part of all nodes and links in a food supply chain. This reflects assemblage and network-based perspectives. A specific study by Araújo (2019) in this vein uses assemblage

thinking to understand the construction of the Brazilian Halal meat and poultry industry through multiple sites and human and non-human agents in the production–consumption chain, from processing factories to urban sites of trading and consumption.

Understanding current and future transformations in food supply chains

Food supply chains are deeply affected by some of the "changing contours of globalization" identified by Gereffi (2018: 17) before the 2020 COVID-19 pandemic, including the rise of emerging market economies, growth in regional value chains and South–South trade, increasing protectionism, and digitalisation. Such shifts have all in different ways contributed to a reshaping of food supply chains, changing forms of governance, and transforming challenges that have seemingly exacerbated since the beginning of the pandemic.

Considering the increasing digital influences on food supply chains, literature often refers to a range of developments including the Internet of Things, big data, blockchain (distributed ledger) technologies, and artificial intelligence (AI) (Morella et al., 2021). Prause et al. (2021) address how digitalisation across the whole supply chain affects forms of power and governance. They argue that digital technologies enable not only the persistence of long-present corporate purchasing power including big capital agribusiness, but also the rise of a suite of tech players capitalising on data-driven and platform-based forms of governance.

With respect to the challenges posed by the pandemic, research on food supply chains since 2020 has captured multiple ways in which COVID-19 has affected food production, trade, and consumption, from the impacts at the start of lockdowns across the globe to reverberating effects on trade and livelihoods (Davila et al., 2021). Mahajan and Tomar (2020) demonstrate from research in India that geographically longer food supply chains were less resilient to the effects of the pandemic than shorter supply chains. And looking at the combined effects of geopolitical change and the shock of the pandemic, Blessley and Mudambi (2022) discuss an example of how the US–China trade war led to food originally intended for export to be re-routed to domestic food banks in the USA.

ALEX HUGHES

Given that food is a vital commodity, the project of tracing its journeys through the supply chain from production to consumption is arguably more important now than ever before. Doing so enables us to understand not only how food is bound up in contemporary challenges associated with changing "contours" of the global economy and recent intersecting crises, but also how it might be a part of more hopeful and progressive social and ecological arrangements in the future.

References

Anderson B, Kearnes M, McFarlane C and Swanton D (2012) On assemblages and geography. *Dialogues in Human Geography* 2, 171–189.

Appadurai A (1986) Introduction: commodities and the politics of value. In: Appadurai A (Ed.) *The Social Life of Things: Commodities in Cultural Perspective*. Cambridge, Cambridge University Press, pp. 3–63.

Araújo S H (2019) Assembling halal meat and poultry production in Brazil: agents, practices, power and sites. *Geoforum* 100, 220–228.

Atkins P J (2013) Why is there horsemeat in our food? *Geography Review* 27(1), 38–41.

Barrientos S (2020) *Gender and Work in Global Value Chains: Capturing the Gains? (Development Trajectories in Global Value Chains)*. Cambridge, Cambridge University Press.

Blessley M and Mudambi S M (2022) A trade war and a pandemic: Disruption and resilience in the food bank supply chain. *Industrial Marketing Management* 102, 58–73. https://doi.org/10.1016/j.indmarman.2022.01.002.

Bush S R (2010) Governing 'spaces of interaction' for sustainable fisheries. *Tijdschrift voor Econmische en Sociale Geografie* 101(3), 305–319.

Clarke N (2008) From ethical consumerism to political consumption. *Geography Compass* 2, 1870–1884. https://doi.org/10.1111/j.1749-8198.2008.00170.x.

Coe N M (2021) *Advanced Introduction to Global Production Networks*. Cheltenham, UK and Northampton, MA, USA, Edward Elgar Publishing.

Cook B (2019) Organic rural development: barriers to value in the quest for qualities in Jordanian olive oil. *Journal of Rural Studies*, 27–42.

Cook I et al. (2017) From 'Follow the thing: papaya' to followthethings.com. *Journal of Consumer Ethics* 1(1), 22–29.

Crang P (1996) Displacement, consumption, and identity. *Environment and Planning A: Economy and Space* 28(1), 47–67. https://doi.org/10.1068/a280047.

Davila F, Bourke R M, McWilliam A, Crimp S, Robins L, van Wensveen M, Alders R G and Butler J R A (2021) COVID-19 and food systems in Pacific Island Countries, Papua New Guinea, and Timor-Leste: Opportunities for actions towards the sustainable development goals. *Agricultural Systems* 191, 103137. DOI: 10.1016/j.agsy.2021.103137.

Fine B, Bayliss K and Robertson M (2018) The systems of provision approach to understanding consumption. In: Fine B, Bayliss K and Robertson M (Eds.), *The SAGE Handbook of Consumer Culture*. London, Sage, pp. 27–42.

Freidberg S (2017) Big food and little data: the slow harvest of corporate food supply chain sustainability initiatives. *Annals of the Association of American Geographers* 107(6), 1389–1406.

Friedmann H (1993) The political economy of food: a global crisis. *New Left Review* 197, 29–57.

Gereffi G (2018) *Global Value Chains and Development: Redefining the Contours of 21st Century Capitalism*. Cambridge, Cambridge University Press.

German L A, Bonanno A M, Foster L C and Cotula L (2020) "Inclusive business" in agriculture: evidence from the evolution of agricultural value chains. *World Development* 134(C), 105018.

Henry M and Roche M (2013) Valuing lively materialities: bio-economic assembling in the making of new meat futures. *New Zealand Geographer* 69, 197–207.

Hughes A and Reimer S (2004) *Geographies of Commodity Chains*. London and New York, Routledge.

Jackson P (2010) Food stories: consumption in an age of anxiety. *Cultural Geographies* 17(2), 147–165.

Kissi E A and Herzig C (2020) Methodologies and perspectives in research on labour relations in global agricultural production networks: a review. *The Journal of Development Studies* 56, 1615–1637.

Lang J, Ponte S and Vilakazi T (2022) Linking power and inequality in global value chains. *Global Networks* 23(4), 755–771. https://doi.org/10.1111/glob.12411.

Little P and Watts M (1994) Introduction. In Little P and Watts M (Eds.) *Living under Contract: Contract Farming and Agrarian Transformation in Sub-Saharan Africa.* Madison, WI, University of Wisconsin Press, pp. 3–20.

Mahajan K and Tomar S (2020) COVID-19 and supply chain disruption: evidence from food markets in India. *American Journal of Agricultural Economics* 103, 35–52.

Matheis T V and Herzig C (2019) Upgrading products, upgrading work? Interorganizational learning in global food value chains to achieve the Sustainable Development Goals. *GAIA – Ecological Perspectives for Science and Society* 28(2), 126–134.

Mentzer J T, DeWitt W, Keebler J S, Mon S, Nix N W, Smith C D and Zacharia Z G (2001) Defining supply chain management. *Journal of Business Logistics* 22, 1–25. https://doi.org/10.1002/j.2158-1592.2001.tb00001.x.

Mieres F and McGrath S (2021) Ripe to be heard: worker voice in the Fair Food Program. *International Labour Review* 160, 631–647. https://doi.org/10.1111/ilr.12204.

Miller D (Ed) (1998) *Material Cultures: Why Some Things Matter.* UCL Press.

Morella P, Lambán M P, Royo J and Sánchez J C (2021) Study and analysis of the implementation of 4.0 technologies in the agri-food supply chain: a state of the art. *Agronomy* 11, 2526. https://doi.org/10.3390/agronomy11122526.

Ouma S (2015) *Assembling Export Markets: The Making and Unmaking of Global Food Connections in West Africa.* Wiley Blackwell.

Ponte S (2022) The hidden costs of environmental upgrading in global value chains. *Review of International Political Economy* 29(3), 818–843. doi:10.1080/09692290.2020.1816199.

Ponte S, Sturgeon T J and Dallas M P (2019) Governance and power in global value chains. In: Ponte S, Gereffi G and Raj-Reichert (Eds.) *Handbook on Global Value Chains.* Cheltenham, UK and Northampton, MA, USA, Edward Elgar Publishing, pp. 120–137.

Prause L, Hackfort S and Lindgren M (2021) Digitalization and the third food regime. *Agriculture and Human Values* 38(3), 641–655. doi: 10.1007/s10460-020-10161-2.

Pye O (2021) Agrarian Marxism and the proletariat: a palm oil manifesto. *The Journal of Peasant Studies* 48(4), 807–826. doi:10.1080/03066150.2019.1667772.

Raynolds L T (2004) The globalization of organic agro-food networks. *World Development* 32(5), 725–743.

Strube J, Glenna L L, Hatanaka M, Konefal J T and Conner D S (2021) How data-driven, privately ordered sustainability governance shapes US food supply chains: the case of field to market. *Journal of Rural Studies* 86, 684–693.

Vicol M, Fold N, Hambloch C, Narayanan S and Pérez Niño H (2022) Twenty-five years of *Living Under Contract*: contract farming and agrarian change in the developing world. *Journal of Agrarian Change* 22(1), 3–18. https://doi.org/10.1111/joac.12471.

Werner M (2022) Geographies of production III: global production in/through nature. *Progress in Human Geography* 46(1), 234–244. https://doi.org/10.1177/03091325211022810.

Further reading

González-Ramírez M, Santoyo-Cortés V, Arana-Coronado J J and Muñoz-Rodríguez M (2020) The insertion of Mexico into the global value chain of berries. *World Development Perspectives* 20, 100240.
This paper applies the GVC framework to an evaluation of control and influence in the contemporary global fresh berry trade. It demonstrates corporate forms of power and governance linked to the pattern of supply chain interactions between influential US markets and production and work in Mexico.

Donaldson A (2022) Digital from farm to fork: infrastructures of quality and control in food supply chains. *Journal of Rural Studies* 91, 228–235.
This paper notes the ways in which digital technologies and devices enable forms of transparency and traceability through the food supply chain, changing how information flows and who controls it.

ALEX HUGHES

68. Food systems

GIANLUCA BRUNORI, SABRINA
ARCURI AND FRANCESCA GALLI

Introduction

Ensuring food security and nutrition for all, and providing livelihoods to farmers and other operators in the food chain and rural development, while remaining within safe planetary boundaries, are widely recognised as the 'triple challenges' of our time (OECD, 2021). Evidence shows that, far from attaining these goals, 'the food system is failing us' (Béné et al., 2019) and an unprecedented effort – or what some term a 'Great Food Transformation' towards more sustainable and just food outcomes (Willett et al., 2019) – is needed to move towards sustainability.

Until recently, much research and policy has been devoted to agricultural production, processing, and trade. One major consequence of the focus on specific, fragmented activities is that less attention has been paid to the linkages among activities and the implications of these relationships. The importance of studying connections between activities and actors involved in food provisioning has now been recognised and the 'food system' has rapidly become a key concept in both academic and policy circles. To embark on the food system's transformation, new knowledge must replace the old paradigms, which are co-responsible for the current failures. However, as the 'food system' concept increases in popularity, there is a risk of the trivialisation of its meaning and a subsequent lack of clarity.

The value of food system approaches lies in the potential to capture and unravel complexity and to provide policymakers with a tool to navigate trade-offs and synergies and to inform and guide policymaking in the efforts required to pursue meaningful sustainability. In agri-food studies, the journey towards this major understanding has been marked by many theoretical and practical attempts to improve the food system's representational capacity.

System approaches as a way out of reductionism

System approaches address one of the main weaknesses of reductionism, the most adopted approach in contemporary sciences, that consists in splitting-up problems into their smallest possible components (Toffler, 1984). Through this approach, scientists set up experiments, reject or confirm hypotheses, and generalise statements on how, assuming all other variables remain unchanged, the observed variables behave. The approach has proved to be very successful, as it has allowed important practical advancements in the field of science and technology. Its success, however, has resulted in a loss of interest in interrelations between the parts and the whole, and has supported simplistic representations of reality and unwarranted optimism on change.

System approaches aim at studying interconnected entities. A system can be defined as 'any group of interacting, interrelated, or interdependent parts that form a complex and unified whole that has a specific purpose' (Kim, 1999: 2). System approaches seek to provide an explanation for complex problems, i.e., problems with a multiplicity of causes and effects. Different systems have different levels of explanatory power. In mechanical systems, each event is determined by the initial conditions, so the system's events are predictable, and the study of these systems is comparable to the reductionist method. In contrast, living systems are characterised by disorder, instability, diversity, disequilibrium, and nonlinear relationships. In general, 'system thinking' refers to the second type, and is evoked when cause-effect relationships do not give plausible or satisfactory explanations.

With the emphasis on interactions between entities, system thinking aims to understand how things influence each other within a whole. Important features of system approaches are nonlinearity (reactions not proportional to the action), feedback (consequences of an action that affect its source), and emergent properties (properties generated by repeated interaction). System approaches help to highlight the root causes of problems, the distant and retarded effects of choices, adaptation to the environment, and self-organisation (Holland, 1992). In living systems, social, technical, and biological components interact and influence each other.

Positioning the system concept in agri-food scholarship

The earliest system approaches to food were proposed to provide alternative views to the dominant approach to agricultural policies. Supporters of system approaches aimed to show that agricultural production was not the outcome of the market's 'invisible hand', but rather the visible hand of concrete agents, namely the state and agribusiness companies. Since then, systems have been studied to show that food-related activities are linked to each other. An early step towards food system studies was made with the introduction of the 'supply chain' concept, which encompasses all actors and activities involved in, and contributing to, the creation of the final product, in this case food commodities. While it allows researchers to assess and foresee the indirect and unintended consequences of events affecting food-related activities, the supply chain concept overlooks, by definition, the multiplicity of connections that each component of the chain could have.

A further step has been made using the network metaphor, which highlights the multiple and hybrid (i.e., material and immaterial, social and economic) relationships that characterise actors and activities related to food. Networks, and more recently related work on assemblage theory and food assemblages (defined broadly as associations of food-related practices and socio-material relations), are employed to explain agency, multicausality, and multifunctionality. These approaches are used to analyse how actors can (re-)define their identities (as consumers, citizens, co-producers) through their relations, and how they can build alliances with other actors. In this way the links between food, tourism, gastronomy, culture, environmental protection, and social justice claims have been studied (Goodman et al., 2012).

More nuanced frameworks are used to appraise the hybridity of the components of food systems and the multiplicity of relational configurations that characterise food systems. For instance, socio-ecological system perspectives explore the relations between social practices, governance patterns, and natural resources. Socio-technical studies aim to understand how social interaction and technology development influence one another. Political ecology focuses on power relations within systems. Based on these frameworks, the identities, functions, and course of activities related to food are seen as effects of localised configurations of actors, rules, artifacts, and natural resources.

Defining and representing food systems

With the advent of sustainability as a generally agreed policy frame, system approaches are increasingly promoted as the way to overcome the barriers imposed by reductionism to academic disciplines, and to address the interconnected dimensions of current food-related challenges. However, although there are plenty of 'food system thinking' exercises in the literature, attempts to define what a food system is, and to provide methods to describe its complex interconnections, are still in progress.

In the context of global food security, Ericksen (2008) defines food systems in terms of (a) the actors and activities related to food; (b) the social, economic, and ecological outcomes of these activities, which determine systems' performance; and (c) the political, environmental, and technological factors ('the drivers') that affect food systems' activities but cannot be controlled by food systems' actors. The definition provides a guide to the characterisation of contextualised food systems, which implies the selection of the components to be considered and the definition of system boundaries. Since systems are mental representations of reality, these operations are arbitrary and depend on the goals of the observers and on the purposes of the analysis. It is the observers who decide what to include and exclude in their representation. For example, choosing nutrition as the observed outcome brings attention to households, nutritionists, media, retailers, school canteens, and health authorities. Likewise, defining the boundaries of a system is arbitrary, since the observers decide whether a component is external to the system or internal to it, based on their estimated ability to influence the system's course of action.

Adopting the same approach, the HLPE (2017: 23) provides the following definition: 'A food system gathers all the elements – environment, people, inputs, processes, infrastructures, institutions, etc. – and activities that relate to the production, processing, distribution, preparation and consumption of food, and the outputs of these activities, including socio-economic and environmental outcomes.'

Food systems analysis can produce maps, typologies, causal patterns, and scenarios that are useful for policy purposes. For instance, in its typologies, the HLPE distinguishes between modern and traditional food systems, depending on the role of supermarkets and the food industry. Classification into specialised or diversified food systems is based on the number and weight of supply chains in food system activities. The study of the localised interaction of food system components enables the description of emergent food system properties, such as food environments, that help explain systemic influences on individual food choices.

Mobilising food systems approaches for sustainability

The development of food systems studies has a strong policy-related focus. The power of food system approaches, in fact, is linked to their capacity to help a community identify and remove barriers to change, formulate food-related challenges, and anticipate the consequences of given choices. System approaches highlight that transformation goals require efforts to redesign routines, infrastructures, and mental models. Food system approaches facilitate communication between stakeholders to establish common views on food-related problems. As stakeholders are themselves actors of the system, their perspectives contribute to more accurate representations of the system and to actionable knowledge.

Food systems approaches can support the framing of sustainability problems, linking together social, economic, and ecological dimensions. For instance, urging policy actors to look at the problems' complexity, system approaches encourage collaboration between knowledges and between administration sectors, fostering inter- and trans-disciplinarity, social learning, and cross-sectoral cooperation.

A food systems approach can be disruptive of the dominant problem definitions and of the incumbent institutional configurations. For a long time, food policies have been subsumed into agricultural policies, and have focused on food availability, disregarding access – and access rights – and nutrition. A system approach to food security in a sustainability framework allows the interdependence between agriculture, health, welfare, and environmental policies to be established, assisting in the pursuit of policy coherence.

Food systems thinking also highlights the trade-offs between systems' outcomes and activities. In a policy process, different values and interests can make these trade-offs as sources of potential tensions and conflict; awareness of these differences can suggest the involvement of different actors in the appraisal of the system, in turn providing more accurate system representations and more effective policies.

Developing food systems research

Because agricultural and food sciences have traditionally been shaped by reductionist or mechanistic paradigms, the emergence of a 'food systems science' has the potential to overcome hyper-specialisation and foster more problem-centred research. This implies the need to build a solid body of theory and methodology, to address the emerging themes (such as global and local food security, power distribution, sustainable diets, circularity, sustainable transitions, urban food policies, etc.) with a solid empirical base. We suggest here that a 'food systems science' can develop along four main system properties: diversity, interdependence, self-organisation, and choice.

Diversity

Food systems approaches assume that diversity is a key asset. Diverse components ensure redundancy and the fulfilment of system functions. Social, economic, and biological diversity are connected to each other: a diversified diet implies diversified agri-food systems; biodiversity degradation has strong causal links with the increasing concentration of food business. Diversity is key to sustainability solutions: the diversity of transformation processes is the condition for circular economies, as it allows for a matching between production and re-utilisation of residues. Diverse breeds and varieties can respond differently to climatic stresses; likewise, different business models may differ in their response to economic shocks, making systems more resilient to adverse conditions and providing the necessary resources for adaptation. Diverse systems also provide multiple outputs and outcomes, and this implies that system activities generate co-benefits – such as private and public goods – but also trade-offs, spill overs, and unintended consequences. Food systems science should explore the mechanisms that reduce or increase diversity across sectors, identify co-benefits and trade-offs, and develop win-win or compromise solutions to stop and reverse the processes of degradation and compensate the actors who lose out in the process.

Interdependence

One of the key tasks of food systems scientists is to detect indirect effects, feedback loops, emergent properties, and trade-offs between activities and outcomes. The study of feedback loops can yield important insights for more effective policies. Most sustainability-related food systems problems are linked to actors' unawareness of indirect links, as in the relation between food consumption and resource depletion, or trade and social inequalities, between soil degradation and human health. Much of the debate on 'the true cost of food' is related to the measurement of these invisible links. One example is antibiotic resistance, which arises from feedback loops between antibiotic use and selection pressure. Antibiotics kill sensitive microbes while allowing resistant ones to survive and multiply, accelerating the development of resistance. Resistant microorganisms that emerge in livestock can then spread to humans through multiple pathways. Feedback loops are also at the origins of 'rebound effects', by which improved efficiency eventually increases the pressure on resources, and of 'fixes that fail', like sugar or fat taxes introduced with the purpose of discouraging overconsumption of junk food, which may end up increasing inequalities by raising food prices for low-income groups, i.e., those most affected by higher incidence of obesity. Policies that support carbon removal on farming might be harmful for biodiversity, e.g., by sustaining monocultures with high carbon storage.

Self-organisation

Self-organisation consists of processes whereby some form of order arises out of a disordered environment. Such an emergent property is generated by repeated interaction between entities, which brings learning and adaptation to the environment. Self-organisation occurring at low levels can generate patterns that eventually affect higher levels of organisation: radical innovation occurs when current paradigms and

routines are abandoned by visionary and pioneer actors, who create new rules and routines that eventually spread over the system. Grassroot civil society initiatives are self-organisation processes that challenge the rules of the system and provide the seeds for change. Food systems studies are particularly rich in examples of self-organisation: alternative food network studies from the last twenty years revealed the capacity of local actors to activate new patterns of interaction between consumers, producers, local administrations, and civil society organisations, with the purpose of gaining autonomy from large retailers or the food industry. These initiatives have scaled up by aggregation and scaled out by replication and, in some cases, their success has influenced the innovation pathways of 'conventional' food system actors.

Choice

The difference between living systems and mechanical systems is that in living systems entities can choose multiple courses of action. Studying choice implies understanding how interdependence can be coupled with agency. Food systems are characterised by strong power imbalances, and often food systems activities are heavily influenced by the choices of big players that local actors cannot control. However, local actors may find in their own environment the opportunities to create coalitions and mobilise resources that allow them to detach from big players, developing resistance, innovation, or growth strategies in hostile market contexts. Choice is also coupled with responsibility, which implies being accountable for one's own choices.

Understanding food systems as arenas of choice and responsibility, power, and conflict also brings attention to the potential of system representations. Consumers' awareness of the systemic impacts of their choices empowers them to influence big players. Accountability mechanisms and transparency may provide system feedbacks to regulate corporate behaviour. Innovation policies may give technology development a direction towards equitable solutions. Participation at all levels of the system can provide leverage points for system innovation.

Concluding remarks

Sustainable food systems require a change of paradigm in the way science addresses food.

GIANLUCA BRUNORI, SABRINA ARCURI AND FRANCESCA GALLI

Sustainability is about reconnecting environment, society, and the economy, and gaining awareness of the interdependencies between the activities, actors, and outcomes in these three domains. In this entry, we argue that a food systems science is needed—one that offers the theoretical and methodological tools to explain the identity, behaviour, and performance of food-related activities in relation to system properties.

A food systems science is strongly policy-related: it encourages a holistic view on the variety of causes, outcomes, and variables underpinning a policy problem, helping system actors make sense of the complexity of the problem. Food systems science provides a guide to understanding the hybridity of material and immaterial components that constitute food systems, including relations between social, economic, and political domains. It also shows that effective solutions to policy problems are linked to shared representations and negotiation of goals, for which participation is indispensable.

Food systems scientists have an important role in food systems transformation. They provide evidence to critically engage in discovering how food systems work, are organised and are represented in multiple narratives, uncover the values and interests behind these different representations, and develop tools for assessment and comparison both within and across food systems. Their work can also bridge different representations by proposing syntheses that generate consensus in efforts to create more sustainable food production and consumption. Researchers who adopt food systems approaches are aware that they themselves are components of the system rather than external observers: their research therefore influences relationships within food systems, making them responsible agents of positive and sustainable change.

References

Béné C, Oosterveer P, Lamotte L, Brouwer I D, de Haan S, Prager S D, ... & Khoury C K (2019) When food systems meet sustainability: Current narratives and implications for actions. *World Development*, 113, 116–130. https://doi.org/10.1016/j.worlddev.2018.08.011.

Ericksen P J (2008) Conceptualizing food systems for global environmental change research. *Global Environmental Change*, 18(1), 234–245. https://doi.org/10.1016/j.gloenvcha.2007.09.002.

Goodman D, DuPuis E M, and Goodman M K (2012) *Alternative food networks: Knowledge, practice, and politics.* London: Routledge.

HLPE (2017) *Nutrition and food systems: A report by the High-Level Panel of Experts on Food Security and Nutrition of the Committee on World Food Security.* Rome: FAO. https://www.fao.org/documents/card/en/c/I7846E.

Holland J H (1992) Complex adaptive systems. *Daedalus*, 121(1), 17–30. https://www.jstor.org/stable/20025416.

Kim D H (1999) *Introduction to systems thinking.* Pegasus Communications, Innovations in Management Series. https://thesystemsthinker.com/wp-content/uploads/2016/03/Introduction-to-Systems-Thinking-IMS013Epk.pdf.

OECD (2021) *Making better policies for food systems.* Paris: OECD Publishing. https://doi.org/10.1787/ddfba4de-en.

Toffler A (1984) Introduction. In: Ilya Prigogine and Isabelle Stengers (Eds.), *Order out of chaos: Man's new dialogue with nature.* London: Verso.

Willett W, Rockström J, Loken B, Springmann M, Lang T, Vermeulen S, ... & Murray C J (2019) Food in the Anthropocene: The EAT–Lancet Commission on healthy diets from sustainable food systems. *The Lancet*, 393(10170), 447–492. https://doi.org/10.1016/S0140-6736(18)31788-4.

Further reading

Ericksen P J (2008) Conceptualizing food systems for global environmental change research. *Global Environmental Change*, 18(1), 234–245. https://doi.org/10.1016/j.gloenvcha.2007.09.002.
One of the earliest and most complete attempts to conceptualise food systems and provide a framework for food-related policies.

HLPE (2017) *Nutrition and food systems: A report by the High-Level Panel of Experts on Food Security and Nutrition of the Committee on World Food Security.* FAO: Rome. https://www.fao.org/documents/card/en/c/I7846E.
Provides an internationally recognised definition of food system and a conceptual framework addressing the link between food system components and nutrition.

GIANLUCA BRUNORI, SABRINA ARCURI AND FRANCESCA GALLI

Sage C (Ed.) (2022) *A research agenda for food systems.* Cheltenham, UK and Northampton, MA, USA: Edward Elgar Publishing.

The book examines some of the most relevant issues that confront current food systems and discusses in a critical way the proposed solutions.

GIANLUCA BRUNORI, SABRINA ARCURI AND FRANCESCA GALLI

69. Food taxes

PHILIPPA SIMMONDS

Introduction to food taxes

Food taxes have been levied in societies around the world for millennia. Purposes include generating revenue, improving public health, and, more recently, reducing environmental harm.

A key concept related to food taxation is 'price elasticity of demand'. If demand for a product is elastic, then it increases and decreases in response to prices going up and down, while if demand is inelastic, then it stays similar even when prices fluctuate. For example, demand for meat tends to be relatively inelastic, though this varies by geographic region (Andreyeva et al., 2010). Meanwhile, progressive taxation accounts for varying income levels between households, and takes a similar proportion of income from both wealthy and less wealthy households. Taxes are regressive if they take a greater proportion of income from low-income households compared with wealthier households.

"Pigouvian" taxes, named after British economist Arthur Pigou, are those levied on a product or activity that generates negative externalities, meaning a harmful effect occurs to persons or places other than the direct consumer. In the case of food taxes, the negative externality in question is often harm to public health, or sometimes harm to the environment. Food taxes are sometimes labelled as "sin taxes", meaning they are levied at the point of purchase to discourage consumption of a specific product, which is likely to have moral connotations (Hoffer et al., 2014). Those critical of food taxes are likely to make accusations of paternalism, in which decisions are made on one's behalf by a more powerful actor. Such accusations are a common response to state intervention and private food regulation initiatives.

Current issues: health-motivated food taxes

Many current issues in food taxation can be illustrated via taxes on sugar-sweetened beverages (SSBs), which have been introduced in over 40 countries globally (Cawley and Frisvold, 2023), and meat taxes, which are often discussed as a mechanism to reduce high meat consumption in industrialised Western countries such as the UK and the USA. Both these taxes are health-motivated, with meat taxes also having an environmental motivation.

Critics of taxation argue that the regressive nature of these food taxes makes them unfair to people on lower incomes. Ideological arguments such as the "nanny state critique" are also levelled at "sin taxes", suggesting that these are inappropriate state interventions into the affairs of private citizens. Critics also tend to highlight uncertainty in the literature and the risk of unintended consequences. Research has demonstrated similar types of arguments used by sectors whose products may be taxed, including sugar, tobacco, and alcohol industries. These arguments are underpinned by the message that the industry comprises socially responsible firms who are working to reduce harmful consumption of their product (Hilton et al., 2019). A parallel to the latter has also been identified in debates on meat taxes, in which livestock sector stakeholders have argued that they are working rapidly to reduce greenhouse gas emissions from cows and sheep (Simmonds and Vallgårda, 2021). Some also argue that introducing a meat tax could force grazing livestock farmers to leave the sector, negatively impacting land use, supply chains, and rural communities (Lee et al., 2021).

Meanwhile, advocates of health-motivated food taxes argue that taxation will reduce consumption of the product in question, leading to improved population health. There is evidence that SSB taxes reduce purchases of SSBs; however, evidence of reduced consumption or health benefits remains sparse (Cawley and Frisvold, 2023). Although SSB taxes are generally regressive, advocates argue that they are progressive in terms of health benefits, because those on lower incomes consume more SSBs and thus stand to gain more benefits from reduced consumption (Goianada-Silva et al., 2020). Furthermore, advocates of meat taxes have argued that taxation is not strongly paternalistic, because private companies already influence consumer behaviour through strategies such as pricing, advertising, and product placement (Simmonds and Vallgårda, 2021). In the case of SSBs, ringfencing of tax income for specific programmes has been shown to alleviate concerns about regressivity (Cawley and Frisvold, 2023). For example, revenue from the Mexican SSB tax was used to expand access to drinking water in schools (Véliz et al., 2019).

Future directions

Debates around food taxes are likely to continue as we seek solutions to interconnected health and climate crises (Swinburn et al., 2019). Further research is needed to understand the impacts of health-motivated food taxes on consumption and health. Modelling studies have begun to assess the potential impact of dietary change on the agriculture sector (Rieger et al., 2023), and further research is needed to explore potential impacts of a meat tax on rural livelihoods and how these impacts might be mitigated. Future research should consider food taxes as part of a package of measures, including food subsidies and broader action to address unequal access to healthy and sustainable diets.

References

Alsukait, R., Bleich, S., Wilde, P., Singh, G. and Folta, S. (2020) Sugary drink excise tax policy process and implementation: case study from Saudi Arabia, *Food Policy* 90, 101789. https://doi.org/10.1016/j.foodpol.2019.101789.

Andreyeva, T., Long, M.W. and Brownell, K.D. (2010) The impact of food prices on consumption: a systematic review of research on the price elasticity of demand for food, *American Journal of Public Health* 100 (2), 216–222. https://ajph.aphapublications.org/doi/abs/10.2105/AJPH.2008.151415.

Cawley, J. and Frisvold, D. (2023) Review: taxes on sugar-sweetened beverages – political economy, and effects on prices, purchases, and consumption, *Food Policy*, 117, 102441. https://doi.org/10.1016/J.FOODPOL.2023.102441.

Childress, J.F., Faden, R.R., Gaare, R.D., Gostin, L.O., Kahn, J., Bonnie, R.J., Kass, N.E., Mastroianni, A.C., Moreno, J.D. and Nieburg, P. (2002) Public health ethics: mapping the terrain, *Journal of Law Medicine and Ethics* 30 (2), 170–178. https://doi.org/10.1111/j.1748-720X.2002.tb00384.x.

Goiana-da-Silva, F., Cruz-e-Silva, D., Bartlett, O., Vasconcelos, J., Morais Nunes, A., Ashrafian, H., Miraldo, M., Machado, M.C., Araujo, F. and Darzi, A. (2020) The ethics of taxing sugar sweetened beverages to improve public health, *Frontiers in Public Health* 8, 110. https://doi.org/10.3389/fpubh.2020.00110.

Hilton, S., Buckton, C.H., Patterson, C., Vittal Katikireddi, S., Lloyd-Williams, F., Hyseni, L., Elliott-Green, A. and Capewell, S. (2019) Following in the footsteps of tobacco and alcohol? Stakeholder discourse in UK newspaper coverage of the Soft Drinks Industry Levy, *Public Health Nutrition*, 22 (12), 2317–2328. https://doi.org/10.1017/S1368980019000739.

Hoffer, A.J., Shughart, W.F. and Thomas, M.D. (2014) Sin taxes and sindustry: revenue, paternalism, and political interest, *The Independent Review* 19 (1), 47–64.

Lee, M.R.F., Domingues, J.P., McAuliffe, G.A., Tichit, M., Accatino, F. and Takahashi, T. (2021) Nutrient provision capacity of alternative livestock farming systems per area of arable farmland required, *Nature Scientific Reports* 11, 14975. https://doi.org/10.1038/s41598-021-93782-9.

Rieger, J., Freund, F., Offermann, F., Geibel, I. and Gocht, A. (2023) From fork to farm: Impacts of more sustainable diets in the EU-27 on the agricultural sector, *Journal of Agricultural Economics* 74 (3), 764–784. https://doi.org/10.1111/1477-9552.12530.

Simmonds, P. and Vallgårda, S. (2021) "It's not as simple as something like sugar": values and conflict in the UK meat tax debate, *International Journal of Health Governance* 26 (3), 307–322. https://doi.org/10.1108/IJHG-03-2021-0026.

Stroud, R.S. (1998) The Athenian Grain-Tax Law of 374/3 B.C., *Hesperia Supplements*, 29, iii. https://doi.org/10.2307/1354031.

Swinburn, B.A., Kraak, V.I., Allender, S., Atkins, V.J., Baker, P.I., Bogard, J.R., Brinsden, H., Calvillo, A., De Schutter, O., Devarajan, R., Ezzati, M., Friel, S., Goenka, S., Hammond, R.A., Hastings, G., Hawkes, C., Herrero, M., Hovmand, P.S. ... and Dietz, W.H. (2019) The global syndemic of obesity, undernutrition, and climate change: the Lancet Commission report, *The Lancet* 393 (10173), 791–846. https://doi.org/10.1016/S0140-6736(18)32822-8

Véliz, C., Maslen, H., Essman, M., Taillie, L.S. and Savulescu, J. (2019) Sugar, taxes, and choice, *Hastings Center Report* 49 (6), 22–31. http://doi.wiley.com/10.1002/hast.1067.

Further reading

The following two articles use political science approaches to better understand conflict around SSB taxes.

Buckton, C.H., Fergie, G., Leifeld, P. and Hilton, S. (2019) A discourse network analysis of UK newspaper coverage of the 'sugar tax' debate before and after the announcement of the Soft Drinks Industry Levy, *BMC Public Health* 19 (1), 490. https://doi.org/10.1186/s12889-019-6799-9.

Sainsbury, E., Magnusson, R., Thow, A.M. and Colagiuri, S. (2020) Explaining resistance to regulatory interventions to prevent obesity and improve nutrition: a case-study of a sugar-sweetened beverages tax in Australia, *Food Policy* 93, 101904. https://doi.org/10.1016/j.foodpol.2020.101904.

PHILIPPA SIMMONDS

70. Food loss and waste

Jonas Cromwell

Introduction: an overview of the problem

The issue of food loss and waste (FLW) has gained significant attention due to its social, environmental, and economic implications. The growing focus on FLW is highlighted by the UN's Sustainable Development Goal (SDG) 12.3, which aims to halve global food waste at retail and consumer levels and reduce food loss along supply chains by 2030.

FLW occurs throughout the food supply chain, yet the actual scale of the problem remains unclear. The Food and Agriculture Organisation (FAO) of the United Nations estimated in 2019 that nearly 14% of food produced in 2016 was lost before reaching retail and consumer levels. However, a recent World Wide Fund for Nature (WWF-UK) report (2021) identified primary production as a major hotspot for global food losses, estimating that global FLW onfarms alone amounts to 1.2 billion tonnes per year, representing 15.3% of global agricultural production. An earlier estimate by FAO in 2011 put annual global FLW accross all stages of the supply chain from farm to forkat 1.3 billion tonnes. In Europe, 21–33% of food is lost during agricultural production, 21–25% during manufacturing, storage, processing, and distribution, and over 40% at retail and consumer stages (Zeinstra et al., 2020). In the Global North, much of the FLW occurs at the consumption stage, while in the Global South, it primarily happens on farms and during harvesting, storage, and distribution. Roots, tubers, oilbearing crops, and fruits and vegetables experience the highest levels of FLW.

FLW represents a significant waste of resources used in food production, processing, distribution, and preparation. Globally, FLW contributes 10% of greenhouse gas emissions (WWF-UK, 2021), with consumer FLW alone accounting for trillions of megajoules of energy and 82 billion cubic metres of water lost annually (Coudard et al., 2021). Additionally, FLW leads to income losses for farmers, processors, manufacturers, retailers, and consumers, drives up food prices, and threatens global food security. The FAO (2024) estimates that between 713 and 757 million of the world's population faced hunger in 2023, with 582 million people projected to be chronically undernourished by the end of the decade. Reducing FLW will not only help improve food and nutrition security for millions of people globally, but also contribute to other SDGs (zero hunger SDG 2, sustainable water management SDG 6, climate action SDG 13, marine resources including "blue foods" SDG 14, and terrestrial ecosystems SDG 15).

Complexities in the conceptualisation of FLW

No universal definition of FLW exists, despite several in the literature. The World Resources Institute (WRI, 2016) defines food "loss" as the unintended result of agricultural processes or technical limitations in storage, infrastructure, packaging, or marketing, while "waste" occurs during storage, processing, and distribution. Definitions vary across dimensions such as what qualifies as food, whether only edible parts should be considered, whether food diverted to other uses (e.g., animal feed) is included, and which stages of the food supply chain are considered.

Some definitions consider FLW only after crops are ready for harvest, excluding pre-harvest losses and resources used in agricultural production. Others define FLW as all agricultural products intended for human consumption but not consumed, even if they have other final uses. Therefore, products removed from the food chain or repurposed for animal feed, bioenergy, or biomaterials are not considered FLW. Even overconsumption, or luxus consumption, has been conceptualised as food waste (Smil, 2004; Blair and Sobal, 2006).

Different conceptualisations highlight the various aspects of FLW that stakeholders and researchers focus on. Most definitions focus on quantitative FLW, as this is easier to define and measure than qualitative FLW. For instance, should the measure taken be in terms of volume, caloric or other nutritional content, or economic value? The varying definitions can obscure the true magnitude of FLW and hinder efforts to identify causes and design effective interventions.

Distinguishing between "food loss" and "food waste" by supply chain stage adds further complexity. Food loss is typically associated with the pre-consumer stage, while food waste is linked to retail and consumer stages. This distinction is crucial from a policy perspective, as different interventions may be required for different actors. However,

Table 70.1   Different conceptualisations relating to food loss and waste

Terms	Conceptualisation
Food loss	A decrease in the quantity or quality of food resulting from decisions and actions by food suppliers in the chain, excluding retail, food service providers, and consumers.
Food waste	A decrease in the quantity or quality of food resulting from decisions and actions by retailers, food services, and consumers.
Quantitative (physical) FLW	Physical decrease in the mass of food destined for human consumption but removed from the food supply chain due to decisions and actions by food suppliers.
Qualitative FLW	A decrease in food attributes that reduces its value in terms of intended use- reduced nutritional value (e.g., reduced vitamin C in bruised fruits) or reduced economic value due to non-compliance with quality standards.
Avoidable food waste	Edible food that is discarded due to misunderstanding portion sizes, lack of cooking or storage skills, overbuying, and confusion over expiration dates.
Possibly avoidable food waste	Edible food parts (such as potato skins, fish heads, or food that is subject to personal preference) that some people might choose to eat while others would discard.
Unavoidable food waste	Inedible parts of food products not intended for human consumption (meat bones, eggshells, fruit peels, and tea bags).

Source: Adapted from FAO (2019).

in practice, the distinction is nuanced. For example, FLW can occur during agricultural production due to decisions or actions at both retail and production stages, such as a farmer overproducing or not harvesting due to low prices. Retailer decisions are often strongly influenced by consumer behaviour, blurring the line between loss and waste. The binary approach often reduces FLW to inefficiency or lack of technology, leading to a focus on technological solutions while neglecting structural and institutional causes like market conditions and local norms (Cromwell, 2022). There is a need to conceptualise FLW as arising from social relations and macro-structural and institutional forces across multiple scales. This approach allows FLW to be understood as issues of power dynamics and inequalities.

Studying food loss and waste

FLW has been explored through quantitative and qualitative approaches. Quantitative methods focus on understanding "what" and "how much", while qualitative methods address "how" or "why". Quantitative methodologies play a critical role in addressing food waste by providing consistent measures

to track FLW against reduction targets. In quantitative studies, modelling approaches, such as life cycle assessments and circular economy, have been employed to assess the environmental impact (greenhouse gas emissions of FLW), economic impact, and the sustainability of various FLW valorisation options, including diverting waste from landfills to compost, animal feed, and energy recovery.

Quantitative approaches

Quantitative methods used in food waste studies vary but commonly include surveys, audits, and technologies like radio frequency identification (RFID), geographic information systems (GIS) and food photography. Food waste audits involve separating waste into categories, and sorting and weighing each category. Audits have been widely applied in households, communities, schools, and businesses to evaluate sorting behaviours, provide baseline data, and test interventions and waste management strategies. Although audits are costly and resource-intensive, they offer accuracy by avoiding the under-reporting issues often seen in surveys or diaries. On the other hand, surveys are extensively used to estimate food waste across the supply chain, collecting data on attitudes, beliefs, and self-reported behaviours through various designs. However, field surveys are more expensive than lab-based ones, which can produce different behavioural responses due to their artificial settings.

Digital photography is increasingly being used to quantify food waste. For example, the remote food photography method (RFPM) has been employed to estimate portion sizes and waste, offering cost-effective and accurate data collection. However, RFPM is currently limited to plate waste and does not account for household waste from over-preparation/poor storage and is often restricted to lunchtime meals despite evidence suggesting higher waste during evening meals. RFID and GIS have been used for route optimisation, billing, and waste data transmission.

Most quantitative FLW studies focus on the retail and consumer levels, often neglecting farm-level FLW. However, inconsistencies in quantification methods have prompted international efforts to standardise measures. The World Resources Institute's Food Loss and Waste Protocol, launched in 2013, aims to standardise FLW quantification with ten defined methods and guidelines.

Qualitative approaches

While quantitative methods provide data on the extent of food waste, they do not explain why FLW occurs. Understanding the reasons behind FLW is essential for designing effective policies and interventions. This involves exploring both the material and the social aspects that influence everyday food practices. At the consumer level, behavioural theories like the theory of planned behaviour (TPB) and transtheoretical model of behaviour change have been applied to study determinants of food waste, such as planning and shopping behaviours, intentions related to waste reduction, and perceptions of changeability. TPB offers a linear model of behaviour applicable to quantitative modelling but focuses on individual actions rather than the interconnected behaviours that contribute to food waste.

There is a growing call to shift focus from individual contexts to broader social contexts where food waste occurs. Sociological theories of practice have been used to examine the

social, cultural, and contextual factors that shape food waste behaviours. This approach views food waste as a social phenomenon influenced by shared meanings, practices, and material interactions. Researchers like Evans (2012) and Watson and Meah (2013), among others, have applied practice-based approaches to study different aspects of domestic food waste. In upstream supply chains, practice-based approaches have been used to investigate farmers' decisions regarding what produce to harvest or not (Johnson et al., 2019), and how institutions, materiality, and practices interact to produce FLW on farms and wholesale/distribution stages (Cromwell, 2022). These studies often employ ethnographic methods, such as participant observations, diaries, and interviews, to gain in-depth insights into FLW practices. However, this approach is time-consuming and costly due to the extensive data collection required.

Interventions to reduce FLW

Various interventions have been implemented at different stages of the food supply chain to reduce FLW. In the Global North, a significant portion of food waste occurs at the consumption stage, and consequently interventions have focused on changing consumer behaviour, addressing barriers or drivers like meal planning, shopping lists, leftover reuse, social norms, storage, concerns about dates, labels, and environment. Interventions in the Global South focus on harvesting, storage, and distribution. At the consumer stage, interventions generally fall into three categories: information-based, technological solutions, and policy/system/practice changes.

Information-based interventions

Information-based interventions, while widely used, are relatively less effective compared with interventions like changing portion or plate sizes. They involve providing information (to increase knowledge and skills) to enable change of behaviour in the target group, e.g., households, hotel managers and diners, etc., through methods such as campaigns, prompts, cooking classes, and tips for household practices. The effectiveness of these interventions varies. For instance, a student-focused education campaign led to a 33% reduction in waste, a "Home Labs" intervention resulted in a 28% reduction, while portion size advertising increased the uptake of smaller portions from 3.5% to 6% (see Reynolds et al., 2019).

Furthermore, the use of prompts like signage in hotels was found to reduced food waste by 20% while e-newsletters and social media prompts to provide tips on leftover reuse and storage achieved a 19% reduction in self-reported household food waste. However, prompts have shown limited effectiveness, primarily in public spaces like buffets, and there is little evidence of their impact in private settings. While information-based interventions are relatively effective, they are more successful when combined with other interventions.

Technological interventions

Technological solutions involve introducing or modifying technologies to alter behaviour related to FLW. Popular interventions at the consumption stage include changes in plate or portion sizes, fridge cameras, thermometers, smart fridges, and mobile apps. Only plate and portion size studies have effectively quantified waste reduction. For example, switching from disposable to permanent plates reduced food waste by 51%, while smaller portions reduced French fry waste by 31%. Mobile apps like Social Recipes, which suggest recipes using ingredients at risk of becoming waste, have raised awareness but did not directly reduce food waste. However, combining these apps with waste-reduction interventions could improve their effectiveness (see Reynolds et al., 2019).

Policy/systems/practice changes

Policy interventions often follow the FLW hierarchy, prioritising actions from most to least preferable: preventing FLW, redistributing surplus food, composting, energy recovery, and landfilling. Surplus food is technically "food loss and waste" diverted from the commercial sector due to overproduction, sub-optimal shape/size, mis-labelling and packaging, or food nearing the end of its shelf-life through initiatives like the UK's Courtauld Commitment 2030 and France's Food Waste Law. These efforts mandate and encourage the donation of unsold food to charities, aiding community kitchens, clubs (breakfast/lunch), food banks, food pantries, and social supermarkets. In this case 'surplus' food associated with food redistribution efforts by community food aid organisations making use of the suplus food can be viewed as waste. However, such redirection helps mitigate landfill waste and supports low-income and food-insecure or food-poor individuals with access to necessary nutrition.

However, a lack of infrastructure and investment in surplus redistribution chains can lead to unintended disposal issues within the food aid sector rather than in supermarkets. Additionally, navigating the legal aspects of food redistribution requires compliance with food safety regulations.

Policy interventions involving updating menus, changing dietary guidelines, or revising how nutrition and FLW education are taught have been effective in reducing waste. For example, changing school dietary guidelines led to a 14% and 28% reduction in fruit and vegetable waste, respectively, while increasing the consumption of fruits (23%) and vegetables (16.2%) despite the increased portion size (Cohen et al., 2014). Furthermore, changing how food waste is taught in schools has proven effective, resulting in a 33% reduction in waste.

Future directions

While cooking classes, mobile apps, advertising, and information sharing have all been reported to be effective, there is a need for robust evidence to back the claims by testing these interventions with accurate measurement methods as they are being proposed as strategies to reduce food waste. Also, many interventions that feature advertising, or an information campaign, do not provide enough detail to analyse and correlate the content type, and tone (positive, negative, shocking, etc.), with the effectiveness of the campaign. Furthermore, there is lack of evidence regarding the ease with which these interventions can be scaled up. These are important evidence gaps for researchers, policy makers, and practitioners working to prevent food waste at the consumption level. Studies on longitudinal and larger sample size interventions are needed to strengthen current evidence of effectiveness. Future intervention studies will benefit from standardised guidelines consisting of the intervention design, monitoring and measurement, moderation and mediation, reporting, and systemic effects (Reynolds et al., 2019).

JONAS CROMWELL

Due to the complex nature of the causes and drivers of FLW, addressing the issue requires taking a food system approach that involves multiple stakeholders across the entire food chain. Taking a food system approach to FLW policy development and interventions is necessary as varying levels of waste are generated at each stage, influenced by the food types, processes, and geography in question. Moving towards a system approach will enhance understanding of the interconnected impacts and potential trade-offs of policy measures, promoting more sustainable and efficient practices.

Acknowledgement

I acknowledge the support from the Food System in Southern Africa for One Health (FoSTA-Health) project, supported by the European Commission's Horizon Europe programme (project number 101060887) for the time spent on authoring this entry.

References

Blair D and Sobal J (2006). Luxus consumption: Wasting food resources through overeating. *Agriculture and Human Value* 23(1), 63–74. http://doi10.1007/s10460-004-5869-4.

Cohen J F, Richardson S, Parker E, Catalano P J and Rimm E B (2014). Impact of the new US Department of Agriculture school meal standards on food selection, consumption, and waste. *American Journal of Preventive Medicine* 46(4), 388–394. https://doi.org/10.1016/j.amepre.2013.11.013.

Coudard A, Corbin E, de Koning J, Tukker A and Mogollón J M (2021). Global water and energy losses from consumer avoidable food waste. *Journal of Cleaner Production* 326, 129342. https://doi.org/10.1016/j.jclepro.2021.129342.

Cromwell J (2022). Understanding food loss and waste in Tanzania's avocado production systems: A case study of domestic and export avocado supply chains. Doctoral dissertation, University of Sheffield.

Evans D (2012). Beyond the throwaway society: Ordinary domestic practice and a sociological approach to household food waste. *Sociology* 46(1), 41–56. https://doi.org/10.1177/0038038511416l.

FAO (2024). *The State of Food Security and Nutrition in the World 2024: Financing to end hunger, food insecurity and malnutrition in all its forms.* https://doi.org/10.4060/cd1254en.

FAO (2019). *The State of Food and Agriculture 2019: Moving forward on food loss and waste reduction.* https://openknowledge.fao.org/server/api/core/bitstreams/11f9288f-dc78-4171-8d02-92235b8d7dc7/content (Accessed 2 August 2024).

Johnson L K, Bloom J D, Dunning R D, Gunter C C, Boyette M D and Creamer N G (2019). Farmer harvest decisions and vegetable loss in primary production. *Agricultural Systems* 176, 102672.

Reynolds C, Goucher L, Quested T, Bromley S, Gillick S, Wells V K, Evans D, Koh L, Kanyama A C, Katzeff C and Svenfelt A and Jackson P (2019). Consumption-stage food waste reduction interventions: What works and how to design better interventions. *Food Policy* 83, 7–27.

Smil V (2004). Improving efficiency and reducing waste in our food system. *Environmental Sciences* 1(1), 17–26.

Watson M and Meah A (2013). Food, waste and safety: Negotiating conflicting social anxieties into the practices of domestic provisioning. *The Sociological Review* 60, 102–120. https://doi.org/10.1111/1467-954X.12040.

WRI (2016). *Food Loss and Waste Accounting and Reporting Standards.* Washingston, DC World Resource Institute.

WWF-UK (2021). *Driven to Waste: Global Food Loss on Farms.* https://wwf.panda.org/discover/our_focus/food_practice/food_loss_and_waste/driven_to_waste_global_food_loss_on_farms/(Accessed 01/09/2024).

Zeinstra G, van der Haar S and van Bergen G (2020). Drivers, barriers and interventions for food waste behaviour change: A food system approach. *Wageningen Food & Biobased Research.* https://doi.org/10.18174/511479.

Further reading

Evans D, Campbell H and Murcott A (2013). *Waste Matters: New Perspectives on Food and Society.* Oxford, John Wiley and Sons. This collection delves into the sociological aspects of food waste, examining its cultural, political, and economic impacts, and discusses the regulation, social practices, materiality, and valuation of food, offering theoretical and empirical insights from various perspectives.

Reynolds C, Soma T and Lazell J (2020). *Routledge Handbook of Food Waste.* Abington, Routledge.

The book offers a thorough exploration of food waste, examining its systemic causes, potential solutions like social innovation and technology, and the importance of various approaches including spirituality and activism, making it vital for those involved in addressing this complex issue.

71. Gastronomy

MICHAELA DESOUCEY

Introduction: towards a critical understanding of gastronomy

Gastronomy is an important topic for critical food studies. It holds a double conceptual meaning, with implications for the cultural and political dynamics of food and cuisine.

First, the term translates lexically as rules (*nomos*) of the stomach (*gaster*) and is oft-characterised as the scientific and artistic pursuit of culinary excellence. This definition allies with the professional culinary arts and class-based consumption practices that together constitute the creation and enjoyment of fine and delicious foods. Inherent in it is pleasure; a "gastronome" is well-versed in sophisticated or fashionable food, has a discriminating palate, and is sometimes referred to as a gourmet, epicure, or foodie.

Second, the term – and perhaps, today, most commonly – centres the relationship among food, place, and culture: ingredients, dishes, and cooking techniques that are considered characteristic of regions, time periods, or social groups (Gillespie and Cousins, 2012), sometimes referred to as foodways. Gastronomy in this way elicits notions of heritage, authenticity, and tradition, connoting that "a" gastronomy has a defining set of ingredients, flavours, and cooking techniques. Here, gastronomy is similar to cuisines, which historians (Belasco, 2008) and anthropologists (Douglas, 1984) have argued can be analogous to language or grammar – a shared set of protocols (core ingredients, seasonings, and flavour principles), preparations, etiquette codes, utensils, meal structure, and market infrastructures. Indeed, cuisine operates as a system of communicating identity claims (Brulotte and Di Giovine, 2016) that can situate, connect, and differentiate people through time and space. In other words, cuisines are socially constructed *structures* of cooking and eating that help meals and foods make cultural sense.

Gastronomy and cuisine differ in terms of the social implications of each idea. While the culinary arts can be traced to ancient times (Flandrin et al., 1999), gastronomy as a modern sociopolitical phenomenon was only established at the turn of the 19th century, in France (Fantasia, 2018; Pitte, 2002). It was then that French cuisine's self-styled superiority was institutionalised, and gastronomy formalised as a "cultural field" (Ferguson, 2004). This new ideological form grew through the rise of the restaurant as a ubiquitous part of French public life (Spang, 2000), the elevation of cooking and (male) chefs from servitude to an esteemed profession, and the copious writings of new culinary professionals – cookbooks by prominent chefs and culinary treatises by elite thought leaders and critics (Ferguson, 2004). The ensuing codification of a set of (formerly regional) ingredients and dishes emplaced gastronomy as a facet of French nation-building. It also created a template for others, using print and now online media, to link gastronomy to distinctive techniques, such as "molecular gastronomy", or to the social visibility of particular places.

Gastronomies – and thus ideologies and institutions undergirding diverse culinary cultures – are necessarily constitutive of group identities and cultural conventions: not just who we are, but how we want to be seen. They can also typecast or test groups, as well as become fraught political issues that both unite and divide.

Current issues in gastronomic politics

As a concept and practice, "gastronomy" layers institutional, market-based, and political elements onto cuisines. Gastronomic practices have become codified by texts like cookbooks and travel guides, as well as through international organisations like Slow Food, the World Tourism Organization, and UNESCO. Here, gastronomies do more than identify special culinary practices: they provide guiding and systematic ways for people to see, experience, and disseminate the food practices of others (von Bremzen, 2023). For example, the relationship between gastronomy and tourism has developed rapidly in recent decades, with food-related experiences shifting from a peripheral to a central concern of much destination travel. For tourists, food is a domain where ideas about culture are represented as an experiential part of learning about "authentic" places and people. "Authenticity" here denotes social expectations – specifically around ingredients, dishes, and customs adhering to idealised, supposedly original, culinary forms (DeSoucey, 2010, 2016). For hospitality industries and stakeholders across cities, regions, and countries, gastronomy serves as a means of place-branding (Rinaldi,

2017) and is seen to have immense potential for both local economic development and community pride.

Gastronomic attractions – restaurants, food festivals, open-air markets, cooking classes, agritourism, and others – are now highly valued by stakeholders globally (Dixit, 2021). Some countries, such as Denmark, Spain, and Peru, endorse the global fame of their restaurant scenes and prestigious chefs. UNESCO has inscribed multiple dishes (e.g., French baguette, Korean kimchi, Neapolitan pizza, and Ukrainian borscht) on its Intangible Cultural Heritage List and has declared Cities of Gastronomy around the world (the current two in the United States, interestingly, are Tucson, Arizona, and San Antonio, Texas). This process necessarily blends "local" and "cosmopolitan" gustatory elements into "haute traditional" gastro-touristic cuisines (Sammells, 2016), though such initiatives can occasionally trap gastronomies into rigid, museum-like forms, halting creative culinary pursuits.

Affective connections between foods and geography are impossible to refute. Yet, the places associated with particular gastronomies are not, and have never been, closed containers of culture or people. Significant dishes represent the settings they were popularised in in the past. Moreover, as people worldwide have become increasingly cognisant of the moral and environmental implications of industrialised food systems, assertions of collective identity via promoting and eating (or eschewing) foods associated with specific gastronomies have become more complex and fraught, even for many who might prefer to remain apolitical. Namely, in the last few decades, fears of global cultural homogeneity have spurred projects purporting to protect "local" dishes, defending gastronomies from perceived external influences and regardless of the veracity of their origin stories or of the culinary or demographic shifts occurring in those places today (von Bremzen, 2023).

A gastro-political perspective, drawing from theories of symbolic politics, highlights not only how groups perceive their own foodways, but how, why, and for whom certain "edible identities" (Brulotte and Di Giovine, 2016) become emboldened and/or controversial (DeSoucey, 2016). Gastropolitical issues foreground attempts to claim cultural and moral authority about food, meshing the everyday with formal policies and laws that shape food systems. Gastronomy is politically compelling because it can validate claims-making around group identity projects (Appadurai, 1988). As Bourdieu (1984: 56) aptly noted, "Taste is first and foremost distaste… of the taste of others." Three sub-categories to discuss here are gastronationalism, gastronativism, and gastrodiplomacy. Each helps elucidate why and how a food's cultural potency can change dramatically; how gastronomy is utilised to mark group boundaries (Parasecoli, 2022); and why culinary "traditions" are often invented, consecrated, and reified during moments of political difficulty or turmoil (Ranta and Ichijo, 2022).

First, gastronationalism is a type of identity politics responding to the consolidation of agri-food industries alongside open trade markets. DeSoucey (2010: 433) coined the term as the double-sided "use of food production, distribution, and consumption to demarcate and sustain the emotive power of national attachment" alongside "nationalist sentiments to produce and market food". Indeed, legally protecting foods and drinks as national emblems – helping people classify where they and others are from – is but a recent chapter in a longer history of nation-states recognising the cultural power of collective belonging. For example, DeSoucey's (2016) work on foie gras politics in France and Gaytán's (2014) research on tequila in Mexico each show how these objects became legally codified assets in their respective national cultural treasuries.

However, it is an underlying gastronationalist presumption that critiques of, or opposition to (symbolic or otherwise), a place's renowned foods are challenges to its heritage. In such cases, state actors intervene in markets as agents and brokers for foods as symbols of history and identity. One important example is the European Union's (EU) programme of geographic origin labels (DeSoucey, 2010), which now extends to thousands of items around the world, often in the wine and spirit sectors (Ranta and Ichijo, 2022). In the late 20th century, the EU recognised dilemmas inherent in the new "common market" agricultural trade policies for artisanal food producers and instituted a programme for producer collectives to register certain foods and drinks as national-level "exceptions", allowing stakeholders to articulate the uniqueness of localised gastronomies and prohibiting others from making similar claims. Some legal battles over foods'

MICHAELA DESOUCEY

provenance—for example, between Greece and Denmark over "feta" cheese—have spent years in the European Court of Justice. Gastronationalist dilemmas have similarly emerged elsewhere through transnational conflicts over differing food safety standards (Ranta and Ichijo, 2022), as well as through other institutions. For example, diplomatic tensions arose between Morocco and Algeria and Tunisia when Morocco left a joint application and received a UNESCO inscription solely for "Moroccan couscous" in 2021.

The second, gastronativism, is gastronationalism's cousin. Parasecoli (2022) depicts it as the strategic use of food as a political tool to define who does or does not belong to a community, and to act, sometimes divisively, based on those assumptions. Gastronativism can thus connect food practically and ideologically to racism, ethnocentrism, and religious intolerance. Gastronativist disputes and debates have become particularly visible in the last two decades, amplified by resurging xenophobic movements across the world. Examples include European politicians denouncing kebob stalls and pork-free school lunches to rally anti-immigrant energies; and populist politicians in Brazil, India, the United States, and elsewhere deploying specific food images on their social media accounts and imposing new, targeted import tariffs to convey "us versus them" ideologies. Involving such food issues in political demonstrations becomes a way to frame perceived threats writ large. What matters is how the food in question figures into specific political narratives. Importantly, Parasecoli's (2022) account of gastronativism also includes related initiatives and protective measures by groups that claim to be non-exclusionary in practice, such as food sovereignty and anti-globalisation organisations.

Finally, gastrodiplomacy illustrates countries' efforts to raise their international profiles by promoting gastronomy, especially abroad (Passidomo, 2017), in what Ray (2016) has called a global "hierarchy of taste". It has been characterised by scholars and practitioners alike as diplomatic "soft power" designed to "share" or "export" a country's cuisine, as well as increase gastronomic tourism at home, and is sometimes described colloquially as winning foreigners' affections through their stomachs. Proponents imagine reputational benefits of economic competitiveness and national pride at home, as well as international tolerance and support that can lead to very real outcomes, from food security to economic prosperity.

The term was first used by *The Economist* in 2002 to describe Thailand's "Global Thai" campaign, which poured resources into expanding the number of Thai restaurants across Western countries and exporting high-level chefs (with legal agreements to facilitate work visas) to raise the international prestige of Thai gastronomy. Such governmental campaigns and export strategies are becoming more common, dependent on investment and marketing professionals, as well as social media. More recently, a widely shared *New York Times Style Magazine* article (Mishan, 2022) detailed a 20th-century campaign by South Korea's government to safeguard Korean royal cuisine under cultural property preservation acts and then, in the 21st century, to disseminate an international Korean food programme. Kimchi, a fermented cabbage dish, received a UNESCO Intangible Heritage inscription in 2013. Similarly, a "gastronomic revolution" in Peru has absorbed national elites' financial and political resources at home and abroad. This includes claims of civil reconciliation after decades of political violence in the interests of turning Peru into a prestigious food nation on the global stage (Matta, 2023). For these and other, often midsized countries, gastrodiplomacy has become deemed a way to enhance how international audiences – consumers, companies, and investors, as well as governments – perceive them.

Looking to the gastronomic future

Gastronomy is a rich and foundational concept for much research and theory in critical food studies. Materially, it brings together the acts of producing, preparing, cooking, serving, and eating food. Socially, it includes discussion, evaluation, and strategy, deigning to nourish our minds as potent symbols of place, purpose, cultural aspiration, and group identities. Initially, it coalesced as an ideology through relatively purposive and programmatic statements of new ways of thinking about food within a larger cultural shift in 18th century France. As such, its emergence reflected the philosophical and political notions of that period, similar to other facets of modern national cultures: language, art, literature, architecture. Since then, what delineates a gastronomy is more than simply ingredients, tools, or techniques; it is also a project of cultural, national, and even transnational politics in a rapidly changing global foodscape.

Namely, gastronomies continue to be reinforced by the ways that designations of authenticity and heritage are performed in economic and cultural spaces around the world. They are embedded in the global flows of goods, ideas, practices, capital, and people, and they reveal how ingredients and dishes may become significant objects through which people make sense of – and try to influence – the world around them. Indeed, tourism associations and policymakers around the world have latched on to promoting places' gastronomies through "traditional" dishes and the cultural construction of food-related historical narratives (even if those stories turn out to be "fakelore" [von Bremzen, 2023]), contributing to a sense of inimitable shared – and shareable – experiences.

This matters for food studies scholars moving forward for two reasons. First, gastronomy matters in understanding the politics of cultural representations, and how gustatory norms can evoke strong affective responses about the relative morality of related activities. A sociological approach to gastronomy emphasises the social organisation of meanings and not necessarily seeing significance as embedded in the food objects themselves. For example, in spring 2020 as the Covid-19 pandemic began, different national governments in Europe beseeched citizens to consume even more of their gastronational symbols than they already did: cheese in France, fries in Belgium, beef in Great Britain. This was not to stymie rising infection rates, of course, but to show solidarity with one's compatriots.

Second and relatedly, gastronomy is significant for our conceptions of how foods – and frictions around food – connect to politics. Alongside historical significance as symbols of belonging, gastropolitics can trigger public discussions and policy negotiations around meaning-making and its limitations. As such, clashes over food's symbolic and material realities lay bare *why* people are willing to defend or fight over food as well as *how* they marshal resources to do so. For example, we may likely see increasing gastropolitical volatility in the coming years with more extreme weather events and climactic shifts affecting what kinds of food production will

no longer be, or be newly, possible in certain geographies.

Future concerns for those engaged in gastronomy must include sustainability, with land availability, energy prices, soil depletion, and water competition likely making food production more expensive. Most food scholars agree that food should be understood as part of a system, wherein all components between the field and the plate influence each other. Future research must also incorporate impacts of the financial industry and new technologies on the domain of food. Just as "molecular gastronomy" captivated the world of haute cuisine at the beginning of the 20th century and lab-grown meats are now making their way onto restaurant menus and grocery shelves, what might be next? For gastronomes of all types, the future will indubitably hold new cultural codes, controversies, and critical reflections.

References

Appadurai A (1988) How to Make a National Cuisine: Cookbooks in Contemporary India. *Comparative Studies in Society and History* 30(1): 3–24.

Belasco, W (2008) Food: The Key Concepts. New York: Berg.

Bourdieu P (1984) *Distinction: A Social Critique of the Judgment of Taste.* Cambridge, MA: Harvard University Press.

Brulotte RL and Di Giovine MA (2016) *Edible Identities: Food as Cultural Heritage.* New York: Routledge.

DeSoucey M (2010) Gastronationalism: Food Traditions and Authenticity Politics in the European Union. *American Sociological Review* 75(3): 432–455.

DeSoucey M (2016) *Contested Tastes: Foie Gras and the Politics of Food.* Princeton, NJ: Princeton University Press.

Dixit SK (2021) *The Routledge Handbook of Gastronomic Tourism.* London: Routledge.

Douglas M (1984) *Food in the Social Order: Studies of Food and Festivities in Three American Communities.* New York: Russell Sage Foundation.

Fantasia R (2018) *French Gastronomy and the Magic of Americanism.* Philadelphia: Temple University Press.

Ferguson PP (2004) *Accounting for Taste: The Triumph of French Cuisine.* Chicago: University of Chicago Press.

MICHAELA DESOUCEY

Flandrin JL, Montanari M and Sonnenfeld A (1999) *Food: A Culinary History From Antiquity to the Present.* New York: Columbia University Press.

Gaytán MS (2014) *¡Tequila!: Distilling the Spirit of Mexico.* Stanford, CA: Stanford University Press.

Gillespie C and Cousins J (2012) *European Gastronomy into the 21st Century.* London: Routledge.

Matta R (2023) *From the Plate to Gastro-Politics: Unravelling the Boom of Peruvian Cuisine.* New York: Palgrave McMillan.

Mishan L (2022) When a Country's Cuisine Becomes a Cultural Export. *The New York Times Style Magazine.* Oct 12. https://www.nytimes.com/2022/10/12/t-magazine/korean-food-national-royal-cuisine.html

Parasecoli F (2022) *Gastronativism: Food, Identity, Politics.* New York: Columbia University Press.

Passidomo C (2017) "Our" Culinary Heritage: Obscuring Inequality by Celebrating Diversity in Peru and the U.S. South. *Humanity & Society* 41(4): 427–445.

Pitte J-R (2002) *French Gastronomy: The History and Geography of a Passion.* New York: Columbia University Press.

Ranta R and Ichijo A (2022) *Food, National Identity and Nationalism: From Everyday to Global Politics.* 2nd ed. London: Palgrave McMillan.

Ray K (2016) *The Ethnic Restaurateur.* New York: Bloomsbury.

Rinaldi C (2017) Food and Gastronomy for Sustainable Place Development. *Sustainability* 9(10): 1748.

Sammells C (2016) Haute Traditional Cuisines: How UNESCO's List of Intangible Heritage Links the Cosmopolitan to the Local. In: Brulotte RL and Di Giovine MA (eds) *Edible Identities: Food as Cultural Heritage.* New York: Routledge, pp. 141–158.

Spang RL (2000) *The Invention of the Restaurant: Paris and Modern Gastronomic Culture.* Cambridge, MA: Harvard University Press.

von Bremzen A (2023) *National Dish: Around the World in Search of Food, History, and the Meaning of Home.* New York: Penguin.

Further reading

DeSoucey M (2016) *Contested Tastes: Foie Gras and the Politics of Food.* Princeton, NJ: Princeton University Press.

Sociological monograph using the case of foie gras to show how "gastropolitics" reflects issues of national identity, social class, markets, ethics, and culture in France and the United States.

Parasecoli F (2022) *Gastronativism: Food, Identity, Politics.* New York: Columbia University Press.

A critical scholarly perspective on gastronomy's ideological uses and deployments across various countries and types of political projects.

MICHAELA DESOUCEY

72. Gender and food

ADELE WYLIE

Introduction: food production, consumption, and gender

Food is intertwined with society through social and cultural norms, production and consumption practices, and material and virtual spaces, as well as acts of care, solidarity, and mutual aid. There are various ways in which food is gendered ranging from our everyday food practices to the discourses surrounding it, which tend to portray food through the lens of hegemonic masculinities and femininities. Who carries out certain food practices such as cooking, preparing, shopping, growing, animal rearing, planting, harvesting, is determined by uneven power dynamics and norms which reflect underlying hierarchies of gender, race, class, and ethnicity. Food is therefore political, and analysing the power dynamics embedded within foodscapes across different food geographies can illuminate the connections between food, power, and gendered inequalities. In this entry, gender is socially constructed. As highlighted by feminist philosopher Judith Butler (1988), gender is something that is performed to consolidate the gender identities assigned to us by society in relation to our biological sex – male or female. Overall, gender is a loaded word and concept, contested by many who reject it as a binary and conceptualise it more as a continuum with man and woman at each end of the spectrum, and more fluid identities in between. Overall, this contested nature of gender is part of the politics that calls for it to be further explored in relation to food.

Viewed through a wide lens, food production practices reflect the capitalist and patriarchal societies we live in, with the most marginalised being exploited for their paid and non-paid labour to generate wealth for the most powerful elites. Women's roles in both urban and rural agriculture are integral in global food production. In the Global South, women's foodwork in agriculture ranges between 43% and 80–90% in some countries in Africa (Glazebrook et al., 2020). In rural agriculture, the labour of women encompasses many aspects of food production beyond growing crops, such as collecting food, water, and firewood for the home, tending to the livestock, and most post-harvest processing work. Yet, although women's agriculture is vital for food security, their labour is perpetually undervalued at societal, domestic, and economic levels.

Globally, the roles of paid food workers are gendered throughout the food system. In the Global North, women within the food service industry tend to work as servers of food, kitchen assistants, and pastry chefs whereas men are dominant in the roles of head chefs and other leadership positions within professional kitchens. Professional kitchens are typically characterised by toxic masculinity, sexism, and misogyny, to the extent that they have been compared with the military. They are built upon masculine traits and a hierarchy which favours men. Female chefs who do progress must work harder and endure more stress to show they are as capable as male chefs. However, given the anti-social, long working hours that chefs work, female chefs tend to change careers or maintain lower status positions once they have children. This allows for the reproduction of the male dominance and toxic masculinity that kitchens are characterised by (Wylie, 2020).

Celebrity chefs such as Gordon Ramsey and Marco Pierre White thrust professional kitchens into the limelight through their television shows such as *Hell's Kitchen*, *Kitchen Nightmares*, and *The Chopping Block*, which were particularly popular in the US, Australia, and the UK between 2004 and 2014. The aggressive and abusive behaviour of the celebrity chefs towards the contestants revealed how violence and abuse become normalised as the way to run a professional kitchen. Overall, these chefs have been associated with the glamourisation and a resurgence of the "old school" abuse and toxic masculinity chefs endure in the industry.

More recently, digital media influencers have overtaken celebrity chefs as the authority on good food. They play a key role in shaping contemporary food norms and practices through the medium of digital media platforms. These online spaces have been conceptualised by Goodman and Jaworska (2020: 3) as "digital foodscapes" where "digitized food – in all its forms and functions – has colonized all corners and platforms of the Internet and played a key role in facilitating the construction of contemporary digital societies and food-based capitalism".

Concerns about the climate emergency and animal welfare have become mainstream in food-based capitalism. The methane emissions and environmental impacts of consuming meat have led to a proliferation of food trends and lifestyle choices, and animal-based produce is being replaced with more environmentally conscious options. In response to vegetarian and vegan lifestyles and increased consumption of plant-based alternatives to meat, the media and popular cultural imagery around meat has become more sexualised and exploitative of women, whilst placing more emphasis on the virility of male meat eaters (Adams, 2003). Men are being invited by these marketing campaigns to reaffirm their masculinity through the consumption of meat. Ecofeminist writer Carol Adams (2003) noted that the notion of selling women's bodies has become more normalised through the mainstreaming of pornography. This sexualisation of meat consumption reflects the wider speciesism and misogyny experienced by women and non-human animals in patriarchal capitalist Western societies.

Gender, bodies, and food in a capitalist society

Uneven power relations associated with food and gender have generated decades of feminist scholarship within food studies and food geographies. This work has explored women's food labour in the formal, informal, and care economies, including their reproductive labour and the construction and performativity of gendered identities through food practices and well-being choices. More recently, intersectionality, which stemmed from Black feminist theory, has become an important lens through which to study the gendered and racialised politics of food (Swan, 2020). Intersectionality encapsulates the political underpinnings shaping the lived experiences of women from a diversity of backgrounds, impacted by structural inequalities and oppressions throughout the food system which extend beyond those associated with one's gender or gender alone.

Women as food caregivers in the Global North

When it comes to the gendered division of food-related labour, or what is better known as foodwork, no space has been studied more than the domestic sphere. Reproductive labour in relation to food practice was of particular

interest to DeVault (1991). She argued that reproductive food labour was both mentally and physically laborious for women, yet not validated as work nor financially rewarded. The underlying societal assumption was that women undertook foodwork as an act of care for others.

Domestic foodwork has been widely researched, mostly focusing on heteronormative couples exploring how heteromasculinities and heterofemininities shape domestic foodwork, with little attention to same sex or gender non-conforming families. Concepts such as maternal foodwork and intensive mothering have arisen to capture the expectations and motivations of mothers who undertake uneven amounts of domestic foodwork as compared with their male partners and dedicate themselves to their babies' and children's growth. From a food perspective, this means showing love and nurturing by providing healthy, nutritious, and ethically sourced home cooked meals. As this requires a mother to sacrifice her time and career, it is a privilege generally reserved for middle- to upper-class mothers. Many want a shift away from this oppressive "anti-kitchen bias" representative of the middle-class, Western white woman (Christie, 2006: 1). By overlooking the cultural significance and value in women's foodwork beyond the Global North, this research has overlooked the fact that women can be empowered through food preparation. For diasporic women, cooking can help enhance and preserve their ethnic and gendered identities and shape gendered social ties through cooking and sharing food knowledges carried through the process of migration. Consuming "traditional" food has shown impacts at a visceral level, a sensory response which reaffirms an emotional and physical connection to cultures and places of origin.

Yet, DeVault's (1991) early research on questions of gender and food in American households overlooked the significance of race and ethnicity in women's foodwork. She did, however, touch upon class, where she found that working class women would rely on learning to cook traditional meals that they grew up with. However, over thirty years later, working class and low-income women are turning to food banks. Many mothers are going hungry to ensure their children are fed as the ingredients they once relied on are now unaffordable. In the face of financial destitution as a result of decades of austerity policies in the UK, low-income domestic food workers who now "shop" at food banks must endure being the targets of media culinary saviours – i.e. television chefs and social media influencers – demonstrating how to cook on a budget. These culinary performances can reaffirm common assumptions that low-income households do not know how to cook or how to budget properly and need to be shown how to live in poverty to be able to manage. This narrative fundamentally deflects governments' responsibilities and overlooks the systemic failures and economic and social oppression low-income women are confronted with.

Women as producers of food in the Global South

In the Global South, women play a central role in agriculture through subsistence farming and livestock keeping. Yet even though their food labour is essential for food security, it is undervalued. Female farmers have significantly less access to land, financial, and technological resources than male farmers, and they are compensated significantly less for their labour. These gendered inequalities and patriarchal agricultural norms keep hundreds of millions of rural women farmers in the Global South in positions of poverty. In the face of climate change – a major threat to agriculture globally – women rural farmers in the Global South are the most vulnerable. In comparison to the Global North, where farming is a business protected though insurance or government welfare, many rural women farmers in the Global South are subsistence farmers who grow crops to feed themselves and their families with produce that is not sold or traded through markets. In the event of climate-induced shocks such as crop failures, female farmers and their communities are likely to face severe food insecurity or hunger.

Approaches to urban agriculture, albeit with some differences, tend to reproduce these gendered roles, with women undertaking subsistence farming (e.g. small garden plots; small farms which produce beans, maize, herbs; rearing small animals), and men producing food for commercial purposes (large scale farming such as sugar cane and the rearing of livestock), and processing and marketing it. Even though women's foodwork might feed urban dwellers, it too is very often undervalued because it is less profitable than

that performed by men. This results in women having limited decision-making power and resources, as well as an inadequate participation in policy decisions.

Climate change-induced food insecurity has placed attention on adaptation and sustainable agriculture. Gendered inequalities in both rural and urban agriculture highlight the significant role of gender in a farmer's adaptive capacity and priorities. Women, caught up in a cycle of low productivity tend to prefer crops that reflect their domestic foodwork needs, such as nourishing their families, in that they tend to be simple to cook and high in nutrients, and taste good. Men prefer crops that are economically viable and that have a high yield. Whilst they are more concerned with large-scale technical interventions, women tend to make small, practical changes and work to ensure food security for themselves, their families, and their communities.

Gendered bodies in the digital foodscapes

Digital foodscapes are significant in shaping and influencing everyday food practices and choices. Digital media have taken body imagery and the cultural politics of eating to extraordinary levels in that practically anyone can accrue a large following through their social media posts, images, videos, blogs, etc. In turn, digital food influencers have now replaced food celebrities and chefs as the gatekeepers of what constitutes good food.

Media and celebrities have long shaped our expectations of the perfect feminine and masculine physiques. Women for decades were held to impossible and problematic standards of ultra-thin supermodels, leading to an explosion of eating disorders such as anorexia and bulimia. More recently, the ideal man is portrayed as a muscular, fitness buff who consumes a great deal of protein, supplements, and, perhaps, is a vegan, or a "hegan" – a contested label intended to portray veganism as masculine. Food trends and dietary choices are associated with gendered norms and expectations, prompting many to consider which food and lifestyle choices they must make to perform their gender correctly.

The cultural politics of eating is entrenched in power relations which go beyond gender to include race and class. This has raised the question of who is being represented in food narratives and from what perspective. For example, vegan diets can be elitist, steeped

ADELE WYLIE

in privilege and inaccessible for low-income eaters, while the food choices of low-income women (opting for cheaper processed, high-sugar foods) and people of colour (opting for culturally significant cuisines such as soul food) have acted as scapegoats as the drivers of obesity crises (Slocum, 2011). Such misrepresentations and blame have reinforced white-privileged neoliberal ideals of good food. Meanwhile, they overlook both the socio-economic constraints faced by low-income women in contemporary consumer societies, and the importance of eating culturally significant food for one's identity and pleasure.

Ecofeminist Carol Adams (1990; 2003) connected the cultural imagery of meat eating, which displays the feminisation of farmed animals (e.g., feminised proteins) and vice versa, to the violence, exploitation, and oppression that women and non-human animals suffer under the patriarchy and capitalism of Western societies. More recently, whilst analysing food in the digital sphere, Lupton (2018: 1) found that meat was celebrated in an almost pornographic tone, detrimental to women and non-human animals: "men are depicted as aggressive meat eaters and animals and women as objects for men's carnal appetites."

Gendered food futures

Going forward, the capitalist nature of our food system will continue to reproduce power dynamics that exploit women throughout the care economy and marginalised groups, throughout formal and informal food economies. Couple this with the climate emergency and it becomes clear that resisting the gendered and intersectional socio-economic inequalities throughout the food system is and will be vital in the future. The 2020 Covid-19 pandemic was the biggest shock the global food system has felt since the 2008 global financial recession. The pandemic exposed the food system as exploitative, racist, misogynist, unjust, and vulnerable. It also provided a lens into what needs to change to forge a more equal and resilient food system in the face of future crises.

Gendered foodwork and Covid-19

The Covid-19 pandemic has had far-reaching impacts on societies and the geographies of food across the world. In the Global North, the pandemic has generated an increase in food insecurity and reliance on food banks and community kitchens. Access to food networks was restricted during lockdowns and self-isolation. The restrictions placed upon the food service industry generated vast unemployment and job insecurity for food workers.

Research by feminist and food justice scholars has highlighted the gendered dimension of Covid-19 through a food lens, as women were unevenly burdened in both the formal and care economies. Women's unpaid foodwork increased along with domestic care duties, greatly impacting women in low-income households, single mothers, and women in minority groups such as asylum seekers (Swan, 2020). Throughout the food service industry, unemployment and job insecurity impacted women as they held the most casual, insecure roles going into the pandemic. Furthermore, as childcare facilities closed during lockdowns, working mothers had to prioritise caring roles over paid work.

In the UK, furlough payments were provided to workers in the food industry. Such welfare and employment reforms re-enforced labour precarity through the normalisation of zero-hour contracts, reduced and unpredictable working hours, and mass unemployment, with many employers refusing to provide food workers with a paid salary.

To continue operating during the pandemic, many restaurants turned to online delivery platforms creating a demand for informal food workers – delivery drivers and riders. This work is male dominated, it is intense, and it is precarious as the wages are low and worker rights and job protection are limited. In addition, these food workers were some of the most exposed to the Covid-19 virus. Furthermore, as the delivery service aimed to reduce human interaction during the pandemic, the drivers suffered from loneliness and isolation. The gender burdens faced by food workers reflect the precariousness and vulnerability embedded in pre-pandemic foodscapes.

Gender, food, and solidarity in a changing climate

In the face of future crises, there is a need to organise food systems around notions of solidarity, care, and empowerment for both women and men who are exploited and marginalised. Anarchist geographer Springer (2020: 1) argues that, at its core, capitalism creates societies which are selfish, and it "alienates us from all other life on this planet". It generates environmental degradation and social inequalities, thriving on consumption and deprivation. Yet, during the Covid-19 pandemic both men and women showed solidarity as they came together voluntarily through food to feed homeless and food-insecure people and essential workers. The roles were gendered as men were highly represented in the delivery component and women through cooking and food preparation. This compassion and food aid mutualism was a sign that community cooperation is essential in tending to the failures of capitalism such as precarity, austerity, and inequality. However, what occurred during Covid-19 were mostly de-politicised actions devoid of any notion of deconstructing the systemic capitalist injustices which generate the need for food aid to begin with. Gaps in societal responsibility left by the state were filled, and opportunities to instigate long-term systematic changes were overlooked, and as society reopened voluntary workers returned to their normal jobs and lives.

There are a few examples of what a gender-contextualised sustainable and equitable food system could look like. For instance, women-led community food initiatives in Aotearoa are forging their own food system based on traditional knowledge and Māori cultural values. Female rural farmers in the Global South are playing a key role in food secure futures through food diversification innovation. In the digital sphere, hashtag activism, a term reflecting the role of digital protest such as #arabspring, #MeToo, and #BlackLivesMatter, is breaking down dominant discourses around food. In Australia, for example, food security activists have used it to strategically raise awareness, create new narratives, and promote new food security policy imaginaries. Going forward from a feminist perspective, both women and men must come together to forge something never seen before – a sustainable and equitable food system. This entails rejecting existing norms which oppress women, exploit urban poor people, reinforce poverty and precarity, and leave rural poor people vulnerable to climate change.

References

Adams Carol, J., 1990. *The Sexual Politics of Meat: A Feminist-Vegetarian Critical Theory.* New York: Continuum.

Adams, C., 2003. *The Pornography of Meat.* London: Continuum.

Butler, J., 1988. Performative Acts and Gender Constitution: An Essay in Phenomenology and Feminist Theory, *Theatre Journal, 40*(4), 519–531.

Christie, M. E., 2006. Kitchenspace: Gendered territory in central Mexico. *Gender, Place and Culture, 13*(6), 653–661.

DeVault, M. L., 1991. Family discourse and everyday practice: Gender and class at the dinner table. *Syracuse Scholar (1979–1991), 11*(1), 2.

Glazebrook, T., Noll, S. and Opoku, E., 2020. Gender matters: Climate change, gender bias, and women's farming in the global South and North. *Agriculture, 10*(7), 267.

Goodman, M. K. and Jaworska, S., 2020. Mapping digital foodscapes: Digital food influencers and the grammars of good food. *Geoforum, 117*, 183–193.

Lupton, D., 2018. Vitalities and visceralities: Alternative body/food politics in digital media. In Phillipov, M., and Kirkwood, K. (Eds.), *Alternative Food Politics: From the Margins to the Mainstream* (pp. 151–168). Routledge.

Slocum, R., 2011. Race in the study of food. *Progress in Human Geography, 35*(3), 303–327.

Springer, S., 2020. Caring geographies: The COVID-19 interregnum and a return to mutual aid. *Dialogues in Human Geography, 10*(2), 112–115.

Swan, E., 2020. COVID-19 foodwork, race, gender, class and food justice: An intersectional feminist analysis. *Gender in Management: An International Journal, 35*(7/8), 693–703.

Wylie, A., 2020. Climate conscious professional kitchens? Analysing the Scottish food sector through a feminist lens. *Feminismo-s, 35*, 95–125.

Further reading

Cairns, K. and Johnston, J., 2015. *Food and Femininity.* Bloomsbury Publishing. The authors discuss the many dimensions of food and femininity. It unpacks how femininity is performed through food choices and practices in contemporary societies.

Reese, A. M. and Cooper, D., 2021. Making spaces something like freedom: Black feminist praxis in the re/imagining of a just food system. *ACME: An International Journal for Critical Geographies*, 20(4), 450–459.

These authors consider the role of Black feminist thought and action in the food justice movements. The book highlights the leadership roles and resistances of Black women throughout the food system and their vision of building a more just and equitable food system.

Schneider, T., Eli, K., Dolan, C. and Ulijaszek, S. (eds.), 2017. *Digital Food Activism*. Routledge.

The authors explore the digital media technologies that are currently shaping the food choices, practices, and identities of both men and women through their interaction within the digital sphere.

ADELE WYLIE

73. Health and food

Lauren T. Williams

Introduction

Health and food have long been seen as inextricably linked. First Nations peoples traditionally value their strong connection to the lands and waters that provide them with food, nourishment and wellbeing (Robin, 2022). There is documented evidence that the ancient civilizations of Egypt, China and Greece appreciated the link between health and food, with foods such as garlic used as a source of medicine (Metwaly et al., 2021). Around 400 BC, eating was seen as an act subject to health advice by Hippocrates, who espoused the application of dietetics (the modification of foods eaten to treat illness): 'I will apply dietetic measures for the benefit of the sick according to my ability and judgment; I will keep them from harm and injustice' (Cardenas, 2013; e261).

Given the widely accepted link between health and food, a rational approach would see people eat foods that optimise their health and minimise illness. This relies on people possessing an understanding of the relationship between food and health, and then being willing and able to act on this knowledge through a behaviour termed 'healthy eating'. This entry explores how discourses of the relationship between health and food are created within a social context and examines the extent to which individuals possess agency to enact healthy eating behaviour within a food system structured to maximise economic profit. Alternatives to the dominant discourses are considered and insights provided into possible futures in this field.

The relationship between health, food and healthy eating

Definitions

Food can be defined as a substance that provides a living organism with nutrients for growth and energy. Eating food is essential to life in humans, and continued absence of food results in illness and eventual death. While food is physically material, the meanings around food, including what constitutes healthy eating, are socially constructed. Eating is arguably the most frequently performed and complex health behaviour (Williams and McMahon, 2019). The act of eating comprises multiple decisions that include when we eat, who we eat with, how we procure and prepare our food, and what foods we choose to consume.

Health is more complex to define. The definition of health most widely quoted was documented in 1948 by the World Health Organization (WHO): 'Health is a state of complete physical, mental and social wellbeing and not merely the absence of disease or infirmity' (WHO, 1948: 100). Absence of illness is thus an essential, but not sufficient, requirement for health. Inherent in the WHO definition is an aspirational quality ('complete'), and a sense of health as an holistic concept. Health cannot be reduced to any singular discrete measurable factor. Rather, the concept of health has meaning that is negotiated and renegotiated within complex social systems. This social construction of health means that the concept varies between social groups. Likewise, the value that people place on achieving health through behaviours like healthy eating varies. Those who seek to enact healthy eating behaviour need to understand what that entails. The next section considers the ways in which healthy food messages are constructed and communicated.

Scientific and social constructions of healthy eating: risk discourse, healthism and the rise of mass misinformation

In the second half of the 20th century, governments of developed nations became concerned about the rapid rise in the 'diseases of affluence', chronic diseases such as cardiovascular disease, type 2 diabetes and cancers. Chronic diseases were found to have complex causal pathways and to develop over long time periods, making them difficult to cure, resulting in expensive, ongoing treatments for a growing proportion of the population. This led to a call for prevention of chronic disease and scientists began the challenging task of investigating the contribution of lifestyle behaviours, including eating, to chronic disease development. The dominant discourse linking food and health thus became focused on empirical evidence, predominantly from the discipline of epidemiology, expressing the relationship between food and health in terms of disease risk.

Medical and health professionals began to communicate these research findings by engaging in 'risk discourse', promoting healthy eating behaviours to reduce the risk of illness and/or optimise health. This medicalised the relationship between health and food. By the beginning of the 1980s, Robert Crawford noted that the aspirations for health had become a societal trend, with its pursuit raised to a moral virtue or 'supervalue' (Crawford, 1980). He described the privileging of health above other life goals as 'healthism', the '-ism' positioning it as a type of prejudice. Society had internalised the risk discourse.

Presuming the public wanted to strive for healthy eating (acknowledging that not everyone places the highest value on health), what information was available to guide them? Scientists, who typically present their research findings in the scientific literature in terms of the statistical likelihood of disease development within a population, found that they needed to work with traditional media to communicate these findings to the public. The media in turn had their own agenda and, at best, over-simplified messages and, at worst, sensationalised findings. Further confusion arose from conflicting messages released by sectors of the food industry designed to prevent healthy eating messages from affecting sales of their products.

From the turn of the century, the internet and social media revolutionised access to information on healthy eating. The results of food and health research could be made widely available by scientists and health authorities. The emergence of these media has helped to increase personal agency over health (Lupton and Maslen, 2019) and has allowed the public to join the conversation. However, these new media also introduced the potential for widespread diffusion of healthism and misinformation. While the traditional media might sensationalise headlines, they are at least bound by a code of ethics to verify the truth of the findings and to seek critical opinions on the results. Social media is not thus constrained, resulting in the potential for mass communication of misinformation. The effects of the latest technological advance, generative artificial intelligence (AI), on creating and sharing understandings of health and food have yet to be realised (Allman-Farinelli, 2023).

Individual understandings of health and food discourses: good and bad foods

How have these various communications around healthy eating been received by the public? We can obtain insights on this from qualitative studies of healthy eating discourses. The relationship between food and health tends to be expressed in a discourse of a 'good' or 'bad' dichotomy, with good foods being consistent with healthy eating and bad foods with health risk (Lupton, 2005). In the 1990s, a focus group study of Australian women interested in controlling their weight found that they constructed 'good' foods as those that are non-fattening (Germov and Williams, 1996)). An Australian interview study found that people reported that they were trying to eat 'good' food and avoiding too much 'bad' food – with the latter being described by participants as foods with a high fat content leading to overweight, with negative health and aesthetic consequences (Lupton, 2005).

Being socially constructed, these discourses change over time. A more recent qualitative analysis of messages by social media influencers located in the United Kingdom showed that the dominant discourse around 'good' foods now emphasises eating 'clean' foods, that is, those free from undesirable components (Goodman and Jaworska, 2020). Interestingly, sugar has now taken over from fat as the main public concern. People may also form understandings of the link between health and food based on their personal experience of risk. When the effect of food on health can be felt immediately, as in the case of an allergic reaction, or a drop in blood sugar levels in a person with type 1 diabetes, the link between food and health is readily understood and motivates behaviour change. People are understandably less willing to make changes to the way they eat without proof of health benefit within a reasonable time frame. For example, despite good evidence that the food pattern referred to as the Mediterranean diet protects against the chronic diseases of cardiovascular disease and cancer, an individual feels no different after a day or a week of following the diet. In fact, they may never 'feel' the benefit given effective prevention means that the chronic disease does not eventuate.

While the public may have internalised the concept of health risk, there are barriers to the enactment of healthy eating behaviour. A limitation of the dominant healthy eating discourse, whether promulgated by health professionals or the digital environment, is that it posits healthy eating as an individual responsibility, with illness perceived as a consequence of actively choosing unhealthy practices (Lupton, 2005). This denies the structural contributions to ill-health by society and absolves governments from responsibility for the health of its citizens.

Enacting healthy eating: the structure–agency debate

The ability of people to enact healthy eating behaviour relies on the extent to which they possess agency (freedom to act) within social structures (recurring patterns of social interaction linking people through social institutions and social groups) (Germov and Williams, 2017).

Factors influencing healthy eating: individual agency

Food choice is an important part of our identity, and what we eat is one of the ways in which we signify who we are and our membership of certain groups in society. This includes the physical food we eat and the way in which we perform our foodways in a digital space. An individual needs to be willing and able to privilege health as an aspiration to change their eating behaviour, but other values and aspirations may take priority. Such choices may be gendered. For example, there is evidence that women tend to put their own health needs last to meet their caring responsibilities for others (Britton et al., 2023). Some people will knowingly sacrifice health in the pursuit of the ideal body (Williams and Germov, 2017). Others attempt to meet psychological needs at the expense of health in the case of emotional eating. The pace of life is often cited as a reason for eating takeaway and convenience foods, despite knowing that these foods can be detrimental to health.

Factors influencing healthy eating: social structures and the dominant food system

Social structures have strong impacts on food choice (Williams and McMahon, 2019). The key structure influencing food and health in society is the dominant food system, which was designed to maximise economic profit

rather than achieve population health. Mass production and globalisation of food has resulted in food being one of the most important internationally traded commodities (Germov and Williams, 2017). This makes the food industry a powerful lobby group and one which seeks to influence government policy in the direction of their corporate interests, which may conflict with the best interests of the population and the natural environment. Governments obtain income from agricultural production and the food industry and thus have a vested interest in continuing to support the current dominant food system.

The link between the industrialised food system and health is a complex one. On the one hand, the food system ensures an abundant food supply to provide food security needed for survival, but on the other hand its use of resources decreases the health of the population and of the planet. A globalised food system incurs high food miles, significant waste and extensive environmental costs. Food production, particularly animal food production, continues to grow at a pace that is unsustainable for the planet. Individuals are not the only actors to bear the consequences of poor health outcomes. Societies and their governments bear the cost through healthcare costs and loss of productivity. Thus, governments find themselves in tension between making money from agriculture and the food industry and having to spend money on health services and environmental repair. Given the implications for population health and environmental sustainability, it is important to explore possible alternatives to the current industrialised food complex.

Alternatives to the dominant food system: changing the meaning of 'good' food

Alternative food system structures, such as farmers markets and the Slow Food movement, have arisen in response to the issues with the dominant food system. Slow Food is the name of a movement that arose in the mid-1980s in reaction to the growth of fast food that evolved from industrialised food production, with a slogan of food that is 'good, clean and fair'. Founded by food activist Carlo Petrini, the Slow Food movement incorporates features of pre-existing and parallel food movements, such as organic agriculture and fair trade. Through its highly effective use of the media, Slow Food promotes local culinary tourism events that bring together academics, chefs, farmers and 'foodies' to support non-standardised and re-localised food production (Williams et al., 2015). The Slow Food movement promotes enjoyment of eating locally produced food, and repositions consumers as co-producers, through interactions with food growers, enhancing individual agency over food and eating. These principles are similarly espoused by local farmers markets aimed at creating alternative food networks that decrease food miles and enhance environmental sustainability. However, while they provide individuals with the ability to exert their agency over the ethics and sustainability of their food supply, these alternative food networks are no challenge to the dominant food system.

Future directions: towards informed individuals and a planetary perspective on health and food systems

The future for informing people about healthy eating is promising if technology and political will can be appropriately harnessed. Digital disruption through AI has the potential to revolutionise the ability of individuals to directly evaluate the health impacts of their eating. Technology is emerging that uses visual data to calculate the nutrient content of foods in real time. For people with type 1 diabetes, this information can immediately be used to automatically adjust the amount of insulin released by a wearable pump. AI can assist with recording a person's dietary intake (a record of everything they eat and drink) in real time over a 24-hour period (Allman-Farinelli, 2023). This puts monitoring in the hands of the owner, enhancing agency over their food–health relationship.

At the food system level, development of a more productive food–health relationship, perhaps even the continued existence of life on Earth, depends on an emerging approach known as planetary health. This is an ecological perspective which sees the biological systems of living creatures, including humans, as inextricably linked to the health of Earth's biosphere, including the climate of our planet. From this perspective, food production and consumption form a link between the earth's ecosystem and human health (The Lancet Planetary Health, 2019). Heavy reliance on animal sources of food comes with a high, and unsustainable, cost to the Earth's ecosystem and to population health. The United Nations' Sustainable Development Goal 2, to eliminate hunger, can be achieved with predominantly plant-based diets. Cultural aspects of food and eating need to be considered in this approach which would ideally see social scientists work with health scientists to advocate for a balance between the needs of the planet and the needs of its population. The integration of personal and planetary health provides hope for a sustainable future.

References

Allman-Farinelli M (2023) Digital dietetics and the era of artificial intelligence. *Nutrition and Dietetics*, 80(4): 334–337.

Britton LE, Kaur G, Zork N, Marshall CJ and George M (2023) 'We tend to prioritise others and forget ourselves': How women's caregiving responsibilities can facilitate or impede diabetes self-management. *Diabetic Medicine*, 40(3): e15030.

Cardenas D (2013) Let not thy food be confused with thy medicine: The Hippocratic misquotation. *e-SPEN Journal*, 8(6): e260–e262.

Crawford R (1980) Healthism and the medicalization of everyday life. *International Journal of Health Services: Planning, Administration, Evaluation*, 10(3): 365–388.

Germov J and Williams L (2017) Exploring the social appetite. In: Germov J and Williams L (eds) *A Sociology of Food and Nutrition: The Social Appetite*, 4th ed. Melbourne, Oxford University Press, 3–18.

Germov J and Williams L (1996) The sexual division of dieting: women's voices. *The Sociological Review*, 44(4): 630–647.

Goodman MK and Jaworska S (2020) Mapping digital foodscapes: Digital food influencers and the grammars of good food. *Geoforum*, 117: 183–193.

Lupton D (2005) Lay discourses and beliefs related to food risks: an Australian perspective. *Sociology of Health & Illness*, 27(4): 448–467.

Lupton D and Maslen S (2019) How women use digital technologies for health: Qualitative interview and focus group study. *Journal of Medical Internet Research*, 21(1): e11481.

Metwaly AM, Ghoneim MM, Eissa IH, Elsehemy IA, Mostafa AE, Hegazy MM,

Afifi WM and Dou D (2021) Traditional ancient Egyptian medicine: A review. *Saudi Journal of Biological Sciences*, 28(10): 5823–5832.

Robin T (2022) Food as relationship: Indigenous food systems and well-being. In: Greenwood M, de Leeuw S, Stout R, Larstone R and Sutherland J (eds) *Introduction to Determinants of First Nations, Inuit and Metis Peoples' Health in Canada*. Canadian Scholars, Ontario.

The Lancet Planetary Health (2019) More than a diet. *The Lancet Planetary Health*, 3(2): e48.

Williams L and Germov J (2017) Gender, food and the body. In: Germov J and Williams L (eds) *A Sociology of Food and Nutrition: The Social Appetite*, 4th ed. Melbourne, Oxford University Press, 232–258.

Williams L and McMahon A (2019) Social and behavioural aspects of food consumption. In: Tapsell L (ed) *Food, Nutrition and Health*, 2nd ed. Melbourne, Oxford University Press, 494–519.

Williams LT, Germov J, Fuller S and Freij M (2015) A taste of ethical consumption at a Slow Food festival. *Appetite*, 91: 321–328.

World Health Organization (1948) *Summary Reports on Proceedings, Minutes and Final Acts of the International Health Conference held in New York from 19 June to 22 July 1946*. World Health Organization, available from: https://apps.who.int/iris/handle/10665/85573. (Accessed 8 July 2024).

Further reading

Germov J and Williams L (2017) *A Sociology of Food and Nutrition: The Social Appetite*, 4th ed. Melbourne, Oxford University Press.
This interdisciplinary reader and academic text uses a sociological perspective to examine food structures and food consumption in relation to nutrition and health.

Willett W, Rockström J, Loken B, Springmann M, Lang T, Vermeulen S, Garnett T, Tilman D, DeClerck F, Wood A, Jonell M, Clark M, Gordon LJ, Fanzo J, Hawkes C, Zurayk R, Rivera JA, De Vries W, Sibanda LM ... and Murray CJL (2019) Food in the anthropocene: The EAT-Lancet Commission on healthy diets from sustainable food systems. *Lancet*, 393(10170): 447–492.
This provides the detail of the first report by the EAT-Lancet Commission on the challenges of achieving food systems that are environmentally sustainable and beneficial for human health.

LAUREN T. WILLIAMS

74. Identity and food

Barbara Parker

Introduction to identity and food

Tell me what you eat, and I'll tell you who you are. (Brillat-Savarin in *La Physiologie du gout,* 1826)

Philosophers have long considered food and diet, and the question of *what one should eat* holds the public imagination because of the complex relationship between food and identity. In globalised and plural societies, discourses about food, diet, nutrition, the environment, migration and health circulate widely informing us how to think about bodies and ourselves. Although we eat to satisfy hunger and sustain our physical health, food also nurtures social connections and our emotional well-being; eating therefore effects our mental health, bringing us pleasure and fulfilment, especially when food is shared with family and friends. Food can also, however, be viewed with fear or scepticism, perceived as risky, or even mundane, and not worthy of critical inquiry.

Food scholars insist that food and identity be studied because of the complexity of relationships we have with food and our food practices. Food practices refer to all the meanings and everyday actions, routines, and habits that we carry out or perform in relation to the consumption and production of food, which also assign and encourage identities and subjectivities (Lupton, 1996). Drawing on Caplan (1997), Guptill et al. (2017) explain that through food and identity-work, we define and differentiate ourselves from one another, constructing ourselves as "distinct" individual eaters and as members of collective social groups. Thus, it is through the social meanings we give to foods and to our food practices that we establish our identity and our subjectivities, or how we think about and experience ourselves. These processes are material, symbolic, relational, and structured so food and food practices act as a mechanism to create acceptance (inclusion) and differences (exclusion) from others (Guptill et al., 2017: 20–21). This means that we construct belonging and social hierarchies through food based on nationality, place (or where we live), gender, race, and class, among other social positionalities.

Although it may seem that what and how we eat is a matter of individual choice, for most of us, our food practices consist of familiar foods that we have learned to enjoy through socialisation processes in our families based on our socio-cultural background, ethnic heritage, religious beliefs, and social class, and the communities in which we live. We consume foods we have access to geographically and locally, eating what we consider and recognise to be culturally, symbolically, and materially safe and healthy, perhaps even choosing foods that are deemed *good for us* or *good for the planet.*

Key dimensions of identity and food

Identity, food, and place

Food identities may be assigned through citizenship, or living in a particular region, holding membership of an ethnic or cultural group, in which case shared collective meanings are ascribed to specific foods that signify belonging to this particular group. This means that Canadians may eat maple syrup (if they can afford it!), or a British subject may choose to eat a curry, or prefer Marmite on toast, while the Australian will resolutely choose Vegemite. These taste preferences are shared because of collective social meaning, and, as one might imagine, acts of food choice are performed (Caplan, 1997). That is, individuals exercise agency in how they will either take up or resist the collective food meanings by choosing to eat, or not eat, specific foods. The shared meanings of these foods are in constant tension as social forces such as globalisation, neoliberalism, and migration lead to a plurality of peoples and foods, which shift food discourses over time, in different socio-historical contexts.

Our choice of diet and what we eat is organised and structured through social processes and the symbolic meanings we give to food based on our upbringing and the social and cultural norms mentioned above. For example, the meanings we attach to a "meal", from what foods are served, to who does the serving, are constituted through the family but are also structured by social class (Mennell, 1996; Murcott, 1983). Eating local or organic foods, for instance, is not necessarily a choice for everyone because of the cost, nor does everyone believe them to be better than industrially produced foods, because of shared meanings about their goodness. Some might prefer chips or crisps and the convenience of fast food. Norms around food develop through powerful food ideologies, structured identities such as our gender, social class, or ethnicity, and overlapping discourses that influence what we eat while also defining who we are.

Food ideologies emerge through the power of social, political, and cultural food discourses, which influence how we think about food and how we perform everyday food practices (Lupton, 1996). Food discourses are the systems of language and social practices around particular foods or eating, and the body. Importantly, food ideologies and discourses are contextual and always shifting. For instance, foods that were once deemed *good* may no longer be, causing confusion for eaters (e.g. eggs or butter, or beef). These changing food discourses represent new and emerging social meanings and, importantly, also highlight the connections between food and morality, or that some foods are good while others are bad, and, significantly, that there may be *right ways to eat* for members of particular social groups, with whom we identify. This is because for omnivorous humans, food is never just food, but is layered with meanings about nutrition or health, social status, or other food discourses, through which power circulates. For individual eaters, our food choices reflect who we are, our identities and subjectivities, which also transpose meaning onto the body.

Identity, food, and the body
Collective and shared social meanings about food shape who we are as individuals giving way to food identities through the act of eating and ingesting food (or *not* eating in the case of someone with disordered eating) or making a meal as mentioned above. The body is centred in this relationship between food, identity, and the self because food is liminal. That is, food moves between the "outside" and "inside" of our bodies (Fischler, 1988: 279). Moreover, our emotions, memories, and tastes are experienced through our bodies, such that we embody the foods we eat viscerally and materially (think about the smell of freshly baked bread or bacon sizzling in the pan and your hunger may spark). It is through these visceral materialities and social processes, which also function in relation to power and morals, that *we become what we eat*, through

our decisions to consume or reject foods that we consider either safe and delicious or dangerous and disgusting.

The purity/danger and clean/dirty binaries are experienced and practised by the self through bodily acts of ingestion (Douglas, 2002). These discourses are taken up by individuals in contemporary society through "technologies of the self", with its obsession on hygiene, germs, and personal cleanliness (Lupton, 1996; Foucault, 1988). Specifically, individuals are expected to pursue a healthy body through food and diet, constructing their subjectivity or identity in the process. For instance, consider orthorexia, or the obsession with "clean" eating. Individuals choose to eat foods in a raw or whole food state, for their natural, organic qualities and overall "wholesomeness", as the eater pursues purity of the body (and mind) through foods and food practices perceived as "clean". In the process, they constitute themselves as a healthy subject, or citizen, which is a prized identity.

However, because the body is liminal and can be breached through the practice of eating, our identities are also fraught as foods are highly moralised and our food choices and food practices become a way to manage belonging and social difference. That is, the morals associated with foods and the body become a way to maintain social order, creating distinctions between us and them, or ourselves and the Other (Caplan, 1997). Thus, individuals do not simply govern themselves and their individual bodies through food choice. Rather, we are also governed collectively through assigned and active identification with different social groups (gender, race, ethnicity, religion, etc.) and their specific food practices, such as halal when following Islamic dietary laws.

The body marks and reflects our identities and defines us to ourselves (our subjectivities) and others. The body is viewed as a project, or in the process of becoming; it is dynamic and subject to conscious and unconscious moulding (Caplan, 1997). Individuals are expected to act in enterprising ways and self-govern their bodies carefully through food in the neoliberal society. To this end, there are numerous body projects that individuals take up in relation to food and food practices. For example, the performance of gender as a body project with bodily ideals for thinness or muscularity can strongly influence an individuals' relationship with food and their body. Moreover, food is highly medicalised across societies, meaning that another dominant discourse about food is in relation to the health and functionality of bodies.

Identity, food, and nutrition: managing health risks

The medicalisation of foods as healthy/ unhealthy through biomedicine and public health nutrition represents dominant food discourses in Western societies. These medicalised food discourses, or ways of knowing and thinking about foods and food practices, position foods as either good for us and our bodies, or not good for us, and potentially even dangerous or risky. Central to discourses that medicalise food, there is an accompanying disgust and fear of fat bodies, which are presumed unhealthy because of poor lifestyle choices, or making bad food and diet choices (Lupton, 1996). Health, as achieved through food, is presumed controllable, and the body is viewed as malleable, and for these reasons overweight or larger bodies are stigmatised. Individuals are held responsible for their bodies and may experience shame in relation to food and eating habits if they eat fatty or unhealthy foods. Bodily ideals are enforced through social sanctions and social institutions such as healthcare and education. Individuals experience their health and bodies through the medicalisation of food and dietary risks, taking up identities and subjectivities reflected in food practices.

An emerging ideology is nutritionism, or the reductive belief that it is the nutrients in food alone that are more beneficial and functional to individuals and their bodies than the foods themselves (Scrinis, 2008). Nutritionism works in tandem with healthism, a food ideology that positions individuals as responsible for their own health. Nutritionism encourages us to think about macro and micro nutrients, like protein or the omega 3s and 6s in our food, rather than the taste of food or who we are eating with. Healthism and nutritionism require individuals to take responsibility for their own health and body by eating foods with nutrients that will promote health and functionality.

For food identities, the implication of medicalisation, healthism, and nutritionism is that foods and food practices reinforce a moralising "right" way to eat without recognising the wider consequences for individuals and social groups, who may not be able to access purported healthier and functional foods (e.g. yoghurt with probiotics or fortified foods such as orange juice with calcium and iron) (Parker, 2020). Moreover, public health nutrition guidelines and health promotion and dietary advice tend to prioritise the foods of the dominant social group (the white middle class), overlooking important health-giving foods of Black, Latinx, Asian, or Indigenous communities. Significantly then, not everyone has access to certain foods and the food discourses that they represent; thus, socially, some bodies are constituted as unhealthy. These food–health–risk discourses are strengthened by ideologies of social difference, and classism, racism, and settler colonialism perpetuate harm and injustice for individuals whose communities experience food insecurity or stigma relating to bodies that do not fit an ideal shape, size, or form.

Identity, food, and the environment

There is a growing awareness of the impacts of our diets and food practices on the environment. With the climate emergency and environmental pollution and degradation deepening, there is just cause to think about food and nutrition in relation to sustainability and the environment. Many individuals identify with ethical environmental food discourses and take responsibility for the health of the planet through their food choices and food practices (Parker, 2020). Specifically, some foods are labelled or viewed as energy or carbon intensive, such as the production of beef or dairy, the farming of cash crops such as quinoa or avocados, or the transportation of food in the globalised food system.

Some individuals, particularly those living in the Global North, are highly attuned to these environmental food discourses, and are changing how they eat, making "green" food choices and thinking about sustainable food practices as part of sustainable food systems and sustainable diets. This looks different depending on the context (place, food system), as individuals take up ethical food identities such as vegetarianism and veganism, or pursuing local foods and claiming "locavore" as a food identity. Social status can play a role, as individuals pursue ethical food consumption that aligns with their different foodie identities (Huddart Kennedy et al., 2019). Beyond making social change through food practices, individuals take up ethical food identities to signify their moral relationship to the valuing of the environment, environmental justice, and animal welfare.

Identity, food, and gender

Gender and discourses about femininities, masculinities, and bodies also inform how we eat, and perform food identities. This is why some women might choose lighter foods such as salads or fish and eat smaller portions and some men might prefer heavier foods choosing to eat steak and potatoes while not fearing a second serving. Of course, this example represents gender stereotypes of femininity and masculinity, and the gender binary, yet it remains salient because cultural ideas about gender, food, and the body are deeply embedded within patriarchal and heterosexual society (Cairns and Johnston, 2015; Lupton, 1996). Recently, Contois (2020) pointed to "dude" food identities demonstrating how ideas about male bodies (muscularity) and masculinities are taken up via food and food practices. As mentioned above, constructions of femininity and masculinity are connected with hegemonic bodily ideals through discourses that maintain normative ways of eating that conform to these gendered bodily ideals.

While some individuals embrace these ideals and their associated femininities or masculinities, others actively resist these norms and the dominant or hegemonic discourses about food, performing instead alternative queer food identities while at the same time constructing counter discourses about vegetarian and vegan foods (Overend, 2019).

Food futures: belonging and social justice

Food identities are never just individual; instead, they are structured collectively, are symbolic of the social order, and are experienced materially through our bodies, constituted and reconstituted through food ideologies and food discourses. Through our food practices and by making decisions about what to eat, we actively construct identities, subjectivities, and bodies. In so doing, we intentionally and unintentionally create social belonging while also differentiating ourselves from one another and actively positioning us

as different from the Other (Caplan, 1997). Food identities and subjectivities are shared through specific foods and food practices, and it is through repeated food performances that we attach or resist dominant social meanings about food and individual or collective bodies.

Our individual and collective identities are informed by food, our food practices and the intersecting social positionalities we occupy including our gender, race or ethnicity, social class, sexuality, age, and nationality, among other aspects of being and belonging. An intersectional understanding of food identities enables us to explore how power is operating at the micro level to create complex relationships between food, identity, the body, and the self, and at the macro level of society to understand how food identities privilege some groups while marginalising other groups. As much as food can bring us together, it is also a powerful force in dividing us into social groups and is a marker of social difference. Looking towards food futures, social justice must be centred in our understanding of the power of food identities to create belonging and food justice.

References

Brillat-Savarin (1826) *Physiologie du Goût ou, Méditations de Gastronomie Transcendante*. Paris: A. Sautelet.

Cairns K and Johnston J (2015) *Food and Femininity*, London and New York: Bloomsbury.

Caplan P (ed) (1997) *Food, Health and Identity*, London and New York: Routledge.

Contois E (2020) *Diners Dudes & Diets*, Chapel Hill: University of North Carolina Press.

Douglas M (2002) *Purity & Danger: An Analysis of Concepts of Pollution and Taboo*, London: Routledge.

Fischler C (1988) Food, Self and Identity. *Social Science Information*, 27(2), 275–292.

Foucault M (1988) Technologies of the Self. In Martin L H, Gutman H and Hutton P H (eds) *Technologies of the Self: A Seminar with Michel Foucault,* London: Tavistock, 16–49.

Guptill A E, Copelton D A and Lucal B (2017) *Food & Society*, 2nd ed., Cambridge and Malden: Polity Press.

BARBARA PARKER

Huddart Kennedy E, Baumann S and Johnston J (2019) Eating for Taste and Eating for Change: Ethical Consumption as a High-Status Practice. *Social Forces*, 98(1), 381–402. https://doi.org/10.1093/sf/soy113.

Lupton D (1996) *Food, the Body and the Self*, London, Thousand Oaks, New Delhi: Sage Publications.

Mennell S (1996) *All Manners of Food: Eating and Taste in England and France from the Middle Ages to the Present*, Urbana: University of Illinois Press.

Murcott A (1983) Cooking and the Cooked: a Note on the Domestic Preparation of Meals. In A Murcott (ed) *The Sociology of Food and Eating*, Aldershot, England: Gower, 178–185.

Overend A (2019) Is Veganism a Queer Food Practice? In Parker B, Brady J, Power, E and Belyea, S (eds) *Feminist Food Studies: Intersectional Perspectives*, Toronto and Vancouver: Women's Press, 91–121.

Parker B (2020) Consuming Health, Negotiating Risk, "Eating Right": Exploring the Limits of Choice through a Feminist Intersectional Lens. *Journal of Critical Dietetics*, 5(1), 45–57. https://doi.org/10.32920/cd.v5i1.1336.

Scrinis G (2008) On the Ideology of Nutritionism. *Gastronomica*, 8(1), 39–48.

Further reading

Johnston J and Baumann S (2015) *Foodies: Democracy and Distinction in the Gourmet Foodscape*, 2nd ed., New York: Routledge.
This highly readable book explores foodie identities as these are constructed through everyday food consumption practices and the pursuit of pleasure, authenticity, or localism through food. The authors provide a rich historical accounting of gourmet food, and its more recent turn towards the multicultural, following patterns of migration and globalisation and sustainable foods. As demonstrated, foodie discourses are symbolic and material, and function to create social belonging, status, and exclusion.

Tovares A and Gordon C (eds) (2022) *Identity and Ideology in Digital Food Discourse: Social Media Interactions Across Cultural Contexts*, London and New York: Bloomsbury Academic Press.
This edited book examines how identities are constructed through food ideologies. The collection authors pay close attention to various social media contexts and the digital platforms of Facebook, Youtube, Instagram, and Twitter, where they show how individuals express, communicate, and perform various food identities in relation to health, nutrition, food production, and food movements.

BARBARA PARKER

75. Indigenous food systems

Lopamudra Patnaik Saxena

Introduction

Indigenous food systems (IFSs) are integral to the cultural food use patterns of Indigenous peoples, who are ethnic groups native to traditional lands with unique cultures and relationships with the natural environment (Kuhnlein and Turner, 1991; UN, 2009). These food systems include the food practices of almost 500 million Indigenous peoples living in over 90 countries in territories covering almost a quarter of the world's land surface, who belong to 5000 different peoples and linguistic groups (FAO & Alliance of BI & CIAT, 2023: 9). They also include the socio-cultural meanings, techniques, use, composition, and nutritional outcomes for the people consuming the food (Kuhnlein et al., 2001).

IFSs are thus culturally diverse and unique food systems that exist within various social and ecological contexts, ranging from the Amazon rainforest to the Arctic. They include wild food harvesting, hunting, gathering, herding, fishing, shifting cultivation, agroforestry, small-scale farming, pastoralism, and various combinations of these practices, which have developed and adapted over centuries, rooted in the history, culture, spirituality, ancestral links, and traditional knowledge systems of Indigenous peoples.

Despite their significance, globally IFSs have been severely impacted by colonisation, urbanisation, industrialisation, globalisation, extreme weather events, and environmental degradation, resulting in widespread impoverishment, lack of food security, malnutrition, and chronic diseases among Indigenous communities. However, in the last two decades, there has been a growing public interest and policy attention on revitalising IFSs.

This entry explores the key focus areas, challenges, and threats to IFSs, and their future. It concludes by highlighting the need for decolonial approaches to food governance that recognise the significance of IFSs beyond sustenance in fostering sustainable, culturally sensitive, and equitable approaches to climate-resilient, diverse, and inclusive food systems.

Revitalisation of indigenous food systems – key areas

Food, nutrition, and health of Indigenous people

Indigenous communities are facing disproportionately high levels of food insecurity, malnutrition, obesity, and chronic health issues such as diabetes and cardiovascular diseases. These challenges largely stem from disparities in food access, nutrition, and health caused by increased integration into market economies and changing lifestyles. To tackle these issues, the revitalisation of IFSs is considered essential for improving food and nutrition security and promoting positive health outcomes in Indigenous communities.

Biodiversity and biocultural heritage for environmental stewardship

Indigenous communities have been instrumental in protecting and conserving almost 80% of the world's remaining biodiversity, both cultivated and wild (FAO & Alliance of BI & CIAT, 2023: 9). Their practices, knowledge, and beliefs promote soil health, biodiversity, water conservation, and ecological resilience. This food-related 'biocultural diversity' (Bridgewater and Rotherham, 2019) comprising of crops, livestock, forest products, marine resources, and more, along with the associated knowledge of cultivation, harvesting, preparation, and cooking, is essential for building local resilience and environmental stewardship. Moreover, it is the 'biocultural heritage' (Swiderska et al., 2022) of Indigenous peoples that has sustained this diversity, and its revitalisation is considered vital for the health of the planet and for human well-being.

Resilience and adaptation for climate change

IFSs that have survived environmental changes over the decades have brought attention to the valuable knowledge, skills and practices of Indigenous communities that can help in adapting to changing climatic conditions. In agriculture, for example, it is crucial to identify, store, and conserve seeds with desired traits, such as water conservation or pest resistance, maintain diverse crop and livestock varieties, and cultivate climate-resilient varieties to mitigate various risks, including the unpredictable effects of climate change.

Food sovereignty and community-based governance

In contrast to food systems dominated by market entities and global food chains, IFSs prioritise local decision-making and collective management under community-based governance structures. These systems have a deep connection to the land and territory, where food is not only a source of sustenance but also a vital component of cultural identity, self-determination, livelihoods, health, and cultural and spiritual heritage. The reclaiming and revitalisation of IFSs have brought food sovereignty to the forefront, emphasising the right of Indigenous communities to have culturally appropriate, ecologically sustainable, and socially just practices in food production and consumption.

Indigenous cosmovision

The Indigenous cosmovision that emphasises the interconnectedness of all living and non-living things, including plants, land, food, and health, is rooted in a worldview where humans and nature are co-dependent rather than separate entities. Agriculture in an IFS is therefore not just about producing food and livelihoods. It is also central to belief systems, ceremonial traditions, and cultural activities. Kimmerer (2013: 115), an Indigenous botanist, describes the human–environment relationship as 'cultures of reciprocity' that bind humans and non-human entities to each other, and establish duties and responsibilities for both. Understanding the concept of reciprocity is crucial to maintaining a harmonious balance between humans and nature, thereby supporting both present and future generations.

Challenges and threats to Indigenous food systems

Land dispossession and exploitative resource extraction

The forced displacement of Indigenous communities from their land for commercial agriculture, mining, energy, and infrastructure projects has been a longstanding issue that has severely impacted IFSs. IFSs are not only a source of sustenance but also deeply connected to the land, culture, ecology, and community. The dispossession of land and exploitative extraction of resources fundamentally disrupt these food systems, making it challenging for Indigenous communities to access traditional foods and maintain their cultural practices. Moreover, Indigenous communities encounter complex legal and political barriers when attempting to assert their land rights and protect their practices.

Commodification of Indigenous foods and introduction of non-Indigenous food

The commodification of Indigenous foods poses a threat to IFSs in three ways. Firstly, the focus on profitability and marketisation undermines the socio-cultural-ecological values and practices that ensure balance and harmony with the environment over time. Secondly, the ultra-processing of commodified Indigenous foods, alongside the introduction of non-Indigenous processed foods result in dietary shifts among Indigenous communities, leading to health and nutritional disparities. Thirdly, a loss of food sovereignty occurs when Indigenous communities become disconnected from their land, foods, cultural knowledge, and associated health and 'wellness' (Burnette and Figley, 2017). Furthermore, the appropriation of Indigenous knowledge by large multinational corporations – such as patenting indigenous medicinal plants, seeds, and genetic resources, along with branding traditional foods for mass consumption without Indigenous consent – marginalises Indigenous food producers (Imran et al., 2021).

Climate change and environmental degradation

IFSs are facing multiple risks due to the climate emergency, environmental degradation, and biodiversity loss. These risks are impacting land use and access to essential resources such as land, water, and forests.. As a result, the livelihoods of Indigenous communities are being affected, leading to changes in their dietary patterns, which have caused an increase in food and nutrition insecurity. Extreme weather events, unpredictable changes in temperature and precipitation patterns, and coastal erosion are some of the factors that are disrupting traditional harvesting and farming practices, making food less accessible and available to these communities.

Changing livelihoods and out-migration of Indigenous peoples

The migration of Indigenous peoples, specifically the younger generation, to urban centres presents a significant challenge to the sustainability of IFSs. This is driven by various factors, such as educational and forced assimilation programmes, conflicts and persecution, climate change, dispossession of lands, better employment opportunities, and other economic prospects. As a result, traditional connections of Indigenous peoples to their territories, culture, spirituality, languages, food habits, customs, and preferences are undermined. This trend is a threat to the intergenerational transfer of Indigenous knowledge, skills, and practices that are essential for participating in traditional food system activities.

Loss of Indigenous/traditional knowledge

Indigenous or traditional knowledge (IK/TK) refers to the cumulative local body of knowledge, practices, and beliefs that are passed down through generations within local communities. This knowledge is generated in response to the social, economic, and environmental contexts in which these communities are embedded. Studies show that IK is being lost at an alarming rate, particularly in relation to medicinal, nutritional, agricultural, harvesting, storing, and preparation practices. This loss is largely due to the integration of Indigenous communities into the global market economy and forced acculturation through development-induced displacement programmes. The consequences of losing IK are significant, as it undermines food sovereignty, biocultural diversity, and environmental sustainability.

Future of Indigenous food systems

IFSs remain at the margins of global food governance. They encounter systemic barriers and challenges to their autonomy and endure a lack of access to land and territory and to nutrient-rich and healthy foods. What lies at the core of IFSs, however, is that they promote (place-based) ecological and socioeconomic sustainability that interlocks food, nutrition, and health with biodiversity, seeds, lands, cultural values, ecological knowledge, sustainable practices, and community governance. This holistic ecosystemic approach is increasingly recognised as an alternative vision for transforming food systems, which is essential to countering the negative environmental and social outcomes of the industrial food system.

The future of IFSs depends on a paradigmatic shift away from unsustainable and 'extractive' food systems towards 'regenerative' agri-food systems (Anderson and Rivera-Ferre, 2021). This transition requires decolonial approaches that confront the legacies of colonialism, dispossession, and anti-Indigenous racism, while challenging the dominant neo-liberal narrative of 'productivism' (Swiderska et al., 2022).

The revitalisation of IFSs will require recognising Indigenous peoples' rights to their land and culture, establishing partnerships that prioritise Indigenous voices and knowledge, and promoting international cooperation to support regenerative food systems. This includes land restitution, policy reform, community-led initiatives, robust legal frameworks, ethical guidelines, and mechanisms to ensure that Indigenous peoples can control and benefit from their food systems. These approaches must be participatory and interdisciplinary, tailored to the specific social-ecological and cultural context.

References

Anderson M D and Rivera-Ferre M (2021) Food system narratives to end hunger: extractive versus regenerative. *Current Opinion in Environmental Sustainability* 49, 18–25.

Bridgewater P and Rotherham I D (2019) A critical perspective on the concept of biocultural diversity and its emerging role in nature and heritage conservation. *People and Nature* 1, 291–304.

Burnette C E and Figley C R (2017) Historical oppression, resilience, and transcendence: can a holistic framework help explain violence experienced by Indigenous people? *Social Work* 62, 37–44.

FAO and Alliance of Bioversity International and CIAT (2023) *In Brief: Indigenous Peoples' food systems – Insights on sustainability and resilience from the front line of climate change.* Rome, FAO.

Imran Y, Wijekoon N, Gonawala L, Chiang, Y-C and De Silva K R D (2021) Biopiracy: abolish corporate hijacking of indigenous medicinal entities. *The Scientific World Journal*, 8898842.

Kimmerer R W (2013) *Braiding sweetgrass: Indigenous wisdom, scientific knowledge, and the teachings of plants.* Minneapolis, Milkweed Editions.

Kuhnlein H V, Receveur O and Chan H M (2001) Traditional food systems research with Canadian Indigenous Peoples. *International Journal of Circumpolar Health* 60, 112–122.

Kuhnlein H V and Turner N J (1991) *Traditional Plant Foods of Canadian Indigenous Peoples: Nutrition, Botany and Use.* London, Gordon and Breach Science Publishers.

Swiderska K, Argumedo A, Wekesa C, Ndalilo L, Song Y, Rastogi A and Ryan P (2022) Indigenous peoples' food systems and biocultural heritage: addressing Indigenous priorities using decolonial and interdisciplinary research Approaches. *Sustainability* 14, 11311.

United Nations (2009) *State of the World's Indigenous Peoples.* New York, UN.

Further reading

Gilio-Whitaker D (2019) *As long as grass grows: The indigenous fight for environmental justice, from colonization to Standing Rock.* Boston, Beacon Press.

This book by an Indigenous researcher and activist provides both a historical account of Indigenous resistance to land theft and cultural erasure and new approaches to environmental justice activism and policy.

FAO (2021) *The White/Wiphala paper on Indigenous Peoples' food systems.* Rome, FAO.

This is based on contributions from Indigenous peoples to global discussions leading up to the UN Food Systems Summit 2021. It includes sections on key concepts, core principles, and rights relevant to Indigenous peoples' food systems.

Settee P and Shukla S (2020) *Indigenous food systems: Concepts, cases, and conversations.* Canadian Scholars.

This provides a good understanding of the barriers and challenges to a diverse range of Indigenous food systems from Canada, using contributions from researchers, practitioners, and community members to develop key insights for cross-cultural dialogues and the development of policy and practice.

LOPAMUDRA PATNAIK SAXENA

76. Industrial food systems

Raquel Ajates

Introduction: the spread of industrial food systems

Farming: from self-sufficiency to a global economic activity

The expansion of industrial food systems is closely intertwined with the unfolding of industrial revolutions (IR). Over the last two centuries, farming has been gradually transformed into a commercial activity and an industry sector with a decreasing role in national economies (Goodman et al., 1987). The UK was the first country in the world to undergo the first IR, and to industrialise and globalise its food system. By the end of the 19th century, the importance of farming to the UK economy had already dramatically decreased, employing no more than a quarter of the population (Hobsbawm, 1999), a sign of things to come. As a result, a significant proportion of the redundant rural workforce moved to cities, reducing the amount of labour available to rich landowners. This farm labour shortage triggered a higher demand that raised agricultural wages for almost the first time in history, and elicited an interest in labour-saving methods, starting the still ongoing transition towards mechanised, and more recently automated, farming (Hobsbawm, 1999). Other countries followed the same pattern, and this 19th-century European industrial specialisation model spread around the Western world, starting a race to apply factory methods to food production with the objectives of reducing unpredictability and increasing capital accumulation and efficiency (Friedmann and McMichael, 1989). This transformation resulted in the re-structuring of agriculture, the consolidation of farmland into bigger farms, and the creation of the processing and distribution industries. This was the beginning of a long process of division of labour promoted by elites and governments in the name of capitalist efficiency, moving from a history of food self-sufficiency to the separation of roles and distancing of stakeholder groups in the supply chain, i.e. farmers, processors, retailers, and consumers.

New dynamics of international food trade began, with relations – some still ongoing today – between colonised and colonising countries, based on the notion of competitive advantage that triggered the globalisation of food production and commercialisation. This development was championed by the emerging industrial classes who were keen on cheap food options for their workers. Control of food production gave wider control in other areas of society, and well-established "food regimes" started to, and still do, determine the rules of what humans and farmed animals eat, and how food and feed are produced, processed, distributed, wasted, and disposed of (Friedmann and McMichael, 1989).

Unravelling the relationship between industrial revolutions and industrial food systems

The evolution of the food system can be linked to the technological paradigms of the uneven IRs that modern societies have undertaken. During the first IR, dating back to the 1760s, mechanisation through coal and the invention of the steam engine caused the replacement of agriculture by industry as the backbone of national economies. A century later, the second IR was characterised by new sources of energy, i.e. electricity, gas, and oil, which resulted in the development of the internal combustion engine, steel, chemical synthesis, and new methods of communication and transport. The introduction of synthetically produced fertilisers and pesticides was a game-changer in farming. While the steam engine of the first IR did not have many applications in agriculture, the internal combustion engine of the second IR allowed the first tractors and mechanised harvesters, which dramatically reduced the need for human labour, and incorporated so-called "factory methods" in farmers' fields.

A century later, the discovery of nuclear energy triggered a third IR. Genetic modification, pest control using sterilisation, food preservation, and water usage control are some of the areas of nuclear application in agriculture (Chaurasia et al., 2023). These are highly debated applications due to their safety risks and the complexity of nuclear waste management. This revolution also brought forth the rise of electronics, telecommunications, computers, and the first robots. For food systems, this third IR meant the beginning of digitalisation, biotechnology, and the rise of an era of high-level automation.

Currently, we are entering the so-called fourth IR, based on the internet and the increasing digitalisation of all aspects of society and nature, which is starting to blur the boundaries of physics and biology as we know them (Ajates, 2023; Goodman, 2023). Building on the third IR's use of electronics and information technology to automate production, the crosscutting effects of the fourth IR's automation in food systems involves disruptive technologies that aim to control the building blocks of animal and plant organisms, as well as the wider farming environment. The aim is to tackle a variety of issues both created by and threatening industrial food systems – ranging from stagnated yields to diet-related disease and the current climate emergency.

Food as commodity: the challenges facing the food system in the fourth industrial revolution

The application of an industry lens to the natural ecosystems that underpinned food systems

The control over and appropriation of elements from natural environments such us woods, land, and water – all key to food production – began with enclosures of common land during the aforementioned first IR. Early enclosures robbed the poorest of their shares in the commons, and paved the transition from feudalism to capitalism (Polayni, 2001), dispossession processes still ongoing today in many countries (e.g. land grabs).

Industrial methods pushed food systems to produce cheaper foods without taking into account naturally interrelated cycles with uncountable feedback loops. It is not only the simplified cycles of industrial methods that increase food system vulnerability, but also their financialisation. Since the 1846 Corn Laws – the poster law for second IR industrialists demanding cheap food for their factory workers – a myriad of financial mechanisms have been used in food policy, from the troublesome entry of agriculture in the World Trade Organization, to farming subsidies financing unsustainable methods and futures trading (Clapp, 2023). These economic control tools shape offer and demand in world markets, and determine which countries benefit from competitive advantage, financial if not climatic, for key cash crops.

From battle fields to cultivated fields: the transfer of war technologies to food systems

The application of industrial methods to food has popularised industrial terminology, reframing and rebranding the natural environments on which the food system depends, and our place within them. Rivers, fields, and forests became labelled as "natural resources" to be exploited for irrigation, pastures, and wood; domesticated animals became *livestock*, complementing material stock. These were resources to be controlled and competed for.

The new energy sources of each IR changed welfare as well as the food system. War technologies found new markets in agriculture and food processing.. Food and farming technologies, in turn, fed the war effort. The first caterpillar tractors that used treads instead of wheels – able to operate in rough terrains and shell craters – were used in an adapted version in World War I, replacing horses in the front line. The reverse, i.e. the application of war technology to the food system, counts many more numerous examples and accelerated the industrialisation of food production and processing. For example, at the end of the 18th century, the French Society for the Encouragement of Industry ran a competition to find better ways for preserving food to give France a war advantage, resulting in the invention of canning (Janes et al., 2019). Canned food played a crucial role in 19th-century conflicts, such as the Crimean War, the US Civil War, and the Franco-Prussian War, as well as feeding explorers and colonialists. The Haber–Bosch process for synthesising ammonia, invented shortly before the outbreak of World War I, was used to make both gunpowder and fertilisers (Janes et al., 2019). The organophosphates-based pesticides still used today are nerve gases related to chemical weapons but in a diluted form (Vallianatos, 2018). Nowadays, commercial drones first developed for war operations are finding their ways to fields as automated shepherds and crop surveyors. Over the centuries, even to this day, food itself has been used as a weapon of war, e.g. through hunger or starvation (WFP, 2022).

As always, legal frameworks lag behind societal and industry practices. There is an ongoing race in which regulatory and governance frameworks fail to keep up with new ways of food producing, processing, trading, conserving, fortifying, advertising, and so on. From establishing "safe" pesticide trace levels, to banning BPA in tins, to introducing "food to feed" regulations, and regulating new genome editing techniques, governments, industry, and civil society are always in an arm-wrestling contest to achieve a balancing act between cost saving methods, technological innovations, and safety measures.

Human, animal, and environmental impacts of industrial food systems

Through its insertion in industrial cycles, food has been rebranded as a commodity, rather than a human right or a common good. This commercial focus is generating unaccounted externalities that have become too obvious to ignore, too complex to calculate (see the complexity of true cost accounting for food), and too large to sustain (see the global cost of diet-related diseases). Concerns about the way food is intensively produced, highly processed, and unequally distributed have intensified since the beginning of the Green Revolution, and especially since the third IR, when food trade became progressively globalised and food supply chains expanded at an unprecedented rate.

From a public health perspective, the industrial food system has failed to end hunger and is aggravating obesity and malnutrition numbers. More than 828 million people (c. 10% of the world's population) were undernourished in 2021, and one third of the world's population was malnourished. At the same time, 2.5 billion adults were overweight (43% of the population) and of these 890 million were obese in 2022. This "quintuple burden" of malnutrition is now considered the "new normal" and is compounded by environmental factors and the worsening of non-communicable diseases associated with unhealthy diets, such as diabetes, cardiovascular diseases, or certain types of cancer (Ajates, 2023).

Environmentally, the food sector is responsible for about 30% of all anthropogenic greenhouse gas emissions, the ongoing erosion in wild and cultivated biodiversity, water pollution, and soil degradation, while wasting about a third of all food produced. Farming is both culprit and victim of climate change and environmental collapse. From a rights perspective, the industrial food system has perpetuated the use and abuse of free, cheap and hidden labour of hidden animals, as well as the less visible and less valued labour of low paid, temporary, landless agricultural workers who appear and disappear with the harvest cycle, and the unpaid labour of women managing family food shopping, planning, cooking, washing up, etc. The apparent infinite choice of products in supermarkets hides a severe loss of diversity, which decreases the resilience of food systems, diverse diets, and traditional knowledge. The main aim is perpetual growth and expansion, which requires crossing frontiers, both geographical and technical, with inputs from everywhere to reach consumers from anywhere.

The unprecedented challenge ahead: fourth industrial revolution technologies

Technologies always amplify their impact when implemented in a coordinated manner, generating both challenges and opportunities. Whilst it is not the first time in history that new innovations have coincided, the fusion of technologies of the fourth IR is unfolding at a degree and pace never seen before. The importance of synergetic applications of technologies can be traced by analysing the sectors in which mergers and acquisition take place. The convergence of mechanical and chemical innovations towards the end of the Second IR created powerful modern-day corporations – John Deere, Monsanto, Bayer, AstraZeneca, etc. As the fourth IR fuels the convergence between agrochemicals and digitalisation, these giant corporations are now merging and collaborating with technology companies (Goodman, 2023). The result is an ever more consolidated market controlled by a handful of players with well-funded interdisciplinary scientific, marketing, legal, and lobbying teams that hinder other alternatives and reinforce path dependence in food policy and practice (Ajates, 2023).

The original processes of physical enclosure are now turning digital (Ajates, 2023). The material corporeality and unpredictability of animals (including humans) and natural cycles have always been a return-on-investment risk to an industrial system that thrives on homogenous and consistent production. Thus, industrial capital has strived to reduce these sources of risks, through the appropriation and substitution of natural cycles and living beings (Goodman et al., 1987) – e.g. by removing workers and animals from fields, developing in vitro meat, or indoor aquaponics systems. With the fourth IR's fusion of disruptive technologies that traverse digital, physical, and biological domains, the food system is entering an era of dematerialisation and fragmentation of biological agents of production, replaced by an increased materialisation of industrial and lab-synthesised inputs: i.e., replacing animals with tractors and cultured meat, seeds with digital sequence information, or shepherds with drones. The digitalisation of food services is also creating new hidden labour fuelled by automation and new distribution channels: from "dark" factories to "dark" kitchens, and the labour behind still-not-so-autonomous AI.

All these technologies are based on big data, laden with biases hidden in the algorithms increasingly used to make policy and practice decisions (Bronson, 2022), exacerbating quantophrenia – the misapplication of quantitative methods and factors that can be easily measured to sociology (Ajates, 2023). The unravelling of these links between technologies and industry reveals how foodways have always been socially constructed, offering us a glimpse into their likely evolution. These technological developments are introduced throughout the world as neutral advances but are the result of socio-economic and political choices of investors and industrial actors in high income countries.

Conclusions: food governance for post-automated futures

IRs and war developments have shaped food and farming for centuries. Despite all the buzz words – e.g. precision agriculture, smart farming, or sustainable intensification – the industrial food system is failing to provide healthy and sustainable diets without damaging the planet. Public policies are not moving fast enough, and current subsidy allocations perpetuate damaging practices. The digital and economic divides are increasing exponentially in the fourth IR. At the same time, the complexity of living beings and ecosystems remains a barrier to complete the full industrialisation of food. The food system is the canary in the coal mine of increasingly automated societies. This raises complex questions on how to provide healthy and meaningful livelihoods for the foreseen growth of "spare labour".

Previous models of food policy and governance that merely focused on increasing yields are no longer adequate. New governance and research methodologies are needed to keep up with desires for more inclusive approaches and new technologies that are aligned with responsible innovation. Food systems in the fourth IR have reached a stage in which technology and data democracy are irremediably interwoven with food democracy, opening debates on how to transition to post-automated food futures centred around ethical artificial intelligence and open-source technology and biological data (e.g. genetic sequences of seeds) (Ajates, 2023), amongst other developments that we cannot yet imagine. These challenges are accelerating the case for reframing food not as an industrial good, but as a public service and a common good, an objective that has become an urgent necessity rather than a distant utopia.

References

Ajates, R. 2023. From land enclosures to lab enclosures: digital sequence information, cultivated biodiversity and the movement for open source seed systems. *The Journal of Peasant Studies*, 50(3), pp.1056–1084.

Bronson, K. 2022. *The immaculate conception of data: agribusiness, activists, and their shared politics of the future.* McGill-Queen's Press.

Chaurasia, J., Tripathi, V.K. and Tripathi, R. 2023. Nuclear technology in horticulture: boosting productivity, controlling pests, conserving water. *Asian Journal of Agricultural and Horticultural Research*, 10(4), pp.178–182.

Clapp, J. 2023. Concentration and crises: exploring the deep roots of vulnerability in the global industrial food system. *The Journal of Peasant Studies*, 50(1), pp.1–25.

Friedmann, H. and McMichael, P. 1989. Agriculture and the state system: the rise and decline of national agricultures, 1870 to the present.. *Sociologia Ruralis*, 29(2), pp.93–117..

Goodman, D. 2023. *Transforming agriculture and foodways: the digital-molecular convergence.* Policy Press.

Hobsbawm, E. J. 1999. *Industry and empire: From 1750 to the present day.* New York: The New Press.

Janes, L., Merleaux, A., Veit, H.Z., Weinreb, A. and Yamashita, S. 2019. World War I and the origins of the modern food system. *Global Food History*, 5(3), pp.224–238.

Polanyi, K. 2001. *The great transformation: the political and economic origins of our times*. Boston: Beacon Press.

Vallianatos, E. 2018. Pesticides, tear gas and history: from WW1 to today's streets. ARC. https://www.arc2020.eu/pesticides-tear-gas-and-history-from-ww1-to-todays-streets/.

WFP 2022. The day the UN barred using hunger and starvation as weapons of war. WFP: https://www.wfp.org/stories/un-barred-using-hunger-and-starvation-weapons-war

Further reading

Ajates, R. 2023. From land enclosures to lab enclosures: digital sequence information, cultivated biodiversity and the movement for open source seed systems. *The Journal of Peasant Studies*, *50*(3), pp.1056–1084.

This article presents seeds as a case study of physical and digital enclosures in food systems throughout the last century, including the latest governance debates on the digitalisation of plant genetic materials.

Goodman, D., Sorj, B. and Wilkinson, J. 1987. *From farming to biotechnology: a theory of agro-industrial development*. Basil: Blackwell.

This publication from 1987 is as timely as ever. Recommended reading for unpacking the industrial food systems' strategies of appropriationism and substitutionism mentioned in this entry.

Friedmann, H. and McMichael, P. 1989. Agriculture and the state system. *Sociologia Ruralis*, *39*(2): pp.93–117.

This key work introduces the "food regime" theory, essential reading to explore the role of agriculture in the development of the capitalist world economy, and in the trajectory of the state system.

77. International food aid

JANE MIDGLEY

Introduction

International food aid has historically been organised around three main objectives: economic, political and humanitarian (Clapp, 2012). These objectives are usually outlined from the aid donor's perspective and work to fulfil their domestic policy interests while ostensibly attempting to meet the food needs of impacted regions and populations. Discussions of international food aid often began in the late 1940s and early 1950s as the world was beginning to address the food inequalities between large-scale food-producing nations (such as Canada, United States and Australia) and those nations who were food insecure. The latter included countries still coming to terms with post-war reconstruction in Europe (i.e., Marshall Plan) and initiatives for cooperative economic development in South and South East Asia (i.e., Colombo Plan). These approaches saw the transfer (usually sale) of donor countries' domestic surplus agricultural stocks to supply food that would fuel populations to achieve regional economic development objectives elsewhere in the world. Surplus domestic stocks were traded on favourable terms (below market price or through loans agreed with low interest rates and lengthy repayment schedules) to generate export incomes for the donor country and its agricultural sector. Food aid (as trade) was also used strategically by donors to fulfil other domestic policy interests such as strengthening international relations – by building regional alliances and showing the productive strength of capitalist economies – in addition to alleviating hunger (Friedmann, 1982). Criticisms of stock dumping and global grain export markets being undermined by this approach led to the United Nations (UN) intervening to create a formalised global food aid system. The UN Committee on Commodity Problems and its principles of surplus disposal were established in 1954 and provided the institutional basis for international food aid transfers for the latter half of the twentieth century. The principles intended that food aid was provided for additional direct consumption rather than displacing other food sources or distorting markets (Clapp, 2012). Major donors/suppliers (national and regional governments) through a series of Food Aid Conventions (1969–1999) committed to make available a predictable amount of food for emergency situations or food security outcomes, and to supply international humanitarian organisations (IHOs, UN agencies – including UN World Food Programme – and non-governmental organisations). International food aid moved from serving the disparate economic and political interests of donors towards a shared global responsibility for addressing hunger. Yet it remained controversial; foundering World Trade Organization agriculture negotiations (Doha Round 2001–2010) until it was resolved that donor agricultural surpluses could supply emergency food aid if this did not impact on receiving country/domestic producers.

From food aid to food assistance

The role and modality of international food aid have continued to move towards humanitarian agendas, encompassing both emergency response and resilience-building objectives (discussed by Harvey et al., 2010). Today, externally sourced and imported foods are only provided in the most extreme crises or sudden emergencies: the emergency status justifying the exceptional circumstances that warrant in-kind provision. Otherwise 'international food assistance' is arranged by IHOs who following assessments may source foods locally or provide impacted populations with the means to purchase food through cash-based transfers. Transfers enable people to buy their preferred foods, offering access to culturally appropriate and familiar products, and supporting the livelihoods of local producers and traders whilst maintaining local and regional markets and infrastructures.

Consistent dedicated funding for food assistance is provided by member states of the Food Assistance Convention (FAC, 2012 to date) that commit to an annual minimum contribution. The activities supported by the FAC now work across a range of global policy discourses and agendas – nutrition and education goals, food security and livelihoods, building resilience to shocks that could trigger crises – and supporting emergency responses delivered by IHOs. This is indicative of efforts to improve coordination between national and regional donors and IHOs, and greater transparency as each donor provides a narrative overview of the amount and type of assistance and how this aligns with its domestic policy (FAC, 2022).

Future concerns

In 2016 the global humanitarian community agreed on a 'Grand Bargain' to improve the effectiveness and efficiency of humanitarian action. This included supporting greater localisation of aid decision-making, i.e., global south national and domestic authorities and organisations would receive a greater share of funding and control its disbursement (Inter-Agency Standing Committee, 2023). Changing the locus of power and creating inclusive practices is part of the humanitarian sector's attempt to address its Western dominance and colonial legacy that has marginalised 'local' knowledge and expertise. Consequently, what form future food aid and assistance may take as expressed through greater locally determined sourcing remains to be seen, including how this may change donor practices and reporting requirements. For example, FAC (2022) donors work with 'trusted partners'; this hints at the traceability and financial accountability structures that donors have built with IHOs in the search for the best value for money and greater efficiency and effectiveness of aid (following the Grand Bargain) that may prevent rapid or extensive change (Midgley, 2024).

Another concern relates to the promotion of specialised and 'ready to use' food products to save lives in emergency settings by IHOs and donors over recent decades. This family of fortified food products include cereals, milk powders, biscuits and pastes, with the most fortified 'ready to use therapeutic food' (RUTF) classed as a 'food for special medical purposes'. Used as short-term intensive treatments to combat undernutrition in vulnerable populations, particularly children, these products are viewed as essential to meeting global nutrition outcomes and Sustainable Development Goals. Despite their medical efficacy, these products are contentious, especially RUTFs. It is argued that by separating short-term nutrition gains from long-term food security, they fail to address the structural inequalities in which they are provided and serve the interests of manufacturers, donors and humanitarian organisations (Scrinis, 2020). IHOs have responded to this critique and work to procure these commodities from local and regional producers and

manufacturers (WFP, 2021). IHOs are also dependent on external funding which remains orientated towards emergency interventions rather than multi-year financing which would offer aid actors flexibility to support the growing numbers of ongoing complex crises facing the most vulnerable and food insecure (WFP, 2021). The Grand Bargain attempts to reduce the specificity and short-termism of aid funding towards longer-term resourcing and flexible outcomes, along with promoting other outcomes and mechanisms such as localisation and cash-based assistance. Despite the expansion of the humanitarian sector to include actors and expertise beyond the global north, the provision of aid and assistance remains dependent on donor interests. The challenge remains to address the structural and food system inequalities that have resulted.

References

Clapp J (2012) *Hunger in the balance: The new politics of international food aid.* Ithaca, NY, Cornell University Press.

Food Assistance Convention (FAC) (2022) *Food Assistance Convention 2021 annual narrative report.* Available at: https://www.foodassistanceconvention.org/en/reports.aspx (Accessed 11 April 2023).

Friedmann H (1982) The political economy of food: The rise and fall of the postwar international food order, *American Journal of Sociology* 88, S248–S286. https://www.jstor.org/stable/3083245.

Harvey P, Proudlock K, Clay E, Riley B and Jaspars S (2010) *Food aid and food assistance in emergency and transitional contexts: A review of current thinking.* London, Overseas Development Institute. https://interagencystandingcommittee.org/grand-bargain

Inter-Agency Standing Committee (2023) *The grand bargain.* Available at: https://interagencystandingcommittee.org/grand-bargain (Accessed 11 April 2023).

Midgley J (2024) Engaging the humanitarian marketplace: Values, valuations and the making of humanitarian geographies, *Environment and Planning F* 3(4), 305–322. https://doi.org/10.1177/26349825231163142.

Scrinis G (2020) Reframing malnutrition in all its forms: A critique of the tripartite classification of malnutrition, *Global Food*

Security 26, 1000396. https://doi.org/10
.1016/j.gfs.2020.100396.

World Food Programme (WFP) (2021)
Strategic plan 2022–2025. https://docs.wfp
.org/api/documents/WFP-0000132205/
download/ (Accessed 20 October 2023).

Further reading

Scott-Smith T (2020) *On an empty stomach:
Two hundred years of hunger relief*. Ithaca,
NY, Cornell University Press.

This accessible book provides a genealogy of
food aid and discusses the changing social,
cultural and political sensitivities that have
informed humanitarian approaches to
addressing hunger.

JANE MIDGLEY

78. International trade and food

ELIZABETH SMYTHE

Introduction: international trade and food

As Peter Rosset (2006) noted, food is not a typical traded commodity; it *is* different. Eating food is the most intimate act of consumption, necessary to our survival and well-being, tied up in culture and community. But a global food system has emerged as a result of liberalised markets, new technologies and financialisation, which has increased the distance between producers and eaters of food and seen high levels of corporate concentration in production. Despite these developments food and agricultural products have remained sensitive in trade negotiations. This was reflected from the outset in the decision of the main trade negotiating forum in the post World War II period, the General Agreement on Tariffs and Trade (GATT), to exempt agriculture from GATT trade principles. Even after negotiations were finally launched, they reached an impasse in certain areas. Moreover, where limited rules have been developed they pose a threat, in the context of food crises, to food security in many countries highly dependent on food imports.

Trade rules have also affected national regulations and standards on food and agricultural production. Since food is vital to our health and well-being, governments have, over time, developed regulations and standards on food production and imported food designed to ensure it is safe for human consumption and produced in a way that conforms with prevailing societal values (for example, regarding animal welfare or the environment). Recognising that national regulations can impact international trade, the World Trade Organization (WTO) and other trade agreements have rules to ensure national regulations do not create non-tariff barriers designed to protect domestic production from imports which would undermine trade liberalisation. Determining what is permissible in domestic regulations that might impact trade is covered by two WTO agreements and an international standard setting body. Once again, however, agreement on what is permissible and what those standards should be has proven especially difficult and led to numerous, protracted trade disputes among countries.

International trade agreements and food

The Agreement on Agriculture (AoA), which resulted from the final GATT Uruguay Round of negotiations in 1994, ended the exemption of agriculture from GATT principles. Thus agriculture and food production became subject to the norms of neo-liberalism which saw state intervention in markets as negative and suspect. The key goal of WTO agricultural rules was to increase efficiency, liberalise markets and reduce redundancy. Policies of subsidising production or supporting prices or farmers' incomes were seen to cause surplus production and distorted markets which new rules sought to limit. The negotiations that followed reflected the reality that members of the WTO were reluctant to treat agriculture in the same way as other traded products. The AoA reforms focussed on three 'pillars' of commitments: increased market access for agricultural products, the elimination of export subsidies, and ending trade-distorting domestic subsidies for food and agricultural production (where the US and EU were in competition and most culpable). Members also agreed to continue further negotiations. The 2001 WTO Ministerial meeting incorporated the AoA into the Doha round of trade negotiations. The implementation of the AoA, however, was uneven, both in advancing trade liberalisation and in fairly distributing its benefits among countries.

Limits to export subsidies saw some reductions and the transparency of non-tariff trade barriers was increased, but progress on reducing domestic subsidies for production was much slower. The agreement categorised support for domestic agriculture and food production into boxes: amber (trade distorting), blue and green (trade neutral). The latter includes government programmes, such as food aid to vulnerable groups, or research services which do not affect levels of agricultural production. Amber measures, however, such as governments buying agricultural production from farmers at a guaranteed price, which might increase production and lower prices, were to be subject to restrictions and negotiated reductions. Opening developing country markets to imports, however, given the slow movement of large Northern countries on reducing domestic subsidies, led to those countries dumping products abroad where cheap imports destroyed local food and agricultural production in the South. Countries in the South were pushed by international financial institutions and the WTO to focus on export-oriented production, often of a single or limited number of commodities. The result was very high levels of dependence on food imports among many low-income developing countries (Margulis et al., 2023). This dependence, combined with WTO rules on subsidies, price supports and stockpiling food nationally, set the stage for major threats to food security in the context of food crises and climate change.

Social movements and civil society were active in both the global South and the North in resisting the rules and policies of the international trade system. One of the most significant, La Via Campesina (LVC), developed out of a network of peasant and farmer organisations from South, Central and North America as well as Europe. LVC played an important role in challenging international trade rules of the WTO and other trade agreements and articulating an alternative vision of agricultural production based on the concept of food sovereignty in 1996. A second group of organisations addressing the global food system and trade rules is what has been called the Food Justice Advocates (Clapp, 2020)

Harmonisation of food standards and trade disputes

The efforts to harmonise national food standards and regulations to minimise their impact on international trade are reflected in two agreements at the WTO and in other regional trade agreements. These are the agreement on Sanitary and Phytosanitary Standards (SPS) and Technical Barriers to Trade. They cover standards related to food safety and food labelling and impose obligations on states to be transparent in their regulations and justify any that impact trade based on scientific evidence or relevant international standards. In the case of food, these agreements reference the international food standards setting body the Codex Alimentarius.

Role of the Codex Alimentarius

Founded in 1963 as a joint body of the Food and Agriculture Organization (FAO) and the World Health Organization (WHO), the mandate of the Codex Alimentarius is to develop and harmonise food standards both "protecting consumer health and promoting fair practices in the food trade" (FAO, 2023) With the creation of the WTO and its agreements on restricting barriers to trade, Codex standards took on increased significance for states. National rules that deviate from (i.e exceed) Codex standards in response to consumer safety concerns or other civil society demands could become the subject of trade disputes and targets for WTO-authorised trade retaliation. On the other hand, if a state's regulatory practice becomes the Codex standard, it is insulated from challenges to that regulation as an unjustified trade barrier. Because Codex standards can reduce or expand the national policy space for food regulation, standard-setting processes have become more politicised. However, establishing standards and having states adopt and adhere to them has proven difficult in relation to food production, most notably in the use of genetically modified organisms (GMOs) and various drugs as growth promoters in the production of milk and meat (Smythe, 2014). Conflicts were often based on different views of the safety of these products for human consumption or other values.

In the case of GMOs, countries, like the US, heavily invested in GM crops were, after a 20-year battle at the Codex Committee on Food Labelling, unable to stop adoption of a standard permissive of the EU's mandatory labelling regulation. Equally protracted have been conflicts over the use of antibiotics and drugs called beta agonists (ractopamine and zilpaterol) to promote animal growth in the production of pork and beef. In both cases residue remains in the meat after slaughter and it fell to the Codex Committee on Residues of Veterinary Drugs in Food to determine what maximum levels of residue (MRLs) were safe for human consumption. In its work on risks to human safety the committee sought the advice of scientists of the FAO-WHO Joint Expert Committee on Food Additives (JECFA). Despite JECFA's determination of safe residue levels in meat, the Codex had great difficulty agreeing on a standard. Concerns about the adequacy of the scientific assessment and safety and, in the case of beta agonist drugs, animal welfare continued to divide Codex members.

Food scares and growing consumer concerns about the provenance of food in the EU and elsewhere meant that EU restrictions on imports of meat using growth promoters increased over time despite potential threats of trade retaliation. In the case of hormones, despite the US, Canada and others winning a dispute at the WTO, which found that the EU had violated the SPS agreement, and 10 years of trade retaliation, they failed to secure access to the EU market. Similarly the adoption of standards for MRLs for ractopamine by a two-vote margin at the Codex Commission in 2012 did not lead to market access for meat produced using ractopamine (Smythe, 2014). Although at the time of writing, MRLs for zilpaterol are making their way very slowly through the Codex process, agreement on a standard is unlikely to result in increased market access for meat produced using it.

Food supplies and food security in an era of conflict and climate change

The global food crises in 2007–8 and 2010–11, with large price spikes for major traded commodities, pushed millions into hunger and put the issue of domestic measures to address food security front and centre at the WTO (Smythe, 2014). However, the inability to reach consensus meant that efforts to ensure food security through policy tools such as price supports and domestic stockpiling of reserves continued to fall under the amber box category of subsidies limiting the ability, especially of net import dependent developing countries, to take effective measures to ensure food security (Margulis et al., 2023). Import dependence, the concentration of control of production of key commodities among a few countries and corporations (Clapp, 2023), led to vulnerability for many due to the lack of resilience in the food chain as a result of the WTO's rules (Margulis et al., 2023).

Concerns about food insecurity have become more acute in the context of the climate emergency and geo-political conflict. Agriculture and food production are especially sensitive to climate change as warming temperatures lead to drought, crop failures and, in the case of "natural disasters", destruction of distribution infrastructure and food supply chains. Rules that limit state intervention to ensure a local food supply and resilience in the food system risk exposing millions globally to extreme food insecurity.

Consumer concerns about the provenance and safety of their food, the unjustness of the existing food system and the looming threats to food security, especially from climate change, mean that concerns about food are likely to augment, not diminish. Food is indeed different when it comes to international trade and will continue to challenge the future and legitimacy of trade institutions and agreements, which have been premised on neo-liberal ideas which limit the policy space for states to ensure food security and promote local, sustainable food production.

References

Clapp, J. (2023) Concentration and crises: exploring the deep roots of vulnerability in the global industrial food system. *The Journal of Peasant Studies*, 50:1, 1–25. https://doi.org/10.1080/03066150.2022.2129013.

Food and Agriculture Organization (FAO) (2023). https://www.fao.org/fao-who-codexalimentarius/en/.

Margulis, M.E., Hopewell, K. and Qereshniku, E. (2023) Food, famine and the free trade fallacy: the dangers of market fundamentalism in an era of climate emergency. *The Journal of Peasant Studies*, 50:1, 215–239. https://doi.org/10.1080/03066150.2022.2133602.

Rosset, P. (2006) *Food is Different: Why We Must Get the WTO out of Agriculture*. New York: Zed Books.

Smythe, E. (2014) Food is different: globalization, trade regimes and local food movements. In: D. Deese (ed.) *Handbook of the International Political Economy of Trade*. Cheltenham, UK and Northampton, MA, USA: Edward Elgar Publishing, pp. 471–497.

Further reading

Clapp, J. (2020) *Food*, 3rd ed. New York: John Wiley and Sons.
Provides an accessible overview of the global food system highlighting the concentration of corporate control, global trade rules and the financialization of food and agricultural land and their impact on food producers, eaters and the planet.

Margulis, M.E., Hopewell, K. and Qereshniku, E. (2023) Food, famine and the free trade fallacy: the dangers of market fundamentalism in an era of climate emergency. *The Journal of Peasant Studies*, 50:1, 215–239. https://doi.org/10.1080/03066150.2022.2133602.

This article provides an overview of the WTO's rules on domestic support and how they pose a threat to food security in the context of climate change.

79. Just transitions and food in the Global South

Laxmi Prasad Pant

Introduction: towards a critical understanding of food system transitions

Transition to net zero in food and agriculture has been prioritised as this sector accounts for one-third of global emissions. However, net zero transitions can cause social injustices. Just transition initiatives aim to uphold social justice while mitigating greenhouse gas emissions. Since the existing 'sustainability transition' frameworks are Eurocentric in origin, their application in peripheral regions needs an approach to decolonising this idea (Ghosh et al. 2021). Although the sustainability transition literature is well established in the energy, transport, and buildings sectors, it is still emerging in food and agriculture, more so in the Global South (Wieczorek 2018).

The just transition literature challenges the colonial divide between developing and developed regions in favour of a non-dual core–periphery idea (Munro 2019). Regardless of the sectoral focus, low-carbon transitions in the geographical peripheries require rethinking transition theory, practice, and movements for two reasons (Pant et al. 2015). First, peripheral areas in the Global South primarily depend on subsistence agrarian economies, often with a desire to adopt modern technologies because of the dominant high modern colonial narrative that the centre is always superior to peripheries. Second, these areas are disproportionately affected by the affluence in geographic cores that are primarily responsible for political and ecological crises of modernity, such as extractive industries, greenhouse gas emissions, the climate emergency, and extreme events. This entry develops a novel transition typology to challenge the dominant narrative that the 'periphery' should 'catch up' with the core in innovation, growth, and prosperity. It serves as a boundary object (i.e., a way to translate just transition ideas across cultural boundaries and contexts) to engage in the discourse to decolonise the Eurocentric idea of sustainability transition.

Food system transitions

Innovation and just food transition

Just transition ideas in food and agriculture can build on science and technology studies literature that identifies three innovation framings – innovation for growth, innovation systems, and innovation for transformation (Schot and Steinmueller 2018). The first framing focuses on technology transfer from the centre to the peripheries. The industrial food system emerged from the global economic shocks of the 1970s and 1980s and subsequent neoliberal capitalist expansion to peripheral regions (Holt-Giménez and Shattuck 2011). Before the Second World War, cheap food and raw materials from the tropical and temperate settler colonies fuelled economic growth in Western Europe. The emerging settler states, including the United States and Canada, provided Europe with wheat and meat, which became the dietary staples of the working class, replacing traditionally grown crops, such as legumes (Cusworth et al. 2021). India served as a major source of cotton, tea, and sugarcane. After the Second World War, settler colonies focused on reversing the flow in the form of international food aid, a transfer of surpluses to the newly independent states. The dominant innovation for growth framing subsequently led to large-scale transformations, such as the Green Revolution in the 1960s and 1970s, but such interventions ended up with unintended consequences, such as the consolidation of resources into fewer hands, class struggle, gender inequity, social exclusion, and deepening regional inequalities.

The innovation systems framing argues that knowledge and technology do not transfer freely over geographic and cultural distances because of their tacit and sticky nature, particularly when it relates to experiential learning and Indigenous knowledge. The emphasis is on catching up and competitiveness based on comparative advantage in trade, as seen, for example, in the successes of Japan, the so-called four 'tigers' in East Asia (Taiwan, Korea, Singapore, and Hong Kong), and most recently China and Vietnam. The growth oriented agricultural intensification in these countries caused social and environmental injustices. These countries failed to learn enough from the critical lessons from the Green Revolution and similar approaches to modernisation and industrialisation (Agyeman and McEntee 2014).

The innovation for transformation framing is one possible transition pathway. Transitioning from one equilibrium state to another is a process, whereas transformation is not only both a process but also signifies desired societal outcomes (Hölscher et al. 2018). This framing addresses the shortcomings of the earlier two frames, especially social and environmental injustices. Sustainability transitions can aggravate existing injustices, generate new ones, or limit genuine participation – raising questions like who decides what is sustainable, who bears the costs, and who enjoys the benefits (Tribaldos and Kortetmäki 2022).

Just food transitions in the Global South

The proposed transition typology in Figure 79.1 includes two axes: core–periphery relationships (Munro 2019) and human–nature interactions (Muradian and Pascual 2018). These axes are important, particularly to understand how core areas exploit peripheries through extractive practices, including natural resource extraction and labour migration (Contesse et al. 2021). The Eurocentric concept of 'sustainability transition' does not adequately translate into peripheral regions that are already low-carbon and bear a disproportionate adaptation burden. Obsession with scale and scope in transition is often understood as large-scale, long-lasting transformations primarily involving politically top-down and technocratic interventions toward efficiency and growth (Scoones et al. 2020). The high modern techno-optimist pathway does not sufficiently consider either space and place in sustainability transitions (Coenen et al. 2012), or minority identities and the role of non-human species (Contesse et al. 2021).

The idea of 'just transition' to avoid social and environmental injustices in industrialised countries led to outsourcing production in areas where there are less stringent environmental regulations and cheap labour, often perpetuating historical injustices. The growing popularity of regenerative agriculture, agroecology, and other alternative food movements in the Global North can lead to the intensification of food systems in the Global South as happened in other economic sectors. The research on just food transition in already low-carbon peripheral regions involves the idea of 'adaptive transition' – adaptation to socio-ecological changes (e.g., climate change and extreme events) and co-designing transitions to net-zero futures (Pant et al. 2015). Vulnerable communities in peripheral areas are unfairly forced to adapt to socio-ecological changes on an everyday basis – autonomous adaptation or even maladaptation – while also holding a responsibility to build sustainable futures for themselves, their children, and the environment.

The idea of 'adaptive just transition' (see Figure 79.1) is useful to include personal, political, and practical spheres in the transformation process (O'Brien 2018) and challenges the dominant transition frameworks that promote human-nature dualism and are primarily developed for core areas (Martiskainen and Sovacool 2021). Alternative transition frameworks like the one proposed here serve as a boundary object to introduce epistemic diversity in transition policy and practice, particularly to reintroduce more-than-human non-dual ideas involving the affective and spiritual domains (Coe and Coe 2023).

Just food futures

The just transition literature calls for not only low- or zero-carbon but also just food systems. However, the separation of nature from humans does not necessarily help to translate the established transition frameworks into food and agriculture, particularly in peripheral areas. Regenerative agriculture and agroecological farming emerged in the Global North, which is less relevant in peripheral areas that are already low carbon and yet unfairly shoulder the burden of adaptation to climate change and extreme events. Nor should the Eurocentric idea of sustainability transition motivate large players to move their extractive operations and practices to peripheral regions to benefit from less stringent environmental regulations and cheap labour. A just transition for food and agriculture should address injustices for people and the planet.

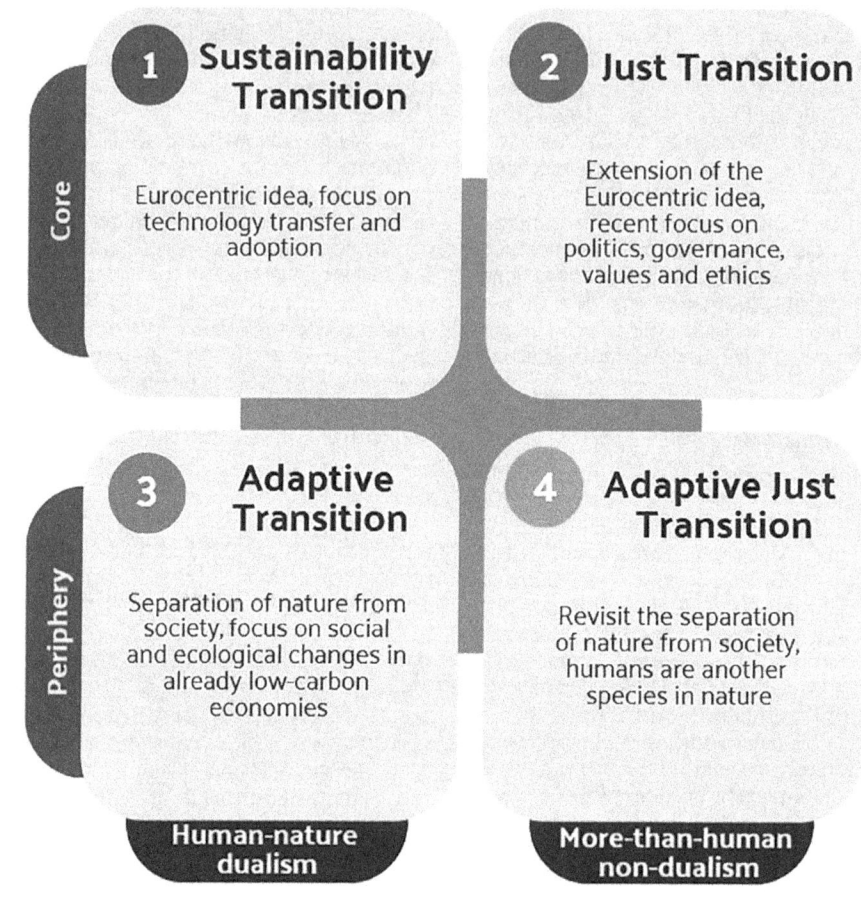

Source: Author.

Figure 79.1   A transition typology

References

Agyeman, J., and J. McEntee (2014) Moving the field of food justice forward through the lens of urban political ecology. *Geography Compass* 8(3): 211–220.

Coe, E. S., and R. Coe (2023) Agroecological transitions in the mind. *Elementa: Science of the Anthropocene* 11(1): 00026.

Coenen, L., P. Benneworth, and B. Truffer (2012) Toward a spatial perspective on sustainability transitions. *Research Policy* 41(6): 968–979.

Contesse, M., J. Duncan, K. Legun, and L. Klerkx (2021) Unravelling non-human agency in sustainability transitions. *Technological Forecasting and Social Change* 166: 120634.

Cusworth, G., T. Garnett, and J. Lorimer (2021) Legume dreams: The contested futures of sustainable plant-based food systems in Europe. *Global Environmental Change* 69: 102321.

Ghosh, B., M. Ramos-Mejía, R. C. Machado, S. L. Yuana, and K. Schiller (2021) Decolonising transitions in the Global South: Towards more epistemic diversity in transitions research. *Environmental Innovation and Societal Transitions* 41: 106–109.

Hölscher, K., J. M. Wittmayer, and D. Loorbach (2018) Transition versus transformation: What's the difference?

Environmental Innovation and Societal Transitions 27: 1–3.

Holt-Giménez, E., and A. Shattuck (2011) Food crises, food regimes and food movements: Rumblings of reform or tides of transformation? *The Journal of Peasant Studies* 38(1): 109–144.

Martiskainen, M., and B. K. Sovacool (2021) Mixed feelings: A review and research agenda for emotions in sustainability transitions. *Environmental Innovation and Societal Transitions* 40: 609–624.

Munro, F. R. (2019) The geography of socio-technical transitions: Transition–periphery dynamics. *The Geographical Journal* 185(4): 447–458.

Muradian, R., and U. Pascual (2018). A typology of elementary forms of human-nature relations: A contribution to the valuation debate. *Current Opinion in Environmental Sustainability* 35: 8–14.

O'Brien, K. (2018) Is the 1.5°C target possible? Exploring the three spheres of transformation. *Current Opinion in Environmental Sustainability* 31: 153–160.

Pant, L. P., B. Adhikari, and K. K. Bhattarai (2015) Adaptive transition for transformations to sustainability in developing countries. *Current Opinion in Environmental Sustainability* 14: 206–212.

Schot, J., and W. E. Steinmueller (2018) Three frames for innovation policy: R&D, systems of innovation and transformative change. *Research Policy* 47(9): 1554–1567.

Scoones, I., A. Stirling, D. Abrol, J. Atela, L. Charli-Joseph, H. Eakin, A. Ely, P. Olsson, L. Pereira, R. Priya, P. van Zwanenberg, and L. Yang (2020) Transformations to sustainability: Combining structural, systemic and enabling approaches. *Current Opinion in Environmental Sustainability* 42: 65–75.

Tribaldos, T., and T. Kortetmäki (2022) Just transition principles and criteria for food systems and beyond. *Environmental Innovation and Societal Transitions* 43: 244–256.

Wieczorek, A. J. (2018) Sustainability transitions in developing countries: Major insights and their implications for research and policy. *Environmental Science & Policy* 84: 204–216.

Further reading

Agyeman, J., and J. McEntee (2014) Moving the Field of Food Justice Forward Through the Lens of Urban Political Ecology. *Geography Compass* 8(3): 211–220.

This article examines power and politics in food justice studies.

Ghosh, B., M. Ramos-Mejía, R. C. Machado, S. L. Yuana, and K. Schiller (2021) Decolonising transitions in the Global South: Towards more epistemic diversity in transitions research. *Environmental Innovation and Societal Transitions* 41: 106–109.

This article identifies the need for a fresh and alternative approach to sustainability transition in peripheral areas.

LAXMI PRASAD PANT

80. Labelling and food

Beth Clark, Sharron Kuznesof, Albert Boaitey and Luca Panzone

Introduction: food labelling

Food labels provide a range of information on food product attributes. They sit at the interface between consumers' decision-making at the point of purchase, market regulations and commercially marketed products (Moreira et al., 2019). Whilst labelling legislation varies by country, the General Standard for the Labelling of Pre-packaged Foods as adopted by Codex Alimentarius is followed around the world (Food and Agricultural Organization of the United Nations, 1991). Mandatory food-labelling regulations typically seek to ensure the safety, transparency and accurate representation of foods to protect consumers' health and inform their food choices. 'Use-by' dates and instructions for food storage, preparation and cooking all safeguard against the growth of pathogens and bacteria that may cause foodborne illness. Allergen listings protect consumers with intolerances or immune system responses to ingredients such as wheat, nuts, soy and milk. The listing of food additives can inform consumers about the presence of ingredients they seek to avoid such as phosphorous-based additives for the dietary management of chronic kidney disease. These interactions between food and health have led to food labels becoming an important policy instrument to drive large-scale changes in behaviour (Meijer et al., 2021). In many countries, quantified nutrition information has demonstrated efficacy in nudging some consumers into making healthier dietary choices (Cecchini and Warin, 2016). Although nutrition information panels are most commonly mandatory on the back of packaging (BoP), some food manufacturers and retailers within the UK and Europe voluntarily place their 'RAG-rated' (red, amber, green) panels on the front of packaging (FoP) to communicate the health attributes of their products.

For food businesses, food labels provide an opportunity to differentiate products from those of competitors, including through nutrition and health claims, and environmental and production standards (e.g., animal welfare credentials, Fairtrade, organic). Nutrition claims relate to ingredient descriptors such as 'sugar free', 'low in salt', 'high in fibre' and 'source of calcium', the meanings of which are legally defined. Health claims occur where substantiated claims between an ingredient and health impact have been approved, e.g., 'calcium is needed for the maintenance of normal bones', and provide an opportunity to develop 'health halos' and promote brand values with the intention of encouraging purchase. The presence and enforcement of legislation on labelling and nutrition and health claims ensures competitive fairness.

For consumers, labels on foods reduce the information asymmetry that exists between themselves and manufacturers. Labels can signal quality differences between brands through cues that communicate attributes such as price, brand name, production method, country of origin, dietary suitability (e.g., for those on vegetarian or vegan diets), and nutrition and health claims. As interest grows in a widening range of quality dimensions that cannot be evaluated before or after consumption, referred to as credence attributes, which typically rely on third party certification (for example Fairtrade or UK Soil Association for organically produced foods), consumers' trust in labels and the regulatory environment becomes increasingly important (Tonkin et al., 2015).

Criticisms of food labelling

To achieve their informative aims, food labels need to be clear and easy to read, understandable, visible and not misleading. Criticisms of food labels can be levelled at each of these factors (Temple and Fraser, 2014), and the effectiveness of labels requires an understanding of people's individual differences (e.g., beliefs, perception), their decision-making environments (e.g., time constraints) and the food labels themselves, including competition from different attributes.

Labelling needs to be visible to be effective, yet labelling information is abundant and often complex, particularly when providing a large amount of technical information that needs to be processed by the consumer in a narrow time window. Means of information simplification, e.g., FoP logos, colour coding, etc., are often used to help with clarity. However, there is debate around the effectiveness of colour coding (e.g., RAG) versus full information as a means to facilitate label use, for both environmental and health grounds

(Meijer et al., 2021; Cecchini and Warin, 2016).

Consumers may also interpret labelling information differently to as intended. It is not uncommon for consumers to evaluate a product in its entirety by using a single piece of information on the label, for example considering a dairy ice cream as lower calories (hence healthier) if lactose-free (that is, healthier for those with lactose intolerance), irrespective of whether the association is true. This is referred to as the halo effect. Halos impact consumer judgements by leading to inferences about underlying product attributes beyond what the label intends to communicate, and serve as cues that impact consumer valuation of different attributes. Using another example, research has found that consumers associate labels which communicate ethical and environmental attributes with healthier food. The concern is that these halos may induce consumers to behave in a way contrary to what the label intended. For instance, the health halo may serve as pretext for the underestimation of attributes such as calorie levels, whilst the eco-friendly halo can lead to undesirable environmental behaviours. For example, consumers associate greater healthfulness with fair trade labelled products and subsequently increase their consumption by up to 30% in some cases (Berry and Romero, 2021). Labelling information can also have paradoxical effects where a 'positive' label reduces the likelihood of purchasing the product. For example, consumers may refrain from consuming products labelled as healthy, because they think they are less tasty.

The future of food labelling

The extent to which food labels are an expression of social, political, public health and commercial aspirations means labels will evolve and change in response to multiple drivers. Consumers' use of nutritional profile labels to simplify decision-making and promote healthier choices suggests changes to mandatory labelling. Consultations on the repositioning of BoP nutritional labels to FoP are beginning in some countries. Moreover, as evidence-based links between diet and disease are published, food labels and linked information sources (such as via QR codes) are likely to reflect relevant health benefits and warnings such as a widening list of allergens.

As sustainability and social justice concerns increase, the demand for information on the impact of food production is likely to see an increase in labels indicating carbon footprint, water usage, marine conservation, deforestation impact and the identification of certification schemes, which address these concerns. The most useful format for these labels is, however, unclear.

One response to the anticipated increase in demand for information in the above is through digital technologies. QR codes, barcodes and smart labels can provide supplementary and detailed information on allergens, customisable and personalised nutrition information, and real-time information on origin, farming practices, product certifications and supply chain audits. This information could increasingly be linked to foods purchased online as well as offline.

Finally, we can also expect the continued global harmonisation of labels (Meijer et al., 2021) facilitated by the Codex Alimentarius' development of international food standards, guidelines and codes of practice. This process is, however, lengthy, requiring extensive co-ordination and agreement among multiple stakeholders which need to reconcile differences in national food cultures, trade policies and regulatory enforcement.

Whilst the content and format of labels will be dynamic moving forward, their importance as a communication device will remain.

References

Berry, C. and Romero, M. (2021). The fair trade food labeling health halo: Effects of fair trade labeling on consumption and perceived healthfulness. *Food Quality and Preference*, 94, 104321.

Cecchini, M. and Warin, L. (2016). Impact of food labelling systems on food choices and eating behaviours: A systematic review and meta-analysis of randomized studies. *Obesity Reviews*, 17(3), pp.201–210.

Food and Agricultural Organization of the United Nations (1991). Codex Alimentarius: Codex general standard for the labelling of prepackaged foods. Available at: http://www.fao.org/3/Y2770E/y2770e04.htm. Accessed: 30 August 2023.

Meijer, G.W., Detzel, P., Grunert, K.G., Robert, M.C. and Stancu, V. (2021). Towards effective labelling of foods. An international perspective on safety

BETH CLARK, SHARRON KUZNESOF, ALBERT BOAITEY AND LUCA PANZONE and nutrition. *Trends in Food Science & Technology*, *118*, pp.45–56.

Moreira, M.J., García-Díez, J., De Almeida, J.M.M.M. and Saraiva, C. (2019). Evaluation of food labelling usefulness for consumers. *International Journal of Consumer Studies*, *43*(4), pp.327–334.

Temple, N.J., and Fraser, J. (2014). Food labels: A critical assessment. *Nutrition*, *30*(3), pp.257–260.

Tonkin, E., Wilson, A.M., Coveney, J., Webb, T. and Meyer, S.B. (2015). Trust in and through labelling: A systematic review and critique. *British Food Journal*, *117*(1), pp.318–338.

Further reading

Meijer, G.W., Detzel, P., Grunert, K.G., Robert, M.C. and Stancu, V. (2021). Towards effective labelling of foods. An international perspective on safety and nutrition. *Trends in Food Science & Technology*, *118*, pp.45–56.
This article reviews research into food safety and nutrition labelling information providing insights into how this information is read and understood by consumers and how this impacts their purchasing decisions.

Tonkin, E., Wilson, A.M., Coveney, J., Webb, T. and Meyer, S.B. (2015). Trust in and through labelling: A systematic review and critique. *British Food Journal*, *117*(1), pp.318–338.
This article gives an introduction to the role of trust in and through food labelling. It provides a useful framework for the consideration of trust in a food labelling context.

BETH CLARK, SHARRON KUZNESOF, ALBERT BOAITEY AND LUCA PANZONE

81. Meatification

CHI-MAO WANG

Introduction

According to the Food and Agriculture Organization (FAO), global meat production increased by 5% in 2021, amounting to 339 million metric tons, with a 34% rise in pig meat production recorded in China following the outbreak of African swine fever (OECD/FAO, 2022). It is predicted that the world's per capita consumption of animal protein will increase to 35.6 kg/year by 2031. Fast-growing meat consumption and production rates are occurring on a global scale and are interwoven with increasing flows of oilseeds and feed grains, such as soybeans, coarse grains, and maize. As the world's largest producer and consumer of pork in 2021, China imported over 99 million tonnes of soybeans from countries such as Brazil, contributing to a significant areal expansion of feed crops globally (FAO, 2023). Informed by the political economy approach, geographer Tony Weis coined the term 'meatification' to capture animal protein's dramatic shift 'from the periphery of human food consumption patterns … to the centre' (Weis, 2013: 67). Weis' meatification theory also contends that global food and environmental crises are entangled with 'the cheap surpluses of the industrial grain-oilseed-livestock complex' (Weis, 2013: 66).

Meatification: environmental risks and animal welfare

According to Weis, volatile global food prices are entwined with industrial livestock sectors, which demand a large amount of soybeans and maize. Based on statistics produced by the FAO, the US and Brazil are leading soybean producers worldwide, accounting for over two-thirds of global soybean production in 2021. However, in the 1960s, Brazil was not a significant supplier of global soybean, producing only 1.5 million tonnes of soy per year. Its production increased steeply to 134.9 million tonnes per year in 2021 (FAO, 2023). Weis contends that the growth of global soy production has negative impacts on society, the environment, and animal welfare, with each of these aspects analysed independently below.

First, global reliance on cheap grains has undermined food security in countries in the Global South. Encouraged by development planners, countries of the Global South have become heavily dependent on the importation of cheap grains, with substantial areas of what was previously arable land now used for tropical commercial products, such as coffee and palm oil. However, dependence on cheap food imports is leaving poor farmers vulnerable to market fluctuations in commodity prices and national economies susceptible to price spikes and food insecurity. Industrial animal feed production requires standardised and simplified environments, thus exacerbating multiple biophysical problems. For example, monoculture reduces soil health, increases water consumption, and decreases soil biodiversity, making cheap industrial agriculture vulnerable to environmental disturbance. The global industrial agricultural system's vulnerability and food dependency are putting Global South farmers' livelihoods at risk. Moreover, the expansion of grain production is synonymous with the concentration and agglomeration of global livestock production.

Second, Weis' analysis highlights the environmental problems associated with meatification. In addition to the arguments above regarding biophysical problems, we know, for example, that global industrial meat industries are heavily reliant on cheap grains. Fertilisers and pesticides are widely used in industrial crop production. Derived from petrochemicals, these fertilisers are a significant contributor to greenhouse gases (GHGs) (Willett et al., 2019). Moreover, while Weis' work has identified cattle ranching as a significant force in deforestation of the Amazon, other more recent studies have shown the causality between human dietary changes and deforestation. For example, Brazil became the leading global beef producer in 2021, and a recent study published in *Science* (Tyukavina et al., 2017) has found that Brazil's soy production and pasture expansion for cattle are closely linked to deforestation in the Brazilian Legal Amazon.

Third, meatification calls for reconsideration of the relationships between humans and other species. For instance, chickens are often raised under poor environmental conditions in the industrial poultry sector, where these animals' bodies do not easily accommodate confinement and sensory deprivation. Moreover, to increase the protein efficiency ratio, broiler chickens are overfed to meet the market weight, causing substantial physical and biological damage to their bodies. In short, Weis' work on meatification also alludes to animal welfare issues. Recent studies of animal geographies have sought to expand this body of work, and this will be discussed in further detail below.

Meatification of diets: political debates and health concerns

Critical studies of food and agriculture have recently sought to expand the discussion on meatification by focusing on the environmental and health risks associated with growth rates in the production and consumption of meat. This work also highlights the way in which the expansion of livestock sectors animates political debates, generating defensive politics from livestock industries. While concerns have varied, in general, they have been largely focused on issues relating to infectious zoonotic diseases, GHG emissions, and animal welfare.

First, rooted in science and technology studies, social scientists have been critical of the industrial livestock sectors' intensification and expansion, suggesting that it creates ideal 'disease situations' for novel emerging infectious diseases (Hinchliffe et al., 2013, Hinchliffe et al., 2017). They argue that disease is not simply an outcome of microbes infecting a host, but it occurs due to the interaction between people, materialities, animals, and ways of managing diseases. From this perspective, the focus of attention shifted from a single pathogenic agent and its incursion into a host, to the diverse relations or 'disease situations' that make microorganisms more or less likely to cause diseases and the wider meat production consumption systems that underpin those relations. For example, poultry farms in the UK often employ a range of biosecurity measures to prevent the invasion of pathogens, such as reduced contact between farmers and animals, and clean rooms for changing clothes. However, despite implementing strict procedures, industrial chicken farms have encountered difficulties in tracing the sporadic outbreak of a food poisoning bacterium, *Campylobacter*, responsible for approximately 100 deaths annually in the UK.

Reports have shown that the disease risk is embedded within just-in-time industrial poultry production systems rather than emanating from the 'outside'. The confined environments of industrial poultry production, wherein thousands of animals are raised under intensive conditions, pose significant risks for the circulation, amplification, and mutation of microbial lives. The situation is exacerbated by the overuse of antibiotics within modern poultry farming. In 2016, studies found that strains of bacteria, such as *Campylobacter* and *Salmonella*, had developed resistance to various types of antibiotics due to their excessive use within European farms (Hinchliffe et al., 2017). Barrier systems, designed to prevent the incursion of pathogenic agents, become less effective, while a large number of birds raised in confined spaces seem to create 'a ready-made disease incubation chamber' (Hinchliffe et al., 2017: 99). Based on this relational understanding of the disease, meatification exacerbates the incubation of infectious zoonotic diseases. For example, the 2009 swine flu pandemic appeared to be linked to intensive pig farms in Mexico.

Second, the fast-growing expansion of livestock sectors worldwide is regarded as responsible for increased GHG emissions. According to an EAT-Lancet Commission report, food production industries, particularly ruminant livestock farms, are the prime source of GHGs, such as methane and nitrous oxide, which 'have 56 times and 280 times the global warming potential (over 20 years) of carbon dioxide, respectively' (Willett et al., 2019: 462). Thus, this report calls for reducing meat consumption and transforming existing food production systems. However, studies of the impacts of livestock farming have triggered political debates revolving around the contribution of livestock to anthropogenic warming. Opponents have argued that the prevailing assessment of carbon footprint for livestock sectors, as outlined in the EAT-Lancet Commission report or based on global warming potential metrics, has exaggerated the impacts of livestock industries on climate change (McGregor and Houston, 2018, Cusworth et al., 2022). Meat industries have used different discourses to counterbalance standard scientific metrics, with attention focusing explicitly on one pollutant—methane. Recent studies, for example, have shown how the concept of 'nature' is mobilised to naturalise methane emissions throughout the Earth's history. Other narratives focus on issues such as replacing meat with artificial meat, veganism, or using science and technology to produce more efficient cattle

(McGregor and Houston, 2018). Debates are ongoing, and further work is warranted in order to investigate the way in which meatification shapes political disputes.

Third, industrial livestock production often intentionally obscures the animals' lived experiences and takes farm animals' lives for granted. The intensification and expansion of animal husbandry accelerates the process that detaches animals from animal products. Since the 1970s, public attention has been directed to animal cruelty and animal rights, which endeavours to promote standard animal welfare and universal ethical protocols through objective and scientific methods. However, universal animal welfare regulation is often unable to attune to the embodied human–animal interactions. Social scientists have sought to foster animal welfare by drawing attention to farmed animals' sensory experiences (see e.g. Buller and Roe, 2018). Animal geographers suggest, for example, that attention needs to be paid to farmers' existing care practices and their ability to attend to the nonhuman animals in their care (Bear, 2021). Nevertheless, challenges remain, including how to attend to the non-representational nature of human–animal encounters.

Future concerns and questions

The concept of meatification significantly contributes to studies of food and agriculture in society, emphasising that fast-rising meat production and consumption rates have become the drivers of the global food crisis. This analysis focuses on the biophysical and environmental contradictions associated with capitalist agriculture development models. While Weis' meatification theory is insightful, recent work draws on a more-than-human approach to extend the discussion and explore what Tsing (2015: 22) describes as 'multispecies world making'. Humans, insects, microbes, and elements change everyone's world. A more-than-human approach to agriculture and food reorients people's attention and opens up new directions for future research. In light of this, the following questions warrant academic attention: how do farming practices react to the new climate regime which aims to reduce meat consumption; how do livestock industries respond to or prepare for the next pandemic; and what type of knowledge or technologies are being applied to gain insight into or understanding of the animal embodied experience?

References

Bear C (2021) Making insects tick: Responsibility, attentiveness and care in edible insect farming. *Environment and Planning E: Nature and Space* 4, 1010–1030. https://doi.org/10.1177/2514848620945321.

Buller H and Roe E (2018) *Food and animal welfare*. London, Bloomsbury Academic.

Cusworth, G., Lorimer, J., Brice, J., & Garnett, T. (2022). Green rebranding: Regenerative agriculture, future-pasts, and the naturalisation of livestock. *Transactions of the Institute of British Geographers*, 47(4), 1009-1027. https://doi.org/https://doi.org/10.1111/tran.12555

FAO (2023) FAOSTAT. https://www.fao.org/faostat/en/#rankings/countries_by_commodity_imports (Accessed 16 February 2023).

Guthman J (2019) *Wilted: Pathogens, chemicals, and the fragile future of the strawberry industry*. Oakland, University of California Press.

Hinchliffe S, Allen J, Lavau S, Bingham N and Carter S (2013) Biosecurity and the topologies of infected life: From borderlines to borderlands. *Transactions of the Institute of British Geographers* 38, 531–543. https://doi.org/10.1111/j.1475-5661.2012.00538.x.

Hinchliffe S, Bingham N, Allen J and Carter S (2017) *Pathological lives: Disease, space and biopolitics*. Chichester, West Sussex, Wiley Blackwell.

Lorimer J (2020) *The probiotic planet: Using life to manage life*. Minneapolis, University of Minnesota Press.

McGregor A and Houston D (2018) Cattle in the Anthropocene: Four propositions. *Transactions of the Institute of British Geographers* 43, 3–16. https://doi.org/10.1111/tran.12193.

OECD/FAO (2022) *OECD-FAO Agricultural Outlook 2022–2031*. Paris, OECD Publishing.

Tsing A L (2015) *The mushroom at the end of the world: On the possibility of life in capitalist ruins*. Princeton, NJ, Princeton University Press.

Tyukavina A, Hansen M C, Potapov P V, Stehman S V, Smith-Rodriguez K, Okpa

C and Aguilar R (2017) Types and rates of forest disturbance in Brazilian Legal Amazon, 2000–2013. *Science Advances* 3. https://doi.org/10.1126/sciadv.1601047.

Weis T (2013) The meat of the global food crisis. *Journal of Peasant Studies* 40, 65–85.

Willett W, Rockstrom J, Loken B, Springmann M, Lang T, Vermeulen S, Garnett T, Tilman D, DeClerck F, Wood A, Jonell M, Clark M, Gordon L J, Fanzo J, Hawkes C, Zurayk R, Rivera J A, De Vries W, Sibanda L M … & Murray C J. L (2019) Food in the Anthropocene: The EAT-Lancet Commission on healthy diets from sustainable food systems. *Lancet* 393, 447–492. https://doi.org/10.1016/S0140 -6736(18)31788-4.

Further reading

Weis T (2013) The meat of the global food crisis. *Journal of Peasant Studies* 40(1), 65–85.

Weis' (2013) article offers a political and economic critique of the global rise in meat consumption. It argues that industrial livestock production, including the cycling of large volumes of grains and oilseeds to feed this industry, is the key driver behind rising meat consumption globally, as well as exacerbating climate change.

Guthman J (2019) *Wilted: Pathogens, chemicals, and the fragile future of the strawberry industry.* Oakland: University of California Press.

Lorimer J (2020) *The probiotic planet: Using life to manage life.* Minneapolis: University of Minnesota Press.

Lorimer (2020) and Guthman (2019) both draw on a more-than-human perspective to critically investigate the anthropocentric domination of nature. Their findings demonstrate that the separation of species, which is a critical aspect of industrial agriculture, has undermined future agricultural production conditions.

82. Media and food

JONATAN LEER AND STINNE GUNDER
STRØM KROGAGER

Introduction: towards a critical understanding of food and media

The contemporary consumer's relationship to food is shaped by and unfolds through the media. One might even say that contemporary food consumption (almost) always involves some form of media use. The relationship between media and food is nonetheless nothing new.

In a European context, the earliest cookbooks can be traced back to medieval times. With the development of the printing press and new media like the magazine, food media were increasingly popularised in the 19th century and even more so in the 20th century with mass communication through radio, newspapers, and television where food was featured. Since the turn of the century, food has seen an unprecedented growth in digital content, including the many consumer-oriented apps that are integrated into everyday cooking.

While food media have existed for a long time, it is only in the 21st century that we really see them being the subject of serious academic scrutiny, notably concerning food media's relationships to power, normativity, aesthetics, moral, identity, economics, and their integration in everyday life.

The politics and impacts of food media and discourses

Food media are highly integrated in contemporary everyday life, but food media do not just convey practical information (Rousseau 2012). They are also vehicles of ideological discourses which are embedded in political and economic structures, moral economies, social identities, and consumer cultures (Leer and Povlsen 2016, Lewis 2020).

Gender and identity in food media

There are numerous studies that highlight the gendered character of food media across genres and time periods (Hollows 2022, Leer 2017, Contois 2022). These genres have developed from the cookbook to contemporary social media with its ever-expanding catalogue of content increasingly founded on visual forms of representation.

In cookbooks and food television, there has been a tendency to associate men with professional cooking (Harris & Giuffre 2015, Leer 2016) and more exclusive forms of food, while women have been more associated with everyday cooking (Devault 1991, Nathanson 2009). This distinction was often spatialised so that professional restaurant kitchens were masculinised and domestic kitchens were associated with women's cooking (Black 2021). Similarly, subgenres were gendered, so that travelogue cooking shows were dominated by men (Heldke 2015, Leer & Kjær 2015) while women were dominant in shows on health and domestic cooking (Magee 2007). These patterns reflect traditional gendered hierarchies in food culture (Szabo 2013, Devault 1991).

These gendered distinctions are not absolute (Neuman 2016). As men are increasingly undertaking more domestic food work, there are changes in traditional gender roles as related to food (Holm et al. 2015). These do, however, often involve some negotiations, for instance, establishing men's home cooking as distinct from women's home cooking (Leer 2019). Notably, the rise of social media has increased the gendered diversity of food media and has allowed for gender non-conforming, LGBT+ foodies to come to prominence (Lewis 2020, Vester 2020).

As numerous studies have also highlighted, gender often correlates with other social categories, most importantly race and class (Cruz 2013). Similarly, food media have been criticised for reproducing a male gaze and white middle-class gaze on subjects from working classes (Hollows and Jones 2010) and romanticising and stereotyping the "ethnic other" (Leer and Kjær 2015, Heldke 2015). There are also some examples of food media notably on social media as sites for more subversive narratives of food and gender, such as female food bloggers and Instagrammers subverting the stereotypes of food porn (Dejmanee 2016).

Food celebrities and influencers

Since the turn of the century, there has been a great deal of attention paid to the changing role of the figures of food media and their roles in society. Many chefs have become public figures (Hollows 2022). For instance, the Danish chef René Redzepi was prestigiously featured on the cover of *Time* magazine in 2012, a space previously reserved for politicians, pop stars, and iconic business figures (Leer 2016). Celebrity chefs have also become active on social media platforms as political voices and as a way of extending their brand to new audiences (Lee 2014).

It has been suggested that the term "celebrity chef" should be replaced by the broader term of "food celebrity" (Johnston and Goodman 2015), as this covers more than just chefs. For instance, Michelle Obama, with no background in food, became an important voice on food and children in the US. Obama also demonstrated the potential impact of food celebrities as she was a central force in a ban on unhealthy food commercials on the Disney Channel (Kjær 2016).

Despite examples of how food celebrities have been able to raise important issues and spark public awareness on important food issues, various forms of criticism have been levelled against the impact and voice of food celebrities (Rousseau 2012). Indeed, rather than addressing structural issues related to food systems and inequality, they tend to reproduce "unequal power relations" (Hollows 2022). More recently, studies have increasingly focused on food influencers who "construct, curate and share the meanings of good food" and reproduce "a form of white, hetero-normative middle- and upper-class privilege that produces particular grammars of good food" (Goodman and Jaworska 2020: 183).

At the same time, food celebrities' roles as cultural and political intermediaries are used to tackle issues related to food ethics and sustainability and to form consumers' food choices (Phillipov & Gale, 2020). For example, Friedlander & Riedy (2018) studied meat reduction campaigns on Facebook, Instagram, and Twitter led by influencers such as Jamie Oliver. They conclude that social media makes it possible to reach a much broader audience with these "inconvenient" messages than if they had to go through gatekeepers in traditional news media.

Digital food media and consumers' everyday life

With the rise of digital media, food media are increasingly integrated into and becoming inseparable from everyday food practices (Lewis 2020, Leer & Krogager 2020). Hence,

the contemporary food consumer is increasingly a "prosumer" (Rousseau 2012), for instance as a co-creator through sharing recipes, comments, and photos. Also, new modes of exchange have occurred in digital food consumption where personal information or attention is used as a means of transaction—a form of emerging "surveillance capitalism" (Zuboff 2015)—where powerful corporate players monetise creative food work on, for example, SoMe (Lewis 2020: 9).

At the same time, digitalisation has facilitated a democratisation in food media. Here a striking example is the reviewing of restaurants. Reviewing used to be an occupation for specialists. It is now a mundane practice that every consumer can engage in and is often encouraged to do so. These "amateur" reviews are what many orient themselves towards and they can have a great impact on restaurants' economy and survival (Luca 2016), and they allow for interaction between restaurateurs and consumers (Vásquez 2021).

Furthermore, digital media have facilitated various forms of digital food activism where digital platforms work to unite consumers and activists against powerful corporate players and food inequality (Schneider et al. 2018), for instance via hashtag activism such as #foodpoverty that has been used as a "'catch-all' phrase for food insecurity" (Mann 2021: 92). This form of digital activism might be efficient in connecting people across geographies, but it can also simplify the challenges and work to stigmatise a large and very heterogeneous population.

Food media futures

Social media, sustainability, and activism

Social media plays a vital role in setting the public agenda, especially with respect to sustainability issues such as food waste. According to Närvänen et al. (2018), social media campaigns are an effective tool to raise awareness and inform consumers about food waste. For example, Teoh et al. (2022) have shown that social media usage has a significant impact on attitudes and norms regarding food waste, and that intentions to reduce food waste constitute an important predictor in preventing food waste. Also, in terms of reconfiguring eating, social media is important. Laakso et al. (2021) conclude that discussions in a vegan social media community potentially support and facilitate social change towards veganism and that this can also reach outside the vegan community.

Thus, digital media has altered consumers' engagements with food, eating, and sustainability issues, and has also provided new forms of food activism. Digital platforms and consumers have become key mediators of the directives of food corporations and government actors, changing both everyday practices around food consumption and ethics and aesthetics central to the field.

Social media futures

Different affordances in media enable diverse kinds of content and the many digital, social, and mobile media platforms sustain different aesthetic, political, and social content.

Instagram offers a platform for sophisticated aesthetics preoccupied with ethical concerns in relation to food consumption (Contois & Kish, 2022; Leer & Krogager, 2022, McDonnell, 2016; Paddock, 2011). The platform has lent its name to the new adjective "Instagrammable" that is used to signal highly elaborate and idealised aesthetics in the context of food (Kusumasondjaja & Tjiptono, 2019). Facebook, on the other hand, houses a more diverse media food landscape that is less ruled by aesthetic and ethical dogmas. For example, users gather in Facebook groups to share unpretentious photos of prefabricated dinners (Krogager & Leer, 2020). YouTube provides a very diverse platform in regard to food aesthetics, ethics, and themes. The genre of "how-to videos" showing people's "ordinary expertise" is very popular on YouTube (Lewis, 2020), as are videos and channels of a more grotesque and carnivalesque character (Lupton, 2020; Forchtner and Tominc, 2017), sexualised and gendered videos (Braun & Carruthers, 2020; Contois, 2018). In addition, professionalised cooking channels are also on the rise, which contribute to the continuing monetisation of the platform (Simonsen & Krogager, 2021). Twitter has been used for celebrity chefs' controversies on, e.g., ethics and plagiarising of recipes and various discussions of food politics and sustainability (Rousseau, 2012, Pilăr et al. 2019). Research on TikTok has explored pro-recovery communities, that is, how the platform provides shared spaces for people recovering from eating disorders (Herrick et al., 2021; Brooks et al., 2022).

As these examples show there is an increasing interconnectedness between media and food. It might even be argued that—for better or worse—the smart phone is the most important tool in contemporary kitchens and for contemporary food consumers (Krogager & Leer, 2021). Future food studies need to monitor and reflect on this development and always have an eye for the importance of media in all domains of food.

References
Black, R.E. 2021. *Cheffes de Cuisine*. University of Illinois Press.

Braun, V. & Carruthers, S. 2020. Working at self and wellness. In D. Lupton & Z. Feldman (eds.) *Digital Food Cultures* (pp. 82–96). London: Routledge.

Brooks, R., Christidis, R., Carah, N., Kelly, B., Martino, F. & Backholer, K. 2022. Turning users into 'unofficial brand ambassadors': marketing of unhealthy food and non-alcoholic beverages on TikTok. *BMJ Global Health*, 7(6): e009112.

Contois, E.J. 2020. *Diners, Dudes, and Diets*. University of North Carolina Press.

Contois, E.J.H. 2018. The spicy spectacular: Food, gender, and celebrity on Hot Ones. *Feminist Media Studies*, 18(4): 1–4.

Contois, E.J.H. & Kish, Z. (eds.) 2022. *Food Instagram: Identity, Influence, and Negotiation*. University of Illinois Press.

Cruz, A. 2013. Gettin' Down Home with the Neelys: Gastro-Porn and Televisual Performances of Gender, Race, and Sexuality. *Women & Performance: A Journal of Feminist Theory, 23*(3): 323–349. https://doi.org/10.1080/0740770X.2013.853916.

Decorte, P., Cuykx, I., Teunissen, L., Poels, K., Smits, T., Pabian, S., van Royen, K. & De Backer, C. 2022. Everywhere you look, you'll find food. *Ecology of Food and Nutrition, 61*(3): 273–303.

Dejmanee, T. 2016. 'food Porn' As Postfeminist Play: Digital Femininity and the Female Body on Food Blogs. *Television & New Media, 17*(5): 429–448. https://doi.org/10.1177/1527476415615944.

DeSollier 2013. Food and the Self. Bloomsbury: London.

Devault, M. 1991. *Feeding the Family*. University of Chicago Press.

Forchtner, B. & Tominc, A. 2017. Kalashnikov and cooking-spoon. *Food, Culture & Society*, 20(3): 415–441.

Friedlander, J. & Riedy, C. 2018. Celebrities, credibility, and complementary frames. *Communication Research and Practice*, 4(3): 229–245.

Goodman, M.K. & Jaworska, S. 2020. Mapping digital foodscapes. *Geoforum*, 117: 183–193.

Harris, D.A. & Giuffre, P. 2015. *Taking the Heat*. Rutgers University Press.

Heldke, L. 2015. *Exotic Appetites*. Routledge.

Hepp, A. 2020. *Deep Mediatization*. Routledge.

Herrick, S.S.C., Hallward, L. & Duncan, L.R. 2021. This is just how I cope. *International Journal of Eating Disorders*, 54(4): 516–526.

Hollows, J. 2022. *Celebrity Chefs, Food Media and the Politics of Eating*. Bloomsbury Publishing.

Hollows, J. 2003. Oliver's twist: Leisure, labour and domestic masculinity in The Naked Chef. *International Journal of Cultural Studies*, 6(2): 229–248.

Hollows, J., & Jones, S. 2010. 'At least he's doing something': Moral entrepreneurship and individual responsibility in Jamie's Ministry of Food. *European Journal of Cultural Studies*, 13(3), 307-322.

Holm, L., Ekström, M.P., Hach, S. & Lund, T.B. 2015. Who is cooking dinner? *Food, Culture & Society*, 18(4): 589–610.

Johnston, J. & Goodman, M.K. 2015. Spectacular foodscapes. *Food, Culture & Society*, 18(2): 205–222.

Kjær, K.M. 2016. Just a happy housewife? In Leer, J. & Povlsen, K.K. (eds.), *Food and Media: Practices, Distinctions and Heterotopias* (pp. 62–77). Routledge.

Krogager, S. G. S., & Leer, J. 2021. Mad og medier. Samfundslitteratur.

Krogager, S.G.S. & Leer, J. 2020. Mad uden filter. In Jessen, I.B. & Graakjær, N.J. (eds.), *Medieæstetik: politik, hverdagsliv og forbrugskultur* (pp. 207–229). MÆRKK – Æstetik og kommunikation, Aalborg Universitetsforlag.

Krogager, S.G.S., Leer, J., Povlsen, K.K. & Højlund, S. 2020. The amalgamation of media use practices and food practices in a school setting. *Communication Research and Practice*, 6(2): 79–94.

Kusumasondjaja, S. & Tjiptono, F. 2019. Endorsement and visual complexity in food advertising on Instagram. *Internet Research*, 29(4): 659–687.

Laakso, S., Niva, M., Eranti, V. & Aapio, F. 2021. Reconfiguring everyday eating. *Food Culture & Society*, 25(2): 268–289.

Lee, N., 2014. *Celebrity Chefs: Class Mobility, Media, Masculinity*. Doctoral Dissertation, University of Sydney. Available at: https://ses.library.usyd.edu.au/handle/2123/11727?show=full

Leer, J. 2016. What's cooking, man? *Feminist Review*, 114(1): 72–90.

Leer, J. 2017. Gender and food television. In Lebesco, K. and Naccarato, P. (eds.) *The Bloomsbury Handbook of Food and Popular Culture* (pp. 13–26). Bloomsbury.

Leer, J. 2019. New Nordic men. *Food, Culture & Society*, 22(3): 316–333.

Leer, J. 2022. Gender and barbecue. *Anthropology of Food, 16*. DOI: https://doi.org/10.4000/aof.12915

Leer, J. & Kjær, K.M. 2015. Strange culinary encounters. *Food, Culture & Society*, 18(2): 309–327.

Leer, J. & Krogager, S.G.S. (eds.) 2021. *Research Methods in Digital Food Studies*. Routledge.

Leer, J. & Krogager, S.G.S. 2022. Transgressive Food Practices on Instagram. The case of Guldkroen in Copenhagen. In Contois, E.J.H. & Kish, Z. (eds.) *Food Instagram: Identity, Influence, and Negotiation* (pp. 205–220). Chicago: University of Illinois Press.

Leer, J. & Povlsen, K.K. (eds.) 2016. *Food and Media*. Routledge.

Leer, J., Krogager, S.G.S., Povlsen, K.K. & Højlund, S. 2019. Gender and children's food practices. *NORA*, 27(3): 181–193.

Lewis, T. 2020. *Digital Food*. Bloomsbury Publishing.

Luca, M. 2016. Reviews, reputation, and revenue: The case of Yelp.com. March 15, 2016. *Harvard Business School NOM Unit Working Paper* (12-016).

Lupton, D. 2020. Carnivalesque food videos. In D. Lupton & Z. Feldman (eds.) *Digital Food Cultures* (pp. 35–50). London: Routledge.

McDonnell E.M. 2016. *Food Porn*. Palgrave Macmillan.

Magee, R.M. 2007. Food puritanism and food pornography.*The Journal of American Popular Culture*, 6(2): 1–13.

Mann, A. 2021. Beyond the hashtag: Social media ethnography in food activism. In

J. Leer & S. Krogager (eds.) *Research Methods in Digital Food Studies* (pp. 86–98). Routledge.

Närvänen, E., Mesiranta, N., Sutinen, U. & Mattila, M. 2018. Creativity, aesthetics and ethics of food waste in social media campaigns. *Journal of Cleaner Production*, *195*: 102–110.

Nathanson, E. 2009. As easy as pie: Cooking shows, domestic efficiency, and postfeminist temporality. *Television & New Media*, *10*(4): 311–330.

Neuman, N. 2016. *Stories of Masculinity, Gender Equality, and Culinary Progress* (Doctoral dissertation, Acta Universitatis Upsaliensis).

Paddock, J. 2011. *Class, Food, Culture: Exploring "Alternative" Food Consumption* (Doctoral disseration, University of Cardiff).

Parasecoli, F. 2016. Manning the table. In J. Leer & K. Povlsen (eds.) *Food and Media* (pp. 95–109). Routledge.

Pearson, D., Mirosa, M., Andrews, L. & Kerr, G. 2017. Reframing communications that encourage individuals to reduce food waste. *Communication Research and Practice*, *3*(2): 137–154.

Phillipov, M., & Gale, F. 2020. Celebrity chefs, consumption politics and food labelling: Exploring the contradictions. *Journal of Consumer Culture*, *20*(4), 400-418.

Pilǎr, L., Stanislavská, L.K., Pitrová, J., Krejčí, I., Tichá, I., & Chalupová, M. 2019. Twitter analysis of global communication in the field of sustainability. *Sustainability*, *11*(24). DOI: https://doi.org/10.3390/su11246958

Rousseau, S. 2012. *Food Media: Celebrity Chefs and the Politics of Everyday Interference*. Berg.

Schneider, T., Eli, K., Dolan, C. & Ulijaszek, S. (eds.) 2018. *Digital Food Activism*. Routledge.

Simonsen, T.M. & Krogager, S.G.S. 2021. How to approach food texts on YouTube. In J. Leer & S.G.S. Krogager (eds.) *Research Methods in Digital Food Studies* (pp. 54–68). Routledge.

Szabo, M. 2013. Foodwork or foodplay? Men's domestic cooking, privilege and leisure. *Sociology*, *47*(4): 623–638.

Teoh, C.W., Koay, K.Y. & Pei Sun Chai (2022). The role of social media in food waste prevention behaviour. *British Food Journal*, *124*(5): 1680–1696.

Vásquez, C. 2020. What if the customer is wrong? Debates about food on Yelp and TripAdvisor. In Tovares, A. & Gordon, C. (eds.) *Identity and Ideology in Digital Food Discourse* (pp. 111–135). Bloomsbury.

Vásquez, C. & Chik, A. 2015. "I Am Not a Foodie…": Culinary capital in online reviews of Michelin restaurants. *Food and Foodways*, *23*(4): 231–250.

Vásquez, C., & Chik, A. 2021. How to study online restaurant reviews. In Leer, J. & Krogager, S.G.S. (eds), *Research Methods in Digital Food Studies* (pp. 127–140). Routledge.

Vester, K. 2020. Queering the cookbook. In Coghlan, J.M. (ed.) *The Cambridge Companion to Literature and Food* (pp. 131–145). Cambridge University Press.

Zuboff, S. 2015. Big other. *Journal of Information Technology*, *30*(1): 75–89.

Further reading

Leer, J. & Krogager, S.G.S. 2021. *Research Methods in Digital Food Studies*. Abingdon: Routledge.
This collected volume provides thoughtful ideas for how to work with digital food and it is the first methodological synthesis of digital food studies bringing together contributions from leading scholars in food and media studies.

Lewis, T. 2020. *Digital Food: From Paddock to Platform*. London: Bloomsbury.
This book provides an introduction and in-depth treatment of digital food politics through an analysis of the tensions around digital engagement in increasingly commercialised spaces, the changing nature of politics in a social media context, the growing naturalisation of digital devices and data monitoring, and the role and impact of digitalisation on social relations.

83. Medicalisation and food

ALISSA OVEREND

Introduction

The concept of medicalisation—where relatively normal human functioning is defined and treated as a medical issue—grew out of the anti-psychiatry movement of the 1960s (Szasz, 1961/2010) and developed through the critical sociology of health and illness of the 1970s (Conrad, 1975; Foucault, 1973; Zola, 1972). In contemporary Western societies, virtually no facet of human functioning is outside the scope of medicalisation, including food and eating. The medicalisation of food has taken place alongside the growth of market-based food economies, broader advances in food science, the proliferation of food advertising, an increase in chronic diseases of adulthood, and an increase in psychological explanations for diet- and food-related diseases. The medicalisation of food is summarised through two related trends: (1) the medicalisation of food's biochemical properties and (2) the medicalisation of eating and feeding processes.

Current issues

While food as long been used as a form of medicine, the language and corollary understanding of food in contemporary Western contexts is dominated by biomedical framings. The language of vitamins, minerals, macronutrients, proteins, omega 3s, unsaturated fats, and calories is increasingly used in food guides, front of package food labelling, food advertisements, and nutritional facts tables. It has also crept into the common vernacular. Under a medicalised food paradigm, "a cool, creamy glass of milk [has become] 150 calories and a measurable ratio of fat, proteins, and carbohydrates" (Mudry, 2009: p. 22). In a relatively short period, scientific understandings have almost entirely replaced long-standing traditional, cultural, and holistic accounts of food. So much so that statements like "drink orange juice, which is high in vitamin C, antioxidants, and micronutrients to improve heart health" are ubiquitous in broader understandings of disease prevention. Such medicalised accounts of food have given rise to an understanding of functional nutrition, where singular aspects of food are valued for their perceived disease-fighting effects. Without negating the advances made by nutritional science, medicalised (and by extension, functional) accounts of food individualise issues that are systemic. In short, they oversimplify complex epidemiological aspects of disease and in doing so detract from social, cultural, and political causes of disease and ill-health.

Also medicalised are an increasing number of feeding and eating disorders. Defined by psychologists and others in the Diagnostic and Statistical Manual (DSM) of Mental Disorders 5 as "a persistent disturbance of eating or eating-related behaviour that results in the altered consumption of food and that significantly impairs health or psychological functioning" (APA, 2013: 329), eating disorders include anorexia nervosa, bulimia nervosa, binge eating disorder (BED), and avoidant/restrictive food intake disorder (ARFID), among others. These classifications and related diagnoses mark a distinct shift in historical understandings of eating. In the Middle Ages, self-restricted food intake was an act of fasting, described in theological terms, and in the Freudian psychopathology of the early 20th century, it was a symptom of an underlying condition, not a disease in and of itself (Fixsen & Cheshire, 2022). Over-eating is equally medicalised. BED was added to the DSM-5, furthering the medicalisation of obesity in Western contexts. Commonly diagnosed by the often-skewed body mass index (BMI), critics point out that obesity is not a disease, though it may be a risk factor for other diseases (Mayes, 2014). The medicalisation of over-eating also hyper-focuses on individual food choice, while detracting attention from economic and food inequalities and the effects of neoliberal market forces that require over-consumption and produce cheap, calorie-dense foods (Guthman & DuPuis, 2006). ARFID, sometimes referred to as orthorexia, medicalises picky eating, health consciousness, and veganism (Fixsen & Cheshire, 2022). By expanding definitions of disordered eating, the American Psychological Association and its related organisations expand what Gusfield (1989) refers to as the "troubled persons industries"—the medical agencies (clinics, hospitals, and rehabilitation centres) and measures (surgery, pharmaceuticals, and therapy) through which disordered eating is treated.

Future concerns

The risks of medicalisation are well documented and include expensive and often dangerous procedures, the pharmaceuticalisation of society, a blurring of boundaries between the normal and the pathological, the use of medicine as an agent of social control, the medicalisation of social deviance, and the loss of traditional and cultural understandings of health and eating (Busfield, 2017). Many of these risks are exacerbated in neoliberal economies, where there is creeping privatisation and an increase in globalised food production, and where consumers are ever more disconnected from food production, and by extension food knowledge. As a counterbalance to the medicalisation of food and eating, critical food studies scholarship highlights food's most essential component: the social and political contexts in which food is produced, sold, and consumed. It is these frameworks that will help us mitigate disease far more effectively than any one vitamin or nutrient component.

References

APA (2013) *Diagnostic and statistical manual of mental disorders: DSM-5* (5th ed.). American Psychiatric Association.

Busfield J (2017) The concept of medicalisation reassessed. *Sociology of Health & Illness* 39(5), 759–774.

Conrad P (1975) The discovery of hyperkinesis. *Social Problems 12*(1), 12–21.

Fixsen A and Cheshire A (2022) Orthorexia nervosa: The medicalization of extreme healthy eating practice. In M Harbusch (ed.), *Troubled Persons Industries*, 141–171. https://doi.org/10.1007/978-3-030-83745-7_7.

Foucault M (1973) *The birth of the clinic*. Tavistock.

Gusfield J R (1989) Constructing the ownership of social problems: Fun and profit in the welfare state. *Social Problems 36*(5), 431–441.

Guthman J and DuPuis M (2006) Embodying neoliberalism: Economy, culture and the politics of fat. *Environment and Planning D: Society and Space 24*(3), 427–448.

Mayes C (2014) Medicalization of eating and feeding. In P B Thompson and D M Kaplan (eds.), *The Encyclopedia of Food and Agricultural Ethics*, 1371–1378. https://doi.org/10.1007/978-94-007-0929-4. Dordrecht: Springer.

Mudry J (2009) *Measured meals: Nutrition in America*. State University of New York Press.

Szasz T (1961/2010) *The myth of mental illness: Foundations of a theory of personal conduct*. Harper Perennial.

Zola I (1972) Medicine as an institution of social control. *Sociological Review 20*(4), 487–504.

Further reading

Conrad P (2007) *The medicalization of society: On the transformation of human conditions intro treatable disorders*. Johns Hopkins University Press.

One of the most cited sources on the topic, this is a landmark book that covers foundational concepts, cases, constraints, and consequences of medicalisation.

Harusch M (ed.) (2022) *Troubles persons industries: The expansion of psychiatric categories beyond psychiatry*. Palgrave MacMillan.

This edited collection is a contemporary discussion of medicalisation that examines the discipline of psychiatry, the political contexts of neoliberalism, and the cases of mental health governance in schools, pregnancy, ADHD, and cannabis use.

ALISSA OVEREND

84. Migration and food

Laura Terragni

Introduction

According to the latest report published by the International Organization for Migration (IOM), there are 281 million international migrants. This is about 3.5% of the entire population in the world. Of these, 87 million headed to Europe and 59 million to the United States (IOM, 2022). A large proportion of the world population therefore has experience with food in the context of migration.

When people leave their country and resettle in a new one many things change in their lives. People have to get accustomed to a new language, different kinds of housing, and the different organisation of the school system and health care. Food is one of the important aspects of everyday life that is affected by migration (Abbots et al., 2016; Koc and Welsh, 2001; Ward, 2008). The food that is available, the way it is prepared, the organisation of meals, and what is considered healthy and unhealthy food differ to various degrees from the country one originally comes from (Terragni et al., 2014).

Food and good nutrition are essential for our health and well-being. Knowledge about the impact of migration on dietary habits is therefore relevant from a public health perspective. However, food is more than nutrients. Food is also an important part of our social life and identity. Knowing how people navigate in a new food environment can provide insights into the new life after migration. Finally, food in the context of migration can provide a lens for understanding the relationship between immigrant groups and the society they resettle in and provide an indication of the integration process.

Key dimensions of the food–migration relationship

The process of dietary acculturation

Studies investigating food in the context of migration tend to agree that food habits in the new country reflect some continuity with the original food culture together with the incorporation of new elements from the food culture of the country of resettlement (Osei-Kwasi et al., 2016).

'Dietary acculturation' is the most widely used concept for approaching food habits and dietary changes in the context of migrations. Dietary acculturation refers to the process that occurs when members of a minority group adopt the eating patterns of the host country (Satia, 2010). The concept of dietary acculturation builds on the concept of acculturation developed by Berry (1992). He stated that the process of acculturation occurs according to two independent dimensions. The first one considers the maintenance and development of one's ethnic distinctiveness in society. The other involves the desirability of inter-ethnic contact. The interweaving of these dimensions gives a four-fold typology of acculturation: marginalisation, separation, assimilation, and integration. Marginalisation indicates the case in which groups lose cultural and social contact with both their traditional culture and larger society; separation happens instead 'when there are not substantial relations with the larger society, accompanied by a maintenance of ethnic identity and traditions; assimilation has been defined as relinquishing ones' cultural identity and moving into the larger society; finally, integration implies some maintenance of the cultural integrity of the group as well as the movement to become part of a larger societal framework' (Berry, 1992: 70–71).

Immigrants may experience unfamiliarity with a new food environment and previous knowledge about food may be challenged (Osei-Kwasi et al., 2016). For instance, language barriers can make it difficult to shop for food, basic ingredients may not be available, and competencies like recognising the quality of food by taste and smell may not be an option in supermarket chains. Fear of eating food that is not allowed by religion (for instance food that is not halal) may also be experienced (Osei-Kwasi et al., 2016). Because of these uncertainties, immigrants may restrict the variation of their diets (Osei-Kwasi et al., 2016), which may have consequences for their health (Abubakar et al., 2018).

Diets and health after migration

Deterioration of diets after migration has been shown in several studies and the immigrant population is more likely to suffer from food-related non-communicable diseases such as type 2 diabetes, cardiovascular diseases, and obesity (Agyemang and van den Born, 2019). The larger availability and affordability of calorie-dense food in host countries (the so-called nutrition transition) has been regarded as one the main reasons for the deterioration of diets after migration (Osei-Kwasi et al., 2023). The appeal of this kind of food as a way of renewing social identity and strengthening the feeling of belonging in the new country needs also to be considered (Parasecoli, 2014; Vignola et al., 2021).

Recent studies have, however, started questioning whether dietary habits do actually deteriorate after migration. It has been noted that increased attention to nutritional health in many destination countries (such as Europe) may have contributed to the creation of healthier food environments that may also benefit immigrant populations (Berggreen-Clausen et al., 2022). Moreover, aspects related to the nutrition transition are nowadays more common in many of the countries immigrants come from, weakening the assumption that unhealthy diets start after migration (Holdsworth et al., 2020).

Food as a form of inclusion and exclusion

It is not only immigrants who change their food habits after migration. The immigrants' food culture has an impact on the country of resettlement as well. As the immigrant community grows, so does the availability of ethnic food, grocery shops, and restaurants. While initially serving the immigrant communities, these have become part of the food habits of the host population and enriched the variety of ingredients and dishes in their food culture For instance, a study conducted among Ghanaians in London indicated that in the beginning they had trouble finding food from their own culture and therefore established food businesses to provide familiar food to the community (Tuomainen, 2009). A study conducted on the same population a few years later showed that Ghanian food and restaurants had become popular among British consumers wanting to try something new (Tuomainen, 2018).

Future directions

Globalisation of food cultures, digitalisation, and transnationalism tend to make the distinction between food habits in the country of origin and host country more fluid and the definition of dietary acculturation becomes more complex (Ward, 2008). Several scholars thus talk about the creolisation of food cultures (Parasecoli, 2014; Tibère, 2016).

Parallel with trends toward a 'melting pot food culture', other processes occur. Immigrant groups are at higher risk of poverty and food insecurity also in countries with a well-established welfare state (Ahmed et al., 2023; Henjum et al., 2019; Maynard et al., 2019). Another issue that needs to be considered when talking about food in the context of migration is the potential politicisation of 'immigrant food', exemplified – for instance – by the commercialisation of halal food (Ayyub, 2015). On the other hand, food can also become a way to show solidarity and strengthen multiculturalism, as illustrated by initiatives to provide food and experience of commensality among refugees and undocumented immigrants (Starck and Matta, 2022).

Food is a powerful lens for understanding society, our well-being, and collective identity. The encounters between different food traditions can lead to the transformation not only of food cultures but also of societies. To understand food in the context of migration, different perspectives are required, from social science to history, to health sciences, each providing a unique contribution to understanding the impact of migration on food habits and the transformations in our societies.

References

Abbots, E.-J., Klein, J., & Watson, J. (2016). Approaches to food and migration: Rootedness, being and belonging. In Klein, J.A. and Watson, J.L.*The handbook of food and anthropology*, 115–132, Bloomsbury Academic.

Abubakar, I., Aldridge, R. W., Devakumar, D., Orcutt, M., Burns, R., Barreto, M. L., Dhavan, P., Fouad, F. M., Groce, N., & Guo, Y. (2018). The UCL–Lancet Commission on Migration and Health: the health of a world on the move. *The Lancet*, *392*(10164), 2606–2654.

Agyemang, C., & van den Born, B.-J. (2019). Non-communicable diseases in migrants: an expert review. *Journal of Travel Medicine*, 26(2), tay107.

Ahmed, D., Benavente, P., & Diaz, E. (2023). Food insecurity among international migrants during the COVID-19 pandemic: A scoping review. *International Journal of Environmental Research and Public Health*, 20(7), 5273.

Ayyub, R. M. (2015). An empirical investigation of ethnic food consumption: a perspective of majority ethnic group. *British Food Journal, 117*(4), 1239–1255.

Berggreen-Clausen, A., Pha, S. H., Alvesson, H. M., Andersson, A., & Daivadanam, M. (2022). Food environment interactions after migration: a scoping review on low- and middle-income country immigrants in high-income countries. *Public Health Nutrition, 25*(1), 136–158.

Berry, J. W. (1992). Acculturation and adaptation in a new society. *International Migration, 30*, 69–69.

Henjum, S., Morseth, M. S., Arnold, C. D., Mauno, D., & Terragni, L. (2019). "I worry if I will have food tomorrow": a study on food insecurity among asylum seekers living in Norway. *BMC Public Health, 19*, 1–8.

Holdsworth, M., Pradeilles, R., Tandoh, A., Green, M., Wanjohi, M., Zotor, F., Asıkı, G., Klomegah, S., Abdul-Haq, Z., & Osei-Kwasi, H. (2020). Unhealthy eating practices of city-dwelling Africans in deprived neighbourhoods: evidence for policy action from Ghana and Kenya. *Global Food Security, 26*, 100452.

IOM (2022). *World migration report 2022*. https://worldmigrationreport.iom.int/wmr-2022-interactive/.

Koc, M., & Welsh, J. (2001). Food, foodways and immigrant experience. *Toronto: Centre for Studies in Food Security, 2*, 46–48.

Maynard, M., Dean, J., Rodriguez, P. I., Sriranganathan, G., Qutub, M., & Kirkpatrick, S. I. (2019). The experience of food insecurity among immigrants: a scoping review. *Journal of International Migration and Integration, 20*, 375–417.

Osei-Kwasi, H., Boateng, D., Asamane, E. A., Akparibo, R., & Holdsworth, M. (2023). Transitioning food environments and diets of African migrants: implications for non-communicable diseases. *Proceedings of the Nutrition Society, 82*(1), 69–79.

Osei-Kwasi, H. A., Nicolaou, M., Powell, K., Terragni, L., Maes, L., Stronks, K., Lien, N., Holdsworth, M., & Consortium, D. (2016). Systematic mapping review of the factors influencing dietary behaviour in ethnic minority groups living in Europe: a DEDIPAC study. *International Journal of Behavioral Nutrition and Physical Activity, 13*, 1–17.

Parasecoli, F. (2014). Food, identity, and cultural reproduction in immigrant communities. *Social Research, 81*(2), 415–439.

Satia, J. A. (2010). Dietary acculturation and the nutrition transition: an overview. *Applied Physiology, Nutrition, and Metabolism, 35*(2), 219–223.

Starck, E., & Matta, R. (2022). More-than-human assemblages and the politics of (food) conviviality: cooking, eating, and living together in Germany. *Food, Culture & Society, 27*(3), 734–753.

Terragni, L., Garnweidner, L. M., Pettersen, K. S., & Mosdøl, A. (2014). Migration as a turning point in food habits: the early phase of dietary acculturation among women from South Asian, African, and Middle Eastern Countries living in Norway. *Ecology of Food and Nutrition, 53*(3), 273–291.

Tibère, L. (2016). Food as a factor of collective identity: the case of creolisation. *French Cultural Studies, 27*(1), 85–95.

Tuomainen, H. M. (2009). Ethnic identity, (post) colonialism and foodways: Ghanaians in London. *Food, Culture & Society, 12*(4), 525–554.

Tuomainen, H. (2018). Ghanaian cuisine entering the cosmopolitan stage: the role of women, meal formats, and menu adaptations in the shaping of Ghanaian restaurants in London. *Anthropology of Food*, S12. https://doi.org/10.4000/aof.9149.

Vignola, E. F., Nazmi, A., & Freudenberg, N. (2021). What makes ultra-processed food appealing? A critical scan and conceptual model. *World Nutrition, 12*(4), 136–175.

Ward, C. (2008). Thinking outside the Berry boxes: new perspectives on identity, acculturation and intercultural relations. *International Journal of Intercultural Relations, 32*(2), 105–114.

Further reading

Matta, R., de Suremain, C. E., & Crenn, C. (Eds.) (2020). *Food identities at home and on the move: explorations at the intersection of food, belonging and dwelling*. Routledge.
This book is recommended for further exploration of the relationships between food, migration, and identity.

85. Mutual aid and food: feeding radical politics

Oli Mould

Introduction

Mutual aid, as a political praxis, is about providing reciprocal support while fostering understanding about the structural inequalities that create the conditions of vulnerability and need in the first place (Firth, 2022). The term originates from the works of Peter Kropotkin, a prominent anarchist, and spiritual and radical thinker who wrote 'Mutual aid: a factor of evolution' in 1902. Mutual aid underscores the innate human inclination towards cooperation and solidarity. Kropotkin's thesis challenges the accepted doctrine of social Darwinian 'survival of the fittest' that was pervasive in evolutionary and indeed socio-economic paradigms of the time (and indeed still pervades today). Instead, he posited that individuals, rather than relying solely on hierarchical institutions, competitiveness, or market mechanisms, are more inclined to engage in voluntary acts of aid and solidarity to address shared *mutual* needs and collective challenges. Kropotkin's work is foundational within anarchist ideology in that it directly, and radically, critiques contemporary narratives of capitalist social relations that are based on class hierarchy, extraction, and oppression and the enrichment of the few. Mutual aid, as part of that anarchist praxis, instead focuses on how people can create radical new modes of sociality and solidarity that provide what is needed for the many (Spade, 2020). As Kropotkin was at pains to emphasise, mutual aid is a basic part of human practice that stretches back throughout human history. Its radicality today therefore stems from how 'buried' it has become within prevailing modern capitalist societies (Mould, 2021), particularly in the UK and the US. That is not to say, however, that mutual aid is not a thriving practice in other parts of the world. In many indigenous communities of the global majority world, mutual aid is simply a given; it is a fundamental driving force of how societies function (Gahman, 2017). To emphasise the radicality of mutual aid then is to focus in on the areas in which it has become such an anathema to how contemporary capitalist society functions, namely in the US and

the UK (which will be the focus of this chapter). In addition, while the broader mutual aid movement, and indeed the academic scholarship that surrounds it, is about more than just feeding people (and includes provision of shelter, emotional support, healthcare, etc.). However, during the recent COVID-19 pandemic, the provision of one of the most basic of human needs – food – gave mutual aid networks the important visibility that they had (Mould et al., 2022a).

Mutual food aid: before and during COVID-19

Mutual aid and food provision has an intricately tied history. In the US (where it has a more radical political edge than in other Western nations), the Black Panthers famously created the breakfast clubs for Black school children in the 1960s, and in feeding many hungry, poor young people, they were able to critique the lack of state provision and the structural racism that underpinned it (Heynen, 2009; Potorti, 2017). More recently, the activist group in the US Food Not Bombs (FNB) cooks vegan and vegetarian food in US cities' public squares and parks – often illegally and in the face of urban officials attempting to continually shut them down – in order to feed homeless and urban poor people (Parson, 2014). As such, with the Black Panthers and FNB (and many other besides) the groups' radical mutualism is deliberately tied to their anti-capitalist politics: indeed, as Heynen (2010: 1233) argued, having conducted an in-depth activist ethnography with the group, 'unlike much charity, FNB works hard not to be complicit in the perpetuation of the capitalist states' biopolitics, but seeks to radically transform it'.

The political potency of the mutual aid movement in the UK is not as pronounced, yet many of the mutual aid groups recognised the urgency of addressing food insecurity during the pandemic, because of how entrenched it was beforehand due to ongoing governmental policies of austerity (Firth, 2022). At first during the onset of the pandemic, often via social media groups, many neighbourhoods across the country swiftly organised food parcel initiatives to ensure vulnerable individuals and families had access to essential ingredients and/or ready-made meals. One notable case study is the Cook to Care programme in South London. Starting simply as a furloughed individual (who could cook), it quickly became an established food distribution programme, with a garden that grew the ingredients and a kitchen that cooked all the culturally appropriate food fresh, and a team of over 200 volunteers that were mostly prison-leavers and gang-affiliated youths. At its height, Cook to Care was delivering over 2,000 food parcels to vulnerable households each week (Badger et al., 2022). By leveraging local partnerships and community support, the group successfully provided immediate relief to those facing food insecurity. Nationally, research by the Food Foundation (2021) highlights the significance of food parcels during the pandemic, revealing that 15% of UK households experienced food insecurity during lockdown. Mutual aid groups therefore stepped in to bridge this gap, addressing the inadequacies of existing welfare systems and food poverty. These groups mobilised quickly and were able to adapt and respond to the needs of their communities before local councils or charities could act (Mould et al., 2022a).

Tackling food waste

Another feature of the community response (that included mutual aid groups, but also bled into more charity and institutional forms of support as the pandemic rolled on) recognised the opportunity to address both food insecurity *and* food waste simultaneously. Community fridge networks were already in place, notably by the charity Hubbub and the Coop supermarket, but during the pandemic they became more prevalent as a means of distributing food in a way that existing food provision systems under capitalism do not. They emerged as innovative solutions, offering a space where surplus food from local businesses, supermarkets, and individual donations could be shared with those in need (Mould et al., 2022b). An example would be The Real Junk Food Project in Brighton that started in 2014, but initiated a nationwide network of community fridges, often operating in collaboration with mutual aid groups, particularly during the pandemic. The project estimates that their network saved over 500 tons of food from being wasted during the pandemic (Midgley & Slatcher, 2021).

The community fridge initiative, while often brought about via charity models of food justice (rather than bottom-up mutual aid practice that is more prevalent in the US; see Morrow, 2019), not only reduced food waste but also empowered vulnerable individuals to access fresh and nutritious food. The slogan often accompanying community fridges being 'give what you can and take what you need'. But also, community fridges fostered social connections, with participants reporting a sense of belonging and community cohesion and often became a site of 'quiet' or 'soft' solidarity, causing people to consider the wasteful practices of supermarkets, as well as the reciprocity and consciousness raising that comes from simply sharing food outside of a marketised system (Kispert, 2022).

Future directions

Mutual aid activists provided supermarket deliveries, cooked food, delivered emotional support on the doorstep, and conducted other activities which not only meet immediate food needs but also created ongoing relationships that offered solidarity and alleviated social isolation. These relations cut to the heart of the radical politics of mutual aid in action, in that they evidence the class consciousness-raising that goes with the provision; in other words, this is the prefigurative politics of mutual aid (Mould et al., 2022b). It is more than simply providing food in a charitable way. Mutual aid brings together the provision of food and political awareness of why that food is needed in the first place.

Through their unwavering commitment, these grassroots organisations provided vital food parcels, established community fridge networks, and facilitated supermarket deliveries to the most vulnerable. Those on the left and right (well, mostly) of the political spectrum would find it difficult to argue for people going hungry and starving. Access to food is a universal, basic human right, but as the mutual aid provision during the pandemic showed, it was a way to raise political consciousness, particularly in the UK (to a level perhaps closer to that which has been seen in the US over the decades). Going forward as the cost of living continues to plunge many more people into food poverty, the political potential of mutual aid networks will only continue to affect more people, and begin to foster consciousness of the critique of the injustices of state power: in that sense, food plus mutual aid equals a highly political weapon.

References

Badger, A., Brown, P., Cole, J., Kispert, M., & Mould, O. (2022). Manifesto for mutual aid. Available at mutualaid.uk/manifesto.

Firth, R. (2022). *Disaster anarchy: Mutual aid and radical action*. Pluto Press, London.

Food Foundation (2021). A crisis within a crisis: The impact of Covid-19 on household food security. Available at https://foodfoundation.org.uk/publication/crisis-within-crisis-impact-covid-19-household-food-security.

Gahman, L. (2017). Building 'a world where many worlds fit': Indigenous autonomy, mutual aid, and an (anti-capitalist) moral economy of the (rebel) peasant. In Duncan, J. and Bailey, M. (eds.) *Sustainable food futures* (pp. 103–116). Routledge, London.

Heynen, N. (2009). Bending the bars of empire from every ghetto for survival: the Black Panther Party's radical antihunger politics of social reproduction and scale. *Annals of the Association of American Geographers*, 99(2): 406–422.

Heynen, N. (2010). Cooking up non-violent civil-disobedient direct action for the hungry: 'Food Not Bombs' and the resurgence of radical democracy in the US. *Urban Studies*, 47(6): 1225–1240.

Kispert, M. (2022). *From below*. Documentary film.

Kropotkin, P. (1902). *Mutual aid: A factor of evolution*. Heinemann, London.

Midgley, J., & Slatcher, S. (2021). Cafe society: Transforming community through quiet activism and reciprocity. In Steer, M., Davoudi, S., Shucksmith, M. and Todd, L. (eds.) *Hope under neoliberal austerity: Responses from civil society and civic universities* (pp. 73–88). Policy Press, Bristol.

Morrow, O. (2019). Community self-organizing and the urban food commons in Berlin and New York. *Sustainability*, 11(13): 3641.

Mould, O. (2021). *Seven ethics against capitalism*. Polity, London.

Mould, O., Cole, J., Badger, A., & Brown, P. (2022a). Solidarity, not charity: Learning the lessons of the COVID-19 pandemic to reconceptualise the radicality of mutual aid. *Transactions of the Institute of British Geographers*, 47(4): 866–879.

Mould, O., Cole, J., Badger, A., & Brown, P. (2022b). Mutual aid: Can community fridges bring anarchist politics to the mainstream? Available at: https://theconversation.com/mutual-aid-can-community-fridges-bring-anarchist-politics-to-the-mainstream-174491.

Parson, S. (2014). Breaking bread, sharing soup, and smashing the state: Food Not Bombs and anarchist critiques of the neoliberal charity state. *Theory in Action*, 7(4): 33.

Potorti, M. (2017). "Feeding the revolution": The Black Panther party, hunger, and community survival. *Journal of African American Studies*, 21(1): 85–110.

Spade, D. (2020). *Mutual aid: Building solidarity during this crisis (and the next)*. Verso Books, London.

Further reading

Conroy, W. (2019). The (im)mobilities of mutual aid: Occupy Sandy, racial liberalism, and the making of insurgent infrastructures. *ACME: An International Journal for Critical Geographies*, 18(4): 875–891.

Grubacic, A., & O'Hearn, D. (2016). *Living at the edges of capitalism: Adventures in exile and mutual aid*. University of California Press, Berkeley.

These texts go deeper into the idea of mutual aid beyond just food distribution to think about how it can help sustain communities in the longer-term. The aftermath of Hurricane Sandy has been written about as an important event in mutual aid's prefiguration in the US, and is worth exploring. Grubacic and O'Hearn's text goes into detail about three specific groups' food aid experiences highlighting their trials and tribulations.

86. Nutrition and food

Lauren T. Williams

Introduction

Let food be thy medicine and medicine be thy food. – Hippocrates

The secret of success in life is to eat what you like and let the food fight it out inside. – Mark Twain

Whether you agree with Hippocrates that food should be eaten for its health value, or with Mark Twain that food should be eaten for pleasure, it is important to consider the role of food and nutrition in society. The term 'nutrition' has been in use from the early 15th century to describe '[t]he action or process of supplying, or of receiving, nourishment or food', and 'that which nourishes; food, nourishment' (Oxford English Dictionary 2024). Eating food is one of the most commonly performed human behaviours and in an abundant food supply eating is enacted for motivations beyond the fulfilment of essential biological needs. Our food-related behaviours or food-ways – including how we choose, procure and prepare our food and where and with whom we consume it – occur within the complexity of the social environment. While hunger provides a biological drive to eat, our foodways are socially constructed. Social science concepts are therefore useful in examining contemporary food and nutrition issues and their possible solutions.

A social science approach to the study of food and nutrition

Despite the universality of eating, little was written about food by social scientists until the late 20th century. With the notable exception of earlier works including Georg Simmel's *Sociology of the Meal* (1910), Lévi-Strauss's *The Raw and the Cooked* (1964), and Mary Douglas's *Deciphering a Meal* (1972), it was not until the 1980s that there was a substantive increase in food studies, with landmark texts such as Pierre Bourdieu's *Distinction: A Social Critique of the Judgement of Taste* (1979/1984) and a series of books by Murcott (1983), Mennell et al. (1992), and Mennell (1996) (see Williams and Germov, 2015).

In 1999, my sociologist colleague John Germov and I added our own perspective to this burgeoning literature though publishing the text *A Sociology of Food and Nutrition* (Germov and Williams 1999). In it we argued for food and nutrition issues to be considered from the perspective of what we termed 'The Social Appetite'. This term is used to describe the social patterning of food production, distribution and consumption and answer the question of why we eat the way we do. The Social Appetite provides a lens for considering how social factors influence nutrition issues in societies.

Key to exploring these issues is recognising the tension between structure and agency. This sociological concept examines human behaviour (such as eating) as the outcome of an individual's freedom to act (agency) and the social structures (recurring patterns of social interaction linking people through social institutions and social groups) within which the behaviour occurs (Germov and Williams 2017). It should be noted that structure and agency are inextricably linked. They operate together to influence food choice within the structures of food regulations, the food system, economic resources, religion, education and cultural beliefs, to name a few. The extent to which structure and agency operate in current food and nutrition issues is considered next.

Current issues in food and nutrition

The commodification of food, nutrition and dietary advice by the food industry

Food and nutrition behaviours occur within the complexity of an abundant food supply in wealthy nations and dietary advice is designed to assist in navigating that complexity. Dietary advice is based on the science of nutritional epidemiology, which examines the extent to which foods and nutrients either cause or prevent disease (Tapsell 2019a). While food has been traded as a commodity for millennia, the commodification of nutrition, or more specifically, commodification of the scientific evidence base that underlies dietary advice, is more recent. This has been driven by the structural interests of food corporations in the pursuit of profit at the expense of health and other societal needs (Nestle 2013) and is a major factor limiting agency in food and nutrition.

The food industry co-opts nutrition expertise and evidence to enhance product sales. When the food industry has a product that they want to argue possesses a health promoting quality – whether naturally occurring or deliberately added in food processing – they seek to have that information clearly displayed on the food label in the form of a 'health claim' (Lawrence and Germov 2008). Health claims are statements regulated by government agencies that link nutrients in food products with health outcomes. The food industry has capitalised on its ability to use health claims by developing the category of 'functional foods'. These are food products altered or formulated by the deliberate addition of ingredients designed to provide a therapeutic effect (Lawrence and Germov 2008). One example is the fortification of breakfast cereals with the vitamin folate, designed to be eaten by women of childbearing age to prevent neural tube defects in newborns. Functional foods have the effect of medicalising the food supply, that is to imply that food can act like a drug in order to achieve a particular health outcome. Among the many public health concerns about functional foods is their potential to actually cause harm – for example, overconsumption of folate in older people may mask the signs of vitamin B12 deficiency (Lawrence and Germov 2008). The medicalisation of food not only adds to food costs but limits agency over what nutrients are being consumed.

Conversely, where food products are not eligible to claim a health benefit because there is evidence that the product is detrimental to health (as in the case of sugar-sweetened beverages), the food industry provides only mandated information on food labels. With some notable exceptions, countries do not require the food industry to apply warning labels to their products (Jones et al. 2019). Instead, it is left to governments and expert bodies to advise the public to 'eat less' of such products (Bragg and Nestle 2017). Due to the complexity of measuring nutrients in foods, food behaviours and health outcomes, nutritional epidemiology is far from an exact science (Tapsell 2019b). When industry wants to sell a product that runs counter to dietary advice, it seeks to undermine dietary guidance by questioning the epidemiological evidence on which the advice is based (Nestle 2013). This is disingenuous given it is the same evidence-base that is invoked in claiming positive health benefits for other products. As seen in the next section on sugar, the food industry has a history of exerting its power to directly influence the wording of dietary advice that might affect product sales. It invokes terms like 'nanny state' pejoratively to imply that the government is using dietary advice to limit people's agency (Bragg and Nestle, 2017). The food industry does this not to defend personal freedoms, but rather to optimise profits. The economic profitability of manufactured food provides the sector with power and political influence, making the food industry a dominant structural influence on our foodways.

When structure limits agency: how much sugar are you forced to eat?

Sugar is a food component whose pervasiveness in the food supply has a major impact on nutrition internationally. Sugars are chemicals whose names end in '-ose' (such as sucrose, fructose, glucose) and belong to the group of nutrients known as carbohydrates (Tapsell 2019b). Sugar provides no nutritive value beyond providing energy to the body in the form of kilojoules (calories). Sugar occurs naturally in some plant foods (such as sugarcane, sugar beets and fruit) but the majority of sugar in the industrial food system is added during food processing (Tapsell 2019b). It has been cultivated for millennia and its history is a story of how power is wielded and abused by structural interests, from slave traders and colonisers from the 1500s up to the modern-day food industry.

The success of sugar is multifactorial. Humans are born with a strong taste preference for sweet food (Williams and McMahon 2019). This was of biological advantage in a hunter-gatherer food supply naturally low in carbohydrates and energy. In that setting, sweet foods provided an important energy source. Unfortunately, the modern food supply is drenched with sugar, providing the population with too much energy. Humans have not lost the taste preference for sugar, but it is no longer of biological advantage. In fact, our preference for sweetness is a disadvantage given excess sugar causes dental caries and creates an 'obesogenic' environment – one that encourages population weight gain, obesity and associated health problems. As an agricultural commodity, sugar is cheap and easy to grow, process and store. Its price, chemical stability and other properties make it a desirable ingredient for the food processing industry to use in 'value-adding' to food products.

The sugar industry has long been part of the powerful food industry lobby, seeking to influence the nutritional image of its product and to control health messages and recommendations that might threaten the high level of sugar consumption (Bragg and Nestle 2017). Efforts by governments and non-government organisations to decrease the amount of sugar in the food supply are not aimed at decreasing agency by taking away treat foods or making food so bland as to be unenjoyable. In fact, it's difficult to argue that individuals possess much agency within a food supply that encourages over-consumption of foods that 'taste good' but aren't 'good for you'. In recognition of the health problems associated with sugar, a strong trend toward no-sugar or low-carbohydrate diets have emerged over the past decade. Within the context of a high-sugar food supply it requires significant time, effort and expense to exert the agency to eat a low-sugar diet.

Nutrition academic and advocate Marian Nestle has written extensively on the political power of the food industry, and how it has directly influenced nutrition and dietary advice at the highest level – most notably the World Health Organization (WHO) (Bragg and Nestle 2017). The WHO develops international dietary guidelines aimed at optimising health, but the process of guideline development has been subject to influence by political and economic stakeholders. By making threats to remove funding from the WHO, the US government successfully lobbied to weaken the wording of the sugar recommendation in the 2004 WHO document 'The Global Strategy' from a quantitative target for sugar intake of less than 10% of total energy to a qualitative goal to 'limit the intake of free sugars' (Bragg and Nestle 2017:78). By the next revision the scientific evidence was stronger and more difficult for industry to refute, and the wording for the quantitative goal of 10% was finally established.

Bragg and Nestle (2017) similarly describe the attempts by the industry lobby group, the Australian Food and Grocery Council, to influence the wording on the 2013 Australian Dietary Guideline for sugar. The body responsible for developing the guidelines, the National Health and Medical Research Council, was able to minimise the impact of industry by basing the guidelines on the synthesis of 55,000 scientific journal articles including evidence on the negative effects of sugar-sweetened beverages on health (Bragg and Nestle 2017). Thus, vigilance and considerable effort are required to limit the structural influence of the food lobby on the food supply. The next section considers ways in which these initiatives can be strengthened.

What are the alternatives? Social interventions for food and nutrition

There is a clear need to change the obesogenic environment rather than expect individuals to effectively manage their own nutrition in the context of the existing food supply. The food and nutrition system is regulated by national and international agencies, with some components enshrined in law. Governments are the agencies with most potential to limit the structural dominance of the food industry, and they have voluntary and mandatory tools at their disposal.

Dietary guidelines and food and nutrition policy

As we have seen, dietary guidelines aimed at reversing undesirable trends in food consumption are subject to interference by industry. Continuing to strengthen the evidence base, through research that has not been conducted, funded or influenced by the food industry, is the best chance for achieving meaningful guidelines. The WHO actively encourages individual countries to develop food-based dietary guidelines (WHO 1998), in recognition of the fact that people eat food rather than nutrients. This approach not only makes the guidelines easier to understand, but also makes it more difficult for industry to obfuscate the messages.

Governments and other agencies develop policies relevant to food and nutrition that could potentially be used to influence food consumption. The complexity of the food system (which spans production, processing and transport before consumption is even considered) means that governments tend to have multiple policies within different portfolios (including agriculture, transport and the environment), separate from nutrition which is usually part of a health portfolio. This artificially divides food from nutrition. In 1992, Australia was one of the first countries to combine food *and* nutrition into a single national policy (Commonwealth of Australia 1994). The policy spanned issues from food transport to remote areas to developing curricula for nutrition education. Unfortunately, that version was rescinded long ago and, despite strong advocacy from the public health sector, at the time of writing a new version is still not on the horizon. Policies that link food and nutrition have the potential to address issues such as food security and malnutrition in poorer countries, and the overnutrition that results from an over-abundant food supply in wealthier countries.

Mandating change through government regulation

Governments can make structural change to influence food and nutrition through mandatory strategies such as food law and food taxes. According to the 2023 WHO report, there are 108 countries throughout the world that levy a tax on sugar-sweetened beverages, although the majority did not introduce that tax for health reasons (WHO 2023). In 2014, Mexico was one of the first countries to implement a tax levied at the point of purchase aimed at reducing the consumption of sugar-sweetened beverages by making them more expensive to purchase (Colchero et al. 2015). Industry opposition to this move was fierce, but the tax effectively decreased consumption of these products, and the associated level of sugar and calories (Pedraza et al. 2019). In 2018, the United Kingdom introduced a Soft Drinks Industry Levy, which was a charge paid by industry on products that exceeded set sugar limits (Smith et al. 2018). This had the beneficial effect of encouraging manufacturers to reformulate products to reduce sugar content to avoid the tax (Scarborough et al. 2020). This removed an estimated 45 million kg of sugar from soft drinks annually (Rogers et al. 2020). There are several large, industrialised countries, notably the United States and Australia, which are yet to design and implement a sugar-sweetened beverage taxation strategy despite the evidence of its effectiveness in reducing sugar in the food supply.

The United Kingdom has also introduced reformulation initiatives to further reduce the amount of sugar that industry adds to food, with significant potential health impacts (Amies-Cull et al. 2019). Despite their progress, the Australian government has resisted the introduction of mandatory strategies that would significantly impact the food industry. Instead, government representatives formed a coalition with public health agencies and the food industry to establish voluntary sugar reformulation targets (Coyle et al. 2021). Unfortunately, but unsurprisingly, modelling has shown that the targets were set so low that even if they are fully implemented (and there are no penalties if they are not), they are likely to be ineffectual, given they would reduce sugar intake by less than 1 gram per capita per day or 1.5% of the total sugars provided by packaged foods and beverages (Coyle et al. 2021). Governments who let the food industry control the nutrient content of the food supply may gain a short-term economic advantage. However, they are also creating a looming health crisis by limiting the agency of people who want to pursue healthy eating.

Future directions: why do you eat the way you do?

This entry has mainly considered food and nutrition issues from the structural perspective. This is not because agency doesn't play a role in food choice, but because changes in the food supply have the greatest potential to significantly impact food and nutrition. However, the processed food industry poses a potential barrier to implementing wide-scale change as it uses its power to block government efforts. The argument used by industry is that it produces products that 'consumers' want to buy, implying that voluntary or mandated product changes will detract from people's agency. Yet the nutrition profile of the current food supply already limits the agency of those seeking good nutrition. There is also increasing public awareness of the impacts of food production and retail on environmental sustainability. Finding out what drives the complex decisions behind food choice requires qualitative social research that explores individual perspectives. This research needs to be unbiased, in that it is not funded, conducted or influenced by the food industry. Structural initiatives by governments and health agencies to change the food supply need to be based on research that aims to enhance people's agency in food and nutrition.

References

Amies-Cull B, Briggs ADM and Scarborough P (2019) Estimating the potential impact of the UK government's sugar reduction programme on child and adult health:

modelling study. *British Medical Journal* 365: 1417.

Bourdieu P (1984) [1979]. *Distinction: A Social Critique of the Judgement of Taste*. London, Routledge and Kegan Paul.

Bragg M and Nestle M (2017) The politics of government dietary advice: the influence of Big Food. In: Germov J and Williams L (eds) *A Sociology of Food and Nutrition: The Social Appetite*, 4th ed. Melbourne, Oxford University Press, 75–90.

Colchero MA, Salgado JC, Unar-Munguía M, Molina M, Ng S and Rivera-Dommarco JA (2015) Changes in prices after an excise tax to sweetened sugar beverages was implemented in Mexico: evidence from urban areas. *PLoS One* 10(12): e0144408.

Commonwealth of Australia (1994) *Food and Nutrition Policy*. Canberra, Australian Government Publishing Service.

Coyle DH, Shahid M, Dunford EK, Louie JCY, Trieu K, Marklund M, Neal B and Wu JHY (2021) Estimating the potential impact of the Australian government's reformulation targets on household sugar purchases. *International Journal of Behavioral Nutrition and Physical Activity* 18(1): 138.

Douglas M (1972) Deciphering a meal. *Daedalus: Journal of the American Academy of Arts and Sciences* (Winter) 61–82.

Germov J and Williams L (1999) *A Sociology of Food and Nutrition: The Social Appetite*. Melbourne, Oxford University Press.

Germov J and Williams L (2017) Exploring the social appetite. In: Germov J and Williams L (eds) *A Sociology of Food and Nutrition: The Social Appetite*, 4th ed. Melbourne, Oxford University Press, 3–18.

Jones A, Neal B, Reeve B, Mhurchu CN and Thow AM (2019) Front-of-pack nutrition labelling to promote healthier diets: current practice and opportunities to strengthen regulation worldwide. *BMJ Global Health* 4(6): e001882.

Lawrence M and Germov J (2008) Functional foods and public health nutrition policy. In: Germov J and Williams L (eds) *A Sociology of Food and Nutrition: The Social Appetite*, 3rd ed. Melbourne, Oxford University Press, 147–175.

Levi-Strauss C (1969) [1964] *The raw and the cooked*. New York, Harper and Row.

Mennell S (1996) *All Manners of Food: Eating and Taste in England and France from the Middle Ages to the Present*, 2nd ed. Chicago, University of Illinois Press.

Mennell S, Murcott A and van Otterloo AH (1992) *The Sociology of Food: Eating, Diet and Culture*. London, Sage.

Murcott Anne ed. (1983) *The Sociology of Food and Eating*. Aldershot, Gower.

Nestle Marian (2013) *Food Politics: How the Food Industry Influences Nutrition and Health*. Berkeley, University of California Press.

Oxford English Dictionary. *Nutrition*. https://www.oed.com/dictionary/nutrition_n?tl=true. (Accessed 14 March 2024).

Pedraza LS, Popkin BM, Batis C, Adair L, Robinson WR, Guilkey DK and Taillie LS (2019) The caloric and sugar content of beverages purchased at different store-types changed after the sugary drinks taxation in Mexico. *International Journal of Behavioral Nutrition and Physical Activity* 16(1): 103.

Rogers NT, Pell D, Penney TL, Mytton O, Briggs A, Cummins S, Rayner M, Rutter H, Scarborough P, Sharp SJ, Smith RD, White M and Adams J (2020) Anticipatory changes in British household purchases of soft drinks associated with the announcement of the Soft Drinks Industry Levy: A controlled interrupted time series analysis. *PLoS Medicine* 17(11): e1003269.

Scarborough P, Adhikari V, Harrington RA, Elhussein A, Briggs A, Rayner M, Adams J, Cummins S, Penney T and White M (2020) Impact of the announcement and implementation of the UK Soft Drinks Industry Levy on sugar content, price, product size and number of available soft drinks in the UK, 2015–19: A controlled interrupted time series analysis. *PLoS Medicine* 17(2): e1003025.

Simmel G 1997 [1910] Sociology of the Meal. In: Frisby D and Featherstone M (eds.) *Simmel on Culture: Selected Writings*. London, Sage, 130–136.

Smith E, Scarborough P, Rayner M and Briggs ADM (2018) Should we tax unhealthy food and drink? *Proceedings of the Nutrition Society* 77(3): 314–320.

Tapsell L (2019a) Food and health: Working with nutrition. In: Tapsell L (ed.) *Food, Nutrition and Health*, 2nd ed. Melbourne, Oxford University Press, 2–27.

Tapsell L (2019b) Carbohydrates and phytochemicals: Major components of plant foods. In: Tapsell L (ed.) *Food,*

Nutrition and Health, 2nd ed. Melbourne, Oxford University Press, 87–118.

Williams LT and Germov J (2015) Food. In: Cook DT and Ryan JM (eds.) *The Wiley-Blackwell Encyclopedia of Consumption and Consumer Studies*. Wiley-Blackwell. https://doi.org/10.1002/9781118989463.wbeccs122.

Williams L and McMahon A (2019) Social and behavioural aspects of food consumption. In: Tapsell L (ed.) *Food, Nutrition and Health*, 2nd ed. Melbourne, Oxford University Press, 494–519.

World Health Organization (1998) *Preparation and Use of Food-based Dietary Guidelines: Report of a Joint FAO/WHO Consultation*. WHO technical report series 880. Geneva, WHO.

World Health Organization (2023) *Global Report on the Use of Sugar-sweetened Beverage Taxes*. Geneva, WHO.

Further reading

Germov J and Williams L (2017) *A Sociology of Food and Nutrition: The Social Appetite*, 4th ed. Melbourne, Oxford University Press.

This interdisciplinary reader and academic text considers public health nutrition issues of international significance from a sociological perspective.

Nestle M (2013) *Food Politics: How the Food Industry Influences Nutrition and Health*. Berkeley, University of California Press.

This is a revised and updated edition of the groundbreaking book that examined the evidence that Big Food (the food industry) promotes over-consumption of their products through marketing, philanthropy, lobbying and partnerships, at the expense of the health of the population.

Nestle M (2015) *Soda Politics: Taking on Big Soda (and Winning)*. New York, Oxford University Press.

In this book, Marion Nestle focuses on the ways in which the 'soda' (soft drink) industry forms a powerful lobby group to resist attempts to regulate their products, despite the evidence that they cause extensive harms to health in adults, and even more concerningly, to their main target audience of children.

LAUREN T. WILLIAMS

87. Nutritionism

ISABEL FLETCHER

Introducing nutritionism

The concept of nutritionism in its modern form was initially developed by Gyorgy Scrinis. Where 'nutrition' is generally considered to be the process by which living organisms obtain the food necessary for healthy growth and development, the concept of *nutritionism* is much more specific and critical in its focus. In Scrinis' words, nutritionism is an approach whereby:

> [p]articular nutrients, food components, or bio-markers—such as saturated fats, kilojoules, the glycemic index (GI), and the body mass index (BMI)—are abstracted out of the context of foods, diets, and bodily processes. Removed from their broader cultural and ecological ambits, they come to represent the definitive truth about the relationship between food and bodily health. (Scrinis, 2008: 40)

He describes nutritionism as both an 'ideology' and a 'reductive' approach that has come to dominate contemporary understandings of the complex relationship between food and health. Scrinis developed his critical model of nutrition research (see below) deploying a Foucauldian-inspired terminology to analyse the operation of nutritionist discourses over the last century, including the 'nutritionist gaze' and the 'nutricentric person' (Scrinis, 2013: 259–60).

Nutritionism provides a critical lens on the processes through which advice on eating well by authoritative actors – such as research institutions and governments – is created, and how these processes shape public understandings of food–diet–body relationships. It builds on and develops previous social science research describing the prominent role scientific and medical research plays in determining what 'good' eating looks like, and how such ideas have come to dominate everyday discussions about food choice – even if people do not always act on them. These dietary guidelines also have very real material effects on contemporary foodscapes; they shape the food offered in state institutions (e.g. schools, hospitals), and the level of food assistance provided by states to their citizens.

This entry traces the idea of nutritionism from Scrinis' original conceptualisation,

through to its popularisation and subsequent critiques, before concluding with suggested directions for future work.

A critique of food in the modern era

Scrinis divides the history of nutrition into three paradigms and historical eras: *quantifying nutritionism* (mid-19th to mid-20th century); *good-and-bad nutritionism* (1960s to mid-1990s); and *functional nutritionism* (mid-1990s to the present) (Scrinis, 2013: 261). He argues that these paradigms "essentially define the nutritional zeitgeist of each era" (Scrinis, 2013: 47).

In the quantifying era, the focus of nutrition researchers and governments was on using this knowledge to prevent nutritional deficiencies. In the good-and-bad era, nutrition researchers began to focus on the relationship between diet and chronic disease, and to categorise nutrients – particularly fats and sugar – as good or bad. Finally, the era of functional nutritionism is characterised by an increased focus on measuring the effects of specific nutrients and the development of 'functional foods' that aim to deliver targeted health benefits to consumers.

The first two of these eras align well with existing historical accounts (e.g. Rothstein, 2003), which describe a major shift in medical and nutrition science research in the US and the UK beginning in the 1950s. Concerns with undernutrition and deficiency diseases, such as rickets and scurvy, that had dominated the first hundred years of research into diet and health were abruptly replaced by a focus on *over*nutrition – specifically in the Minority world. However, Scrinis' third era is less fully established, and it is not clear whether the phenomena he describes constitute a new 'paradigm' within nutrition research or merely the development of existing approaches within research and marketing, a point returned to later in the entry.

Scrinis' concept and the wider critique of modern food production, marketing and retailing were popularised by the food writer Michael Pollan (2009) in his best-selling book *In Defense of Food*. Pollan provides a slightly different account to Scrinis, concluding that nutritionism – the reduction of dietary advice to recommendations about avoiding single nutrients – is ultimately misleading since it does not address the key problem with a 'Western Diet' largely composed of processed foods. Scrinis and Pollan's critiques of the contemporary food industry and its products continue a long and vibrant tradition of alternative food politics in places like Australia, the UK and the US. They represent a fundamental pillar of critical and vociferous debates that have been ongoing in both academic and public fora since at least the 1970s about the influence of the food industry on how (or if) we eat well (Belasco, 1989).

Interactions between nutrition research and policy: tensions and limitations

Scrinis' work on nutritionism is part of a larger body of critical social science analyses of biomedical accounts of the relationship between diet, nutrition and health, sometimes labelled critical nutrition studies (Biltekoff, 2012). This scholarship highlights the selective ways that scientific research has been taken up by governments and industry, demonstrating the influence of changing beliefs and norms in the development of both dietary advice and guidelines (Biltekoff, 2013; Mudry, 2010), and models of the relationships between health and weight (Gard and Wright, 2005). These authors argue that unacknowledged aesthetic, economic, gendered and racial judgements are embedded in these accounts of what people should and should not eat, and/or in what amounts particular foods should be eaten, e.g., when white middle-class ideals of appearance and appropriate eating (such as the 'clean eating' trend [Wilkes, 2024]) are used to judge those of other classes and ethnicities who cannot easily achieve them. They also articulate alternative, and less exclusionary, narratives that acknowledge the role of structural injustice in shaping individual diet, body size and health status. For example, Gard and Wright (2005: 183) argue that conventional accounts of body weight often do not acknowledge that "people's lives are not always organized in situations where they are free to 'choose' active leisure or 'healthy' planned eating".

As part of this scholarship, the nutritionism approach has provided a new critical tool for analysing some of the ways that nutrition research is shaped and put to use by governments and the food industry. Existing studies (e.g. Watts, 2011) confirm that the processes underlying the uptake of nutrition research specifically by governments are often highly politicised and contested, with many actors lobbying governments, advisory bodies and individual researchers to ensure that advice is crafted with their interests in mind; a process that does not always result in the most equitable public health outcomes.

However, a limitation of the nutritionism critique has been a tendency to conflate the *conduct* of nutrition research (i.e. the methods used) with the wider *uptake* of that research by governments or the food industry (i.e. how the research is used by other actors). Methodological criticisms of nutrition research are not new (Ioannidis, 2018) and elements of them are acknowledged by nutrition researchers (e.g. Nestle, 2002) who argue that it is not possible to control for confounding factors in the way that can be done in other forms of medical research. Wide variation in the composition of diets, and the biochemical complexity of foods and their interactions, combined with the long timescales needed to understand the causes of chronic diseases, also mean that if nutrition research is not to be largely observational, complexity must somehow be managed. Reductionism as a part of a scientific method is one important way of creating manageable problems for researchers to investigate. Yet it is important to note that nutrition research typically involves re-introducing complexity back into the picture. As such, reductionism as a tool in nutrition research is not an end point in itself. Nevertheless, too often it is the reduced nutrient-focussed understanding of diets that ends up leading government advice and food industry advertising.

Looking forward: food as one of the commercial determinants of health

Contemporary research related to Scrinis' nutritionism critique has broadened its focus to examine the health impacts of the food industry approaches developed in public health policy (see Gilmore et al., 2023). Such analyses of the commercial determinants of health see the activities of businesses, especially large powerful corporations, as an important influence on the health of populations. The use of the term 'determinants' demonstrates how these activities are now given a similar weight to factors such as class, ethnicity and gender, whose effects on health have historically been studied in the field of public health.

Isabel Fletcher

Research on the commercial determinants of health compares the lobbying activities of multinational food corporations to those of the tobacco and alcohol industries, and argues for corporate exclusion from public health policymaking. Scrinis' development of the nutritionism concept in more recent work contributes to these arguments. This work describes how large corporations reformulate existing, often ultra-processed, products to improve their nutritional profiles (e.g. creating 'low fat' or 'high protein' products), which fragments the market for specific products rather than improving the nutritional content of their overall ranges (Clapp and Scrinis, 2017). Food manufacturers have been using nutrition research findings in the development and marketing of new products since the beginning of modern nutrition in the late nineteenth century (e.g., Horrocks, 1995) but the increasing importance of their products in modern diets adds urgency to these analyses.

Recent work also reveals how these large food companies use their resulting market dominance to influence government policies (Scrinis, 2020), and that the food industry has a long history of funding nutrition research which invariably serves their commercial interests. As such, critics like Marion Nestle (2018) argue that the findings of industry-funded studies should be considered as a form of marketing rather than robust science, and that nutrition researchers should instead use different sources of funding to go beyond unhelpful 'single nutrient' studies.

These new approaches highlight the wider influences shaping why and what we eat, and this is an important way in which research and policy can go beyond narrow nutritionist accounts of food, diet and health.

References

Belasco, W.J. (1989) *Appetite for Change: How the Counterculture Took on the Food Industry*. New York: Pantheon Books.

Biltekoff, C. (2012) 'Critical Nutrition Studies', in Pilcher, J.M. (ed.), *The Oxford Handbook of Food History*, Oxford Handbooks (online ed., Oxford Academic, 21 Nov. 2012). https://doi.org/10.1093/oxfordhb/9780199729937.013.0010.

Biltekoff, C. (2013) *Eating Right in America: Food, Health and Citizenship from Domestic Science to Obesity*. Durham: Duke University Press.

Clapp, J. & Scrinis, G. (2017) Big Food, Nutritionism, and Corporate Power. *Globalizations*, 14(4), 578–595. https://doi.org/10.1080/14747731.2016.1239806.

Gard, M. & Wright, J. (2005) *The Obesity Epidemic: Science, Morality and Ideology*. Abingdon, Oxon and New York: Routledge.

Gilmore, A.B., Fabbri, A., Baum, F., Bertscher, A., Bondy, K., Chang, H-J., Demaio, S., Erzse, A., Freudenberg, N., Friel, S., Hofman, K.J., Johns, P., Karim, S.A., Lacy-Nichols, J., de Carvalho, C.M.P., Marten, R., McKee, M., Petticrew, M., Robertson, L. ... & Thow, A.M. (2023) Defining and Conceptualising the Commercial Determinants of Health. *Lancet*, 401(10383): 1194–1213. https://doi.org/10.1016/S0140-6736(23)00013-2

Horrocks, S.M. (1995) 'The Business of Vitamins: Nutrition Science and the Food Industry in Inter-war Britain', in Kamminga, H. and Cunningham, A. (eds.), *The Science and Culture of Nutrition 1840–1940* (pp. 53–75). Amsterdam: Rodopi.

Ioannidis, J.P. (2018) The Challenge of Reforming Nutritional Epidemiologic Research. *JAMA*, 320(10), 969–970. https://doi.org/10.1001/jama.2018.11025.

Mudry, J. (2010) *Measured Meals: Nutrition in America*. Albany: State University of New York Press.

Nestle, M. (2002) *Food Politics: How the Food Industry Influences Nutrition and Health*. Berkeley: University of California Press.

Nestle, M. (2018) *Unsavory Truth: How Food Companies Skew the Science of What We Eat*. New York: Basic Books.

Pollan, M. (2009) *In Defense of Food: An Eater's Manifesto*. New York: Penguin Press.

Rothstein, W.G. (2003) *Public Health and the Risk Factor: A History of an Uneven Medical Revolution*. Rochester, NY: University of Rochester Press.

Scrinis, G. (2008) On the ideology of nutritionism. *Gastronomica: The Journal of Food Studies*, 8(1), 39–48. https://doi.org/10.1525/gfc.2008.8.1.39.

Scrinis, G. (2013) *Nutritionism: The Science and Politics of Dietary Advice*. New York and Chichester: Columbia University Press.

Scrinis, G. (2020) Ultra-processed foods and the corporate capture of nutrition: An essay by Gyorgy Scrinis. *BMJ* 371(m4601). https://doi.org/10.1136/bmj.m4601.

Watts M.L., Hager M.H., Toner C.D., & Weber J.A. (2011) The Art of Translating Nutritional Science into Dietary Guidance: History nd Evolution of the Dietary Guidelines for Americans. *Nutrition Reviews*, 69(7), 404–12. https://doi.org /10.1111/j.1753-4887.2011.00408.x.

Wilkes, K. (2024) Eating, Looking, and Living Clean: Techniques of White Femininity in Contemporary Neoliberal Food Culture. *Gender, Work & Organization*, 31(3), 916–936. https://doi.org/10.1111/gwao.12620.

Further reading

Nestle, M. (2018) *Unsavory Truth: How Food Companies Skew the Science of What We Eat*. New York: Basic Books.

One of the most respected US commentators on food and nutrition policy. This book explains why commercial funding of nutrition research is so damaging and what should be done about it.

Mayes, C.R. & Thompson, D.B. (2015) What Should We Eat? Biopolitics, Ethics, and Nutritional Scientism. *Bioethical Inquiry,* 12, 587–599. https://doi.org/10.1007/s11673 -015-9670-4.

Two bioethicists provide philosophical context for debates about the role nutrition research should play in our decision-making, highlighting the ethical implications of what they label 'nutritional scienticism'.

ISABEL FLETCHER

88. Nutrition transition

Lucy Aphramor

Introduction

Nutrition transition outlines a historical perspective on broad changes in patterns of human diet and disease that are observed at a large group or population level across time and space. Barry Popkin proposed the term in 1993, suggesting five stages to the transition. These were (1) food gathering, (2) famine, (3) receding famine, (4) degenerative diseases (renamed nutrition-related non-communicable diseases (NR-NCDs) (see Brady 2019), and (5) behavioural change toward a 'healthy, balanced diet'.

Although differences in stage and pace of change in diet and disease between high-income countries (HICs) and low- and middle-income countries (LMICs) are documented, the general trend epidemiologically is that a pattern of high fertility and high mortality is replaced by one of low fertility and low mortality.

Nutrition transition is explained by economic and other forces entangled with globalisation, seen in shifts in the agricultural system, an expansion of industrial food systems, a reduction in physical activity, and urbanisation. As a result, people shift from eating traditional diets high in starchy staples and local crops, fruits, legumes, and other vegetables, to a diet of (often) reduced diversity consisting of more refined carbohydrate foods and extrinsic sugar, vegetable oils, animal-source foods, and other foods associated with industrial food systems.

Nutrition transition theory uses a biomedical model that tracks the increased prevalence of NR-NCDs through a pathway of causation where changes in nutrient profile and reduced physical activity lead to population weight increase and higher rates of NR-NCDs/PRDs. (Power-related diseases)

For example, the World Health Organization reports that the number of people with diabetes rose from 108 million in 1980 to 422 million in 2014 and project the figure to rise to 592 million in 2035. While NR-NCDs are a global concern, LMICs are experiencing a disproportionate increase in rates due to a reduction in mortality from infectious disease and the nutrition transition. This means that diabetes and other NR-NCDs/PRDs that were once understood as diseases of affluence are now of significant concern in LMICs, where they often co-exist with deficiency diseases and hunger.

A key focus in nutrition transition studies involves understanding how to intervene to prevent and remedy undernutrition (lack of specific nutrients and/or overall energy deficit) and how to prevent people eating 'excess calories', called 'over-nutrition' (pathologised as overweight and obesity). The term 'malconsumption' is also used to capture the fact that fat people can be poorly nourished. At a population level researchers describe the double or twin burden, naming a situation where undernutrition and 'over-nutrition' co-exist.

Nutrition transition also describes trends in macronutrient intake, noting a consistent rise in calories from protein, for example, that is unevenly distributed across HICs and LMICs, and a rise in calories from refined and 'low quality' carbohydrate.

Getting critical: shifting understandings of nutrition transition

The terminology of nutrition transition is used by a wide range of food scholars to measure and understand trends and to think with and strategise from, and so it shapes research and policy directions, and hence domestic and personal food intake. It is also of interest for what it reveals about the interpretive frameworks that dominate the field and for highlighting generative avenues for inter-disciplinary engagement.

Researchers in the field critique the calorie-burning model as oversimplified, referencing work on epigenetics that demonstrates the influence of parental and early childhood nutrition in adult health which complicates the model's instrumental logic. This is an important point. However, the field's foundational premise – namely, that changes in energy intake overwhelmingly account for changes in NR-NCDs/PRDs mediated by a rise in population body mass index (BMI) – remains uncontested.

A more critical analysis of this premise, constructed at the nexus of fat liberation, fat studies, and critical food studies (Brady et al., 2023), reveals epistemological, ontological, and axiological norms that embed healthism, ableism, nutritionism, and racism. For example, a key point made by Black fat scholar Da'Shaun Harrison is that anti-fatness, intrinsic to nutrition transition's BMI-based agenda, exists as an ideology coherent with anti-Blackness (Harrison, 2021).

Work that critically engages the social sciences and biomedicine helps extend this critique by fracturing the linear path from high BMI/poor diet to NR-NCDs/PRDs. This includes work that incorporates social and economic inequity, and racism, into the lifestyle theorisation of increased incidence of diabetes (Hatch, 2016; Doucet-Battle, 2021).

Building accountable knowledge: nutrition transition for health equity and food sovereignty

Through an uncritical embrace of hegemonic understandings of nutrition, nutrition transition's narrative can be linked to fatmisic and racist positions. The conventional lifestyle framing it reproduces (mis)represents the role of nutrients in health inequity by erasing non-nutrient pathways involved in metabolic dysregulation. For instance, narrowing inquiry to nutrients fails to account for the ways that oppression and poverty, among other interlinked structural and ecological factors, metabolically predispose people to diseases such as diabetes and heart disease beyond any impact of diet and activity patterns. Specific examples relying on biomedical empiricism include research on racism and hypertension (Krieger and Sidney, 1996), and fat oppression as a health hazard (Muennig, 2008).

Within this, the individualistic framing of 'health' acts as a lock-in to coloniality, side-lining subaltern framings approximately translated to 'health' that refer to a synergy of earth-care, spirituality, human and nonhuman relationship and reciprocity, ancestral connection, and more. Thus, despite attention to myriad non-nutrient forces that shape human and planetary vitality, nutrition transition's epistemic allegiance to energy balance and the logics of coloniality obstructs a transition to food sovereignty and perpetuates scientific imperialism.

Exchange between fat studies and critical scholars in geography, dietetics and food studies holds enormous potential for an expanded reframe of nutrition transition. Work from within the food sovereignty movement and feminist political ecology that draws attention to the role of gender and power in shaping who gets heard, who eats, and what we eat, is also highly relevant. This remapping of nutrition transition's terrain of enquiry could radically alter what questions get asked, what strategies are written, what Othered voices are subsequently heard, and what new worlds are imagined (Harrison, 2021).

References

Brady J (2019) Naming nutrition justice: how might dietitians articulate a socially just dietetic practice? *Journal of Critical Dietetics* 4, 6–17. http://doi:10.32920/cd.v4i2.1321.

Brady J, Potvin L, Bombak A, Kirkham A, Fraser K-L and Gingras J (2023) Fat food justice: where fat studies meets food studies. *Fat Studies* 12, 1–8. http://doi:10.1080/21604851.2021.1968667.

Doucet-Battle J (2021) *Sweetness in the Blood: Race, Risk, and Type 2 Diabetes.* Minneapolis, University of Minnesota Press.

Harrison D (2021) *Belly of the Beast: The Politics of Anti-Fatness as Anti-Blackness.* Berkeley, CA, North Atlantic Books.

Hatch AR (2016) *Blood Sugar: Racial Pharmacology and Food Justice in Black America.* Minneapolis University of Minnesota Press.

Krieger N and Sidney S (1996) Racial discrimination and blood pressure: the CARDIA Study of young black and white adults. *American Journal of Public Health* 86, 1370–1378. http://doi:10.2105/ajph.86.10.1370.

Muennig P (2008) The body politic: the relationship between stigma and obesity-associated disease. *BMC Public Health* 21, 128. http://doi:10.1186/1471-2458-8-128.

Further reading

Popkin BM (1998) The nutrition transition and its health implications in lower-income countries. *Public Health Nutrition* 1, 5–21. http://doi:10.1079/phn19980004.

Popkin's work outlines the theory of nutrition transition, with particular reference in this paper to LMICs.

Strings S (2019) *Fearing the Black Body: The Racial Origins of Fat Phobia.* New York, New York University Press.

Sabrina Strings' work shows how BMI is rooted in eugenics such that anti-fatness campaigns (i.e. geared to tackling overweight or obesity) are inherently also anti-Black.

LUCY APHRAMOR

89. Obesity

Rachel Colls

Introduction: defining 'obesity'

'Obesity' and 'obese' are terms used to describe both the size of a body and a 'disease' state. Over the past twenty years, terms such as 'the obesity epidemic' or the 'obesity crisis' have been used to describe the increase, globally, of people's body size (and under- and mal-nutrition) and to make claims for a range of associated risks to people's health including cardiovascular disease, diabetes, musculoskeletal disorders and some cancers. Food (and drink) are central to explanations of 'obesity' causation through an imbalance between calorie consumption and the amount of energy expended through physical activity. Moreover, connections are made between people's increased body size due to their (over)consumption of particular types of food and drink (high fat, high sugar, high salt and energy dense) and their access or 'exposure' to them within different 'food environments'. These arguments are often contextualised within broader societal inequalities as well as exploring how 'obesity' prevalence aligns across axes of difference according to gender, ability, age, class, race and ethnicity. The term 'globesity' is used as a means to highlight the effect of a 'Western' diet on different countries whereby inherently healthy eating practices have been corrupted through the expansion of development and/or the resultant poverty.

However, whilst there might be an apparent consensus across the medical literature about the health risks of being 'obese' and thus an imperative to treat and manage 'obesity' at global, population, local and individual levels, critical obesity studies and at tudies (see Gard and Wright 2005) call into question the efficacy of science which designates 'obesity' as a cause of ill health. This work also challenges weight stigma and fat discrimination and adopts a 'Health at Every Size' (HAES) approach to health, which includes the practice of intuitive eating. It also highlights the often harmful and moralising assumptions made about 'obese' people, and thus their relationships with food, and thus the need to explore the detrimental effects of 'anti-obesity' discourses and interventions. Integral to this approach is centring the voices and experiences of 'obese' or fat people, some of whom question the very use of the terms 'obesity' and 'obese', instead preferring terms such as 'fat' or 'larger bodied'.

Categorising 'obesity'

'Obesity' is defined and deployed differently depending on the academic, policy and popular context. The most widely used measure of body size, and thus categorisation of bodies as 'obese', is the body mass index (BMI). The BMI is calculated by dividing body weight (kg) by height (m), and categorises people as 'underweight' (below 18.5), 'normal' (18.5–24.9), 'overweight' (25–29.9), 'obese' (30–39.9) and 'severely obese' (40 or above). Its use is justified because of the ease with which it can be calculated and its capacity to be used comparatively across different contexts.

The BMI is used frequently across research, health care and government contexts to map obesity rates across different scales (e.g. country, region, city, neighbourhood, school), which can help to identify 'the problem' and thus develop targeted policies and initiatives. It is also used to correlate the relationships between 'obesity' and specific illnesses and health conditions, and as a screening tool to identify people who are 'obese' or at risk of becoming obese, which can lead to interventions to maintain or attain a 'healthy' weight, some of which are concerned with food consumption.

Critiques of the BMI are rooted in its use as a 'proxy' for ill health and its inability to measure adipose tissue on a body nor distinguish it from muscle mass. Moreover, it does not take account of people's differences in body composition, for example according to age, race and ethnicity (although there are adjusted BMI cutoffs for Asian people, who have a higher risk of metabolic diseases at a lower BMI). Indeed, far from being a neutral descriptor of body size, the BMI has the potential to harm individuals through labelling them as 'obese' and making assumptions about their behaviours and capacities alongside specific populations and places. In short, the BMI makes 'obesity' political.

The politics of 'obesity'

This section explores two key issues related to the political significance of 'obesity' and its specific relationship to food (and drink): causation and responsibility.

Causation

Access to food and food consumption are often implicated as causes of 'obesity' despite a broader recognition that causes of 'obesity' are multi-factorial. A commonly used model to help explain this relationship is the 'obesogenic environment', first described by Swinburn et al. (1999: 564), as "the sum of influences that the surroundings, opportunities or conditions of life have on promoting 'obesity' in individuals and populations". This ecological approach to 'obesity' reinforces an energy balance model by explaining high weight and weight gain as an imbalance between food consumption (energy intake) and physical activity (energy expenditure). Thus, food environments (sites of energy intake) and/or physical activity environments (sites for energy expenditure) are used to both identify and classify particular locations as being 'obesogenic', according to a range of explanatory components and qualities. Specific attention has been paid to how race and ethnicity, poverty and low household income correlate with the quality of the food environments and thus the propensity of a person living there to be obese.

Measurable characteristics of food environments include numbers of and proximity to fast food or takeaway restaurants, supermarkets and convenience stores or corner shops; the availability of certain 'healthy' or 'unhealthy foods', including fruit and vegetables; self-reported nutritional intake; and the accessibility of and transportation to supermarkets. A similar categorisation of 'consumer' food environments is used to consider what consumers encounter within individual food retail outlets (e.g., stores or restaurants), as well as other organisational environments where food is available, such as workplaces, hospitals, homes, schools and universities. The term 'food swamp' is used to identify areas with a concentration of high calorie 'unhealthy' food options, often as a result of depleted retail food provision. The 2020 Covid-19 pandemic also drew attention to online and home food delivery fast-food provisioning.

Such an understanding of 'obesity' causation has been subject to critique (see Colls and Evans, 2014). The categorisation of food environments identify and imply mostly 'Western' and urban features and tend to 'map' 'obesity' prevalence to focus on correlation rather than cause and effect. Consequently, relationships between people and food environments and their practices of food consumption, are overlooked. There is also a tendency to categorise food as 'healthy' and 'unhealthy' and not attend to *how* bodies and food interact, and often without a sensitivity to ethnic and religious food preferences. Finally, by designating locations as 'obesogenic' or 'swamps', entire places and thus the populations who live there become stigmatised as 'obese' and 'unhealthy'.

Responsibility

Integral to understanding causation is the imperative to determine (a) who or what is responsible for 'obesity', and consequently (b) to design and implement interventions designed to slow or reverse 'obesity' rates. Responsibility in relation to food access and consumption is attributed to a range of actors and across scales. These include national and local governments, charities and NGOs, food and drink manufacturers and retailers, workplaces, schools, households, families and parents. Moreover, 'obesity' represents a financial cost to governments associated with the assumed 'risks' to health and the treatments and interventions which may be required. Thus, an 'obese' person, in order to be a deserving and productive citizen, needs to be managed and controlled, as well as encouraged and supported to become responsible for their own and, in some cases, others' (e.g. their children's) body weight.

National and local government interventions include taxation and restrictions placed on the promotion of high calorie food and drink, alongside curbs on advertising. For example, in 2013, Mexico passed an 8% tax on a wide range of non-essential foods as part of its efforts to tackle soaring levels of 'obesity'. Similarly, in 2018, England and Wales introduced a soft drinks levy to reduce the consumption of sugar. Local planning is also used to manage the availability and location of fast-food outlets. In England so-called 'exclusion zones' of 400m are maintained when reviewing planning applications for new fast-food outlets and their proximity to schools and areas of high deprivation or with high 'obesity' levels. Moreover, schools monitor the nutritional value of school meals, young people's lunchboxes and the content of vending machines whilst families are targeted to improve the provision of food and drink to their children through public health campaigns or, in England and Wales, through medical referrals made after children are weighed and measured in school.

Future concerns

A focus on the causes of and responsibilities for 'obesity' provides a context for critically engaging with the effects of positioning 'obesity' as a 'problem' and the assumptions made about 'obese' people's relationships to food and drink. Indeed, critical obesity studies and fat studies approaches draw out a number of concerns which need further interrogation.

Firstly, critical scholars consider the associated moralities attached to fat people and their relationships with food, as gluttonous, out of control and addicted to 'unhealthy' food. This begins with acknowledging the colonial legacy of demonising fatness and the relative moral superiority of thinness and whiteness as a form of anti-blackness (see Strings, 2019). It also centres how specific populations, notably women, parents, people on low incomes and black and ethnic minorities, and particular food types and choices (highly calorific, fast food and processed) are targeted and thus deemed '(ir)responsible'. Here, weight stigma, also named as fat discrimination, has social, economic and psychosocial consequences for fat people, as well as exacerbating poor health and contributing to weight gain and disordered eating (see Puhl and Suh, 2015). For example, in April 2022, the UK introduced new legislation for large food retailers to provide the calorie content of food and drinks on menus and apps alongside daily recommended calorie intakes. This anti-obesity measure was critiqued for encouraging dieting, as well as exacerbating and initiating symptoms of disordered eating through drawing attention to the relative 'values' of different food and drink. Indeed, the healthism of such interventions, which align eating 'healthy' foods with 'fixing' 'obesity, only intensifies the stigmatisation of fat bodies and the assumption that fat bodies can and should lose weight.

Secondly, and relatedly, it is important to consider the ways that eating and drinking are managed inside of the body through the increase in surgical and pharmaceutical interventions. Bariatric surgery involves the permanent or temporary reduction of a person's stomach, which reduces the amount of food a person can consume. Medication, such as the type 2 diabetes drug semalglutide (Ozempic), reduces appetite and the speed at which food is digested. Side effects and subsequent surgeries and complications are common and these interventions do not always result in permanent weight loss. Alternative approaches to eating and drinking are offered by proponents of HAES and intuitive eating, which disconnects health from body size or weight loss. Such approaches involve acknowledging a person's hunger cues and feelings of fullness; avoiding food restriction; not demonising foods as 'good' or 'bad'; and being kinder to our bodies.

Finally, following Brady et al. (2023), 'health sovereignty', an approach which centres fat people's right to health and thus nutritious and affordable food, is a useful framework to develop more compassionate and social justice-orientated approaches to understanding the relationships between fatness, food and society. It provides the conceptual space in which to decouple weight from health and acknowledges the potential harm of anti-obesity discourses and interventions on fat people themselves. Undoubtedly systemic injustices and inequalities, such as weight stigma, poverty, hunger, austerity measures and cost of living crises, permeate fat people's everyday lives in ways which already place limits on the affordability and consumption of food. However, everyone, regardless of body size, should have the right and opportunity to be able to access and enjoy a range of nutritious and affordable food without stigma or judgement.

References

Brady, J., Potvin, l., Bombak, A., Kirkham, A., Fraser, K-L. & Gingras, J. (2023). Fat food justice: where fat studies meets food studies. *Fat Studies*, *12*(1), 1–8. DOI: 10.1080/21604851.2021.1968667.

Colls, R. & Evans, B. (2014). Making space for fat bodies? A critical account of 'the obesogenic environment'. *Progress in Human Geography*, *38*(6), 733–753. https://doi.org/10.1177/0309132513500373.

Gard, M. & Wright, J. (2005). *The Obesity Epidemic: Science, Morality and Ideology*. London: Routledge.

Puhl, R. & Suh, Y. (2015). Health consequences of weight stigma: implications for obesity prevention and treatment. *Current Obesity Reports*, *4*, 182–190.

Strings, S. (2019). *Fearing the Black Body: The Racial Origins of Fat Phobia*. New York: New York University Press.

Swinburn, B., Egger, G. & Raza, F. (1999). Dissecting obesogenic environments: the development and application of a framework for identifying and prioritizing environmental interventions for obesity. *Preventative Medicine*, *29*(6 Pt 1), 563–570. doi: 10.1006/pmed.1999.0585. PMID: 10600438.

Further reading

Durocher, M. (2023). "Healthy" food and the production of differentiated bodies in "anti-obesity" discourses and practices. *Fat Studies*, *12*(1), 37–54. DOI: 10.1080/21604851.2021.1980281.

This article provides a critical analysis of discourses of 'healthy food' and fatness found across a range of anti-obesity initiatives in Quebec, Canada.

Guthman, J. (2014). Doing justice to bodies? Reflections on food justice, race, and biology. *Antipode*, *46*(5), 1153–1171.

This article utilises a food justice approach to demonstrate the significance of 'race' and epigenetics for considering obesity causation and inequalities.

Pausé, C. & Taylor, S.R. (Eds.) (2021). *The Routledge International Handbook of Fat Studies*. London: Routledge.

This edited collection provides an introduction to the field of Fat Studies across a wide range of topics and disciplinary perspectives with contributions written by scholarly writers and activists. Topics include embodiment, public health, intersectionality and activism.

RACHEL COLLS

90. Organic agriculture

Lukáš Zagata

Introduction

The concept of organic agriculture encompasses a complex system of farming. In general terms, organic farming is defined as a specific production system that sustains 'the health of soils, ecosystems, and people' (IFOAM, 2008). In a broader sense, the concept also includes agronomic, ecological, political, social and ethical issues of food production and consumption.

Organic agriculture as we know it today is the result of long-term development patterns—its origins date back to the late 19th century. From its inception, organic agriculture has represented an alternative approach to conventional agriculture, criticising modern (industrialised) farming methods (Stinner, 2007). Proponents of organic agriculture have sought to create a fully fledged agricultural system that respects and uses ecological processes instead of industrial inputs, thus reducing the negative impact of farming on nature and society.

This entry describes the development and circumstances of organic agriculture, which has grown from a marginal social movement into a recognised agricultural system. The important question is: what are the long-term values of organic agriculture and what factors have allowed it to succeed in a changing social context? Understanding this question is crucial in terms of discussing future developments and assessing the ability of organic agriculture to respond to major sustainability challenges of the 21st century.

The origins and development of organic agriculture

Organic agriculture first emerged at the turn of the 19th and 20th centuries. Historical overviews tend to mention schools established in German- and English-speaking countries, with leading figures like the UK's Albert Howard and Eve Balfour, Germany's Rudolf Steiner and the USA's Jerome I. Rodale. The initial organic farming concepts were based on biologically oriented agricultural sciences and the values of reform movements (e.g., German *Lebensform* and American *Food Reform*), and took inspiration from farming practices in India and other Asian countries (Vogt, 2007).

Despite having diverse approaches, advocates of organic agriculture have always shared a common mission—to create an alternative to industrial agriculture.

This pioneering period lasted until the 1970s—that is when the original social movement started to formalise, and local organic farmer organisations began to emerge in countries around the globe. An important milestone was the founding of the International Federation of Organic Agriculture Movements (IFOAM) in 1972. One of the main goals of the organisation was to set up consistent standards for organic food products as well as to create programmes for the inspection and certification of organic farmers. In the 1990s, the organic agriculture concept was formally integrated into official policy. In the European Union, for example, organic agriculture began to be formally recognised and incorporated into food policy (Regulation No. 2078/92).

From a lay perspective, organic agriculture is understood as farming that conserves nature while providing better quality food than conventional farming. This belief is now shared by consumers around the world, particularly in Europe, with around 80% of EU citizens indicating support for organic farming (EC, 2022: 142).

Official statistics indicate that over 76 million hectares of land are currently farmed organically worldwide (Willer et al., 2023). Although this is a negligible portion of the global agricultural land area (1.6%), there are relatively large differences in the percentages between individual regions. There are now twenty countries in the world where over 10% of agricultural land is farmed organically, fifteen of which are in Europe. Globally, analysis indicates that the area of organically farmed land has been increasing over the long term (see e.g. Willer et al., 2023).

Historical and spatial analysis of available data indicate, then, that organic agriculture has become a successful and widespread alternative to mainstream agriculture. This status is the result of developments that started at the beginning of the 20th century. Organic agriculture has come a long way since then, growing from a marginal social movement into a recognised farming system that now fulfils official policy objectives in sustainable development.

Current issues

Organic agriculture as a social movement

Organic agriculture can be understood as a social movement. Over the course of the 20th century, this social movement underwent a significant transformation as new issues emerged and changed the status of organic agriculture. The transformation is mainly owed to the agricultural crises of the inter-war period (1930s) and the subsequent rural decline, as well as the later (1960s) environmental crisis, which was directly associated with modern industrial agriculture. Societal reflection and debate on environmental risks and a newly emerged interest in the sustainability of agriculture became a major factor in the success of organic agriculture in the last quarter of the 20th century.

In the pioneering period, the concept of organic agriculture was promoted through an informal social movement, meaning that 'being an organic farmer' meant *subscribing to* the basic principles and values of the organic movement.

The question of farmers' motivations changed fundamentally as the social movement became more formalised. With the codification of the rules for organic farming, a formal framework was developed that defined organic farming standards. Being an organic farmer meant being obligated to *adhere* to these formal standards.

The process of formalising the organic movement provided a significant boost to the successful spread of organic farming methods into mainstream agriculture. Producers who were motivated and could meet the formal standards could now join the organic agriculture system. This innovation diffusion mechanism—the development of production standards—presents also a paradox to the organic movement's success (Dabbert et al., 2004), in that as the concept diffuses so too does the potential waning of its core values.

Mainstreaming and the 'conventionalisation' thesis

The 'paradox of growth' and associated concerns about the organic movement's ability to realise its transformative potential (i.e., to make the food production and consumption system more sustainable) have resonated in organic farming research since the mid-1990s, with a particular focus on the expansion of organic agriculture and food supply chains into mainstream markets and in particular the so-called 'conventionalisation' thesis. Conventionalisation argues that the values of organic farming wane as the sector grows, and that organic farming slowly ceases being an alternative to conventional farming, instead resembling more and more the features of the system it dialectically opposes (Darnhofer et al., 2010).

Research on conventionalisation has given rise to numerous studies in countries around the world, providing empirical findings that place farmers as well as their practices under scrutiny, including examining their personal values and motivations for organic farming as well as the growth in conventional retail chain arrangements, and overall corporatisation of organics.

The organic sector, which since the mid-1990s has become highly professionalised and commercialised, has undergone significant transformations from production adoption and innovation diffusion through to retail uptake and governance through standards and certification. Organic sector advocates do not oppose the modernisation of organic agriculture as such, but rather processes that underpin conventional agriculture (intensification, substitution and appropriation). For some sector advocates, these processes are seen as malignant in the sustainable development of organic farming.

There are no simple answers to questions and critiques associated with the conventionalisation thesis, but nevertheless the position of the organic sector has been and is strengthening rather than weakening vis-à-vis global environmental challenges, as discussed in the sections below.

Organic food consumers

Consumer demand for organic food products has been an essential driver of the sector's growth and innovation. In the 1990s organic foods were a niche food commodity but are now much more mainstream. According to official statistics, the world market for organic food and drink exceeded €120bn in 2020 (European Commission, 2023). The demand for organic food products has therefore grown significantly, and particularly in more affluent market economies.

A key main driver of this growth is the consumer 'turn to quality' (Murdoch and Miele, 2004), which in response to growing environmental concerns saw consumers, particularly from the late 1990s onwards, starting to pay more attention to food sourcing and process-oriented qualities of food production, i.e., how food products are produced. This trend was initially associated with Western diets and consumption trends, but in fact has globalised over time, as seen through global consumption data and patterns of organic consumption in China and other parts of Asia (Si et al., 2015).

The sale of organic food products on a commercial scale, including in supermarkets and other main food retail and food service outlets, would not be feasible without a sophisticated certification and labelling system. The credibility of the claim of origin and quality of organic food products is directly related to the credibility of the certification system itself.

European research shows that consumers have relatively little knowledge of the rules of organic farming (Piracci et al., 2024). Trust and integrity thus play a much greater role in purchasing organic food products than one might expect, and in essence substitute the knowledge that consumers lack.

The main motivations for buying organic food products are consistent across countries around the world (Arbenz et al., 2017). Health benefits are the principal concern, even though positive impacts on health are to some extent a socially constructed attribute that stems from consumer trust only—there is no mention of it in the official definition of organic food products. Environmental aspects are an inevitable part of consumers' motivations, but they are not as high on the priority list as one might expect.

Future issues: seeking a new strategy

The global organic movement has recently introduced a new vision and strategy for the development of the organic sector titled Organic 3.0 (Arbenz et al., 2017). In this reimagining of organic farming futures, the first phase of development, it argues, was completed thanks to the pioneers of the organic movement, who, as seen in early sections of this entry, raised questions regarding the need to support more environmentally friendly food production systems (1920–1970). The second phase is then associated with the successful growth of the sector, thanks largely to the growth and development of standards, which enabled a process of mainstreaming in terms of sales and reach (1970–2010). In the third (ongoing) phase, the organic movement seeks to deepen the basic principles of organic agriculture. There is a new emphasis on making the rules of organic farming descriptive rather than prescriptive. In practice, this means that instead of enforcing minimum standards for farming, the organic movement defines binding outcomes and gives farmers the freedom to find their own ways of reaching them (Arbenz et al., 2017). This gives more scope, it is argued, for innovation, adaptation and the empowerment of key actors.

Going forward, there are likely to be increasingly high expectations for organic agriculture to respond to new sustainability challenges. One of the main issues will be figuring out how to use the concept of organic agriculture to combat the global climate emergency, which from a production perspective has seen a rise in wider associated systems of production, including agroecology (Gliessman, 2013) and regenerative agriculture, which are increasingly discussed as a means to contribute to climate action plans (Newton et al., 2020). A key challenge will be to maintain the innovative status of organic production as new styles of farming and associated markets emerge, including those which espouse agroecological principles but in ways that do not disrupt conventional models of food and farming.

References

Arbenz M, Gould D and Stopes C (2017) ORGANIC 3.0: the vision of the global organic movement and the need for scientific support. *Organic Agriculture* 7, 199–207.

Dabbert S, Haring A M and Zanoli R (2004) *Organic farming: policies and prospects.* Zed Books.

Darnhofer I, Lindenthal T, Bartel-Kratochvil R, and Zollitsch W (2010) Conventionalisation of organic farming practices: from structural criteria towards an assessment based on organic principles. A review. *Agronomy for Sustainable Development* 30, 67–81.

European Commission (2022) Special Eurobarometer 520 report: Europeans, agriculture and the CAP.

European Commission (2023) *Agricultural market brief No 20: Organic farming in the EU. A decade of organic growth.* https://europa.eu/eurobarometer/surveys/detail/2665https://agriculture.ec.europa.eu/media/news/organic-farming-eu-decade-growth-2023-01-18_en#more

Gliessman S (2013) Agroecology: Growing the roots of resistance. *Agroecology and Sustainable Food Systems* 37, 19–31.

Guthman J H (2000) *Agrarian dreams? The paradox of organic farming in California.* University of California, Berkeley.

IFOAM (2008) *Definition of organic agriculture.* IFOAM General Assembly 2008. https://www.ifoam.bio/why-organic/organic-landmarks/definition-organic.

Murdoch J and Miele J (2004) A new aesthetic of food? Relational reflexivity in the 'alternative' food movement. In: Harvey M, McMeekin A and Warde A (eds) *Qualities of food.* Manchester: Manchester University Press, 156–175.

Newton P, Civita N, Frankel-Goldwater L, Bartel K and Johns C (2020) What is regenerative agriculture? A review of scholar and practitioner definitions based on processes and outcomes. *Frontiers in Sustainable Food Systems* 4, 1–11.

Piracci G, Lamonaca E, Santeramo F G, Boncinelli F and Casini L (2024) On the willingness to pay for food sustainability labelling: a meta-analysis. *Agricultural Economics* 55, 329–345.

Regulation (EEC) No 2078/92 of 30 June 1992 on agricultural production methods compatible with the requirements of the protection of the environment and the maintenance of the countryside. https://eur-lex.europa.eu/eli/reg/1992/2078/oj/eng

Si Z, Schumilas T and Scott S (2015) Characterizing alternative food networks in China. *Agriculture and Human Values* 32, 299–313.

Stinner D H (2007) The science of organic farming. In: Lockeretz W (ed) *Organic farming: An international history.* Wallingford: CABI, 40–72.

Vogt G (2007) The origins of organic farming. In: Lockeretz W (ed) *Organic farming: An international history.* Wallingford: CABI, 9–29.

Willer H, Schlatter B and Trávníček J (2023) *The world of organic agriculture: Statistics and emerging trends 2023.* Research Institute of Organic Agriculture FiBL, Frick, and IFOAM.

Further reading

Lockeretz W (2011) (ed) *Organic farming: An international history.* Wallingford: CABI.
This book provides an excellent overview of the historical development of organic agriculture, as well as its role and evolution in modern society to increase the sustainability of agriculture.

Arbenz M, Gould D and Stopes C (2016) *Organic 3.0 for truly sustainable farming and consumption: A landmark document of organic movement.* Approved by the 2017 General Assembly (New Delhi, India). IFOAM Organics International.
This paper provides an overview of the Organic 3.0 concept, representing a new vision and future strategy for the organic movement in the 21st century.

LUKÁŠ ZAGATA

91. Peasants and peasant agriculture

SERGIO SCHNEIDER

Introduction

Peasant agriculture, often also characterised by small-scale farming and family farming, has been the backbone of rural communities and food production systems for centuries. Unlike large industrial farms, peasant agriculture relies on traditional knowledge, diverse crop production, and a deep connection to the land. Despite its ancient origins, peasant agriculture remains relevant today, particularly in discussions about sustainable and equitable food systems and more broadly on rural development too. This entry aims to explore the intersection between peasant agriculture and contemporary food systems. By examining the historical context, current challenges, and potential future directions, it will highlight the crucial role of peasant agriculture in promoting sustainable and resilient food systems in the twenty-first century.

Characteristics of peasant agriculture

Peasant agriculture is characterised by small-scale, family-oriented farming operations that focus on subsistence and local markets rather than large-scale commercial production. These farms often involve diverse cropping systems and mixed livestock, often with a reliance too on manual labour. Peasant farmers maintain a deep connection to the land, using traditional knowledge passed down through generations to manage their resources sustainably. The primary objective is to produce enough food to meet the needs of the household, with any surplus being sold or traded within the local community.

According to Jan Douwe van der Ploeg (2008), peasant farming is not merely a historical remnant but a dynamic, evolving form of agriculture that adapts to changing circumstances while retaining its core principles of sustainability and autonomy. The term "peasant farming" is historically and sociologically loaded. It often refers to traditional, subsistence-oriented farming systems that have existed for centuries, particularly in regions with feudal or colonial histories. According to Shanin (1990), peasants are typically seen as part of a broader social class that is distinct from urban and industrial workers, and they often have a unique cultural identity tied to their land and local traditions.

Given these histories and sociologies, the concept of peasant farming is often linked to notions of autonomy, resistance, and resilience against external pressures, such as market forces, state policies, or land grabs. Peasants are frequently depicted as resisting the encroachment of industrial agriculture and maintaining traditional practices and knowledge systems (Shanin, 1990). In many cases, peasant farming can be seen also as a subset of family farming (Schneider and Niederle, 2010). All peasant farms are family farms, but not all family farms are peasant farms (Ploeg, 2023). The distinction largely depends on the degree of market integration, historical context, and the farm's orientation towards subsistence versus commercial production (Ellis, 1988).

Background and definitions

The origins of peasant agriculture can be traced back to the early stages of human civilisation, when hunter-gatherer societies transitioned to settled farming communities. This shift, often referred to as the Neolithic Revolution, marked the beginning of agricultural practices that formed the foundation of most societies. Peasant farming became the dominant mode of production in many regions, with its structure and techniques adapted to local environmental conditions and cultural practices (Mazoyer and Roudart, 1998).

In early food systems, peasant agriculture played a central role in sustaining local populations. It provided a stable food supply, contributed to local economies, and supported cultural and social structures. The diversity of crops and farming techniques used by peasant farmers helped to build resilient agricultural systems that could withstand environmental fluctuations and pest outbreaks. Moreover, peasant agriculture fostered a deep sense of community and shared responsibility for the land, ensuring that resources were managed sustainably for future generations.

In order to distinguish peasants from family farmers, smallholders, or small-scale farmers, it is necessary to know what a peasant farmer or peasant farming is (Ploeg, 2017). In the languages of the Iberian Peninsula, a peasant is anyone who lives or resides in the countryside. The French term *paysan* and the English term *peasant* are the same, both originating from the Latin word *pays*, which comes from the Latin *pagus*, meaning a land subdivision and tribal restriction, adopted from the subdivision of Gallo-Roman cities. The inhabitant of a *pays* is a *paysan*. Studies on peasant farmers and peasant farming began to spark the interest of social scientists in the twentieth century, especially when those in the fields of anthropology and sociology became interested in the processes of social integration of traditional societies and cultural changes.

According to Silverman (1979), studies of peasant farming gained momentum in the 1950s, highlighting two significant themes. First, Redfield (1960) was interested in understanding the processes of integration of peasant farmers within modern societies. He defines peasant farmers as "folk societies" which are characterised as having their own lifestyle, which greatly contrasts with the city lifestyle. This particular way of life is marked by cultural characteristics, based on tradition and community life. The second theme relates to the definition of peasant farmers, which favours an interpretation of peasant farmers as a type of community that differs from primitive groups. The emphasis is thus understanding the relationship between cultures and the environments in which they were created. Wolf (1955) in this context defines peasant farmers in terms of "horizontal sociocultural segments" which have three fundamental characteristics: agricultural cultivation, control of the land, and subsistence farming.

There are differences between the peasant farmers of the past and present that cannot be ignored. Peasant farming implies a rural community and way of life that is relatively autonomous in relation to cities and markets. Sociologists like Henri Mendras stated that local collectivity (community) and relationships of solidarity and reciprocity are key to the characterisation of peasant farming societies. Wolf too referred to peasants as social groups with little internal distinction, reduced social mobility, and few ties to the cities and markets. However, as the small rural community or isolated population loses its influence over the social and economic reproduction of peasant farmers and their external relations (whether these are technological, cultural, informational, commercial, etc.), peasant farmers then become appropriated and redefined and are given new meaning (Friedmann, 2021). Peasant farmers therefore transform

themselves and change their social characteristics. They are no longer quasi-isolated and semi-autonomous and become part of the dynamics of a broader society (Bernstein, 2018).

In contemporary contexts, the fundamental distinction between family farmers and peasant farmers is that family farmers are highly integrated in the social division of labour and in the more general economic dynamic, whereas peasant farmers have a partial and incomplete relationship with the surrounding society (Ellis, 1988; Brunori and Bartolini, 2016). The social reproduction of family farmers depends on the intensity (more or less autonomous) and the manner (more or less diversified) in which they are included in the market economy and capitalist society as a whole; while the social reproduction of peasant farmers depends on the conditions and replication potential of their local community.

There are four main elements that define a peasant family farmer or peasant agriculture: (a) the predominant use of family labour in the production process of the economic activities from which the family obtains the necessary resources for their livelihood; (b) the management of the family establishment and activities, which means that there is no external recruitment for activities; (c) the output from production, along with other forms of income, are common property resources, belonging to the domestic group; and (d) access to the means of production is generally carried out by the transfer of family wealth through inheritance. Thus, peasant agriculture is essentially a "family business", subject to the culture, habits, and community way of life in the place they are located.

Peasant agriculture and rural development

Peasant agriculture, with its emphasis on diversity, sustainability, and local markets, offers a valuable alternative to the dominant industrial agricultural model. Unlike industrial agriculture, which prioritises high yields and efficiency, peasant farming focuses on maintaining the health of the ecosystem and the well-being of the community. This approach often results in lower yields per hectare but contributes to greater resilience in the face of environmental and economic challenges. Peasant agriculture also supports biodiversity by cultivating a wide variety of crops and livestock, which helps to maintain genetic diversity and reduce the risk of crop failure. In contrast, industrial agriculture's reliance on monoculture has led to the erosion of biodiversity and increased vulnerability to pests and diseases.

Peasant agriculture, biodiversity, and sustainability

Peasant farmers play a crucial role in preserving agricultural biodiversity, which is essential for the resilience of food systems. By growing diverse crops and maintaining traditional farming practices, peasant farmers contribute to the conservation of heirloom varieties and landraces, which are often more resistant to local pests and diseases. This diversity also supports ecosystem services, such as pollination, soil fertility, and water regulation, which are vital for sustainable agriculture.

Moreover, peasant agriculture often employs agroecological practices that minimise the use of external inputs and enhance the sustainability of farming systems (Ploeg, 2008). These practices include crop rotation, intercropping, agroforestry, and organic farming. By working with nature rather than against it, peasant farmers can produce food in a way that is environmentally sustainable and socially just.

Peasant agriculture and food sovereignty

Peasant agriculture is closely linked to the concept of food sovereignty, which emphasises the right of communities to control their own food systems, including the production, distribution, and consumption of food. It advocates for the protection of local food traditions, the empowerment of small-scale farmers, and the promotion of sustainable agricultural practices.

By supporting local economies, peasant agriculture helps to build resilient communities that are less dependent on global markets and more capable of withstanding economic and environmental shocks. Local food systems, which prioritise short supply chains and direct relationships between producers and consumers, can also reduce the carbon footprint of food production and distribution.

Policy recommendations to strengthen peasant agriculture

Current discussions of the value of peasant agriculture emphasise policy recommendations including:

1. Land Reform: Implementation of land reform policies that ensure secure access to land for small-scale farmers and promote equitable land distribution.
2. Market Access: Improving market access for peasant farmers by investing in infrastructure, such as roads, storage facilities, and markets, and by promoting fair trade practices.
3. Subsidies and Support: Redirecting subsidies and support from industrial agriculture to small-scale farmers, including access to credit, extension services, and research support.
4. Agroecology: Promoting agroecological practices and providing training and support for farmers to adopt sustainable farming methods.
5. Food Sovereignty: Recognising and supporting the rights of communities to control their own food systems, including the protection of local food traditions and the promotion of local food systems.
6. Climate Adaptation: Supporting peasant farmers in adapting to climate change by providing access to climate-resilient seeds, technology, and information.

Challenges faced by peasant agriculture in the twenty-first century

Economic pressures and market access

Peasant farmers often face significant economic pressures, including limited access to markets, credit, and resources (Arulingam et al., 2022). The dominance of industrial agriculture and the concentration of market power in the hands of a few large corporations have made it increasingly difficult for small-scale farmers to compete. Additionally, global trade policies and subsidies for industrial agriculture have further marginalised peasant farmers, leading to lower prices for their products and reduced income.

Market access is a critical challenge for peasant farmers, particularly in remote or rural areas (Ploeg and Schneider, 2022). Without access to markets, farmers are unable to sell their produce at fair prices, which can lead to economic hardship and food insecurity. Additionally, the lack of infrastructure, such as roads and storage facilities, further hinders the ability of peasant farmers to participate in the market economy (Schneider and Cassol, 2021).

Climate change and environmental degradation

The climate emergency poses a significant threat to peasant agriculture, as small-scale farmers are often more vulnerable to the impacts of extreme weather events, changing precipitation patterns, and rising temperatures. These changes can lead to crop failures, reduced yields, and increased susceptibility to pests and diseases.

Environmental degradation, including soil erosion, deforestation, and water scarcity, also poses challenges for peasant farmers. The degradation of natural resources reduces the productivity of agricultural land and increases the difficulty of sustaining livelihoods in rural areas. Additionally, the encroachment of industrial agriculture and extractive industries has led to the displacement of peasant communities and the loss of traditional farming practices.

Policy and institutional barriers

Peasant farmers often face significant policy and institutional barriers that hinder their ability to thrive. Many governments prioritise industrial agriculture and large-scale agribusinesses in their agricultural policies, providing them with subsidies, infrastructure, and research support. In contrast, peasant farmers often lack access to these resources and are excluded from decision-making processes.

Land tenure insecurity is another major challenge for peasant farmers. In many regions, land ownership is concentrated in the hands of a few, while small-scale farmers lack secure access to land. This insecurity makes it difficult for peasant farmers to invest in their farms and adopt sustainable practices. Additionally, the lack of access to education, extension services, and technology further limits the ability of peasant farmers to improve their productivity and adapt to changing conditions.

Peasant agriculture in a sustainable food future

Peasant agriculture has the potential to play a crucial role in creating a more sustainable and equitable food system. By promoting biodiversity, supporting local economies, and adopting agroecological practices, peasant farmers can contribute to the resilience of food systems and help mitigate the impacts of climate change. Additionally, the emphasis on food sovereignty and the empowerment of small-scale farmers can lead to more just and inclusive food systems.

To realise this potential, there must be a shift in agricultural policies and practices to better support peasant agriculture. This includes recognising the value of traditional knowledge, providing access to resources and markets, and promoting sustainable farming practices. Additionally, efforts must be made to address the structural inequalities that have marginalised peasant farmers.

Peasant agriculture remains a vital component of the global food system, offering valuable lessons in sustainability, resilience, and food sovereignty. While the contemporary food system is dominated by industrial agriculture, there is growing recognition of the need to diversify and support alternative models of food production. By embracing the principles of peasant agriculture and promoting policies that support small-scale farmers, we can create a more just, sustainable, and resilient food system for future generations.

The intersection of peasant agriculture and contemporary food systems presents both challenges and opportunities. It is essential to recognise the importance of supporting diverse agricultural practices and to create an environment which enables peasant farmers to thrive. By doing so, we can build a food system that is not only productive but also equitable, sustainable, and resilient.

References

Arulingam, I., Brady, G., Chaya, M., Conti, M., Kgomotso, P. K., Korzenszky, A., Njie, D., Schroth, G. and Suhardiman, D. (2022). *Small-scale producers in sustainable agrifood systems transformation*. Rome: FAO.

Bernstein, H. (2018). The "peasant problem" in the Russian revolution(s), 1905–1929.

Journal of Peasant Studies, 45(5–6): pp. 1127–1150.

Borras, S. M. Jr. and Franco, J. C. (2012). Global land grabbing and trajectories of agrarian change: a preliminary analysis. *Journal of Agrarian Change*, 12(1): pp. 34–59.

Brunori, G. and Bartolini, F. (2016). The family farm: model for the future or relic of the past? In: Shucksmith, M. and Brown, D. L. (Eds.), *Routledge international handbook of rural studies*. London: Routledge, pp. 192–204.

Chayanov, A. V. (1966). The theory of peasant economy. In: Thorner, D., Kerblay, B. and Smith, R. E. F. (Eds.), *The American Economic Association translation series*. Homewood, IL: Richard Irwin for the American Economic Association (first published 1925).

Chayanov, A. V. (1991). *The theory of peasant co-operatives*. London: I. B. Tauris (first published 1919).

Ellis, F. (1988). *Peasant economics: Farm households and agrarian development*. Cambridge: Cambridge University Press.

Friedmann, H. (2021). Origins of peasant studies. In: Akram-Lodhi, A. H., Dietz, K., Engels, B. and McKay, B. M (Eds.), *Handbook of critical agrarian studies*. Cheltenham, UK and Northampton, MA, USA: Edward Elgar Publishing, pp. 15–24.

Hayami, Y. (1996). The peasant in economic modernization. *American Journal of Agricultural Economics*, 78(December): pp. 1157–1167.

HLPE (2013). *Investing in smallholder agriculture for food security: A report by the High Level Panel of Experts on Food Security and Nutrition of the Committee on World Food Security*. Rome: HLPE.

Lowder S. K., Sánchez, M. V. and Bertini, R. (2021). Which farms feed the world and has farmland become more concentrated? *World Development*, 142: pp. 105455.

Mazoyer, M. and Roudart, L. (1998). *Histoire des agricultures du monde, du Néolithique à la crise contemporaine*. Paris: Editions du Seuil.

Ploeg, J. D. van der (2008). *The new peasantries: Struggles for autonomy and sustainability in an era of empire and globalization*. London: Earthscan.

Ploeg, J. D. van der (2017). *The importance of peasant agriculture: A neglected truth*.

Wageningen: Wageningen University and Research.

Ploeg, J. D. van der (2023). *The sociology of farming: Concepts and methods*. London: Earthscan/Routledge.

Ploeg, J. D. van der and Schneider, S. (2022). Autonomy as a politico-economic concept: peasant practices and nested markets. *Journal of Agrarian Change*, 22(3): pp. 529–546.

Redfield, R. (1960). *Peasant society and peasant culture*. Chicago: Phoenix Books and The University of Chicago Press.

Schneider, S. and Cassol, A. (2021). Food and markets: the contribution of economic sociology. In: Duncan, J., Carolan, M. and Wiskerke, H. (Eds.), *The Routledge handbook of sustainable and regenerative food systems*. London: Routledge, pp. 171–187.

Schneider, S. and Niederle, P. A. (2010). Resistance strategies and diversification of rural livelihoods: the construction of autonomy among Brazilian family farmers. *Journal of Peasant Studies*, 37(2): pp. 379–405.

Shanin, T. (1973). The nature and logic of the peasant economy 1: a generalisation. *Journal of Peasant Studies*, 1(1): pp. 63–80.

Shanin, T. (1990). *Defining peasants: Essays concerning rural societies, exploratory economies, and learning from them in the contemporary world*. Oxford: Basil Blackwell.

Silverman, S. (1979). The peasant concept in anthropology. *Journal of Peasant Studies*, 7(1): pp. 49–69.

Thorner, D. (1988). Peasant economy as a category in history. In: Shanin, T. (Ed.), *Peasant and Peasant Societies*. London: Penguin Books, pp. 202–218.

Wolf, E. (1955). Types of Latin American peasantry: a preliminary discussion. *American Anthropologist*, 57(3): pp. 452–471.

Further reading

Bernstein, H. and Byes, T. J. (2001). From peasant studies to agrarian change. *Journal of Agrarian Change*, 1(1), pp. 1–56.
This essay surveys three decades of work in peasant studies and agrarian change, from 1973 to 2000, providing a useful overview of peasant farming and political economy.

SERGIO SCHNEIDER

Ploeg, J. D. van der (2013). *Peasants and the art of farming. A Chayanovian manifesto.* Halifax: Fernwood.

Inspired by Chayanov, this book provides an important account of peasant farming and wider links with labour, production, and governance.

Akram-Lodhi, A. H. and Kay, C. (Eds.) (2009). *Peasants and globalization: Political economy, rural transformation and the agrarian question.* London: Routledge.

This volume brings together essays on the trajectory of agrarian change and the impact of neoliberal globalisation on peasant farms.

SERGIO SCHNEIDER

92. Pedagogy, education and food

Elaine Swan

Introduction

Scholars use the term food pedagogy to bring together theories of food with theories of teaching and learning through foregrounding the analytic of pedagogy. This examination of education matters because of the proliferation and intensification of food related reforms of various kinds. Although scholars, activists and policy makers interested in food reform initiatives use phrases like food education, food learning and taste education, food pedagogy academics are distinctive in that they draw on educational and cultural theories of pedagogy. One definition of food pedagogies is 'attempts by a range of agencies, actors, institutions and media to 'teach about growing, provisioning, cooking, eating, and wasting food' (Flowers and Swan, 2012: 425). Educators, or pedagogues, who seek to 'educate' about food include food activists, farmers, food producers, sports and diet professionals, community members, school-teachers and a growing litany of cultural intermediaries such as celebrity chefs, food writers, food bloggers, health practitioners and advertisers (Flowers and Swan, 2015; Park, Yeatman, Russell and MacPhail, 2022). Food studies and adult education scholar, Jennifer Sumner (2013), who taught the first master's subjects called Food Pedagogy at the University of Toronto, has popularised the term and insists that studies of food pedagogies are not simply describing teaching and learning processes but foregrounding power, injustice and sustainability.

Since the 1970s, scholars have extended the term pedagogy to examine teaching and learning outside of educational institutions (Luke 1996; Hickey-Moody, Savage & Windle, 2010; Sandlin, O'Malley and Burdick, 2011). Anna Hickey-Moody, Glen Savage and Joel Windle (2010) gloss this as 'pedagogy writ large'. Broadly speaking, theorists use pedagogy as an analytic to study social and cultural processes beyond the classroom which attempt to modify or transform how we act, feel and think (Watkins, Noble and Driscoll, 2015). For instance, feminist theorist Carmen Luke (1996) shows how toys, books and media teach gendering. For Megan

Watkins, Greg Noble and Catherine Driscoll (2015), using pedagogy as an analytical lens means examining the pedagogical processes underpinning theoretical concepts such as socialisation, reproduction and interpellation, which imply learning or transformation.

Accordingly, food pedagogy scholars seek to explore how cultural and social processes inside and outside of formal, institutionalised education attempt to shape the feelings, thoughts, practices, embodiments and imaginings of children and adults in relation to food. Going beyond the classroom means scholarly attention turns to food education across institutions such as museums, universities and public health bodies; media such as women's magazines, cookbooks and social media platforms; genres such as TV cooking shows, food memoirs and travel documentary films; and policy instruments such as national food plans, school curricula reform, labelling and nutrition guidelines.

Many food pedagogy writers focus on the teaching of children and younger people about food in school. Examples include school classroom teaching on food health, especially 'obesity' educational initiatives (Leahy and Pike, 2015); school lunch times (Lalli, 2019); school lunch boxes (Pluim et al., 2018); school lunches (Leahy and Pike, 2015); and school gardens (Hayes-Conroy, 2014).

Others use the analytic lens of pedagogy to examine institutionalised, formal and informal education and learning beyond the classroom aimed at adults. Such research covers a wide range of curricula, educational processes and aims, media and domains. Examples of formal food pedagogies include cooking courses, health education, nutrition workshops and culinary tours; informal food pedagogies encompass activities such as museum food exhibitions, TV cooking shows, community gardening projects, food activist campaigns and food marketing; and incidental food pedagogies cover learning from eating and drinking at work, at home, in restaurants, at farmers' markets and at large-scale food events such as festivals (Sumner, 2013, Etmanski, 2015, Flowers and Swan, 2015); home cooking (Janhonen et al., 2018); community gardens (Hake, 2017); food exhibitions in museums (Swan et al., 2019); and food social movements (Hayes-Conroy, 2014).

A second element of the study of food pedagogies is that scholars insist on the politics embedded in their discourses and practices.

Some problematise food related curricula for a lack of attention to structural inequalities, the experiences of racialised food workers (Yamashita and Robinson, 2016) and the destruction caused by the industrialised food system (Sumner, 2013). Many problematise the moralism underpinning food education. For instance, 'healthy cooking classes', school lunchbox policies and obesity campaigns target particular groups: women in their roles as mothers and carers – especially people of colour and Indigenous and working-class mothers – and women or school children designated as 'obese' or 'unhealthy'.

Moreover, food pedagogies can have an explicit political intent such as activist pedagogies from food sustainability, food sovereignty, vegetarianism, veganism and ethical food consumption, the health properties of organic foods, the environmental benefits of local foods, permaculture techniques, the inequalities of food production and the importance of food justice, and questions of food supply and food security, to name but a few.

Current issues, concerns and areas of focus

Moralism

Food pedagogies have been shown to reproduce hierarchies and inequalities of race, gender, class, settler-colonialism and heteronormativity, especially around normative notions of food conduct, social distinction and middle-class whiteness (see for example, Gagliardi 2022; Flowers and Swan, 2019; Jones, 2019). The North American food studies theorist Julie Guthman (2008) argues that much food reform based on education and food pedagogy is a classed project and she problematises the privileging of white middle-class do-gooders who want to 'educate' those they feel do not understand how to eat properly. Naya Jones (2019) stresses how Black young people are often the targets of food pedagogies, which reproduce binaries of good and bad foods, and stigmatise their existing food lives.

A dominant concern for most food pedagogy scholars is the moral economy of food education interventions, especially those which focus on hegemonic nutrition and public health through 'nutritionism' and 'healthism'. Certain food pedagogies stigmatise women's domestic provisioning, shopping, cooking, eating and food waste practices.

Thus, because of transformations in the food system, food policy and food health, women are incited to take on board complicated prescriptions on nutrition, health, food waste, environmentalism and food safety, many of which are based on narrow racialised, cultural and classed knowledges (Jones, 2019; Martin, 2018). Food reform based on 'eco-nutritionism' and 'healthism' creates extra burdens on minoritised mothers and can be found across so many different domains from community initiatives, TV programmes and women's magazines (Martin, 2018; Parker, 2020). With the increasing impoverishment of women, and intensified health expectations promulgated by food initiatives, new types of labour and inequalities are created which reinforce heteronormative, gender, race and class hierarchies (Brenton 2017). These prescriptions circulate in food and health media, popular culture and public health creating extra burdens for maternal feeding work, especially for women of colour and low-income white women, for whom many are cruelly inaccessible (Martin, 2018).

Women are expected to keep their babies and children healthy and safe, and to produce healthy citizens, through incitations to buy healthy, organic and local foods, even though what these mean, and the ethics of how they are produced, is not so straightforward (Koch, 2019). For instance, many poorly paid farmworkers, often women of colour, can't afford to buy fresh locally sourced food (Koch, 2019). The stress, stigmatisation and burden of hegemonic healthism on women of colour and women on low budgets cannot be underestimated (Koch, 2019; Jones, 2019). Food sustainability pedagogies create new burdens in recommending 'sustainable foodwork' (Swan and Perrier, 2019) – managing domestic food waste and shopping from alternative food systems – which require more labour-intensive practices (Fraser & Parizeau, 2018).

At the same time, white middle classes take on certain kinds of so-called sustainable and healthy food practices such as eating local, fresh, unprocessed and organic food and can draw on these practices as cultural distinction and distance themselves from 'unhealthy Others' (Guthman, 2008; Johnston, Szabo, & Rodney, 2011). Scholars, activists and mothers roundly critique 'eating for change' or 'eating for good' pedagogies (Johnston, Szabo, and Rodney 2011), which recommend localism, organic foods and fair trade, for their elitism, moralism, whiteness and classism, and which add to women's already overburdened workload (Guthman, 2008; Parker, 2020).

Visceral learning and hierarchies

A related theme is, as feminist scholars note, that because food education initiatives often ignore the sensory, embodied and visceral meaning of food they are doomed to fail and reproduce inequalities. For example, in their work across many food pedagogical sites aimed at children and adults, such as school gardens, vegetarian activism, cooking programmes and the Slow Food movement, Alison Hayes-Conroy and Jessica Hayes-Conroy (2010) insist that we need to understand the significance of the visceral 'feelings' associated with how people grow to like or dislike certain foods. Visceral responses are not authentic, automatic or spontaneous but are processes which can be educated, taught, trained and shaped. Rather than being innate and pre-social, visceral responses can be nurtured by society and influenced by cultural norms and pedagogies (Hayes-Conroy and Hayes-Conroy, 2010). At the same time, visceral learning and training in food activism for instance can reproduce inequalities and hierarchies. Through food pedagogies, oppressive regimes may become 'internalised' and 'embodied' (Hayes-Conroy and Hayes-Conroy 2010: 1276). Bodies are where cultural patterns, socio-economic hierarchies and structures impact on people (Hayes-Conroy and Hayes-Conroy, 2010).

A key question for these researchers is how food pedagogies prime (i.e. make ready) bodies to be affected by food discourses, activities and their milieux (Hayes-Conroy & Hayes-Conroy, 2010). The point is not simply to describe bodily sensations and movements but to do so to support social justice. The political focus means asking how thesensory, as part of body–environment relations, 'materially, physically "activates" people', turning them on and off food activism, often through racism and classism (A. Hayes-Conroy, 2017: 51) To illustrate, they study how, in Slow Food activism, bodily practices such as touching and eating food get entangled with ideologies of localism and heritage food, and the sense of belonging within a discerning group affects how Slow Food tastes and events feel.

In a ground-breaking article, Emilia Sanabria (2015) examines the 'sensorial pedagogies' of health promotion practitioners to reduce obesity in France, which promote pleasure and sensuality in their strategies where simply informing eaters is deemed ineffective. In a study of Australian Vietnamese tour guides, Flowers and Swan show how they teach middle class white tourists how to appreciate Vietnamese dishes sensorially and aesthetically (Flowers and Swan, 2019). Anthropologist David Sutton (2001) researches the transmission of memories and learning through women's cooking in Greece; and geographer Ben Highmore (2003) writes of the alimentary pedagogies of the ingestion of ingredients which he sees as active agents transforming bodies and emotions. These studies have much to offer research on how food pedagogies – from food activism to health promotion – mobilise, train and prohibit senses; and how race, gender, heteronormativity and class are reproduced and performed through visceral and sensory practices via food education.

Future concerns, issues and questions

A range of scholars from different national contexts have mobilised food pedagogy as an analytical lens in the study of a variety of sites and educational initiatives but often they don't attend closely to what makes them 'pedagogical'. As public pedagogy theorists Jenny Sandlin, Michael O'Malley and Jake Burdick (2011) ask, how do educational sites and practices beyond the classroom actually work to teach the public? They argue that more work needs to be conducted on how the various sites, spaces, products and places identified as public pedagogy actually operate as pedagogy (Sandlin et al., 2011: 359).

For Hickey-Moody et al. (2010), the answers can be found in the common elements across classrooms and beyond classroom education. Namely, researchers can examine: pedagogical intent or aims; the substance or curriculum; and processes or teaching and learning approaches. But school-based metaphors and meanings aren't enough for Sandlin and colleagues. They seek theories which show how meanings are generated via active, sensate, embodied interactions, the post-human and affect.

This means food pedagogy research needs to examine more closely how, for instance, cooking classes or food media educate.

Drawing on the work of Watkins, Noble and Driscoll, we would explicate how forms of food subjectivity and food conduct are 'capacitated', 'regulated' and 'shaped' (Watkins, Noble and Driscoll, 2015). On this view, key questions for future scholarship include: what are the pedagogical processes, mechanisms and modes, situated practices, interactions and relations that produce learning, new knowledge and transformation in relation to food (Watkins et al., 2015)? Through which processes and practices are food-related capacities such as food shopping and cooking brought about? This also raises issues about the specificities of food: how do the symbolic, cultural and material qualities of food inflect education and learning? How do food pedagogies through these practices and relations constitute and reproduce gendered, racialised, heteronormative and classed hierarchies?

A second under-researched issue is how food pedagogies can offer resistance and disrupt power (Gagliardi, 2022; Jones, 2019). Thus, critical race food feminists insist that food practices can offer sustenance, spaces for anti-racism, gendered connectivity and environmental activism (Jones, 2019, Nettles-Barcelon et al., 2015). Food pedagogies do not always oppress, stigmatise or discriminate. Food scholarship which attends to race stresses the significance of food as a means of self and cultural expression. Women use food practices as survival politics: building community with other women, nurturing cultural connections, challenging hegemonic healthism and sustaining a ballast against racism (Jones, 2019; Nettles-Barcelon et al., 2015). On this view, cooking food 'creates a locus for work, creativity and pleasure that transcend realms of human reproduction as shaped by the market, patriarchy and alienating labour' (Lewis, 2016: 6). Scholars argue that Indigenous food pedagogies can rupture settler-colonial logics (Gagliardi, 2022); and co-designing food health pedagogies can be liberating (Hess, 2021). Black food geographer Naya Jones (2019) shows how critical embodied food pedagogies can be designed which do not marginalise people of colour and their food. In this vein, critical race and Indigenous feminisms will be vital for designing and evaluating future food pedagogies especially those associated with science and bio technologies or aimed at creating more sustainable and just food systems.

References

Brenton, J. (2017). The limits of intensive feeding: Maternal foodwork at the intersections of race, class, and gender. *Sociology of Health & Illness*, *39*(6), 863–877.

Etmanski, C. (2015). Introduction to adult learning and food. *Studies in the Education of Adults*, *47*(2), 120–127.

Flowers, R. and Swan, E. (2012). Introduction: Why food? Why pedagogy? Why adult education? *Australian Journal of Adult Learning*, *52*(3), 419–433.

Flowers, R. and Swan, E. (2015). Food pedagogies: Histories, definitions, and moralities. In R. Flowers and E. Swan (Eds.) *Food pedagogies* (pp. 1–29). New York: Routledge.

Flowers, R. and Swan, E. (2019). 'Sauce in the bowl, not on your shirt': Food pedagogy and aesthetics in Vietnamese ethnic food tours to Cabramatta, Sydney. In C. Leong-Salobir (Ed.) *Routledge* handbook *of food in Asia* (pp. 85–101). New York: Routledge.

Fraser, C. and Parizeau, K. (2018). Waste management as foodwork: A feminist food studies approach to household food waste. *Canadian Food Studies/La Revue canadienne des études sur l'alimentation*, *5*(1), 39–62.

Gagliardi, L. M. (2022). Noticing and rupturing settler-colonial logics with fooding pedagogies: Thinking with children-food relations and more-than-human worlds. In D. Ruge, I. Torres and D. Powell (Eds.) *School food, equity and social justice: Critical reflections and perspectives*. New York: Routledge.

Guthman, J. (2008). 'If only they knew': Colour blindness and universalism in California alternative food institutions. *The Professional Geographer*, *60*(3), 387–397.

Hake, B. J. (2017). Gardens as learning spaces: Intergenerational learning in urban food gardens. *Journal of Intergenerational Relationships*, *15*(1), 26–38.

Hayes-Conroy, J. (2014). *Savouring alternative food: School gardens, healthy eating and visceral difference*. New York: Routledge.

Hayes-Conroy, A. (2017). Critical visceral methods and methodologies: Debate title: Better than text? Critical reflections on the practices of visceral methodologies in human geography. *Geoforum*, *82*, 51–52.

Hayes-Conroy, A. and Hayes-Conroy, J. (2010). Visceral difference: Variations in feeling (slow) food. *Environment and Planning A, 42*(12), 2956–2971.

Hess, M. J. (2021). *Liberating .public food pedagogy: Principles for co-developing health equity* Doctoral dissertation, University of Colorado at Denver.

Hickey-Moody, A., Savage, G. C. and Windle, J. (2010). Pedagogy writ large: Public, popular and cultural pedagogies in motion. *Critical Studies in Education, 51*(3), 227–236.

Highmore, B. (2008). Alimentary agents: Food, cultural theory and multiculturalism. *Journal of intercultural studies, 29*(4), 381–398.

Johnston, J., Szabo, M., & Rodney, A. (2011). Good food, good people: Understanding the cultural repertoire of ethical eating. *Journal of Consumer Culture, 11*(3), 293–318.

Janhonen, K., Torkkeli, K. and Mäkelä, J. (2018). Informal learning and food sense in home cooking. *Appetite, 130*, 190–198.

Jones, N. (2019). "It tastes like heaven": Critical and embodied food pedagogy with Black youth in the Anthropocene. *Policy Futures in Education, 17*(7), 905–923.

Koch, S. L. (2019). *Gender and food: A critical look at the food system.* London: Rowman & Littlefield.

Lalli, G. (2019). *Schools, food and social learning.* London: Routledge.

Leahy, D. and Pike, J. (2015). 'Just say no to pies': Food pedagogies, health education and governmentality. In R. Flowers and E. Swan (Eds.) *Food pedagogies* (pp. 169–182). New York: Routledge.

Lewis, D. (2016). Bodies, matter and feminist freedoms: Revisiting the politics of food. *Agenda, 30*(4), 6–16.

Luke, C. (Ed.) (1996). *Feminisms and pedagogies of everyday life.* Albany: State University of New York Press.

Martin, M. A. (2018). "Sometimes I feel like I'm counting crackers": The household foodwork of low-income mothers, and how community food initiatives can support them. *Canadian Food Studies/ La Revue Canadienne Des Études Sur L'alimentation, 5*(1), 113–132.

Nettles-Barcelon, K. D., Clark, G., Thorsson, C., Walker, J. K. and Williams-Forson, P. (2015). Black women's food work as critical space. *Gastronomica, 15*(4), 34–49.

Park, S. J., Yeatman, H., Russell, J. and MacPhail, C. (2022). Food pedagogy – key elements for urban health and sustainability: A scoping review. *Appetite, 168*, 105672.

Parker, B. (2020). Consuming health, negotiating risk, eating right: Exploring the limits of choice through a feminist intersectional lens. *Journal of Critical Dietetics, 5*(1), 45–57.

Pluim, C., Powell, D. and Leahy, D. (2018). Schooling lunch: Health, food, and the pedagogicalization of the lunch box. In S. Rice and A. G. Rud (Eds.) *Educational dimensions of school lunch: Critical perspectives* (pp. 59–74). Basingstoke: Palgrave Macmillan.

Sanabria, E. (2015). Sensorial pedagogies, hungry fat cells and the limits of nutritional health education. *BioSocieties, 10*, 125–142.

Sandlin, J. A., O'Malley, M. P. and Burdick, J. (2011). Mapping the complexity of public pedagogy scholarship: 1894–2010. *Review of Educational Research, 81*(3), 338–375.

Sumner, J. (2013). Food literacy and adult education: Learning to read the world by eating. *The Canadian Journal for the Study of Adult Education, 25*(2), 70–92.

Sutton, D. (2001). *Remembrance of repasts: An anthropology of food and memory.* Oxford: Berg.

Swan, E. (2020). COVID-19 foodwork, race, gender, class and food justice: An intersectional feminist analysis. *Gender in Management: An International Journal, 35*(7/8), 693–703.

Swan, E. and Perrier, M. (2019). Foodwork: Racialised, gendered and classed labours. Available at https://futuresofwork.co.uk /2019/12/09/foodwork-racialised-gendered -and-class-labours/.

Watkins, M., Noble, G. and Driscoll, C. (2015). *Cultural pedagogies and human conduct.* London: Routledge.

Yamashita, L. and Robinson, D. (2016). Making visible the people who feed us: Educating for critical food literacy through multicultural texts. *Journal of Agriculture, Food Systems, and Community Development, 6*(2), 269–281.

Further reading

Flowers, R. and Swan, E. (Eds.) (2015). *Food pedagogies.* New York: Routledge.

ELAINE SWAN

This is an edited volume which introduces food pedagogy via a range of authors, case studies and perspectives.

Park, S. J., Yeatman, H., Russell, J. and MacPhail, C. (2022). Food pedagogy – key elements for urban health and sustainability: A scoping review. *Appetite*, *168*, 105672.

This provides a thorough literature review on studies of food pedagogies to date.

Jones, N. (2019). "It tastes like heaven": Critical and embodied food pedagogy with Black youth in the Anthropocene. *Policy Futures in Education*, *17*(7), 905–923.

Jones challenges food pedagogies from a Black geographies and embodied point of view.

93. Place and food

Fernando Bosco

Introduction to place and food

It is difficult to think about food or study food without considering place. Place immediately invokes location: geographic space somewhere. For that reason, it has been argued that food itself is a geographic fact, since food must be produced and consumed somewhere (Joassart-Marcelli and Bosco, 2018).

One relationship between place and food involves the physical environment where food is grown. Climate, soil conditions, growing seasons, and other environmental variables impact the availability and taste of food as well as people's diets. Another fundamental relationship between place and food involves the different human characteristics of locations—or the human geographies of food—impacting how food is produced, distributed, and consumed. Places are filled with cultural meaning, and traditions around food practices vary geographically. Places also are parts of economic systems, and they are embedded in different social and political networks, leading to a complex mosaic of human practices connected to food. In other words, the specific human geographic characteristics of the locations where food is produced, distributed, sold, and consumed directly impact food practices and how food is experienced. For example, food cooked and consumed at home might taste different than food from a street vendor or a high-end restaurant; eating produce grown on a small farm with specific growing practices might elicit different sensations than consuming produce grown on large-scale commercial farms. Place matters to food because it is through place that we can contextualise food's connections to the physical environment, social relations, economic structures, cultural practices, and political institutions.

At the same time, food practices, from production to consumption, create, impact, and transform places in multiple ways. Farms transform places by the way they impact the physical and cultural landscape of a region. The transformation of an empty city lot into a small growing garden for the local community is a visible process of urban change. Clusters of ethnic restaurants in a particular neighbourhood immigrant enclave or working-class neighbourhood give particular flavours and atmosphere to parts of a city. Food trucks, pop-up restaurants, a traditional bistro, and other unexpected food places have the same effect. In fact, many would argue that food seemingly tastes better when it comes from a specific place, leading some consumers, in particular foodies and gastro-tourists, to move across their own cities and countries or travel the world searching for food experiences, altering everyday places in the process. The connections between place and food, then, are not just about the impacts of location on our food and food practices, but they are also about how food makes places. Food practices connect us to the places where food is grown, processed, sold, prepared, served, and consumed and, in the process, the same food practices transform places, and even make new ones. Place and food are mutually constitutive.

Unpacking place in relation to food

The different components of place and food

The relationship between place and food is complex because place itself is a complex concept. Place, as a key geographic concept, consists of at least of three components: location, locale, and sense of place (Agnew, 1987). Food is connected to all these elements of place.

Location refers to the specific objective position of a place in the world. Place as location can refer to a city block, a village, a city, a region, or a country. Thinking of place and food in terms of location is about positioning food somewhere and examining how that somewhere impacts food. There are several food-specific concepts that speak directly to locational attributes of place and food. *Terroir* refers to a location with specific soil, climate, and topography characteristics, which in turn impart specific qualities to a food product. Terroirs can also define a place in terms of its gastronomic identity and create regional distinctiveness for food. The *food environment* also refers to place as location in terms of the material context in which people obtain food. The food environment includes food retailers, places of alternative food production and procurement such as community gardens and allotments, and community resources for food such as food pantries. An *obesogenic food environment* refers to a location that is said to contribute to obesity and other adverse health effects because it contains establishments where fast and junk food are prevalent. *Food deserts* are defined as locations with limited access to affordable and nutritious food and tend to be associated with lower income neighbourhoods and communities (Guthman, 2013).

Place can also refer to a *locale*, indicating the setting and context of people's everyday lives, which is itself produced through social relations. Locale also refers to the physical and cultural landscape of a place, a combination of natural and human-made elements including buildings, infrastructure, and open spaces. Thinking of place and food in terms of locale leads to a focus on how food practices differ, change, and evolve as they take place or move through different physical settings: farms, home kitchens, grocery stores, restaurants, food banks, and so on. Place as locale connects to the concepts of *food landscapes* or *foodscapes*, which refer not just to the locations under which food is grown, produced, distributed, or consumed but also to the conditions under which these happen as well as to the ways in they are seen and experienced by people immersed in them. The concept of foodscape also permits focusing 'on the mutually constitutive relationship among various aspects of a food system, rather than on its separate, quantifiable or mappable attributes' (Miewald and Mccann, 2014: 540). *Foodsheds* refer to places with specific boundaries and physical geographic characteristics in which social and political decisions about food take place (Feagan, 2007). Food deserts can simultaneously be examined as locations where access to nutritious and affordable food is limited, but also as locales where specific socio-economic, cultural, and political processes and practices allow such food deserts to develop.

Place as locale in connection to food plays a major role in contemporary studies that look at the relationship between food and gentrification. Scholars have examined the myriad ways in which food can play a major role in the gentrification of urban neighbourhoods and lead to the displacement of lower-income residents, including people of colour and immigrants (Alkon et al., 2020). *Foodification* describes the transformation of the retail landscape of urban neighbourhoods into food-centred functions and is connected to the taste of gentrification, a notion that captures the unique foodscape aesthetics that attract middle-class and higher-income consumers and visitors to low-income areas that are being transformed, often drawing on notions of cosmopolitanism, sustainability, and localism (Joassart-Marcelli and Bosco, 2020). Food places reflect such notions not only through the food being offered—(cosmopolitan, farm to table, local)—but also through the physical environment, architectural styles, and décor of the food places themselves—industrial or vintage vibes, communal spaces, and open kitchens. These are aesthetic strategies to create places through stories and experiences around food.

Sense of place points to the subjective elements of place and the meanings that people attach to it. It refers to settings that are made meaningful by human activity and to the contexts where people experience a sense of belonging or, on the other hand, feel 'out of place'. Sense of place helps structure the connections between food and identity. Cafes and restaurants are not only settings for the provisioning of food but places where meaningful social interactions and cultural exchanges develop and to which some people might feel spatially attached. Ethnic foods are often linked to their places of origin and to immigrants' efforts to create a taste of home in new places (Ray, 2016). Thus, ethnic restaurants and stores are important places of both nostalgia and belonging. Cooking traditional foods might also inspire a feeling of connection to a distant homeplace, showing there is relationship between food, affect, and belonging that can be recreated in places such as home kitchens (Joassart Marcelli and Bosco, 2018).

Place and food from a relational perspective

Place is an important concept in the interdisciplinary field of food studies, which examines how economic, political, environmental, social, and cultural variables come together through food. Many scholars in food studies examine the connections between food and place from the perspective of place as location. This is prevalent in public health research that examines food behaviours and their impact on human health by focusing on the food environment. A significant body of work suggests that many contemporary urban environments are correlated with what some call an 'obesity pandemic', especially in Western societies. Much of this research sees place as a physical container where one can identify specific patterns of the food environment. Such patterns are used in making assumptions and inferences about food access and health. For example, a neighbourhood is defined by specific geographic boundaries, and places of food production and provisioning can be mapped using addresses or geographic coordinates. Questions of food access can then be approached by measuring households' distances from food stores, using different thresholds of travel time and accessibility depending on the modality of mobility—walking, driving, or using public transportation. The maps produced can be useful to find out what areas of the city lack supermarkets or other types of food stores—food deserts—and the distance that people must travel to access food. Additionally, these data can be correlated with other demographic and economic data, such as race, ethnicity, and household incomes, to further reveal how patterns of food access vary across populations and areas.

This type of research has received criticism because it presents a static view of the food environment that cannot explain how and why these patterns emerge in the first place. Critical urban and health geographers have been at the forefront of the critique (Lever et al., 2022), arguing that these approaches are decontextualised and that they treat different components of the food environment in isolation from each other—such as when the neighbourhood food environment is analysed separately from the home food environment or from the school food environment (Bosco and Joassart-Marcelli, 2018). This compartmentalisation fails to consider how different components of the food environment relate to each other and how they influence people's attitudes and practices around food. They fail to reflect how people experience place in their daily lives, and how place itself is continuously produced by those who inhabit it (Shannon, 2014). Different people have different mobility patterns and food provisioning strategies, and these cannot be homogenised or reduced to considerations of distance. These types of studies also are limited in how they account for the larger structural political, social, and economic factors that shape the connection between places and food. For example, in the United States, suburbanisation and 'white flight', capital disinvestment, and political neglect must be included in any discussion of the problems of food access that

lead to the emergence of food deserts. This view of the food environment also contributes to the stigmatisation of places and people as unhealthy, one of the main criticisms of the obesogenic environment thesis (Guthman, 2013).

To counter these tendencies, scholars draw from critical notions of place that offer a more dynamic and relational perspective of its connections to food, which in turn allows them to ask and answer more complex questions about the relationship between people, place, and food. The inspiration comes from human geographers who reformulated and refined the concept of place as something open, porous, and networked that simultaneously touches down in different locations (Massey, 2005). Places are seen as the products of relations between various kinds of entities including social relations and non-human entities. Thus, even though places are certainly located somewhere, they cannot be reduced to locations. Places do not have essential characteristics, they are not closed or contained, but rather they are always in contact with other places. These relational characterisations ask that we consider places as meaningful locales of human activity where many social networks come together. It is in those locales where people experience their own sense of place through their bodies, emotions, and affects. As constellations of social relations, places bring together different power relations, so that they are also political.

Thinking along these lines about place and food means emphasising the social, political, and relational construction of food. Instead of locations on a map, food-specific sites such as supermarkets, gardens, or restaurants can be seen as parts of economic, social, political, and cultural networks that influence our relationships to food in multiple ways. One can ask: how do places reproduce or contest the unevenness of the food environments in different locations? How can places be transformed into locales of contestation and resistance to certain food practices and food policies (Bosco and Joassart-Marcelli, 2018)? The relational definition of place has also inspired research on local and alternative food networks, critically interrogating the 'local' and the 'community' as it attempts to counter the negative effects of the conventional and globalised food system. The local is something fluid and not easily delineated, and it is not separated from the community but rather is interdependent and often mutually constitutive. However, 'local' places cannot be artificially blocked off from other 'local' places, and the local might have connections to the global despite the negative connotation that global processes sometimes have for local food system scholars. Thus, a relational view of place asks that notions of local resilience, community food security and the re-territorialisation of food systems be critically examined. While there is a need to re-engage with place and community to create a more just food system, there will always be an interconnectedness of places. This recognition is important to avoid place-based food projects that can become anti-democratic and xenophobic because of excessive and exclusionary localisms (Feagan, 2007).

Digital places and food futures

The relational understanding of place also relates to our new digital reality. We are spending much more of our time in digital environments and we are experiencing place digitally while still being located somewhere in the physical world. These digital environments are meaningful places for our daily interactions and a new component in the process of place-making. Digital places are transforming our relationship with food, which is increasingly taking place through online platforms and mobile technologies: what and where we decide to eat, where we shop for food, how we cook, what we understand as healthy food, and even how we fashion our identities around food practices. The present and future of the relations between place and food will continue to be impacted by digitalisation of everyday life.

Digital platforms and technologies around food are shaping cities in new ways. The global COVID-19 pandemic in 2020 accelerated the ongoing digitalisation of food, leading to the appearance of a new food lexicon, the transformation of our relationship with food, and a remaking of urban and other places. 'Ghost kitchens' are created for the purpose of housing food preparation operations for multiple virtual restaurants, from which we order food from tablets and phones using digital menus. 'Dark' grocery stores—grocery stores that close their doors to customers and become fulfilment centres for digital orders to be home delivered—dot urban streetscapes and suburban spaces. These changes and their full impacts are still largely unexplored. There is a real possibility that dark grocery stores could replicate the problem of food deserts in new ways, such as by limiting access to food to those who have good internet access, technology, and the ability to subscribe and pay for food digitally, or even by locating in places where they can reach the best market, which would leave disenfranchised areas uncovered (Shapiro, 2022).

Digital food platforms and food experienced through social media are influencing our mobility and lifestyle, creating new urban imaginaries that draw people and resources to neighbourhoods. The digitalisation of food also creates virtual places that are highly symbolic but that hide the material relations of production in connection to food, in particular work in food systems. Because we no longer interact with waiters, hosts, or others in restaurants and eateries, food labour is hidden behind digital platforms and becoming more invisible—just as cooks and others who work in the kitchen and behind the scenes have generally been hidden. Digitalisation should lead to new questions and investigations on the changing relationships between place and food, as well as to the development of new methodologies that can capture this more complex relationship.

References

Agnew J A (1987) *Place and politics: The geographical mediation of state and society*. London, Routledge.

Alkon A H, Kato Y and Sbicca J (Eds.) (2020) *A recipe for gentrification: Food, power, and resistance in the city*. New York, New York University Press.

Bosco F and Joassart-Marcelli P (2018) Relational space and place and food environments: geographic insights for critical sustainability research. *Journal of Environmental Studies and Sciences* 8, 539–546. https://doi.org/10.1007/s13412-018-0482-9

Feagan R (2007) The place of food: mapping out the 'local' in local food systems. *Progress in Human Geography* 31, 1, 23–42. https://doi.org/10.1177/0309132507073527.

Guthman J (2013) Too much food and too little sidewalk? Problematizing the obesogenic environment thesis. *Environment and Planning A* 45, 1, 142–158. https://doi.org/10.1068/a45130.

FERNANDO BOSCO

Joassart-Marcelli P and Bosco F (2020) The taste of gentrification: difference and exclusion in San Diego's urban food frontier. In Alkon A H, Kato Y and Sbicca J (Eds.) *A recipe for gentrification: Food, power, and resistance in the city.* New York, New York University Press, 31–53.

Joassart-Marcelli P and Bosco F (Eds.) (2018) *Food and place: A critical exploration.* Lanham, MD, Rowman & Littlefield.

Lever J, Blake M, Newton D, and Downing G (2022) Working across boundaries in regional place-based food systems: triggering transformation in a time of crisis. *Cities* 130, 103842. https://doi.org/10.1016/j.cities.2022.103842.

Massey D (2005) *For space.* London, Sage.

Miewald C and Mccann E (2014) Foodscapes and the geographies of poverty: sustenance, strategy, and politics in an urban neighborhood. *Antipode* 46, 2, 537–556. https://doi.org/10.1111/anti.12057.

Neil M A M (2017) Affective migration: using a visceral approach to access emotion and affect of Egyptian migrant women settling in the Region of Waterloo, Ontario, Canada. *Emotion, Space and Society* 25, 37–43. https://doi.org/10.1016/j.emospa.2017.10.005.

Ray K (2016) *The ethnic restauranter.* London, Bloomsbury Academic.

Shannon J (2014) Food deserts: governing obesity in the neoliberal city. *Progress in Human Geography* 38, 2, 248–266. https://doi.org/10.1177/0309132513484378.

Shapiro A (2022) Platform urbanism in a pandemic: dark stores, ghost kitchens, and the logistical-urban frontier. *Journal of Consumer Culture* 23, 1, 168–187. https://doi.org/10.1177/14695405211069983.

Further reading

Joassart-Marcelli P (2021) *The $16 taco: Contested geographies of food, ethnicity, and gentrification.* Seattle, University of Washington Press.

This accessible book explores how food and place are co-produced, focusing on extensive fieldwork and rich ethnographic accounts of food projects in gentrifying neighbourhoods and paying attention to the impacts on minoritised residents and immigrants.

Parham S (2015) *Food and urbanism: The convivial city and a sustainable future.* London, Bloomsbury.

The book explores the connections between place and food in urban spaces, focusing on the impacts of food in urban design and advancing ideas of the way urban futures can consider gastronomic possibilities in the shaping of cities and regions.

FERNANDO BOSCO

94. Planetary boundaries and food

Dieter Gerten

Introduction: Planetary boundaries in the Anthropocene

The current 'Anthropocene' is characterised by multiple, exponentially increasing human pressures on the Earth system. These include the global climate emergency, widespread land cover conversion, resulting dramatic losses of terrestrial and aquatic fauna and flora, excessive freshwater use, and contamination with many different novel substances. These compound impacts are increasingly likely to redirect the Earth system onto a new and dangerous trajectory and into territory unknown to human civilisation. If this development continues, societies' well-being and even survival is at serious risk (Kemp et al. 2022).

Against this backdrop, the scientific framework of "planetary boundaries" aims to represent and quantify nine global processes that together regulate the functioning and stability of the Earth system in a unified and internally consistent manner, namely: climate change, stratospheric ozone depletion, atmospheric aerosol loading, loss of biosphere integrity (biodiversity), land-system change, freshwater change, biogeochemical (nutrient) flows, novel entities, and ocean acidification (Richardson et al. 2023, Rockström et al. 2009, Steffen et al. 2015). To articulate the criticality of their anthropogenic modifications, the framework also defines and quantifies planetary boundaries (and in some cases corresponding subglobal boundaries) for each of these processes. The boundaries are positioned to represent the status during the Holocene period (i.e. the past ~11,700 years after the last Ice Age), thereby distinguishing a Holocene-like "safe operating space" from a domain of increasing danger. Choosing the Holocene as a baseline reflects the fact that this epoch is the only known – and quasi-stable – biophysical and biogeochemical state of the Earth system able to support billions of people. It also reflects the "precautionary principle", suggesting that the planetary boundaries should be maintained so as to avoid gradual or abrupt aggravation of impacts once one or more boundaries are transgressed. Assessments indicate that six out of the nine planetary boundaries are already overstepped, i.e. all of them except aerosol loading, ocean acidification, and ozone depletion after the recent recovery (Richardson et al. 2023 with updates by Persson et al. 2022, Wang-Erlandsson et al. 2022). In view of this worrying status, it is imperative to identify the drivers of this development and to urgently avoid further transgressions in the future by respective measures.

Agriculture as main driver of boundary transgressions

Several studies have found that food production – especially resource-intensive, industrial agriculture in its various forms – is by far the most important driver of planetary boundary transgressions, causing widespread land cover and land use change, nitrogen and phosphorus release into soils and waterbodies, diminution of freshwater resources, and biodiversity loss. Campbell et al. (2017) estimate that the fractional share of agriculture to the current transgression of both the planetary boundaries for land-system change (e.g. loss of pristine forest biome area) and biosphere integrity (loss of genetic and functional biodiversity in terrestrial ecosystems) is about 80%, induced by large-scale conversion of forest to cropland or grazing land. Moreover, they find that agriculture contributes even more than 80% to the transgression of both the boundaries for freshwater change (water consumption and depletion) through crop irrigation and, respectively, biogeochemical flows (nitrogen and phosphorus loads in waterbodies) through fertilisers. Regarding the transgression of the climate change boundary (defined by an atmospheric CO_2 concentration >350 ppm), agriculture-driven land use change currently contributes approximately 25% of the global greenhouse gas emissions (the remainder stemming from other processes such as fossil fuel combustion). These findings are basically in line with the large body of evidence demonstrating that agriculture is a main cause of multiple environmental problems across the planet.

Food production dependence on boundary transgressions

A more comprehensive study based on spatial modelling and data analysis – including explicit representation of the regional patterns of planetary boundary constraints and conditions – demonstrated that no less than 49%

of current global food production depends on planetary boundary transgressions (Gerten et al. 2020). For example, 19% of food production depends on the transgression of the boundaries for biosphere integrity and land-system change, respectively. In other words, this share of food is being produced in regions where forests and biodiversity should have been actively protected according to the planetary boundaries framework's precautionary principle. Another 4% of agricultural production depends on irrigation with water that should not be used (to preserve the respective aquatic ecosystems) according to the freshwater boundary. A further 25% relies on application of nitrogen fertiliser above the allowed (regional) limits. This analysis also shows that different regions are affected differently: excess nitrogen use prevails in parts of Europe, the US, and China; large parts of the tropics are hotspots of biodiversity loss and land-system change; and freshwater overuse happens especially in the subtropics. In certain regions, e.g. in Asia, often three boundaries are transgressed simultaneously (also see Rockström et al. 2023 for synchronous transgression of similarly defined "Earth system boundaries").

Potential of sustainable food systems to maintain planetary boundaries

Further analysis suggests that more sustainable ways of food production and consumption could – at least from the perspective of biophysical potentials – enable the supply of healthy food for up to about 10 billion people while staying within the four relevant planetary boundaries (land-system change, biosphere integrity, freshwater change, biogeochemical flows). The radical measures required for achieving this ambitious goal include (i) reallocation of food production to areas where the planetary boundary constraints would still allow for expansion of cropland, irrigation, or nitrogen application; (ii) significant improvement of water and nutrient use efficiency; (iii) halving of food losses; and (iv) dietary change towards a maximum 25% share of animal-based proteins. All these measures combined would yield a global food supply of 53% above the year 2005 value. For example, more efficient on-farm use of water resources by covering bare soil results in higher crop water uptake and biomass production, and can be complemented by the collection of rainwater for later use in dry spells, ideally involving a switch from sprinkler irrigation to more efficient drip irrigation. Field studies and model simulations have shown that crop production could be doubled or even quadrupled by such measures without requiring more land, water, or fertiliser. In a further example, restricting the share of animal proteins in the diet would shrink the required global agricultural area, and land for pasture or production of animal feed could be freed for cultivation of food that is directly consumable by humans. A similar conclusion – that the health of both the planet (in terms of planetary boundary maintenance) and people (in terms of their diets) can be reconciled – is also reached by other studies working with sophisticated nutrition scenarios (e.g. Springmann et al. 2018).

Implementation challenges and opportunities

It must be emphasised that the above-mentioned measures need to be implemented collectively, as single solutions would not be sufficient to produce enough food for a growing world population within planetary boundaries. Moreover, the effects of anthropogenic climate change – very likely to intensify in the coming decades – may not only directly impact crop growth and production (e.g. via heat mortality) but also indirectly by worsening the status of other planetary boundaries (such as by depletion of streamflow especially during droughts, limiting irrigation potentials). Beneficial direct effects of the higher atmospheric CO_2 concentration on plants may partly counteract these impacts due to increased water use efficiency of plants, but their effectiveness eventually also depends on sufficient nutrient and water availability. The situation is further complicated by the fact that the likely demand for large-scale biomass plantations – extracting additional CO_2 from the atmosphere as a contribution to climate change mitigation or to achieve "negative emissions" – would strongly narrow the scope for sustainable water, land, and nutrient use. These examples illustrate that the planetary boundaries and their underlying Earth system processes strongly interact, and that their maintenance requires synergistic solutions that address all boundaries as a whole (Gerten & Kummu 2021, Chrysafi et al. 2022).

DIETER GERTEN

The actual implementation of these radical transformations affecting different action areas is a grand challenge, as ultimately also envisaged in the United Nations' Sustainable Development Goals. It requires the cooperative participation of policy-makers, companies, and civil society across all sectors, scales, and levels. Meanwhile, the concept of planetary boundaries is increasingly recognised as a powerful framework in political and corporate contexts, being applied to analyse and promote more sustainable food production and consumption modes. This involves, for example, determining the environmental "footprints" of food commodities in life-cycle assessments and translating them to the planetary boundary values, based on which countries and companies can explore options to reduce their multi-faceted global environmental pressures. An example from the European Union of possible harmonisation across scales and policy/business fields is the protection of river environmental flow requirements, which are a component of the freshwater planetary boundary and compliance with which is demanded by the European Water Framework Directive. Analogously, there are opportunities for linking the EU Nitrates Directive to the boundary for biogeochemical flows. Overall, the framework of planetary boundaries can help to support the configuration of globally consistent pathways towards sustainable food systems (e.g. Jones et al. 2023) by explicitly bringing in the perspective of long-term Earth system stability.

References

Campbell B M, Beare D J, Bennett E M and Hall-Spencer J M (2017) Agriculture production as a major driver of the Earth system exceeding planetary boundaries. *Ecology & Society* 22(4), 8. https://doi.org/10.5751/ES-09595-220408.

Chrysafi A, Virkki V, Jalava M, Sandström V, Piipponen J, Porkka M, Lade S J, La Mere K, Wang-Erlandsson L, Scherer L, Andersen L S, Bennett E, Brauman K A, Cooper G S, De Palma A, Döll P, Downing A S, DuBois T C, Fetzer I … and Kummu M (2022) Quantifying Earth system interactions for sustainable food production via expert elicitation. *Nature Sustainability* 5, 830–842. https://doi.org/10.1038/s41893-022-00940-6.

Gerten D and Kummu M (2021) Feeding the world in a narrowing safe operating space. *One Earth* 4, 1193–1196. https://doi.org/10.1016/j.oneear.2021.08.020.

Gerten D, Heck V, Jägermeyr J, Bordirsky B L, Fetzer I, Jalava M, Kummu M, Lucht W, Rockström J, Schaphoff S and Schellnhuber H J (2020) Feeding ten billion people is possible within four terrestrial planetary boundaries. *Nature Sustainability* 3, 200–208. https://doi.org/10.1038/s41893-019-0465-1.

Jones S K, Monjeau A, Perez-Guzman K and Harrison P A (2023) Integrated modeling to achieve global goals: lessons from the Food, Agriculture, Biodiversity, Land-use, and Energy (FABLE) initiative. *Sustainability Science* 18, 323–333. https://doi.org/10.1007/s11625-023-01290-8.

Kemp L, Xu C, Depledge J and Lenton T M (2022) Climate endgame: exploring catastrophic climate change scenarios. *Proceedings of the National Academy of Sciences USA* 119, e2108146119. https://doi.org/10.1073/pnas.2108146119.

Persson L, Almroth B M C, Collins C D, Cornell S, de Wit C A, Diamond M L, Fantke P, Hassellöv M, Macleod M, Ryberg M W, Jørgensen P S, Villarrubia-Gómez P, Wang Z and Hauschild M Z (2022) Outside the safe operating space of the planetary boundary for novel entities. *Environmental Science & Technology* 56, 1510–1521. https://doi.org/10.1021/acs.est.1c04158.

Richardson K, Steffen W, Lucht W, Bendtsen J, Cornell S E, Donges J F, Drüke M, Fetzer I, Bala G, von Bloh W, Feulner G, Fiedler S, Gerten D, Gleeson T, Hofmann M, Huiskamp W, Kummu M, Mohan C, Nogués-Bravo D … and Rockström J (2023) Earth beyond six of nine planetary boundaries. *Science Advances* 9. DOI: 10.1126/sciadv.adh2458

Rockström J, Gupta J, Qin D, Lade S J, Abrams J F, Andersen L S, McKay D I A, Bai X, Bala G, Bunn S E, Ciobanu D, DeClerck F, Ebi K, Gifford L, Gordon C, Hasan S, Kanie N, Lenton T M, Loriani S … and Zhang X (2023) Safe and just Earth system boundaries. *Nature* 619, 102–111. https://doi.org/10.1038/s41586-023-06083-8.

Rockström J, Steffen W, Noone K, Persson Å, Chapin F S III, Lambin E, Lenton T M, Scheffer M, Folke C, Schellnhuber H J, Nykvist B, de Wit C A, Hughes T, van der Leeuw S, Rodhe H, Sörlin S, Snyder P K, Costanza R, Svedin U … and Foley J (2009) Planetary boundaries: exploring the safe operating space for humanity. *Ecology & Society* 14(2), 32. http://www.ecologyandsociety.org/vol14/iss2/art32/.

Springmann M, Clark M, Mason-D'Croz D, Wiebe K, Bodirsky B L, Lassaletta L, de Vries W, Vermeulen S J, Herrero, M, Carlson K M, Jonell M, Troell M, DeClerck F, Gordon L J, Zurayk R, Scarborough P, Rayner M, Loken B, Fanzo J … and Willett W (2018) Options for keeping the food system within environmental limits. *Nature* 562, 519–525. https://doi.org/10.1038/s41586-018-0594-0

Steffen W, Richardson K, Rockström J, Cornell S E, Fetzer I, Bennett E M, Biggs R, Carpenter S R, de Vries W, de Wit C A, Folke C, Gerten D, Heinke J, Mace G M, Persson L M, Ramanathan V, Reyers B and Sörlin S (2015) Planetary boundaries: guiding human development on a changing planet. *Science* 347, 1259855. https://doi.org/10.1126/science.1259855.

Wang-Erlandsson L, Tobian A, van der Ent R, Fetzer I, te Wierik S, Porkka M, Staal A, Jaramillo F, Dahlmann H, Singh C, Greve P, Gerten D, Keys P W, Gleeson T, Cornell S E, Steffen W, Bai X and Rockström J (2022) A planetary boundary for green water. *Nature Reviews Earth & Environment* 3, 380–392. https://doi.org/10.1038/s43017-022-00287-8.

Further reading

Rockström J and Gaffney O (2021) *Breaking Boundaries: The Science of Our Planet.* London, Dorling Kindersley.
This accessible book, addressed to the general public and accompanying a same-titled film, summarises current planetary boundary science and presents a vision of how people can rethink their relationship with planet Earth.

95. Plastics and the food system

JACK PICKERING

Introduction: plastics as ubiquitous

Plastics are ubiquitous throughout food production, distribution, and consumption and are present in food itself as micro-plastics. The term 'plastics' describes an incredibly wide range of generally composite materials that can be formed to perform useful functions successfully, but some parts of these substances are biologically disruptive and environmentally persistent (Liboiron, 2016). Plastic use in the food system further contributes to plastic pollution, but it is often difficult to replace. This entry will therefore address how plastic use in food production contributes to plastic pollution directly, while food packaging occupies a critical mediating position between production and consumption. For this reason, this entry will focus on the problem of disposability and attempts to reconfigure retail systems in response. Ultimately, the harm that plastics cause is diffuse and still uncertain, making their socio-economic revaluation a critical task.

Plastics in food production

Plastic use in food production contributes directly to plastic pollution. Discarded fishing gear is a prime example of this, as it makes up 10% of the overall total marine plastic pollution (Thomas et al, 2019) and is a by-product of inevitable accidents and damage. Micro-plastics are perhaps a more concerning pollutant, since they are invisible and result from chemical and mechanical degradation of plastics in use and as waste. For example, crop covering and mulching in agriculture commonly involves plastic sheeting. In outdoor conditions with lots of direct sunlight, many plastics are more likely to fragment into micro-plastics. Biodegradable and bio-based alternatives are available but connections between the durability and neatness of conventional plastic sheeting and social norms of good farming prevent easy adoption (Dentzman and Goldberger, 2020). Plastics can perform many functions successfully and this explains their ubiquity in agriculture and other sectors; their impact and influence is largely limited to this context, however.

Plastics and food packaging

Unlike the plastics used in agriculture, the development and widespread adoption of plastics for use in food packaging is an integral part of the historical trajectory of food systems over the last 50–100 years (Parsons, 2022). Many of the technical and logistical achievements of modern, industrialised food systems, particularly for fresh food, would be more difficult or impossible without plastic packaging. Packaging occupies a critical role mediating relations between production and consumption in food systems because of the especially wide range of functions it performs. In addition to logistical functions and the contested role it plays in preventing food waste, plastic packaging provides important practical support for retailers and supply chain logistics (Sattlegger, 2021), and it has specific affordances for marketing that other materials do not share (Evans et al., 2020). The economic mediation work that it performs is so pervasive that plastic is seen as enabling key aspects of food retail. While waste management systems are able to process and recycle some plastics, complex social, technical, and economic barriers hinder recovery efforts, and the sheer volume and variety of plastics in production contribute to this difficulty. Systems of returnable and refillable packaging are of particular interest to those aiming to reduce plastic pollution as they 'detach' packaging and retail from plastics where possible (Hawkins, 2018; 2021).

Understanding and responding to the impacts of plastic pollution from the food system

Awareness of the growing impacts of marine plastic pollution on wildlife has been rising, increasing general public concern worldwide. This and the ever-increasing quantity of consumer waste has stimulated the growth of the zero-waste lifestyle movement on social media (Lu, 2023) and associated package-free retail (Fuentes et al., 2019), which has been trialled in major supermarkets in the UK and is already in place for some retailers in Australia, the US, and France. There are also numerous legislative efforts from governments around the world to ban or limit the use of single-use plastics in food retail (coffee cups, for example) or to enforce fully recyclable packaging designs or reusable packaging systems.

Alongside their ubiquity, the other part of the problem with tackling plastic pollution relates to the durability of plastics. Measuring the harm from micro-plastics and associated substances presents a challenge because their durability means they are now so pervasive that it is impossible to find unaffected control groups (Liboiron, 2016). This touches on the socio-economic paradox underlying the disposability of plastic packaging. Plastics are industrially produced, durable materials with remarkable qualities, which are often disposed of immediately after use. Removing plastics from the environment seems impossible, but while removing them from disposable packaging and agricultural production appears difficult, it also challenges fundamental connections between food production and consumption.

References

Dentzman, K., & Goldberger, J. R. (2020). Plastic scraps: biodegradable mulch films and the aesthetics of 'good farming' in US specialty crop production. *Agriculture and Human Values*, *37*(1), 83–96. https://doi.org/10.1007/s10460-019-09970-x

Evans, D. M., Parsons, R., Jackson, P., Greenwood, S., & Ryan, A. (2020). Understanding plastic packaging : The co-evolution of materials and society. *Global Environmental Change*, *65*(March), 102166. https://doi.org/10.1016/j.gloenvcha.2020.102166

Fuentes, C., Enarsson, P., & Kristoffersson, L. (2019). Unpacking package free shopping: Alternative retailing and the reinvention of the practice of shopping. *Journal of Retailing and Consumer Services*, *50*, 258–265. https://doi.org/10.1016/j.jretconser.2019.05.016

Hawkins, G. (2018). The skin of commerce: Governing through plastic food packaging. *Journal of Cultural Economy*, *11*(5), 386–403. https://doi.org/10.1080/17530350.2018.1463864

Hawkins, G. (2021). Detaching from plastic packaging: Reconfiguring material responsibilities. *Consumption Markets and Culture*, *24*(4), 405–418. https://doi.org/10.1080/10253866.2020.1803069

Liboiron, M. (2016). Redefining pollution and action: The matter of plastics. *Journal of Material Culture*, *21*(1), 87–110. https://doi.org/10.1177/1359183515622966

Lu, D. (2023). Performing zero waste: lifestyle movement, consumer culture, and promotion strategies of social media influencers. *Environmental Sociology*, *10*(1), 12–29. https://doi.org/10.1080/23251042.2023.2267829

Parsons, R. (2022). The role of plastic packaging in transforming food retailing. *British Food Journal*, *124*(4), 1285–1300. https://doi.org/10.1108/BFJ-04-2021-0407

Sattlegger, L. (2021). Making food manageable: Packaging as a code of practice for work practices at the supermarket. *Journal of Contemporary Ethnography*, *50*(3), 341–367. https://doi.org/10.1177/0891241620977635

Thomas, K., Dorey, C., & Obaidullah, F. (2019). Ghost gear: The abandoned fishing nets haunting our oceans [pdf]. Greenpeace Germany. Available at: https://www.greenpeace.org/static/planet4-international-stateless/2019/11/8f290a4f-ghostgearfishingreport2019_greenpeace.pdf

Further reading

Nielsen, T. D., Hasselbalch, J., Holmberg, K., & Stripple, J. (2020). Politics and the plastic crisis: A review throughout the plastic life cycle. *Wiley Interdisciplinary Reviews: Energy and Environment*, *9*(1). https://doi.org/10.1002/wene.360
This review provides a broad overview of recent research on the politics of plastics.

96. Poverty and food

Megan K. Blake

Introduction: poverty and food

Ending hunger, food insecurity and all forms of malnutrition is a United Nations Sustainable Development Goal (SDG) to be achieved by 2030. Approximately 38% (3.1 billion people) of the world's population is estimated to struggle to get the food they need to live a healthy life (FAO et al., 2022). Food security is defined as the ability, now and in the future, to access, afford and utilise food of a sufficient quantity that is safe, healthy and culturally appropriate. It is widely recognised that poverty strongly predicts vulnerability to food insecurity.

Poverty itself is a somewhat contested term. Some understand it as being defined in absolute terms based on a single monetary dimension such as income level (heretofore referred to as the economic model of poverty). Others understand it as a relative phenomenon linked to the ability to achieve well-being and health, although an individual may or may not exercise that ability in action (Nussbaum, 2011). This later view of poverty is known as the capabilities approach. According to Amartya Sen, who first developed the approach, addressing poverty must consider people's diverse needs and characteristics and their inability to achieve key 'beings and doings' that are basic to human life, such as feeding oneself and one's family (Sen, 1999).

How poverty is conceptualised has implications for understanding its effects individually and cumulatively and addressing poverty and its effects. The economic model sees the effects of poverty as it relates to food security as the inability to afford food and measures it as going without. In this framing, the solution is to give people food or money to purchase food. Because it is multi-dimensional, the capabilities approach focuses on what people can or cannot do and gives room for understanding the implications of those constraints on the ability to do as the effects of poverty (Conconi and Viollaz, 2018). Concerning food, this is calculated according to the ability to be food secure, which might include the ability to purchase healthy food, but also has other possibilities, such as the ability to grow food, cook it or carry it home from where it is obtained. The approach also leaves room to consider how identity dimensions such as race, class, ethnicity, disability and gender are institutionally structured to create systematic inequalities for specific groups and intersectional disadvantages for individuals. These different possibilities work together to determine the capacity of someone to be nourished or well fed. This approach also gives room to understand how a person's circumstances (e.g., being in good mental and physical health), their geographical contexts (local and national) and their orientations toward certain doings shape their capabilities. Addressing food security within this more complex and multi-dimensional understanding means enhancing people's access to the necessary tools to avoid food insecurity.

The United Nations Development Programme adopts the capabilities approach to addressing poverty, and capabilities directly inform how food security is conceptualised. How poverty and food security is predominantly understood and measured in affluent nations follows the economic model. This is evidenced by the questions used in the USDA food security module that emphasise the affordability of food and do not consider other aspects that also influence the ability to be food secure. There is also a prevailing myth that countries commonly conceived of as high income (e.g., the United States and Canada, most European countries, Australia and New Zealand) are food secure. However, among these nations, there is significant variation. For example, in England, an economically wealthy nation, one in five adults was classified as having low or very low food security in 2022 (Armstrong et al., 2023). In Sweden, a country typically understood as having high levels of food security, evidence suggests food insecurity is still relatively low but increasing (Rost and Lundalv, 2021). Given that there is food insecurity in wealthy countries, research and interventions need to be implemented in these countries as well as the countries that have traditionally been the focus.

Food poverty or the capability to be food secure

While we may intuitively understand poverty, it is often not a term people use to describe themselves. People can apply it to others whose life experience is worse than their own: that person living on the street, the child who comes to school in old clothes and is chronically hungry, the people living in a shelter rather than a home, someone somewhere else.

This section outlines the economic model that casts food insecurity as food poverty and highlights some of the limitations of this approach. The section then turns to a discussion of the capability approach as applied to food security and sketches out the need for a systems perspective that considers the different forms of resources or tools needed to achieve food security beyond just the finances. The section argues that interventions must focus on multiple scales, not just individuals or households, to address food security.

Food Poverty

Food poverty is a sub-category within the economic understanding of poverty. In this approach, poverty is the lack of sufficient income necessary to purchase a bundle of goods to guarantee survival, and food poverty is the lack of income to purchase enough food. Rowntree (2000 [1902]) defined poverty as mere physical existence in what is arguably the subject's first scientific exploration. When income is inadequate to meet all needs, the only recourse is to cut back on food. This, he argued, sacrifices physical health because food intake is insufficient. *Food poverty* is frequently used by researchers, policymakers, the press and charities in economically developed nations.

The economic model reduces food to calories, whereby food insecurity equates to insufficient calories to maintain energy (Burchi and De Muro, 2012). Rowntree's study was undertaken in an era before highly processed foods, characterised by high calories and low nutrients, were available at prices often considerably lower than those that help maintain a healthy life. The transition to a food system that has introduced these high-calorie, low-nutrient foods means that the physical manifestation of undernourishment is no longer reducible to being underweight. The food–poverty nexus is manifested as an increased risk of diet-related health outcomes that disproportionately affect those who struggle financially. These health inequalities, in turn, deepen poverty. They do so by undermining the physical energy needed to maintain or improve one's circumstances, extending the duration and magnitude of the harm caused by poor health and increasing the financial burden that living with poor health extracts (Dowler, 1998).

Acknowledging the importance of sufficient nutrients as a critical aspect of the food–poverty nexus is an area of investigation by nutrition, medicine and public health scholars. However, it sits awkwardly in the economic model. This approach reduces food to a financial exchange. Focusing on the ability to make a transaction (e.g., buy food) in each moment does not consider the cumulative effects that transactions can have (e.g., purchase of low-nutrient food leading to poor health). When people purchase low-quality food, the public health response assumes they are making poor choices because they do not understand what healthy food is or its importance. However, within economic rationality, people purchase low-nutrient foods. They provide better value for money than high-nutrient foods because they are filling, taste good and are less likely to be wasted (Blake, 2019).

Another way that the economic model positions itself awkwardly is the underlying presumption that the economic market is the ideal location to source food. Not only does this approach discount the other ways that people access food, but it promotes a solution to engage with the same market that contrived a food system dominated by cheap, unhealthy food. Nothing in the economic model directly challenges the contributing role that market actors who commercially supply food play in producing poor nutritional outcomes and lack of food access for people in places with a concentration of poverty. Indeed, it is possible that providing a cash transfer so that people can purchase food may result in deepening health inequalities as there is little incentive to re-introduce healthy foods into these localities. There is little evidence that providing cash increases diet diversity.

Changing what people understand to be food, shifting diets and increasing diet diversity are critical for addressing the climate emergency and improving health. Because of its transactional focus, the economic model does not acknowledge the issues presented by entrenched food cultures among people experiencing poverty. In wealthy countries, where highly commercial food systems have long operated, these food cultures are characterised by narrow diets and low uptake of fruits and vegetables (Dowler and Turner, 2001). Nor does it halt the transition from more traditional diets toward high environmental impact diets that are also highly processed and occurring in countries considered less economically developed, such as Uganda (Auma et al., 2019). These transitions are caused by introducing convenient, low-cost, shelf-stable, low-nutrient foods combined with a positive lifestyle narrative that makes these foods attractive.

Finally, the economic model takes the household and what happens with food within it as a black box. It assumes that food allocation within households is equal. However, evidence shows that parents feed children first, and mothers are likelier to skip meals to ensure other family members are fed (Dowler and Turner, 2001). There is also no acknowledgement that other demands, values and emotions may influence what and how much is eaten. For example, poor mental health makes planning difficult, poor physical health makes it difficult to stand at a cooker, addictions divert resources and living alone can lead to a lack of motivation to cook.

The capability to be food secure

In *Hunger and Public Action*, Dreze and Sen set out the capabilities approach and its links to hunger when arguing a shift from instrumental control over commodities toward a focus on human capabilities. They argued that means, rather than ends, are important, as ends operate in the immediate timeframe, whereas means allow for addressing needs now and in the future. Thus, for them, "[a] more reasoned goal would be to make it possible to have the capability to avoid undernourishment and escape the deprivations associated with hunger" (1989: 13). In doing so, the approach acknowledges all four original pillars of food security identified by the UN as well as the two new pillars of sustainability and agency (HLPE, 2020).

The four original food security pillars include access, availability, utilisation and stability. While a narrow conceptualisation of access as affordability is acknowledged in the economic model, the other aspects are not. In the capabilities framing, access also comprises other means, such as the absence of legal or religious barriers or the presence of social networks through which food is given. Availability is the presence of food in the place where people are. If there is no food close enough to where people are, it will not be available regardless of cost. Utilisation, a vital component of the capabilities approach, involves knowing how and being able to process, store and cook food safely. It also includes knowing if certain things are edible or will cause personal harm; for example, they will not be poisonous, cause an allergic reaction or induce an otherwise adverse reaction. Utilisation also includes access to complementary inputs, for example, cooking equipment, fuel or electricity, sanitation and water. Stability means having all these all of the time and is what offers security. This means having national and local-scale policies and infrastructures in place to ensure food is produced or imported to meet population needs and provide people with opportunities to acquire the resources needed to access food.

Resources in this context extend beyond money that can be exchanged for food to include other elements that enhance the capability of someone to be able to achieve food security. We can think of money as a communicative resource that enables smooth exchange between buyer and seller. Money in the household context must be exchanged for its use value to be realised and then replenished. Social capital, although potentially less efficient than money, is also a communicative resource that requires replenishment. A second form of resource, assets, contribute their utility not by being exchanged but by being used. Assets are both intangible and tangible. Intangible assets include but are not limited to health, knowledge, motivation, inventiveness and know-how. Tangible assets include things such as land or equipment, including cooking equipment. Selling one's cooking utensils may enable food to be purchased now, but the problem of how to cook food today and tomorrow arises instead and undermines security. There are also place-based resources that enable food security and that support both communicative resources and assets. Local resources that enable the replenishment of communicative resources include a local labour market that provides good jobs that pay sufficient wages for the time spent working and is open to all. Linked to this is childcare that supports people to take advantage of that labour market while protecting their children. Community spaces and activities enable the development of social networks, as do opportunities to participate in social life. Those that enhance assets include, for example, a foodscape that provides the diversity of food needed to live a healthy life and does so without bias and with few limitations, a health and welfare system that protects people when they need support, an education system that enhances people's knowledge and know-how, and safe outdoor spaces that facilitate good health.

The UN argues that all the pillars must be present for food security to be achieved and maintained. Vulnerability to food insecurity arises when communicative resources are not replenished and assets and local resources are not maintained. Sen clearly states that different people have different abilities to be food secure based on their unique circumstances, the resources they control, and their contexts. Place plays a central role in food security capability. Physical, social, legal, political and economic processes determine what is in a place and how resources are available to people to access, make decisions about and utilise food to maintain health and well-being. Geographical concentrations of people with few resources lead to the creation of unhealthy or barren foodscapes. An inability to socialise, linked to the inability to share food, leads to isolation. This isolation, in turn, increases social divisions and fear of crime. At the same time, anti-social behaviour that arises from feelings of anger that result from hunger and disadvantage reinforces this fear, leading ultimately to community breakdown. Thus, to increase the capability to be food secure, both people and places must be developed so that they can act in ways that ensure their food security.

Food and poverty futures

As the previous section argued, poverty and its interlinked food security capability is complex, and it is not sufficient to focus only on access to food in the immediate term. Basic capabilities such as achieving or maintaining good health, being educated and having the opportunity to participate in household decisions and community life are also needed (Burchi and De Muro, 2012). In short, we must develop human capability, including in high-income nations. This suggests several future challenges and needs that shape how we understand and act on this relationship going forward.

To know where to provide support, better data that captures these capabilities is needed. As mentioned above, many wealthy countries collect food security data based on affordability. While this data is only a partial picture of food security, it is made more partial by the lack of a fine enough geographical scale and small sample sizes. Local-scale data linked to administrative units provides insights that can inform policy and interventions that repair the localities within which struggling people live.

We know that different approaches to addressing poverty and food insecurity vary in their effects; for example, considerable stigma is associated with charity food parcels. People who use low-cost food clubs, food hubs or so-called social supermarkets that are place-based report greater connectivity with their communities, increased diet diversity and increased uptake of fruits and vegetables. Provider evaluations of voucher schemes for fruits and vegetables report dietary improvement and increased diversity. Children's school meals and breakfast clubs are linked to children's readiness and ability to learn, which are key to overcoming deprivation and poverty. There is a need to understand what other interventions would support and be acceptable for people who struggle to achieve food security. There is also little systematic research examining how different interventions enhance access to the resources needed to achieve food security. There is a lack of research that systematically compares outcomes from other interventions. This research would support those seeking to improve population health and well-being and increase food security to make informed decisions regarding services to introduce and support.

To meet the SDGs, household capabilities and the contexts that help shape those capabilities must be addressed. A considerable body of research and innovation has focused on countries where food insecurity is recognised. Research and activity are also needed that consider how existing learning and innovation could be adapted for economically wealthy countries.

References

Armstrong B, King L, Clifford R, Jitlai M, Jarchlo A I, Meers K, Parnell C, and Menasah D (2023) Food and You 2: Wave 5. [Available Online: https://www.food.gov.uk/research/food-and-you-2/food-and-you-2-wave-5] Food Standards Agency (Date Accessed 12 July 2023).

Auma C, Pradeilles R, Blake M, and Holdsworth M (2019) What can dietary patterns tell us about the nutrition transition and environmental sustainability of diets in Uganda, *Nutrients* 11(2), 3422. https://doi.org/10.3390/nu11020342.

Blake M K (2019) More than just food: food insecurity and resilient place making through community self-organising, *Sustainability* 11(10), 2942. https://doi.org/10.3390/su11102942.

Burchi F and De Muro P (2012) A human development and capability approach to food security: conceptual framework and informational basis. [Available Online: https://www.undp.org/sites/g/files/zskgke326/files/migration/africa/Capability-Approach-Food-Security.pdf] UNDP (Date Accessed 14 June 2023).

Conconi A and Viollaz M (2018) Poverty, inequality and development: a discussion from the capability approach's framework. In BBVA OpenMind (eds) *The age of perplexity: Rethinking the world we knew.* [Available Online: https://www.bbvaopenmind.com/en/articles/poverty-inequality-and-development-a-discussion-from-the-capability-approach-s-framework/] Penguin House Group Editorial (Date Accessed 14 June 2023).

Dowler E (1998) Food poverty and food policy, *IDS Bulletin* 29(1), 58–65.

Dowler E and Turner S (2001) *Poverty bites: food health and poor families.* London, Child Poverty Action Group.

Dreze J and Sen A (1989) *Hunger and public action.* Oxford, Oxford University Press.

FAO, IFAD, UNICEF, WFP and WHO (2022) *The state of food security and nutrition in the world 2022* [Available Online: https://www.fao.org/documents/card/en/c/cc0639en] Rome, FAO (Date Accessed 12 July 2023).

HLPE (2020) *Food security and nutrition: building a global narrative towards 2030* [Available Online: https://www.fao.org/3/ca9731en/ca9731en.pdf] Rome, the High Level Panel of Experts on Food Security and Nutrition of the Committee on World Food Security (Date Accessed 29 August 2023).

Nussbaum M (2011) *Creating capabilities: the human development approach.* Cambridge and London, Harvard University Press.

Rost S and Lundalv J (2021) A systematic review of the literature regarding food insecurity in Sweden, *Analysis of Social Issues and Public Policy* 201, 1020–1032. https://doi.org/10.1111/asap.12263.

Rowntree B S (2000) *Poverty: a study of town life*, Centennial Edition (Reprinted edition). Bristol, Policy Press.

Sen A (1999). *Commodities and Capabilities.* Oxford, Oxford Univerisity Press.

Further reading

Conconi A and Viollaz M (2018) Poverty, inequality and development: a discussion from the capability approach's framework. In BBVA OpenMind (eds) *The age of perplexity: Rethinking the world we knew* [Available Online: https://www.bbvaopenmind.com/en/articles/poverty-inequality-and-development-a-discussion-from-the-capability-approach-s-framework/] Penguin House Group Editorial (Date Accessed 14 June 2023).

Provides a plain English description of the capabilities approach and how it links to different dimensions of well-being.

Hick R (2011) The capability approach: insights for a new poverty focus, *Journal of Social Policy* 41(2), 291–308. doi:10.1017/S0047279411000845.

This summary article explains the problems associated with different conceptions of poverty and how the capabilities approach can help overcome these.

MEGAN K. BLAKE

97. Prisons and food

WILL McKEITHEN

Introduction: food, eating, and carceral power

Food is central to any institution whose social function is to discipline, punish, or warehouse human beings. This includes criminal-legal institutions like prisons, jails, and juvenile detention centres; immigration jails; and congregate care settings like psychiatric hospitals and nursing homes. For these carceral institutions, what, where, when, and how people eat pose serious logistical, political economic, sociocultural, health, legal, and philosophical questions. While prisons and food have historically been understood in isolation, mass incarceration – for example more than 1.9 million people, mostly Black, Brown, and poor, are incarcerated in the United States on any given day – is forcing new conversations and political movements.

The politics of food and eating behind bars

Prison food from the modern penitentiary to mass incarceration

The modern penitentiary emerged in late-eighteenth-century Western Europe. Reformers hoped to "rehabilitate" individuals through social isolation and hard labour (Davis, 2003). As the Industrial Revolution created new crises and states created new crimes, prison populations ballooned. The typical British or American prison meal consisted of bread served alongside barley, potatoes, beer, or nothing (Camplin, 2016).

In the late-nineteenth century, three organising principles emerged that still define prison food today. First, administrators emphasised a standardised, ration-based diet. Second, prison reformers saw diet as central to balancing rehabilitation and punishment in a capitalist society. Rations were designed to keep prisoners "strong enough to compete for honest work" without appearing to coddle convicts (Carpenter, 2006: 1). Third, the rise of nutrition science recast prison food within a managerial discourse of intangible nutrients and professional control. Indeed, British nutritionists developed their earliest theories in prisons, which they saw as the ideal natural experiment.

Prison diets remained largely unchanged for much of the twentieth century. Beginning in the 1970s, however, neoliberal policies of organised disinvestment, mass criminalisation, and budget austerity created new crises (Aviram, 2015). Prisons became increasingly "overcrowded, underfunded, and offering fewer and poorer quality services" (Gibson-Light, 2018: 203). This includes prison food that is lower quality, cheaper, malnutritious, and served in smaller portions at fewer meals (Smoyer and Lopes 2017).

Food and carceral control

Prison food serves as a tool of discipline and punishment. For example, many US prisons still serve nutraloaf – a bland mush of vegetables, beans, oatmeal, and oil – to people in solitary confinement (Zoukis, 2016). Despite dozens of lawsuits by incarcerated people, US courts have ruled nutraloaf constitutional and said "the Eighth Amendment requires only that prisoners receive food that is adequate to maintain health" (LeMaire v. Maass, 1992).

Prisons also use food to punish in everyday ways. Exposés abound describing prison food that is paltry, unthawed, maggoty, bland, and repetitive. Administrators control not only people's diets but also meal times, frequency, portions, and serving methods. For example, during the 2020 COVID-19 pandemic, many prisons delivered pre-packaged meals to people's cells. This kept incarcerated people isolated, but also increased administrative control and cut costs. Many prisons have continued this practice even while ending other pandemic-era policies. The loss of bodily autonomy over eating, combined with poor quality food, reinforces incarcerated people's sociopolitical status as criminals.

Prison food and health

Prison food has numerous impacts on incarcerated people's health (Herbert et al., 2012). US prisons are not subject to food safety law or health inspection. People in US prisons are six times more likely to suffer an outbreak-related foodborne illness compared with non-incarcerated people (Marlow et al., 2017). Poor nutrition also increases incarcerated people's risk of diabetes and heart disease. Poor nutrition especially burdens incarcerated people who are pregnant, older, disabled, non-white, poor, and women – groups already exposed to unhealthy foodscapes outside prison.

The prison-food-industrial complex

Angela Davis defines the prison-industrial complex (PIC) as an "array of relationships linking corporations, government, correctional communities, and media" that reproduces mass incarceration (2003, 84–85). Agri-food corporations stock prison kitchens, commissaries, vending machines, and mail-order food packages. An entire industry of vendors, expos, and consultants exists to help wardens feed incarcerated people, cut costs, and avoid lawsuits.

More than half of US prisons host some animal, food, or plant production (Chennault and Sbicca, 2022). The vast majority of prison food, however, is produced off-site. Half of US prisons have outsourced food production to corporations like Aramark (Neate, 2016). In the other half, incarcerated people are paid cents by the hour to manufacture and quick-freeze meals, which are then shipped, reheated, and served across the prison system. As a result, incarcerated people play an increasingly marginal and deskilled role in food production.

Prison foodways and resistance

Incarcerated people have developed a cornucopia of practices for acquiring, preparing, distributing, and eating food. Prisoners have fought for religious meals (e.g., iftar during Ramadan) and culturally significant foods (e.g., frybread for many Indigenous people). Those with resources may supplement the mainline diet with snacks or foodstuffs purchased at exorbitant rates from the prison commissary, while those without may forage from prison kitchens or trade with fellow prisoners. Prisoner cookbooks document their culinary ingenuity with recipes like "Donald D's Jailhouse Pizza" (Marek, 2022). These foodways shape people's sociocultural relations along and across lines of gender, race, ethnicity, religion, disability, class, indigeneity, and nationality.

Incarcerated people also use food practices to "resist institutional efforts to deny their humanity" (Smoyer, 2016: 205). In the US and Canada alone, people in prisons, juvenile detention centres ("juvies"), military jails, and immigration detention centres undertake dozens of hunger strikes every year (Perilous Chronicle, n.d.). For incarcerated people, refusing to eat represents a rare avenue to assert bodily autonomy (Shah, 2018). Better food is also a perennial demand in prison insurrections.

Future research: expansive and abolitionist agendas

The intersections of carceral power and food are ripe for further study. First, agri-food scholars could examine carceral food relations beyond the Anglophone minority world, while also tracing transnational (dis)continuities between, for example, the climate emergency, farmer displacement, and migrant policing. Second, agri-food scholars could consider carceral food relations across the "carceral continuum" (Foucault, 1995): not just prisons, but also schools, military bases, Indian reservations, borders, ghettos, and food deserts. Finally, scholars, practitioners, and activists could explore and work to create "carceral-free food systems" (Reese and Sbicca, 2022). For example, how have the twinned structures of racism and capitalism shaped both agriculture and mass incarceration? How might prison food reforms also reinforce carceral domination (see McKeithen, 2022)? And how can food justice movements collaborate with fights for PIC abolition? This research agenda is both theoretical and practical and is critical for creating more just systems to protect, heal, and feed one another.

References

Aviram H (2015) *Cheap on Crime*. Oakland, CA: University of California Press.

Camplin E (2016) *Prison Food in America*. Lanham, MD: Rowman & Littlefield.

Carpenter K J (2006) Nutritional Studies in Victorian Prisons. *The Journal of Nutrition* 136(1), 1–8.

Chennault C and Sbicca J (2022) Prison Agriculture in the United States: Racial Capitalism and the Disciplinary Matrix of Exploitation and Rehabilitation. *Agriculture and Human Values* 40(1), 175–191.

Davis A (2003) *Are Prisons Obsolete?* New York: Seven Stories Press.

Foucault M (1995) *Discipline & Punish*. New York: Random House.

Gibson-Light M (2018) Ramen Politics. *Qualitative Sociology* 41(2), 199–220.

WILL MCKEITHEN

Herbert K, Plugge E, Foster C, and Doll H (2012) Prevalence of Risk Factors for Non-Communicable Diseases in Prison Populations Worldwide. *The Lancet* 379(9830), 1975–1982.

Marek E U (2022) Recipes for Resistance and Abolition. *Food and Foodways* 30(1–2), 82–102.

Marlow M A, Luna-Gierke R E, Griffin P M, and Vieira A R (2017) Foodborne Disease Outbreaks in Correctional : InstitutionsUnited States, 1998–2014. *American Journal of Public Health* 107(7), 1150–1156.

McKeithen W (2022) Carceral Nutrition. *Food and Foodways* 30(1–2), 58–81.

Neate R (2016) Prison Food Politics. *The Guardian*, September 30.

Perilous Chronicle (n.d.) A Chronicle of Prisoner Unrest Across the US and Canada. www.perilouschronicle.com.

Reese A M and Sbicca J (2022) Food and Carcerality. *Food and Foodways* 30(1–2), 1–15.

Shah N (2018) Feeding Hunger-Striking Prisoners. In Happe K E, Johnson J, and Levina M (eds) *Biocitizenship*. New York: NYU Press, 178–203.

Smoyer A B (2016) Making Fatty Girl Cakes. *The Prison Journal* 96(2), 191–209.

Smoyer A B and Lopes G (2017) Hungry on the Inside. *Punishment & Society* 19(2), 240–55.

Zoukis C (2016) Use of Nutraloaf on the Decline in U.S. Prisons. *Prison Legal News*, March 31.

Further reading

Camplin E (2016) *Prison Food in America.* Lanham, MD: Rowman & Littlefield.
While this accessible and short read lacks a critical lens, it nonetheless provides newcomers an introduction to the key issues of prison food, including its history, the role of for-profit businesses, sample menus, and incarcerated people's practices of resistance.

Reese A M and Sbicca J (2022) Food and Carcerality. *Food and Foodways* 30(1–2), 1–15.
This essay introduces a wider special issue that takes a critical approach to questions of food and eating, carceral power, and the abolition of the PIC and racial capitalism more broadly. This collection aims to bring together agri-food studies, critical prison studies, and abolitionist scholars and develop a shared conceptual language and political horizon.

Chatterjee D and Chatterjee S C (2017) Food in Captivity: Experiences of Women in Indian Prisons. *The Prison Journal* 98(1), 40–59.
Drawing on interviews with women in three Indian prisons, the author analyses the state's use of prison food as a tool of punishment, identity formation, and resistance.

WILL MCKEITHEN

98. Public food procurement

Kevin Morgan

Introduction

Public procurement is the mechanism through which governments and public sector bodies purchase goods, services and works and it represents a highly significant part of every national economy. The worldwide value of the public procurement market is estimated to be as much as $13 trillion, over $10 trillion of which (77% of the total) is spent by just 16 countries (OCP, 2020).

Public food procurement (PFP) may not be the biggest category in financial terms, but its social significance is so much greater than its monetary value would suggest. This is due to the unique status of food. Since we ingest it, food is vital to human health and wellbeing in a way that other commodities are not and herein lies its unique status. Another notable feature of PFP is its beneficiaries. Although pupils, patients, pensioners and prisoners are very different people, and their institutional settings are also radically different, they have one thing in common: they are all vulnerable people whose wellbeing depends on a nutritious diet (Morgan and Morley, 2014).

The public procurement process is embedded in a highly intricate regulatory landscape which has been designed to ensure integrity and accountability. This means that procurement officers are legally obliged to respect the principles of non-discrimination, equal treatment and transparency when they are awarding public contracts to ensure that the process is open and fair to all bidders. This obligation applies to all EU countries and to all countries that are signatories to the World Trade Organization's Agreement on Government Procurement (WTO, 2012).

However, the purpose of procurement is undergoing a sea change. Over the past decade in particular, the procurement process has been caught between two radically different regulatory philosophies. The dominant philosophy since the 1980s has been *neoliberalism*, which seeks to minimise the role of the state and maximise the scope of the market, subjecting the public sector to competition to reduce costs. More recently an alternative philosophy has emerged around *sustainability*, one that is closely associated with the United Nations' (UN) Sustainable Development Goals, and this champions a more holistic conception of development. The tension between these two regulatory philosophies has enormous significance for the role of PFP because it has considerable potential to influence both food consumption and food production patterns and deliver multiple social, economic, environmental, and nutritional and health benefits for a multiplicity of beneficiaries, including food producers, food consumers and the wider community (FAO, 2021; WHO, 2022).

Current issues: sustainable public food procurement

Tapping the multifunctional potential of the food system – especially its capacity to promote social justice, public health and ecological integrity, the quintessential values of sustainability – is arguably the central issue facing the global food policy community and therein the governance of public food provisioning. If *sustainability* in the capacious sense is the central issue facing PFP for the foreseeable future, then the question becomes: what needs to be done to realise the vision of a sustainable foodscape?

At least five critical issues need to be addressed as a matter of urgency by those responsible for PFP if we are to see a systemic transition to a more sustainable foodscape.

The first issue is to render visible the *real costs and benefits* of food because many of the costs of food-related harms are externalised (i.e. not reflected in market prices) and PFP has a major role to play in exposing the true cost of food. A report to the 2021 UN Food System Summit documented the scale of the problem and proposed a solution. Externalities and other market failures generate a host of unintended consequences for present and future generations by, among other things, precipitating premature death and other diet-related diseases, destroying nature and perpetuating social injustices such as low pay for workers. To establish the real costs of food, the report recommended the use of *true cost accounting*, a policy tool to measure the costs of externalities (Hendriks et al., 2021).

The quest to calculate 'true cost' in PFP requires a more robust and *enabling regulatory philosophy*, one that ensures that low price can no longer masquerade as best value, as it frequently did in the heyday of neoliberal regulation. Therefore, the second critical issue is to ensure that the multidimensional values of sustainability are embedded in all regulations, but especially in PFP regulations given the social significance to consumers of public food provisioning (FAO, 2021).

Another critical issue concerns atrophied *public sector capacity*. One of the most debilitating effects of forty years of neoliberalism has been to denude governments and public sector bodies of the capacity and capability to fashion sustainable foodscapes through the medium of their PFP policies. The damage wrought by neoliberalism was most evident in the degradation of the school meals service in the UK, where its effects included: the imposition of a low-cost contracting culture among buyers and suppliers; a reliance on ultra-processed foods; the de-skilling of the (largely female) catering staff; and, most egregiously of all, the abolition of nutritional standards for children's food. PFP officers have had to wean themselves off a low-cost contracting culture, in which value for money was framed in the desiccated terms of low price, and to learn to design public tenders which allow contracts to be weighted towards quality considerations such as the social and environmental impact of school food (Morgan and Sonnino, 2008).

Spatial scale is a fourth critical issue. Good practice PFP policy has been confined to a minority of local municipalities and for various reasons – largely concerning political will and institutional capacity – it has not diffused beyond the locality, leaving the mainstream food system intact. The transition to a more sustainable foodscape requires localities to work in concert to aggregate their demand-side powers of purchase to re-shape the supply side. In the USA, for example, six of the country's largest urban school districts joined forces to create a purchasing collaboration that will buy only chickens that are free of antibiotics. The agreement creates a larger national market for antibiotic-free chicken and provides participating schools with more bargaining power (Freudenberg, 2016).

The significance of spatial scale is also evident in the city region food systems (CRFS) approach, through which urban areas are enabled to re-connect with their rural hinterlands and where the power of purchase can be enhanced through inter-municipal collaboration. The CRFS lens also enables planners to integrate flows across sectors and resources, like the water/food/energy nexus for example, ensuring that PFP policy becomes less of a silo-based activity and part of an integrated suite of planning policies for sustainable place-making (FAO, 2016; Blay-Palmer et al., 2018; Morgan, 2025).

The fifth critical issue concerns *accountability*. This issue highlights the role of citizens and civil society organisations in their collective struggles to fashion a food system that is accountable and democratic – the social and political aspects of sustainability that deserve much more prominence. One of the most striking features of the food policy landscape over the past thirty years or so has been the rapid growth of local food movements. Although they are focused on a bewildering array of food-related issues, they are all trying to fashion a more sustainable foodscape in one way or another (Pollan, 2010). The proliferation of Food Policy Councils (FPCs) in North America and Europe is perhaps the most tangible expression of this trend and, whatever their differences, these FPCs invariably aim to harness the power of the public plate in schools, hospitals and care homes to render the food system more accountable to local communities and their vulnerable members (Morgan, 2025). Although FPCs are often portrayed as vehicles for empowering citizens and increasing citizen engagement, critics allege that there is too little diversity in council membership to equip them "to address race, class and other equity issues related to food systems and food democracy" (Schiff et al., 2022: 9).

Future concerns: leveraging the power of the public plate

Of all the pressing concerns facing the global PFP community, perhaps the most important is the extent to which PFP policy can be leveraged into a tool for sustainable development for the sake of people and planet (Morgan, 2025). Although this distinction is clearly artificial, since the fates of people and planet are inextricably interwoven, it is worth making because food movements tend to foreground one or the other in their political campaigns: the primary focus being 'people' in campaigns for social justice and public health and the 'planet' in campaigns to decarbonise the food system, for example.

On the people front, healthy-food procurement is one of the few nutritional interventions that can address the double burden of malnutrition, namely hunger *and* obesity, a problem that is no longer confined to the Global South. A PFP strategy that can unite global policy makers, health providers and NGOs warrants more attention and more resources, as they are working on goals that are often posed as contradictory but arguably have much in common (Freudenberg, 2016).

On the planetary front, PFP has yet to be fully exploited as a tool to decarbonise the food system in the face of the climate emergency. In a special report *Climate Change and Land*, the Intergovernmental Panel on Climate Change (IPCC) said that up to 37% of total greenhouse gas (GHG) emissions are attributable to the food system – that is from agriculture and land use, storage, transport, packaging, processing, retail and consumption. For adaptation and mitigation throughout the food system, the IPCC stressed that enabling conditions need to be created through a combination of policies, markets, institutions and governance. Recognising the inter-dependence of people and planet, the IPCC recommended that PFP policies should be deployed to change the composition of demand to promote healthier outcomes, reduce healthcare costs and contribute to lower GHG emissions (IPCC, 2019).

Designing policies that promote public health whilst being climate-friendly at the same time is imperative if sustainable foodscapes are to become a reality, and PFP policies have a central role to play in meeting this societal challenge (FAO, 2021). Paradoxically, the greatest potential for securing the multiple dividends of a sustainable foodscape would seem to be in the United States, where three quarters of health care spending is devoted to treating chronic diseases, most of which are preventable and linked to diet. This health care crisis cannot be addressed without addressing "the catastrophe of the American diet, and that diet is the direct (even if unintended) result of the way that our agriculture and food industries have been organized" (Pollan, 2010: 31).

Cities have become the catalysts for deploying their PFP policies to address the multiple goals of social justice, public health and ecological integrity. Prominent examples include New York City's ten-year food policy plan, *Food Forward NYC*, which aims to integrate PFP policies with a suite of other food security policies to address the needs of people and planet (NYC, 2021). In Europe, Malmo City in Sweden is a good example of a municipality that has designed its PFP policies to reduce the carbon footprint of the public plate and promote public health and social justice goals at the same time (Moragues-Faus and Morgan, 2015).

To make a difference to the mainstream food system, however, these examples of progressive localism need to be leveraged through national and international networks of cities, city-regions and municipalities – such as the Milan Urban Food Policy Pact and the C40 network of mayors (Moragues-Faus, 2021). This is arguably the major political priority for PFP policymakers and food system reformers: to use the power of purchase at scale to help make sustainable foodscapes the norm rather than the exception.

References

Blay-Palmer, A., Santini, G., Dubbeling, M., and Renting, H. (2018) Validating the City Region Food System Approach. *Sustainability* 10(5). https://doi.org/10.3390/su10051680

FAO (2016) *City Region Food Systems*. FAO, Rome.

FAO (2021) *Public Food Procurement for Sustainable Food Systems and Healthy Diets*, Volume 1. FAO, Rome.

Freudenberg, N. (2016) Healthy food procurement: using the public plate to reduce food insecurity and diet-related diseases. *The Lancet*, 4(5), 383–384.

Hendriks, S., de Groot Ruiz, A., Acosta, M. II., Baumers, H., Galgani, P., Mason-D'Croz, D., Godde, C., Waha, K., Kanidou, D., von Braun, J., Benitez, M., Blanke, J., Caron, P., Fanzo, J., Greb, F., Haddad, L., Herforth, A., Jordaan, D., Masters, W. … and Watkins, M. (2021) *The True Cost and True Price of Food*. UN Food Systems Summit. https://sc-fss2021.org.

IPCC (2019) *Climate Change and Land*. IPCC.

Moragues-Faus, A. (2021) The emergence of city food networks. *Food Policy*, 103. https://doi.org/10.1016/j.foodpol.2021.102107

Moragues-Faus, A. and Morgan, K. (2015) Reframing the foodscape: the emergent world of urban food policy. *Environment and Planning A*, 47(7), 1558–1573.

Morgan, K. (2025) *Serving the Public: The Good Food Revolution in Schools*,

Hospitals and Prisons. Manchester University Press, Manchester.

Morgan, K. and Morley, A. (2014) The public plate: harnessing the power of purchase. In T. Marsden and A. Morley (eds) *Sustainable Food Systems.* Routledge, London, pp. 84–102.

Morgan, K. and Sonnino, R. (2008) *The School Food Revolution: Public Food and the Challenge of Sustainable Development.* Routledge, London.

NYC (2021) *Food Forward NYC.* New York.

Open Contracting Partnership (2019) *How Governments Spend: Opening up the Value of Global Public Procurement.* OCP, London.

Pollan, M. (2010) The food movement, rising. *New York Review of Books,* 57(10), 31–3.

Schiff, R., Levkoe, C. Z., and Wilkinson, A. (2022) Food Policy Councils: A 20-year scoping review (1999–2019). *Frontiers in Sustainable Food Systems* 6, 868995. doi: 10.3389/fsufs.2022.868995.

World Health Organization (2022) *How Together We Can Make the World's Most Healthy and Sustainable Public Food Procurement.* WHO, Copenhagen.

World Trade Organization (2012) *Agreement on Government Procurement 2012.* WTO, Geneva.

Further reading

FAO (2021) *Public Food Procurement for Sustainable Food Systems and Healthy Diets,* Volumes 1 + 2. FAO, Rome.

This resource provides an excellent overview of the linkages between public procurement and sustainable development, and the key instruments, enablers and barriers for public food provisioning.

Gemmill-Herren, B., Baker, L. E. and Daniels, P. A. (eds.) (2021) *True Cost Accounting for Food: Balancing the Scale.* Routledge, Abingdon.

The volume provides an important overview of 'true cost accounting' as an approach and method, including why this is important for a 'values-based' approach to (public) food.

Morgan, K. (2025 ,) *Serving the Public: The Good Food Revolution in Schools, Hospitals and Prisons.* Manchester University Press, Manchester.

This book explains why public procurement is essential to delivering sustainable foodscapes, emphasising the social value of food and the need to leverage this power for a 'good food revolution'.

Morgan, K. and Sonnino, R. (2008) *The School Food Revolution: Public Food and the Challenge of Sustainability.* Routledge, Abingdon.

This book provides a detailed analysis of school food procurement, with international case studies and a framework for sustainable school meal provisioning.

KEVIN MORGAN

99. Race and food

AQEEL IHSAN

Introduction

Race is a social construct that categorises people based on perceived physical traits, which were once erroneously believed to reflect fundamental biological differences. The classification of people into races contributed to the development of racism, a belief system and institutional practice where one race is deemed inherently superior to others, leading to social, economic, and institutional inequities. Racism is embedded in cultural norms and everyday practices, such as those surrounding food, where the cuisines of minority groups can be devalued by dominant cultures, thereby reinforcing racial hierarchies. The significance of food as a marker of racial identity is often trivialised by researchers and members of ethnic and racial communities themselves, which can contribute to the erasure of cultural heritage and identity.

At its most basic level, food is any substance consumed by the human body for sustenance. However, when one looks beyond the material function of food, foodstuffs and foodways function as important identity markers for different ethnic and racial groups because they are imbued with a history and cultural meaning that different groups carry and persist with across different generations. Sociologist John Burdick argues that food and the socio-cultural act of eating "have been significant markers of racial identity throughout colonial and American history" (Burdick, 2014: 1574). When one looks at the concept of race within the field of food studies more broadly and analyses all the processes involved in producing, processing, transporting, marketing, and selling food, one can see distinct power dynamics at play that have racial implications and have had for centuries. Racial discrimination as a process requires the presence of power and privilege, and this entry argues that this power not only was used historically by white people to control the foodways of and exploit Indigenous peoples, enslaved Africans, and non-white immigrants, but continues to permeate food inequalities and food poverty in different parts of the world. This entry, therefore, highlights this relationship between food and race through three specific food processes: the growing of crops, the transportation of food, and food consumption.

Race in the study of food

Geographer Rachel Slocum argues that race is critical to understanding "all the processes that make animal, vegetable or mineral into something to eat and then all that is involved in what happens next to bodies and societies" (2011: 303). Thinking of food in this way allows one to go beyond the materiality of food itself, and instead focus on the power structures of systemic and structural racism in which food revolves. Slocum argues that reproducing ethnic cuisines is of importance when maintaining connections to the homeland and in producing and maintaining one's racial identity. The cooking and eating of ethnic foods gives people a sense of belonging to an imagined community, and this becomes even more important in the case of groups that lack other cultural markers. One such group are African Americans who have embraced soul food "because it reclaims foods previously despised" by white slaveowners, but were consumed by enslaved Africans themselves in the absence of other options (2011: 306). Soul food is the ethnic cuisine traditionally associated with African Americans in the Southern United States, and it often consisted of the undesirable parts of animals which plantation owners did not eat. Another example is that of Goans, who in a way similar to enslaved Africans, because of the varied origins and places they migrated from, placed importance in the consumption of Goan food because it linked them to an ancestral homeland with which they identified (D'Sylva and Beagan, 2011: 284).

Moreover, food belonging to non-white groups has been exoticised and racialised for being unclean, unhealthy, and unfit for European consumption. According to historian Rebecca Earle (2014), this connection between diet and health saw the development of a racial discourse articulated by Europeans sailors which suggested that European bodies were radically different from Indigenous bodies because they consumed different foodstuffs. Chinese food, for a long time, was seen as a threat to the bodily health of the Canadian nation-state (Chen, 2012: 434). Spaghetti as an immigrant foodway was only accepted in American diets after the replacement of pungent cheeses with milder cheeses that were better suited to the American palates (Iacovetta, 2000: 15). Historian Jeffrey Pilcher credits the rise of taco shops in Southern California for creating opportunities whereby non-Mexicans were able to develop a taste for Mexican cuisine without necessarily having to venture into ethnic communities themselves (Pilcher, 2008: 35). Also, South Asian cuisine, heavy in spices, was considered a sensory assault on white people's noses, and a health hazard because it was believed to be prepared by "cooks [who were] dirty and their dishes permeated by germs" (Buettner, 2008: 874). As such, racism permeates many different facets of food. The one most seen has to do with the ingestion of food; however, the processes behind the growth, transportation, and purchasing of food are also racialised.

Current concerns in food and race

Growing food: rice and sugar plantations

Studies of the transfer of plants and animals between the Old World of Europe and Africa and the New World of the Americas often draw attention to the role Europeans played in revolutionising the food systems of places in Asia and Africa with the introduction of Amerindian seeds, but less attention is given to the role Africans played in the domestication of several cereals, namely rice, in the Americas. Geographer Judith Carney argues that *glaberrima* (African rice) and enslaved people played a crucial role in the expansion of rice cultivation in the Americas during the early period of the Atlantic slave trade. As rice became a major cash crop, Africans from West Africa were imported as slaves due to their knowledge of rice cultivation in order to cultivate this crop in the Carolinas. In total, the Western African rice region contributed "more than 40% of the slaves delivered to colonial South Carolina" (Carney, 1998: 530).

Enslaved Africans who were accustomed to growing rice in Africa found themselves growing the same crop in the Carolinas, and in turn became part of a capitalist system that they did not profit from. Not only were they labouring to grow crops, but they were being stripped of knowledge as they were informally teaching Americans their techniques to grow and harvest rice. These enslaved peoples, along with providing menial labour, also provided colonies like South Carolina with a cash crop that their masters had failed to grow. Along with growing rice, some enslaved women were assigned to 'the big house' kitchens and were also tasked with using their knowledge of the crops to turn native African ingredients into meals for their white masters. Many of the meals commonly recognized by Americans today as "Southern"—such as cornbread, biscuits, fried chicken, pork dishes, greens, gumbo, and jambalaya—were a direct result of African slave foodways (Burdick, 2014, 1577). Enslaved people benefited little from rice growing and food production as a capitalist enterprise and received little compensation for establishing rice as a viable crop in the Americas.

In *Sweetness and Power: The Place of Sugar in Modern History*, Sidney Mintz (1985) posits that sugar, or, to be more precise, the sucrose extracted from cane sugar, was first domesticated in New Guinea around 8000 BC and it was in the 18th century that sugar became increasingly popular as a sweetener in European households, and by the 19th century, a necessity. Sugar cane was grown by enslaved Africans, who were brought over shortly after Columbus's arrival, and hence it was Spain that pioneered sugar production in the plantation form in the Americas, with the help of African enslaved labour. The first English colony in the New World was Jamestown, founded in 1607, and sugar cane was brought to the colony in 1619, along with the first wave of enslaved Africans. Attempts to grow sugar cane here failed, and it would not be until 1655 that Barbados, a newly claimed British territory, would become a major source of sugar for Britain. According to Mintz, "England fought most, conquered the most colonies, imported the most slaves, and went furthest and fastest in creating a plantation system. The most important product of that system was sugar" (1985: 38). As part of this plantation economy, Britain also used its maritime power to transport and exploit over 900,000 enslaved Africans to the Caribbean from 1701 to 1810, all to be able to fulfil the consumption habits of the British working class (Mintz, 1985: 53). As such, there is long, racial legacy in the Americas of African slave labour and enslaved people's knowledge of the crops being exploited as part of the commodity production and trade process that enabled the rapid development of capitalism for Europeans, and had little to no benefit for the Africans themselves.

Transportation of and access to food

Along with controlling the growth of crops, Slocum argues that the transportation of and access to food itself was also racialised. An example of this is how the entry of food into the Gaza Strip and West Bank has historically been policed, specifically as it has related to Israel's 'hydro-hegemony', "consisting of the dispossession and usurpation of water for Jewish settlements" (Slocum and Saldanha, 2016: 5). The Israeli government has also had policies in place where they studied how many calories Palestinians would require in order to avoid malnutrition. This had the end goal of ensuring that the means for survival of the Palestinians were controlled, and that they would be given just enough nutrients so that they would not die of hunger (Urquhart, 2006). Restricting access to food and water is an extreme measure; more subtle forms of racism, as described by anthropologist Ashanté Reese, can be observed through the availability and quality of the foodstuffs themselves.

Racism in America permeates food inequalities and food poverty, and this can be observed through the disinvestment of grocery stores, or grocer redlining, in America, specifically in neighbourhoods with higher Black populations. Reese states that the last remaining grocery chain closed down in Detroit in 2007, while in Oakland there is an average of one grocery store for every 93,000 residents (Reese, 2019: 5). This means that Black neighbourhoods have lesser access to grocery stores and fresh, healthy, affordable food options than their white counterparts. This lack of access to healthy food is understood through the term 'food desert', popularised in the UK in the 1990s to describe the lack of access to healthy and affordable food. However, Reese says this term is inadequate because it implies an empty place, when in reality the issue in Black neighborhoods is the overabundance of corner stores, fast-food restaurants, and liquor stores (2019: 6). The lack of access to healthy food options makes it difficult for Black Americans to meet their food wants and needs, as healthy food options are less accessible and less affordable (2019: 65). If one wants to purchase these healthier foodstuffs, one needs to drive to different neighbourhoods, which comes with a considerable cost. For many, this process is further complicated due to their reliance on public transportation. As such, race and racialisation in this case shape the shopping experience of Black shoppers and in turn reflect racial inequalities in America when it comes to one's health.

Future concerns: preserving ethnic foodways in future generations

Migration results in social and economic challenges that are often reflected in foodways, and this was true for many immigrant families who were trying to preserve their culture in America. Migration also sees a shift in identity when old foodways encounter new food elements and consumption patterns. Reflecting the intersection of race with gender, it is often women who act as gatekeepers in balancing traditional foods and cuisines with foodways of the host nation. This legacy today persists with immigrant women through a 'culinary capital', which refers to the knowledge and mastery of ethnic foodways that allowed women to transfer a culture that could only be transmitted through food to take their families and especially children to places they "had come from but never been" (D'Sylva and Beagan, 2011: 287). This idea is echoed by different food scholars who essentially arrived at similar conclusions in explicating the role that cooking and eating 'ethnic' food plays in maintaining one's identity. However, a big issue for immigrant communities in the future is that mothers are facing increasing challenges in trying to continue to serve as gatekeepers in balancing their traditional cuisine with the new tastes being developed by their children. This in turn has resulted in new challenges for immigrants who are struggling with instilling that culture that was reflected through foodways, in a time when they are failing to maintain control over their children's evolving tastes and dietary preferences.

Iacovetta discusses how the children of European immigrants in Canada were increasingly becoming embarrassed of eating 'ethnic' foodstuffs in schools. They were embarrassed of their spicy salami or sausage sandwiches on dark bread that their mothers prepared when they compared their lunches with those of Canadian children who ate white bread sandwiches with peanut butter and jelly, and other odourless meats (Iacovetta, 2006: 168). European mothers are having to deal with their children declaring their love for Canadian food like 'hamburgers, hot dogs, potato chips', and this created a conflict at home because the parents would like 'ethnic' foodstuffs, but would have to concede some food preparation choices to accommodate the changing tastes of their children. South Asian mothers are finding that their children are rejecting traditional cuisines like curries in favour of pizza and spaghetti. As such, second- and third-generation immigrant children's resistance to traditional foods, or even preference for Western ones, can be interpreted as a rejection of traditional foodways that have been passed down for generations by their parents, while for the younger generation, it can be seen as the fusion of new culinary cultures and identities between the ethnocultural heritage of the places their ancestors migrated from and that of their adopted homes.

As this entry has highlighted, food and race are inextricably linked. The various processes involved in food, including farming and provisioning, transporting and purchasing, cooking and eating, can be understood through a racial lens. The different groups discussed in this entry preserved their culinary traditions and maintained a cultural connection to their homeland through food. Beyond culinary techniques, minority groups also brought with them a culinary capital that allowed them to preserve and reproduce some semblance of their food cultures. This process in the present is complicated due to issues around accessibility and affordability. Other challenges exist in trying to produce and reproduce familiar foodways for immigrants and their families in the absence of other sources of familiarity. For the current generation of immigrant mothers and their children, the challenge is not a unique one, but it is one that can be observed in this entry as being a challenge that has racial implications and needs ongoing study.

References

Buettner, E. (2008) "Going for an Indian": South Asian Restaurants and the Limits of Multiculturalism in Britain. *The Journal of Modern History*, 80(4), 865–901.

Burdick, J.M. (2014) 'Race, Racial Identity, and Eating'. In Thompson, P.B. and Kaplan, D.M. (Eds), *Encyclopedia of Food and Agricultural Ethics*. Dordrecht: Springer, 1573–1583. doi:10.1007/978-94-007-0929-4_53.

Carney, J. (1998) The Role of African Rice and Slaves in the History of Rice Cultivation in the Americas. *Human Ecology*, 26(4), 525–545.

Chen, Y. (2012) 'Food, Race, and Ethnicity'. In Pilcher, J.M. (Ed), *The Oxford Handbook of Food History*. New York: Oxford University Press, 428–443.

D'Sylva, A. and Beagan, B. (2011) 'Food is Culture, but it's Also Power': The Role of Food in Ethnic and Gender Identity Construction among Goan Canadian Women. *Journal of Gender Studies*, 20, 279–289.

Earle, R. (2014) *The Body of the Conquistador: Food, Race and the Colonial Experience in Spanish America, 1492–1700*. Cambridge: Cambridge University Press.

Iacovetta, F. (2000) Recipes for Democracy? Gender, Family, and Making Female Citizens in Cold War Canada. *Canadian Woman Studies/les cahiers de la femme*, 20, 12–21.

Iacovetta, F. (2006) *Gatekeepers: Reshaping Immigrant Lives in Cold War Canada*. Toronto: Between the Lines.

Mintz, S.W. (1985) *Sweetness and Power: The Place of Sugar in Modern History*. New York: Viking.

Pilcher, J.M. (2008) Was the Taco Invented in Southern California? *Gastronomica*, 8(1), 26–38.

Reese, A. (2019) *Black Food Geographies: Race, Self-Reliance, and Food Access in Washington, D.C.* Chapel Hill: University of North Carolina Press.

Slocum, R. (2011) Race in the Study of Food. *Progress in Human Geography*, 35(3), 303–327.

Slocum, R. and Saldanha, A. (2016) *Geographies of Race and Food Fields, Bodies, Markets*. New York: Routledge.

Urquhart, C. (2006) 'Gaza on brink of implosion as aid cut-off starts to bite.' *The Guardian*. Available at: https://www.theguardian.com/world/2006/apr/16/israel.

Further reading

Epp, M., Iacovetta, F. and Korinek, V.J. (2012) *Edible Histories, Cultural Politics: Towards a Canadian Food History*. University of Toronto Press.
This book examines the cultural and historical dimensions of Canadian food practices.

AQEEL IHSAN

Gabaccia, D.R. (2000) *We Are What We Eat: Ethnic Food and the Making of Americans.* Harvard University Press.

This book explores the role of 'ethnic' food in shaping American identity.

Reese, A. (2019) *Black Food Geographies: Race, Self-Reliance, and Food Access in Washington, D.C.* University of North Carolina Press.

This book investigates the intersection of race, self-reliance, and food access within the context of Washington, DC.

Slocum, R. and Saldanha, A. (2016) *Geographies of Race and Food Fields, Bodies, Markets.* New York: Routledge.

This book explores how racial inequalities shape our food and how race influences where food comes from, who has access to it, and how it is sold.

AQEEL IHSAN

100. Regenerative agriculture

George Cusworth

Introduction: regenerative agriculture

Regenerative agriculture is founded on the assertion that the ecological systems involved in the production of food need to be restored, not just sustained. Its practices and principles are organised around the delivery of this restoration. Under its ministrations, so its advocates claim, farming can be changed from one of the major driving forces behind the interlinking socio-ecological crises of climate emergency and biodiversity loss into one of its salves. These promises have seen a wide variety of food system actors begin to deploy the language of regeneration. As its supporters multiply, though, what regenerative agriculture means is changing.

This entry will introduce regenerative agriculture as a growing force in the food system, and as an area of study for agri-food researchers. It defines what regenerative agriculture is, presents some areas of contention, and poses some open questions about its future.

Definition

Regenerative agriculture was born of an anxiety about the socio-ecological costs of intensive agricultural management. Although the term has been in circulation since the 1980s – coined at the Roedale Institute in Pennsylvania in the US – it was not until the 2010s that its uptake by farmers, policy makers, academics, environmental NGOs, and corporate sustainability officers exploded (Giller et al., 2021).

Five practices lie at the heart of regenerative agriculture: (1) reduced or no-till management; (2) maintaining soil cover; (3) increasing agricultural diversity; (4) keeping living roots in the soil; and (5) livestock–arable integration. Although regenerative agriculture works towards the restoration of the many different ecosystem functions implicated in crop growth and animal husbandry, it pays particular attention to soil health (Schreefel et al., 2020). By reducing soil disturbance, by ensuring its surface is always covered by photosynthesising plant matter, and by introducing greater levels of agro-ecological complexity through diverse crop rotations and alternating grass-arable leys, regenerative agriculture works to improve soil biodiversity, structure, drainage, and organic content.

Regenerative agriculture is marked by its emphasis on context specificity and adaptability. It encourages farmers to reflect on the suite of practices that lead to the attainment of regenerative outcomes on their specific farms and to iterate on their farm management regimes. This is part and parcel of the regenerative enthusiasm for trial and error and peer-to-peer knowledge-exchange (Cusworth et al., 2021). Participating farmers share experiences and data about the practices that have and have not worked for them as a way of assisting others in the pursuit of agricultural regeneration.

The regenerative model encourages farmers to introduce piecemeal practices on the farm before making more wholesale changes to their management programme. This lowers the barrier to entry to regenerative farming and, compared with, say, agroecology or organic agriculture, has made it attractive for large and commercial operations. The focus on farm business profitability has also made it amenable to mainstream farming interests. The regenerative 'profitability over yield' maxim encourages farmers to reduce costly inputs as far as possible (fuel, pesticides, fertilisers, etc.) whilst attempting to keep yields as high as possible (LaCanne and Lundgren, 2018).

Particularly for its farming practitioners (rather than, say, its new multinational food businesses advocates), the regenerative agricultural model goes beyond a set of practices that can be applied on the farm. It aims to catalyse a more meaningful connection between human and other-than-human life, to create high levels of rural employment, and to close the spatial and emotive gaps that have opened up between producers and consumers of food (Newton et al., 2020). These goals amount to a sixth principle that many add to the five outlined above: social regeneration (Soloviev and Landua, 2016).

Current issues

With a growing cohort of political and commercial actors looking for nature-based solutions to climate change, the carbon sequestration gains delivered through regenerative practices have been an important part of the rise of the regenerative movement. The evidence supporting these carbon claims is, however, fiercely contested (Briske et al., 2011). There are concerns that the reversibility of soil carbon sinks makes them an unreliable warming mitigation measure (Bossio et al., 2020), and that soils quickly reach a 'plateau' after which they can store no more carbon (West and Six, 2007). In sum, there is concern that the offsetting promises of regenerative agriculture have been oversold (Reinhart et al., 2022).

In spite of this empirical patchiness, many multi-national agri-food businesses and accreditation start-ups are piecing together what regenerative agriculture is, and how it might be called on to help service their political, commercial, climate, or biodiversity objectives. This interest is meshing with ongoing national governmental efforts to incentivise farmers to adopt practices that lead to soil carbon sequestration and other environmental public goods (USDA, 2022).

Particularly for some of its earlier adopters and advocates, these arrivals are complicating what it means to be a regenerative practitioner. These anxieties can be distilled into two related worries: dilution and greenwash. Given the lack of robust legalistic definition, there is concern that the version of regenerative agriculture that will be pushed by these actors will include only the aspects most amenable to corporate rollout, and those with clearest consumer- and investor-facing traction. The celebration of farmers' emotional attunement with the nonhuman world might, for example, be lost to a focus on the adoption of a handful of management practices designated as regenerative.

This is, relatedly, causing anxiety about the susceptibility of regenerative agriculture to greenwash. Like the term sustainability before it (Parguel et al., 2011), large multi-nationals (including McDonald's, Nestle, and Danone) are looking to use the regenerative discourse, in part to pacify consumer and investor anxieties about the environmental footprint of their upstream portfolios. Although their strategies are inchoate, the danger is that regenerative agriculture will shore up the food system that created the socio-ecological crises we are reckoning with today, rather than precipitate a more radical overhaul.

The ambiguous stance of regenerative agriculture towards broader food system justice is most problematic in relation to the topic of decolonialisation. The food system is defined by its historical links with – and contemporary enactments of – land dispossession, racialised coerced labour, capital accumulation, and the uneven distribution of the environmental loads associated with food production (Davis et al., 2019). Some argue that the regenerative model represents little more than an underacknowledged and exploitative repackaging of food production practices long-championed by Indigenous people and peasant farmers (Fassler, 2021). Without a more explicit focus on food justice, race, and (de)colonialisation, regenerative agriculture will be unable to meaningfully grapple with these issues (Sands et al., 2023).

The ambivalence of the regenerative model towards broader food system transitions can also be seen in its treatment of livestock sustainability. Owing to the outsized greenhouse gas and land use footprint of livestock systems, concern over the desirability of meat and dairy in sustainable diets is now widespread (Willett et al., 2019). By framing livestock animals as carbon sequestration ecosystem engineers whose place in the farmed landscapes is natural and inevitable, some argue that the regenerative movement is problematically unengaged with efforts to reduce meat and dairy consumption. Indeed, some industry actors are beginning to proactively leverage regenerative messages as part of a pro-environmental rebranding for livestock animals (Cusworth et al., 2022).

Future concerns

With its boosters, critics, and practitioners proliferating, the future of regenerative agriculture is uncertain (Gordon et al., 2023). This section outlines several questions that need to be subject to critical and empirical study over the coming decades.

The first relates to the regenerative route to market. Will it follow in organics' footsteps and seek to expand its spatial coverage of the world's farmland by appealing to consumers to pay a premium for regenerative produce? Many lament how the political ambitions of early organics pioneers have given way to a model of food production as reliant on economies of scale, poor labour conditions, and long supply chains as the conventional systems they sought to replace (Guthman, 2004). Empirical studies need to assess the extent to which these lessons have or have not been learnt by those seeking to develop a similar regenerative niche.

It also remains to be seen how the involvement of large agri-businesses will continue to shape the regenerative movement. It is hard to see, for example, how corporate articulations of regenerative agriculture will be sufficiently pliable to honour its valorisation of local specificity and adaptability whilst remaining sufficiently prescriptive to be clear and credible to downstream buyers. There is a danger that a handful of management practices (like no-till) that are most compellingly (semiotically) regenerative will be rolled out, whether or not doing so pertains to good agro-ecological outcomes. The substantial literature around commercial sustainability management and environmental social and corporate governance (ESG) investing will be key for understanding how the regenerative model resists/succumbs to the threat of greenwash and corporate capture.

These questions hint at a more general research imperative that might be directed to many aspects of regenerative agriculture (*inter alia* its relationship with meat and dairy, its relationship with technology, and its relationship with nature): that is, the extent to which regenerative agriculture amounts to an attempt to improve the upstream socio-environmental efficiencies of food production, or whether it is about trying to catalyse a more holistic, just, and radical change in the food system. Whatever the answers to these questions may be, it seems clear that regenerative agriculture will be a prominent topic for agri-food scholars for many years to come.

References

Bossio, D. A., Cook-Patton, S. C., Ellis, P. W., Fargione, J., Sanderman, J., Smith, P., Wood, S., Zomer, R. J., von Unger, M., Emmer, I. M. & Griscom, B. W. 2020. The role of soil carbon in natural climate solutions. *Nature Sustainability,* 3, 391–398.

Briske, D. D., Sayre, N. F., Huntsinger, L., Fernandez-Gimenez, M., Budd, B. & Derner, J. D. 2011. Origin, persistence, and resolution of the rotational grazing debate: Integrating human dimensions into rangeland research. *Rangeland Ecology & Management,* 64, 325–334.

Cusworth, G., Garnett, T. & Lorimer, J. 2021. Agroecological break out: Legumes,

crop diversification and the regenerative futures of UK agriculture. *Journal of Rural Studies,* 88, 126–137.

Cusworth, G., Lorimer, J., Brice, J. & Garnett, T. 2022. Green rebranding: Regenerative agriculture, future-pasts, and the naturalisation of livestock. *Transactions of the Institute of British Geographers,* 47, 1009–1027.

Davis, J., Moulton, A. A., Van Sant, L. & Williams, B. 2019. Anthropocene, Capitalocene, … Plantationocene? A manifesto for ecological justice in an age of global crises. *Geography Compass,* 13, e12438

Fassler, J. 2021. Regenerative agriculture needs a reckoning. *The Counter.* Available: https://thecounter.org/regenerative -agriculture-racial-equity-climate-change -carbon-farming-environmental-issues/.

Giller, K. E., Hijbeek, R., Andersson, J. A. & Sumberg, J. 2021. Regenerative agriculture: An agronomic perspective. *Outlook on Agriculture,* 50, 13–25.

Gordon, E., Davila, F. & Riedy, C. 2022. Transforming landscapes and mindscapes through regenerative agriculture. *Agriculture and Human Values,* 39, 809–826.

Gordon, E., Davila, F. & Riedy, C. 2023. Regenerative agriculture: a potentially transformative storyline shared by nine discourses. *Sustainability Science,* 18, 1833–1849.

Guthman, J. 2004. *Agrarian Dreams: The Paradox of Organic Farming in California.* University of California Press.

LaCanne, C. E. & Lundgren, J. G. 2018. Regenerative agriculture: Merging farming and natural resource conservation profitably. *PeerJ,* 6, e4428.

Newton, P., Civita, N., Frankel-Goldwater, L., Bartel, K. & Johns, C. 2020. What Is regenerative agriculture? A review of scholar and practitioner definitions based on processes and outcomes. *Frontiers in Sustainable Food Systems,* 4, 577723.

Parguel, B., Benoît-Moreau, F. & Larceneux, F. 2011. How sustainability ratings might deter 'greenwashing': A closer look at ethical corporate communication. *Journal of Business Ethics,* 102, 15–28.

Reinhart, K. O., Sanni Worogo, H. S. & Rinella, M. J. 2022. Ruminating on the science of carbon ranching. *Journal of Applied Ecology,* 59, 642–648.

Sands, B., Machado, M. R., White, A., Zent, E. & Gould, R. 2023. Moving towards an anti-colonial definition for regenerative agriculture. *Agriculture and Human Values.* 40, 1697–1716

Schreefel, L., Schulte, R. P. O., de Boer, I. J. M., Schrijver, A. P. & van Zanten, H. H. E. 2020. Regenerative agriculture: The soil is the base. *Global Food Security,* 26, 100404.

Soloviev, E. & Landua, G. 2016. Levels of regenerative agriculture. Terra Genesis International. https://ethansoloviev.com/wp-content/uploads/2019/02/Levels-of-Regenerative-Agriculture.pdf

USDA 2022. USDA to invest $1 billion in climate smart commodities, expanding markets, strengthening rural America. Press Release No. 0038.22. https://www.usda.gov/media/press-releases/2022/02/07/usda-invest-1-billion-climate-smart-commodities-expanding-markets

West, T. O. & Six, J. 2007. Considering the influence of sequestration duration and carbon saturation on estimates of soil carbon capacity. *Climatic Change,* 80, 25–41.

Willett, W., Rockström, J., Loken, B., Springmann, M., Lang, T., Vermeulen, S., Garnett, T., Tilman, D., DeClerck, F., Wood, A., Jonell, M., Clark, M., Gordon, L. J., Fanzo, J., Hawkes, C., Zurayk, R., Rivera, J. A., De Vries, W., Sibanda, L. M. … & Murray, C. J. L. 2019. Food in the Anthropocene: The EAT-Lancet Commission on healthy diets from sustainable food systems. *Lancet,* 393, 447–492.

Further reading

Giller, K. E., Hijbeek, R., Andersson, J. A. & Sumberg, J. 2021. Regenerative agriculture: An agronomic perspective. *Outlook on Agriculture,* 50, 13–25.

To understanding how regenerative agriculture is (re)shaping the food system, agri-food scholars need to understand its scientific principles. This article presents regenerative agriculture from the 'agronomic perspective'.

Gordon, E., Davila, F. & Riedy, C. 2022. Transforming landscapes and mindscapes through regenerative agriculture. *Agriculture and Human Values,* 39, 809–826.

This article reviews practitioner materials and academic literature to codify the main discourses underpinning regenerative agriculture. These reflect the ecological, financial, agronomic, social, and political aspects of the movement.

101. Religion and food

John Lever

Introduction: religion and food

Food is central to the religious traditions and beliefs of people in diverse contexts and circumstances worldwide, and there are many rules about what foods are acceptable (or not) for people of faith to eat and about when they should be eaten. Evident in numerous creation stories, food symbolises the ecstasy of paradise, the torment of hell, and the longing of exile (Feeley-Harnik, 1995). As a mode of ritual activity, eating is sacred, uniting believers with gods and ancestors, as in the case of feasting and fasting. Food and eating practices thus reflect wider religious ideals and provide telling insights into religious traditions, cosmologies and societal worldviews.

Early insights from sociology and anthropology

Although there are exceptions, some of the most important understandings of the relationships between religion and food have emerged in anthropology and sociology rather than through the study of religion. Early insights came from the work of William Robertson Smith (1894) in the sociology of religion, who interrogated the connection between sacrifices and communal feasts in the religion of the Semites. Focusing on ancient religious practices in early biblical writings, Smith claimed that animal sacrifices were always followed with a lavish communal meal, and that commensality shaped a living bond between the Semites and their god. From Adam and Eve's apple to Brahmans cooking the world into being, religious peoples have always related to their gods and each other through food, making meaning through a plethora of ritual practices, including Christian communion, Hindi diets, and kosher and halal food codes.

Mary Douglas' anthropological work on food, communal identity, and order in *Purity and Danger* (1966) is perhaps the most well-known study of religion and food. In a context where the identity of the Israelites was being threatened by the presence of other tribes, Douglas argued that Hebrew dietary laws, especially the prohibition against eating pork, outlined what it meant to be 'holy' and 'clean' within the bounds of the conditional promises made by God. As Douglas (2002 [1966]: xv) states: "the prohibitions on unclean animals are not based on abhorrence but are part of an elaborate intellectual structure of rules that mirror God's covenant with his people."

In sociology, Emile Durkheim (1912) famously pondered social distinctions between the sacred and the profane, asking why wine was considered profane in non-religious contexts but sacred during Christian Communion or Jewish Seder (a religious meal served to commence the festival of Passover). In *The Sacred Cow and the Abominable Pig* (1985), Marvin Harris explored similarly how and why religious groups came to avoid particular foods and consume others. In early Vedic texts from around 2000 BC, Harris shows that the slaughter and consumption of cattle was permitted, and that their meat was eaten at ceremonial feasts overseen by Brahman priests. The worship of cows has thus evolved over time, he claims, and reverence for them is not irrational, as many in the West suggest, but an important cultural recognition of the extraordinarily usefulness of the cow in Indian society.

The most notable contemporary source on these issues is Freidenreich's (2011) *Foreigners and Their Food: Constructing Otherness in Jewish, Christian, and Islamic Law*, which cuts across numerous disciplinary boundaries. Not only does Freidenreich explore how food codes developed in classical and medieval Judaism, Christianity, and Islam, but he also examines how they have functioned within specific religious contexts to demarcate and maintain religious boundaries. For example, in rejecting Jewish dietary laws and most food restrictions, he shows that early Christian authorities proclaimed that they had in effect been freed, and that because all foods were edible and pure, it followed that Christians themselves were essentially pure. We can see the impact of these arguments today, where 'good' food is often represented as clean, pure, and natural, as opposed to foods that are seen as unnatural, processed, and bad for us.

Current issues

Most religions have something to say about pure/impure food, sacred food, food taboos, feasting/fasting, symbols, and sacrifices and offerings. In this sense, studies of proscription and prescription are perhaps the most common theme in studies of religion and food, particularly though not only across studies of traditional 'religions' such as Judaism, Christianity, Islam, Buddhism, and Hinduism. This can be seen in contemporary studies of religious food markets and religious food cultures, where many of the religious food codes and classifications identified by Freidenreich are still evident.

Religious food markets

Elements of market thinking can be found in the work of the sociologist Max Weber, but it was not until the neoliberal period that the market metaphor emerged as a way of understanding religion. In the 1990s, both halal and kosher food were made available in the American fast food chain McDonald's for the first time: halal initially in Singapore in 1992 and kosher a few years later in Israel in 1995. Both were underpinned by new forms of standardisation and regulation governing market transactions, which numerous studies in anthropology and sociology have since focussed on (Lytton, 2013; Bergeaud-Blackler et al., 2015; Lever and Fischer, 2018).

The impact of these developments can be seen in the discourses of *Us and Them* now evident across the diverse contexts in which neoliberal markets operate. In Singapore and Malaysia at the end of the last millennium, halal was lifted out of its traditional community base into standardised supermarket and hypermarket contexts, where strict halal regulations kept halal and non-halal products separate (Fischer, 2011). A similar situation emerged in Western countries in the early 21st century, but here it was halal products that were kept separate. In some countries, labelling was omitted for commercial reasons, and this led to social and political controversy, with traditional halal (and kosher) animal slaughter practices being questioned and sometimes prohibited on moral grounds (Lever and Fischer 2018). Malaysia has also been criticised for putting forward a simplified approach to halal ritual and practice in their international halal standards, which has bypassed many contentious theological issues to facilitate market access. As more conservative interpretations would have lessened the appeal of the standards in global markets, this has created tensions between different schools of Islamic thought worldwide (Armanios and Ergene, 2018).

Vegetarianism

Vegetarianism is another widely discussed topic in the literature on religion and food (Stuart, 2006; Walters and Portmess, 2001). Within Hinduism and Jainism, the concept of reincarnation, whereby the human soul may return in nonhuman form, encourages compassion for all living beings and hence vegetarianism. In advising care for even the smallest creatures, Buddhism also teaches that the consumption of meat and fish produces negative karma. Comparable debates are evident in work on religious food markets in contemporary India, where Fischer (2023) has looked at how relationships between vegetarians and meat eaters are being redefined by neoliberal reforms. Examining the interface between the state, markets, and politics, he focusses on the controversy between Hindu priests (Brahmins) who promote vegetarianism and cow veneration and lower caste untouchables (Dalits) who eat beef. Highlighting how local and transnational manufacturing companies and hypermarkets respond to the expansion of neoliberal markets by marketing and positioning meat (although kept separate) more openly *vis-à-vis* vegetarian products, Fischer (2023) argues that powerful political discourses continue to promote and uphold the national myth that India is a vegetarian nation.

Religious food cultures

Turning to work on contemporary religious food cultures further illustrates the changing nature of debates about religion and food. While ancient religious animal slaughter and meat consumption practices are on the rise globally, Markowitz and Avieli (2022) note that in the midst of concerns about the climate emergency and pressure from animal rights activists to ban these sacrificial practices, veganism is also becoming popular. In this sense, as they point out, while "ritual animal sacrifice and veganism may seem ideologically opposed, they share a fundamental approach to eating" that evolves "in specific cultural contexts" (2022: 641).

Markowitz and Avieli (2022) provide various examples. One is culinary redemption, where cooking and eating not only reflect theology and cosmological considerations, but provide an important space for socioreligious innovation and deliverance. Here, they point to the consumption of watermelon by African

Hebrew Israelites, which commemorates their exodus from the US *and* the physical and spiritual rejuvenation, and sense of belonging, this group receives by eating watermelon in Israel. Another example revolves around more nuanced approaches to sacrifice and commensality, where Markowitz and Avieli (2022) illustrate the move away from animal sacrifice towards more abstract forms of sacrifice. Looking to the Cao Dai religion in Vietnam, they draw attention to the ways in which elders sacrifice strong tasting vegetables in their quest for higher levels of spirituality. Their final example comes from the field of gastropolitics. One strand here revolves around the practices of Muslim Palestinian citizens of Israel working as butchers and restaurateurs, which are explored to illustrate how these groups negotiate Jewish dietary laws to produce food suitable for Jewish customers.

Markowitz and Avieli (2022) position these examples and insights as a critique of Feeley-Harnik's "Religion and Food: An Anthropological Perspective" (1995). They argue that while Feeley-Harnik viewed food as a constantly moving symbol with a transformative nature, she left religion uninterrogated as a static, implicitly understood phenomenon. Arguing for a more nuanced understanding of 'eating religiously', they suggest that religion and food now interact "to constitute, confirm, and challenge each other as symbolic and material practices" (2022: 642).

Future concerns

Religious food codes and classifications have had great longevity and continue to evolve over time in line with changing external conditions. We can see this in Fischer's (2023) work on India and through the cultural insights provided by Markowitz and Avieli (2022). In the midst of growing climate related concerns, both in their own way highlight the growing intersection between religious food ethics and support for environmental sustainability. To go back to the first human transgression in the Garden of Eden, Wirzba (2011) argues that humanity is experiencing separation from the garden on a number of levels. Highlighting ecological, economic, and bodily forms of separation, he stresses the negative role played by a small number of large corporations in relation to environmental degradation and human dietary requirements. Invoking the symbolic ritual of offering Christ's body and blood as a shared meal of bread and wine in the Eucharist, Wirzba argues that privileged Christians in the developed world can heal these broken, sinful relationships by showing more care for land, other species, and the less well off in the Majority World. In many diverse cultural contexts, such arguments and the practices they engender will continue to raise important questions about the fundamental relationship between religion and food.

References

Armanios, F. and Ergene, B.A. (2018). *Halal Food: A History.* Oxford University Press.

Bergeaud-Blackler, F., Fisher, J. and Lever, J. (eds) (2015). *Halal Matters: Islam, Politics and Markets in Global Perspective.* Routledge.

Durkheim, E. (1995 [1912]). *The Elementary Forms of Religious Life* (trans. K. Fields). Free Press.

Douglas, M. (2002 [1966]). *Purity and Danger: An Analysis of Concepts of Purity and Taboo.* Routledge Classics.

Feeley-Harnik, G. (1995). "Religion and Food: An Anthropological Perspective 1." *Journal of the American Academy of Religion* LXIII (3): 565–582. doi: 10.1093/jaarel/LXIII.3.565.

Fischer, J. (2011). *Proper Islamic Consumption: Shopping Among the Malays in Modern Malaysia.* NIAS Press.

Fischer, J. (2023). *Vegetarianism, Meat and Modernity in India.* Routledge.

Freidenreich, D.M. (2011). *Foreigners and Their Food: Constructing Otherness in Jewish, Christian, and Islamic Law.* University of California Press.

Harris, M. (1985). *The Sacred Cow and the Abominable Pig: Riddles of Food and Culture.* Touchstone Books.

Lever, J. and Fischer, J. (2018). *Religion, Regulation Consumption; Globalising Kosher and Halal Markets.* Manchester University Press.

Lytton, T.D. (2013). *Kosher: Private Regulation in the Age of Industrial Food.* Harvard University Press.

Markowitz, F. and Avieli, N. (2022). "Eating Religiously: Food and Faith in the 21st Century." *Food, Culture & Society* 25 (4), 640–646.

Robertson Smith, W. (1894). *Lectures on the Religion of the Semites,* new ed. London: Adam and Charles Black. e-book.

Stuart, T. (2006). *The Bloodless Revolution: Radical Vegetarianism and the Discovery of India*. HarperPress.

Walters, K.S. and Portmess, L. (eds) (2001). *Religious Vegetarianism: From Hesiod to the Dalai Lama*. State University of New York Press.

Wirzba, N. (2011). *Faith & Food: A Theology of Eating*. Cambridge University Press.

Further reading

Douglas, M. (2002 [1966]). *Purity and Danger: An Analysis of Concepts of Purity and Taboo*. Routledge Classics.

This classic text should be the starting point for any investigation of religion and food.

Markowitz, F. and Avieli, N. (2022). "Eating Religiously: Food and Faith in the 21st Century." *Food, Culture & Society* 25 (4), 640–646.

In this introduction to a special issue of the journal *Food, Culture & Society*, invaluable historical and contemporary insights are provided into debates about religion and food.

Fischer, J. (2023). *Vegetarianism, Meat and Modernity in India*. Routledge.

Fischer's most recent book highlights contemporary debates about religion and food in all their complexity.

JOHN LEVER

102. Resilient food systems

Jennifer Hodbod

Introduction: resilience and food systems

Resilience has become an increasingly popular concept in recent decades when thinking about the need for environmental and social sustainability while simultaneously dealing with shocks from increasingly connected and changing systems. Food systems are in no way immune to external shocks – they are systems composed of elements connected across geographical and governance scales, both creating and responding to change in the environment, while aiming (yet failing) to support global food security (Hodbod and Eakin 2015). Therefore, the food systems literature increasingly discusses resilience, particularly in light of the 2020 COVID-19 pandemic (Béné 2020; Zurek et al. 2022).

Given this interconnected nature, a social-ecological resilience (SER) perspective based in complex systems science is commonly used when framing food system resilience (Hodbod and Eakin 2015; Tendall et al. 2015; Zurek et al. 2022). The ecological theory underpinning SER defines resilience as the capacity to absorb disturbance and reorganise while undergoing change to retain essentially the same identity and form (Folke 2016). This approach was adopted in early definitions of food system resilience, such as that elaborated by Tendall et al. (2015), as the capacity of a food system (and its associated units at multiple levels) to provide sufficient, appropriate, and accessible food to all, in the face of various and even unforeseen disturbances. This definition incorporates adaptability (actions that sustain development on the current pathway) but misses an additional component of SER – transformability.

Social-ecological resilience is the capacity of a system to respond to change through adaptation or transformation while maintaining structure, function, and identity and continuing to develop (i.e., to support positive and proactive change) (Brown 2015; Folke 2016). By including transformability (actions that shift development into new pathways), SER thinking captures the capacity of people in a system to learn, innovate, and adjust responses and institutions to changing external drivers and internal processes, even to create fundamentally new systems if current structures make the existing system untenable (Folke 2016). Given the complex nature of food system sustainability challenges, such as addressing food in/security and concomitantly minimising environmental degradation while adapting to the climate emergency, transformation is increasingly called for.

Critical perspectives on desirable and undesirable food system resilience

The theoretical framing of SER is appropriate for food systems as complex systems (Ericksen 2008) – the structure, function, and identity of food systems are well theorised. Additionally, as resilience science has evolved, so too has its translation into guidelines for management of social-ecological systems (SES), including food systems, meaning there are both theoretical and practical lessons to take from the SER literature for food systems. However, there is one core element to address where food system resilience and SER diverge. Food systems are fundamentally normative in nature – humans need food to survive (Hodbod and Eakin 2015). In other words, there is a clear desirable state associated with a resilient food system, where food security is achieved. In the SER literature, as a system property, resilience is neither good nor bad (Folke 2016); resilient regimes might maintain desirable or undesirable outcomes. These two perspectives can be reconciled by going back to adaptation and transformation as mutually non-exclusive aspects of system change that unify resilience as both a goal and an emergent phenomenon. By grounding more specific resilience conceptualisations (such as food system resilience) within SES, different definitions of resilience are complementary, whether or not resilience has a normative connotation (Allen et al. 2019). In particular, this underlines the importance of considering adaptability and transformability when analysing resilience of food systems.

SER assessment tools use participatory approaches to both study and facilitate resilience and are designed to support adaptive management of the focal system, remaining open to both adaptation and transformation (Enfors-Kautsky et al. 2021). A key guiding question is resilience of what, to what, for whom (Lebel et al. 2006). Both SER and thus food system assessments should take a cross-scale approach across spatial and governance levels, and also study a system over time. Looking back in time supports an understanding of how the food system has evolved to its current state; looking forwards allows for the designing and envisioning of a future system that achieves multiple functions (e.g. productivity, food security, environmental sustainability) in an equitable way (Hodbod et al. 2023). This requires a participatory approach to ensure multiple perspectives are included, including those of marginalised actors. In Hodbod et al. (2023) this means integrating ethnically diverse participants in urban agriculture, not just female, well-educated, and white or Asian decision makers. The result of this visioning allows the assessment of whether this is a food system its actors want to preserve, or whether it is a system that is failing to achieve multiple food system goals. For example, actors access food system resources differently, creating inequities in food security that can be both undesirable and resilient. Therefore, it might be salient to deliberately disrupt the system to address the inequities (often related to power dynamics and resulting in issues such as structural racism) and transform the system to create a regime that is both resilient and desirable (Folke 2016). If the food system achieves its goals (ideally diverse ones such as minimal food insecurity, financially viable livelihoods in agriculture, and support of biodiversity), then the focus for management should be on boosting adaptive capacity to respond to disturbance and to maintain system structure, function, and identity. In this context, the food system is resilient if it can do so. If it is not achieving its goals, then the focus for management should be on boosting transformative capacity and supporting intentional change towards a more desirable state. In this case, the food system is resilient if it can transform intentionally to support a new identity and structure. This might include removing monopolies in sectors like meat processing or switching from monocultures to polycultures. Either way, the food system will demonstrate a lack of resilience if in response to disturbance it goes through an unintentional change in regime, e.g., if farms go bankrupt after a market shift and the land moves out of production.

Future concerns, issues, and questions

Resilience trade-offs

Creating food systems that are resilient and desirable is challenging. Food systems are generally managed to achieve two functions: productivity and profit, with stability in both a primary policy objective (Hodbod and Eakin 2015). To achieve stable productivity and profit goals we have adjusted food system structures, creating an increasingly connected and globalised system. Optimising productivity maximises efficiency but has trade-offs for risk management, as being resilient requires food system elements to be duplicated. Duplication ensures a diversity of responses or back-up plans and thus continued productivity (adaptation). The 2020 COVID-19 pandemic exposed the globalised food system's vulnerabilities, with trade restrictions, food supply chain disruptions, and reduced access to markets and labour initially resulting in decreased food security (Béné 2020; Zurek et al. 2022). Simultaneously, the efficiency in food systems is not achieving other critical functions, such as equitable food security (given one sixth of the population is food insecure) or environmental sustainability (given the food system is responsible for surpassing multiple planetary boundaries (Campbell et al. 2017). Therefore, and as called for by food system stakeholders (Zurek et al. 2022), more work is needed to study efficiency and resilience trade-offs to address the global and timely challenge of transforming our food system to support a growing population whilst remaining within environmental limits and being resilient to social, economic, and environmental shocks.

Operationalisation of resilience in our future food systems

The call for food system transformation has been increasingly echoed by policy makers and non-profit organisations and it is optimistic to see resilience thinking being employed in the management of food systems to support their capacity to respond to change as they continue to develop. Moving forwards, there are two main areas where SER theory should be bolstered in those discussions and management of our food systems.

Firstly, given that inequity is often a characteristic of resilient but undesirable food system regimes, a focus on equity should be embedded within SER assessment through its focus on resilience for whom (Lebel et al. 2006). Understanding which actors the current regime is working for and against, and how, is necessary to avoid inequity in the future. If equity analyses reveal balanced benefits, adaptive capacity should be supported; if they instead reveal imbalanced benefits, transformative capacity should be supported to shift to a new, more equitable regime that supports wellbeing for the most marginalised actors. Transformative capacity of a system may be supported by existing actors and resources (Walker et al. 2004), but given the consolidated powers held within the food system, it will likely require external interventions so actions do not reinforce power structures and inequitable outcomes.

Secondly, as sub-fields develop (i.e., food system resilience, agroecosystem resilience, supply chain resilience) their approach to resilience assessment often becomes more specialised. A review of community resilience assessment tools identified four major approaches – scorecards, indices, models, and toolkits (Sharifi 2016), which aligns with what is seen in food systems. It is critical that specialisation of approaches to resilience assessment in food systems does not lose the systems framing core to SER and reduce resilience to a narrow set of indicators, as this will block the deeper understanding of system dynamics needed to apply resilience thinking and inform management actions, particularly for transformation (Enfors-Kautsky et al. 2021; Quinlan et al. 2015).

References

Allen C R, Angeler D G, Chaffin B C, Twidwell D and Garmestani A (2019) Resilience reconciled. *Nature Sustainability* 2, 898–900. https://doi.org/10.1038/s41893-019-0401-4.

Béné C (2020) Resilience of local food systems and links to food security: A review of some important concepts in the context of COVID-19 and other shocks. *Food Security* 12 (4), 805–22. https://doi.org/10.1007/s12571-020-01076-1.

Brown K (2015) *Resilience, Development and Global Change*. London: Routledge.

Campbell B, Beare D, Bennett E, Hall-Spencer J, Ingram J, Jaramillo F, Ortiz R, Ramankutty N, Sayer J and Shindell D (2017) Agriculture production as a major driver of the Earth system exceeding planetary boundaries. *Ecology and Society* 22 (4). https://doi.org/10.5751/ES-09595-220408.

Enfors-Kautsky E, Järnberg L, Quinlan A and Ryan P (2021) Wayfinder: A new generation of resilience practice. *Ecology and Society* 26 (2). https://doi.org/10.5751/ES-12176-260239.

Ericksen P J (2008) Conceptualizing food systems for global environmental change research. *Global Environmental Change* 18 (1), 234–245. https://doi.org/10.1016/j.gloenvcha.2007.09.002.

Folke C (2016) Resilience (Republished). *Ecology and Society* 21 (4), 44. https://doi.org/10.5751/ES-09088-210444.

Hodbod J and Eakin H (2015) Adapting a social-ecological resilience framework for food systems. *Journal of Environmental Studies and Sciences* 5 (3), 474–84. https://doi.org/10.1007/s13412-015-0280-6.

Hodbod J, Goralnik L, Vicari L and White S (2023) From theory to transdisciplinary practice: Community-based resilience visioning in urban agriculture. *Society and Natural Resources* 37 (1), 143–167. https://doi.org/10.1080/08941920.2023.2228264.

Lebel L, Anderies J M, Campbell B, Folke C, Hatfield-Dodds S, Hughes T P and Wilson J (2006) Governance and the capacity to manage resilience in regional social-ecological systems. *Ecology and Society* 11 (1), 513–530. http://www.ecologyandsociety.org/vol11/iss1/art19/.

Quinlan A, Berbes-Blazquez M, Haider L J and Peterson G D (2015) Measuring and assessing resilience: Broadening understanding through multiple disciplinary perspectives. *Journal of Applied Ecology* 53 (3), 677–687. https://doi.org/10.1111/1365-2664.12550.

Sharifi A (2016) A critical review of selected tools for assessing community resilience. *Ecological Indicators* 69, 629–647. https://doi.org/10.1016/j.ecolind.2016.05.023.

Tendall D M, Joerin J, Kopainsky B, Edwards P, Shreck A, Le Q B, Kruetli P, Grant M and Six J (2015) Food system resilience: Defining the concept. *Global Food Security* 6, 17–23. https://doi.org/10.1016/j.gfs.2015.08.001.

Walker B H, Holling C S, Carpenter S R and Kinzig A (2004) Resilience, adaptability and transformability in social-ecological systems. *Ecology and Society* 9 (2), 5. http://www.ecologyandsociety.org/vol9/iss2/art5/.

Zurek M, Ingram J, Sanderson Bellamy A, Goold C, Lyon C, Alexander P, Barnes A, Bebber D P, Breeze T D , Bruce A, Collins L M, Davies J, Doherty B, Ensor J, Franco S C, Gatto A, Hess T, Lamprinopoulou C, Liu L … and Withers P J A (2022) Food system resilience: Concepts, issues, and challenges. *Annual Review of Environment and Resources* 47 (1), 511–534. https://doi.org/10.1146/annurev-environ-112320-050744.

Further reading

Hodbod J and Eakin H (2015) Adapting a social-ecological resilience framework for food systems. *Journal of Environmental Studies and Sciences* 5 (3), 474–484. https://doi.org/10.1007/s13412-015-0280-6.

Early article offering context on the reasoning for and practice of integrating food systems and social-ecological resilience thinking.

Zurek M, Ingram J, Sanderson Bellamy A, Goold C, Lyon C, Alexander P, Barnes A, Bebber D P, Breeze T D , Bruce A, Collins L M, Davies J, Doherty B, Ensor J, Franco S C, Gatto A, Hess T, Lamprinopoulou C, Liu L … and Withers P J A (2022) Food system resilience: Concepts, issues, and challenges. *Annual Review of Environment and Resources* 47 (1), 511–534. https://doi.org/10.1146/annurev-environ-112320-050744.

Review article on integrating resilience thinking from multiple disciplines into food system resilience.

Béné C (2020) Resilience of local food systems and links to food security: A review of some important concepts in the context of COVID-19 and other shocks. *Food Security* 12 (4), 805–822. https://doi.org/10.1007/s12571-020-01076-1.

Application of resilient food system ideas to the 2020 COVID-19 pandemic and implications for food security.

JENNIFER HODBOD

103. Restaurants

I-LIANG WAHN

The commodification of eating out

Eating in restaurants has become a part of daily life for people around the world, allowing opportunities to enjoy different cuisines and socialise. Historically, commercial eating out emerged during the breakdown of feudalism and accelerated during the industrial revolution. Urbanisation and the separation of work from home created the need for travel, accommodation and eating outside of home. In Europe, commercial eating out started with coffee houses, taverns and street food stalls serving a variety of foods and social classes (Beardsworth and Keil, 1997). As a market sector, the development of restaurants was also stimulated by political changes (exemplified by the French Revolution) that prompted private cooks formerly serving wealthy households to start their own establishments, and Prohibition in the US also drove restaurants to expand their service offerings after losing profits from the sale of alcohol. Thus, social and economic changes stimulated and shaped the development of restaurants.

Restaurants are now an important part of the food system in many places and, along with supermarkets, have become one of the main ways people come into contact with food as they are increasingly disconnected from the origin of the food they eat. Restaurants are thus an important part of the commodification of food and eating, along with related services and supporting environments.

With the further commodification of food, restaurants gained considerable influence on food production and consumption processes. In terms of production, restaurant cooks, waiters and managers from mostly working class and immigrant backgrounds created different food works. Restaurant services increasingly became a form of performance combining aesthetic and emotional labour to hide the commercial nature of restaurant eating (Fine, 2008). Moreover, as restaurants came to control a growing proportion of demand for food, they had a greater say in food standards and qualities.

In terms of consumption, restaurants configure social practices of sharing a meal with others, and these practices gradually became more informal and were valued not just for the food but also for their entertainment and companionship components. They also exert significant influence on food culture, emphasising food aesthetic, diversity and authenticity. Food presentation and restaurant decoration have emerged as crucial aspects of the dining experience, and an increasingly diverse range of restaurant types provide various national and experimental cuisines, while the variety of venue type has expanded to include bistros, pubs, cafés, food trucks and others. This variety increasingly serves a growing range of customers and provides venues for celebrations and the marking of different occasions and events. Modern restaurants are also shaped by the globalisation of food culture that has seen the spread of Western food cultures to the rest of the world. At the same time, immigrants have brought their home cuisines to more cities and countries, constituting an important aspect of multiculturalism and cosmopolitanism.

Restaurants thus provide a unique angle from which to understand the embeddedness of food and eating in society. From their influence on food provision and consumption practices to the globalisation of food cultures, restaurants reflect social, economic and political changes and shape both social relations and spaces.

How restaurants shape eating, inequality and spaces

Researchers have developed different theories to explore the power of restaurants in food culture and how they influence taste and hierarchy, along with foodscape inequalities and politics.

Restaurants exert an increasingly powerful impact on shaping the contents and experiences of eating out. The theory of McDonaldization (Ritzer, 2009) explains how fast food chains use set menus, self-service and the design of dining spaces to standardise the experience of eating out. Customers are offered near-identical eating experiences around the world, allowing restaurants to calculate, control and expand operations to different countries. This has also led to standardisation and has rationalised control over food production, as chain restaurants have considerable market power to dictate what kinds of food are grown, as well as where and how foods are grown and processed, exerting a strong impact on agriculture and farmers around the world.

Restaurants are also powerful through the work of famous chefs and food advocates promoting healthy eating and sustainable foods through various food media. However, celebrity chefs and their restaurants are also widely criticised for furthering the commodification of food as part of product and brand development (Joassart-Marcelli and Bosco 2018), and these chefs and their brands rarely challenge the power relations and inequalities of the food system.

Researchers have also analysed how restaurants facilitate social differentiation along class, race, age and gender lines. In general, highly educated professionals tend to eat out more often. In Western societies, 'haute cuisine' restaurants are luxurious places for elites and 'nouvelle cuisine' reflects the new taste of the middle class. Despite a general preference for variety, people with more cultural capital are more likely to develop omnivorous eating habits and frequent ethnic restaurants (Warde et al., 2020). Besides classifying cuisines, legitimising certain tastes and facilitating social differentiation, restaurants can also help construct collective identities, for example, through the construction of national cuisines as part of nation building and market formation. Another example is the construction and reinvention of food traditions that help form and maintain the identity of specific social groups.

Social differentiations are also manifested in restaurant spaces as places of cultural encounter where consumers learn about different cultures (Joassart-Marcelli and Bosco 2018). While consumers tend to perceive ethnic restaurants as representing their authentic cultural antecedents, ethnic cuisine is socially constructed and fluid. This raises issues of appropriation, with ethnic cuisine being socially constructed by others and used to draw boundaries of inclusion and exclusion. In addition, ethnic restaurants not only bring foreign traditions to the host country but also hybridise cuisines. For example, Chinese food and Vietnamese food in the US combine elements from different cultures and sometimes invent new dishes adapted to local tastes (e.g., 'General Tso's chicken'). In other words, restaurants bring diversity and options for certain social groups but also reflect as well as produce and maintain racial, class and gender inequalities.

The spatial politics surrounding restaurants is also reflected by the foodscape, the socially and politically produced environment and spaces that give food meaning. Restaurants can produce a trendy atmosphere and their presence can increase a neighbourhood's attractiveness. While 'creative cities' frequently use restaurants for development, Zukin (2015) argues that restaurants can foster gentrification processes that normalise elite lifestyles and exclude older and poorer residents. Moreover, ethnic restaurants tend to be clustered in ethnic enclaves such as Chinatowns, that reflect social differences and inequalities.

While many of the studies on restaurants are focused on Western societies, works from non-Western societies can enrich our understanding of restaurants, their roles and influences. Taking Taiwan as an example, restaurants have played a key role in creating and defining Taiwanese cuisine (Chen, 2020). This construction was initially driven by a need to distinguish Taiwanese foods from Japanese foods during Japan's colonial rule. Following the end of Japanese rule and the arrival of the Chinese nationalist government after WWII, there arose a need to reposition Taiwanese cuisine as a variation of broader Chinese cuisines. Through this history, restaurants have developed a distinctive Taiwanese cuisine by incorporating elements of Japanese, Cantonese and Fujian cuisines, creating a unique foodscape and cultural identity. Restaurants thus play a political role in repositioning food and eating in different political contexts.

Taiwan's restaurants have also shaped tastes and hierarchy, serving as meeting venues for intellectuals, politicians and businesspeople, and the tastes of these cultural and economic elites have had an influence on the wider society. Furthermore, changing political contexts have shaped the cultural status of different restaurant types. The arrival of the Nationalist government from Mainland China drove the emergence of restaurants specialising in cuisines from Zhejiang, Beijing and Sichuan, and these venues enjoyed higher status because they catered to the tastes of high-level government officials. Following Taiwan's democratisation in the early 2000s, restaurants reinvented Taiwanese cuisine by incorporating and elevating ordinary dishes and street food, using local ingredients to establish a local food culture and identity.

This history demonstrates how restaurants are part of Taiwan's nation-building process

I-LIANG WAHN

and also played a key role in forming markets for local agricultural produces. Opening and working in restaurants also was an important means by which the arriving immigrants supported themselves and was key to facilitating cultural encounter. They served as centres for innovation of food cultures, and the reformulation of identity, tastes and cultural hierarchy associated with political change.

The future of restaurants and the food system

Several developments are currently reshaping restaurants and eating out. First, digital technologies provide new ways of interacting with restaurants, and present both opportunities and challenges for restaurant owners. For example, online reviews, ratings and maps are increasingly important for restaurant reputation and competitiveness. With the rise of digital ordering services and delivery platforms, restaurants are also increasingly catering to consumers who eat at home and work, which has required adaptation to on-site work and service practices, along with location selection. In addition, digital food culture has changed the way consumers choose and talk about restaurants, along with social practices involving sharing meals and interacting with others. The impact of such digital technologies on restaurant work, the social practices of consumption, and foodscapes are critical questions with significant implications for the future of restaurants.

Secondly, restaurants are assuming new roles in addressing challenges associated with the pursuit of sustainability, through supporting alternative food networks, farmers' markets, local food hubs and communities to provide for different social groups. New initiatives also certify 'green restaurants' that source from local producers, designing seasonal, healthy and environmentally friendly dishes and devising ways to reduce food waste. Other restaurants may specialise and promote alternative protein or vegetarian and vegan diets. How restaurants shape food content and tastes, and how they interact with experts, advocates, local communities and policy makers in these processes are interesting questions to explore for imagining the future of food systems.

Finally, the development of restaurants in non-Western countries also adds new dynamics to foodscape development and cultural

politics. As the example of Taiwan illustrates, restaurants can combine local elements with regional influences to actively construct local food cultures and identities. The local foodscape reflects both cultural encounter and the political economy of local food systems. How restaurants in different societies assert their identities and interact with local food systems and global food cultures will be important for understanding the shifting global foodscape, as well as taste hierarchies in different countries, with implications for meeting sustainability challenges.

Restaurants connect food provision and consumption, and changes to restaurant operations reflect changes in food and society. Restaurant interactions with technology, sustainability discourse and cultural and spatial dynamics raise key issues for the organisation of urban society.

References

Beardsworth, Alan and Keil, Teresa (1997) Eating Out. In A. Beardsworth and T. Keil (eds), *Sociology on the Menu: An Invitation to the Study of Food and Society.* Routledge, pp. 100–122.

Chen, Yu-Jen (2020) *The Cultural History of Taiwanese Cuisine: The Embodiment of a Nation in Food Consumption.* Linking Publishing.

Fine, Gary Alan (2008) *Kitchens: The Culture of Restaurant Work.* University of California Press.

Joassart-Marcelli, Pascale and Bosco, Fernando J. (eds) (2018) *Food and Place: A Critical Exploration.* Rowman & Littlefield.

Ritzer, George (2009) *The McDonaldization of Society.* Pine Forge Press.

Warde, Alan, Paddock, Jessica and Whillans, Jennifer (2020) *The Social Significance of Dining Out: A Study of Continuity and Change.* Manchester University Press.

Zukin, Sharon (2015) *Naked City: The Death and Life of Authentic Urban Places.* Oxford University Press.

Further reading

Joassart-Marcelli, Pascale and Bosco, Fernando J. (ed.) (2018) *Food and Place: A Critical Exploration.* Rowman & Littlefield.

The book explores a collection of critical food issues focusing on place and space.

It provides in-depth discussions on food regime, foodscapes and bodies that contextualise the roles of restaurants.

Murcott, Anne (2019) *Introducing the Sociology of Food and Eating.* Bloomsbury. This is a comprehensive textbook that introduces the sociology of food with a focus on eating. It covers topics from eating at home, in public and in institutional settings, and relates eating to cooking, packaging and nutrition. It also discusses how ethnicity, food waste and poverty link restaurants to different issues.

I-LIANG WAHN

104. Right to food

JASBER SINGH

Introduction

The Universal Declaration of Human Rights (1948) and the International Covenant on Economic, Social and Cultural Rights (1967), Article 11(1), affirm the right to food, whereby 'every human being has, alone or in community with others, the right to be free from hunger and malnutrition, to have physical and economic access at all times to adequate food – in quality and quantity – that is nutritious and culturally acceptable' (FIAN, 2016). Yet, hunger affects 828 million people across the world, mainly farmers from small-holdings, landless communities, and mostly women and girls from rural regions in the global south (FAO, 2010; WHO, 2022). Hunger is also a growing problem in the global north.

Whilst the right to food has been recognised since the late 1940s, food security narratives dominated discussion in the 1970s (Mechlem, 2004), when the prevailing view was that food insecurity and famines were caused by a lack of food availability and could be tackled through increasing agricultural productivity (Mechlem, 2004; Elver, 2016). Sen (1981), however, argued that famines and food insecurity were caused by lack of entitlements and capabilities to produce, procure, or access food, indicating that poverty related to food insecurity.

The right to food is more than ending food insecurity; it is fundamentally about changing the relationship between the state and people, so that everyone lives with dignity. It draws from a rich tradition of human rights which are premised on achieving human dignity, obliging states to be transparent, accountable, and non-discriminatory and recognises that all human rights, such as the right to housing, income, and education, are interrelated, universal, and inalienable. Human rights also aim to empower rights holders to claim their rights and to bring the state to account if inalienable rights are breached (Mechlem, 2004).

The right to food was taken more seriously after the World Food Summit in 1996, partly because of pressure from civil society organisations and social movements, such as La Via Campesina, which compelled nation states to ratify a human rights approach to tackling food insecurity (Elver, 2016; Lambek et al., 2018). Two recent developments furthered the realisation of the right. In 2000, the Commission for Human Rights established the United Nations Special Rapporteur on the Right to Food. The role aims to investigate hunger and food insecurity, which includes invited state visits (Elver, 2016). In 2004, at the Committee of World Food Security, all member states of the FAO adopted The Voluntary Guidelines to Support the Progressive Realisation of the Right to Adequate Food in the Context of National Food Security. The FAO uses these guidelines to support governments to develop strategies and legislation to realise the right (Lambek et al., 2018).

Realising the right to food

To ensure that individuals and communities are not deprived of access to adequate food, the right seeks to impose obligations on states to respect, protect, and fulfil the right to food (Sampson et al., 2021). Yet, without incorporating the right into domestic law, state obligations remain voluntary. Hence, incorporating international treaties on the right to food into domestic law effectively compels nation states to act. By doing so, claimants can use the judiciary to make the case that right to food violations are unlawful, therefore forcing the state to tackle hunger.

The right to food has successfully been incorporated into domestic law or the constitution in several countries. At the time of this writing, the right to food is recognised in the constitution and law in South Africa, Brazil, Ecuador, Nepal, and Mexico (Boyle and Flegg, 2022). Latin America has arguably made the most progress in advancing the right to food, with many countries adopting laws with right to food elements (Elver, 2016). In India, the supreme court has ruled on right to food matters and compelled the government to address right to food violations (Lambek et al., 2018). The legal realisation of the right to food is also being developed in Bangladesh and Scotland (Boyle and Flegg, 2022). A key challenge is internationalising the right to food in law in all countries.

Hunger is gendered and disproportionately affects communities that face structural discrimination, for example, Dalits and oppressed castes in India, African heritage communities in parts of Latin America, or racialised and other marginalised groups in the global north (Sampson et al., 2021) Furthermore, women can face discrimination for their gender and their race, caste, disability or ethnicity, and these intersectional forms of discrimination underscore the importance of why the right to food needs to centre non-discrimination in its strategies and monitoring (Singh, 2022).

There are also concerns that the right to food has limitations. Food entitlements are often separate from other interconnected rights that affirm human dignity, such as the right to housing, and other rights (Lambek et al., 2018; Boyle and Flegg, 2022). Critically, the right to food, like other human rights, is mediated between the state and its citizens. However, people who are claiming their international right to asylum are not considered citizens of that state, and thus the right would not apply to non-citizens. Non-citizens, therefore, do not have 'rights to have rights' and this undermines the universality of the right to food (Singh, 2022).

All human rights, whilst needed in the contexts of rightlessness, could limit the political imagination to radically transform society. Right to food law, for example, does not change uneven corporate power relations with the food system, facilitate access to land to grow food, transform ecologically degrading agricultural production, or tackle the global neoliberal food and trade relations, patriarchy, caste oppression, structural racism, or ableism that are arguably some of the root causes of poverty.

Future concerns

Incorporation of the right to food into law needs to be complemented with the other human rights, such as the right to housing and more. Given that hunger is gendered and disproportionally affects marginalised groups, gender rights and non-discrimination need to be at the centre of strategies to fulfil the right. Right to food strategies will also need to face that a right is not only about the individual and foster collective community rights, address unequal power relations in the food system and land access, foreground the root causes of poverty, and be inclusive to non-citizens.

References

Boyle, K and Flegg, A (2022) The Right to Food in the UK: An Explainer. Stirling: University of Stirling. https://dspace .stir.ac.uk/retrieve/67b40252-e5a0-420f -849e-2662d682f3da/05-Briefing4-food _18MAY22.pdf (Accessed: 27 June 2024).

Elver, H (2016) The challenges and developments of the right to food in the 21st century: Reflections of the United Nations Special Rapporteur on the Right to Food. *UCLA Journal of International Law and Foreign Affairs*, 20(1), 1–43.

FAO (2010) Fact Sheet No. 34: The Right to Adequate Food. https://www.ohchr.org/en /publications/fact-sheets/fact-sheet-no-34 -right-adequate-food.

FIAN (2016) The Right to Food and Nutrition: Beyond Food Security, Towards Food Sovereignty. FIAN International. https://www.fian.org/fileadmin/media/ Publications/30th_Anniversary/Right _to_Food_and_Nutrition_Beyond_Food_ Security__towards_Food_Sovereignty.pdf.

Lambek, N, Mattheisen, E and Cordova, D (2018) Civil Society Report on the Use and Implementation of the Right to Food Guidelines. https://www.csm4cfs.org/wp -content/uploads/2018/10/EN-CSM-LR -2018-compressed.pdf.

Mechlem, K (2004) Food security and the right to food in the discourse of the United Nations. *European Law Journal*, 10(5), 631–648. https://doi.org/10.1111/j.1468 -0386.2004.00235.x.

Sampson, D, Marcela, C, Barbara, G, Nicholas B, Annelie, B, Rachel, B, Jennifer, B, Evan, B, Mackenzie, F, and André, G (2021). Food sovereignty and rights-based approaches strengthen food security and nutrition across the globe: A systematic review. *Frontiers in Sustainable Food Systems*, 5. https://doi.org/10.3389/fsufs .2021.686492.

Sen, A (1981) *Poverty and Famines. An Essay on Entitlement and Deprivation.* Oxford, Oxford University Press.

Singh, J (2022) Monitoring Social Inclusion and the Right to Food and Nutrition in Europe. FIAN. https://www.fian.org/files /is/htdocs/wp11102127_GNIAANVR7U/ www/files/Module_3_Social%20Inclusion _English.pdf.

WHO (2022) UN Report: Global Hunger Numbers Rose to as many as 828 Million in 2021. https://www.who.int/news/item /06-07-2022-un-report--global-hunger -numbers-rose-to-as-many-as-828-million -in-2021 (Accessed: 23 August 2024).

Further reading

Lambek, N, Mattheisen, E and Cordova, D (2018) Civil Society Report on the Use and Implementation of the Right to Food Guidelines. https://www.csm4cfs.org/wp -content/uploads/2018/10/EN-CSM-LR -2018-compressed.pdf.
Drawing from UN bodies and social movement analysis, this NGO report shows the need for the right to food, describes multiple societal and environmental challenges to fulfil the right to food, and offers recommendations to strengthen the right to food internationally and within nations.

Mander, H (2012) Food from the courts: The Indian experience. *IDS Bulletin*, 43, 15–24. https://doi.org/10.1111/j.1759-5436.2012 .00342.x.
This article provides interesting insights on how communities took their case to the judiciary and describes how the Indian Supreme Court mandated and enforced the right to food.

105. Schools and food

GURPINDER SINGH LALLI AND
ELLEN BISHOP

Introduction

This entry provides an overview of critical debates about school food globally with reference to equity and social justice (Torres et al., 2022). School food serves a dual purpose, highlighting both the nutritious value of food and its social learning potential. In the Global North, a survey conducted by the Food Foundation (2023) revealed that the number of households where children experienced food insecurity almost doubled from 11.6% in January 2022 to 21.6% in January 2023, highlighting the vital nature of school meals. In the Global South, efforts to transform children's lives are underway with the United Nations and the World Food Programme leading the School Meals Coalition (UN, 2021). In 2020, school meals programmes delivered more meals than ever before, serving 388 million children, which was exacerbated by the pandemic. Efforts to improve school food policy continue to progress with 161 countries having school feeding policies (OECD, 2022). In March 2020, schools around the world closed their doors to limit the spread of COVID-19, resulting in 370 million children missing out on nutritious school meals. These statistics highlight the importance of the place of food in school.

Why school food matters

School food has the potential to make key contributions in addressing social inequities for children who may be going hungry by 'improving nutrition across the population and by removing the structural barriers … [facing] those experiencing the worst health outcomes' (Pike and Colquhoun, 2009: 59). At the same time, school food also has the potential to create spaces for social learning opportunities (Lalli, 2019). For example, school meals are an opportunity to socialise children around communal eating and food practices (McIntosh et al., 2010). It is also said, however, that 'food practices in schools may act as a means for social reproduction and normalisation, inclusion and exclusion, alienation and discrimination, empowerment and oppression' (Torres et al., 2022: 1). Therefore, food is a matter of social justice with the

potential to provide and empower young people with opportunities to make choices for the social good. School food involves a complex network of political actors with economic demands which have an impact on key stakeholders such as students, parents, public procurement of food and teachers.

A healthy school meal not only is a solution for nutrition and health concerns, but also offers the potential for harnessing social, academic and environmental issues. School food directly affects students' health, learning and lifelong wellness habits and simultaneously plays a key role in driving positive change. Delivery of school meals has the potential to promote future healthy eating habits (Morgan and Sonnino, 2008); however, 'evidence suggests that school food messages do not intersect with family food contexts and practices, limiting the possibility … to impact positively on current and future family food practices' (Maher et al., 2020: 81–2). Research on the role socialisation plays in relation to young people and school food is lacking, although the work that has been done shows us how gender, race, social class and the foodscape intersect and work together to include or exclude specific groups (Lalli, 2023). Food in school goes beyond the plate and also has a place in the curriculum, where learning takes place, and school grounds, such as school gardens where students are able to learn about food growing. The social, rather than nutritional, aspects of school lunchtimes are arguably more important to children themselves (McIntosh et al., 2010), with opportunities to socialise with friends in dining halls and playgrounds with different contestations of power relations compared with classrooms.

The School Meals Coalition highlights significant findings on the importance of school meals, including how 'providing school meals contributes to higher rates of school attendance, particularly in countries where girls' participation in education has been traditionally low' (Bundy, 2023). Furthermore, investment in school meals means an investment in future society, as school meals are connected to academic benefits (Cribb et al., 2023). School meals programmes provide value for money in the resulting educational and societal benefits that they enable (Bundy, 2023). In the Global South, school meals provide food security at times of crisis and help children to become healthy and productive adult citizens, breaking the cycle of poverty and hunger. In the Global North, cost of living crises, the nutritional value of school meals and child obesity rates (Maher et al., 2020) are key considerations in current policy debates and practices around school food. As Morgan and Sonnino (2008) argue, school food has the capacity to enact a 'public ethic of care' challenging mainstream economic models of procurement and addressing health and well-being of children based on principles of justice and rights (moral economy) and social food service relations that prioritise care and sustainable development.

The future of school food

More empirical evidence documenting the situations of those experiencing hunger would be valuable in supporting policy debates and decisions. This is true in both the Global North and South. Through the amplification of such voices, it is possible and realistic to enact change around food and education. After all, it is the future generations who will be leading the way, championing enacting change and advocating for a more equitable society. Doing so through food will be critical to support a better school meals service and influence positive activities around social justice and climate change.

References

Bundy D (2023) School meals: What does the evidence tell us? https://www.globalpartnership.org/blog/school-meals-what-does-evidence-tell-us (Accessed 23 May 2023).

Cribb J, Farquharson C, McKendrick A and Waters T (2023) The policy menu for school lunches: Options and trade-offs in expanding free school meals in England. https://ifs.org.uk/publications/policy-menu-school-lunches-options-and-trade-offs-expanding-free-school-meals-england (Accessed 1 June 2023).

Food Foundation (2023) Child food insecurity doubles fuelling calls for urgent expansion of free school meals. https://foodfoundation.org.uk/publication/child-food-insecurity-doubles-fueling-calls-urgent-expansion-free-school-meals (Accessed 25 April 2023).

Lalli G (2023) *Schools, Space and Culinary Capital.* London, Routledge.

Lalli G (2019) *Schools, Food and Social Learning.* London, Routledge.

Maher J, Supski S, Wright J, Leahy D, Lindsay J and Tanner C (2020) Children, 'healthy' food, school and family: The '[n]ot really' outcome of school food messages. *Children's Geographies, 18*(1), 81–95. https://doi.org/10.1080/14733285.2019.1598546.

McIntosh I, Emond R and Punch S (2010) Discussant piece: Food and schools. *Children's Geographies, 8*(3), 289–90. https://doi.org/10.1080/14733285.2010.494868.

Morgan K and Sonnino R (2008) *The School Food Revolution: Public Food and the Challenge of Sustainable Development.* London, Earthscan.

OECD (2022) How to make better policies for school meals. https://www.oecd.org/agriculture/events/howtomakebetterpoliciesforschoolmeals.htm (Accessed 25 April 2023).

Pike J and Colquhoun D (2009) The relationship between policy and place: The role of school meals in addressing health inequalities. *Health Sociology Review, 18*(1), 50–60. DOI: 10.5172/hesr.18.1.50.

Torres I, Powell D and Ruge D (2022) International perspectives on school food: A matter of equity and social justice. In Ruge D, Torres I and Powell D (eds), *School Food, Equity and Social Justice.* London, Routledge, pp. 1–7.

UN (2021) School meals coalition: Link-up aims to transform the lives of children. https://www.wfp.org/stories/un-food-systems-pre-summit-rome-school-meals-coalition (Accessed 25 April 2023).

Further reading

Lalli G, Turner A andRutland M (2023) *Food Futures in Education and Society.* London, Routledge.

This book engages with critical debates on the future of food and how this has an impact on food insecurity and the environment.

106. Slow Food

EMANUELE AMO

Introduction: Slow Food

Slow Food is a social movement founded in Italy in 1989 to prevent the disappearance of local food cultures and traditions through the promotion of artisanal food production and consumption. Initially established as an anti-fast food and anti-consumerist organisation, in the early 2000s Slow Food evolved from a gastronomic to an eco-gastronomic movement, reflecting its growing concern with social and environmental issues affecting localities at different scales (Van Bommel and Spicer, 2011). Officially present in 160 countries, today, Slow Food counts tens of thousands of supporters, making it one of the most influential agri-food movements worldwide.

The movement's philosophy is synthesised in its commitment to "good, clean, and fair" food (Petrini, 2013). "Good" is quality, flavourful food that is culturally appropriate. "Clean" means sustainable food that helps preserve rather than destroy the environment. "Fair" refers to food that is produced in socially sustainable ways with fair wages for producers and accessible prices for consumers.

The projects managed by the movement involve different actors such as farmers, chefs, journalists, and academics. Its work relates therefore to a multitude of different topics including (but not exclusively) gastronomy, the climate emergency, food and health, sustainability, and migration. Some of the most important initiatives developed by the organisation include:

Ark of Taste: A catalogue of foods that are at risk of disappearing, launched in the 1990s.

Convivia: Local groups of Slow Food members involved in activities such as tastings, conferences, and visits to producers.

Earth Markets: International network of local markets created in the early 2000s.

Presidia: Groups or communities of Slow Food producers related to a specific product linked to tradition, region, culture, and agricultural history.

Terra Madre: Global network of Slow Food activists linked through methodological, theoretical, and material exchanges.

Gardens in Africa: International project aimed at creating 10,000 gardens in African schools and other public spaces.

Current issues

Due to its heterogeneous nature, Slow Food has been an object of interest for different scholars. A significant number of investigations have examined Slow Food as a social movement, attempting to understand the cultural, economic, or political value of its projects with highly diverse conclusions. On the one hand, the movement has been criticised for elitism, resistance to innovation, and a romanticisation that, some analysts argue, obscures the complexity of historical food practices and knowledges (see, e.g. Simonetti, 2012; Grasseni, 2012; Littaye, 2015). On the other hand, the organisation has been praised for its ability to mobilise large numbers of people, fostering a global community dedicated to sustainable and ethical food practices. Studies also point to Slow Food's strong collaborations with intergovernmental agencies, and with national governments, which enhance its influence and reach (Amo, 2023; Siniscalchi, 2023).

Today Slow Food defines itself as an organisation for food sovereignty (Petrini, 2009). Indeed, the movement aligns with notions of horizontal democracy and agroecology involving various stakeholders beyond just producers, and promoting sustainable practices rooted in local traditions. In terms of horizontal democracy, the movement is linked to the socio-political framework of food sovereignty on two levels: (1) the recognition that producers are an important, but not exclusive component of the agri-food system; and (2) the attempt to spread the responsibility for change among civil society and the various layers of the food chain, empowering social categories and expanding democratisation processes on food-related issues. Regarding agroecology, agroecological practices are often implemented by Slow Food groups and are promoted by the movement as practical means and favoured production methods that enable food sovereignty.

The movement therefore seeks to defend "the right of peoples to healthy and culturally appropriate food produced through ecologically sound and sustainable methods, and their right to define their own food and agriculture systems" (La Via Campesina, n.d.), and can be ascribed to the growing number of initiatives that oppose the monopoly of agri-food corporations. However, contrary to traditional organisations for food sovereignty, Slow Food does not seem to be interested in promoting any ideology deriving from experiences limited in time and space, but encourages instead sharing between different traditions and cultures to avoid any uniform or pre-established view. Where this approach can lead to contradictions within the organisation, potentially weakening the common effort of activists and producers to achieve an alternative food system, it mindfully considers the multiplicity of the cultural and productive contexts from which the various parts of the movement come. In this sense, Slow Food represents an original and unconventional organisation for food sovereignty.

Future issues

A significant challenge faced by Slow Food is managing the decentralisation of the movement due to its increasingly global nature, which will require embracing more and more non-Western cultures without losing its popularity in Europe, where most of its initiatives still take place. Another challenge lies in including activists who promote non-animal products while simultaneously defending food traditions that are based on animal production and consumption, such as pastoralism. Finally, Slow Food must maintain collaborations with intergovernmental organisations like the European Union, balancing the promotion of anti-corporatist and anti-capitalist discourses linked to food sovereignty with the need for financial and political support to sustain its projects.

There are also critical open questions about the future of the movement. For example, what will happen to Slow Food when its founders and historic managers retire? Will Italy maintain its central role in the organisation despite its growing global presence? This transition period will test the resilience and adaptability of the movement, highlighting the importance of cultivating new leaders and decentralised governance structures capable of upholding its core values and mission on a global scale.

References

Amo, E., 2023. The Slow Food Movement and the Terra-Madre project: food sovereignty and translocal assemblages. *Globalizations*, 20(4), pp.644–660. https://doi.org/10.1080/14747731.2022.2149158.

Grasseni, C., 2012. Re-inventing Food: The Ethics of Developing Local Food. In Carrier, J. G. and Luetchford, P. G. (Eds), *Ethical Consumption: Social Value and Economic Practice* (pp. 198–216). Berghahn Books. https://doi.org/10.1515/9780857453433-013.

La Via Campesina, n.d. https://viacampesina.org/en/.

Littaye, A., 2015. The role of the Ark of Taste in promoting pinole, a Mexican heritage food. *Journal of Rural Studies*, 42, pp.144–153. https://doi.org/10.1016/j.jrurstud.2015.10.002.

Petrini, C., 2009. *Terra Madre: Forging a new global network of sustainable food communities*. Chelsea Green Publishing.

Simonetti, L., 2012. The ideology of slow food. *Journal of European Studies*, 42(2), pp.168–189. https://doi.org/10.1016/j.jrurstud.2015.10.002.

Siniscalchi, V., 2023. *Slow food: The economy and politics of a global movement*. Bloomsbury Publishing.

Van Bommel, K. and Spicer, A., 2011. Hail the snail: Hegemonic struggles in the slow food movement. *Organization Studies*, 32(12), pp.1717–1744. https://doi.org/10.1177/0170840611425722.

Further reading

Andrews, G., 2008. *The Slow Food story: Politics and pleasure*. Pluto Press.
Offers a comprehensive history of the movement and detailed analysis of some of the most important Slow Food projects.

Petrini, C., 2013. *Slow Food nation: Why our food should be good, clean, and fair*. Rizzoli Publications.
Explores the Slow Food philosophy through the words of one of its founders.

107. Soil and food

Anna Krzywoszynska

Introduction: soils, food production, and societies

The overwhelming majority of human food comes from soils. Different soil types support different kinds of food webs, and this influences the variety of food and agrarian cultures. Soils are not uniform. Distinct soils are created as climatic conditions and living organisms, including humans, break up the various parent materials of the bedrock and decompose organic matter. Soils are also not static: they change over time. While some soil qualities, such as texture, are more permanent, other qualities, such as fertility, can be purposefully altered within human time-scales. The practices of adapting to as well as transforming soils are therefore central to societies, and soil diversity influences the variety of historical and contemporary agri-food systems (Salazar et al., 2020). The centrality of soils to food cultures is recognised in the European concept of *terroir*, originally created to express the impact of soil on the distinctive flavours of wines, and subsequently extended to underpin the idea of territory-based food qualities. Soils can also be a food-stuff themselves through the often medicinal practices of earth-eating, or geophagy.

The centrality of soils to food means that ways of using, knowing, and valuing soils inform all aspects of social life. A central dynamic influencing the interplay between societies, soils, and foods is the provision of soil nutrients. In pre-industrial Europe and Asia, additional soil nutrition was derived from human and animal manure, shaping rural land use patterns and human diets, and linking cities and the countryside. In the 19th century, the import of guano (accumulated excrement of seabirds) to fertilise fields of industrialising states such as the US and the UK destroyed island soils in the Pacific and the Caribbean and undermined the food systems of their populations. The current global food system depends on the addition to soils of mined (potash) and synthetic (nitrogen) fertilisers. These capital-intensive nutrient sources produce high yields in combination with specific crops and soil management practices (often mechanised ones, demanding the use of fossil fuels). Where traditional food plants were adapted to local soil conditions and the local systems of soil work, modern cultivars of dominant crops depend mainly on synthetic fertilisers and mechanised soil labour, allowing for cultivation with less concern for soil type (Blakie and Brookfield, 1987). These forms of soil management have changed foods and societies, enabling the production of internationally traded, uniform food crops. While increasing the yields of specific plants, this change in soil management has also decreased the variety of food crops, and so of agricultural practices. It further gave rise to a vicious cycle in which continued use of soil inputs is now required to sustain food production.

Changing soils, changing societies

The links between agronomic and soil knowledges

Knowledge of agriculture and knowledge of soils go hand in hand. Much of the traditional soil knowledge was and continues to be rooted in agricultural practice, and to be held in local communities. More systematic and centralised ways of producing knowledge about soils, for example through soil mapping, first arose to enable states to manage the tax and agricultural resource base of domestic and colonial territories (Brevik et al., 2016, Van Sant, 2021). Soil sciences rose to prominence in Europe and the USA after the Second World War, when the fear of hunger spurred a desire for greater agricultural productivity (Montanarella, 2015). As soil science became more embedded in governance, pre-existing local soil knowledges were increasingly marginalised and even disappeared. Indeed, the discounting of indigenous soil knowledges contributed to one of the most impactful environmental catastrophes of the early 20th century: the 1930s Dust Bowl in the USA. There, the use of tillage by colonial settler societies caused drastic soil degradation, causing a collapse of the food system with profound social and ecological consequences. There is a lack of research on traditional and local soil knowledges, especially beyond the Western cultural sphere (although the discipline of ethnopedology seeks to address this gap). Indigenous soil practices were and continue to be discounted and even obliterated in colonial, neo-colonial, and authoritarian regimes (Engel-Di Mauro, 2014). Some important examples persist, however, such as the knowledge of making rich soils for food production from the slow burning of organic materials, resulting in the South American *terra preta* soils and in the African "dark earths". The use of terracing to enable long-term sustainable soil use is also well documented, most notably in Asia.

Soil degradation, food security, and the political ecology of land

Soil degradation is a long-standing societal concern, historically linked to fears about the loss of agricultural productivity and its societal consequences. Food security and soil conservation policies therefore typically go hand in hand, and the first global soil protection policy was issued by the Food and Agriculture Organization of the United Nations (FAO) in 1982. The negative impacts of intensive, modern forms of agriculture on soils are increasingly well documented in various contexts (Montanarella, 2015, Lal et al., 2004). There is a growing interest in safeguarding agricultural soils, as evidenced e.g. by the formation of the FAO's Global Soil Partnership in 2012. The uptake of various soil-improving and soil-conserving practices is the subject of many studies within the wider field of research on farmers' innovation adoption. The variability of soils and farming systems means that sustainable soil management requires ongoing and situated learning: Skaalsveen et al. (2020) show that such learning can be well supported by farmer peer-to-peer networks. The importance of policy frameworks to act on reducing soil degradation is also often stressed (Montanarella and Vargas, 2012), and there is a growing focus on soils in European policy (e.g. the Soil Health Law, introduced in 2023).

Soil degradation concerns should not, however, be seen as a simple reaction to an objectively observed change in soil qualities. Soil degradation is contextual (Warren, 2002): designating soils as "degraded" implies the loss of a desired function not just in the soil itself, but also in relation to the use of that soil in society. Concerns about soil degradation are therefore also expressions of certain ideas about how soils should be used, and so about how societies should function. In land struggles, claims that soils are being degraded by certain groups or by certain forms of land use often play a role, and they have been used to justify land grabs and other forms of oppression. A much-cited historical example is the forcing of peasants from the land through enclosures in the name of soil improvement in 16th century UK , and the consequent destruction of commons-based forms of soil management and social organisation (Krzywoszynska, 2020). In the early 20th century USA, the US Cooperative Soil Survey expressed and reinforced racialised prejudices against black farmers as "undesirable" soil managers (Van Sant, 2021). Today, claims of soil improvement in the name of national or even global food security are still driving land dispossession in many countries (White et al., 2013). Although well-meaning, some soil degradation campaigns have therefore been criticised for reproducing Euro-centric and capital-intensive food production methods while overlooking the diversity of food obtaining practices adapted to different socio-ecological conditions (Lyons, 2014). Political ecologists studying soils continue to stress that soil degradation is a societal issue, and cannot be addressed without attention to the socio-economic systems which inform agricultural land use, such as land rights and power relations within food systems (Blakie and Brookfield, 1987).

Soil carbon, food, and societal responses to climate change

In soil governance and related debates, attention is shifting from a nearly exclusive focus on soils' productive capacity to a wider concern with soils' environmental functions (see for example the policy recommendations of the Global Soil Partnership). Overall, the concept of "soil quality" is giving way to the idea of "soil health", referring to soil as a living ecosystem with a dynamic "health" which needs careful attention. This shift recognises that it is soil fauna, flora, and fungi, especially on micro-scales, who create a habitat for all other forms of terrestrial life (Montanarella, 2015). Many groups are particularly interested in enhancing soils' capacities to sequester and store atmospheric carbon (at times underplaying the scientific uncertainties around soil carbon dynamics (Granjou and Salazar, 2019)). In policy, this is driving a transition in land use from agriculture to conservation, with an interest in re-wetting highly productive drained peatlands, and in planting forests on "marginal" soils such as upland pastures. Such changes have significant impacts on agri-food systems and farming communities. Different groups, including farmer-led

ANNA KRZYWOSZYNSKA

movements such as regenerative agriculture, policy and pressure groups such as the French government's "4/1000" (a policy initiative advocating land use change to increase soil carbon by four parts per thousand each year), and large food companies such as Danone and Nestle, are also promoting changing farming methods to enhance soil carbon sequestration. In many cases this is linked with the rise of carbon markets as an income stream for farmers; in turning agriculture into "carbon farming", soils are expected to produce both crops *and* carbon credits. While sequestering carbon can be combined with food production, there are concerns that this may also lead to new forms of land grabbing, further financialisation of land, and an undermining of local communities' food security (Granjou and Salazar, 2019).

Soil and food transformations: the challenge of socio-environmental justice

It is clear that a better relation between societies and soils is needed: the shift to viewing soils as socio-ecologies. For some, this transformation should be achieved through the combination of appropriate technologies and governance frameworks (Montanarella and Vargas, 2012), with even a role for soil-less food production (Muller et al., 2017). Others suggest a more fundamental shift in agricultural and social systems towards a better alignment between societal demands and soils' ecological capacities, including through less anthropocentric forms of engagement with soils (Puig de la Bellacasa, 2015). Different de-growth, de-colonial, and alternative food systems movements are united by their desire for soil management and food systems that do not depend on fossil fuels and other resource extraction. Notably, the organic agriculture movement first arose from concerns about the financial dependencies created by using synthetic fertilisers in subsistence and small-scale agriculture, although the "conventionalisation" of organic practices has been seen to weaken the movements' concern with social justice as inseparable from sustainable soil management (Guthman, 2004). Agroecology, which is historically linked to the struggles for peasant rights by the organisation La Via Campesina, similarly centres socially just food systems on ecologically sensitive ways of managing soil fertility (Nyéléni, 2015), while

in India the Zero Budget Farming movement advocates the use of local microbial resources (Münster, 2021). Within more intensive forms of agriculture, the regenerative agriculture movement is also promoting a de-coupling of production from inputs through a focus on soil health. The rising popularity of home and small-scale composting, feeding into urban and peri-urban agriculture, is also highlighting the ways in which all people can act as soil recuperators and carers (Abrahamsson and Bertoni, 2014). For the influential scholar and activist Vandana Shiva, a focus on soil ecology as the primary source of fertility is fundamental for a post-consumerist, localised, and democratic future (Shiva, 2008). These debates share a concern with soils as objects of care and responsibility, rather than as resources existing independently of social bonds and freely available for exploitation (Krzywoszynska, 2020), and are pointing the way for more sustainable relations and more-than-human connections between soils and societies.

References

Abrahamsson S and Bertoni F (2014) Compost politics: Experimenting with togetherness in vermicomposting. *Environmental Humanities*, 4, 125–148. https://doi.org/10.1215/22011919-3614962.

Blakie P and Brookfield H (1987) *Land degradation and society.* London: Methuen.

Brevik E C, Calzolari C, Miller B A, Pereira P, Kabala C, Baumgarten A and Jordan A (2016) Soil mapping, classification, and pedologic modeling: History and future directions. *Geoderma*, 264, 256–274. https://doi.org/10.1016/j.geoderma.2015.05.017.

Engel-Di Mauro S (2014) *Ecology, soils, and the left: an ecosocial approach.* New York: Palgrave Macmillan.

Food and Agriculture Organization of the United Nations (2015) *Status of the world's soil resources.* http://www.fao.org/3/ai5199e.pdf. Accessed 6/12/2023.

Granjou C and Salazar J F (2019) The stuff of soil: Belowground agency in the making of future climates. *Nature and Culture*, 14, 39–60. https://doi.org/10.3167/nc.2019.140103.

Guthman J (2004) The trouble with 'organic lite' in California: A rejoinder to the 'conventionalisation' debate. *Sociologia*

ANNA KRZYWOSZYNSKA

Ruralis, 44, 301–316. https://doi.org/10 .1111/j.1467-9523.2004.00277.x.

Krzywoszynska A (2020) Nonhuman labor and the making of resources: Making soils a resource through microbial labor. *Environmental Humanities*, 12, 227–249. https://doi.org/10.1215/22011919-8142319.

Lal R, Sobecki T M, Ilvari T and Kimble M (2004) *Soil degradation in the United States: extent, severity, and trends.* Boca Raton, FL: Lewis Publishers.

Lyons K M (2014) Soil science, development, and the "elusive nature" of Colombia's Amazonian plains. *The Journal of Latin American and Caribbean Anthropology*, 19, 212–236. https://doi.org/10.1111/jlca .12097.

Montanarella L and Vargas R (2012) Global governance of soil resources as a necessary condition for sustainable development. *Current Opinion in Environmental Sustainability*, 4, 559–564. https://doi.org /10.1016/j.cosust.2012.06.007.

Montanarella L, Badraoui M, Chude V, Costa I D S B, Mamo T, Yemefack M, Aulang M S, Yagi K, Hong S K, Vijarnsorn P, Zhang G L, Arrouays D, Black H, Krasilnikov P, Sobocá J, Alegre J, Henriquez R, Mendonça-Santos M d L, Taboada M ... McKenzie N (2015) Status of the World's Soil Resources (SWSR) – Main Report. Food and Agriculture Organization of the United Nations and Intergovernmental Technical Panel on Soils, Rome, Italy (FAO and ITPS, 2015). https://openknowledge.fao .org/server/api/core/bitstreams/6ec24d75 -19bd-4f1f-b1c5-5becf50d0871/content

Muller A, Ferré M, Engel S, Gattinger A, Holzkämper A, Huber R, Müller M and Six J (2017) Can soil-less crop production be a sustainable option for soil conservation and future agriculture? *Land Use Policy*, 69, 102–105. https://doi.org/10.1016/j .landusepol.2017.09.014.

Münster D (2021) The nectar of life: Fermentation, soil health, and bionativism in Indian natural farming. *Current Anthropology*, 62, S24, S311–S322. https:// doi.org/10.1086/715477.

Nyéléni Center (2015) *Declaration of the international forum for agroecology.* https:// ag-transition.org/wp-content/uploads/2015 /10/NYELENI-2015-ENGLISH-FINAL -WEB.pdf. Accessed 6/12/2022.

Puig De La Bellacasa M (2015) Making time for soil: Technoscientific futurity and the pace of care. *Social Studies of Science*, 45(5), 691–716. https://doi.org/10.1177 /030631271559985.

Salazar, J F, Granjou C, Kearnes M, Krzywoszynska A, and Tironi M (Eds.) (2020) *Thinking with soils: material politics and social theory.* London: Bloomsbury Publishing.

Shiva V (2008) *Soil not oil: environmental justice in a time of climate crisis.* Berkeley, CA: North Atlantic Books.

Skaalsveen K, Ingram J and Urquhart J (2020) The role of farmers' social networks in the implementation of no-till farming practices. *Agricultural Systems*, 181, 102824. https://doi.org/10.1016/j.agsy.2020 .102824.

Van Sant L (2021) "The long-time requirements of the nation": The US Cooperative Soil Survey and the political ecologies of improvement. *Antipode*, 53, 686–704. https://doi.org/10.1111/anti .12460.

Warren A (2002) Land degradation is contextual. *Land Degradation & Development*, 13, 449–459. https://doi.org /10.1002/ldr.532.

White B, Borras S M Jr, Hall R and Wolford W (2013) *The new enclosures: critical perspectives on corporate land deals.* London: Routledge.

Further reading

Engel-Di Mauro S (2014) *Ecology, soils, and the left: an ecosocial approach.* New York: Palgrave Macmillan.

Where soils have traditionally been studied separately by social and natural scientists, this book shows both the power and the necessity of a combined and critical soil research. The "ecosocial" approach to soils proposed by Engel-Di Mauro demonstrates soils as both natural and social phenomena, and that approaching soils in this way changes how we think about the role soil knowledges play in social dynamics.

Shiva V (2008) *Soil not oil: environmental justice in a time of climate crisis.* Berkeley, CA: North Atlantic Books.

To achieve food security, it is commonly argued, we need more technology and more globalised markets. Conversely, Shiva argues that to achieve secure and just societies we need to transition from resource-intensive agricultures and food systems to a "living economy" of "biodiverse, organic and local food systems … based on living soil" (p. 109). This book is a key text for de-colonial and de-growth perspectives on food–soil–society relations.

ANNA KRZYWOSZYNSKA

108. Street food

ANDRZEJ KOWALCZYK AND
MAGDALENA KUBAL-CZERWIŃSKA

Introduction: towards understandings of street food

Street food is defined as food or drinks sold in public places (streets, markets, fairs, parks, etc.). The snacks or meals are usually sold by a vendor (often by a hawker), from a food stand, food cart, or food truck, or through a window in a bar, pastry shop, etc. Street food is usually for immediate consumption. Despite street food being popular on every continent, it is most prevalent in countries with warm or temperate climates. It originated in products that were readily available in each geographical zone and became associated with a particular cultural tradition (Civitello, 2008). Currently, these geographical and cultural relationships are less clear, due to migration, progressive globalisation (the transfer of consumption patterns and cultures, for example), and changes in food storage and preparation technologies.

The history of street food

Street food origins

In pre-agricultural times, it was common to eat in open spaces. As archaeological excavations of ancient Egyptian sites suggest, the shepherd economy, and especially sedentary farming, transformed food preparation and consumption. An increased number of meals were prepared and eaten at home or nearby. What is now commonly known as 'street food' rarely occurred in closed rural communities. Street food only began to spread with trade and the development of cities. The food offered in marketplaces was eaten by both buyers (customers) and the people who sold the products. This was the case not only in Egypt, but also in the cities of the Indus civilisation, Mesopotamia, and ancient China. The inhabitants of Athens who visited the agora eagerly ate lentil soup; and the consumption of small bread loaves called koulori and cheese pies was popular not only in ancient Greece but also in Byzantium (Matalas and Yannakoulia, 2000). It was common for food hawkers to sell bread, biscuits, and sausages across the urban landscape of ancient Rome (Holleran, 2016). This phenomenon, also occurring in the cities of Asia, Europe, and the Americas, gained strength in Europe in the following centuries alongside the progression of urbanisation. This was the case in the Middle Ages and at the beginning of the modern era. For example, in Chinese cities, during the Song dynasty (10th–13th century), baked sweet potatoes became a popular street food (Hall, 2008: 28). In Europe, this was true not only of cities located in regions with a warm climate, such as 18th-century Naples (Calaresu, 2007), but also in northern Europe (London, for example) (Taverner, 2019).

Street food and modern capitalism

The emergence of capitalism reinforced the tendencies already noticeable in the 18th century. The rapid development of street food was fostered not only by the development of industry and transport (which, among others, resulted in long stays away from home), but also by migration to cities. With the rise of industry in the 19th century, cities sprung up throughout Europe, North America, and later Asia and South America. The influx of young men and women into cities who were living away from their families influenced the demand for street food. An additional factor conducive to the development of street food in cities in the 19th century and at the beginning of the 20th century was migration, including from Europe to North America. Migrants brought many snacks and cultural dishes with them that then gained popularity as 'street food'. Through their diverse experiences as migrants and workers, street vendors selling street food, including those operating illegally, gained a sense of citizenship and belonging. As Bhimji (2010) notes, street vendors in this period were agents of social justice.

Street food in contemporary form: food cultures around the globe

In relation to street food's form and place in contemporary foodscapes and food cultures, there are several issues to note. Street food is of the greatest importance to the daily diet of residents of Asia, Africa, and Latin America. For many people in cities, eating on the street and/or in the market is often the primary form of consuming food. Eating snacks offered by hawkers takes place not only while shopping or travelling, for example, but also during lunch breaks and in the evenings. Street food often replaces lunch that could otherwise be eaten at home or in a restaurant. This is especially true for young and single people. In countries of the Global South, the preparation of snacks and simple dishes as well as their sale in public places is important and sometimes the primary source of income for women and even entire families (Tinker, 1997; Acho-Chi, 2002). It is also a very important way of eating for people from social groups with lower incomes (Civitello, 2008). The availability, affordability, and nutritional value of street food also makes it important to urban food security (Etzold, 2014). In fact, a wide range of cultural traits are preserved through street food vending, including traditional professions and food items rooted in a region's history and consumption culture (Matalas and Yannakoulia, 2000).

The street food renaissance

Street food meanings and manifestations

Street food in wealthier countries also has a long tradition and has recently been undergoing a renaissance. The growing popularity of this form of food is related to several key factors.

Firstly, among young people, street food is associated with a lifestyle. This also applies to school-age children, although in their case snacks might replace school meals. Another factor contributing to street food is the urban consumption model, in which people spend a significant part of their leisure time shopping. The popularity of street food is also supported by advertisements on digital platforms. Potential customers receive texts and view photos on social media that promote this type of consumption, which is related to new forms of marketing (pop-up experimental marketing combined with the power of word-of-mouth marketing, for instance). The drive-thru system used by fast food restaurants is another factor in the spread of street food cultures of consumption.

Secondly, street food offers an increasing number of snacks and dishes tailored to people who follow a specific diet (including vegetarians and vegans), prefer biodegradable packaging, and are interested in supporting local products.

Thirdly, the dynamic shape and influence of global migration has meant that inhabitants of destination countries, guided by a desire to experience new flavours, are very eager to eat dishes brought by immigrants, and these are often dishes typical of street food. Examples include tacos and burritos (Mexican cuisine), kebabs and falafels (Middle Eastern cuisine), and gyros (Greek cuisine).

Fourthly, street food has taken on a new role in the urban food system and foodscape, not just as a fashion, but also as a way for residents and tourists to eat cheaper meals. This allows consumers to reduce consumption time, discover a variety of flavours, and ultimately connect with foreign places, thus combining experiences of new cuisines with touristic emotions (Priviteraa and Nesci, 2015), preserving tradition and history through the coexistence of old and new flavours.

Street food and the city

The presence of street food in urban space means that this issue is often reflected in the politics of cities (Henderson, 2016). In addition to striving to ensure that street food vendors meet appropriate sanitary conditions (te Lintelo, 2009), in some cities, the authorities not only support but initiate the creation of food streets, food courts (sometimes believing that this kind of policy leads to the regeneration of neglected districts), and street food markets (based on pop-up retailing). For example, municipal authorities can treat street food, as in Singapore during the 2020 COVID-19 pandemic (Radomskaya and Bhati, 2022), as an important part of social policy.

References

Acho-Chi C (2002) The mobile street food service practice in the urban economy of Kumba, Cameroon. *Singapore Journal of Tropical Geography 23* (2), 131–148. https://doi.org/10.1111/1467-9493.00122.

Bhimji F (2010) Struggles, urban citizenship, and belonging: the experience of undocumented street vendors and food truck owners in Los Angeles. *Urban Anthropology 39* (4), 455–492.

Calaresu M (2007) From the street to stereotype: urban space, travel and the picturesque in late eighteenth-century Naples. *Italian Studies 62* (2), 189–203. https://doi.org/10.1179/007516307X227659.

Civitello L (2008) *Cuisine and culture: a history of food and people.* Hoboken, NJ, John Wiley & Sons, Inc.

ANDRZEJ KOWALCZYK AND MAGDALENA KUBAL-CZERWIŃSKA

Etzold B (2014) Towards fair street food governance in Dhaka: moving from exploitation and eviction to social recognition and support. In: de Cassia Vieira Cardoso R, Companion M and Marras S R (Eds.) *Street food: culture, economy, health and governance*. New York, Routledge, pp. 61–82.

Hall K (2008) Agriculture: Asia and the Pacific. In: Crabtree P J (Ed.) *Encyclopedia of society and culture in the medieval world, facts on file*. New York, Infobase Publishing, pp. 24–29.

Henderson J C (2016) Foodservice in Singapore: retaining a place for hawkers? *Journal of Foodservice Business Research 19* (3), 272–286. https://doi.org/10.1080 /15378020.2016.1175900.

Holleran C (2016) Representations of food hawkers in ancient Rome. In: Calaresu M and van den Heuvel D (Eds.) *Food hawkers: selling in the street from antiquity to the present*. London, Routledge, pp. 19–42.

te Lintelo D J H (2009) The spatial politics of food hygiene: regulating small-scale retail in Delhi. *The European Journal of Development Research 21* (1), 63–80. https://doi.org/10.1057/ejdr.2008.10.

Matalas A L and Yannakoulia M (2000) Greek street food vending: an old habit turned new. *World Review of Nutrition and Dietetics, 86*, 1–24. doi: 10.1159/000059738.

Priviteraa D and Nesci F S (2015) Globalization vs. local: the role of street food in the urban food system. In: *2nd International conference 'economic scientific research – theoretical, empirical and practical approaches'*. ESPERA 2014. 13–14 November 2014. Bucharest, Romania. *Procedia Economics and Finance 22*, 716–722.

Radomskaya V and Bhati A S (2022) Hawker centres: a social space approach to promoting community wellbeing. *Urban Planning, 7* (4), 167–178. https://doi.org/10 .17645/up.v7i4.5658.

Taverner C (2019) *Selling food in the streets of London, c. 1600–1750* [dissertation]. Department of History, Classics and Archaeology Birkbeck, University of London.

Tinker I (1997) *Street foods: urban food and employment in developing countries*. New York, Oxford, Oxford University Press.

Further reading

de Cassia Vieira Cardoso R, Companion M and Marras S R (eds) (2014) *Street food: culture, economy, health and governance*. New York, Routledge.

A comprehensive social scientific perspective on street food, illustrating its enormous cultural diversity and economic significance around the world.

Kowalczyk A and Kubal-Czerwińska M (2020) Street food and food trucks: old and new trends in urban gastronomy. In: Kowalczyk A and Derek M (Eds.) *Gastronomy and urban space: changes and challenges in geographical perspective*. Cham, Springer, pp. 309–327.

Describes the evolution of ready-to-eat food vendors within city districts. It explores the location of food tracks during the week (particularly business and corporate districts) and on weekends (free-time districts) in Warsaw and Krakow in Poland.

ANDRZEJ KOWALCZYK AND MAGDALENA KUBAL-CZERWIŃSKA

109. Superfoods

Jessica Loyer

Introduction: situating superfoods

Superfoods are not a regulatory category, but a distinctive creation of market-driven consumer cultures that reflect intersecting desires for novelty, nostalgia, and nutrition. Gaining popularity over the past several decades, the term refers to foods with purported superior nutritional and/or medicinal properties, "natural" or "authentic" qualities, and histories of traditional use (Loyer and Knight 2018). As the category is largely defined by lifestyle media and pseudo-scientific marketing (MacGregor et al. 2021), commentators frequently overlook the materiality of the foods themselves, including how they interact with people and places. Yet McDonnell and Wilk's (2020, 12) observation that "superfoods do not exist a priori" underscores the creative production and consumption work that transforms the mundane into the magical, from the mainstreaming of marginalised Global South staples, such as quinoa, to the repositioning of familiar Global North foodstuffs, such as blueberries. While many scholarly and media texts are concerned with confirming or debunking health claims, the social significance of superfoods extends beyond marketing to considerations of people and places impacted by their production and contested cultural and consumer politics surrounding their consumption.

Production: people, places, and impacts of consumer demand

Before they are symbolically and materially transformed, superfoods have agricultural origins. Increased consumer demand due to the superfood label unevenly affects people and places of production. Many superfoods, such as açai, quinoa, and maca, are products of the Global South with complex histories of Indigenous use. As these foods enter global commodity chains, they simultaneously provide opportunities for producers to expand their livelihoods and disrupt traditional socioecological balances.

Quinoa in Bolivia provides an example of how, as Global North demand increased, farming communities embraced renewed opportunities for land-based livelihoods and rural repopulation, yet found their staple had become too expensive for their own consumption. Increased demand threatened historical communal land management practices and sparked ownership disputes, while negatively impacting environments through expanded and intensified cultivation (Kerssen 2015). Growing demand for maca, an Andean root vegetable with purported fertility enhancing properties, has led to similar environmental and social impacts, as well as international biopiracy, indigenous intellectual property theft, and market share concerns (Loyer and Knight 2018). These concerns are mirrored by rapid increases in demand for the Amazonian superfruit açai, whose producers benefit from an expanded local economy yet miss out on the largest share of the market: the physical and symbolic transformation of the berry occurs at a distance from areas of primary production (Brondizio 2020), and thus economic value is not captured by those growing it. These issues reflect common consequences of global food provisioning systems, but are of particular concern due to romantic representations of production in superfoods marketing.

Consumption: contested cultural and consumer politics

Superfood consumers are predominantly located in the Global North and are largely affluent, urban, white, and female (Sikka 2019). Their superfood consumption can be understood as normative identity performance as health-conscious citizens in a neoliberal, postfeminist context that emphasises individual responsibility (Sikka 2019). The popularity of superfoods, as distinct from other types of consumer-focused health foods, relies on their discursive positioning between science and tradition. Superfoods marketing and media representations synthesise two competing knowledge frameworks for understanding foods' healthfulness: functional nutritionism, whereby foods are primarily understood in terms of nutrient contents and valued for biophysical effects on bodily health; and nutritional primitivism, whereby health benefits are conferred by a food's history of traditional use by ancient or indigenous cultures (Loyer and Knight 2018). These representations emphasise favourable nutrient contents, such as omega-3 fatty acid for chia seeds or antioxidants for blueberries, often relying on industry-funded scientific research to bolster health claims. Closely tied to superfoods' rise in the

Global North is the allowance of certain types of health benefit and nutrient content claims on product packaging in countries such as the United States, Japan, and Australia. However, unlike fortified functional foods, superfood representations also emphasise "natural" and "authentic" qualities. Marketing materials highlight associations with remote, ancient, or exotic Others, employing primitivist discourse and imagery placing superfood production outside of intersubjective time and space. These representations reflect consumer dissatisfaction with contemporary corporate food provisioning systems, but gloss over the impacts of neoliberal globalisation on people and places of production. Further, the emphasis on individual health in superfoods marketing precludes deeper engagement with questions of equity and access.

Future directions

Taking a broad sociohistorical view, superfoods belong to a long tradition of seeking immortality and/or social change via consumption. Future critical research should consider superfoods' materiality and symbolism within a broader framework of substances that defy precise categorisation, crossing cultural boundaries between food, medicine, and drug. Ongoing scholarship and activism regarding more equitable production of individual superfoods contribute to food sovereignty efforts, particularly among Global South producer communities. Attending to the range of drivers and impacts throughout superfood production–consumption networks provides entry points for challenging nutritional hegemony and constructing genuinely healthy and equitable foodscapes.

References

Brondizio E (2020) The global açaí: a chronicle of possibilities and predicaments of an Amazonian superfood. In: McDonnell E and Wilk R (eds) *Critical Approaches to Superfoods*. London, Bloomsbury, 149–168.

Kerssen T M (2015) Food sovereignty and the quinoa boom: challenges to sustainable re-peasantisation in the southern altiplano of Bolivia. *Third World Quarterly* 36(3), 489–507. https://doi.org/10.1080/01436597.2015.1002992.

Loyer J and Knight C (2018) Selling the 'Inca superfood': nutritional primitivism in superfoods books and maca marketing. *Food, Culture & Society* 21(4), 449–467. https://doi.org/10.1080/15528014.2018.1480645.

McDonnell E and Wilk R (2020) Tracking superfoods: an introduction. In: McDonnell E and Wilk R (eds) *Critical Approaches to Superfoods*. London, Bloomsbury, 1–16.

MacGregor C, Petersen A and Parker C (2021) Promoting a healthier, younger you: the media marketing of anti-ageing superfoods. *Journal of Consumer Culture* 21(2), 164–179. https://doi.org/10.1177/1469540518773825.

Sikka T (2019) The contradictions of superfood consumerism in a postfeminist, neoliberal world. *Food, Culture & Society* 22(3), 354–375 https://doi.org/10.1080/15528014.2019.1580534.

Further reading

McDonnell E and Wilk R (eds) (2020) *Critical Approaches to Superfoods*. London: Bloomsbury.

This edited volume provides diverse critical perspectives on the production, consumption, and semiotics of superfoods as both health food category and individual food products.

JESSICA LOYER

110. Supermarkets and food

LISA JACK

Introduction

A supermarket is a self-service shop that sells food and usually a wide range of other goods, including household goods, clothing, stationery and fuel. Typically, supermarkets are owned and operated by large corporations as chains of stores in multiple towns and cities; however, smaller, independent stores and chains can also be found. Multiple shop formats are used, from smaller convenience stores in towns and cities, through to very large superstores or hypermarkets sited out of town centres. Perhaps the most contentious aspect of supermarkets is that they are largely profit-making businesses, with the perception that shareholders and CEOs benefit unfairly from dividends and bonuses at the expense of their customers. There is, though, a range of ownership models, including share ownership, private ownership, private equity, co-operatives and partnerships.

The first supermarkets were established in the USA in the 1930s, and the format spread throughout Canada, Europe and elsewhere after the Second World War. Into the 21st century, the supermarket model has spread across all inhabited continents. Three phases have been identified in the origin of the model: establishment of the initial model and an expectation of low prices; a battle for dominance over other food retail models; and the development of a category management-led, consumer-focused, multiple-format international business (Tillotson, 2007/8).

The supermarket model has come to dominate the buying and selling of food in the majority of the world's countries. For 2021, it is estimated that globally 64% of all food bought for consumption at home was purchased in a supermarket (GVR, 2023). In the UK, the percentage of people buying at least some of their food in supermarkets is as high as 84% of the population (Statista, 2025).

The importance of supermarkets lies in their dominance. As the place where consumers make most of their decisions about what to buy and to eat, they have shaped food cultures and supply chains. More than that, they have helped to habituate society to convenience, acted as a conduit for the consumption of unhealthy food and created a reliance on a small number of multinational corporations throughout the food system, which exhibits economic concentration more widely. They have controversially shaped urban and rural landscapes by obtaining planning permissions for the development of large out-of-town stores, distribution and, more recently, in-town convenience format stores.

The institutionalisation of the supermarket model has come about because they aim to meet certain perceived needs. They came to prominence in the USA during the depression of the 1930s, when low prices were a boon. In the UK, supermarket owners combatted high prices charged by manufacturers and drove down costs, acting as a voice for consumers (McClelland, 1962). The convenience food on offer and the perceived time saving of one-stop shopping drew in shoppers as more women entered the workplace, and more men shopped for themselves, among other social trends.

The reasons supermarkets became institutionalised appear to go beyond the ready availability of cheap and convenient food. Supermarkets can also be seen as places of anonymity, where neighbours and shop staff are less able to pass judgement on choices and ability to pay. Elsewhere, this anonymity is described as associated with 'non-places' in a time of supermodernity, somewhere individuals can go 'under the radar'. However, Goidanich and Rial (2012) challenge this in their ethnographical account of Brazilian supermarkets. They found supermarkets to be both personal places, almost a private store cupboard, and social places, where one can, if one chooses, be part of a social group chatting and taking refreshments.

Another factor is the extent to which supermarkets have replaced employment of kitchen staff in homes and businesses to source and prepare meals, and possibly a reduction in the reliance on vendors of prepared foods. The irony is that by selecting, carrying and checking out goods, shoppers are providing their own labour for free to the supermarket.

Current issues, concerns and areas of focus

The aim of a supermarket is to sell basic foods very cheaply. It was recognised early in the development of the model that profits would come from selling in volume to regular customers. However, it very quickly became

447

clear that profits only really materialised if the same customers bought non-necessary groceries and non-grocery items that could be sold alongside the basic foods but at a slightly higher margin. Stores are deliberately designed to entice shoppers to make additional and impulse purchases. Supermarkets employ one of two strategies to encourage additional spending. High–low pricing strategies involving special offers such as 'buy one get one free' and vouchers or loyalty card schemes are known to add an element of excitement through bargain hunting and create brand loyalty to a supermarket. Everyday low pricing strategies aim to keep all prices lower than or equal to those of competitors. Supermarkets accept that they will have low net profit margins and low rates of return on investment, and that higher profits result from gaining a bigger market share than competitors.

The business models of supermarkets have institutionalised the way in which societies think about food. They have ingrained an expectation that food should be cheap and this is encouraged by governments who see higher GDP from purchases of cars, white goods and entertainment, for example, from the discretionary spending released by the availability of cheaper foods for those on moderate or high incomes. Governments are also then able to attempt to put the responsibility for feeding those on low incomes onto multinational corporations or more locally run supermarkets.

However, because the model also relies on the purchase of non-necessities and a high volume of shoppers to achieve any profit margin, many of the top sellers in most supermarkets are alcohol, soft drinks, confectionery and snack foods sold at competitive prices. Supermarkets rapidly became the conduit for new product development and for long-life, processed (including ultra-processed), non-essential foods. It is the case that supermarkets have made more varied and nutritious foods available to more people. They have also made less healthy foods more readily available at lower prices, allegedly contributing to the epidemic of obesity and chronic diseases in many Western countries and elsewhere.

The supermarket business model relies also on its only economy of scale: bargaining power with its suppliers (Jack, 2021). Although there is an illusion that large corporations must be more cost effective, in reality each store and each product sold adds costs to the business. From the beginning, supermarkets have used their bargaining power to achieve significant volume discounts and low prices from suppliers on the promise of high-volume sales. In the second phase of supermarket development, manufacturers and supermarkets battled to set the prices for goods, but with the emergence of category management in the mid-1990s (the third phase), nearly all the bargaining power across food supply chains sits with the corporate multiple retailers.

Intuitively, it is usually assumed that supermarkets make profits from what they charge consumers. What few consumers realise is that supermarkets charge their suppliers too. To keep prices very low for consumers, it is these 'suppliers' payments' that can help the supermarkets to achieve a profit on an item. There are three main ways in which supermarkets charge suppliers. The first is to negotiate volume discounts. The second is to charge fees for the supermarket's services in marketing and for the space occupied by the goods in their marketplace. Third, the current supermarket model also runs on a system of 'on time in full and to specification' agreements for deliveries and this allows penalties to be charged if these agreements are not met. The payments from suppliers to supermarkets in the form of discounts given, marketing fees and penalties are termed 'commercial income'. In many cases, supermarket profits would be significantly reduced or even eliminated, without payments from suppliers (Jack, 2021).

Big food corporations may be able to absorb demands for suppliers' payments, although disputes between the major manufacturers and the supermarkets over payments have been reported in the press. Suppliers' payments are a significant problem for small- and medium-sized manufacturers and farmers, and ultimately this has an impact on the rural economy as food production becomes unprofitable. It also highlights a fundamental unfairness in the system which has also relied on low wages and low returns throughout the supply chains to keep food prices down. Although egalitarian in the sense that everyone is offered the same choice of food at the same prices, by not ensuring living wages for all the problems of low incomes and lower equality of opportunity for those working within the agri-food industry, social inequalities can be further exacerbated.

LISA JACK

A further current concern is the food waste engendered by supermarket systems. It is estimated that from farm to fork, between 30% and 50% of food is thrown away. The supermarket model facilitates and has encouraged the over-purchase of food by shoppers (Cardello, 2009). Supermarkets understandably forecast their own purchases on products sold rather than products eaten. The current consumer expectation nurtured by the retailers is to have on-shelf availability of all products all day, every day, to a high-quality standard. Therefore, producers and manufacturers are under pressure to overproduce, and to provide products with a long shelf life. Initially, supermarkets avoided selling fresh produce because it had a short shelf life and was easily damaged. However, supermarkets in the 1980s and 1990s experimented with providing cleaned, unblemished and conveniently prepared fresh produce, and, controversially, appear to have normalised the idea in consumers that this is how fresh produce should be produced and sold. Despite the overhead costs involved, mitigated by putting pressure on suppliers to keep prices low, supermarkets in developed countries have become the source of fresh produce for consumers, 24 hours a day, all year around (Jack, 2021; Jack et al., 2018).

Supermarkets are gradually accepting the responsibility to reduce systemic food loss and waste due to social and financial pressures. Handling excess product incurs costs, adding to the price of food and drink and reducing profits. Food can be redistributed through charities to those on lower incomes and repurposed to create energy and animal feed, but to a great extent these mask fundamental problems with food systems based on the current supermarket model of wide choice and low price (Caraher and Furey, 2018).

Future concerns, issues and questions

Supermarkets have a rather confused role in modern society. They are usually profit-making businesses who also profess to provide the population with food at near cost. They have positioned themselves as the place to buy fresh produce yet are also perceived, as seen in the Covid-19 crisis in 2019–2022, as a nation's emergency stores. They are the custodians of safe food and put stringent requirements on suppliers in terms of food safety

incident and food fraud prevention, yet this builds additional overhead costs into the price of food.

As champions of cheap basic food and affordable luxuries, they have created an expectation among shoppers that food prices should remain low. This leads to accusations of profiteering in times of price rises in fuel and labour costs. It also becomes very difficult for supermarkets to address low returns to farmers and growers; a reliance on imported foods; lack of investment in environmental, public health and social initiatives; and the need for higher wages. However, in Europe and the UK in the 2020s, there is evidence that the larger corporate chains are investing profits in programmes to address some of these issues, whilst keeping basic food prices at near cost. There is also a wave of emerging, independent 'ethical' supermarkets run as social enterprises which aim to provide fair returns and fair wages and to reduce food loss and waste. These smaller, community-based stores adopt the self-service model, and also aim to be a one-stop shop covering fresh produce to non-groceries. They tend to be not-for-profit enterprises offering value for money and ethical products rather than everyday low pricing.

The most important question, though, is whether the business model itself is sustainable or still desirable. In the early stages, the choice for shoppers was to buy from a supermarket, or from a local business or market. During the late 20th century, supermarkets displaced many of the local businesses in Western countries. In the 21st century, there has been a rise in other retailers offering food alongside household goods and clothing; a resurgence of small manufacturers, farmers markets and local shops in some areas; and a rapid growth in online shopping. There are more places for people to buy food and drink cheaply, or to source affordable premium products. Supermarkets are competing with these trends, providing bulk buys and special lines, but the more changes and additions, the greater the overhead cost to the businesses.

The supermarket model continues to spread, and is almost universal. For example, Carrefour started to operate in the Middle East in the mid-1990s, with local businesses becoming established from around 2000. The spread of supermarkets in Africa, South America and Asia also began in the mid-1990s. This supermarket revolution (Das

Nair, 2020) follows similar patterns in each wave: increasing urbanisation, a rising middle class and more women in the workplace, coupled with foreign direct investment and incursions by global multinational retailers. The same patterns of buyer power, displacement of local businesses and use of suppliers' payments appear to be repeated. Although now taken for granted as the primary means of distributing food to a large population, serious debate is needed about the role of supermarkets in a more equitable food system.

References

Caraher M and Furey S (2018) *The economics of emergency food aid provision.* Cham: Springer Books.

Cardello H (2009) *Stuffed: an insider's look at who's (really) making America fat.* New York, Ecco.

Goidanich M E and Rial C (2012) A Place Called Supermarket. *International Review of Social Research*, 2(1), 143–156.

GVR (2023) Food & Grocery Retail Market Size, Share & Trends Analysis Report By Product (Food Cupboard, Beverages), By Distribution Channel (Supermarkets & Hypermarkets, Online), By Region (APAC, Europe), And Segment Forecasts, 2022–2030. https://www.grandviewresearch .com/industry-analysis/food-grocery-retail -market/toc.

Jack L (2021) *The secrets of supermarketing: A model balanced on a knife-edge.* Food Research Collaboration Discussion Paper. https://foodresearch.org.uk/publications /the-supermarket-system-balanced-on-a -knife-edge/.

Jack L, Florez-Lopez R and Ramon-Jeronimo J M (2018) Accounting, performance measurement and fairness in UK fresh produce supply networks. *Accounting, Organizations and Society*, 64, 17-30.

McClelland W G (1962) Economics of the Supermarket. *The Economic Journal*, 72(285), 154–170.

Das Nair R (2020) The 'supermarket revolution' in the South. In Crush J, Frayne B and Haysom G (eds) *Handbook on urban food security in the global South.* Cheltenham, Edward Elgar Publishing, pp. 113–144.

Statista (2025) Grocery shopping by store type in the UK as of December 2024 [Graph]. Statista, January 30. Retrieved May 27, 2025, from https://www.statista .com/forecasts/997923/grocery-shopping -by-store-type-in-the-uk

Tillotson J E (2007/8) *Supermarkets in the 21st Century: Parts 1–3.* Nutrition Today.

Further reading

Charvat F J (1961) *Supermarketing.* New York, The Macmillan Company.

This book is essential reading to understand the business model of supermarkets, and the maths behind the decision making. Although there have been changes since 1961, the rationale for how to bring in and keep customers, and make a profit, is the same now. The key is the practice of (super)marketing, and why that is different to running a grocery store.

Deutsch T (2010) *Building a housewife's paradise: Gender, politics, and American grocery stores in the twentieth century.* Chapel Hill, University of North Carolina Press.

Whilst Charvat (1961) is a history from within supermarkets, Deutsch is one of several writers looking at supermarkets from the consumer point of view.

Reardon T, Timmer C P and Berdegue J (2012) The rapid rise of supermarkets in developing countries: Induced organizational, institutional and technological change in agri-food systems. In McCullough E B, Pingali P L and Stamoulis K G (eds) *The Transformation of Agri-Food Systems.* London, Routledge, pp. 71–90.

This is an excellent choice as a starting place to read about the more recent transmission of the supermarket model in Africa.

111. Sustainability transitions and food

GIUSEPPE FEOLA

The unsustainability of industrial food systems

Industrial food systems, which include the production, consumption, processing, packaging, and transport of food, are predominantly characterised in modern capitalist societies by high levels of external input (e.g., synthetic pesticides and fertilisers), an extractive approach to the natural environment, reliance on markets, increasing financialisation, growth, and capital accumulation. Despite the increasing affordability of "recommended diets" (as defined in country-specific guidelines), food systems "are falling short of delivering optimal nutrition and health outcomes, environmental sustainability, and inclusion and equity for all" (Ambikapathi et al., 2022: 764).

Campbell et al. (2017) found that agricultural production contributes substantially to the transgression of so-called planetary boundaries (e.g., freshwater use, ocean acidification, atmospheric aerosol loading, and climate change). Jones et al. (2010) also identified multiple negative environmental effects, such as the "destruction of biodiversity and environmental service systems ...; animal welfare issues; [and] excessive levels of waste and carbon footprints" (p. 93). Industrial food systems have also had negative social, economic, and socio-ecological repercussions. These include an obesity pandemic and its associated health conditions (e.g., cardiovascular diseases and type 2 diabetes); poor quality of food in terms of taste, human nutrition, and limited access (as indicated by the increasing prevalence of urban food deserts and food banks); labour exploitation, especially of undocumented and seasonal migrant workers; the expulsion of smallholders and peasants from the land and markets; and the loss of often diverse and traditional practices and cultivars (Jones et al., 2010). Food systems are being homogenised and land and resources are becoming ever more concentrated.

Food systems are not only drivers of negative impacts; they are also vulnerable to them. Climate change is a case in point: it has had numerous adverse consequences for water security and food production in every region of the world, but agricultural systems are responsible for around one-third of global greenhouse gas emissions (Pörtner et al., 2022). Extreme events and disruptions such as droughts and inland flooding damage the land systems and infrastructure on which food systems depend. Limited water availability, poor soil properties, and the slower, less visible, yet hard-to-reverse losses in crop and pasture suitability and productivity are all associated with worsening climatic conditions. Meanwhile, food insecurity, loss of income and rural livelihoods, and reduced outdoor labour productivity (due in part to heatwaves and increasingly unfavourable weather conditions) are causing social and economic disruption (Pörtner et al., 2022).

The COVID-19 pandemic, which peaked between 2020 and 2021, exposed the unsustainability and vulnerability of food systems (Blay-Palmer et al., 2020; Leeuwis et al., 2021). Problems with long supply chains, consumption infrastructures (locked-down supermarkets and grocery stores), and mobility (of produce, as well as of seasonal workers) quickly became apparent. The vulnerability of farm workers (especially seasonal, migrant, and undocumented ones), who lie at the bottom of or below the social security pyramid, as well as farming enterprises dependent on migration flows, was revealed (albeit temporarily addressed, e.g., by removing barriers to freedom of movement, as was the case in some European countries). Unequal access to healthy, nutritious food and food insecurity were also magnified, as was the vulnerability of those with diet-related diseases (e.g., cardiovascular diseases and type 2 diabetes): such individuals were subject to higher morbidity and mortality rates from COVID-19. More generally, the pandemic has shown the ineffectiveness of piecemeal policy approaches and has reinforced the call for a systemic approach that prioritises healthy, equitable, resilient, and ecologically sustainable and regenerative food systems characterised by shorter food supply chains and a greater sensitivity to ecological and social contexts (see, for example, Blay-Palmer et al., 2020).

The well-evidenced shortcomings of industrial food systems, which have been laid bare by the COVID-19 pandemic, call for a food system sustainability transition. The latter has been defined as "a transformation process in which food systems are reconfigured to produce more desirable outcomes" (Leeuwis et al., 2021: 775), including healthy and nutritious food, food security, environmental sustainability, and justice. Such sustainability transitions involve "non-linear, long-term, multi-actor processes with struggles and tensions between actors" (Leeuwis et al., 2021: 775), potentially resulting in the reconfiguration of, for instance, food production, distribution, and consumption practices, regulatory and governance regimes, technologies, values and institutions, industrial structures, and power relations.

However, food system sustainability transitions are highly contested political processes rather than matters of rational design (Leeuwis et al., 2021). Stark differences exist between national and international organisations, social movements, business organisations, and consumers and citizens alike regarding the prioritisation of outcomes (e.g., ecological sustainability, adaptation to climate change, nutrition, and food sovereignty); visions (e.g., sustainable intensification, nature-inclusive agriculture, climate-smart agriculture, permaculture, and agroecology); and the role of technologies (e.g., cultured meat and digitalisation). More generally, a diverse range of imaginaries and discourses (e.g., ecocentric, anthropocentric, ecomodernist, commons and degrowth-orientated) inform, to varying degrees, both policy-making processes and experimentation in transitions at the local level through business innovation, public–private partnerships, and grassroots, community-led initiatives, which together represent a broad spectrum of coexisting conventional and alternative practices.

Food system sustainability transitions: schools of thought and crucial concerns

Research on food system sustainability transitions is informed by schools of thought and paradigms that defy any stringent classification (Melchior and Newig, 2021). Two commonly adopted and mutually contrasting paradigms are those of sustainability transitions (ST) and food regimes.

The ST paradigm is a widely recognised approach to the study of "long-term, multi-dimensional, and fundamental transformation processes through which established socio-technical systems shift to more sustainable modes of production and consumption" (Markard et al., 2012: 956). Although

sustainability transitions vary between domains and countries, they are ordinarily expected to take several decades and involve four phases: experimentation, stabilisation, diffusion and disruption of incumbent structures, and institutionalisation and anchoring. Sustainability transition scholars have tended to employ frameworks such as the multi-level perspective and technological innovation systems to explore the dynamics that drive socio-technical change. When observed through these theoretical lenses, food systems can be conceptualised as socio-technical regimes, that is, relatively stable and persistent sets of rules that orientate and coordinate the activities of the social groups that reproduce the various elements of socio-technical systems. This results in the relatively stable and persistent alignment of knowledge, regulations, infrastructures, and values across multiple interrelated domains (e.g., policy, industry, technology, markets, science, and culture).

Sustainability transitions entail a reconfiguration of socio-technical regimes with an objective to improve, in some capacity, sustainability performance. This may ensue, for example, from deliberate interventions on innovation systems (e.g., through policy incentives for more sustainable food production practices or the generation and targeted diffusion of knowledge about nature-inclusive agricultural practices) or from the dynamic interaction of innovation niches and landscape trends. In the latter case, the macro landscape level (e.g., macroeconomics, deep cultural patterns, macro-political developments, and climate change) of slow-moving trends that are beyond the direct influence of regime actors exert pressure on the regime. They may create an opportunity for bottom-up pressure from so-called "innovative niches" that diffuse through and disrupt the existing system, resulting in regime reconfiguration. Niches come from outside the dominant socio-technical regime; they incubate and protect innovation (e.g., in organic or agroecological agriculture) and aim to transform the existing regime. Niche innovations are carried and developed by small networks of dedicated actors, who are often outsiders (e.g., networks of frontrunner farmers, scientists and investors, or of community-based movements and new peasants) (Leeuwis et al., 2021).

The ST approach can be used to analyse transition processes in food systems, as well as informing articulated strategies for governing them. Nevertheless, as a paradigm historically rooted in innovation, evolutionary economics, and science and technology studies—and more recently encompassing issues relating to power, politics, gender, and justice—ST research on food systems has only dealt marginally with crucial drivers and outcomes of food sustainability transitions, namely: (i) social justice, equity, and inclusion in food systems, which have given way to concerns over socio-technical processes; (ii) food security and nutrition; (iii) the spatiality, place-specificity, and geography of food systems, and the specificity of sustainability transitions of food systems in low- and middle-income countries; (iv) cross-scale dynamics regarding trade flows, information transfer, and species dispersal; (v) agency (e.g., the role of social movements, civil society, firms, and industries) and associated power relations; and (vi) the political economy of food sustainability transitions (El Bilali, 2019a, 2019b; Hebinck et al., 2021). Increasing the cross-fertilisation of ST research and other paradigms, such as social-ecological systems research, may be particularly useful when addressing blind spots regarding the ecological and multi-scale dynamics of food transitions (Leeuwis et al., 2021; Ollivier et al., 2018).

In contrast with ST, the food regimes (FR) approach has placed political-economic concerns at the front and centre of analyses of agriculture and food systems (McMichael, 2009; Friedmann, 2005). FR scholars have examined changes to regime institutions and power relations in distinct capitalist formations over time. From an FR perspective, a regime transition or transformation entails the reconfiguration of capitalism. This view foregrounds formal and informal institutions, actors (e.g., governments, corporations, and civil society), and power relations.

A food regime, a historically specific phenomenon in the global political economy of food, is characterised by the formal and informal institutions of capital accumulation. It is made stable by the international linking of agrifood production and consumption relations in accordance with global capital accumulation patterns. McMichael (2009) refers to capitalist industrial agriculture as "the corporate food regime", and suggested that understanding this concept is "a key to unlock not only structured moments and transitions in the history of capitalist food relations, but also the history of capitalism itself" (p. 163).

McMichael (2009) argues that food systems cannot be considered to be external to capitalism because they reflect and reproduce dominant capitalist elements in particular historical periods. According to Friedmann (2005), capitalist industrial agriculture reinforces two key pillars of capitalism, namely commodification (i.e., of nature, labour, and food) and capital accumulation.

The FR approach has advanced the understanding of the pivotal role of the food regime in the broader global capitalist political economy across time and space from a historical perspective. In particular, it brings to the fore the political-economic, cultural, and power structures that sustain industrial food systems, while offering a critical entry point for thinking about the transformation of those structures (Friedmann, 2017). The FR approach tends, however, to take a totalising view of capitalism; it provides less systematic and empirically informed analyses of transition processes at levels other than the global, which has created certain simplistic dichotomies (e.g., between unsustainable global agribusiness capital and small scale sustainable farmers). Furthermore, it is not easy nor perhaps possible to derive insights from the past that are convincing and relevant to future food system sustainability transitions.

In sum, research on food sustainability transitions is informed by a variety of schools of thought and paradigms. The two outlined herein are marked by specific concerns, analytical perspectives, and blind spots. Further exploration of their theoretical, analytical, and methodological complementarities, as well as paradigms such as social-ecological systems and sustainability transformation, would advance our understanding of the complexity of food systems and possible sustainability transitions (Melchior and Newig, 2021; Ollivier et al., 2018).

The agroecological transitions literature has managed to cut across the divides between approaches. Scholars in this field have examined the institutionalisation and scaling of agroecology at the national level in countries such as Brazil, Cuba, Nicaragua, and France. They have documented concrete cases in which agroecological practices have become institutionalised in policies and political and administrative structures and adopted by large numbers of people across different regions. Their studies have also distilled lessons from drivers and processes to take agroecology to scale; agroecological transitions depend on effective agroecological practices, the recognition of the need for alternatives to current food systems, favourable markets and policies, and—crucially—relationships based on social organisation, learning, and adaptation in real-world situations (Mier y Terán Giménez Cacho et al., 2018).

The agroecological literature has, however, also exposed the limitations and difficulties in the institutionalisation and scaling of agroecology. Incentives and policies are often only weakly implemented; they do not always lead to the reconfiguration of food systems because they are often added to food policy mixes and coexisting logics without the deliberate destabilisation and phasing out of pre-existing unsustainable agrifood practices, institutions, and structures. Furthermore, the agroecological discourse is often co-opted by incumbent actors and vested interests that effectively resist or slow down the transition and dilute the transformative potential of agroecology in the political and other arenas (Schiller et al., 2020).

Food system sustainability transitions: future prospects

Research on food system sustainability transitions can inform policy and action, but the question of how to govern—and, ultimately, realise—food system sustainability transitions in the face of path dependency and the problem of overseeing change in complex systems has yet to be answered (Leeuwis et al., 2021).

The long-standing emphasis on ecological sustainability in food system sustainability transitions has narrowed the space in which food security, sovereignty, justice, coloniality, and nutrition can be discussed, even though these issues remain on the agendas of social movements, international organisations, governments, and researchers, who tend to be disconnected from debates concerning the socio-technical and social-ecological perspectives of sustainability transitions. Diverse conceptualisations of sustainability in food sustainability transitions need, therefore, to be integrated. This would shift the focus from technological and ecological to social, political, and health outcomes in food system sustainability transitions, diversifying transition policy interventions, and encouraging policy integration across conventionally separated policy domains (e.g., nutrition and health, ecology, technological and economic development, and rural planning; Hebinck et al., 2021). Matters of food security and sovereignty, nutrition, food justice and food democracy, access to land, land use conflicts, and the livelihoods of rural poor people are likely to trigger normative stances, make food system sustainability transitions more contentious, and pose an obstacle to change. On the other hand, integrated conceptualisations of sustainability in food sustainability transitions offer the opportunity to establish diverse advocacy and political coalitions and pursue change by multiplying political opportunities as discourses around food system problematics converge. Also, it is crucial that interested parties explore the potential of emerging critiques of capitalism (e.g., degrowth); cast new light on the systemic roots of the flaws manifested in industrial food systems; and bridge distinct but aligned analyses of food systems and their possible sustainability transition (Guerrero Lara et al., 2023).

Another issue is the need to understand how sustainability transitions are connected to trends beyond the regime level. For example, despite recent insightful analyses of the benefits and risks of agriculture and food system digitalisation, the effects of advanced technologies on sustainability transitions and their governance have been under-researched. Other topics that merit more attention in future research include: (i) the ageing farming population; (ii) ongoing migration from rural to urban areas (as well as larger international migration flows that are altering the social fabric of many societies); (iii) the persistent (and in some instances accelerating) trend towards flexibilisation and unregulated (and unprotected) work; and (iv) increasing corporate concentration and power in the global food system (Hebinck et al., 2021). These issues are as prevalent in the Global North as they are in the Global South, where they more evidently intersect the legacy and present experience of (neo)colonisation, dependency, and exploitation.

References

Ambikapathi R, Schneider K R, Davis B, Herrero M, Winters P, Fanzo J C (2022) Global food systems transitions have enabled affordable diets but had less favourable outcomes for nutrition, environmental health, inclusion and equity. *Nature Food* 3, 764–779. https://doi.org/10.1038/s43016-022-00588-7.

Blay-Palmer A, Carey R, Valette E, Sanderson M R (2020) Post COVID 19 and food pathways to sustainable transformation. *Agriculture and Human Values* 37, 517–519. https://doi.org/10.1007/s10460-020-10051-7.

Campbell B M, Beare D J, Bennett E M, Hall-Spencer J M, Ingram J S I, Jaramillo F, Ortiz R, Ramankutty N, Sayer J A, Shindell D (2017) Agriculture production as a major driver of the Earth system exceeding planetary boundaries. *Ecology & Society* 22(8). https://doi.org/10.5751/ES-09595-220408.

El Bilali H (2019a) Research on agro-food sustainability transitions: where are food security and nutrition? *Food Security* 11, 559–577. https://doi.org/10.1007/s12571-019-00922-1.

El Bilali H (2019b) Research on agro-food sustainability transitions: A systematic review of research themes and an analysis of research gaps. *Journal of Cleaner Production* 221, 353–364. https://doi.org/10.1016/j.jclepro.2019.02.232.

Friedmann H (2005) From colonialism to green capitalism: social movements and emergence of food regimes. *Research in Rural Sociology and Development* 11(5), 227–264. https://doi.org/10.1016/S1057-1922(05)11009-9.

Friedmann H (2017) Paradox of transition: two reports on how to move towards sustainable food systems. *Development and Change* 48, 1210–1226. https://doi.org/10.1111/dech.12329.

Guerrero Lara L, van Oers L, Smessaert J, Spanier J, Raj G, Feola G (2023) Degrowth and agri-food systems: a research agenda for the critical social sciences. *Sustainability Science* 18, 1579–1594. https://doi.org/10.1007/s11625-022-01276-y.

Hebinck A, Klerkx L, Elzen B, Kok K P W, König B, Schiller K, Tschersich J, van Mierlo B, von Wirth T (2021) Beyond food for thought: directing sustainability transitions research to address fundamental change in agri-food systems. *Environmental Innovation and Societal Transitions* 41, 81–85. https://doi.org/10.1016/j.eist.2021.10.003.

Jones O, Kirwan J, Morris C, Buller H, Dunn R, Hopkins A, Whittington F, Wood J (2010) On the alternativeness of alternative food networks: sustainability and the co-production of social and ecological wealth. In Fuller D, Jonas A.E, Lee R. (Eds), *Interrogating Alterity: Alternative Economic and Political Spaces*. Ashgate Publishing, Farnham, pp. 95–109.

Leeuwis C, Boogaard B K, Atta-Krah K (2021) How food systems change (or not): governance implications for system transformation processes. *Food Security* 13, 761–780. https://doi.org/10.1007/s12571-021-01178-4.

Markard J, Raven R, Truffer B (2012) Sustainability transitions: an emerging field of research and its prospects. *Research Policy* 41, 955–967. https://doi.org/10.1016/j.respol.2012.02.013.

McMichael P (2009) A food regime genealogy. *Journal of Peasant Studies* 36(1), 139–169. https://doi.org/10.1080/03066150902820354.

Melchior I C, Newig J (2021) Governing transitions towards sustainable agriculture: taking stock of an emerging field of research. *Sustainability* 13, 528. https://doi.org/10.3390/su13020528.

Mier y Terán Giménez Cacho M, Giraldo O F, Aldasoro M, Morales H, Ferguson B G, Rosset P, Khadse A, Campos C (2018) Bringing agroecology to scale: key drivers and emblematic cases. *Agroecology and Sustainable Food Systems* 42, 637–665. https://doi.org/10.1080/21683565.2018.1443313.

Ollivier G, Magda D, Mazé A, Plumecocq G, Lamine C (2018) Agroecological transitions: what can sustainability transition frameworks teach us? An ontological and empirical analysis. *Ecology & Society* 23(5). https://doi.org/10.5751/ES-09952-230205.

Pörtner H-O, Roberts D C, Poloczanska E S, Mintenbeck K, Tignor M, Alegría A, Craig M, Langsdorf S, Löschke S, Möller V, Okem A (eds.) (2022) *Summary for Policymakers*. In IPCC, *Climate Change 2022: Impacts, Adaptation and Vulnerability. Contribution of Working Group II to the Sixth Assessment Report of the Intergovernmental Panel on Climate Change*. Cambridge University Press, Cambridge, UK and New York, 3–33. https://doi:10.1017/9781009325844.001.

Schiller K, Godek W, Klerkx L, Poortvliet P M (2020) Nicaragua's agroecological transition: transformation or reconfiguration of the agri-food regime? *Agroecology and Sustainable Food Systems* 44, 611–628. https://doi.org/10.1080/21683565.2019.1667939.

Further reading

Breaking away from industrial food and farming systems. Seven case studies of agroecological transition, 2018. IPES-Food. https://ipes-food.org/report/breaking-away-from-industrial-food-and-farming-systems/

An analysis of concrete examples of how, in spite of barriers to change, people around the world have been able to fundamentally rethink and redesign food systems around agroecological principles.

Klerkx L, Rose D (2020) Dealing with the game-changing technologies of Agriculture 4.0: how do we manage diversity and responsibility in food system transition pathways? *Global Food Security* 24, 100347. https://doi.org/10.1016/j.gfs.2019.100347.

An overview of the development of digitalisation in food systems, and a discussion of its implications for sustainability transitions.

GIUSEPPE FEOLA

112. Sustainable agriculture

JULIE INGRAM

Introduction

The concept of sustainable agriculture first rose to prominence in the 1980s and has progressively gained scientific legitimacy. At the time, the concept emerged in response to a fundamentally unsustainable model of agricultural production. The multiple environmental and social impacts of this production model have been widely documented, including loss of biodiversity, widespread pollution by fertilisers and pesticides, and degradation of natural resources, with associated human health risks. These impacts include also the social justice and food security issues inherent in a more industrial food system. Since then, there have been growing debates about the need to re-orientate food production towards more ecological, social and environmental goals to address the growing demands from society on agricultural systems.

Sustainable agriculture is often described as a set of ideal objectives aligned to the three sustainability pillars: a healthy environment, economic profitability, and social and economic equity. This is captured in the FAO's definition: "To be sustainable, agriculture must meet the needs of present and future generations for its products and services, while ensuring profitability, environmental health, and social and economic equity" (FAO, 2014: 12). However, sustainability issues in agriculture qualify as so-called 'wicked problems', and are poorly defined or even resist conventional definition. The term 'sustainable' can evoke diverse concepts (e.g. financial profitability, mitigating environmental impact, maintaining natural capital, building resilience). The notion of sustainable agriculture is accordingly vague and this has led to the emergence of a great variety of different discourses, views, models and paradigms. These are reflected in the plurality of values in different sustainable agriculture models, their forms of organisation and the institutions governing them (Plumecocq et al., 2018). As such, multiple definitions and understandings have emerged and evolved over time, going through a sequence of 'semantic shifts' as new challenges and opportunities arise (Struik and Kuyper, 2017). Now, it is generally agreed that, rather than seek one correct, universal definition, we need to adapt the definition of sustainable agriculture to the respective context. This can be done according to a number of critical principles for sustainable agriculture that have been identified (for example: Pretty 2008), namely: (1) improving efficiency in the use of resources; (2) conserving, protecting and enhancing natural ecosystems; (3) protecting and improving rural livelihoods and social well-being; (4) enhancing the resilience of people, communities and ecosystems; and (5) promoting good governance of both natural and human systems (FAO, 2014).

At its simplest, sustainable agriculture is often defined in opposition to conventional agriculture although there are no criteria that clearly delineate the two and the variety of definitions highlights the fluidity of these boundaries. Conventional agriculture typically involves highly specialised systems that emphasise yields achieved by high inputs (fertilisers, pesticides). In contrast, sustainable agriculture is characterised by low inputs and multiple objectives, systems and practices. Sustainable agricultural systems are framed by multiple concepts (e.g., natural capital, ecosystems services, multifunctionality, resilience, stewardship) associated with different farming approaches and principles (e.g., agroecological farming, sustainable intensification, ecological intensification, smart and precision farming, regenerative agriculture), addressing different foci (carbon farming, agroforestry, integrated pest management). These systems are in turn enacted according to repertoires of different best management practices (e.g. non-inversion tillage, nutrient management, cover crops, rotational grazing, intercropping, polyculture); assessed with reference to a number of different metrics and indicators; and subject to multiple synergies and trade-offs at farm and landscape scale. They are also underpinned by different values and ideologies which consider to varying degrees the social, economic and ethical context within which food production activities take place.

Sustainable agriculture is interpreted and implemented differently across the world, depending on different challenges and settings. In the EU, for example, a range of sustainable agriculture policies have supported agricultural production alongside agri-environment and rural development schemes. In a Global South context, food and agriculture are central to the United Nations' Sustainable Development Goals (SDGs), specifically SDG2: "[to] [e]nd hunger, achieve food security and improved nutrition and promote sustainable agriculture". Here the notion of sustainable food and agriculture has also been advanced by FAO. This contributes to all four pillars of food security – availability, access, utilisation and stability – and the three common dimensions of sustainability (environmental, social and economic) (FAO, 2014). Poverty alleviation, smallholder livelihoods, inclusion, gender, tenure and labour rights, and empowerment of farmers are also emphasised in sustainable agriculture concepts in Global South contexts, and are integral to agroecology approaches characterised by farmer-led social movements such as La Via Campesina. More recently, the climate emergency has entered the sustainable agriculture lexicon, with climate smart agriculture being promoted, and the COP26's Policy Action Agenda to Transition to Sustainable Food and Agriculture lists agricultural practices that sequester or minimise greenhouse gas emissions as one of its seven principles for a sustainable agriculture approach.

Towards a critical understanding of sustainable agriculture

Two positions

Seen as a contested concept, the debate about what constitutes sustainable agriculture is largely framed by two contrasting positions. First, the *techno-economic* position is characterised by economic goals and technological solutions and viewed as a production issue on the level of the farm. Also known as the *bio-economic* model, it has a focus on agricultural development in the form of precision and smart farming, and technical and genetic crop improvement. Second, the *ecocentric* position takes a strong alternative agroecological position, which considers overarching values, proposes the application of alternative approaches and promotes action in arenas beyond the farm gate. This ecocentric position is also called the *eco-economy* model and is based on a broad variety of local practices, projects and farmer initiatives, illustrating a more locally embedded agriculture, adapted to natural assets and based on a diversity of agro-ecological approaches (Horlings and Marsden, 2011; Velten et al., 2015). These so-called conceptual dichotomies are

characterised in other literatures as: weak or strong (shallow or deep) sustainability, relating to the extent of substitutability of natural capital (; Hill and Macrae, 1996); weak versus strong ecological modernisation, according to the extent of systemic change (Horlings and Marsden, 2011); and weak versus strong multifunctionality, according to a productivist/ non-productivist spectrum of multifunctionality (Wilson, 2008).

In these sustainability frameworks, the entry point is to understand that farming practices are embedded in different agri-food systems. Weak sustainability is therefore associated with perpetuating the market and scientific dominance of the current agri-industrial food paradigm. Weak versions of sustainable agriculture address environmental problems by technocratic and corporatist modes of policy-making. Strong versions of sustainability, on the other hand, are seen as more aligned with restructuring the capitalist political economy and with farmer and consumer participation (Horlings and Marsden, 2011). These competing visions have also been described as 'life sciences versus an agroecology vision' based on epistemological differences between the two knowledge systems and patterns of innovation. The first relies heavily on technical change, whereas in the second vision a large role is also played by organisational and institutional change (social innovation), system optimisation and system innovation respectively (Levidow et al., 2018).

This dichotomy is also explored with reference to high or low territorial embeddedness (Therond et al., 2017). Embeddedness is low when farming systems are embedded in industrial, globalised, commodity-based food systems and social relationships are driven mainly by globalised market prices. Conversely, territorial embeddedness is high when farming systems are involved in place-specific approaches (or initiatives), like circular economies or alternative food networks, and they are in systems which meet multiple socioeconomic and environmental objectives at the local or regional level.

This debate is also played out in Global South contexts. In particular, scholars note how the SDG2 goal conceals substantial differences in perspective regarding what precisely is the challenge and how it can best be resolved due to inconsistency in SDG targets and different agendas (McNeill, 2019). While high level international organisations and agencies have criticised the productionist approach, the industrial agriculture approach continues to maintain a very powerful position through some international agencies, donor countries and foundations. Aligning the principles of sustainable agriculture with the need to invest in agriculture for development to address declining yields and increasing poverty is a challenge. This economic imperative is articulated in the Bill and Melinda Gates Foundation's goal with respect to agricultural development, which aims "[t]o support farmers and governments in sub-Saharan Africa and South Asia that are seeking a sustainable, inclusive agricultural transformation—one that creates economic opportunity, respects limits on natural resources, and gives everyone equal access to affordable, nutritious food" (Bill and Melinda Gates Foundation, n.d.).

Appropriation

This range of understandings and ambiguities allows for exploitation of the sustainable agriculture concept by vested interests who use the notion for their own purposes. This so-called appropriation is reinforced by a framing of future food shortages and population growth, which is used to justify more intensive models of farming and perpetuates weaker forms of sustainable agriculture.

In practice, what this means is that sustainability is effectively co-opted by neoliberal forms of capitalism, leading to the promotion of ecological modernisation or sustainable intensification, which at a concept-level are well intended but may become too aligned with the dominant agri-food paradigm. Some interpretations of 'sustainability' are seen as a vehicle to 'smuggle' into sustainable agriculture potentially harmful technologies. As sustainable agriculture has evolved, different terms have emerged and are often bundled together in the policy and corporate literature, with prefixes like 'ecological', 'climate' or 'smart' or suffixes of 'intensification' or 'modernisation', which are then used to justify productivist approaches (Struik and Kuyper, 2017). There is evidence, for example, where agribusinesses position themselves as a necessary part of the solution and use the concept to advance their preferred technologies and strategies as well as seek to re-package them in ways which access new financial and revenue streams. As sustainable agriculture proponents shift toward market-based relationships with penetration of profit-driven rationality, there are concerns that this will dilute or alter what sustainable agriculture means and, crucially, that social and ecological sustainability values become of secondary importance.

Achieving a sustainable transition

A shift or transition from a system characterised as having the goal of producing food and increasing productivity, to one built around the wider principles of sustainable production and rural development, resilience and food security requires radical transformations in the social and economic organisation of agriculture, based on equitable distribution, individual empowerment and social justice. However, while certain groups of researchers, NGOs, social movements and activists argue that transition means major changes and a complete overhaul of existing farming and agri-food systems, stakeholders active in various sectors in the agri-food system claim that they are already largely sustainable, and that small and incremental improvements can bring, and are bringing, about sustainability. This debate about radical and incremental change reflects the competing visions for sustainable agriculture discussed above.

Transition requires challenging the dominant agri-food regime which is maintained in institutions and is held together by strong lobbies. Innovative forms of agriculture are emerging which can potentially contribute to such a transition, often associated with groups and networks of social actors advocating alternatives to mainstream agri-food systems. However, these niches tend to encounter difficulties in achieving transformative change due to the strong status of the regime. These niche actors can penetrate the regime and gain legitimacy by conforming to prescriptive practices and standards, and acquiring network relationships with mainstream individuals and organisations, but this can risk dilution of values. The efficiency-substitution-redesign framework developed to support the transition from conventional to sustainable agriculture suggests a linear process (Hill and Macrae, 1996). However, others, such as Pretty (2008), argue for a complete redesign process to bring about ecological, economic, social and political conditions change across whole landscapes through cooperation and collective action. This highlights the difference between *goal-prescribing* approaches where certain types of management, measures or prescribed techniques are defined as being sustainable (such as standards for organic farming) and *system-describing* approaches which focus on balancing social, economic and ecological goals, in a process of continuous optimisation (Siebrecht 2020).

Future concerns, issues and questions

The rationale and arguments for further supporting high input agriculture continue with a rising population and increasing demand for food. However, the capacity of ecosystems to deliver essential services to society is under increasing stress and the additional effects of climate change and targets for net-zero amplify this. Many of the future agri-food system missions and visions are framed as contributing to sustainable agriculture. These envision novel forms of agriculture (e.g. urban agriculture, vertical agriculture, cellular agriculture), employ a suite of new technologies (e.g. satellite technology, robot technology, artificial intelligence), and claim transformative concepts and new styles of farming (nature-based solutions, ecologically regenerative solutions, circular farming, smart farming, protein transitions). However, these will need to be accompanied by reframing agriculture to foster and incorporate social justice, stronger nature–society ties, fairer trade, and more deliberative forms of food democracy. Achieving a transformation to sustainable agriculture therefore requires societal debates about values and norms, and more democratic and transparent decision-making with respect to the many trade-offs this transformation entails (Struik and Kuyper, 2017).

References

Bill and Melinda Gates Foundation (n.d.) https://www.gatesfoundation.org/our-work/programs/global-growth-and-opportunity/agricultural-development (Accessed 1 November 2023).

FAO (2014) *Building a common vision for sustainable food and agriculture: principles and approaches.* Food and Agriculture Organization of the United Nations (FAO) Publications, Rome, Italy. ISBN 978-92-5-108471-7.

Hill S B and Macrae R J (1996) Conceptual framework for the transition from conventional to sustainable agriculture. *Journal of Sustainable Agriculture,* 7, 81–87.

Horlings L G and Marsden T K (2011) Towards the real green revolution? Exploring the conceptual dimensions of a new ecological modernisation of agriculture that could 'feed the world'. *Global Environmental Change,* 21, 441–452.

Levidow L, Nieddu M, Vivien F D and Béfort N (2018) Transitions towards a European bioeconomy: life sciences versus agroecology trajectories. In Allaire G and Daviron B (Eds), *Ecology, Capitalism and the New Agricultural Economy* (pp. 181–204). Routledge.

McNeill D (2019). The contested discourse of sustainable agriculture. *Global Policy,* 10, 16–27.

Plumecocq G, Debril T, Duru M, Magrini M B, Sarthou J P and Therond O (2018) The plurality of values in sustainable agriculture models. *Ecology and Society,* 23, 21.

Siebrecht N (2020) Sustainable agriculture and its implementation gap: overcoming obstacles to implementation. *Sustainability,* 12, 3853.

Struik P C and Kuyper T W (2017) Sustainable intensification in agriculture: the richer shade of green. A review. *Agronomy for Sustainable Development,* 37, 39.

Therond O, Duru M, Roger-Estrade J and Richard G (2017) A new analytical framework of farming system and agriculture model diversities. A review. *Agronomy for Sustainable Development,* 37, 1–24.

Velten S, Leventon J, Jager N and Newig J (2015) What is sustainable agriculture? A systematic review. *Sustainability,* 7, 7833–7865.

Wilson G A (2008) From 'weak' to 'strong' multifunctionality: conceptualising farm-level multifunctional transitional pathways. *Journal of Rural Studies,* 24, 367–383.

Further reading

Pretty J (2008) *Sustainable agriculture and food: history of agriculture and food,* Earthscan.

These four volumes provide a comprehensive overview of sustainable agriculture and food. With selected examples, overview chapters and historical contexts, the collection draws together a large body of knowledge and offers a useful reference and entry point for this diverse and complex field.

Leal Filho W, Kovaleva M and Popkova E (eds) (2022). *Sustainable agriculture and food security*. Springer Nature.

This book provides a global perspective on sustainable agriculture, describing initiatives and concrete examples on sustainable food production. It provides a comprehensive and interdisciplinary understanding of the cross-cutting issues related to sustainable agriculture, including the intersection with food security.

JULIE INGRAM

113. Sustainable diets

Paolo Prosperi and Kathleen
Kevany

Introduction

The term "sustainable diets" was developed by American nutritionists Gussow and Clancy (1986), with their foundational article "Dietary Guidelines for Sustainability" published in the *Journal of Nutrition Education*. A "sustainable diet" was explicitly defined three years later by Herrin and Gussow (1989:270), as "a diet composed of foods chosen for their contribution not only to health, but also to the sustainability (the capability of maintenance into the foreseeable future) of the U.S. agricultural system". When Gussow and Clancy introduced the term sustainable diets, their aim was to improve consumer education about the hazards of the "agricultural and food processing system" (1986:4), by associating challenges of agricultural sustainability with nutrition messages. In this work, Gussow and Clancy (1986:2) provided a definition of sustainable agriculture as "uses human and natural resources to produce food and fiber in a manner that is not wasteful of such finite resources as topsoil, water, and fossil energy". This underscored the intertwined systemic and dynamic connections between agricultural problems (i.e., energy inefficiency, geographic concentration, pesticide resistance, water depletion) and increasing consumption of unsustainable diets. It is of particular interest that Gussow and Clancy (1986) stressed the need to link agriculture and global resources to nutrition education, by building on early and mid-20th-century observations of Sherman (1919, 1950), who was advocating – even back then – for the consumption of local fresh products to avoid energy and transportation costs, grains for humans instead of livestock feeding, and dairy products instead of meat to reduce waste of resources. Gussow and Clancy further articulated a comprehensive picture and systems-thinking of the critical role of nutrition to avert undesirable environmental, economic and social impacts on agricultural and food systems sustainability. Based on scientific evidence, they drew up key dimensions for a sustainable diet which suggested that for nutrition and the environment people should: (a) consume a variety of foods that offer nourishment and also serve to protect biodiversity; (b) maintain ideal weights to avoid waste linked to overconsumption; (c) reduce the use of fat, saturated fat and cholesterol to reduce the energy costs and soil degradation linked to animal production; (d) promote foods with adequate fibre to improve consumption of starch, fibre and vitamin sources and to avoid processed products rich in sugar, salt and fat, and to add value to farmer primary products; (e) reduce sugar consumption to decrease the use of energy for production, processing and packaging; (f) reduce sodium to promote fresh products for sustainability and health instead of processed foods; and (g) moderate alcoholic beverage consumption to reduce environmental and health costs of production and consumption. While Gussow and Clancy provided sound nutritional foundations and insights on multiple dimensions within sustainable diets, importantly they offered critical analysis of the complex dynamics that link nutrition and agricultural sustainability in food systems and showed that industrialised food production systems: (a) generate overconsumption and waste of natural resources, (b) build on inefficient use of energy, (c) lead to inequalities between population groups, with some living in areas of concentrated production and some living in areas with concentrated consumption, and (d) include economics that fail to produce sustainability. They highlight that sustainable practices are needed all along the food value chain, particularly with governments, producers, practitioners and consumers.

Current issues and trends in sustainable diets

Gussow and Clancy urged nutrition educators to incorporate agricultural sustainability issues into food guides for "long-term stability of the food system" (1986:4), and the use of sustainability, in ways that were consistent with the contemporary work of the United Nations World Commission on Environment and Development: The Brundtland Commission. Between 1983 and 1987 this Commission developed the report *Our Common Future*, which formulated an interdisciplinary and integrated approach to global and interlinked current and future economic, environmental and social concerns and identified the objective of sustainable development as that which "meets the needs of the present without compromising the ability of future generations to meet their own needs".

With growing concerns of the international community around sustainability, sustainable diets and sustainable development became frequently leveraged strategies for contending with needs (food, nutrition, livelihood, etc.) and limitations (natural resources, ecosystem parameters). The Brundtland report also highlighted multiple strategies for sustainable food security that were incorporated into a holistic vision including government interventions, natural resource management, agricultural productivity and socio-economic equity.

In 1996, however, food security itself was defined by the World Food Summit of the United Nations as a condition that "exists when all people, at all times, have physical, social and economic access to sufficient, safe and nutritious food which meets their dietary needs and food preferences for an active and healthy life" (United Nations, 1996). The sustainability vision for agricultural and food systems – the concept of the Sustainable Diets arising from Gussow and Clancy in 1986 – was not encompassed in this more recent United Nations food security definition despite having the power to guide the world towards more sustainable food systems. Simultaneously, during the 1990s, the international community was preparing the Millennium Development Goals that, in the end, were extremely fragmented into so-called sectoral "silos" – such as health, education, environment – and thus resulted in several lost opportunities to improve multidimensional development outcomes (Waage et al., 2010).

Following this period, on the way to the 2010s, passing through the oil and food price global spike in 2007–8, and heading towards the 2030 Agenda for Sustainable Development and the Sustainable Development Goals (SDGs), the necessary holistic and pluralistic character of strategies for human development and global sustainability regained the attention of the international community. In 2012, 26 years after the Gussow and Clancy article, the Food and Agriculture Organization of the United Nations and Bioversity International – including forty-six participants in the related symposium – agreed on the new and common definition of sustainable diets as "those diets with low environmental impacts which contribute to food and nutrition security and to healthy life for present and future generations. Sustainable diets are protective and respectful

of biodiversity and ecosystems, culturally acceptable, accessible, economically fair and affordable; nutritionally adequate, safe and healthy; while optimising natural and human resources" (FAO and Bioversity International, 2012: 7).

The current conceptualisation of sustainable diets (FAO and Biodiversity International, 2012) highlights the primary purpose of food systems, which is to ensure the health and food security of individuals, emphasising the importance of quality rather than simply quantity or accessibility. It advocates for a research and policy agenda that incorporates nutrition as a core element and stands for economically, socially and environmentally sustainable food systems, and the role of governance and politics needing attention. Importantly, sustainable diets discourse provides food and nutrition security-oriented perspectives with critical reviews of economic and equity implications (Allen et al., 2014). Compared with the current FAO definition, the first Sustainable Diet definition by Gussow and Clancy is still extremely relevant as it encourages systems critiques, yet global sustainability problems continue and are worsening. Scientists continue collecting and presenting evidence that food and diet are directly related to and interact with interlinked challenges such as undernutrition, malnutrition, overnutrition and obesity, food safety, the climate emergency and water scarcity, soil erosion and biodiversity loss, food waste and global poverty. In this respect, major works organised by Johnston with Fanzo and Cogill (2014), Downs with Payne and Fanzo (2017) and Mason and Lang (2017) furnish substantial evidence to feed a policy agenda for sustainable diets according to the classification of interdependent categories of actions that consist of nutrition and health; food security, food quality and agriculture; environment and ecosystems; markets, trade and value chains (food economics); and socio-cultural, equity and political factors (culture and society). Diets that are sustainable are able to foster human health while supporting environmental sustainability, as identified by the EAT–Lancet Commission on healthy diets from sustainable food systems (co-chaired by Willett and Rockström, involving 37 scientists). They define and quantify a safe operating space for food systems. The EAT-Lancet Commission – building on quantitative evidence from a global food system modelling framework – categorises a universal healthy reference diet that should be composed of "vegetables, fruits, whole grains, legumes, nuts, and unsaturated oils ... low to moderate amount of seafood and poultry ... no or a low quantity of red meat, processed meat, added sugar, refined grains, and starchy vegetables", in order to nourish an approximate human global population of 10 billion within food production and planetary boundaries by 2050 (Willet et al., 2019:459). The notion of a "universal" healthy diet has been critiqued as it may fail to recognise sufficient access, affordability and cultural diversity in diets (Hirvonen et al., 2020). This scenario aims to achieve the SDGs and the Paris Agreement, which is a legally binding international treaty from 2015 on climate change designed to hold the increase in the global average temperature to well below 2°C above pre-industrial levels and work to limit the temperature increase to 1.5°C above pre-industrial levels. These involve specific management strategies based on healthy dietary patterns, strong reductions in food loss and waste, and radical advances in food production practices, in the face of climate change, land-system change, freshwater use, biodiversity loss, and nitrogen and phosphorus cycles.

New questions and future actions for sustainable diets

The Routledge Handbook of Sustainable Diets (2023), edited by Kevany and Prosperi, develops and gathers findings, new questions and future actions for Sustainable Diets with the contributions of 148 co-authors, scientists, and health and development practitioners. Building on a plethora of previous studies, field evidence, transdisciplinary collective reflections and scientific initiatives – including many pivotal works as cited above – Kevany and Prosperi (2023) provide the first systemic model of Sustainable Diets (p.7) that illustrates how food-related human activities, and in particular consumer dynamics, interact within local and global contexts, and draws the essential role of sustainable practices to achieve the SDGs, across production systems and value chains. The value of this handbook on sustainable diets is revealed through a strong pluralistic approach and the mobilisation of diverse scientific disciplines and food system stakeholders, and by the call to action for sustainable diets through operational and

ethical engagement of the international community. Practical, promising, non-prescriptive contributions are made by the co-authors and editors of the handbook to accelerate the communication and implementation of sustainable diets. Many questions still need attention and action. How might societies move more expeditiously to the adoption of sustainable diets? What are the impediments to its widespread implementation and how might levers be pulled to advance the goals of critical improvements for human, animal and planetary health? To effectively advance this work, it is critical to share stories of the meaningful engagement of leadership by Indigenous Peoples, women and youth. Goals to advance sustainability through food necessitate strong environmental strategies for sustainable agriculture practices, including agroecology, low carbon production, and reduction of inputs, loss and waste. Given the improved state of understanding of how food impacts health and the environment, citizens, industry, educators and policy makers are urged to position food for optimal health and well-being. Specialists also are urged to recognise the diversity among regional food systems and consider affordability, while striving for minimal adverse environmental impacts. Governments are called upon to ensure regulations and supports enable food environments that increase accessibility of sustainable diets. Leaders and supporters of food movements also are critical in bringing about *a great food transformation* as the EAT–Lancet report urges. To ensure access to sustainable diets for all in the community, providing food prescriptions or vouchers for fruit and vegetables is one example of public investment that can increase consumption of these essential, nutritious foods. Greater attention also needs to be placed within business and governance approaches to reduce adverse environmental and social externalities. Citizens should not have to pay the price for corporate profits arising from practices that extract resources or conduct business beyond planetary boundaries. More creative ideas are needed to incorporate virtuous sustainable practices such as circular bioeconomy and digital innovation. Optimising artificial intelligence in the food system will be key to monitoring and evaluating the advances and the setbacks, along with the many outcomes from supporting the proliferation of sustainable diets.

References

Allen T, Prosperi P, Cogill B and Flichman G (2014) Agricultural biodiversity, social–ecological systems and sustainable diets. *Proceedings of the Nutrition Society* 73(4), 498–508.

Downs S M, Payne A and Fanzo J (2017) The development and application of a sustainable diets framework for policy analysis: a case study of Nepal. *Food Policy* 70, 40–49.

FAO and Biodiversity International (2012) *Proceedings of the International Scientific Symposium: Biodiversity and Sustainable Diets United Against Hunger*. Rome, FAO.

Gussow J D and Clancy K L (1986) Dietary guidelines for sustainability. *Journal of Nutrition Education* 18, 1–5.

Herrin M and Gussow J D (1989) Designing a sustainable regional diet. *Journal of Nutrition Education* 21, 270–275.

Hirvonen Bai Y, Headey D and Masters W A (2020) Affordability of the EAT–Lancet reference diet: a global analysis. *The Lancet Global Health* 8(1), e59–e66.

Johnston JL, Fanzo JC and Cogill B (2014) Understanding sustainable diets: a descriptive analysis of the determinants and processes that influence diets and their impact on health, food security, and environmental sustainability. *Advances in nutrition*, 5(4), 418-429.

Kevany K and Prosperi P (eds) (2023) *Routledge Handbook of Sustainable Diets*. London and New York, Taylor & Francis.

Mason P and Lang T (2017) *Sustainable Diets: How Ecological Nutrition Can Transform Consumption and the Food System*. London and New York, Taylor & Francis.

Sherman HC (1919) Permanent gains from the food conservation movement. *Columbia University Quarterly* 21(1), 1-14.

Sherman HC (1950) *The nutritional improvement of life*. New York, Columbia University Press.

United Nations (1996) *Rome Declaration on World Food Security. World Food Summit Plan of Action*. Rome, FAO.

Waage J, Banerji R, Campbell O, Chirwa E, Collender G, Dieltiens V, ... and Unterhalter E (2010) The Millennium Development Goals: a cross-sectoral analysis and principles for goal setting after 2015: Lancet and London International Development Centre Commission. *The Lancet* 376(9745), 991–1023.

Willett W, Rockström J, Loken B, Springmann M, Lang T, Vermeulen S, ... and Murray C J (2019) Food in the Anthropocene: the EAT–Lancet Commission on healthy diets from sustainable food systems. *The Lancet* 393(10170), 447–492.

Further reading

Kevany K and Prosperi P (eds) (2023) *Routledge Handbook of Sustainable Diets*. London and New York, Taylor & Francis.

This handbook offers the most comprehensive, strategic and timely actions in all components needed to advance sustainability in food production and consumption.

Mason P and Lang T (2017) *Sustainable Diets: How Ecological Nutrition Can Transform Consumption and the Food System*. London and New York, Taylor & Francis.

This text was the first to provide substantial analyses of the essential elements of sustainable diets in a compelling and accessible manner.

114. Sustainable food systems

Katerina Psarikidou

Introduction

"All food systems are sustainable" (UN, 2015, p.1). This is the statement that the United Nations High Level Task Force on Food and Nutrition Security chose to open their 2015 report on 'Zero Hunger'. It is an ambitious albeit ambivalent statement, which, in many ways, concretely summarises a key controversy and contestation that lies at the heart of understanding as well as pursuing 'sustainable food systems': are *all* food systems sustainable?

Since the Brundtland Commission's report in 1987, a lot of debate has revolved around the contested nature of sustainable development as a concept. Discussions have also focused on the contradictions within the concept itself: can development and sustainability go hand in hand? The three sustainability pillars have been put under scrutiny, especially questioning dominant narrow conceptualisations of 'the economic' and 'the environmental' as well as the marginalisation of 'the social' in configuring the 'tripartite' vision of and for sustainability (Boström, 2012). Of course, here, understanding the politics of sustainable development is also key, in terms of understanding dominant sustainability framings and narratives, and the role of specific actors and institutions in such processes.

Defining sustainable food systems

A quick web search provides a strong indication of the diversity of definitions on 'sustainable food systems', manifesting the diversity of contested visions and agendas for agrifood sustainability. One of the most commonly used definitions is that of the UN's Food and Agriculture Organization, describing a sustainable food system as "a food system that delivers food security and nutrition for all in such a way that the economic, social and environmental bases to generate food security and nutrition for future generations are not compromised" (FAO, 2018). Key aspect in this definition is the direct link of a 'sustainable food system' to the debated ideas of 'food security' and 'nutrition security'. This adds not only to the contestations of the definition itself but also to the perpetuation of some narrow productivist and nutritionist techno-fix approaches to addressing agrifood sustainability challenges through the production of more food (Psarikidou, 2022).

Such ideas are also further demonstrated through the ways 'economic', 'social' and 'environmental' sustainabilities are explicated in understanding 'sustainable food systems'. These confirm earlier critiques of prioritisation of the economic and the environmental, the first being narrowly associated with the neoliberal logic of profitability and fiscal viability and the second with natural resource efficiency, but also with the narrow economocentric conceptualisations of 'the social', mainly defined by levels of equity in the distribution of economic value. Thus, despite calls for more 'systemic' approaches to thinking about agriculture and food by considering the broader spectrum of agrifood sub-systems (and other systems), 'sustainable food systems' as a concept appears to still resemble what Francis and colleagues (1988) attributed to 'sustainable agriculture', that is 'a management strategy' that aims to reduce input costs, while minimising environmental damage and providing production and profit over time. And, by doing so, it also falls into the trap of what Altieri (1988) described as the neglect of questions of social justice, both substantive and procedural, in configuring 'sustainability' in food systems.

Positioning the sustainable food system

Repositioning (as well as redefining) 'the social' in sustainability thinking and practice can be key in enacting more 'sustainable food systems'. Within academic and policy advocacy circles, there has been a lot of discussion about social justice and equity as guiding principles for rethinking sustainability for 'sustainable food systems'. As early as 1984, anthropologist Gordon Douglass proposed approaching 'social sustainability' as a whole new way of thinking about agrifood sustainability that would not only help us move beyond ontological separations between 'the environmental', 'the economic' and 'the social', but also acknowledge the ever-present and continuous entanglements of the economy and the environment in the social. Such ontological entanglements are key for realising more systemic thinking in relation to 'sustainable food systems', encompassing also a greater diversity of actors from civil society and social movements.

Thus, sociologists and geographers of agriculture and food have turned to 'alternative food networks' (AFNs) as a way of understanding as well as reconfiguring agrifood sustainability. And, in this context, unpacking 'the alternative' is also important, in not only understanding the ways they can 'oppose' industrial food systems and its sustainability configurations, but also by repositioning social justice and equity at the heart of 'sustainable food systems' thinking and practice (Psarikidou and Szerszynski, 2012): for example, by raising questions of ownership of land and food production in food systems, evidencing relations of solidarity enabled through those networks, but also raising questions about how to overcome the class, race and gender injustices also embedded in some of those 'short-food' or 'local' food systems.

Beyond sustainable food systems?

The work of organisations, such as La Via Campesina, is key here not only in learning from agro-ecological practices and farmer struggles but also for developing alternative conceptualisations, such as that of 'food sovereignty', that could help us overcome the challenges, ambiguities and limitations of 'sustainable food systems'. So, would there be a need to move beyond 'sustainable food systems' as a concept, and could this be the solution to the challenge of the unsustainabilities embedded in current food systems?

From the above analysis, it can be understood that there is not a clear definition of and for 'sustainable food systems'. It is a concept that can be used by many different actors – from agro-industrial corporations to governance bodies and civil society organisations – representing different visions and justifying different agendas for agriculture and food. However, what becomes clear is that we cannot configure future food systems without understanding or even possibly moving beyond those contestations. Re-embedding 'the social' in sustainability can also be key, in terms of raising questions of social justice in relation to agrifood practices but also in relation to processes of inclusion in 'sustainable food systems' thinking and framing.

References

Altieri M (1988) Beyond agroecology: making sustainable agriculture part of a political agenda. *American Journal of Alternative Agriculture* 3(4), 142–143. https://doi.org/10.1017/S0889189300002411.

Boström M (2012) A missing pillar? Challenges in theorizing and practicing social sustainability: introduction to the special issue. *Sustainability: Science, Practice and Policy* 8(1), 3–14. https://doi.org/10.1080/15487733.2012.11908080.

FAO (2018) *Sustainable food systems: concept and framework*. https://openknowledge.fao.org/server/api/core/bitstreams/b620989c-407b-4caf-a152-f790f55fec71/content (Accessed 30 May 2025)

Francis C, King J, Nelson D and Lucas L (1988) Research and extension agenda for sustainable agriculture. *American Journal of Alternative Agriculture* 3(2–3), 123–126. https://doi.org/1.1017/S0889189300002290.

Psarikidou K (2022) *Reclaiming the knowledge economy: the case of alternative agro-food networks*. Singapore, Palgrave MacMillan.

Psarikidou K and Szerszynski B (2012) Growing the social: alternative agrofood networks and social sustainability in the urban ethical foodscape. *Sustainability: Science, Practice and Policy* 8(1), 30–39. https://doi.org/10.1080/15487733.2012.11908082.

UN (2015) *All food systems are sustainable*. Compendium Final Report, Zero Hunger Challenge Working Groups. https://www.un.org/en/issues/food/taskforce/pdf/All%20food%20systems%20are%20sustainable.pdf (Accessed 27 November 2022).

Further reading

Agyeman J & Evans B (2004) Just sustainability: the emerging discourse of environmental justice in Britain? *The Geographical Journal* 170(2), 155–164. https://doi.org/10.1080/00330120802013679.

This article introduces 'just sustainability' as a framework that underlines the interlinkages between environmental justice and sustainability.

Douglass G (1984) The meanings of agricultural sustainability. In Douglass G (Ed.), *Agricultural sustainability in*

a changing world order. Boulder, CO, Westview Press, 3–29.
This chapter introduces 'social sustainability' as a new way of thinking about agrifood sustainability beyond ontological separations between 'the environmental', 'the economic' and 'the social'.
Guthman J (2008) "If they only knew": color blindness and universalism in California alternative food institutions. *The Professional Geographer* 60(3), 387–397. https://doi.org/10.1080/00330120802013679.
This article problematises the colour-blindness and whiteness implicated in alternative food discourses and spaces.

KATERINA PSARIKIDOU

115. Sustainable intensification

Niamh Mahon

What is sustainable intensification?

During the late twentieth century, the call to advance global food security was met by a recognition of the need to reduce the negative impacts of agriculture. One potential solution to these problems was via the 'sustainable intensification' of agriculture (SI). SI has been promoted as a third way between highly productivist, industrialised forms of agriculture and the approaches promoted as part of the alternative agriculture movement (Mahon et al., 2017). Its aim is to increase or maintain agricultural productivity while concurrently reducing its negative environmental impacts. As such, SI does not necessarily promote any particular methods to achieve these aims.

The term was coined by Jules Pretty in the 1990s in the context of smallholder, African agriculture (Pretty, 1997). Pretty's definition emphasises the use of local knowledge, farmer participation and the application of a range of technologies to increase crop yields, reduce agricultural pests and manage natural resources. However, Pretty identified 'scaling up' as a potential challenge – that is, how to learn from and build on the small-scale examples identified, and subsequently implement SI on larger scales. Interest in SI increased in the late 2000s thanks, in part, to the UK Royal Society's *Reaping the Benefits* report (Royal Society, 2009). This focused on issues surrounding ensuring future food security at the global scale, and how the application of biotechnologies, such as genetic engineering, could achieve through these particular forms of SI greater food security. However, the authors acknowledged that, although outside their remit, issues of food access and availability also needed to be addressed in order to achieve long lasting food security. SI was further promoted by organisations such as the UN-FAO, USAID, the World Bank and various agricultural transnationals. Each group has defined and described SI differently based on their particular worldviews and ideologies, leading to growing contradictions and confusion about the term and what it means in terms of agricultural practice. Nevertheless, SI has found continued relevance within recent debates on the relative merits of land sparing versus land sharing approaches to agriculture (see Benton & Harwatt, 2022).

Questions and complexities

Despite being widely promoted, questions about SI remain, especially in terms of what SI means in practice. During its history, the emphasis on the different dimensions of SI has changed depending on which stakeholders are using the term and for what purpose. This has led to significant criticism of different uses of the term from NGOs such as Friends of the Earth and the UK's Food Ethics Council, amongst others, and growing confusion as to what SI really means. Queries have been raised as to the relative emphasis placed on both sustainability and intensification and how this changes depending on who is defining the term. Thus, an important first question is whether it should be sustainability or intensification that is accorded more emphasis when putting SI into practice, or should they be accorded an equal emphasis? This then leads to further questions around how to respond to the multiple facets of sustainability – environmental, economic, social and, more recently, institutional and ethical. SI has often been thought of in terms of reducing the environmental impacts of agriculture; however, some suggest all facets of sustainability need consideration for SI to fully embrace the concept. In addition, there are questions around what exactly is being sustained and what is being intensified. SI is commonly described as more from less. But more what? Food, calories or, in terms of the application of technologies, knowledge and labour? And similarly, less of what? External inputs, land, labour? This then raises a set of related questions around the idea of intensification. Does this relate to the inputs of agricultural systems, e.g., the use of technologies, knowledge, labour; or the outputs, e.g., food, fuel and fibre; or both? Finally, the concept is most commonly used in discussions around arable agriculture, but more recently some have raised concerns about the moral and ethical implications of SI when it is discussed in relation to animal agriculture, especially around the consequences of the intensification of farming animals.

It is unlikely a single definition of SI will be applicable everywhere and there is a growing recognition that the meaning of SI in practice is likely to be context-specific. Thus, action towards SI will need to be adaptable, depending on where and how it is employed and at which scale it is operationalised. However, this will require significant coordination between the different sites and scales at which SI is implemented in order for it to be effective. It is also likely that putting the concept into practice anywhere and at any scale will necessitate trade-offs to be made between the different dimensions that make up the term. These trade-offs will need to be carefully considered in order for SI in its varied forms to be employed in ways that are socially acceptable.

Is sustainable intensification still relevant?

SI alone is unlikely to be the 'silver bullet' that solves all the problems related to achieving global food security. Coupled with issues around food production and the impact this has on the environment (and potentially other facets of sustainability) addressed by SI, there is also a corresponding need to focus on the equitable distribution of food, reducing food waste and promoting more sustainable consumption patterns. So, is SI still relevant? Fads and fashions come and go: is it the case that SI was just a fashionable buzzword that has now lost relevance? Other concepts are attracting increased interest and are often promoted as alternatives to SI and with (slightly) less baggage attached. Examples include ecological intensification, regenerative agriculture, agroecology, precision agriculture and climate smart agriculture. If SI is to remain a viable concept some of the questions posed here will need to be addressed in more concrete

terms, including elucidation of the particular scales and farming systems certain forms of SI could be operationalised in.

References

Benton T G and Harwatt H (2022) *Sustainable agriculture and food systems: Comparing contrasting and contested versions.* Research Paper, Royal Institute of International Affairs, London.

Mahon N, Crute I, Simmon E and Mofakkarul Islam M (2017) Sustainable Intensification: "oxymoron" or "third way"? A systematic review. *Ecological Indicators* 74, 73–97.

Pretty J (1997) The sustainable intensification of African agriculture. *Natural Resources Forum* 21(4), 247–256.

Royal Society (2009) *Reaping the benefits. Science and the sustainable intensification of global agriculture.* The Royal Society London, UK.

Further reading

Weltin M, Zasada I, Piorr A, Debolini M, Geniaux G, Perez O, Scherer L, Marco L and Schulp C (2018) Conceptualising fields of action for sustainable intensification: A systematic literature review and application to regional case studies. *Agriculture, Ecosystems & Environment* 257, 68–80.

A systematic review of the current literature on SI that identifies and acknowledges the contradictions and confusions around the concept and develops a framework for areas of action required for operationalising SI.

Niamh Mahon

116. Taste and food

PAUL FREEDMAN

Introduction: taste and food

In English, the word "taste" has two meanings. First, it refers to an embodied ability to sense flavour. Second, it implies a culturally attributed sense of discrimination; "good taste" as opposed to inept judgement ("bad taste"). The sense of taste is obviously related to the consumption of food while the second extends to art, literature, material culture and indeed every aspect of life. Crucially important for considering the latter definition is that taste-making and the diffusion of what are considered to be correct or stylish forms express and reinforce social hierarchy and the calculus of prestige.

The human sense of taste is biologically fixed in certain respects such as the identification of bitter, salty or sweet foods and this was in an evolutionary sense vital to identifying nutritious versus dangerous plants. But taste varies greatly across different cultures as is obvious in the very different attitudes towards such factors as fermentation or spiciness. These norms are not as fixed as people often believe and there are many examples, such as raw fish (in sushi most obviously), of foods that at one time seemed unpleasantly foreign to Americans and Europeans that later become well liked and taken for granted. Sometimes the fondness for a food considered noxious by outsiders reinforces cultural identification of those who consume it: lutfisk (Scandinavian dried and cured fish) and durian (a Southeast Asian fruit) are famous and comical examples of what is presented as impossible tastes that, amazingly, some nations enjoy. The border between rottenness and delight is perceived as clear but is in fact permeable.

The production of taste

It might seem that within culturally accepted standards, how food tastes would be the most important factor in acceptance and consumption, but the evolution of modern (i.e. industrial) food goes against this intuitive logic. The use of the word "homemade" (which only came into existence when a considerable amount of food was *not* prepared at home) shows an assumption that painstaking effort produces a tastier product. Other factors, however, notably price and convenience, induce people to opt for food that is not as sensuously rewarding. Another factor interfering with pleasure is the perception of health. The development of modern food is linked to the identification of carbohydrates, vitamins and other ingredients and measurements that are invisible and imperceptible. Foods that are good for you, or advertised as such, are often inferior in taste, but successfully marketed, nonetheless. Cold breakfast cereal and artificial sweeteners are historical examples (Levenstein 1988, 10–109)

In every culture the social elite prizes certain dishes and styles of cooking and they are considered as signs of prestige. Often highly ranked dishes are delicate, theatrically presented or difficult to prepare. Sugar sculptures, shimmering aspic or exotic animals such as giraffe or flamingo, for example. Sophisticated taste might tip over into excess or absurdity. The comic meal depicted in the Latin *Satyricon* attributed to the first-century imperial courtier Petronius involves nouveau-riche gastronomic effects intended to amaze that are in fact vulgar (dormice smothered in honey and the like). Eating wild game has been a mark of social privilege in many societies, but such distinction often has overlapped the hunting practices of the rural lower classes, and thus in the American South, raccoon, squirrel and opossum were thought of as rural poor people's food.

In terms of actual taste, opinions surrounding prestige change slowly but ultimately sharply. In medieval Europe, aristocratic food and fashionable recipes emphasised spices, an example of exoticism but also of a certain set of taste preferences for complex aromatic effects. The development of modern French cuisine in the seventeenth and eighteenth centuries banished most spices from haute-cuisine and they often came to be identified with foreign or immigrant tastes. In recent decades, there has been a shift back towards spiciness with the globalisation of Mexican, Indian and Korean cuisines (Panayi 2008).

For most of modern history, the upper classes have established, at least in their own opinion, the definitions of culinary preference. Opinions shift over time, so that in nineteenth-century American high-end cuisine, organ meats, turtles and game were popular while, either through species depletion or a radical alteration of taste, these are now either forgotten or avoided. Not content with making rules for social distinction, elites have often defined, with variable inaccuracy, a set of lower-class tastes that they find either amusing, unpleasant or both. Medieval European stories often made fun of the rustics' preference for porridge, root vegetables, dairy products and other lowly foods; the sordid history of American racism built up a dossier of supposedly comical stereotypes of African American food practices.

Current issues

Taste is thus a weapon of discrimination that can go beyond the tolerant relativism of common observations on the order of "there's no accounting for taste". "Polenta, si; couscous, no!" is an Italian anti-immigrant slogan. Any child of immigrants who has ever brought homemade lunch to school will have experienced the narrow definitions of acceptable tastes and the cruel comedy of the majoritarian imagination.

With globalisation, contemporary societies experience a great range of food options. While the number of ingredients available to those with some choice in what to eat has increased, interconnections, tourism, marketing and communication have homogenised taste: one finds pizza everywhere. Today there is, as always, a gastronomic elite, but its tastes are harder to identify in comparison to a time, not so long ago, in which caviar, foie gras, lobster and a few other ingredients were widely recognised as constituting the highest forms of taste. Essential to all forms of fashion, including taste in food, is change, a separation between high and low, and some kind of snobbery, recognised or not. That we are officially in an age of gastronomic experimentation and acceptance hasn't altered the reality of in-groups and out-groups. It is just that the path from hip status to derision is shorter: avocado toast covered this ground in just a few years (Johnston and Baumann 2010)

References

Johnston, J and Baumann, S (2010) *Foodies: Democracy and Distinction in the Gourmet Foodscape.* New York and London, Routledge.

Levenstein, H (1988) *Revolution at the Table: The Transformation of the American Diet.* Oxford and New York, Oxford University Press.

Panayi, P (2008) *Spicing up Britain: The Multicultural History of British Food.* London, Reaktion.

Further reading

Cohen, B R, Kideckel, M S, and Zeide, A, eds. (2021) *Acquired Tastes: Stories About the Origins of Modern Food.* Cambridge, Massachusetts and London, MIT Press. Provides good examples of the imposition of expert, scientific and pseudo-scientific ideas about the modernisation of food in the late-nineteenth and twentieth centuries.

Freedman, P (ed.) (2007) *Food: The History of Taste.* London, Thames and Hudson. Emphasises culture rather than natural environment in creating food preferences. Prehistory to the present.

Levenstein, H (2003) *Paradox of Plenty: A Social History of Eating in Modern America.* 2nd ed. Berkeley and Los Angeles, University of California Press. Describes the shifting notions of taste and social distinction from 1930 to the end of the twentieth century.

Mintz, S W (1985) *Sweetness and Power: The Place of Sugar in Modern History.* New York, Viking Penguin. A foundational work on the cataclysmic impact of food fashions and choices. How the European taste for sugar created the Caribbean plantation system and the transatlantic slave trade.

PAUL FREEDMAN

117. Technology and food

KUSHANG MISHRA, MASCHA
GUGGANIG AND KARLY BURCH

Introduction

This entry examines the trajectory of technological innovation in agriculture and food. After introducing this interdisciplinary field, we give a brief history of technological innovation in agriculture and food with respect to mechanisation, transportation, chemical inputs, biotechnology, and digitalisation. The entry ends with a reflection on what this means for food and farming today and into the future.

A critical lens on farming, food, and technology

When researchers and corporations present their new food and agricultural technologies (foodtech and agritech) innovations, they often pitch them as the solution to food security, labour security, and other pressing issues (Burch and Legun, 2021). Yet these techno-solutions can ignore key social and biological dimensions of the problems they claim to solve (Gugganig, 2024; Guthman and Butler, 2023).

Critical scholars do not allow these social and biological dimensions to go unnoticed. They study the interrelationships between scientific innovation, technology development, and society by interrogating how power shapes science and technology, and how science and technology manifest and distribute power. Thus, a critical agrifood technoscience lens (Gugganig et al., 2023) can help uncover the assumptions and obfuscations embedded within techno-optimist rhetoric. For example, it can examine how many techno-solutions are embedded with both capitalist and colonial logics. Capitalist logics appear in the ways foodtech and agritech developments hyped as 'productive' and 'efficient' often favour the monetary interests of a few big corporations, scientists, engineers, and governments at the cost of ecosystems, food producers (including peasant farmers), and people's abilities to access healthy food in sustainable ways (Clapp, 2016). Colonial logics appear in the ways in which technology developers assume access to Indigenous lands, waters, bodies, and data to accomplish their goals (Liboiron, 2021; Taiuru et al., 2022).

Technological innovation in farming and food

Mechanisation in farming

Around the 6th millennium BCE, with the commencement of agricultural settlements, the first irrigation systems were invented in ancient Iran, allowing people to engage in agriculture and settle in one place (Torfi et al., 2021). From around 3500 BCE, the plough began rapidly expanding and quickening people's abilities to sow seeds. Other early mechanical hand tools used in agriculture were sickles, scythes, and knives, and with the subsequent transformative shift from stone and copper to iron-based tools, farmers "could penetrate harder soils, allowing for more efficient and extensive cultivation of land" (Kaur et al., 2023: 4).

Many centuries later, the onset of the Industrial Revolution and capitalist modes of production in the late 19th century in Europe brought about a major transformation in agriculture, where enclosures confiscated collectively owned lands and mechanisation began replacing farmers (Caunce, 2006). This growing mechanisation was driven by capitalist logics: a desire to make farming more productive, efficient, and less labour-intensive. More 'efficient' farming relied on specialised machines, standardised processes and managerial expertise as opposed to the artisanal expertise of the farmer to produce standard products (Liu and Sengers, 2021).

Over time, crops were bred in ways to support machines, while at the same time machines increasingly formed food production. A classic example is the mechanical tomato harvester developed in the late 1940s, where tomatoes were specially bred to endure the rougher harvester (unlike handpicking), leading to a "hardier, sturdier and less tasty" tomato, which also affected taste and nutritional value (Winner, 1980: 126). While these processes of mechanisation benefitted large growers, they had an adverse impact on farmworkers (especially undocumented migrants), where machines often became valued more than workers' skills and knowledge (Baur and Iles, 2023).

Domestic food technologies

Kitchens and cooking are domestic areas that also rely on technology. From domestic refrigerators to cooking apps, kitchen technologies have long shaped people's understanding of and relationship to food. For instance, the idea of 'fresh' food, which was initially (at the turn of the 20th century) controversially debated, is now unthinkable without refrigerating technology (Freidberg, 2009). Is it possible to comprehend food and cooking without technology anymore?

Tackling this question requires understanding people's relationship to food, cooking, and technologies as deeply cultural and social. For instance, researchers have shown how kitchen technologies help to foster social ideals of a 'good cook'. This is particularly so with regard to the gender roles of the good, nurturing mother. These are not so much disrupted, but rather maintained through kitchen technologies, like the Bimby (or Thermomix) cooking machine in Italy, which is a food processor that combines numerous cooking functions in one (Ascione, 2013).

Some scholars argue that many mundane (digital) cooking technologies, such as the kitchen robot Thermomix, have already transformed people into *cyborg cooks* (Graf, 2023). In other words, cooking technologies, even omnipresent ones such as microwaves or electric ovens, do not displace all experiential knowledge and senses of a cook: people still engage creatively with cooking as they use these technologies (Silva, 2000). Moreover, while cooking technologies, especially in the post-war period of the 1950s in the United States, were marketed to women in terms of making cooking easier for them, this often resulted in new forms of labour for women and confined them to the kitchen, as a cog in the wheel of the larger capitalist system (Holliday, 2001). It is therefore important to think of cooking technologies as interrelated with existing (food) knowledge, (cooking) practices, and people's identities, and how this interrelationship creates new, hybrid forms of knowing, practicing, and being.

Transporting and processing food

Today, refrigeration technologies – constituting what is known as the 'cold chain' – allow food to be processed, packaged, and transported across long distances from farms to supermarkets and onto plates. The cold chain maintains the safety and freshness of perishable food (e.g., fruits, vegetables, meat, and dairy products), storing and transporting them through "a temperature-controlled supply chain" (Hosseini Bamakan et al., 2021: 3).

Food processing is another technology developed to preserve foods for longer, allowing them to travel long distances without compromising their nutritional value or taste. Preservation through processing dates back to the Neolithic period (c. 7000–1700 BCE), where people used salt to preserve their food. However, food preservation and processing underwent a major transformation during the Industrial Revolution when the introduction of steam power led to the mass production of flour and heating was established as a novel method of preservation from microbes through pasteurisation. Fast forward to the 20th century, where the capitalist logic driving the liberalisation of global trade has supported an emerging processed food sector with its own transportation routes across the world (Huebbe and Rimbach, 2020).

Today, food transportation and processing use artificial intelligence (AI) and blockchain technologies to monitor and trace food throughout the supply chain in an attempt to improve food safety and quality assurance (Dedeoglu et al., 2023). However, these technologies are often only affordable for industry giants like Walmart and Cargill and so may disadvantage small-scale retailers and farmers (Reisman, 2021).

Chemical application in food and farming

In its organic form, the use of fertilisers in agriculture can be traced back 8,000 years, when farmers in Europe were using animal excrement as fertiliser (Bogaard et al., 2013). However, the foundations of modern inorganic fertilisers were laid in the early 19th century, starting with phosphorus and, later, potassium- and nitrogen-based fertilisers. After the Second World War, large-scale nitrate factories that had been used to make bombs were converted to produce nitrogen for agricultural use (Philpott, 2013). The popularity of chemical-based fertilisers and pesticides further increased with the so-called Green Revolution, which drastically increased food production through mixing a capitalist logic of productivism with colonial entitlements to lands in places like India (Kumar, 2016). This resulted in an increase in fertiliser use in agriculture across the world, from 46.3 million metric tons in 1965 to 195.38 million tons in 2021 (Statista, 2023).

This escalating development has had an adverse impact on the environment, as the production of fertilisers and pesticides contributes significantly to greenhouse gas (GHG) emissions, and phosphorus, pesticides, soil sediment, pathogens, and nitrate are polluting soil and water (Parris, 2011). The excessive use of fertilisers and pesticides has also created an imbalance in predator and prey pests, leading to the usage of even stronger pesticides to tackle those pests (John and Babu, 2021). The use of pesticides has, further, had an adverse impact on human health, affecting the endocrine, immune, nervous, and reproductive systems, particularly of farmers and farmworkers in many countries of the Global South like India, who often do not wear personal protective gear like safety masks or gloves (John and Babu, 2021). This lack of safety is largely due to the underestimation of the long-term health effects of these chemicals by the farmers, who are stuck with unsustainable agricultural practices where pesticides form an integral part of commercial agriculture, which has been promoted over the years under the capitalist logic (Wilson and Tisdell, 2001).

Biotechnology in food

Biological modification in food systems began 10,000 years ago in southwest Asia when humans started selective breeding to increase yield, modify plants' chemical composition to enrich certain nutrients, and increase the shelf life for food processing (Raman, 2017). In the 20th century, scientists began experimenting with genetic engineering by manipulating the genetic material of living organisms (crops, fruits, or animals) by inserting specific genetic information into a host organism, thereby making the plant more resilient to pests or applied pesticides (Raman, 2017). Genetic engineering became popular as conventional breeding was deemed too slow to provide food for a growing population (Zhang et al., 2016). It allowed for a new level of genetic modification, with the first successful genetically modified organism (GMO) being engineered in 1973 by Herbert Boyer and Stanley Cohen (Rangel, 2015).

The difference between the millennia-old practice of improving the genetic stock of plants through selective breeding and GMOs is that "the genetic material (DNA) has been altered in a way that does not occur naturally by mating and/or natural recombination" (WHO, 2014). However, while in the

short term genetic engineering might reduce the use of toxic pesticides or use less labour, in the long run weeds and insects might evolve to disrupt such human-made solutions (Zhang et al., 2016). Like other technologies, genetic engineering is also guided by capitalist logics, which allow companies to monopolise research in ways that have been repeatedly shown to exclude the interests of farmers (Bronson, 2015). Colonial logic has also underpinned attempts by corporations and others to patent and intellectually protect seeds that are Indigenous to certain places and key parts of Indigenous food systems (Taiuru et al., 2022).

Digitalisation of farming and food

In recent years, influential actors have created hype in foodtech and agritech circles about the potential of AI or big-data-based machine learning systems to transform agriculture. While data collection and analytics to assist farmers in bringing more 'precision' into their farming are over two decades old, unlike those technologies, data-driven farming is based on the "real-time" nature of data and technologies that allow for a faster rate of data collection (Steup et al., 2019: 1505). Digital agriculture received a public relations boost around the 2010s with the massive influx of technologies like "cheap and improved sensors, high bandwidth cellular communication, cloud-based ICT systems, and Big Data analysis" (CEMA, 2017). This has resulted in an increased range of uses, from input supply, precision farming, on-farm mechanisation, and robotics to supply chain management and agricultural financing, with an oft-heralded potential to transform agrifood systems completely.

Following capitalist logics, major agritech companies promise to make farming systems more productive and sustainable through 'precision'. However, this precision can only be achieved through collecting vast amounts of data, highlighting the colonial logics driving these technologies: technology developers assume access to data collected from all farming lands, often without concern for Indigenous data sovereignty (Taiuru et al., 2022). Furthermore, these data systems emerged to address the adverse effects of chemical-intensive agriculture on the environment and human health, as discussed in the previous section (Bronson and Sengers,

2022). In other words, data-driven technologies are pitched as the solution to the problems created by chemical technologies, with little questioning about the capitalist and colonial logics underlying both of these technological developments and their negative impacts.

Future concerns

This entry has outlined some of the key issues when it comes to technological innovation in food and farming. What connects these issues is the capitalist and colonial logics driving them, which are often overlooked as promises of increased productivity, efficiency, and precision frame new technologies as inherently good (Tomlinson, 2013).

Often presented as the next frontier in food and farming, corporations and governments are framing digital agriculture as the silver bullet solution for securing enough global food supply in an increasingly turbulent world. As with technological innovations that came before, many scholars have questioned the 'revolutionary' claims of digital agriculture technologies, as they do not address the underlying social, economic, and political problems associated with agriculture. Likewise, it has been shown repeatedly that global food insecurity is not primarily an issue of quantity but rather of food quality and unequal distribution and access (Clapp, 2016). Instead, these issues are reduced to mere technical problems that can be solved by technology while actually perpetuating the same capitalist and colonial logic that created the problems in the first place.

Not questioning underlying capitalist and colonial logics is problematic since business as usual is shifting power away from farmers, workers, and Indigenous communities into the hands of technology developers and data owners (Taiuru et al., 2022). Creating more sustainable and just food and farming systems through technology will require continued critical analysis of how particular people and power relations shape technology design and use. For instance, grassroots farmer collectives around the world have redefined agricultural technologies as corporatist extensions of agritech companies by developing their own GPS systems to collect, interpret, and own such farming data – such as the collective FarmHack in the United States – or offering farmers a platform to build and distribute farming tools as commons, including

the pioneering efforts of L'Atelier Paysan in France (see https://farmhack.org/welcome and https://www.latelierpaysan.org/English). A critical lens on farming, food, and technology will be required to understand how technology is shaping food and farming and find ways to strategically disrupt the capitalist and colonial logic threatening true food security.

References

Ascione, E. (2013). Mamma and the totemic robot: towards an anthropology of Bimby food processors in Italy. In M. McWilliams (ed.), *Food & Material Culture: Proceedings of the Oxford Symposium on Food and Cookery* (pp. 62–69). Prospect Books.

Hosseini Bamakan, S. M., Ghasemzadeh Moghaddam, S., & Dehghan Manshadi, S. (2021). Blockchain-enabled pharmaceutical cold chain: Applications, key challenges, and future trends. *Journal of Cleaner Production, 302*, 127021. https://doi.org/10.1016/j.jclepro.2021.127021

Baur, P., & Iles, A. (2023). Replacing humans with machines: A historical look at technology politics in California agriculture. *Agriculture and Human Values, 40*(1), 113–140. https://doi.org/10.1007/s10460-022-10341-2.

Bogaard, A., Fraser, R., Heaton, T. H. E., Wallace, M., Vaiglova, P., Charles, M., Jones, G., Evershed, R. P., Styring, A. K., Andersen, N. H., Arbogast, R.-M., Bartosiewicz, L., Gardeisen, A., Kanstrup, M., Maier, U., Marinova, E., Ninov, L., Schäfer, M., & Stephan, E. (2013). Crop manuring and intensive land management by Europe's first farmers. *Proceedings of the National Academy of Sciences, 110*(31), 12589–12594. https://doi.org/10.1073/pnas.1305918110.

Bronson, K. (2015). Responsible to whom? Seed innovations and the corporatization of agriculture. *Journal of Responsible Innovation, 2*, 62–77. https://doi.org/10.1080/23299460.2015.1010769.

Bronson, K., & Sengers, P. (2022). Big tech meets big ag: Diversifying epistemologies of data and power. *Science as Culture, 31*(1), 15–28. https://doi.org/10.1080/09505431.2021.1986692.

Burch, K. A., & Legun, K. (2021). Overcoming barriers to including agricultural workers in the co-design of new agtech: Lessons from a COVID-19-present world. *Culture, Agriculture, Food and Environment, 43*(2), 147–160. https://doi.org/10.1111/cuag.12277.

CEMA (2017). Digital farming: What does it really mean? Available at: https://www.cemaagri.org/images/publications/position-papers/CEMA_Digital_Farming_-_Agriculture_4.0__13_02_2017_0.pdf.

Caunce, S. A. (2006). Mechanisation and society in English agriculture: The experience of the North-East, 1850–1914. *Rural History, 17*(1), 23–45. https://doi.org/10.1017/S0956793305001585.

Clapp, J. (2016). *Food*. Polity Press.

Dedeoglu, V., Malik, S., Ramachandran, G., Pal, S., & Jurdak, R. (2023). Blockchain meets edge: AI for food supply chain traceability and provenance. In J. L. D. Nelis & A. S. Tsagkaris (eds.), *Comprehensive Analytical Chemistry* (Vol. 101, pp. 251–275). Elsevier. https://doi.org/10.1016/bs.coac.2022.12.001.

Freidberg, S. (2009). *Fresh: A Perishable History*. Cambridge University Press.

Graf, K. (2023). Cyborg cooks: Mothers and the anthropology of smart kitchens. *Digital Culture & Society, 9*(1), 49–70.

Gugganig, M. (2024). Vanguard visions of vertical farming: Envisaging and contesting an emerging food production system. *Science, Technology and Human Values*. https://doi.org/10.1177/0162243924124079.

Gugganig, M., Burch, K. A., Guthman, J., & Bronson, K. (2023). Contested agri-food futures: Introduction to the Special Issue. *Agriculture and Human Values, 40*(3), 787–798. https://doi.org/10.1007/s10460-023-10493-9.

Guthman, J., & Butler, M. (2023). Fixing food with a limited menu: On (digital) solutionism in the agri-food tech sector. *Agriculture and Human Values, 40*(3), 835–848. https://doi.org/10.1007/s10460-023-10416-8.

Holliday, L. S. (2001). Kitchen technologies: Promises and alibis, 1944–1966. *Camera Obscura, 16*(2), 1–131.

Huebbe, P., & Rimbach, G. (2020). Historical reflection of food processing and the role of legumes as part of a healthy balanced diet. *Foods, 9*(8), 1056. https://doi.org/10.3390/foods9081056.

John, D. A., & Babu, G. R. (2021). Lessons from the aftermaths of green revolution on food system and health. *Frontiers in Sustainable Food Systems, 5*, 1–6.

Kaur, B., Mansi, S. D., Singh, J., Mishra, S., Chauhan, N., Kukreti, T., Sharma, B., Singh, S. P., Arora, S., Uniyal, D., Agrawal, Y., Akhtar, S., Rather, M. A., Naik, B., Kumar, V., Gupta, A. K., Rustagi, S., & Preet, M. S. (2023). Insights into the harvesting tools and equipment's for horticultural crops: From then to now. *Journal of Agriculture and Food Research, 14*, 1–29.

Kumar, R. (2016). *Rethinking revolutions: Soyabean, choupals, and the changing countryside in Central India*. Oxford University Press.

Liboiron, M. (2021). *Pollution Is Colonialism*. Duke University Press. https://doi.org/10.1215/9781478021445.

Liu, J., & Sengers, P. (2021). Legibility and the legacy of racialized dispossession in digital agriculture. *Proceedings of the ACM on Human–Computer Interaction, 5*(CSCW2). https://doi.org/10.1145/3479867.

Parris, K. (2011). Impact of agriculture on water pollution in OECD countries: Recent trends and future prospects. *International Journal of Water Resources Development, 27*(1), 33–52.

Philpott, T. (2013). A brief history of our deadly addiction to nitrogen fertilizer. *Mother Jones*. https://www.motherjones.com/food/2013/04/history-nitrogen-fertilizer-ammonium-nitrate/.

Raman, R. (2017). The impact of Genetically Modified (GM) crops in modern agriculture: A review. *GM Crops & Food, 8*(4), 195–208.

Rangel, G. (2015). From corgis to corn: A brief look at the long history of GMO technology. *Science in the News*. https://sitn.hms.harvard.edu/flash/2015/from-corgis-to-corn-a-brief-look-at-the-long-history-of-gmo-technology/.

Reisman, E. (2021). Sanitizing agri-food tech: COVID-19 and the politics of expectation. *Journal of Peasant Studies, 48*(5), 910–933. https://doi.org/10.1080/03066150.2021.1934674.

Silva, E. B. (2000). The cook, the cooker and the gendering of the kitchen. *The Sociological Review, 48*(4), 612–628.

Statista (2023). Global fertilizer consumption by nutrient 1965–2021. https://www.statista.com/statistics/438967/fertilizer

-consumption-globally-by-nutrient/ (accessed 26 March 2024).

Steup, R., Dombrowski, L., & Su, N. M. (2019). Feeding the world with data: Visions of data-driven farming. In *Proceedings of the 2019 on Designing Interactive Systems Conference*, 1503–1515.

Taiuru, K., Burch, K., & Finlay-Smits, S. (2022). Realising the promises of agricultural big data through a Māori data sovereignty approach. *New Zealand Economic Papers*, 57(2), 172–178. https:// doi.org/10.1080/00779954.2022.2147861.

Tomlinson, I. (2013). Doubling food production to feed the 9 billion: A critical perspective on a key discourse of food security in the UK. *Journal of Rural Studies*, 29, 81–90.

Torfi, K., Albaji, M., Naseri, A. A., & Boroomand Nasab, S. (2021). An introduction to the ancient irrigation structures upon Karun River in Shushtar City. *Iranian Journal of Science and Technology, Transactions of Civil Engineering*, 45, 815–831. https://doi.org /10.1007/s40996-020-00490-x.

WHO. (2014). World Health Organization. Frequently asked questions on genetically modified foods – May 2014. https:// www.who.int/news-room/questions-and -answers/item/food-genetically-modified. Accessed 23 May 2025.

Wilson, C., & Tisdell, C. (2001). Why farmers continue to use pesticides despite environmental, health and sustainability costs. *Ecological Economics*, 39(3), 449–462. https://doi.org/10.1016/S0921 -8009(01)00238-5.

Winner, L. (1980). Do Artifacts Have Politics? *Daedalus, 109*(1), 121–136.

Zhang, C., Wohlhueter, R., & Zhang, H. (2016). Genetically modified foods: A critical review of their promise and problems. *Food Science and Human Wellness*, 5(3), 116–123.

Further reading

Biltekoff, C. (2024). *Real Food, Real Facts: Processed Food and the Politics of Knowledge*. University of California Press. https://doi.org/10.1525/luminos.198.
This book looks at the knowledge politics around processed food, which is at the centre of the friction between the public and the food industry. It also explores the role which science and authority play in the food industry's responses to concerns about what we eat and how it is made.

Gugganig, M., & Bronson, K. (2022). Digital agriculture, and the promise of immateriality. In D. Szanto, A. Di Battista, & I. Knezevic (eds.), *Food Studies: Matter, Meaning & Movement* (pp. 648–664). Rebus Press, https://ecampusontario .pressbooks.pub/foodstudies/chapter/ digital-agriculture/.
This chapter is part of a textbook for undergraduate students and offers a more detailed account of how digital technologies have reshaped farming and whether the promise of reaching more sustainable agriculture is, in fact, feasible.

KUSHANG MISHRA, MASCHA GUGGANIG AND KARLY BURCH

118. Terroir

ENRIC CASTELLÓ

Introduction

Terroir is a French word with strong cultural resonances, and it is difficult, if not impossible, to translate it into other languages. Therefore, in different languages the original word *terroir* is often used. In short, it means land, earth (*terre*), soil, but more broadly it refers to the conditions under which specific foods or drinks are produced in places which confer upon them particular characteristics that consumers should be able to appreciate. Terroir is traditionally applied to vineyards and wine and the Cambridge Dictionary (2023) defines it as "the special character that a wine is thought to get from the particular place where the grapes were grown to make it".

The concept originated in the Middle Ages and historical readings attached the notion to French identity (Parker, 2015). Before being considered a valuable label to market wine and promote food product origins, it had a pejorative meaning, expressing the "earth taste" of local and poor-quality wines (Matthews, 2015). However, the development of specific regions like Champagne and promotional storytelling around the product (Guy, 2003) contributed to current understandings of the notion.

Current issues

There are diverse approaches to defining terroir, but there is consensus that both physical and sociocultural aspects of wine and food production need to be considered. Although some orthodox understandings can be reluctant to see its application outside the wine industry or the French context, in practice, there is a growing use of terroir applied to a diversity of food products, in different cultural and geographical contexts.

One influential work in the geological and oenological study of the French terroir was by James E. Wilson (1998). Agronomic and viticultural elements are of relevance and, for a long time, researchers have remarked on the importance of soils, climate, mineral supply, or geological elements (e.g.Falcetti, 1994; van Leeuwen et al., 2018), although others emphasise ripening conditions and water availability for the plants, rather than the minerality of soils (e.g. Meinert, 2018).

For marketing purposes, terroir is considered as differentiating a product, communicating authenticity, or attaching food to a genuine place of production; here we find interconnections with the notions of geographical indications. This can provide opportunities for raising prices, an added value that can be transferred (but not necessarily) to primary producers. In this sense, terroir can be seen as an elitist, gourmet device to which only wealthy consumers could have access. It can also drive the reduction of terroir as part of place branding strategies. However, although the relationship between terroir and market rationales can be highlighted, cultural and geographical complexities play a role in its constitution. Here, Charters (2006) remarks that place marketing is just one of the elements in the definition of terroir, among others like viticultural environment or place as identity.

Socio-cultural, anthropological, and geographical perspectives on terroir stress the importance of human factors and the sociological construction of terroir (Moran, 2001; Demossier, 2011; Unwin, 2012). "People are responsible for the idea of terroir", remarks Warren Moran (2006:1), reflecting on the human factors attached to the concept. Here, the cultural and sociological nature of terroir has a preeminence over physical conditions. As such, its socially constructed value can be an important part of the contribution of speciality foods and drinks to rural development strategies (Prévost et al., 2014) which utilise ideas of gastronomy and may be linked to the promotion of 'alternative' food networks. Finally, terroir can be also studied as a communicative object within social interaction, so it would require a "will for terroir" from producers to consumers (Castelló, 2021). This idea implies a need for individuals, rural communities, and institutional agents to believe in and positively promote a collective idea of terroir as commons, as a collective good.

Future concerns

Because terroir is such a complex and multifaceted concept, it is used and manipulated in many different sectors with diverse purposes. One concern from marketing studies revolves around 'terroir awareness', or how consumers appreciate terroir in products and whether this could influence their purchase decisions.

Terroir risks being reduced to marketing, using storytelling tools to increase value and justify higher prices. Another growing issue is related to better translation of the market value of terroir to local communities and rural areas, thus promoting rural development. Intermediaries and supply chain complexities can mean that the efforts put in by communities and small producers in the construction of terroir go unrewarded. Here there is the peril of the commodification of terroir or its appropriation under straightforward unidimensional commercial premises. The frictions between environmental sustainability and market rationales, production systems – intensive vs extensive – and food quality, and distribution and supply chain complexities are shaping the current understandings of terroir. In that sense, and in a similar way to what can happen with geographical indications and other food labels, a more culturally embedded and commonly understood notion of terroir is needed at all levels. Added to the required physical elements, , terroir can be a valuable sociocultural object which generates a return for rural communities, or it can become another advertising device put to the service of consumerism and the global markets.

Acknowledgements
Grant PID2021-122696NB-I00 funded by MICIU/AEI/10.13039/501100011033 and "ERDF A way of making Europe".

References
Cambridge Dictionary (2023) 'Terroir', in *Cambridge Advanced Learner's Dictionary & Thesaurus*. Cambridge: Cambridge University Press. https://dictionary.cambridge.org/dictionary/english/terroir.

Castelló, E. (2021) 'The will for terroir: A communicative approach', *Journal of Rural Studies*, 86, pp. 386–397. https://doi.org/10.1016/j.jrurstud.2021.06.007.

Charters, S. (2006) *Wine and Society. The Social and Cultural Context of a Drink*. Amsterdam: Elsevier.

Demossier, M. (2011) 'Beyond terroir: Territorial construction, hegemonic discourses, and French wine culture', *Journal of the Royal Anthropological Institute*, 17(4), pp. 685–705. https://doi.org/10.1111/j.1467-9655.2011.01714.x.

Falcetti, M. (1994) 'Le Terroir. Qu'est-ce qu'un terroir? Porquoi l'etudier? Porquoi l'enseigner?' *Bulletin de l'OIV*, 757–758, pp. 246–275.

Guy, K.M. (2003) *When Champagne Became French: Wine and the Making of a National Identity*. Baltimore & London: John Hopkins University Press.

van Leeuwen, C., Roby, J.-P. and de Rességuier, L. (2018) 'Soil-related terroir factors: A review', *Oeno One*, 52(2), pp. 173–188. https://doi.org/10.20870/oeno-one.2018.52.2.2208.

Matthews, M.A. (2015) *Terroir and Other Myths of Winegrowing*. Oakland (CA): University of California Press.

Meinert, L.D. (2018) 'The science of terroir', *Elements*, 14(3), pp. 153–158. https://doi.org/10.2138/gselements.14.3.153.

Moran, W. (2001) 'Terroir: The human factor', *Australian and New Zealand Wine Industry Journal*, 16(2), pp. 32–51.

Moran, W. (2006) 'Crafting terroir: People in cool climates, soils, and markets', in the proceedings of the Sixth International Cool Climate Symposium for Viticulture and Oenology. Christchurch, 17 p.

Parker, T. (2015) *Tasting French Terroir: The History of an Idea*. Oakland (CA): University of California Press.

Prévost, P., Capitaine, M., Gautier–Pelissier, F., Michelin, Y., Jeanneaux, P., Fort, F., Javelle, A., Moïti-Maïzi, P., Lériche, F., Brunschwig, G., Fournier, S., Lapeyronie, P. and Josien, E. (2014) 'Le terroir, un concept pour l'action dans le développement des territoires', *Vertigo: La revue électronique en sciences de l'environnement*, 1, pp. 1–25.

Unwin, T. (2012) 'Terroir: At the heart of geography', in P.H. Dougherty (ed.) *The Geography of Wine*. Dordrecht: Springer, pp. 37–48. https://doi.org/https://doi.org/10.1007/978-94-007-0464-0_2.

Wilson, J.E. (1998) *Terroir: The Role of Geology, Climate and Culture in the Making of French Wines*. Berkeley, Los Angeles & London: University of California Press.

Further reading

Trubek, A.B. (2008) *The Taste of Place: A Cultural Journey into Terroir*. Berkeley

& Los Angeles: University of California Press.

This book offers a cultural approach to the term and provides a grounded analysis to food and cultural debates and the links between taste and place. It is an entertaining and, at the same time, scholarly insightful discussion around food, culinary issues, and terroir realities.

Patterson, T. and Buechsenstein, J. (2018) *Wine and Place: A Terroir Reader.* Oakland (CA): University of California Press.

This book examines the pros and cons of the concept of wine terroir. Not necessarily addressed to an academic public, the authors propose a "definitive definition" with ten influential elements "that shape terroir": soil, site, climate, weather (seasons, etc.), inputs (irrigation, etc.), the human element, biotics, grapevine (varieties, etc.), yeast and wine (as expressed in flavour).

ENRIC CASTELLÓ

119. Tourism and food

SALLY EVERETT

Introduction

Given that up to 40% of tourist expenditure is spent on food and drink (Choe and Kim, 2019), and 53% of tourists are motivated by food (WFTA, 2023), it is undeniably a core part of the tourism experience. Whether enjoyed as a 'peak experience' (Quan and Wang, 2004) or for essential sustenance, destinations have been keen to capitalise on food's potential to generate economic benefits and utilise it to celebrate local communities and traditions (Everett and Aitchison, 2008). Culinary engagement allows tourists to come into close contact with local cultures and food-related experiences (Carvalho et al., 2023).

People have always travelled in search for food; however, explicit food-related tourism can be traced back to early fifteenth century explorers (often at the brutal expense of others), and more latterly during the Grand Tour of Europe. Today, travelling to explicitly experience a destination's food offering can foster close social interactions between visitors and local people, building 'a relationship between the insider and outsider created via food as culture' (Park et al., 2019:253). Given it is one of the few experiences to involve all five senses, tourists can actively immerse themselves in the culture and flavours of their host destination (Everett, 2019).

Hall and Mitchell (2001: 308) define food tourism as 'primary and secondary food producers, food festivals, restaurants and specific locations for which food and tasting and/or experiencing the attributes of a specialist food production region are the primary motivating factors for travel'. However, terminology varies and includes 'culinary tourism', 'foodways tourism' (Long, 2013), and 'gastronomy tourism' (WTO, 2017). Food tourism ranges from tours to cookery schools, from specific restaurants to markets, from food festivals to vineyards. Typologies include the 'gastronome' who intentionally pursues diverse ethnic cuisines and existential experiences, to the 'recreational' tourist with little interest in food (Cohen, 1979). Hall and Sharples (2003) note the differing levels of interest from high interest (gourmet) to moderate interest (culinary tourism) to low/ no interest, where tourists simply satisfy biological needs.

Current issues

Research generally falls into two main themes: supply (marketing, revenue, and production) and demand (experience, emotional value, and culinary adventure). Inevitably, tourism is a revenue-generating industry so studies have tended to prioritise economic analyses, food supply chains, strategies, and quantitative impacts; however, a more cultural focus drawing on social and cultural geographies, philosophy, and cultural studies has emerged in addition to analyses of how it can sustain place and people (Everett, 2015; Sims, 2010). It has become a strategic priority for many destinations, with investment in branding campaigns celebrating everything from the humble potato (Giampiccoli et al., 2023) to gourmet cuisine.

From the supply side, destination marketing organisations increasingly harness food-motivated travel, given food gives place a unique identity and brand (Antón et al., 2019). One increasingly popular way has been via food events, ranging from local farmer-led events to large annual celebrations (Tran et al., 2023). Usually linked to historic traditions, food events have become significant generators of visitors, bolstering community pride whilst simultaneously bringing economic and social benefits. Examples include La Tomatina in Bunol in Spain; Ivrea Orange Fest in Italy; Potato Days Festival in Minnesota; and other festivals built around eating chilli, garlic, hotdogs, melons, and asparagus. Competitions and challenges with unusual foods have become tourism attractions (Gyimóthy and Mykletun, 2009), and staged food celebrations (especially in places with few natural tourism attractions) such as cheese rolling (in the UK) have become part of a dramaturgical performance in created carnivalesque spaces.

In terms of demand, food tourism addresses a desire for escape from a world seemingly in crisis, providing nostalgic resurrection (Everett, 2009) and memorable experiences (Sthapit et al., 2019). It is a search for authenticity in an inauthentic world; an alternative to the homogenisation of everyday life. Food helps link a tourist to the land, its people, and its history. Beyond the visual, people seek unique and niche experiences in multisensory tastescapes where there is sensory and cognitive stimuli, coupled with behavioural and affective engagement (Everett, 2012).

Another issue is the role of social media in shaping food tourism. The extensive use of smart devices to instantaneously share experiences across the plethora of social network platforms, apps, and review sites has transformed engagement with food. We see the creation of 'culture vultures' through digital transformations (Okumus, 2021), fuelled by the rise of generative artificial intelligence (AI) – fostering digital and interactive food experiences using chatbots, virtual assistants, and AI algorithms to identify and offer personalised and bespoke food-related content (Filimon and Fusté-Forné, 2023).

Tourism occupies a paradoxical societal position, surfacing psychological, behavioural, and demographic tensions (Robinson et al., 2018). Whilst much work focuses on specific food-motivated travel (Everett, 2015), it is important to consider the broader role of food in the tourism experience. Food tourism is not the same thing as looking at the role of food in tourism. An effective 'food' and 'tourism' partnership has been found to help sustain cultures, heritage, and local economies (Everett and Aitchison 2008), but a tension exists in the carbon footprint of the tourist travelling (often by air) to enjoy a 'local' food in a destination. Tourists are privileged members of the planet who have disposable income and passports so they can access cultural and culinary experiences. Furthermore, food tourism is growing despite a background of global food scarcity, increasing levels of obesity, unequal access to food, habitat destruction to produce ingredients (e.g. palm oil), depleted fish stocks, and high energy and transport demands.

The challenge for the tourism industry is how it might alleviate poverty (via pro poor tourism) in an economically and culinarily divided world. One must ask how compatible food tourism is with current food concerns, structural inequality, and agriculture crises. We need to scrutinise food and tourism supply chains and explore who is really benefiting. Recent scholarship advocates interrogation of the supply chain in terms of how food is provided to tourists and where it comes from – does tourism complement or compete with local food systems? Likewise, there remains a tension given the promotion of culinary tourism (where food experiences often attract a premium) to fulfil recreational wishes that can also fuel inequality and a wealth divide. Consequently, Hall (2020:284) urges researchers to 'improve the recipe of food tourism' given people may be undernourished and hungry in the very same places we visit.

The future of tourism and food

Tourists will always need to eat, and food-motivated tourism will remain one of the fastest-growing sectors of the tourism industry (Yeoman et al., 2015). Whilst the challenges of the climate emergency, food security, energy source scarcity, and geopolitical upheaval will affect its future, the desire to 'taste the other' will remain insatiable. After the 2020 Covid-19 pandemic, tourism is once again becoming a key driver of economic growth and vehicle to enhance social progress in developing nations (WTTC, 2021), with countries including China, Cambodia, Rwanda, and Sri Lanka seeing annual tourism GDP growth exceed 8% between 2011 and 2020 (compared with a global rate for tourism GDP at 4.1%). Given food is around a third of tourism spend, it requires attention when overall tourism is worth 10% of global GDP (US$10 trillion) and international visitor spending is about US$1.9 trillion.

As destinations continue to seek new streams of revenue based on their agriculture, history, and traditions, we will see a growing demand for more unusual items and unique food experiences. The search for 'authentic' experiences, and the 'pursuit of personal identity' will certainly increase. The search for culinary traditions so sought after by tourists (Horng and Tsai, 2012) will inevitably trigger increasingly innovative and co-created tourism experiences between producer and consumer. For example, Carvalho et al. (2023) suggest food tours are rarely discussed in the academic literature yet facilitate closer contact between local community and local stakeholders and directly prompt revisits.

Food tourism experiences should be balanced alongside concerns about the gap between rich and poor, the need for mechanised production to feed the world's population, and sustainability goals. This 'evolution of fault lines' where a gap has emerged between the need to feed the world and the search for the unique and distinctive in food tourism will remain a conundrum (Hansen, 2015). Destinations will need to ensure experiences reduce external leakages via shorter supply chains, promote ethical consumption, foster sustainability, and build local economic development through stronger relationships between producer and consumer. Strategies should shift from how food can be shaped into a commercial tourism product to attract visitors, towards better understanding of waste and energy use – to the point where food tourism might need to embrace a more significant move to vegetable-based diets and less intensive agriculture.

The future of food tourism will inevitably involve technological innovation including AI, food photography, culinary medicine, molecular gastronomy, and the expansion of social media (Okumus 2021). There is little doubt that food and tourism will continue to thrive as intertwined sectors and experiences; after all, it is through tasting, experiencing, and purchasing that tourists can access the cultural and historic identity of a place. It will always offer visitors to a destination a way to engage in something unique, immersive, and delicious.

References

Antón, C., Camarero, C., & Laguna, M. (2019) Impacts of authenticity, degree of adaptation and cultural contrast on travellers' memorable gastronomy experiences. *Journal of Hospitality Marketing & Management* 28(7), 743–764.

Carvalho, M. (2023) Co-creation of food tourism experiences: Tourists' perspectives of a Lisbon food tour. *Tourist Studies* 23(2), 128–148. doi/10.1177/14687976231168941.

Carvalho, M., Kastenholz, E., Carneiro, M. J., & Souza, L. (2023). Co-creation of food tourism experiences: Tourists' perspectives of a Lisbon food tour. Tourist Studies, 23(2), 128–148.

Choe, J. Y. J., & Kim, S. S. (2019) Development and validation of a multidimensional tourist's local food consumption value (TLFCV) scale. *International Journal of Hospitality Management* 77, 245–259.

Cohen, E. (1979) A phenomenology of tourist experiences. *Sociology* 13(2), 179–201. https://doi.org/10.1177 /003803857901300203.

Ellis, A., Park, E., Kim, S. & Yeoman, I. (2019) What is food tourism? *Tourism Management* 68(1), 250–263.

Everett, S. (2019) Theoretical turns through tourism tastescapes: The evolution of food tourism research. *Research in Hospitality Management* 9(1), 3–12.

Everett, S. (2015) *Food and Drink Tourism Principles and Practice*. London, Sage.

Everett, S. (2009) Beyond the visual gaze? The pursuit of an embodied experience through food tourism. *Tourist Studies* 8(3), 337–358.

Everett, S. (2012). Production places or consumption spaces? The place-making agency of food tourism in Ireland and Scotland. *Tourism Geographies,* 14(4), 535–554.

Everett, S., & Aitchison, C. (2008) The role of food tourism in sustaining regional identity: A case study of Cornwall, South West England. *Journal of Sustainable Tourism* 16(2), 150–167.

Filimon, N., & Fusté-Forné, F. (2023) Exploring tourists and local consumers' attitudes on service automation in restaurant industry: The Spanish fast-food experience. In F. Xavier Medina, D. Conde-Caballero and L. Mariano-Juárez (eds), *Food, Gastronomy, Sustainability, and Social and Cultural Development*, pp. 95–115. Cambridge, MA: Academic Press.

Garibaldi, R., & Pozzi, A. (2018) Creating tourism experiences combining food and culture: An analysis among Italian producers. *Tourism Review* 73(2), 230–241.

Giampiccoli, A., Mzobanzi Mnguni, E., Dłużewska, A., & Oliver, M. (2023) Potatoes: Food tourism and beyond. *Cogent Social Sciences* 9(1), 2172789. DOI: 10.1080/23311886.2023.2172789.

Gyimóthy, S., & Mykletun, R. J. (2009) Scary food: Commodifying culinary heritage as meal adventures in tourism. *Journal of Vacation Marketing* 15(3), 259–273.

Hall, C. M. (2020) Improving the recipe for culinary and food tourism? The need for a new menu. *Tourism Recreation Research* 45(2), 284–287. DOI:10.1080/02508281.20 19.1694243.

Hall, C. M., & Mitchell, R. (2001) Wine and food tourism. In N. Douglas, N. Douglas and R. Derrett (eds), *Special Interest Tourism: Context and Cases*, pp. 307–329. Brisbane, John Wiley & Sons.

Hall, C. M., & Sharples, L. (2003). The consumption of experiences or the experience of consumption? An introduction to the tourism of taste. In Hall, C.M., Sharples, L., Mitchell, R., Macionis, N. & Cambourne, B. (Eds), *Food tourism around the world* (pp. 1–24). London: Routledge.

Hall, C. M., Sharples, L., Mitchell, R., Macionis, N., & Cambourne, B. (eds) (2004) *Food Tourism around the World.* London, Routledge.

Hansen, K.V. (2015) Investigating food development in an area of Norway: An explorative study using a grounded theory approach. *The Qualitative Report* 20(8), 1205–1220.

Horng, J. S., & Tsai, C. T. (2012) Culinary tourism strategic development: An Asia-Pacific perspective. *International Journal of Tourism Research* 14(1), 40–55.

Long, L. M. (2013) *Culinary Tourism.* Dordrecht, Springer.

Okumus, B. (2021) Food tourism research: A perspective article. *Tourism Review* 76(1), 38–42. https://doi.org/10.1108/TR-11-2019 -0450.

Park, E., Kim, S., & Yeoman, I. (2019) Eating in Asia: Understanding food tourism and its perspectives in Asia. *Food Tourism in Asia*, 3–13.

Quan, S., & Wang, N. (2004) Towards a structural model of the tourist experience: An illustration from food experiences in tourism. *Tourism Management* 25(1), 297–305.

Robinson, R.N., Getz, D., & Dolnicar, S. (2018) Food tourism subsegments: A data-driven analysis. *International Journal of Tourism Research* 20(3), 367–377.

Sims, R. (2010). Putting place on the menu: The negotiation of locality in UK food tourism, from production to consumption. *Journal of Rural Studies*, 26(2), 105–115.

Sthapit, E., Coudounaris, D., & Björk, P. (2019) Extending the memorable tourism experience construct: An investigation of memories of local food experiences.

Scandinavian Journal of Hospitality and Tourism 19(4–5), 333–353.

Tran, A., Le, A. D., Bui, L., Le, V., & Vu, L. (2023) Food festival research review in contemporary tourism. *International Journal of Tourism Cities* 9(2), 325–347. https://doi.org/10.1108/IJTC-01-2022 -0009.

World Food Travel Association (WFTA) (2023) *What Is Food Tourism.* https://www .worldfoodtravel.org/what-is-food-tourism.

World Travel and Tourism Council (WTTC) (2021) *Travel and Tourism as a Catalyst for Social Impact.* https://wttc.org/Portals/0/ Documents/Reports/2021/Travel%20and %20Tourism%20as%20a%20Catalyst %20for%20Social%20Impact.pdf?ver =2021-02-25-183248-583.

World Tourism Organization (UNWTO) (2017) *Second Global Report on Gastronomy Tourism.* https://www.e-unwto .org/doi/pdf/10.18111/9789284418701.

Yeoman, I., McMahon-Beattie, U., Fields, K., Albrecht, J., & Meethan, K. (2015) *The Future of Food Tourism.* Bristol, Channel View Publications.

Further reading

Dixit, S. K. (Ed.) (2019) *The Routledge Handbook of Gastronomic Tourism.* London, Routledge.

A wide-ranging and eclectic collection of contributions by several scholars from thirty-one countries offering critical perspectives of gastronomic tourism. Covers everything from slow food to hospitality issues, from marketing to festivals, and from intellectual property to wine tourism.

Everett, S. (2016) *Food and Drink Tourism: Principles and Practices.* London, Sage.

An accessible and comprehensive textbook covering key aspects of the food and drink tourism experience from its history, to marketing approaches, to supply chains and its future.

SALLY EVERETT

120. Ultra-processed foods

Sinéad Furey and Martin Caraher

NOVA classification

A system that categorises food into one of four groups according to the degree of processing it undergoes.

Introduction: what are ultra-processed foods?

Ultra-processed foods (UPFs) for the food industry are profitable, value-added foods that are shelf-stable, often ready to eat (Monteiro et al., 2019) and less expensive than minimally processed foods (Gupta et al., 2019). The concept was introduced in the 1980s when they became widely available in supermarkets. As UPFs have increasingly come to dominate people's food consumption they are contributing to the 'nutrition transition' (Baker et al., 2020), accompanied by declining consumption of whole grains, fruits and vegetables, and increasing consumption of animal food products and processed, high fat and sugar foods (Popkin and Ng, 2021). The nutrition debate over UPFs in the diet is not about individual products but rather that, increasingly, in many countries, they account for the majority of calories consumed, impacting on nutritional health and contributing to the development of diet-related chronic disease such as heart attacks. They are ubiquitous in developed economies mirroring the increased prevalence in obesity.

Over time with the increasing concentration and industrialisation of the food system, more and more of the food we eat has become processed and increasingly ultra-processed. This is due to changes in the distances food travels to the consumer, in how we source our food (supermarkets) and in consumer demands for convenience. This has resulted in reductions in the consumption of fresh food and increases in foods that have been through a process that changes their fundamental properties and is often accompanied by the addition of preservatives, flavour enhancers and stabilisers.

The US Department of Agriculture defines any agricultural product whose fundamental nature has been changed – by heating, freezing, dicing, juicing – as a processed food. The taxonomy most applied in the scientific literature is the NOVA food classification system due to its conceptual coherence and wide operational usefulness and acceptance in dietary public health research and policy (Lawrence and Baker, 2019).

The NOVA classification was developed by Carlos Monteiro and places food into one of four groups according to the nature, extent and purpose of processing applied (see Table 120.1) (Monteiro et al., 2019). It is important to note that UPFs are Group 4 under this classification.

UPFs equate with the terms unnatural, unhealthful and of low-nutritional value (Aguirre et al., 2019). It is important to recognise that UPFs are not just "junk foods"; they also can include foods sold as having healthy properties such as low-fat margarine and vitamin fortified breakfast cereals. There are also links between UPFs and a food's sustainability credentials with, generally, the more processing a food has undergone, the greater the environmental damage (see also Mason and Lang's [2017] eco-nutrition [or sustainable diets] discussion, which helpfully links health and eco-sustainability agendas). UPFs also threaten sustainability goals due to their combination of low-cost ingredients, environmental processing costs and consequent increased consumption worldwide (Fardet and Rock, 2020).

The proliferation of UPFs in modern consumer society

Studies from countries in the Global North show UPFs consistently account for more than 50% of dietary energy (Adams et al., 2020). UPFs tend to be purchased and consumed in larger amounts, making them a significant contributor to rising obesity levels. Martinez Steele et al. (2016) reported that UPFs are the main source (58%) of calories eaten in the US and contribute almost 90% of the energy ingested from added sugars. An analysis of UK dietary data concluded that men, younger people and those in the lowest occupational social class consumed a higher percentage of energy from UPFs than women and older people. There is, however, some ambiguity across current analyses from different countries, with some studies suggesting an inverse relationship between UPF consumption and socio-economic status (Schnabel et al., 2019), while others report high UPF consumption amongst all socio-economic groups (Simões et al., 2018). This

Table 120.1   The NOVA classification

Group	Description	Examples
1	**Unprocessed or natural foods**	Edible parts of plants (fruit, leaves, stems, seeds, roots) or from animals (such as muscle, offal, eggs, milk) and also fungi, algae and water.
2	**Processed culinary ingredients**	Can include oils, butter, lard, sugar and salt. These are substances derived from Group 1 foods via processes such as pressing, refining, grinding, milling and drying, often to remove impurities and improve storage and shelf life.
3	**Semi-processed food**	Made by the addition of salt, oil, sugar to ingredients from Groups 1 and 2. Also includes canned or bottled vegetables or legumes (pulses) in brine; whole fruit in syrup; tinned fish in oil; some types of processed animal foods (e.g., bacon and smoked fish); most freshly baked breads; and simple cheeses to which salt is added. Like Group 2, this helps improve storage and shelf life.
4	**Ultra-processed foods (UPFs)**	Ranges from carbonated soft drinks; sweet, fatty or salty packaged snacks; confectionery; mass-produced packaged bread and cakes; margarine and other spreads; sweetened breakfast cereals; fruit yoghurt and "energy" drinks; pre-prepared meat, cheese, pasta and pizza dishes; poultry and fish "nuggets"; sausages, burgers and other reconstituted meat products; powdered milk; most prepacked microwave meals and packaged instant soups, noodles and desserts; baby formula.

Source: Adapted from Monteiro et al., 2018; Monteiro et al., 2019.

may be related to individual countries being at different stages in their respective nutrition transitions – for example, in 2008 in Portugal, consumption of fast and processed foods was greater among high-income consumers as the country was at an early stage of the nutrition transition (Rodrigues et al., 2008). Now while the overall population consumption of UPFs is still low in Portugal, compared with other European countries, it has increased and consumption of UPFs has spread across the population (Popkin and Ng, 2021). At the time of writing, over one billion people worldwide are obese, with estimates that approximately 167 million people will become less healthy due to being overweight or obese by 2025.

UPFs are increasingly common in emerging economies, particularly in Latin America and South Asia (PAHO and WHO, 2019). There is evidence of the UPF industry gaining a foothold in Africa (Kruger et al., 2023). This nutrition transition will impact on lower-income countries' prevalence of obesity and diabetes.

The UK Scientific Advisory Committee on Nutrition (SACN, 2023) and some academics remain concerned that the research results should be interpreted with caution (Gibney et al., 2017; Sadler et al., 2021). This is despite a growing body of research linking UPFs with low diet quality and increased risk of noncommunicable diseases including cancer, cardiovascular disease, diabetes, stroke, obesity and cognitive decline (Adams et al., 2020; Gomes Gonçalves et al., 2023). UPFs are contributing to obesity, principally because they are "cheap" sources of calories, less satiating and readily available. They are also associated with pervasive, aggressive and well-funded advertising that perpetuates both their increasing consumption and their disproportionate expenditure within household food budgets (Hall et al., 2019).

Future issues

There is a need for more recognition of the negative contributions that UPFs make to nutrient intake. Some suggest revisiting the nutritional profile of UPFs and reframing the narrative away from a binary lens, asking instead whether there is potential for UPFs

SINÉAD FUREY AND MARTIN CARAHER

to be reformulated healthily. US researchers created a healthy diet plan, compliant with the 2020–2025 Dietary Guidelines for Americans, with 91% of the calories coming from UPFs (Hess et al., 2023). However, this ignored more general healthy eating advice and sustainability issues such as seasonality.

Another approach is to recommend limiting UPF consumption (and increasing consumption of minimally processed foods) in any revised obesity prevention strategies or public health messaging (inter)nationally. However, to do so necessarily involves strategising around ensuring affordable food is accessible to all.

Due to the negative impacts of the UPF industry in Africa, researchers have called for UPF industry regulation in the same way as "harmful industries such as tobacco, alcohol and arms and ammunition" (Kruger et al., 2023: 535). The UN Food and Agriculture Organization has stated that "a great concern exists on high consumption of ultra-processed food, obesity and the need for rules and regulations that encourage the consumption of healthy and nutritious foods" (quoted in Romani and De Lessa Carvalho, 2021: 5).

Research indicates that up-stream regulatory measures to offset UPF exposure are necessary to effect change in supply and demand given the dominance of supermarkets and the predominance of UPFs within them (Popkin and Ng, 2021). Attention is turning to whether supermarkets could be mandatorily required to report UPF sales as a proportion of all sales in order to help judge the balance between healthy unprocessed foods and processed foods. Transparent criteria (e.g., front of pack nutrition labelling or health star ratings) could be used for industry, regulators and consumers to assess nutritional quality and increase the proportion of sales from nutritious food by making healthy foods more accessible. In this scenario, however, assurance would be required that reformulation efforts do not simply replace one "problematic" ingredient (e.g., removing fat) with another (introducing or increasing sugar). Instead, a "nutrients-to-limit" reformulation model should be pursued that concentrates on reducing key nutrients of public health interest (e.g., fat, saturated fat and salt).

There is ongoing debate over taxing UPFs across many nations. In 2023, Colombia introduced a "junk food law" under which a levy will gradually be introduced on UPFs starting at 10%, rising to 15% in 2024 and 20% in 2025. Another interesting development is whether UPFs fall short of World Trade Organization commitments to facilitate better health protection and trade expansion by ensuring that rules and regulations encourage the availability of healthy foods. As Romani and De Lessa Carvalho (2021: 1) note, "trade restrictions should not be justified based only on the industry process but rather in [sic] the ingredients and quality of those food contents".

Returning to Mason and Lang's eco-nutrition philosophy, evidence indicates the many merits of eating a sustainable and healthy diet, with benefits to both population and environmental health. To reduce reliance on UPFs within a healthy eating lifestyle that re-traditionalises eating practices, it is necessary to prioritise, subsidise and promote unprocessed and minimally processed foods and tax UPFs (Popkin and Ng, 2021). Differentiation between energy-dense and nutrient-dense UPFs, coupled with food education, is key for policymakers who are responsible for dietary health. Industry involvement in regulatory deliberations should be limited, given their ongoing tendency to "impede political commitment for strong regulatory action" and governance arrangements (Baker et al., 2020: 17).

References

Adams J., Hofman K., Moubarac J. and Thow A.M. (2020) Public health response to ultra-processed food and drinks, *British Medical Journal* 369, m2391. https://doi.org/10.1136/bmj.m2391.

Aguirre A., Borneo M.T., El Khori S. and Borneo R. (2019) Exploring the understanding of the term "ultra-processed foods" by young consumers, *Food Research International (Ottawa, Ont.)* 115, 535–540. https://doi.org/10.1016/j.foodres.2018.09.059.

Baker P., Machado P., Santos T., Sievert K., Backholer K., Hadjikakou M., Russell C., Huse O., Bell C., Scrinis G., Worsley A., Friel S. and Lawrence M. (2020) Ultra-processed foods and the nutrition transition: Global, regional and national trends, food systems transformations and political economy drivers, *Obesity Reviews* 21(12), e13126. https://doi.org/10.1111/obr.13126.

Fardet A. and Rock E. (2020) Ultra-processed foods and food system sustainability: What are the links? *Sustainability* 12, 6280. https://doi.org/10.3390/su12156280.

Gibney M.J., Forde C.G., Mullally D. and Gibney E.R. (2017) Ultra-processed foods in human health: A critical appraisal, *American Journal of Clinical Nutrition* 106(3), 717–724. https://doi.org/10.3945/ajcn.117.160440.

Gomes Gonçalves N., Vidal Ferreira N., Khandpur N., Martínez Steele E., Levy R.B., Lotufo P.A., Bensenor I.M., Caramelli P., de Matos S.M.A., Marchioni D.M. and Suemoto C.K. (2023) Association between consumption of ultraprocessed foods and cognitive decline. *JAMA Neurology* 80(2), 142–150. https://doi.org/10.1001/jamaneurol.2022.4397.

Gupta S., Hawk T., Aggarwal A. and Drewnowski A. (2019) Characterizing ultra-processed foods by energy density, nutrient density and cost. *Frontiers in Nutrition* 6, 70. https://doi.org/10.3389/fnut.2019.00070.

Hall K.D., Ayuketah A., Brychta R., Cai H., Cassimatis T., Chen K.Y., Chung S.T., Costa E., Courville A., Darcey V., Fletcher L.A., Forde C.G., Gharib A.M., Guo J., Howard R., Joseph P.V., McGhee S., Ouwerkerk R., Raisinger K. … and Zhou M. (2019) Ultra-Processed diets cause excess calorie intake and weight gain: An inpatient randomized controlled trial of ad libitum food intake. *Cell Metabolism* 30(1), 67–77.e3. https://doi.org/10.1016/j.cmet.2019.05.008.

Hess J.M., Comeau M.E., Casperon S., Slavin J.L., Johnson G.H., Messina M., Raatz S., Scheett A.J., Bodensteiner A. and Palmer D.G. (2023) Dietary guidelines meet NOVA: Developing a menu for a healthy dietary pattern using ultra-processed foods. *Journal of Nutrition* 153(8), 2472–2481. doi.org/10.1016/j.tjnut.2023.06.028.

Kruger P., Wynberg R., Mafuyeka M., Laar A., Mialon M., Lake L., Witten C., Nisbett N., Baker P., Hofman K. (2023) The ultra-processed food industry in Africa, *Nature Food* 4(7), 534–536. https://doi.org/10.1038/s43016-023-00802-0.

Lawrence M.A. and Baker P.I. (2019) Ultra-processed food and adverse health outcomes. *British Medical Journal* 365, l2289. DOI: 10.1136/bmj.l2289.

Martínez Steele E., Baraldi L.G., Louzada M.L.D.C., Moubarac J-C., Mozaffarian D. and Monteiro C.A. (2016) Ultra-processed foods and added sugars in the US diet: Evidence from a nationally representative cross-sectional study. *BMJ Open* 6, e009892. https://doi.org/10.1136/bmjopen-2015-009892.

Mason P. and Lang T. (2017) *Sustainable Diets: How Ecological Nutrition Can Transform Consumption and The Food System*, Routledge, London.

Monteiro C.A., Cannon G., Moubarac J.C., Levy R.B., Louzada M.L.C., Rauber F., Khandpur N., Cediel G., Neri D., Martinez-Steele E., Baraldi G. and Jaime P.C. (2018) The UN decade of nutrition, the NOVA food classification and the trouble with ultra-processing, *Public Health Nutrition* 21(1), 5–17. https://doi.org/10.1017/S1368980017000234.

Monteiro C.A., Cannon G., Levy R.B., Moubarac J., Louzada M.L.C., Rauber F., Khandpur N., Cediel G., Neri D., Martinez-Steele E., Baraldi G. and Jaime P.C. (2019) Ultra-processed foods: What they are and how to identify them, *Public Health Nutrition* 22(5), 936–941. https://doi.org/10.1017/S1368980018003762.

Pan American Health Organization and World Health Organization. (2019) *Ultra-processed Food and Drink Products in Latin America: Sales, Sources, Nutrient Profiles, and Policy Implications*. PAHO, WHO: Washington, DC, USA.

Popkin B.M. and Ng S.W. (2021) The nutrition transition to a stage of high obesity and noncommunicable disease prevalence dominated by ultra-processed foods is not inevitable. *Obesity Reviews* 23(1), e13366-n/a. https://doi.org/10.1111/obr.13366.

Rodrigues S., Caraher M., Trichopoulou A. and de Almedia M.D.V. (2008) Portuguese households' diet quality (adherence to Mediterranean food pattern and compliance with WHO population dietary goals): trends, regional disparities and socioeconomic determinants, *European Journal Clinical Nutrition* 62, 1263–1272. https://doi.org/10.1038/sj.ejcn.1602852.

Romani N.C. and De Lessa Carvalho F.L. (2021) Restrictions on ultra-processed foods: Challenge for compliance with World Trade Organization commitments, *Seqüência – Legal and Political Studies* 42(89), 1–29. https://doi.org/10.5007/2177-7055.2021.e83028.

Sadler C.R., Grassby T., Hart K., Raats M., Sokolović, M. and Timotijevic, L. (2021) Processed food classification: Conceptualisation and challenges, *Trends in Food Science & Technology* 112, 149–162. https://doi.org/10.1016/j.tifs.2021.02.059.

Schnabel L., Kesse-Guyot E., Allès B., Touvier M., Srour B., Hercberg S., Buscail C. and Julia C. (2019) Association between ultraprocessed food consumption and risk of mortality among middle-aged adults in France, *JAMA Internal Medicine* 179, 490–8. https://doi.org/10.1001/jamainternmed.2018.7289.

Scientific Advisory Committee on Nutrition. (2023) *SACN Statement on Processed Foods and Health: Summary Report.* Available: SACN-statement-on-processed-foods-and-health-summary-report-GOV.UK_23.pdf (foodpolitics.com) (Accessed 8 August 2023).

Simões B.D.S., Barreto S.M., Molina M.D.C.B., Luft V.C., Duncan B.B., Schmidt M.I., Benseñor I.J.M., de Oliveira Cardoso L., Levy R.B. and Giatti L. (2018) Consumption of ultra-processed foods and socioeconomic position: A cross-sectional analysis of the Brazilian Longitudinal Study of Adult Health (ELSA-Brasil). *Cad Saude Publica* 34, e00019717. https://doi.org/10.1590/0102- 311x00019717.

Further reading

van Tulleken C. (2023) *Ultra-Processed People: Why Do We All Eat Stuff That Isn't Food … and Why Can't We Stop?* Cornerstone Press, London.
This is an up-to-date, accessible text that outlines the science, economics, history and production of UPFs.

Hässig A., Hartmann C., Sanchez-Siles L. and Siegrist M. (2023) Perceived degree of food processing as a cue for perceived healthiness: The NOVA system mirrors consumers' perceptions, *Food Quality and Preference* 110, 104944. https://doi.org/10.1016/j.foodqual.2023.104944.
This article investigates consumers' associations with, and perceptions of, processed foods concluding that consumers use the perceived degree of processing as a shortcut to their decision making when evaluating the healthiness of foods. The research also found a strong association between laypeople's perceived level of processing and the NOVA classification system.

Kruger P., Wynberg R., Mafuyeka M., Laar A., Mialon M., Lake L., Witten C., Nisbett N., Baker P. and Hofman K. (2023) The ultra-processed food industry in Africa, *Nature Food* 4(7), 534–536. https://doi.org/10.1038/s43016-023-00802-0.
This article presents a useful overview of the availability of UPFs in emerging economies and future possibilities for food regulation using the tobacco and alcohol industries as the predecessors for UPFs.

Lawrence M. (2023) Ultra-processed foods: A fit-for-purpose concept for nutrition policy activities to tackle unhealthy and unsustainable diets, *Public Health Nutrition* 26(7), 1384–1388. https://doi.org/10.1017/S1368980023000605.
The article critiques UPFs' usefulness in the development of food-based dietary guidelines and nutrition policy actions while assessing the polarised nature of the concept and debate.

121. Urban agriculture

Han Wiskerke

Introduction

In urban and peri-urban settings, agricultural production encompasses a wide spectrum of activities, including cultivating crops, raising livestock and fish, and nurturing trees. These endeavours serve multiple purposes, ranging from food production to the cultivation of non-food items like flowers and fodder. But it also encompasses activities related to the transportation, processing, and marketing of agricultural products, as part of a wider urban food system. Moreover, it extends to the provision of services such as agrotourism, urban greening, and water storage. A distinctive feature of urban agriculture, setting it apart from rural agriculture, lies in its deep integration within the urban socioeconomic, ecological, and legal framework. In essence, urban agriculture effectively harnesses urban resources, supplies goods and services to urban consumers, and operates under the sway of urban regulations and market dynamics (Wiskerke, 2020).

Urban agriculture is practised in both the Global North and South. There are many similarities in the characteristics of urban agriculture across different geographical areas, but also many differences. Urban agriculture exhibits a wide array of forms, resulting in a rich tapestry of practices, organisational structures, and business models (Van der Schans, 2015). This diversity is influenced by various dimensions (RUAF, 2023):

1. Location: Urban agriculture can take root within city confines (intra-urban agriculture) or on the outskirts of urban areas (peri-urban agriculture). These agricultural activities may occur outdoors, encompassing plots, rooftops, and balconies, or indoors within buildings and greenhouses. Locations span different spectra: from formal to informal, from legitimised to illegal, and from privately owned properties to public spaces.
2. Types of Production: The range of production encompasses diverse offerings, including crops for human consumption and animal feed, trees bearing fruits and nuts, and animals raised for meat,

milk, and eggs. Additionally, non-food products such as aromatic and medicinal plants, as well as ornamental plants, are cultivated. Typically, the emphasis is on producing perishable, nutritionally rich, and relatively high-value goods.

3. Scale: The size of production units exhibits significant variation, ranging from very small, occupying just several square metres (e.g., balconies or home gardens), to larger entities, contingent on their location. Peri-urban areas tend to house larger fields and farms.
4. Individual or Collective: Urban agriculture can be an individual pursuit or a collective endeavour, with collectives taking the form of family units, community groups, or cooperatives.
5. Degree of Market Orientation: In many urban settings, food is produced primarily for household consumption, with any surplus either exchanged for other food items or sold. However, a substantial proportion of urban farms (partially) operate on a commercial basis, vending fresh and processed products directly at the farm, local markets, and nearby shops, or even supplying supermarkets.
6. Technological Approach: Some production units rely heavily on manual labour, using basic tools like hoes and spades. In contrast, others employ sophisticated, automated systems, incorporating LED lighting and hydroponics. And there is a multitude of possibilities in between.
7. Integration with other Activities or Services: Some operations specialise in the production of a particular item, while others produce a variety of crops, engage in product processing, and offer diverse services. These services may encompass composting organic waste, food literacy, healthcare provisions, water storage, and the management of public spaces.

Recent data about the number of people involved in urban farming are lacking. This also holds true for the proportion of urban dwellers who partially (or fully) rely on urban agriculture for their daily food needs. However, specific case studies do indicate that urban agriculture can satisfy the needs of the majority of urban eaters for some specific foods. For example, a study across nine cities in Asia and Africa showed that urban farms supplied 70–100% of all leafy vegetables consumed by urban dwellers (Mostier and Danso, 2006).

The UN Food & Agriculture Organization states that 800 million people are involved in urban farming (FAO, 2023), but this is an estimation dating back to 1996 (Gallaher and Njenga, 2014). The highest percentage of urban dwellers practising urban agriculture is found in sub-Saharan Africa, primarily in the form of subsistence and small-scale commercial farming. In Asia the focus lies on the intensive urban production of perishable high-value commodities, such as green leafy vegetables and milk. In Latin American cities, a combination of subsistence and small-scale commercial food production can be found, with a focus on horticulture, dairy, and poultry (Van Veenhuizen and Danso, 2007). In Central and Eastern European countries, food self-provisioning (eggs, poultry, potatoes, vegetables, fruits) is a common practice, in both urban and rural areas (Jehlicka et al., 2020). In Western European countries and North America there is a resurgence of urban agriculture, either for food self-provisioning (mainly vegetables and fruits) in the form of allotment and community gardening or for achieving societal impact (community building) and providing ecosystem services (Orsini et al., 2020).

Current issues, concerns, and areas of focus

The growth of the world's urban population poses a number of interlinked challenges that are related to urban agriculture (Wiskerke, 2020): the climate emergency, food waste, diet-related ill-health, and urbanisation of poverty. In this section these challenges will be briefly discussed to understand how they relate to urban agriculture.

Numerous emerging climate change risks, such as urban heat islands and flooding, are concentrated in cities and metropolitan areas, with a particular focus on urban deltas (Scown et al., 2023). The increased frequency and severity of extreme climate events (flooding and droughts) are anticipated to yield adverse impacts on food production and food security, affecting various facets such as food availability, accessibility, utilisation, and the stability of food systems. The swift process of urbanisation will amplify the risks to urban

communities that are vulnerable to the effects of climate change, predominantly comprising urban poor people.

Trend analyses over the past fifty years indicate that urbanisation also coincides with a change in diet: an increase in the calorie intake per capita, a higher share of animal protein in diets, and a shift towards more processed food (Ruel et al., 2017). This also means more food packaging. This contributes to two urban challenges: diet-related ill-health and climate change. Diet-related ill-health (hunger, malnutrition, and obesity) is more prevalent among urban poor people as they generally face more challenges regarding the availability of, access to and affordability of food. Moreover, the 'empty' calories – e.g., soft drinks, energy drinks, and fast food – are generally cheaper than nutritious food items (Drewnowski, 2020). The aforementioned dietary changes also imply that the energy needed per urban dweller for food production increases, and as this is largely fossil energy, these changes in diet also contribute to climate change. Moreover, approximately 30% of all food produced is wasted, which means that significant amounts of fossil energy needed to produce food and its packaging are wasted. In relation to these and other urban challenges, urban agriculture provides a multitude of (potential) benefits, in particular for urban poor people (Dubbeling et al., 2011):

1. Social: This category encompasses factors such as food security, poverty reduction, fostering social inclusion, and community cohesion. Typically, these social advantages are attained through subsistence urban agriculture, wherein individuals, households, or community groups cultivate food and medicinal plants for their own consumption, but also engage in food sharing. This practice aids in reducing food and healthcare expenses, thereby freeing up funds for other necessities like housing, education, and clothing.

2. Economic: The economic dimension entails income generation, job creation, and the development of small and medium enterprises. Economic benefits come to fruition in market-oriented or commercially driven urban agriculture ventures. By producing both food and non-food products and directly selling

them to consumers (at farm gates and markets) or through retail outlets and supermarkets, this form of agriculture generates employment opportunities and income streams.

3. Health and Environment: Mental and physical health gains and ecological benefits are primarily achieved through the myriad services provided by urban agriculture, such as urban greening, recreational spaces, waste recycling, and actions aimed at climate change mitigation and adaptation. By cultivating food in close proximity to its consumption, there is a reduction in the need for long-distance food transport, and often less necessity for extensive food storage and packaging. This translates into decreased energy consumption and reduced greenhouse gas emissions, thereby serving as a means to combat climate change. Urban agriculture also contributes to urban greening efforts, assisting in mitigating the urban heat island effect, curbing air pollution, and enhancing the local urban microclimate and water retention capacity of cities.

One of the biggest barriers to sustainable urban development is that urban policymakers and planners do (or did) not understand why urban agriculture should be on the urban policy agenda (Pothukuchi and Kaufman, 1999). For many decades, food security was seen as a production challenge and hence as belonging to the realm of agricultural and thus rural policies. This urban–rural dichotomy has seriously delayed research on and policy interventions in the domain of urban food security. Moreover, not understanding the relationship between food and challenges such as social inequality, climate change, and nutrition-related health problems implies that urban agriculture is (or has been) missing on the urban policy agenda (Wiskerke, 2020). If space for urban agriculture is created and supported by municipalities it is quite often of a temporary nature. Urban agriculture, in particular in its 'traditional' form, is regularly regarded as an outdated or even illegal activity that should be banned from the 'modern' city (Smit, 1996). This discourages further development of and support for urban agriculture, thereby not seizing its full potential. However, in the last decades, starting in the Global South, more and more cities have begun to develop urban or city-region food policies in which considerable attention is paid to urban agriculture as a means to enhance food security, adapt to and mitigate climate change, and provide ecosystem services. The Milan Urban Food Policy Pact, which was launched in 2015 and had 300 signatory cities by mid-2025, has been key to putting urban agriculture on the urban policy agenda globally.

In recent years there has also been a growing interest in new forms of high-tech urban agriculture. This refers to technologies such as rooftop greenhouses, aquaponic systems, and vertical farming, including indoor farming using LED lights (Despommier, 2020). Quite a few cities are (keen on) supporting the development of vertical farming as part of their food security strategy. This especially holds true for cities that are very reliant on global food imports and that do not have space or fertile land within the city borders or in the urban fringe for the more traditional land-based forms of urban agriculture. Examples of such cities are Dubai and Singapore. Generally speaking, indoor vertical farming is a commercial, high-investment type of urban agriculture that is very efficient in the use of water and free of pesticide use, yet is also a form of urban agriculture that requires a lot of energy (Lubna et al., 2022). Typically, this implies that food items cultivated in vertical farms tend to be more expensive compared with those grown outdoors, benefiting from free natural sunlight. While the development of high-tech forms of vertical urban farming may be an interesting component of a city's food strategy, it is important to realise that these forms of urban agriculture commodify and privatise food, reduce the affordability of food for urban poor people and do not allow for commoning of urban food production and greening of cities. However, as architects excel in creating fancy designs of vertical farms, they tend to become the showcase projects of modern urban agriculture that urban policymakers like to identify with, yet quite a few fail because of too low a return on investment (Butturini and Marcelis, 2020).

Future concerns, issues, and questions

To improve our understanding of the multiple social, economic, ecological, and health benefits of urban agriculture, it is of the utmost importance that the impacts of different forms of urban agriculture are systematically monitored and evaluated over longer periods of time. This also holds true for the impact of specific interventions aimed at supporting the development of specific forms of urban agriculture. Questions to be addressed through monitoring, evaluation, and comparative analyses include:

- Does urban agriculture really help to keep food affordable for urban poor people in times of economic crises?
- Which forms of urban agriculture help to mitigate climate change and adapt to the negative effects of climate change?
- Are cities with urban agriculture in flood zones less prone to flooding than cities without urban agriculture?
- Under which conditions are high-tech forms of urban agriculture, such as vertical indoor farming, economically and environmentally sustainable?
- Is indoor vertical farming capable of serving the food needs of all urban dwellers?
- What are the food safety risks, and for whom, in situations where crops are being produced in contaminated soils or when urban wastewater is used for irrigation or sewage sludge as a source of nutrients?

A key component of long-term monitoring and evaluation of the multiple (assumed) benefits of urban agriculture will have to be cost–benefit analyses, especially as space in urban environments is scarce and thus expensive and cities have to fulfil multiple spatial functions to meet the needs of urban dwellers. When undertaking cost–benefit analysis, it is crucial to do so in a comprehensive and integral way as financial investments or other incentives or interventions to achieve a particular benefit (e.g. increased food availability for urban poor people) may have other positive economic (e.g. reduced health care costs due to better nutrition and physical activity) and non-economic (e.g. social cohesion, community empowerment, increased youth

food literacy) impacts. Hence, cost–benefit analyses of urban agriculture should not be a narrow-focused financial exercise, but should focus much more on broader understandings of impact such as wellbeing and quality of life.

Overall, this calls for the importance of recognising and legally protecting urban agriculture as an urban ecosystem service. This has been successfully implemented in Rosario (Argentina) where the municipal government decided to protect 800 hectares of urban and peri-urban land, 400 hectares since 2000 as part of its food security programme and another 400 hectares since 2014 as part of its climate action programme and metropolitan green belt project (Dubbeling and Terrile, 2016). This relates not only to the provisioning service of urban agriculture (food) but also to the regulating, cultural, and supporting services it provides, such as enhancing biodiversity, mitigating and adapting to climate change, reducing health inequalities, and empowering communities.

References

Butturini M and Marcelis L F (2020) Vertical farming in Europe: present status and outlook. In: Kozai T, Niu G and Takagaki M (eds) *Plant Factory: An Indoor Vertical Farming System for Efficient Quality Food Production*, London, Academic Press, 77–91.

Despommier D (2020) Vertical farming systems for urban agriculture. In: Wiskerke J S C (ed) *Achieving Sustainable Urban Agriculture*, Cambridge, Burleigh Dodds Science Publishing, 143–172.

Drewnowski A (2020) Analysing the affordability of the EAT–Lancet diet. *The Lancet Global Health* 8, e6–e7.

Dubbeling M and Terrile R H (2016) Rosario, Argentina: Operationalising urban-rural linkages through the preservation and improved use of peri-urban agricultural land. In: Dubbeling M, Bucatariu C, Santini G, Vogt C and Eisenbeiss K (eds) *City Region Food Systems and Food Waste Management*, Bonn and Eschborn, Deutsche Gesellschaft für Internationale Zusammenarbeit, 72–81.

Dubbeling M, De Zeeuw H and Van Veenhuizen R (2011) *Cities, Poverty and Food: Multi-stakeholder Policy and*

Planning in Urban Agriculture. Rugby, Practical Action Publishing Ltd.

FAO (2023) Urban and peri-urban agriculture. Food and Agriculture Organization of the United Nations. https://www.fao.org/urban-peri-urban-agriculture/en (accessed 1 September 2023).

Gallaher C and Njenga M (2014) Urban agriculture. In: Thompson B P and Kaplan D M (eds) *Encyclopedia of Food and Agricultural Ethics,* Dordrecht, Springer, 1775–1782.

Jehlička P, Grīviņš M, Visser O and Balázs B (2020) Thinking food like an East European: a critical reflection on the framing of food systems. *Journal of Rural Studies* 76, 286–95.

Lubna F A, Lewus D C, Shelford T J and Both A J (2022) What you may not realize about vertical farming. *Horticulturae* 8, 322. https://www.mdpi.com/2311-7524/8/4/322.

Mostier P and Danso G (2006) Local economic development and marketing of urban produced food. In: Van Veenhuizen R (ed) *Cities Farming for the Future: Urban Agriculture for Green and Productive Cities,* Ottawa, International Development Research Centre, 174–195.

Orsini F, Pennisi G, Michelon N, Minelli A, Bazzocchi G, Sanyé-Mengual E and Gianquinto G (2020) Features and functions of multifunctional urban agriculture in the global north: a review. *Frontiers in Sustainable Food Systems* 4, 562513. https://doi.org/10.3389/fsufs.2020.562513.

Pothukuchi K and Kaufman J L (1999) Placing the food system on the urban agenda: the role of municipal institutions in food systems planning. *Agriculture and Human Values* 16, 213–224.

RUAF (2023) Urban agriculture: what and why? RUAF foundation, https://ruaf.org/our-work/how-we-work/ (accessed 1 September 2023).

Ruel M T, Garrett J, Yosef S and Olivier M (2017) Urbanization, food security and nutrition. In: De Pee S, Taren D and Bloem M W (eds) *Nutrition and Health in a Developing World,* Cham, Springer Nature, 705–735.

Scown M W, Dunn F E, Dekker S C, Van Vuuren D P, Karabil S, Sutanudjaja E H, Santos M J, Minderhoud P S, Garmestani A S and Middelkoop H (2023) Global change scenarios in coastal river deltas and their sustainable development implications. *Global Environmental Change* 82, 102736. https://doi.org/10.1016/j.gloenvcha.2023.102736.

Smit J (1996) Urban agriculture, progress and prospect: 1975–2005. *Cities Feeding People Series Report* 18, 1–33.

Van der Schans J W (2015) *Business Models Urban Agriculture.* Wageningen Economic Research.

Van Veenhuizen R and Danso G (2007) *Profitability and Sustainability of Urban and Peri-urban Agriculture.* Rome, Food & Agriculture Organization.

Wiskerke J S C (2020) Creating a supportive public policy framework for urban agriculture. In: Wiskerke J S C (ed) *Achieving Sustainable Urban Agriculture,* Cambridge, Burleigh Dodds Science Publishing, 3–22.

Further reading

De Zeeuw H and Drechsel P (eds) (2015) *Cities and Agriculture: Developing Resilient Urban Food Systems.* Routledge.
This edited volume provides an overview of the crucial aspects of urban agriculture in both the Global South and North.

Viljoen A and Böhn K (2014) *Second Nature Urban Agriculture: Designing Productive Cities.* Routledge.
This book reviews research, design, and planning projects, and concrete actions on introducing and incorporating urban agriculture as an essential element of sustainable urban development.

Wiskerke J S C (ed) (2020) *Achieving Sustainable Urban Agriculture.* Burleigh Dodds.
This edited volume reviews research on building urban and peri-urban agricultural networks and the use of technologies such as rooftop and vertical farming systems, as well as providing case studies of particular products from urban farming.

HAN WISKERKE

122. Urban food

JANE BATTERSBY AND ANA
MORAGUES-FAUS

Introduction

Urban food has been increasingly present on the research and policy agenda since the 1990s. While authors at the time flagged the conspicuous absence of food from critical urban fields of study, like planning (Pothukuchi and Kaufman, 2000), there is, in fact, a far longer history of urban research and policy work focussing on food. For example, food was a central consideration of urban planners like Ebenezer Howard (1902). Walter Hedden's seminal 1929 text, *How Great Cities Are Fed*, provided a deep analysis of the functioning of New York City's food system within the city, and its relationship to local and distant food sources. However, throughout much of the latter part of the twentieth century, urban food fell off the research and policy agenda.

The re-emergence of the field in the 1990s came from the recognition of particular sets of challenges and opportunities that had emerged. Within the global south context, rapid urbanisation and the associated urbanisation of poverty raised questions about how to feed urban populations and how the relationship between urban and rural areas would change. In the global north, critical questions emerged about urban inequality and access to healthy foods, and at the same time the sustainability and justice of increasingly globalised food systems were being debated. In terms of governance, the 1992 United Nations Conference on Environment and Development in Rio focused attention on city or local government action as an entry point for systemic transformation, on the basis that many of the world's sustainable development challenges had roots and solutions at the local scale. Since then, international food governance agendas have evolved, converging in key spaces and declarations such as Habitat III, where urban food and nutrition are highlighted or the 2030 Agenda and the Sustainable Development Goals (see Forster et al., 2023, for an analysis of this evolution). The role of cities in creating key socio-ecological challenges and developing solutions is widely recognised, increasingly alongside their role in transforming food systems (Hawkes, 2023). Not least, to date, more than 280 cities have signed the Milan Urban Food Policy Pact, a protocol established in 2015 where cities commit to developing sustainable urban food systems. This range of global and local actions, as well as co-emerging concerns, has sparked research and policy interest in urban food issues for researchers working across various disciplinary fields.

Responses to these disparate challenges and opportunities set up diverse research interests from various disciplinary traditions. Within the global south, concerns with food security and developmentalist responses initially focused on urban agriculture and the role of cities in feeding people (see Egziabher, 2014). Within the global north, many studies have focused on food deserts and, more recently, on urban food environments and their health impacts; analysing urban food community projects, including urban agriculture; and studying urban food as part of a broader environmental slant, although dialogue across these strands of work is scant (Roberts, 2024). In the last two decades, an increasing number of contributions have interrogated how food can be integrated into urban planning and focused on the development of participatory urban food governance processes and spaces. Understanding distinct urban food dynamics has, therefore, brought together planners, political scientists, sociologists, public health specialists and geographers, among others, in conversation. The result of these different disciplinary and ideological entry points means that the same research topics are often analysed from very different positions. For example, urban agriculture in the African context is frequently purely understood from a developmental perspective and, in many instances, depoliticised (Maxwell, 1998). In contrast, in research and advocacy spaces in North America, urban agriculture was more likely to be framed in terms of community engagement, cultural continuity and even spaces of resistance (Battersby and Marshak, 2013). However, these distinctions have blurred over time, and more complex readings have developed cross-fertilising distinct conceptual frameworks, case studies and geographies (McClintock, 2018; Siebert, 2020).

Contributions to the urban food field have now expanded across disciplines, theories, frameworks, geographies and practices (see Moragues-Faus et al., 2023). However, despite the diversity of research entry points, one common thread across the field is the co-development of research and governance actions. Within the urban food field, many actors in the research and governance fields overlap, with academics often serving as key members of local food policy councils, working as activists in food advocacy organisations, or in partnership with NGOs and development agencies conducting urban food programmes.

Key concepts and contributions on urban food

Urban food research and practice is experiencing a rapid expansion; however, key concepts to delineate the field are still highly debated. An unresolved and undertheorised question within urban food research is what "urban food" actually means. Is the urban simply the location where food system activities take place, and people engage with food? Is the urban food system the components of the food system located within an urban area or is it the system feeding into an urban area? Moragues-Faus and Battersby (2021: 4) propose urban food governance scholars view the urban as a trialectic, "in which the urban is viewed simultaneously as a spatial container, a conceptual terrain and a governance structure". This means that the urban should be viewed as a physical space, but also as a site of politics, a site of economic activity and livelihoods, a location where the presence or absence and distribution of infrastructures shapes urban form and function, and a space in which social relationships shape systems and governance. The urban is also a space where there are important flows of materials, energy and resources within and beyond its borders (HLPE, 2024). A shared and debated understanding of what is meant by "urban food" is required to advance the field of scholarship.

However, to date, different definitions have been proposed by academics and practitioners to delineate the field. First, defining and, therefore, establishing the boundaries of *urban food systems* is challenging. Do they refer to the activities that happen within cities? Or also those that are necessary to feed cities and happen beyond their boundaries? How do we account for the interconnections that happen across scales, places and actors that ultimately affect what and how food-related activities happen in a city? And not least, how do we define what is urban? A current working definition of *urban food systems*

is provided by the HLPE report (2024), which states that urban and peri-urban food systems incorporate both food system activities (production, processing, distribution, marketing, preparation, consumption and disposal of goods) that take place within a given urban or periurban area and their interaction with other systems, and food system activities that take place outside the urban or peri-urban context, but which flow into the given urban or periurban area, and their interaction with other systems. Notwithstanding, mapping these activities and their impacts is challenging, as well as identifying interventions to reshape urban food system outcomes towards delivering sustainable food systems.

A second set of key concepts in the field revolves around urban food governance. *Urban food policies* have become increasingly present in urban areas across the globe, and are broadly defined as a deliberate process endorsed by city governments of developing urban interventions to address food-system challenges (IPES-Food, 2017; Moragues-Faus and Battersby, 2021). Cities have been signalled as food policy innovators in the last decades, given their integration of different actors (from planners to caterers), activities (from production to waste) and policy domains and departments (from health to environment or economy) in developing urban food policies. While urban food policies highlight the city council role, the term *urban food strategy* has also been mobilised to refer to a broader process of "how a city envisions change in its food systems, and how it strives towards this change", which might be supported by governments or not (Moragues et al., 2013: 6). In many instances, these processes lead to the creation of multi-actor spaces of deliberation and collaboration, such as food policy councils or partnerships. In this regard, and given the increasingly participatory approach to the development of urban food policies and strategies, it is important to note that *urban food governance* is wider than these deliberate policy-making spaces (Moragues-Faus and Battersby, 2021), which do not engage all the powers that shape urban food systems, such as hedge funds or real estate developers that actively shape urban food environments. Consequently, it is important to adopt a critical approach to analyse power in urban food dynamics, not least within co-governance platforms and processes (Drimie, 2023).

Finally, another recent urban food governance innovation revolves around the emergence of *city food networks* at the national, regional, and international levels (Moragues-Faus, 2021). These networks bring together cities to support transitions towards more sustainable food systems through peer-to-peer learning, collaboration in specific projects and advocacy at different scales. Key networks include Milan Urban Food Policy Pact (MUFPP), C40 and CITYFOOD-ICLEI operating globally; EUROCITIES; or national examples such as Food Policy Networks in the US, the UK Sustainable Food Places or the Spanish Network Cities for Agroecology. This translocal urban food governance landscape is contributing to the multiplication of local and global efforts in transforming urban food systems.

Future trajectories

While there has clearly been considerable research on urban food issues, there has not conventionally been much dialogue across the different clusters of food researchers, due to different disciplinary entry points and geographic focal areas. However, the presence of researchers within food policy networks has begun to create opportunities for deeper cross-disciplinary and cross-regional research collaborations. There have therefore been efforts to consolidate research and policy work across different contexts, and to develop common tools and metrics to engage urban food (e.g. MUFPP, C40, etc.). However, these are often designed by scholars and practitioners from the global north and are sometimes not well designed to address Southern food systems and governance systems. The importance of urban food as a critical challenge has been reinforced by the production of major reports and strategies on the topic by World Bank, World Food Programme, UN Habitat, UNEP, FAO and the HLPE-FSN.

As the field matures there are four dominant strands of research. These include research on (i) urban food governance structure and networks, (ii) strengthening local and territorial food systems, (iii) urban food environments, and (iv) research linking urban food to other urban issues (such as infrastructure, housing inequality, livelihoods, etc.; see LOGIC et al., 2024). Given the heterogeneity of entry points, it is difficult to project future research directions; however, given

the fragility of urban systems and food systems in the context of the climate emergency it is likely that urban food systems and climate vulnerability, adaption and resilience will strengthen as a critical entry point for researchers and policy makers (Glasgow Food and Climate Declaration, 2021).

References

Battersby, J. and Marshak, M. (2013). Growing communities: Integrating the social and economic benefits of urban agriculture in Cape Town. *Urban Forum, 24,* 447–461. Springer Netherlands.

Drimie, S. (2023). The Role of the Private Sector in Urban Food Governance. In A. Moragues-Faus, J. Battersby, J.K. Clark & A. Davies (eds.), *Routledge handbook of urban food governance* (pp. 311–324). Oxon and New York, Routledge.

Egziabher, A.G. (2014). *Cities feeding people: an examination of urban agriculture in East Africa.* IDRC.

Forster, T., Egal, F. and Puhac, A. (2023). International Agendas and Urban Food System Governance: Informing, integrating and operationalizing the SDGs. In A. Moragues-Faus, J.K. Clark, J. Battersby & A. Davies (eds.), *Routledge handbook of urban food governance.* Oxon and New York, Routledge.

Glasgow Food and Climate Declaration (2021). https://www.milanurbanfoodp olicypact.org/wp-content/uploads/2021 /10/31f564_844a2e58e94a439cab38beb 97fe114fd.pdf.

Hawkes, C. (2023). Leveraging Urbanization for Food Systems Transformation. Presentation at UN Food Systems Summit +2 Stocktaking Moment, 2023, Rome. https://www.youtube.com/watch?v =L3uDlRakK0w.

Hedden, W.P. (1929). *How great cities are fed.* New York, DC Health.

HLPE (2024). *Strengthening urban and peri-urban food systems to achieve food security and nutrition in the context of urbanization and rural transformation.* Rome, CFS HLPE-FSN.

Howard, E. (1902). *The garden city of to-morrow.* London, Swan Sonnenschein & Co.

IPES-Food (2017). *What makes urban food policy happen? Insights from five case studies.* International Panel of Experts on Sustainable Food Systems. https://ipes-food.org/wp-content/uploads/2024/03/Cities_full.pdf

Living Off-Grid Food and Infrastructure Collaboration (LOGIC), Battersby, J., Brown-Luthango, M., Fuseini, I., Gulabani, H., Haysom, G., Jackson, B., Khandelwal, V., MacGregor, H., Mitra, S., Nisbett, N., Perera, I., te Lintelo, D., Thorpe, J. and Toriro, P. (2024). Bringing together urban systems and food systems theory and research is overdue: understanding the relationships between food and nutrition infrastructures along a continuum of contested and hybrid access. *Agriculture and Human Values, 41*, 437–448. https://doi.org/10.1007/s10460-023-10507-6.

McClintock, N. (2018). Urban agriculture, racial capitalism, and resistance in the settler-colonial city. *Geography Compass, 12*(6), e12373.

Maxwell, D. (1998). The Political Economy of Urban Food security in Sub-Saharan Africa. FCND Discussion Paper No. 41. Washington DC: IFPRI.

Moragues-Faus, A. (2021). The emergence of city food networks: rescaling the impact of urban food policies. *Food Policy, 103*, 102107. https://doi.org/10.1016/j.foodpol.2021.102107.

Moragues-Faus, A. and Battersby, J. (2021). Urban food policies for a sustainable and just future: concepts and tools for a renewed agenda. *Food Policy, 103*, 102124.

Moragues-Faus, A. Battersby, J., Clark, J.K. and Davies, A. (eds.) (2023). *Routledge handbook of urban food governance*. First edition. London, Routledge.

Moragues, A., Morgan, K., Moschitz, H., Neimane, I., Nilsson, H., Pinto, M., Rohracher, H., Ruiz, R., Thuswald, M., Tisenkopfs, T. and Halliday, J. (2013). Urban Food Strategies: The Rough Guide to Sustainable Food Systems. Document developed in the framework of the FP7 project FOODLINKS (GA No. 265287).

Pothukuchi, K. and Kaufman, J.L. (2000). The food system. *Journal of the American Planning Association, 66*(2), 113–124. https://doi.org/10.1080/01944360008976093.

Roberts, W. (2024). Toward City- and People-Centered Food Policy. In S. Raja, M. Caton Campbell, A. Judelsohn, B. Born and A. Morales (eds.), *Planning for equitable urban agriculture in the United States: future directions for a new ethic in city building* (pp. 491–503). Springer. https://library.oapen.org/bitstream/handle/20.500.12657/90407/978-3-031-32076-7.pdf?sequence=1.

Siebert, A. (2020). Transforming urban food systems in South Africa: unfolding food sovereignty in the city. *The Journal of Peasant Studies, 47*(2), 401–419.

Further reading

HLPE (2024). *Strengthening urban and peri-urban food systems to achieve food security and nutrition in the context of urbanization and rural transformation.* Rome, CFS HLPE-FSN.

This report by the High Level Panel of Experts on Food Security and Nutrition (HLPEFSN) challenges prevailing narratives, revealing that over three quarters of the world's food insecure population lives in urban and periurban regions, providing a unique compilation of data and the state of the art on urban food systems knowledge. It provides an in-depth analysis of the unique challenges and opportunities of urban and peri-urban areas in delivering equitable, accessible, sustainable and resilient food systems, for the realisation of the right to food.

Moragues-Faus, A., Battersby, J., Clark, J.K. and Davies, A. (eds.) (2023). *Routledge handbook of urban food governance*. First edition. London, Routledge.

This handbook is the first collection to reflect on and compile the currently dispersed histories, concepts and practices involved in the increasingly popular field of urban food governance.

Steel, C. (2008). *Hungry city: how food shapes our lives.* London, Chatto & Windus.

This book contributed to situate cities back at the centre of how we understand food systems and their transformations. The book traces the historical development of cities – such as Rome or London – to the present day and how food systems have shaped urban spaces and vice versa.

JANE BATTERSBY AND ANA MORAGUES-FAUS

123. Vegetarianism and veganism

Andrew McGregor

Introduction

Vegetarianism and veganism pose fundamental questions about the relationships between humans and the animals that are used for food and other purposes. Vegetarianism opposes the consumption of meat while veganism seeks to avoid, as much as possible, the use of animal products of any form, including eggs and animal milks, but also leather, fur, gelatine, and other animal-derived substances. They reject taken-for-granted norms that the flesh and organs of non-human animals should be eaten and, in the case of veganism, that their reproductive systems, skins, and other body parts should be systematically harvested for human use. In doing so they aim to disrupt local and global political ecologies based upon the ongoing and accelerating violent exploitation and commodification of human and non-human animals. By rejecting the positioning of animals as food they challenge social norms, tastes, and values, and pursue widespread social change.

Motivations

The rationales for vegetarianism and veganism are multiple and often overlapping. While both are commonly associated with animal rights concerns, the range of motivations is much more diverse. Vegetarian practice, for example, has long been associated with spiritual asceticism and piety in Hindu and Buddhist traditions. In the West it also has spiritual roots, being known as the Pythagorean diet until the mid-19th century, inspired by the Greek philosopher's concern about the transmigration of souls between human and non-human animals and the spiritual benefits of abstinence. Spiritual wellbeing is still prominent in some interpretations of contemporary vegetarianism; however, it is now more commonly associated with concerns about animal cruelty and the health and environmental impacts of eating meat.

Veganism is a more recent concept that is sometimes associated with Jainism, which emerged in western India in 570 BC. However, the link is not strong, as Jainism believes all things, including rocks, have life, and the goal of living is to liberate that life through practising austerity and avoiding harm at all times. Modern veganism focuses on animal life only, emerging in its modern form after vegetarians in the UK disagreed with the appropriateness of eating eggs and dairy. They formed The Vegan Society in 1944, pre-dating the modern animal rights movement by about three decades, striving to end "the use of animal[s] by [hu]man[s] for food, commodities, work, hunting, vivisection, and all other uses involving exploitation of animal life by [hu]man[s]" (The Vegan Society, 2014). Veganism was also associated with health and environmental issues from its inception, both of which, as is the case with vegetarianism, have become more prominent over time.

Vegetarianisms and veganisms

What defines vegetarianism and veganism, then, is not shared motivations or political subjectivities but shared practice. At its simplest, to be vegetarian is to practice a diet that does not involve meat, and to be vegan is to practice a lifestyle that avoids as much as possible the consumption or use of animal products. However, beyond this common baseline there are multiple "vegetarianisms" and "veganisms" that range from those experimenting with plant-based diets for personal health reasons through to activists involved in blockades and public protests striving to bring about more caring and less exploitative societies. Greenebaum (2018: 680) catches this diversity well when referring to veganism as "a diet, lifestyle, and social movement that centres on animal rights, environmental protection, and human health". Researchers reflect this diversity by studying vegetarianism and veganism in a variety of ways including as a diet, an alternative food network, a market, a lifestyle or social movement, a form of political or ethical consumerism, a form of prefigurative politics, and a philosophy. What these studies show is that animals are so entrenched and normalised in food and other production systems that their disentanglement through vegetarian and vegan practices has significant implications for human and non-human bodies, lifestyles, subjectivities, economies, environments, and politics.

Popularity and its challenges

The growing popularity and diversity of plant-based diets

Growing awareness about the environmental and health implications of eating animals, as detailed in high profile publications like the FAO's *Livestock's Long Shadow* report (Steinfeld, et al. 2006) and the Eat-Lancet Commission's (2019) Planetary Health Diet, alongside popular documentaries like *Cowspiracy: The Sustainability Secret* (2014: Dir. Kip Anderson and Keegan Kuhn), *Forks Over Knives* (2011: Dir. Lee Fulkerson), and *The Game Changers* (2018: Dir. Louis Psihoyos), has underpinned an unprecedented rise in popularity and visibility of plant-based diets. Veganism, in particular, has undergone a transformation from a fringe counterculture movement to a trendy, accepted, and even desirable lifestyle choice in some contexts. While both remain at the margins of most societies, they are much more popular than ever before.

New subjectivities that similarly trouble the use of animals as food have also emerged, such as flexitarian, referring to a reduced meat diet; climatarian, referring to those who choose low carbon diets; and plant-based "food tribes" that may or may not include small amounts of animal-based products. A profusion of apps, cookbooks, events, pledges, webpages, social media groups, documentaries, and celebrities, as well as restaurants, meals, and food products have added to the acceptability of new and old subjectivities and the ease through which people can become involved. While most veg*ns (a term used to refer to vegetarians and vegans) welcome this shift, their growing popularity and visibility has also attracted concerns about the changing composition, meanings, and politics associated with each term.

Shifting meanings and definitions

A commonly voiced concern is that the meanings, practices, and politics originally associated with veganism and vegetarianism are being hollowed out and transformed in ways that weaken their association with animal rights. Researchers have shown, for example, that some people are drawn to veganism primarily for health and environmental reasons, alongside or instead of animal concerns (e.g. Kalte 2020). Health

vegans are unlikely to engage in the same sorts of political actions an animal rights vegan might practise, nor avoid animal products outside diets in quite the same way. Similarly, an environmental vegan may find that some animal products cause less environmental harm than synthetic products, creating dilemmas about what to use. Gheihman (2021) argues that as veganism has grown in popularity it has shifted from being a social movement based on political protest to being a lifestyle movement focused on individual consumption. The politics that emerge are much more passive and iterative rather than social and confrontational, something that is criticised as having limited impacts but nevertheless may assist in prefiguring less violent worlds.

A problem with the animal rights argument is that vegetarianism, and to a lesser extent veganism, have always incorporated a broader range of concerns than just animal rights. Any attempt to limit the definition of either term to singular motivations risks ostracising people who are drawn to veg*nism for different reasons but are nevertheless practising diets that align with efforts to halt the systematic exploitation of animals in food systems. One of the critiques of the recent rise of veganism, for example, is that it is becoming associated with whiteness and privilege. Harper (2011) has criticised a "colourblind" approach whereby race and class have been deemed irrelevant to the pursuit of veganism and animal rights more generally, resulting in uncritical proliferation of thin white vegan stereotypes. By not engaging in race and class and the very different reasons people may be interested in avoiding animal foods, vegan events and campaigns can become exclusionary, not only deterring people of colour from participating but also exposing them to critiques from friends and associates when they do participate. Indigenous scholars have echoed these concerns, calling for Indigenous veganisms that are responsive to cultural differences and place-specific human–animal relations that may involve the use of animals as food (Dunn, 2019; Yandarra et al., 2022).

Plant-based capitalism

Accompanying these critiques has been the rise of what Sexton et al. (2022) call Big Veganism, referring to the extraordinary proliferation of businesses seeking to profit from the popularity of plant-based foods. Much of this work has focused upon the development of meat substitutes, not in the form of tofu or chickpeas, but in the form of plant-based meat analogues that look and taste like meat, and cellular meat grown from animal cells, or animal products, including dairy, grown from yeast through precision fermentation. A huge range of startups funded by substantial amounts of venture capital are involved in the research, development, and production of these foods. These alternative protein companies are engaging in diverse strategies to not only make their products edible and acceptable, but also desirable in terms of taste, health, animals, environments, and food security.

This shift towards "plant-based capitalism" (Giraud, 2021) has made the transition away from animal-based foods much easier by not only expanding the range of alternative foods that can be eaten but expanding them in a way that requires little or no new cooking skills or knowledge, nor even retraining taste buds given the similarity these products have with animal products. It also democratises access to plant-based alternatives, with many fast food franchises and supermarkets now providing plant-based meat options. However, critics are also concerned that these emergent industries are often supported by corporations whose primary business model relies on the widespread exploitation of animals. As alternative proteins expand, a challenge will be to increase the number of producers alongside the number of products, otherwise it risks further enhancing the influence and profits of large agri-corporations (Sexton et al., 2022). Perhaps most troubling is how alternative proteins promulgate a politics that assumes a shift away from animal industries can be driven by small shifts in consumer choices rather than the more confrontational and activist politics traditionally associated with social movements and political change.

Going forward

Vegetarianism and veganism are likely to continue growing and evolving as the full social and environmental impacts of animal agriculture become more well-known and the impacts of the Anthropocene become more severe. However, growth is likely to be constrained, remaining at the margins of society rather than widespread and normalised. The challenge proponents face is how to upscale their appeal and transition societies away from animal products in ways that are inclusive and respectful of the diverse human and non-human interests involved, including just transitions for those working in animal industries. A passive politics of abstinence based on product substitution can only go so far; however, it provides a launching pad for more active and creative strategies opposing industrial animal agriculture. Climate scientists, for example, have lobbied for a staged reduction from nationally declared levels of "peak livestock" (Harwatt et al., 2019), whereas Dominick (2015) has called for structural change by lobbying for increased government regulation of animal cruelty, labelling of animal welfare and environmental impacts, direct action to disrupt production, and costing of the health and environmental externalities of animal industries. Food scholars, critical animal studies, more-than-human theorists, public health proponents, environmental researchers and religious leaders all have a role to play in challenging the hegemony of animal agriculture by developing an inclusive politics oriented at realising food systems where the lives of animals and those negatively affected by animal food production, whether by environmental degradation, food insecurity, colonisation, poor health, or spiritual corruption, actually matter.

References

Dominick B (2015) Anarcho-veganism revisited. In: Nocella A, White R and Cudworth E (eds) *Anarchism and Animal Liberation: Essays on Complementary Elements of Total Liberation*. Jefferson, McFarland and Company, 23–39.

Dunn K (2019) Kaimangatanga: Maori perspectives on veganism and plant-based kai. *Animal Studies Journal* 8, 42–65.

Eat-Lancet Commission (2019) *Food in the Anthropocene: The EAT-Lancet Commission on Healthy Diets From Sustainable Food Systems Summary Report*. Available: https://eatforum.org/eat-lancet-commission/eat-lancet-commission-summary-report/ (Accessed 21/8/2023).

Gheihman N (2021) Veganism as a lifestyle movement. *Sociology Compass* 15, 5, e12877. https://doi.org/10.1111/soc4.12877.

Giraud E (2021) *Veganism: Politics, Practice, and Theory.* London, Bloomsbury.

Greenebaum J (2018) Vegans of color: managing visible and invisible stigmas. *Food, Culture & Society* 21, 680–697 https://doi.org/10.1080/15528014.2018.1512285.

Harper A (2011) Vegans of Color, Racialized Embodiment, and Problematics of the "Exotic". In: Alkon A and Agyeman J (eds) *Cultivating Food Justice: Race, Class and Sustainability.* Cambridge. The MIT Press, 221–238.

Harwatt H, Ripple W, Chaudhary A, Betts M, and Hayek M (2019) Scientists call for renewed Paris pledges to transform agriculture. *The Lancet Planetary Health* 4, 1, E9–E10 https://doi.org/10.1016/S2542-5196(19)30245-1.

Kalte D (2020) Political veganism: an empirical analysis of vegans' motives, aims, and political engagement. *Political Studies* 69, 814–833 https://doi.org/10.1177/0032321720930179.

Sexton A, Garnett T, and Lorimer J (2022) Vegan food geographies and the rise of Big Veganism. *Progress in Human Geography* 46, 605–628 https://doi.org/10.1177/03091325211051021.

Steinfeld H, Gerber P, Wassenaar T, Catel V, Rosales M and de Haan C (2006) *Livestock's Long Shadow: Environmental Issues and Options.* Rome: Food and Agricultural Organization.

The Vegan Society (2014) *Ripened by Human Determination: 70 years of The Vegan Society.* The Vegan Society.

Yandarra, Smith S, Smith N, Hodge P, Daley L, and Wright S (2022) Ngurrajili – "continued giving". In: Hodge P, McGregor A, Springer S, Véron O and White R (eds) *Vegan Geographies: Spaces Beyond Violence, Ethics Beyond Speciesism.* Brooklyn: Lantern Publishing and Media, 83–106.

Further reading

Hodge P, McGregor A, Springer S, Véron O, and White R (eds) (2022) *Vegan Geographies: Spaces Beyond Violence, Ethics Beyond Speciesism.* Brooklyn, Lantern Publishing and Media.

This edited collection provides an introduction to some of the ways in which veganism has manifested across space and how people are coming together to contest and disrupt the normalisation of animal agriculture.

ANDREW MCGREGOR

124. Water and food

Amanda Shankland

Introduction

In 1995, vice president of the World Bank, Dr Ismail Serageldin, remarked: "Many of the wars of the 20th century were about oil but wars of the 21st century will be about water unless we change the way in which we manage it" (Connell, 2013). Increases in population, drought, deterioration of critical ecosystem services, and poor water resource governance have all contributed to a situation where water scarcity threatens critical food supplies. These problems have created a looming crisis of unparalleled proportions (Pereira and do Rosario Cameira, 2019). The climate emergency is perhaps the biggest driver, with significant direct and indirect influences on water resources and agriculture. Shifts in average temperatures, changing precipitation patterns, and increases in the frequency and intensity of extreme weather events present significant challenges for agriculture. For instance, water availability will be substantially reduced in semi-arid and arid areas, particularly in sub-Saharan Africa (de Fraiture et al., 2010).

Discussing the relationship between food and water requires some key definitions. The 'water footprint' of a product quantifies the amount of freshwater used to produce a product over the entire supply chain. The water footprint is important for assessing social, economic, and environmental sustainability (Muthu, 2020). 'Beneficial use' of water refers to water use with clear and tangible benefits, such as in households, irrigation, industrial processing and cooling, hydropower, recreation, and navigation (United Nations Economic and Social Commission for Western Asia, 2022). 'Consumptive use' refers to water that is no longer available for such use because it has evaporated, transpired, been incorporated into products and crops, or been consumed (European Environmental Agency, 2002).

Current issues, concerns, areas of focus

Some of the most productive agricultural lands in the world were developed through massive hydrological projects that began in the 20th century, including the Hoover in the United States, Kariba in Zambia, Bhakra in India, and the WAC Bennett dam in Canada (see Hiltzik, 2010; Matanzima, 2022; Rangachari, 2006). These projects radically transformed ecological landscapes, damaging and destroying wetlands and displacing people. Alongside the chemical and technological innovations of the 'green revolution', they dramatically increased food production in the 20th century.

Today, the advantages of modernisation projects are overshadowed by many problems. Irrigation diverts water from essential aquatic ecosystems, including lakes, rivers, and wetlands. It contributes to salinisation, erosion, biodiversity decline, increases in invasive species, and reduced habitats for inland and coastal fish species (de Fraiture et al., 2010). Pollution associated with irrigation agriculture contributes to massive algae blooms and die-offs (Swihart, 2011). While animal farming provides valuable manure for crops, modern intensified practices have led to the pollution of rivers with various substances, including nitrogen, phosphorus, and pathogens like oocysts. This slurry finds its way into rivers primarily through surface run-off from fertilised crop fields (Yanan et al., 2022). The future of irrigation farming is also threatened because many of the largest dams in the world are drying up (Leslie, 2021). Over-extraction and climate change have contributed to severe water shortages and droughts. Further, the increased demand for scarce water resources challenges established political relationships and contributes to the emergence of 'water wars' (Nash, 2007).

One of the most difficult challenges we currently face is how to manage the demands of farms, wetlands, wildlife, and development (balancing 'beneficial' and 'consumptive' use). The 310-square-mile Pontine Marsh in Italy is demonstrative of this challenge. The marsh developed as several streams where access to the sea was impeded by 28 miles (45km) of dunes along the shore. Before the 20th century, nomadic communities lived on the plains during the summers and returned to the Lepini mountains in winter. These nomads were the only people who ventured into this swampy, malaria-infested land. Kings and popes, for centuries, tried to reclaim the land for cultivation with no success. It was only under the leadership of Mussolini, in what was known as the Fascist Battle of the Swamps (1928–1939), that the marshes were turned into farmland. A complex system of roads, canals, and treelines created an orderly grid which separated nature from production and wilderness from civilization (Metta and Onorati, 2019).

Numerous problems with this transformation of the land have since surfaced. The range of agricultural activities in the Pontine plains has caused considerable pollution, with high levels of nitrates and phosphates contaminating the land and water and poisoning the Mediterranean Sea. Given the diminished quality of surface water, irrigators have resorted to deep groundwater extraction, which increases saline seepage and undermines soil quality and ecosystems. The need for water quality monitoring has increased, and the roughly 10,000 miles (16,000km) of drainage canals crossing the plains need constant maintenance through dredging and repairing (Metta and Onorati, 2019).

Elsewhere, pastoral farming is endangered by diminishing water supplies. Pastoralism in the Sahel and the Horn of Africa has historically provided a substantial portion of dietary needs and is an effective way to use limited water resources. Pastoralists comprise over half of the population in Somalia and South Sudan and between ten and forty percent in other countries in the region. These pastoralists make use of scarce water resources by continuously moving to where water is available. However, ancient trading and droving routes have been disturbed by the regulatory and revenue-generating demands of the modern state. Further, growing populations and climate change have meant pastoralists are increasingly in competition with other farmers for scarce water resources. Mineral exploration companies and transnational human and drug trafficking also contribute to conflicts over water (Anon, 2018).

Water scarcity is also caused by the diversion of water for commercial purposes. Commercial enterprises do not just include irrigation agriculture. Consumer beverage production, particularly bottled water, competes with agriculture and has an enormous 'water footprint'. Water that was once readily available to all people is increasingly commodified, which exacerbates the growing divide between rich and poor (Nash, 2007).

The commercialisation of water has been progressing for hundreds of years. In Mexico, the Spanish conquerors drained and diverted the abundant waters in the Aztec capital and then introduced commercialised sugar cane and maguey, which was used to produce rum and tequila. During colonial times and the period following independence, Indigenous pueblos adapted rum and tequila to be used in libation ceremonies as offerings to the saints and divine powers. Eventually, the demand for water was expanded to soft drink companies. Today, in San Cristobal de Las Casas, Chiapas, most of the groundwater extraction is done by the Coca-Cola Company. The company bottles the water, sells it worldwide, and also back to the people it was taken from (Nash, 2007).

Modernised management of water is a double-edged sword. Projects have allowed us to extract and utilise water for growing crops more effectively. At the same time, these projects have often contributed to water contamination, drought, and unfair distribution in the hands of elites. As a result, water for farming has been significantly reduced, contributing to a loss of food security in much of the world.

Future concerns

Water availability has become the most significant constraint to agricultural production in much of the world. Physical water scarcity is when there is insufficient water to meet all demands, including environmental flows. Economic scarcity is when there is insufficient water to meet financial, human, or institutional demands (Seckler, 1998). More than 1.2 billion people live in river basins that suffer from physical water scarcity, while another 1.5 billion live in economically scarce basins (Molden et al., 2007). Millions of small-scale farmers work under conditions of physical or economic water scarcity, or both. Water storage and management investments are needed to improve access to irrigation water and reduce economic scarcity, and resources must be distributed to reduce physical scarcity (de Fraiture et al., 2010).

Despite this dismal picture, solutions are being explored. Agroecology is a philosophy that emphasises the connections between plants, animals, humans, and *all* the natural elements, in growing food that supports the historically prevalent ecology of a given area. In my chapter, 'Farming Innovations in Agroforestry and Agroecology', in the *Routledge Handbook of Sustainable Diets* I explore two such examples. The first explores a deep-rooted farming technique called *chinampas* that emerged in the pre-colonial Mexico City area. The second looks at how Anishinaabeg Indigenous farmers are trying to re-establish traditional rice varieties known as *manoomin* (Shankland, 2023).

In the Pontine marshes described above, an ancient Italian agro-ecological practice known as 'marcite' is being revived. 'Marcite' is the cultivation of a stable irrigated grassland. In areas of the Pontine rich in spring waters, grass crops are being cultivated. The practice of marcite differs significantly from traditional irrigation methods, as these water meadows are under continuous and slow-running water, which prevents the problems associated with stagnation. Water flows are controlled through channel gates and natural earth ridges, which provide variable irrigation supply for sections of the marshes. These soaked fields widen the range of traditional crops that can be grown and support plants that help clean polluted water (Metta and Onorati, 2019). While the legacy of modernisation presents many problems, agroecology combines both ancient and modern methods to address these issues.

Tackling the problems associated with the water–agriculture–food nexus will be challenging. Nonetheless, there are many opportunities to effectively address this challenge. Practitioners are working to build integrated approaches to water and food policies and practices, improve water management in agriculture, enhance agricultural systems to use water more efficiently and productively, ensure sustainable management and conservation of ecosystems, and foster participative and inclusive governance of water.

References

Anon (2018). Pastoralism and conflict in the Horn of Africa and the Sahel. *Population and Development Review, 44*(4), 857–860.

Connell, D. (2013). Water wars, maybe, but who is the enemy? *Global Water Forum.* https://www.globalwaterforum.org/2013/04/10/water-wars-maybe-but-who-is-the-enemy/

de Fraiture, C., Molden, D., and Wichelns, D. (2010). Investing in water for food, ecosystems, and livelihoods: An overview of the comprehensive assessment of water management in agriculture. *Agricultural Water Management, 97*(4), 495–501. https://doi.org/10.1016/j.agwat.2009.08.015

European Environmental Agency (2002). *Consumptive Use (of Water).* https://www.eea.europa.eu/help/glossary/eea-glossary/consumptive-use-of-water

Hiltzik (2010). *Colossus: Hoover Dam and the making of the American century* (1st ed.). Free Press.

Leslie, J. (2021). *As Warming and Drought Increase, A New Case for Ending Big Dams.* Yale Environment 360. https://e360.yale.edu/features/as-warming-and-drought-increase-a-new-case-for-ending-big-dams

Matanzima, J. (2022). "We were displaced several times since 1956": the Tonga-Goba involuntary resettlement experiences at the Kariba Dam. *Water International, 47*(8), 1249–1266. https://doi.org/10.1080/02508060.2022.2085851

Metta, A. and Onorati, D. (2019). Modern rural-scape and contemporary ideology: The case of the Pontine Plain. *SHS Web of Conferences, 63.* 12002. https://doi.org/10.1051/shsconf/20196312002

Molden, D., Oweis, T. Y., Pasquale, S., Kijne, J. W., Hanjra, M. A., Bindraban, P. S., ... and Upadhyaya, A. (2007). Pathways for increasing agricultural water productivity. In D. Molden (ed), *Water for food, water for life: a Comprehensive Assessment of Water Management in Agriculture* (pp. 279–310). Earthscan.

Muthu, S. S. (2020). Calculating the water and energy footprints of textile products. In S. S. Muthu (ed.), *Assessing the Environmental Impact of Textiles and the Clothing Supply Chain* (2nd ed., pp. 77–93). Woodhead Publishing.

Nash, J. (2007). Consuming interests: Water, rum, and Coca-cola from ritual propitiation to corporate expropriation in Highland Chiapas. *Cultural Anthropology, 22*(4), 621–639. https://doi.org/10.1525/can.2007.22.4.621

Pereira, L. S. and do Rosario Cameira, M. (eds) (2019). Innovation issues in water, agriculture and food. *MDPI.* https://doi.org/10.3390/books978-3-03921-166-1

Rangachari (2006). *Bhakra-Nangal Project: Socio-economic and Environmental Impacts.* Oxford University Press.

Seckler, D.W. (1998). *World Water Demand and Supply, 1990 to 2025: Scenarios and Issues* (Vol. 19). IWMI Research Report.

Shankland, A. (2023). Farming Innovations in Agroforestry and Agroecology. In K. Kevany and P. Prosperi (eds), *Routledge Handbook of Sustainable Diets.* Routledge.

Swihart, T. L. (2011). Florida's water: A fragile resource in a vulnerable state. *RFF Press.* https://doi.org/10.4324/9781936331932

United Nations Economic and Social Commission for Western Asia (2022). *Beneficial Use of Water.* https://www.unescwa.org/sd-glossary/beneficial-use-water

Yanan, L., Mengru, W., Xuanjing, C., Shilei, C., Nynke, H., Carolien, K., Lin, M., Wen, X., Qi, Z., Fusuo, Z., and Maryna, S. (2022). Multi-pollutant assessment of river pollution from livestock production worldwide. *Water Research, 209.* 117096. http://doi.org/10.1016/j.watres.2021.117096

Further reading

Classens, M. (2021). *From Dismal Swamp to Smiling Farms.* Vancouver: University of British Columbia Press. https://doi.org/10.14288/1.0398733

This book looks at the historical evolution of one of Canada's most profitable farmlands, the Holland Marshes. This agricultural area just north of Toronto has been the site of intense political debate as developers, environmentalists, and farmers compete for space. Classens argues that capitalist and liberal notions of nature have imperilled the marshes and the long-term sustainability of agriculture in the region. This book offers a compelling case study detailing the challenges of managing marshlands alongside farmlands.

Pereira, L. S. and do Rosario Cameira, M. (2019). *Innovation Issues in Water, Agriculture and Food.* MDPI. https://doi.org/10.3390/books978-3-03921-166-1

This book provides a valuable overview of issues in the water–agriculture–food nexus. Leading experts and scholars address the challenges of producing enough food for an ever-increasing population in the face of increasing competition for scarce water resources. The relationship between water, agriculture, and food security is explored through multiple disciplinary approaches offering an overview of innovations in modelling, crop water use and saving, systems design, mapping and remote sensing, and governance tools.

AMANDA SHANKLAND

125. Wild food

Mikelis Grivins

Introduction: the unnoticed part of the food system

Domestication, arguably one of the most influential innovations of all time, signifies a turning point in human history, particularly from a food system perspective. In modern society, agriculture has replaced hunting and foraging as the main source of food. However, while foraging has lost its prominence, it has not disappeared and in both the Global South and the Global North some groups continue to nurture and collect wild products using various picking, fishing, and hunting techniques. Furthermore, with the growing interest in alternatives to existing food systems and emerging food-related lifestyles, wild foods have been rediscovered by new groups (Grivins 2021). Foraging and wild food provisioning offers a completely different interaction with nature and as such represents an opportunity to rethink the ways we think about where we our food comes from, how we perceive nature surrounding us, and how we can organise food production.

The challenge of foraging's increasing popularity

The growing popularity of foraging and the trade of wild products has illuminated problems as well as opportunities that are linked with these products – such as the threat of overharvesting, ownership of wild food products, tensions between groups relying on these products, and difficulties in regulating the practice, particularly as it becomes more popular and commercially viable.

The threat of overharvesting

It is close to impossible to keep a record of the extracted quantity of wild products (Schulp et al. 2014). However, there have been reports warning of the threats of overharvesting of certain species (see Groner et al. 2022). On the one hand, this is linked to the growing number of people interested in foraging. On the other hand, this is also strongly connected to commercial foraging that, thanks to global food supply chains, can extract wild products on an almost industrial scale (Grivins and Tisenkopfs 2018). Furthermore, constant human presence in 'wild' areas is also having an impact on wildlife habits. Thus, increased human engagement with wild products can have devastating effects on ecosystems. Yet, while there have been attempts to regulate wild product extraction (see Peintner et al. 2013; Laird et al. 2012), the success of these attempts is debatable.

Ownership of the wild

Wild product foraging traditionally can be linked to communities looking for wild products in their surrounding territories. Foraging has been an additional link between local communities and the areas they inhabit, offering communities both food and a source of income. These communities in most cases have worked out a balance between the wild product yields generated by the territory and how much is picked. However, this is changing because of commercial foragers (often focusing on quick extraction) (Malin et al. 2019) and because of new, much more mobile groups of people engaging in foraging. These more recent practices are creating tensions between traditional foraging communities and newcomers. These tensions raise an important question regarding the ownership of wild products. Across the EU (Peintner et al. 2013) and elsewhere (Laird et al. 2012), there are different regulations addressing wild product ownership. Some of them attach the rights to forage to the ownership of the land, while others separate ownership of the land from the rights to pick wild products, stating that people must be able to benefit from the wild environment surrounding them.

Cultural knowledge

The engagement of various groups with foraging and 'the wild' has been very different across cultures. Communities maintain a diverse wildlife-related knowledge that can be used as a basis for innovations in the areas of agroecology, medicine, ecosystem restoration, diets, etc. This knowledge could support the transition to more sustainable agriculture. However, the differences in cultural practices can also be a potential source of conflict. Groups migrating to new locations carry their ways of engaging with nature with them, which can create tensions with communities living in destination territories.

How to govern invisible activity

Wild product foraging is important in the fields of conservation, ecosystem services, and agricultural innovations, and a potential source of knowledge and inspiration. Interest in wild products is likely to grow among all stakeholder groups in the future. This interest should be supported because engagement with wild products can foster new understandings and care of surrounding ecosystems and wilderness. This could be a gateway to repairing the broken relations consumers have with food production and re-establishing an understanding of natural processes. On the one hand, landscape planning, including urban landscape planning, should consider foraging as a way people can positively interact with the surrounding environment. On the other hand, public engagement with wild products must be more conscious – there needs to be a strategy on how foraging-related data will be collected, how the rights and the needs of the engaged actors will be protected, and what instruments could be developed to support interest in these products.

References

Grivins, M. (2021). Are all foragers the same? Towards a classification of foragers. *Sociologia Ruralis*, 61(2): 518–539. https://doi.org/10.1111/soru.12335.

Grivins, M. and Tisenkopfs, T. (2018). Benefitting from the global, protecting the local: The nested markets of wild product trade. *Journal of Rural Studies* 61: 335–342. https://doi.org/10.1016/j.jrurstud.2018.01.005.

Groner, V.P., Nicholas, O., Mabhaudhi, T., Slotow, R., Akçakaya, R., Mace, G.M. and Pearson, R.G. (2022). Climate change, land cover change, and overharvesting threaten a widely used medicinal plant in South Africa. *Ecological Applications*, 32(4): e2545. https://doi.org/10.1002/eap.2545.

Laird, S.A., McLain, R.J. and Wynberg, R.P. (eds.) (2012). *Wild Product Governance*. Earthscan, Routledge.

Malin, S.A., Ryder, S. and Lyra, M.G. (2019). Environmental justice and natural resource extraction: Intersections of power, equity and access. *Environmental Sociology*, 5(2): 109–116. https://doi.org/10.1080/23251042.2019.1608420.

Peintner, U., Schwarz, S., Mešić, A., Moreau, P.A., Moreno, G. and Saviuc, P. (2013). Mycophilic or mycophobic? Legislation and guidelines on wild mushroom commerce reveal different consumption behaviour in European countries. *PLoS ONE* 8(5): e63926. https://doi.org/10.1371/journal.pone.0063926.

Schulp, C.J.E., Thuiller, W. and Verburg, P.H. (2014). Wild food in Europe: A synthesis of knowledge and data of terrestrial wild food as an ecosystem service. *Ecological Economics*, 105: 292–305. https://doi.org/10.1016/j.ecolecon.2014.06.018.

Further reading

Laird, S.A., McLain, R.J. and Wynberg, R.P. (eds.) (2012). *Wild Product Governance*. Earthscan, Routledge.
This book offers an overview of the issues related to wild products from across the globe.

126. Working in food systems

HANNAH PITT

Introduction

Everything we eat involves countless people labouring to produce, prepare, move and sell it. But this work and these workers are entangled in contradictions, meaning their value is often under-appreciated. Work in food systems involves three contradictions which foreground pervasive injustices and perverse thinking. Food work is (1) everywhere but nowhere; (2) essential but undervalued; and (3) desirable – except as waged jobs. Food work includes all tasks associated with food systems: production, processing, distribution, retail and hospitality. This includes unwaged work, not least domestic labour, but the emphasis here is waged work, to show how unfair employment relations are inevitable in systems dominated by global, industrialised, commodity foods. Without cheap food there is no capitalism, and there is no cheap food without cheap labour.

Food work – everywhere but nowhere

Food work has significance by force of volume, having always been the world's largest labour force: 1 billion people globally are engaged in farm work alone. In the USA, jobs across the food system represent at least 10% of employment, with the largest group being in food service (USDA 2022). Food work is extensive and inescapable, touching everyone and everywhere. However, these workers are typically hidden from or ignored by consumers, rarely receiving due social attention. Those who study food for too long neglected food systems' labour dimensions; although everywhere, food work is often nowhere in our consciousness.

This contradiction is highly connected to a second: work so essential to society has been under-valued and consequently under-rewarded with low pay and poor conditions. For example, the Food Chain Workers Alliance investigation of food workers' experiences in the USA repeatedly finds widespread hard work, low pay and poor work conditions (FCWA and SRC 2016). UK food sector workers report concerns about food

insecurity, and experiences of shortages at home (BFAWU 2022). Women and racialised and migrant populations are disproportionately likely to be in low paid jobs, so represent a majority in food work. Marginalised groups are favoured by employers because of their vulnerability, leaving them open to sexual and racist abuse. Exploitation of food workers crosses space and time, even in well-regulated European countries (Corrado et al. 2017). The fight for more just food systems therefore centres on seeking fair pay, protection and rights for workers, recognising them as disempowered actors. But this means challenging structural problems of racial capitalism and patriarchy, which shape food work and hide its problems.

Why don't we know who works with our food?

Any idea how many hands your breakfast passed through to reach your plate? Unlikely, as food may be the ultimate fetishised commodity, carrying multiple untold stories far beyond the consumer (Cook 2004). The rise of industrialised, globalised food systems stretched production away from consumption, through spatial fixes in which colonising nations exploited the workforce of peripheral nations, including enslaved people (Corrado 2017). Separation between workers and those they feed, combined with capitalism's need to veil workers from consumers, has rendered workers 'invisible' (Gerbeau and Avallone 2016). These dynamics continue through export-driven production in majority world countries, and worker migration to higher income countries. Inequalities of racial capital and labour-capture typical of colonialism remain endemic. American farmers replaced freed slaves with migrant workers until the industry became dominated by Latinx, many undocumented. Intensive horticulture expanded around the Mediterranean *because* of migrant worker availability (Corrado et al. 2017). Food production and human migration are so symbiotic, one makes no sense without the other (Agyeman and Giacalone 2020). These racialised trends demonstrate how working in food systems is driven by powerful actors' interests.

Food workers on the margins

In migration's apparent win–win–win, employers get willing workers, migrant workers get jobs, and their home country gets remittances; but this dynamic leaves workers hidden, and therefore exploitable. As production is concentrated in remote rural locations, migrants are hidden from the domestic population and regulatory agencies. Hidden workers are easier to underpay and overwork, only revealed for marketing purposes: a smiley face on the packaging justifying a higher price. Migrants make good – i.e. more amenable – employees because temporary recruits lacking residency rights lack power. Migration law varies globally but is frustratingly similar in enabling abuse of migrant agricultural workers, with even well-regulated worker programmes enabling forced labour.

Immigrants and people of colour dominate food work and racist abuse of food workers remains pervasive (FCWA and SRC 2016). Early 20th-century Chinese migrants fuelled the rise of California's agriculture, but employers argued their work was unskilled work, so paid them less, a dynamic replicated through the region's switch to Mexican labour (Gray 2013). Associations between low pay and migrant workers are global, drawing on similar justifications that immigrants suit physical labour which the domestic population will not do. But constructions of workers' ethnicities are entwined with those which justify low pay and limited rights; employers desire 'good migrants', meaning those willing to over-deliver and be under-rewarded. In this vicious cycle, employers rely on exploitable employees, so marginalised groups dominate. Vulnerability arising from ethnicity and migration are often confounded by gender as the food workforce is highly feminised. Women have long been favoured for roles requiring 'nimble fingers' to handle fragile produce, whilst their part-time roles are seen to supplement 'duties' as homemakers. These narratives persist, particularly in association with migrant workers in seasonal horticulture, where 'feminine' traits – patience, attentiveness – make them valued employees, masking their *real* value as more exploitable employees (de Castro et al. 2020).

Perhaps the most invisible food work remains that in the home, by women who take on the majority of caring responsibilities and are blamed when a family is under-fed. As feminist scholars and activists highlight, domestic work is crucial to capitalist society, but goes unremunerated. Cooking, shopping or growing food for a household *is* essential food work, *and* underpins other food system work: feeding farmers and workers, caring for their children (Medland 2021). Producing cheap food requires cheap labour; workers remain cheap because their reproduction costs are externalised (Gerbeau and Avallone 2016). This reproduction–production nexus results in women being paid less in more precarious jobs; gendered and racialised marginalisation of waged and unwaged food workers continues despite their essential roles.

Why are food jobs so under-valued?

Marginalisation of food work is entangled with its reliance on marginalised people, and because marginal groups are so associated with food jobs these became socially devalued. Many food jobs are termed manual or physical, categorised as unskilled, supposedly requiring minimal education or intelligence (Pitt 2025). But anyone who has served in restaurants knows it is mentally demanding, whilst 'unskilled' agricultural work requires stamina, dexterity, knowledge of plants or animals, and manipulation of equipment; both involve negotiating workplace relations. Certain roles are imagined as 'unskilled' to serve the needs and profit of certain groups, rather than because the work is inherently simple or the workers ignorant. This is particularly true of roles dominated by women and people of colour, further reason they earn low pay.

Under-valuing of food work developed not despite food being essential to human life, but because it is. Everyone must eat so capitalist agri-food systems tend to over produce to keep prices low, hence low incomes for producers and workers. Food also benefits from agrarian exceptionalism:

> farm businesses are exempt from many of the standard labour protections governing other businesses on the premise that they meet society's basic need for food through self-sacrifice. (Weiler 2022: 68)

Pre-industrial agriculture relied on farmers' self-exploitation, creating a myth that their hard work is central to food production. This perpetuates veiling of other labourers and fuels expectations of hard work for little reward. Further, biophysical properties of perishable food and seasonal growth cycles lend agri-food employers special dispensation as crops must be gathered just-in-time. But farm owners also lobbied for farm work's exclusion from regulations offering worker protection, minimum pay and collective bargaining (Gray 2013). Food workers' precarity makes it difficult for them to resist, hence limited unionisation.

Worker exploitation has featured across successive agri-food regimes because of capitalism: cheap food is required to feed the urban workforce, and cheap commodities can only be produced by cheap labour (Gerbeau and Avallone 2016, 128). Industrialised food production arose with insecure cheap employment, and just-in-time food supply chains arose with just-in-time labour: the flexible and impermanent workforce enabled by neoliberal governments' laissez faire employment law and low regulation. But flexibility for employers constitutes vulnerability for workers. Neoliberal employment trends reach their nadir in food work where precarity through temporary or no contracts and third-party employment agents are prevalent. Some argue this is inevitable in industries with highly seasonal production, but the real driver is profit margins. Retailer competition squeezes the price producers receive, so they minimise costs, with labour often the only input where they can achieve savings, hence paying as little as possible for as short a time as possible. The quintessential precarious food worker must be the Deliveroo courier: a gig economy worker, often an immigrant, given as little pay and as few rights as possible. The technology platform capitalists rely on may be new, but the way they extract value from workers is not.

Lifting the veil, fighting for change

The veil obscuring food workers occasionally lifts, for example during the 2020 Covid-19 pandemic. Travel restrictions spread just as producers in Europe expected seasonal migrant workers to arrive, prompting predicted shortages of a million workers. Food work continued, with farmers and supermarket staff celebrated as essential workers (King and Melossi 2021). They received unprecedented appreciation, whilst new recruits offered labour to 'feed the nation'. Some hoped this would prompt re-appreciation of food work and workers, but a second pandemic trend suggests otherwise. Outbreaks of coronavirus

in food production settings revealed workers' vulnerability, poor conditions and health inequalities. This was one driver of a 'great resignation' from food jobs, which employers have struggled to rectify. In high employment economies like Western Europe and North America, food work struggles to compete with other industries.

Critical food scholars have argued that cases of worker maltreatment as revealed by the pandemic are not bad apples amongst a healthy harvest; the whole barrel is rotten. Worse, it is not that the system has broken allowing infection by exploitation and precarity; rather it was fixed to be so (Guthman 2014). There are always some winners in the race to the bottom. Even food production driven by sustainability and localism harbours unjust work relations (Gray 2013). Farmers adhering to agro-ecological values do not always extend justice to workers because it is so hard to make a viable income. Artisanal products celebrated for their craftwork also require cheap, precarious labour (Weiler 2022). Restaurants which promote sustainability do not necessarily include treatment of staff in these credentials (Jayaraman and Schlosser 2013). Alternative food movements are not so alternative when it comes to labour justice, but activists were long silent on labour; workers – particularly service and hospitality workers – remained hidden.

Food justice movements brought workers' rights further to the fore, but most food workers lack adequate protection and are largely forgotten by consumers. International regulations which should protect them are poorly enforced; even best practice seasonal worker programmes offer workers weak protection (Klassen et al. 2023). Sadly, it often takes tragedy to drive change, such as the deaths of 21 illegally employed cockle pickers in 2004, which urged politicians in England to regulate gang labour. Other steps towards greater protection include certification schemes which require minimum work conditions. However, auditing of certified products is often inadequate, and standards are designed without workers' input so do not pursue their priorities.

Demands for higher pay soon encounter a false impasse: producers and workers cannot be paid more without prices rising, purportedly untenable when many face food insecurity. But poverty is what makes food unaffordable, not price. This perniciously false zero-sum equation is highlighted by impacts on food workers who are

> particularly poorly paid and therefore suffer doubly, as both workers and consumers, in the food system. (Guthman 2014: 224)

Low pay and food poverty are different outcomes of the same unjust, racist, neoliberal capitalist systems.

Workers are the least powerful people in food systems, which points to food work's third contradiction. Food work is not inherently bad; tending and preparing food are not necessarily unpleasant or dangerous tasks. Doing such work voluntarily is socially celebrated, but as waged jobs it is not. Food movements promote gardening to enhance wellbeing, or cooking to strengthen community, celebrating practical work for 'reconnecting people to food'. Stars of the Netflix series *Chef's Table* are lauded for the artistry of *their* cooking, and paid much more than the brigade toiling out of shot. Physical work in market gardens, artisanal bakeries, craft brewers and butchers attracts highly educated middle-class recruits who could work elsewhere (Weiler 2022). Exalted positions and ownership in craft-food enterprises remain dominated by privileged groups, whilst their labouring class is largely migrants or people of colour. Popularisation of food work hobbies and gentrification of manual food skills indicate the work itself is not undesirable; it is unfair employment and unjust power relations which are.

Resolving these three food work contradictions requires fairer food systems. Replacing workers with robots and AI is a misguided solution for three reasons. Firstly, affordable technology to replace mass labour doing tasks like picking delicate fruits is years away. Secondly, investing in technology is only feasible for the richest producers, meaning further concentration with corporate, white-owned businesses. Thirdly, technology does not remove all work; it just changes it and the socio-political dynamics. New technology will feature in future food production but impacts on workers must be integral to its advancement (Klassen et al 2023).

One trend is more hopeful. December 2021 the first USA Starbucks branch unionised, initiating a movement across locations and companies, countering a history of low unionisation in food service. Perhaps buoyed by recognition during the pandemic and a favourable labour market, food workers are mobilising. The Coalition of Immokalee Workers remains a prominent influence on worker movements, having mobilised consumer support to secure retailer commitment to better pay and standards for tomato pickers in the USA (Mieres and McGrath 2021). But movements need legislation protecting workers, plus enforcement of international standards. It is heartening that decent work features within recent reforms to EU agricultural policy (European Commission n.d).

As the pandemic's impacts suggest, making food workers more visible is insufficient to drive change. Visibility often excludes roles in distribution and catering, rarely foregrounding migrants. Consumer awareness of workers struggles to influence purchasing habits – an individualised solution to systemic problems (Guthman 2014). The veil must be pulled back further because fetishisation also obfuscates ownership of the means of production and power distribution, or how alternatives could begin with common good (Pettenati et al. 2019). Worker cooperatives prefigure fairer food systems but, unless inequalities entrenched in conventional food systems are confronted, they remain side-shows. Systemic problems need systemic solutions, connecting capitalism, neoliberalism, colonialism, racism and patriarchy to food. Achieving better food systems work needs multiple solidarities: unions linked with consumer campaigns, producer cooperation, food activists collaborating with labour, migrant and anti-racism movements. And movements crossing borders – exactly as many food workers do.

References

Agyeman, J. and Giacalone, S. (2020), *The immigrant-food nexus: Borders, labor, and identity in North America.* The MIT Press.

Bakers Food and Allied Workers Union (BFAWU) (2022), *The Right to Food: A law needed by food workers and community across the UK.* BFAWU https://www.bfawu.org/campaign/right-to-food/.

Cook, I. (2004), 'Follow the Thing: Papaya.' *Antipode* 36(4), 642–64. https://doi.org/10.1111/j.1467-8330.2004.00441.x.

Corrado, A. (2017), 'Agrarian Change and Migrations in the Mediterranean from a

Food Regime Perspective.' In A. Corrado, C. de Castro and P. Domenico (eds), *Migration and Agriculture* (pp. 313–31). London: Routledge.

de Castro, C., Reigada, A., and Gadea, E. (2020), The devaluation of female labour in fruit and vegetable packaging plants in Spanish Mediterranean agriculture. *Organization* 27(2), 232–250.

European Commission (n.d), *Factsheet – A Greener and Fairer CAP*. https://agriculture.ec.europa.eu/document/download/89b607ec-8a43-4073-bafd-f2493da7699e_en?filename=factsheet-newcap-environment-fairness_en.pdf.

Food Chain Workers Alliance and Solidarity Research Cooperative (2016), *No Piece of the Pie: US Food Workers in 2016*. Los Angeles: Food Chain Workers Alliance. https://foodchainworkers.org/wp-content/uploads/2011/05/FCWA_NoPieceOfThePie_P.pdf.

Gerbeau, Y. and Avallone, G. (2016), 'Producing Cheap Food and Labour: Migrations and Agriculture in the Capitalistic World-Ecology.' *Social Change Review* 14(2), 121–48. https://doi.org/10.1515/scr-2016-0025.

Gray, M. (2013), *Labor and the Locavore: The Making of a Comprehensive Food Ethic*. Berkeley: University of California Press.

Guthman, J. (2014), *Agrarian Dreams: The Paradox of Organic Farming in California*, Second ed. Oakland: University of California Press.

Jayaraman, S. and Schlosser, E. (2013), *Behind the Kitchen Door*. Ithaca, NY: ILR Press.

King, R. L. A. and Melossi, E. (2021), 'New Perspectives on the Agriculture–Migration Nexus.' *Journal of Rural Studies* 85, 52–8. https://doi.org/10.1016/j.jrurstud.2021.05.004.

Klassen, S., Medland, L., Nicol, P., and Pitt, H. (2023), 'Pathways for Advancing Good Work in Food Systems: Reflecting on the Good Work for Good Food International Forum.' *Journal of Agriculture, Food Systems, and Community Development* 12(2), 249–65 https://doi.org/10.5304/jafscd.2023.122.004.

Medland, L. (2021), '"There is No Time": Agri-food Internal Migrant Workers in Morocco's Tomato Industry.' *Journal of Rural Studies*, 88, 482–90. https://doi.org/10.1016/j.jrurstud.2021.04.015

Mieres, F. and McGrath, S. (2021), 'Ripe to Be Heard: Worker Voice in the Fair Food Program.' *International Labour Review* 160(4), 631–47. https://doi.org/10.1111/ilr.12204.

Pettenati, G., Toldo, A., and Ferrando, T. (2019), 'The Food System as a commons.' In J. L. Vivero Pol, T. Ferrando, O. de Schutter and U. Mattei (eds), *Routledge Handbook of Food as Commons* (pp. 42–56). Oxford and New York: Routledge.

Pitt, H. (2024). *Revaluing Horticultural Skills: The Knowledge and Labour of Growing Food*. Taylor & Francis.

US Department of Agriculture (USDA) (2022), 'Ag and Food Sectors and the Economy.' https://www.ers.usda.gov/data-products/ag-and-food-statistics-charting-the-essentials/ag-and-food-sectors-and-the-economy/#:~:text=In%202020%2C%2019.7%20million%20full,percent%20of%20total%20U.S.%20employment.

Weiler, A. (2022), 'Seeing the Workers the Trees: Exalted and Devalued Manual Labour the Pacific Northwest Craft Cider Industry.' *Agriculture and Human Values* 39(1), 65–78. https://doi.org/10.1007/s10460-021-10226-w.

Further reading

Corrado, A., de Castro, C., and Perrotta, D. (eds) (2017), *Migration and Agriculture*. London, Routledge.

Perspectives from industrialised horticulture around the Mediterranean demonstrate how precarious labour and migration are integral to food regimes. It provides historic context on the evolution of working in food systems, demonstrating how migration underpins intensive production regimes.

Gray, M. (2013), *Labor and the Locavore: The Making a Comprehensive Food Ethic*. Berkeley: University of California Press. https://doi.org/10.1525/9780520957060.

This work was highly influential in highlighting contradictions within alternative food movements, illustrating problematic employment conditions across production models including organic farms.

Minkoff-Zern, L-A. and Mares, T. (2025), *Will Work for Food: Labor Across the Food*

System. Berkeley: University of California Press.

Taking a systems approach to food work, this book argues that workers across agri-food roles face inter-connected pressures, and argues for a systemic approach to change.

HANNAH PITT

Index